JOHN GRAY

I & II KINGS

Second, Fully Revised, Edition

JOHN GRAY

I & II KINGS

[3-4 Kings in Catholic versions]

A Commentary

Second, Fully Revised, Edition

The Westminster Press
PHILADELPHIA

ISBN-0-664-20898-3
LIBRARY OF CONGRESS CATALOG CARD NO. 73-134271

PUBLISHED BY THE WESTMINSTER PRESS ®
PHILADELPHIA 7, PENNSYLVANIA
PRINTED IN GREAT BRITAIN

To
The late Rev. Professor H. H. Rowley
in token of gratitude
for his continued help and encouragement as a colleague
and friend
for the stimulus of his many publications
for his loyal support of our present project
in his failing health
and as a parting tribute
this book is inscribed

CONTENTS

MAPS

PREFACE TO SECOND EDITION

THE WRITER has taken the opportunity of a second edition of this commentary to modify certain parts of the first edition and to expand it by a fuller study of certain problems such as 'Ahab's' campaigns in I Kings 20 and 22, the date of the fall of Samaria, Sennacherib's invasion of Judah in Hezekiah's reign and the question of a pre-Deuteronomistic prophetic source for the history of the monarchy in North Israel. The author had isolated such topics for further study since his first edition, and the interim has been a welcome opportunity to reach more satisfactory conclusions. The reviews of the first edition have been most helpful not only in confirming the writer in certain conclusions, but even more in focussing his attention on outstanding problems and giving fresh orientation to his thought. The publication of the late Professor Noth's commentary on Kings has been a most fruitful stimulus to revision, and the author takes this opportunity to pay his humble tribute to the whole of Professor Noth's work as a formative influence on his own. The interruption of this great commentary by the sudden death of Professor Noth will be a lasting regret among scholars, the more so as evidently he left nothing except the manuscript of one fascicule already in the hands of his publishers, Neukirchener Verlag des Erziehungsvereins, to whom the writer acknowledges his indebtedness for the readiness with which they supplied proofs of this unpublished fragment. Further modification of the first edition of *I and II Kings* has been demanded by the most recent excavations in Jerusalem by the French and British Schools of Archaeology in Jerusalem, in the light of which a new map of the city has been prepared by Mrs Heather Lyall MA, Cartographer in the Department of Geography in the University of Aberdeen, whose patience and expert co-operation the writer gladly acknowledges.

In the preparation of this edition the writer's thanks are due also to the Rev. John Bowden of SCM Press and his editorial staff, to the editors of the Old Testament Library series, Professor James Barr of the University of Manchester and Professor Peter R. Ackroyd of King's College, the University of London, who have, with the assistance of Mr Richard Coggins, Lecturer in King's College, London, revised the proofs of the work. The writer is especially grateful to his former principal in the University of Manchester, the late Professor H. H. Rowley, DD, D.Theol., FBA, who kindly volunteered to read both manuscript and proofs, a kindness the more gracious in his declining health. It gives peculiar satisfaction that he consented to accept the dedication of this edition as a token of gratitude and esteem. The revision of proofs, which only the suffering of his last few days interrupted, has been carried on by my colleague the Rev. William Johnstone MA, BD, of whose careful and pure scholarship the late Professor Rowley would certainly have approved, and for this the latest of his kind services the writer is most grateful.

King's College
University of Aberdeen
Michaelmas, 1969

ABBREVIATIONS

AASOR	*Annual of the American Schools of Oriental Research*, New Haven
AfO	*Archiv für Orientforschung*, Berlin
AJ	*Antiquaries Journal*, London
AJA	*American Journal of Archaeology*, Princeton
AJSL	*American Journal of Semitic Languages and Literature*, Chicago
ANEP	*The Ancient Near East in Pictures*, ed. J. B. Pritchard, London, 1954
ANET	*Ancient Near Eastern Texts relating to the Old Testament*, ed. J. B. Pritchard, London, 1950
AO	*Der Alte Orient*, Leipzig
ARA	*Ancient Records of Assyria and Babylonia*, see Bibliography: Luckenbill
ARE	*Ancient Records of Egypt*, see Bibliography: Breasted
Arch. Or.	*Archiv Orientální*, Prague
ARW	*Archiv für Religionswissenschaft*, Leipzig
AS	*Anatolian Studies*, London
ASAE	*Annales du Service des Antiquités d'Égypte*
AT	Das Alte Testament
A und S	*Arbeit und Sitte in Palästina*, see Bibliography: Dalman
AV	Authorized Version
BA	*Biblical Archaeologist*, New Haven
BASOR	*Bulletin of the American Schools of Oriental Research*, New Haven
BDB	Brown, Driver and Briggs, *Hebrew and English Lexicon to the Old Testament*, rev. ed., Oxford, 1957
BHT	Beiträge zur historischen Theologie, Tübingen
BJ	*La Sainte Bible traduite en français sous la direction de l'École Biblique de Jérusalem*, Paris, 1956
BJRL	*Bulletin of the John Rylands Library*, Manchester
BMB	*Bulletin du Musée de Beyrouth*
BWA(N)T	Beiträge zur Wissenschaft vom Alten (und Neuen) Testament, Leipzig
BZAW	Beihefte zur Zeitschrift fur die alttestamentliche Wissenschaft, Giessen and Berlin
CAH	*Cambridge Ancient History*, ed. J. B. Bury, S. A. Cook and F. E. Adcock, Cambridge, 1923–39; revised ed., vols. I–II, ed. I. E. S. Edwards, C. J. Gadd and N. G. L. Hammond, 1961ff.

CB	Century Bible, Edinburgh, 1901–22; new series, London, 1966ff.
CBQ	*Catholic Biblical Quarterly*, Washington
CIS	*Corpus Inscriptionum Semiticarum*, Paris, 1881ff.
CRAIBL	*Comptes rendus de l'Académie des Inscriptions et Belles Lettres*, Paris
DR	*Deutsche Rundschau*, Berlin
ET	English translation
ETL	*Ephemerides Theologicae Lovanienses*, Louvain
EVV	English Versions
ExpT	*Expository Times*, Edinburgh
FuF	*Forschungen und Fortschritte*, Berlin
G	Septuagint Version of the Old Testament
G^{A}	Septuagint Version, Codex Alexandrinus
G^{B}	Septuagint Version, Codex Vaticanus
G^{h}	Hexaplaric Greek Versions of the Old Testament
GK	Gesenius-Kautzsch, *Hebrew Grammar*, 2nd English ed., rev. A. Cowley, Oxford, 1910
G^{L}	Lucian's recension of the Septuagint
GP	*Géographie de la Palestine*, see Bibliography: Abel
HDB	*Hastings' Dictionary of the Bible*, Edinburgh, 1898–1901; one-volume ed., Edinburgh, 1963
HKAT	Handkommentar zum Alten Testament, ed. W. Nowack, Göttingen, 1892–1933
HTR	*Harvard Theological Review*, Cambridge, Mass.
HUCA	*Hebrew Union College Annual*, Cincinnati
HSAT	*Die Heilige Schrift des Alten Testaments*, ed. E. Kautzsch; 4th ed., A. Bertholet, Tübingen, 1922–23
ICC	International Critical Commentary, Edinburgh, 1895ff.
IEJ	*Israel Exploration Journal*, Jerusalem
IP	*Die israelitischen Personennamen*, see Bibliography: Noth
JA	*Journal Asiatique*, Paris
JAOS	*Journal of the American Oriental Society*, New Haven
JBL	*Journal of Biblical Literature*, Philadelphia
JCS	*Journal of Cuneiform Studies*, New Haven
JEA	*Journal of Egyptian Archaeology*, London
JMUEOS	*Journal of the Manchester University Egyptian and Oriental Society*, Manchester
JNES	*Journal of Near Eastern Studies*, Chicago
JPOS	*Journal of the Palestine Oriental Society*, Jerusalem
JQR	*Jewish Quarterly Review*, London
JRAS	*Journal of the Royal Asiatic Society*, London
JSS	*Journal of Semitic Studies*, Manchester

JTS	*Journal of Theological Studies*, Oxford
K	*K^e^tîb*
KS	*Kleine Schriften zum Alten Testament*, see Bibliography: Alt
L	Old Latin versions of the Old Testament
MT	Massoretic Text of the Old Testament
NF	Neue Folge (new series)
NGT	*Norsk Geografisk Tidsskrift*, Oslo
NSI	*A Textbook of North Semitic Inscriptions*, see Bibliography: G. A. Cooke
NTT	*Norsk Teologisk Tidsskrift*, Oslo
OIC	Oriental Institute of Chicago
OLZ	*Orientalistische Literaturzeitung*, Berlin
OTS	*Oudtestamentische Studiën*, Leiden
PEF	Palestine Exploration Fund
PEFQS	*Palestine Exploration Fund Quarterly Statement*, London
PEQ	*Palestine Exploration Quarterly*, London
PJB	*Palästinajahrbuch*, Berlin
PRU	*Le palais royale d'Ugarit*, see Bibliography: Nougayrol and Virolleaud
Q	*Q^e^rē*
QDAP	*Quarterly of the Department of Antiquities of Palestine*, Jerusalem
RA	*Revue d'Assyriologie et d'Archéologie Orientale*, Paris
RB	*Revue Biblique*, Paris
RES	*Revue des Études Sémitiques*, Paris
RHPR	*Revue d'Histoire et de Philosophie Religieuses*, Strasbourg
RHR	*Revue de l'Histoire des Religions*, Paris
RSV	Revised Standard Version of the Bible
RV	Revised Version of the Bible
S	Syriac Version of the Bible (Peshitta)
SAT	Die Schriften des Alten Testaments in Auswahl, ed. H. Gunkel, 2nd ed., Göttingen, 1920–25
SEÅ	*Svensk Exegetisk Årsbok*, Uppsala
S^h	Syriac Version of the Hexapla
SVT	Supplements to *Vetus Testamentum*
T	Targum
TLZ	*Theologische Literaturzeitung*, Leipzig
TR	*Theologische Rundschau*, Tübingen
TWNT	*Theologisches Wörterbuch zum Neuen Testament*, Stuttgart, 1933ff.
UH	C. H. Gordon, *Ugaritic Handbook*, Rome, 1947
UL	id., *Ugaritic Literature*, Rome, 1949
UM	id., *Ugaritic Manual*, Rome, 1955
UT	id., *Ugaritic Textbook*, Rome, 1965

UUÅ	*Uppsala Universitets Årsskrift*, Uppsala
V	Vulgate
VT	*Vetus Testamentum*, Leiden
ZA	*Zeitschrift für Assyriologie*, Leipzig
ZAW	*Zeitschrift für die alttestamentliche Wissenschaft*, Giessen and Berlin
ZDMG	*Zeitschrift der Deutschen Morgenländischen Gesellschaft*, Leipzig
ZDPV	*Zeitschrift des Deutschen Palästina-Vereins*, Leipzig
ZTK	*Zeitschrift für Theologie und Kirche*, Tübingen

QUMRAN SCROLLS

1QIs[a]	Isaiah: First Scroll from Qumran Cave I
1QIs[b]	Isaiah: Second Scroll from Qumran Cave I
4QSam[b]	Samuel: Second Scroll from Qumran Cave IV
5QK	Fragments of a MS of Kings from Qumran Cave V
6QK	Fragments of a MS of Kings from Qumran Cave VI

I

INTRODUCTION

1. THE COMPOSITION OF KINGS

KINGS IN THE CANON OF THE OLD TESTAMENT

THE BOOKS OF KINGS were divided into two roughly even parts in G, probably for the sake of convenience when MS rolls were still in use. In Josephus and the Talmud, however, the original Hebrew version was visualized as one undivided book, and there is no indication of division in Hebrew until the late fifteenth or early sixteenth centuries. In spite of the division, Kings was obviously regarded as a unity with Samuel in G, which classifies I and II Kings as III and IV *Basileiai* ('reigns' or 'dynasties'), certain MSS of G carrying II *Basileiai* (MT II Sam.) forward to MT I K. 2.11 (the death of David) and others to I K. 2.46 (the establishment of Solomon's throne). The same unity is indicated by the common source used in II Sam. 9–20 and I K. 1 and 2 in the story of the Davidic succession, and by the fact that the whole work is arranged and interpolated by the same compiler of the Deuteronomistic school.

In a larger context, Kings, with Samuel, is the culmination of the second division of the Jewish canon, the Former Prophets, including Joshua and Judges. The classification of Joshua, Judges, Samuel and Kings as 'the Former Prophets' emphasizes their character as primarily the theological interpretation of the history of Israel from the settlement of Israel in Palestine until the Exile. The work is developed from the conviction of the operation of the word of God expressed in the adjurations with which the ritual and social implications of the covenant were accepted in, as we believe, the days of the judges in the covenant-sacrament at the central shrine of the sacral confederacy of Israel (Deut. 27.15–26) and presented in public proclamation in the same context (Deut. 28.15ff.). Deuteronomy is properly the introduction to Joshua, Judges, Samuel and Kings, aptly called by Noth, who first recognized the unity of this great work, the Deuteronomistic History.[a] Owing to the fact that large portions of the work are from original sources, there is no stylistic unity to indicate a single self-contained work. But the self-contained character is shown by the consistent theology which governed the choice and use of sources in all parts of the work. Stylistically, too, its unity is indicated by the punctuation of the history at significant crises with passages in familiar Deuteronomic style, reviewing the past and adumbrating the future, with all problems set in perspective and duly emphasized from the standpoint of Deuteronomic theology. These may be either in narrative form, as the summary of Joshua's conquests (Josh. 12), the programme of the book of Judges (Judg. 2.11–3.6) and the review of the tragic past of the Northern kingdom at its fall in 722 BC (II K. 17.7ff.), or in speeches from the protagonists, e.g. of Yahweh to Joshua on the eve of the occupation (Josh. 1.2–9), the address of Joshua on the completion of the occupation, which anticipates the problems of the next phase in Judges (Josh. 23f.), the speech of Samuel, which marks the end of the period of the judges (I Sam. 12), the divine oracle by Nathan, which heralds the hereditary monarchy under the house of David and the building of the Temple (II Sam. 7.18–29), and the prayer of Solomon at the dedication of the Temple (I K. 8.14ff.).

More particularly significant, in view of the development of the theme of this great historical work from the standpoint of the consequences of Israel's commitment as a sacral community in the context of the ancient covenant-sacrament expressed in Deut. 26.16–28.68, is the renewal of the covenant at significant junctures in the history, as in Josh. 24; I Sam. 7.3–9, which is also implied in the introductions to the deliverances by the great judges (Judg. 3.7–11, 12–15a, 30; 4.1a, 2a, 23f.; 5.31c; 6.1–2a, 7–10; 8.28, 33–35; 10.6–16; 11.33b; cf. I Sam. 7.3–9, which reflects God's contention with his people in a public fast with relation to the covenant-sacrament).[b] This central theme of the covenant is sustained in the divine covenant with the king of the house of David as representative of the people (II Sam. 7.8–16; I K. 2.2–4; 8.25f.), in the light of which the

[a] *Überlieferungsgeschichtliche Studien*, 1957.

[b] This has been recognized by W. Beyerlin, 'Gattung und Herkunft des Rahmens im Richterbuch', *Tradition und Situation*, ed. E. Würthwein and O. Kaiser, 1963, pp. 1–29.

Deuteronomistic historian explains God's forbearance with the nation under her kings and the ultimate fall of the house of David and the nation.

The unity of Joshua, Judges, Samuel and Kings, with Deuteronomy as an introduction, is further indicated by overlaps in subject-matter. Thus forty-five years span the time between Joshua's reconnaissance of Canaan, visualized as immediately after the Exodus, and his apportionment of the land, allowing five years for the conquest of the land East and West of the Jordan; Josh. 23f. anticipates the problems of the settlement in Judges; the Philistine oppression, stated in Judg. 13.1 to have lasted forty years, is still the theme of I Sam.; and I K. 1f. continues the theme of the establishment of a hereditary monarchy under the house of David, which is the subject of II Sam. 7ff.

Finally, this impression of the unity of this historical work seems to be confirmed by the schematic chronology which is so marked a feature of Joshua, Judges, Samuel and the reigns of David and Solomon in the beginning of Kings. The statement that the Temple was begun in Solomon's fourth year, 480 years after the Exodus (I K. 6.1) seems to be connected with the periods of forty, twenty and eighty years which recur in Judges, and Noth has used this as an argument for the unity of Joshua, Judges, Samuel and Kings according to the following chronological scheme:[a]

The death of Moses 'in the 40th year', sc. after the Exodus (Deut. 1.3)	40
The completion of the conquest under Joshua forty-five years after his reconnaissance of Canaan, visualized as immediately after the Exodus (Josh. 14.10)	5
Eight years of oppression from which Othniel delivered the people (Judg. 3.8), followed by forty years' rest	48
Moabite oppression for eighteen years (Judg. 3.14) and eighty years' rest (Judg. 3.30)	98

[a]M. Noth, *Überlieferungsgeschichtliche Studien*, pp. 18–27. We cite this chronology, not because of its historical probability, which has obvious limitations, though there is in the odd numbers a basis of historical fact, but simply to emphasize the schematic character of the whole as an element in Noth's argument for the unity of Joshua-Judges-Samuel-Kings. On the difficulties and problems of this chronology and our proposed solution see J. Gray, *Joshua, Judges and Ruth*, Century Bible, 1967, pp. 4–7. Beyond the relevance to the unity of the Deuteronomistic History, this schematic chronology concerns only the reigns of David and Solomon, and so does not demand further discussion here. See further, pp. 8f.

Oppression under Sisera for twenty years (Judg. 4.3) followed by forty years' rest	60
Midianite oppression for seven years (Judg. 6.1) followed by forty years' rest	47
Abimelech's reign: three years	3
Tola as judge: twenty-three years (Judg. 10.2)	23
Jair as judge: twenty-two years (Judg. 10.3)	22
Ammonite oppression for eighteen years (Judg. 10.8)	18
Jephthah as judge: six years (Judg. 12.7)	6
Ibzan as judge: seven years (Judg. 12.9)	7
Elon as judge: ten years (Judg. 12.11)	10
Abdon as judge: eight years (Judg. 12.14)	8
Philistine oppression for forty years (Judg. 13.1), including the latter part of Eli's forty-year office (I Sam. 4.18), Samson's leadership (Judg. 16.31) and Samuel's career until the elevation of Saul, or until his death (time unspecified)	40
Saul's reign: two years (I Sam. 13.1)	2
David's reign: forty years (I K. 2.11)	40
The foundation of the Temple in Solomon's fourth year (I K. 6.1), his first year perhaps coinciding with David's last (I K. 1)	3
Total	480

In this essentially theological work, the largely schematized presentation of Israel's occupation of Palestine serves the purpose of the Deuteronomistic historian to emphasize the success which followed when Moses' influence was still felt in holding Israel to obedience to her covenant commitment, as Josh. 1 emphasizes, in accordance with the promise of blessing in the public proclamation in the covenant-sacrament in Deut. 28.1–14, which we may regard as the text of which the book of Joshua is an amplification. In Judges, Samuel and Kings, phases in the history of Israel are adduced to illustrate the theme of Deut. 28.15ff., the disastrous consequences of disloyalty to the law of God. The books of Samuel lead up to the main theme, the establishment of the monarchy, which under David is visualized as a sacred trust, where the king represents the people as the sacral community, the people of God, expressed in the conception of the divine covenant with the house of David (II Sam. 7.8–16). Thus it is that the books of Kings are not, as the Assyrian annals, full and detailed objective history, but an account of the vicissitudes of the kings of Israel and Judah, which involve those of their people, according as they notably exemplify the principles of reward and retribution following fidelity to, or flouting of, the covenant commitment.

In Kings, the fidelity of the kings to the covenant commitment is assessed by the somewhat mechanical criterion of cultic orthodoxy. Thus the various kings of Israel are condemned for their addiction to the cult established by Jeroboam the son of Nebat, and the kings of Judah are appraised according to their fidelity to the central shrine, the Temple in Jerusalem, all being stigmatized for their tolerance of the local 'high places' except Hezekiah and Josiah. Here the editor applies the principles of the Deuteronomic reformation under Josiah, though the circles which preserved that tradition flourished for a long time after the reform, continuing the work of editing the Deuteronomistic History at least to 561, the last event recorded being the favour shown to Jehoiachin by Evil-Merodach on his accession in that year. The hand of the Deuteronomist, though most obvious in the main framework of Kings in editorial introductions to, and conclusions of, the various reigns, is evident besides in characteristic stereotyped language, figures and norms of appraisal in commentaries on events in the particular reigns of the kings.

Again it must be emphasized that the record in Kings is not an objective history, nor is the interest centred in individual reigns. This part of the Deuteronomistic history is primarily concerned with the monarchy and its failure in large perspective, and might well be entitled 'The Hebrew Monarchy: its Rise, Decline and Fall'. Hence the materials for the history have been treated selectively according to theological principles. The result is a philosophy, or theological interpretation, of history, which Jewish tradition recognized by including Kings in that division of the canon of Scripture known as the Prophets.

THE CONTENT OF KINGS

The Books of Kings begin with an account of David's last days, the circumstances of Solomon's succession and his reign, continuing with the disruption of the kingdom at his death, and giving the parallel histories of the kingdoms of Judah and Israel until the collapse of the latter in 722 BC and of the former in 586. The last event referred to, however, is the alleviation of the lot of the exiled king Jehoiachin on the accession of Evil-Merodach to the throne of Babylon in 561, this being, we believe, an exilic supplement by a redactor.

KINGS A COMPOSITE WORK

In the Deuteronomistic history, Kings is a composite work like the Pentateuch, though the indications of this are different in the case of Kings. Here we are not so much concerned with ill-edited parallel sources in the account of the same events, which betray their presence by doublets and discrepancies. The underlying sources may rather be detected by the different nature of their subject-matter and their style. Indeed there is explicit reference to various sources of information, all obviously written sources, e.g. the Book of the Acts of Solomon (I K. 11.41), the Book of the Chronicles of the Kings of Israel, and the Book of the Chronicles of the Kings of Judah. It is not difficult to conjecture with a fair degree of probability the amount of the content of Kings drawn from these respective sources, though the references to these sources indicate beyond doubt that they contained more matter than was actually incorporated in the Books of Kings.

PRE-EXILIC COMPILATION AND EXILIC REDACTION

The critical view of the Deuteronomistic Book of Kings is that it is a pre-exilic compilation with exilic redaction and expansion. This has been questioned, particularly by Hölscher,[a] who dates the whole of the compilation of Kings *c.* 500, mainly because he dates the Book of Deuteronomy and the work of the school that produced it in the post-exilic period, but before Nehemiah. This view that the Deuteronomistic compilation of Kings is an exilic work is supported by Noth (*op. cit.*). More recently A. Jepsen[b] has proposed a pre-exilic compilation on the basis of a synchronistic chronicle of Israel and Judah with excerpts from the annals of both kingdoms. This he terms R1, ascribing it to a priest towards the end of the monarchy.[c] Jepsen further proposes that the main redaction, which incorporated prophetic sources with traditions from Solomon's reign and the

[a]'Das Buch der Könige, seine Quelle und seine Redaktion', *Eucharisterion* (Gunkel Festschrift) I, 1923, pp. 158ff.

[b]*Die Quellen des Königsbuches*, 1953, pp. 76ff.

[c]Priestly authorship is suggested by the fact that the characteristic feature is criticism of the cult in the monarchy and that generally the only persons named besides kings and queen-mothers are priests.

Story of the Davidic Succession (I K. 1–2), was exilic. This (R2) he terms the Nebiistic redaction, or the Deuteronomistic redaction proper with its distinctive theology, as distinct from the earlier priestly redaction (RI). Like Noth, Jepsen admits later adjustments, which he terms the Levitical redaction. While admitting such late hands in Kings, we question if this can be termed a full-scale redaction. The view that the extant Books of Kings are a pre-exilic work of the Deuteronomistic compiler with exilic redaction from the same circles is taken in Fohrer's revision of Sellin's *Introduction*.[a] Fohrer would date the pre-exilic Deuteronomistic compilation between 622 BC, the initiation of Josiah's reform, and the king's death in 609, on the grounds that the compiler is apparently unaware of the violent death of Josiah. This view is based, however, on the prediction of the prophetess Huldah (II K. 22.20), and strangely ignores the factual statement in II K. 23.29. So it may be doubted. Our own view is that the pre-exilic Deuteronomistic compilation ended between the outbreak of Jehoiakim's revolt against Nebuchadrezzar in 598 and his death in 597 (see below, p. 753.), from which point the history is continued, possibly by the exilic redactor.

There is no doubt that, whether we agree with Hölscher, Noth, and Jepsen, or regard Kings as a pre-exilic compilation with exilic redaction, there is a consistency in the main theme, that of Israel's sin and retribution. There are, however, in our opinion, clear signs that the body of the work was pre-exilic. In a study of this problem W. Nowack[b] conveniently summarized such evidence. After Solomon's prayer of dedication of the Temple (I K. 8.14ff.), for instance, the divine promise is naturally expected, and is in fact given to the king (9.1–5); this, however, is followed somewhat incongruously by a threat to the people, which foresees the Exile (vv. 6–9). Here the address to the king as representative of the Davidic house and also, presumably, as representative of the people is natural in the pre-exilic period, when the community was intact, whereas the abrupt change to the address to the people in the second person plural reflects a later period with the development of the consciousness of the individual, as Mowinckel has noticed in the case of psalms of lamentation.[c] In the note on the liquidation of the Northern kingdom as retribution for the sins of Jeroboam in II K. 17.18ff. this theme is

[a]E. Sellin-G. Fohrer, *Introduction to the Old Testament* (ET 1968), p. 248.
[b]*Deuteronomium und Regum*, BZAW XLI (Marti Festschrift), 1925, pp. 221–31.
[c]*The Psalms in Israel's Worship* I, 1962, p. 38.

rudely interrupted by vv. 19f., an obvious exilic note on the sin which brought about the final destruction of Judah, which is prompted by the statement in v. 18b that Judah survived the fall of Samaria. The suggestion is surely that the note on the fall of Samaria which continues at vv. 21ff. after the interruption is from an earlier compilation than vv. 19f., which are certainly from an exilic redactor. This is also the natural conclusion from the oracle on the disruption of Solomon's kingdom (I K. 11.29–39), where it is stated (vv. 32–35) that one tribe shall be left to the scion of David 'that David my servant may have a lamp always before me in Jerusalem . . .' (v. 36). The last evidence cited by Nowack, the reference to Edom in revolt from Judah 'to this day' (II K. 8.22), is less convincing. 'To this day' usually indicates the compiler or redactor, and if that were so in this case it would indicate the former rather than the latter and point to a time when Judah still stood as an independent state which remembered its claim on Edom. In this context, we are not convinced that the statement is from the Deuteronomist rather than from the original annalistic source he was handling, especially if this source was a literary one prepared from state archives, and so itself a compilation. This apart, however, there seems to us sufficient evidence for a pre-exilic compilation and an exilic redaction.

The *terminus post quem* for this redaction would most naturally be the note on the alleviation of the lot of the captive Jehoiachin in 561 (II K. 25.27).[a] The chronological system in the Deuteronomistic History, however, as is emphasized by Mowinckel,[b] in reckoning from Exodus, regards the foundation of Solomon's Temple as the middle point of its period, thus visualizing 537/6 as the end of that period, when, presumably, worship was resumed by the first group of exiles to return after the fall of the neo-Babylonian Empire. We think that the silence regarding this significant event, in which Zerubbabel, a prince of the royal house of Judah, was probably involved, is an insuperable obstacle to the view that the chronological scheme is an essential part of the main Deuteronomistic redaction. The

[a]This is the only thing that suggests a Mesopotamian origin for the Deuteronomistic history, which is urged by Sellin (*Einleitung*, ed. L. Rost, 1950, p. 77). Noth, on the contrary, takes the full and accurate topographical notes throughout to indicate that the compilation was done in Palestine, possibly about Bethel or Mizpah (*Überlieferungsgeschichtliche Studien*, 1957, p. 110, n.1). Jepsen (*op. cit.*, pp. 95ff.) also regards the work as produced in Palestine, possibly at Mizpah.

[b]Die Chronologie der israelitischen und jüdischen Könige', *Acta Orientalia* X, 1932, pp. 168–70.

basis of the chronological scheme is the reference in I K. 6.1 to the foundation of the Temple 480 years after the Exodus. This, as an examination of the text shows, is certainly post-exilic, and is, we maintain, a post-redactional gloss certainly from after 537/6. Late redactional notes of a minor character, showing sensitivity to Levitical qualifications for the priesthood and the reflection of the sanctuary of Bethel on the status of the Temple in Jerusalem, reflect the standpoint of P and the Chronicler. This matter suggests to Jepsen a third redaction, called by him 'the Levitical redaction'.[a] He plausibly takes this to reflect the Levitical protest against the degradation of the order proposed by such programmes as that in Ezek. 44.9ff. We are less convinced by his view[b] that this redaction reflects antipathy to the renewed claims of a revived sanctuary at Bethel after 516, which is, of course, pure conjecture.

TREATMENT OF SOURCES

The Deuteronomistic compiler handled various older sources, generally most faithfully. His subject and his theology, however, determined his selection of sources. Some of these were admitted into his work virtually as they stood; others were used selectively. Deuteronomistic comment and interpretation is added, but in such a way as to leave little doubt as to what is source and what is editorial comment.

PRINCIPLES OF SELECTION AND TREATMENT OF SOURCES: CULTIC ORTHODOXY

The major interests of the Deuteronomistic compiler are at once obvious, namely, first, cultic orthodoxy according to principles familiar in the Book of Deuteronomy, centred in the Temple in Jerusalem, as the criterion of fidelity to the will of God for Israel, secondly, the fulfilment of the word of God in prophecy, and thirdly, divine retribution occasioned by infidelity to Deuteronomistic orthodoxy, foreshadowed by the curses in the sacrament of the renewal of the covenant in the ancient tribal amphictyony (Deut. 27–28) and later in prophecy. This dominating theme occasions the selection of material from the various sources, and dictates the length and detail in which certain elements are treated. This gives a definite

[a]*Die Quellen des Königsbuches*, pp. 102ff.
[b]*Ibid.*, p. 104.

unity to Kings, which is the culmination of the Deuteronomistic presentation of the history of Israel in Palestine.[a]

In contrast to scanty treatment of certain themes of major importance from the point of view of secular history and in his sporadic citations of annalistic sources in such matters, the Deuteronomist expatiates on other themes of less importance from a strictly historical point of view. He omits reference, for instance, to anything in the first ten years of Josiah's reign and proceeds straight to the reformation, which he dates from his 18th year (II K. 22.3–23.28). Important political events in the history of Western Asia involving Egypt and Babylon are mentioned in 23.29 simply because, incidentally, they involved the death of the reformer Josiah (vv. 29f.), whose motives, to be sure, in opposing Necho at Megiddo are not mentioned. Here we detect one of the main interests of the Deuteronomistic compiler. He is interested in cultic orthodoxy according to those principles which conditioned the reformation of Josiah and which the Book of Deuteronomy emphasizes. Notable instances of adherence to those principles occasion lengthy treatment, as in the case of Hezekiah (II K. 18–20), though the length at which his reign is treated is largely owing to the incorporation of sources on which the compiler of the traditions of Isaiah of Jerusalem also drew. On the other hand, notable instances of aberration from Deuteronomic orthodoxy occasion similar treatment at length, the most notable instance being the reign of Manasseh (II K. 21.1–18), where nothing at all is said of the most important political aspect of his reign, his personal involvement in Assyrian politics in Egypt, which we know only through Assyrian annals. It is this principle of retribution for aberration from Deuteronomic orthodoxy that conditioned the particular presentation of the reign of Solomon; the disorders of his reign, the revolts of Edom (I K. 11.14–22), Damascus (vv. 23–25), and Jeroboam (vv. 26–40), whatever their sources, being presented as the consequence of his tolerance of alien cults (ch. 11). The disruption of the kingdom (ch. 12) merits similar treatment at comparative length not merely because of its significance in the politics of Israel, but mainly because it emphasizes the principle of retribution on Solomon's defection from Deuteronomic principles and from the moral obligations of the Davidic covenant (II Sam. 7.12ff.), which is another recurrent theme in the Deuteronomistic compilation (I K. 11.32–39). The reign of Jeroboam, though such matters of

[a]So Noth, *Überlieferungsgeschichtliche Studien*, pp. 100–10.

political significance as his actual relation with Egypt and his constitutional relationship to the various elements in Israel are entirely ignored, is dealt with at length (12.25–14.20) because of his violation of Deuteronomic principles in patronizing the cults at Dan and Bethel, a baneful legacy which, in the eyes of the Deuteronomist, he bequeathed to all his successors on the throne of Israel, whose disasters until the final calamity were regarded as its consequences. This conditions the comparatively lengthy treatment of the final collapse of the Northern kingdom (II K. 17.4–23), and the sequel (vv. 24–41), where the new cult at Bethel owes its place and prominence to the dominating ecclesiastical interest of the Deuteronomist.

The decline and fall of Judah, probably a matter of personal experience to the compiler, is presented also as retribution for infidelity to Deuteronomic principles of orthodoxy, being anticipated by the stigma which Judah shared with Israel in II K. 17.19f., though this passage is from the exilic redactor rather than from the pre-exilic compiler (see p. 8).

PROPHECY AND FULFILMENT

In the unusually lengthy treatment of the reign of Jeroboam I another guiding principle in the method of the Deuteronomistic compiler emerges, namely the interest in the fulfilment of the word of God in prophecy. The steady decline and final ruin of Israel is presented as according to the divine economy. No doubt the incident of Ahijah's acclamation of Jeroboam (I K. 11.29ff.), with its fulfilment in 12.1–20, was treated at length because the tradition was already found by the Deuteronomist in an independent prophetic source, and because it represented the extent of native Israelite opposition to Solomon, but the passage as it stands, with its peculiar style, language, and thought, emphasizing the moral obligations of the Davidic covenant, is indisputably Deuteronomistic. The incident, we feel, was elaborated by the Deuteronomist in anticipation of the defection and final ruin of Israel according to the word of God. This also plainly determines the Deuteronomist's selection and elaboration of the activity of Ahijah (I K. 14.1–18) and an unnamed prophet (13.1–10) in the sequel. This theme of prophecy and fulfilment gives coherence to the Deuteronomistic presentation of the history of Israel through the dynasties of Jeroboam I (especially I K. 15.27–30), Baasha (especially 16.1–14), and Omri, and it is significant for the standpoint of the Deuteronomist that it is only as subsidiary to this theme that he condescends to introduce historical details in the various *coups d'état* of the usurpers, as Noth points out.[a] The disorders, decline, and final fall of the house of Omri are represented as the consequence of defection from Deuteronomic standards in the tolerance of the Baal-cult under the influence of Jezebel and her family (II K. 9), hence the prominence given to the famous trial by ordeal on Carmel (I K. 18) and to the dramatic extirpation of the Canaanite fertility cult by Jehu (II K. 10.18–28). Again the Deuteronomist, out of respect to the prophet as the representative of the native Israelite tradition over against the fertility cult, incorporates a substantial amount of the Elijah saga, some of it simply to ennace the authority of the prophet, e.g. I K. 17, as the final v. 24 indicates: 'Now do I know that you are a man of God and that the word of Yahweh in your mouth is truth.' Thus introduced, the prophet leads the attack on Baalism (ch. 18), and in the context of his protest against the absolution of Ahab in the affair of Naboth's vineyard, a corollary of his tolerance of the amoral cult of Baal, Elijah utters his famous oracle on Ahab and his house (21.19ff., with variation in vv. 23 and 24). This, with its fulfilment in the revolt of Jehu (II K. 9.7–10, 26, 30–37), gives coherence to the account of the dynasty of Omri, though the unity is disrupted by other variations on the theme of prophetic opposition to the house of Omri (e.g. I K. 20.35–43) and prophecy and fulfilment, e.g. the incident of Micaiah ben Imlah (I K. 22.2ff.). Other matter from prophetic saga, especially the passages concerning Elisha in II K. 2–7; 8.7–14; 9.1ff., which seems less relevant to the Deuteronomistic presentation of history, secured a place, possibly by mere attraction to the major prophetic theme, but possibly in order to enhance the authority of the prophet. The eclipse of Israelite power by Hazael (II K. 10.32; 13.3ff.), a decisive step to final ruin, is seen as the object of prophetic foresight (II K. 8.7–15), which is treated at the length we expect the Deuteronomist to treat such a theme, and the rally of Israel culminating in the glorious reign of Jeroboam II, regarded by the Deuteronomist as an interval of respite merely, is heralded by a word of God from the prophet Elisha (13.14–19), to which the Deuteronomist gives due prominence, together with an oracle by the prophet Jonah, the son of Amittai (14.23–27). Another motable instance where the Deuteronomist expatiates is the reign of Hezekiah, where his treatment is conditioned partly by the tradition of the meritorious orthodoxy of Hezekiah

[a] *Überlieferungsgeschichtliche Studien*, pp. 74f.

(II K. 18.4–7) and partly by his association with the prophet Isaiah, whose word of encouragement was fulfilled in the survival of Jerusalem. It is characteristic of the Deuteronomistic treatment, however, that of the various significant political incidents of Hezekiah's eventful reign, only one (possibly the telescoping of two) is selected for full treatment (II K. 18.13–19.34), being incorporated from a source shared with the Book of Isaiah. The incident of Hezekiah's sickness and that of the Babylonian embassy (20.1–19) have been incorporated with the previous passage, mainly owing to the prophecy of the exile to Babylon (vv. 17f).

INTEREST IN JERUSALEM AND THE TEMPLE

In this incident we discern another of the major themes of the Deuteronomist, which determines his selection of material from his sources and the length of his treatment of it, namely that of the significance of Jerusalem as the place chosen by God as the site of the Temple. Anything concerning the Temple and Jerusalem as the seat of Yahweh tends to be treated at a disproportionate length, to the exclusion of what seem to us more important political issues.

This is particularly marked in the Deuteronomist's arrangement and treatment of matter concerning the reign of Solomon, which begins properly with the legitimization of Solomon's succession in the dream of Gibeon (I K. 3.4–15). In the seven chapters devoted to Solomon's reign by far the most important single theme is his building of the Temple (6.1–38) and its furnishing (7.13–51) and dedication (ch. 8). In comparison with this single sustained theme other matter is introduced almost sporadically and dealt with comparatively briefly. Much of it, indeed, is presented as subsidiary to the description of the building and furnishing of the Temple. By contrast to 38 verses in which the building of the Temple is described (6.1–38), verses (7.1–12) suffice for the notice of all the other buildings of Solomon in Jerusalem; the metal-work in the Temple is described in detail (7.13–51), but though the other buildings and the palace were also no doubt filled with similar works and *objets d'art*, only passing notice is taken of the amount of gold in the shields in the House of the Forest of Lebanon (I K. 10.16f.), a general reference is made to the drinking vessels of gold (10.21), and three verses (10.18–20) describe the throne of ivory and gold. The relations between Solomon and Hiram of Tyre and the organization of forced labour in Israel occupy a chapter indeed (ch. 5), but not because of their inherent political significance in the reign of Solomon, but simply because of their relation to the major theme of the building of the Temple.

Again, in any matter derogatory to the status of the Temple as the sole seat of Yahweh we find the same tendency to expatiate, as in Jeroboam's adaptation of the cult of Yahweh at Bethel and Dan (II K. 12.28–33), the unforgivable sin for the Deuteronomist, and the prophetic denunciation of the Bethel-cult (13.1–10), with its sequel (vv. 11–32). The cultic innovations of Ahaz are noted at length (II K. 16.10–18). The appropriation of Temple treasure for war-indemnity never fails to be recorded, e.g. by Shishak (I K. 14.26–28), Asa (15.18), Jehoash (II K. 12.18), Amaziah (14.14), Hezekiah (18.16), and Nebuchadrezzar (24.13; 25.13–17). The same interest explains the length at which Jehoash's reform of Temple finance (II K. 12.4–16 [5–17]) is treated; we may contrast the scanty reference to Hazael's invasion of Judah (vv. 17[18]f.). For such matter a Temple history has been postulated, and there may well have been such a work based on Temple archives, on which the Deuteronomist drew. In view of the critical attitude to the priesthood in the account of Jehoash's reform of Temple finance (II K. 12.4–16 [5–17]) and the wider interest in the constitution (II K. 11.1–12, 18b–20; 22; 23), this probably belongs to a literary history of the kingdom of Judah, though from priestly hands, the critical attitude to the establishment in Jehoash's time reflecting the Deuteronomists or their precursors. In the passage just cited we appreciate the wider perspective in contrast to the dominating ecclesiastical interest in the accounts of the appropriation of Temple resources for war indemnities, where this detail is presented at the expense of matters of major political importance.

SOURCES: THE STORY OF THE DAVIDIC SUCCESSION

Kings opens with an account of David's last days and the circumstances of Solomon's succession by the agency of Nathan the prophet and Zadok, who now under royal patronage had supplanted the old Levitical priesthood formerly invested in the family of Abiathar. The note in I K. 2.46, 'So was the kingdom established in the hand of Solomon', suggests that this was the end of a certain self-contained block of tradition, and its obvious connection with the court history of David in II Sam. 9–20 suggests that it belongs to the source which is generally designated in studies of Samuel as the Court History.

This affinity, recognized on grounds of style and content by Klostermann in his commentary on Samuel and Kings, and more recently the subject of a penetrating study by Rost, *Die Überlieferung von der Thronnachfolge Davids*, 1926, is now generally accepted. The theme of this work, implicit throughout, is almost certainly expressed in I K. 1.20 in the words of Bathsheba to David, 'The eyes of all Israel are upon you that you should tell them who shall sit upon the throne of my lord the king after him.' To this question Rost sees the final answer in I K. 2.46, 'and the kingship was established in the hand of Solomon', which almost certainly marks the conclusion of the source.

This source, however, though one of those which the compiler of Kings allowed to stand virtually untouched, has received certain accretions. The most notable of these is the final charge of David to Solomon (I K. 2.1–4), with the practical injunctions to eliminate certain adversaries (vv. 5–9), and the notice of David's death and the accession of Solomon (vv. 10–12). In the first of these passages the language and the conception of a written law of Moses as the norm of the king's conduct are obviously from the Deuteronomistic compiler. This is clearly indicated when we examine the content of the oracle of Nathan (II Sam. 7.12–16) to which this passage refers. There the emphasis is laid on general obedience of the king to Yahweh as father to son; whereas in I K. 2.3 the king's conduct must be governed by 'that which is written in the law of Moses'. The obituary on David conforms to the regular style of the Deuteronomistic editor in Kings, while the notice of the succession of Solomon anticipates the statement of the establishment of Solomon as king in I K. 2.46, thus impairing the dramatic effect of this last statement in the context of the work. This is quite out of character with such an artistic production, one of the chief features of which is the suspense in which the author holds the reader concerning the final solution of the problem of the succession. The passages I K. 2.1–4 and 10–12 at least are thus certainly secondary. The practical testament of David (vv. 5–9) must also be suspect in such a context, and it does seem odd that David, who is obviously in his dotage in the intrigue of Nathan and Bathsheba in ch. 1, should now evince such shrewd political interest and insight. These practical injunctions concerning Joab and Shimei, his own contemporaries, may reflect the fixations of an old man, or they may have been fathered on David by the author of the source in order to justify the decisive and somewhat unscrupulous action of Solomon. In either case they may well belong to the original source. There is more than a suspicion, however, that the passage has been worked over. The reason for the death of Joab (vv. 5, 31–33) seems rather specious, and does not really accord with the account of his death in vv. 28–30, where his action in seeking sanctuary indicated that he knew he was foredoomed for the part he had played in the abortive *coup* of Adonijah. The unity of I K. 2.5–46, moreover, is seriously impaired by the statement that 'Solomon's kingdom was firmly established' (2.12b), which ends vv. 5–9 on David's dying instructions, and by a summary after v. 35 of Solomon's wisdom and achievements in G (Swete, vv. 35a–o). 2.12b anticipates 2.46b, 'And the kingdom was firmly established in the hand of Solomon', which after Rost we regard as the dramatic conclusion of the Story of the Davidic Succession. So we agree with Noth[a] in regarding the passages on the elimination of Adonijah (I K. 2.13–25), Abiathar (vv. 26–35) and Shimei (vv. 36–46a) as a secondary elaboration of the Story of the Davidic Succession, probably by a younger contemporary and in the same style, and the passage on David's last instructions to Solomon (vv. 5–9) as secondary to that.

The question is raised by Rost[b] as to whether the work in II Sam. 9–20, I K. 1–2 is complete as it stands or is abbreviated by the compiler from a fuller work. Klostermann had already limited the work to the story of the elimination of Solomon's elder brothers, beginning in II Sam. 13, but had extended it to include the career of Solomon to I K. 9. We agree with Rost in seeing in I K. 2.46 the end of the work, the theme of which is not the career of Solomon but the question of the Davidic succession. Rost seems certainly right in carrying the source back to include the oracle of Nathan in II Sam. 7, and even further. The note on the barrenness of David's wife Michal the daughter of Saul in II Sam. 6.23, eliminating as it does any succession from Saul, agrees with the theme of this work and is possibly incorporated from the same source in the more extended form for which Rost argues. To this view von Rad has lent the weight of his support in his appraisal of this first and finest flowering of history-writing in Israel.[c] Rost's assumption, however, that the appropriation of the Nathan oracle of II Sam. 7.11b by Solomon as a personal revelation (I K. 2.24) indicates a part of the work omitted in Kings

[a] *Könige*, Biblischer Kommentar, 1964, *ad loc.*

[b] *Op. cit.*, pp. 104ff.

[c] 'Der Anfang der Geschichtsschreibung im alten Israel', *Gesammelte Studien*, 1958, pp. 148–88; ET in *The Problem of the Hexateuch and Other Essays*, 1966, pp. 166–204.

seems to us unwarranted, being readily explained on the grounds of the ancient Semitic conception of the solidarity of the family, which would make the oracle to David applicable to each and all of his descendants.[a] Actually we doubt if much of this work has been omitted by the compiler, particularly in Kings. The accretions to it are generally easily recognized, and the impression is that of a self-contained work of distinctive style, subject-matter and treatment, which is so convincingly authoritative as to invite speculation about the identity of the author with an eyewitness, a contemporary of David and Solomon.

The work has often been put in the category of the novel (Caspari, Gressmann, Eissfeldt), and there is no doubt that in the vivid depiction of character and episode, with the wealth of colourful, circumstantial detail, dramatic direct speech and striking imagery, there is the substance of the novel. There are also features of the epic with the leisurely unfolding of events and the emphasis gained through repetition. The *coup d'état* of Adonijah, for instance, is described four times over, once in the event (I K. 1.5–10), then in Nathan's instructions to Bathsheba (vv. 11–13), in Bathsheba's report to David (vv. 17–19), and finally in Nathan's confirmation of this (vv. 24–26). This is reminiscent of the epic style in the Ras Shamra texts. In the Baal-myth the question of a house for Baal is discussed several times over in the same language, and when it is decided to build the house details are mentioned which are similarly repeated in the description of the actual building. In the Krt legend the royal wooing is outlined in a dream before it is described in the same terms in the event, and similarly in the 'Aqht text the son the king desires is described three times: in supplication to El, in the birth of the son, and in the king's rejoicing. The author of our source in Kings was obviously familiar with this literary convention, probably through the art of the professional story-teller, who until recently was an age-long institution in the Near East. Rost has emphasized the significance of direct speech in this work. This lends life to characters, but it is further used specifically here to mark the culmination of episodes in the story, which, as scenes in a drama, are recapitulated in dialogue or report. That

[a]In this connection the divine authentication of Solomon's succession in his dream at Gibeon (I K. 3.4–15), based on the oracle of Nathan, may be considered as a possible extension of the Story of the Davidic Succession. We prefer, however, to regard this as the real introduction to the reign of Solomon and a reflection rather than an extension of the Story of the Davidic Succession, the oracle of Nathan here being really secondary. See further, pp 22f.

part of the work which is included in Kings, the report of Jonathan to Adonijah and his company at En Rogel (I K. 1.42–48), emphasizes the decisive nature of the step taken by Solomon, adds the information that it was by David's authority and hence was final, and so serves as the prelude to the account of the collapse of Adonijah's attempt. The author knows the value of suspense to heighten his dramatic effect, and the circumstantial detail of persons and places, while here probably indicating the eyewitness and contemporary, is also part of the equipment of the narrative artist. Indeed, all the dramatic technicalities of the work may be illustrated in the art of the Arab *rāwī*, or professional story-teller, as in ballad-literature in most languages. This being so, we are prepared to find historical detail rearranged with particular emphasis, or perhaps even omitted in the interest of dramatic effect. The fact, however, that the writer was a contemporary, and that through his association with the court he well appreciated the significance of the events he was describing means that the work was more than a novel; the sense of historical perspective is well preserved throughout. If facts are used selectively, they are selected according to their bearing on the major theme; the work is described by Rost[a] as that of a historian with artistic susceptibility, and, provided that it is understood as concerning a particular dynastic problem, it stands out as one of the finest examples of historical narrative in the Old Testament and, indeed, in the whole of antiquity.

The fact that it reveals no knowledge of the disruption of the kingdom almost certainly dates the work in the lifetime of Solomon, and the intimate detail strongly suggests a contemporary. More particularly the optimistic tone regarding the reign of Solomon and the complacency of the final statement that 'the kingship was established in the hand of Solomon' suggests that the work was completed in the early part of his reign before the disturbances in the latter part. The intimate account of the events and personalities suggests that the author was of the court circle, if not actually personally involved, and he has been the subject of conjecture. Duhm, followed more recently by Auerbach,[b] has suggested the priest Abiathar; but that is hardly likely in view of the obvious sympathy with Solomon, and the general humanistic, or secular, viewpoint of the work. We think it far more likely that Abiathar was the author, or at least the source,

[a] *Thronnachfolge Davids*, p. 127.
[b] *Wüste und gelobtes Land*, I, 1932, p. 34.

of the account of the adventures of David as an outlaw from Saul, in which Abiathar was personally involved as the bearer of the ephod, which plays such an important part in that tradition. The conjecture of Klostermann is much more probable that the author was Ahimaaz the son of Zadok, who was personally involved with David in his flight from Absalom (II Sam. 15.36; 18.19ff.), and was probably the same person as the prefect in the district of Naphtali in Solomon's administration, and who was a son-in-law of the king (I K. 4.15). He, however, was probably too young in the reign of Solomon, in view of the practical, didactic nature of the work. Nathan may have composed the work as a justification of the role he played in sponsoring the claims of the young Solomon, his protégé, over against those of his older brothers and, in portraying the life and character of David in his strength and weakness, to instruct Solomon in the perils and duties of a ruler. Only such as he could have used such freedom in the treatment of David, particularly in the origin of Solomon from the union of David and Bathsheba after the discreditable affair of Uriah the Hittite, for which Nathan castigated David, and the harem intrigue which set Solomon on the throne. The broad moral principle which unifies the whole work may be represented, as von Rad[a] maintains, after J. Hempel,[b] as that of natural retribution. David's immorality with Bathsheba brings its own nemesis, first in Amnon's rape of Tamar, then in Absalom's bloody vengeance for his sister, and then in Absalom's violation of the sanctity of the harem of David 'before the eyes of all Israel', a sin which, at least technically and in intention, was the final undoing of Adonijah. The criticism of David, which is thus implicit throughout, is natural from Nathan in view of the role he played in the affair of Uriah and Bathsheba, or at least from one of his age and authority at court.

The humanism of this work has often been emphasized. Action is not determined by *deus ex machina* through the medium of miracle or charismatic leaders, but by human propensities and character. This, standing in marked contrast to the tone of the J narrative in the Pentateuch, which, though not, to be sure, disregarding such motivation of events, emphasizes direct divine intervention, a feature also of the sagas of the judges, is surely a reflection of the wider cultural contacts and the secularization of Solomon's reign, in which the work must surely be dated. The humanistic tone of this not insub-

[a]*Gesammelte Studien*, pp. 179ff.; *The Problem of the Hexateuch*, pp. 176ff.
[b]*Das Ethos des Alten Testaments*, BZAW LXVII, 1938, p. 51.

stantial part of Samuel and Kings is a potent argument against the view of Hölscher[a] that the J source of the Pentateuch is continued in Kings to the disruption of the kingdom at I K. 12.19. We admit that the sagas of Elijah and Elisha, in which Benzinger, Smend, and Hölscher find the E sources of the Pentateuch, were not uninfluenced by the contemporary literary crystallization of the E tradition, and we are disposed to admit similar influence of J in the Story of the Davidic Succession. The part of J and E in the Books of Kings is, however, in our opinion, limited to this general literary influence. While we should emphasize the humanistic tone of the story we should not forget that it is informed throughout by a deep faith in Providence, and is theologically much more mature and realistic than any other source in Kings, not excluding the Deuteronomistic compilation and redaction. Here the opinion of von Rad[b] is worth recording, that the great theological contribution of the author of the first literary history in the literature of the world was that he emphasized the working of God not through direct intervention, miracle, special agents, human or supernatural, nor through sacred institutions, but through ordinary personalities and their individual idiosyncrasies in the secular sphere, where every man has his part to play.

Owing to artistic embellishment, such as the private conversations with colourful figures which are a marked feature of the work, it is not altogether easy to assess the historical worth of its material, the more so as the events described are not attested elsewhere. R. N. Whybray[c] has in fact rightly emphasized that, with the exception of the passage on the Ammonite war in II Sam. 10.1–19; 11.1; 12.26–31, which is incidental to the episode of David and Bathsheba, the mother of Solomon, there is practically no reference to the international affairs of the important reign of David, while the internal situation, which conditioned the vicissitudes of the house of David which the work describes, is left to be inferred rather than explicated. Nevertheless, the vivid portrayal of the *dramatis personae* in the critical junctures of the eventual establishment of David's dynasty under Solomon, e.g. in the revolt of Absalom, suggests a contemporary. This shrewd ability to assess character and motive is evidence of historical insight, and, if the work lacks the wider perspective of the

[a]'Das Buch der Könige, seine Quellen und seine Redaktion', *Eucharisterion* (Gunkel Festschrift), I, 1923, pp. 158ff.

[b]*Gesammelte Studien*, p. 188; *Problem*, p. 204.

[c]R. N. Whybray, *The Succession Narrative: A Study of II Sam. 9–20 and I Kings 1 and 2*, 1968, pp. 11–19.

international situation and important internal issues of David's eventful reign, this is less a defect than the natural consequence of the limited objective of the author, the question of the succession.

As to the purpose of the work, most engaging as it is, this is not mere entertainment, despite the essential features of a novel or drama. Its limited historical perspective relates it to the constitutional issue of dynastic succession as a crucial issue in Israel, where, as it proved, the majority still held to the tradition of the charismatic leadership of an individual designated by a prophet in the name of God and popularly acclaimed. The Succession Narrative in fact expresses the same concern in this vital issue as the oracle of Nathan in II Sam. 7.12ff. and, as S. Herrmann has suggested,[a] the tradition of Solomon's dream at Gibeon and the divine promise of wisdom, in which the successor of David, already appointed, is invested with the charisma in virtue of the evidence of his wisdom according to the tradition of leadership in Israel. The oracle of Nathan, however, probably reflects the creation of a mystique of dynastic authority, which was to be propagated in the official cult (cf. Pss. 89.28ff. [29ff.]; 132.11ff.); the dream at Gibeon (I K. 3.4–15) may be the adaptation of the Egyptian 'Königsnovelle', the narrative of a theophany to authenticate royal authority, often followed by a freely composed historical narrative by way of vindication. This we conceive to be a popular justification of the accession of Solomon. The psychological maturity and masterly art of the Story of the Davidic Succession, however, and the penetrating analysis of human character and motives and their consequences suggest that the work came from the hand of one interested in empirical morality studied and taught for practical purposes in the training of a ruling class[b] as in Egypt.

Such a work might have been written by a royal tutor of Solomon, designed for the instruction and admonition of the young ruler. It could conceivably have been the work of Nathan, who had a peculiar interest in Solomon, but it is more likely to have been the work of an official tutor of the royal family of wider cultural interest. The intimate picture of court life and particularly of the life of David may indicate a senior member of his family, but the psychological and

[a]S. Herrmann, 'Die Königsnovelle in Ägypten und Israel', *Wissenschaftliche Zeitschrift der Karl Marx-Universität Leipzig* III, 1953–4, pp. 51–62.

[b]Whybray, *op. cit.*, pp. 56ff., supports this thesis by citing the emphasis on practical 'wisdom' (*ḥokmā*), the themes of sin and retribution and the ultimate divine control of human destiny, sometimes in accord with, and sometimes in despite of, human activity and intention.

literary maturity of the work stamps it as from a professional tutor well versed in moral philosophy and probably in the international wisdom tradition, particularly Egyptian, as Whybray suggests.[a] The great responsibility of the tutor's office as one who stood *in loco parentis* would explain the extraordinary frankness which does not spare David's delinquencies, though in this he may have been supported by the authority of the prophet Nathan.

THE LEGITIMIZATION OF SOLOMON'S SUCCESSION: THE DREAM AT GIBEON

The second section, describing the reign of Solomon, is prefaced by the account of his dream at the sanctuary of Gibeon (I K. 3.4–15). This seems at first sight to be no more than an introduction to the wisdom of Solomon, which, in its various aspects, is the theme of the sequel, at least until ch. 10. It probably has a greater significance as an independent source. Herrmann has noted the affinities of the thought-sequence in this passage with a definite literary type found in Egyptian inscriptions where the Pharaohs from the Middle Kingdom to the New Empire introduce accounts of their innovations and exploits by an account of special revelation, often in a dream, where the reign of the Pharaoh and his immediate policy are legitimized by the assurance of divine election before his birth or while he was still very young. By the same convention the extraordinary accession of Solomon is legitimized.[b] The judges in ancient Israel, Saul, and David had been raised to authority by general acclaim or consent inspired by their obvious possession of the *b^erākā* or divine blessing, manifested in their ability to govern (*šāpaṭ*). Similar ability to govern (*šāpaṭ*) and to make decisions and guide them to a successful issue (*ḥokmā*), of which Solomon had given no evidence, is here represented as being given by special divine assurance and grace. Within the framework of this divine authentication a further appeal is made to the divine covenant with David, which guaranteed the foundation of a dynasty, implemented in the accession of Solomon (I K. 2.46). The Story of the Davidic Succession, of which this is the theme, would have itself have been sufficient authentication of Solomon's succession.[c] Hence I K. 3.4–15, which authenticates Solomon's

[a]*Op. cit.*, pp. 96ff.

[b]So also G. Fohrer, 'Der Vertrag zwischen König und Volk in Israel', *ZAW* LXXI, 1959, p. 7.

[c]Noth, 'Die Gesetze im Pentateuch', *Gesammelte Studien*, 1957, pp. 27ff., ET

accession by the convention of special endowment assured through the dream-revelation, though incorporating the conception of the Davidic covenant, seems an independent introduction to the reign of Solomon. This may have been the introduction to an independent account of the reign proper as distinct from the accession, which, as the conclusion of the Story of the Davidic Succession, where the conception of the Davidic covenant as sufficient legitimization of Solomon is properly at home, obviously terminates with the words 'thus was the kingship established in the hand of Solomon' in I K. 2.46. The conception of the Davidic covenant in I K. 3.4–15, though we regard it as secondary to the main theme, is complementary to that rather than contradictory.

OTHER SOURCES AND TREATMENT OF THE REIGN OF SOLOMON

The sequel in I K. 3.16–11.43 describes the reign of Solomon and the building of the Temple and palace-complex in Jerusalem, and contains various traditions of his reign, the relevance of which to history, and particularly to the Deuteronomistic interpretation of history, is not always easy to determine. In virtue of the miscellaneous matter here it is unlikely that we are dealing with a self-contained work. Apart from the technical account of the building of the Temple, which bulks so large in the account of the reign of Solomon (I K. 6.2–7.51) and which is doubtless drawn ultimately from Temple archives, a source fuller than the others on which the compiler drew here was probably 'the Acts of Solomon' (I K. 11.41). This reference ought particularly to be noted, 'And the rest of the acts of Solomon and all that he did, *and his wisdom*, are they not written in the book of the acts of Solomon?' It may be that 'his wisdom' means the success which was the fruit of Solomon's practical administrative sagacity, for the Hebrew *ḥokmā* may have this connotation. In view of the content of the account of Solomon's reign in Kings, however, it is unlikely that this exhausts the meaning of 'wisdom'. The statement suggests that the source was more than an annalistic or strictly historical record of the reign of Solomon,[a] but

The Laws in the Pentateuch and Other Essays, 1966, p. 16, emphasizes the legitimization of Solomon's accession through the Davidic covenant, without apparently appreciating this significance of the passage concerning the dream at Gibeon, though he comes very near to this in his note on p. 27.

[a]This is further suggested by the absence of all dates of events in Solomon's reign except for the building of the Temple and palace, where an archival source is most probably used in I K. 6.1b.

included instances, both anecdotal and reported sayings, no doubt, of the reputed wisdom of Solomon, such as, for instance, the celebrated story of the judgement between the two women who claimed the same child (I K. 3.16–28). The fact that a similar instance occurs as an Indian folk-tale may indicate that here we have an instance of miscellaneous wisdom anecdotes collected by the authority of Solomon, whose trading ventures down the Red Sea brought so many foreign novelties to Jerusalem. There is much of this nature in this section, e.g. the visit of the Queen of Sheba (I K. 10.1–13), and the rest of ch. 10 describing the fabulous wealth and magnificence of the king. This reads less like annals or history than saga, and it may well be that there was a Solomon-saga; but it is uncertain how far this coincided with the Book of the Acts of Solomon cited in I K. 11.41. In view of the civil service of Solomon (I K. 4.2ff.), there must certainly have been state archives of his reign which recorded the administrative organization of the realm, as in I K. 4.2–19, 22f., 26–28 [5.2f., 6–8], but the extent to which these were incorporated, if at all, in the Acts of Solomon is uncertain. Such matters would come into the category of annals or *dibᵉrē hayyāmīm*, and it may not be irrelevant to note here that the Book of the Acts of Solomon (*sēper dibᵉrē šᵉlōmō*) seems wider in connotation, a saga of Solomon rather than an official 'daily record' or chronicle. Official archives of Solomon's reign would certainly contain a description of his building including the Temple, though the description of the Temple and its furnishing in I K. 6; 7.13–51 is possibly elaborated from a more detailed description from Temple archives.

In this section the hand of the Deuteronomist is more in evidence than in I K. 1–2. In describing Solomon's experience at Gibeon, which was a notable pre-Israelite sanctuary, for instance, the editor mentions that 'Solomon loved Yahweh, walking in the statutes of David his father; only he sacrificed and burned incense in high places', thereby asserting the well-known Deuteronomic principle that the only legitimate sanctuary was at Jerusalem. Solomon's speech at the dedication of the Temple is also heavily impregnated with Deuteronomic language and ideas (I K. 8.14ff.). The hand of the exilic redactor is particularly evident in this passage in vv. 44–51, where the Exile is visualized as the chastisement for national sin. The same is true of the divine response to Solomon in I K. 9.1–9, where the confirmation of the Nathan oracle (vv. 3–5) is from the pre-exilic Deuteronomistic compiler, and vv. 6–9, which visualize the

Exile, from the exilic Deuteronomistic redactor. The introduction to the disorders of Solomon's reign, which are presented as the consequence of his liberalism in religion and later apostasy (I K. 11.1–13), and the note on the Nathan oracle in the light of the disruption (I K. 11.32b–39), with the obituary on Solomon (vv. 41–43), are also from the Deuteronomistic compiler.

This section, which is mainly composed of the Acts of Solomon and annals of his reign selected and arranged with comment first by the Deuteronomistic compiler, and then retouched by the exilic redactor with the same viewpoint, with other sources to be considered in more detail in the critical introduction to individual sections in our commentary, presents a number of textual problems. In G^B the order varies from the MT at the following points: 4.17–5.18 [32]; 6; 7; 9.15–22; 10.23–29; 11.3–8; and after 12.24. In these variations, G is somewhat fuller than the MT. This points to a certain fluidity in the tradition, which was not yet finally fixed by the third or second century BC, when Ben Sirach attests the Prophets as canonical Scripture.

SOURCES AND TREATMENT OF THE HISTORY OF THE DIVIDED MONARCHY

The third section of the Books of Kings (I K. 12–II K. 17) describes the disruption of the kingdom after the death of Solomon, for which the ground is prepared in I K. 11, which is very critical of Solomon. In this section the framework of Kings is most obvious. The main pattern here is a description of such events as suited the purpose of the Deuteronomistic compiler from this history of the now divided kingdoms of Israel and Judah. The fortunes of Israel in a certain reign are thus followed, then the contemporary history of Judah is given in outline, always with a slight overlap. Stereotyped formulae give clear indication of the editing of the work. The reign of each king of Israel is introduced by a note of his accession according to the regnal year of his Judaean contemporary; the length of his reign is then noted, and finally judgement is passed on him, the norm being Deuteronomic orthodoxy. All the kings of Israel are roundly condemned for walking 'in the ways of Jeroboam the son of Nebat who made Israel to sin'. Fuller information is given in corresponding formulae which introduce and conclude the reigns of the kings of Judah. In the introduction, beside the synchronism of his accession with the regnal year of his Israelite contemporary, the length of his reign, and judgement on it, the king's age is given at his accession, or, as we believe, at his designation as heir-apparent,[a] and his mother's name and home is noted, which was, of course, of interest, in view of the status of the queen-mother as first lady in the realm and since the kings of Judah were polygamous. In the closing formula we are referred to other sources of information on the reigns of the kings of Israel and Judah, a significant note, which clearly indicates that what we have before us does not pretend to be an exhaustive objective history. Further we are told of the king's burial and the name of his successor.[b] As on the kings of Israel, so judgement was summarily passed on the kings of Judah, the norm of judgement being their devotion to the central shrine of Jerusalem as the only legitimate sanctuary and their attitude to the provincial 'high places', a sure characteristic of the Deuteronomistic circle.

ANNALISTIC SOURCES

In this section there are certain clear traces of the sources which the Deuteronomistic compiler used so selectively. There are the Annals, or Books of the Chronicles of the Kings of Israel and of Judah, independent bodies of annals, or works based on these, and, of course, written sources. Eissfeldt thinks of these as literary compositions based on actual annals and circulated for private reading. They may, however, have been copies or digests of the actual annals, officially circulated to maintain the royal authority, as Darius's Behistun inscription was circulated in the provinces of the Persian Empire as far as Upper Egypt, as we know from an Aramaic copy in the Elephantine papyri. Jepsen[c] postulates a synchronistic chronicle which may be reconstructed almost completely from introductions to reigns of the kings of Israel and Judah to the time of Hezekiah, with short notices of main events in their reigns. This was, he supposes, a Judaean work designed to contrast the permanence of the Davidic dynasty with the instability of the dynasties in Northern Israel. Jepsen's main argument is unity of vocabulary, style, and

[a]See p. 57 below.

[b]Exceptions for obvious reasons are the lack of a concluding formula in the case of Joram of Israel and Ahaziah of Judah, who were killed by Jehu (I K. 9.24, 27), and of Hoshea of Israel and Jehoahaz, Jehoiachin and Zedekiah of Judah, who were removed by their suzerains. In the case of the usurping queen Athaliah, whose death is described at length in II K. 11, there is neither introductory nor concluding formula.

[c]*Die Quellen des Königsbuches*, 1953, pp. 30–40.

substance. This, however, may just as well be the mark of the Deuteronomistic compiler. The historical details, such as the names of the queen-mothers of Judah, which Jepsen rightly takes to point to a written source, and notes of the main historical events, are just as likely to be summarized by the compiler from the annals of both kingdoms as to be the work of Jepsen's assumed chronicler. It is true that the Babylonian Chronicle takes note of contemporary events and dates in neighbouring countries, but this analogy, far from supporting Jepsen's theory of a synchronistic chronicle in Judah, rather suggests that the synchronisms in Kings were a feature of the respective annals of Israel and Judah.

Fohrer[a] objects that a synchronistic chronicle of Judaean origin such as is assumed by Jepsen would not have been characterized by chronological discrepancy as Kings seems to be. If, however, we assume that Jepsen's synchronistic chronicle was itself a composite work composed from annalistic sources, from both kingdoms, where the kings of Judah generally acceded officially at the New Year Festival after the death of their predecessor and the kings of Israel generally immediately, and assume further 'partisan dating' (see below, p. 67) in the Israelite source, Fohrer's argument has less force. A more serious objection to Jepsen's theory of a Judaean synchronistic chronicle from the end of the eighth century BC is the author's occasional confusion of the annalistic note of a king's adoption as heir apparent and co-regent with his father and his accession as sole king (see below, p. 57). This mistake is most unlikely in the case of a compiler during the monarchy, when the convention of co-regency was familiar, and is much more likely after the fall of the monarchy.

Besides his synchronistic chronicle, Jepsen would see a composite annalistic work of a single author, who, he supposes, was a priest in the time of Manasseh. This he supposes to have been combined with the synchronistic chronicle by priestly redactors in Palestine about 580 BC. Here there is more substance in Fohrer's objection[b] that the specific mention of various historical sources fuller than the annals and their partial, but often extensive, incorporation in Kings militates against the theory of a self-contained annalistic source for which Jepsen contends. In view of the continuance of annalistic matter and historical narrative beyond the terminus of Jepsen's annalistic source to the end of the monarchy, it is difficult to subscribe

[a]Sellin-Fohrer, *Introduction*, p. 229. [b]*Ibid.*

to this theory. In our opinion, the summary references to historical events, drawn from the annals of both kingdoms, and the unity of subject-matter and vocabulary, are more probably due to the Deuteronomistic compiler. Jepsen's view, in fact, remains an interesting hypothesis, but nevertheless one which as yet wants conclusive proof, and the most probable view is that the general synchronism, as the introductions and epilogues to the several reigns indicate, was the work of the Deuteronomistic compiler.

There are indications that these annals, like those of Assyria and Babylon, were dry and factual, as is suggested by the abrupt way in which concise notes of certain events are introduced, e.g. the invasion of Tiglath-pileser III (II K. 15.19), often with dates, e.g. 'In the fifth year of King Rehoboam came Shishak King of Egypt' (I K. 14.25), etc. Such matter, communicated in a series of asyndetic clauses, is often introduced by the adverb 'then' (*'āz*), which Montgomery[a] has recognized as a feature of the annalistic style, or by 'in his days' or 'in that day', which generally introduces a specific event. Such events are frequently introduced asyndetically by the pronoun 'he' (*hū'*), 'he it was who . . .', which reflects the style of inscriptions of the type 'I am he who . . .', e.g. those of Mesha, Azitawadd, and various Aramaic inscriptions from Northern Syria. A. van den Born[b] suggests that one source of this matter was inscriptions. But nothing of the kind has so far been found in Palestine to bear this out. He argues that if historical inscriptions were found in small states like Moab it is much more likely that there were royal inscriptions of comparable length and content in Israel and Judah. That, in our opinion, does not follow, since in these more mature and stable states, particularly in Judah, written archives and annals for local circulation may well have taken the place of monumental inscriptions, though these are not excluded. Such fuller sources were likely to be used by the compiler of Kings rather than the hypothetical inscriptions.

SOURCES FOR THE HISTORY OF THE HOUSE OF AHAB

In this section, in the account of the reign of Ahab, the Syrian wars during and after his reign, and the fall of his house in the revolt of Jehu, the narrative is suddenly expansive and circumstantial. The explanation is twofold.

[a]'Archival Data in the Book of Kings', *JBL* LIII, 1934, pp. 46–52.
[b]*Koningen uit de grondtext vertaald en uitgelegd*, 1958, p. 9.

SAGAS OF ELIJAH AND ELISHA

First a large body of saga had gathered about two great prophetic figures, Elijah and Elisha, the former the contemporary of Ahab and the latter, according to a tradition (II K. 9.1ff.) which there is no reason to doubt, the inspiration of the revolt of Jehu. The involvement of both in affairs of state, especially in the case of Elijah, who opposed the king in a major religious and social crisis in the national history, accounts for the fullness in which the Deuteronomistic compiler cites such sources of prophetic tradition. In certain passages the prophets play a major role in historical and social crises, e.g. I K. 18 (the ordeal on Carmel), ch. 19 (Elijah at Horeb, anticipating the commissioning of Elisha and prophetic support for the forces of opposition to the house of Omri, which were to find a leader in Jehu), ch. 21 (Naboth's vineyard), perhaps II K. 8.7–15 (Elisha and the *coup d'état* of Hazael of Damascus), and 9.1–6 (Elisha and the *coup d'état* of Jehu). Such passages might well be part of a genuine historical work, though the role of the prophet and the bias against the monarchy indicates prophetic authority of sobriety and reliability. We shall deal with this matter much more fully in our commentary, but we may state our view meanwhile that the passages of this type concerning Elijah owe their character to the fact that they were transmitted by his contemporary Elisha, while such matter concerning Elisha as we have cited, together with II K. 6.24–7.20 (Elisha at the siege of Samaria), and 13.14–19 (Elisha's encouragement of the king of Israel on his deathbed), stem from a mature prophetic authority associated personally with Elisha, probably in Samaria.

HAGIOLOGY OF ELIJAH AND ELISHA

Together with this matter, which is of real historical value, there is included in the record of the times, solely on grounds of contemporaneity, a mass of prophetic tradition concerning Elijah and Elisha of quite a different order. These are reminiscences of a more personal nature, e.g. I K. 17 (Elijah miraculously (?) fed in famine), II K. 1 (Elijah calls down fire upon the emissaries of Ahaziah), 2.19–22 (Elisha and the water of Jericho), vv. 23–25 (Elisha and the children of Bethel), 4.1–7 (Elisha and the widow's oil), 4.8–37 (Elisha and the Shunammite's son), 4.38–41 (death in the pot), 4.42–44 (Elisha and the multiplication of food), 6.1–7 (Elisha and the floating axe), 6.8–23 (Elisha and the blinding of the Syrians), and perhaps ch. 5

(the healing of Naaman). Most of these incidents are quite trivial and indicate an authority of little discrimination. They are, in the case of Elisha, associated for the most part with prophetic, or dervish, communities of various localities, and it is possible to see a certain local rivalry in claiming association with the great prophet. This is the breeding-ground of miracle, and it is noteworthy that here, in contrast to the first group of traditions of the prophets, miracles abound. The conclusion is then suggested that in the second group of traditions concerning Elijah and particularly Elisha the source is a concatenation of local hagiology, or folk-lore of the prophets.

PROPHETIC ADAPTATION OF HISTORICAL NARRATIVE

The second notable expansion of the narrative in this section of Kings concerns the Syrian wars in which the kings of Israel were engaged (I K. 20.1–34, ending with a prophetic anecdote, vv. 35–43, and 22.1–37), the Moabite campaign of Jehoram the son of Ahab, (II K. 3.4ff.), the famine in Samaria and the defeat of Benhadad (6.24–7.20), the *coup d'état* of Jehu (9.1–10.27), and the last meeting of Elisha and King Joash (13.14–19). In the first two passages, a special source, 'the Acts of Ahab', has been conjectured.[a] This, however, is very doubtful, partly because the anonymous 'king of Israel' in chs. 20 and 22 was probably not originally Ahab, and partly because those are not historical narrative *simpliciter*, but historical narrative adapted by prophetic circles, to whom Ahab, as the opponent of Elijah, was the classical opponent of the will of Yahweh through the prophets, like Pharaoh in the Exodus tradition or Herod in English mystery plays. The fact, however, that this expansive historical narrative is not limited to events which occurred in Ahab's reign, but extends to the reign of his son Jehoram, and in the account of Jehu's revolt adopts quite a different attitude to Ahab and his house, suggests that there was much more of this historical narrative than the hypothetical 'Acts of Ahab'. Here, in fact, we may have a substantial fragment of a narrative history of the kingdom of Israel. This would presumably be from a period of security when a dynasty was relatively established and may have been begun under Ahab. The full description of the revolt of Jehu, however, indicates that if there was such an historical work it was continued under the house of Jehu, probably

[a]Oesterley and Robinson, *An Introduction to the Books of the Old Testament*, 1934, p. 97.

in the time of Jeroboam II. Whatever the origin of this matter, whether in historical narrative or in briefer annals, there may be other reasons for its fullness. First, it is noteworthy that I K. 20.1–34 leads up to the account of the prophetic rebuke of Ahab (vv. 35–43); the account of Ahab's campaign at Ramoth Gilead in ch. 22 may be regarded as an instance of prophecy and fulfilment; the account of Jehu's revolt may be regarded as an elaboration of the fulfilment of Elijah's prophecy on the doom of the house of Ahab and Jezebel, and the theme of prophecy and fulfilment in the famine and relief of Samaria (II K. 6.24–7.30) is dominant. Hence original historical or annalistic sources may well have been adapted and elaborated here by the more reputable prophetic authorities of the historical traditions of Elijah and Elisha and others. So adapted, this prophetic work probably comprised also the tradition of the encounter of Ahijah and Jeroboam in I K. 11.29ff.; 14.1ff., and that of the prophet Jehu and Baasha in I K. 16.1–4.

A significant feature of this historical narrative is the critical attitude to the kings of Israel from Jeroboam I to Jehoash maintained by prophets, and particularly the succession of oracles of doom on the successive dynasties. Those differ from the stereotyped and colourless Deuteronomistic condemnations of the various kings in their striking, and indeed coarse, imagery, declaring that none of the royal family who piss against the wall should be spared in the final reckoning (I K. 14.10; cf. 16.11; 21.21; II K. 9.8), and that whoever of them should die in the city would be eaten by dogs and whoever should die in the open country by the birds of the air (I K. 14.11; cf. 16.11; 21.24; II K. 9.10). Such an oracle of doom on the house of Baasha is attributed to the prophet Jehu, the son of Hanani (I K. 16.1–4, 12), to whom II Chron. 20.34 ascribes a book which it associates with historical records of North Israel. This may be the prophetic adaptation of historical narrative on the vicissitudes of the short-lived dynasties of North Israel, reflecting prophetic opposition to hereditary monarchy as against the traditional ideal of charismatic authority of those so marked out by obvious signs of God's favour (*b^erākā*) and popularly acclaimed by the sacral community, such opposition to the monarchy in fact as was voiced in Israel by the prophet Hosea. This was a source which accorded so well with the view of the Deuteronomistic historian that it could be incorporated practically without modification and *in extenso*. Possibly the incident of Elijah and Naboth's vineyard, culminating with the distinctive imagery we have noted

(21.21), originally belonged to this source before it was incorporated in the Elijah cycle.

JUDAEAN HISTORICAL NARRATIVE

The sources just considered are specifically North Israelite, though the role played by Jehoshaphat of Judah in the accounts of 'Ahab's' campaign at Ramoth Gilead (I K. 22) and of Jehoram's Moabite campaign (II K. 3) suggests that the sources have been reworked by a Judaean authority. There are in the same section of Kings two similar historical narratives of like detail and proportion which are Judaean in origin. These are the account of Athaliah's usurpation and her suppression, with the elevation of Joash (II K. 11) and Joash's reform of Temple finance (12.4–16 [5–17]). The latter, owing to its preoccupation with the Temple and its lack of wider historical perspective, probably comes from a priestly authority, as Wellhausen suggested, contending for a Temple history as a separate source, to which he assigned the account of Athaliah's usurpation and the elevation of Joash (11.1–12, 18b–20), the religious innovations of Ahaz in subservience to Assyria (16.10ff.), and Josiah's reformation (chs. 22 and 23 excluding Deuteronomistic expansions). The objection to the hypothesis of a priestly source of ch. 12 is the critical attitude to the priestly administration of Temple finance. Nevertheless, if we may suppose that the work came from a priest after the reformation of Josiah, this need not be an insuperable objection. To such a work certain statistics may have belonged, such as the amounts drawn from the Temple treasury to pay political indemnities at sundry times by Rehoboam (I K. 14.25–28) and Joash (II K. 12.17f. [18f.]), and the bribe sent by Asa to the king of Damascus (I K. 15.18). Such a composition would also have contained a description of the Temple, such as that in I K. 6f., and the baffling combination of detail and vagueness in that account would be admirably explained on the assumption that this account is a description in retrospect from a time late in the monarchy after the reformation of Josiah. To the same source the inventory of Temple furnishings destroyed by the Babylonians in II K. 25.13–17 may also belong. It is generally admitted on internal evidence that the suppression of Athaliah and the accession of Joash comprise two distinct sources, one a priestly account, represented in II K. 11.1–12 and 18b–20, which probably belongs to the Temple history we have just noted, and the other the popular or secular account of the same events (vv. 13–17). The real objection to the assignment of II K. 11.1–12 and 18b–20 and chs. 22f. as they stand to a Temple history is that these passages are, constitutionally and politically, much wider in scope than a Temple history would be; hence our conclusion is that as they stand these passages are from a history of the house of David by a priestly authority who had access to Temple archives, from which he drew matter concerning events such as the death of Athaliah and the accession of Joash, which happened in the Temple, and in which the Temple personnel were involved.

The notable expansion of the narrative at such points as the *coup d'état* of Athaliah and her subsequent suppression (II K. 11) and the reign of Hezekiah (chs. 18–20) doubtless reflects the full citation of sources, such as secular historical narrative (e.g. II K. 11.13–18a) and a Temple record (e.g. II K. 11.1–12), prophetic legend (e.g. II K. 18. 17–19.7, 36f.; 20.1–7, 9–11, 12–19), which is combined with the edifying legend of the good king Hezekiah (II K. 19.9b–35). But they probably owe their fullness in the Deuteronomistic compilation to the peculiar interest of the Deuteronomistic theologian, who thus, according to Noth,[a] emphasized his principle that the fidelity of such a man as Hezekiah to Deuteronomic ideals led on to success, while apostasy or religious liberalism like Athaliah's brought due retribution.

JUDAH ALONE: THE DEUTERONOMISTIC HISTORY

After the collapse of Samaria, from II K. 18, the record of events in Judah is much fuller, though still not complete. From the reformation of Josiah in 622 the Deuteronomistic compiler, if not describing events which he had personally witnessed, was certainly dealing with history which his 'school' had helped to make. The Deuteronomic 'school' is generally and correctly associated with 622, but it must be remembered that this is but the date when the circle emerged articulate and effective. There is no reason to suppose that the Deuteronomic movement was newly born in 622. Indeed, the fact that the Deuteronomists already had a book and were sufficiently strong to oblige the king to carry through a reform not only of religion but of the constitution indicates that they had a not inconsiderable history behind them. In fact, a similar measure of reform, though on a much smaller scale, associated with Hezekiah a century before, may reflect the crystallization of opinion which is associated

[a] *Überlieferungsgeschichtliche Studien*, pp. 85f.

with the Deuteronomic circle, the moment for this being the collapse of the Northern kingdom, which, as A. C. Welch[a] maintained, prompted a revival and reformation in Judah, where the rallying-point for refugees from North Israel was a new presentation of the best in their ancestral legal and religious tradition. If this is so, then the lengthy, but still not detailed, account of the reigns of Hezekiah (II K. 18–20), Manasseh and Amon (ch. 21), and Josiah (chs. 22–23.35), where the Deuteronomistic passages are long and continuous, e.g. 18.1–8, 12: 21.1–22, is a matter of personal reminiscence and interest within the Deuteronomic circle, and even to the compiler himself.

ANNALISTIC SOURCES AND PROPHETIC TRADITION

Here again, however, the compiler found sources ready to hand. Apart from the brief notices which recur throughout the account of the remaining period of the monarchy of Judah and are drawn from the annals of the kingdom, the source of the bulk of the account of the reign of Hezekiah (II K. 18.13–20.21) is suggested by its close verbal correspondence with Isa. 36–39. The first impression is that here the compiler of Kings drew on prophetic biography from the Isaiah tradition, but the matter is not quite so simple, as a detailed analysis will show.[b] From such an investigation it is apparent that one of these passages depends on the other, and there seems little doubt that that in Kings must have priority, except perhaps in the collection of oracles in 19.21–34 and 20.1–11, 12–19. Here there are ostensibly three episodes in which the prophet is involved, that of Sennacherib's menace to Jerusalem (18.17–19.37), Hezekiah's sickness and Isaiah's sign of the shadow (20.1–11), and the legation of Merodach-baladan and Isaiah's oracle of doom (20.12–19), which probably antedates the former episodes.[c] In the last two episodes the focus of interest is the prophet, and it is likely that the ultimate source was tradition regarding Isaiah, possibly on the periphery of the main Isaianic tradition, as its position as an appendix to the first section of the Book of Isaiah indicates. In the first of these episodes we would distinguish a prose account of Sennacherib's legation (18.17–19.7, 36). This is introduced by an annalistic digest (18.13–16) and culminates in a rather restrained oracle of Isaiah to the effect that Sennacherib will withdraw because of bad news from his own land and

[a]*Post-exilic Judaism,* 1935, pp. 17ff.
[b]See pp. 659f. below.
[c]See p. 668 below.

die a violent death (19.6f.), an oracle which is confirmed in 19.36f., the latter verses being perhaps a later gloss. This seems at first sight an excerpt from a history of the kingdom of Judah, where the prophet, as in the case of Elisha in the account of the Moabite campaign (II K. 3), does not dominate the scene, though his influence is admitted. This may be part of the history of Judah or of the Davidic house from a priest after the Josianic reformation, which we have already postulated as one of the sources of the narrative of the suppression of Athaliah and the accession of Joash (II K. 11), and his reform of Temple finance (II K. 12). The difference, however, in style and matter between the account of what is probably the same situation in 18.13–16 and 18.17–19.7,36 indicates that, despite the relation of the latter passage to historical facts, it is not of the literary category of history, but is part of a prophetic legend of Isaiah. 19.9b–35, on the other hand, belongs essentially to the popular edifying legend of the good king Hezekiah, whose exemplary piety was rewarded in relief from the Assyrian menace. Each passage, however, has influenced the other in the process of transmission and compilation. Thus both emphasize the humility and piety of Hezekiah, and the latter includes oracles traditionally ascribed to Isaiah (19.21–34). In this context, the theme of the inviolability of Zion as the seat of the Divine King reflects the theme of the Feast of Tabernacles in the Temple (cf. Ps. 46). The speech of the Assyrian officer (19.10–13) is a digest of the diplomatic arguments in 18.19–21, 22, 23–25, 31–32a and 30, 32b–35 and therefore later work. It expresses the conscious theological theme of God's vindication of his sovereignty which is the motive of the deliverance of Jerusalem. Thus the digest of the diplomatic arguments may be the contribution of the Deuteronomistic compiler, but it may equally well have belonged to his source, the legend of the good king Hezekiah.[a]

ANNALS OF JUDAH AND DEUTERONOMISTIC EXPANSION

The end of the kingdom of Judah from the time of Manasseh (ch.21) to the destruction of Jerusalem and the Temple is composed mainly of excerpts from the annals of the kingdom liberally amplified by Deuteronomistic comment and expansion, which is natural considering the fact that the Deuteronomistic compiler, and after him the redactor, were writing of contemporary matters in which they were personally involved and hence were independent of other sources.

[a]For detailed analysis, see further pp. 662ff.

THE END OF THE DEUTERONOMISTIC COMPILATION AND REDACTIONAL APPENDICES

In this section, as indeed throughout Kings, a distinction is to be observed between the pre-exilic Deuteronomistic compilation and the exilic Deuteronomistic redaction (see pp. 6–9). Of the two, only the latter visualizes the fall of the Davidic monarchy. The precise point at which the compilation ended, however, is uncertain. We believe, for the reasons stated below (pp. 753f.), that the work was concluded before the first capture of Jerusalem in March 597, and was continued by the redactor, first possibly to 25.21b, where the words, 'So Judah was carried away captive out of his land' have the appearance of a conclusion, and later to the alleviation of the lot of the captive king Jehoiachin in 561 (25.27–30), this passage and that on the fortunes of the remaining Jews under Gedaliah (vv. 22–26) being appendices. The latter passage shows a close verbal correspondence with the historical appendix in Jer. 40.7–41.18, but the fact that the passage in Jeremiah is so much fuller and more circumstantial suggests that the passage in Kings is a summary of this source.

LIMITATIONS AND SCOPE OF KINGS

With Kings that part of the Jewish canon known as 'the Former Prophets' is concluded. Though these are generally termed 'historical books', they have serious limitations as history, and this applies also to Kings. We expect a much more systematic presentation of the reign and administration of Solomon rather than laudatory passages and a somewhat trivial instance of his 'wisdom' and expatiation on the building and dedication of the Temple, which was but one event in his reign. We should have appreciated fuller information on the achievements of Omri and Ahab, who made their impression on the records of the greatest imperial power of their day, and of the campaigns of Jeroboam II, who rehabilitated Israel after Aramaean domination. Only sporadic incidents in the reign of Hezekiah are mentioned. The bulk of the space devoted to his reign ostensibly concerns but one incident in his 14th year, and his sickness and treatment with a fig-plaster is of no political significance. By contrast, his political intrigues and the resulting alliance which provoked the invasion of Sennacherib in 701 are entirely ignored, nor is anything said of the truncation of his realm, which the Assyrian records attest. In the account of the reign of Manasseh, too, we should prefer to hear less of his ritual 'abominations' and more of his political relations with Assyria, which the Assyrian records attest. We might also have expected a detailed account of the various steps by which Josiah effected his reformation, and an indication of its political and constitutional significance. But the Deuteronomistic compilation of Kings does not purport to be an objective history. The objective records which a historian seeks lie behind the compilation, and what the Deuteronomist has given us is an interpretation of history from his own theological viewpoint, an indication of which is the selective use of material from the sources as much as the actual treatment of the material selected.

THE THEOLOGY OF THE DEUTERONOMISTIC HISTORY IN KINGS

The general perspective in which the Deuteronomists present the history of the monarchy in Israel and Judah is taken from the point at which the school emerges into the light of history in the reign of Josiah. The superficial impression made upon the reader is that they were primarily interested in the cultic purity and centralization of worship in Jerusalem, and judge kings from the time of Solomon mechanically by a standard which came into actual force only late in the history of Judah, and which, consequently, was unknown to the predecessors of Josiah. Actually closer study of the vital passage describing the Josianic reformation and the whole Deuteronomistic history in the light of that passage reveals a much more penetrating philosophy of history, which is fully discerned when we study the kernel of the Book of Deuteronomy itself, particularly chs. 27f., in the complex of Israel's *Heilsgeschichte*.

From such a study it is apparent that the Deuteronomistic history of Israel is presented as the continuation of the history of the confederate tribes, who realized their essential status and destiny as the people of Yahweh in the covenant-sacrament at Shechem. The exclusive worship of Yahweh in its primitive austerity and the observance of the principles of social equity revealed in the law was demanded as the condition of the fulfilment of Israel's status as the people of his election, redeemed by his grace and power for a divinely appointed destiny. In this presentation of the law in the complex of the *Heilsgeschichte* Israel was given the opportunity of good or evil, peace or suffering, life or death (Deut. 30.15), of which she was made pointedly aware in the blessings and curses to which she said Amen (Deut. 27.15–26). This for the Deuteronomists was not ancient history, an obsolete custom. The word of God, declared in those ancient blessings and curses, was active, the judgements of God were abroad in the earth, and von Rad is undoubtedly right in characterizing the theme of the Deuteronomistic history as 'the operation of the word of God in history'.[a] So the sufferings and degradation of Israel and Judah under the monarchy were appreciated as the operation of the curse upon a broken covenant-engagement, of which the addiction to the many local sanctuaries was only a symptom. This might be a simple philosophy of history, but it was sober and realistic, and even if it went no further, betokens a commendable self-discipline and moral vigour, which singles Israel out from her contemporaries in antiquity.

Despite the superficial impression of a rather sketchy history in which the Deuteronomist stigmatizes in a broad, mechanical, and somewhat offhand way the various kings of Israel and Judah, his judgement is not a mere particularist animadversion on individual delinquency. He accepts the institution of the monarchy and the unique significance of the king as representative of the people before God[b] and the custodian *par excellence* of the Mosaic tradition, e.g. II K. 23, where Josiah, as Moses and Joshua, dispenses the covenant.[c] The sins of the king, then, are the sins of the people, and in animadverting on those the Deuteronomist is but emphasizing his main theme of the tragedy of his people as the supreme example of divine retribution.

The day had long passed when the good and evil in consequence of the blessing and curse were put before Israel so pointedly as in the covenant-sacrament at the ancient amphictyonic assembly. But the word of God was still active in Israel, and in all but the most abandoned ages men were confronted by the prophets with the same pointed alternatives and their inevitable consequences. We find it strange that of the great canonical prophets who spoke and devoted themselves to the ministry of the word of God in Israel and Judah only part of the work and words of Isaiah have been noted by the Deuteronomist. The reason is probably twofold. It reflects the reserve

[a] *Studies in Deuteronomy*, 1953, pp. 89ff.

[b] So G. von Rad, *Old Testament Theology* I, 1962, p. 339: 'He does in fact ascribe to the monarchy the crucial key-position between Jahweh and Israel, since it was in the kings' hearts that the decision whether Israel was to be saved or rejected had to be taken.'

[c] Noth, 'Die Gesetze im Pentateuch', *Gesammelte Studien*, pp. 61ff.; *The Laws in the Pentateuch*, pp. 46ff.

which priests felt over against the fiery and less conventional prophet, and the Deuteronomist, with regard to his public, probably sought advisedly to make a more general impression of the operation of the word of God in history by selecting more obvious cases of prophecy and fulfilment which pertained directly to kings and dynasties, and using prophetic sagas such as those of Elijah and Elisha, which by their very nature were popularly known. A further explanation is suggested by Noth:[a] that the activity of the great prophets was naturally not the subject of the historical annals on which the Deuteronomist drew, and the literary compilation of the traditions of the canonical prophets had not yet begun. The general interest of the Deuteronomist in prophecy and fulfilment, however, is clearly apparent.

The interest of the Deuteronomist in the continuing activity of the word of God in history indicates that he was not a mere antiquarian. He was a man of his own generation, and his repeated reference to the Davidic covenant (II Sam. 7.12ff.), so assiduously propagated on regular cultic occasions in Jerusalem throughout the monarchy, had had its effect. He accepted the monarchy, and, as his opinion of Hezekiah and Josiah shows, was ready to welcome a king who fulfilled the ideal which David was regarded as embodying. This belief in the Davidic covenant as the guarantee of stability in Judah seems at first sight to accord ill with the critical attitude to the monarchy which characterizes the Deuteronomistic history, but the same ardent hope in the covenanted house of David is an element in the faith of the prophets of Judah, Isaiah (9.6ff.[5ff.]; 11.1ff.), Micah (5.2ff.[1ff.]), and towards the end of the monarchy and perhaps contemporary with the Deuteronomistic compiler, Jeremiah (33.21); yet not even the Deuteronomist was stauncher to the democratic tradition of Israel or more critical of the monarchy than the prophets. So for the Deuteronomist, David as the recipient of the covenant was a great ideal, to be realized in one of his line according to the oracle of Nathan (II Sam. 7.12ff.). Thus it is that the Deuteronomist is almost pathetically ready to acclaim this ideal in Hezekiah and Josiah and, even in his foreboding, holds the hope almost to the end of his compilation.

We may question von Rad's view,[b] however, that there is evidence

[a]*Überlieferungsgeschichtliche Studien*, pp. 97f.

[b]*Old Testament Theology* I, p. 343. K. D. Fricke, in the Introduction to the posthumous commentary of J. Fichtner, takes a more sober view in referring to the

of the persistence of this hope, which he ventures to call, in a qualified sense, messianic, in the note on the alleviation of the lot of Jehoiachin in exile (II K. 25.27–30), with which the book ends. This isolated note on the amelioration of the lot of Jehoiachin without comment seems tenuous evidence for such a hope as von Rad assumes, especially in view of the opinion of the monarchy throughout the Deuteronomistic history from Deuteronomy to the end of Kings. In such passages as Josh. 23.15b–16, I Sam. 12.25, II K. 17.7ff. and 21.12ff. the fate of the old order, in which the monarchy was admitted as a temporary expedient, seems sealed, and we agree with Noth (*op. cit.*, pp. 107–10) that, whatever beliefs his contemporaries may have held, the Deuteronomistic redactor in the work he presents is preoccupied with the sins and retribution of Israel, which finds its consummation in the liquidation of state and crown, beyond which the chastened philosophy of the Deuteronomistic redaction does not penetrate. It is, of course, true that the hope of the realization of the covenanted grace of God to the House of David (*ḥasᵉdē dāwīd*) was not dead in the Exile, as appears from Isa. 55.3, from which the messianic hope develops. This, too, from circles who, like the Deuteronomists, had a keen sense of Israel's sin and due retribution (Isa. 40.2). But if this hope through the Davidic line was shared by the Deuteronomists, our opinion is that it finds no expression in their final redaction of Kings.

We look in vain in Kings for any consciousness of the positive destiny of Israel among the peoples of the earth. This is surprising in the Deuteronomistic compiler in view of his sympathy with the prophets, the negative aspect of whose message he certainly grasped. It is surprising, too, in the case of the redactor in view of the fact that his work dates from as late as 561 or soon after, when the Isaianic circle was already feeling the way to a solution of the problem of Israel's supreme suffering in the realization of her mission, expressed in the passages on the Suffering Servant. Even admitting that these passages are later than, and distinct from, the rest of Deutero-Isaiah, in which we do not find this positive sense of missionary purpose, it is still difficult to believe that this fair hope had no antecedents among responsible Jews contemporary with the Deuteronomistic redaction of Kings. There was at the same time, however, a deep sense of pessim-

release of Jehoiachin from close confinement as 'the first gleam of hope in a dark time' (J. Fichtner, *Das erste Buch von den Königen*, Die Botschaft des AT, ed. K. D. Fricke, 1964, p. 31).

ism and resignation to divine retribution, against which Ezekiel had to strive hard (Ezek. 33).

The Deuteronomistic History as a whole, however, does not share this extreme pessimism. It is a purposeful and positive work for Israel at the nadir of her fortunes, and this is reflected in the theme of the forgiveness and renewed grace of God throughout. Moses may only see the Promised Land from Mount Nebo, and his contemporaries who tried God in the desert never entered it; but their children did with Joshua and Caleb. In the period of the judges, God is always ready to hear Israel when she turns to him contritely in fast and penance, and to give her a deliverer and new courage in adversity. In spite of the suspicion of kingship and the failure of Saul, God had himself hallowed the status of David and his house by covenant as responsible representatives of his people, and at repeated junctures during the monarchy had shown mercy. The effect of this accumulation of mercy may be to emphasize the progressive decline in Israel's allegiance, which such grace deserved, as Fricke[a] maintains. We believe, however, that this recurrence of the theme of repentance and mercy has more significance than mere literary effect. The compiler of the Deuteronomistic History was the heir of the tradition of the sacral community which found its solidarity in the covenant-sacrament. He was probably from the class of priests or Levites familiar with the address to the covenant community on the subject of blessing or curse consequent upon fidelity to, or apostasy from, the principles of the covenant, e.g. Deut. 28.1–14, 15–68, and with the office of advocate for God in the indictment of the people in the fast liturgy, which we believe to be the origin of the distinctive office of the prophet in Israel.[b] It is most significant that this was the framework of what we believe to be the pre-Deuteronomistic collection of the narratives of the great judges,[c] which the Deuteronomist found so

[a]K. D. Fricke, Introduction to J. Fichtner, *Das erste Buch von den Königen*, Die Botschaft des Alten Testaments, pp. 30f.

[b]This view is based on the role of the prophet in the fast-liturgy in the introduction to the Gideon cycle in Judg. 6.6b–10, which W. Beyerlin, 'Geschichte und heilsgeschichtliche Traditionsbildung im Alten Testament', *VT* XIII, 1963, pp. 10ff., has demonstrated to be distinct from the Deuteronomistic introduction in 6.1, 2a, 6a.

[c]This work is taken to comprise Judg. 3.7–11.33, the story of Jephthah's daughter, excluding the notices of the 'minor judges' and the Samson cycle (chs. 13–16), in a framework reflecting the liturgy of the divine contention in public fast and penance in the context of the covenant-sacrament. See further, W. Beyerlin, 'Gattung und Herkunft des Rahmens im Richterbuch', *Tradition und Situation*, ed. E. Würthwein and O. Kaiser, 1963, pp. 1–29.

congruous with his purpose that he incorporated it in his great history. Thus the Deuteronomistic compiler could not be oblivious to the prospect of grace, and if as the work progresses the shadows darken, the fact that such a work was composed indicates a hope that it might achieve the purpose, if not of inspiring a sanguine hope in the revival of the kingdom, under the Davidic house, at least of stimulating a sober moral amendment and a steady faith that Israel's distress was not fortuitous or arbitrary, but was the evidence of the nature of her God, who in judgement and mercy was consistent with his self-revelation in the covenant.

H. W. Wolff,[a] who points to the recurrence of the verb *šūb*, denoting turning again to God with the purpose of renewed grace, as the key to the prospect and purpose of the Deuteronomistic History, adduces evidence from Kings in the ideal expressed in the case of Josiah (II K. 23.25) and particularly in Solomon's prayer at the dedication of the Temple, in what is in our opinion an addition by the redactor at I K. 8.46–53, where provision is made for a merciful hearing of whoever would sincerely petition God, even in exile. Here we should emphasize the prospect of the grace of God available to 'his people'. We are directed back to the deliverance from Egypt (vv. 51, 53), and the experience of God's grace in election and covenant is implied in the conception of 'God's people'. God's people and the divine purpose for and through this community had by his grace survived the failures of the desert wandering and the lapses in the time of the judges; they should also survive the expedient of monarchy with its frequent abuses. The sins of the past, of which cultic aberrations were merely symptomatic, with their grim consequences, should serve as an admonition in the future, which lay with the people of God now independent of kings, of state, and even of Temple and traditional cult. The people of God would now be conserved by their fidelity to the Mosaic tradition, the fundamental social, ethical and religious demands of the covenant on which the Deuteronomistic historian repeatedly insists. We should agree with Wolff that in this sober prospect, the note on the alleviation of the lot of king Jehoiachin in captivity, though far from betokening a messianic hope, may be adduced to encourage the people of God that security with honour was still possible and that fidelity to ancestral principles of the people of God's election might still raise Israel, even

[a]H. W. Wolff, 'Das Kerygma des deuteronomistischen Geschichtswerks', *ZAW* LXXII (1961), pp. 171–86, esp. pp. 179ff.

in political obscurity, above the ruck of peoples, as Jehoiachin was given preference above his fellows in captivity (II K. 25.28).[a] Thus God's initial grace in the election of Israel (Deut. 4.7–8) might find positive fulfilment.

2. THE TEXT

MASSORETIC TEXT

The text of Kings is reasonably well preserved, but there are notable exceptions. In the list of Solomon's fiscal officials in I K. 4.8—19 the mention of the officers by their fathers' names only in vv. 8–11 points to the use of an official document, the right edge of which was broken off. In the description of the Temple and its furnishings in I K. 6f. certain technical terms which have become obsolete by the time of the compiler and the scribes who transmitted the text have given rise to corruptions, not all of which may be restored. Kings presents, of course, the usual difficulties of texts which have been standardized after centuries of transmission by the hands of scribes, and the textual notes to this commentary will reveal corruptions in detail throughout the work, few of which, however, are beyond restoration by various aids which are ready to hand.

First there are parallel passages in Isaiah, Jeremiah, and in Chronicles. Here the parallels in Isaiah and Jeremiah are very close and are cases of passages from the Kings-compilation used directly in the compilations of the prophetic books or *vice versa* (see critical introduction to II K. 18–20, and II K. 24.18–25.26, pp. 657ff.; 767). The parallel accounts in Chronicles must be used with very great caution owing to the tendentious nature of that work, its particular ecclesiastical bias, and its anachronistic tendency to safeguard the sanctity of the Temple and priestly monopoly of sacral office. Nor is the text of Kings itself exempt from this tendency on the part of later redactors, who reflect the views of the priestly circle. These passages, however, which post-date the main Deuteronomistic recension of Kings, are easily recognized, and may often be corrected by the aid of the Greek versions, especially the Septuagint. A case in point

[a]Wolff suggests that the relief of Jehoiachin and the preferential treatment he received may indicate the Deuteronomist's sense of Israel's responsibility to give testimony to her distinctive calling in the world. We think of the responsibilities and prospects of a figure like Daniel. But, as Wolff is careful to state (*op. cit.*, p. 185), this is at the best implicit, rather than stated, in the books of Kings.

is the account of the installation of the ark in the Temple (I K. 8.3f.), where MT, as against the Septuagint in Codex Vaticanus (G^B) and Lucian's recension (G^L), associates the Levites with the priests, and for the simple 'all Israel' of G^{BL} reads 'all the congregation of Israel' (*kol-ʿadat yiśrā'ēl*), a phrase which is peculiar to P. The ancient versions are particularly valuable, especially the Greek and the Syriac. In certain passages which are notoriously corrupt, and even, in certain cases, meaningless, we may in the last resort have recourse to conjectural emendation, an expedient of which British scholars are generally chary. Conjectural emendation, however, must be controlled by the internal evidence of the Old Testament, other ancient Semitic literatures, and the context of the ancient Near East, which becomes increasingly clear and vivid with the progress of modern archaeology.

Though to all ends and purposes the unvocalized consonantal text of the Old Testament was standardized about AD 100, complete standardization, with agreement in vocalization, was not achieved till the ninth or tenth century, and as far as Kings is concerned the earliest Hebrew MS of the books in full is not earlier than the Aleppo Codex from the first half of the tenth century. This represents the same textual tradition as the Leningrad Codex from the Ben Asher family of MSS. The date of the latter MS is 1008, and it is this Hebrew text of Kings, printed in the third edition of R. Kittel's *Biblia Hebraica*, which is the basis of our study.

THE SEPTUAGINT (G)

If the MS authority for the Hebrew text is so very late, however, there is evidence for the text over half a millennium earlier in the Greek versions, the best known of which is the Septuagint, G in our textual notes. This, according to tradition, originated with the translation of the Law in Alexandria in the middle of the third century BC, and, according to the prologue to Ecclesiasticus, apparently included the Prophets—hence Kings—by the beginning of the second century BC. It is not, however, as variants show, a direct translation of the Hebrew text which was later standardized. In our textual notes variants of individual words and phrases will be noted. The most notorious discrepancy is in the account of the origin and career of Jeroboam I, the incident of the rending of the new robe, and the rejection of Rehoboam by the Northern tribes at Shechem. Having followed MT without serious divergence in this matter up to I K.

12.24, G follows with an account (v. 24 a–z in Swete's edition) which has no counterpart here in MT. Some of this matter corresponds to I K. 11.26–28, 40; 14.1–18, which has no counterpart in G here; 12.1; 11.29–31; 12.3–14, 16, 21–24, with variations of time, place and personalities, see pp. 288ff., 301f., 310f., 335f. The complexity arises from the use by Judaean editors, possibly of different periods, of traditions of these events stemming respectively from Israel and Judah. At I K. 2.35 there is a similar case, G (Swete, v. 35 a–o) giving a summary of Solomon's reign which does not correspond to anything in MT at this point, but which is composed of statements in I K. 4.29ff. [5.9ff.]; 3.1ff.; 9.24ff.; 5.15 [29]; 2.8ff., with less exact versions of 7.23–30 and 9.15b, 19a. In the account of Solomon's administration in I K. 4.17–5.8, the order of G varies from MT, and in 5.1–8 the omission in G of certain obviously later redactional passages in MT almost certainly brings us nearer to the archival source of the compiler.

Apart from those discrepancies, there are two notable transpositions. I K. 20 and 21 are transposed to give the juxtaposition of 20 and 22, which are certainly part of the prophetic adaptation of a historical narrative which the compiler used as a source for his account of the house of Omri, ch. 21, the incident of Naboth's vineyard being inserted in its position in MT in immediate anticipation of the fulfilment in ch. 22 of the oracle of doom on Ahab, which is the culmination of the story of Naboth's vineyard (21.19ff.). After I K. 16.28 the account of the reign of Jehoshaphat of Judah is transposed in G (Swete, v. 28 a–h) from I K. 22.41–50 (MT), where it follows the account of Ahab's reign in the endeavour to achieve chronological harmony after the statement (G, v. 28a) that Jehoshaphat became king in the 11th year of Omri the father of Ahab.

The chronological notes of the accessions and reigns of kings of Israel and Judah are also a notable point of divergence, but here in general it may be said that the numbers of G represent efforts by late redactors of the Hebrew text, if not of the Greek itself, at harmonization of chronology of notorious complexity. Usually they simply complicate the problem and reveal ignorance of the systems of dating in Israel and Judah. See Introduction: Chronology.

These discrepancies and transpositions of text in Kings alone indicate that the tradition of the Hebrew text was fairly fluid when G was made. Here it must be borne in mind that it has never been seriously claimed that the Hebrew text of the Old Testament was standardized before the end of the first century AD, and G in that part which includes Kings is about three centuries before that. Nevertheless, in spite of such divergence, the measure of agreement of MT and G in essential matter and even in order is remarkable, and if it is true that there was no such thing as a generally authoritative *textus receptus* at that early date, it just as surely indicates that there was a strong tendency in that direction.

Apart from earlier fragmentary evidence of G, as in citations in Philo in the first half of the first century AD and Josephus (*c.* AD 70–100), the oldest MSS of the Old Testament approaching fullness are the great uncials Sinaiticus (א) and Vaticanus (B) from the first part of the fourth century AD. Of these only B contains Kings, which is also attested in Codex Alexandrinus (A) from the following century.

HEBREW MSS FROM QUMRAN

The evidence of G that, though there was no single authoritative Hebrew text of the Old Testament in the pre-Christian era, there was nevertheless a definite tendency in that direction is strikingly corroborated by the recent discoveries in the Judaean desert about Qumran. Here at last are MS fragments of practically all books of the Old Testament, including books almost complete, which antedate the great Greek uncials א, B, and A actually by almost half a millennium. Some of these, including fragments of Kings from Caves 5 and 6, are almost as old as the earliest papyrus of G, the John Rylands Papyrus of Deut. 23.24–24.3; 25.1–3; 26.12, 17–19; 28.31–33, which is dated in the middle of the second century BC. Indeed, fragments of a MS of Samuel from Cave 4 (4QSam^{b}) have been dated on palaeographic grounds to the third century BC.[a] This may well antedate G of the Prophets, including Samuel and Kings, and in view of the agreement with G rather than MT in Samuel, where G and MT notably diverge, there is a strong probability that we have at last arrived at the Hebrew text from which the translation of G was made. This must lend great weight to the Qumran fragments of Kings where these agree with G rather than with MT on the score of antiquity alone. It must also affect our judgement on the variations in G, which have often been too lightly assumed to be paraphrases not based on an original Hebrew text. This at the same time should

[a]F. M. Cross, 'A New Qumran Biblical Fragment related to the Original Hebrew underlying the Septuagint', *BASOR* 132, 1953, pp. 15–26; 'The Oldest Manuscripts from Qumran: IV', *JBL* LXXIV, 1955, pp. 165–72.

not obscure the fact that in the Qumran texts in general, and also in certain passages in the fragments of Kings, the MT is strongly supported. Unfortunately for our present purpose Kings is represented so far only by a few fragments from Qumran.

From Cave 5 there are three fragments on leather from the first column of I K. 1, containing parts of vv. 1, 16, 17, 27, 28, 29, 30, 31, 32, 33, 34, 35, 36, and 37. They are dated palaeographically to the late second century BC, and, except for spelling, agree with MT and G.

More interesting and useful are the fragments of Kings from Cave 6 (6QK) on rather coarse papyrus and palaeographically contemporary with 1QIs[a] in the late second century BC. Of the 24 fragments, however, seven yield only single words or parts of a word or two, and, their location in Kings not being certain, they are of very limited value. The remaining 17 fragments contain many lacunae, the length of some of which, as will be noted in our critical apparatus, indicates a text generally shorter than MT. What remains is certainly identified. I K. 3.12b–14; 12.28b–31; 22.28–31 and II K. 5.26 and 6.32 agree with MT, except that I K. 22.31 must have read, as the spacing suggests, *wayeṣaw melek 'arām* for MT *ūmelek 'arām ṣiwwā*, with no difference in meaning. The fragments of II K. 9.1–2 and 10.19–21, which contain only a few words, agree also with MT. In the rest of the fragments, however, there is a certain divergence from MT, both in the comparatively few words which have survived and in the length of the text as indicated by the lacunae. In II K. 7.8–10, for instance, a certain minor variation agrees with the Syriac version (S); in II K. 7.20–8.5 at certain points the Qumran text agrees with G, S, and the Targum (T), and is generally shorter than MT and the versions at other points, which will be noted in detail in the textual notes in the commentary.

Of major value for the restoration of the text of K. are the passages in Isa. 36.1–39.8, cf. II K. 18.13–20.19; Jer. 52.1–34, cf. II K. 24.18–25.30; Jer. 39.1–10, cf. II K. 25.1–21; Jer. 28.2b–7, cf. II K. 25.3–7; and Jer. 40.7–10; 41.1–3, 16–18, cf. II K. 25.22–36. Here again the Qumran discoveries in prophetic texts have a bearing on the text of Kings, as is indicated in our textual notes on the Isaiah MSS from Cave 1. Unfortunately there is no comparable discovery for Jeremiah.

HEXAPLAR G AND OTHER GREEK VERSIONS

G is of undoubted value as a witness to the original Hebrew text though, as a translation for the practical purpose of making the Old Testament intelligible to congregations unfamiliar with Hebrew, whose thought-world was far removed from that of the biblical writers, it had its inevitable limitations. Both the importance and the limitations of G were recognized by the great Alexandrine scholar Origen, who in Caesarea in Palestine *c.* AD 240 prepared his great Hexaplar, including the Hebrew text, by then standardized (MT), a transliteration into Greek letters, the Greek translation of Aquila, an Anatolian proselyte to Judaism *c.* AD 130, another Greek translation from *c.* AD 170 by Symmachus, probably an Ebionite or Jewish-Christian sectary, Origen's own recension of G and a Greek text by Theodotion, a proselyte to Judaism *c.* 200 AD, which was really the revision of one of the current Greek translations, either G (so Rahlfs) or another Greek translation (so Kahle). Fragments of other Greek translations, Quinta, Sexta, Septima, were also included, so far as they were available. The texts appear in the Hexaplar in the above order. Disturbed by the number of variants of G, Origen set out in the Hexaplar to collate variants and to produce a text which should directly reproduce the standard Hebrew text. His resultant recension of G notes additions and deficiencies of G vis-à-vis MT by signs used in textual criticism of classical texts in Alexandria, the omissions being supplemented by Origen chiefly from Theodotion. Hexaplar G is attested in the Codex Colberto-Sarravianus from the fourth or fifth century, containing Gen. 31.5–Judg. 31.12. A similar work, the Tetraplar, in four columns comprising Aquila, Symmachus, another recension of G by Origen, and Theodotion, was produced, probably later (Rahlfs). Here Origen treats the Greek text even more critically, with further emendations on the basis of MT. This recension of G is known in a Syriac translation made in 617 by Paul, Bishop of Tello, and is termed, not quite correctly, the Hexaplar Syriac (S^h).[a]

AQUILA

Of the Greek versions apart from G that of Aquila, best known from a sixth-century palimpsest from the Qaraite Geniza in Old Cairo,[b] is of the greatest value for the recovery of the text of Kings.

[a]Other fragments from citations of Hexaplar variants are included in F. Field's *Origenis Hexaplarum quae supersunt*, 1875.

[b]C. Taylor, *Hebrew-Greek Cairo Genizah Palimpsests from the Taylor-Schechter Collection*, 1900; F. C. Burkitt, *Fragments of the Books of Kings according to the Translation of Aquila*, 1897.

Literal to the extent of barbarism, it is a very faithful witness to its original Hebrew text, and indeed its very inelegance is its chief merit for the textual criticism of the Old Testament. It is furthermore of greater value than G as evidence of the MT, which had been standardized about half a century before. This fact, according to Kahle,[a] necessitated the new translation.

LUCIAN'S RECENSION OF G

The G text of Origen's Hexaplar was only one recension current in contemporary Christendom, and Jerome, writing *c.* 400, mentions three authoritative recensions of G, that of Hesychius, which was esteemed in Egypt, that of Origen in Palestine, and Lucian's recension in North Syria (Antioch) and Asia Minor. Of these the Hesychian recension is known only by name, but the Lucianic (G^L) is of definite value in the restoration of the text of Kings, though owing to a tendency to simplification, smoothing out according to the canons of Greek grammar and style, and expansion to facilitate understanding, it must be used with care and never independently of other textual evidence. The author Lucian was martyred in AD 312, and his recension has peculiarities in common with several early citations from the Greek translations of the Old Testament, particularly in Justin Martyr, Philo, Josephus, the John Rylands Papyrus 458 (*c.* 150 BC) and now in fragments of the Minor Prophets from Qumran.[b] Lucian, it appears, used these early Greek translations in his recension of G. The early date of these and the fact that they were made by Jews directly from the Hebrew text at a time before its standardization give the variations in G^L a quite peculiar value.

LATIN VERSIONS

The Old Latin version, originating probably in North Africa and first attested in the writings of Tertullian in the latter half of the second century AD, is made from G, and is of value chiefly as evidence for G before the recensions which we have just mentioned. The proliferation of recensions and indeed of independent translations from G belongs to a special department of study of the Old Latin texts. Of immediate relevance to our study is the fact that this situation dictated the need for a sound, single, and authoritative Latin ver-

[a] *The Cairo Geniza*, 1947, p. 117.
[b] P. Kahle, *TLZ* LXXIX, 1954, cols. 83ff.

sion, for which Pope Damasus (366–384) commissioned Jerome. Eventually between 390 and 405 Jerome produced a Latin translation from the Hebrew, which he, like very few of the Roman Church, knew. But even with his knowledge of Hebrew and of local customs and topography from long residence in Bethlehem, where he accomplished his work, much in those ancient texts was strange to him, and he was obliged to have recourse to Greek translations, G, Aquila, Symmachus, and Theodotion. This was imposed on him not merely by limitations in his own knowledge, but by the pressure of opinion in Western Christendom, where Augustine particularly was alarmed at the possibility of a translation from Hebrew which would rest on the authority of one man, who was beyond the reach of criticism.

SYRIAC VERSIONS

G of Origen's Tetraplar was, as we have mentioned, translated into Syriac in 617. More familiar, however, was the Peshitta, first attested in the Codex Ambrosianus (sixth or seventh century AD) and accessible in Walton's Polygot. Philologically 'Peshitta' may mean either 'simple' or 'diffused'. If the latter is the meaning this version would be tantamount to a Syriac Vulgate. If the former is the correct meaning it would signify a simplification in comparison with an earlier text, perhaps the Syriac translations of the Tetraplar G. On the other hand, the word may simply mean simplification in the sense of 'translation', or translation direct from the Hebrew into Syriac independent of the medium of Greek. The direct translation seems natural in view of the fact that Syriac is a cognate Semitic language with Hebrew and the thought-forms and ethos of Syriac-speaking Aramaeans and Israelites were fundamentally the same. It is a matter of dispute as to whether this was the work of Jews or Christians. It seems natural that, as a Greek translation was necessary for the Greek-speaking Jews of Egypt and as Aramaic targums (translations), first oral, were used among Palestinian Jews as early at least as the beginning of the Christian era,[a] Syriac targums may have been used in North Syria and Mesopotamia, where communities of

[a]The standard Targums to the Old Testament were several centuries later, but there is a reference (Bab. Talmud, *Shabbat* 115a) to an Aramaic Targum on Job before the middle of the first century AD, and a Targum on Job was found in Cave 11 at Qumran, which must antedate the abandonment of the settlement by the sect in AD 68, and probably dates to the last century BC (A. S. van der Woude, 'Das Hiobtargum aus Qumran', SVT IX, 1963, pp. 322–33).

Jews had been long established. It is, in fact, feasibly suggested that an impetus to such a translation of the Hebrew Old Testament may have been the conversion of the Aramaean royal house and many subjects of Adiabene in the middle of the first century AD.[a] Such was possibly the beginning at least of the Syriac translation which was to emerge as the Peshitta, which as a Semitic rendering and interpretation of the Hebrew text has its own value, though in its final form it is the product of various hands and traditions and is not quite independent of G, a fact which somewhat impairs its worth. The adoption of Lucian's recension of G at Antioch in the beginning of the fourth century may have occasioned a harmonization of the Syriac and Septuagint versions, as W. Wright[b] feasibly suggests.

HEBREW SCRIPTS

In restoring the Hebrew text in the light of variant readings in parallel passages of the MT in Isaiah, Jeremiah and Chronicles, in Qumran fragments of these parallels and fragments of Kings, and in the versions we have mentioned, we must, of course, test the feasibility of such variants in the light of the context. Occasionally we may understand a corruption by seeing the possibility of homoeoteleuton, the lapse of a word or phrase because of a similar word- or line-ending. Or we may see how one Hebrew letter or more may have been mistaken for another and omitted (haplography) or added (dittography), or have been substituted for the letter it resembled. This confusion may often seem quite unlikely or even impossible so long as we confine our attention to the familiar square Hebrew script of the printed Hebrew Old Testament. But it must be remembered that this marks the final stage in the evolution of the Hebrew script. The Qumran MSS introduce us to this script in a somewhat different, though substantially the same, form. Here the most significant calligraphic feature for purposes of textual criticism is the similarity between *w* and *y*, both shaped alike, the former appreciably shorter than *w* in our standard texts and the *y* definitely longer than the later *y*. A case in point is I K. 4.12, where *mibbēt* is a scribal corruption of *m*[e]*bō' bētō*, where the corruption of the text is further complicated by haplography. We may trace the development of the alphabet back much further, thanks to inscriptions from Syria and

[a]Kahle, *The Cairo Geniza*, pp. 184ff.
[b]*A Short History of Syriac Literature*, 1894, p. 4.

Palestine, where it is attested in its various stages of development from the proto-Hebraic, or Phoenician, linear alphabet to a cursive version of that in the sixth and fifth centuries BC. We shall not digress on the subject of short inscriptions painted, incised, or stamped on pottery from various sites in Palestine, funerary inscriptions from the tenth century in Syria, legends engraved on seals from the monarchic period or the legends in the proto-Hebraic script and its variations on Jewish coins of the Hasmonaeans, Herods, and insurgents of AD 66–70 and 132–35. We may, however, single out certain inscriptions which are contemporary with significant phases of Hebrew literature. The inscription of Mesha, the contemporary of Jehoram of Israel and Jehoshaphat of Judah, on the famous stone from Diban in Moab, enables us to visualize the script and perhaps even the idiom in which the Story of the Davidic Succession (ending in I K. 1 and 2) was written, or the Acts of Solomon, or the historical narrative of Israel under the house of Omri, or the J source of the Pentateuch. The Samaritan ostraca, fiscal dockets on potsherds from the palace of Jeroboam II at Samaria, are in substantially the same script as the Moabite Stone, and the E source of the Pentateuch and the Elijah saga, if it was written down so early, the historical narrative relating the fall of the house of Ahab and the revolt of Jehu, the ancestor of Jeroboam, and the annals of the kingdom of Israel would be written in that script. This persisted without appreciable development until the reign of Hezekiah, when it is attested in the famous inscription at the mouth of the Siloam tunnel, probably the work of Hezekiah. This, then, was the script in which the oracles of Isaiah, if any of them were written down in his lifetime as Isa. 8.16 could imply, have to be visualized in their earliest form, together with contemporary written sources used by the compiler of Kings such as the annals of the kingdom of Judah. This script, already showing signs of developing almost into a cursive, is attested at the end of the independent monarchy of Judah in the Lachish Letters, written on a dozen and a half potsherds, mostly from a chamber in the ruined gateway of Lachish, from which Baruch's record of the oracles of Jeremiah, who lived at this time, probably did not much differ. Up to this point we find that *k*, *m*, *n*, and *w* are quite easily confused if written hastily, *p* and *r* are often hard to distinguish and *r* and *d* may be easily mistaken one for the other if the short downward stroke on the right is prolonged a little in the case of *d* or shortened in *r*. Both *ṭ* and ʿ are round circles, *ṭ* having a small, not always distinct, cross in the centre. Now in the fully developed square script only in the case of *r* and *d* is there serious danger of any of these letters being mistaken for the other. For instance *ṭ* and ʿ could not possibly be confused. But in the proto-Hebraic script this could easily happen. In the Lachish letters the letters became somewhat less distinct, the script approximating to the cursive and being written with a broad-pointed reed pen. In this thick lettering it is not always easy to distinguish *y*, *d*, and *g*, or *k* and *m*, while *d* and *r* are readily confused, especially if, as often, the long downward right-hand stroke of *r* is written shorter than usual.

In the Aramaic papyri from Elephantine in the fifth century BC, this script is already developing into the square character finally assumed in the Hebrew MSS of the Old Testament. The fluency which the papyrus surface facilitated encouraged a certain stylization which made for confusion between certain characters, e.g. *t* and *m*, and *y*, *w*, *k*, *n*, *p*, and *r*.

The Elephantine papyri carry us down to the beginning of the fourth century,[a] and by the third century BC the familiar square script has evolved, the earliest attested specimen being probably the inscription from the tomb of the Tobiad family at Iraq al-Amir in Transjordan from the early second century BC. The earliest Qumran MS so far distinguished, one of the texts of Samuel, from Cave 4 (4QSam[b]), has been dated on palaeographic grounds to the third century BC. By that time the MSS of the books of the Old Testament are written in the square character, virtually the same as that with which we are familiar in the printed texts, with minor calligraphic variations which are easily recognized.

Thus in reading any Hebrew text of MT, where the *apparatus criticus* indicates variants and where, as often, the text is either grammatically wrong or even makes no sense, in seeking to recover the consistent grammar and meaning that the text undoubtedly once bore we must visualize the ancient MSS in these various scripts. This mental transliteration often immediately suggests sense and the obvious meaning even without the corroborating evidence of the ancient versions.

ARCHAEOLOGY AND ANCIENT SEMITIC LITERATURES

It goes without saying that the more we may assimilate ourselves to

[a]One papyrus from those in the Brooklyn Museum published by E. G. Kraeling refers to events after the end of the reign of Amyrtaeus, and so is to be dated in 399 (*The Brooklyn Aramaic Papyri*, 1953, pp. 113, 284ff.).

the environment, life, and mentality of the ancient East contemporary with the events of which we are reading or the words and work of the *dramatis personnae*, the more able we are to decide between variant readings and select the correct one, and, in the last resort, to divine the reading by conjecture. Here archaeology has come to the aid of the textual critic by building up a picture of the life of the ancient East in its various regions and periods by the aid of material remains amplified by ancient literatures in cognate languages. Apart from providing and filling out this general background, passages in those ancient literatures often help directly in the restoration of doubtful texts in the Old Testament, as in various instances in the Ras Shamra texts. Many words in the Old Testament, occurring only once, have been suspected on that account when their meaning was not clear from a familiar root. Often in such cases scholars have resorted to emendation. Certain of these words, however, have been found in the Ras Shamra texts and other ancient literatures recovered by archaeology. In many cases these are not *hapax legomena* there, and, occurring in various contexts, their meaning is beyond doubt. Indeed, even where the meaning is not immediately apparent, or when the word is as rare in the Ras Shamra texts as in the Old Testament, the fact that so many of the Ras Shamra texts are poetic in form, observing the same principles of parallelism of phrase and idea as Hebrew poetry, means that the word in question may be recovered often beyond doubt. In the light of such cases many a doubtful word in the Old Testament which the critics in their haste had rejected and emended, often with commendable skill, has been vindicated, and a strict and detailed study of such cases in the Old Testament in the light of the Ras Shamra texts has satisfied us that the MT is vindicated in this way more often than discredited. A case in point will be found in II K. 4.42, where *wᵉkarmel bᵉṣiqlōnō* is such a problem. Commentators after Jerome proposed to emend to *wᵉkarmel bᵉqalʿātō* ('and fruit in his wallet'). In the Ras Shamra texts, however (*UT* 1 'Aqht, VI, 61–66), *biṣqᵉlōn* of our text is attested in the non-diminutive form *bṣql*, which is found in parallelism with *'ur*, which is known in Hebrew as 'plants', 'vegetables', or the like. Hence no emendation of MT is needed except metathesis and omission of *w* after *biṣqᵉlōn*, *w* resembling the preceding *n* and the following *k* in the proto-Hebraic script. The resulting *ūbiṣqᵉlōn karmillō* means 'and plants from his orchard' (see pp. 501f.). It is only just, however, to state that there are also cases where variants from MT suggested in the ancient versions have been confirmed by those extra-biblical texts, and in certain cases where the versions give no help such passages in those texts suggest an obvious emendation. In all such cases, however, the reading adopted must be demonstrably derivative from the corrupted MT passage, and in such emendations as we adopt in our text of Kings, it will be found that they usually correspond closely to the consonants of the MT, confusion occurring in the cases that we have noted in our section on the evolution of the Hebrew script.

3. CHRONOLOGY

FIRM CHRONOLOGY IN THE HEBREW MONARCHY

In the period of the Monarchy, for the first time in the history of Israel, we find a chronology which is more than merely relative. The reigns of David and Solomon, to be sure, are suspect as round numbers, 40 being the conventional indefinite number and length of a generation in Semitic folklore. Even here, however, a certain degree of particularization is possible through the synchronism of the reigns of David and Solomon with that of Hiram of Tyre (II Sam. 5.11; I K. 5.1ff.[15ff.]). Dating Hiram *c.* 970–940 (Josephus, *Contra Apionem* I, 18, after Menander of Ephesus),[a] the accession of Solomon would be normally dated within a decade after 970, and his death in the beginning of the reign of Shishak I (935–914), who sheltered Jeroboam after the failure of his revolt. Actually this agrees with the evidence of Kings, which suggests 931 as the date of Solomon's death.

The reigns of the subsequent kings of Israel and Judah are noted by their duration and are synchronized with one another. We might thus expect chronological accuracy, but on the sole evidence of Kings these precise figures often confuse rather than elucidate chronology, which in consequence is one of the notorious problems of Old Testament scholarship.

SCHEMATIC CHRONOLOGY

The chronological notes in Kings occur in the introduction to the reigns, where the accession of a king is synchronized with the regnal year of his contemporary in the sister kingdom during the period of the divided monarchy, and the duration of his reign given. This

[a]Kittel, *Die Bücher der Könige, HKAT*, 1900, p. 42; cf. E. Meyer, *Geschichte des Altertums* II, 1921–31, pp. 79f.: *c.*969–926; A. T. Olmstead, *History of Palestine and Syria*, 1931, p. 319: 981–947.

obviously belongs to the editorial framework of Kings, and on this account has been suspect to certain critical scholars, such as J. Wellhausen and I. Benzinger, who regard both synchronisms and duration of reigns as the work of a late redactor, hence artificial and unreliable. R. Kittel, on the other hand (HKAT, pp. X–XIII), while admitting that the redactor took considerable freedom with both synchronisms and duration of reigns, regards both as represented in original annalistic sources. Difficulties and discrepancies are admitted by all who have concerned themselves with the chronology of Kings, and, on the basis of the biblical evidence alone, taken at its face value, no final certainty may be achieved in the chronology of Kings.[a] The duration of the reigns of various kings may be suspected as being the work of the redactor, and the note on the foundation of Solomon's Temple 480 years after the Exodus and the schematic chronology of the earlier part of the Deuteronomistic history rouses natural suspicion of the chronology of Kings.

THE RELATIVE VALUE OF SYNCHRONISMS

Here, however, synchronisms supply a clue to the facts. Synchronisms with the reigns of neighbouring kings were a feature of ancient annals, e.g. Babylonian and Assyrian,[b] and were no doubt also a feature of the historical sources on which the compiler of Kings drew. This emphasis on the synchronisms, as apart from the duration of reigns, marks the work of J. Lewy,[c] J. Begrich,[d] and S. Mowinckel.[e] Here, however, it is not possible to tell immediately whether a synchronism is an element in a genuine old source or the work of a schematizing redactor. There are certain unmistakable cases of the latter, but each synchronism must be treated on its own merits.

REDACTIONAL AND TEXTUAL DIFFICULTIES: THE QUESTION OF CO-REGENCIES

Begrich and Mowinckel proceed, with the help of variant readings

[a]Thus Jepsen ('Noch einmal zur israelitisch-jüdischen Chronologie', *VT* XVIII, 1968, pp. 31–46) argues from the redactional adjustments in G to similar adjustments in MT, which would render any attempt to find an original systematization of the data vain.

[b]Gressmann, *Altorientalische Texte und Bilder zum Alten Testament*, 1926–27, pp. 359 and 333.

[c]*Die Chronologie der Könige von Israel und Juda*, 1927.

[d]*Die Chronologie der Könige von Israel und Juda*, 1929.

[e]'Die Chronologie der israelitischen und jüdischen Könige', *Acta Orientalia* X, 1932, pp. 161–275.

in the versions, relying, in our opinion, rather too much on Greek MSS of secondary value, and frequent assumption of deliberate falsifications and scribal errors, to draw up a chronology which actually does not differ widely from that which we have independently determined, except in the time between Jeroboam II and Ahaz. Both repudiate the hypothesis of co-regencies in Israel and Judah, except in the case of Jotham, to which R. de Vaux[a] adds Solomon's co-regency with David as the only instances of this practice explicitly mentioned in the Old Testament, regarding the hypothesis of co-regency as a desperate effort to reconcile the notorious discrepancies. The practice is assumed by Lewy and E. R. Thiele.[b] Certainly the only cases which are explicitly noted are those of Solomon and Jotham, but the latter case, in our opinion, may be stronger evidence for the general practice than an isolated case would suggest. We are certainly told without qualification that Jotham 'became king' in the second year of Pekah and reigned 16 years (II K. 15.32f.). An actual reign of this length can on no reckoning be fitted in between the death of Azariah in 740 and the accession of Ahaz before the end of the next decade, hence the 16 years, if not a scribal error for six, must refer to his reign together with his co-regency, of which we have explicit notice in II K. 15.5. This instance gives us a reasonable justification for assuming that in certain other instances of apparent discrepancy in the chronology of Kings the practice of co-regency similarly solves the difficulty. We formulate our chronological scheme on this hypothesis, which seems to be substantiated by the fact that usually the date at which a prince was adopted as co-regent coincides with particular political circumstances which make this step imperative. Moreover in a polygamous society, as the case of David's family indicates, the designation of an heir-apparent and his association with the reigning king was a natural measure to obviate civil strife, as regularly in Egypt and the later Assyrian Empire.[c]

RELATIVE WORTH OF SYNCHRONISMS AND NOTICES OF DURATIONS OF REIGNS

So far we agree with Lewy, Begrich, and Mowinckel that, though certain synchronisms may be the effort of a late redactor at har-

[a] *Ancient Israel*, 1961, p. 101.
[b] *The Mysterious Numbers of the Hebrew Kings*, 1951.
[c] H. Frankfort, *Kingship and the Gods*, 1948, pp. 101f., 143f.

monization in the interest of his schematization, the synchronisms were an element in the sources. Like them we should emphasize the significance of the synchronisms rather than the notices of the length of the reigns. There may, however, still be original annalistic matter here, and on this assumption we have worked. After all, if the synchronisms and duration of reigns were wholly the creation of the redactor there would be a consistency, which is lacking in the chronology of Kings. In view, however, of the undoubted schematization by the late redactor our efforts at a firm chronology on the basis of this matter may still be suspect, and it is notable that such an authority as de Vaux[a] can declare that the synchronisms in Kings set a problem which is perhaps insoluble. Within certain limitations, however, the biblical data may be controlled by more reliable evidence.

SYNCHRONISMS WITH EXTRA-BIBLICAL CHRONOLOGY

Fortunately there are certain synchronisms with Assyrian and Babylonian history. Here is a firm chronology based on accurate lists of Assyrian eponym officials (*limmu*), *limmu* annals recording events in the eponym's year of office, royal annals, which often record the same events as are mentioned in the *limmu*-chronicles, and finally lists of kings with the duration of their reigns. Of the last the most significant is the Khorsabad kinglist,[b] which, though noting only the names and sequence of the first 32 kings of Assyria, continues with the duration of the reigns until 738. Into these records dates may be introduced relatively to the eclipse of the sun noted in the *limmu*-chronicle in the month *Simanu* in the *limmu*-ship of Pur-Sagale in the ninth year of the King Ashur-dan III. This may be astronomically calculated, and is dated 15 June 763. Calculating backwards and forwards from the accession of Ashur-dan on the basis of the Assyrian kinglists we may establish a firm Assyrian chronology from a period contemporary with the foundation of the Hebrew monarchy to the year of the last *limmu* recorded (649). This chronological scheme is supplemented and continued by that of the great Alexandrine scholar Ptolemy (AD 70–161), who utilized local annals and astro-

[a]*Op. cit.*, p. 194.

[b]A. Poebel, 'The Assyrian Kinglist from Khorsabad', *JNES* I, 1942, pp. 247–306, 460–92; II, 1943, pp. 56–90. The accuracy of this list is corroborated in spite of minor variations by another kinglist bought in Mosul and now in the Seventh Day Adventist Seminary in New York, I. Gelb, 'Two Assyrian Kinglists', *JNES* XIII, 1954, pp. 209–30.

nomical observations to give a chronology from 747 BC to the Roman imperial period. Within the framework of Assyrian history there are determinable synchronisms with Hebrew history, which are amplified for the last phase of the history of Judah by the evidence of the Babylonian chronicles of Nabopolassar and Nebuchadrezzar.[a]

THE CAMPAIGNS OF SHALMANESER III AND THE REIGNS OF AHAB AND JEHU

Of these synchronisms the first and most significant is the Battle of Qarqar on the Orontes in the sixth year of Shalmaneser III (853), who mentions Ahab of Israel among his opponents. The same king lists Jehu among his tributaries in his 18th year (841). Now between Ahab and Jehu fell the reigns of Ahaziah and Joram, given respectively as two (I K. 22.51) and 12 years (II K. 3.1). This appears to sum up to 14 years, but if we assume that parts of a year in the last year of a king's reign were reckoned as full years both to the new king and to his predecessor we are left with reigns of part of two years for Ahaziah and so 12 years between 852 and 841, reckoning inclusively. Thus 853, when the Assyrian inscription of Shalmaneser mentions Ahab as present at Qarqar, was Ahab's last year, and 841 was the first year of Jehu.[b] From those two fixed points in Hebrew chronology it is possible to work out a scheme backward to the death of Solomon and forward to the final destruction of Jerusalem by the Babylonians. Here we may use the synchronisms and notices of the durations of reigns in Kings, though only with great caution. The critical use of such evidence, however, is facilitated by other notable synchronisms with Assyrian history attested in Assyrian records.

THE CAMPAIGNS OF TIGLATH-PILESER III AND THE REIGNS OF MENAHEM, AZARIAH, PEKAH, AHAZ, AND HOSHEA

Tiglath-pileser III, in the account of his campaigns in the West,[c] in his third year (743), records tribute from 'Menahem of Samaria' and 'Azriyau of Jauda', probably Azariah of Judah. Since Tiglath-pileser was active in the West till 738 the older chronologists, such as

[a]C. J. Gadd, *The Fall of Nineveh*, 1923; Sidney Smith, *Babylonian Historical Texts*, 1924; D. J. Wiseman, *Chronicles of Chaldaean Kings (626–556 BC) in the British Museum*, 1956.

[b]Our conclusion is that here the accession of Ahaziah and Joram is reckoned as automatic after the death of their predecessors, and not from the next New Year festival, as assumed by the editor after the Judaean custom.

[c]A. L. Oppenheim, in *ANET*, pp. 282f.

Mowinckel and Begrich, dated Menahem's payment of tribute in that year. This, however, necessitated a drastic revision of the chronological data on Menahem and his successors in Kings, which the use of variants in minor Greek MSS and the large assumption of scribal errors or redactional manipulation most certainly does not recommend. More recent scholars see in this inscription a comprehensive account of events of several years at the end of this phase of activity in 738, which was after the death of Menahem, which we reckon independently of the inscription in 742. Oppenheim, for instance, dates the reference to Azariah in 743, three years before his death in 740, on our reckoning from biblical data. He leaves Menahem's subjection, however, undated. E. R. Thiele[a] dates the subjection of both in 743, which supports our dating; cf. H. W. F. Saggs,[b] who dates that of Azariah in 742 and that of Menahem in 741.

The account of Tiglath-pileser's activity in Palestine between 734 and 732[c] with the references to the death of Pekah, the installation of Hoshea and the vassal status of Ahaz, supports our dating, on biblical evidence, of the death of Pekah in 732, the elevation of Hoshea in 732–1, and the recognition of Ahaz, who had already acceded in 732, in 731.

THE FALL OF SAMARIA

The date of the fall of Samaria has been one of the cruxes of biblical scholarship, owing to the fact that II K. 18.9f. attributes it to Shalmaneser V, who died at the end of 722 or the beginning of 721, whereas Shalmaneser's successor, Sargon II, claims it as his exploit in his few and fragmentary inscriptions which are relevant. Since he dates it in his *rēš šarrūti*, the year of his accession, this suggests 722–1, the year during which Shalmaneser died. The biblical statement further particularizes in dating the fall of Samaria in the ninth year of king Hoshea and the sixth year of Hezekiah, which, we claim, dates from his adoption as co-regent in 729. This suggests 723, after a siege of almost three years which began in 725, when the Assyrian records attest an expedition by Shalmaneser. If the biblical statement is authoritative, the discrepancy between II K. 18.9f. and Sargon's inscriptions might possibly be solved by positing that the writer of the biblical passage assumed that the city fell when Hoshea was arrested, whereas the siege may have continued after his arrest (so Begrich, Mowinckel). But there is good reason to doubt the accuracy of

[a] *The Mysterious Numbers . . .*, ch. 5. [b] *Iraq* XVII, 1955, pp. 144ff.
[c] *ANET*, pp. 282a, 283f.

Sargon's statement regarding the fall of Samaria in his *rēš šarrūti*. A. T. Olmstead, in his important study of Assyrian historiography,[a] has noted that display inscriptions to embellish buildings, in giving a résumé of a king's exploits, are less accurate than the annals, which are their source, enumerating local successes geographically rather than chronologically, and occasionally, as notoriously in the case of Ashurbanipal, expropriating the exploits of the previous king. Olmstead has further demonstrated that the annals recorded a campaign immediately after success and were edited on the occasion of the next notable success, being thoroughly reliable only for contemporary events, the former events being rendered in résumé and less accurately. The statement that Sargon took Samaria in the beginning of his reign in his first year comes from the Khorsabad Annals of his seventh year, a fragmentary source restored from his Display Inscription (*ANET*, p. 284) late in his reign. Olmstead therefore doubts Sargon's statement regarding the reduction of Samaria in his first year and dates the fall of the city to Shalmaneser V in 723 BC,[b] in which he is followed by Thiele.[c] This is borne out by the fact that, since Sargon was a usurper, his first year was preoccupied with domestic affairs and his first *palu* (campaign-year) was not until 720, when, however, he did deal with a revolt in the West involving Samaria. A further constructive attempt to solve the problem is undertaken by H. Tadmor,[d] who contends that Sargon's fragmentary Khorsabad Annals and the Display Inscription and the Nimrud Prisms discovered in 1952 and 1953[e] had telescoped details of the fall of Samaria in 723 or 722 and Sargon's campaigns in 720 and 716, the account of the campaigns being geographical rather than chronological. This is suggested to Tadmor by the fact that the fall of Samaria is associated with the victory over the army of Egypt and the subjugation of the Arabs in the West, events which occurred in 720 and 716 respectively. While Sargon's claim to have reduced Samaria in the first year of his reign must be frankly dismissed as an inaccuracy, the involvement of Samaria in the revolt which he suppressed in 720 and of the tribes in 716 probably entitled him to to suppose that he, rather than Shal-

[a] A. T. Olmstead, *Assyrian Historiography: a Source Study*, University of Missouri Studies, Social Science Series III, 1916.

[b] *Id.*, *AJSL* XXI, 1906, pp. 179–82. [c] *Op. cit.*, pp. 122–8.

[d] H. Tadmor, 'The Campaigns of Sargon II of Assur', *JCS* XII, 1958, pp. 22–40, 77–100, esp. 33–9.

[e] C. J. Gadd, 'Inscribed Prisms of Sargon II from Nimrud', *Iraq* XVI, 1954, pp. 173–201.

maneser, was responsible for the complete subjugation of Samaria. Under the latter, as the revolt of 720 indicated, it had only been partially successful. Tadmor argues plausibly[a] that the resettlement of the province of Samaria had begun by the beginning of Sargon's reign, which was complicated by domestic troubles and a revolt by Merodach-Baladan of Babylon, supported by the Elamites. This explains the settlement of people from Southern Mesopotamia in the province of Samaria (II K. 17.24). Sargon's preoccupation in the homeland and in Southern Mesopotamia in 721 not only precluded his activity against Samaria, but gave the Israelites in Samaria the opportunity of joining in the revolt, headed by Ilubi'di of Hamath, which Sargon suppressed in 720. It may be added that not only may the inscriptions of Sargon telescope events of 723–716, but that the very succinct statement of II K. 18.9–11 may also telescope events between the fall of the city of Shalmaneser V in 723–2 and the final deportation and resettlement of the district which was complete under Sargon in 715.

SARGON'S CAMPAIGNS AND THE REIGN OF HEZEKIAH

Mowinckel[b] shrewdly adduces the evidence of Sargon's accounts of his campaigns in the Philistine plain in 720[c] and in 711 in support of the dating of Hezekiah's accession in 714, which is suggested by the biblical dating of Sennacherib's campaign in 701 in Hezekiah's 14th year (II K. 18.13) and by the statement of II K. 16.2 that Ahaz reigned 16 years. On the evidence of the Old Testament and Assyrian records Ahaz was never anything but a subservient Assyrian vassal, while Hezekiah on the same evidence was a rebel. Dating Hezekiah a decade or more earlier, as is still done by Montgomery (ICC, pp. 52ff.), after the older chronologists on the basis of the synchronism of the apparent accession of Hezekiah with the third year of Hoshea (II K. 18.1), it might still be said that the fact that Judah is not mentioned in the account of Sargon's campaign to Philistia in 720, but is an enemy in 711, might indicate a change of policy on the part of Hezekiah. The greater likelihood is that this represents rather a change of government. The very circumstantial account in the Assyrian records of the part that Hezekiah played in Sennacherib's campaign of 701 is, of course, the direct corroboration of the synchronism of this campaign in the 14th year of Hezekiah (II K. 18.13).

[a]Tadmor, *op. cit.*, p. 38. [b]*Acta Orientalia* X, pp. 198f. [c]*ANET*, pp. 284–6.

THE BABYLONIAN CHRONICLES OF NABOPOLASSAR AND NEBUCHADREZZAR AND THE REIGNS OF JOSIAH AND HIS SUCCESSORS, AND THE CAPTURE OF JERUSALEM IN 597 AND 586

From the death of Josiah, synchronisms with the Babylonian Chronicles of Nabopolassar and Nebuchadrezzar yield a very accurate chronology. Nabopolassar's Chronicle dates Necho's expedition from Tammuz to Elul (June–July to August–September), 609. Hence it is clear that the death of Josiah at the hands of Necho at Megiddo *en route* for Mesopotamia (II K. 23.29; cf. II Chron. 35.20ff.) was in Tammuz. The three months' campaign of Necho in Northern Mesopotamia seems thus to coincide with the three months' reign of Jehoahaz, whom the people elevated to Josiah's place (II K. 23.31), so it is likely that Jehoahaz's brief reign is to be dated 609, the emergency accounting for the lack of an accession-year. Since the Pharaoh so far respected Jewish tradition as to give his nominee a Yahweh-theophoric Jehoiakim, it would not have been strange if he had observed the convention of accession at the New Year festival. This seems precluded, however, by the subsequent chronology, which suggests that the 11 years' reign of Jehoiakim (II K. 23.36) is dated 607–597. Our explanation is that though Jehoahaz was removed at the end of 609 (Elul) and Jehoiakim appointed by Necho at the New Year festival in 608, the records of Judah ignored this appointment, regarding 608 as Jehoiakim's accession-year and his formal accession as the New Year festival of 607. The three months' reign of Jehoiachin is accurately dated from the Babylonian Chronicle of Nebuchadrezzar, which dates the expedition which culminated for Judah in the fall of Jerusalem from Kislev (November-December) to Adar (February–March), 597.[a] The official reign of Zedekiah is thus dated according to Jewish custom from his accession at the New Year festival in 596 to the fall of Jerusalem in his 11th year (II K. 24.18; 25.3) in 586.

HISTORICAL INFORMATION BEHIND APPARENT DISCREPANCIES IN THE CHRONOLOGY OF KINGS

The synchronisms and notices of the length of reigns in Kings are apparently full of discrepancies. We believe, however, that there is real historical information underlying them. Thus the figures must be seriously considered and apparent discrepancies patiently investi-

[a]D. J. Wiseman, *op. cit.*, pp. 72f.

gated. Here three considerations regulate our reckoning. The reckoning of an event in the reign of a king may be not from his accession but from some other event. The note of a king's elevation or of his reign may relate not to his accession as sole king, but to his adoption as heir-apparent or co-regent with his father. Then it must be remembered that, though this chronology was doubtless based on annalistic records from Israel and Judah, it has been communicated in the extant synchronistic system by Judaean scribes working after the fall of the Northern kingdom, hence not fully conversant with North Israelite eras of reckoning, especially in the dark period of Assyrian domination, nationalist rebellion, and civil war under Menahem, Pekah, and Hoshea.

EXAMPLES OF DISCREPANCIES: BAASHA, OMRI, PEKAH

The first notable discrepancy is in the reign of Baasha, the third king of Northern Israel. It is stated that he died in the 26th year of Asa of Judah (I K. 16.6, 8); but in II Chron. 16.1 he is said to have raided Judah in the 36th year of Asa. Here obviously the first date is reckoned from the accession of Asa and the second from the disruption of the kingdom, the synchronism with Asa being an editorial inadvertency. So, too, in the case of Omri. Counting back 12 years inclusively from Ahab's accession in 874, 22 years before his death in 853, we date Omri's accession in 885. This agrees with the statement that Zimri, his ephemeral predecessor, slew king Elah in the 27th year of Asa (I K. 16.10, 15), i.e. in Elah's second year (I K. 16.8) after Baasha's death in Asa's 26th year. In I K. 16.23, however, Omri's reign is dated from the 31st year of Asa. The first date is from the time that Omri ruled with a rival Tibni (16.22); the second relates to the establishment of Omri as sole ruler, which we date in 881. Notorious difficulties in the chronology of Israel in the last two decades of her independence may be similarly resolved. II K. 15.27 states that Pekah became king in the 52nd year of Azariah of Judah, which we date 740, and reigned 20 years. That is on the face of it absurd, since it carries his reign down to 721, ignoring the reign of Hoshea, who slew Pekah in 731. The accession of Pekah as undisputed king was, we believe, in 740, as the text states, but his 20 years may be reckoned not from that date, but from an earlier date in the life of Pekah, presumably from the time he headed an abortive nationalist rising against Menahem, who was an Assyrian vassal (II K. 15.19f.), having come to the throne as the victor in a civil war (15.16). In this case the presumable rising of Pekah, which is not mentioned in Scripture, may have occurred in 750, which, in view of the disorders of Menahem's reign, is quite feasible. When Pekah eventually came to the throne in 740 this earlier date was probably the point from which he dated his archives, which are one of the ultimate sources for the chronological notice we are considering.

CO-REGENCIES

Illustrative of the second principle, the practice of co-regencies, is the period of Joash of Judah and his successors Amaziah and Azariah. Their reigns amount to 121 years. Since the death of Azariah cannot be after 740 nor the 40 years of Joash reckoned from earlier than 841,[a] there is here an overplus of at least 20 years which can best be accounted for by the assumption that the given duration of the reigns included co-regencies.[b] In this period an apparent discrepancy in the chronology of Jehoahaz of Israel and his son Jehoash at II K. 13.10 and 14.1 suggests the same solution in the practice of co-regencies. In the first passage, Jehoash of Israel is said to have become king in the 37th year of Joash of Judah. Since the latter is said to have reigned 40 years (12.1), the accession of his son Amaziah in the 2nd year of Jehoash of Israel (14.1) would seem to have been in the 38th year of his father's reign, i.e. before his death. According to our calculation (see p. 72) the year of the accession of Jehoash of Israel was 796, the year of the death of Joash of Judah, so that if we allow Amaziah an accession year, his formal accession was in 795, the second year of his Israelite contemporary. But the 37th year of Joash of Judah was 799, when II K. 13.10 notes the beginning of the reign of Jehoash of Israel; hence we conclude that the reference here is to the co-regency of Jehoash of Israel, the note of his reign of 16 years being really independent, referring to the period from his accession as sole king to his death. It is possible that the reference to the elevation of Amaziah in the second year of Jehoash of Israel refers to the adoption of Amaziah as co-regent in 798. This is not unlikely in view of the general unpopularity of Jehoash at the end of his reign, which was

[a]Even admitting that the reign of Joash included the six years of his grandmother Athaliah, as is confidently stated by Mowinckel, 'Die Chronologie . . .', p. 235.

[b]Mowinckel solves this problem drastically by suggesting that the redactor in the interests of his schematic chronology assigned Azariah ten years too many, *ibid.*, pp. 238–43.

increased after his humiliation at the hands of the Aramaeans (12.17f.), closely associated with his death in II Chron. 24.24f. The elevation of Jeroboam II again is dated from the 15th year of Amaziah of Judah (II K. 14.23). Even if we reckon this from the earliest possible date, the presumable co-regency of Amaziah in 798, the 41 years of Jeroboam would carry us down too late, to 744, precluding the reigns of Menahem and his two predecessors. The 41 years must therefore include a co-regency of Jeroboam. Here, however, as in 13.10 and 14.1 and often in such notices, the Judaean compiler has confused two facts. He notes the number 41, which can only date from the adoption of Jeroboam as co-regent in 794, but with this he misleadingly associates the accession of Jeroboam as sole king in the 15th year of Amaziah, reckoning from the date of Amaziah's accession as sole king in 795.

CO-REGENCIES IN THE FAMILIES OF AHAB AND JEHOSHAPHAT

Recognizing the fact that co-regencies occurred regularly, though not invariably, and that these, or the elevation to the status of heir-apparent, were noted in the archives of both kingdoms, and were often confused by the later compiler with the dates of accession as sole king, we may consider one of the most perplexing periods in the chronology of Kings, that from the end of the reign of Omri to the time of his grandson Jehoram and Joram the son of Jehoshaphat. The reigns of Ahab and Jehoshaphat may be fixed as respectively 874–853 and 871–847, dating back from Ahab's last year 853 and in agreement with earlier synchronisms in the reigns of the kings of Israel and Judah. Now it is said in I K. 22.51 [52] that Ahaziah the son of Ahab became king in the 17th year of Jehoshaphat and reigned two years, his brother Jehoram succeeding him in the 18th year of Jehoshaphat and reigning 12 years. But the 17th year of Jehoshaphat was 855, three years before the death of Ahab, while, since Jehoram was killed by Jehu in 841, his reign must be dated 852–841, and that of Ahaziah 853–852. The most likely solution is that the editor had a record of the appointment of Ahaziah as co-regent with Ahab in 855, a natural measure in view of Ahab's political involvements, and that he wrongly combined with this the notice of his two years' reign. This having been done, he rightly noted the succession of Jehoram a year later than the accession of Ahaziah, but wrongly dated it in the 18th year of Jehoshaphat in agreement with the former synchronism. A further complication here is that the accession of

Jehoram the son of Ahab is dated in the second year of Joram the son of Jehoshaphat (II K. 1.17). Taking 852 as the firm date for the accession of Jehoram of Israel would give 853 for the first year of Joram the son of Jehoshapat, seven years before his father's death. The explanation may be that the compiler had a notice of the elevation of Joram the son of Jehoshaphat to co-regency in that year, which is most feasible considering Jehoshaphat's probable implication in Israelite politics in the eventful year of Qarqar (cf. I K. 22; II K. 3.7ff.). The matter seems further complicated by the statement that Joram of Judah began to reign in the fifth year of Jehoram the son of Ahab (II K. 8.16f.) and reigned eight years. Since his son Ahaziah was killed in his first year in 841, apparently before his formal accession though after his father's death, we have a double check here, which fixes the reign of Joram of Judah as 848–841. Now, according to our reckoning by I K. 22.41f., Jehoshaphat reigned 871–847. Our conclusion is that he withdrew from public life in 848, when Joram was invested with the supreme authority. This would accord with the curious note that 'In the fifth year of Jehoram the son of Ahab . . . *Jehoshaphat being then king of Judah*, Joram the son of Jehoshaphat king of Judah began to reign' (II K. 8.16.).

FURTHER CASES OF CO-REGENCY AND 'PARTISAN DATING'; AHAZ'S ACCESSION

The case of the chronology of Jeroboam (II K. 14.23) suggests a further solution of the vexed problem of the chronology of Kings. Here it is obvious that the compiler was using two sources of information which did not agree in their system of dating. Figures were available from the independent records of Israel and Judah, the length of the reigns referring to the whole period from the time that the king was designated as co-regent till his death, but occasionally the synchronism, especially if it was made by the compiler,[a] was made with reference to the accession of a king as sole ruler on the death of his father. Here the matter is complicated by the use of the verb *mālak*, which apparently means 'to act, or be adopted, as co-regent' as well as 'to accede as king'. The task of the compiler was further complicated by a local system of dating, which, as in the instance of Pekah's chronology, we may term 'partisan dating'. In

[a]The extent to which synchronisms entered into the archives of Israel and Judah is quite uncertain, but cannot be excluded from our reckoning.

Pekah's case the political party which had opposed Menahem's pro-Assyrian policy and had been temporarily suppressed by him ignored his reign when their champion Pekah finally rose to power, hence events in his reign were dated from the time of his abortive rising. An excellent instance of the confusion caused by such local 'partisan dating' in the original records is the chronology of Ahaz of Judah, which, incidentally, is good evidence of the practice of co-regency. Hoshea, according to Tiglath-pileser's annalistic account of his Palestinian campaign of 732, was appointed vassal king in Samaria in 732. Taking the conclusion of the siege of Samaria as in his ninth year (II K. 17.6) his reign must be reckoned from 731. This may be because he was not able to establish his authority until then, or it may be a case of the Judaean compiler allowing an accession-year according to the practice familiar in Judah. The first explanation appeals more to us. Thus 731 was the second year of Ahaz, which 17.1 (emended, see p. 70 below) gives as the year of Hoshea's accession. Hence Ahaz must have acceded in 732. But 16.1 suggests the year 734, which must refer to his adoption as co-regent. But if Hezekiah acceded in 714 at the New Year festival following the death of Ahaz in 715, as 18.13 taken with Sennacherib's account of his 701 campaign suggests, and Ahaz reigned 16 years (16.2), Ahaz's accession must be regarded as in 730. Our explanation is that there are three different chronological systems here. Ahaz was adopted as co-regent with Jotham shortly before his death in 734 (15.32; 16.1). Since Tiglath-pileser III was then in Palestine, Ahaz did not formally accede as an independent king; cf. Tiglath-pileser's curtailment of the royal dignity implied in 16.18. Nevertheless Tiglath-pileser accorded him some recognition of authority in 732, and North Israelite records, drawn upon in 17.1, regard this as his formal accession. But not until 730 was Ahaz free to assume his full royal authority at the New Year festival according to the tradition in Judah. From this date his reign runs in the chronology of Judah.

ACCESSION IN ISRAEL AND JUDAH

On the principles just set out it is not difficult to determine a chronological scheme which is reliable and generally accurate. Those who have interested themselves in this problem, however, are vexed to find that discrepancies of an odd year persist. To this difficulty E. R. Thiele proposes a solution by presuming that in Judah the king's official reign did not begin till the first New Year festival after the death of his predecessor, his first year, therefore, not being reckoned. This he regards as the practice from Rehoboam to Jehoshaphat and from Amaziah to Zedekiah, the reign of the usurper Athaliah being reckoned according to the practice in North Israel, where the king's official reign began immediately after the death of his predecessor, and the reign of her successor Joash, who acceded as the result of a nationalist *coup d'état*, likewise beginning with no accession-year. In the Northern kingdom Thiele assumes a non-accession system from Jeroboam I to Jehoahaz, the son of Jehu, but an accession-system from Jehoahaz's successor Jehoash to Hoshea, this being possibly assumed by Judaean editors in their use of North Israelite sources. We venture to doubt the validity of this assumption. There is no doubt that an accession-year was generally observed in Judah, but not in Israel, but we question if it were so regularly observed as Thiele claims. Asa is stated to have reigned 41 years, having acceded in the 20th year of Jeroboam (I K. 15.9f.). He died therefore in the third year of Ahab. Since his son Jehoshaphat acceded in the fourth year of Ahab (I K. 22.41), the convention of the accession-year must have been observed in the case of Jehoshaphat. Again, the apparent discrepancy of II K. 9.29, where the accession of Ahaziah of Judah is dated in the 11th year of Jehoram the son of Ahab, with the statement that he acceded in the 12th year of Jehoram (8.25) is explicable on the assumption that the second statement is taken directly from North Israelite archives, which did not recognize an accession year, and the first represents a modification by a scribe or editor who was familiar with the Judaean accession system and subtracted an accession-year from the reign of Jehoram. On the other hand Abijah the son of Rehoboam acceded in the 18th year of Jeroboam I (I K. 15.1ff.) and reigned three years, hence to the 20th year of Jeroboam (15.9). But Asa is stated to have acceded in Jeroboam's 20th year (15.9), hence no accession-year seems to have been observed in the case of Asa. Our conclusion is, then, that in Judah the accession of a king at the New Year festival after the death of his father was *de rigueur*, but if his predecessor died soon before the New Year festival there was in effect no accession-year. This is admittedly a conjecture which lacks conclusive proof, but it would account for apparent exceptions to the rule of an accession-year in Judah in the case of Asa at least. In any case, though the assumption of the practice of an accession-year in Judah is generally well founded, it cannot be automatically applied, and each case demands special consideration.

SCRIBAL ERRORS IN THE CHRONOLOGY OF KINGS

Finally we must reckon with simple scribal errors in the transmission of the text. Again the most notable examples are, incidentally, from the period of Jotham and Ahaz, which on other grounds poses the greatest problems to chronologists. In II K. 15.32f. it is stated that Jotham reigned 16 years from the second year of Pekah. Dating from the actual accession of Pekah in 740, the reign of Jotham on this reckoning would extend well down into the sole reign of Ahaz, to 724. If the dating, on the other hand, is from 750, from which point we have seen the reign of Pekah to be reckoned elsewhere, when presumably he first rose unsuccessfully against Menahem, the death of Jotham would be in 734, when we have calculated the co-regency of Ahaz just before his father's death. In the latter case the accession of Jotham in the second year of Pekah might refer to his adoption as co-regent with Azariah in 749. But it seems simpler to regard 16 in II K. 15.32f. as a scribal error for 6 and to date Jotham's reign 739 to 734. Another instance of a similar scribal error from the same period is II K. 17.1. Here the nine years' reign of Hoshea, the last king of Israel, is dated from the 12th year of Ahaz. But, dating back nine years from his arrest during the siege of Samaria in 723, the accession of Hoshea is in 731, the second year of Ahaz, dating from his accession as sole king in 732, according to North Israelite reckoning.

In the light of these principles we now proceed to a reconstruction of the chronology of Kings.

RECONSTRUCTION, FROM THE DEATH OF AHAB TO THE DISRUPTION

Starting with the date 853 for the death of Ahab we fix the beginning of his reign of 22 years (I K. 16.29) in 874. Since the same passage states that this was the 38th year of Asa, the latter must have acceded in 911. Asa acceded in the 20th year of Jeroboam (I K. 15.9), whose reign is thus dated from 930. This would agree with the evidence for the reigns of Asa's predecessors Abijah, 3 years, acceding in the 18th year of Jeroboam, i.e. 913, and Rehoboam, 17 years, if we allow 914–913 as an accession-year for Abijah. Here, however, there is an apparent discrepancy, since, if we count back from the death of Ahab on the basis of the biblical chronology, we reach 931 for the beginning of Jeroboam's reign. We suggest that this reckoning depends on North Israelite records, which dated the beginning of Jeroboam's reign from the time he was called home from Egypt or from the Shechem assembly, whereas Judaean scribes reckoned his accession from the New Year festival in 930, when his contemporary Rehoboam formally acceded. Jeroboam's successor Nadab acceded immediately on his father's death in 910, the second year of Asa (I K. 15.25), and was killed by Baasha the following year in the third year of Asa (I K. 15.28, 33), having reigned for parts of two separate years, which were reckoned as two years. Baasha then reigned 24 years (I K. 15.33), from 909 till 886, the 26th year of Asa, when he was succeeded by Elah (I K. 16.8), who was killed the following year, the 27th of Asa, hence reigning during parts of two years (I K. 16.10), 886–885. After the suppression of his assassin Zimri, who reigned seven days, Omri's official reign according to North Israelite records begins in 885, though his reign was disputed by a rival, Tibni (I K. 16.21), and he was not undisputed ruler till the 31st year of Asa (I K. 16.23) in 881. The 12 years of his reign, however, were dated in his archives from 885, and Ahab acceded on his death in 874, the 38th year of Asa (I K. 16.29).

ASA TO JEHU'S REVOLT, 841

Turning now to Judah, Asa was succeeded after a reign of 41 years (I K. 15.10) by Jehoshaphat in the fourth year of Ahab (I K. 22.41), in 871. In this case therefore there was no accession-year. We have already explicated the confused chronology of Israel and Judah from this point to the accession of the usurper Jehu (see pp. 66f. above) concluding that Jehoshaphat reigned 871–847, possibly withdrawing from public life in 848, Joram his son 848–841, and Ahaziah was killed by Jehu in 841, the year that he succeeded, but before his formal accession. In Israel in this period Ahaziah, who had been named as co-regent in 855, the 17th year of Jehoshaphat of Judah (I K. 22.51), succeeded Ahab in 853 and died in 852, his reign being reckoned as two years, and his brother Jehoram succeeded immediately. We have suggested that the synchronism of the accession of Jehoram in the second year of Joram the son of Jehoshaphat (II K. 1.17) may be occasioned by the note in Judaean records that Joram was appointed co-regent in 853 when Jehoshaphat was involved in Ahab's foreign politics. The 12 years' reign of Jehoram of Israel ended with his death at the hand of Jehu in 841.

JEHU AND JOASH OF JUDAH

In Israel Jehu reigned 28 years (II K. 10.36) from 841 to 814, and was succeeded by Jehoahaz in the 23rd year of Joash of Judah (II K. 13.1). Dating from the accession of Joash in 835 this would be in 813, the year after the death of Jehu. Such an interval was contrary to the rule of Israel, but the exception might be explained by the circumstances of Aramaean domination at that time. The beginning of Jehoash's reign is given as the 37th year of Joash of Judah (II K. 13.10), which is 799 if reckoned from 835. Here, however, when we reckon back from the end of the monarchy, taking as our starting-point the Assyrian invasion of 701 in the 14th year of Hezekiah (II K. 18.13), we reach the date 781 for the accession of Jeroboam as sole king on the death of Jehoash in the 15th year of Amaziah (II K. 14.23), which would give Jehoash a reign not of 16 years (II K. 13.10) but of 19 years. Here we conclude that behind the chronology of II K. 13.10 there lie two independent notices, one that Jehoash became co-regent in 799 in the 37th year of Joash of Judah and the other that he reigned 16 years, from 796 to 781.

FROM ATHALIAH TO AMAZIAH OF JUDAH

In this period in Judah Athaliah reigned 6 years (II K. 11.6), from 841 to 836, being succeeded by Joash, who was elevated by a *coup d'état* probably on the occasion of the New Year festival (see commentary) in 835, and reigned 40 years (II K. 12.1). It is stated that Amaziah began to reign in the second year of Jehoash of Israel and reigned 29 years. If the date of his elevation is from the year of Jehoash's co-regency, this is 798, and refers to the adoption of Amaziah as co-regent. If it dates from the accession of Jehoash as sole king in 796 the reference is to Amaziah's accession as sole king in 795, which is the year after his father's death, thus allowing for an accession-year. In any case the reign of Amaziah as sole king is 795–767.

FROM JEROBOAM II AND AZARIAH TO PEKAH AND JOTHAM

The accession of Jeroboam II of Israel is given as the 15th year of Amaziah (II K. 14.23). If this is dated from 795 it falls in 781, but the subsequent chronology indicates that, apart from this fact, the passage notes an independent fact that an earlier elevation of Jeroboam as co-regent is indicated. That is in 794, from which, misleadingly, the compiler numbers his 41 years. Hence the reign of

Jeroboam as sole king is from 781 to 754, when he was succeeded by his son Zechariah, who reigned six months in the 38th year of Azariah (II K. 15.8). The last dating is from 791, when Azariah, called also Uzziah, became co-regent with Amaziah, whom he succeeded in 766, after an accession-year. Since this is stated to have been in the 27th year of Jeroboam, i.e. from his co-regency, there is a slight discrepancy, since that date would be 792. The explanation may be that the Judaean editor assumed that the date referred to the accession of Jeroboam as sole king and wrongly allowed an accession-year. A further complication may be that the North Israelite New Year began a month after that of Judah, as I K. 12.32 suggests. Hence we date the reign of Azariah of Judah 766–740, allowing an accession-year. His 52-year reign (II K. 15.2) dates from 791, when he became co-regent. The month-long reign of Shallum fell in the 39th year of Azariah, hence 753, when, according to II K. 15.17, the reign of Menahem began. Here again there seems a discrepancy, his reign being given as ten years. This apparently lasts till 744, but as Menahem was succeeded, evidently peaceably, by his son Pekahiah in Azariah's 50th year, he must have reigned to 742. The explanation lies in the context. Menahem came to the throne as the result of a very savage civil war (II K. 15.16), and the asyndetic statement 'ten years in Samaria' (II K. 15.17) probably means that though his reign is dated in his own archives from 753, he was not able to establish himself in Samaria till 751. His son Pekahiah succeeded him in 742 and died the following year (II K. 15.23), but Pekah was not able to assert himself till the 52nd year of Azariah (II K. 15.27), i.e. 740, which is easily understood in view of the fact that this involved fighting. We have already demonstrated that Pekah's 20 years of office must date from 750, the date of an abortive rising against Menahem. Hence his violent death at the hands of Hoshea (II K. 15.30) was in 731. As this is dated in the 20th year of Jotham, the latter must have been appointed co-regent in 750, his actual reign as sole king being six years (II K. 15.33, reading 6 for 16, see p. 70 above), from the second year of Pekah, 739, after an accession-year, to 734, when, in the intensification of Assyria's interest in Palestine, he may have abdicated in favour of his son Ahaz, who, however, did not immediately accede, owing to the intervention of Assyria.

AHAZ, HOSHEA, AND HEZEKIAH

We have already dealt with the problems of the reigns of Jotham and Ahaz of Judah and Hoshea, the last king of Israel, whose reigns we have dated as follows: Jotham, 739–734; Ahaz co-regent 734, the 17th year of Pekah (II K. 16.1), sole king in Judah 732 (Hoshea becoming king in Ahaz's second year, II K. 17.1, emended, see p. 70 above), recognized as king by Tiglath-pileser, 732, and formally acceding at the New Year festival according to Judaean custom, 730; Hoshea, 731–723. Here one of the vital keys to the problem is the chronology of Hezekiah, the Assyrian expedition in his 14th year (II K. 18.13) being dated in the annals of Sennacherib in 701. Hezekiah must then have acceded as sole king in 714, one accession-year after the death of Ahaz in 715. Since Ahaz reigned 16 years (II K. 16.1), his formal accession must have been in 730. In II K. 18.1 it is stated that Hezekiah began to reign in the third year of Hoshea, a statement which has influenced II K. 18.9, where Shalmaneser's expedition against Samaria is dated 'in the fourth year of Hezekiah', which was the seventh year of Hoshea. This can only refer to the adoption of Hezekiah as heir-apparent in 729 at the age of ten. The 29-year reign of Hezekiah as sole king therefore is from 714 to 686.

From this point on there are no synchronisms with Israelite rulers; hence we work backwards from the death of Josiah, now to be accurately dated by a reference to the campaign of Pharaoh Necho in the Babylonian Chronicle of Nabopolassar, in the summer (the month Tammuz) of 609.[a] His reign must therefore date from 639. In the circumstances of his elevation after a popular rising against Amon he may not have had an accession-year, but this is doubtful, since Amon's two years (II K. 21.19) must date from 641–640 or 640–639. The 55 years ascribed to Manasseh (II K. 21.1), allowing for Amon's accession-year, would carry us back to 695 or 694, hence before the death of Hezekiah. Thus Manasseh must have been adopted as heir-apparent or co-regent then, acceding in 685, after an accession-year following the death of his father Hezekiah.

FROM THE DEATH OF JOSIAH TO THE FALL OF JERUSALEM IN 586

For our reconstruction of the chronology of this period see p. 63.

[a]D. J. Wiseman, *Chronicles of Chaldaean Kings . . .*, pp. 62f.

4. CHRONOLOGICAL TABLE

Death of David *c.* 970–960
Death of Solomon 931

ISRAEL		JUDAH	
Jeroboam I	931–910	Rehoboam	930–914
Nadab	910–909	Abijah	913–911
Baasha	909–886	Asa	911–871
Elah	886–885		
Omri (rule disputed by Tibni)	885–881		
(undisputed ruler)	881–874		
Ahab	874–853	Jehoshaphat	871–847
		(probably withdrawing from public life in 848)	
Ahaziah co-regent	855		
sole king	853–852		
Jehoram	852–841	Joram co-regent	853
		sole king	848–841
Jehu	841–814	Ahaziah	841
		Athaliah	841–836
Jehoahaz	813–797	Joash	835–796
Jehoash co-regent	799		
sole king	796–781	Amaziah co-regent	798
		sole king	795–767
Jeroboam II co-regent	794	Azariah (Uzziah) co-regent	791
sole king	781–754	sole king	766–740
Zechariah	754–753		
Shallum	753		
Menahem's rising	753	Jotham co-regent	750
Menahem established	751–742	sole king	739–734
Pekahiah	742–741	Ahaz co-regent	734
Pekah	740–732/1	recognized by Tiglath-pileser	732
Hoshea	731–723		
Fall of Samaria	723/2	formal accession	730
		reign	730–715
		Hezekiah co-regent	729
		sole king	714–686
		Manasseh co-regent	695
		sole king	685–641
		Amon	640–639
		Josiah	639–609
		Jehoahaz (3 months)	609
		Jehoiakim, possibly appointed by Necho	608
		but dated by Jewish reckoning	607–597
		Jehoiachin (3 months)	597
		Zedekiah	596–586
		Fall of Jerusalem	586

II

THE HEBREW EMPIRE: I KINGS 1–11

1. THE LAST DAYS OF DAVID AND THE ACCESSION OF SOLOMON: 1.1–2.46

FOR THE LITERARY INTRODUCTION to this passage from the Story of the Davidic Succession, see Introduction, pp. 14ff.

In contrast to the general style of Kings, this history is presented in racy narrative style, with dramatic representation of the characters and keen awareness of the relation of men and motives to events.

(*a*) THE ADOPTION OF SOLOMON AS HEIR-APPARENT AFTER THE FINAL CRISIS IN THE STRUGGLE FOR THE SUCCESSION: 1.1–53

(i) THE OLD AGE OF DAVID: 1.1–4

This section gives the account of Abishag's introduction to court in anticipation of Adonijah's request after David's death to marry her, a request which was the immediate cause of his own death (2.16–22). It may, like 2.13ff., be a secondary elaboration of the Story of the Davidic Succession.

1 [1]Now king David was old, advanced in years, and they covered him
with clothes but he got no heat. [2]So his servants said, Let them seek out
for the king[a] a girl, a virgin, and let her stand before the king and care
for him and lie in his bosom,[b] and the king[c] will get heat. [3]And they

[a]In MT *la'dōnī hammelek* ('my lord, the king'), the sing. pronom. suffix does not agree with the subject of the main verb of the sentence, which is plural. The direct speech of MT may be retained as the statement of each of the 'servants', but we prefer the reading of G^{B}, which omits *'adōnī*.

[b]G^{BA} suggest that *beḥēqō* should be read for MT *beḥēqekā*. Though we follow G^{BA}, the second person is intelligible in spite of the previous reference to the king in the third person, which is, of course, characteristic of deferential address.

[c]So G^{L} for MT *la'dōnī hammelek*, but cf. n[a].

sought out a beautiful girl in all the land of Israel and found Abishag the Shunammite and brought her to the king. [4]And the girl was very beautiful and cared for the king and served him, but the king had no intercourse with her.

1.1 In this verse 'bed-clothes' rather than 'robes' might seem the more natural reading, and, in fact, the singular *beged* is used in I Sam. 19.13 apparently of bed-clothes. In both cases, however, we may reasonably question if the text did not originally read *r*[e]*bādīm* ('coverlets') and *rebed* for *b*[e]*gādīm* and *beged*.

2. 'His servants', *'*[a]*bādāw*, is a general term the precise significance of which is not always easy to determine. It refers in Kings to four categories: slaves, feudal retainers, and courtiers, both feudal and independent, who have the status almost of privy counsellors, e.g. II K. 5.6 (Naaman the Syrian); 22.12 (Asaiah). In II K. 25.8 *'ebed* as the designation of Nebuzaradan, the chief of the guard, who destroyed Jerusalem, probably denotes his feudal status. In the present passage the interest in the intimacies of the royal bed-chamber probably indicates that the 'servants' were of the third category. Lastly it may refer generally to subjects of the realm.

3. The status of Abishag is uncertain. Nothing in vv. 1–5 suggests that she was more than a nurse who also slept with the king. This may have been the survival of a primitive rite of contactual magic to convey the health and heat of the young body to the old king, and Josephus[a] adds that it was a medical prescription, and it is so attested in Greek medicine by Galen. On the other hand, field anthropology among primitives indicates that the authority and even the life of the king depends on his virility, and there may be more than coincidence in David's appointment of a co-regent after he failed to pass the test of virility, cf. the Krt text from Ras Shamra, where the sickness of the king is assumed to disqualify him from reigning.[b] In view of the significance of the adoption of the late king's harem, as in the case of Abner's claim to Saul's concubine Rizpah (II Sam. 3.7ff.) and the rebel Absalom's public adoption of David's harem (II Sam. 16.21ff.), Solomon's mortal resentment at Adonijah's request for Abishag ('Ask the kingship also for him!') suggests that Abishag was a regular concubine of the king. The verb *sākan*, which describes her capacity and activity, is attested in Job 15.3, meaning 'to be of service', being in parallelism with the verbal root *yā'al* ('be profitable').

[a]*Ant.* VIII, 19.3.
[b]Gordon, *UT*, 127, 35–38.

The identity of the 'Shunammite' with the 'Shulammith' of the Song of Songs, itself phonetically possible, has been held by various scholars from W. Erbt[a] to F. Dornseiff.[b] J. Goodspeed[c] explains the term Shulammith in the Song of Songs as the feminine form of Solomon in the wedding songs, where the bridegroom is hailed as 'Solomon' and the bride as Shulammith. The present passage, however, as H. H. Rowley points out,[d] does not associate Abishag the Shunammite with Solomon. There is no reason to take the term otherwise than as referring to the home of Abishag, Shunem, which till lately was the Arab village of *Sulem*, on the west side of *Jebel ad-Dāhī*, seven miles south-east of Nazareth, later known in II K. 4.12ff. as the home of the woman whose son Elisha restored to life.

1.4 The name Abishag is interesting, though of uncertain import. The connection with the verb *šāgā*, 'to err, or stray', is immediately suggested, in which case the name may have been given by the mother with reference to the father's personal history or character. If, as often in such names, the first element refers to the god of the bearer's family, the second element may be the name or attribute of a local deity now lost. The reference may be to some astral god 'the wanderer' once worshipped at Shunem, but we prefer our first suggestion.

(ii) THE PRETENSIONS OF ADONIJAH: 1.5–10

1 5Now Adonijah the son of Haggith exalted himself, saying, I will be king. So he prepared for himself chariotry and horses[e] and fifty outrunners, 6and his father never restrained him,[f] saying, Why do you so? He was, moreover, of very handsome appearance, and his mother bore[g] him after Absalom. 7And he had talk with Joab the son of Zeruiah and with Abiathar the priest and they gave their support to Adonijah. 8But

[a] *Die Hebräer*, 1906.

[b] 'Ägyptische Liebeslieder, Hohelied, Sappho, Theokrit', *ZDMG* XL, 1936, pp. 589–601.

[c] 'The Shulammite', *AJSL* L, 1934, pp. 102–4.

[d] 'The Meaning of the Shulammite', *AJSL* LVI, 1939, p. 89.

[e] Reading *perāšīm* for MT *pārāšīm* ('mounted horsemen'). Chariots and horses were still in the time of David a comparative novelty in Israel; when David had captured horses from the Aramaeans at Rabbath Ammon he had hamstrung all but a few. Mounted cavalry came into use in the tenth century, but only in Assyria, and so far was Israel from using mounted cavalry at the time of David that even in Ahab's time Israel used only chariots in the Battle of Qarqar in 853.

[f] Reading *ʿaṣārō* with G^{BA} for MT *ʿaṣābō* ('vexed, punished him'). G^L *epetimēsen* ('he rebuked') supports either reading.

[g] We suppose that *'immō* has dropped out after *yāledā*. The Qal of the verb is supported by all the versions except G^L, which is given to smoothing out and simplification of the Hebrew text where difficulties occur, and which reads *hōlīd* here, the subject assumed (but not named) being David.

Zadok the priest and Benaiah the son of Jehoiada and Nathan the prophet and Shimei, the Friend of David,[a] and the professional soldiers of David were not with Adonijah. [9]Then Adonijah slaughtered sheep and cattle and fatlings by the Stone of Zoheleth, which is by En Rogel, and he invited all his brothers, the royal princes,[b] and all[c] the men of Judah, the king's servants. [10]But Nathan the prophet and Benaiah[d] and the professional soldiers and Solomon his brother he did not invite.

1.5 Adonijah, the fourth (II Sam. 3.4) and apparently oldest surviving son of David, born in Hebron in the active years of David as king of Judah, assumes the status of heir-apparent and is supported by the older and more conservative elements: Joab, the commander of the free militia of Israel, and the kinsman of David (I Chron. 2.16), and Abiathar, who had survived Saul's massacre of the priests at Nob and had been the companion and consultant priest of David when he was an outlaw from Saul in the wild country of Judah (I Sam. 22.20). With these were numbered 'the men of Judah', these being distinct from the inhabitants of Jerusalem, which was the crown possession of David. On the reading *pᵉrāšīm* and its significance see p. 78 n.[e]. The training of war-horses was a specialized trade and had already in the beginning of the second millennium in Syria and Palestine given rise to a privileged class of feudal barons of greater and less status, with their own feudal retainers, a system attested in the administrative texts from Ras Shamra and Atchana. Formerly in Israel war had been waged by free levies, who had rallied in the time of a crisis; under Saul and David a new standing army had developed to meet national emergencies; now Adonijah employs a personal chariot-force and retainers, ostensibly to enhance his prestige, but probably in anticipation of a *coup d'état*. The action of Adonijah indicates the nature of the problem of succession in the new state of Israel, for which apparently David had made no provision. The state of Israel and the

[a]*wᵉšimᵉʿī rēʿe dāwīd* with Josephus for MT *šimᵉʿī wᵉrēʿī* as two proper names. Since the well-known figures Zadok and Nathan are designated by their function it would be odd if the two unknowns 'Shimei and Rei' were designated simply by their proper names without further qualification. From 4.5 it is known that *rēʿe hammelek* was an officer of state, probably a privy counsellor, in the time of Solomon. Nearer to MT would be *hārēʿe*, 'the Friend', but the institution was not yet well enough established for this absolute use of the noun.

[b]G[B] rejects MT *bᵉnē hammelek* as tautological after *'eḥāw*.

[c]Probably, with ten Hebrew MSS, *wᵉ'et-kol* . . . should be read for MT *ūlᵉkol* . . . The latter, however, would be admissible, *lᵉ* being either the particle introducing the accusative, as in Aramaic, or the preposition introducing the dative. In the interests of consistency *wᵉ'et-kol* is preferable in the context.

[d]*'et* before Benaiah as before the other proper names in the context.

institution of the monarchy were young enough for this to be a real problem. The native tradition of Israel was still that of the judges, where authority was invested in a man whose response to a given situation at the prompting of Yahweh marked him out as one who had the blessing (*b^e^rākā*) of Yahweh and therefore should be followed in his undertakings. This authority, however, was strictly *ad hoc* and personal, and in the one instance in the case of the judges where son (Abimelech) attempted to follow father (Gideon), the attempt was abortive. Adonijah, therefore, could not presume on the right of primogeniture, though his experience of the monarchy from the early days in Hebron might have given him priority over Solomon. While Israel was slow to outgrow the tradition of the temporary authority of the judges, of which the tribes of the North probably never quite divested themselves,[a] David had provided for the transmission of his authority to one of his family in his crown possession of Jerusalem. Here the authority of the king was as head of a feudal order, and this Adonijah seemed to appreciate to a degree in attaching to himself Joab and a personal bodyguard. He failed, however, in being unable to secure the support of the commanders of the new feudal forces, especially Benaiah, whose command had apparently largely superseded that of Joab. Adonijah apparently relied on the support of the more conservative elements in Jerusalem, through whom he hoped, not without some encouragement, to win the support of the people at large (I K. 2.15). The sequel shows that there were now strangers in the new order in Jerusalem, where the dominating elements were those attached to David's own person, the local priest Zadok, the king's seer Nathan, and the professional commander of the heterogenous mercenaries in David's standing army, Benaiah. The problem of transmission of authority in a society in transition from a religious to a political community is illustrated in Islam between the death of the Caliph Omar (AD 644) and the accession of the Umayyad Caliph Marwan (AD 684). Omar had ordered the election of a new Caliph by a council of six notable Muslims, and Uthman, of a different Meccan clan, was elected, to be succeeded by Ali of a different clan of the Quraysh, and a dynasty was not established until his successor Mu'awiyah of the Umayyad family designated his son Yezid, with the approval of his privy council. On the death of Yezid (684) the Caliphate passed to Marwan of a collateral branch

[a]A. Alt, 'Das Königtum in den Reichen Israel und Juda', *KS* II, 1953, pp. 123ff.; ET 'The Monarchy in Israel and Judah', *Essays*, pp. 246ff.

of the Umayyad family, who undertook to designate the young son of Yezid as successor, but actually designated his own son, Abd al-Malik, who succeeded in 685. An inscription of Esarhaddon (680–669) states that the problem of succession in his case was settled by oracles through Shamash and Adad after his selection as heir-apparent by his father. The king bound the community to allegiance to the heir by oath before the god of Assyria, and he was installed in the House of Succession (*bīt ridūti*), the palace of the heir apparent, where he was inducted into the mysteries and technique of the royal office.[a]

1.6 The fact that David did not restrain Adonijah may indicate his tacit approval; on the other hand, in the light of the sequel, the reason may have been the king's senility. This is a further note of David's fatal indulgence towards his family, as in the case of Amnon, whose rape of his half-sister Tamar had merely roused David's ineffective anger (II Sam. 13.21), and of Absalom, for his solicitude for whom Joab roughly rates him (II Sam. 19.1–8). The aside on the handsome appearance of Adonijah is characteristic of this source, where shrewd insight and appreciation of the significance of political issues is interspersed with lively and graphic narrative details.

7. *wayya‘ z*^{e}*rū ’aḥ*^{a}*rē ’*^{a}*dōnīyyā* (lit. 'and they supported after A.') is a pregnant construction characteristic of Hebrew, cf. *ḥār*^{e}*dū ’aḥ*^{a}*rāw* 'they trembled after him'. (I Sam. 13.7).

8. The forces of opposition are described in anticipation. Zadok the priest is first mentioned after David's occupation of Jerusalem (II Sam. 8.17), along with the representative of the line of Eli, 'Ahimelech the father of Abiathar', for which we should probably read, after S, 'Abiathar the son of Ahimelech', cf. II Sam. 20.25. Noting *ṣādōq* or *ṣedeq* as an element in names of rulers of pre-Israelite Jerusalem, S. Mowinckel,[b] followed by A. Bentzen[c] and H. H. Rowley,[d] regarded him as the hereditary priest of the local pre-Israelite cult of Jerusalem. R. de Vaux, on the other hand,[e] noting that Zadok is never mentioned in the Old Testament except in connection with the Ark and the Tent of Meeting, suggests that he had been a Levite of a family other than Eli's, who had been the custodian of the Ark at

[a]H. Frankfort, *Kingship and the Gods*, 1948, pp. 243f., after Theo Bauer, *ZA* XLII, 1934, pp. 170ff.

[b]*Ezra den Skriftlærde*, 1916, p. 109n.

[c]*Studier over det zadokidiske præsteskabs historie*, 1931, pp. 8–18.

[d]'Zadok and Nehushtan', *JBL* LVIII, 1939, pp. 113–41.

[e]*Ancient Israel*, pp. 372–4.

Kiriath Jearim and subsequently at Gibeon (cf. I Chron. 16.39), where, according to II Chron. 1.3, the Tent was kept. This is a feasible view, but the association with Gibeon may be a late pious fiction on the part of the Chronicler, to give Zadok and his family a more legitimate title to office than they actually possessed. Benaiah, the general of David's new standing army of professional soldiers detached from all ties with their local communities and owing their status entirely to the king, is first mentioned, like Zadok, in the account of David's administration in Jerusalem (II Sam. 8.18). Nathan the prophet (*hannābī'*), always closely associated with the king, emerges also after David's occupation of Jerusalem (II Sam. 7.2). Possibly his office was the mediation of divine revelation, of which in more primitive times in Canaan the king himself was the channel. Whether or not in this particular, as apparently in certain others, David was adapting the Canaanite conception of royalty, the fearless criticism of Nathan, who was in effect the king's conscience, as in the affair of Bathsheba (II Sam. 12), is a measure of the extent to which the native faith and tribal democracy of Israel persisted after the desert had been left behind. This was the effect, no doubt, of the sacrament of the deliverance from Egypt and the renewal of the covenant, which was regularly celebrated in Israel.

On Shimei, who had the status of king's Friend (cf. 4.5), see p. 79 n.[a].

David's professional soldiers, *gibbōrīm*, generally translated 'mighty men', naturally followed their general Benaiah. *gibbōr* has an Arabic cognate *jabbār*, meaning 'giant' or 'bully'. In Hebrew it means primarily 'man of substance', more fully *gibbōr ḥayil*, and under Saul it comes to mean one able in virtue of his property to equip himself, and possibly also followers, for war. Eventually, as in the present context, it means those who were enabled to do so under David's organization of the feudal system indicated in I Sam. 8.11ff.[a]

1.9 The verb *zābaḥ*, like its Arabic cognate *ḏabaḥa*, means primarily 'to slaughter', cf. the calf slaughtered by the witch of Endor for the entertainment of Saul with no implication of sacrifice (I Sam. 28.24). Generally in Hebrew sacrifice is intended and, as all slaughter was a breach of the mysterious life given by God, blood-letting was done with a certain degree of ceremony, as, when an Arab kills a beast for entertainment of a guest, he cuts its throat, turning its head towards

[a]See J. Gray, 'Feudalism in Ugarit and Early Israel', *ZAW* LXIV, 1952, pp. 49–55.

Mecca. The occasion was a common meal, which, as still among the primitive sort of Arabs, has the effect of integration of the company participating. Such a common meal was also apparently the beginning of Absalom's rising (II Sam. 15.11ff.). The locus of Adonijah's feast is significant, En Rogel, which, like most rare springs, had a certain sanctity, though not to the same degree as Gihon higher up the Kidron Valley. En Rogel, which has been variously explained as 'the Spring of the Fuller' (Targum) and 'the Spring of the Treadwheel', or 'the Spring of the Spy', means probably 'the Spring of the Stream' (Aramaic *ragōlā*),[a] so called since its rock-drilled shaft, if it is identical with *Bīr Ayyūb*, taps a subterranean stream just below the confluence of the dry valleys of the Kidron and Hinnom (*Wādī ar-Rabābī*), probably draining from the latter. En Rogel, as indicated in the description of the tribal boundary between Benjamin and Judah (Josh. 15.7; 18.16), and in the description of David's espionage system in the revolt of Absalom (II Sam. 17.17), is the present *Bīr Ayyūb* (Job's Well), used by the inhabitants of the southern part of the village of *Silwān* (Siloam). Here native tradition confuses the patriarch Job with Joab the confederate of Adonijah, as Goliath (*Jālūṭ*) is confused with Gideon in the place-name *'Ain Jālūṭ* on the slope of Mount Gilboa near the source of Gideon's famous exploit. The adjacent Stone of Zoheleth might mean 'the Serpent-Stone', *zōḥēl* meaning 'serpent' or possibly 'worm', lit. 'gliding one', in Micah 7.17, in which case the identity of En Rogel with the Dragon (*tannīn*) Well of Neh. 2.13 is suggested, and this is accepted by J. Simons.[b] The latter, however, though in the general vicinity of En Rogel, was probably much higher up the Valley of Hinnom, and is possibly now blocked by the displacement of rock in an earthquake. The verb *zāḥal* means primarily 'to slip' and the participle means only secondarily, 'worm, serpent', as in Micah 7.17. By coincidence a certain steep, slippery track leading down from *Silwān* to the Kidron is called *az-zaḥweileh*, but as this is opposite the Spring of Gihon, it cannot be the Stone of Zoheleth. Since in Arabic the verb is used of landslides,[c] the Stone of Zoheleth might signify some rock mass detached from the overhanging cliffs by an earthquake such as brought down a great mass of rock in the reign of Uzziah according to Josephus.[d]

[a]So G. A. Smith, *Jerusalem* I, 1907, pp. 108ff.
[b]*Jerusalem in the Old Testament*, 1952, pp. 158–62.
[c]G. R. Driver, *ZAW* LII, 1934, pp. 51ff.
[d]*Ant.* IX, 10.4.

Driver takes *zōḥelet* as a participle agreeing with *'eben* from which the definite article is omitted, as commonly from the noun in place-names (*GK*, § 126w).[a]

'All the men of Judah', as the appositional phrase *ʿab^{e}dē hammelek* indicates, does not refer to the general population of the province, but to the Judaean elements in David's professional army, the striking-force of his own clansmen, who under Joab had laid the foundation of the king's power, as apart from the new professional army of heterogeneous elements under Benaiah.

1.10. The pointed exclusion of Nathan, Benaiah and his officers (*haggibbōrīm*) and Solomon from the meal at En Rogel indicates that Adonijah was not prepared for 'peaceful coexistence', to which, by ancient Semitic convention, he would have been committed by such a meal. He obviously trusted in the strength of his party to liquidate the opposition (cf. v.12), the strength of which, to say nothing of the weakness of the king, he much underrated. *haggibbōrīm* denotes the new class of professional soldiers introduced by David (II Sam. 23) where the limited number of 37 indicates an officer corps. Their personal allegiance to the king in the new feudal order in Israel is indicated by the inclusion of Uriah the Hittite (II Sam. 23.39) and Ittai of Gath (II Sam. 18.2.).

(iii) THE COUNTER-CLAIMS OF SOLOMON: 1.11–40

1 [11]Then Nathan said to Bathsheba the mother of Solomon, Have you
not heard that Adonijah the son of Haggith has assumed royal estate
and our lord David does not know? [12]So come now, and let me give
you advice, and save your life and the life of your son Solomon. [13]Come,
go in to king David and say to him, My lord the king, did you not
swear to your handmaid saying, Surely Solomon your son shall be king
after me and he will sit upon my throne? Why, then, has Adonijah
become king? [14]And[b] lo! while you are yet speaking there with the
king I shall come in after you and corroborate your words. [15]So
Bathsheba went in to the king in the privacy of his chamber—now
the king was very aged and Abishag the Shunammite was tending the
king—[16]and Bathsheba prostrated herself and bowed down to the king,
and the king said to her,[c] What ails you? [17]And she said to him, My
lord, you swore by Yahweh your God to your maidservant, Surely

[a]So also M. Noth, *Könige*, Biblischer Kommentar, 1964, p. 6.

[b]Reading *w^{e}hinnē* with 21 Hebrew MSS and the Versions for MT *hinnē*, *w* being omitted by haplography after *w* at the end of the previous word.

[c]Reading with G^{L} and S *lāh*, which is omitted in the MT. The emendation, like most suggested by G^{L}, makes the meaning more explicit, but is not strictly necessary.

Solomon your son shall be king after me and he shall sit upon my throne. [18]But now here Adonijah has assumed kingship and you,[a] my lord the king, know nothing about it. [19]And he has slaughtered oxen, fatlings, and sheep in abundance, and he has invited all the royal princes and Abiathar the priest, and Joab the commander of the host, but Solomon your servant he has not invited. [20]And now,[b] my lord the king, the eyes of all Israel are upon you to declare to them who shall sit upon the throne of my lord the king after him. [21]And it will happen when my lord the king lies down with his fathers that I and my son Solomon shall be found at fault. [22]And behold! while she was yet speaking with the king there came Nathan the prophet. [23]And they told the king saying, Here is Nathan the prophet, and he came in to the presence of the king and prostrated himself to the king on his face to the ground. [24]And Nathan said, My lord the king, Did you yourself say, Adonijah shall be king after me and he shall sit upon my throne, [25]that he has gone down today and slaughtered oxen and fatlings and sheep in abundance and has invited all the royal princes and the commander[c] of the host and Abiathar the priest, and there they are eating and drinking in his presence and they have said, Long live king Adonijah! [26]and me, even me your servant, and Zadok the priest and Benaiah the son of Jehoiada and Solomon your servant[d] he has not invited? [27]Or has this matter been effected by my lord the king and he has not let your servant[e] know who shall sit on the throne of my lord the king after him? [28]And king David answered and said, Call Bathsheba to me. So she came into the presence of the king and stood before him.[f] [29]Then the king swore an oath and said, By the life of Yahweh who redeemed my life from all adversity, [30]as I swore to you by Yahweh God of Israel saying, Certainly Solomon your son shall be king after me and he shall sit upon my throne in my place, even so shall I surely carry it into effect this day. [31]Then Bathsheba bowed down her face to the ground and did obeisance to the king and said, Life to my lord king David for ever! [32]Then king David said, Call to me Zadok the priest and Nathan the prophet and Benaiah the son of Jehoiada, and they came into the presence of the king. [33]And the king said to them, Take with you the retainers of your master and mount Solomon my son on

[a]Reading *weʾattā* with many Hebrew MSS and the Versions for MT *weʿattā* ('and now').

[b]Reading *weʿattā* with many Hebrew MSS and T for MT *weʾattā* ('and you').

[c]There has been no mention of any commander of the host among Adonijah's party except Joab, hence Josephus in his version reads simply 'the commander of the host', G^{L} adding 'Joab'. The singular must be read, the final *y* of *śārē(y)* in MT being a dittograph of the *h* in *haṣṣābāʾ*, which it resembles in the proto-Hebraic script.

[d]G^{L}, again making the matter more explicit, reads *binekā* ('your son') for MT *ʿabdekā*.

[e]Reading singular with Q, for K, which gives the consonants of the plural. The expression is, of course, 'me' of deferential address.

[f]Reading *lepānāw* with G^{BA} and V for MT *lipenē hammelek*, which is possible, but an ugly repetition.

my mule and take him down to Gihon. 34And there let Zadok the priest
anoint[a] him king over Israel, and you shall blow the trumpet and say,
Long live king Solomon! 35And you shall come up after him and he
shall come in and sit upon my throne, and he shall be king in my place,
and it is my last testament that he shall be leader over Israel and Judah.
36Then Benaiah the son of Jehoiada answered the king and said, Sure!
Even so may Yahweh the God of my lord the king make it effective.[b]
37Even as Yahweh was with my lord the king, may he be[c] with Solomon
to make his throne even greater than the throne of my lord king David.
38Then down went Zadok the priest and Nathan the prophet and
Benaiah the son of Jehoiada, and the Kerethites and Pelethites, and
they mounted Solomon on king David's mule and escorted him[d] down
to Gihon. 39And Zadok the priest took the horn of oil from the tent and
anointed Solomon, and they blew the trumpet, and all the people said,
Long live king Solomon! 40And all the people came up after him performing dances[e] and rejoicing exceedingly, and the earth was cleft with
the sound of them.

In this section we may note as a feature of the literary style of the source the frequent verbal repetitions, e.g. in vv. 9f. Adonijah's doings are described as they took place, and they are reported twice in the same words (vv. 17–19, 25). In the Ras Shamra myths and legends this is a regular feature of the epic style, and here we may have an indication of one of the main formative influences on the Hebrew narrative style which developed in the story of David's escapades as a fugitive from Saul and in the Story of the Davidic Succession, of which the present passage is a secondary elaboration, and culminated in the J source of the Pentateuch. Such repetition is, of course, a feature of popular narrative and is found in ballad literature.

[a]G^{B} reads the plural, understanding Nathan as an associate with Zadok in the act of anointing. This office was here performed by the priest, as v. 39 clearly indicates, and this passage suggests that *w^{e}nātān hannābī'* of MT should be omitted, though G^{B} obviously read it. In v. 45 the plural of the verb is read with Zadok and Nathan as subjects, and it may be that in both passages Nathan is visualized as an assessor of Zadok.

[b]Reading *ya'^{a}śe* with three Hebrew MSS and S for MT *yō'mar*. G^{L} and certain MSS of the Old Latin versions read, feasibly, *ya'^{a}mēn yhwh et-dib^{e}rē '^{a}dōnī hammelek*.

[c]K suggests the jussive, which we read, but Q suggests the imperfect, which is also feasible, this being then an assurance instead of a wish.

[d]It is also possible, with no practical difference of meaning, to read *wayyēl^{e}kū 'ittō* ('and they went with him'), with no change of the consonants of MT, as G^{L} suggests.

[e]Reading with G^{BA}, S and T *m^{e}ḥōl^{e}līm bim^{e}ḥōlōt* for MT *m^{e}ḥal^{e}līm baḥ^{a}līlīm* ('piping with pipes'), surely a more spontaneous expression of joy than piping on pipes, which, in any case, would not apply to 'all the people'.

1.11. It is somewhat surprising to find Nathan the prophet, who had played such an honourable part in rebuking David in the affair of Bathsheba and the murder of Uriah (II Sam. 11.1–17), a party to this intrigue, and one would have expected his sympathies to be with the conservatives.[a] Did he feel that the outrage to Bathsheba ought to be made good by the elevation of her son? Probably as tutor to the young Solomon (II Sam. 12.25) he hoped that he would be better able to govern his counsels than those of his much older brother Adonijah. Nathan exploits the influence of Bathsheba, to whom the king might well feel a sense of debt. The name is interesting. It has been explained as referring to the birth of Bathsheba on the seventh day, cf. Shabbethai and Shabbathith of later Judaism. Alternatively the name might signify the seventh of a family, or a child born in fulfilment of an oath, perhaps bearing on the confirmation of the status of the mother, as in the former British custom of provisional marriage or 'hand-fasting'.

The perfect of the verb *mālak*, here obviously the equivalent of the Greek Aorist, is relevant to the use of the key-phrase *yhwh mālak* in the 'Enthronement Psalms' (Pss. 93, 96–99, cf. Ps. 47.8[9]), where the phrase is taken variously as 'Y. has become king' (Mowinckel) and 'Y. is royal'.[b] The usage of the perfect in the notice of the accession of Absalom (II Sam. 15.10) and Jehu (II K. 9.13) suggests that Mowinckel is right, though the other meaning is grammatically possible. How adroitly Nathan plays upon the instincts of Bathsheba as a mother and rival wife in his reference to Adonijah as 'the son of Haggith'!

12. Nathan adds a note of urgency to his intrigue. The omission of Solomon and his supporters from Adonijah's ceremonial meal at En Rogel was more than discourtesy or wilful neglect. There were obviously already two rival parties in Jerusalem, and Adonijah was not going to grant his rivals immunity by eating a communal meal with them.

The verb 'Save!' (*mallᵉṭī*) is the intensive with causative and transitive force from the root from which Malta is derived, the island being a port of refuge in the long sea stage in Phoenician navigation, which preferred coasting. The life (*nepeš*), often mistranslated in EVV 'soul', means essentially 'life-breath' and generally 'life' or

[a]Hempel (*Geschichte und Geschichten im Alten Testament*, 1964, p. 131) has proposed that two different Nathans are indicated, but for this there is insufficient ground.
[b]Eissfeldt, 'Jahwe als König', *ZAW* XLVI, 1928, p. 85.

the 'total vitality' of an animated body, a consideration which ought to condition our exegesis of many a scriptural 'proof-text'. There was no such dualism in Hebrew anthropology as in Platonism.

1.13. 'My lord the king . . . your maidservant' is the usual polite and deferential address, 'my lord' meaning 'you', and 'your servant' meaning 'I'. The statement 'Solomon your son shall be king' is introduced by the Hebrew conjunction *kī*, which before direct speech has the force of a strong asseverative 'indeed'. Since this is the first notice of an oath on the elevation of Solomon, this is probably a case of auto-suggestion, Nathan exploiting the dotage of the king.

14. 'I shall corroborate your words', lit. I shall fill out. . . .

15. The Hebrew word *bā'* means both 'arrive' and 'enter'.

m^{e}šārat ('tending'), for *m^{e}šāretet*, is the Piel participle feminine singular active from the verbal root *šrt*, which is often used of serving in the sanctuary. The assimilation of the final dental to the *t* termination of the feminine is well attested in Hebrew orthography (GK § 80d), cf. Ugaritic *ylt* for *yldt*.[a]

16. Prostration, from the verbal root *qdd*, and obeisance, from the root *šḥh*, originally final *w*, are the gestures of deference to human authority and of the worship of God, still exemplified in the prostrations of Muslim prayer, where the brow and the nose must touch the ground.

19. *šōr* ('oxen'), *m^{e}r'ī*, ('fatlings'), and *ṣō'n* ('sheep') are collective singulars.

20. The request is not for the abdication of David and the immediate elevation of his successor to sole regal state, but for the appointment of a co-regent or for the designation of his successor. The action of David was a precedent for this practice in Israel (see Introduction, pp 65ff.). Probably the chronological notices of the king's age *b^{e}mol^{e}kō* usually refer to his designation as successor.

21. 'Lying down with one's fathers' means being dead and buried, originally, though not in the case of David, in the family tomb, usually one of the caves in the soft white limestone rock with which Palestine is honeycombed. R. H. Pfeiffer[b] has pointed out that this phrase only once seems to refer to a violent death, that of Ahab (I K. 22.40), which is one reason adduced for doubting the historicity of the account of Ahab's death. The present instance, however, indicates how loose the meaning of a phrase might become.

[a]Gordon, *UT* 52.60.
[b]*Introduction to the Old Testament*, 1948², p. 398.

ḥaṭṭā'īm means often 'sinners', but primarily it means 'those who have missed the mark' (e.g. with a sling, Judg. 20.16) or come short in the matter of pledge (as Judah when he persuades Jacob to entrust him with Benjamin, Gen. 43.9) or payment, hence 'defaulters'. Such may be the victims of circumstances, as Bathsheba and Solomon would doubtless have been if Adonijah had come to power. The word *ḥēṭ'* is used for venial sin, for which amends, *ḥaṭṭā't* ('sin-offering'), are admitted. Such 'sins' are often unwitting offences, often ritual, and the implication here is that some such captious interpretation of the law would have been found for putting Solomon and his mother out of the way, as was actually done in the case of Joab and Shimei.

1.25. 'Life to the king!', the acclamation of royalty since time immemorial, refers in Semitic court-etiquette to the association of the king with the sacral community he represents, which lives in, or in fellowship with, its god, whose mediator the king is. In Egyptian royal ideology the emphasis was on the association of the king with the god and, in fact, on his identity with the god Horus, whose incarnation he was in life, and with Osiris, the father of Horus, with whom the Pharaohs were identified after death.[a] Early in the Davidic monarchy the royal office was invested with the aura of sanctity, but though the court etiquette (Gunkel's '*Hofstil*')[b] was drawn upon, probably after Solomon had set the fashion, the ideological emphasis in Israel lay rather on the king as the representative *par excellence* of the sacral community. See further the article on the phrase by P. A. H. de Boer,[c] who emphasizes the significance of the king as the channel of divine power or vitality. Bearing in mind the significance of *ḥāyā* and *ḥayyīm* in Hebrew thought as 'vitality' rather than the span of human life, the acclamation might well be paraphrased: 'May the divine vitality be particularized in the king, including, of course, all his line, for ever.'

27. The best explanation of *'im* here seems to us to be that this is the interrogative particle introducing the alternative question to the one asked, though without an interrogative particle, in vv. 24–26; cf. Gen. 24.21; 27.21; Ex. 16.4; Num. 13.18 (*GK* § 150i).

29. *pādā* ('redeemed') signifies the ransom of a captive or the redemption of a slave. Here the conception is that Yahweh himself

[a]H. Frankfort, *Kingship and the Gods*, 1948.
[b]*Einleitung in die Psalmen*, 1933, pp. 160ff.
[c]'Vive le Roi', *VT* V, 1955, pp. 225–31.

has undertaken to deal with the adversity which claimed the life of David. There seems to be a tacit admission here attributed to the king of his deliverance from a just retribution. The word *ṣārā* ('adversity') means literally 'that which constricts', the verb in the Hiphil meaning 'to besiege'. On the meaning of *nepeš*, literally 'life', see on v. 12.

1.31. On the phrase 'May . . . the king live for ever', see on v. 25. The implication of hereditary royal power is a measure of the development of the constitution under David.

32f. David from personal experience knew the value of his personal retainers, especially the professional soldiers under their commander Benaiah. In view of the formal consecration of Solomon, Zadok the priest was summoned, also Nathan the prophet, in virtue probably of the personal relationship in which he stood to Solomon, but also, no doubt, in order to give an auspicious oracle assuring the new king of the favour of God. An example of such an oracle on the occasion of a royal accession or the anniversary of such is Ps. 110. Solomon was to be mounted on the king's mule, a symbol of royalty, of which Mowinckel,[a] perhaps overpressing the evidence, would see a reflection in Zech. 9.9 and Matt 21.5, where the Messiah rides into Jerusalem on an ass. The scene of Solomon's anointing was to be the Spring of Gihon ('Gusher', so called from its intermittent flow). This is the present *ʿAin Umm ad-Darāj* ('Spring of the Mother of the Steps') in the upper part of the Kidron Valley under the north part of the fortified area of Jebusite Jerusalem occupied by David on the south-east hill. The spring is named again in the Old Testament only in II Chron. 32.30; 33.14, but its strategic significance is indicated by the tunnel which carried its waters within the walls to the Pool of Siloam, almost certainly the work of Hezekiah (see on II K. 20.20). It probably played a part in local ritual and pre-Israelite mythology, of which Ezekiel's vision of the fertilizing river from beneath the throne of God (Ezek. 47.1–12; cf. Joel 3.18[4.18]; Zech. 14.8) is an adaptation. The reference in Ps. 110.7 to the king drinking from the wadi, if the questionable text is geniune, may be an allusion to the role of Gihon in the ritual of accession.[b]

34. The anointing with consecrated oil, which was kept in the sanctuary, was an act whereby the king was brought into intimate

[a] *The Psalms in Israel's Worship* I, 1962, p. 62.

[b] See further G. Widengren, 'Psalm 110 och det sakrala kungadömet i Israel', *UUÅ* 1941, pp. 9, 12ff.; S. Mowinckel, *He That Cometh*, 1956, pp. 63ff.

relationship with God, and became his intermediary with the community. Anointing was known in Egypt as a rite whereby the authority of the Pharaoh was delegated to officials and to vassal kings in Syria in the fifteenth century, and it has been argued that it symbolized the strengthening of the person anointed with special ability. It is also known in Egypt and among the Hittites as a rite in marriage and betrothal, and among the Amorites at Mari in the eighteenth century in business transactions and conveyance of property. This is also the significance of anointing as a rite in emancipation of slaves, now attested in a deed from the palace at Ras Shamra,[a] where it signifies severance of former associations.[b] This is the conception underlying the anointing of a priest, who is thus set apart for exclusive service of, and association with, God, and is corroborated by the use of *qiddēš* in Ex. 28.41; 30.30; 40.13 as a synonym for *māšaḥ* ('anoint'), *qiddēš* meaning 'to remove from the sphere of the profane to the sacred'. The fact that inanimate objects such as the tabernacle and its furniture were anointed indicates that separation was the significance of the rite, and not the conferring of ability or the delegation of authority. By this rite the king was removed from secular to sacral status as the dedicated executive of God. This ceremony was performed by the priest (in this verse 'and Nathan the prophet' is probably an interpolation, see textual note). The trumpet, or ram's horn (*haššōpār*), is regularly associated with the epiphany of God as King in the Psalms and was a feature of the autumnal New Year festival, of which this epiphany was an element. In this particular as in general the accession of the king reflected the liturgy of the Enthronement of Yahweh, e.g. Pss. 2, 110.

1.35. Noth (*op. cit.*, p. 24) rightly emphasizes the sacral connotation of 'Israel'. The meaning of *ṣiwwā* in this context is not so much 'to order' or 'to appoint' as 'to dispose as a last will or testament', as in Arabic *waṣṣā*, whence *waṣiyya*, 'last disposition'; see further on 2.1.

nāgid, a passive form, means one who is set over against, as leader or president.[c] Its use may indicate the status of Solomon as co-regent and not yet fully king, or it may indicate David's deference to conservative opinion in Israel, to which kingship with all its

[a] F. Thureau-Dangin, 'Trois contrats de Ras Shamra', *Syria* XVIII, 1937, pp. 249–51.

[b] E. Kutsch, *Salbung als Rechtsakt im Alten Testament und im alten Orient*, BZAW LXXXVII, 1963.

[c] Alt, *KS* II, 1953, p. 62, takes it to mean one appointed by God over Israel.

Canaanite associations was still repugnant. Since this title is applied to Saul at his anointing in I Sam. 10.1 and to David in I Sam 7.8, Noth (p. 25) feasibly conjectures that it may reflect the liturgy of anointing. Dynastic succession was an innovation in Israel. Both Saul and David had been elected king by popular acclaim when they, like the charismatic judges, had proved themselves by their success in crises to be endowed with the divine blessing (*bᵉrākā*), and of special aptitude. Each had been confirmed in his office at a shrine *coram populo*, Saul at Gilgal and David at Hebron, as a party to a tripartite covenant between God, king, and people. Now a young, unproved prince is designated co-regent by the royal fiat. Saul had been king only over Israel; David had been king first over Judah and then over Israel also by two separate transactions. Now he does not forget the uneasy union of the two elements in his kingdom, having had to suppress an Israelite rising in his own day under Sheba (II Sam. 20) and another in Judah under Absalom (II Sam. 15–19), hence Solomon is designated leader of Israel *and* Judah.

1.36. The lead in the response to the king's declaration is taken by Benaiah with a solemn 'Amen'! ('Sure!'), the legal term of endorsement of a declaration, as at the declaration of the principles of the Law and the blessings and curses attendant on their observation or infringement (Deut. 27.15ff.).

38ff. Note the description of the anointing of Solomon in almost the same words as David's directions, a feature of the style of the saga or epic antecedents of Hebrew historical narrative.

38. Note the accurate local notes of direction in the Old Testament. They *went down*, i.e. from the residential quarters of the palace on the highest point on the south-eastern hill of Jerusalem into the deep cleft of the Kidron Valley. Palestine is a land of very diversified contour and that is always reflected in the verbs of 'going'.

Kerethi and Pelethi are singular in both cases in Hebrew and are used collectively. The latter suggests the Philistines, Pulusatu of Egyptian records from the fifteenth to the twelfth century, one of the elements of the 'Sea-peoples', who broke the maritime power of Crete at the end of the fifteenth century. Some of those were employed by the Egyptians and the Hittites as mercenaries until *c.* 1200, when they became too numerous and powerful, destroyed the Hittite empire in Anatolia and north Syria, and settled in the coastal plain of Palestine, mainly south of Jaffa, possibly as vassals of Egypt under five feudal lords in Ekron, Gath, Ashdod, Ashkelon, and Gaza. David, out of favour with Saul, had eventually taken feudal service with Achish of Gath (on the location of which see on I K. 2.39), and had received the fief of Ziklag in perpetuity (I Sam. 27.6). David's feudal retainers from this service were apparently the nucleus of his standing army in Hebron and later in Jerusalem, and were now under the command of Benaiah (II Sam. 20.23). *keretī* suggests Crete as the immediate provenance of some of the Philistines or their associates. The ultimate home of the 'Sea-peoples', however, was much farther afield, probably in the northern Balkans or the Lower Danube.

1.39. 'The horn of oil' was not *a* horn, but the specific horn of olive-oil kept for the purpose of anointing the king. As the medium of consecration, it was kept apart from common use in the sanctuary, which at that time was the tent which housed the ark after David's restoration of that sacred palladium of the tribes to Jerusalem (II Sam. 6.17). This was apparently pitched in 'the city of David', i.e. his citadel on the south-eastern hill (I K. 8.1), though from the statement that Benaiah 'went up' from the palace to the sanctuary (2.34), a site in the future Temple area is indicated.

The popular acclamation (*terūʿā*), which is noted in the accession of Saul (I Sam. 10.24) and Joash (II K. 11.12), is emphasized by Alt[a] as an essential element in the accession ritual, which conserved the democratic constitution in Israel.

40. On the reading 'performing dances' see textual note. It is not to be supposed that the public were well enough informed beforehand of the transactions afoot to provide themselves with pipes as MT suggests. But the dance was something in which they might express themselves impromptu. This activity might involve extravagant leaping, as when David installed the ark in Jerusalem (II Sam. 6.14), in which they might vent their exuberance, or controlled, stilted marching accompanied by handclapping, which is the 'dancing' we have witnessed by the males of Arab villages. Their rejoicing, like the dancing, had a ritual significance, to obviate all possible malevolent influence apprehended at such a crisis. In later Judaism there were certain days of auspicious memory when mourning was forbidden.[b]

'And the earth was cleft with the sound of them' is a hyperbolic

[a]A. Alt, 'Das Königtum in den Reichen Israel und Juda', *KS* II, 1953, pp. 116–34; ET, 'The Monarchy in Israel and Judah', *Essays*, pp. 239–59.

[b]G. Dalman, 'Die Fastenrolle', *Aramäische Dialektproben*, 1927, pp. 1–3.

phrase, perhaps recalling the association of the displacement of rocks with the crash in earthquake.

(iv) THE FAILURE OF ADONIJAH'S ATTEMPT: 1.41–53

1 41 And Adonijah heard and all the guests who were with him—they
had finished eating—and Joab heard the sound of the trumpet, and he
said, What is the meaning of the sound of the city in uproar?[a] 42 While
he was still speaking there came Jonathan the son of Abiathar the priest
and Adonijah said to him, Come, for you are a worthy man and must
bring good news. 43 Then Jonathan answered and said to Adonijah, On
the contrary; our lord king David has made Solomon king. 44 And the
king sent with him Zadok the priest and Nathan the prophet, and
Benaiah the son of Jehoiada, and the Kerethites and Pelethites and they
mounted him on the king's mule. 45 And they have anointed him, [b]even
Zadok the priest and Nathan the prophet,[b] as king[c] at Gihon, and they
have gone up from there rejoicing, and the city is in an uproar. That is
the noise you have heard. 46 Yes, and Solomon has taken his seat upon
the throne of the kingdom. 47 Moreover the king's servants came to congratulate our lord king David saying, May your God[d] make the renown
of Solomon even greater than your renown, and may he make his throne
greater than your throne. Then the king bowed down on the couch.
48 And further the king spoke thus, Blessed be Yahweh God of Israel,
who has given this day one of my seed[e] to sit upon the throne of Israel,
and my eyes see it. 49 And all Adonijah's guests trembled, and rose, and
went their several ways. 50 And Adonijah was afraid of Solomon, and he
rose and went[f] and laid hold on the horns of the altar. 51 Now it was

[a] At first sight the participle *hōmā* appears to demand either the definite article in agreement with *haqqiryā* ('the city') or the masculine form in agreement with *qōl* ('sound'). Actually cases are attested in Hebrew where the predicate of a compound phrase, though pertaining strictly to the first noun, the construct, agrees in number and gender with the following absolute, e.g. *qešet gibbōrīm ḥattīm* (I Sam. 24), lit. 'the bow of the mighty is broken'; see *GK* § 146a.

[b] It is proposed to omit this phrase, but there is no support for the omission in the Versions, nor is the plural of the verb *wayyimšeḥū* ('they have anointed') questioned. Since the only objection to the phrase could be the inclusion of Nathan as one who anointed Solomon, this scarcely seems valid, since the plural of the verb obviously visualizes assessors, cf. v. 34.

[c] G^{BL} and S omit *lemelek*, presumably considering such an admission of the royal estate of Solomon tactless in the ears of his rival, but, however Adonijah and his friends chose to ignore this, it was a fact.

[d] So with K and S, Q, G^{BA} and V reading *ʾelōhīm*.

[e] Reading with S and the Hexaplar S (S^h) *mizzarʿī*), which is omitted in MT. Since someone had to succeed David in any case, there seems no particular point in his gratification at being succeeded; the point is that it gratified him to be succeeded by one of his sons, which he had regarded as the crowning blessing (II Sam. 7.12ff.).

[f] G^L adds *ʾel-ʾōhel yhwh* ('to the tent of Yahweh'), another instance of the tendency of G^L to explication.

reported to Solomon, Behold! Adonijah is afraid of king Solomon, and has grasped the horns of the altar, saying, May[a] Solomon now swear by oath that he will not put his servant to death with the sword. [52]So Solomon said, If he behaves worthily there shall not fall a single hair of of his to the ground, but if ill be found in him he is a dead man. [53]Then king Solomon sent and they brought him down from the altar, and he came in and prostrated himself before[b] Solomon, and Solomon said to him, Go home.

1.41–48. Note again the verbal repetition of the earlier account of these events.

41. The ear of the old warrior Joab is quick to hear the trumpet, a dramatic touch of this literary source. The word *qiryā* is rare in the Old Testament, but is attested in the Ras Shamra texts and later Phoenician inscriptions, and occurs in variant forms in the Moabite Stone. It properly means a walled fortress, a citadel rather than a city.

42. Jonathan the son of Abiathar had already proved serviceable to David as a swift-footed intelligence agent in Absalom's revolt (II Sam. 15–17), to which, no doubt, Adonijah alludes by calling him a bearer of good news (*beśōrā*). The designation of Jonathan as *'îš ḥayil* ('a worthy man') refers primarily to his social and economic status as a man with his own property, not dependent on the king, and secondarily to his independence of spirit, a valuable asset in those days when a new class was emerging, like the Mamelukes of the Sultans of medieval Egypt, who were the tools of the ruling power.

45. The verb *wattēhōm* ('is in an uproar') is the Niphal imperfect with *w* consecutive from *hmm*, a by-form of the more regular *hāmā*, which conveys the sound as well as the confused motion of an excited crowd or a swarm of bees.

47. The particular identity of the 'servants' of the king here is, as usual, hard to determine, and may denote the courtiers, his feudal retainers swearing their allegiance to Solomon, or his subjects in general, particularly the people of Jerusalem, who, as inhabitants of a crown estate, were the king's 'servants'. To 'bless' means to congratulate and invoke the blessing of God upon David in his son Solomon. 'Name' means 'renown' or 'repute', in which a man lives,

[a]G[B] omits *hammelek*. The abject situation of Adonijah as a suppliant to the mercy of Solomon, however, may have constrained him to address Solomon as king, as 'his servant' may imply.

[b]Again G[B] omits *lammelek* of MT.

the medium by which the force of his personality makes itself felt; it is his *alter ego*.

1.48. David's response is to bless God, i.e. to thank him, on the realization of the promise of dynastic succession, a new conception in Israel, and one henceforth assiduously propagated within the cult as the conception of God's covenant with the house of David (II Sam. 23.5; Pss. 89.3f.[4f.], 28ff.[29ff.]; 132.11f.; Isa. 55.3) on the basis of an oracle delivered by the prophet Nathan (II Sam. 7.12ff.).

50. Adonijah, apprehending severe treatment from Solomon, which he himself was probably prepared to mete out to his rival had he been successful, laid hold on the 'horns of the altar', the protuberances at the corners where the blood of sacrifice was smeared (Ex. 27.2; Ezek. 43.20), and which afforded sanctuary *par excellence*, cf. Amos 3.14, where the reference to the breaking off of the horns of the altar is thus a prophecy of relentless wrath. The fugitive from vengeance, having thus made contact with the part of the altar where union with God was effected by the blood of sacrifice, was regarded as *gēr 'elōhīm*, the protected sojourner with God, cf. Arabic *jār Allāh*, who has similar rights. The hand of the avenger was thus stayed till his case was considered and settled if possible without bloodshed. The right was widely practised throughout the ancient Near East and indeed was abused to such an extent that it was abolished in many cases by the Emperor Tiberius, as the temples were overcrowded with the worst criminals of the Empire.[a] The location of the altar is not mentioned, but doubtless it was by the tent which housed the ark (v. 39).

51. 'To swear' in Hebrew means 'to lay oneself under seven (oaths)'. Note the expression of a negative in Hebrew after the oath formula expressed or understood, lit. 'if he slays', which is actually affirmative, the phrase being the protasis of a conditional sentence, the apodosis understood, and often expressed, being 'So may Yahweh do to me and more also . . .' Conversely a strong asseverative is expressed by the protasis in the negative.

52. On the meaning of *ben ḥayil* ('a man of worth') and *'īš ḥayil* see on v. 42, referring primarily to the possession of property and independent status and secondarily to the character which such property or social status obliges a man to support. A not inapt analogy is that of the Arab sheikh, who, in virtue of his status, has

[a]Tacitus, *Annals* III, 60ff.; W. R. Smith, *The Religion of the Semites*, 1894, p. 148n.

the obligation to his tribesmen to entertain them and to maintain their cause. Montgomery (ICC, p. 81) felicitously renders 'If he behaves like a gentleman'.

In the phrase *lōʾ yippōl miśśaʿarātō* ('there shall not fall a single hair'), the singular *śaʿarātō* with the partitive *min* emphasizes the adjective 'single', cf. the declaration in the Qur'an *wamā yaśquṭu min waraqatin ʾillā biʿilmihi*, 'and there falls not a single leaf save by his knowledge'.

1.53. Fichtner[a] takes the order 'Go home' to indicate that Adonijah was banished from court. This can hardly be so, however, since his request for Abishag (2.13–18) shows that he still had access to the palace and indeed to the harem.

(*b*) THE END OF DAVID, HIS FINAL CHARGES TO SOLOMON, AND THE ACCESSION OF SOLOMON AS SOLE KING: 2.1–12

See critical introduction in Introduction, pp. 15ff. The passage is interpolated with general Deuteronomistic phraseology (vv. 2b–4), which recalls the Deuteronomistic description of the divine exhortation to Joshua (Josh. 1). In vv. 10f. we have the first case of the Deuteronomistic editorial epilogue on the late king, followed by the notice of the establishment of the royal authority of his successor. The conjunctions *wegam* ('and moreover') at the beginning of vv. 5–9 may suggest that the last charges of David were preceded by others of a like tenor in the original source, which was probably independent of the Story of the Davidic Succession; so Noth, *Könige*, p. 9.

2 [1]Then the time of David's death drew near, and he gave his last charges to Solomon his son, saying, [2]I am going the way of all the earth, so be strong and play the man, [3]and keep the charge of Yahweh your God to walk in his ways and[b] to keep his statutes and his commandments and his judgements and testimonies according to what is written in the law of Moses in order that you may prosper in all that you do and[c] wherever you turn[c], [4]so that Yahweh may establish his word which he spoke to me[d] saying, If your sons keep my ways to walk before me in truth with all their heart and all their vitality there shall not be cut off

[a]J. Fichtner, *Das erste Buch von den Königen*, p. 44.

[b]Inserting *we* with certain Hebrew MSS.

[c]The subordinate clause, which is strictly an adverbial clause introduced by *ʾet*, is rather awkward. G[AB] read *kekol-ʾašer-ʾaṣawwekā* ('according to all that I charge you' for MT *ʾet-kol-ʾašer tipne šām*, which we read.

[d]Reading *ʾēlay* for MT *ʿālay* ('concerning me'), which G[B] omits.

a man from you from the throne of Israel. [5]And further, you know what Joab the son of Zeruiah did to me in what he did to the two commanders of the armies of Israel, even to Abner[a] the son of Ner and to Amasa the son of Jether, slaying them and taking vengeance[b] in peace for blood shed in war and putting blood gratuitously[c] on [d]my girdle which is upon my loins and on the sandals which are upon my feet.[d] [6]So act according to your wisdom and do not suffer his grey hair to go down unscathed to Sheol. [7]But with the sons of Barzillai the Gileadite deal loyally, and let them be among those that eat of your table, for they rallied to me when I fled before Absalom your brother. [8]Now with you is Shimei the son of Gera the Benjamite from Bahurim. He it was who cursed me with a blighting curse when I was going to Mahanaim, but he came down to the Jordan to meet me, and I swore an oath to him by Yahweh, saying, I shall not put you to death with the sword. [9]But do not you[e] hold him guiltless, for you are an astute man. So take note how you may deal with him, and bring his grey hair with blood down to Sheol. [10]So David slept with his fathers and was buried in the city of David. [11]And the years that David was king over Israel were forty years; he reigned seven years in Hebron and in Jerusalem he reigned thirty-three years. [12]And Solomon took his seat upon the throne of David his father and his royal authority was firmly established.

2.1. It will always be a problem as to how far the legacy of bloody vengeance on the faithful Joab and on the hostile Shimei, whom David had already pardoned under oath, was really due to David, otherwise depicted as so chivalrous. It seems more likely that these measures were decided upon by Solomon, but since amnesties were regularly proclaimed as auspicious beginnings of new reigns, the political murders were imputed to David, with some technical justification. In virtue of the ancient superstition regarding the potency of the curse and the solidarity with his kin and posterity,

[a]G and I Sam. 14.50 suggest that the name should be pointed as Abiner, which was no doubt the original pointing, though as a later development Abner is possible.

[b]Reading *wayyiqqōm* with G^L for MT *wayyāśem* ('setting'). Noth (*op. cit.*, p. 30) cites *śām dāmīm babbayit* in Deut. 22.8 in the sense of 'bringing blood-guilt upon', but as *śām dāmīm* is followed by a preposition, this is hardly a valid analogy, unless *śām dāmīm . . . b^{e}šālōm* means 'bring guilt for blood shed in war upon peaceful relations'.

[c]Reading *dām ḥinnām* with G^A and S^h (cf. I K. 2.31) for MT *d^{e}mē milḥāmā* ('blood of war'), which is obviously the repetition of an earlier phrase in the same verse by scribal inadvertency.

[d]Reading the pronominal suffixes throughout in the first instead of the third person, as in MT.

[e]Reading *w^{e}ʾattā* with G^L for MT *w^{e}ʿattā* ('and now'). The point is that David was hindered by his oath from dealing summarily with Shimei, but Solomon was free.

David might well have given Solomon the charge to eliminate Shimei, which he himself could not undertake, but the alleged offence of Joab, valid enough in itself, would not normally affect David, unless under some feudal convention on which, in this particular, we are not sufficiently informed. Strong men like Joab who have laid the royal house under obligation are notoriously embarrassing in the infancy of a dynasty, and the sordid drama of Solomon's reign was re-enacted in the first decade of the Abbasid dynasty, when the protection given by Abu Salamah to the Abbasid pretender in Iraq and the invaluable service in propaganda, war, and government by Abu Muslim of Khorasan did not save them from the bloodthirsty policy of the first two Caliphs. The present passage has a perfect analogy again in Arab history in the last injunctions (*waṣiyya*) which the first Caliph of the Umayyad dynasty, Mu'awiyah, laid upon his son Yazid, which concerned political enemies.[a] The Arabic verb *waṣiya* (form II) 'to make a last testament' 'to give parting charges', suggests that the Hebrew *ṣiwwā*, which has this connotation here and in Gen. 49.29 (Jacob) and II K. 20.1 (Hezekiah), may be connected with the Arabic verb.

2.2. The Deuteronomistic preface to David's last charges re-echoes the sentiment and phraseology of Moses' farewell exhortation to Joshua, 'Be strong and of good courage' (Deut. 31.23), and the divine exhortation to Joshua to the same effect (Josh. 1.6, 9, 18).

3. The keeping of the ways of Yahweh, 'his statutes, commandments, judgements and testimonies' according to what is written in the law of Moses, is also the theme of Josh. 1. Apart from obvious Deuteronomistic interpolations by the compiler of Kings there is no mention of such a formal law-book associated with Moses until the reign of Josiah. Yahweh's 'statutes' (*ḥuqqōtāw*, lit. 'things engraved'), and 'commandments' (*miṣwōtāw*) signified direct orders in the form 'thou shalt . . .' or 'thou shalt not . . .' as opposed to casuistic laws which admitted qualifications and refinements reflecting the complexities of sedentary life as opposed to the grand simplicity and moral austerity of nomad society.[b] 'Judgements' (*mišpāṭim*) means properly *ad hoc* decisions which are accumulated as legal precedents. The word may also mean 'customs', lit. the order which is maintained by a *šōpēṭ*, which, as the Ras Shamra texts show, means

[a]Ibn aṭ-Ṭiqṭaqa, *Al-Fakhri*, ed. W. Ahlwardt, 1860, p. 132.

[b]A. Alt, 'Die Ursprünge des israelitischen Rechts', *KS* I, 1953, pp. 279–332: ET, *Essays*, pp. 79–132.

primarily 'ruler', being found in parallelism with *zbl*, 'prince', and *mlk*, 'king'. 'Testimonies' (*ʿēdōt*) means 'solemn charges' in which God is called upon as a witness (*ʿēd*), adjuration being a further feature of the transaction. The specific reference here is to the terms of the law traditionally associated with the Sinai covenant.

In a study of *maśkīl* in the heading of Pss. 32–42, 55, 74, 78, 88, 89, 142, in all of which the essential elements of the Plaint of the Sufferer are prominent, G. W. Ahlström[a] maintains that the verb *śākal* denotes success after suffering, achieved through prudent submission to divine discipline, as in the fast-liturgy, hence the meaning 'wisdom', which the root often signifies. 'Success' as the sense of the root *śākal* is certainly suggested by the passages he cites, Deut. 29.8; Josh. 1.7; Jer. 50.9; Isa. 44.18; 53.15; and possibly also Gen. 3.6. Those passages significantly indicate success after suffering or ordeal, hence the relevance of *maśkīl* to the Plaints of the Sufferer in the Psalms, though in the *epithalamium* Ps. 45 it possibly means merely a skilful composition. Insofar as the verb *śākal* connotes wisdom or prudence, as it often does, that is wisdom gained from hard experience.

2.4. 'That Yahweh may establish his word' (lit. . . . cause to stand . . .) is a further reference to the covenant with the house of David (II Sam. 7.12ff.) (see on I K. 1.48). The condition that David's successors should 'keep his way to walk before him in truth with all their heart and all their vitality' is a typical Deuteronomistic addition to the original oracle of Nathan. There the insistence is upon the preservation of the father-son relationship of Yahweh and the king; here it is upon the keeping of 'all that is written in the law of Moses', which certainly bears the impress of the Deuteronomist.

5. 'Taking vengeance in peace for blood shed in war' refers to Joab's murder of Abner in the gate of Hebron (II Sam. 3.22–27) in requital for the blood of his brother Asahel (II Sam. 3.27). Abner had, however, slain him in war near Gibeon (II Sam. 2.12–23), actually in self-defence. The 'innocent blood' was that of Amasa, one of David's commanders, whom Joab slew treacherously out of jealousy (II Sam. 20.4–10). Since Amasa held David's commission and Abner was in negotiation with him, David is here depicted as being responsible for their deaths, hence 'what Joab did to me'. An Arab sheikh would, incidentally, assume the same responsibility for

[a]G. W. Ahlström, *Psalm 89, eine Liturgie aus dem Ritual des leidenden Königs*, 1959, pp. 21–26.

the murder of one who had the temporary protection of his tribe. The blood thus shed and claiming requital could be said to be 'upon the girdle' of David; the strength of David, symbolized by his girdle, or his loins, could be said to be impaired. The girdle on his loins might alternatively symbolize his progeny, which would inherit his bloodguiltiness. Blood on the sandals indicates that David and his issue would be dogged with blood until it was avenged. There is some legal justification, if somewhat specious, for the death of Joab, but there is no doubt that his death was owing to the part he took with Adonijah against Solomon, for which he stands self-condemned in his taking refuge at the altar. We should therefore take this verse as an instance of later elaboration of the narrative of the Davidic succession.

2.6. 'Wisdom' (*ḥokmā*) in ancient Israel, and specifically in the account of the reign of Solomon, falls into three categories. As in the tradition of Solomon's revelation at Gibeon and its sequel (I K. 3.4ff.), the famous judgement between the two mothers, it denotes the capacity of discernment and the ability to decide a case, which, as in the Ugaritic texts Krt and 'Aqht, was the function of the ancient king. In this connection we should note that the Arabic verb *ḥakama* means 'to decide', the participle *ḥākim* meaning 'governor'. 'Wisdom' in this sense therefore is knowledge of relevant fact and power of discrimination in the use of it, resulting in administrative ability crowned with success. Wisdom in I K. 4.29–34[5.9–14] has a different connotation, not, however, quite unrelated to the first sense of the word. Here it connotes encyclopaedic knowledge not related to practical administration. The content of this knowledge of Solomon, however, of the details of natural phenomena, suggests an analogy with the classified lists of natural phenomena in Mesopotamian and Egyptian wisdom exercises.[a] The principle of classification here implies knowledge of the facts and discrimination, which was the essence of administrative wisdom. In both cases, empirical familiarity with facts is essential, and wisdom is a secular asset, a gift of God perhaps, but only in the same objective sense as riches. In emphasizing this fact, Noth[b] indicates that often *ḥākām* is used in the derogatory sense of practical, worldly *savoir-faire*, meaning '*klug*' (astute) rather than '*weise*' (wise), '*ja vielleicht sogar schlau*' ('sly'). In the present

[a]A. Alt, 'Die Weisheit Salomos', *KS* II, 1953, pp. 90–99.

[b]'Die Bewährung von Salomos "Göttlicher Weisheit"', *Wisdom in Israel and the Ancient Near East*, SVT III, 1955, pp. 232ff.

passage it is suggested that Solomon used his practical *savoir-faire* to get rid of his adversaries, 'wisdom' being beyond doubt the practical and even unprincipled path to success.

'Unscathed' is our rendering of *b^e^šālōm*. The last word, from the root *šālēm*, 'to be whole', means primarily 'wholeness', of which 'wellbeing' is one aspect. The meaning 'peace' is secondary. As G. von Rad has pointed out, it denotes primarily a relationship between man and man, or man and the community, or between both and God.[a] In the greeting *šālōm* one wishes that a person in the state of *šālōm* with one may share one's wellbeing, hence the derivative meanings of 'wellbeing' and 'peace'. 'Concord' is perhaps the best comprehensive translation of *šālōm*.

Sheol is the shadowy, insubstantial underworld, the destination of all, good and bad without discrimination, where existence is wholly undesirable. The Hebrews in the classical period had no comfortable prospect of the hereafter.

2.7. The provision for the sons of Barzillai may well have been made by David. Montgomery (ICC, p. 90) cites biblical and extra-biblical evidence for the significance of eating at the king's table as a method of pensioning, cf. I K. 18.19 (Jezebel's Baal-prophets). Under Solomon this entertainment might have been designed to hold men as guarantors for the allegiance of Israelites in Transjordan, as David detained Saul's grandson Mephibosheth by him (II Sam. 9.11–13). The Aramaic form of the name Barzillai ought to be noted with reference to the dialect spoken by the Israelites in the north part of Transjordan. The name is explained by Noth[b] as denoting a physical or mental characteristic ('the man of iron'). It might, however, be an appellative referring to the status of the man as head of a smith-caste, who might the more readily have been induced to leave Transjordan to settle in Jerusalem, since such are not usually attached to ancestral lands. Metallurgy was anciently practised in the vicinity of Succoth (possibly *Ḫirbet Deir ʿAllā*) and Zarethan (I K. 7. 46), and the local explorations of H. Franken have discovered deposits of metal slag at various mounds in the vicinity of *Deir ʿAllā*, where he has excavated blast-furnaces from various periods from the Late Bronze Age onwards, through the Iron Age.[c] Glueck also notes the abundance of iron slag at Ajlun.

[a] *TWNT* II, p. 401; 'Die falschen Propheten', *ZAW* LI, 1933, pp. 109ff.
[b] *IP*, 1928, p. 225.
[c] 'The Excavations at Deir ʿAllā in Jordan', *VT* X, 1960, pp. 386–93.

The word *ḥesed*, generally translated 'mercy', is much fuller, and means primarily firmness or loyalty to the terms and spirit of a covenant. It is used of the loyalty of God to the covenant with Israel in which of his free grace he revealed his nature and will to Israel, whom he had chosen and delivered; it expresses the loyalty to God demanded of Israel as debtors to his grace; and it expresses the loyalty of one member of Israel to another as the covenanted people of God. The word is so pregnant of meaning as to defy translation. It is generally translated *charis* ('grace') in G, but that is too narrow and misses the association with the covenant. G. A. Smith's translation 'leal love' is the most felicitous, though unfortunately not relished to the full outside Scotland.

2.8. Shimei's cursing of David when he withdrew in Absalom's revolt (II Sam. 16.5ff.) is remembered. In the Book of the Covenant, cursing a ruler of the people was a capital offence (Ex. 22.28[27]), and David, in sparing the life of Saul, had shown himself very scrupulous in respecting the sanctity of the Lord's anointed (I Sam. 24.6). Bahurim, the home of Shimei, was just north of Bethany on the east slope of the Mount of Olives on the way to Jericho, and it is noticed as the scene of the escape of David's spies during the revolt of Absalom (II Sam. 17.18). It is noted here by the sixth-century pilgrim Antoninus Martyr, and is probably to be located at *Rās at-Tamīm*, where pottery of the Davidic period is found.[a] The curse of Shimei is said to have been 'crippling' (*nimreṣet*), lit. 'sick' (cf. Arab. *marīḍ*). The Niphal indicates that the curse (*qᵉlālā*) had in it the germ of disability, which was infectious. L. Kopf[b] aptly cites *rāʿā ḥōlā* (Eccl. 5.13[12]). In the mind of the oriental the curse, like the blessing, had an objective effect, cf. the irrevocable nature of Isaac's blessing (Gen. 27.33ff.).[c] David had been restrained by oath from nullifying the curse of Shimei by putting him to death, so the curse was still potent and could harm David in his descendants according to the ancient oriental conception of the solidarity of the family and a man's survival in his descendants.

9. On the force of the reading *wᵉʾattā* ('but you') see textual note. This is a pointed commentary on the Hebrew conception of wisdom,

[a]Abel, *GP* II, 1938, p. 260.

[b]'Arabische Etymologien und Parallelen', *VT* VIII, 1958, pp. 161–215, esp. 163.

[c]See the writer's article on 'Blessing and Curse' in *HDB*², 1963, pp. 109ff., and J. Pedersen, *Israel*, I–II, 1926, pp. 437ff.

see on v. 6. The hint is that Solomon by some subtlety should find some legal pretext on which to eliminate Shimei.

2.10. David, like men of property in Israel, was buried in his own domain, 'the city (or rather 'citadel') of David'. The walled city of the Jebusites was taken not by the free levies of Israel and Judah, but by the personal striking-force of David led by his kinsman Joab, hence it remained the crown property of David and his successors, crown property within the State of Israel, and later of Judah.[a] House-burial is well known from excavations in Syria and Palestine, and the kings of Ugarit were buried in vaults in the palace. Ezekiel in referring to the defilement of the Temple by the bodies of the kings of Judah (Ezek. 43.7–9) implies that at least the later kings, probably from Hezekiah's time, were buried in the Solomonic palace-complex north of the old Jebusite city, which formed a unit with the Temple. The tomb of David was still shown *c.* AD 30 (Acts 2.29), but there is no guarantee that this was authentic. Josephus records that the antechambers of the tomb were opened for their treasures by John Hyrcanus and Herod the Great,[b] but that the tomb containing the body was left intact. The precise location of the tomb, however, is today quite unknown because of Roman quarrying, though probably located generally at the southern extremity of the south-eastern hill.

11. On David's forty-year reign see Introduction, p. 55, Chronology. The number may be a round one, the conventional length of a generation and the indefinite number in Semitic folklore, e.g. forty days and forty nights and Ali Baba and the Forty Thieves.

12. This verse, the second half of which is repeated with slight variation in v. 46b, is taken as the beginning of *Basileiai* 3 in G^L, a division which is defended by H. St J. Thackeray[c] and accepted by Montgomery.[d] Eissfeldt, however, is much more reserved in his judgement,[e] and we regard the verse as borrowed and adapted from 46b in conformity with the pattern of the Deuteronomic epilogue on the reign of the late king, which notes his successor. In view of the theme of this source as the succession of Solomon, our opinion is that the statement that the kingship was established under

[a] Alt, 'Jerusalems Aufstieg', *KS* III, 1959, p. 254.
[b] *Ant.* VII, 15.3; XVI, 7.1.
[c] *JTS* VIII, 1907, pp. 262–78.
[d] 'The Supplement at the end of 3 Kingdoms 2 (1 Reg 2)', *ZAW* L, 1932, pp. 124–9.
[e] *The Old Testament: an Introduction*, 1965, p. 298; so also Noth, *Könige*, pp. 9f.

Solomon (v. 46b) must be taken with what precedes rather than with what follows. See further on v. 46b.

(*c*) SOLOMON'S PURGE: 2.13–46

This is so to speak an addendum to the Story of the Davidic Succession in the same graphic and detailed narrative style. Here, as in the narrative of Solomon's *coup d'état*, a stylistic feature is verbal repetition and direct speech. There is no question that the author favoured Solomon, for whose action he is at pains to find legal justification. He treats his subject, however, remarkably objectively for a partisan, and he even succeeds in engaging our sympathy for Adonijah in the peculiar circumstances of his death. His art prevails over his politics.

(i) THE END OF ADONIJAH: 2.13–25

2 [13]Now Adonijah the son of Haggith came to Bathsheba the mother of Solomon, and she said, Do you come in concord? And he said, In concord. [14]And he said, I have a matter to discuss with you. So she said, Speak. [15]Then he said, You know that the kingship was to have been mine, and on me all Israel set their expectations that I should be king, but the royal power was given on the contrary to my brother, for Yahweh so disposed it for him. [16]Now then, I make one request of you; do not repulse me. So she said to him, Speak. [17]Then he said, Tell king Solomon, please, for he will not repulse you, and let him give me Abishag the Shunammite to wife. [18]And Bathsheba said, It is well, I shall speak on your behalf to the king. [19]So Bathsheba went in to king Solomon to speak with him on the matter of Adonijah, and the king rose to meet her and he did obeisance to her[a] and sat down on his throne and [b]had a seat set[b] for the queen-mother, and she sat at his right hand. [20]And she said, There is one small request which I make of you; do not repulse me. And the king said, Ask it, mother, for I shall not repulse you. [21]Then she said, May Abishag the Shunammite be given to Adonijah your brother as wife. [22]Then king Solomon answered and said to his mother, Why then do you ask for Abishag the Shunammite for Adonijah? You may as well ask for the kingship for him, for he is my older brother, and he is supported by Abiathar[c] the priest and

[a]G reads *wayyiššāqehā* ('and he kissed her') for MT *wayyištaḥū lāh*. The queen-mother in the ancient Near East enjoyed great respect, and a royal epistle among the Ras Shamra texts (Gordon, *UT*, 1965, 117, 5), where the king declares, 'At the feet of my mother I bow down', seems to authenticate the MT over against the G variant.

[b]G and S^h read the passive *wayyūśam* ('and a seat was set'), cf. S *wayyāśīmū* ('and they set'). We may read MT, with Solomon as the ultimate subject.

[c]Reading *w^{e}lō 'ebyātār hakkōhēn w^{e}lō yō'āb* with G and S for MT *w^{e}lō ūl^e'ebyātār hakkōhēn ūl^{e}yō'āb* ('and for him and for Abiathar the priest and for Joab').

by Joab the son of Zeruiah. [23]And Solomon swore by Yahweh saying, So may God do unto me and more also, but Adonijah has spoken this word at the cost of his life. [24]And now, as Yahweh lives who has established me and set me on the throne of David my father and made him[a] a house just as he has said, Adonijah shall certainly be put to death today. [25]So king Solomon sent by the agency of Benaiah the son of Jehoiada, and he fell upon him and he died.

2.13ff. The request of Adonijah for the hand of Abishag is variously treated as a romance and as the indirect claim to the throne, the appropriation of the harem of the late king having this significance (II Sam. 16.21ff.). It was certainly taken by Solomon as signifying the latter, and on this pretext, too eagerly sought by Solomon, Adonijah was put to death.

13. *šālōm* is used adverbially here. The analogy of Arabic usage suggests that this is an adverbial accusative. For the sense of *šālōm*, indicating a social relationship, hence our translation 'concord', see on v. 6.

14. *dābār* according to context signifies in Hebrew 'an event', 'a matter', as well as 'a word', cf. Arabic *'amr*, 'a command' and 'a matter'. It is of importance to bear this in mind in view of the concrete and objective significance of 'the word of Yahweh', of which the prophets were the agents in word and deed. The word of Yahweh so communicated brought men into palpable contact with realities, with relation to which it had a creative effect.

15. Adonijah here alludes to the native Israelite elements, apart from the new feudal class, which had supported his claims to the succession. *wattissōb hammelūkā* means literally 'the kingship has turned round', i.e. David's intention in the matter was revoked. Adonijah's resignation is typically oriental. He accepts the unpalatable situation which he cannot amend as a Muslim would accept it *min 'allāh*, 'from God'.

19. The status of the queen-mother is evident from Solomon's reception of her (see textual note). She is further seated at the king's right hand as he in the cult was seated at the right hand of God (Ps. 110.1). The queen-mother was the first lady (*haggebīrā*) in the realm, taking precedence over any lady of the royal harem while she lived. See further on 15.13.

[a]The reference to the covenant with David in II Sam. 7.12ff. suggests that *lō* should be read for MT *lī* ('to me'), in spite of the fact that the versions unanimously support MT.

2.22. Here Solomon seems to accept the weakness of his own position *vis-à-vis* his older brother in a society where, even if the hereditary principle in the new institution of the monarchy was not accepted, the right of primogeniture was generally presumed (cf. the case of Esau and Jacob); Solomon further admits that Adonijah had the support of the free elements of Israel, such as Abiathar and Joab, over against the feudal retainers of the king.

23. Here the physical meaning of *nepeš* is obvious.

24. According to MT, Solomon apparently appropriates the promise given to David. We should, however, perhaps read 'has made him a house', i.e. a family or dynasty. See p. 106 n.[a]. The oracle of Nathan on the subject of the covenant with David was successfully propagated in the litany (e.g. Pss. 89.3f.[4f.]; 132.11f. [12f.]) to such an extent as may be gauged by the fact that it was a dogma for the compiler of Kings, for all his Deuteronomic ideals, till the eve of the Exile.

25. Nothing is recorded of the death of Adonijah except the bare fact. For such work Benaiah, a feudal retainer removed from social context and conventions, was a fit instrument.

(ii) THE ELIMINATION OF ADONIJAH'S PARTY: 2.26–35

2 [26]Then the king said to Abiathar the priest, Go to Anathoth (to live) on[a] your land, for you deserve death, but just now I shall not put you to death, for you carried the ark of my lord Yahweh before David my father, and suffered in all the hardships of my father. [27]So Solomon expelled Abiathar from the status of priest to Yahweh, fulfilling the word of Yahweh, which he had spoken against the house of Eli in Shiloh. [28]And the rumour reached Joab, for Joab had sided with Adonijah, though he had not sided with Absalom,[b] and Joab fled to the tent of Yahweh and laid hold of the horns of the altar. [29]And it was reported to king Solomon, Joab has fled to the tent of Yahweh, and there he is by the altar. Then Solomon sent[c] Benaiah the son of Jehoiada saying, Go and strike him down. [30]Then Benaiah came to the tent of Yahweh and said to him, Thus says the king, Come out! And he said, No! but I shall die here. So Benaiah reported back to the king saying, So spoke Joab and so did he answer me. [31]And the king said to

[a]'*el* ('to') is proposed here for MT '*al* ('on'), but the latter is to be retained in the pregnant phrase, where the words 'to live on' are to be understood.

[b]G^L, S, S^h, and V read 'Solomon' for MT 'Absalom', but Montgomery (ICC, p. 49) justly remarks that the verb *nāṭā*, which signifies declension from the right party, would not have been used with Solomon.

[c]An addition to MT is suggested by G, the passage having been doubtless omitted through homoeoteleuton through the words *wayyišlaḥ š*[e]*lōmō* ('and Solomon sent').

him, Do as he has said, and strike him down, and bury him, and remove innocent blood which Joab shed from me and from my father's house. [32]And Yahweh will cause [a]the blood of his crime[a] to recoil on his own head, in that he struck down two men more innocent and better than himself and slew them with the sword, though my father David was not privy to it, Abner the son of Ner, the commander of the host of Israel, and Amasa the son of Jether, the commander of the host of Judah. [33]And let their blood recoil on the head of Joab and on the head of his seed for ever, and let David and his seed, his house and his throne have security from Yahweh for ever. [34]So Benaiah the son of Jehoiada went up and fell upon him and killed him, and he was buried in his house[b] in the country. [35]And the king appointed Benaiah the son of Jehoiada in his place over the host, and the king appointed Zadok the priest in place of Abiathar.

2.26. Anathoth, the family home to which Abiathar is now rusticated, is by *Kefr Anātā*, about three and a half miles north-east of Jerusalem. The Iron Age settlement is located more particularly about half a mile south of the modern village at *Rās al-Ḫarrūbeh*.[c] The prophet Jeremiah was of a priestly family from this community, hence in his oracle on the destruction of the Temple (Jer. 26) he may be echoing the traditional local resentment of the Temple and its parvenu priesthood.

In the recounting of the service of Abiathar we may seriously consider the possibility that *'ēpōd* should be read for MT *'ᵃrōn*, particularly in view of the reference to David's hardships as an outlaw from Saul. Abiathar then had the ephod for divination, but not the ark, which was still in the Philistine country, or at least had not been restored to a sanctuary in Israel. If 'the ark' is read, the reference is presumably to the restoration to Jerusalem by David, when Abiathar might have officiated. The ephod, Akkad. *epadatu*, was a garment which might be laid over some symbol of the divine presence at a shrine, or worn by a priest. It was used for divination (I Sam. 23.9f.; 30.7f.), and probably contained pockets holding the sacred lots, the Urim and Thummim (Ex. 28.28–30). It survived as a relic in the high priest's pectoral set with its twelve precious and semi-

[a]Reading *dam riš'ō* with G for MT *dāmō* ('his blood'). If *dāmō* were retained it would signify not Joab's own blood, but the blood of others which he had shed. This, as v. 33 indicates, is the blood which recoils on the head of the slayer.

[b]G[L] and S read *qibrō* ('his tomb') for MT *bētō* ('his house'), quite unnecessarily, since burial in private houses and their adjuncts is well enough attested; cf. the case of Samuel (I Sam. 25.1). See note on v. 10.

[c]Abel, *GP* II, pp. 243ff.

precious stones. The reading *'ēpōd* has no support in the versions, though it differs from *'ªrōn* by only two letters, of which one, *p*, in the proto-Hebraic script closely resembles *r*.

2.27. This verse, which notes the degradation of Abiathar as a fulfilment of the prophetic oracle against the House of Eli at Shiloh (I Sam. 2.27ff.), is a Deuteronomistic aside, reflecting one of the main interests of the Deuteronomistic compiler. Here the authority of the king over the priest is to be noted; cf. Jeroboam's installation of priests at Bethel and Dan. The priesthood, as distinct from the office of judge or prophet, is not a charismatic calling, but an office filled automatically by heredity or by royal appointment.[a]

28. On the right of sanctuary at the altar see on I K. 1.50. Joab, a realist, anticipated the consequences of his 'turning after Adonijah', which is introduced here, perhaps hinting at the real reason for his death apart from the cause alleged in v. 5. *nāṭā* is used of swerving from the path of loyalty, cf. 11.9. The fuller text in v. 29 implied in G, which is rejected by Stade, Šanda, and Burney, but admitted by Thenius, Kittel, and Eissfeldt, emphasizes, as Montgomery has pointed out,[b] the bad conscience of Joab over his part in Adonijah's abortive attempt, and so advances the narrative by citing a further justification for his death.

30. Joab refuses to leave the altar, but is determined to embarrass Solomon and his henchman Benaiah, who, for the moment frustrated, appeals to Solomon, who urges specious reasons (v. 31, cf. v. 5) for refusing the right of sanctuary. The case of Joab is interesting inasmuch as refuge was not sought because he was conscious of bloodguiltiness, but because he had supported the wrong political party. Solomon's apparent violation of the right of asylum was probably because the sanctuary was under his jurisdiction, and pardon and punishment at the royal discretion (cf. the case of Adonijah, 1.51, 53), as N. M. Nicolsky has pointed out.[c] Joab's slaughter of Abner and Amasa, which is alleged as justification for his death (v. 31), is probably no more than a specious reason for the removal of this embarrassingly strong subject, but it was technically in accord with Hebrew law, which admitted refuge only in the case of unintentional homicide, the slayer who lurks deliberately for his victim, as Joab

[a]See further M. Noth, *Amt und Berufung im Alten Testament*, 1958; ET, 'Office and Vocation in the Old Testament,' *The Laws in the Pentateuch*, pp. 229–49.

[b]ICC, p. 95.

[c]'Das Asylrecht in Israel', *ZAW* LXVIII, 1930, p. 149.

had done for Abner in the gate of Hebron, being under the curse (Ex. 21.14; Deut. 27.24).

2.31. Solomon's instruction to bury Joab was not only a case of giving Joab a decent and honourable burial; it was important to 'cover up' blood shed violently lest it cry out for vengeance, cf. Gen. 4.11; Job. 16.18. A. M. Honeyman has pointed out that Abimelech's sowing of Shechem with salt (Judg. 9.45) was designed to cover the blood of his kinsmen and to allay the baneful influence.

34. Samuel also had been buried in his house (I Sam. 25.1), see on v. 10. Joab's home was at Bethlehem, where Asahel his brother had been buried (II Sam. 2.32). The 'country' means not quite 'the wilderness' of EVV, but the open country over which flocks may graze, usually land too stony for cultivation, from a root *dbr*, 'to graze', now well attested in the Ras Shamra texts,[a] cf. Isa. 5.17; Micah 2.12.

35. Solomon replaces Joab by Benaiah as commander-in-chief of the army, including the free levies of Israel and Judah, and Abiathar by Zadok. This notice indicates that Zadok was a parvenu in office in Israel. The priestly supremacy remained in Zadok's family till Menelaus of the tribe of Benjamin outbid Jason for the high-priesthood in 171 BC (II Macc. 4.24). The Qumran sect may have come out over the issue of the high-priesthood, either on this occasion or when the office, as a political bribe, was accepted by Jonathan, the brother of Judas Maccabaeus, who was not of this family.

(iii) THE DEATH OF SHIMEI: 2.36–46a

2 [36]Then the king sent and called Shimei and he said to him, Build yourself a house in Jerusalem and settle there and you may not go out anywhere from there. [37]And it shall be that on the day when you go out and cross the Kidron Wadi, know of a certainty that you shall surely die, and your blood shall be on your own head.[b] [38]And Shimei said to the king, The matter is fair. Just as my lord the king has said, so will your servant do. So Shimei settled in Jerusalem many days.[c] [39]Now at the end of three years two slaves of Shimei ran off to Achish the son of Maacah the king of Gath, and they told Shimei saying, See, your slaves are in Gath. [40]And Shimei arose and saddled his ass and went to Gath to Achish to seek his slaves, and Shimei went and brought his slaves from

[a]E.g. Gordon, *UT* 49. II, 19–20; 67. V, 18.

[b]G adds 'and the king made him swear an oath that day', which may be justified by the reference to the oath in v. 42.

[c]G states 'three years', which may be a secondary reading suggested by the statement in v. 39.

Gath. [41]And it was reported to Solomon that Shimei had gone from Jerusalem to Gath, and had returned. [42]So the king sent and called Shimei and said to him, Did I not adjure you by Yahweh and testify against you saying, In the day that you go out and proceed anywhere, know of a certainty that you shall surely die? And you said to me, The matter is fair. I have heard it. [43]Why then have you not kept the oath by Yahweh and the order which I have laid upon you? [44]And the king said to Shimei, You yourself know all the ill [a]of which you are secretly conscious[a] which you did to David my father, and Yahweh will cause your ill to recoil on your own head. [45]And king Solomon has the blessing, and the throne of David will be established before Yahweh for ever. [46]So the king gave Benaiah the son of Jehoiada the order and he went out and fell upon him and he died.

2.36ff. The end of Shimei is an example of the astuteness (*ḥokmā*) of Solomon. In obliging Shimei to reside in Jerusalem, Solomon deprives him of the influence of his own kinsmen in his home at Bahurim, where his ancestral land is now managed by his slaves. The fact that two of them ran off indicates how much the influence of Shimei was undermined. Nothing better illustrates the relative status of the Israelites living on their ancestral land among their own kinsfolk, safeguarded by the traditional Israelite social conventions, for which the whole kinship held themselves responsible, and those who lived without any such guarantees in the crown property of Jerusalem.

37. The mention of the Kidron Wadi, which Shimei, confined to Jerusalem for strict observation, was forbidden to cross on pain of death, indicates that it was Solomon's intention to keep him isolated from his kinsmen of Benjamin, who had been the spearhead of the revolt against David under Sheba (II Sam. 20). In effect, when he left Jerusalem, Shimei went south and did not actually cross the Kidron, but the tributary Valley of Hinnom (modern *Wādī ar-Rabābī*). Thus he did not violate the letter but the spirit of Solomon's ban. The name *qidrōn* may be derived from the verbal root *qādar*, 'to be black', referring to the shadow in the deep ravine of the Kidron Wadi between Jerusalem and the Mount of Olives. On the other hand, shut off from the prevailing wind by its depth, it is intensely hot, the sun at its height being reflected from the bare rocks of the escarpments, so that the Wadi may owe its name to the heat, the

[a]It is suggested that this phrase is tautological and is an interpolation. Alternatively *'ašer yēraʿ lᵉbābᵉkā* ('the evil which your heart perpetrates') is proposed. The MT is intelligible, however, and is not questioned in any of the versions.

name being derived from another verb *qādar*, which A. Büchler[a] has shown on convincing evidence from post-biblical Hebrew to mean 'to glow, reflect heat'. There is possibly a reminiscence of this significance of the name *qidrōn* in the modern name of the Wadi from its confluence with the *Wādī ar-Rabābī*, *Wādī an-Nār* ('the Wadi of Fire').

2.39. Shimei's runaway slaves, like David as an outlaw from Saul, had joined Achish of Gath, who was one of the five 'lords' of the Philistines and probably the son of David's former master. The Philistines had a feudal organization and were not nice in their recruitment. B. Mazar has done well to note that there were a number of towns compounded with Gath, e.g. Gath-Karmel (Ginti-Kirmil of the Amarna Letters), Gath-Rimmon north of Jaffa, Gath-Padallu, Gath-Hepher in Galilee and 'Gath of the Philistines'. One Gath was associated with Ashdod and Ekron and Jabneh in an inscription of Sargon II,[b] and was apparently a point at which an expedition might deviate from the west to Jerusalem, as in the account of Hazael's expedition (II K. 12.17). Mazar identifies this Gath with a large low mound, an early Iron Age site, *Rās Abu Ḥamīd* by Ramleh, which, however, shows no surface pottery from an earlier period. The inclusion of Gath in Rehoboam's fortifications on the border of Judah and Benjamin in the Shephelah, where it is listed between Adullam and Marishah, suggests a location further south, possibly at the Iron Age site of *Tell Burnāṭ*,[c] but this does not rule out Libnah at *Tell aṣ-Ṣāfī* ('Gleaming Mound') on a spur of the western foothills of the Shephelah commanding the passage to and from the interior by way of the Vale of Elah (*Wādī as-Sanṭ*),[d] which is the location we prefer as commanding the access to Jerusalem by the Vale of Elah, as II K. 12.17 suggests. The Crusaders appreciated the strategic significance of the site, which they fortified against Saracen attack from Ashkelon, naming it Blanchegarde after the conspicuous white bluff which gave the place its Canaanite and Arab names, Libnah and *Tell aṣ-Ṣāfī*. Gath of Achish, however, as is indicated by the outlying fief of Ziklag, *Tell al-Ḫuweilefeh*, *c.* 11 miles north-north-east of Beersheba,[e] was another Gath further south, in the vicinity of, if not

[a] *ZAW* XXXII, 1912, pp. 56–64.
[b] Luckenbill, *ARA* II § 62, cf. II Chron. 26.6; I Sam. 17.52.
[c] So Albright, *BASOR* 15, 1924, p. 9.
[d] So K. Galling, *Biblisches Reallexikon*, 1937, pp. 170f.
[e] So Alt, *KS* III, 1959, pp. 29f., cf. Josh. 15.31.

identical with, *Tell an-Nājileh*.[a] Neither the fortification nor the pottery of this site, however, nor that of *ʿIrāq al-Manshīyeh*, *c*. 6 miles west-north-west of Lachish (*Tell ed-Duweir*), suggests one of the five great Philistine fiefs.

2.40. Shimei recovered his slaves according to a well-established convention in the ancient Near East, attested in the Ras Shamra texts in the case of a charioteer of the king of Ugarit, who had absconded to the neighbouring kingdom of Alalakh (about Aleppo) and against whom the king of Ugarit appeals for extradition.[b] In Deut. 23.16ff., on the contrary, foreign slaves fleeing to Israel were regarded as having sanctuary.[c]

45. With the declaration of the blessing on Solomon, the curse of Shimei on David is formally annulled.

(iv) CONCLUSION TO THE STORY OF THE DAVIDIC SUCCESSION: 2.46b

And the kingdom was established in the hand of Solomon.

The problem again arises as to whether this passage, which is repeated in substance and with slight verbal modification in v. 12, ends the preceding account of the succession of Solomon or is the heading of the account of his reign which follows. The later view is taken by G, which, apparently regarding the elimination of Solomon's rivals as distinct from his reign, proceeds (Swete, *Basileiai* III 2.35a–o) to give a miscellaneous summary of the reign of Solomon, which is supplemented by a collection of similar miscellaneous matter in Swete, v. 46 a–l, this matter being found for the most part in I K. 4.20–29[5.9]. Montgomery[d] is probably right in regarding the origin of this matter as summaries of the reign of Solomon. As to the purpose of the miscellanies, J. Hänel[e] has contended that they were a regular listing of variant traditions of the reign of Solomon, which seems a feasible suggestion. We question, however, if he is right in seeing the purpose of that list as the intention of disposing of them so that the following account of the reign of Solomon could proceed smoothly without such complication. If that were so, the sequel would be much more systematic than it is. Our

[a]So S. Bülow and R. A. Mitchell, *IEJ* XI, 1961, pp. 109f.
[b]Albright, *BASOR*, 63, 1936, p. 24.
[c]See further R. de Vaux, *Ancient Israel*, p. 87.
[d]*ZAW* L, 1932, pp. 125ff.
[e]*ZAW* XLVII, 1929, pp. 76–79.

opinion is that the miscellanies took their origin as Montgomery suggests, but they were designed as preliminary notes, which were incorporated in the MT in their present position. They were placed in the Hebrew original of G partly after v. 35, following the establishment of Solomon's throne after the death of Adonijah and Joab, and partly at 46b after the account of the death of Shimei, which is associated with the elimination of Joab in the testament of David (vv. 1–9), but which happened three years after Solomon became sole king (v. 39), as a summary of Solomon's reign. This matter was then incorporated *en bloc* at 4.20–28[5.8] in the passage describing Solomon's fiscal administration, with which part of it (4.22ff.[5.2ff.]) has some affinity of subject. Unfortunately the worth of the passages in G for the textual criticism of the MT is impaired by much overworking in the Greek.

2. SOLOMON IN ALL HIS GLORY: 3.1–11.43

This section consists of miscellaneous matter from various sources, public archives, royal annals, and possibly also a Solomon saga. A source explicitly cited is 'the Acts of Solomon' (11.41), but the precise scope and nature of this is not certainly known, and it was probably of miscellaneous content.

The length at which the reign of Solomon is treated is not owing to its significance in external and internal politics, but to the fact that he was the builder of the Temple. The building, furnishing, and dedication of the Temple is the largest single theme of this section (chs. 6–8), and 5.1–18[15–32] concerns the preparation for this. The wisdom of Solomon in its various aspects also occupies a large place, partly in honour of the founder of the Temple, and partly because it was probably the theme of a popular saga. The miscellaneous data on the wealth and magnificence of Solomon, like that on his wisdom, are subsidiary to his building and dedication of the Temple.

No longer is a major narrative source of the dramatic power and maturity of the Story of the Davidic Succession used. The account of Solomon's reign is composed from several sources differing widely in subject-matter, nature, and historical worth, varying with the themes handled. After the account of Solomon's fiscal administration (4.1–19) there is some indication of his status in the contemporary Near East in 4.21–28[5.1–8], but the note of his political significance is vague and general, and the passage is very much glossed over by late redaction. At the end of the reign of Solomon, however, matters of real political significance are dealt with, such as Solomon's fortifications in Palestine and his trading enterprises with Hiram of Tyre in the Red Sea (9.10–28), the revolt of Edom under Hadad (11.14–22), the rise of Rezon of Damascus (11.23–25), and the abortive rising of Jeroboam (11.26–32, 40), which has a large Deuteronomistic amplification (11.33–39), on the theme of retribution for Solomon's ritual laxity. The arrangement is that of the Deuteronomistic editor.

In general we may say that, after the divine authentication of Solomon's succession (3.4–15), the theme is first the wisdom of Solomon (3.16–28; 4.29–34[5.9–14]), which is amplified by an account of his administration (4.1–28[4.1–5.8]), his magnificence attested by his buildings (5.1–9.9[5.15–9.9]) and his trading enterprises and foreign contacts (9.26–10.29). The troubles of his reign conclude the account (ch. 11), being a judgement upon his lapses.

In the section 3.1–10.29, the great difficulty is to distinguish objective fact from legend in the sources, apart from the account of the Temple and its furniture (chs. 6 and 7), which is in the former category, and its dedication (ch. 8) which, like its sequel (9.1–9), is largely and obviously Deuteronomistic, though doubtless based on actual fact.

The tradition of Solomon's wisdom is so intimately bound up with that of his magnificence, which is so often obviously the theme of legend and hyperbole, that the tradition of his wisdom is also suspect as belonging to the same category. This is particularly true of the tradition of Solomon's encyclopaedic wisdom and skill in proverbs (4.29–34[5.9–14]; 10.1–10, 13, 23f.), which is intimately related to his fabulous magnificence. The secondary nature of this tradition, though perhaps based on the fact of an interest in classification of natural phenomena at his court parallel to similar scientific interest evidenced by classified word-lists in Mesopotamia and Egypt,[a] is suggested by its insertion along with the incident of the Queen of Sheba in such a way as to interrupt the more sober historical account of Solomon's trading ventures with Hiram through the Red Sea, and much of the phraseology has been demonstrated by R. B. Y. Scott[b] to be distinctive of post-exilic sources. Here then, in 4.29–34[5.9–14]; 10.1–10, 13, 23–25, there is either late embellishment of a

[a] Alt, 'Die Weisheit Salomos', *KS* II, 1953, pp. 90–99.

[b] 'Solomon and the Beginnings of Wisdom in Israel', *Wisdom in Israel*, SVT III, 1955, pp. 267ff.

historical tradition based on a feature of humanistic education in the court of Solomon to provide for the new administrative class, or the adaptation of a Solomon saga.

In 3.16–28, however, which deals with a different category of wisdom, namely that faculty of discrimination in judgement and administration which was the attribute of a successful ruler, we have a different tradition of the wisdom of Solomon, and one which is, in our opinion, much more closely related to the actual facts. This presentation of wisdom is connected by Scott[a] with the Deuteronomist, whose impress is strong in this passage. Here, however, the Deuteronomist seems to be handling an older tradition, as is indicated by the association of the gift of wisdom with the local sanctuary of Gibeon, which causes the Deuteronomistic reviser some embarrassment, but which is apparently accepted tacitly by the Deuteronomistic compiler. Noth[b] sees here two distinct traditions: that of the revelation at Gibeon, and the tradition of Solomon's juridical wisdom, to which the incident at Gibeon serves artificially as an introduction. Of these we consider the revelation at Gibeon (3.4–15), doubly attested here and in 9.2, as primary and connected with the king's *ḥokmā* in the sense of his fitness for administration. The sequel, however (3.16–28), the famous judgement of Solomon, to which Gressmann[c] has cited parallels in later folk-tales from India to China, has all the appearance of a popular tradition; such a case, as Noth points out, being normally provided for in traditional Israelite practice by the oath of purgation at the shrine (Ex. 22.9f.), divine oracle (Ex. 22.7f.), ordeal (Num. 5.11ff.), or lots (Josh. 7.14ff.; I Sam. 14.38ff.).

The prelude to this matter is the dream at the sanctuary of Gibeon (3.4–15), which caused some embarrassment to the reviser, who allowed worship only at Jerusalem. Hence he added v. 2, where Solomon, the builder of the Temple, is exonerated from worship at local shrines at the expense of the people. The Deuteronomistic compiler introduces the reign of Solomon proper by noting the extent and limitation of his orthodoxy (v. 3), and it is possibly in part the association in his mind of Solomon's liberality in religion with his marriages with foreign women which prompted him to insert

[a] *Op. cit.*, p. 270.

[b] 'Die Bewährung von Salomos "Gottlicher Weisheit" ', *Wisdom in Israel*, pp. 227ff.

[c] 'Das Salomonische Urteil', *DR* CXXX, 1907, pp. 212–28.

from the annals of Judah, quite out of context at 3.1, the note on his marriage with the daughter of the Pharaoh.

This matter, though arranged according to a general system, is either less skilfully executed than conceived or it has been worked over and retouched, since there are many repetitions, e.g. 4.20f. [4.20–5.1], cf. 4.24f.[5.4f.]; 4.26–5.16[5.6–30], cf. 9.10–23; 10.23–26. This suggests the overlapping of sources which the editor used, not taking the trouble to omit matter already incorporated in his work, a situation with which we are familar in Arab historians, who, however, do name the various sources. Again it may indicate that the form and content of the section was for long rather fluid, a fact suggested by G with its amplifications at I K. 2.35 and 46 and 12.24, with miscellaneous matter from other parts of this section in MT.

The section on Solomon is further complicated by unskilful insertions in the text, which disrupt the account even when that is drawn *en bloc* from a single source, e.g. the general statement of the prosperity in Israel and the somewhat exaggerated note of the extent of Solomon's dominion, and miscellaneous amplifications of statements in the main source (4.20f.[4.20–5.1]), which interrupt the account of the fiscal organization of Solomon (4.2–19; 4.27ff.[5.7ff.]). Another such case is the episode of the Queen of Sheba (10.1–10), which seems to interrupt the account of Solomon's joint enterprises in the Red Sea with Hiram of Tyre (9.26–28; 10.11). This may, like certain details in 4.20–26[4.20–5.6], be a case of later amplification from general knowledge or popular tradition, but it seems rather a case of the compiler himself, on the clue of the mention of South Arabia and the 'gold of Ophir', inserting part of a saga of Solomon.

(*a*) SOLOMON'S MARRIAGE WITH THE DAUGHTER OF PHARAOH: 3.1

The inclusion of this note here, anticipating the information in 9.24, is probably suggested by the mention there that the lady had been living in the city of David until the completion of Solomon's building of the Temple, etc. Since this was begun in his fourth year it is assumed that the marriage was before that, and the fact that the last incident described, the death of Shimei, is dated in Solomon's third year (2.39) determines the note on the marriage of Solomon at this particular point. That this is a somewhat arbitrary editorial effort at chronological arrangement is indicated by the fact that

G[BL] insert the note on the marriage among miscellaneous matter after 2.46a.

3 [1]Then Solomon affianced himself with Pharaoh king of Egypt, for he married Pharaoh's daughter, bringing her[a] in to the city of David until he should finish his building of his palace and the Temple of Yahweh, and the wall of Jerusalem round about.

3.1. This was strictly, as the language suggests, a diplomatic alliance. It reflects, moreover, the Near Eastern conception of marriage, which was an arrangement between two families, courtship being not respectable. The verb *ḥātan*, with the bride's father as direct object, is similarly used in one of the Ras Shamra texts (*UT* 77, 25–26). The 'City of David', according to a gloss on II Sam. 5.7, was 'the stronghold of Zion' at the north end of the south-east hill. There is no mention of the identity of the Pharaoh. It is well known from the Amarna Tablets[b] that in the XVIIIth Dynasty no Egyptian princesses married foreigners, hence it is generally concluded that the Pharaoh was one of the decadent XXIst Dynasty (so Šanda, Kittel, Meyer, Noth, Bright, and Malamat[c]). Alt, Breasted, and Olmstead regard the Pharaoh as Shishak. Alt,[d] on the basis of the statement in 9.16 that Gezer was given as the dowry of the daughter of the Pharaoh, argues that Egyptian aggression in the Philistine plain suggests the time of Shishak rather than the weak XXIst Dynasty. Noth,[e] however, questions the reliability of the note on the capture of Gezer in 9.16, which comes in adventitiously to interrupt the account of Solomon's corvée and public works in 9.15ff., and thinks it highly improbable that Gezer should have maintained its independence when certainly Solomon, if not David, was incorporating the Canaanite cities in his territorial state. J. Bright,[f] following Albright,[g] suggests that Gerar, north-west of Beersheba, be read for Gezer. An Egyptian expedition against Gerar off the beaten track between Asia and Africa seems to have little point, whereas Gezer was a key-point on the trunk highway, and a *démarche* here would

[a]On the variant in G[BL] see immediately above in the introduction to this passage.
[b]Esp. J. A. Knudtzon, *Die El-Amarna Tafeln*, no. 3.
[c]A. Malamat, *JNES* XXII, 1963, pp. 11f.
[d]*Israel und Aegypten*, BWAT I.6, 1909, pp. 19ff.
[e]*The History of Israel*, 1960², p. 216 n.1.
[f]*A History of Israel*, 1960, p. 191 n.
[g]*Archaeology and the Religion of Israel*, 1953, pp. 213ff.; *JPOS* IV, 1924, pp. 142–4.

rehabilitate the prestige of Egypt among the Philistines and also with the new power of Israel. Noth's remark that it is strange that Gezer stood independent at a time when other Canaanite cities were being absorbed by Israel seems the key to the solution of the problem, suggesting a date early in the reign of Solomon, which rules out the identity of the Pharaoh with Shishak, who came to the throne in 935 BC, five years before the death of Solomon.[a] In spite of the weakness of the XXIst Dynasty the advantage of an alliance with the new nationalistic power in Palestine may well have stimulated the attack on Gezer, the Philistine defeats under David inviting this enterprise. In any case the Egyptian affiliation with Hadad of Edom, which it is natural to associate with the same statesmen, must certainly be dated in the XXIst Dynasty before the death of David, which encouraged the return of Hadad to his own country (11.14–22).

Montet[b] is in little doubt that the Pharaoh in question was Siamun, the penultimate Pharaoh of the XXIst Dynasty, who is depicted[c] in a fragmentary sculpture from his capital at Tanis slaying a foreign enemy, whose double axe-head suggests one from the Philistine country in Palestine rather than from elsewhere in the neighbourhood of Egypt. Malamat,[d] who accepts this identification, cites possible evidence of a campaign in the Philistine country before the expedition of Shishak after Solomon's death in levels of destruction at *Tell Mor* near Ashdod and Bethshemesh II, which actually is not named in Shishak's list of places he overran in this campaign. Malamat goes on to suggest that the Pharaoh's real objective was the conquest of Israel, a task which he found beyond him. Solomon, according to Malamat, was able to negotiate a favourable peace, which was cemented by the marriage of a daughter to Solomon and the cession of Gezer, in addition to which Solomon was able to annex other districts west of this place. This view, however, depends on the identification of Baalath, one of Solomon's fortifications mentioned with Beth-Horon and Tamar in the Steppe (9.18), south-east of Beersheba, with which we identify it (see on 9.18). Our opinion is

[a]M. B. Rowton, *JEA* XXXIV, 1948, pp. 57–74; 'The Date of the Founding of Solomon's Temple', *BASOR* 119, 1950, pp. 20–22; W. F. Albright, 'New Light from Egypt on the Chronology and History of Israel and the History of Judah', *BASOR* 130, 1953, pp. 4–8; P. van der Meer, *The Chronology of Ancient Western Asia and Egypt*, 1947, p. 83.

[b]*L'Égypte et la Bible*, 1960, pp. 39–42.

[c]*Op cit.*, fig. 5.

[d]'Aspects of the Foreign Policies of David and Solomon', *JNES* XXII, 1963, pp. 12ff.

that, as Siamun's sculpture from Tanis shows, he was eager to control the south of the coastal plain of Palestine occupied by the Philistines, probably to tap the trade route from southern Arabia at its Gaza terminal, but, conscious of the military limitations of Egypt in the time of tension between the Theban priesthood and the parvenu XXIst Dynasty in the Delta, he was glad to show the flag as far as Gezer, which he committed to Solomon, with whom he affianced himself, thus placing the Philistines between two potential enemies.

(*b*) EDITORIAL NOTE ON WORSHIP AT HIGH PLACES: 3.2f.

See critical introduction to this section. This Deuteronomistic note is suggested by Solomon's experience at the high place of Gibeon described in the sequel, and v. 2 is a later gloss explanatory and palliative of v. 3.

> **3** [2]But the people sacrificed at the high places, for no temple was built for the name of Yahweh until[a] those days. [3]And Solomon loved Yahweh, walking in the statutes of David his father, only he sacrificed at the high places and sent up the smoke of his sacrifice.

3.2 The conjunction *raq*, 'only' (lit. 'empty'), in this particular context indicates that the passage is secondary to v. 3. The high places, *bāmōt*, lit. 'backs', i.e. of men or animals, as now known from the Ras Shamra texts, were open-air sanctuaries on eminences throughout the land associated with the Canaanite fertility-cult; see further on 11.7.

(*c*) THE DIVINE AUTHENTICATION OF SOLOMON'S SUCCESSION IN THE DREAM AT GIBEON: 3.4–15

This passage, introducing the actual reign of Solomon, repeats the theme of the Story of the Davidic Succession, which ends in ch. 2. The theme is the legitimization of the succession of Solomon after his anomalous elevation to the throne without obvious aptitude for leadership, such as the people had recognized by spontaneous acclaim in the case of the judges, and without the covenant, such as David had made with the people of Israel at Hebron. Hence the claim of Solomon was given a new basis, the covenant of Yahweh

[a]Possibly an improvement would be to read *ʿōd* ('yet') for *ʿad*, and possibly *bayyāmīm hāhēm*.

with David and his house. This, however, as G. Fohrer[a] rightly stresses, is specifically stated (v. 8) to be within the economy of Yahweh's chosen community, a by-product, as it were, of Yahweh's covenant with Israel. This revelation also anticipates the administration of Solomon, which is first of all, and most emphatically, presented in its more successful aspects. As one who was fit to rule and was to introduce so many innovations, Solomon is the recipient of the divine assurance of 'wisdom' in a dream at Gibeon. Here S. Herrmann[b] recognizes in vv. 4–15 the pattern of the preamble to Egyptian accounts of significant events, usually royal innovations, from the Middle Kingdom onwards. There the Pharaoh receives his revelation, often in a dream, after which he makes sacrifices and communicates publicly to his nobles and officials, just as Solomon after his dream at Gibeon repairs to Jerusalem and holds a feast for his 'servants', at which presumably he communicated his revelation and his plans for administration to his 'servants'. The closest parallel is the account of the dream revelation to Thothmes IV at the Sphinx at Gizeh, which was also a holy place (*ANET*, p. 449). This communication in the Egyptian royal texts cited by Herrmann from inscriptions of Sesostris I, Thothmes III and Thothmes IV stresses the divine election of the king to his peculiar task before he was born and the divine preservation of him to the present end while he was yet young, a theme which is almost certainly re-echoed in Solomon's reference to Yahweh's making him king (probably in anticipation) when he was 'a little child' (v. 7). Furthermore the Pharaoh in his communication is often at pains to emphasize tl c legitimacy of his succession, which is the theme of vv. 6–8. In view of the Egyptian prototype of this literary category and the principle of the permanence of the Davidic house according to the divine covenant, which finds striking expression in the revolt against Athaliah (II K. 11), Herrmann contends for a Solomonic date for this passage. Rost[c] would date it to the period after the fall of Samaria, with the Nathan oracle, which it recalls, excepting II Sam. 7.11b–16, which he takes as Davidic, and v. 13, which he regards as Deuteronomistic. Certainly the affinities of I K. 3.4–15, particularly vv. 6, 9, 11ff., with the so-called 'messianic' passages in Isa. 9 and 11 are striking (see on vv.

[a] 'Der Vertrag Zwischen König und Volk in Israel', *ZAW* LXXI, 1959, pp. 7ff.

[b] 'Die Königsnovelle in Ägypten und Israel', *Wissenschaftliche Zeitschrift der Karl Marx-Universität, Leipzig* III, 1953–54, pp. 51–62.

[c] *Thronnachfolge Davids*, pp. 63ff.

6, 9, 11ff.), but Herrmann's view[a] that I K. 3.4–15 is the legitimization not only of the Solomonic succession but of the Davidic ideology of kingship, which finds expression in those passages in Isaiah and in the messianic ideology proper of later times, is, in our view, more probable.

3 [4]Then the king went to Gibeon to sacrifice there, for that was the greatest 'high place'. A thousand whole burnt-offerings would Solomon offer up on that altar. [5]At Gibeon[b] Yahweh appeared to Solomon in a dream at night, and Yahweh[c] said, Ask what I shall give you. [6]Then Solomon said, Thou hast dealt most loyally with thy servant David my father; according as he walked before thee truly and rightly and with uprightness of heart towards thee, so thou hast kept this great faith with him in giving him a son to sit upon his throne as at present. [7]So now, Yahweh my God, thou hast made thy servant king in place of David my father, while I am yet a little child; I know not how to go out or come in. [8]And thy servant is in the midst of thy people whom thou hast chosen, a numerous people, which cannot be numbered or counted, so numerous are they. [9]So give thy servant a receptive heart to judge thy people, understanding between good and evil. For who is able to judge this thy great people? [10]Now the speech pleased the Lord, that Solomon made this request. [11]And Yahweh[c] said to him, Because you have asked this thing and have not asked for yourself long life, nor have asked wealth, nor asked the life of your enemies, but have asked for yourself understanding in hearing judgement, [12]behold! I shall do as you say. Lo! I have given you a wise and understanding heart, such that there has been none like you before you, nor shall any arise after you like you. [13]Yes, moreover, that which you have not asked have I granted you, even wealth, and honour too, such that there shall not have been any among the kings like you [d]all your days.[d] [14]And if you walk in my ways, keeping my statutes and my commandments according as David your father walked, I shall give you length of days. [15]Then Solomon awoke and, behold! it was a dream, and [e]he arose[e] and came to Jerusalem, and he stood before[f] the ark of the covenant of the Lord, and he offered up holocausts and made communion-offerings, and made a drinking-feast to all his servants.

3.4. Gibeon is probably modern *al-Jib*, some seven miles north-

[a]*Op. cit.*, p. 60.

[b]G and S read *b^e gib^c ōn* with the preceding sentence, and introduce the following verb with a conjunction.

[c]G reads *yhwh* for MT *'^e lōhīm*, which seems more natural after the mention of Yahweh already in the verse.

[d]This phrase is omitted in G^BL. If this reading is followed the verb of the last clause, which we have translated as a future perfect, would be best rendered as a perfect.

[e]Inserting *wayyāqom* with G.

[f]G, perhaps correctly, inserts '(before) the altar which was before . . .' *hammizbēaḥ '^a šer lip^e nē*.

west of Jerusalem, where J. B. Pritchard in his recent excavation found several jar-handles stamped *gbʿn*.[a] In the tradition of the Hebrew penetration under Joshua the Gibeonites made a separate peace (Josh. 9), and subsequently had the duty of supplying wood and water for the Temple services (Josh. 9.21, 27). This may have been really a privilege rather than a duty, reflecting the former status of Gibeon, as in the present passage. The place, lit. 'little hill', may have been 'the hill', where the ark lay at 'the house of Abinadab' (II Sam. 6.3, cf. I Chron. 16.37f., which locates the last resting-place of the ark before its removal to Jerusalem at the house of Obed-Edom, possibly at Gibeon). 'A thousand whole burnt-offerings' is probably hyperbolic, a feature of saga rather than of sober history. Noth[b] emphasizes that, since Solomon's association with the pre-Israelite sanctuary of Gibeon was not suppressed by D, whose principles it contravened, and whose impress is otherwise strong in this section, the tradition, with that of Solomon's wisdom, must be ancient.[c] R. B. Y. Scott[d] is much more critical of the tradition which associated wisdom with Solomon. In the case of 3.4ff. he notes the formal speech, which, as 2.3f.; 5.3–5, 7[17–19, 21]; 6.12f.; 8.14–30, 46–51; 9.3–9, is a feature of the Deuteronomist. He emphasizes the generally critical attitude of the Deuteronomist to Solomon, and regards the tradition of his wisdom as generally late, originating ultimately from 3.12ff. and crystallizing in the reign of Hezekiah, when, on the evidence of Prov. 25.1 and Isa. 5.21; 29.13–16; 30.1–5 and the stylistic features of gnomic wisdom in Isaiah's oracles, there was an efflorescence of wisdom literature. After Sellin[e] he regards this rather than the era of Solomon as the period of Egyptian influence on Hebrew wisdom. Scott rightly emphasizes the association here, as in the late books of Esther and Daniel, of wisdom and royal grandeur, and points out late analogies for linguistic features in the tradition of Solomon's wisdom in 4.29–34[5.9–14] and 10.1–10, 13,

[a]See *Hebrew Inscriptions and Stamps from Gibeon*, 1959; 'More Inscribed Jar-handles from el-Jib', *BASOR* 160, 1960, pp. 2–6; cf. Albright, *BASOR* 159, 1960, p. 37, who notes the association of *gbʿn* in these jar-handles with *gdr*, probably Gedor, which is associated with Gibeon in I Chron. 8.31; 9.37, which supports the identification of *al-Jīb* with Gibeon.

[b]*Wisdom in Israel . . .*, pp. 228ff.

[c]So also A. van den Born, *Koningen*, 1958, p. 32, who treats it as a genuine local tradition of Gibeon.

[d]*Wisdom in Israel*, pp. 262–79.

[e]*Einleitung in das Alte Testament*, ed. Rost, 1950, p. 156.

23f.,[a] which he regards as post-Deuteronomistic interpolations from a source independent of D. His arguments against the genuine attribution of encyclopaedic and gnomic wisdom to Solomon, however, though valid, if not conclusive, in the case of 4.29–34[5.9–14] and 10.1–10, 13, 23ff., fail to reckon seriously with the tradition of his administrative wisdom in 3.5–28, which, to be sure, was in accord with the traditional association of juridical ability with the king in Canaan half a millennium before Solomon, cf. the Krt and 'Aqht texts from Ras Shamra.

3.5. In accordance with a custom well established in the ancient Near East, where the king was the channel of divine blessings and revelation, Solomon may have gone to the shrine of Gibeon with the express purpose of obtaining a revelation through a dream. Such cases of ritual incubation of ancient kings are known in the two royal sagas from Ras Shamra, the Krt and 'Aqht texts, and the Mesopotamian royal texts,[b] and the dream was recognized as one of the regular means of revelation (I Sam. 28.6), particularly in the E tradition of the Pentateuch.

This passage conforms to an Egyptian literary prototype where the Pharaohs introduce accounts of their innovations and exploits by alleging special divine revelation.[c] More specifically the present tradition of the revelation in a dream at Gibeon at some distance from the court in Jerusalem is closely paralleled by the sphinx-stele inscription of Thothmes IV,[d] where the Pharaoh receives his revelation in a dream in the shadow of the Sphinx at Gizeh, near Memphis, which he divulges only after he has hastened to the city. Here, like Solomon, he sacrifices before communicating the divine purpose to his court and officials.

6. 'Rightly' for the general rendering of EVV 'with righteousness', which invests *ṣ*ᵉ*dāqā* with a moral connotation which is secondary to the root meaning of the word. *ṣ*ᵉ*dāqā* is conduct which is 'right' in the sense of measuring up to a given standard, the right (*ṣedeq*). This word might denote any standard, e.g. the proper tools for any given job are 'tools of *ṣedeq*'. In the conduct demanded of Israel by her covenanted God the norm is the divine revelation in the law accompanying the covenant. Hence secondarily the word

[a] *Op. cit.*, pp. 267ff.

[b] R. Labat, *Le caractère religieux de la royauté assyro-babylonienne*, 1939, p. 147; H. Frankfort, *Kingship and the Gods*, 1948, pp. 252f.

[c] This has been noted by S. Herrmann, *op. cit.*

[d] *ANET*, p. 449.

has a moral connotation, which comes to dominate in the Old Testament. 'Uprightness' (*yešārā*) means literally 'straightness', cf. Arabic *rašīd* ('straight'), with both physical and moral connotations. The loyalty (*ḥesed*) which God has fully kept with David presupposes a covenantal relationship, here not the covenant with Israel, but the newer conception, perhaps now first promulgated, of God's covenant with David, guaranteeing the permanence of his dynasty, 'a son to sit upon his throne', though this was within the scope of the covenant with Israel (v. 8). The language here and in v. 14 does, as R. B. Y. Scott holds,[a] suggest the Deuteronomist, but, while this may be the source of v. 14, v. 6 may well be an original tradition concerning the legitimization of Solomon's accession. The emphasis in this whole passage on *ṣedāqā*, *'emet* (v. 6), *'emūnā* (v. 9), *bīnā* (vv. 9, 11, 12) and *ḥokmā* (v. 12) recurs in the so-called 'messianic' passage in Isa. 11.2, 4, 5 in such a way as to suggest that the passage in Kings, as well as legitimizing Solomon's succession on the basis of the Davidic covenant, either reflected or, more probably, set the pattern of, the regular accession-liturgy of the house of David. Hence we would discount Scott's opinion, at least as far as concerns all in this passage, except possibly v. 14, that this is a Deuteronomistic expansion, and follow Herrmann[b] in regarding the passage as genuinely Solomonic.

3.7. Solomon was certainly young, though, if we accept the tradition of his 40 years' reign and the statement that his son Rehoboam was 41 at his accession (I K. 14.21), Solomon was old enough, as Kittel pointed out,[c] to be married at his accession. Hence his reference to himself as 'a little child' could be merely the conventional humility of prayer. This attitude recalls the representation of himself by Ramses II in a sculpture at Pi-Ramses (*Ṣān al-Ḥagar*), squatting like a young child and sucking his finger under the protection of Horus as a giant stone falcon.[d] Actually this feature in our passage is paralleled in the Egyptian royal preamble cited by Herrmann,[e] where the Pharaoh refers to his divine election before birth or to the favour of God shown to him when he was still young, e.g. Thothmes IV in the inscription already cited. Hence Herrmann's translation

[a] *Op. cit.*, pp. 262–79.
[b] *Op. cit.*, pp. 55ff.
[c] HKAT, p. 6.
[d] P. Montet, *L'Égypte et la Bible*, 1959, pl. II.
[e] *Op. cit.*, p. 55.

'you have made your servant king . . . when I am yet a little child'. This convention also is a feature of the accession-ritual of Jerusalem as pointed out by Herrmann,[a] being expressed in the adoption-formula in Ps. 2.7, with which Alt[b] would associate the reference to the royal child (*yeled*) and son (*bēn*) of Isa. 9.5.

3.8. To be taken with what precedes, the Davidic covenant being within the wider context of the covenant with Israel.

9. 'A receptive (lit. hearing) heart' implies patience to hear a case and understand it fully, the heart (*lēb*, *lēbāb*) for the ancient Semite being the seat of the understanding. Here again there is a close parallel with Isa. 11.3, 'he will not decide by what he hears with his ears'. From the Ras Shamra texts we learn that the root *šāpaṭ* (Ugaritic *ṯpṭ*) had the primary connotation 'to rule', judgement, the usual sense of the verb in Hebrew, being but one of the essential functions of the ruler. Thus the great judges of Israel were primarily those who upheld Yahweh's community against the menace of the political forces of disorder, and only the minor judges may have been givers or expounders of the law, as Noth suggests.[c] Here, however, the reference is to hearing cases (v. 11), so the meaning is 'judgement' rather than 'ruling'.

11. This is a good example of the primary meaning of Hebrew *nepeš*, often mistranslated 'soul'.

12. The adjective *ḥākām*, though referring, like its Arabic cognate, to discrimination in judgement, also connotes familiarity with the facts of a case and their relative significance (see on 2.6); *nābōn* ('understanding') refers rather to discrimination in judgement, being etymologically related to the preposition *bēn* ('between').

13. 'Honour' (*kābōd*, derived from the verb *kābēd*, 'to be heavy') may be applied to God, signifying 'glory', or to man, signifying 'honour'. Emphasizing the literal meaning 'weight', we might render *kābōd* 'effectiveness'.

14. This reflects the ethos of Israel, the moral condition of the fulfilment of the covenant to David and his house. The language here, with the addition of personal long life to Solomon as the reward of obedience, may be a Deuteronomistic expansion, though the thought is quite typical of early Israel.

15. 'And he arose and came to Jerusalem, and he stood before the

[a] *Op cit.*, p. 60.
[b] *KS* II, 1959, pp. 218ff.
[c] *Festschrift A. Bertholet*, 1950, pp. 404ff.

ark of the covenant of the Lord' at least is probably, as Hölscher held,[a] a later intrusion to redeem the orthodox reputation of the builder of the Temple. Solomon's offerings and feast are the natural conclusion of the events at Gibeon. *šelāmīm* is derived from the verb *šālēm*, 'to be whole', hence our rendering 'communion-offerings', i.e. sacrifices by which the community was reintegrated with God and the various members with one another by partaking of parts of the same victim, in contrast to the 'whole burnt-offerings' (*'ōlōt*), which were wholly offered to God. We agree with the view of W. R. Smith[b] that the basis of this conception of *šelāmīm* is the common meal, the bread and salt of desert convention, which similarly integrates the company participating, but we doubt if we may further interpret this sacrifice as the absorption of the god by the killing and eating of the totem-animal as Smith maintained.[c] The social function of *šelāmīm* is noted among the duties of the head of the community in the 'Aqht text from Ras Shamra (*UT* 2 'Aqht, I, 32f.). There the successor of the king is one

Who may eat his slice in the temple of Baal,
His portion in the temple of El.

In Solomon's case the common meal had the practical purpose of communicating to the people the blessing which the king had been given.

(*d*) SOLOMON'S ARBITRATION BETWEEN THE TWO HARLOTS: 3.16–28

Now follows an instance of the practical sagacity of Solomon, 'that blending of insight, shrewdness and tact which penetrates the disguises of human action and plays deftly on the true motives which lie beneath' (Skinner, CB, p. 88). *ḥokmā* in this instance preserves the nuance of 'decision, arbitration', which underlies the Arabic root *ḥakama*. The story is a familiar one in folk-tale, its closest parallel being an Indian one,[d] and Gressmann[e] notes 22 versions of the same theme from various parts of the world, suggesting that the Indian version, where the women are wives of the same man, is more original than the Hebrew one. The narrative style, with vivid direct speech and frequent repetition, suggests the folk-tale.

[a]'Das Buch der Könige', *Eucharisterion* (Gunkel Festschrift) I, 1923, pp. 158ff.
[b]*The Religion of the Semites*, 1894², pp. 269ff.
[c]*Op. cit.*, pp. 295f.
[d]J. G. Frazer, *Folklore in the Old Testament*, 1918, ch. 11.
[e]*Die älteste Geschichtsschreibung und Prophetie Israels*, 1921², p. 198.

3 [16]Then there came two women, harlots, to the king and stood before him. [17]And one said, May it please you, my lord, I and this woman occupy the same house, and I gave birth[a] in the house. [18]And it happened on the third day after I had given birth that this woman also gave birth, and we were together, there was no stranger with us,[b] but only we two were in the house. [19]Now the child of this woman died during the night because she overlaid it. [20]So she got up during the night and took my child from beside me,[c] and your maidservant was asleep, and she laid it in her bosom, and she laid the dead child in my bosom. [21]And I arose in the morning to suckle my child, and there he was dead, and I considered him closely in the morning, and lo! it was not my child which I had borne. [22]And the other woman said, No, but the living child is mine and the dead one is your child, and the other said, No, but the dead child is yours and the living one is mine, and they stated their case before the king. [23]And the king said, This woman says, This is my son who is alive, and the one who is dead is your son, and the other woman says, No, but the one who is dead is your son, and the living one is my son. [24]Then the king said, Bring me a knife, and they brought a knife before the king. [25]And the king said, Divide the living child in two and give the half to one woman and the half to the other. [26]Then the women whose child was the living one said to the king, since her bowels were moved on account of her child, Please, my lord, give her the living child; you must by no means kill him. The other said, Neither you nor I shall have him. Divide him. [27]Then the king answered and said, Give her the living child, do not on any account kill it. She is the mother. [28]And all Israel heard of the judgement which the king had given, and they stood in awe of the king, for they saw that he had preternatural sagacity in giving judgement.

3.16. Note the direct access which the litigants had to the king, as in the case of the woman of Tekoa and David (II Sam. 14), and the comparable ideal of royal justice in the sagas of Krt and 'Aqht in the Ras Shamra texts, where the kings personally sit in the place of public access and judge the case of the widow, the orphan, and the oppressed. Arab rulers, too, until the time of Abd al-Malik (AD 685–705) were accessible to the public,[d] and still are to a certain extent. Nevertheless, the case before Solomon may be more ideal than real in this respect, an indication of saga rather than sober history in the source. Harlots (*zōnōt*, which has an Arabic cognate) were a regular institution of the ancient Near East, about which the Hebrews had apparently no inhibitions; for instance, it is recorded unashamedly that the Hebrew spies visited Rahab at Jericho (Josh.

[a]Omitting *ʿimmāh* with G.
[b]Omitting *babbayit* with G[B] as tautological.
[c]G reads *mē'aṣṣīlay* ('from my armpits') for MT *mē'eṣlī* ('beside me').
[d]Ibn aṭ-Ṭiqṭaqa, *Al-Fakhri*, ed. Ahlwardt, 1860, p. 146.

2.1) and Judah's intercourse with Tamar in the guise of a harlot is not condemned (Gen. 38).

3.17. *bī*, 'may it please thee', is probably the imperative of the verb *'ābā* 'to be willing, consent', with the survival of the original final consonant.[a]

18. The participle *zār* in Deut. 25.5 denotes a man outside the family to whom a widow may not be married if a kinsman of her late husband is alive. In the light of this passage, *zār* in the present context denotes the clients of the prostitutes, who alone of the women in the ancient Near East would entertain intimately any man who was not of their family. A woman of this status, who alone was free of her company outside the family, is termed *'iššā zārā* (Prov. 2.16; 5.3, 20; 7.5, etc.).

21. In *wā'etbōnēn* ('and I considered him closely'), the intensive reflexive of the root, close scrutiny is implied.

22. *kī* here has its adversative sense.

25. The verb *gāzar* ('divide') is also used of the dividing of the sea at the Exodus (Ps. 136.13).

26. The bowels (*raḥ^a^mīm*; cf. 'womb', *reḥem*) were the seat of the emotions in the reckoning of the ancient Hebrews. The phrase means literally 'her bowels were in a ferment', or 'grew hot', cf. Lam. 5.10, *'ōrēnū k^e^tannūr nikmārū* ('our skin is hot as an oven'). By the unusual form of the common root *yālad*, here a passive participle, found only here and in Job 14.1; 15.14; 25.4, and I Chron. 14.4, meaning 'the borne one', i.e. 'the bairn', the mother recalls the bearing of the child whom she cannot see suffer.

28. Judgement (*mišpāṭ*) is here used in its forensic sense. *wayyīr^e^'ū*, lit. 'and they feared', denotes awe, since his sagacity was more than natural or human, it was preternatural sagacity, lit. 'sagacity of God'. *'^e^lōhīm* is often used in this qualifying sense denoting 'preternatural' or 'awful', e.g. *hār^a^rē 'ēl*, 'awful mountains' (Ps. 36.7), *'ar^e^zē 'ēl*, 'mighty cedars' (Ps. 80.11). The usage is found also in the Ras Shamra texts, e.g. *mdbr 'el*, 'the awful desert'.

(*e*) THE ADMINISTRATION OF SOLOMON: 4.1–28[4.1–5.8]

This section, which, for purposes of present treatment, falls into two parts, 4.2–6, a list of Solomon's ministers of state, and 4.7–28 [4.7–5.8], Solomon's fiscal administration, is drawn ultimately from

[a]See A. M. Honeyman, *JAOS* LXIV, 1944, pp. 81f.

archival sources. This is particularly apparent in the list of Solomon's fiscal officers and their administrative districts (4.7–19), where the names of the officers in vv. 8–13 with one exception have been lost, only their fathers' names remaining. Possibly the compiler of an earlier account of Solomon's reign used a copy, originally excerpted from public records, which has been damaged, the right edge having been broken off. This Albright[a] explains by its being frequently copied. It is not possible to tell whether this document was the original record or a copy. If the latter, the fact of its being used in its damaged state suggests respect for a source which was known to be official. Alt, on the other hand,[b] proposes that here, as in administrative lists from the palace of Ras Shamra, persons named without the patronymic were hereditary officers. We agree with Noth[c] that it is unlikely that this system was established long enough in Israel for hereditary office to have developed by the time of Solomon, under whom the fiscal administration was obviously an innovation, and it is less likely that two of these officials, Abinadab (v. 11) and Ahimaaz (v. 15), would have been able to marry daughters of Solomon. This official matter, however, has been glossed, expanded and interrupted in 4.20 and 4.21–26[5.1–6]. In the list of Solomon's ministers of state the fact that, with the exception of Jehoshaphat (v. 3) and the doubtful reference to Zadok and Abiathar as priests (v. 4), the officials are sons of men in office under David, suggests that the list is from a later date in Solomon's reign than it purports to refer to.[d] In view of the demotion of Abiathar (2.26) it is most unlikely that he bore office under Solomon again, and doubtless this point must also cast a certain doubt on the mention of Zadok. The list is generally taken to be influenced by the list of David's officers of state in II Sam. 8.15ff.; 20.23–25, being introduced in the same way by the statement that the king reigned over all Israel. It was doubtless owing to such influence that Abiathar was introduced into the list in Kings.[e]

The fiscal division of the realm (4.7–28[5.8]) visualizes only the territory occupied by Israel in Palestine, a notable limitation which,

[a]'The Administrative Divisions of Israel and Judah', *JPOS* V, 1925, p. 26.

[b]'Menschen ohne Namen', *AO* XVIII, 1950, pp. 21ff.

[c]*Könige*, p. 60.

[d]Cf. Šanda, I, pp. 71ff., who dates the list broadly in the first half of Solomon's reign.

[e]For a reconstruction of the passage on the basis of variants in G^{BL} here and in G^{B} at 2.46 see J. A. Montgomery, 'The Year Eponymate in the Hebrew Monarchy', *JBL* XLIX, 1930, pp. 311–19 and *Kings*, ICC, pp. 112–18.

at variance with the extravagant claims in 4.21, 24 [5.1, 4], bears the stamp of a sober official document. Alt,[a] by careful study of the localities described, has demonstrated that the administrative divisions were based on the old Canaanite city-states now incorporated in Israel as well as on tribal territories. This sober and methodical division for fiscal and administrative purposes supports the view that the passage rests on the authority of an official document and modifies the view often advanced that the administrative division of Solomon was designed to reduce the independence of the tribes of Israel. Alt points out[b] that the six tribes omitted as separate units from the new system are Levi, which never had any political status in historical times, Simeon, which was included in Judah for all practical purposes, as Reuben was in Gad, while Dan, which had only one considerable town, was grouped together with Naphtali, as Zebulun was probably counted in Asher. With this in the main we agree, except that we would suggest that Zebulun was included rather in the district of Megiddo, the latter owing to its strategic position being an obvious district centre and, because of its ancient significance as one of the foremost Canaanite city-states, having a well-organized fiscal system, which was readily taken over in the Solomonic administration.

(i) SOLOMON'S MINISTERS OF STATE: 4.1–6

4 1Now king Solomon was king over all Israel. 2And these were his
chief officers: Azariah the son of Zadok, the priest; 3Elihoreph and
Ahijah the sons of Shisha, scribes; Jehoshaphat the son of Ahilud,
herald; 4and [c]Eliab the son of Joab,[c] over the army;[d] 5and Azariah[e] the
son of Nathan, over the district prefects; and Zakur[f] the son of Nathan,[g]
king's Friend; 6and Ahishar,[h] chamberlain; and Adoniram the son of
Abda, over the corvée.

4.2. These high officers are termed with relation to the king his

[a]'Israels Gaue unter Salomo', *KS* II, pp. 76–89.

[b]*Op. cit.*, p. 88.

[c]So G^{L} for MT *ūb^{e}nāyāhū ben y^{e}hōyādā'*.

[d]Omitting *w^{e}ṣādōq w^{e}'ebyātār kōh^{a}nīm* ('and Zadok and Abiathar, priests') as a secondary addition, since Abiathar was in any case demoted and Zadok's son already priest, according to MT (v.2).

[e]For Azariah (MT) G reads 'Orneia', which seems a corruption of Adonijah.

[f]Reading Zakur with G^{L}, though MT Zabud ('bestowed') is not impossible.

[g]Omitting *kōhēn* with G^{BL}.

[h]Ahishar, which is otherwise unattested as a Hebrew proper name, but is still not impossible, must be in doubt, cf. alternatives in G^{B} (Acheim) and G^{L} (Achiel).

'servants' (*ʿabādīm*); with relation to the people they are called 'princes' (*śārīm*), a designation of local notables at Succoth in the time of the judges (Judg. 8.6, 14). The fact that so many of these were sons of David's ministers indicates a tendency to build up hereditary offices under the authority of the king, which Alt has noticed in the administrative texts from the palace of Ras Shamra (p. 130).

4.3. Montgomery (ICC, pp. 113–15) proposes that in place of the proper name Elihoreph, which is not attested as a Semitic name,[a] we should read a title of Azariah 'who is over the year' (*ʿal-haḥōrep*), lit. 'over the autumn', when the year began, this recalling the *limmu* official in Assyria, who gave his name to the year (see above, pp. 58f.). This has the support of one Greek reading that Azariah was 'over the sundial' (*epi tou plinthiou*), which, like the instrument *basīṭa* among the Arabs, determined the seasons as well as the hours of the day.[b] This, however, involves not only the emendation of *'elīḥōrep* to *ʿal-haḥōrep*, but the reading of sing. for plur. in MT *bene* and *sōperīm*. Noth (*Könige*, p. 13) argues plausibly that in the new administration under Solomon, which was modelled so largely on the Egyptian bureaucracy, there would have been scope for two chief secretaries for internal and external business. He would retain MT *šîšā'* (cf. *šeyā'*, the scribe, in II Sam. 20.25), which was probably Egyptian *šš* ('scribe'). Perhaps Elihoreph and Ahijah were the sons of an actual Egyptian official in the latter period of David's administration, who was known by his title rather than by his proper name. The scribe was private as well as State secretary, and had certain fiscal duties (II K. 12.10[11]). Eventually he became one of the chief officers of State, e.g. II K. 18.18; cf. Isa. 36.3ff., where, with the royal chamberlain and the royal herald, he meets the representatives of Sennacherib at Jerusalem. Jehoshaphat is the herald (EVV 'recorder'). The Hebrew *hammazkīr* indicates 'he who names' or 'causes the name (here the king's name) to be heard', and/or 'he who brings to notice' (i.e. brings public affairs to the king's notice or makes the king's mind known to the people). De Vaux[c] cites an Egyptian official title with the same significance designating an official who regulated the ceremonies of the palace and introduced people to royal audiences,

[a]So Noth, *IP*, p. 237.

[b]Montgomery, 'The Year Eponymate in the Hebrew Monarchy', *JBL* XLIX, 1930, pp. 311–19.

[c]De Vaux, *Ancient Israel*, p. 132.

was also the master of ceremonies on an official tour, reported affairs to the king, and transmitted and explained royal commands.

4.4. G^B omits 'Benaiah, the son of Jehoiada, over the army', but the list demands some notice of the commander. G^L reads 'and Eliab the son of Joab was commander-in-chief', a reading so startling after the notice of Joab's death that it must surely be genuine. Noting that the other officers are nearly all sons of those in office under David or in the beginning of Solomon's reign, we may well credit that Benaiah was succeeded by Joab's son. This would be one office where the concentration of influence in one family might be dangerous. The mention of a commander of *ṣābā'* alone, apart from the mercenaries, seems to indicate a concentration of command, at first probably under Benaiah, then under Eliab. Was a son of Joab perhaps reinstated in command after the return of Hadad of Edom on the strength of his father's prestige in Edom?

5. In view of Nathan's part in the elevation of Solomon it is not surprising to find two of his sons, Azariah (see p. 131 n.[e]) and Zakur (or Zabud) in office. The former was 'over the district prefects' (*hanniṣṣābīm*), whose functions were apparently fiscal (vv. 7ff.). The latter may have supported the king in his sacral office. This person is named also king's 'Friend', an honorific title once held by Hushai (II Sam. 15.37), David's faithful friend and counsellor. The title disappears after Solomon's time, but the office may be referred to in II K. 10.11, which refers to the 'familiars' (*m[e]yuddāʿīm*) of Ahab. The title *rēʿe hammelek* may be a loanword from Egypt, where the noun *rḫ* is found in a phrase meaning 'one whom the Pharaoh wished to notice'.[a]

6. Ahishar (for variants see textual note) was royal chamberlain (lit. over the house, i.e. palace). This person is unique in this list as having no patronymic, indicating perhaps his foreign, or humble, origin, and the inferior nature of his office as major-domo of the royal palace. The title later designated a very high office, which was discharged by the prince Jotham in the illness of his father Azariah (Uzziah) (II K. 15.5) and Eliakim, who, with the scribe and royal herald, met Sennacherib's officer at the walls of Jerusalem (II K. 18.18; Isa. 36.3). The title, with the name Gedaliah, probably the friend of Jeremiah, whom the Babylonians appointed as governor at Mizpah after the fall of Jerusalem (II K. 25.22), was found on a clay seal-impression at the excavation of Lachish. Adoniram, Adoram of

[a]De Vaux, *Ancient Israel*, p. 123.

II Sam. 20.24, apparently held the same office under David, but this is unlikely, since Adoniram, in full vigour, survived Solomon and was put to death at Shechem (I K. 12.18), where he is called Adoram. With the disappearance of this person from the administration of David it is doubtful if the corvée (*mas*) was instituted at all under David. In the administrative and legal texts from the palace of Ugarit (Ras Shamra) it is apparent that lands were held subject to certain burdens to the king, including that of labour of men and beasts. In the Canaanite cities now incorporated into the kingdom of Israel the system had probably been in practice, but in extending it to Israel Solomon gravely affronted the dignity of the free tribesmen, and it was the immediate cause of the disruption of his kingdom on his death (I K. 12.4ff.). On the distinction between the corvée applied to Israelite and non-Israelite subjects, see below on 5.13[27].

(ii) SOLOMON'S FISCAL SYSTEM: THE OFFICERS AND THEIR DISTRICTS: 4.7–19

4 [7]Now Solomon had twelve district prefects[a] over all Israel, and
they would supply provisions for the king and his household; each had
the responsibility to supply provisions for one month of the year. [8]And
these are their names: ( )[b] the son of Hur in the hill-country of
Ephraim. [9]( )[b] the son of Deker in Makaz and in Shaalbim and
Bethshemesh and Aijalon and [c]Beth-hanan. [10]( )[b] the son of
Hesed in Arubboth: he had Socoh and all the land of Hepher.
[11]( )[b] the son of Abinadab: all the Heights of Dor.[d] He had as
wife Taphath the daughter of Solomon. [12]Baanah the son of Ahilud:
Taanach, and Megiddo even to[e] Bethshean, from the descent[f] of

[a]Sixteen Hebrew MSS have the passive participle, *n*^{e}*ṣībīm* for MT Niphal *niṣṣābīm*. Both are possible.

[b]In all cases the right-hand edge of the copy of the source from which this passage was compiled seems to have been broken off and the names of the individuals lost.

[c]G reads 'as far as (*ʿad*) Beth-hanan'. A variant in the Ginsburg Masora has *ūbēt* . . ., *w* being easily omitted by haplography after the final *n* of Aijalon.

[d]Reading plural for singular of MT, see note.

[e]Reading *'el-bētš*^{e}*'ān* for MT *w*^{e}*kol b* . . ., *w* being a dittograph of the last letter of *m*^{e}*giddō*, and *k* being a mistake for ' in the proto-Hebraic script. In this verse it is suggested that transpositions have occurred. See Albright, *JPOS* V, 1925, p. 26, and Montgomery, ICC, p. 121. 'Which is by Zarethan' certainly should be transposed from its present position in MT to after 'as far as Abel-Meholah' (*ʿad-'ābēl m*^{e}*ḥōlā*), but we find that otherwise the order of MT may be retained with almost the minimum of emendation. The district is described from Taanach and Megiddo, first east and south-east by Jezreel and Bethshean to Abel Meholah, then from Taanach or Megiddo north-west to Jokmeam.

[f]Reading *naḥat* (cf. Isa. 30.30) for MT *taḥat* ('beneath').

Jezreel on the approach[a] to Bethshean as far as Abel-Meholah, which is by Zarethan[b] and[c] to beyond Jokmeam. 13( )[d] the son of Geber in Ramoth[e] Gilead (he had the tent agglomerations of Jair the son of Manasseh which were in Gilead)[f]; he had the district of Argob [g](which was in Bashan, sixty great cities with wall and bronze bar).[g] 14And Ahinadab the son of Iddo: Mahanaim. 15Ahimaaz was in Naphtali; he also took to wife Basemath the daughter of Solomon. 16Baanah the son of Hushai was in Asher and the Uplands.[h] 17Jehoshaphat the son of Paruah was in Issachar. 18Shimei the son of Ela was in Benjamin. 19(Geber the son of Uri was in Gilead/Gad[i] the land of Sihon the king of the Amorites and Og the king of Bashan.) And there was one prefect who was over the home district.[j]. . .

(Here the passage is interrupted, to be resumed at 4.27 [5.7].)

4.7. 'Prefects', *niṣṣābīm* (lit. 'those appointed'), is found in the variant form *n*^{e}*ṣībīm* for the commandants of garrisons in occupied countries, e.g. the hill-country of Israel under the Philistines (I Sam. 10.5, probably) and in Damascus (II Sam 8.6) and Edom (I Chron. 18.13) under David. Solomon's prefects are fiscal officers. The 12 districts suggests the 12 tribes of Israel, originally an amphictyony,[k] but the verse indicates that the division was suggested rather by the 12 months of the year. It is noteworthy that the division of the country, if not ignoring the old tribal boundaries, was not rigidly

[a]Reading *m*^{e}*bōʼ bēt* for MT *mibbēt,* the corruption of *w* to MT *y* and ʼ to MT *t* occurring when the text was written in the script exemplified in the Qumran texts, and *m*^{e}*bōʼ* having then dropped out by haplography.

[b]This is the only phrase we admit as being displaced, see p. 134 n.[e].

[c]Reading *w*^{e}*ʿad* for MT *ʿad.* [d]See p. 134 n.[b].

[e]G^{B} suggests here and later the singular instead of the plural, which may well be correct despite the common tradition of the MT.

[f]Omitted in G^{BL}, probably a later Deuteronomistic expansion after Deut. 3.4, 14.

[g]Another expansion after Deut. 3.4, 14, which probably suggested the expansion noted in n.[f].

[h]Reading with G^{A} *ūma*^{ʿa}*lōt*, a common noun, for MT *ūb*^{e}*ʿālōt,* which suggests a place-name unknown in this district, see on v. 16.

[i]G^{BL} read *gād* for MT *gilʿād* (so Kittel, Stade, Šanda, Abel, Noth). On the basis of MT it is held that MT *geber ben ʼūrī* in v. 19 is a variant of *ben geber*, the prefect of Gilead in v. 13 (so Albright, *op. cit.*, pp. 26 ff., Montgomery, ICC, *ad loc.*, de Vaux, *BJ*, *ad loc.*, and van den Born, p. 37). This would give 12 officers including the one who was 'over the land', i.e. the homeland, Judah. Otherwise we must regard the last prefect as over the crown estates in Judah, hence distinct from the other 12 (so Alt, Abel). Since the district of Mahanaim (v. 14) was in Transjordan and actually in Gad (Josh. 21.38), v. 19a would seem certainly to be superfluous, as Albright maintains, 'the land of Sihon the king of the Amorites and Og the king of Bashan' being an obvious gloss from a later Deuteronomistic hand.

[j]The absolute use of *hā ʼāreṣ*, meaning 'the homeland', is apparently attested in I K. 9.18, and certainly in Assyrian. In view of the fact that the next word in the present text is *y*^{e}*hūdā*, however, this may be a case of haplography.

[k]So M. Noth, *Zwölf Stämme*, 1930, pp. 85ff.

bound by them. This portended a social revolution in Israel, but it is doubtful if, as is often asserted, it was deliberately precipitated by Solomon.[a] Solomon's administrative division and the consequent social revolution were both conditioned by the incorporation of the Canaanite towns such as Megiddo, Taanach, Bethshean and others. Solomon's fiscal organization probably applied particularly to the territory of Canaanite cities, now crown lands under an administration to which, on the evidence of administrative texts from the palace of Ras Shamra, they had been long accustomed. The administrative texts from Ras Shamra show that in Ugarit the population was organized for fiscal purposes by localities and by classes rather than by families or tribes. Albright sees a relic of this fiscal organization, with modification after the disruption of the kingdom, in the fiscal dockets found in the storehouses of the palace of Samaria, now dated in the eighth century, and in the jar-handles from various Judaean sites stamped *lmlk* with the names Hebron, Socoh, Ziph, and *mmšt*, which, after Clermont-Ganneau[b] and Macalister,[c] he regards as fiscal centres, dating the inscribed jar-handles to 750–590.[d]

The verb *kilkēl* is the Pilpel, a variant of the intensive of *kūl*, 'to contain' (of capacity), and means regularly in Hebrew 'to sustain, nourish'. A tablet from the palace of Ras Shamra,[e] which is a receipt for the consignment of poultry by the hundred and a quantity of quarters of beef, may be relevant to the present passage. Note the idiomatic use of the preposition *ʿal* signifying, as in Arabic, liability. The *w* consecutive with the perfect indicates frequency. The king's 'house' means his family and all his servants and officials.

4.8. First district: the hill country of Ephraim, stretching from about ten miles north of Jerusalem probably to just beyond Shechem, and from the Jordan to beyond the western foothills about 15 miles from the sea. The personal name Hur is attested in Num. 31.8 and I Chron. 2.19. On the analogy of Arabic it would signify 'free'.

9. Second district: roughly coinciding with the original settlement of Dan, from the western foothills of the central highlands (Aijalon and Bethshemesh) to within about ten miles from the sea south of Jaffa, including Shaalbim (modern *Selbīt*, about seven miles south-

[a]Alt, *KS* II, p. 88.
[b]*Receuil d'archéologie orientale* IV, 1888–1907, pp. 1–24.
[c]*Excavations in Palestine, 1898–1900*, 1902, p. 114.
[d]'The Administrative Divisions . . .', *JPOS* V, 1925, pp. 17–54.
[e]Virolleaud, *PRU*, II, 1957, pp. 162f., no. 129.

east of Lydda), Bethshemesh (*Tell Rumeileh*), Aijalon (modern *Jalu*), and Beth-hanan (modern *Beit ʿAnan*, about two and a half miles north-west of *al-Qubeibeh*). Makaz may be *Ḫirbet Maqqūṣ* just north of Ashkelon. The Hebrew name suggests *Deir Muḥeisin*, about seven miles north-west of Bethshemesh, or possibly *al-Muḥeisin*, about four miles farther west.[a] The name Deker may be attested in the patronymic of Jehu's charioteer Ben Deker (II K. 9.25).

4.10. Third district: western central highlands of Manasseh including the southern part of the Plain of Sharon. Socoh, a fairly common place-name in Palestine, is the modern *aš-Šuweikeh*, two miles north of Tulkarm, mentioned in Crusading sources and topographical lists of Thothmes III and Shishak as on the trunk highroad north through the coastal plain, where it was joined by the road from the interior by Shechem.[b] Arubboth is *Arabbah*, 12 miles north-east of *aš-Šuweikeh*. 'The whole land of Hepher' may refer to the district occupied by the Manassite clan of Hepher (Josh. 17.2), possibly the unbroken land in the central part of the Plain of Sharon, where cultivation was difficult because of the drainage from the interior being hindered by sand-dunes, and which in consequence was grazing land (I Chron. 27.29).[c] A Canaanite city Hepher, however, is noted here in Josh. 12.17, feasibly located by B. Maisler[d] at Tell Ibsar, *c.* 8 miles north-west of Tulkarm. The administrative centre of this land was Arubboth. The region is possibly mentioned in the Samarian ostraca.[e]

11. Fourth district: adjacent to the last on the north-west, where the foothills (*nāpōt*) of the central highlands close in on the coast. *nāpat*, in form the fem. sing. participle of *nūp*, is attested in MT in Josh. 12.23, where Naphath Dor is given as the city of a Canaanite king. But in the enumeration of districts by physical characteristics in Josh. 11.2, the plural is used, which we read here in the sense of 'heights overlooking', cf. Arabic *nāfa, yanūfu*. D. W. Thomas[f] has proposed that the sing. means 'hill sanctuary' or 'high place', but this is not elsewhere attested. If the sing. is to be read, following Josh.

[a]Abel, *GP* II, p. 377.
[b]Alt, *KS* II, pp. 78ff.
[c]For a good description of this region and the problems of its drainage see D. Baly, *The Geography of the Bible*, 1957, pp. 133–7.
[d]*ZDPV* LVIII, 1935, pp. 82f.
[e]R. Dussaud, 'Samarie au temps d'Achab', *Syria* VI, 1925, pp. 314–38; J. W. Jack, *Samaria in Ahab's Time*, 1929, p. 73.
[f]*PEFQS*, 1935, p. 89.

12.23, a citadel on the heights immediately west of the coastal settlement would be more appropriate, though one is not known to archaeology. Dor is the modern *Ḫirbet al-Burj* by the modern *Ṭanṭūrah* on the coast, mentioned in the Golenischeff Papyrus, recording the misadventures of Wen-Amon *c.* 1110 BC, as a port of the *Ṯekel*, a people kindred to the Philistines. This was apparently the administrative centre. The high rank of the prefects is indicated by the fact that the prefect of the district was married to a daughter of Solomon, and the prefect of Naphtali to another (v. 15). This note, probably secondary, though doubtless authentic, indicates that the list is from the second half of Solomon's reign. The name Tapath is connected by Noth[a] with *nāṭap*, 'to drop'. We think it more likely that it is from a verb cognate with Arabic *ṭāfa, yaṭīfu*, 'to appear in a vision', alluding to the experience of the mother at birth or during gestation.

4.12. Fifth district: the southern part of the great central plain from Jokmeam in the north-west to Bethshean and south-east to the narrowest part of the Jordan Valley east of Abel-Meholah, modern *Tell Abū Sifrī*, about ten miles south of Bethshean (see p. 134 n.[e]). Jezreel (the former Arabic *Zerʿīn*), the point where the plain dips sharply eastwards, hence 'the descent' ((see p. 134 n.[f]), was the site of royal demesnes in the time of Saul (II Sam. 2.9) and Ahab (I K. 21.1 ff.), and may have been the home of the family of Omri. Taanach (*Tell Taʿnik*), Megiddo (*Tell al-Mutasallim*), and Jokmeam (*Tell Qeimūn*) are all well-known fortress cities commanding passes through the mountains from the great central plain to the Plain of Sharon. Bethshan (*Tell al-Ḥuṣn*) commanded the eastern end of the central plain. Abel-Meholah was the home of Elisha (19.16), and Zarethan, which is mentioned with Abel-Meholah in Judg. 7.22, is near the ford of the Jordan at Adamah (modern *ad-Dāmīyeh*).

13. Sixth district: Gilead (see p. 135 n.[i]). Ramoth Gilead, as the account of the Aramaean campaigns suggests, is to be located in the northern part of Transjordan either at *Tell al-Ḥuṣn* near Irbid (Dalman) or at *Tell Rāmit*[b]. Towards the north the district included 'the tent-agglomerations of Jair' (possibly a later extension, see p. 135 n.[f]), and 'the district of Argob' ('the mound') about the headwaters of the Yarmuk, the largest tributary of the Jordan, in the region of Bashan. A locality *ḥawwōt yāʿīr* in the north part of Trans-

[a] *IP*, p. 226.
[b] N. Glueck, *BASOR* 92, 1943, pp. 10ff.; P. W. Lapp, *BA* XXV, 1963, p. 128.

jordan is known from the passage on the settlement of Manasseh, and Judg. 10.3 transmits the tradition of a judge Jair with wide local affinities in Gilead. The place-name is rather to be associated with the Manassite clan Jair mentioned in Num. 32.41; I Chron. 2.22. G variously transliterates (as here) as a place-name and renders as a common noun *epauleis* ('encampments') or *kōmai* ('villages'). It is almost certainly a common noun cognate with Arabic *ḥiwā'* ('a cluster of houses or tents'). This passage is certainly glossed over by the Deuteronomists (see p. 135 n.[f]).

4.14. Seventh district: Mahanaim, probably *Tell al-Ḥajjāj* in the foothills of Transjordan just south of the lower Jabbok,[a] which is archaeologically more suitable than *Ḫirbet Maḥneh* just north of *'Ajlūn*, where Glueck[b] proposed to locate it. It was in the tribal territory of Gad (Josh. 13.26, 30), which extended to the southern part of Transjordan, the administrative centre of which it apparently was. It had been the seat of Saul's family after Gilboa (II Sam. 2.8ff.) and the fortress where David rallied his forces in Absalom's revolt (II Sam. 17.24).

15. Eighth district: Naphtali, the eastern part of Galilee. The prefect Ahimaaz, who was married to Solomon's daughter, may have been the son of Zadok (II Sam. 15.27), and is thought by some to have been the author of the Story of the Davidic Succession (see Introduction, p. 19). The name Basemath may mean 'fragrant', being connected with Hebrew *bōśem*, Arabic *bašam*, 'balm' (so Montgomery). We think it more probable that it is cognate with Arabic *basama*, 'to smile', the name being given from an early emotional reaction of the child. That it is to be derived from a verbal root *bāśam* is indicated by the proper name *yibśām* (in the kinship of Issachar, I Chron. 7.2).

16. Ninth district: Asher, the western slopes of Galilee. For the unidentified 'Bealoth' or 'Aloth' of the MT read *ma'alōt* with G. This means either 'upper parts' or 'steps'. The latter might refer to the configuration of western Galilee which rises from the coastal plain about Acco to an upland plain from *Majd al-Kurūm* to *Rāma* and to a higher level above a steep escarpment to the north. The prefect was the son of Hushai, perhaps 'David's Friend' (II Sam. 15.37).

[a]So De Vaux, *Vivre et Penser* I, 1941, pp. 30ff.; Noth, *PJB* XXXVII, 1941, pp. 82–86.

[b]N. Glueck, *AASOR* XXV–XXVIII, 1951, p. 230.

4.17. Tenth district: Issachar, the northern part of the eastern and central part of the great central plain.

18. Eleventh district: Benjamin, immediately north of Jerusalem, extending almost ten miles north, and east to the Jordan from the watershed of the central highlands.

19a. See p. 135 n.[h].

19b. Whether or not 'Judah' is read after 'the land', the district of Judah is certainly meant. Assyrian evidence may be cited for the usage 'the land' to denote the homeland. The name of the prefect is not included. This may be because the fiscal arrangements in Judah were under the hand of Ahishar, the royal chamberlain (v. 6). This is suggested to us by the case of Ahab's chamberlain, Obadiah, who, like the prefects of Solomon's realm, was responsible for provender for the chariot-horses (I K. 18.3–5).

(ii) MISCELLANEOUS INSERTIONS ON THE EXTENT OF SOLOMON'S REALM, THE GENERAL WELL-BEING OF HIS TIME, AND HIS PROVISIONS AND HORSES 4.20–26[4.20–5.6]

As the reference to 'these prefects' in v. 27 [5.7] suggests, v. 26 [5.6] (Solomon's horses) is secondary matter here, as, indeed, the obvious exaggeration indicates. Verse 25 [5.5] is probably of the same nature, the combination 'Judah and Israel' suggesting a post-exilic gloss, cf. Jer. 23.6; II Chron. 16.11; 35.18.[a] Here we may note the divergence of G from MT. After the list of fiscal officers, where I K. 4.17–19 is read by G in the order vv. 19, 17, 18, G continues with I K.4.27[5.7] (the monthly provision by 'these prefects' for the king's table), 4.28[5.8] (fodder for the horses), 4.22f.[5.2f.] (the daily provision for the palace), and 4.24[5.4] (the extent of Solomon's realm 'beyond the river', but omitting 'from Tiphsah to Gaza' of MT). This matter from G. following on naturally from a list of fiscal officers (omitting such verses of MT as 1, 5, and 6, where either 1 or 4 must be considered superfluous and 5 is an expansion of 4, which is suspect through the reference to 'beyond', i.e. west of, 'the river' from a Mesopotamian point of view, and the reference to the horses in v. 6 is another gloss prompted by the reference to fodder in v. 8), is worthy of serious consideration. It has all the appearance of a better text than MT, reproducing more closely and without so much late redactional interpolation the archival source from which all admit the list of fiscal officials to have been taken.

[a]So A. van den Born, *op. cit.*, p. 38.

4 [20]And Judah and Israel were as numerous as the sand which is on the seashore,[a] eating and drinking and rejoicing.
[21]And Solomon ruled over all the kingdoms from the river[b] to the land of the Philistines[b] and to the border of Egypt. They brought tribute and were subject to Solomon all the days of his life. [22]Now Solomon's daily provisions were thirty *kors* of fine flour and sixty *kors* of wheat, [23]ten fattened oxen and twenty oxen from the pastures, and one hundred sheep, besides deer, gazelles, roebucks, and cribbed geese. [24]For he ruled over all the land Beyond-the-River[c] from Tiphsah as far as Gaza over all the kings of Beyond-the-River,[c] and he had security on all his borders[d] round about. [25]And Judah and Israel dwelt in security, each under his own vine and under his own figtree from Dan to Beersheba all the days of Solomon.[e] [26]And Solomon had 40,000[f] stalls of horses for his chariotry and 12,000 horsemen.

4.21. The rule of Solomon from the River (i.e. Euphrates) to the border of Egypt (generally taken as 'the river of Egypt', probably the *Wādī al-Arīsh*) is contradicted by the more sober historical statement in 11.23ff. that the Aramaeans of Damascus successfully revolted after the death of David, but see p. 142. If *weʿad* (restored from II Chron. 9.26, see textual n. b) has strictly the local sense and does not signify 'including', the statement might refer to Solomon's control of the northern part of the Philistine plain through his occupation of Gezer (see on 3.1). In this case, 'and to the border of Egypt' may be a later accretion by a glossator who took the reference to 'the land of the Philistines' as inclusive. The basis of this claim is possibly the fact that Aramaean traders from the north-east paid transit dues to Solomon. This may be indicated by the 'tribute' (*minḥā*) mentioned

[a]Nine Hebrew MSS add *śepat* ('shore'), which is generally used in this conventional expression, though MT is quite intelligible.

[b]The passage suggests II Chron. 9.26 and I K.2.46k (G), where it is stated that 'Solomon ruled over all the kings from the river to the land of the Philistines and the border of Egypt'. If MT 'the land of the Philistines' is not originally a gloss, which it may well be, the variants in Chronicles and G suggest that the phrase should be introduced by *weʿad*.

[c]This, repeating the statement of Solomon's rule over all Beyond-the-River in the beginning of the verse, seems certainly a later gloss, the note on Tiphsah and Gaza, wanting in G, probably amplifying the statement of Solomon's rule from the river (Euphrates) to the Egyptian border.

[d]*ʿabārāw*, rendered 'his borders', is a *hapax legomenon*, and, if not unintelligible, its meaning must still be doubtful. Certain MSS read *ʿabādāw* ('his subjects').

[e]G^L adds 'and there was no adversary all the days of Solomon'.

[f]This is evident exaggeration and is a generalization, as the number 40 suggests. MT in I K. 10.26 and G^B and II Chron. 9.25 give a much more sober estimate of 4,000 horses. Twelve thousand horsemen agrees with II Chron. 9.25, though 'horsemen' in the time of Solomon, if, as normally, it means 'mounted cavalry', suggests an anachronism.

in v. 21 [5.1]. This word means 'tribute' in the Old Testament and Ras Shamra texts; in Gen. 43.11 the word means a 'present'; and as a cultic term it came eventually to mean a bloodless offering, though as a sacrifice it has the general meaning of bloody sacrifice as in I K. 18.36 and II K. 3.20. It has been argued[a] that the Aramaean Hadadezer, a native of Rehob, who became king also of Zobah, was apparently suzerain of the Aramaean principalities as far as, and even beyond, the Euphrates (II Sam. 10.16), which, on Hadadezer's defeat, acknowledged David as suzerain (II Sam. 10.19; cf. 8.3–8). The rapprochement of Toi of Hamath on the Upper Orontes may also have been an acknowledgment of Israelite suzerainty, and Malamat would see in the name of the prince Joram a throne-name given by David as suzerain, cf. the installation of Eliakim-Jehoiakim and Mattaniah-Zedekiah (II K. 23.34; 24.17), where the change of names betokened vassalage. In the case of Joram, the Yahweh element may imply an oath to Yahweh, the God of the suzerain power. The prince of Hamath may have been reared at the court of David, as Syrian princes had been at the court of the Pharaohs of the XVIIIth Dynasty, and may possibly have been adopted into the House of David. This may be the explanation of the Yahweh theophoric Yaubidi (var. Ilubidi), king of Hamath, mentioned in the Assyrian account of the revolt of Hamath in 720 BC.

4.22. The daily provision of Solomon's palace is possibly an antiquarian gloss, though instances cited by Montgomery (ICC, p. 128) from Persia (after E. Meyer) and mediæval Egypt (after P. K. Hitti) indicate that this is no exaggeration here and may be an excerpt from official records. The *kōr* was a measure of dry capacity equivalent to the *ḥōmer*, or 'ass-load' of 10 ephahs, 'basketfuls', an Egyptian loanword. The *ḥōmer* refers to loads which could be visualized or generally estimated; the *kōr*, as here and at 5.11[25], is used in more accurate accounts. It is reckoned at 6·3 imperial bushels by R. B. Y. Scott.[b] *sōlet* is probably 'fine flour', possibly an Egyptian loanword *trt*, unless the Egyptian word was a Canaanite loanword. It is used of the most delicate food, as indicated in Ezek. 16.13, 19, hence hardly 'unhusked barley', as Arabic *sult* may suggest.

23. The stall-fed oxen may have been for the table of the palace, and those direct from the pasture for the feudal retainers and palace

[a] E. g. Malamat, *JNES* XXII, 1963, pp. 3ff.

[b] R. B. Y. Scott, 'Weights, measures, money and time', *Peake's Commentary on the Bible*, ed. M. Black and H. H. Rowley, 1962, § 34k.

guards. These would doubtless be straight from the herds pastured in the Plain of Sharon, which is noted in I Chron. 27.29 as ranching country. The roebucks (*yaḥmūr*), 'red beasts', may also have come from this jungle-country. The word *barbūrīm* is of uncertain derivation and meaning. It may be derived from *bārar*, 'to be white', and may indicate geese. G. R. Driver[a] takes the word as a cognate of Arabic *birbir* ('young hen'), though there is no evidence for the domestication of hens till the end of the Davidic monarchy, and Noth (*Könige*, p. 58), after L. Köhler, proposes that it is cognate with Arabic *abū burbur* ('the cuckoo'), presumably referring to a titbit like the Roman dish of larks' tongues.

4.24. For vv. 24f. see n. on v. 21. 'Beyond-the-River' refers to Syria west of the Euphrates, used first in Assyrian records from the middle of the seventh century and throughout the Persian period (539–331 BC) as the official description of the fifth Persian satrapy including Palestine, hence it probably indicates a late interpolation in the text. Tiphsah is the Greek Thapsacus (modern *Qalʿat ad-Dibs*) at the great western bend of the Euphrates. It has been derived from *pāsaḥ* 'to hop over',[b] and, with more probability, from the same verb in the sense of 'to bend' (the knee) by de Vaux.[c] Insofar as this may correspond to historical fact, it denotes the Israelite hegemony over the Aramaeans to the Euphrates which resulted from David's victories in Ammon. The picture of unbroken security ignores the successful rising in Damascus and the return of Hadad the prince of Edom (I K. 11) in the time of Solomon.

25. 'From Dan', at the headwaters of the Jordan, 'to Beersheba', on the verge of the southern steppe, is the conventional description of the Israelite homeland.

26. The meaning of the rare word *'ūrᵉwōt* ('stalls') is indicated in II Chron. 32.28, and is supported by Akkadian, Aramaic, and Arabic cognates. 'Horsemen' (*pārāšīm*) generally refers to mounted cavalry, which was only now coming into use in Assyria. In the campaign against Assyria at Qarqar Ahab contributed no mounted cavalry, but put the largest chariot-contingent into the field, namely 2,000. This number suggests that the present account of Solomon's chariot-force is an exaggeration, and that 'horseman' either has a general reference or, if meaning 'mounted cavalry', is a later un-

[a] *PEQ*, 1955, pp. 133ff.
[b] W. A. Heidel, *The Day of Yahweh*, 1929, p. 185.
[c] 'Les prophètes de Baal sur le mont Carmel', *BMB* V, 1941, pp. 9–11.

critical insertion. 12,000 'horsemen' might mean a warrior, a driver and a groom for each pair of 4000 pairs. See further on 9.19.

(iv) SOLOMON'S FISCAL ADMINISTRATION: 4.27f.[5.7f.] (continued from 4.19)

4 [27]And these prefects[a] used to supply provisions for king Solomon and all who were admitted to king Solomon's table, each man in his month; they let nothing be lacking. [28]And the barley and the chopped straw for the horses and the chariot-steeds they used to bring to the place where each (prefect) was according to his established office.

4.28. Barley (*śeʿōrîm*) and chopped straw (*teben*) indicates how well these studs were cared for, cf. the drought in Ahab's time, when fodder for the chariot-horses was a priority (I K. 18.3–5). Straw chopped small as the result of the primitive method of threshing by sledge is the staple provender in the Arab East. The word *rekeš* ('chariot-steeds') is used by Micah (1.13) in a punning reference to Lachish. If we must discriminate between two kinds of horses, the first might be stud horses and *rekeš* trained chariot-teams. The centres to which the provender was brought were, no doubt, the places mentioned in the list of fiscal officers. *mišpāṭ*, derived from *šāpaṭ*, which, as the Ugaritic cognate indicates, means 'to rule' as well as 'to judge', means occasionally 'regulated order' or 'custom'. Here we prefer to regard it as the verbal noun of 'to rule', hence 'established office'.

(*f*) THE WISDOM OF SOLOMON: 4.29–34[5.9–14]

Further elaboration of the legendary greatness and specifically the wisdom of Solomon in general terms from a late popular source, probably the same as that which lauds the power and wisdom of Solomon in 4.20f. 24f. [4.20; 5.1, 4f.] as suggested by similar large and conventional round numbers, and by the mention of the apparently legendary paragons of wisdom. In support of his thesis that this source is late R. B. Y. Scott[b] points out certain late features in the phraseology and vocabulary of this passage, of which we may note the following outstanding instances:

'Judah and Israel' in that order (4.20, 25[4.20; 5.5]) is found in II Chron. 16.11; 25.26; the description of the region west of the Euphrates as 'Beyond-the-River' (4.24[5.4]) is found only in Ezra-Nehemiah and was obviously written either in Mesopotamia or at a time when the

[a]See on 4.7.
[b]*Wisdom in Israel* . . ., pp. 262–79, esp. 267ff.

Persian satrapy in the west was so designated; *tᵉbūnā* ('discernment') and *rōḥab lēb* ('breadth of understanding') (4.29[5.9]) are attested besides only in post-exilic sources; Ethan, Heman, Calcol, and Darda are mentioned besides only in I Chron. 2.6 and the psalm titles in Pss. 88 and 89.

While this may be true, the transmission of the tradition in a late source does not disprove the antiquity of the tradition itself, and Scott himself suggests that the tradition of Solomon's wisdom reflects the revival of the glory of his reign in the time of Hezekiah, when there was a tradition of wisdom literature (Prov. 25.1). Alt,[a] however, emphasizes the affinity of the nature-wisdom ascribed to Solomon with the classified lists of mainly natural phenomena in Mesopotamia,[b] where they go back to the early third millennium, and in Egypt, where such a list[c] goes back conceivably a century or so earlier than Solomon. Noting further that the Hebrew interest in nature for its own sake, evidenced in Job 38–41, Prov. 30.15ff., 18–20, 24–28, etc., has been eventually overshadowed by the human or ethical interest, he concludes that the naturalistic interest in those passages goes back to an early date, probably that of Solomon. Associating the gnomic wisdom and poetry with the classification of mainly natural phenomena known in Mesopotamia and Egypt, Alt makes the further suggestion that the tradition that Solomon excelled his neighbours in natural lore signified that he or the persons associated with him first expressed the characteristics and common features of these in gnomic poetry. For the traditional skill of Solomon in riddles (ch. 10, also transmitted in a late popular source), and for the particular illustration of the juridical wisdom of Solomon in 3.16–28, Gressmann[d] plausibly suggests affinities with Arabia and India, which points to the time of Solomon, when Israel had such contacts.

4 29Now Yahweh[e] gave wisdom to Solomon and very great discernment and breadth of understanding as abundant as the sand which is upon the seashore. 30And the wisdom of Solomon was greater than the wisdom of all those of the East and of all the wisdom of Egypt. 31And

[a]'Die Weisheit Salomos', *KS* II, pp. 90–99.

[b]L. Matouš, *Die lexikalischen Tafelserien der Babylonier und Assyrer in den Berliner Museen* I, 1953; W. von Soden, 'Leistung und Grenze sumerischer und babylonischer Wissenschaft', *Die Welt als Geschichte* II, 1936, pp. 417–64.

[c]G. Maspero, 'Manuel d'hiérarchie égyptienne', *Journal Asiatique* 8 sér., 11, 1888, pp. 250–80; A. H. Gardiner *Ancient Egyptian Onomastica*, 1948.

[d]*ZAW* XLII, 1924, pp. 282ff.

[e]Reading 'Yahweh' with GTS[h] for MT *'ᵉlōhīm*.

he was wiser than all men,[a] wiser than Ethan the Ezrahite and Heman and Calcol and Darda the sons of Mahol, and his repute was among all the peoples round about. [32]And Solomon[b] spoke three thousand proverbs and his songs were [c]a thousand and five.[c] [33]And he spoke of trees from the cedar which was in Lebanon to the hyssop which sprang from the wall, and he spoke of beasts and birds and reptiles and fishes. [34]And they came from all peoples to hear the wisdom of Solomon[d] even from all the kings of the earth, who heard his wisdom.

4.29. On 'wisdom' (*ḥokmā*) and 'discernment' (*tᵉbūnā*) see Commentary on 3.12, the latter being attested, like *rōḥab lēb* (lit. 'breadth of heart', i.e. understanding), only here and in later sources, see introduction to this section. The nature of *ḥokmā* here is not defined, and it may be of a more liberal, humanistic character than that implied in the knowledge of natural phenomena in v. 13.

30. The wisdom of the men of the East was proverbial among the Hebrews. It might signify the wisdom of Mesopotamia expressed in such documents of humanism as the Gilgamesh epic, the Myth of Adapa, which pose the problem of the ultimate limitation of man, and other collections of proverbs. In view of the nature of 'wisdom' as practical sagacity, however, 'the men of the East' may have been Arabs of the steppe, where intertribal relations make constant demands on the ability to understand men and take practical decisions, and a sheikh succeeds to his position in virtue of manifest ability of this sort. The word *qedem*, however (lit. 'before'), denotes time as well as place, and the allusion may be to the proverbial wisdom of the ancients. The men of Edom were also proverbial for wisdom (Jer. 49.7; Obad. 8). The wisdom of Egypt is well attested from the Wisdom of Ptah-hotep in the first half of the third millennium to the 11th century. Actually the incorporation of a section of the Wisdom of Amen-em-ope (probably *c.* 1000 BC) in the Book of Proverbs (22.17–23.12) indicates the extent of the influence of Egyptian wisdom, which is of an essentially prudential nature, like most of the Hebrew

[a]Šanda feasibly suggests the reading *hā'ᵃdōmīm* ('the Edomites') for MT *hā'ādām*, the final *m* in this case having dropped out before the initial *m* of the following word; so Gressmann, Montgomery and van den Born.

[b]Inserting *šᵉlōmō* with G^B, which has probably been omitted in MT by haplography before the following word *šᵉlōšet* ('three').

[c]Perhaps *ḥᵃmēšet 'elep* ('five thousand') should be read, as in G and 12 MSS of V.

[d]G^L and S insert 'and he received tribute', cf. II Chron. 9.23ff. Burney understands 'deputed by (all the kings . . .)'. In view of wisdom as a manifestation of divine favour, the association with Solomon through gifts (rather than 'tribute') would be natural, as in the case of the Queen of Sheba (10.10).

Proverbs.[a] Solomon's 'wisdom' may have included riddles and word-plays, such as those with which the Queen of Sheba is said to have tried Solomon (I K. 10.1), of which Samson's riddle in Judg. 14 is the classic example in the Old Testament. This type of word-play in poetry Gressmann[b] associated with the Arabs, among whom it is a point of honour to be proficient to the point of preciosity in language. The date of the incorporation of the Wisdom of Amen-em-ope in Hebrew Proverbs is uncertain, but may well be early. This type of wisdom was used in the education of Egyptian scribes, and pre-occupation with Egyptian wisdom may reflect the training of Solomon's new bureaucracy.

4.31. The names of the sages are known from a genealogy of the progeny of Judah and Tamar in the hill-country of Judah about Hebron (I Chron. 2.6, 8), which suggests their antiquity, if little else. The names Ethan and Heman have been taken to be Arabic in form,[c] but the form is attested in the Ras Shamra texts from Canaan, e.g. 'Aqht and 'Al'eyn. De Vaux,[d] however, after Albright,[e] takes *bᵉnē māḥōl* to mean 'choristers', hence those families responsible for psalmody in the Temple, in which connection the family of Heman is already known in psalm headings. If this were so, the fact that they are listed not among the Levites but among the descendants of Judah and the Canaanite Tamar probably points to a pre-Israelite origin of psalm-tradition. Calcol suggests Egyptian Kerker, Kurkur or Kulkul, the singer of Ptah, who apparently had a temple at Ashkelon, named on an ivory pencase from Megiddo (*c.* 1350–1150 BC).[f] *māḥōl* certainly means dancing rather than psalmody, but the two were not independent. Mowinckel[g] further emphasizes that wisdom and poetic skill, both manifestations of the spirit, were often combined, especially in such a serious calling as that of the temple singer.

32. The round numbers suggest saga or popular tradition. *māšāl* may indicate 'figure of speech' or 'proverb'. The root meaning is

[a] H. Gressmann, *ZAW* XLII, 1924, pp. 272–96, and more recently W. Baumgartner, *Israel und die altorientalische Weisheit*, 1933; J. Fichtner, *Die altorientalische Weisheit in ihrer israelitisch-jüdischen Ausprägung* (BZAW LXII), 1933.

[b] *Op. cit.*, p. 282.

[c] H. Gressmann, *op. cit.*, p. 282; R. H. Pfeiffer, 'Edomite Wisdom', *ZAW* XLIV, 1926, p. 13.

[d] *Ancient Israel*, p. 382.

[e] *Archaeology and the Religion of Israel*, 1953, p. 127.

[f] G. Loud, *The Megiddo Ivories*, Oriental Institute Publications LII, 1939, pls. 62f., pp. 11–13.

[g] *The Psalms in Israel's Worship* II, 1962, p. 96.

'likeness', which might be expressed in a simile or metaphor or in a proverb which employed such a figure to reflect an inherent truth. Such gnomic wisdom was usually couched in poetry. The root *maṭala* is used in Arabic in the reflexive of the intensive (Vth form) for poetic citation à propos of a relevant situation. Solomon's 'songs' refers to lyric poetry, such as love-lyrics known in ancient Egypt and among modern Arab peasantry, and possibly also psalms of praise. On the number of the songs see p. 146 n.[c]. The figure 'one thousand and five', denoting 'more than a thousand', recalls the 'Thousand and One Nights'.

4.33. The precise significance of the tradition of Solomon's sayings or discourses about natural phenomena is uncertain. It may signify the figurative language of proverbs, e.g.

The ants are a people not strong,
yet they prepare their meat in the summer;
the conies are but a feeble folk,
yet they make their houses in the rocks (Prov. 30.25f.).

It may refer to parables or animal fables, e.g. Jotham's parable of the trees (Judg. 9). For the analogy which Alt draws with the classified lists of natural phenomena in Mesopotamia and Egypt see the critical introduction to this section. Since such lists were used in Egypt as exemplars in the training of young scribes, a similar scribal training under Solomon may be the source of the tradition which associates this type of wisdom with Solomon, but we should rather emphasize the verb 'and he spoke' as referring to figures of speech in gnomic wisdom. On Alt's view of Solomon's original contribution to the development of natural wisdom see the critical introduction to this section.

The cedars of Lebanon were proverbial for their height and grace; there is abundant evidence from Mesopotamia and Egypt that the wood was much valued as early as the third millennium. The hyssop, a small wall-plant, is contrasted with the lofty cedar. It was used for ceremonial sprinkling (Ex. 12.22).

34. The wisdom of Solomon is taken as that which vindicated for him pre-eminence among contemporary kings, thus serving as an introduction to Solomon's dealings with Hiram in preparation for the building of the Temple, and the visit of the Queen of Sheba. The reference to non-Israelite peoples as *'ammīm* and not *gōyīm* should be noted. *'am*, as pointed out by E. A. Speiser,[a] denotes properly a

[a] *JBL* LXXIX, 1960, pp. 157–60.

religious group with a common god, with whom they stand in a kin-relation, at least ethically; *gōy*, on the other hand, is primarily a political unit. Since the immediate neighbours of Israel were Aramaeans, tribal confederacies which had grown from single kin-groups, the term *ʿammīm* is strictly proper here.

(*g*) THE BUILDING AND DEDICATION OF THE TEMPLE 5.1–9.9 [5.15–9.9]

(i) SOLOMON'S NEGOTIATIONS WITH HIRAM FOR MATERIALS AND ARTISANS: 5.1–12[15–26]

The narrative style and the elaboration of the theme of Yahweh's covenant with the house of David (vv. 3–5[17–19]; cf. Nathan's oracle in II Sam 7.12ff.) suggests secondary elaboration, but the conventions and phraseology of royal correspondence, known in the Old Testament (e.g. II Sam. 10) and the Amarna Tablets, suggest that, if the actual correspondence was not available, it was reconstructed with fair verisimilitude. The reference to the covenant with the house of David and the building of the Temple by the son promised to the late king (vv. 3–5 [17–19]), though skilfully wrought into the context, is probably part of an early narrative history, like the Story of the Davidic Succession. Verse 12 [26], in so far as it mentions the pact between Solomon and Hiram after the statement that their exchange of materials and provisions had been in effect on a yearly basis (vv. 10ff., [24ff.]), appears to be a later insertion by one who saw in the pact the practical result of Solomon's (administrative) wisdom. The bulk of this passage is probably from the Acts of Solomon.

In the general plan of the Deuteronomistic History, Solomon's preparation thus early in his reign for the building of the Temple is an instance of his wisdom (4.29–34[5.9–14]).

5 [1]Then Hiram king of Tyre sent his servants to Solomon, for he had
heard that they had anointed him king in place of his father, for Hiram
was always friendly with David. [2]And Solomon sent to Hiram saying,
[3]You know that David my father could not build a temple for the name
of Yahweh his God because of the enemies[a] by whom he was surrounded,
until Yahweh had put them under the soles of his feet.[b] [4]But now

[a]Inserting *'anᵉšē* before *hammilḥāmā*, the personal plural being suggested by the pronominal suffix in *'ōtām* in the following clause. The reading *sᵉbābattū* in one Hebrew MS and *hammilḥāmōt* in another emphasize the particular difficulty rather than solve it.

[b]Reading *raglāw* with G for K of MT *raglō*, Q *raglāy*.

Yahweh my God has given me relief from all around; there is no adversary nor baneful mischance. [5]So here I propose to build a temple for the name of Yahweh my God just as Yahweh spoke to David my father saying, Your son whom I shall put after you upon your throne, he shall build the temple for my name. [6]So now give the order that they may fell for me cedars[a] from Lebanon, and let my subjects be with your subjects, and I shall give you the hire of your subjects, just as you say, for you know that there is none among us skilled in tree-felling like the Sidonians. [7]And it happened that, when Hiram heard the words of Solomon, he was very glad and said, Blessed be Yahweh[b] today in that he has given David a wise son (to be) over this great people. [8]And Hiram sent to Solomon saying, I have heard (the message) which you have sent to me; I shall do all that you desire in the matter of the cedar trees and fir trees. [9]My subjects[c] shall bring them down[d] from Lebanon to the sea and I shall make them into tow-rafts that I may bring them[e] to wherever you direct me and shall break them up there and you shall take them up, and you for your part do what I want and give me food for my household. [10]So Hiram would give Solomon cedar trees and fir trees, as many as he wanted. [11]And Solomon gave Hiram twenty thousand *kors* of wheat as food[f] for his household and twenty thousand *baths*[g] of pure olive oil, so much would Solomon give Hiram year by year. [12]And Yahweh gave Solomon wisdom according as he had said to him, and there was concord between Hiram and Solomon, and the two of them made a covenant.

5.1. 'Hiram' is an abbreviation of Ahiram ('My brother is exalted'), which is the name of a king of Byblos *c.* 1200 BC, whose inscribed sarcophagus was found at Byblos. Tyre was the most famous of the Phoenician settlements on the shore of Syria in the second millennium. The ancient settlement was on the mainland, but the main settlement in historical times was on a rocky island half a mile off shore,[h] and its empire was a mercantile one, its merchants founding Carthage in the latter half of the ninth century. In 333 it was reduced

[a]G reads *ʿēṣīm* (trees) for MT *ʾarāzīm*.

[b]G[BA] reads 'God' (*ʾelōhīm*) for MT *yhwh*, it being thought inappropriate for an alien to admit the power of Yahweh.

[c]It is suggested, though on no authority of MSS or versions, that *ʿabādekā* ('your subjects') should be read here. The handling of heavy timber, however, was as much a province of the Phoenicians as felling it.

[d]Reading *yōrīdūm* with G for MT *yōrīdū*, the final *m* having been omitted by haplography before the initial *m* in the following word.

[e]Reading *waʾabīʾēm* for MT *bayyām*, which G[BL] omit.

[f]Reading *maʾakōlet* for MT *makkōlet*, as suggested by G[A], which reads *maʾakāl*.

[g]Reading *ʿeśrīm ʾelep bat* with G for MT *ʿeśrīm kōr, kōr* being a dry measure, unlike *bat*, which was a liquid measure.

[h]Actually four stades, Q. Curtius, IV 2.

by Alexander the Great, who built a mole from the mainland. This caused sanding up so that the place is today not an island but a peninsula. In the time of Solomon, Tyre was a rising power and was soon to dominate its sister city Sidon and the whole of southern Phoenicia. Hiram had entered into friendly relations with David soon after his establishment in Jerusalem as king over all Israel, and had supplied the materials and artisans to build his palace (II Sam. 5.11). Doubtless Hiram was anxious to conciliate the new power which now held command of the vital trade-routes through Palestine and could supply important agricultural commodities to supplement the limited resources of the narrow Phoenician littoral (cf. Acts 12.20 and the inscription of Eshmunazzar of Sidon, which records the gift by 'the lord of kings' [of Persia] of corn-lands in the Plain of Sharon).[a] Such an exchange of greetings at the accession of a king was a regular courtesy in the ancient Near East. Here it was a convenient prelude to negotiations for mutual advantages.

5.3. Solomon's reason for David's not building the Temple was preoccupation with war. In II Sam 7.12ff., however, in the passage concerning Nathan's oracle, which is actually cited now, no mention is made of war as the prevention of David's building the Temple, and, in fact, it is said that he had relief from war (II Sam. 7.1). Yet another reason is adduced in I Chron. 22.8ff.; 28.2ff., namely that David's hands were stained with blood. The statement of Kings has the most authentic ring.

'Putting under the soles of the feet' is a common and most natural expression for subjection, e.g. Ps. 110.1, '. . . until I make your enemies your footstool'. The allusion is to the gesture of the victor setting his foot on the neck of his prostrate enemy.

4. Note the use of *śāṭān* as a common noun here and in Num. 22.22; I Sam. 29.4; II Sam. 19.22[23]; I K. 11.25. The noun is used with the definite article to denote 'the adversary' *par excellence*, the public prosecutor in the heavenly court in Job 1.6ff. and Zech. 3.1–2, which is translated in Greek as *ho diabolos* ('the devil' of the New Testament). Eventually in the late passage in I Chron. 21.1 (cf. II Sam. 24.1) the word becomes a proper noun without the article, Satan, who prompts David to take a census of Israel. From this point onwards until the Christian era Satan, the Adversary of man, is a common figure in Jewish apocalyptic.

5. The verb *'āmar* generally means 'to say' in Hebrew; the Arabic

[a] G. A. Cooke, *NSI*, no. 5, 18ff.

cognate means 'to order'. Occasionally in Hebrew the meaning, as here, is 'to think' or 'intend'.

The 'name', which in Semitic practice had usually some reference to the circumstances of one's birth or anticipated one's future, had a much greater significance for the Israelite than for moderns. It was a manifestation or reflection of one's personality, one's *alter ego*. The name of God signified the actual divine presence, which might be invoked or addressed. Christian theology, as Montgomery (ICC, on 8.16) points out, would regard the 'name of God' in ancient Israel as one person of the Godhead. Canaanite thought was also conscious of the paradox between the transcendent deity and the deity whose presence might be invoked and addressed, as is indicated by the term *šm bʿl* in the Ras Shamra text *UT* 127.56 and *pᵉnē baʿal* ('presence', lit. 'face' of B.) on coins of Ashkelon in the Roman imperial period.[a] The reference to Yahweh by his 'name' is Deuteronomic and represents a refinement of thought since the anthropomorphism of J.[b]

The presumption of man's provision of a temple for God is felt to demand the sanction of a special divine oracle, which is the theme of the passage on the Davidic covenant in II Sam. 7.4ff., which is invoked here. Gudea of Lagash in the second half of the third millennium BC felt the same diffidence, and was encouraged to proceed only after the interpretation of an elaborate dream.[c] Another such work was undertaken by Nabonidus in the Neo-Babylonian period after such oracles by Shamash, Adad, and Nergal.[d]

5.6. 'And now . . .' is the regular introduction to the substance of a letter after the preliminary greetings.

We agree with Noth (*Könige*, p. 91) that *'erez*, though perhaps generally denoting the cedar, which was the pride of Lebanon, is not particularly adapted, as a branching tree with a comparatively short trunk, for rough building, for which pine would be more suitable. It may be that the Cilician pine is visualized here. This long-trunked timber, however, is specifically mentioned in v. 23, so that we may retain 'cedar', which was to be used rather for panelling.

[a] G. F. Hill, *A Catalogue of the Greek Coins of Palestine in the British Museum*, 1914, pp. lxiff.

[b] On the theological implications of the 'name' of Yahweh, particularly as denoting God's accessible presence in the Temple, see von Rad, *Studies in Deuteronomy*, 1953, pp. 37ff.

[c] T. Jacobsen, *Before Philosophy*, 1949, pp. 205f.

[d] H. Frankfort, *Kingship and the Gods*, 1948, pp. 269–71.

In view of the numbers involved, *ʿabādīm* here indicates subjects in general rather than serfs on crown lands and in the recently incorporated Canaanite cities, or feudal retainers, to which the term might properly apply. The administrative texts from the palace at Ras Shamra demonstrate a feudal system where crown lands carried burdens of personal service, see esp. the Akkadian administrative texts from the palace.[a] Tyre, too, had this system, no doubt, but it was a novelty in Israel and was the eventual cause of the revolt of the North from the house of David.

'The Sidonians', denoting Hiram's subjects, reflects conditions somewhat later than the time of Solomon, when Sidon was subject to Tyre; cf. I K. 16.31, where Jezebel's father is designated 'King of the Sidonians'.[b]

5.9. As the position of the subject *ʿabāday* indicates, Hiram rejects Solomon's proposal that Israelites should be employed in the Lebanon, and undertakes all responsibility for felling and transport of the timber to the coast and to Palestine. This must modify the statement in the appendix in vv. 13–18, especially in v. 14.

The word *dōberōt* ('tow-rafts') is the participle of a denominative verb, 'to follow', cf. Arabic *dubr*, 'the back'. This is also the derivation of *debīr* 'inmost shrine'. The parallel account in II Chron. 2.15 specifies Joppa as the port of landing. We should perhaps particularize more specifically since B. Maisler's excavation of *Tell Qasīleh* on the River Jarkon (*Nahr al-ʿAwjā*) on the northern ourskirts of Tel Aviv, where two inscribed potsherds found on the surface of the mound indicate that it was an entrepot of foreign trade about two centuries after the time of Solomon.[c]

11. The provisions asked by Hiram 'for his household' were probably for those engaged in the lumbering and transport, whose maintenance while on public works was provided from the king's commissariat. Solomon now agreed to defray those expenses and so relieve the economic burden on the resources of the realm, which were limited (see note on v. 1). Nevertheless, the excessive amount. if not exaggeration in oral tradition, and the fine quality of the oil suggests that the commodities were probably, as Šanda suggests, for

[a]J. Nougayrol, *Mission de Ras Shamra VI. Le palais royal d'Ugarit III, Textes accadiens et hourrites des archives est, ouest, et centrales*, 1955.

[b]In Josephus he is correctly styled 'King of Tyrians and Sidonians', *Ant.* VIII, 13.1.

[c]B. Maisler, *The Excavation at Tell Qasile. A Preliminary Report*, 1951.

export. In 'pure olive oil' (lit. beaten olive oil; cf. Ex. 27.20; Num. 27.5) the olives were beaten by hand-pestle in a mortar. The crushing of the olives in large cylindrical stone presses mixed pulverized stones with oil, which in consequence was less pure than that from the hand-mortar.

5.12. This is a good illustration of the primary meaning of *šālōm*. Since there was no question of war between Israel and Tyre the meaning 'peace' has little point here. The word indicates primarily 'wholeness', hence our translation 'concord'. As von Rad emphasizes,[a] a social relationship is denoted, conditions of well-being, security, and peace being secondary to the social relationship. The phrase *kārat b^e^rīt*, lit. 'cut a covenant', refers to the sacrifice by which a covenant was ratified. The ritual of the covenant may be reflected in Abraham's sacrifice in Gen. 15.9–17, where Abraham divided sacrificial animals, and fire and smoke symbolizing Yahweh's presence passed between the pieces, and a covenant was made (v. 18). Another explanation of the verb is suggested in Jer. 34.18ff., where the parties lay themselves under the adjuration to be severed as the sacrifice if they break the covenant.

(ii) THE CORVÉE IN ISRAEL IN PREPARATION FOR THE BUILDINGS OF SOLOMON: 5.13–18[27–32]

This passage seems to be a continuation of the preceding account of the agreement between Solomon and Hiram, but being more detailed, it may be closer to archival sources. Montgomery, in urging the archival origin of the statistics of this passage, apart from vv. 15f., which are certainly secondary (see below on vv. 15f.), cites royal inscriptions noting the vast amount of provisions for workmen engaged on the construction of the famous Maʿrib dam in the Yemen, which indicates a concentration of labour analogous to that here described as a subject of official record. In view of the implication of v. 9, v. 14 is suspect as a later expansion.

5 13And king Solomon levied forced labour from all[b] Israel, and the corvée consisted of thirty thousand men. 14And he sent them to Lebanon, ten thousand a month in relays, one month they were in

[a] *TWNT* II, pp. 400–5.

[b] The phrase *wayyaʿal mas mikkol-yiśrāʾēl*, lit. 'and he imposed forced labour from all I.', is not unintelligible provided that *wayyaʿal mas* is understood as 'and he called up'. The variant in about twenty Hebrew MSS *ʿal* ('upon') for *min* ('from'), however, is to be seriously considered.

Lebanon and[a] two months they were at home,[b] and Adoniram was in charge of the corvée. [15]And Solomon had seventy thousand porters and eighty thousand quarrying in the hill-country, [16]apart from the officers of Solomon's prefects who were in charge of the work, 3,300[c] who had control over the people who laboured in the work. [17]And at the king's order they quarried great stones, split stones to lay the foundation of the Temple, dressed stones. [18]And the builders of Solomon and Hiram hewed them and dressed their edges,[d] and prepared the timber and the stones for the building of the Temple.

5.13. On the levy for forced labour (*mas*) see note on 4.6. On the relative numbers involved see n.[c] below. This statement that the levy was 'from all Israel' to the extent of 30,000 men is apparently contradicted by 9.20–22, where the Israelites are exempted, being reserved for military service. The language of the relevant passages, however, must be carefully noted. In 5.13[27] it is stated that Solomon subjected all Israel to the corvée (*mas*); in 11.28 it is said that Jeroboam had charge over 'all the *sēbel* of the House of Joseph'. The significance of *sēbel* in this context is uncertain, and it is safer to take it literally as 'porter service' (so Noth, *Könige, ad loc.*) after the obvious meaning in Ps. 81.6[7] and Neh. 4.10[11], where it denotes labourers to the skilled masons. In 9.22 it is stated that no Israelite was made a serf (*ʿebed*) as distinct from the non-Israelites in the kingdom who were subject to state servitude, *mas ʿōbēd* (9.21). We should probably distinguish between *mas ʿōbēd*, permanent serfdom, or liability to the corvée, which applied to non-Israelites, and *mas*, occasional regimentation after the Canaanite system, but *ad hoc*, as in Solomon's public works in Jerusalem, to which Israelites were exceptionally subjected, but which did not involve the status of serfdom. It has been suggested (Fichtner, *op. cit.*, p. 99) that 9.22 is an aside by the Deuteronomist, who found it inconceivable that Israelites should be relegated to serfdom. Deut. 17.14–20, however,

[a]Reading with many Hebrew MSS *ûšᵉnayim*; others lack the conjunction.

[b]Assuming a dittography of *w* in *bᵉbētō* and reading *babbayit*, cf. G, which reads *bᵉbētām* ('in their homes').

[c]The 3,300 supervising officers is at variance with the much more reasonable 550 of 9.23. Assuming the latter to be original, the number in the present verse is obviously the result of editorial calculation after a secondary reading of the numbers of Solomon's labourers as 150,000 (v. 15) added to the 30,000 of v.13. The ratio of supervising officers to labourers is then 3,300 : 180,000, exactly the same as 550 : 30,000, one officer to between 50 and 55 men. Thus vv. 15ff. in their present form are secondary.

[d]Reading *wayyagbīlūm* for MT *wᵉhaggiblīm* ('and the Giblites'), the position of which in MT makes it suspect. G^B apprehended a verb here in which it conjectured 'cast down' (*ebalan*), a *pis aller*, see commentary.

without specifically mentioning the corvée, obviously visualizes this feature of absolutism (esp. v. 20). We suggest that 9.22 combines two facets of the truth, that Israelites were not subject to permanent serfdom like non-Israelite subjects, and that military service was reserved for them.[a]

5.14. The word *ḥ^a^lîpôt*, here used adverbially, is from the same root as the Arabic *ḫalīfa* (Caliph), lit. 'successor' (i.e. of Muhammad). The singular is used in Job 14.14 as a military term signifying 'relief from duty' (*ṣābā'*).

15. Besides the labour-gangs stated to be in Lebanon there were, according to these verses, porters and quarrymen working in the hill-country, i.e. the limestone hills of Palestine. The local stone varies in colour and hardness, some very easily cut, but hardening on exposure to the weather. The verb *ḥāṣab* denotes the splitting of blocks from the living rock rather than the more skilled operation of hewing or dressing (*pāsal*). Only the timber was procured from Lebanon, Palestine providing the stone which was dressed by Israelite and Phoenician craftsmen.

16. *śārē hanniṣṣābîm* is doubtful. In view of the large number, even accepting 550 of 9.23, to which the present passage is certainly secondary, the subordinates seem certainly *śārîm*, these apparently being under Solomon's district prefects (*niṣṣābîm*), of 4.7ff., who thus also had responsibility for a census for labour conscription (so Noth, *op. cit.*, p. 93).

17. The causative form of the root *nāsa'* is found in the sense 'to quarry' in Eccl. 10.9; I K. 6.7. In the phrase *'abānîm yeqārôt* (EVV 'costly stones'), the root *yāqar* is probably a cognate of the Arabic verb *waqara*, 'to split', with an Ethiopic cognate of the same meaning.

18. The verb *pāsal*, 'to hew', is commonly used of the chiselling of a graven image (*pesel*).

If the MT is correct, *haggiblîm* would denote the men of Gebal, the famous Phoenician city of Byblos, which was known as a timber port to the Egyptians as early as *c.* 3000, cf. the bronze axe-head with the name and title of Cheops belonging to an Egyptian lumber-gang found at the mouth of the *Nahr Ibrāhîm* near Byblos.[b] The site,

[a]See further I. Mendelsohn, 'State Slavery in Ancient Palestine', *BASOR* 85, 1942, pp. 14–17.

[b]A. Rowe, *A Catalogue of Egyptian Scarabs . . . in the Palestine Archaeological Museum*, 1936, Addendum A, p. 283.

intensively excavated, is *Jubeil*, just 20 miles north of Beirut. This would be the only reference to the men of Gebal as stone-masons. G (see p. 155 n.[d]) reads the word as a verb 'and they threw them', which sounds like a despairing transliteration of a Hebrew verb. Following this clue, Thenius suggested *wayyagbīlūm*, 'and they provided them with borders', a reference to the margin-drafted masonry, which archaeology attests as a Phoenician feature, with the function of facilitating the marking, dressing and fitting of the blocks. A good example is the fortification of the citadel of Samaria under Omri and Ahab.[a]

(iii) THE BUILDING OF THE TEMPLE AND RELATED PUBLIC BUILDINGS: 6.1–7.51

The most striking feature of this section is the contrast between the detail in which the Temple and its fittings are described (6.2–36; 7.13–51) and the vagueness of the description of the palace complex (7.1–12). This suggests that the writer was more familiar with, or more interested in, the Temple than the palace, and was probably a priest. The ultimate source of the description of the Temple and its furniture has been thought to be the Temple archives,[b] but we might expect an account based on these to be much clearer and more coherent than chs. 6f. Noting that the focus of attention is on measurements (vv. 2, 3, 6a, 10a, 16a, 17a, 20a, 23b, 24–26), materials (vv. 7, 9b, 10b, 15, 16a, 20b, 21b, 23a, 31a, 32a, 33, 34a, 35b, 36) and technique (vv. 7, 9b, 10b, 29a, 32b, 35b, 36), rather than on the more generally interesting and important details of site, orientation, foundations, thickness of walls, method of roofing and general appearance, and that this matter is largely arranged according to materials used, Noth[c] makes the interesting suggestion that the account of the Temple in ch. 6 was based on the oral tradition of instructions to the various craftsmen, which was eventually included in the annals of Solomon's reign in the general form in which the Deuteronomistic historian has included it in chs. 6f. This most feasible suggestion would certainly account for the obviously incomplete source-material, the many technical terms which have so often been misunderstood by the compiler and later glossators, and would

[a]J. W. Crowfoot, K. M. Kenyon, E. L. Sukenik, *Samaria-Sebaste I, The Buildings*, 1942, pp. 18–20, pl. 32, 2.
[b]Eissfeldt, *The Old Testament. An Introduction*, p. 289.
[c]Noth, *Könige*, pp. 104–6.

admirably account for the remarkable fact that the statement of the foundation and actual building comes at the end (vv. 37f.), after which 6.1 has been adapted by the compiler as an introduction. The furnishing of the Temple also (7.13–50) shows a similar construction. This becomes the basis for a description of the Temple which, however, was restricted by the limitations of the source and is still deficient in significant detail, partly because of actual ignorance of technicalities and features which never visualized a description for the benefit of those like ourselves to whom details were important.

The Deuteronomistic redactor added his editorial heading in 6.1, adapted from 6.37, with the significant schematic dating 480 years after the Exodus, and other obvious asides, e.g. 6.11–14, where with regard to the whole theme of the Deuteronomistic History, he recapitulates on Nathan's oracles and the Davidic covenant (II Sam. 7.12ff.; so also 6.7, cf. Deut. 27.5).

A theme like the Temple was bound to attract accretions, and such post-Deuteronomistic matter may be observed in 6.18. Eissfeldt in fact maintains[a] that additions in MT as compared with G indicate that overworking continued beyond the time that Kings was completed in G (before *c.* 190 BC), but after the evidence from Qumran for Hebrew texts of Samuel from the third century BC (see above, p. 4), near to G but both more and less full than MT, this does not follow.

The parallel passage on the Temple in II Chron. 3.1–14 is of little use in the evaluation of the account in Kings, since it is not independent, but itself based on the Kings passage, while visualizing the Second Temple. Nor is Ezekiel's description of the temple (Ezek. 40–42) in his visionary blueprint of the new Jerusalem of much help in solving the problem of the obscure technical details in the construction of the First Temple, which nevertheless the prophet did visualize. But it is hardly to be supposed that there had been no developments in the structure and decoration of the Temple in the four centuries since Solomon's building.

The description of the palace-complex (7.1–12) is placed by G at the end of the description of the Temple furnishings (7.51) on the assumption that palace and Temple were distinct. Josephus also reserves this description until after the dedication of the Temple.[b] Wellhausen, however, followed by Eissfeldt,[c] contended for the order

[a] *HSAT*, p. 504.
[b] *Ant.*, VIII 5.1–2.
[c] *HSAT*, p. 504.

in the MT, and he is undoubtedly right since palace and Temple belonged to the same complex, directly communicating, as Ezekiel (43.7ff.) objected, the point of contiguity being the great court, sometimes called 'the outer court' of the Temple and sometimes called 'the middle court', with reference to the Temple and palace (II K. 20.4; 23.12). Here, however, in contrast to the passage on the Temple furnishings, the writer confines himself practically to the bare structural features, as in the House of the Forest of Lebanon (7.2–5), the Hall of Pillars (v. 6) and the Hall of the Tribunal (v.7); the private quarters of the palace and the palace of Pharaoh's daughter are barely noted as being 'of the same construction' (v. 8), with a general note on the masonry of the whole (vv. 9–12). The more detailed account of this matter, as in the account of the House of the Forest of Lebanon and the two halls, was probably based on annals of Solomon's reign, but the mere note on the two palaces may reflect the alteration of the royal palace in the course of history and the disappearance of the palace of Pharaoh's daughter.

(*a*) *Late chronological gloss*: 6.1. *Editorial introduction, adapting* 6.37 *from the annalistic source*

The character of this is betrayed by the conventional figure 480, which may either be suggested by the number of the tribes of Israel, multiplied by 40, the conventional length of a generation, or the period from the fourth year of Solomon, reckoning on the duration of reigns in Kings (430) and adding 50 years from 586 to the return from Exile under Zerubbabel, the foundation of the Temple being considered the middle point of the history of Israel from the Exodus to that date. G reads 440 for MT 480, probably representative of the 11 generations (each 40 years) which intervened between Aaron and Zadok (I Chron. 5.29) reckoning inclusively. Another indication of the late date of this passage is the numbering of the months according to the Babylonian system from the Spring New Year, the word *ḥōdeš* for 'month' being much later than *yeraḥ* (6.37ff.; 8.2, and the Gezer calendar from the tenth century BC). This note on the month is obviously a late interpolation in the verse, breaking the natural sequence between *baššānā hārebî'ît* and *limlōk šelōmō*.

6 1 And it came to pass in the four hundred and eightieth year[a] from the Exodus of the Israelites from the land of Egypt, in the fourth

[a]G^BA read 440; see critical introduction to this section.

year of Solomon's reign over Israel in [a]the month of Ziv, that is[a] the second month, that he built the Temple to Yahweh.

6.1. In contrast to the dating according to the regnal year of Solomon and the citation of the months (lit. 'moons') Ziv and Bul (vv. 37ff.) in which the work was begun and completed, the date relative to the Exodus is not convincing (see critical introduction to this section). It has nevertheless been taken as the cardinal clue to the date of the Exodus by older orthodox scholars and by modern conservatives, who, assuming that Solomon acceded *c.* 960, arrive at a date *c.* 1440 BC for the Exodus. A date for the Exodus in the thirteenth century, however, accords much better with the political situation in Egypt in the XIXth Dynasty and in Palestine in the period of the Judges, and with archaeological data from the Delta, Palestine, and Transjordan. The dates of the accession of Solomon and David on the basis of their reigns of 40 years are open to suspicion owing to the conventional significance of 40. Thus, though we may calculate the death of Solomon accurately in 931, working back from the death of Ahab in 853,[b] the duration of Solomon's reign of 40 years seems an approximation and the precise date of his accession is therefore unknown. Josephus,[c] on the contrary, on the authority of Menander, who claims to cite a Tyrian king-list from the accession of Hiram to the foundation of Carthage, dates the foundation in the twelfth year of Hiram of Tyre, which E. Meyer[d] gives as *c.* 957, working on the basis of the foundation of Carthage in 814. This, however, does not accord with the date in the fourth year of Solomon's reign, unless the 40 years attributed to him include 10 years' co-regency with David and the foundation of the Temple was in Solomon's fourth year as sole king, which is possible. Working from a synchronism between a recently discovered text of Shalmaneser III[e] which cites Baʿli-ma-AN-zeri of Tyre as a tributary in 841 with Jehu of Israel and 'Belozorus', whom Menander notes as reigning six years after Ithobalos, the father of Jezebel, J. Liver[f] arrived at the date 825 for the founding of Carthage. Classical authorities differ on the date

[a]G omits, indicating a secondary gloss; see critical introduction.
[b]See Introduction, Chronology, pp. 70ff.
[c]*Contra Apionem* I, 18.
[d]*Geschichte des Altertums* 2.2, 1921–31, pp. 79ff.; so also M. B. Rowton, 'The Date of the Founding of Solomon's Temple', *BASOR* 119, 1950, pp. 20–22.
[e]F. Safar, 'A Further Text of Shalmaneser III', *Sumer* VII, 1951, pp. 11f.
[f]J. Liver, 'The Chronology of Tyre at the Beginning of the First Millennium BC', *IEJ* III, 1953, pp. 113–20.

of this event, but it may be noted that at least one, Pompeius Trogos, gives 825 BC, which, accepting the foundation of the Temple in the fourth of Solomon's 40 years, indicates a date 968/7 for the founding of the Temple. We may compare this chronological note with that in v. 37a, which records the foundation of the Temple simply in the fourth year of the reign of Solomon (not 480 years after the Exodus) and in the month (*yeraḥ* not *ḥodeš*) of Ziv (not 'the second month', which dates from the vernal equinox, thereby betraying its editorial character from the Babylonian period). This suggests that v. 37 may be drawn directly from an early record.

(β) *Description of the structural features of the Temple*: 6.2–10

6 [2]Now the Temple which king Solomon built to Yahweh was sixty[a] cubits in length and twenty[b] in breadth and thirty[c] cubits in height, [3]and the vestibule before the nave of the Temple was twenty cubits in length along the front of the breadth of the Temple, its breadth (i.e. depth) along the front of the Temple being ten cubits. [4]And he made for the Temple windows of close lattice-work. [5]And he built against the wall of the Temple a platform[d] around[e] the nave and the back part, and he made storeys round about, [6]and the lowest storey[f] was five cubits in breadth, and the middle was six cubits in breadth, and the third was seven cubits in breadth, for he made rebatements in the Temple all round on the outside, so that (sc. the side-wings) were not bound into the walls of the house. [7]And the Temple when it was being built was built of complete stones, quarry hewn, and there was not heard any hammer or adze,[g] nor[h] any iron tool in the Temple when it was

[a]G[BL] reads 40, obviously excluding the back part, the inmost shrine (*d[e]bîr*), which was a cube of 20 cubits. G[A] and Josephus support MT.

[b]Five Hebrew MSS and G and S insert *'ammā* ('cubits'), which should probably be read in conformity with the next dimension, where *'ammā* is read after the number.

[c]G[BL] reads 25 for the height of the nave (*hêkāl*), though G[A] supports MT, and Josephus actually doubles the height. Since the inmost shrine (*d[e]bîr*) was a cube of 20 cubits, this would allow for an elevation of 5 cubits from the floor of the nave to that of the inmost shrine, unless indeed the roof of the latter was lower than the roof of the rest of the Temple. The comparative elevation of the floor of the inmost shrine would be in conformity with temple architecture in Palestine and Mesopotamia, though an elevation of 10 cubits would be excessive, as de Vaux points out (*Ancient Israel*, p. 314).

[d]Q *yāṣîa'* for MT *yāṣûa'*.

[e]Omitting MT *'et-qîrōt habbayit sābîb* ('the walls of the house around') as a gloss with G[BL] and T, as the grammatical structure of the sentence demands.

[f]Reading *haṣṣēlā'* with G, a reading confirmed by the feminine singular adjectives *taḥtōnā*, *tîkōnā*, and *š[e]lîšît*, instead of MT *hayyāṣîa'* ('the platform'), which is masculine.

[g]Omitting the definite article with G.

[h]Inserting the conjunction with certain Hebrew MSS, G and S.

being built. [8]And[a] the door of the lowest[b] storey was by the right fore-corner and by trap-doors men went up to[c] the middle storey, and from the middle one to the third.[d] [9]And he built the Temple and finished it and ceiled the Temple [e]in coffers and aligned beams[e] in cedar. [10]And he built the platform all round against the Temple, its height being five cubits, and it was bonded to the Temple by cedar beams.

6.2. The dimensions of the Temple, 60 by 20 cubits on the ground plan, inside measurement, strike us as comparatively modest in comparison with the House of the Forest of Lebanon, which is given as 100 by 50 cubits (7.2). The relative proportions and location of Solomon's palace and Temple are illustrated in the association of palace and temple in Mesopotamia and Syria, and particularly from the ninth-century level at *Tell Taināt*, where the temple is scarcely a quarter of the size of the palace. This shrine reproduces the tripartite plan, the proportions, and certain significant details of Solomon's Temple.[f] This has suggested that the Temple took its origin as a royal chapel. Certainly the association of the king with the Temple is not to be gainsaid in view of the freedom with which the kings of Judah introduced novel cultic features and removed others from the Temple area (e.g. Ahaz, Hezekiah, Manasseh, Josiah) and controlled Temple finance (e.g. Joash, Josiah). God and king were particularly closely associated as evidenced by the divine covenant with the house of David and by the reflection of the ideology of the kingship of God on the status of the king (e.g. Pss. 2, 110). In spite of his sacral status, however, the king was still, in the words of H. W. Robinson, a societary figure, who represented the whole community, so that the Temple had a public significance. We must never forget that, in spite of the fact that it was built as an adjunct to the palace and its administration was always under

[a]Inserting the conjunction with G and S.

[b]Reading *hattiḥtōnā* with G and T for MT *hattīkōnā* ('middle').

[c]Reading *'el* with certain Hebrew MSS and G, instead of MT *'al* ('upon'); cf. *infra*, *'el-haššelīšīt*.

[d]Reading *haššelīšīt* ('the third', fem. sing.) for MT *haššelīšīm* ('the thirds', masc. pl.) with certain Hebrew MSS, S and V.

[e]G[BL] omits the phrase *gēbīm ūśedērōt*, which is not without its problems, *gēbīm* in the sense of 'coffers', i.e. recessed panelling, being a *hapax legomenon*, and *śedērōt* a doubtful phonetic variant of *sedērōt* ('rows'), though *śedērōt* in this sense is apparently attested in II K. 11.8, 15.

[f]W. M. McEwan, 'The Syrian Expedition of the Oriental Institute of the University of Chicago', *Bulletin of the Oriental Institute of the University of Chicago*, 1937, no. 1, p. 13; *AJA* XLI, 1937, p. 9, fig. 4.

royal influence, the Temple was, as de Vaux emphasizes,[a] built to house the ark. As such it was the new amphictyonic shrine, where Israel expressed her solidarity, and as it was designed primarily for the simple ritual of such an occasion, the actual shrine was small, not being designed for a congregation, who were accommodated in the spacious open court. Of the actual building the nave (*hēkāl*) was reserved for cultic personnel and the side-wings for their accommodation and for the storing of equipment, offerings, and treasure. L. Waterman, in fact, regards the *hēkāl* primarily as a treasury, the cherubim in the *debīr* being originally only the guardian genii of the royal treasure.[b] Though we cannot agree, we admit that the side-adjuncts of the *hēkāl* were used partly for this purpose, but the main reason for the comparatively modest proportions of the Temple was that the main part of the cult at which the public assisted was in the open court, reducing the role of the building to the minimum, as the repository of the ark and dedicated offerings.

The cubit (*'ammā*) was the distance from the tip of the elbow to the tip of the middle finger. This gives a mean distance of a foot and a half. R. B. Y. Scott[c] has deduced from the specification in the inscription in the Siloam tunnel that the official cubit in Israel, as distinct from the natural cubit ('the cubit of a man', Deut. 3.11), was derived from the Egyptian cubit of 17·7″, and was 17·5″. On this basis the modest dimensions of Solomon's Temple were 87′ 6″ long, 29′ 2″ wide and 43′ 9″ high, possibly excluding the vestibule (*'ūlām*), which measured 10 cubits in depth (see on v. 3) and the back-chamber, or inmost shrine (*debīr*), which was a cube of 20 cubits (v. 20).

6.3. *'ūlām*, which is merely transliterated in LXX, is translated by Symmachus as *propulon* and by Josephus as *pronaion*. Etymologically the word would seem to be derived from a root *'wl*, 'to be in front', cf. Arabic *'awala*, 'to be first'. The transliteration of LXX, *ailam*, suggests the form *'ēlām*, which is read in MT of Ezek. 40. This has suggested the Akkadian cognate *ellamu*, but, as Ezek. 8.16 and II Chron. 3.4 read *'ūlām*, this is probably the correct form of the word, *'ēlām* of Ezek. 40 being a scribal corruption owing to the similarity of *w* and *y*, as in the Qumran MSS. *hēkal habbayit*, which is to be pre-

[a] *Ancient Israel*, pp. 320ff.; so also Noth, *Könige*, p. 192.

[b] 'The Damaged "Blueprints" of the Temple', *JNES* II, 1943, pp. 284–94.

[c] R. B. Y. Scott, 'Weights and Measures of the Bible', *BA* XXII, 1959, pp. 24–26, 39f.

ferred to *hēkāl* alone (G and V), indicates that *hēkāl*, Sumerian *egallu*, 'the great house', refers to the main hall, or nave, of the Temple rather than the whole. The length, *'orkō*, is given in the MT as 20 cubits 'along the front of the breadth of the house' (*'al-pᵉnē rōḥab habbayit*), 'its breadth (*roḥbō*, i.e. its depth) all along the front of the house' being 10 cubits. The difficulty of this statement is that *rōḥab* is apparently used in different senses in the one passage. Josephus, however, states that the length (i.e. projection from the front of the *hēkāl*) was 20 cubits, *and so it was ordered that it might agree with the breadth of the house*, a statement which agrees with LXX, the breadth of the vestibule being omitted as unnecessary after the statement that it was flush with the side-walls of the *hēkāl*. Possibly *'eśer* ('ten') is a corruption of *'eśrīm* ('twenty'), though this is not attested in any Hebrew MS.

6.4. The words *'ᵃṭūmīm* and *šᵉqūpīm* are both passive participles of verbal roots, meaning respectively 'to stop up' (lips, Prov. 17.28; ears, Prov. 21.13; Isa. 33.15) or 'contract', and 'to look' or 'peep' (through a window, e.g. Jezebel, II K. 9.30, 32). The latter, however, may be derived from a root cognate with the Arab. *saqīfa*, 'a rib, plank, or splint', hence 'slatted'. G gives us no help, and Josephus does not even mention windows. G^L reads *dediktuomenas*, 'netted, latticed', which would support our suggestion 'slatted'. S reads 'windows open and closed', T specifying 'open inside and closed outside', which is obviously understood by V, *obliquas fenestras*, i.e. embrasured windows, so AV and RV (margin). Whether we regard the windows as latticed or embrasured, or both, the purpose is the same, to admit air and to tone down the heat and strong light.

5. See p. 161 n.[d]. The problematic word is *yāṣīa'*, which is generally taken as a side-wing. There is no good philological ground for this assumption, which is really based upon the occurrence of the word with the following adjectives 'lowest, middle, and third' in v. 6, which refers obviously to three storeys. On our reading *ṣēlā'* (G *pleura*) for *yāṣīa'* in v. 6 see p. 161 n.[f], *ṣēlā'* being the technical term for 'storey' in vv. 6 and 8. This being so, *yāṣīa'* is the squared platform on which the storeyed side-wings were built. The word, which means 'bed' in Gen. 49.4, cf. Isa. 14.11 (*taḥtekā yuṣṣa' rimmā*) has an Arabic cognate *waḍa'a*, 'to lay, found', which is specifically used of the levelling off of a foundation for a building. Noth (*op. cit.*, p. 112) thinks rather of the levelling off of the tops of the walls for roofing. The height of this feature is given in v. 10 as 5 cubits, which was also the height of each of the three storeys in the side-wings, which excludes the possibility that *yāṣīaʿ* denotes the side-wing.

6.6. The fact that a total rebatement of 3 cubits in the wall of the Temple was possible gives us a rough idea, the only indication, of the thickness of the wall. The religious interest of the writer is apparent here, since he is so careful to dissociate the Temple from the storage or service chambers in the side-wings. The word for rebatements, *migrāʿōt*, is derived from a root *gāraʿ*, which is well attested in the sense 'to diminish' (e.g. the tally of bricks in Egypt, Ex. 5.8, 19) or 'to withdraw' (e.g. an inheritance, Num. 36.3). The verb *'āḥaz*, lit. 'to hold on to', means 'to be bonded into', the floors and the ceilings of the side chambers being of cedar beams resting on the rebatements. De Vaux[a] suggests that the side-chambers (*ṣelāʿōt*) were added at a later stage, when they and the platform (*yāṣīaʿ*) were together termed *yāṣīaʿ*, but the fact that on the completion of the Temple Solomon deposited treasure (7.51) indicates that these side-chambers for storage were part of the original conception.

7. This is a Deuteronomistic note interrupting the description of the Temple; see critical introduction to this section. The prohibition against the use of iron in constructing the altar (Ex. 20.25; Deut. 27.5; Josh. 8.31) is a long-standing taboo in the religion of Israel, reflecting at once the jealous monopoly of the art of working the metal by the early smiths and the Philistines, who had learned the secret in the days when they and their kindred peoples served the Hittites as mercenaries, and the superstitious fear, perhaps deliberately fostered, of the people who did not possess the secret. This dread is reflected in Celtic folk-lore, where iron is a potent prophylactic against the 'little folk'. 'Complete stones' (*'eben šelēmā*) is possibly a compromise with the principle of the construction of the rude altar in Josh. 8.31. In the construction of the Temple, however, the stones, as the following *massāʿ* indicates, were actually hewn, though not at the building site. On *massāʿ* see on 5.31. *garzen*, which Montgomery translates as 'saw', is rather a type of adze or transverse axe (G *pelekus*). The word *ḫrzn*, read tentatively on an inscribed adze-head at Ras Shamra, was the first clue to the decipherment of the new alphabetic cuneiform script. *barzel*, like the names of various minerals and stones in the Ras Shamra texts, is of non-Semitic and Anatolian origin. The art of working terrestrial iron ore had been known and jealously guarded by the Hittite Empire until the barbarian mercen-

[a] *Op. cit.*, p. 315.

aries of the Hittites learned the secret of the weapons they used and broke the Hittite economic monopoly and political empire at the beginning of the twelfth century. This inaugurated an economic and political revolution in the Near East, resulting in the growth of small independent nations and marking the end of the great empires of antiquity until the rise of Assyria. In the interim the small empire of David and Solomon was founded.

6.8. The right 'fore-corner' (*ketep*, lit. 'shoulder') is vague, meaning either 'right' or 'south', and varying in significance and location according as the prospect was from without or within the Temple. Ezek. 41.11, incidentally, mentions not one, but two entrances from *inside* the nave to the side-chambers, which would be in the interests of greater security, as Waterman[a] suggests. In support of this theory Waterman emphasizes that no door is described in connection with this entrance. In view of the many omissions of quite significant architectural details in the description of the Temple (e.g. roofing, thickness of walls, position, number, and disposal of windows), we cannot press this point, but agree with Waterman that the entrance to the side-chambers was from within. The access to the two upper storeys of the side-chambers raises another problem, that of the meaning of *lūlīm*. For this word, which is a *hapax legomenon* in the Old Testament, G gives *heliktē anabasis* and V *cochlea* (lit. 'snail'), both meaning a spiral staircase. This suggests the Arabic root *lawiya*, 'to be coiled', and is therefore not etymologically impossible. This feature is found in an eighteenth-century palace excavated by Sir Leonard Woolley at Atchana,[b] which removes the objection of B. Stade[c] that, since a spiral, or newel, staircase was unknown in the ancient East, we must visualize a series of trap-doors in the side-chambers of the Temple. We believe, nevertheless, that trap-doors should be visualized, since this is certainly the meaning of *lūlīm* in post-biblical Hebrew.

The ceiling, *sippūn*,[d] may also have served as roofing. The use of cedar beams for roofing, apparently laid horizontally, is well attested in Assyrian and Babylonian inscriptions, e.g. Esarhaddon.[e] This method of roofing must have limited the size of the Temple. 'Coffers'

[a] *JNES* II, 1943, p. 287.
[b] Sir L. Woolley, *AJ* XIX, 1939, p. 14.
[c] *ZAW* III, 1883, pp. 150ff.
[d] Cf. Jer. 22.14; Hag. 1.4; and the Phoenician inscription of Yeḥawmilk of Byblos (fifth century BC), G. A. Cooke, *NSI*, no. 3.6.
[e] Luckenbill, *ARA* II, § 653.

is the technical term for recessed panelling, a style of ceiling suggested by V (*laquear*). *gēbīm* means 'pits', hence 'depressions', e.g. II K. 3.16, of the ditches dug at the suggestion of Elisha in the Moabite campaign. The word is well attested in Akkadian *gubbu* and Arabic *jubb* with the meaning 'well', cf. Arabic *jawba*, 'depression', but as a *hapax legomenon* in the Old Testament it is suspect. On *śᵉdērōt* see textual note. In II K. 11.8, 15 it denotes apparently files of soldiers.

6.10. This verse raises difficult problems. If *yāṣīaʿ* refers, as above, to the platform on which the Temple was built, there seems little probability that it was bound into the Temple by timber. The verse reads as if it were displaced from v. 5, where it was an elaboration.

Deuteronomistic side-note: 6.11–14

This abrupt notice of a divine oracle to Solomon confirming Nathan's oracle to David (II Sam. 7.12ff.), and making the stability of dynasty and Temple conditional upon obedience to the will of God, is a theological interpolation into the factual account of the building and furnishing of the Temple, a conclusion which is confirmed by the fact that the Greek versions omit the passage. It has been taken by Burney to emanate from the P editor, but the language is rather that of the Deuteronomist. The reference to the permanence of the Davidic line (v. 12) suggests a revision from the D standpoint before 586 BC, and seems to preclude so late a hand as P, by which time the line of David was superseded by the Zadokite high-priesthood. This note culminating in v. 14, which repeats the statement of v. 9a that Solomon completed the actual building of the shrine, serves to mark that stage in the work, before the description of the fittings and furnishings (vv. 15ff.).

6 [11]And the word of Yahweh came to Solomon saying, [12]Concerning this Temple which you are building, if you walk in my statutes and carry out my judgments and keep all my commandments to walk in them, then shall I establish my word with you, which I spoke unto David your father, [13]and I shall dwell among the children of Israel and not forsake my people Israel. [14]So Solomon built the Temple and completed it.

(γ) *Interior fittings and decoration of the Temple*: 6.15–22

This passage is disjointed, with many repetitions and elaborations of the same basic detail, suggesting later additions and glosses, probably reflecting the pious antiquarian interest occasionally apparent in P. This has been admirably conveyed at a glance by the arrangement in Montgomery (ICC), which we follow in the main.

Primary	*Secondary*
6 [15]And he built the walls of the Temple within with cedar lining; from the floor of the Temple to the rafters[a] of the ceiling he lined it with wood within, and overlaid the floor of the shrine with fir-planks.	18 And cedar was over the shrine on the inside, carved work of gourds and flower-calyxes; the whole was cedar, no stone being seen.
[16]And he built up twenty cubits in the innermost part[b] of the shrine with cedar lining from the floor to the rafters,[a] and he constructed it within as an inner shrine. [17]And forty cubits was[d] the nave in front of the innermost shrine.[e] [20]And[f] the inner shrine was twenty cubits in length, and twenty cubits in breadth, and its height was twenty cubits, and he overlaid it with fine	19 And an inner shrine in the Temple he prepared to house[c] therein the ark of the covenant of Yahweh. 16b as the holy of holies.
gold, and he made[g] an altar of cedar. [22]And he overlaid the whole Temple with gold, and the whole shrine was completely overlaid.[i]	21 And Solomon overlaid the Temple within with refined gold, and he put chains[h] of gold in front of the inner shrine, and overlaid it with gold.

6.15. *mibbay^{e}tā*, omitted in G[BL], has been suspected by certain commentators, though it seems necessary, meaning 'within'. The form without final *ā* would be more normal, as later in the same verse and in v. 16. *ṣippā* means properly 'to overlay', cf. *ṣapīt* (a cloth or carpet spread for entertainment), Isa. 21.5. Here it means 'to line' a perpendicular wall; in 15b it refers to wood-flooring, which was of

[a]Reading *qōrōt* with G for MT *qīrōt* ('walls').

[b]Reading Q *miyyark^{e}tē*.

[c]Reading *lātēt*, or possibly *lātenet* for the impossible MT *l^{e}tittēn*.

[d]Omitting *habbāyit hū'* ('the house, that is') with G[B]. But for this variation we should have suspected that *habbāyit* was original and *hū' hahēkāl* a gloss.

[e]Reading *lip^{e}nē hadd^{e}bīr* with V, MT suggesting a dittograph of *lip^{e}nē* before the natural sequel in v. 20, where a haplograph of *hadd^{e}bīr* has occurred. In v. 20 we follow V in reading *w^{e}hadd^{e}bīr*.

[f]Omitting MT *lip^{e}nē* with V.

[g]Reading *wayya'aś* with G for MT *way^{e}ṣap* ('and he overlaid').

[h]Q indicates *b^{e}rattūqōt* and K *b^{e}rattīqōt*, both passive forms and equally feasible.

[i]Omitting *w^{e}kol-hammizbēaḥ '^{a}šer ladd^{e}bīr ṣippā zāhāb* ('and he overlaid the whole altar of the inner shrine with gold') with G[BL].

fir (*berōš*), actually the Aleppo pine. Esarhaddon in his building inscription already cited mentions *burašu* in the construction of doors, specially mentioning its pleasant odour. *ṣāleʿōt* (lit. 'ribs') is used both of wainscoting and flooring.

6.16. *yarketē*, as in Amos 6.10, means 'the inmost parts'. From this passage and from the association of the noun with *ṣāpōn* (Isa. 14.13), known from the Ras Shamra texts as the mountain-throne of Baal, and with *bōr* (Isa. 14.15), 'the pit', it is apparent that the word refers to extremity in any direction.

lō is possibly an ethic dative, and is apparently so taken by G^BL, which does not translate it. The Hexaplar variant is *auto*; T and S translate it as a pronoun in the accusative. This is possibly a case of an old Aramaism, *l* introducing the accusative, cf. *hamenaddīm leyōm rāʿ* ('who put far away the evil day') (Amos 6.3).

debīr is not derived from *dābār* ('a word') as implied in EV ('oracle'), Aq. and Symmachus (*chrēsmatērion*), and V (*oraculum*), but means 'the back part' (Arab. *dubr*), hence 'inmost shrine'. G transliterates *dabeir*, thus betraying apparently no consciousness of a connection between the holy of holies and the word of God, the foundation of all reality.[a] The reading *leqōdeš haqqodāšīm*, 'the holy of holies' or 'holiest of all', is not questioned in any of the versions, but is probably a gloss on *haddebīr*. Burney[b] points out that the phrase is peculiar to P and late books influenced by P (e.g. Ezek., Chron., Ezra, Neh., Dan., cf. also I K. 7.50; 8.6).

18. *miqlaʿat* from the context means 'engraved work'. The Arabic cognate means 'to sling forth', but it also means 'to throw into relief', as of an uprooted boulder in a plain, or an eruption of the skin. Perhaps 'relief-work' would be a better translation than the more general 'engraved work'.

In spite of the frequent scribal error of *'el* for *ʿal*, which is actually read here by three MSS, Burney attempts to defend the MT, but the few instances he cites of the use of *'el* (II K. 10.14; Ezek. 31.7; 47.7) are not convincing.

peqāʿīm, used also of the decoration under the rim of the great brazen 'sea' (7.24), is found in the variant feminine form of the fruits of the wild gourd, which brought 'death into the pot' of the prophets of Gilgal (II K. 4.39). Other items of the rather unimaginative decoration

[a]So. J. Barr points out (*The Semantics of Biblical Language*, 1961, p. 136) in his trenchant criticism of T. F. Torrance, *Royal Priesthood*, 1955, pp. 1ff.

[b]*Notes on the Hebrew Text of the Books of Kings*, 1903, p. 71.

were 'open flowers', *peṭūrē ṣiṣṣīm*, lit. 'open parts of flowers', i.e. calyxes.

6.20. It is not certain that *ṣāpā* refers to actual gold-plating; it is rather gilding with liquid gold. Burney[a] aptly cites Prov. 26.23, now to be read in the light of a Ras Shamra passage (2 'Aqht, VI, 36–37) as *kesapsāg meṣuppe ʿal-ḥāreś*, 'as glaze overlaid on earthenware'.[b] The passive participle *sāgūr* qualifying *zāhāb* is found only in this verse and in 10.21, and its precise meaning is uncertain. It is suggested in *BDB*, p. 688, that it refers to gold prized and so 'shut up'. If we may assume a verb *sāgar* as the root of the noun *sagrīr*, 'persistent rain' (Prov. 27.15), the reference might be to liquid gold sprayed on, but since solid gold vessels are so described in 10.21, this seems precluded. The word may be cognate with Arabic *sajara*, 'to heat an oven', hence *zāhāb sāgūr* may mean gold heated in a crucible, hence 'refined gold', cf. Akkadian *ḫuraṣu sagru*.

21. The noun *rattūqōt* or *rattīqōt* is not well attested in the Old Testament, and the meaning is far from certain, e.g. Isa. 40.19 *r. kesep*, and Ezek. 7.23, *ʿaśē hārattōq*, 'make a chain', but this is not certain. The verbal root is better attested, e.g. Nahum 3.10 *ruttequ bazziqqīm*, 'they are bound with fetters', cf. Arabic *rataqa*, 'to close, sew up'. G gives no help. Perhaps a screen is denoted rather than chains, this being later replaced by the veil, *pārōket*, which Šanda, after Thenius, proposed to read.

(δ) *The cherubim in the inner shrine:* 6.23–28

The main textual difficulty here is the displacement of v. 26, which obviously should be read between vv. 23a and 23b, as is done by most commentators since Stade. This is confirmed by the singular pronominal suffix in *qōmātō* in v. 23b, which demands a singular antecedent *hakkerūb haššēnī* in v. 26, and not a plural, as *kerūbīm* in v. 23a. Alternatively, it has been proposed to omit v. 23b (Kittel, de Vaux) or to assume a lacuna after v. 23a (Noth). Verse 27 may also be secondary, explicitly noting that the cherubim were put ready made into the inner shrine and so disposed that their wings touched the opposite walls. Here there seems a desire to avoid the impression that the images had been fashioned *in situ*. The later date of this passage is suggested by the expression *habbayit happenīmī* ('the inmost part of the Temple'), for the more usual *debīr*, the phrase being peculiar to Ezekiel (41.17).

[a] *Op. cit.*, p. 73n.
[b] H. L. Ginsberg, *BASOR* 98, 1945, p. 21 and n.55.

Primary

6 23A And he made in the shrine two cherubs of oil-wood; 26 the height of the one cherub was ten cubits, and so also the second cherub, 23B its height was ten cubits, 24 and five cubits the wing of the one cherub and five cubits the wing of the second cherub, ten cubits from the end of its wing[a] to the end of its wing,[a] 25 and ten cubits the second cherub; the two cherubim had one measurement and one shape. 28 And he overlaid the cherubim with gold.

Secondary

27 And he set the cherubim within the inmost shrine and they spread[b] their wings,[c] and the wing of the one touched the (side) wall and the wing of the second cherub touched the other wall, and their wings in the middle of the shrine were in contact, wing to wing.

6.23ff. The actual appearance and significance of the cherubim is a matter of speculation. In Gen. 3.24 and Ezek. 28.14–16 they are guardians of Paradise, and in the present passage they may have been conceived as guardians of the ark, which rested between them, or, as Waterman has suggested, the guardians of the treasure deposited in the side-wings of the Temple, towards the entrance of which they apparently faced. In this case the function of the cherubim might have been that of the winged composite sphinxes of Assyrian and Babylonian sculpture, the *lamasāti*, often in the form of winged human-faced bulls placed as protecting genii at the entrance to Mesopotamian palaces and temples. Ezekiel was obviously familiar with this protective function of the cherubim, since he speaks of *hakkᵉrūb hassōkēk*, 'the sheltering (lit. 'screening') cherub' (28.14, 16). The winged creatures in the theophany in Ezek. 1 and 10 are obviously inspired by these Mesopotamian figures, and the fact that they are four in number suggests that they had nothing to do with the

[a]Reading singular with the versions for MT plural.

[b]G and S read singular, the subject being possibly the king, who had the cherubim made and arranged.

[c]Reading *'et-kanᵉpēhem* with G for MT *'et-kanᵉpē hakkᵉrūbīm*, but retaining the plural of the verb with the subject *hakkᵉrūbīm* either expressed as in MT or understood.

cherubim of the Temple. The protective aspect of the function of the cherubim is emphasized in the description of the Tabernacle in Ex. 25.18ff. (P), where the cherubim at either end of the ark cover the *kappōret* or lid (EVV 'mercy-seat') with their wings, and they probably have the same significance in the carvings on the panelling of the walls and doors of the Temple (I K. 6.29–35), where they guard the palm-tree as the tree of life (see on 6.31). In view of the employment of Phoenician craftsmen in the construction and decoration of the Temple, however, it is more natural to look for a local Canaanite prototype, and that is found in Phoenician ivory-reliefs from the Late Bronze Age at Megiddo[a] and the throne of Ahiram on his sarcophagus at Byblos from the tenth century.[b] Here winged, sphinx-like figures support the throne of a local king, and this is surely the function of the cherubim in the inmost shrine of the Temple. Their protective function is not excluded, but they are primarily the supports of the throne of Yahweh (Pss. 80.1[2]; 99.1; II K. 19.15; Isa. 37.16; I Sam. 4.4; II Sam. 6.2). The etymology of the word is doubtful, though it may be connected with the Akkad. root *karābu*, 'to be gracious, bless', *kāribu* being regarded in Assyria as the assessor of the great gods and intercessor for the faithful.

6.23. The substance of which the cherubim was made is given as *ʿaṣē šemen*. *šemen* means properly olive oil, but it is probable that we should distinguish between the olive tree (*zayit*) and *ʿēṣ šemen*, 'the oil tree', mentioned with the cedar, acacia, and myrtle, but not with any tree bearing edible fruit, in Isa. 41.19. This is probably *elaeagnus angustifolia*, with leaves and reddish-brown berries resembling the leaves and berries of the olive, hence the name. This tree grows to a height of 15 or 20 feet.[c]

27. The disposition of the figures in the 20-cubit square inner shrine is somewhat vaguely described. There would have been room for the two figures to stand abreast, but whether they were so arranged or stood diagonally facing out from the inner corners is uncertain. The latter arrangement is the more probable.

(ε) *Further details of interior decoration*: 6.29f.

This is probably secondary matter and late, when the Temple was a tradition rather than an actuality. This is suggested by the im-

[a]G. Loud, *The Megiddo Ivories*, 1939, pl. 2a and 2b.

[b]*ANEP*, pl. 456. An earlier example is the throne of Tutankhamen, which reproduces the same somewhat stylized motifs, *ANEP*, pl. 416.

[c]W. Walker, *All the Plants of the Bible*, 1960, p. 152.

practical detail of the gilding of the floor (v. 30). The carving of the Temple, however, outside as well as inside, seems to be implied in Ezek. 41.17, which is generally taken to reflect the pre-exilic Temple.

6 29 And the walls of the Temple round about[a] he carved with reliefs of cherubim and palms[b] both inside[c] and outside. 30 And he overlaid the floor of the shrine with gold inside and outside.

6.29. The overlaying of the floor with gold is unlikely and reflects later extravagant ideas about the legendary splendour of Solomon's Temple. It is not clear what 'within and without' means. Klostermann took it to refer to the inner and outer parts of the shrine (*debīr* and *hēkāl* and also perhaps *'ūlām*).

(ζ) *The doors of the inner shrine and the nave*: 6.31–35

In this section v. 32 at least seems to be secondary, repeating the statement of v. 31. Possibly v. 35 is a later insertion, repeating v. 32b, as suggested by the use of *w* with the perfect of the verbs.

Primary

6 31 And the doorway of the inner shrine he made as doorleaves of oil-wood, the upper projection[d] and[e] the doorposts being a pentagon. 33 And he made likewise for the doorway of the nave doorposts of oil-wood, a square door-frame,[f] 34 and two doors of fir-wood, the one door being two leaves, folding, and the other being two leaves,[g] folding.

Secondary

32 And the two doorleaves were of oil-wood, and he engraved on them reliefs of cherubim, palms, and flower-calyxes, and he overlaid them with gold, and spread the gold out upon the cherubim, and the palms.

35 And he carved cherubim, and palms, and flower-calyxes, and overlaid them in gold applied evenly to the engraving.

[a]Reading *missābīb* for MT *mēsab*.

[b]Omitting MT *ūpeṭūrē ṣiṣṣīm* ('and flower-calyxes') with G^{BL}.

[c]Reading *lipenīmā* for MT *millipenīm*; cf. v. 30.

[d]This word, probably a *hapax legomenon*, is omitted in G^{AL} and V. It may be a corruption of *'ūl* or even *'ūlām*, denoting a projection, either horizontal, in which case the frame of the doorway might be thought of as a small vestibule, or, more probably, vertical to form a gabled lintel.

[e]Inserting *weham* (*ezūzōt*) with G^{AL} and V. MT *ḥamīšit* ('a fifth') should probably be read *ḥamūšōt* ('fivefold'), i.e. a pentagon.

[f]Reading *mezūzōt rebūʿōt* with G, lit. 'doorposts fourfold', i.e. a square door-frame, for the unintelligible MT *mē'ēt rebīʿīt*. The words *ḥamīšit* and *rebīʿīt* may be adverbial in form, as the termination suggests.

[g]Reading *ṣelāʿīm* with G, S, and T for MT *qelāʿīm* ('carvings'), an obvious corruption, *ṣ* resembling *q* in the proto-Hebraic script.

6.31ff. Mesopotamian building inscriptions record many cases of doorways overlaid with bright metal. Montgomery (ICC, p. 158) cites one where Nabonidus in his restoration of the temple of Marduk at Babylon claims to have made the doors 'as bright as day'. The best examples of such work from antiquity are copper sheets ·28 metre broad and ·0015 metre thick from *Tell Balawat* near *Nimrud*, ancient Kalḫu, reputed to have covered the gates of a palace of Shalmaneser III, the contemporary of Ahab and Jehu.[a] These, with their presentation of historical scenes, aspire to a much higher artistic level than the Temple doors with their unimaginative limitation to 'cherubs, palms, and flower-calyxes'. The palm as tree of life in various stylized forms appears as a feature of palace architecture and ornamentation, for instance in the proto-Ionic capitals from columns and pilasters in Jerusalem, Samaria, Hazor and *Rāmāt Rāḥēl* between Jerusalem and Bethlehem, and on an ivory relief from the royal couch in the palace at Ras Shamra,[b] where it is combined with the Egyptian motif of a flourishing lotus (see on 7.19). It is thus at once significant as a pledge of prosperity to the king and as a symbol of his potency as a channel of prosperity to the community. The significance of the king as the divine nominee and medium of divine blessings is admirably illustrated in a remarkable mural painting from the Amorite palace of Mari, which depicts the king's investiture by the goddess Ishtar.[c] The stylized palm-tree, the tree of life, is represented in duplicate for the sake of symmetry in the composition of the picture, and it is guarded by two winged sphinx figures, Hebrew cherubim, which recalls the biblical tradition of the cherubim guarding access to the tree of life in Gen. 3.24. That the doors of the Temple were plated rather than gilded in gold foil is indicated in II K. 18.16, which records how Hezekiah 'cut off' the gold, with which, in a less prosperous age than that of Solomon, he had plated (*ṣippā*) them, as war-indemnity to Sennacherib.

31. *w*^{e}*'ēt petaḥ* ('and the doorway') . . . is taken by Montgomery to be a case of the use of *'et* to emphasize a noun not in the accusative, cf. Num. 5.10; Ezek. 17.21; 44.2; Neh. 9.19, 34; Dan. 9.13; II Chron. 31.17, cited *inter alia* by *GK* § 117m, where it is suggested that the imperative of a verb 'Behold' is understood. In the present

[a]L. W. King, *Bronze Reliefs from the Gates of Shalmaneser*, 1915; *ANEP*, pl. 356–65.

[b]Schaeffer, *Reprises des fouilles de Ras Shamra-Ugarit*, 1955, pl. viii.

[c]A. Parrot, *Mission archéologique de Mari II. Le Palais, 2, Peintures Murales*, 1958.

passage we might take *'ēt* as introducing the accusative *petaḥ* in apposition to *dal^{e}tōt* ('door-leaves'), the predicate of *'āśā*.

6.32. The reading *wyrd* is supported in G^{L}, which, however, reads *kai katebainen* (*wayyēred*). If the word is, as suggested (Burney, Montgomery), a Niphal of *rādad*, it is a *hapax legomenon* in the Old Testament. The versions offer a selection of readings, all suggesting a reading only slightly different from MT, and quite feasible, e.g. S *'asgī* (*wayyāreb*, 'and he made abundant'), T *ūn^{e}sik* (possibly *wayyāreq*, 'and he poured out'). In view of the noun *r^{e}dīdīm*, used of women's garments in Isa. 3.23 and of a veil in S. of S. 5.7, it is possible that the verb is the Hiphil of *rādad*, cognate with the Syriac verb found in the Aphel meaning 'to spread out'. *w^{e}qāla'* ('and he carved'), as in v. 35, is feasibly taken by Burney[a] as an indication of a later retouching of the passage. Noth suggests that the verb means 'hammered in'.

34. *ṣ^{e}lā'īm, var. lect. q^{e}lā'īm* (see p. 173 n.[g]), which is a mis-spelling, possibly under Aramaic influence, has already been used in v. 15 of boards used in wainscoting and flooring. Here it refers to door-leaves, as the qualifying adjective *g^{e}līlīm*, 'rolling', i.e., on hinges, indicates, rather than boards, more than one of which would be used in each door-leaf.

35. In the phrase *m^{e}yuššār 'al-hamm^{e}ḥuqqe*, the verb *ḥāqaq*, the root of *ḥōq* ('decree'), is used in its radical sense, 'to engrave'. *m^{e}yuššār*, 'evenly applied' (Burney), might refer to inlay, the gold being thus flush with the plain surface of the wood. The usual meaning of *ṣippā*, however, suggests overlay of the whole surface rather than inlay.

(η) *The Inner Court*: 6.36

6 [36]And he built the inner court, three courses of hewn stones and a course of cedar beams.

36. This does not mean that the wall enclosing the court was only three courses high coped with cedar, but that, as Montgomery translates, there were three courses of masonry 'to one of cedar beams'. The same proportion of stone and wood courses is noted in Ezra's description of the building of the Second Temple (6.4). The use of timber beams with masonry is attested at Ras Shamra[b] and at Cnossos, Mycenae, Tiryns, Troy (VIth city), and Tell Tainat. This may have been a precaution against earthquake damage.

[a] *Notes on the Hebrew Text . . . of Kings*, p. 77.
[b] C. F. A. Schaeffer, *Ugaritica I*, Paris, 1939, pp. 92–97, pl. XIX.

(θ) *Record of the founding and completion of the Temple:* 6.37f.

The dry, factual style suggests that this section was drawn directly from State archives. There is, however, one late gloss in v. 38, *hū’ haḥōdeš hašš^{e}mīnī*, as is suggested by the word *ḥōdeš* for 'month' (lit. 'new moon'), and the reckoning from the spring equinox customary in Mesopotamia.

6 [37]In the fourth year the Temple of Yahweh was founded in the month of Ziv. [38]And in the eleventh year in the month of Bul [that is the eighth month] the Temple was finished in all its details and in all its order[a] and he built it for seven years.

6.37. The dating is in the fourth year of Solomon's reign. Note the older name for 'month' (*yeraḥ*, lit. 'moon') as in the Ras Shamra texts and the Gezer tablet. The names of the months are the old Canaanite names, 'Flowers' (*zīw*) and 'Moisture' (*būl*, cf. Arabic *wabala*, 'to flow').

38. The noun in *l^{e}kol-d^{e}bārāw* ('in all its details') or *l^{e}kol-d^{e}bārō* (G) is possibly derived from a Hebrew verbal root cognate with the Arabic *dabbara*, 'to dispose, arrange'. *mišpāṭ* ('order') in this context reveals its close relation to the verb *šāpaṭ* in the sense of 'to rule', cf. Ugaritic *ṯpṭ* in parallel to *zbl* ('prince') and *mlk* ('king'). *mišpāṭ* is the order established under the ruler or king, hence the right, or established order, and, in certain contexts, approved custom, which governs a stable society.

(ι) *The palace-complex, including the Royal Palace, the House of the Forest of Lebanon, the Hall of Pillars, the Throne Hall, and the Palace of Pharaoh's Daughter:* 7.1–12

On the arrangement of the text and the sources see critical introduction to the section(chs. 6–7).

General note on the building of the palace-complex: 7.1

7 [1]And Solomon was engaged on the building of his house for thirteen years, and so completed all his house.

7.1. *bētō* refers to the whole complex of buildings to be described in the rest of this section, including the royal residence (*ūbētō ’^{a}šer yāšab šām*). The sequel emphasizes only the more grandiose of the buildings and their peculiar features in a somewhat arbitrary manner.

[a]We prefer K *mišpāṭō* to Q *mišpāṭāw* as more in agreement with Hebrew idiom.

The complexity of palace-buildings has been well illustrated by the extensive palace-complexes which have been excavated in the Near East, e.g. the Amorite city of Mari on the mid-Euphrates, where Parrot uncovered a five-acre complex,[a] Nineveh,[b] Babylon,[c] Alalakh,[d] occupied in the Middle Bronze Age, and Ras Shamra[e] (Middle and Late Bronze Age). At Samaria the palace-complex with courts and esplanades occupied about five acres.[f] The relative proportion of the Temple to the palace is noteworthy. Both may be denoted comprehensively as 'his house', which Solomon completed in 13 years. I K. 9.10, on the other hand, reads 'his house' of v. 1 as Solomon's secular buildings described in the sequel, and reckons seven years for the building of the Temple (6.38) and 13 for the rest, a total of 20 years. This may represent late editorial opinion, reflecting the late consciousness of distinction between the secular and strictly sacred. The relative proportions of the Temple and the rest of the buildings, however, would make seven years and 13 respectively appropriate.

The House of the Forest of Lebanon: 7.2–5

Here, as in the description of the rest of the palace, the writer's attention is arrested by salient features, his description is not systematic or technical, so that only an approximate reconstruction is possible.

> 7 ²And he built the House of the Forest of Lebanon, the length of which was one hundred cubits, the breadth fifty cubits, and the height thirty cubits[g] on four rows[h] of pillars of cedar, and beams[i] of cedar upon the pillars ³and ceiled with cedar above the lofts that were upon the pillars, forty-five, fifteen to each row, ⁴and latticed (or embrasured) windows, three rows facing one another in triplicate; ⁵and all the door-

[a] A. Parrot, *Syria* XVIII, 1937, pp. 54ff.; XIX, 1938, pp. 8ff.; XX, 1939, pp. 14ff.

[b] A. Parrot, *Nineveh and the Old Testament*, 1956.

[c] R. Koldewey, *Das wieder erstehende Babylon*, 1925.

[d] Sir L. Woolley, *A Forgotten Kingdom*, 1953.

[e] C. F. A. Schaeffer, *Le Palais Royal d'Ugarit* III, 1955, Plan in Frontispiece.

[f] J. W. Crowfoot, K. M. Kenyon, E. L. Sukenik, *Samaria-Sebaste I. The Buildings*, 1942.

[g] G^{BL} omits the specification of height.

[h] G reads '3' rows for MT '4', assuming that '45' in v. 3 refers to the total number of pillars (so Stade). But the number refers to the number of side-chambers on each of the two sides, 15 on each of the three storeys (see on 7.2). Hence we see no reason to doubt the MT reading.

[i] G reads *ōmiai* 'struts', lit. 'shoulders' (Hebrew *kitᵉpōt*) for MT *kᵉrūtōt* ('beams').

ways and the doorposts[a] foursquare, with lintels, and [b]facing one another[b] in triplicate.

7.2. The House of the Forest of Lebanon (*bēt yaʿar hallᵉbānōn*) was no doubt so called from its four rows of cedar pillars. Its purpose, to judge from 10.17 and Isa. 22.8, was as a treasury and armoury, the former passage referring to Solomon's deposit of 300 golden shields, and the latter referring to the building as an armoury.[c]

The only explanation of the MT reading '4 rows of pillars (v. 2) . . . 45, 15 to each row' (v. 3) would be that 45 (3 × 15) refers to the number of side-chambers on each long side. In this case, 'rows' (*ṭūrīm*) in the second instance would refer to rows not of pillars but of side-chambers, of which v. 4 indicates that there were three storeys, the doors and windows of which faced one another directly (v. 5). The four rows of pillars may have been disposed either in two rows of pilasters or pillars close to the wall and two rows further into the interior. But we prefer to think of the side-chambers as bonded into the side-walls as in the Temple (6.6) with two rows of pillars supporting the side-chambers further from the walls and two other rows supporting galleries to which the other doors and windows opened. The three rows of pillars of G, the result of the assumption that 45 referred to the pillars, would seem to leave a middle row with no function.

3. *ṣᵉlāʿōt* is already used to denote storeyed side-chambers (6.5) and floor-boards (6.15). Šanda accordingly takes *ṣᵉlāʿōt* here as 'architraves'. The problem is complicated by the fact that there is no further mention of *ṣᵉlāʿōt* in the description of the building. The reference to the three rows of doors and windows facing each other, however, makes it practically certain that there were three storeys of side-chambers. See p. 177 n.[h].

4. *šᵉqūpīm* denotes either 'latticed' or 'embrasured', cf. on 6.4. The Greek versions read *melathra* ('crossbeams'), connecting the word, no doubt, with *mašqōp* ('lintel'), cf. Arab. *saqf* ('ceiling'). This large hall was ventilated by three rows of latticed (or embrasured) windows. *meḥᵉzā 'el-meḥᵉzā* ('prospect to prospect') precludes the interpretation of the Greek versions. See note [b] below.

[a]G reads *chōrai*, 'places, regions' (*mᵉḥōzōt*) for MT *mᵉzūzōt* ('doorposts') apparently confusing *meḥᵉze* ('view') and *meḥōz*, which is found in Ps. 107.30, and is an Assyrian loanword meaning 'place, region'.

[b]*ūmūl* seems tautological before *meḥᵉzā 'el-meḥᵉzā*, lit. 'prospect to prospect'.

[c]A Greek analogy from Athens is cited by C. Watzinger, *Denkmäler Palästinas* I, 1933–35, p. 96.

7.5. *šeqep* must be a defining accusative, a usage common in Arabic. The meaning 'lintel' is suggested by the association of *hammašqōp* with *hammᵉzūzōt* ('doorposts') in the blood-smearing ritual of Passover (Ex. 12.7).

The Hall of Pillars: 7.6

7 [6]And the Hall of Pillars he made,[a] its length being fifty cubits, and its breadth thirty[b] cubits, and a portico [c]before them[c] and pillars and a cornice before them.

6. It is not clear whether this is an extension to the front of the House of the Forest of Lebanon, as its length (50 cubits) suggests, this being also the breadth of the House of the Forest of Lebanon, or a portico abutting elsewhere on the great court. Klostermann's suggestion *wᵉʾūlam hāʿōmᵉdīm* ('and the portico of the courtiers', lit. 'those who stand [before the king]'), or better perhaps 'the waiting-portico', is plausible in view of the fact that the next item to be mentioned is the Hall of Justice.

ʿāb (lit. 'thickness', G *pachos*) apparently denotes a cornice as an extra, or projecting, feature, the word being probably cognate with Arabic *ʿabbā* ('to be superabundant', primarily of liquid).

The Hall of Justice: 7.7

7 [7]And the Hall of the Tribunal where he was to judge (the Judgement portico [d]he made) he panelled[e] with cedar from floor to rafters.[df]

7. The Hall of Justice visualizes the function of the primitive king as the personal dispenser of justice *coram populo*, as the ancient kings in the Ras Shamra texts Krt and Dn'il personally dispensed justice in public, thus publicly vindicating the social order and the tradition of the community. It will be recollected that David also dispensed justice in person (II Sam. 14.3; 15.2). As in the case of the Hall of Pillars, it is uncertain whether this was part of the House of the Forest

[a]G^{BL} omits the verb, possibly correctly, the original text listing the various items of Solomon's building catalogue-fashion.

[b]G^{B} reads '50'.

[c]Perhaps we should omit *ʿal-pᵉnēhem*, assuming homoeoteleuton, the plural pronominal suffix having no suitable antecedent. This, however, has no support in the versions.

[d]G^{BL} omits. Probably only the verb should be omitted, see n. [a] on v. 6.

[e]Reading *sāpān* for MT *wᵉsāpūn*, though, if the verb *ʿāśā* is omitted, the passive participle would suit the catalogue style.

[f]Obviously *haqqarqaʿ* should be emended to *haqqōrōt*, as suggested by S and V.

of Lebanon or a separate building, as Šanda maintains. No detail is given except the cedar panelling, even the dimensions being omitted.

The Palace proper and the Palace of Pharaoh's Daughter: 7.8

7 [8]And his own house, where he was to dwell, [a]the second court[a], was within the portico, of the same construction, and a house for[b] Pharaoh's daughter, whom Solomon took (to wife), was like this portico.

7.8. After the description of the public quarters of the palace, the *selamlik*, characterized by general impressions and overall dimensions, as distinct from the greater detail in which the Temple is described, the private quarters, the royal residence and harem quarters, *ḥaremlik*, are merely noted without dimensions, disposition, or details, except a note on the stonework of these and the public buildings just described.

If MT *ḥāṣēr hā'aḥeret* is correct, this would be an instance of the article before an adjective which has a particularizing or limiting force (*GK* § 126.5*w*), though in this particular case *h* may be omitted by haplography before *ḥ*. The palace was within the portico, *mibbēt lā'ūlām*, not the second court, which we take with Montgomery to be in parenthesis. The second court is distinct from the Temple court. The grouping of apartments round a central enclosed court, still the fashion in the traditional oriental house, is conducive to privacy. 'The second court' here may signify either the court common to Temple and palace, 'the middle court' (II K. 20.4, reading with Q and the versions *ḥāṣēr* for *'īr*), which may have been 'the great court' of v. 9, or a court peculiar to the palace independent of this.

The stonework: 7.9–12

7 [9]All of these were of hewn stones [c]according to the measurements of hewn stone,[c] sawn with the saw both inside and out, and from the foundation to the eaves and outside[d] to the great court. [10]And it was founded with hewn stones, great stones of ten cubits and stones of eight cubits, [11]and above were hewn stones, according to the measurements of hewn stone, and cedar; [12]and the great court[e] round about had three

[a]Reading *heḥāṣēr* for MT *ḥāṣēr*, assuming haplography, but see n. on v. 8.
[b]G[BL] omits MT *ya'aśe*, which seems to be a gloss, signifying that this was yet to be made.
[c]G[BL] omits.
[d]G[BL] omits.
[e]Inserting the definite article before *ḥāṣēr* as suggested by the following adjective with the definite article, but cf. grammatical n. on v. 8.

courses of hewn stone and one of cedar beams [a]as had also the inner court, that of the Temple of Yahweh, to the vestibule[b] of the Temple.[a]

7.9. On *'abānīm yeqārōt* ('hewn stones') see n. to 5.17. The soft white limestone of Palestine may be actually sawn when freshly quarried, hardening with exposure. *ṭepāḥōt*, as the contrast with *massād* ('foundations') indicates, must mean 'eaves' or 'cornices' (G *geisai*) or the like, cf. Isa. 48.13 *yādī yāsedā 'ereṣ wīmīnī ṭippeḥā šāmāyim* ('My hand laid the foundation of the earth, and my right hand spread out the heavens'). The word denotes the width of the border on the ledge of the table of the shewbread in the Tabernacle (Ex. 25.25; 37.12). It is cognate with Arabic *ṭafaḥa* ('to overflow'). In view of the usage in Isaiah and Exodus we cannot agree with de Vaux's suggestion on the basis of a passage in the Amarna Tablets that *ṭepāḥōt* (Amarna *ṭappāti*) refers to timber beams on top of the stonework serving as a base to brick superstructure.[c] The tying of courses of brick or stone masonry with timber beams is well known throughout the ancient Near East in antiquity and is still in use in Turkey. In brickwork, which might absorb rain with consequent disintegration and subsidence, the beams gave stability to the structure, while in stonework it was possibly designed to minimize the effect of earthquake. The feature is admirably illustrated by a layer of carbon in a groove in the stonework of buildings at Ras Shamra.[d]

10. Great quarry blocks of 8 or 10 cubits (about 10 and 15 feet) are not excessive in buildings in the ancient Near East. The colossal hewn blocks of the lower courses of the Wailing Wall, from Herod's construction, are a good instance, some measuring 16 feet 6 inches by 13 feet.

(κ) *The bronze furnishings of the Temple*: 7.13–47

According to the arrangement by materials in vv. 6f. after the note of work in stone and wood, including the gold overlaid on the wood (6.21, 28, 32, 35), the bronze-work of the Temple is next described (7.13–47) and the gold-work (vv. 48–50).

What at first sight seems to be a summary of the bronze-work (vv.

[a]G[BL] omits this phrase, which is awkward.

[b]If the phrase is retained it may be best to follow G[A] and read *welaḥaṣar bēt yhwh happenīmīt*, taking this to refer to the Temple part of the court common to the Palace, and continuing *welaḥaṣar 'ūlām habbayit*, referring to the court exclusive to the Temple.

[c]*Ancient Israel*, p. 316.

[d]Schaeffer, *Ugaritica* I, 1939, Pl. XIX 1, 2, 3, and for a modern example, 4.

41–47), but actually differs in details from the account of the same objects, e.g. the capitals, or objects on top of the pillars Jachin and Boaz, is taken by Noth (*op. cit.*, pp. 146f.) as a check-list of work completed, which turned out to be different in some details from what was originally contemplated in the specifications for workmen, which was the basis of the account in the annals of Solomon, which was later elaborated in vv. 13–39. As the list of articles in vv. 41–47 is combined with the narrative statement that they were made by Hiram (v. 40), who cast them in the Jordan Valley (v. 46), this passage may well have stood immediately after vv. 13f. in the original annalistic source from which it was adapted, being a general note of the completion of the bronze-work, of which vv. 15–39 was an elaboration. The list of bronze-work in vv. 41–47 recalls the list of the spoil from the Temple of Jerusalem in Jer. 52.21–23. Note the displacement of this section and vv. 48–51 in G to before vv. 1–12, which deals with the secular buildings, though the Hexaplar indicates that the order of MT was also known.

Introduction of the craftsman Hiram (var. lect. Huram-abi): 7.13–14

7 [13]And king Solomon sent and brought Hiram (or Huram-abi) from Tyre. [14]He was the son of a widow from the tribe of Naphtali, and his father was a man of Tyre, a craftsman in bronze, and he was full of skill, intelligence, and practical knowledge in working all kinds of bronze-work, and he came to king Solomon and wrought all his work.

7.13. The craftsman is called Huram-abi in II Chron. 2.13[12], where he is said to be the son of a woman of the tribe of Dan. 'Hiram' in Kings seems the simplification and corruption of the name Huram-abi, the latter element of which would be inexplicable in Chronicles except as a genuine element of a theophoric name, which is perhaps a corruption of Ḥoron-abi, attested as the name of a Palestinian or Syrian chief in the Egyptian Execration Texts from the 19th century BC.[a] The fact that this is the only case in the account of the building and furnishing of the Temple and palace-complex where a craftsmen is named leads Noth (*op. cit.*, p. 148) to suspect that v. 13 is a late expansion, with v. 14 later still, the note on the Israelite mother of Hiram being apologetic. He notes further that the description of Hiram's skill in v. 14b reechoes practically verbatim the description of Bezaleel the artisan of the Tabernacle in Ex. 31.3; 35.31

[a]G. Posener, *Princes et pays d'Asie* . . . , 1940, E 17; J. Gray, 'The Canaanite God Horon', *JNES* VIII, 1949, pp. 27–34.

(P). We admit the last fact. But if indeed Hiram had an Israelite affinity, which in the light of Phoenician interest in the region of the upper Jordan (Judg. 18.7) is possible, his skill in metal-work, so rare in Israel, might well merit special notice.

7.14. Naphtali and Dan were both contiguous to territory in the Lebanon and anti-Lebanon where Tyrian influence was strong before the rise of Aramaean states towards the end of Solomon's reign. The interest of the Phoenicians in this region was in the trade-route from the coast to the great trunk highway from Mesopotamia to Egypt via Damascus and Hazor in Upper Galilee, and also to the profitable incense-route from South Arabia to Damascus following the desert edge, the later *Ḍarb al-Ḥāj* (Pilgrim Road). The Phoenicians in their confined coastal settlements were also interested in the corn-lands of the Hauran, which, until comparatively recently, was known as the granary of Palestine.

ḥokmā, *tᵉbūnā*, and *daʿat*, conventionally translated as 'wisdom, understanding, and knowledge', all have a practical connotation. Even in ethics *ḥokmā* is not speculative but empirical wisdom, practical insight and sagacity. The word describes the skill of the seaman (Ps. 107.27), the general (Isa. 10.13), and the artisan (Ex. 28.3), e.g. Bezaleel.

The pillars Jachin and Boaz: 7.15–22

Here vv. 19, 20, and 22 present notorious difficulties. Apart from the unintelligible v. 20, the description of the pillars and their capitals seems to end at v. 18, as the last phrase there, 'and so also he did for the other capital', suggests. From this point it seems natural to pass on immediately to the erection of the pillars (v. 21), and, indeed, vv. 19, 20 appear after v. 21 in G^L, v. 22 being omitted. In the summary recapitulation of Hiram's work in vv. 41f. there is no reference to 'lotus-work' on the capitals of Jachin and Boaz. In this passage *gullā* ('bowl') is taken to be a variant for *beṭen* (lit. 'belly'), cf. v. 20, which was apparently thought of as the bulbous part of the capital; but in vv. 41f. it seems to denote the shape of the capital as distinct from the decoration of trellis-work in relief upon its surface. Thus vv. 19, 20, 22 appear to be later expansions, which themselves possibly include expansions and glosses. Since there is no description of the capitals on the pillars of the pillared portico in v. 6, v. 19 may have been a description of those, their peculiarity being the lotus-design, and their measurement four cubits as against the capitals of

Jachin and Boaz, which are five cubits. Here *bāʾūlām* ('in the porch') may be parenthetic. In v. 20 the fact that only the second pillar is mentioned makes the verse suspect. The sense is further complicated by the similarity of the adjacent words *maʿal* ('above') and *milleʿummat* ('close beside'), and by the preposition *leʿēber* ('beyond'), most unusual in this context. It is very doubtful if the verse as it stands yields sense.

7 15And he cast[a] the two pillars of bronze, the height of the one pillar
being eighteen cubits and its circumference twelve cubits[b] . . . and
so[c] the other pillar. 16And he made two capitals to put on top of the
pillars, bronze-casting, the height of the one capital being five cubits
and the height of the second capital being five cubits, 17and he made
two gratings,[d] [e]trellis-work, festoons, chain-work[e] for the[f] capitals on
top of the pillars, trellis-work[g] for the one capital and trellis-work[g] for
the other capital. 18And he made the pomegranates,[h] and there were
two rows round about on the one trellis-work [i]covering the capitals
which were on top of the pillars[i] [j]and so also the other capital.

Digression on capitals, with glosses

19And the[k] capitals which were on top of the pillars were lotus-fashion
(in the porch), four cubits, 20and there were capitals on the two pillars
and moreover above, connected with them,[l] the bulbous part, which
was free of the trellis-work, and the pomegranates were two hundred in
rows all round, and on the capital, and so[m] the second capital.
21And he set up the pillars at the front of the Temple and set up the
right-hand pillar and named it 'Jachin' ('He establishes') and he set
up the left-hand pillar and named it 'Boaz' ('In/by him is might').

[a]Reading *wayyiṣōq* with G for MT *wayyāṣar* ('and formed').

[b]Reading *ʾōtō* for MT *ʾet-*. Perhaps after G and Jer. 52.21 we should insert 'and its thickness 4 fingers and it was hollow' (*weʿobyō ʾarbaʿ ʾeṣbāʿōt nābūb*).

[c]Reading *wekēn* . . . with S and T, the specification of the second pillar is mentioned before the first, making the MT suspect.

[d]Reading *wayyaʿaś štē* (*śebākōt*) with G for MT *śebākīm*.

[e]G omits these words.

[f]G reads 'to cover the capitals' (*lekassōt ʾet-hakkōtārōt*), which should probably be read.

[g]Reading *śebākā* with G for MT *šibʿā*.

[h]Reading with two Hebrew MSS *hārimmōnīm* for MT *hāʿammūdīm*.

[i]G omits these words, which are possibly a gloss on v. 17.

[j]If MT of v. 18 is retained, *hārimmōnīm* must be emended with S and about fifty Hebrew MSS to *hāʿammūdīm*.

[k]Reading the definite article, which the general sense seems to demand.

[l]A simple emendation of this rare expression would be to emend *m* to *b* and read *milleʿubbat* ('above the swelling'), i.e. of the bulbous part (*habbeṭen*), but the compound prepositional expression is used in P, see Commentary.

[m]Since the first capital has not been described, it would seem that *wekēn hakkōteret* ('and so the capital') has dropped out before *haššēnīt* ('the second').

22a And on the top of the pillars was lotus-fashion,[a] and the work of the pillars was finished.

7.15. *n[e]ḥōšet* is a defining accusative. 'The circumference', lit. 'a line (of 12 cubits) encompassed . . .'

16. *kōtārōt* is a rare word and one might have suspected a corruption of *kaptōr* ('capital'), cf. Amos 9.1; Zeph. 2.14, but for the fact that is is used also in II K. 25.17; II Chron. 4.12f.; cf. also Jer. 52.22. It is conceivably derived from the well-attested verb *kātar* ('to surround') and signifies that which surrounds, like a crown (*keter*), the head of the pillar. Noth, however (*op. cit.*, p. 149), who takes v. 19 to refer to Jachin and Boaz, takes the noun to be cognate with Arabic *kutr* ('hump') and to denote a superstructure, the base of the capital proper. In support of this interpretation it may be noted that G renders *epithema*. *mūṣāq* ('casting'), with the defining accusative *n[e]ḥōšet*, stands in apposition to *kōtārōt*. The breadth of four fingers was a sixth of a cubit, or about three inches.

17. *ś[e]bākā* ('trellis-work') denotes the lattice of a window (II K. 1.2) and is found in parallelism to *rešet* ('net') in Job 18.8. Arabic similarly uses *šabka* ('net') and *šubbāk* ('window'). *g[e]dīlīm* ('festoons') means fringes on a robe in Deut. 22.12. The root is well attested in Arabic and Syriac, meaning 'to plait'. *šarš[e]rōt* means lit. 'twisted work', cf. Assyrian *šaršarratu* and the Arabic cognate *silsileh* ('chain'). The Greek versions do not mention these 'festoons' or 'chains', nor does Jeremiah in dealing with the capitals (52.20–22), though G^L apparently read *g[e]dīlīm*, which it misunderstood and translated by *megala* (Hebr. *g[e]dōlīm*), and II Chron. 3.16 mentions *šarš[e]rōt* in the description of the capitals. This passage indicates that the chains were not moulded reliefs, but were independent fastenings, so probably not decorative but functional.

18. There has apparently been a transposition of *hā'ammūdīm* ('the pillars') and *hārimmōnīm* ('the pomegranates'), as indicated in our translation. The pomegranates recall those hanging independent on the miniature bronze laver-stand from Ras Shamra (*ANEP*, pl. 588). This was probably a fertility symbol, the many seeds of the pomegranate being thrown over the bride in Arab weddings.

19. *bā'ūlām* seems to have been added as an afterthought. The passage is a later addition, a digression prompted by the mention of pillars, see critical introduction to this section. Noth feasibly regards *šūšan* as an Egyptian loanword *ssn* ('lotus-flower'), which, as the lotus-

[a] Perhaps a gloss suggested by v. 19.

bud, was the common order of capital in Egypt. The lotus-flower was a significant emblem of life in Egypt and also in coastal Syria, where, as on the sarcophagus of king Ahiram of Byblos (*ANEP*, pl. 456) a drooping lotus signifies death, cf. the erect lotus-flower in the hand of the victorious king of Megiddo in the famous ivory plaque, *c.* 1350–1150 BC (*ANEP*, pl. 332).

7.20. Here in another later addition we return to the two pillars Jachin and Boaz. If *mill*[e]*ʿummat* of MT is correct it is presumably composed of *min*, *le*, and *ʿummat*. The last two elements are found in the compound preposition *l*[e]*ʿummat* only in P, e.g. Ex. 25.27; 28.27, a fact which may further suggest that the passage is a later expansion. There the preposition means 'connected with', lit. 'in fellowship' (cf. Assyr. *emūtu*, 'family relationship with'). See p. 184 n.[l], above, for our conjectural emendation *mill*[e]*ʿubbat*. *beṭen* is generally taken as 'belly', a bevelled collar on which the capital rested. This is a *hapax legomenon*, its meaning being suggested by its supposed identity with *gullā* (lit. 'bowl') in 7.41 and also its parallel, II Chron. 4.12. Here, however, *gullā* was covered with trellis-work and was apparently the lower part of the capital. Alternatively *beṭen* may be connected with *boṭnīm* ('nuts'), denoting in this case a nut-like bulbous protuberance above the lower part of the capital, which is actually represented in two free-standing pillars in a temple of Aphrodite at Paphos.[a] Another possibility is that *beṭen* denoted a bowl to catch the ashes (reading *'ēper* for *ʿēber*) of a fire which burned in a grating (*ś*[e]*bākā*), the latter feature being functional rather than ornamental, cf. the grating of the altar in Ex. 38.4, where, however, *ś*[e]*baka* is not used, but *rešet* and *mikbār* (lit. 'sieve'). See Commentary p. 187 on Jachin and Boaz. *ṭūrīm* is probably an adverbial accusative. On our assumption of haplography of *hakkōteret* and the omission of *w*[e]*kēn* see p. 184, n.[m] above.

21. The twin pillars were free-standing at the front of the Temple (II Chron. 3.15–17), a feature which is attested in coins from Sidon,[b] on the sculpture of a shrine from *Burj aš-Šamālī* near Tyre from the fifth century,[c] and in the temple of Baal-Herakles at Tyre.[d] The significance of these is uncertain. Lucian[e] suggests that a pair of such pillars, which stood before the temple of the fertility-goddess at

[a]W. R. Smith, *Religion of the Semites*, 1894², p. 488.
[b]G. F. Hill, *Greek Coins*, 'Phoenicia', p. 169, no. 165.
[c]M. Chehab, *Berytus* I, 1934, p. 44, pl. XI, 1.
[d]Herodotus II, 44.
[e]*De Dea Syra*, 28.

Hierapolis (Membij), were phallic emblems, a significance which they also had probably at the shrine of Aphrodite at Paphos. Since W. R. Smith,[a] Jachin and Boaz have been taken by certain scholars as giant cressets where, W. R. Smith suggested, the fat of the sacrifices was burnt. This view has more recently found favour since W. F. Albright lent it his support, citing the representation of two lampstands flanking a tomb at Marisa, which seems to us rather doubtful evidence.[b] One of the pillars before the Baal-temple at Tyre, Herodotus states, held a fire which glowed at night. Hence the twin pillars of Solomon's Temple may have contained the sacred fire of the Temple with the smoke which symbolized the presence of Yahweh as 'the pillar of fire by night and the pillar of cloud by day'. The tradition of the 'pillar of cloud' over the Tabernacle seems to reflect such a feature of the Temple, symbolizing the presence of Yahweh in the Temple, the repository of the ark. The *twin* fires may symbolize the presence and permanence of Yahweh and the king; cf. David as 'the lamp of Israel', cf. II Sam. 21.17. The pillar on the right as one entered the Temple (Jachin) would thus symbolize the presence of Yahweh, while the other (Boaz) on the right of this as one faced outwards, might symbolize by its fire the Davidic House, recalling the station of the king at the right hand of God (Ps. 110.1). The names of the twin pillars may reflect the relationship of God and king, Jachin ('He establishes') referring to the initiative of God, and Boaz ('By him is he mighty')[c] expressing the dependence of the king. Jachin is actually attested as the name of a city gate in a South Arabian inscription,[d] and is an element in the name of the king Jehoiachin. For Boaz G has an interesting reading *Balaz*, suggesting a Hebrew original *ba'al 'az*, 'Baal has rallied his strength', a phrase found thrice repeated in the account of Baal's final conflict with Mot in the Ras Shamra texts.[e] There is admittedly strong evidence of the syncretism of the faith of Israel with the seasonal nature-cult of Canaan, particularly in the great autumn festival, the occasion of Baal's great triumph. The ideology of the kingship of God and the myth and liturgy of the triumph of Cosmos over Chaos was, we believe, borrowed and adapted from this occasion, but in view of the absence

[a]*Op. cit.*, pp. 487–9.

[b]'Two Cressets from Marisa and the Pillars of Jachin and Boaz', *BASOR* 85, 1942, pp. 18ff.; H. G. May, *ibid.* 88, pp. 19ff.

[c]The verb here might be stative or precative, 'May he prevail by him'.

[d]G. Ryckmans, *Les noms propres sudsémitiques*, 1934–35.

[e]*UT* 49, VI, 17–20.

of evidence in the liturgical poetry of Israel for the effective power of Baal along with Yahweh, *Balaz* of G notwithstanding, this view is unlikely. If the names are the initial words of an inscription, or perhaps of a dedicatory prayer, as has been suggested, *bal ʿaz* of G might mean 'There is no might' (sc. apart from Yahweh). Starting from the inscription on a pillar east of Gudea's temple in Lagash which records Enlil's choice of the king as high priest, R. B. Y. Scott[a] proposes that they reproduce the free-standing pillars before ancient Near Eastern sanctuaries, and that Jachin and Boaz, or rather *beʿōz*, are the first words of inscriptions, recalling oracles to royal founders on the subject of God's establishment and sustaining of the dynasty. He notes the significance of the occurrence of *yākīn* in II Sam. 7.12, 13, 16 in Nathan's oracle, with its citation in I K. 2.24; cf. Isa. 9.7[6]; Ps. 89.3f., 21, 36[4f., 22, 37]; also of *ʿōz* in other royal psalms, e.g. Pss. 21.1, 13[2, 14]; 110.2 and psalms on the subject of God as king, e.g. Pss. 93.1; 96.6, 7, 10. On the basis of such oracles, Scott feasibly proposes the inscriptions: *yākīn* (*yhwh*) *kissēʾ dāwīd ūmamlaktō lezarʿō ʿad-ʿōlām* ('He (Yahweh) will establish the throne of David, and his kingdom to his seed for ever') and *beʿōz yhwh yiśmaḥ melek* ('In the strength of Yahweh shall the king rejoice'), cf. Ps. 21.1a[2a]. With one of the pillars which thus commemorated the establishment of the king and his dynasty by royal appointment, Scott connects the pillar by which Joash stood at his coronation (II K. 11.12ff.) and that by which possibly Josiah renewed the covenant (II K. 23.1). It is very significant that, except possibly in such passages, there is no other mention of Jachin and Boaz except in the account of the destruction and spoliation of the Temple. On the evidence of the association of the pillars with the covenant in the two passages in Kings, Jachin and Boaz might be survivals of the standing stones of witness to the covenant at the central sanctuary, cf. Josh. 24.26f., the twin pillars perhaps symbolizing the covenant with the people and with the Davidic king as their representative. Emphasizing the hollow plates (*gullōt*) on each pillar, W. Kornfeldt,[b] after Albright,[c] suggests that they were motivated by the Egyptian *ḏd* pillar, which symbolized the permanence of the life of the king and his descendants. In this view, the lotus motif in the head of the pillars is significant as an acknowledged Egyptian symbol of life. De Vaux has made the

[a]R. B. Y. Scott, 'The Pillars Jachin and Boaz', *JBL* LVIII, 1939, pp. 143–7.
[b]'Der Symbolismus der Tempelsäule', *ZAW* LXXIV, 1962, pp. 55ff.
[c]*BASOR* 85, 1942, p. 26.

further suggestion that these were the names given by the craftsmen who fashioned and set them up.[a]

7.22. Verse 22b, anticipating the statement of the completion of the bronze-work of the pillar in vv. 41f., is secondary.

The bronze 'sea': 7.23–26

The text is fairly plain, except that G[B], probably correctly, transposes v. 26, which, like v. 24, deals with the great basin itself, and v. 25, which describes its base.

7 [23]And he made the 'sea', cast work, [b]ten cubits from rim to rim, quite round, and its height was five cubits, and its circumference was thirty[c] cubits; [24]and gourds under its rim encircling it round about, ten cubits[d] encircling the 'sea',[d] [e]two rows were the gourds, cast in the same mould;[e] [26]and its thickness was a handbreadth and its rim like the work of the rim of a cup, a lotus-flower, [f]holding two thousand *baths*.[f] [25]It stood upon twelve oxen, three facing northwards, and three facing westwards, and three facing southwards, and three facing eastwards,[g] and the 'sea' was upon them,[g] and all their hindquarters were inwards.

23. This is the only case in the Old Testament in which *hayyām* is used in any but its literal sense, though Montgomery cites a possible South Arabian analogy in the use of *mibḥār* (cf. Arabic *baḥr*, 'sea') for a pool, and *yam* was used in late Hebrew for the settling-tank of an oil-press and is apparently used in the copper scroll from Qumran (cols. X, 15; XI, 13) for a settling-tank for water.[h] According to II Chron. 4.6 the 'sea' was used for water for the priests' ablutions, but, standing over seven feet high, it must have been very inconvenient for this purpose. It had probably some symbolic significance, as is suggested by analogous features in sanctuaries elsewhere in the ancient Near East. The closest analogy is a large stone basin from Amathus in Cyprus, now in the Louvre, which measures 2·20 metres in diameter and stands 1·85 metres high, with four false handles in relief encircling bulls' heads.[i] Lucian[j] attests a

[a]*Ancient Israel*, p. 315.
[b]G[BA] omit.
[c]G reads '33', see n.
[d]G[BA] omit.
[e]G[BL] omit.
[f]G[BL] omit. Possibly an antiquarian note.
[g]G[B] reads this phrase at the end of the verse.
[h]J. M. Allegro, *The Treasure of the Copper Scroll*, 1960, pp. 50, 52.
[i]J. L. Myres, 'King Solomon's Temple and Other Buildings and Works of Art', *PEQ* 1948, p. 37.
[j]*De Dea Syra* 45.

sacred lake adjacent to the temple at Hierapolis, and there was an artificial sea (*ta-am-tu*) in connection with the temple of Marduk at Babylon.[a] The name of the 'sea' at Babylon, *ta-am-tu*, suggests Tiamat, the monster of the chaotic waters. Baal's victory over Prince Sea, Ocean-current, the Ruler in the Canaanite version of this myth, made a great impression in Israel, and in the liturgy associated with the New Year ritual in the Psalms there is strong evidence that the theme and its imagery were appropriated in Yahwism. Hence the containing of the waters may have symbolized the triumph of Cosmos over Chaos, the ordering power of Providence in Nature, a theme common in the Psalms, e.g. 74.12ff.; 89.8ff.[9ff.]; 93.3–4; 98.6–9; 104.9; cf. Isa. 40.12 (Qumran text). It has also been suggested that the lavers in the following passage symbolized the distribution of rain, though they had certainly a functional purpose in the Temple ritual, as Eissfeldt maintains.[b] The phrase *'āgōl sābīb* (lit. 'circular all round') is curiously tautological. 'And a line of 30 (by the cubit) surrounded it all round' recalls the similar description of circumference in v. 15. The circumference does not quite correspond to the given diameter; the Greek versions read 33 instead of 30, but this results in even wider divergence. Apparently the MT gives round numbers. Noth (*op. cit.*, p. 155) suggests that the diameter was given from the outflaring rim to the opposite rim and that the circumference was that of the body of the basin at its widest part.

7.24. *y^e ṣūqīm biṣūqāto* (lit. 'cast in its casting') probably means that the decoration was cast in one piece with the basin.

26. *ṭepaḥ* means four fingers' breadth, the thickness of the hollow pillars Jachin and Boaz, about three inches. The *bath* has been variously computed. The most concrete evidence is offered by three large jars from Lachish, of which only one, and that too fragmentary for accurate reconstruction, is inscribed *bt lmlk* ('royal *bath*'). This, however, may reasonably be taken as of like capacity to two similar jars not inscribed, which C. H. Inge[c] estimates to have held 45 or 46 litres. In the Lachish jar, however, the inscription is fragmentary and may have contained a numeral before *bt*. Albright[d] cites a jar from Tell Beit Mirsim marked simply *bt*, which is half the size of the Lachish jar. Accordingly, Albright proposes about 22 litres as the

[a]M. Jastrow, *The Religion of Babylonia and Assyria*, 1898, p. 653; Albright, *JAOS* XL, 1920, pp. 316ff.; A. Parrot, *The Temple of Jerusalem*, 1957, pp. 45–47.
[b]*HSAT*, p. 510.
[c]*PEQ*, 1941, pp. 106ff.
[d]*AASOR* XXI–XXII, 1943, p. 58 n.

capacity of the *bath*, cf. A. G. Barrois'[a] computation of 22·99 litres. Reckoning on the basis of a cubit of 17·5″ derived from the Egyptian cubit of 17·7″ and a bath of 22 litres, R. B. Y. Scott[b] concludes that the scribe in the case of Solomon's 'sea' has computed the capacity of a sphere instead of a hemisphere.

7.25. The oxen, too, may have a symbolic significance, the bull being the cult-animal of Baal, the conqueror of Sea in the Ras Shamra mythology. De Vaux, however, is most sceptical about the symbolic significance of the Temple and its equipment.[c] Our own opinion is that, as de Vaux maintains, the Temple was primarily the seat of the ark, the new shrine of all Israel. In view of the evident syncretism with certain significant elements in the seasonal ritual of Canaan to which the Psalms particularly give evidence we should admit a certain degree of symbolism in certain features of the Temple furnishings, certainly the 'sea', though the dominating influence of Yahwism is beyond doubt. In the evidence from the Psalms of such syncretism we have emphasized that Canaanite motifs are generally not unmixed with Israel's native historical faith.[d]

The wheeled stands and their bases: 7.27–39

In this highly technical passage, which betrays a specialist's interest in a fine piece of craftsmanship, there is apparently a secondary elaboration in vv. 32–36, which we indicate by our arrangement of the translation in two columns. Certain discrepancies have been noticed in the two accounts.

Primary	*Secondary*
7 [27]And he made the stands, ten of bronze. Four cubits was the length of one stand, and four cubits its breadth, and three cubits its height, [28]and this was the fashion of the stands;[e] they had cross frame-pieces, i.e. cross frame-pieces between the socketed uprights, [29]and	

[a]*Manuel d'Archéologie Biblique* II, 1953, p. 251.
[b]'Weights and Measures of the Bible', *BA* XXII, 1959, pp. 29f.
[c]*Ancient Israel*, pp. 328f.
[d]J. Gray, 'The Kingship of God in the Prophets and Psalms', *VT* XI, 1961, pp. 1–29.
[e]Reading plural with G^{BA} and S as suggested by the following *lāhen* (so for MT *lāhem*).

on the cross frame-pieces between
the socketed uprights were lions
and oxen and cherubim, and so
also upon the socketed uprights
and above and below the lions and
oxen guilloches, plated work. [30]And
there were four bronze wheels for
the one stand and bronze axles, and
its four feet[a] with braces under the
laver,[b] cast in a piece, with spirals
beyond each. [31]And the mouth[c] (of
the laver) within the crown and
above was *x*[d] cubits, and its mouth
was round, in the fashion of a stand
one and a half cubits high, and
moreover on its mouth were engravings, and their frames were
square, not round. [37]Like this he
made the ten stands, cast in one
mould, one measurement, one form
for them all; [38]and he made ten
lavers of bronze, each containing
forty *baths*, four cubits each laver,
each laver on a stand for the ten
stands. [39]And he disposed the
stands, five at the fore-corner of the
Temple at the right and five at the
fore-corner of the Temple at its left,
and the 'sea' he placed at the right
fore-corner of the Temple to the
south-east.

32 And (he made) the four
wheels under the cross frame-
pieces, and the axle trees of
the wheels were in the stand,
and the height of each wheel
was one and a half cubits,
[33]and the fashion of the
wheels was like the work of
a chariot wheel, their axle-
trees and felloes and spokes
and hubs were all cast (in the
piece), [34]and the four braces
at[e] the four corners of each
stand, its brace part of the
stand;
35 and at the top of the stand
(and)[f] half a cubit in
height,[g] quite round, and on
the top of the stand its
handles and frames, of one
piece with it; [36]and he engraved upon the panels and
upon the handles[h] and upon
the cross-pieces cherubim,
lions, and palms, as the
clear space on each allowed,
with guilloches round about.

7.27ff. In the descriptions of the lavers and their stands there are many obscurities, chiefly resulting from *hapax legomena*. The subject, however, is greatly elucidated by the description of just such a

[a]Reading *wᵉʾ arbaʿ paʿᵃmōtehā* for MT *wᵉʾarbāʿā paʿᵃmōtāw*, *mᵉkōnā* being feminine.

[b]Omitting *hakkᵉtēpōt*, which is omitted with the rest of v. 30 and v. 31 in G^{BL}.

[c]Reading *pīhā* for MT *pīhū* in agreement with feminine *mᵉkōnā*.

[d]The number has dropped out.

[e]Reading *ʿal* with G for MT *ʾel*.

[f]Some of the text including the number and the conjunction *wᵃ* before *ḥᵃṣī* has been lost.

[g]Reading *qōmātō* with G^{BL} and S for MT *qōmā*.

[h]Reading *wᵉʿal-yᵉdōtēhā*.

laver-stand, the dedication of the Lydian king Alyattes,[a] which illustrates the framework of the stand, and by two actual stands from Enkomi and Larnaka in Cyprus. The latter particularly, a miniature piece, admirably illustrates the decoration and wheeled carriage, as well as details of the framework of Solomon's laver-stands.[b] A miniature model illustrating the conception of a circular frame for the basin on a square undercarriage, but without the exact detail and wheels of the Cyprus models, is the bronze piece from Megiddo (*ANEP*, pl. 587).

These movable lavers were certainly for the distribution of water for the purification of worshippers (II Chron. 4.6) and for the cleansing of the altar and court after bloody sacrifices. It has been estimated that the lavers contained 40 *baths*, which, in addition to their own weight of bronze, would have made them quite unmanageable, and indeed even at the lowest estimate they must have weighed well over a ton. Exact computation, however, is impossible in default of accurate measurement (see vv. 31, 35), and the statement of the capacity of the lavers does not mean that they were quite filled.

7.27. The meaning of *m^e^kōnōt* ('stands') is in little doubt, though, probably by synecdoche, S read *'aganē'* ('basins'). A variant for *m^e^kōnōt* is *kēn* in v. 31, cf. Ex. 30.18; 31.9, which describes the lavers from which the priests washed between the Tabernacle and the altar.

28. The crux of this passage is the meaning of *misg^e^rōt*. It is found in Ex. 25.25, 27, denoting horizontal frame-pieces between the vertical parts of the table of shewbread in the Tabernacle. One difficulty is that the *misg^e^rōt* are said to have been between *š^e^labbīm*, which etymologically means 'ladder-work', i.e. mortised cross-pieces; cf. Pausanias' description of the laver-stand of Alyattes, 'each side of the stand is not solid throughout, but the iron cross-strips are placed *like the rungs of a ladder*'. Unless we regard the corner-posts as part of the *š^e^labbīm*, and indeed in the present passage specifically the *š^e^labbīm*, the description of the *misg^e^rōt* as between these is unintelligible. A greater difficulty is that, since Ahaz is said to have removed the *misg^e^rōt* from the laver-stands (II K. 16.17), these could not have been structurally important, as cross frame-pieces would

[a]In Pausanias, IV. 16, 2.

[b]For illustration see Burney, *Notes on . . . Kings*, figs 1 and 2, and recently A. Parrot, *op. cit.*, pp. 47–50, and, for a detailed study, J. L. Myres, *op. cit.*, pp. 38–41.

certainly have been. This remains the chief difficulty in the interpretation of *misgerōt* as cross frame-pieces, as in the construction of the table of the shewbread. Another view, which has its own peculiar difficulties, is to ignore the evidence of Ex. 25.25, 27, and take *misgerōt* in its radical etymological sense, 'closings', i.e. panels, which close up the framework. This is supported by the later parallel description, vv. 32–36, particularly by v. 36, where the engravings, which in v. 29 are said to be on the *misgerōt*, are said to be on *lūḥōt*, which can mean nothing else than 'panels'. These might well be said to be between the corner-posts, *šelabbīm*, and in this case might quite well have been removed by Ahaz without detriment to the structure of the laver-stands. A certain difficulty is that, though *misgerōt* generally in this passage could quite well mean 'panels', the word in v. 31 apparently means 'framework', so that we are apparently involved in assuming a double sense for the word in the same passage. It is, however, possible that the writer, who wished to convey the rectangular plan of the stand, used 'panels' by synecdoche to describe the horizontal parts. We regard *misgerōt* as referring both to cross frame-pieces at the top and bottom of the stand and panels, and *šelabbīm* as referring to socketed uprights including, perhaps, certain cross-pieces like the rungs of a ladder. Burney[a] boldly conjectures *šelabbīm*, which he translates 'supports', for *misgerōt* in the first occurrence of the latter in MT at v. 28. This is not strictly necessary, but has the support of Josephus,[b] who regards these as 'four small pillars'. *šelabbīm* as a noun is a *hapax legomenon*. The verbal root is found, however, in Ex. 26.17; 36.22, *štē yādōt leqereš 'eḥād mešullābōt 'iššā 'aḥōtā* ('two tenons to each board mortised one to another'). In late Hebrew *šelībā* denotes the rung of a ladder. The passive form, however, indicates that this is a secondary meaning, lit. 'socketed piece'.

7.29. Josephus, whose description of the laver-stands depends upon his personal observation of those used in Herod's Temple, which varied in certain details from Solomon's utensils, attests lions, bulls, and eagles engraved on the uprights as well as on the horizontal pieces.[c] The engraving of sphinxes (cherubim) and stylized palms is illustrated in the Larnaka laver-stand, also the guilloche, or spiral, design (*lōyōt*). *ma'aśē mōrād* posed a problem to commentators

[a] *Op. cit.*, p. 93.
[b] *Ant.* VIII, 3.6.
[c] *Ant.* VIII, 3.6.

from the time of the Greek versions, which translate it *ergon katabaseos*, which has been taken as step-work, or bevelled work. Kittel, Šanda, and Montgomery are certainly right in taking *mōrād* as the Hophal participle of *rādad*, found in the Hiphil in 6.32 of gold-plated work.[a]

7.30. *sarᵉnē* is a *hapax legomenon*, but the meaning is in no doubt, *sarnē* being commonly attested in Syriac meaning 'axle'. *paʿam* in the Old Testament means generally 'footstep', though in the Ras Shamra texts it means the human foot. In Ex. 25.12; 37.3, as here, it signifies the feet of a piece of furniture. *kᵉtēpōt* (lit. 'shoulders') denotes diagonal cross-pieces or braces from the upright to the horizontal cross-pieces under the basin. These are also illustrated in the Larnaka laver-stand, where they terminate in spirals (*lōyōt*) beyond (*mēʿēber*) the junction with the horizontal bar.

31. *kōteret* (lit. 'crown' or 'ring') refers to the circular frame in which the basin was held. Before *bā'ammā* ('cubit' or 'cubits') we should expect a number, which has dropped out, thus rendering an exact computation of the measurement and weight of the laver-cum-stand impossible. *kēn* is a synonym of *mᵉkōnā* in Ex. 30.18; 31.9, etc; see above on v. 27. The laver in its circular frame projected one and a half cubits beyond the rectangular stand (so also v. 35), a feature again illustrated in the Larnaka piece.

32. The precise meaning of *yādōt* (lit. 'hands') is difficult to determine. The commonly accepted meaning 'axles' is suggested by V, which may not be quite accurate. We might naturally take *yādōt* here as referring to the holes or holders, cast in a piece with the legs of the stand, which held the axle, as in the Larnaka laver, but in view of the usage of *yādōt* together with other specific parts of the wheel it is difficult to avoid the meaning 'axle'. In the description of the chariot of Ramses III in the Edinburgh Ostracon a part of the chariot is termed *drt*, lit. 'hands', which is taken by W. R. Dawson and T. E. Peet[b] as an indication of the Asiatic origin of the chariot. Here the fact that the goddesses Anat and Astarte are said to be the 'hands' of the chariot suggests that that part of the chariot was duplicate, as the axles or wheel-sockets.

33. *gabbēhem*, from the root *gābab* ('to be hollow or concave'), is found in the description of a wheel in Ezek. 1.18. Here it presumably

[a]A good example of gold-plating on bronze is the Baal-figurine from Ras Shamra, C. F. A. Schaeffer, *Ugaritica* I, 1939, pl. XXV.

[b]'The So-called Poem on the King's Chariot', *JEA* XIX, 1933, pp. 169, 173.

means 'felloes'. *ḥiššūqīm*, if derived from the root *ḥāšaq* ('to cleave to'), would suggest the spokes which join the felloes to the hub. *ḥiššūrīm*, if not a corruption and dittograph of the previous word *ḥiššūqīm*, may be connected, in spite of imperfect phonetic correspondence, with the Arabic *ḥašara* ('to throng together'), referring to the assembling of the spokes in the hub. *hakkōl mūṣāq* probably refers to casting in the one mould.[a]

7.34. In *min-hammᵉkōnā kᵉtēpehā*, *min* is partitive, the brace or stay being cast in one piece with the stand, as in the Larnaka laver.

35. Apparently some words have dropped out referring to the basin and the height of its projection from the stand, which we may reasonably infer from v. 31 to have been one and a half cubits. The total height must have been some five and a half cubits, almost eight feet, an inconvenient height, which almost certainly involved syphonage.

36. *lūḥōt* (lit. 'boards') were apparently panels, cf. on *misgᵉrōt*, v. 28. In *kᵉmaʿar ʾîš wᵉlōyōt . . .* if the text is correct, *maʿar* would be derived from *ʿārar* ('to be bare'), and so mean 'empty space', cf. *maʿᵃrē gebaʿ* (Judg. 20.33). An alternative reading *mēʿēber* is proposed, i.e. *mēʿēber ʾîš lōyōt . . .* ('beyond each, guilloches'), which is feasible, though the preposition refers to the scroll-work above the figures in the panel, whereas in v. 30 it refers to the spiral finial beyond the junction of the stay and the horizontal bar. Another possibility is to emend *kᵉmaʿar* to *kᵉtōʾar* ('according to the form of each'), assuming the mistake of *ayin* for *aleph* in dictation and *m* for *t* in copying.

39. The location of the bronze 'sea' recalls Ezekiel's vision of the stream rising at the south side of the east door of the Temple (Ezek. 47.1), which, as in Joel 3.18[4.18], and probably in Ps. 46.4[5], probably draws upon pre-Israelite mythology, probably that of the seat of El, the divine king paramount, at the 'out-welling of the rivers' (*mbk nhrm*) in the Ras Shamra texts. This was locally associated with the spring of Gihon.

Summary of Hiram's bronze-work: 7.40–47

This is repeated, with slight variation of single words, in II Chron. 4.11–18. Most of the items, though not systematically listed, are noted in the account of the destruction of the Temple in II K. 25.13ff. On the source, see the Introduction to 7.13–47, on p. 182.

[a]So Burney, *Notes on . . . Kings*, p. 96.

7 40And Hiram[a] made the pots[b] and the shovels and the sprinkling-
vessels, and Hiram finished doing all the work which he wrought for
king Solomon in the House of Yahweh; 41(the) two pillars and the two
bowls of the capitals, which were on top of the pillars, and the two
gratings to cover the two capital-bowls which were on top of the
pillars; 42and the four hundred pomegranates for the two gratings,
two rows of pomegranates for each grating [c](to cover the two capital-
bowls which were upon the two[d] pillars[c]); 43and the ten stands and
the ten lavers upon the stands; 44and the one 'sea' and the twelve oxen
under the 'sea'; 45and the pots and the shovels and the sprinkling-bowls
and all these[e] utensils which Hiram made for king Solomon in the
House of Yahweh, burnished bronze. 46In the plain of the Jordan he[f]
cast them in clay moulds between Succoth and Zarethan. 47[g]And
Solomon deposited all the utensils.[g] Because of the very great abundance the weight of the bronze could not be found out.

7.40. MT *kiyyōrōt* is not unintelligible, since the word is used of a cooking cauldron in I Sam. 2.14. It would be strange, however, to find this word used with this meaning when it had the specific meaning of 'laver' in the same context. Hence we emend to *sīrōt*, as in v. 45 following G and V, and the parallel account in II Chron. 4.11. *sīr* is used of a cooking-pot (Ex. 16.3, II K. 4.38). Of more significance for the present passage is the fact that it is used of a vessel for taking away ashes from the bronze altar of the Tabernacle (Ex. 27.3), which were scooped up in shovels (*yāʿīm*). *yāʿ* is derived from the root *yāʿā*, which is found in the Old Testament only in Isa. 28.17 of hail sweeping away the refuge of delusion (*w^{e}yāʿā bārād maḥsē kāzāb*). It has been connected with Arabic *waʿā*, 'to gather together'. *mizrāqōt*, derived from the verb *zāraq*, were the bowls used for dashing the blood of sanctification on the altar, cf. Ex. 24.6 *waḥ^{a}ṣī haddām zāraq ʿal-hammizbēaḥ* ('and half the blood he dashed against the altar'). It is doubtful if the word is genuine in Amos 6.6, where MT *mizr^{e}qē yayin* ('bowls of wine') should almost certainly be emended to *yayin m^{e}zuqqāq* after G, *oinon diülismenon* ('strained wine'). *bēt yhwh* ('house of Yahweh') is probably an accusative of place, but may be a scribal error of haplography for *b^{e}bēt yhwh* ('in the house of Yahweh').

[a]So G for M *Ḥīrōm*.
[b]Reading *sīrōt* with G and V for MT *kiyyōrōt*.
[c]Probably to be omitted as a dittograph of the last phrase of v. 41.
[d]Reading *š^{e}nē* with G for MT *p^{e}nē*.
[e]Reading Q *hā'ēlle* for K *hā'ēhel*.
[f]Omitting MT *hammelek* ('the king') with G^{BL}.
[g]Probably to be omitted with G as a gloss on v. 48.

7.41. On *gullōt hakkōtārōt* see Commentary on v. 20.

45. The repetition of items from v. 40 suggests that one of the verses is secondary. *m^e^mōrāṭ*, 'burnished', is the Pual participle of *māraṭ*, which is attested in Ezek. 21.15, 16, of a sword scoured and whetted, and in Isa. 18.2, 7, of the shining skin of the Sudanese.

46. *kikkār* (lit. 'round shape') from the verbal root *kārar*, Arabic *karra* ('to move round'), is regularly used of the lower Jordan valley. It possibly denotes the long oval depression of the sunken valley surrounded by the escarpments of the hills of Palestine and Transjordan, and is occasionally visualized as extending to the south of the Dead Sea (Gen. 13.10ff.). If this physical sense of *kikkār* is to be pressed the term might denote the broader part of the lower Jordan valley south of the lower course of the Jabbok (*Wādī Zerqā*), where the valley is narrowest. On the other hand, the word may simply mean 'surrounding district', as in Neh. 12.28, where it refers to the district (Greek *perioikis*) of Jerusalem. Succoth (lit. 'bivouacs') on the east side of the Jordan (Gen. 33.17; Josh. 13.27; Judg. 8.4, 5) has been identified since Talmudic times with *Deir ʿAllā* just north of the Jabbok, where it breaks into the plain.[a] Recent excavation at this site has shown that it was a centre of metallurgy. Deposits of metal slag were found at every level in the Iron Age, and furnaces were sited outside the city wall, in one of which a pottery spout of a crucible was found with a piece of copper still in it. Even so, Franken, the director of the excavation, shows reserve in identifying the site with Succoth, since slag deposits are found in other sites in the vicinity.[b] It is obvious that the whole region was a centre of metallurgy in the Hebrew monarchic period, probably, as Franken suggests, because the clay was suitable for moulds, but also possibly because of the long experience of the local people in the art. What originally attracted metal-workers to this vicinity may have been the clay, the proximity of the scrub forest of Transjordan, still a source of charcoal, and the prevalence of the north wind in the Jordan valley. We suggest that the name Succoth ('bivouacs') may reflect the origin of the place as a settlement of the Kenites or itinerant smiths. Zarethan is of uncertain location, and is described as near Adamah (*ad-Dāmiyeh*) in Josh. 3.16, and by Abel-Meholah (I K. 4.12). If the

[a]Albright, *AASOR* VI, 1926, pp. 46ff.; Abel, *GP* I, pp. 450ff.; Glueck, *BASOR* 90, 1943, pp. 2–23.

[b]H. Franken, 'The Excavations at Deir ʿAllā in Jordan', *VT* X, 1960, pp. 386–93.

latter place is correctly located at *Tell Abū Sifrī* about ten miles south of Bethshan and the same distance north of *ad-Dāmiyeh*, as this passage apparently demands, this would agree with the location of Zarethan twelve miles from Adamah, according to R. Johanan (third century AD), which would exclude the location at *Qarn Sarṭabeh*, which Abel suggests.[a] The site has been feasibly located at *Tell as-Saʿīdīyeh* at the mouth of the *Wādī Kufrinjeh* on the east bank of the Jordan, about eight miles north of *Tell Deir ʿAllā*. Actually the reference to Succoth (*Deir ʿAllā?*) suggests a site considerably farther north than Adamah and the location on the lower course of the *Wādī Fārʿa* proposed by H. Guthe,[b] who explains this name as referring to the narrow ravine where the *Wādī Fārʿa* breaks from the mountains to the plain. It would also rule out the proposal first made by G. F. Moore in his commentary on Judges,[c] and since widely held, that the MT *b^emaʿ^abē hāʾ^adāmā* should be emended to *b^emaʿberet ʾ^adāmā* ('at the ford of Adamah'). The MT apparently means 'in the thickness of the soil', which is translated literally in G, from which V renders *in terra argillosa* ('in the clay soil'). The foundry site was no doubt chosen for its thickness of clay bed in which moulds could be shaped for the huge objects such as the pillars Jachin and Boaz and the bronze 'sea', hence *maʿ^abē* (lit. 'thickness') refers to the depth of the soil rather than its consistency, it being accepted that clay was the only soil suitable for this operation.

7.47. The vast amount of metal came from the escarpments east and west of the Arabah, where copper had been mined by the Egyptians in the middle of the third millennium and was exploited particularly in the early Hebrew monarchy, being mined, crushed, and smelted in primitive furnaces near the mines, as the recent researches of B. Rothenberg[d] and a team of metallurgical experts have convincingly demonstrated, exploding, incidentally, Glueck's view that *Tell al-Ḫaleifeh* (Ezion-Geber) at the north end of the Gulf of Aqaba was a great refinery.[e] The copper of this region is mentioned in Deut. 8.9 as one of the assets of the promised land, and the mines were notorious as penal settlements for Christians in the Roman persecutions in the third century AD.

[a]GP II, pp. 450ff.
[b]*ZAW* XLI, 1925, pp. 105ff.
[c]ICC, 1895, pp. 212ff.
[d]B. Rothenberg, 'Ancient Copper Industries in the Western Arabah', *PEQ*, 1962, pp. 5–71.
[e]Glueck, *BASOR* 71, 1938, pp. 3–18; 75, 1939, pp. 8–22; 79, 1940, pp. 2–18.

(λ) *The gold or gilded furnishings of the Temple*: 7.48–51

This passage, paralleled in II Chron. 4.19–5.1, gives a brief list of various furnishings without detailed description of their construction. In this it contrasts strangely with the elaborate detail of what precedes, and so has been taken as a late elaboration. Certain features appear, which are so far strange in the description of the Temple and its furnishings, such as the incense-altar overlaid with gold in the Temple, which is described in Ex. 30.1ff. (P), and the table for the shewbread, also overlaid with gold, according to Ex. 25.23. These affinities with the Priestly description of the furnishing of the Tabernacle, as against all other pre-exilic evidence, suggest a post-exilic elaboration. Such passages as II K. 12.13; 25.14ff. and Jer. 52.18ff., at any rate, which mention gold utensils, seem to know nothing of the profusion of gold described in this passage, nor are the items mentioned in the account of the gold-plated and gilded furnishings of the Temple in 6.20ff. There is, however, probably a nucleus of original annalistic matter at this point, which we should see in the list of movable smaller objects in v. 50a, as apart from the gold plating of the Temple furnishings. These relate to the service of incense before the inmost shrine. This list of gold objects attracted to itself a number of later gold features, such as the incense-altar and the table for the shewbread (v. 48a) and the *pōtōt* ('front-panels', see text on v. 50) in v. 50b, which is suggested by 6.32, which is also secondary. Noth (*op. cit.*, p. 166) emphasizes the singular *peraḥ* ('flower') in v. 49 as the base of a lamp-bowl, which would hardly be a collective singular even if the ten lampstands in v. 49a were original. Ten lampstands before the inmost shrine are peculiar to this passage and are independent also of P. It may fairly be assumed that, on the clue of the singular *peraḥ*, one lampstand was listed in the original source, and this was subsequently elaborated to ten in the light of a development in the later monarchy. Verse 51a is probably editorial, as is also the note on the disposal of David's spoils in v. 51b, where for the first time 'the treasuries of the Temple' are noted.

7 [48]And Solomon made all the utensils which were in the Temple of
Yahweh, the golden altar and the table whereon was the bread of the
presence, of gold; [49]and the lampstands, five on the right and five on
the left before the inmost shrine, of refined gold, and the flowers, and
the lamps, and the tongs, of gold; [50]and the bowls, and the trimming-
shears, and the sprinkling-bowls, and the ladles, and the firepans, of

refined gold, and the front panels of the doors of the inner house, the Holy of Holies, and of the doors[a] of the main hall,[b] of gold. [51]And all the work which king Solomon wrought in the Temple of Yahweh was completed, and Solomon brought in the dedications of David his father, even the silver and the gold, and the utensils he put into the treasuries of the Temple of Yahweh.

7.48. The only altar so far mentioned is that in I K. 6.20, which was of cedar, not gold. This, however, may well have been overlaid with gold, like all the other wooden objects described in this passage. This was probably the incense-altar described in Ex. 30.1ff., and distinct from the table of the shewbread. The latter, the description of which in this passage agrees with the more elaborate specification in Ex. 25.23, was nevertheless an early feature in Yahwistic sanctuaries, as appears from the incident at Nob, where David and his men ate the shewbread (I Sam. 21.4ff.).

49. *m^enōrōt* are 'lampstands' rather than lamps. The parallel account in II Chron. 4.20 does not specify ten of these, though v. 7 does. *peraḥ*, 'flower-work', is probably ornamental bases on the lampstands on which the oil-bowls were set (Ex. 25.31ff.). *melqaḥayim* ('a pair of prehensile instruments') is found meaning 'tongs' in the vision of Isaiah (Isa. 6.6). Here and in Ex. 25.38; 37.23; Num. 4.9 (P), where the instruments are of gold and are associated with the lamps of the Tabernacle, 'snuffers' would be a more appropriate meaning, but they may denote tongs for incense.

50. *sippōt* ('bowls') is found in association with the same utensils in II K. 12.14, and in Jer. 52.19. The connection with *sap* ('threshold') is suggested by A. M. Honeyman,[c] but in view of the connection and the meaning of *sap* as 'cup' in the phrases *sap raʿal* ('cup of reeling') in Zech. 12.2 and possibly *sap-ḥ^amāt^ekā* ('cup of thy fury') in Hab. 2.15, there is no objection to regarding the word here as 'bowl'. The word is vocalized *sappōt* in II Sam. 17.28. *m^ezamm^erōt*, from the root *zāmar* ('to trim', e.g. by pruning), denotes here trimming shears for the wicks. *kappōt*, variously rendered in EVV as 'spoons' and 'pans', means primarily 'the palm of the hand' or 'the sole of the foot', hence any shallow container, e.g. the pocket of a sling (I Sam. 25.29). It might well indicate a small ladle for oil, incense, or cosmetics, such as the small silver ladle with the handle in the form of a nude

[a]Reading *ūl^edal^etē* with S.
[b]Reading *hahēkāl* with G^BL for MT *habbayit lahēkāl*.
[c]*JTS* XXXVII, 1936, pp. 56ff.

female from the Persian period at *Tell Fārʿa* in the *Wādī Ghazzeh*.[a] *maḥtōt* ('fire-shovels') is derived from *ḥātā* ('to snatch'), which is actually used of snatching fire in Isa. 30.14 (*laḥtōt 'ēš miyyāqūd*) ('to take fire from the hearth') cf. Prov. 6.27. *pōtōt* has been connected with *pōt* in Isa. 3.17, which means *cardo feminae*, cf. Arabic *fawt* ('space between the fingers'), suggesting a meaning here 'hinge-socket'. The word is not otherwise mentioned in the Old Testament. It seems impracticable that the hinge-sockets in the floor and lintel should be of gold, hence we should probably visualize some other part of the door. G. R. Driver[b] has suggested the Akkad. cognate *pūtu* ('forehead'), suggesting that *pōtōt* may refer to the front, or outside of the door. *qōdeš haqqᵒdāšīm* ('holy of holies') is peculiar to P, another indication that the passage is a late elaboration.

7.51. *qodᵉšē dāwīd* ('the dedications of David') included the gifts which David had received from such as Toi of Hamath and the spoils of his wars with Edom, Moab, and the Aramaeans, which he had dedicated to Yahweh (II Sam. 8.10–12). This last campaign was given the aspect of a holy war, since, possibly for the last time, the ark was sent with the army. Hence the spoils of this war were the property of Yahweh. See further on 9.21. This was possibly a modification of the ruder practice of *ḥerem*, where such spoils, including human victims, were destroyed in renunciation of common use, since the war was a 'holy' engagement, hence Yahweh's enterprise, to which both men and weapons were exclusively set apart (I Sam. 21.5[6]). A distinction is made between the bullion to which David's spoils were apparently reduced, and the vessels (*kēlīm*), which Solomon had made specifically for the Temple service. The ancients did not always respect craftsmanship, reducing spoils to bullion, as the Babylonians did with the bronze-work of the Temple (II K. 24.13). The treasures of the Persian Empire suffered the same fate in the Muslim conquest. The *pièce de résistance* of the spoil of the Sassanid palace at Medain was the royal banqueting carpet depicting a garden, the ground being worked in gold and the walks in silver, with lawns in emeralds, rivers in pearls, and trees and flowers in diamonds, rubies, and other precious stones. This fabulous *objet d'art* was cut in pieces by the order of the Caliph Omar and distributed in merit awards and pensions to the Muslims and poor relief.

[a]W. F. Petrie, *Beth-Pelet* I, 1930, pl. 45.
[b]*JTS* XXXVIII, 1937, p. 38.

(iv) THE DEPOSITING OF THE ARK AND THE DEDICATION OF THE TEMPLE: 8.1–66

This section is closely paralleled by II Chron. 5–7. The phraseology and the full, rhetorical style, the admonitory tone and the simple, stern theology of sin and retribution in the prayer of Solomon (vv. 14–61), stamp it as an elaboration of the Deuteronomistic compiler with later expansion by a reviser of the same school during the Exile (e.g. vv. 44–53). Contrasting strongly with this matter in style is the poetic fragment in vv. 12f., which G includes at v. 53 in an expanded form, citing as a source 'the Book of the Song' (*en bibliō tēs ōdēs*). This is certainly anterior to vv. 14–61.

The first section (vv. 1–11) preserves a genuine account of what happened at the dedication of the Temple with due sacrifice proportionate to the occasion and to this epoch-making assembly of the sacral community (v. 5), and the installation of the ark, significantly called simply 'the ark of Yahweh', as in the early narrative source, for instance in Joshua. This narrative, culminating in the poetic citation (vv. 12f.), also early and possibly from the Book of Jashar (see *ad loc.*), is used by the Deuteronomistic compiler as an introduction to Solomon's prayer (vv. 14–61), which in his plan of composition he uses to mark a period with a review and prospect of the scope of his history. The compiler, however, has left his own mark on the narrative, indicated by his characteristic phraseology and theology, e.g. 'the ark of the covenant of Yahweh', i.e. not as a symbol of the divine presence, but, as is stated explicitly and at length in v. 9, as a mere receptacle of the tablets of the law of God, who was above such local limitations. The narrative in vv. 1–11 has been further worked over by a post-Deuteronomistic hand. This is indicated by the addition of *kol-ʿadat yiśrāʾēl* (v. 5a), *qōdeš haqqodāšîm* for *haddebîr* or *debîr habbayit* (v. 6a), and the statement of the exit of the priests from the Temple when the cloud of the glory of God filled it (vv. 10f.), which is obviously suggested by the statement that Moses was not able to enter the Tent of Meeting when the cloud indicated that the glory filled it (Ex. 40.34f.).

The last passage (vv. 62–66) reflects a genuine tradition of the significant assembly of the sacral community Israel at the dedication of the new central sanctuary, but this is the work of the Deuteronomistic compiler, who expatiates on v. 5 in v. 62, his statement 'the king and all Israel were making sacrifice before Yahweh' perhaps reflecting the language of his source in v. 5 before that verse was worked over by himself and the post-Deuteronomistic reviser, who substituted 'all the convocation of Israel' for 'Israel'. The exaggerated numbers of v. 63 are also secondary, elaborating the undoubtedly correct tradition of the great sacrifices of communion offerings demanded on the occasion of the assembly of the sacral community of Israel. Secondary to this note is v. 64 on the consecration of the middle of the court, since the altar was too small for the sacrifices. This is obviously late, and its date and affinity with P is indicated by the threefold classification of the sacrifices. The specific note on the Festival, i.e. the Feast of Tabernacles in the New Year season, and the specification of its seven-day duration and the dismissal of the people on the eighth day (vv. 65f.; cf. Deut. 16.13, 15) is a Deuteronomistic elaboration of the simple statement in v. 2. The omission in G of MT 'and seven days, fourteen days', which is noted more explicitly in I Chron. 7.8f., indicates a late expansion, probably from the Priestly revision.

(a) *The installation of the ark:* 8.1–11

8 1 [a]Then Solomon assembled[b] the elders of Israel, all the heads of
the tribes, the patriarchal chiefs of the children of Israel, to king
Solomon[c] to Jerusalem[d] to bring up the ark of the covenant of Yahweh
from the city of David, that is Zion. 2 [e]And all the men of Israel were
assembled to king Solomon[e] in the month of Ethanim [f]at the (great)
festival, that is the seventh month.[f] 3 [g]And all the elders of Israel came[g]
and the priests lifted up the ark, 4 [h]and they brought up the ark of
Yahweh[h] and the Tent of Meeting and all the holy vessels which were
in the Tent,[i] [j]and the priests and the Levites brought them up[j]; 5 and

[a]There is considerable variation of reading between MT and G, the latter generally omitting phrases in MT which are tautological, most of which are probably later glosses. In the first verse there is a considerable expansion, namely, 'and it happened, when Solomon finished building the house of the Lord and his own house after 20 years'. This statement appears both in MT and G at I K. 9.10.

[b]Forty-seven Hebrew MSS and G, S, and V add 'all'.

[c]Omitted in G^{BL}, and certainly 'to king Solomon' does not seem original after 'Solomon' as subject of the sentence. See further n. on v. 1.

[d]G reads 'Zion'.

[e]G^{BL} omit the phrase, which is tautological after the first clause of v. 1 (MT).

[f]G^{BL} omit. As the numbering of the month after the vernal equinox indicates, this is a post-exilic gloss.

[g]G^{BL} again omit the tautological phrase.

[h]G^{BL} again omit, probably correctly, the phrase being tautological.

[i]Here G adds 'of meeting', a reading which ought to be taken seriously, since it is contrary to the general tendency of G to read a shorter text than MT here.

[j]G^{BL} again omit. The role of the Levites indicates a late priestly expansion of the original text, cf. II Chron. 5.4ff., where the Levites, and not 'the priests' as in this passage, take up the ark.

the king[a] and all [b]the convocation of[b] Israel and [c]those who had kept appointment with him together with him[c] were before the ark sacrificing sheep and oxen, [d]which could not be counted or numbered, they were so many.[d] [6]And the priests brought in the ark of the covenant[e] of Yahweh into its place, even into the inmost shrine of the Temple, into the Holy of Holies under the wings of the cherubim, [7]for the cherubim had their wings spread out over[f] the place of the ark and the cherubim formed a screen over the ark and its staves above; [8]and they had made the staves of such a length that the ends of the staves were seen from the holy place before the shrine, but they were not visible outside, [g]and they have been there unto this day.[g] [9]There was nothing in the ark except the two stone tablets which Moses laid up there at Horeb, [h]the tablets of the covenant[h] which Yahweh made with the children of Israel when they came out of the land of Egypt. [10]And it came to pass, when the priests came out of the holy place, that the cloud filled the Temple of Yahweh, [11]and the priests could not stand to minister before the cloud for the glory of Yahweh filled the Temple.[i]

8.1ff. The fact that the significant omissions of G in this passage are included in G and MT of the parallel passage in II Chron. 5.1–11, suggests that for some time after the final Deuteronomistic redaction the text was fluid and subject to revision in the light of the Priestly account of the Tabernacle in Ex. 25ff., as Noth suggests (*op. cit.*, p. 175), on the basis of which the Chronicler composed his parallel account, with his own significant additions.

A detailed study of these interpolations is found in Burney.[j] His

[a]Omitting 'Solomon' of MT with G^BL.

[b]G^BL omit *ʿadat* of MT, which is a post-Deuteronomistic expansion.

[c]G^BL again omit this phrase, which seems superfluous, a gloss on MT *ʿadat* . . .

[d]For this full, but not unfamiliar, phrase G^BL say simply 'without number'.

[e]G^BL read simply 'the ark', which is probably original, cf. v.3, *habbᵉrīt* being a later explanatory gloss.

[f]Probably the common scribal error of *ʾel* for *ʿal*, which is actually written in II Chron. 5.8.

[g]This phrase, in which 'unto this day' betrays the hand of a late editor with an antiquarian interest familiar in priestly writings, is omitted in G^BL.

[h]After 'the tablets of stone' G adds 'the tablets of the covenant' (*plakes tēs diathēkēs*), obviously feeling the want of an antecedent to the relative clause. The verb *kārat* in the relative clause seems to demand such an antecedent, though the verb is found with the ellipse of *bᵉrīt* in I Sam. 20.16; 22.8, as Burney points out. Burney defends the MT on the grounds that the imperfect connection between the relative clause as it stands in MT and 'the tablets of stone' (*lūḥōt hāʾᵃbānīm*) is due to its stemming from the Deuteronomistic redaction, the ark in the phraseology of D being regularly 'the ark of the covenant'. Burney maintained that the Hebrew reading behind G^BL represents an effort to smooth out the difficulties (*op. cit.*, pp. 108f.). He is clearly right in his view that the verse as it stands in MT could not have come from a single hand.

[i]Reading *habbayit* with G^B for *bēt-yhwh* of MT.

[j]*Notes on . . . Kings*, pp. 104–9.

dating of them in the late exilic or early post-exilic period appears to us insufficient to account for their omission in G.

8.1. *'āz* ('then') refers to a new item or a new step in a narrative. It is taken by Burney, who lists incidences of the particle in Kings,[a] as a trait of the Deuteronomistic reviser, by which he linked his material together. Montgomery's researches[b] suggest to him that it may rather reflect the annalistic style, here of Solomon's court records. Montgomery's evidence notwithstanding, this particular instance is not a case of an annalistic excerpt introduced by *'āz*. After the annalistic note of the year, as well as the month, when the Temple was begun and finished, in the month of Bul (6.37f.), which followed Tishri (here Ethanim), when the great feast fell, we expect a note of the year of Solomon's reign in which the ark was installed (v. 2) and the Temple dedicated. In contrast to the explanatory note 'that is the seventh month', this probably derives from an early narrative source based on Solomon's annals. If the installation of the ark and the dedication of the Temple at the great festival did not take place until the building was fully completed in the eighth month, according to 6.38, eleven months must have elapsed until the following Feast of Tabernacles. This the Deuteronomistic compiler felt to be intolerable, according to Noth (*op. cit.*, p. 176), and accordingly he suppressed the note of the year and substituted the vague *'āz* ('then'). On the other hand, the note in 6.38 may refer to the completion of the adjuncts and equipment which was not essential to the ritual function of the Temple which might then have been dedicated to receive the ark at the Feast of Tabernacles in the seventh year, a month before the completion of the whole complex. In this case, the apparent discrepancy between the note on the completion of the Temple in the month Bul in 6.38 and its dedication and the installation of the ark in the seventh month may have been glossed over by the compiler by the substitution of *'āz* for the note of the year in the source. The verb *hiqhîl*, from which *qāhāl* ('congregation' or generally 'assembly') is derived, occurs most frequently in P, though it is found also in earlier passages. Though late usage in P tended to denote the religious community of Israel as *qāhāl*, the term is not confined to this usage but denotes a number of peoples in general (Gen. 35.11, P), such as the nations associated with Gog and Magog (Ezek. 38.7). The wide scope of the word and its reference to the wicked in general (Ps. 26.5), cf. the

[a] *Op. cit.*, p. 35.
[b] 'Archival Data in the Book of Kings', *JBL* LIII, 1934, pp. 46–52.

Qumran *Manual of Discipline*, seriously modifies the claim that this word has a specific religious connotation, generally supposed to be rendered into *ecclēsia* in its New Testament connotation. See the detailed criticism of this view by J. Barr.[a] The Hebrew term which does denote such a religious assembly, or amphictyony, is *ʿēdā*, which is used in v. 5. This properly means 'those who keep tryst' (*mōʿēd*), but this word also may be used generally, probably in a figurative sense, of a gathering of the wicked (Pss. 22.16[17]; 86.14; Job 15.34) or a swarm of bees (Judg. 14.8).

'All the heads of the tribes, the patriarchal chiefs of the children of Israel', which G omits, but is included in II Chron. 5, is certainly the phraseology of P (cf. Num. 3.30, 35; 7.2; 30.1). In the installation of the ark, the old amphictyonic palladium, it is nevertheless possible that tribal representatives were called. *leha ʿalōt* indicates very precisely the higher elevation of the Temple hill relative to the city of David lower, and farther south, on the south-eastern hill, a situation for the citadel dictated by the Spring of Gihon. Here Zion is identified with the city of David. The fortress at the northern part of the south-eastern hill, which was captured by Joab and his striking-force (II Sam. 5.7–9), is called more specifically 'the fortress of Zion' (*meṣūdat ṣīyyōn*). It is not certain whether Zion was only the citadel, as H. Vincent[b] holds, or the whole settlement, the Hebrew text being patient of both meanings. The name was later transferred to the Temple hill, the seat of the ark (Amos 1.2; Isa. 8.18; Micah 4.2, etc.) and to the whole city (Amos 6.1; Isa. 10.24, etc.).[c]

8.2. On the date see p. 204 n.[f], where 'in the month of Ethanim at the festival' may be original, and 'that is the seventh month' (i.e. from the vernal equinox, by Babylonian reckoning) is a later gloss, as is indicated by the fact that it ignores *beḥāg*. *'ētānīm* means 'regularly flowing', and refers to the heavy rains, which fall regularly in autumn just after the New Year Feast of Tabernacles at the autumnal equinox. The seventh month is also called Tishri, which was used also as the name of this month in the Ras Shamra texts. The adjective, in which the first letter is a radical consonant, is cognate with Arabic *watana* ('to be perpetual, never-failing', of water). In Hebrew it is used primarily of water, e.g. Amos 5.24, *naḥal 'ētān* ('a perennial

[a] *The Semantics of Biblical Language*, pp. 119ff.

[b] *Jérusalem de l'Ancien Testament* II, 1956, p. 632.

[c] See the excellent discussion in J. Simons, *Jerusalem in the Old Testament*, 1952, ch. 3.

wadi'), cf. Ps. 74.15, but it is applied in the general sense of 'enduring', 'stable', e.g. Jer. 5.15, *gōy 'ētān*. On the apparent discrepancy between the statement about the completion of the Temple in the eighth month Bul (6.38) and its dedication in the seventh month, see on 8.1. Van den Born assumes that the dedication was postponed for eleven months so that it should fall on the Feast of Tabernacles at New Year.[a] In the Ras Shamra Baal-myth the completion of the 'house of Baal' is celebrated on the eve of the autumn rains and, in view of the obvious significance of the old Canaanite theme of the kingship of God won in conflict with the forces of Chaos, which the Psalms show to have been adapted by the Hebrews, it seems no mere coincidence that the Temple should have been dedicated at this very season, the most significant crisis in the agricultural year, and as such observed with important ceremonies. This was for the Hebrews the festival *par excellence* (*heḥāg*), when the kingship of Yahweh was celebrated.[b] Unfortunately there is no pre-exilic evidence for the celebration of this festival in the seventh month rather than the eighth. The pre-exilic sources Ex. 23.16 and Deut. 16.13 simply indicate that the great autumn festival was after the harvest, though Deut. 16.13, by mentioning corn and wine and making no mention of olives, may indicate the seventh rather than the eighth month. After the disruption of the kingdom Jeroboam I 'ordained a feast (*ḥag*) in the eighth month on the fifteenth day of the month like the feast which is in Judah'. This remark, however, cannot be taken as conclusive evidence that the corresponding feast in Judah was in the eighth month, but simply that Jeroboam borrowed the theme of the feast, namely the kingship of God. Jeroboam may have altered the date as a gesture of independence, but he may on the other hand have been following custom, which was regularized in the seventh month only after the exile. The truth is that before the centralization of the cult with its syncretism of local nature-worship and native Israelite Yahwism, there was no generally fixed date for the autumn festival, though there was a tendency to regularize it between the new moon of the seventh and eighth months. Jeroboam may have availed himself of this fluidity to fix his feast at Bethel in the middle of Bul (I K. 12.32). In the post-exilic sources (Lev. 23.34ff.; Num. 29.12ff.) the feast, at Jerusalem, of course, is fixed in the middle of the seventh month, but

[a]So van den Born, *Koningen*, p. 54.

[b]J. Gray, 'The Kingship of God in the Prophets and Psalms', *VT* XI, 1961, pp. 1–29.

here, as in many matters of ritual, the late sources may be retailing early traditions. The view of J. Morgenstern[a] might also be mentioned, that the beginning of Solomon's ceremonies was in Ethanim and the climax of the feast in Bul.

8.4. It is suggested that the statement about the bringing up of the tent of meeting (*'ōhel mō'ēd*) is unhistorical, since the sources of Kings know of no sacred tent except that in which David housed the ark, which is not called 'the tent of meeting'.[b] The phrase is almost certainly a priestly gloss, though, as the repository of the ark, this was a tent of meeting, where Yahweh and the community kept tryst. Owing to its association with the ark and other sacred vessels which were taken up to the Temple, the tent would have been physically affected by the 'holiness' of these objects, and would have to be taken in to the Temple, if only to perish decently there. In support of our admission of this reference as historical it should be noted that G, which generally reduces the text of MT here, includes the reference to the 'tent of meeting'. *wayya'ᵃlū 'ōtām hakkōhᵃnīm wᵉhallᵉwīyim* ('and the priests and the Levites brought them up') is omitted by G, correctly, since a distinction is implied between priests and Levites which did not arise until post-exilic times, all Levites in pre-exilic times being priests, but only the Aaronic branch having the full status of priests in P. Here, as in the parallel version in Chronicles, we see the influence of the P redactor, the carrying of the ark and the cult apparatus being the function of the Levites in Num. 4.15.

5. In *'ᵃdat yiśrā'ēl* ('the convocation of Israel') we have another instance of the influence of II Chron. 5.6, the phrase being peculiar to P. The participle *mᵉzabbᵉḥīm* ('sacrificing') may indicate sacrifices at various stages of the progress of the ark to the Temple, as in the case of David's introduction of the ark to Jerusalem (II Sam. 6.13), cf. the sacramental procession and installation of the ark in Pss. 132; 24; and possibly 68, first noticed by Mowinckel.[c]

6. On *qōdeš haqqᵒdāšīm*, which we take as a late gloss from the P redactor, see p. 169. It should be noted that it is included in G.

7. For MT *wayyāsōkkū* ('formed a screen') II Chron. reads *wayᵉkassū* ('and they covered'). MT, however, is defensible, the verb being *sākak* ('to make a hedge, or screen, about'), as the shady trees

[a] *HUCA* I, 1924, pp. 67ff.
[b] Skinner, CB, p. 141.
[c] *Psalmenstudien* II, 1922, pp. 109ff., 141, 332; V, 1924, p. 31 n. 6.

screen the hippopotamus in Job 40.22. The verb is actually used of a cherub in the reference in Ezek. 28.14, 16 to the royal ideology of Tyre. *baddīm* (lit. 'detachable, or projecting, parts') is derived from *bādad* ('to be isolated'), cf. Arabic *badda* ('to cause to withdraw'), whence *bad* ('part') is used of the limbs of a man (Job 18.13) and possibly of the bolts of a gate (Hos. 11.6; Job 17.16). It is the technical term for the staves, or poles, on which the ark and the furniture of the Tabernacle were carried.

8.8. The note on the projection of the staves left in the ark seems to be influenced by the priestly direction in Ex. 25.15 that the staves of the ark should not be removed. *qōdeš* (lit. 'holiness'), describing the place before the inmost shrine from which the ends of the staves were visible, is difficult, and may reflect Ex. 26.34 (P), where a curtain is said to divide the inmost shrine, or 'holy of holies' (*qōdeš haqqᵒdāšīm*), from the 'holy place' (*haqqōdeš*), where it could mean, as in Ugaritic (Gordon, *UT*, 2 'Aqht I, 27, 45; II, 16; Krt, 197; ʿnt III, 27), simply 'sanctuary'. In v. 10 it seems to denote the inmost shrine, but this can hardly be so in v. 8, unless there was a curtain before the ark, cf. Ex. 26.31ff. (P), in the inmost shrine itself, of which there is no mention in chs. 6f. What is obviously visualized is the invisibility of the ends of staves because of the narrow door of the inmost shrine (6.31ff.). If *qōdeš* is not a post-Deuteronomistic gloss, it may be a corruption of *ʿereś* (lit. 'throne'), the dais or top of the steps to the inmost shrine.

9. The statement that nothing was in the ark but the tablets of stone obviously comes from a time when other objects were believed to have been in them, e.g. Aaron's rod and a pot of manna, the source of the tradition in Heb. 9.4, which, however, is not specifically attested in the statement of the deposit of Aaron's rod in Num. 17.10 [25], and the pot of manna in Ex. 16.33.

10. The miracle of the cloud, the symbol of the glory of Yahweh and his presence in the sanctuary, is influenced by the tradition eventually expressed in Ex. 33.9ff.; 40.34ff. At this particular point it may be prompted by the words of the following poetic fragment, *yhwh 'āmar liškōn bāʿᵃrāpel* ('Yahweh has said that he would dwell in thick darkness'), which itself may retain the tradition expressed in P.

11. The verb *šērēt* ('minister') indicates the holy office of the priestly caste in the sanctuary, *ʿābad* ('worship') denoting worship both by priests and by the community.

(β) *Poetic declaration of Solomon, the founder of the Temple:* 8.12f.

This is probably the truncation of the original, which is rendered in G at v. 53,

> Ἥλιον ἐγνώρισεν ἐν οὐρανῷ Κύριος·
> εἶπεν τοῦ κατοικεῖν ἐκ γνόφου.
> Οἰκοδόμησον οἶκόν μου, οἶκον ἐκπρεπῆ σαυτῷ
> τοῦ κατοικεῖν ἐπὶ καινότητος.

G adds that the fragment is taken from 'the Book of the Song',

> οὐκ ἰδοὺ αὕτη γέγραπται ἐν βιβλίῳ τῆς ᾠδῆς;

The peculiar form of the Greek indicates clearly that it is a rather literal translation from a Hebrew original, which itself betrays two versions, *h^alō' hī' k^etūbā b^esēper haššīr* ('Is it not written in the Book of the Song?') and *hinnē kātūb b^esēper haššīr* ('See, it is written in the Book of the Song'). Wellhausen made the further suggestion that the original read *sēper hayyāšār*, which, as we know from the citations in Josh. (10.13) and Samuel (II Sam. 1.18), was in poetry. This saga of the God of Israel, extending as it did at least to the death of Saul (II Sam. 1.18), may well have culminated in the establishment of the Davidic line and the building of the Temple, which is so often mentioned together with Yahweh's covenant with David, fulfilled in the accession of Solomon. If this were so, the first half of Ps. 89 (vv. 1–37 [2–38]) might well incorporate matter from the Book of Jashar. Whether or not this is so, I K. 8.12–13 may be taken from some poetic account of the reign of Solomon, who may be *hayyāšār* ('the legitimate one'), the purpose of the source being to 'legitimize' the claim of Solomon to the throne, though he was one of David's youngest sons. For this sense of *yāšār*, cf. the Krt text from Ras Shamra (Gordon, *UT*, Krt 13). This source would then be a poetic parallel to the prose Story of the Davidic Succession. In view of the content of the poetic declaration in G, the theme may also have been the legitimization of Solomon's step in founding the Temple as the new shrine of the sacral community. This would involve an account of the adventures of the ark from nomadic times to the settlement in Palestine, such as we generally associate with the Book of Jashar.

The mutilated fragment in MT vv. 12f. may be restored on the basis of G:

> *yhwh haššemeš hēkīn* (*or hōpīa'*) *baššāmayim*
> *wayyō'mer liškōn bā'^arāpel*

bānō bānītī bēt zᵉbūl lᵉkā
mākōn lᵉšibtᵉkā ʿōlāmīm

8 12Yahweh has established (or 'caused to shine')[a] the sun in the heavens,
But has said that he would dwell in thick darkness.
13 I have built[b] a royal house for thee,
An established place for thy throne for ever.

8.13. *bēt zᵉbūl* is generally taken as 'an exalted house', for which Schrader cited the Assyrian analogy *bīt zabal*. Certainly in Isa. 63.15 and Hab. 3.11 the root means 'exaltation', but in the Ras Shamra texts the word means also 'prince', being found in parallelism with *ṯpṭ* ('judge'). Since the building and occupation of his 'house' in the Ras Shamra mythology signalized Baal's ascendancy as King, his temple might be said to be 'a royal house'. In view of the place that the 'established dwelling' (*mākōn lᵉšibtᵉkā*) plays in passages which celebrate the kingship of Yahweh and which often reflect Canaanite mythology, we have little hesitation in translating *bēt zᵉbūl* as 'royal house', though admitting the possibility of the translation 'exalted house'. As a parallel to 'royal house' we have taken *šebet* in the pregnant sense of 'throne', cf. *yōšeb* ('he who sits enthroned') in Amos 1.5, where it is parallel to *tōmēk šēbeṭ* ('him who handleth the sceptre').

This poetic fragment, which by its very nature we take as early, indicates the foundation of the Temple and the installation of the ark in the inmost shrine as the symbol of an important religious truth. The God of Israel is at once the Creator of the universe, who has 'established the sun in the heavens', and the God of Israel who has condescended to fix his throne in the midst of his people Israel, but whose nearness and readily-experienced power and grace never exhaust his revelation (cf. v. 27). He dwells still 'in thick darkness' (cf. Pss. 18.11[12]; 97.2), infinitely greater and more mysterious than the sum of his revelation. He is '*mysterium tremendum et fascinans*'.

(γ) *Solomon's address to the assembly, and dedicatory prayer:* 8.14–61

This section, with the exception of the final benediction (vv. 54–61), is found also in II Chron. 6.3–41. It is divided into three parts:

[a]G *egnōrisen* ('he recognized') translates either *hikkīr*, which might be a corruption of *hēkīn*, which is supported by G^L *estēsen*, or *hōdīaʿ*, which might be a corruption of *hōpīaʿ* in the proto-Hebraic script.

[b]G reads the imperative *oikodomēson*, but the personal statement of Solomon is more proper here, as the pronominal suffixes in the sequel suggest. Probably the imperative in G is to be explained by haplography of *bānō bānītī*, only the former being read and taken as an imperative.

Solomon's address to the assembly (vv. 15–21),
the prayer of dedication (vv. 22–53),
the benediction (vv. 54–61).

The rhetorical and hortatory style of the whole and its theology, strongly impregnated with the conception of sin and inevitable retribution, stamps it as Deuteronomistic, and indeed such orations with historical recapitulation and the future prospect at significant crises of the history of Israel are distinctive of the Deuteronomistic history, cf. the speeches of Moses on the eve of the conquest of Palestine (Deut. 1.29–31) and of Joshua at the assembly at Shechem (Josh. 24.1–25), when the tradition represented the conquest as complete. So now at the dedication of the Temple, Solomon's prayer, which is also an admonition to the people in typical Deuteronomistic vein, is prefaced by a historical recapitulation which, though mentioning the Exodus (vv. 16, 21), is really concerned with the project of the Temple since the time of David. Here again, Yahweh's choice of Jerusalem and of David (v. 16), and his covenant with David fulfilled in the succession of Solomon (cf. II Sam. 7.13–16), are propagated as the legitimization of the Davidic monarchy. What is most significant is that these themes are now associated with Yahweh's covenant with Israel in the desert (v. 21). The Davidic house was to capitalize on this association for the duration of the kingdom, as is indicated in Pss. 2; 68; 78; 89.3f., 20–37[4f., 21–38]; 132.11ff.[a] From the evidence of the Deuteronomistic compilation of Kings and from the Psalms, of course, it is not possible to date this combination of the tradition of the Sinai covenant and the Davidic covenant any earlier than the time of Josiah, when Rost[b] dates it, but the association of the theme of the Davidic covenant with the ark as an amphictyonic symbol and with the New Year festival, which was associated with the Feast of Tabernacles, which was the occasion of the renewal of the covenant at Shechem in pre-monarchic times (Deut. 27), makes it most probable that the association was made from Solomon's time.

We have already noted evidence of two hands of Deuteronomistic editorship in Kings, one who apparently did not visualize the collapse of the Davidic dynasty and the destruction of the Temple and the other who knew the experience of the Exile. Here vv. 34, 46 contemplate exile. This, however, might reflect the deportations from

[a]H. J. Kraus, *Gottesdienst in Israel. Studien zur Geschichte des Laubhüttenfestes*, 1954, pp. 72–75; *Worship in Israel*, 1966, pp. 183–8.

[b]'Sinaibund und Davidsbund', *TLZ* LXXII, 1947, cols. 129ff.

the Northern kingdom after 722 or the deportation of Jehoiachin and others in 597, and so be from the first Deuteronomist, the compiler. The resumption of the theme, however, in vv. 44–53 after it had already been dealt with in v. 34, and the prominence of the subject in vv. 44–53, suggests that this is a later expansion by the Deuteronomistic redactor. Burney[a] emphasizes the reference to the Temple as still standing in v. 48 as evidence for the unity of vv. 22–53 in the pre-exilic compilation, but this may simply be a case of the redactor's adaptation of his theme to the literary context of Solomon's address.

Solomon's address to the assembly: 8.14–21

The theme of this introductory passage is thanks to God that Solomon has been able to build the Temple to house the ark according to the divine covenant with David (II Sam. 7.12f.). In view of the importance of the Davidic covenant for authentication of Solomon's rule and such an innovation as the building of the Temple, it is likely that in spite of its Deuteronomistic colouring this does reflect what actually happened in Solomon's dedication of the Temple.

8 [14]And the king turned his face and blessed the whole assembly of Israel, and the whole assembly of Israel was standing. [15]And he said, Blessed be Yahweh, the God of Israel, who spoke by his mouth with David, my father, and has implemented it by his hand, saying, [16]Since the day when I brought my people Israel out of Egypt I did not fix my choice on any city from all the tribes of Israel to build a house where my name might be, [b](but I set my choice on Jerusalem that my name should be there),[b] and on David to be over my people Israel. [17]And it was in the intention of my father David to build a house to the name of Yahweh, the God of Israel, [18]but Yahweh said to my father David, 'In that you have intended to build a house to my name you have done well that it was in your mind. [19]But you shall not build the house, but your son who issues from your loins, he it is who will build the house for my name.' [20]And Yahweh has established his word which he spoke, and I have arisen in place of David, my father, and sit upon the throne of Israel, as Yahweh spoke, and I have built the house to the name of Yahweh the God of Israel; [21]and there have I [c]set a place for the ark,[c] in which is the covenant of Yahweh which he made with our fathers when he brought them out of the land of Egypt.

[a]*Notes on . . . Kings*, p. 14.

[b]This passage, omitted in MT, possibly by homoeoteleuton, is suggested by G^B and the parallel account in II Chron. 6.6.

[c]The reading of S, taking 'the ark' (*hā'ārōn*) as the object of the verb, is probably to be preferred, according much more aptly with the verb (*wā'āśīm*) than MT *māqōm*, and being more strictly relevant to the subject of the previous passage, the installation of the ark.

8.14ff. This is a summary recapitulation of Nathan's oracle to David (II Sam. 7.5ff.), with Deuteronomistic impress, e.g. the 'name' of Yahweh, the covenant as the contents of the ark, and the generally sonorous phraseology. In view of the Deuteronomistic character of the passage, we should seriously consider the insertion we have adopted from G and Chronicles in v. 16, regarding the divine choice of Jerusalem. Note Burney's detailed study of Deuteronomic features in this and the following section.[a]

14. The king in his moment of accomplishment, when the Temple stood as the token of the fulfilment of God's covenant with David, is the manifest possessor of the divine blessing (*b^e^rākā*). As representative of the people he communicates the blessing to the community.

15. *bārūk* as applied to God signifies thanks or congratulation to the source of blessing.

16. On the theological significance of the 'name' of God see on 5.19.

17. *lēbāb* (lit. 'heart'), as usual in Hebrew idiom, signifies the seat of cognition, here of deliberate intention.

The dedicatory prayer: 8.22–53

The theme of the Davidic Covenant in vv. 14–21 is sustained, now with reference to the foundation of the Davidic dynasty with the succession of Solomon, which the present occasion was the appropriate moment to emphasize. This is the theme of vv. 22–26, in the form of prayer.

The prayer continues in vv. 27–53 that the Temple may be the effective guarantee of God's accessibility in Israel's adversity. This section particularly expresses the Deuteronomic theology of the accessible presence ('the name', vv. 16, 18, 19, 20, 29) of God transcendent (vv. 27, 30, 32, 34, 36, 39, 43, 45, 49).

This section, like the preceding, is strongly Deuteronomic in language, style, and thought. In the enumeration of the various calamities the catalogue of curses consequent upon the breaking of the law in Deut. 28.15–68 is at once suggested, as noted by Burney. The intercessory prayers on these occasions are illustrated by the intercessions in Amos 7.1–9 and particularly in the first part of the Book of Joel (1.1–2.27), which is a fast-liturgy on the occasion of drought (cf. I K. 8.25–36) and locusts (cf. I K. 3.37). Many of the

[a]*Op. cit.*, pp. 112ff.

Psalms, too, namely those of public and apparently private lamentation, have their *Sitz im Leben* on such occasions.[a]

8 [22]And Solomon stood before the altar of Yahweh before the whole assembly of Israel and he stretched forth the palms of his hands to the heavens. [23]And he said, 'O Yahweh, God of Israel, there is no god like unto thee in the heavens above or on the earth beneath, who keepest the covenant and loyal love to thy servants[b] who walk before thee with their whole heart, [24]who hast kept unto thy servant David my father all that thou hast spoken to him, yea thou didst speak with thy mouth and thou hast fulfilled it with thy hand even as this day. [25]And now, O Yahweh, God of Israel, keep unto thy servant David my father that which thou didst promise him saying, There shall no man of you be cut off from before me who may sit upon the throne of Israel, if only your sons keep their way to walk before me as you have walked before me. [26]And now, O God of Israel, let thy word[c] be confirmed which thou didst speak to thy servant David my father. [27]For of a truth will God dwell upon the earth? Lo, heaven and the heaven of heavens cannot contain thee, much less this house which I have built. [28]And mayest thou turn unto the intercession of thy servant and unto his supplication, O Yahweh, my God, to hearken unto the cry and unto the prayer which thy servant prays now before thee, [29]that thine eyes may be open towards this house night and day, unto the place concerning which thou hast said, My name shall be there, to hearken unto the prayer which thy servant will address to this place. [30]And mayest thou hearken unto the supplication of thy servant and thy people Israel when they pray unto this place, yea, and mayest thou admit it to thy hearing, even unto[d] the place where thou art enthroned, unto heaven, and mayest thou hear and grant pardon. [31]If[e] a man offends against his neighbour and he imposes an oath upon him, causing him to swear, and he comes under oath[f] before thine altar in this house, [32]then hear thou in heaven

[a]See further H. Gunkel and J. Begrich, *Einleitung in die Psalmen*, 1933, pp. 177ff.; S. Mowinckel, *The Psalms in Israel's Worship* I, pp. 193ff.

[b]In view of the plural participle agreeing with the noun, the MT is to be preferred to G^{BA}, which read the singular. G^{L} also reads the singular, but in agreement with the participle adds 'my father David'.

[c]After the singular of the verb the singular of the noun should be read with Q, G, S, and the parallel passage in II Chron. 6.17 for the plural of MT.

[d]The parallel passage in Chron. reads *min* ('from') for MT *'el* ('to'), but *'el* is attested of rest in, rather than motion to, an object, e.g. Jer 41.12, *wayyimṣeʾū ʾōtō ʾel-mayim rabbīm* ('they came upon him at the great pool'). Here, however, the sense implies that they came to the waters and lit upon him there. So in the present passage the sense is as we have suggested in our translation.

[e]For the inexplicable *ʾēt ʾašer* of the MT read the particle *ʾim* as in the parallel passage in Chron.

[f]For the impossible MT *ūbāʾ ʾālā* we may assume an original *ūbāʾ weʾālā* ('and if he come and swear an oath'), which was read by G and S, or *ūbāʾ beʾālā* ('if he enter into oath'), a phrase which occurs in Neh. 10.30.

and make it effective, and judge thy servants, condemning the wicked, to bring his conduct on his own head, and vindicating the innocent, giving him according to his rights. 33When thy people Israel are smitten before an enemy because they sin against thee, and if they turn again to thee and confess thy name and make prayer and supplication unto thee in this house, 34then do thou admit it to thy hearing, even to heaven,[a] and pardon the sin of thy people Israel and restore them to the land which thou gavest to their fathers. 35When the heavens are shut up and there is no rain because they sin against thee, and they pray towards this place and confess thy name and turn back from their sin because thou dost chasten[b] them, 36do thou admit it to thy hearing in heaven and pardon the sin of thy servant[c] and thy people Israel [d](for thou dost instruct them in the good way wherein they may walk),[d] and give rain upon the land[e] which thou gavest to thy people as an inheritance. 37If there is a famine in the land, if there is a plague, blasting, mildew, locusts, or consuming hoppers, or if one of their enemies besiege them in one[f] of their cities, (if there is) any plague or sickness, 38whatever prayer or supplication be made by any man[g] who shall know each the affliction of his own heart, and shall spread out the palms of his hands to this house, 39then do thou hear in heaven, the established place where thou art enthroned, and grant pardon, and make (the prayer) effective and render unto every man according to his ways;[h] thou knowest his heart (for thou alone knowest the heart of all the sons of men), 40that they may fear thee all the days that they live upon the face of the land which thou didst give to our fathers. 41Moreover, concerning the foreigner, who is not of thy people Israel, and if one come from a far country for thy name's sake—42for men shall hear of thy great name and thy strong hand and thine arm stretched forth—and if one come and pray towards this house, 43then[i] do thou hear in heaven, the established place where thou art enthroned, and bring to

[a]Here and in parallel phraseology in vv. 34, 36, 39, 43, 45, and 49 the absence of a preposition raises a difficulty. G, S and T read 'from' and in the parallel passage in Chron. also this is read. The consistency of the usage without the preposition in this passage, however, is strong evidence for its correctness. Possibly this is an instance of the locative case, usually with final *hē locale*, the sense being 'admit to thy hearing, even to heaven'.

[b]Reading *teʿannēm* with G and V for MT *taʿanēm* ('thou dost answer them').

[c]The singular 'thy servant', i.e. the king as complementary to the people, is certainly to be read here with G instead of the plural in MT.

[d]As the following clause indicates, introduced with a *w* consecutive, this clause is an interpolation of a homiletic nature, though quite in accord with the style and thought of D.

[e]Reading 'the land' with G and S for MT 'thy land'.

[f]Reading *beʾaḥad šeʿārāw* ('in one of their cities', lit. 'gates') for MT *beʾereṣ šeʿārāw* ('in the land of their cities').

[g]Omitting MT *lekol-ʿammekā yiśrāʾēl* ('by all thy people Israel') with G^{BL}.

[h]Omitting *kol* ('all') with G^{B}.

[i]Reading *weʾattā* for MT *ʾattā*, as usual in the recurrence of the phrase in this passage, with certain Hebrew MSS, G, S, and the parallel passage in Chron.

effect all concerning which the stranger calls to thee, so that all the people of the earth may know thy name and fear thee even as thy people Israel, and know that thy name is invoked over this house which I have built. [44]If thy people go forth to war against their enemies[a] in the way wherein thou shalt send them and they pray unto Yahweh towards the city upon which thou hast set thy choice and towards the house which I have built for thy name, [45]then do thou hearken in heaven to their prayer and their supplication and maintain their cause. [46]If they sin against thee—for there is no man who does not sin—and thou art angry with them and deliver them up before their enemy and their captors carry them in captivity unto the land of the enemy far off or near, [47]and if they lay it to heart in the land where they are in captivity and turn again and make supplication unto thee in the land of their captors, saying: We have sinned, we have acted perversely,[b] we have transgressed, [48]and if they turn again to thee wholeheartedly and sincerely in the land of their enemies who have taken them captive, and if they pray unto thee in the direction of their land which thou gavest to their fathers, even unto the city which thou didst choose and to the house which I have built unto thy name, [49]then admit to thy hearing, even unto heaven, thine established dwelling-place, [c]their prayer and their supplication, and maintain their cause,[c] [50]and do thou forgive their sins[d] which they have committed against thee, and all their rebellious acts, which they have perpetrated against thee, and appoint them for mercy before their captors, and may they show mercy unto them, [51]for they are thy people and thine inheritance, whom thou didst bring out of Egypt from the midst of the furnace of iron, [52]that thine eyes and thine ears[e] may be open to the supplication of thy servant and unto the supplication of thy people Israel, hearkening unto them whenever they cry unto thee, [53]for thou hast set them apart for thyself as an inheritance apart from all peoples of the earth, even as thou didst speak through Moses thy servant when thou didst bring our fathers out of Egypt, O my Lord Yahweh.'

8.22. The attitude of Solomon in this ceremony is to be noted. Here he is described as *standing*, an attitude of prayer which is illustrated

[a]Reading plural with Q in the parallel passage in Chron.

[b]Omitting the conjunction *w*[e] as in the parallel passage in Chron.

[c]This phrase is omitted in G^{BL}, and it is generally omitted in the reiterated formula throughout this passage, 'Hear . . . and pardon the sin . . .' (vv. 34, 36). The formula in question, however, is not invariable, cf. vv. 32, 43, and 45, where the phrase in question in v. 49 is included.

[d]Reading *l*[e]*ḥaṭṭō'tām* with G for MT *l*[e]*ʿamm*[e]*kā* ('thy people'). The verb *sālaḥ* ('forgive') with *l*[e] introducing the accusative (as in Aramaic) is found governing both the sin and the sinner, so that there is no grammatical difficulty in MT, the reading of which here is supported by the parallel passage in II Chron. 6.39. Throughout the passage, however, in this formula the verb governs the sin (e.g. vv. 34, 36), so that we prefer to follow G here.

[e]Reading with G and the parallel passage in Chron. *w*[e]*'oznekā*, which is omitted in MT.

by sculptures from all over the ancient Near East, the attitude being that of an inferior before the deity, who is represented as seated. In v. 54 Solomon is represented as *kneeling* in prayer, possibly a reflection of later custom in the time of the Deuteronomistic revision of Kings. The open hand of the supplicant is also illustrated in sculpture, and is referred to in Ex. 9.29 and Isa. 1.15. The altar is here mentioned for the first time in the description of the Temple, an indication that the earlier description, whatever the religious interest, was drawn perhaps indirectly from technical sources, whereas in the Deuteronomistic account of the dedication the religious interest predominates, the altar being tacitly assumed as the place where Solomon prayed. Here there is a faithful reflection of the priestly status of the king in pre-exilic times, when he was the vital link between God and the community. The parallel passage in II Chron. 6.13 significantly omits any mention of the altar and depicts Solomon as officiating on a bronze scaffold some seven feet high in the Temple court. This reflects the increased status and cultic monopoly of the priestly caste in the post-exilic period, which is assumed in the Qumran community, where the *Manual of Discipline* in looking ahead provides for the precedence of the anointed priest ('the Messiah of Aaron') over the anointed king ('the Messiah of David'). As instances of the king *qua* priest J. Morgenstern[a] notes the role of David in the installation of the ark at Jerusalem (II Sam. 6.14–20) and the dedication of the threshing-floor of Araunah (II Sam. 24.25), of Jeroboam at the dedication of the shrine of Bethel (I K. 12.32f.), of Ahaz at the dedication of the new altar (II K. 16.10), and the authority of Joash over the priests. He goes on to propound the view that the priest was the king's surrogate, except at the New Year ceremonies, when the king functioned in person, his specific function, with certain modifications, being taken over by the chief priest in post-exilic times.

8.23. This statement, with which the prayer proper begins, confesses the incomparable nature of God in language which re-echoes the liturgy in Ex. 15.11 and Ps. 86.8 and is ultimately based on the endorsement of the religious obligations of the apodictic law of the sacral community, as in the Decalogue in the context of the covenant-sacrament. The latter half of the verse, in Deuteronomic language (cf. Deut. 7.9), asserts the steadfast love of God to his covenanted community, while emphasizing their obligations. The dedication of the Temple as the new shrine of the sacral community is also an oppor-

[a]'A Chapter in the History of the High-Priesthood', *AJSL* LV, 1938, pp. 5–12.

tunity of self-dedication, and Yahweh's covenant with Israel is recalled, though the thought passes immediately to a new covenant, that of Yahweh with David and his house. As a new element in the religion of Israel this theme is dealt with at greater length (vv. 24–26). There is, however, a reversion to the theme of the deliverance from Egypt and the covenant with Israel (vv. 51–53), which may reflect a certain reaction from the conception of the covenant with David and his house, which, though not superseding the conception of the covenant with Israel, received undue emphasis under the monarchy. Note the association of *ḥesed* with *b^e^rīt* ('covenant') in v. 23. The conception of covenant, and particularly the Sinai-covenant with its moral implications, is inherent in the word *ḥesed*.[a] AV 'mercy' is therefore an inadequate translation. The word denotes God's grace to Israel in taking the initiative in the covenant, by which, in revealing himself more fully after the saving act of the Exodus, he pledged his loyalty to his people and bound them to himself. Not only does *ḥesed* denote God's initial grace in the covenant; it denotes also his loyalty to principles then revealed. To express the fullness of the conception 'loyal love' is a better, if somewhat clumsy translation. The word also expresses the loyalty of the religious community and of the individual to God, the adjective being *ḥāsīd*. The passive form should be noted, meaning 'bound by covenant'. Hence the adjective, usually in the plural, denotes the community of Israel in communion with their covenanted God.[b] A. R. Johnson's translation 'devotees',[c] while implying this relationship, does not make it sufficiently explicit. Finally *ḥesed* denotes the behaviour of one man to another within the covenanted community, implying a respect for a man's personality as God had deemed Israel worthy of his consideration in the covenant. Further, on the pattern of the relationship of people and God, there is the implication of sympathy with a man's needs, and faithful adherence to the principles of the covenant which guaranteed order in human relationships beyond the law of the jungle or even of the legal systems of the ancient Near East, which defined the rights and duties of classes rather than of individuals in a sacral community.

8.25. *w^eʿattā* here and in v. 26 marks the transition to the petition after the introduction.

[a]N. Glueck, *Das Wort ḥesed im alttestamentlichen Sprachgebrauch als menschliche und göttliche gemeinschaftsgemässe Verhaltungsweise*, BZAW XLVII, 1927: ET, *Ḥesed in the Bible*, 1968.

[b]Mowinckel, *The Psalms in Israel's Worship* I, pp. 210ff.

[c]*Sacral Kingship in Ancient Israel*, 1967^2, p. 22n.

8.27. *w* consecutive with the perfect *pānītā* ('may you turn') in v. 28 follows naturally after the verb *yē'āmēn* ('be confirmed') in v. 26, suggesting that v. 27 is parenthetical, and perhaps a later theologizing interpolation. It implies a consciousness that the building of the Temple suggested a limitation of the Deity. The Temple, as the sequel makes clear, is but the meeting-place of man and God, from where and to where man can address his prayers to the divine presence, which has been realized upon the invocation of his 'name'. God's 'name' is the extension of his personality from the remote sphere which is the proper dwelling-place of the Lord transcendent ('heaven'), and it is there that he ultimately receives ('hears') prayer. It has been suggested that 'the heaven of heavens' reflects the cosmology expressed concretely in the Mesopotamian ziggurat or staged tower, where the god occupied the temple on the summit, a conception which lies behind the Jewish belief in a 'seventh heaven' (II Cor. 12.2). We agree with van den Born (*Koningen*, p. 58) that 'the heaven of heavens' signifies 'heaven itself' and does not reflect Mesopotamian cosmology.

28. 'Thy servant' is probably more than the customary form of deferential address, and here denotes specifically one who represents the religious community ('servants' in the sense of worshippers) before their God. As such the title was reserved for the king, e.g. David (v. 25), and the kings Krt and Dn'il in the Ras Shamra texts, who were called *'bd 'il*. The title is given to Moses, too, who represented the religious community before God (v. 53), and to the prophets who fulfilled a similar function. The spiritual nucleus of Israel, too, in so far as it was fulfilling the functions of these earlier 'servants' of Yahweh, could be described as the 'servant', as in the 'Servant Songs' in Deutero-Isaiah.

Though *tᵉpillā*, from the verbal root *pālal*, is used in the Old Testament to denote prayer in general, it may here denote specifically intercessory prayer of the king as the representative of the people, which is the proper meaning of the verbal root, and occasionally of the noun *tᵉpillā*, e.g. II K. 19.4=Isa. 37.4; Jer. 7.16; 11.14. In *tᵉḥinnā*, on the other hand, there is a greater degree of personal involvement, supplication for mercy (*ḥēn*) rather than intercession for another.

hayyōm (lit. 'today') often simply means 'now'.

30. Note the title 'thy servant', referring specifically to the king as apart from, but representing, the people. In the phrase *mᵉqōm šibtᵉkā* ('the place where you are enthroned'), the verbal noun *šebet* may mean either 'dwelling' or 'being enthroned'. As indicating the ultimate seat of divine authority we have taken it in the latter sense. For the peculiar usage of *'el* see p. 216 n.[d]. 'Pardon' was the object of the intercession of Amos (7.2) in cases of natural disasters similar to those mentioned here. The passage in Amos, with Isa. 37.4=II K. 19.4, is a good instance of the intercessory office of the 'servant' of Yahweh in public disasters.

8.31. On the general and neutral import of the verb *ḥāṭā'* see on 1.21. Here the point is that damage had been incurred, but in the hypothetical state of the guilt of the alleged offender such a neutral verb is fittingly chosen. Such oaths of purgation at the sanctuary are attested in cases of default in pledges (Ex. 22.7–12) or alleged adultery (Num. 5.11ff.). The oath, involving a curse (*'ālā*) upon the guilty party, was one of the vital elements in the ceremony of the renewal of the covenant by the tribes of Israel (Deut. 27ff.). The verb *nāśā'* implies a quasi-material conception of the curse which could be lifted up and imposed as a burden (*maśśā'*). The prophets used the same verb of the oracles which they imposed as burdens (*maśśā'ōt*) on the peoples they stigmatized. The blessing also, as instanced by Isaac's blessing of Jacob instead of Esau (Gen. 27), is thought of as something much more substantial than the mere words in which it is expressed. In such instances, as in the invocation of the name of God (v. 43), the Hebrew conception of the creative force of the word is well illustrated.

32. 'Judge' might seem to be used here in a narrow, forensic sense apart from the wider sense which it often bears as the upholding of regular government by authority, *šōpēṭ*, cf. Ugaritic cognate *ṯpṭ*, used in parallelism to *zbl* ('prince'). The proper decision of cases at law, however, was an essential part of the maintenance of ordered rule. The verb is often used in an apparently partial sense of God's deliverance of his people in the crises of history (e.g. v. 45). This, far from being a partial judgement, is to be understood in the new light of the Ras Shamra evidence as the vindication of the rule of God and of his purpose in history, with regard to which he had chosen Israel.

The contrast between 'wicked' (*rāšā'*) and 'innocent' (*ṣaddīq*) is well known in Psalms, where, however, the terms tend to acquire idiomatic meanings in a definite political context.[a] In the present passage, though used in a legal context, the adjectives and their

[a]H. Birkeland, *The Evildoers in the Book of Psalms*, 1955.

derived verbs have a wider application. In the light of evidence from the Ras Shamra texts (Krt) and from later Phoenician inscriptions, the root *ṣdq* signifies primarily not moral righteousness, as in Christian dogmatics, but 'fitness', or 'aptitude to a given purpose' (e.g. *'aṯt ṣdq*), or 'legitimacy' (e.g. *mlk ṣdq*). The meaning of *ṣaddīq* is therefore 'right' and only secondarily 'righteous'. In the present passage it denotes a man who has a right case at law, and the causative of the derived verb means to declare that fact, as the causative *hiršīaʿ* means to make plain the opposite in the case of his adversary, *hārāšāʿ*. In the cultic terminology of the Psalms *ṣaddīq* denotes the true Israelite, and in the plural the community, maintaining the right covenant relationship to Yahweh, while *rāšāʿ* denotes either Israelites who by some act of wrong had put themselves beyond the pale of true worshippers or foreigners who had never been within the covenant fellowship.[a]

8.33–37. This passage provides for prayer and supplication in national calamities in history and nature. In the theology typical of D these are regarded as the just penalty for sin, which, however, may be an unwitting offence (*ḥaṭṭā't*) rather than deliberate rebellion against the divine will (*pešaʿ*). This view of suffering as the consequence of sin was inculcated by the disasters solemnly adjured upon the community in the ceremony of the renewal of the covenant at amphictyonic assemblies from the time of the settlement in Palestine, and the particular disasters now visualized reflect the specific curses invoked in Deut. 28.15ff.

33. *'ašer* may have here the conditional or hypothetical sense, which is rarely, though certainly, attested in the Old Testament.[b] Here, however, in view of the preceding *b*, the last letter of the preceding word *'ōyēb*, it is possible that *kᵉ* has been omitted in error before *'ašer*, so that we should possibly read *ka'ašer yeḥeṭᵉ'ū* ('corresponding to their sin'). The verb *šūb* ('return') is often used in the sense of sincere and effective repentance, cf. Arabic *ṯāba*. In Hebrew it may also signify apostasy. The reference in v. 34 to the restoration of Israel (*wahᵃšēbōtām*) to the land of their fathers raises the problem of date. There were, however, deportations before the Exile of 586 BC, e.g. from Judah in 701, according to Sennacherib's inscriptions, and in 597, and from Israel in 734 and 722. The present passage may refer

[a]Mowinckel, *The Psalms in Israel's Worship* I, pp. 227ff.; cf. K. F. Euler, *ZAW* LVI, 1938, pp. 278ff., who regards the terms as primarily forensic.
[b]E.g. Lev. 4.22; Deut. 11.27; Josh. 4.21; see *GK* § 159cc.

to the deportation from North Israel, the restoration reflecting the hopes of Josiah and his followers, including the Deuteronomists, that a reunion of Israel and Judah might be effected on the obvious decay of the power of Assyria in the last quarter of the seventh century. The reference, therefore, does not obviate the probability that the passage is from the pre-exilic D compilation. Klostermann's proposed emendation of *wahᵃšēbōtām* to *wᵉhōšabtām* ('and settle them'), which seems to be designed to avoid implications of a post-exilic date, is therefore gratuitous.

8.35. The lack, or delay, of the heavy 'early rains' (*yōre*), which make ploughing and sowing possible and replenish the springs, and of the gentle 'latter rains' (*malqōš*) of early spring, which swell the ear of the shooting grain, are a constant menace in Syria. Similar to the description of drought as 'the shutting up of the heavens' is the phraseology of the Canaanite saga of 'Aqht (*UT*, 1 'Aqht, I, 42f.).

37. These natural disasters were peculiar to the geographical situation of Palestine. Plague of man and beast might be the consequence of shortage and pollution of water, but it might also be due to infection from lands beyond, Palestine being the stepping-stone between Mesopotamia and Egypt. Mildew (*yērāqōn* lit. 'greenness', 'paleness') is caused by excessive dew of spring and summer in consequence of the heavy condensation on the high mountains of the interior, or of rain in case of premature ripening, the paleness being caused by a parasite fungus which exhausts the nutritive substances on which the plant depends. 'Blasting' (*šiddāpōn*) is the premature desiccation of the plant in consequence of the sirocco wind from the deserts of the east or south of Palestine, and is explicitly associated with it in Gen. 41.6. In Palestine such winds are normally worst in May and October, sometimes lasting for several days. The siroccos of May usually come after or during the grain harvest, but if they come earlier than usual growth is immediately arrested. This may be the fiery ordeal of Amos 7.4. Locusts are a pest to which Palestine and neighbouring countries are particularly prone through the proximity of the desert, where locusts breed. The wealth of terms for locust in the Old Testament (here *'arbe*, the most common word, and *ḥāsīl*, from *ḥāsal*, 'to consume', e.g. Deut. 28.38, where the subject of the verb is *'arbe*) reflects the common occurrence of the scourge. Such a disaster was the occasion of the fast-liturgy in the first part of Joel. 'Gates' is used by synecdoche for 'cities', being the point at which defence and attack were concentrated. The larger towns in Palestine from the time of Solomon were fortified with great double gateways and inner and outer barriers, flanked with towers and guard-rooms, e.g. Megiddo, Gezer, Lachish, Hazor.

8.38. With the mention of sickness and the prayer of any man we apparently pass from public to private calamities, a fact which G^BL recognizes in omitting 'for all thy people Israel'. Liturgies for such occasions were among those of the psalms characterized by Gunkel as Plaint of the Individual (*Klagelied eines Einzelnen*), which deal in detail with the sickness of the subject, e.g. Pss. 6, 38, 41, etc. It is not easy to determine, however, the extent to which the language of such psalms is figurative.

39. The verb *ʿāśā*, 'to do', here in the sense 'to bring to effect', is used in this sense in contrast to *pāʿal* ('to strive') in Isa. 41.4, *mī pāʿal weʿāśā* ('Who has striven and brought to effect?').

41. 'The stranger' (*nokrī*) is not the protected alien permanently resident in Israel nor a fugitive from blood-revenge who has found asylum in the religious community of Israel, both of whom were classed as *gērīm*, cf. Arabic *jār 'allāh*, but foreigners who were attracted to the worship of Yahweh. In post-exilic times such a movement is well attested, e.g. Isa. 56.6ff., and possibly also in pre-exilic times, e.g. Isa. 2.2f. Apart from representatives of foreign governments and neighbouring aliens, like Naaman and others, whose business led them to Palestine, who may have been attracted to the higher worship of Yahweh, the worshippers from a distant land may have been natives of Mesopotamia who had come under the influence of the better elements of the deportees of North Israel after 734 or 722, or even certain of the descendants of the Mesopotamian and Syrian settlers planted by the Assyrians in North Israel, who served Yahweh (II K. 17.24–28) not as a mere convenience.

42. The Lord's 'great name' may refer to his presence or, more probably, to his fame, cf. II Sam. 8.13 ('David got himself a name'). The 'strong hand' and 'arm stretched forth' recall the Deuteronomic phraseology referring to the deliverance from Egypt; hence it is likely that the foreigner's introduction to Yahweh was the *Heilsgeschichte*, the liturgical recounting of the deliverance from Egypt, the covenant, and the settlement in Palestine, which had a sacramental significance for Israel.

43. The invocation of the name of Yahweh over the Temple is patient of two meanings. The calling of a name over something signified possession, a variant being the setting up of a stele in a conquered place inscribed with the conqueror's name, e.g. that of Ramses VI and Shishak at Megiddo. The pronunciation of the name, on the other hand, evoked the presence of the person named, and this is the sense which we favour here. The effective answer to prayer is a token of the actual presence of Yahweh in the Temple.

8.44–53. The passage, which is preoccupied with defeat in war and deportation, might of itself no more visualize the Babylonian Exile than the reference to deportation in v. 34. The prominence now given to this subject, however, rather suggests the great Exile. This passage is a later expansion by the second Deuteronomist, the redactor, in view of the experience of the destruction of the state and the Babylonian Exile; this is suggested by the fact that, after a comprehensive outline of occasions of prayer, first public (vv. 33–37), including defeat and deportation (v. 34), then individual (vv. 38–40), and the worship of foreigners (vv. 41–43), which shows evidence of orderly classification, the subject of defeat and deportation is resumed. This subject, however, differs in that it is headed by a general provision for supplication in war (vv. 44ff.), and the fact is not to be overlooked that v. 48 implies that the Temple still stood. There are sundry other stylistic variations from vv. 14–53, e.g. the omission of specific reference to Israel in vv. 44–51 and *wešāmaʿtā* in vv. 45, 49 instead of *weʾattā tišmaʿ*, which is used elsewhere. More particularly, the passage should be delimited to vv. 44–51, since vv. 52f. reverts to the supplication for 'thy servant (i.e. the king) and . . . thy people Israel'. Since this passage is sharply divided in subject matter from v. 43 before the later expansion in vv. 44–51, it is probably a still later conclusion of Solomon's prayer fashioned with regard to the beginning of the prayer in vv. 29f. If, as we believe (see below, pp. 753, 755), the first draft of the Deuteronomistic History was completed in 598, vv. 44–51 may have been added after the first deportation from Judah in 597 and vv. 52f. by the exilic hand.

44. In the early days war was the primary expression of the solidarity of the sacral community of Israel, a holy duty, to which the people, reduced to those who were dedicated to the cause and specially consecrated together with their weapons, were directed by Yahweh, hence war was 'the way wherein thou shalt send them', phraseology which recalls the Quranic 'fighting in the way of Allah'. In the monarchy after the development of a professional army this conception of war is no longer a reality, but an ideal. As an expression of the theocratic ideal of the Deuteronomist it indicates the editorial hand in this passage.[a]

8.45. The use of the verb *šāpaṭ* in this context is noteworthy. In so far as 'judgement', the conventional translation, is relevant, God's decision or judgement in the crises of history is in favour of his people. 'Their judgement' here indicates an apparent partiality to Israel, hence our translation of *wᵉʿāśītā mišpāṭām* (lit. 'make their case effective') 'maintain their cause', see on v. 32. A similar usage is *ṣidᵉqōt yhwh* (Judg. 5.11; I Sam. 12.7; Micah 6.5; Dan. 9.16) of God's acts of vindication of his people Israel. These are not primarily 'righteous' acts, but 'right' acts which are 'proper' to, and vindicate, the nature and purpose of Yahweh revealed to and through his chosen people. They are acts which vindicate his chosen people, but always with reference to the divine purpose for which they are chosen.

46. The verb *'ānap* is a denominative verb, referring to the dilation of the nostril (*'ap*) in anger. Hebrew does not deal in colourless abstractions; the original physical connotation of many such expressions indicates the active life of the people and their reaction to the concrete situation. Israel was not alone in the ancient East in attributing disaster to the wrath of God. The conception underlay the practice of fasts and acts of penance to which Mesopotamian psalms of lamentation bear witness in Babylon and Assyria. The Hittites also held the same belief, and King Mesha of Moab in the Dibon stele attributes the sufferings of his people under Omri and his successors to the wrath of the national god Chemosh. The captivity 'far' and 'near' may refer particularly to the deportation of Hebrews to Mesopotamia and the settlement of others in Egypt. Certain of the deportees may, on the other hand, have been posted on garrison-duty in Syria, as men of Hamath were posted in Samaria after 720 (II K. 17.24), as Montgomery (ICC, p. 198) points out.

47. The phrase *wᵉhēšībū 'el-libbām* (lit. 'if they bring [sc. the thought of their sin] back to their heart') illustrates the use of *lēb* as the seat of cognition. The phrase is well rendered by the AV 'if they bethink themselves'. The verb *heʿᵉwīnū* ('we have made perverse'), here used without an object expressed, recalls *heʿᵉwū 'et-darkām* ('they have perverted their way') of Jer. 3.21; cf. Lam. 3.9, and Job 33.27 (*yāšār heʿᵉwītī*, 'I have perverted that which is right'). As indicated by such instances the verb, which may be the root of *ʿāwōn* ('iniquity'), is cognate with Arabic *ʿawā* ('to twist').

[a]See further von Rad, *Studies in Deuteronomy*, pp. 45ff.

8.48. *bᵉkol-lᵉbābām ūbᵉkol-napšām* ('whole-heartedly and sincerely') is a typically Deuteronomic phrase, recalling the Shema in Deut. 6.5. *lēbāb* ('heart') denotes the activity of the mind and *nepeš* the total vitality of man. Here, as in Prov. 19.2, *bᵉlō' daʿat nepeš lō' ṭōb* ('enthusiasm without knowledge is not good'), the meaning of *nepeš* may be 'enthusiasm'.

Prayer in the direction of Jerusalem, or at least of Palestine, is found as a distinctive element of worship after the Exile, e.g. Dan. 6.10[11]; Jonah 2.5.

50. Here a stronger word, *pešaʿ*, is used for 'sin', this being deliberate rebellion against the known will of God, as distinct from *ḥaṭṭā't*, which may denote an unwitting or unwilling delinquency, perhaps even a ritual infringement. The connotation of *pešaʿ* is clearly indicated from its use signifying the rebellion of Israel against Rehoboam (I K. 12.19), of Moab from Israel (II K. 1.1; 3.5, 7), of Edom from Judah (II K. 8.22), and of Israel as sons against the paternal authority of God (Isa. 1.2).

The word for 'mercy' (*raḥᵃmīm*) means literally 'bowels', which to the Hebrews were the seat of emotion. From this the denominative verb *riḥam* is derived, cf. *nikmᵉrū raḥᵃmehā ʿal-bᵉnā* (3.26). See above on 3.26.

51. The conception of the several peoples as the inheritance of their national gods, appointed by a supreme God, is familiar in the Song of Moses (Deut. 32.8f.):

> *bᵉhanḥēl ʿelyōn gōyīm*
> *bᵉhaprīdō bᵉnē 'ādām*
> *yaṣṣēb gᵉbūlōt ʿammīm*
> *lᵉmispar bᵉnē 'ēl*ᵃ
> *kī ḥēleq yhwh ʿammō*
> *yaʿᵃqōb ḥebel naḥᵃlātō*

'When the Most High assigned the peoples an inheritance,
When he divided out the sons of men,
Fixing the bounds of the peoples,
According to the number of the sons of El,
The portion of Yahweh indeed was his people,
Even Jacob his allocated inheritance.'

This is a very forceful way of stating the belief in the divine destiny of Israel, but it also reveals a similar historical faith among Israel's neighbours. This was probably peculiar to the immediate Aramaean neighbours of Israel, and is, in fact, attested in the Moabite stone.

ᵃAfter G, L, Symmachus for MT *yiśrā'ēl*, now supported by a fragment from Qumran (G. von Rad, *Deuteronomy*, 1966, *ad loc.*).

The Aramaeans of Syria were more open to syncretism in religion with the Canaanite fertility-cult, from which Israel herself, on the evidence of the prophets, was not immune.

The deliverance from Egypt was the historical origin of the faith of Israel and the prelude to the revelation of Yahweh in the desert, and the act of commitment which was the basis of the sacral confederacy from which the nation developed, just as the atoning death of Jesus, 'who suffered under Pontius Pilate', is the historical origin of the Christian faith. Doubtless the earlier Hebrew fathers had genuine experiences of God, but the Exodus and the sequel is the effective origin of the common faith in Yahweh, to which the pre-exilic prophets unanimously hark back. This consciousness was kept alive by the regular sacramental experience of this great act of deliverance, followed by the revelation of God's nature and purpose for Israel in the covenant and the law, his guidance of the people in the desert, and their settlement in the land of promise, and this *Heilsgeschichte*, or 'story of deliverance', is repeatedly echoed in the prophets, psalms, and such passages as this. The association of 'the furnace of iron' (i.e. the furnace in which iron is smelted) with the oppression of Israel in Egypt in such divergent categories of Scripture as Deuteronomy (4.20, and the present Deuteronomistic passage) and the prophets (Isa. 48.10 and Jer. 11.4) indicates a common source, probably the liturgy of the sacrament just mentioned, where language tends to be stereotyped.

8.52. Here 'thy servant' is mentioned as distinct from Israel. Usually it denotes the king, though we have already pointed out that prophet or priest may also be so designated. In this case, the possibility of an exilic date is left open, and even if the king is intended, this is not precluded, since it may refer to Jehoiachin after 597. Even later restoration under a prince of the house of David was anticipated in Exile by Ezekiel (34.23f.), if not by Deutero-Isaiah (55.3); Zerubbabel the grandson of Jehoiachin is, in fact, termed 'my servant' (Hag. 2.23).

53. The 'setting apart' (*habdālā*) of Israel here probably reflects the ritual separation imposed on Israel after the great national disaster of 722 and possibly 586, rather than the pre-exilic consciousness of election, though it was in defence of this distinctive status as the covenanted people of Yahweh that Israel organized ritual defence against assimilation to pagan culture. The phrase *beyad mōše* (lit. 'by the hand of M.') ought not to be unduly pressed in its literal sense. It is true that Moses and the prophets, in whose case the same compound preposition is used, mediated revelation not only by word but also by deed, but the preposition is so common as to mean simply 'through' or 'by'. The exclusive relationship between Yahweh and Israel as expressed in the prohibition against intermarriage and even symbiosis with non-Israelites is a feature of Deuteronomy (7.1–6), which was promulgated in the late monarchy under the authority (though not the authorship) of Moses.

The Benediction: 8.54–61

This section is significantly omitted from the parallel passage in II Chronicles, which reflects the development of priestly monopoly of such sacred functions as the blessing of the people, e.g. Num. 6.23 (P); cf. the variant in Chronicles, which denies the king access to the altar in v. 22.

8 [54]And it came to pass, when Solomon had finished making all this prayer and supplication to Yahweh, he rose up from before the altar of Yahweh from kneeling on his knees, and the palms of his hands were stretched forth heavenwards. [55]And he stood and blessed the whole assembly of Israel in a loud voice saying, [56]Blessed be Yahweh who has given rest to his people Israel according to all that he has spoken: not a single word has fallen (void) of all the auspicious word that he has spoken by Moses his servant. [57]May Yahweh our God be with us as he was with our fathers; may he not leave us nor forsake us, [58]inclining our hearts to him to walk in all his ways and to keep his commandments and his statutes[a] which he commanded our fathers. [59]And let these words of mine with which I have made supplication before Yahweh be near to Yahweh our God day and night that he may maintain the cause of his servant and the cause of his people Israel[b] as each day shall require, [60]that all the peoples of the earth may know that Yahweh is God; there is none[c] other. [61]So let your heart be at one with Yahweh our God, walking in his statutes and keeping his commandments as on this day.

[a]Omitting MT *ūmišpāṭāw* ('and his judgements') with G as is demanded by the verb *ṣiwwā* ('he commanded') in the relative clause, which naturally requires a direct antecedent *miṣwōtāw* ('his commandments') of which *ḥuqqāw* ('his statutes') is a near-synonym.

[b]G omits MT *ūmišpaṭ ʿammō* ('and the cause of his people'). Certainly the resulting identity of 'Israel' with 'my servant' is a conception familiar enough in a community where the many is identified with its one representative (e.g. 'Israel my servant' in Deutero-Isaiah) and where Israel is generally designated by the masculine singular personal pronoun. In the foregoing, however, *ʿabdī* ('my servant'), which is mentioned together with Israel, is clearly the king or a representative of the people; hence we retain MT.

[c]G has 'and' before *ʾēn* ('none'), but the acknowledgement of the sole sovereignty of Yahweh is so apparently a cultic response (cf. I K. 18.39) that the asyndetic form, reproducing the ejaculatory form of an audible response, must be retained.

8.54. This is the first mention of the kneeling posture in prayer in this passage, cf. v. 22, where Solomon stands in worship. Kneeling was not unknown in pre-exilic times, but standing was the common posture in prayer, e.g. I Sam. 1.26. On 'bowing the knees to Baal', for which we accept a different interpretation, see on I K. 19.18.

56. 'Rest' or a 'place of rest' (*m^e^nūḥā*) is the culmination of the desert wandering and conquest of Palestine in the *Heilsgeschichte*, and as such is the subject of the 'Mosaic' Deuteronomy. There seems to be a specific reference to Deut. 12.10, though the reference may be to the foundation of the Temple and the peace and security of Solomon's reign after the wars of David.

57. The presence of Yahweh with Israel signifies the unbroken covenant-relationship, which assures the future of Israel. The phrase 'Yahweh our God will be with us' is reminiscent of an audible response in the cult, e.g. Amos 5.14; Ps. 46.7, 11 [8, 12]. It was on this sacramental experience of community with God that Isaiah rallied the faith of Ahaz in his celebrated Immanuel oracle.

59. On *laʿaśōt mišpāṭ* ('maintain the cause') see on v. 45. In *d^e^bar-yōm b^e^yōmō*, 'as each day shall require' (lit. 'in the manner of a day on the day thereof'), *d^e^bar* is an adverbial accusative. Here *dābār*, as frequently in the Old Testament, means 'manner, settlement, disposition', cf. Arab. *dabbara* ('to arrange, manage').

60. *yhwh hū' hā'ᵉlōhīm* ('Yahweh is God') is the confession of faith in the famous ordeal on Carmel (I K. 18.39). There and here it probably reflects a regular audible response in the cult. The adverb *ʿōd*, as in the Ras Shamra texts, means 'over and above'.

61. The adjective or participle *šālēm* might signify 'perfect' in the sense of 'sincere'. The root meaning is 'whole', and might rather signify the unbroken covenantal relationship of the community with its God, as is suggested by the following phrase 'with Yahweh'. This sense of community of purpose may underlie the greeting '*šālōm*'. The infinitives construct with *l^e^* are tantamount to participles denoting circumstances attendant on the finite verb, see *GK* § 114c.

(δ) *The dedicatory sacrifices and the festival:* 8.62–66

The full, rounded, rhetorical style of D, so marked in the preceding section, is lacking here, and the somewhat disjointed succession of factual statements suggests royal annals. These, however, appear to have been worked over by the Deuteronomist, as is indicated by the seven-day duration of the Feast of Tabernacles (*he-ḥāg*) in v. 65 (cf. Deut. 16.13, 15); see further, Introduction to 8.1–66.

8 [62]And the king and all Israel with him were making sacrifice before Yahweh, [63]and Solomon made the sacrifice of [a]communion-offerings, which he made to Yahweh,[a] twenty-two thousand cattle and one hundred and twenty thousand sheep, and the king and all the children of Israel dedicated the Temple of Yahweh. [64]On that day the king consecrated the middle of the court which was before the Temple of Yahweh, for there he made the whole burnt-offering [b]and the meal-offering[b] and the fat of the communion-offerings, for the bronze altar which was before Yahweh was too small to contain the whole burnt-offering [b]and the meal-offering[b] and the fat of the communion-offering. [65]And Solomon celebrated at that time the Feast and all Israel with him, a great convocation from the entrance to Hamath to the Wadi of Egypt before Yahweh our God seven days [c]and seven days, fourteen days.[c] [66]On the eighth day he dismissed the people, and they blessed the king and they went to their tents rejoicing and glad-hearted for all the goodness which Yahweh had done to David his servant and to his people Israel.

8.62. *zābaḥ* means primarily 'to slaughter', like the Arabic cognate *ḏabaḥa*, and secondarily 'to sacrifice'. The shedding of blood remains from the primary sense of the verb, blood, with the fat and entrails, the seat of life, being reserved for the deity.

63. On the significant omission in the parallel passage in Chronicles see n.[a] below. The role of the king and the community, on this reading, is simply that of butchers preparing a feast. The omission of the words may also reflect the changed conception of *šelāmīm* to 'peace-offering' of post-exilic times, which might be offered only by the priest. In pre-exilic times, which were less dominated by sin-consciousness, the word signified the sacrifice of victims for a common meal in which the blood, fat, and entrails were resigned to God and the flesh was eaten by the community.

[a]This phrase of MT is omitted from the parallel version in II Chron. 7.5 in accordance with the view of the late priestly writer that sacrifice was the monopoly of the priests.

[b]This is omitted in G, and in a dedicatory sacrifice of this nature a bloodless offering, which seems to be denoted here in contrast to the bloody offerings *ʿōlā* and *šelāmīm*, seems out of place. It probably reflects later practice at the harvest festival at this season, with which the D reviser was familiar.

[c]Omitted in G, and certainly the first phrase of v. 66 'on the eighth day' suggests that only one seven-day period was mentioned in v. 65. The later account in II Chron. 7.8ff. was familiar with the tradition of two seven-day celebrations, going on to explain that the feast, presumably the Feast of Tabernacles at the New Year, was preceded by a seven-day feast of the dedication of the altar.

This had the effect of integrating, or making whole (*šālēm*) the members of the community one with another, and the community with God. The numbers are probably exaggerated in a later expansion to the text, but since this was essentially a communion-meal on the occasion of the dedication of the new central shrine of all Israel, the sacrifices were doubtless vast. The passage insists throughout that the dedication was the joint action of king and 'all Israel' (vv. 62ff.). This is apparently the earliest instance in the Old Testament of the use of *ḥānak* ('to dedicate'). It is used for dedication generally in later, priestly sources, e.g. Neh. 12.27 (the wall of Jerusalem), Dan. 3.2 (Nebuchadrezzar's idol). It is used, however, in Deut. 20.5 in the general sense of occupying a house for the first time (Scots 'hanselling'), though in this case there may have been a survival of a primitive rite of placation of threshold gods or rites to counteract the mysterious influence of iron tools or the like. The Feast of Hanukkah *par excellence* (*ta enkainia*, John 10.22) commemorated the rededication of the Temple and altar by Judas Maccabaeus in 164 BC after their pollution by Antiochus Epiphanes (I Macc. 4.59), a feast of eight days beginning on the 25th of Chislev (November–December).

8.64. The centre of the court before the Temple was consecrated for the purpose of the colossal sacrifice. It is suggested that the famous rock under the present Dome of the Rock served as an altar, but this cannot be demonstrated, and in any case the rock with the cave beneath was so conspicuous that it can hardly have failed to serve as a place of sacrifice before the time of Solomon. It may have been the site of the altar raised by David on the threshing-floor of Araunah (II Sam. 24.18). In that case it might be thought strange that Solomon had to consecrate it anew. Solomon's special consecration, however, refers to the court around the altar where the exceptionally large number of beasts had to be slaughtered.[a] The bronze altar in the court before the Temple is assumed, but it is strange that there is no mention of it in the list of Hiram's bronze-work (I K. 7.15–46), though it is described in II Chron. 4.1. The parallel account in Chronicles allows seven days for the dedication of the altar before the seven days of the feast, presumably the Feast of Tabernacles. The whole burnt-offering (*ʿōlā*), as distinct from communion-sacrifices (*šelāmīm*), was reserved for God. The bloodless offering (*minḥā*),

[a]For a discussion of the still-disputed question of whether the sacred rock with its underlying cave was the site of the great altar of Solomon's Temple or of the Holy of Holies see de Vaux, *Ancient Israel*, pp. 318f.

which reflects later usage rather than actual practice at the dedication of the Temple, was of meal, oil, fruit, or wine, and was essentially a gift, as in Gen. 43.11 and I Sam. 10.27. On the usage of *minḥā* in the more general sense of 'offering' see on I K. 18.29.

8.65. The Feast (*heḥāg*), written with the definite article and without qualification, is certainly the Feast of Tabernacles (*sukkōt*), which is so called. The festival at the culmination of the year and on the eve of the winter rains was the greatest crisis in the year of the Syrian peasant. It was an auspicious occasion for the dedication of the Temple of Yahweh, to which as King he was entitled. The 'house of Baal' in the Ras Shamra myth was also completed at this time, which suggests that Solomon effected a synthesis of the worship of the power of Providence in nature with the historical faith of Israel expressed in the renewal of the covenant at the same season (Deut. 31.10; cf. 16.13). The view of Mowinckel that the epiphany of Yahweh as King was a feature of the New Year festival seems to us conclusively demonstrated by the passage in Nahum 1.15 (MT 2.1):

> Behold upon the mountains the feet of him that brings good news,
> that proclaims, 'All is well!',
> O Judah keep your solemn feasts (*ḥoggī ḥaggayik*),

taken in conjunction with Isa. 52.7:

> How beautiful upon the mountains are the feet of him that brings good news,
> that proclaims, 'All is well!',
> that says to Jerusalem,
> Your God reigns!

The present occasion when the ark was deposited in the new Temple was a concrete instance of the enthronement of Yahweh and the establishment of his house, characteristic themes of certain of the Psalms which had their *Sitz im Leben* almost certainly at the New Year Feast of Tabernacles. J. Morgenstern[a] from different premises also regards the dedication of the Temple as coinciding with this occasion. *l^ebō' ḥ^amat*, which we render as 'the Hamath approaches', defines the northern boundary of Israel at its maximum extent (e.g. Josh. 13.5; Amos 6.14; II K. 14.25). It probably originated with the description of the area controlled by David, who subjugated the Aramaeans about Damascus and in the Biqʿa between Lebanon and anti-Lebanon but excluding Hamath on the Orontes, whose king Toi

[a] 'The Three Calendars of Ancient Israel', *HUCA* I, 1924, pp. 36ff.; 'A Chapter in the History of the High-Priesthood', *AJSL* LV, 1938, pp. 7ff.

made a timely peace (II Sam. 8.10). It is suggested (so Noth, Eissfeldt, Elliger, Mazar) that *l^ebō'* denotes a place, modern Lebweh, *c.* 70 miles south-west of Hama, which may be that Laba'u of Assyrian royal correspondence, probably from Tiglath-pileser III from Nimrud, published by Saggs.[a] We prefer to render the Hebrew more generally 'the Hamath approaches', cf. *l^ebō' hammidbār* ('the desert approaches', I Chron. 5.9) and *l^ebō' miṣrayim* ('the approaches to Egypt', II Chron. 26.8). In *l^ebō' ḥ^amat*, the region is more precisely denoted by the variant 'Rehob towards Hamath' (Num. 13.21 P), which, according to II Sam. 10.6, 8 and Josh. 18.28, may be located in the southern part of the Biqʿa just north of the present northern frontier of Israel. The Wadi of Egypt (*naḥal miṣrayim*) is rendered Rhinocorura in G, which was *al-ʿArīš*, the last settlement in the south of Palestine on the way to Egypt. The Assyrians knew the place as *Naḥal Muṣri* considerably south of Gaza, as indicated in the account of the expedition of Tiglath-pileser in 734.[b]

8.66. The dispersal of the people on the eighth day of the Feast of Tabernacles was in accordance with Deuteronomic usage (Deut. 16.13, 15) and not with later practice, when the eighth day was a solemn assembly (Lev. 23.36; Num. 28.25). This is reflected in the parallel account in Chronicles. 'To their tents' recalls the revolutionary war-cry, 'Each man to his tent, O Israel' (II Sam. 20.1), hence Montgomery (ICC, p. 199) translates 'went home'. In view of the pilgrimage from all parts of the country to the dedication of the new shrine of all Israel, as formerly to the tribal assembly at Shechem, the tents may indicate the temporary quarters of the pilgrims, cf. Hos. 12.9[10]. A recent analogy was the one-month festival of *Nabī Rūbīn*, when Muslim pilgrims from all over South Palestine used to live in tents in the sand-dunes by the saint's tomb of *Nabī Rūbīn* near the mouth of the wadi of the same name.[c]

(v) THE SECOND APPEARANCE OF THE LORD TO SOLOMON: 9.1–9

This passage, modelled on 3.4–15, is a typical exhortation and admonition such as the Deuteronomist liked to insert at a critical point in the history of Israel, e.g. on the eve of the invasion of Palestine (Deuteronomy and Josh. 1), and on the completion of Joshua's con-

[a] H. W. F. Saggs, *Iraq* XVII, 1955, p. 140.
[b] D. J. Wiseman, 'Two Historical Inscriptions from Nimrud', *Iraq* XIII, 1951, pp. 21–26.
[c] Alt, *PJB* XXI, 1925, pp. 14ff.

quests (Josh. 23f.). The conditional blessing on the house of David (vv. 4ff.) and on the Temple (v. 3), the collapse of neither of which seems to be visualized, might indicate the pre-exilic Deuteronomistic compiler, and the threat of the destruction of people and Temple (vv. 6–9) the post-exilic Deuteronomistic revision (so Burney). The admonitory purpose of the passage, however, requires vv. 1–9 to be treated as a whole, the direct address to Solomon in vv. 1–5 and the optimistic note being due to the nature of this passage as a citation of the oracle on the Davidic covenant, and vv. 6ff. being the Deuteronomist's own expansion, reflecting the decline and fall of the monarchy, which began in Solomon's own reign, now soon (ch. 11) to be described (so Noth, *op. cit.*, pp. 195f.).

9 [1]And it came to pass, when Solomon had finished building the Temple of Yahweh and the palace and all Solomon's desire which he was pleased to do, [2]that Yahweh appeared to Solomon a second time as he had appeared to him at Gibeon. [3]And Yahweh said to him, I have heard your prayer and your supplication which you made before me.[a] I have consecrated this Temple which you have built, to put my name there for ever, and mine eyes and my heart will be there perpetually. [4]And as for you, if you walk before me as David your father walked in integrity of heart and uprightly, doing all that I command you, and[b] keeping my statutes and my rulings, [5]then I shall establish the throne of your kingdom over Israel for ever as I promised to[c] David your father, saying, There shall not fail you a man on the throne of Israel. [6]But[d] if you and your sons shall turn back from following me, and do not keep my commandments, and[e] my statutes that I have set before you, but go and serve other gods and bow down to them, [7]then will I cut off Israel from off the face of the land, which I gave to them, and this[f] Temple which I have consecrated for my name, will I cast away[g] from my presence, and Israel shall be a byword and a taunt among all the peoples. [8]And this Temple shall become ruins;[h] all who pass by it shall be appalled and shall hiss, and they shall say, Why has

[a]MT is intelligible, though the fuller text of G reading 'I have done for you according to all your prayer' gives a smoother reading.

[b]So G.

[c]Reading with G *'el* for MT *ʿal*, cf. *l*^{e}*dāwīd* in the parallel passage in II Chron. 7.18.

[d]Reading *w*^{e} with G, S, V, and the parallel passage in Chron.

[e]So G, S, V.

[f]Reading *habbayit hazze* ('this house') with G for MT *habbayit* ('the house').

[g]Reading with G, V, T and the parallel passage in Chron. *'ašlīk* for MT *'*^{a}*šallaḥ* ('I shall send away'), for which 'Temple' is an unsuitable object.

[h]Reading *l*^{e}*ʿiyyīm* for the unlikely *ʿelyōn* of MT, which is a scribal error of metathesis of *l* and *ʿ* with the corruption of the final *m* to *n*, an easy mistake in the proto-Hebraic script. This reading is supported by the Old Syriac, and Aquila's Greek version, and by the Old Latin, which reads *deserta*.

Yahweh done thus to this land and to this Temple? [9]And they shall say, Because they forsook Yahweh their God, who brought their fathers out of the land of Egypt, and laid hold on other gods and bowed down[a] to them and served them, therefore Yahweh brought all this ill upon them.

9.1. 'When Solomon had finished building the Temple . . .' reflects not the actual chronology but the Deuteronomist's arrangement of the traditions of Solomon's reign. The pious enterprise of building the Temple emphasizes God's undertaking in the Davidic covenant conditional upon Solomon's allegiance; the evils of the latter's secular administration are anticipated in the admonition, to be more specifically described in ch. 11. This schematization does not visualize any other activity or interest in the early part of Solomon's reign than the building of the Temple, despite the statement that the hostile activities of Hadad of Edom and Rezon of Damascus began early in Solomon's reign (11.21, 25).

'And all Solomon's desire' (*ḥēšeq*), a phrase repeated in v. 19 in connection with various building schemes of Solomon, apparently indicates here other buildings which are not listed. The verb *ḥāšaq* is very strong, indicating primarily physical attachment, and secondarily affection, as of man for woman (Gen. 34.8), Yahweh's love for Israel (Deut. 7.7; 10.15), and man's reciprocal love for Yahweh (Ps. 91.14).

2. According to the Canaanite conception of kingship adapted by David and Solomon, the king was the medium of divine influence, here in revelation, as he had been at Gibeon (3.5).

3. The Temple had been effectively consecrated not by the *opus operatum* of human ritual, but by the presence of Yahweh ('to put my name there'), who was thus by his own assurance accessible in prayer.

4f. Here once more the emphasis is laid on Yahweh's covenant with David declared in Nathan's oracle, hence the direct address to the king as distinct from the reference to the people in vv. 6ff.

7. Here the penalty for disobedience is not simply the fall of a dynasty, nor the political subjection of the people, which might reasonably have been anticipated. It is the wholesale deportation of Israel and the destruction of the Temple, particular eventualities which must surely have been imminent possibilities, if not actually experienced. 'A byword (*māšāl*) and a taunt (*šenīnā*)' is an expression

[a]Reading plural with Q.

found in Deuteronomy (28.37), cf. Jer. 24.9, expressive of extraordinary calamity. *māšāl*, which is also found meaning 'a proverb', which was a reflection of life's experience and a principle by comparison with which life's experiences might be judged, means primarily 'likening' or 'comparison', and many proverbs do have the form of similes or metaphors. Referring to Israel after disaster it implies that the experience of Israel would be an example and an admonition to others. It would be a figure for disaster, like the overwhelming of Sodom and Gomorrah (Amos 4.11) or Napoleon's Waterloo. The other word, *šenīnā*, is derived from the denominative verb *šānan* ('to make sharp', lit. 'toothed'). It is found governing 'tongue', referring to the taunts which aggravate the discomfiture of the sufferer in psalms of lamentation, e.g. Pss. 64.3[4] *šānenū kaḥereb lešōnām* ('they sharpen their tongues like swords'); 140.3[4].

9.8. On the reading *le'iyyīm* for MT *'elyōn* see p. 236 n.[h]. The compiler of Chronicles, however, read *'elyōn* here, but paraphrases the passage 'and at this house which was lofty (*'elyōn*) to all passing by, one shall be appalled . . .' T combines both readings 'this house which was lofty shall become desolate'. A Hebrew text *wehabbayit hazzē 'ašer hāyā 'elyōn yihye le'iyyīm* ('and this Temple, which was lofty, shall become ruins') would be quite a possible word-play, though more natural in a prophetic oracle than in the Deuteronomic style. *'iyyīm* is actually used in the famous oracle of Micah on the Temple (3.12), which is quoted in Jer. 26.18. The fact that such an oracle was possible in the time of Micah (*c.* 700 BC) has suggested that the passage need not be post-exilic.

(*h*) SOLOMON'S PUBLIC WORKS AND ENTERPRISES: 9.10-28

Certain statements in this passage suggest that they were drawn from royal annals, e.g. vv. 11b, 14, recording Solomon's financial arrangements with Hiram after the building of the Temple and palace in Jerusalem, the note on Hiram's supply of building materials in v. 11a being a gloss, and the popular etymology of Cabul (vv. 12f.) another. Verse 10, in narrative style, is probably the editorial introduction to the account of the transaction with Hiram, which continues with a citation from the royal annals in 11b, characteristically introduced by *'āz* ('then').[a] Verse 23 and possibly v. 24, recording the moving of Pharaoh's daughter into her palace and the subsequent

[a]So Montgomery, *JBL* LIII, 1934, p. 49.

building of Millo, is probably taken from royal annals. The introduction to the corvée and its object, which really continues with v. 23, is interrupted by a digression prompted by the reference to Solomon's fortification of Gezer in v. 15. The digression moves on from the note on how Solomon acquired Gezer (v. 16) to the rest of his fortifications (vv. 17f.) and his garrisoning of those places (v. 19) and his conscription of the natives in the corvée (vv. 20f.), which in turn suggests a note on the preferential treatment of the Israelites (v. 22). The diffuse nature of this matter indicates that, whatever the historical substratum of it may be, and in spite of its conjunction with archival data in v. 23, it is rather from a narrative source lauding Solomon, and at some remove from his lifetime, though pre-Deuteronomistic, like the note on Solomon's joint naval enterprise with the Phoenicians in the Red Sea (vv. 26–28). Verse 25, which records Solomon's sacrifices thrice yearly, is probably also a scrap inserted here out of its context, as suggested by the concluding statement, 'so he finished the Temple'.

(i) SOLOMON'S FINANCIAL ARRANGEMENT WITH HIRAM: 9.10–14

9 [10]And it came to pass at the end of twenty years in which Solomon built the two houses, the house of Yahweh and the palace, [11](now Hiram the king of Tyre had helped Solomon with cedar trees and fir trees and with gold for all that he desired) that king Solomon gave[a] Hiram twenty cities in the land of Galilee. [12]And Hiram came out from Tyre to see the cities which Solomon had given him, and he was not pleased with them, [13]and he said, What are these cities which you have given me, my brother? And they have called them the land of Cabul to this day. [14]And Hiram sent the king one hundred and twenty talents of gold.

9.10. In 6.38 it is stated that seven years were spent on the Temple and in 7.1 that thirteen years were occupied in building the palace. **11.** The fact that the clause in 11b begins with the annalistic *'āz* ('then') indicates that it is not the grammatical sequence to v. 10, still less to the parenthesis in v. 11a. That v. 10 has no real grammatical sequence indicates that this verse and v. 11a are editorial, thus giving a false impression as to the reason for Solomon's cession

[a]G[A] reads 'built' (*bānā*), and at first sight the perfect seems more fitting after the particle *'āz*. The word *yittēn*, however, may be the preterite tense, familiar in Akkadian, this possibly also being the explanation of what appears formally to be the imperfect with *w* consecutive, which is the narrative tense in the Ras Shamra texts.

of Cabul. From 5.11 it is clear that the expense of the building materials mentioned here and the craftsmen's wages were defrayed by Solomon by an annual contribution to Hiram of grain and oil. This is a fresh transaction, and the reason for the cession of land appears in the extract from the royal annals in v. 14: Solomon needed gold; see further on v. 15. The cities (*ʿārīm*) were mere villages. The etymology of *ʿīr* is uncertain. II Sam. 12.27, *lākadtī ʾet-ʿīr hammayim* ('I have taken the "city" of waters'), might suggest a connection with Arabic *ġawr*, a hole, hence waterhole. A more likely derivation is from a root *ʿīr* cognate with Ugaritic *ġyr* attested in the greeting *ʾilm tġrk tšlmk* ('May the gods protect you and keep you safe'), as Eissfeldt has discerned.[a] The same collocation of *ʿīr* and *šillēm* is found in Job 8.6,

kī-ʿattā yāʿīr ʿālekā
w^e^šillam n^e^wat ṣid^e^qekā
Then he will mount guard over you
And preserve your righteous dwelling intact.

The phrase *ʿīr hammayim* in II Sam. 12.27 may then be translated 'the water-tower'. Galilee, Hebrew *haggālīl*, signifies 'the circuit'. Skinner (CB, pp. 159f.) cites Josh. 20.7; 21.32 and II K. 15.29 as evidence that the term originally denoted practically the tribal territory of Naphtali in Eastern Galilee (so Noth, *op. cit.*, pp. 210f.). But these passages in Joshua mention Naphtali and Galilee in connection with Kedesh in order to distinguish the place from Kadesh in northern Sinai, while II K. 15.29 describes the results of the expedition of Tiglath-pileser in 734. The localities mentioned are certainly in Naphtali, but the fact that Naphtali is specifically mentioned in addition to Galilee, and that the annals of Tiglath-pileser refer to the incorporation of Megiddo and the Plain of Jezreel in the new Assyrian province, suggests that Galilee included more than the land of Naphtali. 'The circuit' may refer to the upland plains of Upper and Lower Galilee such as that north-west of Safed, the Huleh basin, the Plain of Chinnereth, *aš-Šaġūr* about *ar-Rām*, and *Majd al-Kurūm* east of Acco, the Plain of *al-Baṭṭūf*, that about *Turān*, and possibly also the Plain of Jezreel (Esdraelon), which, with its ring of Canaanite fortresses, Alt[b] regarded as the original *g^e^līl haggōyīm*. Such plains and the mountains which encircled them may have suggested the

[a] 'The Alphabetic Cuneiform Texts from Ras Shamra published in "Le Palais Royal d'Ugarit", Vol. II, 1957', *JSS* V, 1960, p. 41.

[b] A. Alt, 'Die Herkunft des Namens Galiläa', *KS* II, 1953, pp. 363–74.

name, which in the present passage included the western foothills south-east of Acco; here there is still a village Cabul, eight miles from Acco and five miles north-west of *Ḫirbet aš-Šafāt*, the site of Jotapata, and this agrees with the statement of Josephus, who was captured there, that Cabul was forty stades from Jotapata.[a]

9.13. The popular but unreliable etymology of Cabul is *ka* ('as') *bul*, fancifully connected with the root *bālā* ('to waste away'), cf. negative *bal*, hence 'as nothing'. In the Talmud (*Shab.* 54a) there are two further efforts to explain the name, (1) 'sterility' and (2) 'bound', the people being chained (*mᵉkubbālīm*) with chains of silver and gold. The use of the Arabic cognate *kabala* suggests that Cabul, as the form indicates, is a passive participle meaning 'mortgaged', this retaining the memory of Solomon's transaction with Hiram. An interesting suggestion of G, but no more, is that the name is a variant of *gᵉbūl*, G *horion*, hence Marchland.[b]

14. The talent (*kikkār*, lit. 'round thing') was the highest unit of weight in the Near East. In the Sumero-Akkadian sexagesimal system, and in Israel, it consisted of 60 minas, the mina (Hebrew *māne*) consisting of sixty shekels in the Babylonian system, and fifty shekels in the Canaanite system (Ex. 38.25ff.; Ezek. 45.12). There have been various computations of the value of this sum, but only the actual weight may be estimated, and that only relatively, since the weights varied at different periods, the talent being as much as 130 lb. in the old Babylonian system and as little as 45 lb. in the latest Jewish system.[c]

(ii) THE CORVÉE AND ITS PURPOSE: 9.15–23

9 [15]And this is the matter of the forced levy, which king Solomon raised to build the Temple of Yahweh and his own house and the Millo and the wall of Jerusalem and Hazor and Megiddo and Gezer. [16]Pharaoh[d] the king of Egypt had come up and taken Gezer and burnt it with fire, and he had slain the Canaanites who dwelt in the city and he had given it as dowry to his daughter, the wife of Solomon. [17]So

[a] *Ant.* VIII, 5.3.

[b] Montgomery, ICC, p. 205.

[c] A. R. S. Kennedy, 'Weights and Measures', *HDB*, pp. 901–6; A. G. Barrois, *Manuel d'Archéologie Biblique* II, 1953, pp. 252–8.

[d] G^L begins this verse with 'then', suggesting Hebrew *'āz* which usually introduces the various items in royal annals (Montgomery, *JBL* LIII, 1934, p. 49). This is quite a feasible reading, and this and the notice of Solomon's marriage with Pharaoh's daughter (3.1), from which this statement has become detached in the compilation of Kings, probably belonged together to royal annals.

Solomon built Gezer and Beth-horon the Lower,[a] [18]and Baalath, and Tamar[b] in the desert in the land (of Judah),[c] [19]and all the store-cities which Solomon had, and the cities for his chariotry, and the cities for his horsemen, and what Solomon was pleased to build in Jerusalem (and in Lebanon),[d] and in all the land of his dominion. [20]As for all the people that were left of the Amorites, the Hittites, the Perizzites,[e] the Hivites, and the Jebusites,[f] who were not of the Israelites, [21]their children who were left after them in the land, whom the Israelites had not been able to exterminate, them Solomon brought up to the levy of servitude, and so to this day. [22]But of the Israelites Solomon made no serfs; but they were warriors, and his personal *attachés*,[g] and officers of[h] his personal corps, and officers of his chariotry and his horsemen. [23]These are the chief officers that were over Solomon's work,[i] five hundred and fifty,[j] who ruled over the people and supervised the work.

9.15. On *d^ebar* in the sense 'the matter of . . . or the manner of . . .' see on 8.59. On the corvée see on 4.6 and 5.24. The object of the forced labour was the building of public works, the Temple, palace,

[a]G reads 'the Upper', but, as these were frontier fortresses, 'the Lower', nearer the plain, is more likely.

[b]Q reads Tadmor, the renowned caravan city Palmyra, still known to the Arabs as Tadmur, a vital stage in the desert-borne traffic between Damascus and the Euphrates. The association with other localities in the context, however, suggests that MT Tamar, on the road between Hebron and the Araba, is correct.

[c]'In the land', without 'of Judah', which we have understood, seems difficult; hence, on the assumption that 'Tadmor' is to be read, 'in Aram' (*ba'arām*) has been proposed. G omits both 'in the desert' (*bammidbār*) and 'in the land' *bā'āreṣ*. We should retain the MT, however. 'In the desert' defines the little-known Tamar, and the absolute 'in the land', as in 4.19, the homeland of Judah.

[d]G[BL] omit 'and in Lebanon', this expansion of Solomon's power being possibly suggested by 4.21[5.1] elaborated in II Chron. 8.6, where the final reviser of Kings may have got the tradition. The realm of Solomon, however, extending 'to the entrance to Hamath', the southern Biqʿa, before the rise of Damascus, could have included the east slopes of the south part of the Lebanon, as suggested in G of 2.46c, where the statement *kai Salōmōn ērxato anoigein ta dunasteumata tou Libanou* ('and Solomon began to capture the strongholds of the Lebanon') suggests a genuine Semitic original, *anoigein* translating *bāqaʿ* ('to capture', lit. 'to cleave', cf. Arab. *fataḥa*, 'to conquer', lit. 'to open'). *bāqaʿ* is attested in this sense in Isa. 7.6; Jer. 39.2.

[e]G includes 'Canaanites' here, obviously repeating the well-known list of peoples in the accounts of the conquest of Palestine.

[f]G includes 'Girgazites', a variant on the more familiar Girgashites from the same sources.

[g]This word is omitted from the fuller passage in II Chron. 8.9 but, since it has the technical significance of personal *attachés*, such as courtiers, privy counsellors, or the like, it suits the sense of the passage, and may be retained.

[h]Omitting *w^e* before *šālīšāw* as a dittograph of final *w* in MT *śārāw*, for which we propose *śārē(y)*.

[i]The verse seems by the syntax to be either the introduction or conclusion to a lost list of the officers in charge of the corvée for public works. The number is uncertain.

[j]The parallel passage in II Chron. 8.10 states 250, and G 3,600, which suggests that accuracy is beyond recovery.

and fortifications in Jerusalem and strategic points in the provinces. Van den Born (*op. cit.*, p. 65), noting that the enumeration of such building is commonly the subject of royal inscriptions in the ancient East, e.g. Mesha, Zakar, and Assyrian inscriptions, makes the interesting suggestion that the present list may be taken from an inscription of Solomon now lost. The mention of the Millo in this connection, and its association with the wall of Jerusalem here and possibly also in 11.27 indicates that it was part of the defence-works of Jerusalem. As such a work, its cognate *mīlu* is used in Akkadian of an artificial earthwork, terrace, or embankment, and even of a wall,[a] and it may refer to the 'filling out', by means of embankment and esplanade, to avoid an awkward bottleneck at the very narrow ridge at the north-west of the south-east hill. II Sam. 5.9 seems at first sight to suggest that the Millo stood in David's time and even in Jebusite days, but that statement might mean no more than that David built from where the Millo later stood. Other views are that the Millo was a tower built in a breach made in the wall by David's men. This is based on an interpretation of I K. 11.27, for which R. A. S. Macalister and G. Duncan claim support in their discovery of the foundation-course of a building between two walls at the north end of the south-east hill.[b] Later archaeologists, however, e.g. J. W. Crowfoot,[c] have shown the walls in question to be much later than David's time, and the extent and nature of the building to be indeterminate. This location is in any case precluded by the fact that the *millō'* is noted as part of Hezekiah's fortifications (II Chron. 32.5), which completely enclosed the north-east hill north of the narrow saddle between the south-east hill and Solomon's palace at the south end of the north-east hill, and Weill's view that the *millō'* was the filling up of this depression[d] is open to the same objection. The latest opinion of Vincent[e] was that the *millō'* was terrace- and buttress-work strengthening the west flank of Solomon's palace, where the sharp east-ward bend of the central valley cut into the north-east hill and the south-east hill at its northern extremity. That the *millō'* involved terracing and buttressing is certainly right, being suggested by LXX on II Chron. 32.5, which renders the word *analēmma* ('raised work'). Such work was occasioned by the steep slopes in Jerusalem. The work

[a] W. Muss-Arnolt, *A Concise Dictionary of the Assyrian Language*, 1905, pp. 544f.
[b] *Annual of the PEF* IV, 1926, pp. 83ff.
[c] *PEQ*, 1945, p. 7 n.1.
[d] R. Weill, *La Cité de David* A II, 1947, p. 31.
[e] L. H. Vincent, *Jérusalem de l'Ancien Testament* II, 1956, pp. 635f.

on the south-west corner of Solomon's palace, however, would not have been so extensive as to prove the notorious burden which the *millō'* evidently was (11.27f.). So we think of a larger work of the same nature in the deep depression east of the north end of the south-east hill, where an esplanade so supported was imperative to provide for Solomon's increased buildings south of the Temple and palace. The *millō'*, then, was in our opinion the 'filling' of the gulf between the City of David on the south-east hill and the Ophel, or 'bulge' to the north-east. This feature immediately east of the palace of Solomon and his successors was probably the site of the barracks for the professional soldiers on whom the Davidic dynasty so largely depended, and may have been 'the house of the *millō'*' at which Joash was assassinated by two of his retainers (II K. 12.20[21]). At this point there have been no excavations to support this conjecture, but the general conception of a *millō'* or terraced embankment is almost certainly attested by the system of terraces supported by massive retaining walls and buttresses to hold buildings on the steep slope of the south-east hill immediately north of the Spring of Gihon, revealed by the excavation of the British and French Schools of Archaeology in Jerusalem.[a]

The precise extent and location of the wall of Jerusalem built by Solomon is uncertain. In the time of David, when Israel was on the offensive, such a fortification was apparently unnecessary, the old Jebusite defences on the south-eastern hill remaining. Excavations by the British and French Schools of Archaeology at Jerusalem in 1961 demonstrated that the pre-Israelite and early Israelite wall on the east of the south-eastern hill did not follow the crest of the escarpment as had previously been thought, but ran along a lower contour, thus including the shaft to the end of the tunnel from the spring of Gihon (*'Ain Umm ad-Darāj*).[b] On the expansion of Jerusalem to include the new Temple on the north-eastern hill with the palace-complex to the south a new system of fortification was necessary. It seems likely to us that the incorporation of these new features necessitated an adjustment at the extreme north-east of the south-eastern hill, where the ridge narrows considerably and where we locate the Millo.

Hazor, *Tell al-Qedaḥ*, also called *Tell Waqqāṣ*, about four miles west of the crossing of the Jordan at *Jisr Banāt Ya'qūb*, was the most

[a]K. M. Kenyon, 'Excavations in Jerusalem, 1961', *PEQ*, 1962, p. 82, pl. XXII; 'Excavations in Jerusalem, 1962', *PEQ*, 1963, pp. 12–14.

[b]K. M. Kenyon, 'Excavations in Jerusalem, 1961', *PEQ*, 1962, pp. 72–89.

significant fortress in northern Galilee, commanding the routes from the north by the crossing of the Jordan between the lakes of Galilee and Huleh and over the low watershed between Lebanon and Hermon. At this most extensive archaeological site, covering about twenty-two acres including outer defences, evidence has been discovered that the place was destroyed not later than the last third of the thirteenth century BC, which supports the Old Testament tradition in Josh. 11.1, 12ff.; 12.19. The Solomonic occupation with double-chambered gateway and casemate walls is attested on the acropolis, but the period of Ahab is much more fully represented, indicating the significance of Hazor as a frontier fortress in the Syrian wars. Evidence of the capture and partial destruction of the city in the eighth century was found, doubtless the result of the expedition of Tiglath-pileser III in 734, when he denuded the Northern Kingdom of Galilee, Gilead and the Plain of Sharon (II K. 15.29).[a] Megiddo, modern *Tell al-Mutasallim*, was the great fortress-town commanding one of the passes through the south-eastern extension of the Carmel range from the great central Plain of Jezreel to the coastal Plain of Sharon. Like Hazor, it was a key fortress on the great trunk highway from the Euphrates to the Nile, and as such was heavily fortified throughout the Israelite monarchy, until it was taken and adapted as the capital of the Assyrian province of Megiddo, including Galilee, in 734. The Solomonic city is well attested (Level IVB), conspicuous features being the fine double-chambered gateway and possible stable-complexes (see on v. 19 and 10.26).[b] The masonry of the time of Solomon and Ahab is noteworthy for its strength and meticulous hewing and jointing, being paralleled by the masonry of Gezer in the same period.[c] Noting the casemate walling of Bethshemesh and *Tell Beit Mirsīm*, Albright assigned them to the same period, probably constructed to a single plan, though particularly he assigned them to the time of David rather than Solomon. Now Yadin's work at Hazor and a smaller excavation at Megiddo have identified similar casemate walling there with Solomon's fortifications as distinct from Ahab's,[d] so that such work at those sites and at Gezer affords concrete evidence of the general fortifications of Solomon which this passage suggests throughout the

[a]Y. Yadin and others, *Hazor I*, 1958; *Hazor II*, 1960.

[b]For a full report on the excavation of Megiddo see R. S. Lamon and G. M. Shipton, *Megiddo I*, 1939, and G. Loud, *Megiddo II*, 1948.

[c]See W. F. Albright, *The Archaeology of Palestine*, p. 125, fig. 33.

[d]*Hazor II*, p. 3.

realm.[a] Gezer, modern *Tell Jezer*, lay on a spur of the Judaean foothills protecting the trunk highway through the coastal plain against marauders from the hills, and serving as a convenient base for the domination of the Philistine plain to the south-west. The place acquired a new significance for Egypt with the rise and consolidation of the kingdom of Israel in the interior, hence the expedition of the Pharaoh, who captured the place and entrusted it to Solomon, to whom he had given his daughter in a diplomatic marriage (v. 16; see further on 3.1). Evidence of the significance of the place under Solomon has been rediscovered by Yadin in a short excavation and a reappraisal of Macalister's report (*The Excavation of Gezer*) where he has shown that what Macalister regarded as 'a Maccabaean castle' was actually a double-chambered gateway which reproduced in plan, and almost exactly in dimension, the Solomonic gateways of Hazor and Megiddo, so that all were, almost certainly, the work of the same architect.[b]

Malamat[c] makes the interesting suggestion that Solomon's fortification of Gezer, Megiddo and Hazor, and we might add the lower Beth-horon, was connected with the aggressive policy of Shishak (961–24) in Palestine, which was indicated by his sponsorship of Jeroboam. He further suggests that those fortifications were the occasion of Solomon's second transaction with Hiram of Tyre, which involved the cession of the district of Cabul (9.11).

9.16. The Pharaoh in question is not named. On the question of his identity, the date of the taking of Gezer, and the possibility that not Gezer, but Gerar, was denoted see on 3.1. The inhabitants of Gezer are here termed 'Canaanites' (collectively *hakkᵉnaʿᵃnī*). *kᵉnaʿan* is the West Semitic form of Akkad. *kinaḫna*, by which the Syrian coast (Phoenicia proper) was designated in Mesopotamia. The name signified 'the purple land', with which Mesopotamian merchants traded for purple dye (*kinaḫḫu*) procured from the local shell-fish (*murex*), hence the meaning 'merchant' for *kᵉnaʿᵃnī* in Isa. 23.8; Zech. 14.21; Job 40.30; Prov. 31.24, a meaning of which the Egyptians were apparently also aware, to judge from the listing of 'Canaanites' as a class in the inscription of the Palestinian campaign of Amenhotep II

[a]See further Y. Aharoni, 'The Date of the Casemate Walls in Judah and Israel and their Purpose', *BASOR* 154, 1959, pp. 35–39, and Y. Yadin, 'New Light on Solomon's Megiddo', *BA* XXIII, 1960, pp. 62–68.

[b]Y. Yadin, 'Solomon's City-wall and Gate at Gezer', *IEJ* VIII, 1958, pp. 80–86.

[c]'Organs of Statecraft in the Israelite Monarchy', *BA* XXVIII, 1965, pp. 60ff.

(*ANET*, p. 246). In the Old Testament the term is found applied specifically to the Phoenician coast, e.g. Josh. 13.4 (the vicinity of Sidon), Isa. 23.11 (Tyre), cf. Judg. 5.19 ('kings of Canaan' in alliance with Sisera in the west of the great central plain by Megiddo). The last reference extends the application of the name to the inhabitants of the urban centres of the plains of Palestine, which maintained contact with the cities of Phoenicia and shared their culture and religion, cf. Num. 13.29, which locates the Canaanites in Palestine in the coastal plain (so including Gezer), and the Jordan, the natural channels of commerce and culture. In view of the racial admixture of Semite and non-Semite evidenced by the Amarna texts, there can be no question of a strictly ethnic connotation of the term 'Canaanite'. A culture rather than a race is denoted, namely that mediated by the Phoenician cities through the Semites, the largest element in the population of Syria and Palestine. This unity of culture is demonstrated by the agreement between the Old Testament references to Canaanite culture, material remains from the various archaeological sites, and the documentary evidence from Ras Shamra. *šillūḥīm* (lit. 'sending-away gifts') is used generally (Micah 1.14) and specifically of a bride's dowry, cf. the Ras Shamra myth of the marriage of the moon-god and the moon-goddess (*UT* 77, 47). Here *ṯlḫ* associated with *mlg* could hardly mean anything else. The phonetic correspondence is not what is expected, but this text has many phonetic variations which reflect the large non-Semitic element in the population.

9.17. Beth-horon the Upper and Lower were on a ridge descending from the plateau north of Jerusalem to the Valley of Aijalon, the names being preserved in the two Arab villages *Beit ʿūr al-Fawqā* and *Beit ʿūr at-Taḥtā* about eight miles north-west of Jerusalem. The strategic significance of these places in one of the comparatively few approaches from the coastal plain to the Judaean highlands, the region from which Jerusalem was most vulnerable, is emphasized by the role the places played in the Hasmonaean struggle with the Seleucids (esp. I Macc. 9.50) and in the great Jewish revolt of AD 66–70.[a] From surface potsherds it appears that the lower settlement was the more significant, and traces of the Iron Age wall are still visible. This is what we should expect, as the defence was organized by a power in the interior against possible assault from the west, and this evidence supports the MT as against G, which reads 'the

[a]Josephus, *War* II, 19.1.

Upper'. The analogy of the use of *bēt* in Hebrew place-names suggests the strong possibility that this element meant 'shrine', and, to be sure, a local god Horon is attested in the Egyptian Execration Texts from the nineteenth century BC.[a] The god is further mentioned in the Krt saga from Ras Shamra, in an Egyptian inscription of Ramses II from *Ṣān al-Ḥagar* (Pi-Ramesse, also called Avaris and Tanis-Zoan),[b] and in a Semitic inscription from the second century BC at Delos.[c] We have suggested that the deity was associated with the power of life and death, like the Phoenician Eshmun.[d] In this connection it is noteworthy that there was a place Irpeel ('God heals') in the vicinity of Beth-horon (Josh. 18.27), identified by Abel with modern *Rafāt*.[e]

9.18. There were several places named Baalath in the south of Palestine, of which two only deserve consideration here. If Baalath is to be taken together with Beth-horon the Lower, as Josephus[f] thinks, the place is the Danite Baalath (Josh. 19.44) south-west of Beth-horon, after which 'the hill-country of Baalath' (Josh. 15.11) was apparently named. From the latter passage this place was east or north-east of *Yibneh*, and Abel's[g] suggested location at *al-Qubeibeh* or *Tell as-Sallaqāt* in the Jewish settlement of Neṣ Ṣiona is feasible. On the other hand, Baalath may be taken together with Tamar in the Steppe, in which case it might be Baalath of Josh. 15.24 or Baalah of Josh. 15.29, which is also ascribed to Simeon (Josh. 19.3). The localities with which this place is associated indicate that it is to be sought east of Beersheba, where Abel[h] suggests the site of *Ḫirbet al-Meḏbaḥ* ten miles south-east of Beersheba. Tamar ('Palms') in the Steppe is mentioned in Ezek. 47.19 and 48.28 as the south-eastern limit of the holy land as Kadesh was the south-western limit. It is again probably mentioned in the same region as Hazazon-Tamar in Gen. 14.7, and as 'the City of Palms' (*'ir hatt*[e]*mārīm*) in Judg. 1.16. Here Eusebius[i] located the place at Thamara, a Byzantine post one day's journey from Mampsis (modern *Kurnub*) on the way

[a] K. Sethe, *Die Ächtung feindlicher Fürsten, Völker, und Dinge auf altägyptischen Tongefässscherben des mittleren Reiches*, 1926; G. Posener, *Princes et pays . . .*, 1940.
[b] P. Montet, *RB* XLIV, 1934, p. 154.
[c] C. Virolleaud, *RES*, 1937, pp. 37ff.
[d] J. Gray, 'The Canaanite God Horon', *JNES* VIII, 1949, pp. 27–34.
[e] *GP* II, p. 92.
[f] *Ant.* VIII, 6.1.
[g] *GP* II, p. 258.
[h] *GP* II, p. 258.
[i] *Onomasticon* 8.8.

between Elath and Hebron. The parallel passage in II Chron. 8.4 gives the name of the place as 'Tadmor' and elaborates on Solomon's activity in Syria, which is not otherwise attested in the Old Testament. This reading is followed by Q on 'Tamar' in I Kings 9.18. On 'in the land', i.e. the home province (Judah), see on 4.19 and p. 242 n.[c].

9.19. Solomon's store-cities (*ʿārē hammiskᵉnōt*) are not specified, but included presumably the provincial capitals, the seats of the fiscal officers listed in ch. 4. The noun, applied also to the store-cities built by the Hebrews in Egypt (Ex. 1.11), recalls Assyrian *maškanu* and the Hebrew verb *sākan* ('to care for'), cf. the similar verbal root *šakānu* in the Amarna Tablets and the noun *zukinu* ('district prefect'), *sōkēn* in Phoenician and in Isa. 22.15. W. F. Albright would see in certain large buildings with raised floors divided into long narrow rooms at certain archaeological sites, such as Bethshemesh and *Tell ad-Duweir* (Lachish), such store-centres,[a] and this is the current interpretation of the rooms with rows of square limestone pillar-bases at Hazor. The depots for the chariotry and for horsemen (MT *pārāšīm*) or horses (*pᵉrāšīm*) are also unspecified here and at 10.26. Guy's discovery of the three stable-complexes with their limestone troughs and tying-posts perforated at the angle with accommodation for 450 animals indicates that Megiddo was such a depot.[b] The attribution of all the Megiddo stables to Solomon, however, has proved to be premature. In a limited excavation east of the main gateway at Megiddo Y. Yadin found that the casemate wall, which was overbuilt by the solid city-wall of Ahab, as well as being associated with the Solomonic gateway, was also associated with a fort in the area excavated, which was the counterpart to the fort on the south side of the city. As the latter had a stable-complex attached, these stables at least are probably Solomonic. The northern fort, however, which was Solomonic, was actually overbuilt by a stable-complex, so that this is definitely not one of Solomon's stables.[c] The great central plain was an excellent ground for training in chariot tactics. At Taanach, too, about four miles south-east of Megiddo, Guy would identify as a stable-complex a double alignment of pillars which E. Sellin[d] described as the standing stones (*maṣṣēbōt*) of

[a] W. F. Albright, cited by G. E. Wright, *Biblical Archaeology*, 1957, p. 130.
[b] P. L. O. Guy, *New Light from Armageddon*, 1931, pp. 37ff., figs. 26–30.
[c] Y. Yadin, 'New Light on Solomon's Megiddo', *BA* XXIII, 1960, pp. 62–68.
[d] *Tell Taʿannek*, 1904, pp. 18, 104, fig. 10.

a sanctuary, and there is a similar alignment of pillars at *Tell al-Ḥeṣī*, possibly Eglon.[a] On the MT *pārāšīm* and the variant see p. 78, n.[e] above.

9.20. The non-Israelite inhabitants of Palestine, now the subjects of the new State of Israel, are designated by the terms familiar from the Deuteronomic source of the Pentateuch, except that only five of the familiar seven terms are mentioned, see p. 242, nn.[e, f]. The participle *nōtār* implies the later, unhistorical view of the Hebrew occupation as a campaign of practical extermination of the natives. This view of the various pre-Israelite inhabitants of Palestine reflects the diversity of races which one would expect from the geographical situation of Palestine. The Semitic element was the Amorites and the Canaanites, the latter specifically designating, perhaps, the inhabitants of the urban settlements along the trunk highways who had most closely assimilated the culture of Phoenicia, or Canaan proper (see on v. 16). The Amarna Tablets name persons in Palestine who had non-Semitic names, some Indo-Iranian and others Hurrian, deriving from North Syria and the Anatolian foothills. It is significant that in the account of Palestine before the Hebrew settlement G at Gen. 34 and Josh. 9.7, 8 reads *ḥōrī* (Hurrian) for *ḥiwwī* (Hivite). There is no evidence of the settlement of the Hittites of Anatolia in Palestine, and at the height of their power they never penetrated beyond the Upper Orontes in Syria. The Assyrians used the designation loosely, denoting by 'the land of the Hatti' (*māt ḫatti*) the West in general, including Syria and Palestine, and there is no reason to think that the Hebrew use of the term is any more accurate. In the Old Testament it may denote the non-Semitic peoples, ultimately from the north, akin to the Anatolian Hittites, like the Armenoid Hurrians. The other terms also, Perizzites, Girgashites, and also possibly the Jebusites, probably all denote descendants of mercenaries from the north-east who had garrisoned Palestine in the Egyptian domination from the fifteenth to the thirteenth century.

21. 'To exterminate them' does not fully translate *l^eh̲aḥ^arīmām*, which signifies extermination as an act of renunciation of common usufruct on the part of warriors in the more primitive stage of the history of Israel. It reflects usage in the time of the militant sacral confederacy of Israel, when war was a holy office and everything consecrated to this purpose was removed from common use. The spoils also were sacrosanct or 'reserved' (*ḥerem*) to God; what was

[a]F. J. Bliss, *A Mound of Many Cities*, 1898, pp. 90ff.

not appropriated for the sanctuary of Yahweh (7.51) was destroyed (e.g. Jericho and its spoil, Josh. 7). The devoted extermination of the Amalekite victims of Saul and the spoils in I Sam. 15 is the last recorded instance in Hebrew history of this crude, fanatical practice, and significantly marks an epoch in the development from the conception of war as a service to Yahweh, divinely inspired and directed through charismatic leadership, to that of action taken in the interests of the state at the dictation of secular politics and carried out by a professional army under the leadership of the king as the head of a feudal order, or by one of his officers. The holy war in the full sense of the term had passed out of use by the time of the Davidic monarchy, though David in his Ammonite campaign, when the ark was taken with the army into the field, revived the practice, probably to enlist the support of all Israel in the campaign, which had the aspect of a holy war as a joint enterprise of the sacral community. In the somewhat idealistic and schematic presentation of the conquest of Palestine and the status of Israel in the narrative and legalistic matter in Deuteronomy and the Deuteronomistic history the holy war is rather an anachronism, reflecting the conception of Israel as a theocracy. At first sight it seems from Mesha's recording of the carrying out of the *ḥerem* in the second half of the ninth century that the practice of the holy war survived longer in Moab than in Israel, but this may be an artificial revival in the war of liberation, and in the lack of further evidence from Moab, we cannot draw definite conclusions.[a] The levy of servitude (*mas ʿōbēd*), as the administrative texts from Ras Shamra show, was a feature of Canaanite life.[b] The term *mas* itself is not so far attested at Ras Shamra, but is known in the form *mazza* in the Akkadian of the Amarna tablets in a reference to the settlement of *amelūti mazza* by Egypt on lands in the centre of the great central plain after a native revolt. This might well refer to the settlement of Issachar, which is noted for service in the *mas* in Gen. 49.14f.[c] On the distinction between *mas*, to which the Israelites were occasionally subject, as in 5.13[27], and *mas ʿōbēd*, which in-

[a]On the primitive practice and development of the holy war see G. von Rad, *Der heilige Krieg im alten Israel* and *Studies in Deuteronomy*, pp. 45–59; R. de Vaux, *Ancient Israel*, pp. 258–65.

[b]See on 4.6 and 5.27, and texts in C. F. A. Schaeffer (ed.), *Mission de Ras Shamra VI, Le palais royal d' Ugarit. Textes accadiens et hourrites des archives est, ouest, et centrales*, which we have summarized à propos of this subject in *The Legacy of Canaan*, 1965², pp. 220f.

[c]Alt, 'Neues über Palastina aus dem Archiv Amenophis IV', *KS* III, 1959, pp. 169–75.

volved permanent serfdom, to which the Canaanites were subjected, see above on 5.13 [27]. The determining word is *ʿōbēd*, and the point of the statement is that, whatever public burdens they might have had to bear occasionally on the Canaanite model, the Israelites were not permanent serfs. The duration of this system of state absolutism, being relevant to the monarchy, 'to this day' surely implies the hand of the Deuteronomist before the liquidation of the state in 586.

9.22. The military service of the Israelites broadly distinguished them from the non-Israelite subjects of Solomon, who retained the permanent liability for state burdens from the feudal system of ancient Canaan. Particularly, however, it may be noted that the military profession was not reserved for Israelites. No doubt the higher commands were, but the instances of Uriah the Hittite and Ittai of Gath in the army of David suggest that in the standing army of Solomon professional soldiers were not limited to native Israelites. In fact, the development of chariotry with its bases in the old Canaanite cities of Hazor, Megiddo and Gezer, though those places are not specifically mentioned in this connection, was probably, like the corvée, a direct development of institutions of the Canaanite city-states incorporated in the new state of Israel, and employing the old feudal personnel. On the various meanings of *ʿebed* see on 1.2. *šālīš* is properly the third man in a chariot apart from the driver and the warrior. He is the shield- and armour-bearer of the latter (Assyrian *šalšu*). The term eventually signifies a royal aide-de-camp, 'he on whose arm the king stayed himself' (II K. 7.2, 17, 19). That the status of the *šālīš* was sufficiently high to stimulate ambition to the throne is indicated by the case of Pekah, the *šālīš* of King Pekahiah, whom he assassinated and supplanted (II K. 15.25).

23. See p. 242 n.[1] above.

(iii) THE REMOVAL OF PHARAOH'S DAUGHTER TO HER NEW PALACE, AND THE BUILDING OF THE MILLO: 9.24

An excerpt from an archival source, here doubtless displaced from its context and included at this point as referring to public works to which the corvée was applied.

9 [24]Then[a] Pharaoh's daughter came up from the city of David to her house that he built for her. Then he built the Millo.

[a]Reading *'āz*, which introduces fresh items in official archives, for MT *'ak* ('only'), which might signify 'then only', but would be barely normal Hebrew. *'āz* is supported by G, which has the substance of the present passage at 9.9.

(iv) MISCELLANEOUS: SOLOMON'S REGULAR SACRIFICES: 9.25

This again may be displaced from its proper context, and may possibly refer, as Montgomery suggested, to Solomon's sacrifices at David's altar (II Sam. 24.25), which Solomon had rebuilt, before the building of the Temple. Nothing in this passage is against this view (see n.[a] below), but the parallel passage in II Chron. 8.12 specifies in the light of later experience that the altar was before the porch of the Temple.

9 [25]And Solomon used to offer three times a year whole burnt offerings and communion-sacrifices on the altar which he had built for Yahweh and he used to burn his offerings[a] before Yahweh, and he used to discharge his vows.[b]

9.25. The perfect *heʿelā* with *wᵉ* denotes frequency, 'used to offer'. The following verb *šillam* ('completed'), also introduced by *wᵉ* with the object *'et-habbayit* ('the house') can only refer to the completion of the Temple, being a late interpolation, when the *w* consecutive was obsolete. But *wᵉšillam* may be frequentative if we understand *nᵉdārāw* ('his vows') as object. On the analogy of Ps. 76.12, where *šillam* means 'paid vows' with the object unexpressed, Montgomery (ICC, p. 215) suggested that the verse ended with *wᵉšillam*, and *'et-habbayit* was added by a late hand accustomed to the use of the perfect with *w* to express past tense. Skinner suggested that *šillam* meant here 'restored the (ceremonial) integrity of' the house (CB, p. 164). This conception, involving the restoration of the association between God and the Temple, is not quite impossible, but a personal object such as 'the people' would be more natural. It is just possible that *habbayit* means 'the family', i.e. of Solomon, though this noun is more naturally understood as 'the Temple'. Montgomery's explanation seems the most feasible. On *ʿōlā* ('burnt offering') and *šᵉlāmīm* ('communion sacrifices') see on 3.15.

The three occasions in the year on which Solomon officiated at the sacrifice were probably the Feast of Unleavened Bread at the beginning of the barley harvest, the Feast of Weeks at the end of the wheat harvest seven weeks later, and the New Year Feast of Tabernacles. On these occasions, when the king exercised his priestly

[a]Reading *'et-'iššō* with Klostermann for the untranslatable *'ittō 'ašer* of MT.
[b]For the absolute use of *šillam* cf. Ps. 76.12; *habbayit* is a late gloss from the time when Aramaic had familiarized men with the use of the perfect of the past tense after *wᵉ*.

prerogative, which at other times he delegated,[a] the community was reintegrated with its God through the communion-offerings (*šelāmīm*). On the subject of these occasions the parallel passage in II Chron. 8.13 particularizes, including daily offerings and offerings on the sabbaths and new moons. This is the only reference in Kings to Solomon building an altar, and, as suggested, may refer to his repair of the Davidic altar before the building of the Temple. II Chron. 8.12 specifies that the altar was before the porch of the Temple. *haqṭēr*, here infin. abs. of Hiphil for the finite verb, denotes primarily, as its Arabic cognate, 'the making of smoke', i.e. of sacrifice (e.g. Amos 4.5). It means only secondarily 'to make (the fumes of) an incense-offering' (Assyrian *quṭrinnu*). In Klostermann's attractive emendation, *iššeʼ*, plural *ʼiššīm*, denoted that part of the sacrifices which was the perquisites of the priests (I Sam. 2.28; Deut. 18.1; Josh. 13.14; Lev. 6.10). Montgomery hesitates to accept this emendation on the grounds that the noun is constructed only with the absolute Yahweh. That is usually so, but in I Sam. 2.28 it is constructed with *benē yiśrāʼēl*. The etymology of the word is uncertain. It may be connected with *ʼēš* ('fire'); G. B. Gray[b] suggested a connection with the root *ʼānaš* (Arabic *ʼanisa*, 'to be sociable'), hence 'fellowship-offering', but nothing in the Old Testament on *ʼiššīm* supports this. We suggest rather a connection with Arabic *ʼaws* ('gift').

(v) SOLOMON'S NAVAL ENTERPRISES IN THE RED SEA: 9.26–28

The dry, factual statement without detail, except for a possible exaggeration of the amount of gold acquired, indicates a summary from a fuller narrative source.

9 [26]And king Solomon made a fleet at Ezion-geber, which is beside Elath[c] on the shore of the Red Sea in the land of Edom. [27]And Hiram sent in the fleet his servants, seamen, who knew the sea, along with the servants of Solomon. [28]And they came to Ophir and brought gold from there, four hundred and twenty[d] talents, and brought it to king Solomon.

[a]J. Morgenstern, 'A Chapter in the History of the High Priesthood', *AJSL* LV, 1938, pp. 1–24.

[b]*Sacrifice in the Old Testament: its Theory and Practice*, 1925, pp. 9–13.

[c]So G for MT Eloth. Elsewhere in the Old Testament the form is usually the singular.

[d]The parallel account in II Chron. 8.18 gives the amount as 450; G[B] gives it as 120, which is much nearer reasonable proportions. Beyond this there is no means of determining the original text.

9.26. The singular *'ᵒnī* is the collective or generic noun, a single ship being *'ᵒnīyyā*, cf. Arabic *ḥajar* ('stone'), *ḥajara* ('a single stone').

There is no reason to suppose, with Guthe, Robinson, and Skinner, that the site of Ezion-geber is to be located at *'Ain al-Ġaḍyān*. The phonetic correspondence is possible, but this site is over fifteen miles inland from the north of the Gulf of Aqaba. Glueck's excavation of *Tell al-Ḫaleifeh* half a mile north of the head of the Gulf proves that the shore-line has receded no more than half a mile since the time of Solomon. Moreover, the surface pottery of *'Ain al-Ġaḍyān* indicates no occupation earlier than Nabataean. Skinner (CB, p. 165) supposes that the location of Ezion-geber with reference to Elath suggests that it was an older settlement eclipsed by Elath. We might suggest that it was rather a new settlement in the time of Solomon, identical with the industrial site of *Tell al-Ḫaleifeh*.[a] The same compound which housed the copper-workers would serve the workmen engaged in shipbuilding, and Glueck records long nails, such as would be used in shipbuilding, lumps of pitch for caulking, and the carbonized remains of thick cables at this site.[b] Elath is mentioned together with Ezion-geber as one of the places passed by the Israelites in their desert wandering (Deut. 2.8). The region, taken from Edom in the time of David, remained in possession of Israel until the time of Jehoram, when it seems to have been lost in the Edomite revolt (II K. 8.20ff.). It was recovered under Amaziah (II K. 14.22), its rebuilding being completed by Uzziah (II Chron. 26.2), but was finally lost in the time of Ahaz (II K. 16.6, where 'Aram' is a scribal error for 'Edom', as Q recognizes, and 'Rezin' a gloss). Strategically important in its situation on the caravan routes from Arabia to Gaza and Egypt, it flourished in Nabataean and Roman times, and in Byzantine, Arab, and Crusading times it was named Aela. These periods of occupation are attested by large deposits of potsherds at a site just over half a mile west-north-west of Aqaba. There is no trace here of earlier occupation, and it is supposed that the Hebrew and Edomite towns were sanded up before the later occupation. The 'Red Sea', *yam sūp* (lit. 'Sea of Papyrus-reeds', Egyptian *twf*), properly refers to marshes including the Bitter Lakes in the depression north of the Gulf of Suez and then to the Red Sea generally. In the earlier traditions of the

[a]F. Frank, *ZDPV* LVII, 1934, pp. 243ff.

[b]'The First Campaign at Tell el-Kheleifeh', *BASOR* 71, 1938, pp. 3–18; 'The Second Campaign . . .', *BASOR* 75, 1939, pp. 8–22; 'The Third Season . . .'. *BASOR* 79, 1940, pp. 2–18.

Exodus, apart from the composite account in the Pentateuch, e.g. the Prophets as against Deuteronomistic passages and later psalms, there is no mention of *yam sūp*, but only of 'the sea'.[a]

The timber for Solomon's merchant fleet was probably drawn from the high escarpment of Edom, which was tolerably well wooded until the Turks devastated the woods for fuel for the engines on the Hejaz Railway.

9.28. The location of Ophir is uncertain. In Gen. 10.29 it is located between Sheba and Havilah, hence in South Arabia. The mention of apes and baboons (see on 10.22) among Solomon's cargoes from Ophir, however, suggests remoter regions, which have been sought in Africa and India. Since such a trading voyage lasted three years (10.22) it has been suggested that Ophir must have been farther away than South Arabia or Somaliland (Punt), which is known in Egyptian inscriptions as a source of gold. In favour of East Africa is the known Phoenician contact with this region between the Zambesi and the Limpopo. The Sanskrit origin of the word for 'apes', however, suggests contacts with India. In view of the biblical tradition that Ophir was in Arabia, known to the Phoenicians as auriferous (Ezek. 27.22; cf. Job. 28.16), it is safest to regard Ophir as South Arabia, and as an important *entrepōt* for merchandise from the further East and also from East Africa. Doubtless the three-year duration of Solomon's trading voyages is to be explained by incidental coasting trade, and the fact that sailing both from Ezion-geber to South Arabia and from more distant regions to South Arabia was confined to a part of the year, being governed by the alternations of the south-westerly and north-easterly monsoons.[b] The G version of Ophir with an initial S has suggested *Sofala*, some 200 miles from the famous ruins of Zimbabwe in East Africa, and *Supara* in Goa on the Malabar coast. This spelling, however, has no basis in MT, and probably reflects the sea-borne trade with India in Ptolemaic times, when G was produced. Josephus[c] also locates Ophir in India. Though it is of no significance for the location of Ophir, we may note the mention of a consignment of 'gold of Ophir' for Beth-horon in an inscribed ostracon found on the surface of *Tell Qasīleh* near the mouth of the Jarkon river (*nahr ʿAwjā*) just

[a]Eissfeldt, *Baal Zaphon, Zeus Kasios, und der Durchzug der Israeliten durchs Meer*, 1932, pp. 65ff.
[b]E. Glaser, *Skizze der Geschichte und Geographie Arabiens* II, 1890, pp. 375f.
[c]*Ant.* VIII, 6.4.

north of Jaffa, which has been dated to the first half of the eighth century BC.[a]

(i) THE VISIT OF THE QUEEN OF SHEBA: 10.1–13
INCLUDING THE PRODUCTS OF SOLOMON'S RED SEA TRADE
(interpolation suggested by the context): 10.11–12

The tradition of the visit of the Queen of Sheba, which has been much elaborated in Jewish, Arab and Christian (Abyssinian) legend, may well rest on a historical basis, the visit possibly being a trade mission. This is suggested by the position of the passage between the note of Solomon's mercantile enterprise in the Red Sea (9.26–28), and his revenue derived from various sources (10.14ff.) including the Red Sea voyages (10.22), and by the interpolation of vv. 11f. concerning produce brought by the Red Sea from the south. Here again R. B. Y. Scott notes the association of Solomon's fabulous wisdom with great magnificence, and would see a later legendary elaboration, citing a number of late, post-exilic usages in the language of the passage.[b] The wisdom here is of a different kind from the administrative *savoir-faire* of ch. 3 and the encyclopaedic nature-lore of ch. 5, and is rather skill in riddles, probably word-plays in verse. Mental gymnastics of this sort were practised at the court of the Umayyad Caliphs, certain of whom affected poetry in conscious preservation of a tradition established among the Arabs before Islam. In this as well as in the problem raised for the mercantile powers of South Arabia by Solomon's enterprises in the Red Sea and his control of the nexus of caravan routes at the head of the Gulf of Aqaba, we may see the germ of historical fact, whatever the later elaboration in this passage, which we freely admit.

10 [1]Now the Queen of Sheba, hearing the report of Solomon,[c] came to test him with enigmatic sayings. [2]And she came to Jerusalem with a very great retinue, camels[d] that carried spices and very much gold and precious stones, and she came to Solomon and spoke to him all that was in her mind. [3]And Solomon explained all her problems; there was nothing hidden from the king which he did not declare to her. [4]And

[a]B. Maisler, *IEJ* I, 1950–1, pp. 209ff.

[b]*Wisdom in Israel*, pp. 267ff.

[c]Omitting with the parallel account in II Chron. 9.1 *l^e^šēm yhwh* ('with respect to the name of Yahweh'), cf. G, S 'and the name of Y.'. The phrase seems obviously inserted for later motives of reverence, and its omission in Chronicles, where it might have been expected, confirms our reading.

[d]The parallel account in Chronicles and in G and S reads 'and camels', which would suggest that *ḥayil* was perhaps a military escort.

the Queen of Sheba saw all the wisdom of Solomon, and the house which he had built, [5]and the food of his table and the seating of his retainers, and the attendance of his servants and his[a] apparel and his drinking-service[b] and the way he went up[c] to the Temple of Yahweh, and she was quite nonplussed. [6]And she said to the king, The word I heard in my own land about your acts and your wisdom has been true, [7]though I did not believe those who told it[d] until I came and my eyes saw, and behold, the half was not told me. You have surpassed in wisdom and in goodliness the report[e] which I heard.[f] [8]Happy are your wives,[g] happy are these your retainers who stand before you continually, hearing your wisdom. [9]Blessed be Yahweh your God, who has pleasure in you, to set you upon the throne of Israel for the love which Yahweh bears to Israel for ever,[h] and has made you king to make effective good order and right. [10]And she gave the king one hundred and twenty talents of gold and a great quantity of spices and precious stones; there came no more such abundance of spices as that which the Queen of Sheba gave to king Solomon. [11]Moreover, the fleet of Hiram, which brought gold from Ophir, brought[i] almug-timbers in great abundance and precious stones. [12]And the king made the almug trees into steps for the Temple of Yahweh and for the palace, and harps and lyres for the singers; there came no almug-timbers like this, nor have any been seen until this day. [13]And king Solomon gave to the Queen of Sheba all that she desired, everything she asked, besides what he gave her, with royal bounty.[j] So she turned and went to her own land, she and her servants.

10.1. Contemporary with the Hebrew monarchy were a number of advanced states in the extreme south of Arabia westwards from the Hadramaut, where the monsoons from the Indian Ocean made cultivation possible in the well-watered highlands towards the

[a]So G for MT 'their apparel'.

[b]Reading a derivative noun (*mašqēhū*) for the plural participle, which, however, would be quite intelligible, though 'his cup-bearers' would doubtless be included in *m^e^šār^e^tāw* ('his servants').

[c]For MT *ʿōlātō* ('his whole burnt-offering') the parallel account in Chronicles reads *ʿ^a^līyātō* ('his upper chamber', i.e. his guest-chamber), but the most suitable reading is the verbal noun *ʿ^a^lōtō* ('his going up'), i.e. the pomp and circumstance with which he headed the procession from the city of David to the new Temple.

[d]Reading *m^e^dabb^e^rīm* with G and V, for MT 'the words'.

[e]A rather better reading is that of G, which inserts 'all' here.

[f]G adds 'in my own land'.

[g]So with G, S, L for MT *ʾ^a^nāšekā*, 'your men', a natural remark from a woman, *ʿ^a^bādekā* ('your retainer') would make *ʾ^a^nāšekā* tautological. Perhaps MT represents an effort to remove the wives of Solomon, which later Deuteronomistic opinion resented.

[h]The parallel account in II Chron. 9.8 reads *l^e^haʿ^a^mīdō l^e^ʿōlām* ('to establish him forever').

[i]Omitting MT *mēʾōpīr* ('from Ophir') with G and the parallel account in II Chron. 10.10.

[j]Omitting MT *š^e^lōmō* ('Solomon') with V, S, and Aquila.

Yemen. Recent exploration and excavation in those regions, particularly by the expeditions of the American Foundation for the Study of Man organized by Wendell Phillips, with the discovery of a great many inscriptions, has revealed the development of those states from theocracy through secular monarchy to oligarchy from the beginning of the first millennium BC to the sixth century AD, with various shifts of power between the Sheban, Minaean, and Qatabanian states, Sheba being the most powerful and durable. More particularly, radio-carbon dating together with palaeographic evidence suggests the period *c.* 900–*c.* 450 BC for the floruit of the Sabaean Empire.[a] Though practising an agricultural economy through the comparatively high rainfall and by advanced works of damming and irrigation, those kingdoms were essentially trading empires, exploiting their situation about 15 miles from Africa across the Straits of Bab al-Mandeb, and as an emporium of sea-borne trade from India and East Africa. Costly luxury commodities, together with incense, which their own land produced, were transported northwards through such oases as Mecca, Medina, Kheibar, and Teima to such terminals as Damascus, the metropolis of the North Arabian steppe, or Gaza by way of the head of the Gulf of Aqaba. A South Arabian clay seal found with ninth-century debris at Bethel, though unfortunately not in a regular stratum, probably bears witness to traffic in incense with the shrine of Bethel in the early Israelite monarchy.[b] Though the visit of the Queen of Sheba has been much elaborated to enhance the glory and wisdom of Solomon, it was probably a historical incident, a trade mission rendered necessary by the Hebrew occupation of the head of the Gulf of Aqaba and their control of Damascus, and possibly also by the threat to South Arabian monopoly of the trade with Africa and India by the naval enterprise of Solomon and the king of Tyre in the Red Sea and Indian Ocean. The numerous inscriptions from South Arabia do not so far attest the pre-eminence of women in the royal line, but Assyrian inscriptions from the eighth and seventh centuries, conveniently listed by N. Abbot,[c] repeatedly mention Arab queens in the northern part of the Arabian peninsula, which suggests a

[a] W. F. Albright, 'A Note on Early Sabaean Chronology', *BASOR* 143, 1956, pp. 9f.; G. W. van Beek, 'A Radio-carbon Date for Early South Arabia', *BASOR* 143, 1956, pp. 6–9.

[b] G. W. van Beek and A. Jamme, 'An Inscribed South Arabian Clay Stamp from Bethel', *BASOR* 151, 1958, pp. 9–16.

[c] 'Pre-Islamic Arab Queens', *AJSL* LVIII, 1941, pp. 1–22.

matrilinear system of succession. The 'Shebans', whom Gen. 25.2ff. and Job. 1.15 locate in the north of the peninsula, may have been tribes in alliance with the southern Sheba along the carvan routes. They may on the other hand, have been independent. The *Wādī aš-Šeba*, north-east of Medina, may be a survival of the name. It is even possible the 'Queen of Sheba' was the ruler of one of these.

It is hardly likely that the main purpose of the queen's visit was to test Solomon (*l^enassōtō*) with riddles (*ḥīdōt*), though such tests of practical sagacity and poetic susceptibility were part of the diplomatic encounters of the day. The tradition of such royal wisdom of the more practical type was a reflection of the conception that the king was the channel of revelation as well as other divine blessing to the community, while his wit and poetic skill were evidence of the extent to which he was conversant with affairs and culture in the world of his day. Relics of this category of wisdom (*ḥīdā*) in the Old Testament, on a particular and local level, are the riddles of Samson (Judg. 14), and, on a universal scale, conundrums in Proverbs with imagery calculated to test the imagination. Josephus[a] records such a battle of wits between Solomon and Hiram.

10.2. If the MT is correct, *g^emallīm* ('camels') must stand in apposition to *ḥayil kābēd m^e'ōd* ('a very great retinue'). If we follow G, S, and the parallel version in Chronicles and read 'and camels', we must understand *ḥayil* as distinct from 'camels'. It is tempting to take *ḥayil* as the Arabic collective *ḫayl* ('horses'), but as this word is not otherwise attested in Hebrew, we must understand it to mean 'retinue', possibly armed. Aromatics (*b^eśāmīm*), probably aromatic gum or incense, was the best-known product of South Arabia, though the term is rather a general one, referring also to a local Palestinian aromatic (S. of S. 5.1.). The balm of Gilead is *ṣ^orī*. On the products of South Arabia see on 9.28. 'All that was in her heart' denotes all that was in her mind, the heart (*lēb*) being the seat of the intelligence, cf. Arabic *'ūli 'l-'albāb* (lit., 'possessors of hearts', i.e. 'intelligent people').

3. 'All her problems' (lit, 'all her words') apparently refers to the questions with which the queen tested Solomon, as is suggested by the statement that 'there was nothing hidden from the king that he did not declare to her'.

4. It is uncertain whether 'the house which he built' signifies the Temple or the palace or both considered as a single complex.

5. 'His servants' might mean either personal, or feudal, retainers

[a] *Ant.* VIII, 5.3.

or courtiers including high-ranking officers of state. At this early stage the former were probably denoted. Mention of the drinking service is significant. The hillsides of Palestine and Syria were famed for the vine since the Egyptian Middle Kingdom, when local wine is mentioned in the Story of Sinuhe. The hills of Judah particularly are celebrated for their vines in the Blessing of Jacob (Gen. 49.11ff.), and until fairly recent times the hills north of Hebron and about Ramallah were the great vine-producing areas. 'She was quite nonplussed' is our somewhat free translation of the phrase meaning literally 'She had no longer any spirit (*rūaḥ*)'. *rūaḥ* is an invasive influence, akin to inspiration, which results in pre-eminence or initiative in action or thought. It is well characterized by N. H. Snaith:[a] 'It stands for the energy and determination which is the main-spring of action.' When the Egyptian fugitive in I Sam. 30.12 came to himself after fainting, it was said that his *rūaḥ* came back to him.

10.9. The establishment of David's dynasty is a pledge of the eternal stability of Yahweh's purpose for and through Israel. The king and the orderly government which he guarantees are the temporal realization of the rule (*mišpāṭ*) of God, and of his standard of right (*ṣᵉdāqā*), a conception which recurs in the Psalms, e.g. 2 and 110, and in the 'messianic' passages in the prophets, e.g. Isa. 9.6f. [5f.]; 11.1–5.

11. *'almug*, a *hapax legomenon* here, cf. II Chron. 2.7; 9.10, 11, *'algum*, has been subject to a wide variety of conjectures in rabbinical and modern commentaries. The reading *'almug* is supported by the listing of thirty pieces of *'almg* along with tribute of olive-oil, iron, cypress-wood, perfume and possibly cinnamon (*qnm*) in an administrative text from Ras Shamra (Gordon, *UT* 120, 8). It is noted as a wood for fine furniture in the Alalakh Tablets,[b] like the *elammaku* wood in the Mari texts from the eighteenth century BC.[c] Unfortunately, none of these texts specifies its nature further, and in mentioning the felling of *elammaku* trees in the mountains of Syria, the Mari text leaves unclear the question of Solomon's *'almug* trees, which in the context it is natural to assume to be a tropical wood. Josephus takes it as pinewood, Symmachus and Jerome (V) suggest '*thyina*', a close-grained African wood used for elegant furniture. It may be red

[a] 'Kings', *Interpreter's Bible* III, 1954, p. 97.
[b] D. J. Wiseman, *The Alalakh Tablets*, 1953, p. 23.
[c] G. Dossin, *Syria* XXXII, 1955, p. 26.

sandal-wood, Sanskrit *mica* with the Arabic definite article, but note the reserve of the Sanskrit specialist W. E. Clark.[a] In a recent study, J. C. Greenfield and M. Mayerhofer[b] note the association with cedar and pine (*berôš*) of Lebanon in II Chron. 2. 8[7]. Thus, in spite of the statement that this cargo came with gold from Ophir, two quite different enterprises in which the fleet of Hiram was involved may be telescoped in this sentence.

10.12. The *'almug*-wood was used apparently for steps (*mis'ād*) (cf. II Chron. 9.11, *mesillōt*) in the Temple. One wonders if *mesillōt* of Chronicles is not a corruption of *sullām* (lit. 'ladder', hence 'steps'). The reference to 'singers' (*šārīm*) and musical instruments, *kinnōrōt*, *nebālīm*, in the Temple is interesting in view of the debated question of the antiquity of the Psalms. In this connection the reference of Amos 5.23 to music in worship is highly significant.

13. 'All that she desired, even what she asked' seems to refer to a specific request of the queen. *keyad hammelek* (lit. 'as the hand of the king') refers to Solomon's entertainment and courtesy gifts given with characteristic munificence. The want of another preposition *b* before *yad* seems strange, though the phrase is not unintelligible. Perhaps the original reading was *kedē hammelek* 'in royal sufficiency' i.e. such as might sustain the prestige of Solomon and be fitting for the queen.

(*j*) MISCELLANEOUS MATTER REGARDING SOLOMON'S REVENUE, WEALTH, AND ITS SOURCES: 10.14–29

Some of this matter is obviously suggested here by the account of the magnificence of Solomon's state which impressed the Queen of Sheba, and some is suggested by the consciousness that the visit of the queen was a trade mission. Some of this is apparently drawn from state archives, e.g. Solomon's imports from the Red Sea trade, also vv. 22f., his other mercantile enterprises and revenues (vv. 28f.), and his development of chariotry (v. 26). The account of Solomon's conversion of gold bullion into ceremonial shields, and of his throne (vv. 16–20) may be from a similar source, but the account of his magnificence (vv. 21, 27), wisdom (vv. 23f.), and the general statement that tribute flowed to him from 'all the earth' (vv. 24f.) has the ring rather of saga than of sober fact, though the details of the tribute (v. 25) suggests a basis in history.

[a]'The Sandalwood and Peacocks of Ophir', *AJSL* XXXVI, 1920, pp. 103–19.
[b]'The *'algummīm/'almuggīm*-Problem Re-examined', SVT XVI, 1967, pp. 83–89.

10 [14]Now the weight of gold that came to Solomon in one year was six hundred and sixty-six talents of gold, [15]besides the taxes[a] on the merchants, and the traffic[b] of the travelling traders, and of all the kings of the Arabs,[c] and the governors of the land. [16]And king Solomon made two hundred[d] shields of beaten gold, six hundred shekels of gold going into each shield, [17]and three hundred targes of beaten gold, three minas[e] of gold going into each targe, and the king put them in the House of the Forest of Lebanon. [18]And the king made a great ivory throne and overlaid it with fine[f] gold. [19]The throne had six steps, and a calf's head[g] behind, and arms on both sides at the place of the seat, and two lions standing by the arms, [20]and there were twelve lions standing[h] on the six steps, on this side and on that; there was not the like made in any kingdom.[i] [21]And all the royal drinking vessels of king Solomon were gold, and all the vessels of the House of the Forest of Lebanon were refined gold, there was no silver; it was of no account at all in the days of Solomon. [22]For the king had a Tarshish-fleet at sea with the fleet of Hiram; once in three years would the Tarshish-fleet come in bringing gold and silver, ivory, ebony, and apes and baboons.[j]

[a]Reading G (*phorōn*, cf. II K. 23.33), i.e. *ʿoneše* for MT *ʾaneše* ('men'). T supports G translating *ʾagar* ('rental').

[b]Reading *ūmissaḥar* for MT *ūmisḥar*.

[c]Reading after Aquila, Symmachus, S, V, and II Chron. 9.14 *ʿarāb* for MT *hāʿereb* ('the West' or 'mixed peoples').

[d]G and L read here 300; MT is supported by II Chron. 9.15.

[e]The parallel account in II Chron. 9.16 reads '300', understanding, no doubt, shekels as in v. 16.

[f]II Chron. 9.17, doubtless paraphrasing, gives the adjective *ṭāhōr* ('pure') instead of MT *mūpāz*. S obviously read *mēʾōpīr* ('from Ophir'), a possible corruption of MT. There seems no compelling reason to discard MT *mūpāz*, the Hophal participle of *pāzaz*.

[g]Reading *ʿēgel* ('calf') after G (*protomai moschōn*) for MT *ʿāgōl* ('rounded'). This was doubtless a Massoretic attempt to gloss over the fact that the bull, the symbol of Baal, was represented on the throne of Solomon. The parallel account in II Chron. 9.18 apparently substituted 'lamb' (*kebeś*) for 'calf' and then altered *kebeś* to *kebeš* ('footstool').

[h]Omitting MT *šām* ('there') with G[BL].

[i]Reading singular after II Chron. 9.19.

[j]The last three items obviously caused the translators of G some difficulty. They apparently read *ʾabānīm* ('stones') for the element *habbīm* in *šenhabbīm* ('ivory'), and rendered, or guessed, the next two words 'carved and cut' (*toreutōn kai pelekētōn*), probably reading *yeqārīm* for MT *qōpīm* ('apes'), and *kerūtōt* for MT *tukkīyīm* ('baboons'). There is a variety of possible readings here, viz. (1) the above; (2) following the clue of G *ʾabānīm*, 'ivory, ebony', (*hobnīm*) (assuming haplography), 'carved and cut', MT *šēnhabbīm* being a *hapax legomenon* in the Old Testament, the element *habbīm* being explained as the Sanskrit *ibhas* ('elephant'); (3) 'ivory, *šēnhabbīm* (or ebony, *hobnīm*), apes and baboons'. A further suggestion was that of Winckler that *sukkīyīm* ('negroes') be read for *tukkīyīm*, which is found in the Old Testament only here and in the parallel passage in II Chron. 9.21. Josephus supports this conjecture, mentioning as the products of this trade 'ivory, Ethiopians, and apes' (*Ant.* VIII, 7.2.)

[23]And Solomon was greater than all the kings of the earth[a] in riches and wisdom. [24]And all the kings[b] of the earth sought the presence of Solomon to hear his wisdom which God had put in his heart. [25]And they brought each his present, vessels of silver and gold, garments, and myrrh, and spices, horses and mules at an annual rate. [26]And Solomon assembled chariots and horses,[c] and[d] he had a thousand and four hundred chariots and twelve thousand horses,[c] which he stationed[e] in the chariot-cities and with the king in Jerusalem. [27]And the king made silver and gold[f] in Jerusalem as stones, and cedars he made as abundant as the sycamores which are in the Shephelah. [28]Now the source of Solomon's horses was Musri[g] and Kue;[h] the king's dealers got them from Kue[h] at a certain price, [29]and a chariot-and-team came up by export from Musri[g] at six hundred shekels of silver and a horse at a hundred and fifty, and so also the kings of the Hittites and the kings of the Aramaeans got them by export through them.[i]

10.14. In spite of the substantial historicity of this matter 666 talents of gold seems both conventional and exaggerated, perhaps being reckoned on the basis of 9.28 (420), 9.14 (120), and 10.10 (120), as van den Born (*op. cit.*, p. 70) suggests.

15. The emendation *ʿonešē*, so well supported by the versions, is almost certainly correct. *ʿōneš* is used in II K. 23.33 for Necho's impost on Judah after his deposition of Jehoahaz. The importance of such tariffs in a caravan emporium is well illustrated by inscriptions from Palmyra.[j] It has been proposed to emend *tārīm* to *taggārīm*, the latter, meaning 'merchant', being common in Aramaic and Arabic. The root *tūr* of which *tārīm* ('merchants') is the participle is not found

[a]G[B] moderates this extravagant claim by omitting 'of the earth'.

[b]Adding 'kings' to the MT with G, S, and the parallel account in II Chron., as the grammar demands.

[c]Reading *perāšīm* for MT *pārāšīm* ('horsemen'), as the numerical proportion demands.

[d]In place of the preceding words in v. 26 of MT G[B] (cf. 4.26[5.6.]) reads 'and Solomon had 4,000 (brood) mares for the chariots and 12,000 horses . . .'. This is an insertion here from 4.26[5.6], *'ūrewōt* ('stalls'), which has cognates in Akkad., Aram., and Arab., being taken from a root cognate with Akkad. *aru* ('to be pregnant').

[e]Reading *wayyannīḥēm* after G, S, T, and Chronicles for MT *wayyanḥēm* ('and he led them').

[f]Adding 'and gold' with G.

[g]Reading *muṣrī* with Winckler for MT *miṣrayim* ('Egypt').

[h]Reading *miqqūwē* for MT *ūmiqwē*, which, with great grammatical awkwardness, was taken variously as 'thread' (AV 'linen yarn', after Rashi and Kimchi), and 'droves' or 'collections' (RV). G (*thekoue*) suggests that the word is really a place-name. Kue in southern Anatolia is well attested in Assyrian records.

[i]G (*kata thalassan*) read *bayyām* ('by sea') in the Hebrew text for MT *beyādām* ('through them').

[j]E.g. G. A. Cooke, *NSI*, pp. 320ff.

in this sense in the Old Testament, though it is used of spies going about the land (Num. 13.16, 17, 21; 14.6). The root is attested in Arabic in the IVth form, meaning 'to repeat', hence 'to go to and fro as a go-between'. We have conjectured its use also in a list of temple employees in the Ras Shamra texts.[a] *rōkēl* ('trader') is used in S. of S. 3.6 of a trafficker in spices, and in Ezek. 27.13ff of Greeks and Anatolians who were agents of the trade of Tyre. The kings of the Arabs, that is to say in the Hejaz and Syrian steppe, were also under impost to Solomon, especially since he controlled the caravan route through Edom to Damascus, where there had been an Israelite governor. For MT *hā'ereb*, for which we read *hā'ᵃrāb*, G reads *tou peran* (*hā'ēber*), 'Over the River'. The 'governors of the land' means probably the provincial governors of the homeland, i.e. the administrative districts of Solomon. *peḥā* ('provincial governor') is seldom used in early passages, and is an Assyrian loanword, e.g. II K. 18.24.

10.16. Solomon had the gold made into, or inlaid upon, shields, which were deposited in the House of the Forest of Lebanon, which was used as an armoury and a treasury. The passive participle *šāḥūt* is difficult, the root being commonly found meaning 'to slay'. It has been suggested that it is cognate with Arab *šaḥaṭa* ('to dilute wine with water'), but in this case the reference would be to an alloy of the gold, to which Solomon would hardly resort in his treasury. It is possible that the verb here and in the parallel passage in Chronicles was *šāṭūaḥ* ('overspread', 'beaten out', lit. 'extended'). Since the bronze shields, with which Rehoboam replaced these gold shields after they had been plundered by Shishak (14.26), were used by the guard when the king went up to the Temple, the gold shields presumably served the same purpose. It is small wonder that the Queen of Sheba was impressed by 'the way he (Solomon) went up to the Temple of Yahweh' (v. 5). The larger shields (*ṣinnōt*) covered the whole body. The smaller (*māginnīm*) being three minas, probably 150 shekels, the weight of gold in each of the larger shields, here given vaguely as '600', was in shekels.

18. The throne was probably of wood inlaid with ivory and plated (*mᵉṣuppe*) in places with gold. *mūpāz* is the Hophal participle of *pāzaz*. This root, meaning 'to be hard, strong', is fairly well attested in the Old Testament, e.g. Gen. 49.24. If *paz*, which is regularly found of gold in the Old Testament, is connected with this root, it would mean 'solid gold'. Like many words referring to

[a] *Legacy of Canaan*, 1965², p. 215.

metals, however, it may be non-Semitic. As suggested by Old Testament incidences, *paz* may mean 'refined gold' from a second root *pāzaz*, from which the *hapax legomenon mūpāz* is derived. This sense is certainly taken by G (*dokimos*) and the parallel passage in Chronicles (*ṭāhōr*).

10.19. The number seven, six steps and the dais, is significant. The seven levels of Babylonian cosmogony find expression in the seven stages of Mesopotamian temple-towers. After this prototype the temple of Baal at Ras Shamra had seven steps up to the inmost shrine. Without committing ourselves to the view that the disposition and furnishing of the Temple and its complex had a symbolic significance which may be consistently worked out to the last detail, we may suggest that, in the conception of the Phoenician architect, the seven stages of Solomon's throne symbolized the Divine Cosmos, of which the king was the temporal guarantor. The head of the calf, or young bull (see p. 269, n.[g]), behind the throne had probably a similar significance. It may be noted, however, that this motif is not attested on any of the thrones of the ancient Near East known in sculpture. The bull was the symbol of Baal, the power of providence in nature. His kingship, won in conflict with the powers of Chaos, is the theme of the Ras Shamra fragments *UT* 129; 137, 68 and, with Yahweh written for Baal throughout, was adapted by Israel in psalms and prophetic passages which re-echo the liturgy of the New Year festival. The king on his throne was the temporal assurance of the power of God. The same relationship of God and king was probably expressed with Jeroboam's establishment of the cult with its bull-symbols at Dan and Bethel, which, in this double sense, was a royal shrine (Amos 7.13). The throne with its arms flanked by lions suggests the ivory relief from Megiddo, where the arms of the throne are supported by sphinxes with the body of a lion.[a] The lions flanking Solomon's throne may have been sphinxes, but it is possible that the lion represented the emblem of Judah (Gen. 49.9).

21. On *zāhāb sāgūr* ('refined gold') see on 6.20.

22. Tarshish in later texts (e.g. Jonah 1.3; 4.2) is a place far from Palestine, probably in the extreme west of the Mediterranean. If Sheba and Dedan stand for the commerce of the East, Tarshish may stand for that of the west (Ezek. 27.25). It is mentioned in Jer. 10.9 as the source of silver and in Ezek. 27.12 of tin, iron, and lead. This indicates Spain and even the regions beyond the Straits of Gibraltar.

[a] *ANEP*, fig. 332.

The Greeks were in touch with Tartessus in the seventh and sixth centuries.[a] Eusebius (*Onomasticon*) refers to *Tharseis hē Baitikē*, which points to the region of the Guadalquivir, anciently the *Baetis*. The name Tarseion occurs in a commercial treaty[b] referring to a Carthaginian city in Spain. The form of the word suggests a verbal noun derived from a root *rāšaš*. This is found in Akkadian in connection with bright metals and mining products, so that *taršīš* was probably originally a common noun, perhaps signifying 'metal refinery' as suggested by Albright.[c] We may further note that one of the copper-smelting sites explored by Glueck in the Araba is called *murašraš*. In any case it is significant that Tarshish and ships of Tarshish are generally mentioned in connection with metal, hence we conclude that 'ships of Tarshish' did not necessarily belong to, or trade with, Tarshish, but signified large ocean-going ships voyaging primarily to the mines and refineries in the far west (Isa. 2.16; 23.1; Ezek. 27.25; Ps. 48.7[8]), but, as in the case of Solomon's navy, sailing south and east *from* Ezion-geber, the port for the refineries.

Here it is stated that Solomon had a fleet of his own in the Red Sea, cf. 10.11, where the fleet of Hiram alone is mentioned, and 9.27, where the fleet is said to have been Solomon's, the navigators being Phoenician. Possibly the fleet and crews were Phoenician, and the merchants Hebrew. The common factor in these passages is the Phoenician seamen, so v. 22 probably represents a late tradition tending to the glory of Solomon. For the objective of these voyages see on 9.28.

On the products of this trade 'ivory (and ebony?)' see p. 263, n.[g] above. Ebony (*hobnīm*) is a *de luxe* import in Ezek. 27.15. It is the heartwood of a tree native to Ceylon and southern India, anciently valued for its smoothness, being much used in the carving of images.[d] Herodotus (III, 114) notes ebony as a product of Abyssinia. We take the element *-habbīm* in *šēnhabbīm* nevertheless as meaning 'elephant', Sanskrit *ibhas*. Ivory, carved in low relief and inlaid, has been abundantly attested in excavations in the Near East. Significant examples are reliefs of the royal family from the palace at Ras Shamra in the fourteenth century,[e] of prisoners and tribute brought

[a] Herodotus I, 163; IV, 152.
[b] Polybius III, 24.
[c] *Archaeology and the Religion of Israel*, pp. 133ff.
[d] W. Walker, *All the Plants of the Bible*, 1960, pp. 74ff.
[e] C. F. A. Schaeffer, *Syria* XXXI, 1954, pp. 1f., pl. VII.

to the king of Megiddo, about the thirteenth or twelfth centuries,[a] and inlays from the palace of Ahab at Samaria, where Phoenician renderings of Egyptian motifs predominate.[b] Also from the ninth century are a number of ivory plaques in low relief of more ambitious and naturalistic design and also in Egyptian motifs from the Assyrian palace at Arslan Tash in north-east Syria.[c] The last two words, *qōpīm* and *tukkīyīm*, are said to be of Indian origin, *kapi* and *togei* ('peacock'), the latter being peculiar to the Malabar coast. W. E. Clarke,[d] however, is sceptical, and W. F. Albright[e] cites Egyptian evidence which indicates that apes (Egyptian *gf*) and baboons (*ky*) were meant, these being noted in the Story of the Shipwrecked Sailor from the Middle Kingdom.[f]

10.25. *minḥā* may signify an *ex gratia* present, e.g. Gen. 43.11, or, as in the Ras Shamra texts (*UT* 120.1, 4), and Judg. 3.15; II Sam. 8.2; II K. 17.4, 'tribute'.

For MT *nēšeq*, which means 'weapons' in Ezek. 39.9, and is attested in Ugaritic, G translates *staktē* ('myrrh'), cf. Arabic *našiqa* ('to smell').

26. On the alleged archaeological corroboration of the statement about Solomon's chariotry, and on the emendation 'horses' for 'horsemen' see on 9.19. In view of the fact that Ahab put 2,000 chariots into the field at Qarqar in 853,[g] the statement that Solomon had 1,400 chariots is no exaggeration. Since three horses (a pair and a led one) were reckoned to a chariot team in Canaan on the evidence of the Ras Shamra texts (*UT* Krt, 128f.), 12,000 horses would number stud-stock and reserves, as well as horses in breaking and trained animals.

27. The sycamore in question (*ficus sycamorus*) is a large, well-rooted spreading tree, which bears an inferior kind of fig. It grows only up to a certain altitude, and is a feature of the Shephelah and the coastal plain.

28. This sober, factual note suggests an official source in the records of Solomon's reign. The reading 'from Kue', suggested by G, denoting the region south of the Taurus, indicates that MT *miṣrayim*

[a] G. Loud, *The Megiddo Ivories*, 1939, pl. 4, 2a, 2b.
[b] Crowfoot and Sukenik, *Samaria-Sebaste II*, *Early Ivories*, 1938.
[c] A. Barrois, *Manuel d'archéologie biblique*, I, 1939, pp. 496–502, figs. 193–7.
[d] 'The Sandalwood and Peacocks of Ophir', *AJSL* XXXVI, 1920, pp. 103 ff.
[e] *Op. cit.*, p. 212.
[f] A. Erman, *Literature of the Ancient Egyptians*, 1927, p. 34.
[g] Luckenbill, *ARA* I, § 611.

(Egypt) is a corruption of *muṣrī*, a region just north of the Taurus. This corruption is the source of the tradition that the king traded men for horses in Egypt (Deut. 17.16). The same confusion between *miṣrayim* and the Anatolian *muṣrī* is made in MT of II K. 7.6, where 'the kings of Musri' are surely to be understood with 'the kings of the Hittites', suspected by the Aramaeans of being suborned by Israel at the siege of Samaria in the time of Elisha. Both regions are named together in an inscription of Shalmaneser III.[a] The same district is known as the home of horsebreeders for half a millennium before the time of Solomon, and in Ezek. 27.14 Togarmah in the same region is noted for its horses. The slopes of the Taurus also would supply wood for the chariots rather than Egypt, which depended on the Lebanon for her timber. Concerning Solomon's alleged traffic in horses and chariots on the grand scale it must be noted that there is little ground in MT for this assumption, and still less in G. All that is said in the former is that the kings of the Aramaeans got their horses and chariots at the same price 'by the agency of' Solomon's dealers, who presumably drove this trade as a sideline to defray their expenses, and possibly to secure safe-conduct through Syria to the far north. All that is said in G is that 'the kings of the Hittites' and the Aramaeans 'of the west' (see p. 264 n.[1]) got their chariots and horses from the same source and at the same price as Solomon. The horses and chariots which Solomon imported to Palestine were for his own use.

10.29. G gives the price of a horse and a *merkābā* as 50 and 100 shekels respectively. MT 150 and 600 is confirmed by a letter from Mari in the eighteenth century BC, mentioning the purchase of two horses from Qatna for 300 shekels each[b] and by the record of the purchase of one for 200 shekels for the royal stud at Ras Shamra in the thirteenth century.[c] To be sure, prices are recorded at Nuzi for as low as 30 shekels for a horse,[d] but trained animals were much dearer. 600 shekels as the price of a *merkābā* seems disproportionate if this means 'chariot', but it may mean a chariot and a pair of matched and trained horses, possibly with a led animal (cf. a chariot and three horses as a unit in the Krt text (Gordon, *UT*, 140f., 252–4)), hence our rendering 'a chariot-and-team'.

[a]Luckenbill, *ARA* I, § 611.
[b]G. Dossin, *Archives royales de Mari* V, 1952, no. 20, 36ff.
[c]J. Nougayrol, *Le palais royal* . . . III, 1955, p. 41.
[d]*Ibid.*, p. 41n.

The 'kings of the Hittites', as in II K. 7.6, if the term is ethnically significant, designates the non-Semitic, possibly Hurrian, elements in northern Syria and southern Anatolia. In so far as 'Hittite' is ethnically accurate, the term may denote the descendants of the great feudal lords who ruled districts there during the Hittite ascendancy and had asserted their independence on the collapse of the Hittite Empire at the end of the Late Bronze Age *c.* 1200 BC. Such a kingdom was that of Danuna, the realm of Azitawadd in the eighth century, revealed in the bilingual Karatepe inscription in Phoenician and in Hittite hieroglyphics.[a] Hittite hieroglyphics from the same period in Hama on the Orontes probably indicate a symbiosis of former Hittite feudatories and Aramaean settlers, the former being the ruling class.[b] This whole question, however, is complicated by the very loose use of the term 'Hittite' by the Assyrians, who designated Syria and even Palestine as 'the Hittite land' (*māt ḫatti*). The mention of Aramaeans along with Hittites in the present passage, however, suggests that the term has a more accurate ethnic significance in this case.

(*k*) THE TROUBLES OF SOLOMON'S REIGN AND ITS END: 11.1–43

The chapter falls into two main divisions, vv. 1–13, which deals with Solomon's toleration of alien cults in the neighbourhood of Jerusalem and the Deuteronomistic censure of this and of his marriages with alien women, and vv. 14–40 which deals with the political troubles of his reign, external and internal, with an obituary notice from the Deuteronomistic editor (vv. 41–43), which anticipates the obituaries which are a feature of the Deuteronomistic compilation of Kings. The superficial impression is that the troubles described in vv. 14–40, culminating in the disruption of the kingdom, were a consequence of Solomon's liberalism in matrimony and his countenancing of alien cults (vv. 1–13). This, however, has been questioned. Actually the Deuteronomistic compiler, after recording the glories of Solomon's reign, ends his account by giving the reverse of

[a] J. Friedrich, 'Eine altphönizische Inschrift aus Kilikien', *FuF*, XXIV, 1948, pp. 77–9; A.M. Honeyman, 'Phoenician Inscriptions from Karatepe', *Le Muséon*, LXI, 1948, pp. 43–57; R. Marcus and I. J. Gelb, 'A Preliminary Study of the New Phoenician Inscription from Cilicia', *JNES* VII, 1948, pp. 194–8; 'The Phoenician Stele Inscription from Cilicia', *JNES* VIII, 1949, pp. 116–20; C. H. Gordon, 'Azitawadd's Phoenician Inscription', *JNES* VIII, 1949, pp. 108–15.

[b] D. G. Hogarth, *Kings of the Hittites*, 1926.

the picture. He records the fact of Solomon's toleration of the cults of Chemosh, Milcom, and Astarte (vv. 6f.) and elaborates the view that this was the consequence of the king's marriages with women of neighbouring peoples, which was itself offensive to Deuteronomic principles. This material, though resting on a basis of historical fact, e.g. vv. 6ff. and possibly vv. 1, 3a,[a] differs markedly in character from vv. 14–40, which is in the style of historical narrative. The author is well informed of his facts, which were probably known through royal annals, but he has filled them out with circumstantial matter, generally reliable, from oral tradition. The Deuteronomistic contribution does not pervade these, but is in the nature of an epilogue (vv. 32b–39). It has been held[b] that the compiler did not intend to present the political troubles of vv. 14–40 as the consequences of Solomon's foreign marriages and his tolerance of alien cults (vv. 1–13), since Solomon's apostasy is dated late in his life, whereas the insubordination of Edom and Damascus is dated early in his reign (vv. 21, 25). This argument, however, ignores the fact that it is only Solomon's personal apostasy that is dated to the end of his life (v. 4). In v. 2 the Deuteronomist makes it clear that the very fact of the marriage of the king, probably at an early age, with local aliens was offensive (cf. Deut. 7.3), and involved the disruption of the kingdom (vv. 11–13), which, if not actually falling in the reign of Solomon, is quite definitely anticipated in the abortive revolt of Jeroboam in vv. 26–32 (note the Deuteronomic epilogue, which re-echoes and elaborates the thought and language of vv. 11–13).

(i) SOLOMON'S MARRIAGES WITH ALIEN WOMEN, HIS TOLERATION OF ALIEN CULTS, AND THE CENSURE OF THE DEUTERONOMIST: 11.1–13

A comparison of G and MT of this section indicates that certain statements in G suggest a source much more objective than MT. The opening sentence in G, for instance, merely states that Solomon was fond of women. No censure is implied as in MT, which states that he loved many *alien* women (v. 1), of the races with whom Israel was forbidden to mix; on the contrary, such a disposition on the part of the king according to G suggests a potency which orientals have always admired. This fact, then, perhaps an element of saga, but resting on the genuine historical basis of political

[a]So Kittel, HKAT, p. 95.
[b]Skinner, CB, p. 174.

marriages,[a] may be taken as belonging to an original text or tradition used, but with adaptation, by the Deuteronomistic compiler. This and the other plain statements of Solomon's delinquency (v. 6) in building shrines for Chemosh and 'Milcom' on the Mount of Olives are feasibly taken by Montgomery as the basis of MT as elaborated in the Deuteronomistic compilation. Though G suggests the initial step in this analysis of the text, it betrays obvious traces of smoothing out of a complex text which had many obvious elaborations and accretions, hence it is to be followed with extreme caution. The text may be reconstructed after Montgomery (ICC, pp. 231ff.) as follows, the left-hand column representing the original tradition and the right the Deuteronomistic elaboration.

11 [1A]And king Solomon loved many alien[b] women, [3]and he had wives of queenly status to the number of seven hundred and three hundred concubines,[c] [1Bd]Moabite, Ammonite, Aramaean,[e] Edomite, Sidonian,[f] Hittite[g] women, [2]of the peoples concerning whom Yahweh said to the Israelites, You shall not come in to them, and they shall not come in to you, lest[h] they turn away your heart after their gods. To them Solomon held fast in love. [4]And it happened, in Solomon's old age, that his wives turned away his heart after other gods, and his heart was not at one with Yahweh his God as the heart of his father David.

6 And Solomon did that which was evil in the sight of Yahweh and did not go fully after Yahweh as his father David.

[a]A. Malamat, 'Organs of Statecraft in the Israelite Monarchy', *BA* XXVIII, 1965, pp. 34–65, emphasizes Solomon's marriages as 'a mainstay of his foreign policy'.

[b]This adjective is omitted, but implied, in G, which states that Solomon was 'fond of women' (*philogunēs*).

[c]Omitting with G *wayyaṭṭū nāšāw 'et-libbō* of MT ('and his wives perverted his heart').

[d]Omitting *wᵉ'et-bat parʿōh* ('and the daughter of Pharaoh') as a gloss and taking the list of foreign wives as defining the numerous harem of the king in v. 3a.

[e]Reading *'ᵃrammīyōt* with G, omitted in MT by haplography before *'ᵃdōmīyōt* ('Edomite').

[f]Pointing *ṣīdōnīyōt*.

[g]G adds 'and Amorite', which we may suspect as a mechanical repetition of the list of pre-Israelite people of Palestine familiar in the Pentateuch. The same might apply to 'Hittite', though in view of the Syrian relationships of Israel, at least in the time of David (II Sam. 8.10), it is possible that Solomon had wives from among the descendants of the old Hittite nobility who had ruled the Aramaean states of the interior of Syria (see on 10.28).

[h]Reading after G, S, and T *pen* for the adversative particle *'ākēn* of MT.

7 Then Solomon built a 'high place' for Chemosh, the god[a] of Moab (on the hill east of Jerusalem)[b] and to 'Molech',[c] the god[a] of the Ammonites.[d]

[5]And Solomon followed after 'Ashtoreth', the deity of the Sidonians, and after 'Milcom', the abomination of the Ammonites,[e] [8]and so he did for all his foreign wives, and they made smoke and slaughter[f] to their gods. [9]And Yahweh was angry with Solomon because his heart was turned away from Yahweh the God of Israel, who had appeared[g] to him twice, [10]and had commanded[g] him concerning this matter not to go after other gods, but he did not keep that which Yahweh commanded him.[h] [11]And Yahweh said to Solomon, Since this is your intention, and you have not kept my covenant[i] and my statutes which I enjoined upon you, I will assuredly rend the kingdom from you, and will give it to your servant. [12]Nevertheless in your days I will not do it for the sake of your father David; from the hand of your son will I rend it.[j] [13]Only I will not rend away all the kingdom; I shall give one tribe to your son for the sake of my servant David, and for the sake

[a]So G for the MT parody *šiqqūṣ* ('abomination').

[b]G omits MT 'on the hill east of Jerusalem', which may well have come into MT under the influence of the passage describing Josiah's reformation in II K. 23.13.

[c]G[B] reads *Malcham*, indicating the word as a title 'their king' in Hebrew. The real significance of the final *m* may be the definite article, as in certain South Arabian dialects.

[d]G[BL] adds 'and to Ashtoreth the abomination of Sidon', possibly under the influence of II K. 23.13.

[e]S reads 'and after Chemosh the abomination of Moab', perhaps influenced by the statement in v. 7 that Solomon built shrines to these gods including Chemosh.

[f]G[L] reads both participles as masculine singular instead of feminine plural of MT.

[g]G reads both verbs as participles.

[h]Reading *ṣiwwāhū* with G for MT *ṣiwwā* ('commanded').

[i]G reads 'my commandments' for MT 'my covenant' (*b*[e]*rītī*).

[j]Here and throughout v. 13 G reads the more prosaic verb *lāqaḥ* ('took') for the graphic and forceful MT *qāraʿ* ('tore').

of Jerusalem[a] which I have chosen.

11.1. Whether we follow MT or prefer G, which does not mention specifically Solomon's harem in v. 1, MT rests on a basis of fact, since the mother of Solomon's heir Rehoboam was an Ammonitess (I K. 14.21), and David had at least one Aramaean wife (II Sam. 3.3). Solomon's marriages, like those of Muhammad, had a political significance. 'And the daughter of Pharaoh', coming between the feminine plural adjectives *rabbōt* ('many') and *mō'ᵃbīyōt* ('Moabite'), etc., is an obvious gloss. There is no specific mention except here of any Phoenician lady in Solomon's harem, but that is quite probable in view of the relations between Hiram and David and Solomon. In the catholic court of Solomon a lady of culture from Phoenicia would be desirable. Actually Menander of Tyre[b] states that Solomon married the daughter of Hiram of Tyre. On 'Hittite' see on 10.29. The Greek text of v. 1, in stating simply that Solomon was 'fond of women', and MT of v. 3, apart from the final clause 'and his wives perverted his heart', which is not in G, are quite neutral, and indeed, complimentary, to Solomon. In the East ancient and modern and in primitive society the virility of the ruler is a happy omen for the welfare of the community. The story is told of Ibn Saud, himself 250 times wedded, that once, having been wounded and the rumour having spread that his virility had been affected, he wedded a virgin from the nearest settlement and consummated his marriage forthwith.

2. *bā' bᵉ* is evidently a variant of *bā' 'el* ('to enter in to'), which refers to entry into the intimacy of the harem quarters, i.e. marriage.

3. *nāšīm* here means 'wives' rather than 'women', as distinct from concubines (*pīlagᵉšīm*). It is not clear whether *śārōt* (G *archousai*) refers to the status of Solomon's wives before or after marriage, but the latter is probably the significance. The Ras Shamra texts make a similar discrimination in private society between *'aṯt 'adrt* ('lady-wife') and plain *'aṯt* (*UT* 119). *śārā* in Esth. 1.18 signifies the principal lady in the royal harem, and is used in parallelism with 'kings' in Isa. 49.23. The fact that David had at least seven wives together with concubines (I Chron. 3.1ff.), whereby he secured relations with various elements in Palestine and beyond, and Rehoboam had eighteen wives and sixty concubines (II Chron. 11.21) suggests that there was a historical basis for the tradition of Solomon's large

[a]G inserts 'the city' (*hāʿīr*) after Jerusalem.
[b]Quoted by Clement of Alexandria, *Stromata* I, 114.2.

harem, though the enormous number and the figure 1,000 suggests that historical fact has been magnified and stylized in saga.

11.4. *šālēm* signifies 'whole', here 'at one with', which is the significance of the greeting *šālōm* rather than 'Peace'. See above on 2.6.

5. 'Ashtoreth' is the deliberate Hebrew misvocalization of the name of the Canaanite fertility-goddess Aṯtarat, known in the Ras Shamra texts and later Phoenician inscriptions, Greek Astarte. The singular form of the name is found in the Old Testament only here and in II K. 23.13. More commonly the plural Ashtaroth is used in general statements about Canaanite paganism, the reference being to various local manifestations of the fertility-goddess. Here and in II K. 23.13 her worship is mentioned together with that of 'Milcom', the god of Ammon, and, in the latter passage, with the cult of Chemosh, the god of Moab. Since there is good reason to believe that 'Milcom' and Chemosh were local forms of the one astral deity, the Venus-star Athtar, this may indicate that 'Ashtoreth' had also been an astral deity, the female counterpart of Athtar. In this connection it is noteworthy that her Mesopotamian counterpart Ishtar retained her character as an astral deity, though at the same time the goddess of love and fertility. Apart from the known astral character of Ishtar and the association of the cult of 'Ashtoreth' with that of 'Milcom' and Chemosh in the passages we have cited, there is no evidence from Canaan that she was an astral deity except that Athtar, of which 'Ashtoreth' is the female form, certainly had this character. In Canaan the goddess is first encountered in the Ras Shamra texts in offering lists and in myths, where she is apparently the ally of Baal in his conflict with the turbulent Sea-and-River (*UT* 68). Unfortunately this text is fragmentary and we cannot tell precisely the role of the goddess. In a later version, however, preserved in an Egyptian papyrus of the XIXth Dynasty,[a] Aṯtarat is claimed by the tyrannical Sea as a bride. From a certain passage in the Krt legend from Ras Shamra where the king invokes a curse in the name of 'Aṯtarat-the-Name-of-Baal', we see that the goddess, at least in the heroic past, was associated with Baal as the giver of life and death. From the Ras Shamra texts generally, however, it would seem that the fertility functions of the goddess were taken over by Anat, the sister of Baal. In Palestine, and probably southern Syria on the evidence of the Phoenician inscriptions of the first millennium BC

[a]A. H. Gardiner, 'The Astarte Papyrus', *Studies presented to F. Ll. Griffith*, 1932, pp. 74–85.

and of the Old Testament, 'Ashtoreth' was much more prominent. The goddess appears in Egyptian inscriptions and sculptures, particularly from the XIXth Dynasty, when a number of Semitic cults were introduced to Egypt. In an inscribed sculpture from the Ptolemaic period at Edfu she is depicted with the head of a lion. The association with the lion suggests that the XIXth Dynasty sculptures, where a naked goddess named Qodshu, holding a papyrus plant and a serpent, stands on a lion between the virile Egyptian fertility-god Min and Reshef, the Semitic god of destruction and death, depicts 'Ashtoreth',[a] as is indicated by the lion, the cult-animal of Ishtar in Assyrian sculpture. Here the goddess wears her hair in the fashion of stylized horns characteristic of the Egyptian cow-goddess Hathor, and bronze figurines from Gezer of a nude female with horns may be representations of 'Ashtoreth'. On such evidence the cult of this goddess seems to have flourished at Bethshan from the fifteenth to the thirteenth centuries. Usually associated with the fertility-cult in Palestine are figurines moulded generally in clay representing nude females with breasts and pudenda emphasized, which are frequently termed Astarte plaques. Though certain of these are modelled on Astarte, however, others exhibit motifs associated with other goddesses,[b] and their great number indicates use in the home as amulets for fertility and childbirth rather than association with the sanctuary. Note the use of the masculine *'elōhē* for the goddess, Hebrew having no feminine term for 'goddess'.

'Milcom' is the deliberate misvocalization of the name of the national god of Ammon, or rather of his title 'the king', as is suggested probably in the oracles against Ammon in Amos 1.15 and Jer. 49.1, 3, which read 'their king'. G generally bears this out, e.g. Lev. 18.21; 20.2–5; Jer. 32.35. The form 'Moloch' used in G, e.g. II. K. 23.10, is interesting in view of the discovery by G. Dossin[c] of a god Muluk in the tablets from Mari on the mid-Euphrates (*c.* 1700 BC). This, however, is an abstract form, a verbal noun, and may be rendered 'kingship'. In spite of G 'Moloch', which is actually used only twice, it seems more likely that the god of the Ammonites was known by his title 'the king'—*mālik* with the final afformative

[a]S. A. Cook, *The Religion of Ancient Palestine in the Light of Archaeology*, 1930, Pl. XXIV, 3.

[b]J. B. Pritchard, *Palestinian Figurines in relation to certain Goddesses known through Literature*, 1944.

[c]*RA* XXXV, 1938, p. 178.

m, which has the force of the definite article. Eissfeldt adduces good evidence from Punic inscriptions that in the phrase 'to sacrifice, or pass a child through the fire, *l^emōlek*', the last word means not 'to Molech', but 'as a votive offering',[a] but that does not exclude the view that in the Old Testament *l^emōlek* denotes the god. From Jephthah's reply to the Ammonites (Judg. 11.24) it seems that the national god of Ammon was identical with Chemosh, the national god of Moab. From the compound divine name Athtar-Chemosh, by which the national god of Moab is named in the Mesha inscription, it appears that the proper name of the god was Athtar—both Chemosh and 'Milcom' being his local titles. This god is well known in Arab paganism as the Venus-star. From the Ras Shamra texts it is apparent that the morning and evening star might be thought of as twins, Shahar and Shalem. From the name of the city we may reasonably infer that the cult of Shalem, and conceivably also his twin Shahar, was practised at Jerusalem in pre-Israelite times, so that when Solomon built shrines for Chemosh and 'Milcom' he was establishing local varieties of a cult already practised at Jerusalem. Apart from the general references to 'Milcom' or 'Molech' in the present passage and Amos 1.15; Jer. 49.1, 3; Zeph. 1.5, the rest of the references to him are associated with human sacrifice (Lev. 20.2–5), specifically by making one's children pass through the fire (II K. 23.10; Lev. 18.21; Jer. 32.35). There 'Molech' is not associated with Ammon, and the view of Eissfeldt is feasible. Human sacrifice in Israel is first explicitly attested under Ahaz in Judah (II K. 16.3) and in Israel under Hoshea (II K. 17.17). In the first passage, though 'Molech' or 'Milcom' is not named, the parallel passage in II Chron. 28.3 adds that the scene of the abomination was the Valley of the Sons of Hinnom, specifically Tophet, which is associated with 'Molech' in Jer. 32.35. Apart from the sacrifice of the son of Mesha (II K. 3.27), which would naturally be made to Chemosh, whom we have identified with 'Molech', human sacrifice was made by the Assyrian military colonists in Samaria after 721. Here the gods so honoured are Adrammelech and Anammelech. The former may signify 'the lordship of Malik', and Anammelech may be a case of syncretism of the local god 'Molech' and Anu, the Amorite sky-god. In spite of the reformation of Hezekiah, which does not mention the cult of 'Molech', this cult survived until the time of Josiah,

[a]'Molk als Opferbegriff im Punischen und Hebräischen und das Ende des Gottes Moloch', *Beiträge zur Religionsgeschichte des Altertums* 3, 1935.

when Zephaniah condemned it (Zeph. 1.5). This passage, associating the worship of 'Milcom' with that of the host of heaven, supports our contention that 'Molech' was primarily an astral deity. In the account of Josiah's reformation the scene of human sacrifices, Tophet in the Valley of Hinnom, was desecrated (II K. 23.10), and the sanctuaries of 'Milcom' and Chemosh, which had survived from the time of Solomon, were destroyed.

11.6. The intransitive use of *millē'* with *'aḥ^a^rē* ('to follow completely') is to be noticed as a Deuteronomistic idiom, e.g. Num. 14.24; 32.11; Deut. 1.36; Josh. 14.8ff.

7. Chemosh, of uncertain etymology, is the name or title of the national god of Moab, 'the people of Chemosh' (Num. 21.29; Jer. 48.46), cf. the theophoric names of Moabite kings, Chemosh(. . .), the father of Mesha, and Kammusu-nadbi in Sennacherib's records. In Mesha's inscription Chemosh is compounded with Athtar, the Venus-star, hence we suppose that Chemosh was the Moabite manifestation of this astral deity.[a] *bāmā*, now attested in the Ras Shamra texts meaning the 'back' of a person or animal (cf. Deut. 33.29), signifies in the Old Testament a provincial sanctuary, being generally used in the plural *bāmōt*, probably an abbreviation of *bēt bāmōt*. Here *bāmōt* probably denotes the memorial pillar to a dead ancestor in the local sanctuary of the kin-group, originally perhaps surmounting the burial cairn, which is exemplified in burials in Sinai in the middle of the second millennium.[b] Instances of such memorials in local sanctuaries are the alignments of pillars at Gezer and Hazor,[c] and the Ugaritic text *UT* 2 'Aqht, I, 27f. refers to the erection of a stele to an ancestor-god in the sanctuary of the clan as a filial duty. This association of the forefathers of the clan with the local sanctuaries gave them a strong appeal for the various kin-groups of Israel in the settlement in Canaan and in the pre-monarchic period, giving them the opportunity to realize the solidarity of the clan and serving the same purpose for ancient Israel as the *wālī* or local saint does for the modern Arab peasants, both Muslim and Christian, who confidently present their petitions at their sacred places and tombs as to intercessory saints and benign *genii loci*. Eventually *bāmōt* came to mean generally local sanctuaries apart from the amphictyonic shrine of

[a]See on v.5 and W. F. Albright, *Archaeology and the Religion of Israel*, pp. 117 ff., and J. Gray, 'The Desert God ʿAṯtr in the Literature and Religion of Canaan', *JNES* VIII, 1949, pp. 72–83.

[b]Albright, 'The High Place in Ancient Palestine', *SVT IV*, 1957, pp. 242–58.

[c]Y. Yadin and others, *Hazor* I, 1958, pl. XXVIII–XXX.

Yahweh, and this is the meaning in the present passage. The hill 'which is before', i.e. east of Jerusalem is, of course, the Mount of Olives, called in II K. 23.13 *har hammašḥīt* ('the Mount of Corruption'), probably a parody of *har hammišḥā* ('the Mount of the Anointing'), which the Targum renders *har zaytā'* ('the Mount of Olives'). The fact that this locality is not named in I K. 11.7 in G suggests that it is a later interpolation in MT under the influence of II K. 23.13. *šiqqūṣ* ('abomination') is a common orthodox parody for 'god' in apposition to the name of an alien god in the Old Testament. In 'Milcom' the vowels of this word are used with the consonants of *mālik-ma*.

11.8. *maqṭīrōt* is ambiguous. It may bear its primary meaning 'to make smoke of sacrifice', being then complementary to *mᵉzabbᵉḥōt*, which primarily denotes killing with effusion of blood. Hence we translate 'making smoke and slaughter', a contemptuous reference on the part of the Deuteronomist. The verb means secondarily 'to make incense-offering'.

9. The language expressing the wrath of God on Solomon's defection as the source of his troubles is re-echoed in Mesha's inscription and in Assyrian and Hittite texts.[a] In anticipation of the disruption of the kingdom as the punishment for Solomon's apostasy the theophanies with their affirmation of the Davidic covenant and their conditional blessings (3.5–15 and 9.1–9) are recalled.

11. *bᵉrītī* ('my covenant'), for which G reads 'my commandments' (*miṣwōtay*), should be retained here as a specific reference to the Davidic covenant, twice affirmed to Solomon, to which reference has just been made. The reference to 'statutes' (*ḥuqqōtay*) doubtless caused the writer to think of 'commandments' in this Deuteronomistic passage. Ps. 2, however, indicates that *ḥōq* had another association, namely with the adoption of the king by God, which was also involved in the Davidic covenant (II Sam. 7.11–16). It is considered that *ḥōq* in Ps. 2 was the divine protocol handed to the king on his accession which was probably 'the testimony' (*hā'ēdūt*) referred to in the accession of Joash (II K. 11.12).[b] The description of Solomon's successor in North Israel as 'your servant' accentuates the tragedy of the secession from the house of David from a Judaean and Deuteronomistic standpoint, and from the same standpoint is derogatory of

[a]See Montgomery, ICC, p. 236, and especially A. Malamat, 'Doctrines of Causality in Hittite and Biblical Historiography: a Parallel', *VT* V, 1955, pp. 1 ff.

[b]See G. von Rad, 'Das judäische Königsritual', *TLZ* LXXII, 1947, cols. 211–6; 'The Royal Ritual in Judah', *The Problem of the Hexateuch*, 1966, pp. 222–31.

Jeroboam. The language recalls the rejection of Saul in I Sam. 15.28. *zō't 'immāk* ('this is your intention') has been rightly noticed by Noth (*op. cit.*, p. 250) as denoting set purpose, as in Job 10.13.

11.13. One tribe is to be left to Solomon's son Rehoboam in fulfilment of the covenant with the house of David, which was diligently propagated together with the divine choice of Jerusalem as a cult-centre, e.g. Ps. 78.68ff. On the number of tribes left to the house of David and on the discrepancy between the present passage and v. 35 see note on that verse.

(ii) THE DISRUPTION OF THE EMPIRE OF ISRAEL: 11.14–40

This section, which, in spite of later expansions and possibly variant traditions, rests on genuine historical sources, falls into three parts: the escape of Hadad of Edom and his insurrection (vv. 14–22, 25b), the rise of Rezon of Damascus (vv. 23–25a) and the abortive revolt of Jeroboam (vv. 26–40).

The first two of these subsections are quite free from Deuteronomistic language and comment and are remarkably objective, the first being quite full and circumstantial. There is little doubt here that a reliable historical source is drawn upon without modification, perhaps the Acts of Solomon, which is mentioned in v. 41, or even, in the case of the Edomite revolt, Edomite annals, which might have become accessible to a Judaean writer in the reign of Jehoshaphat, when Edom was under the domination of Judah (I K. 22.47[48]). The third part harks back to the Davidic covenant and its conditional blessings, and contains much from the Deuteronomistic reviser (vv. 32b–39), but also genuine historical material, possibly from the annals of the Northern kingdom, but more probably, we think, from prophetic tradition.

(a) *The escape of Hadad of Edom and his insurrection:* 11.14–22, 25b

The final verse, 25b, is displaced in MT to the end of the section dealing with the rise of Rezon of Damascus (vv. 23–25a) owing to the fact that the last word, as is indicated in G and S, was corrupted from *'ᵉdōm* to *'ᵃrām*.

The variation of the name of the Edomite prince between Hadad (vv. 14, 17, 19, 21, 25b) and Adad (v. 17), cf. Ader in certain MSS. of G, and the fact that tradition seems to vary about the extreme youth (v. 17) and comparative maturity of the prince (vv. 18ff.) have suggested the view that the passage is a conflation of traditions of two distinct personages, namely Hadad, the prince of Edom, who is taken as a young child to Egypt and returns to claim his throne on the death of David, and Adad, a Midianite, whose son reigned in Midian.[a] This seems, however, a far-reaching conclusion to draw from the tenuous data of variants of the same name and the apparent discrepancy in the statements about the age of the prince. The MT shows a similar variation in the name of Rehoboam's agent at the famous assembly at Shechem, Adoram (I K. 12.18) and Hadoram (II Chron. 10.18), and the narrative of the flight of the young prince and his eventual refuge in Egypt may well be a case of telescoping of different traditions regarding the same person, which is not unfamiliar in the Old Testament. The Midianite episode, which apparently intervenes between v. 17 and the Egyptian sojourn (vv. 18ff.), may indicate a variant tradition of the same events. On the other hand, Midian, the pathless region of *al-Ḥisma* south of Edom, which was at enmity with Edom before the Israelite monarchy (Gen. 36.35), but was not necessarily always hostile, would be a natural refuge for the fugitives, who may have spent several years there before passing on to Egypt. Much would be elucidated if the identity of Hadad's Egyptian patron were known. It would be most natural to assume that the friendly relationship between Egypt and Solomon and between Egypt and Jeroboam dated from the reigns of different Pharaohs, or at least from different periods in the reign of the same Pharaoh, though there is no compelling reason that this should be so. Since Solomon had been married to Pharaoh's daughter before he built Millo (I K. 9.24) and Jeroboam was in charge of the corvée for the building of that feature (I K. 11.27), it is possible that a new Pharaoh had come to the throne, or at least that there had been time for a change in Egypto-Israelite relations. Hadad and his supporters in Midian might have been moved to seek the support that Egypt was so ready to give to curb the power of Solomon. We see no reason to agree with Winckler's view, but we do admit the conflation of two traditions of the Hadad episode, one which briefly recorded his refuge in Egypt and the support of the Pharaoh just before his return, and the other the refuge of the prince and his supporters in Midian in the early days of his exile. The latter may then be secondary in explanation of the former, complementary to it and not contradictory.

11 [14]And Yahweh raised up an antagonist to Solomon, Hadad the Edomite; he was of the royal family in Edom. [15]And it happened that

[a]Burney, *Notes on . . . Kings*, p. 157, after Winckler.

when David defeated[a] Edom, when Joab, the commander of the army, went up to search out the caves,[b] that he struck down every male in Edom. 16For Joab and all Israel stayed there six months until they cut off every male in Edom. 17And Hadad[c] fled, he and Edomites of his father's servants with him, to come[d] to Egypt, and Hadad was a young lad. 18And they rose up from Midian and came to Paran, and they took men with them from Paran[e] and they came to Egypt[e] to Pharaoh the king of Egypt,[f] and Hadad came to Pharaoh,[f] and he gave him a house and he appointed food for him.[g] 19And Hadad found great favour in the sight of Pharaoh, and he gave him as wife the sister[h] of his wife, the *Tahpenes* (the principal lady). 20And the sister of the *Tahpenes* bore him his son Genubath, and the *Tahpenes* brought him up[i] in the family[j] of Pharaoh, and Genubath was in the palace of

[a]The following *'et-'ᵉdōm* demands a transitive verb, *bᵉhakkōt* ('when he defeated') being generally accepted. G and S, however, read 'when he had annihilated', which suggests a stronger Hebrew verb, so that Šanda's proposal (I, p. 307) *bᵉhakrīt* ('when he cut off') may well be the correct reading for MT *bihyōt*.

[b]Following Šanda's plausible conjecture *lᵉbaqqēr 'et-haḥōrīm* for MT *lᵉqabbēr 'et-haḥᵃlālīm* ('to bury the slain').

[c]The name here is spelt *'ᵃdad*. On the relative insignificance of this variant see critical introduction to this section.

[d]G reads 'and he (they) came to Egypt'. If this is the correct reading the following verse, mentioning the sojourn in Midian and Paran, represents a variant tradition. MT simply visualizes the ultimate objective of the refugees. In this case the story is highly condensed and the Midianite episode may be the remains of an explanatory gloss.

[e]G omits 'from Paran' and 'to Egypt'.

[f]So with G for the shorter MT, as is demanded by the singular pronominal suffix in the following clause *wayyitten lō*, to which there is no antecedent in MT.

[g]MT *wᵉ'ereṣ nātan lō* ('and he gave him land') is omitted in G, which we follow. The MT is just possible on the hypothesis that *'ereṣ* means 'district', e.g. *'arᵉṣōt miṣrayim* (Amos 3.9), or even a small landed property, as the appurtenance of the cave of Machpelah (Gen. 23.15).

[h]The repetition of 'sister' in vv. 19, 20 is suspicious, and it is possible that in one place *'ᵃḥōt* is the corruption of a proper name. Klostermann drew attention to the recurrence of this clause with variation in G's extension to MT of I K. 12.24, which gives the name of Pharaoh's wife's sister as Anō, possibly Hebr. *'aḥnō*; hence Kittel (HKAT, p. 97) proposes the reading *wayyitten lō 'iššā 'et-'aḥnō 'ᵃḥōt 'ištō taḥpᵉnēs*. Kittel objects that the title *haggᵉbīrā*, which refers to the queen-mother in Israel (e.g. Maachah, I K. 15.13), is not applicable to the wife of the Pharaoh, hence he reads *haggᵉdōlā* ('the elder') after G (*meizō*). We think it more likely that G misunderstood *haggᵉbīrā* as a title, 'the principal lady'. Kittel's objection on the ground of I K. 15.13 is precarious. The queen-mother was 'the principal lady' as long as she lived. On her decease the title and status naturally passed to the mother of the heir-apparent. The name of the queen is given in G as *Thechemeinah*.

[i]In view of the sequel 'in the family of Pharaoh' *wattᵉgaddᵉlēhū* ('and she brought him up'), which G read, is preferable to MT *wattigmᵉlēhū* ('and she weaned him').

[j]G reads here 'among the sons . . .', but this is not strictly necessary. The preposition *bᵉtōk*, as the Ras Shamra texts indicate, may mean 'in' as well as 'among', and *bēt* in Semitic languages refers to the family as well as the house.

Pharaoh among the sons of Pharaoh. 21Now Hadad heard in Egypt that David rested with his fathers and that Joab the commander of the army was dead, and Hadad said to Pharaoh, Send me away and let me go to my own land. 22And Pharaoh said to him, Nay, but what do you lack with me that, behold, you seek to go to your own country? And he said to him,[a] Nay, but do send me. 25BAnd this was the harm that Hadad did in contempt of Israel, and he became king over Edom.[b]

11.14. Such a passage affords an excellent starting-point for the study of the term *śāṭān* in the Old Testament. Here the word is a common noun meaning an 'adversary' or 'hindrance', as David might have been to the Philistines in the Gilboa campaign (I Sam. 29.4), cf. *śōṭᵉnay*, 'my adversaries' (Ps. 109.20, 29). In Zech. 3.1 the verbal root is used in the sense of 'to provide opposition', and in the vision of a heavenly court the figure of a public prosecutor *haśśāṭān* appears. In Job 1 this figure has substantially the same function, but perhaps a more regular official status as the public prosecutor, somewhat malicious, of all men. Eventually in I Chron. 21.1 the common noun is divested of the definite article and becomes a proper noun Satan, the motivator of every evil impulse. In that passage Satan moves David to take the census in Israel, which was the occasion of the plague. This passage is illustrative of the development of an ethical dualism in Israel in the post-exilic period, doubtless under Persian influence, since in the parallel account in II Sam. 24.1 it is boldly stated that it was Yahweh who moved David to take the noxious census.

Hadad ('the Thunderer', Arabic *hadda*, 'to crash') is known from the Ras Shamra texts as the god manifest in the thunder and rain of winter, whose title was Baal. This divine name is first attested in Palestine as an element in the theophoric names of Amorite chiefs in the Egyptian Execration texts from Saqqara in the late nineteenth century BC.[c] The name of the Edomite prince is a hypocoristicon, or truncation of such a theophoric, and is paralleled possibly by Jehu

[a]Reading with G *lō* for MT *lō'* ('Nay'), which, however, would be possible before the adversative particle *kī*.

[b]Reading with G and S *'ᵉdōm* for MT *'ᵃrām*. The MT corruption occasioned the displacement of this verse (25b) to the end of the passage dealing with Rezon of Aram (vv. 23–25a), and may even have occasioned the inclusion of that passage from archives of Solomon's reign. After this had taken place, the Hebr. text *wᵉzō't hārāʿā 'ᵃšer ʿāśā hᵃdād*, suggested by the versions, was corrupted to *wᵉ'et-hārāʿā 'ᵃšer* (*ʿāśā*) *hᵃdād*, which, not very happily, may be translated 'together with the harm which Hadad did', cf. Noth (*op. cit., ad loc.*), who regards 25b in MT as a gloss which has crept into the text.

[c]G. Posener, *Princes et pays d'Asie* . . .

in Israel and by Baʿalu of Tyre.[a] Two kings of Edom before the Hebrew monarchy were called Hadad (Gen. 36.31–39, Hadar in v. 39 being given as Hadad in I Chron. 1.46f.). The conquest of Edom is mentioned very laconically in II Sam. 8.13ff., with the suggestion of little opposition, though II Sam. 8.12 (G) and I Chron. 18.12 mention the slaughter of 18,000 men. Noth (*op. cit.*, p. 252) considers that the occasion was a later revolt of Edom.

11.15. The rugged nature of Edom and the abundance of natural refuge in such canyons as Petra and in the many caverns of the hills with which the region is pitted makes Šanda's reading, which graphically differs very slightly from MT, very plausible. There is no mention of Joab's extermination of the men of Edom elsewhere in the Old Testament.

17. *ʿabᵉdē ʾābīw* ('the servants of his father') probably refers to his courtiers and high officials rather than to his slaves, though it is, as generally, ambiguous. *naʿar qāṭān* need not signify that Hadad was an infant. Indeed, even allowing for a sojourn of some years in Midian and Paran, his experience in Egypt indicates that he was more than that, though far from mature, when he fled from Edom.

18. G, inserting 'city', visualizes Midian as a town rather than a region, and it has been conjectured (Thenius) that the text originally read Maʿon for Midian. It is very doubtful if Maʿan on the open plateau east of the broken country around Petra would have been adequate refuge for the broken remnants of the Edomites. Actually Ptolemy and the later Arab geographers knew a settlement Midian, *Abū-ʾl-Fedā*, locating it on the coast six days west of Tebuk, and Idrisi placing it five days from Aqaba. It is doubtful, however, if such a town, rather than the region behind Aqaba, is indicated in the present passage. Paran was a desert region settled by Ishmael (Gen. 21.21) and was traversed by Israel after the Exodus (Num. 10.12; 12.16; 13.3–26). It is associated with the wilderness of Zin, from which the spies went up to Palestine (Num. 13.26), and in which Kadesh was located (Num. 20.1; 27.14). Generally the region of Paran apparently corresponds to the inland part of the North Sinai desert of which Kadesh was the centre. The association of the mountain(s) of Paran with Seir in Deut. 33.2 and with Teman in Hab. 3.3 and in the present passage perhaps indicates specifically the eastern edge of the plateau of *at-Tīh*, though Teman may mean the south generally. The district Paran, where David fled after the

[a] Luckenbill, *ARA* II, § 876.

death of Samuel (I Sam. 25.1, where G reads *Maan*), supports this location, though the action is located somewhat farther north.

The verb *'āmar* here, as occasionally in Hebrew, bears the connotation 'order, command', which is regular in Arabic. The phrase is paralleled by the Arab usage *'amara lahu bi* . . . ('he ordered that such a thing should be done to him . . .')[a]

11.19. Tahpenes is probably a corruption of *t.hmt.nsw* ('the wife of the king'), on which *hagg^{e}bīrā* is a gloss. On *hagg^{e}bīrā* as the title of the senior lady of the royal harem, the queen-mother or the mother of the heir-apparent, see p. 282 n.[h]. The status of *hagg^{e}bīrā* is well exemplified in the case of Bathsheba, though the title is not actually applied to her.

21. Hadad's attempt to recover Edom apparently dated from early in Solomon's reign. In the nature of the brief, laconic communication, however, an indefinite period might well have elapsed since the accession of Solomon, with whom the Pharaoh was apparently on good terms. In any case, though the Pharaoh had no scruples about playing the one off against the other, he apparently preferred to detain Hadad a while longer in Egypt. The abrupt end of v. 22, which makes the immediate sequel uncertain, and the equally abrupt and asyndetic resumption of the Hadad story in 25b, precludes a reconstruction and dating of events.

25b. There is no need to emend *wayyāqoṣ* with Kittel (HKAT, p. 98) to *wayyāṣeq* ('and he oppressed'). The verb in the MT denotes 'loathing', with the suggestion of contempt or defiance, cf. Prov. 3.11, *mūsar yhwh b^{e}nī 'al-tim'as w^e'al-tāqōṣ b^{e}tōkaḥtō* ('My son, spurn not the chastening of Yahweh, and despise not his discipline'). It is used to express the contempt of the Egyptians for the Israelites (Ex. 1.12), and the general antipathy of one people for another, as Moab for Israel (Num. 22.3). The success of Hadad must have been limited, as Gressmann points out,[b] since Solomon was able to work the mines of the Edomite escarpment of the Araba and to build a trading settlement at *Tell al-Ḫaleifeh* at the northern end of the Gulf of Aqaba.

(β) *The rise of Rezon of Damascus:* 11.23–25a

Considering the momentous significance of this event in the subsequent history of Israel, it is surprising to find it so briefly noted. Though the present passage states, with great probability, that

[a]L. Kopf, 'Arabische Etymologien und Parallelen . . .', *VT* VIII, 1958, p. 164.
[b]*Die älteste Geschichtsschreibung* . . . p. 220.

Rezon's rise followed upon Zobah's loss of hegemony after her defeat by Israel in Transjordan (II Sam. 8.3), in view of the statement regarding the extent of territory controlled by Solomon in I K. 4.21, it is likely that the present account of the rise of Damascus is foreshortened, a view which is further indicated by the statement that as a reprisal for assistance given to Hadadezer of Zobah, David garrisoned Damascus and reduced it to a tributary condition (II Sam. 8.3–6). The fact that the passage appears at a different place in G (at v. 14), and here also interrupts the narrative regarding Hadad, indicates that it was a later insertion in MT, though substantially historical. As we have suggested, the reason for its insertion may have been the corruption of 'Edom' to 'Aram' in v. 25. We should agree with Jepsen[a] that the notice is a general statement by the editor from popular tradition, the raising up of an antagonist by God indicating the Deuteronomistic theology, but that does not necessarily invalidate the details conveyed, though those are impossible to check.

11 [23]And God raised up an antagonist for him, namely Rezon the son of Eliada, who had fled from his master Hadadezer king of Zobah. [24]And men gathered[b] to him and he was leader of a band when David slew the Aramaeans[c] and he took[d] Damascus and he settled[e] in it and became king in Damascus,[f] [25A]and he was an adversary to Israel all the days of Solomon.

11.23. With great verisimilitude the rise of Damascus is represented as a consequence of the end of Zobah's hegemony of the Aramaeans north-east of Israel. This, however, is represented not as the assertion of independence and power by one tribal confederacy on the downfall of another, but as the personal *coup d'état* of Rezon with the backing of his band of brigands. Doubtless he manipulated these as David manipulated his feudal retainers when, as a vassal of Achish of Gath,

[a]A. Jepsen, 'Israel und Damaskus', *AfO* XIV, 1942, p. 153.

[b]Reading third masculine plural Niphal with G and S for MT third masculine singular Qal.

[c]Reading *'ᵃrām* (collective singular) for MT *'ōtām*, though the whole phrase 'when David slew the Aramaeans' is omitted in G[BL] and may be a later gloss to v. 23, in which case the defection of Damascus may be dated quite late in the reign of Solomon.

[d]Reading with G and L *wayyilkōd* for MT *wayyēlᵉkū* ('and they went to').

[e]Reading singular for plural of MT, as suggested by the preceding and the following verb *wayyimlᵉkū* ('and they became kings'), which must certainly be emended to the singular.

[f]MT 'and he settled in it and became king in Damascus' is omitted in the versions.

he effected a similar *coup*. Malamat feasibly proposes[a] that Rezon may have been first sponsored by Israel as a counterpoise to the Aramaean kingdom of Zobah, which had once held the hegemony in Syria, just as the Philistines were well content to see David promote himself in Judah as a potential rival of Israel. If this were so, the rise of Rezon as an adversary to Solomon might be presented proleptically in 11.23ff. Like David, who became king in Hebron, which was significant as a sanctuary recognized by Kenizzites and men of Judah, Rezon became king in Damascus, which was strategically significant as the metropolis of the North Arabian steppes and southern inland Syria, and, as a great oasis, was probably also a significant cult-centre, as it was certainly in later times. In semi-nomad society much depends on personal prestige. The name Rezon suggests *rōzēn* ('ruler, high official'), which is found in parallelism with *melek* in Judg. 5.3; Hab. 1.10; Ps. 2.2.; Prov. 8.15; 14.28 and with *šōpēṭ* in Isa. 40.23. Thus Mazar[b] makes the feasible suggestion that this was a royal title rather than the proper name of the king, which was Hezion the father of Benhadad I, the contemporary of Asa of Judah (15.18), the great-grandson or grandson of Solomon, but see on 15.18. The noun is cognate with Arabic *razuna* ('to be heavy, dignified'). The name of the father of Rezon signifies 'El notices', El being known in the Ras Shamra texts as the senior god of the Canaanite pantheon, whose sphere was social relations rather than nature. In the theophoric names among the Egyptian Execration Texts from Luxor[c] it is apparent that El was worshipped by the Amorites in Palestine and southern Syria in process of settling down to the sedentary life in the nineteenth century. The Egyptian Execration Texts from Saqqara dating from about half a century later[d] reveal a large number of names compounded with Hadad, now known from the Ras Shamra texts as the Canaanite Baal, whose cult is attested at Damascus, probably on the site of the present Umayyad Mosque, once the site of the Church of St John, and earlier the temple of Jupiter Damascinus[e], by the prevalent royal names Benhadad or Barhadad. The name Hadadezer is thus quite natural in its context.

Zobah, known in Assyrian inscriptions of the seventh century as

[a] *JNES* XXII, 1963, p. 5.
[b] B. Mazar, 'The Aramaean Empire and its Relations with Israel', *BA* XXV, 1962, p. 104.
[c] K. Sethe, *Die Ächtung feindlicher Fürsten. . . .*
[d] G. Posener, *Princes et pays d'Asie. . . .*
[e] R. Dussaud, *Syria* III, 1922, pp. 219ff.

Ṣubaṭe, was located south of Hamath and neighbouring Damascus, hence in the region of Baalbek, which was a cult-centre of the Syrian Baal in his Roman adaptation as Zeus in the early Roman Imperial period and probably much earlier. The pretensions of this Aramaic state in the time of David probably encouraged her neighbour Hamath to seek an alliance with David (II Sam. 8.9f.). The policy of Hamath may have been dictated not so much by local rivalry as by fear on the part of the considerable Hittite element in Hamath of Aramaean domination. One of the settlements of Zobah, Tibhath (I Chron. 18.8, of which Betah of II Sam. 8.8 is a corruption) is Tubiḥi of the Amarna Tablets in this locality.

(γ) *The abortive revolt of Jeroboam*: 11.26–40

This, which is prefaced by a note on the origins of Jeroboam, is a composite passage, which is most likely drawn ultimately from an archival source, probably the annals of the kings of Israel rather than those of the kings of Judah, as is indicated by the attitude to Rehoboam in the sequel. This matter may be a Judaean summary of a primary Israelite tradition. There is a digression (vv. 29–32) which relates the role played by Ahijah, the prophet of Shiloh, in support of Jeroboam. This may be drawn from the annals of the kings of Israel or, like the narrative of the encounter between Ahijah and the wife of Jeroboam (I K. 14.1–18), from a prophetic legend centring upon Ahijah and preserved in prophetic circles. In support of this view is the fact that the matter has much in common with biographical matter in the books of the Prophets, e.g. Isa. 36–39 (cf. II K. 18.13–20.19). This passage is followed by a Deuteronomistic expansion of the oracle of Ahijah elaborating the theme of the defection of the Northern tribes as a punishment for Solomon's religious laxity (vv. 33–39). Since the permanence of the Davidic house is clearly visualized (v. 36), this passage belongs to the Deuteronomistic compilation of Kings before the collapse of the monarchy in 586.

We may well suppose that between Ahijah's encounter with Jeroboam and Solomon's drastic reaction which drove Jeroboam to seek political asylum in Egypt definite acts of insurrection took place to provoke Solomon's reaction. And certainly before Israel summoned Jeroboam from Egypt to head the revolt against Rehoboam (I K. 12.2–3) he must have played a role which marked him out as their natural leader. Here, however, in MT objective history is obscured by Deuteronomistic rationalization. There seems, on the other hand, to be a genuine historical source behind the variant account in G (vv. 24a–z, ed. Swete),[a] which introduces Jeroboam in v. 24b after the notice of Solomon's death and the introduction of Rehoboam with the customary formula for the kings of Judah (v. 24a, cf. MT 11.43, expanded). G then describes in retrospect Jeroboam's open and unsuccessful revolt against Solomon, his flight to Egypt, his return on the death of Solomon, and his preparation for resistance in Ephraim, with his headquarters at 'Sareira' (12.24b–f., cf. MT 11.26–31, 40). Next follows the account of the encounter of Ahijah with Jeroboam's wife, 12.24f–n; cf. MT 14.1–18. G next describes the appearance of Jeroboam at Shechem with a following of the Northern tribes and his encounter with Rehoboam (12. 24n–o). Here there is a variant version of the symbolic rending of the mantle (cf. MT 11.29f.), the prophet Shemaiah, and not Ahijah, being involved, and *all* twelve fragments being given to Jeroboam (12.24o). Rehoboam is petitioned by the Northern tribes and gives his famous rejection of their request (12.24p–s; cf. MT 12.3–14); the people throw off their allegiance to his house, Rehoboam returns with Judah and Benjamin to Jerusalem (12.24t–u; cf. MT 12.16) and 'at the turn of the year' marches against Israel at Shechem (G 12.24x; cf. MT 12.21), but is restrained by the oracle of Shemaiah (12.24y–z; cf. MT 12.16). The framework of this account in G, as suggested by the introduction and the role of the prophet Shemaiah, may well be from the annals of the kings of Judah, but uses matter, as the MT also does, from the annals of the kings of Israel, particularly in what pertains to the abortive rising of Jeroboam (12.24b–d) and the part played by Ahijah, excluding the Deuteronomistic rationalization in MT 11.32–39. The whole, however, including such obvious tendencies to vilify Jeroboam as the statement that his mother was a harlot (v. 24b) and the transference to him of the tradition of marriage with the daughter of Pharaoh (v. 24e), which belongs properly to the story of Hadad of Edom, indicates secondary expansion.

In an appraisal of the historical worth of this matter in 12.22–24 MT, cf. v. 24y–z G, Seebass[b] has emphasized the tradition of the original design for Jeroboam to supplant the house of David over *all*

[a]This applies, however, rather to certain details than to the whole, as recently recognized by H. Seebass, 'Zur Königserhebung Jeroboams I', *VT* XVII, 1967, pp. 325–33.

[b]*Op. cit.*, pp. 327ff.

Israel, regarding the divine purpose to leave the two tribes to the house of David as an accommodation to actual fact, which the prophet Shemaiah communicated as a divine oracle. In this case, Shemaiah would be a prophet of Judah who was actuated by the tradition of the establishment of the Davidic house according to divine covenant, which was already part of the Davidic tradition (II Sam. 7.12ff.) propagated by the liturgy in the Temple (e.g. Pss. 89.28–37 [29–38]; 132.11f.). The tradition of Ahijah's division of his mantle may well have been coloured by that of the oracle of Shemaiah, supported by similar prophetic symbolism. The recurrent reference to the taking of the kingdom (sc. the *whole* kingdom) from the house of David may refer to Ahijah's oracle, perhaps being supported by a rite of prophetic symbolism with his mantle, though not the division of it as described in 11.29ff. The prophetic symbolism involving the division of the pieces of the cloak into ten and two may be properly Shemaiah's later adaptation of Ahijah's symbolism, though such a division is referred to in the case of Shemaiah in G, not in the narrative, but in the reference to Shemaiah's oracle in the end of 12.24o.

11 [26]And Jeroboam the son of Nebat, an Ephraimite from Zeredah, the name of whose mother was Zeruiah, [a] a widow, was a servant of Solomon, and he raised his hand against the king. [b] [27]Now this was the affair of the rising against the king. Solomon built the Millo; he closed the breach of the city of his father David. [28]And the man Jeroboam was a man of substance, and Solomon saw the young man, that he was an apt agent, and he put him in charge of all the porter service of the house of Joseph. [29]And it came to pass at that time that Jeroboam went out from Jerusalem, and the prophet Ahijah of Shiloh met him on the way [c]and took him aside from the road,[c] Ahijah being wrapped in a new mantle, and the two of them were alone in the open country. [30]And Ahijah caught hold of the new mantle which he wore and he tore it into twelve pieces. [31]And he said to Jeroboam, Take to yourself ten

[a]If the name of Jeroboam's mother is really intended it is likely that *Ṣerūʿā* ('leper') is a Jewish perversion of some similar name, possibly Zeruiah, the name of the mother of Joab. The letter-complex is suspiciously like Zeredah, the home of Jeroboam, so that a dittograph with resulting expansion is not improbable. It is noteworthy that G records simply 'from Sareira, the son of a widow woman', cf. the variant version of Jeroboam's origin in I K. 12.24b (G), 'and his mother's name was Sareira, a harlot', omitting the name of his home, though later referring to his building of the city Sareira.

[b]Possibly 'made an attempt at the kingship' (*bammᵉlūkā* for MT *bammelek* 'the king') after G, 12.24b.

[c]The last phrase is suggested by G, having perhaps been omitted by MT by homoeoteleuton of *derek* ('way' or 'road').

pieces,[a] for Yahweh the God of Israel says, See, I am about to rend the kingdom from the hand of Solomon and I will give you the ten tribes.
32And he shall have the one tribe[b] for the sake of my servant David and for the sake of Jerusalem, the city on which I have set my choice from all the tribes of Israel,
33because he forsook[c] me and bowed down[c] to 'Ashtoreth' the god of the Sidonians[d] and to Chemosh the god of Moab and to 'Milcom'[e] the god of the Ammonites and did not walk[c] in my ways to do that which was right in my eyes, and my statutes and ordinances like David his father.
34But I will not take the (whole)[f] kingdom from his hand, but shall assuredly forbear with him[g] all the days of his life for the sake of my servant David, on whom I fixed my choice, who kept my commandments and my statutes,[h]
35but I will take the kingship from the hand of his son and give it to you, [i]that is the ten tribes,[i]
36and to his son will I give one tribe, that there may be a lamp for David my servant all the days before me in Jerusalem, the city I have chosen for myself to set my name there.
37And you will I take and you shall reign over all that your inclination desires and you shall be king over Israel.
38And it shall be, if you listen to all that I

[a]The reference in v. 32 to *one* tribe to be left with the House of David, namely Judah, raised the problem of the MT reading 'ten' here and *vice versa*. The solution lies in the recognition of the complexity of sources, the present passage being from the Deuteronomistic compiler. Hence we retain MT.

[b]See above. G and L refer to *two* tribes, obviously harmonizing.

[c]In view of the reference in the end of the verse to 'David his father' the singular should probably be read for the MT plural.

[d]If this noun were in *scriptio defectiva* we might postulate dittography of *n* and read *Sidon*. Probably the original final *m* was corrupted to *n* in the proto-Hebraic script.

[e]G, probably nearer the truth, reads 'their king', preserving a trace of the use of the word as a title of the god of Ammon, which the orthodox Jewish scribes deliberately perverted to *milkōm,* with the vowels of *šiqqūṣ* ('abomination').

[f]In view of the statement in v. 35 that it was from Rehoboam that the rule should be taken it is likely that the emphasis in v. 34 fell on *his* (Solomon's) hand. We conjecture the omission of *kol* under the influence of what precedes regarding one tribe to be left under the house of David, though the versions do not support this.

[g]G reads 'I will oppose' (*antitassomenos antitaxomai autō . . .*), which is nonsense, as is indicated by the sequel 'for the sake of David my servant, whom I chose'. It does suggest, however, that the translators read *nāśō' 'eśśā' lō* (lit. 'I will assuredly lift up for him', sc. his face) for MT *nāśī' 'ašītennū* ('I will make him a prince'), a singularly inept remark about Solomon, the king 'in all his glory'.

[h]The Deuteronomistic phrase rings superfluous, and is omitted in G^B, but the whole passage is Deuteronomistic and such characteristic redundance in MT may be tolerated.

[i]This phrase, especially after the use of the third feminine singular pronominal suffix agreeing with *hammelūkā* ('the kingship'), seems tautological, and reads like an explanatory gloss referring to the qualification to the deprivation of the Davidic house, already mentioned. It implies, moreover, a misunderstanding of *melūkā* ('kingship') for *mamlākā* ('kingdom'). It is the only place in the Deuteronomistic passage (vv. 32–39) where *ten* tribes are mentioned.

command you and walk in my ways and do that which is right in my eyes, keeping my statutes and commandments as my servant David did, that I shall be with you and shall build up for you an established house, just as I built for David, [a]and I shall give you Israel, [39]that I may make the seed of David suffer for this, yet not for all time.[a] [40]And Solomon sought to kill Jeroboam, but Jeroboam rose and fled to Egypt to Shishak the king of Egypt, and he was in Egypt till the death of Solomon.

11.26. The name, Hebrew *yārobʿām*, is of uncertain significance. Assuming that *ʿam* is the divine element in a theophoric name, certain scholars have equated it with Jerubbaʿal, but, in spite of the popular etymology 'Let Baal uphold his own case', it is not at all certain that this is the explanation of this name, the verb 'to uphold a case' being *rīb* and not *rūb*, though the latter may be a by-form attested only in those two names. From the Massoretic pointing the verb is more likely to be *rābab* ('to be numerous, great'), and on this assumption Kittel (HKAT, p. 99) suggests that the name signifies 'the people is great'. We suggest that an optative of the verb would be more suitable. The people in this case is the clan or kinship group, which *ʿam* properly signifies, rather than the nation, and the birth of a son and heir to an influential member would naturally be regarded as strengthening the community. It is possible that 'Jeroboam' ('may the people be great') may be what Montgomery terms 'a defiant alias' of the throne-name of the rival king of Judah, Rehoboam ('may the people be extended').[b] This question is complicated by the fact that the element *ʿam* may be a divine name or title (lit. 'uncle') indicating the god of a kinship group, as in theophoric names in the Egyptian Execration Texts from Luxor (*c.* 1850 BC) and in such Hebrew names as Ammi-shaddai and Ammi-el (I Chron. 3.5), which is given in II Sam. 11.3 as Eli-am. Such a god seems to be referred to in the Hebrew text behind G of Amos 8.14, where the god of Beersheba is termed *dōd*, lit. 'uncle' (*dōdekā* for MT *darkekā*). In this case the name would signify ' *ʿam* is great'.[c] The name Nebat is apparently the verbal remnant of a theophoric name, such as Nabaṭ-el, which is attested as a South Arabian name, meaning 'El brings, or may El bring, to light', the verbal root with this sense being well attested in Arabic (IVth form). Šanda suggests that Nebat may have been the name of Jeroboam's clan, his father being unnamed, since his mother was a widow. Such

[a]This passage of MT is omitted in G, and is tautological in its context.

[b]So W. F. Albright, *AJSL* XXXVIII, 1922, pp. 140ff., citing the possible analogy of Ḫammu-rabi, *AASOR* XXI–XXII, 1943, p. 67.

[c]So Šanda I, p. 317.

a clan, however, is unattested in Ephraim, though this is no compelling reason to reject Šanda's theory, since the Benjamite clan of Matri, for instance, is mentioned only once in the Old Testament. A more serious objection to Šanda's view is that Jeroboam is said to have been *gibbōr ḥayil* (v. 28), a man of property and so liable for certain services in the community. Such a person would certainly be designated by his father's name.

Ephrah, from which 'Ephrathite' is derived, was apparently a by-form of Ephraim, as is clear from Judg. 12.5, where *'eprātī* certainly means man of Ephraim (collective singular). That the term is coextensive with Ephraim is further indicated by the fact that Elkanah the father of Samuel, from the western foothills of Ephraim, was described as 'an Ephrathite' (I Sam. 1.1).

Zeredah rather than the G Sareisa is the correct reading, the latter being contradicted by G itself at I K. 12.24 n, where the name is given as Sardatha. The locality is indicated by the place-names *'Ain Ṣerīda* and *Wādī Ṣerīda,* and is probably to be more particularly located at *Deir Ģassāneh* in the same vicinity some eleven miles north-west of Ramallah, where there are sherds from all phases of the Iron Age.[a] The fact that this place is some four miles from Rentis, possibly Ramatha, the home of Samuel, suggests that the disruption of the kingdom was possibly largely motivated by the determination of Ephraim to regain the hegemony of Israel rather than a spontaneous revolt of the rest of the Northern tribes.

The name of Jeroboam's mother in MT, Ṣeru'ah ('leper'), and the statement in 12.24b (G) that she was a harlot are probably deliberate efforts of Jewish scribes to vilify the rival house of Israel. See further p. 290 n.[a].

The status of Jeroboam as *'ebed* was that of a special officer of the crown.

11.27. On the nature and location of the Millo at the northern end of the south-eastern hill and of the significance of 'the breach of the city of David' see on 9.15, 24. Since the statement of the closing of the breach in the city of David is introduced asyndetically after that on the building of the *millō'*, Noth (*op. cit.*, p. 257) feasibly suggests that only the one is original and the other secondary and explanatory. The present passage suggests that Jeroboam's first attempt on the monarchy must have been made not earlier than Solomon's twentieth year, since 9.24 states that the Millo was built after the palace of

[a]Abel, *GP* I, p. 459.

Pharaoh's daughter and presumably after the building of the Temple and of his own palace (6.38b–7.1).

11.28. Jeroboam, though a young man in the service of Solomon, had succeeded to the property of his father, who had died early, since his mother is designated as a widow. As a man of property he had obligations in war, and as such he is designated *gibbōr ḥayil* (see on 1.8). *'ōśē mᵉlā'kā* may mean 'industrious' or 'energetic', or, as in II K. 12.11, 'an agent in public works'. On *sēbel*, 'porter service' rather than 'corvée' (*mas*), see above on 5.13. The house of Joseph signifies his immediate kindred of Ephraim and the related clan of Manasseh rather than all the Northern tribes, which were termed 'the house of Joseph' only after the establishment of the Northern kingdom.

29. *māṣā'* means 'to light upon by chance' as well as 'to find' as the result of search.

The association of the prophet (*nābī'*) Ahijah with Shiloh, the ancient amphictyonic shrine, raises the question of the association of the prophet with the cult and the survival of Shiloh as a cult centre after the defeat of Israel by the Philistines and the subsequent destruction of Shiloh attested by the excavations of Kjaer and Schmidt at *Ḫirbet Seilūn*, *c.*12 miles south-south-east of Nablus.[a] Such a guild of prophets as is attested at Bethel in II K. 2.3 might well have survived the destruction of the shrine and the decay of the cult at Shiloh. In view of the role played by the prophets in affairs of state, e.g. Elijah and Isaiah, and especially in changes of dynasty in North Israel, e.g. Jehu and Elisha, the Ahijah incident has the note of authenticity. Šanda (I, p. 318) raises the question as to whether Ahijah voiced his protest on religious as well as political grounds, but rejects the view. In view of the fact that the canonical prophets emphasize the covenant and *Heilsgeschichte* rather than the triumph of God over the powers of chaos in nature in the ideology of the reign of God in the syncretistic New Year liturgy at Jerusalem,[b] and the fact that Hosea, the only North Israelite prophet in the canon, particularly does so, possibly referring to the amphictyonic tent-festival of the renewal of the covenant, we think it not unlikely that in the protest of Ahijah there was involved a conflict between the old cult of the sacral confederacy at Shechem and Gilgal and the new syncretistic cult of Jerusalem.

[a] H. Kjaer, 'The Excavation of Shiloh', *JPOS* X, 1930, pp. 87–174.

[b] J. Gray, 'The Kingship of God in the Prophets and Psalms', *VT* XI, 1961, pp. 14ff.

11.30. The rending of the mantle by Ahijah recalls the incident in I Sam. 15.27ff., where Samuel uses the apparently accidental tearing of his robe to inculcate Saul's deprivation of the kingdom. The one tradition may well have influenced the other. This is the first instance in Kings of prophetic symbolism, so common a method of prophetic teaching. Based on the principle of imitative magic, the attempt to influence the power of providence by autosuggestion, it was used by the prophets to indicate and emphasize the certainty of the divine intention, and so to arrest popular attention.

The note on Ahijah's new mantle is significant. According to the popular conception of acts designed to enlist the activity of the supernatural, new media were important as having had no contact with other agencies which might impair the designed effect, cf. the new bowl used by Elisha in the restoration of the fertility of the spring at Jericho (II K. 2.20), the new ropes and bowstrings with which Samson deceitfully told Delilah that he could be effectively bound (Judg. 16.7–11), and the new cart on which, as fitting to a holy symbol, the ark was sent back by the Philistines, who thus enlisted the immediate activity of God (I Sam. 6.7). The meeting between Ahijah and Jeroboam was not by chance, but the prophet had prepared for his act of imitative magic.

In tearing the mantle into twelve portions. Ahijah shows himself an upholder of the conception of Israel as a twelve-tribe confederacy, a religious rather than a political federation, a fact which seems to us to support our contention that Ahijah voiced a religious as well as a political protest. In view of the disappearance of Levi as a political entity and of the displacement and virtual disappearance of Simeon in the Negeb, the twelve-tribe confederacy seems to have been a schematization, rather than a historic conception, the number twelve being perhaps suggested by the twelve months of the year.[a] The consciousness of twelve tribes was preserved by the recognition of two divisions of Joseph, namely Ephraim and Manasseh, and the solidarity of Simeon with the Northern tribes was preserved long after the disruption of the kingdom by the regular pilgrimage from North Israel to Beersheba (Amos 5.5) and perhaps other shrines in Simeon, possibly referred to by Amos (7.9) as 'the "high places" of Isaac'.

This also involved a conflict between the conception of authority as indicated by the manifest possession of the divine gift, or *charisma*, popularly recognized and acclaimed by the sacral confederacy, and

[a]See Noth, *Zwölf Stämme*; *History of Israel*, pp. 88 ff.

inherited office independent of the sacral confederacy, as in the case of Solomon, elevated by the *fiat* of King David. In the role of prophets in North Israel the hereditary principle is consistently opposed.

11.31f. On the view that originally Ahijah visualized the supplanting of the house of David by Jeroboam over all Israel, see above, pp. 289f. The retention of one tribe by the house of David (vv. 32–35, cf. v. 13) may be part of the original tradition, visualizing the family allegiance of Judah and the retaining of Jerusalem and other districts as heritable crown property. At any rate, the retention of *one* tribe and *two* tribes (v. 31) presents an arithmetical problem for G, which harmonizes, reading *two* tribes in v. 32. The solution of the problem is most easily found by recognizing the eventual settlement. At this time the twelve-tribe sacral confederacy was more ideal than real, since Simeon and Levi had long since ceased to be effective and were in fact respectively incorporated in Judah and taken up into the cult as a sacred guild. The allegiance of Benjamin was divided, part adhering to the kingdom of the house of David more by force of circumstances than by choice. The subsequent fluctuating of the frontier and the fact that such an important place as Jericho remained in the Northern kingdom indicates that the whole tribe of Benjamin did not attach itself to the house of David. The fact that the districts of Benjamin nearest to Ephraim were attached to Israel militates against the view of Seebass[a] that Benjamin joined Judah through local rivalry with Ephraim. It is significant that the territory of Benjamin which adhered to Judah included the old Hurrian city-states of Gibeon, Beeroth and Chepirah, of which Gibeon had been shown preferential treatment by David (II Sam. 21.1ff.) and Solomon (I K. 3.4ff.). The allegiance of the southern part of Benjamin was moreover doubtless secured by the Levitical settlements at Gibeon, Geba, Anathoth and Almon (Josh. 21.17f.), probably established as part of the organization of the kingdom under David.[b]

The Lord's choice of the Davidic house and of Jerusalem is

[a]*Op. cit.*, p. 332.

[b]B. Mazar, 'The Cities of the Priests and Levites', *SVT* VII, 1960, pp. 193–205, sees the origin of the Levitical settlements in Josh. 21 as settlements of Levites as agents of David (I Chron 26.29–32) and Solomon in preserving the Israelite character of the kingdom in the incorporation of Canaanite districts. The Levitical settlements in southern Benjamin may have been designed to counteract the influence of the family of Saul. Perhaps it was the allegiance of the Levites to the house of David that led Jeroboam to exclude them from the cult at Bethel (12.31). See further our development of Mazar's thesis in *Joshua, Judges, Ruth* (Century Bible), 1967, pp. 26–31.

reiterated in the Deuteronomistic elaboration of the Ahijah episode, indicating the Judaean recension before the disaster of 586.

11.33. On the deities of Sidon, Moab, and Ammon see on vv. 5f.

34. In MT *nāśī' 'aśītennū* ('I will make him ruler') Montgomery sees a constitutional limitation of the authority of Solomon, who is not to be a *melek*, but merely a *nāśī'*, a word which is used of the heads of tribes at assemblies of the sacral confederacy, cf. Num. 7.2; Ezek. 46.12, 16. Without disputing this significance of *nāśī'* we prefer to follow G and read *nāśō' 'eśśō' lō* ('I will forbear with him').

35. On 'even the ten tribes' as a gloss see p. 291 n.[a].

36. The 'light' (*nīr*) symbolizes the living representative of the house of the founder David (cf. II Sam. 14.7). The figure is taken by Eissfeldt[a] to be transferred from religious usage, where the light in the dark *penetralia* of the sacred tent symbolized the presence of Yahweh. The form *nīr* for the more usual *nēr* is to be noted, cf. *nyr šmm* ('the luminary of heaven') in the Ugaritic text, *UT* 77.16, 31.

37. *nepeš* here signifies 'enthusiasm' or 'appetite.' 'Israel' denotes the Northern kingdom.

38. This is a Deuteronomistic adaptation, in the case of the house of Jeroboam, of the conditional blessing on the house of David. It may, however, have had an original form in Ahijah's oracle, especially in the covenant obligations of the king.

39. The view that the sufferings of the house of David at the hands of Israel were a divine discipline (*wa'a'anne* for MT *wa''anne*) is characteristic of the Deuteronomistic philosophy of history.

40. This laconic statement of Solomon's successful interference with the plans of Jeroboam and the latter's refuge in Egypt may be filled out from the circumstantial account of the revolt in G (12.24b–c), which may well come from a reliable North Israelite source, quite possibly the annals of the kings of Israel. Here, as distinct from the story of Hadad's refuge in Egypt, the Pharaoh is named, which is the first cross-reference in Kings to contemporary history which may be dated with a fair degree of accuracy. The Pharaoh, as suggested by G, is Shishak I, the Libyan founder of the XXIInd Dynasty (935–914).[b] The possibility that the same Pharaoh gave asylum to Hadad of

[a] *HSAT*, p. 522.

[b] M. B. Rowton, *JEA* XXXIV, 1948, pp. 57–74, and 'The Date of the Founding of Solomon's Temple', *BASOR* 119, 1950, pp. 20–22; W. F. Albright, 'New Light from Egypt on the Chronology and the History of Israel and Judah', *BASOR* 130, 1953, pp. 4–8; P. van der Meer, *The Chronology of Ancient Western Asia and Egypt*, 1955², p. 83.

Edom seems practically ruled out by the late date of his accession in Solomon's long reign.

(ii) THE STANDARD EDITORIAL (DEUTERONOMISTIC) NOTICE OF THE DEATH OF SOLOMON: 11.41–43

This differs from the regular Deuteronomistic epilogues to the reigns of kings in that the duration of Solomon's reign is given in the obituary and not in the introduction to his reign, owing to the incorporation in the record of a more full and circumstantial account of the accession of Solomon from another source, the Story of the Davidic Succession.

11 41And as for the rest of the acts of Solomon and all that he did and his wisdom, are they not written in the book of the annals[a] of Solomon? 42And the years that Solomon reigned in Jerusalem [b](over all Israel)[b] were forty years. 43And Solomon slept with his fathers and he was buried in the city of David his father and Rehoboam his son reigned in his stead.

11.41. As in the regular editorial epilogues to the reigns of kings, reference is made to a fuller source. MT 'book of the acts of Solomon' would suggest a fuller source than annals. If the recorded instances of Solomon's practical sagacity are indeed from this source, then it was rather saga than factual annals. We should probably regard this reference as to annals, 'and his wisdom' being possibly an addition to the original note. There is, however, undoubted evidence of a Solomon legend as a source, so that the annalistic and legendary elements cannot easily or certainly be delimited in the 'book of the acts of Solomon' to which the compiler refers.

42. The number forty for the duration of the reign of Solomon as of David, may be the familiar approximation of Semitic folklore and tradition, e.g. forty days and forty nights, Ali Baba and the Forty Thieves, though, in the case of Solomon, who acceded when quite young, it is probably not far from the truth.

43. Since momentous events were to occur before the official accession of Rehoboam, namely his rejection by the assembly at Shechem and the civil war (12.1–24), the statement concerning his accession in v. 43 is a case of editorial summary. On the name Rehoboam see on v. 26.

[a]Reading with G^L and V *dibᵉrē yᵉmē šᵉlōmō*, for MT *dibᵉrē šᵉlōmō* ('the acts of Solomon'), but the MT here may denote a special source devoted to Solomon as apart from the regular annals of the kings of Judah.

[b]Probably to be omitted with G^B.

III

THE DIVIDED KINGDOM: I KINGS 12–II KINGS 17

1. THE DISRUPTION OF THE KINGDOM: 12.1–24

THE ACCOUNT OF THE actual disruption of Solomon's kingdom (vv. 1–19) is transmitted in an early historical narrative which bears the clear stamp of reliability and a historical sense corresponding to the really important political situation described. This is conveyed in a self-contained narrative account of the rejection of Rehoboam by the assembly of North Israel at the old centre of the sacral confederacy, Shechem (vv. 1, 3b–19 and possibly 20), which the Deuteronomistic compiler has left almost untouched except for the addition of his comment at v. 15 to explain the obtuseness of Rehoboam which caused the breach as the deliberate act of God in fulfilment of the prophetic word through Ahijah.

The sequel, after a late, and probably Deuteronomistic, accretion (vv. 21–24), on the suspension of the civil war between Rehoboam and the tribes of the North (see below, pp. 308f.), continues after a note on Jeroboam's fortifications and the shifting of his capital (v. 25) with his developing and staffing of the cult of Bethel as a rival to Jerusalem and of the New Year festival, which was so important to support his own status as the executive of the divine king, whose enthronement, we believe, was the central feature of the New Year Festival. This in the plan of the Deuteronomistic History leads to the prophetic denunciation of the cult in ch. 13.

The disruption of the kingdom can hardly be described without some cognizance being taken of Jeroboam, who has already been introduced in 11.26–40 in anticipation of the disruption. There v. 40 notes his flight to Egypt, where he remained till the death of Solomon (cf. 12.2–3a, MT). The actual notice of his being made king by the assembled representatives of Israel is given somewhat abruptly at v. 20 after the account of the disruption, but he is already introduced as active in the Israelite assembly at Shechem in v. 12, which is thus at variance with v. 20, where he is called to the assembly only after the Northern tribes had broken with Rehoboam. This suggests that the statement about the return of Jeroboam (see textual note on v. 2) on hearing of the assembly at Shechem in conjunction with the obvious parenthesis on his flight to Egypt, which is suspiciously tautological so soon after 11.40, is secondary, being prompted by the statement about Jeroboam being present at the assembly at v. 12. Therefore 12.2–3a, which interrupt vv. 1, 3bff., like the mention of Jeroboam in v. 12, are secondary glosses to the original narrative in 12.1, 3b–14, 16–19. Verse 18 is probably a genuine historical note from a near-contemporary source, but is probably an addition.

There is little doubt that this tradition of the disruption goes back possibly to within a generation of the event. It is difficult, if indeed at all possible, to tell on the evidence of this account alone if it came from North Israel or Judah, but if, as seems feasible, it is one with vv. 26–32, then it probably comes from a circle in Jerusalem which felt deprived by the disruption but was sufficiently mature to see the fault of Rehoboam, that is to say, Levites who had safeguarded the tradition of Israel in the incorporation of the Canaanite districts under David and Solomon.

We must note the correspondence between 12.2–3a MT and 11.43 G, where the account of Jeroboam's flight and return on hearing of the death of Solomon interrupts the stereotyped obituary for Solomon and notice of Rehoboam's succession. The statement, then, is as suspect here as at 12.1–3 in MT, though that need not, as D. W. Gooding[a] apparently assumes, invalidate the fact that is communicated by 11.43 (G).

Despite the general correspondence between 12.2–3a (MT) and 11.43; 12.24d, f (G), there are significant differences. MT states that on hearing of the death of Solomon, Jeroboam remained (*wayyēšeb*) there and returned only after being called by the assembly of Israel.[b] This may indicate that the assembly had already met and rejected Rehoboam, and now approached Jeroboam to make him king. G,

[a]D. W. Gooding, 'The Septuagint's Rival Versions of Jeroboam's Rise to Power', *VT* XVII, 1967, pp. 173–89.

[b]But note the variant reading of G^A, S^h, V, cf. II Chron. 10.2 *wayyāšob . . . mimmiṣrayim*.

on the contrary, at 11.43b states that, on hearing of the death of Solomon, Jeroboam returned forthwith from Egypt but went to his home town of 'Sereira', Zaredah of MT, and at 12.24 d, f, adds that he gathered all the tribe of Ephraim and fortified the town. This seems natural in view of the confidence which Ahijah's call would have inspired, and might support the reading of G[a], S[h], and V, cf. II Chron. 10.2, *wayyāšob . . . mimmiṣrayim*, which we adopt. Granted that 12.2–3a (MT) and 11.43b (G) are parenthetic and secondary insertions, both G and MT may preserve important facts, G the immediate return of Jeroboam to his home on the death of Solomon, and MT Jeroboam's role in the assembly at Shechem, probably in its later stages, which is natural in view of his career and influence under Solomon, his authority in Ephraim (12.24f. G) and the declared support of prophetic circles. G at 11.43b and 12.24d, f, makes explicit what is implicit in MT at 12.20. The relative vagueness of MT in 12.2f., with the focus of attention put on Jeroboam's advent in the assembly, may be owing to a Judaean version, while G, with the more intimate details about Jeroboam's return, may reflect a Hebrew original which has preserved the Israelite account.

(*a*) THE REJECTION OF REHOBOAM AT THE ASSEMBLY AT SHECHEM: 12.1–19

12 [1]Now Rehoboam went to Shechem, for all Israel had come to Shechem to make him king. [[2]And it came to pass, when Jeroboam the son of Nebat heard (that), he being yet in Egypt, where he had fled from the presence of king Solomon, that Jeroboam returned from Egypt.][a] [3][b]and they spoke to Rehoboam saying, [4]Your father made our yoke hard, but do you lighten the hard service of your father and his heavy yoke which he imposed on us that we may be your subjects. [5]And he said to them, Go for three days and come back to me. And the people went away. [6]Then king Rehoboam took counsel with the elders who had stood in the presence of his father Solomon when he was alive, saying, How do you advise that I answer this people? [7]And

[a]Reading with G[A], S[h], V, and II Chron. 10.2 *wayyāšob . . . mimmiṣrayim* for MT *wayyēšeb b*[e]*miṣrayim* ('and he dwelt in Egypt'). This allows for the return of Jeroboam immediately after the death of Solomon some time before the assembly at Shechem, as suggested by G, and obviates the difficulty of the MT in v. 3, which suggests that Jeroboam was summoned from Egypt on this occasion and arrived before the fateful decision after the lapse of three days.

[b]Omitting 'And they sent and called him and Jeroboam and all the assembly of Israel came' of MT, after G[BL]. Following G here and in 2b, we avoid the discrepancy between the MT here and in v. 20, which states that Jeroboam was summoned after his return from Egypt and after the rejection of Rehoboam. See further the critical introduction to this passage.

they spoke[a] to him saying, If today you will be a servant to this people[b]
and speak fair words to them, then they will be your servants for ever.
8But he abandoned the advice of the elders which they gave him and
took counsel with the youngsters who had grown up with him,[c] that
stood before him. 9And he said to them, What do you advise that I[d]
answer this people who have spoken to me saying, Lighten the yoke which
your father laid upon us? 10And the youngsters who had grown up with
him spoke to him saying, 'Thus shall you say to this people who have
spoken to you saying, Your father made our yoke heavy, but do you make
it lighter upon us, so shall you say to them, My little finger is thicker than
my father's loins. 11And now, my father imposed a heavy yoke upon you,
but I shall add to your yoke; my father chastised you with lashes, but I
shall chastise you with "scorpions".' 12And all the people[e] came to
Rehoboam on the third day as the king had bidden, saying, Come back to
me on the third day. 13And the king gave the people a harsh answer, and
abandoned the advice of the elders which they had given him. 14And he
spoke to them according to the advice of the youngsters saying, My father
made your yoke heavy, but I shall add to your yoke; my father chastised
you with lashes, but I shall chastise you with 'scorpions'. 15And the king
did not listen to the people, for it was a turn of fate by the agency of
Yahweh that he might realize his word which Yahweh had spoken
through Ahijah of Shiloh to[f] Jeroboam the son of Nebat. 16And all
Israel[g] saw that the king did not listen to them, so the people answered
the king saying,

> What portion have we in David?
> We have no inheritance in the son of Jesse.
> To your tents, O Israel.
> Now see[h] to your own house, David.

So Israel went to their tents. [i](17And as for the Israelites who lived in
the cities of Judah, Rehoboam reigned over them.)[i] 18Now king

[a]Pointing the *scriptio defectiva* of the verb with Q.

[b]Omitting *waʿ^{a}badtām* ('and will serve them') of MT with G^{B}. The parallel passage in II Chron. 10 reads *ūr^{e}ṣītām* ('and gratify them').

[c]Omitting *'^{a}šer* with the parallel account in II Chron. 10, the relative particle, if not quite impossible with the participle and the definite article, being certainly highly irregular.

[d]Reading with G, S, and V *w^{e}'āšīb* for MT *w^{e}nāšīb* of the 'communicative plural' (Šanda, I, p. 337), or, less probably, the plural of majesty.

[e]Omitting 'Jeroboam and . . .' of MT with G, consistently with v. 20, which introduces Jeroboam only after the rejection of Rehoboam.

[f]G^{BA} read *ʿal* ('concerning') for MT *'el*, which is equally tenable, though, as the word was privately spoken *to* Jeroboam, the MT must be seriously considered.

[g]G^{L} and V read 'the people' (*hāʿām*) for MT 'Israel'.

[h]G and T read *r^{e}ʿē* ('herd') for MT *r^{e}'ē* ('see', i.e. 'see to'). The conception of the king as the shepherd of his people is familiar in the ancient Near East in Mesopotamian texts and in the Iliad (*poimenes laōn*). In the present passage the reading is feasible, but unnecessary.

[i]G^{L} omits this verse entirely, and in its present position in MT, which is attested first by Aquila, the syntax is just possible, but awkward. It would, on the other hand, fit in admirably at the end of v. 20, which describes the limited realm

Rehoboam sent Adoram[a] the commissioner of the corvée and all Israel stoned him with stones and he died, so king Rehoboam bestirred himself to mount his chariot to flee to Jerusalem. [19]So Israel revolted against the house of David, and so to this day.

12.1. Shechem, at the eastern end of the pass between Mount Ebal and Mount Gerizim, placed as the neck between the shoulders (whence the name, *šekem*, 'shoulder'), was specifically associated with Jacob (Gen. 33.18), whose well (John 4.12) is still shown. It was the scene of the violent reprisals of the tribes Simeon and Levi before the former migrated to the south and the latter lost political status in Israel (Gen. 34), a phase of the Hebrew settlement which may correspond to the activities of the Ḫabiru which the Amarna Tablets note in the vicinity of Shechem.[b] As the reputed burial-place of Joseph (Josh. 24.32) and the scene of Joshua's covenant with Israel (Josh. 24), Shechem played an important part in Israelite religion. It is plausibly argued by Alt and Noth that the incident of Joshua's covenant really reflects the periodic recitation of the law at Shechem and the renewal of the covenant in a solemn assembly, and certainly Deut. 11.26–32; 27.1–26 support this view. No doubt Shechem played a much more important role in Israel than is immediately apparent, this having been obscured first by the concentration of the cult in Jerusalem under David and Solomon and second by the predominance of Jewish tradition in the Old Testament, and lastly because of the enmity of orthodox Judaism to the Samaritan sect. This significance of Shechem is supported by the present passage and by the fact that Shechem was the first capital of the Northern kingdom after the disruption (I K. 12.25).[c] Excavations at *Tell al-Balāṭa*, begun before the First World War and continued at intervals since, have been carried much further under G. E. Wright, who has found traces of settlement from before 3000 BC until the second century BC. There was a recession in the life of the city from about the ninth to the fourth century, no doubt because of the shifting of the capital to Tirzah and

---

of Rehoboam. Hence it may be displaced from there, where it may have originated as a gloss harmonizing the tradition that only Judah was left to the house of David and that which included the tribe of Benjamin. Šanda (I, p. 339), on the other hand, explains the omission in G on the assumption that it was genuine in v. 20, but was mistaken for a gloss and so omitted.

[a]This official is known as Adoniram in I K. 4.6 and 5.14 [28]; this may be, as Kittel suggests (p. 105), a case of popular abbreviation.

[b]Knudtzon, *Die El-Amarna Tafeln*, 289, 1.24.

[c]On Shechem and its traditions see further E. Nielsen, *Shechem*, 1955; G. E. Wright, *Shechem*, 1965.

then to Samaria, but Jeremiah indicates that after 586 there was still an orthodox Israelite community at Shechem. It is significant that there was apparently no destruction of Shechem corresponding to the destruction of Hazor, *Tell Beit Mirsim*, *Tell ed-Duweir* (Lachish), and Bethel about the beginning of the Iron Age, a fact which indicates that the Israelite elements had effected a symbiosis with the local Canaanites before the final phase of the Israelite occupation, as the Jacob tradition in Gen. 34 suggests. In the Christian era occupation shifted slightly westward, especially with the foundation of Flavia Neapolis after AD 70, the name of which survives in Nablus, formerly a vigorous centre of political and religious life.

12.1. The gathering of 'all Israel' at Shechem is analogous to the situation where Abner, on behalf of the tribes of the North, through their elders approached David at Hebron (II Sam 3.17–21) to offer him the kingship over the Northern tribes, and the subsequent covenant between David and 'all the tribes of Israel' through their elders at Hebron (II Sam. 5.1–3). The monarchy was not so long established in Israel as to preclude such a democratic precaution as a covenant, which had been dispensed with in the case of Solomon simply because of his elevation to co-regency with David while the Hebron covenant had been still valid with David in his lifetime. Though this had apparently been accepted by Israel, the measure of traditional democratic opinion in the North may be gauged by the prophetic protest against Solomon's régime which focussed its hopes on Jeroboam (11.29–40) and the forces of revolution which prompted Solomon to take action which resulted in Jeroboam's flight to Egypt (11.40).

4. The yoke (*ʿōl*) was not absolutely resented by the Hebrews. It was not only, as to the Romans and occasionally to the Hebrews, the symbol of servitude (Gen. 27.40; Isa. 9.4 [3]; Jer. 2.20; Ezek. 34.27), but also of government. It is no disparagement for Hosea (10.11) to speak of Israel as a heifer broken to work in harness, implying the yoke, cf. Matt. 11.30, 'my yoke is easy and my burden is light', and the repeated reference in rabbinic literature to 'the yoke of the law' (*ʿōl hattōrā*). Such a concession might reasonably be expected to mark the auspicious beginning of a new reign, rebate of taxes, alleviation of the corvée and general amnesty being attested on such occasions in Mesopotamia.[a]

[a] J. J. Finkelstein, 'Ammiṣaduqa's Edict and the Babylonian "Law Codes"', *JCS* XV, 1961, pp. 91ff.

12.6. *z^e^qēnīm* ('old men' or 'elders') indicates both the age and the status of the persons, which was indicated by *'^a^šer hāyū 'ōm^e^dīm et-p^e^nē š^e^lōmō*, 'who stood in the presence of Solomon', i.e. served him as courtiers or counsellors. Strictly speaking *l^e^hāšīb dābār* ('to return word') requires an indirect object, but, as the phrase is tantamount to the transitive verb *'ānā* ('to answer'), it regularly takes a direct object.

7. As v. 4 indicates, the Northern tribes were prepared for a measure of subjection, hence the counsel of appeasement with the ultimate object of subjection. *ṭōbōt* (lit. 'good things') should be noted as probably an abstract feminine plural with the same sense as *ṭbt'* in the phrase *'dy wṭbt'*, 'a treaty and friendship' in the Sefireh inscription I.1) noted by W. L. Moran,[a] who cites *ṭabutu* as a synonym of *šalmu* ('concord') in the Amarna tablets (Knudtzon, 136) and a tablet from Taanach and from Ras Shamra.[b] On *'dy*, 'treaty', see on II K. 11.12. The use of *'ebed* and *'ābad* of the king in relation to the people is somewhat strange, unless the meaning is that the king should be a servant (of God) for the people. In this case the reading *wa'^a^badtām* would be doubtful, see p. 302, n.[b]. Perhaps a word-play was intended here, the original reading being *'im hayyōm tihye, 'ōbe lā'ām . . . w^e^hāyū l^e^kā '^a^bādīm* ('If you accede to the people now . . . they will be your servants'), the clue to the reading *'obe* being *ūr^e^ṣītām* ('and gratify them') in the parallel account in Chronicles. For this usage of *'ābā l^e^* as equivalent to *šāma'*, see Deut. 13.8 [9]; Ps. 81.11 [12].

8. Note the derogatory use of *y^e^lādīm*. According to 14.21, Rehoboam was 41 when he acceded to the throne, but according to G^B^ (12.24a) he was 16. Malamat (*op. cit.*, pp. 45f.) cites II Chron. 11.18–23, which states that Rehoboam had a family of 28 sons and 60 daughters by his large harem, with Abijah the head (*nāgīd*) of them. *hā'ōm^e^dim l^e^pānāw* has probably the same significance as *'^a^šer hāyū 'ōm^e^dim et-p^e^nē š^e^lōmō* in v. 6, denoting an actual office. This denotes a regular council, a kind of Privy Council of the king, whose interest moreover was very much involved in the constitutional issue raised by the assembly at Shechem. Alternatively, as in Sumerian society as indicated in the epic fragment of the war between Gilgamesh of Uruk and Agga of Kish, the 'young men' may indicate an assembly of those of military age in addition to the assembly of elders.

[a] 'A Note on the Treaty Terminology of the Sefîre Stelas', *JNES* XXII, 1963, pp. 173–6.

[b] Cf. Virolleaud, *RA* XXXVIII, 1941, pp. 1f.

12.10. The disruption is made most graphic by the use of homely hyperbole, of which the Hebrews were very fond, e.g.

My little finger is thicker than my father's loins.

11. The dramatic narrative is sustained by the rhythm of the prose, which may reproduce a poetical version in which the memory of the incident may have survived in oral tradition, e.g.

And now, my father imposed a heavy yoke upon you,
But I shall add to your yoke;
My father chastised you with lashes,
But I shall chastise you with 'scorpions'.

Verse 16 may be another fragment of this version:

What portion have we in David?
We have no inheritance in the son of Jesse.
To your tents, O Israel,
Now see to your own house, David.

14. 'Scorpions' is explained by Ephraem Syrus as a sadistic elaboration of lashes loaded with leather bags stuffed with sand and armed with spikes; but whether this was a purely Roman invention or an adaptation of local Near Eastern usage and appellation is uncertain.

15. The Deuteronomistic historian, true to one of his major themes, represents the disruption as determined in the crisis by God in fulfilment of the prophecy of Ahijah of Shiloh (11.29ff.). The divine 'turn of fate' is described by the rare word *sibbā*, cf. *n^e^sibbā* in the parallel passage in II Chron. 10.15. The word is generally derived from *sābab*, 'to turn about', but we suggest a connection rather with Arabic *ṣāba* ('hit the mark'), cf. *muṣība* ('misfortune').

16. The form and words of the reply of the North Israelites are substantially those of the rebel Sheba (II Sam. 20.1), which suggests that there was an undercurrent of opposition to the house of David not allayed either by David or by Solomon. In the Shechem incident 'to your tents' is generally taken to mean 'home'. We consider that here it may signify the tents where the representatives of the tribes camped during the tribal gathering at Shechem, in which context Malamat (*op. cit.*, pp. 39f.) feasibly suggests that it was the formula for disbanding the sacral community on the occasion of the covenant-sacrament. Here it would denote, as in Sheba's revolt, the renunciation of covenant obligations. Israel on such an occasion was thought of as a military confederacy in the field.

Alt, however, discriminates between a temporary shelter (*sukkā*) and *'ōhel* of the present passage, which means originally 'tent' but has come to mean a permanent home.[a] In the present context it may simply indicate the end of formalities, primarily ritual, but here also political. Here 'David' is used according to common Semitic usage to signify the family, or even tribe (Judah) which he represented.[b] The right of Judah to follow the house of David was apparently unquestioned, and is another indication of the independence of North and South, which probably goes back, as T. H. Robinson suggested,[c] to independent phases of settlement of Palestine. It is noteworthy that there is no tradition of the coercion of Judah by the Northern tribes; on the contrary the aggressive party was Judah.

On the variant reading *reʿē* suggested by G and T see p. 302 n.[h].

12.17. On the relative position of v. 17 (possibly after v. 20) see p. 302 n.[i]. It is not certain whether the reference is to Israelites who preferred to move south into Judah or, as is more likely, Israelites of Benjamin, who had Northern affinities, living in and around Jerusalem, and to whom family and local ties meant more than political allegiance.

18. The choice of Adoram, the commissioner of the corvée, to pacify the assembly was most tactless. Šanda (I, p. 339) suggests that the fact that he had served under David (II Sam. 20.24) determined the choice of Adoram for this mission. The institution of the corvée by David, however, has been doubted, though he may have adapted the system, which, on the evidence of the Ras Shamra texts, was already familiar in Canaan, in his crown estates and in such Canaanite cities as he incorporated in his realm. It may be doubted if Adoram was identical with Adoniram, who had held similar offices under David and Solomon (4.6). In any case, we suggest that Adoram was sent to explain the distinction between the occasional corvée which might be levied on Israel, and the perpetual liability of the non-Israelite subjects. On the distinction between the occasional corvée (*mas*) and the corvée involving permanent serfdom (*mas ʿōbēd*), see above on 5.13 and 9.20.

The verb *hitʾammēṣ* indicates not so much the haste with which Rehoboam mounted his chariot as his rallying of his faculties to do so.

19. This passage affords a good instance of the primary meaning of *pāšaʿ*, 'to rebel', the secondary meaning being to rebel against the known will of God, 'to sin' (deliberately).

[a]Alt, 'Zelte und Hütten', *KS* III, pp. 239–42.
[b]See A. R. Johnson, *The One and the Many in the Israelite Conception of God*, 1961².
[c]*A History of Israel* I, 1932, pp. 119 f.

'To this day' dates the passage before the final liquidation of the Northern kingdom with the fall of Samaria in 722.

(*b*) THE ADOPTION OF JEROBOAM AS KING: 12.20

12 [20]And it happened that, when all Israel heard that Jeroboam had returned, they sent and called him to the assembly and made him king over all Israel. There were none following the house of David except the tribe of Judah[a] alone.

12.20. The assembly (*hāʿēdā*) is used of the religious assembly of Israel in the Pentateuch source P, which also employs the term *qāhāl*. Kittel (HKAT, p. 105) notes its use in this sense in this passage. Our opinion also is that the assembly at Shechem was not an *ad hoc* meeting with Rehoboam, but a tribal gathering based on the ancient assembly of the sacral confederacy on the occasion of a holy tryst (*mōʿēd*), when the historical, legal and religious tradition of Israel was kept alive in sacramental experience of the Exodus, covenant and settlement. As such this was a representative, rather than an actual assembly of 'all Israel'.

(*c*) REHOBOAM'S REPRISALS CHECKED BY PROPHETIC INTERVENTION: 12.21–24

Here it is stated that Rehoboam was supported by Judah and Benjamin (vv. 21–23), whereas in v. 20 it is stated that only Judah supported him. The latter statement may be modified by the transposition of the asyndetic v. 17 to the end of v. 20, but this mentions only 'Israelites who lived in the cities of Judah', not 'the tribe of Benjamin'. Kittel (HKAT, p. 105) takes the statement in vv. 21, 23 to reflect the situation after the Exile, when the country about Jerusalem was settled by Benjamin and Judah. There is also a discrepancy between this passage and I K. 14.30, which states that there was war all the time of Jeroboam and Rehoboam. This suggests that vv. 21–24 come from the hand of one living at a later time, when local differences had been forgotten, and to whom civil war in Israel was intolerable. This may reflect the post-exilic period or perhaps the *rapprochement* of Judah and the Northern elements in the time of Josiah. The role of the otherwise obscure prophet Shemaiah may be authentic, the historical basis being perhaps an abatement in the civil war, which, according to I K. 14.30, lasted the reigns of Jeroboam and Rehoboam. The passage may be from the Deuteronomistic

[a]G adds 'and Benjamin', which the singular 'tribe' renders unlikely.

compiler of the monarchic period or from the exilic redactor. The figure and message of Shemaiah, the man of God giving theological orientation at a historical juncture, seems to anticipate a convention characteristic of history-writing in Chronicles, which von Rad[a] has recognized as a development of the Deuteronomic sermon.

12 [21]And Rehoboam came[b] to Jerusalem and gathered all the house of Judah and the tribe of Benjamin, one hundred and eighty thousand[c] picked warriors, to fight with the house of Israel to restore the kingdom to Rehoboam the son of Solomon. [22]And the word of God[d] came to Shemaiah the man of God saying, [23]Say to Rehoboam the son of Solomon, the king of Judah, and all the house of Judah and Benjamin and the rest of the people, [24]Yahweh says, You shall not go up nor fight with your brothers the Israelites. Return each man to his house, for this thing has been brought about by me. So they obeyed the word of Yahweh, and drew back and suspended[e] the expedition according to the word of Yahweh.

12.22. Shemaiah the man of God, i.e. the prophet, appears only here in Kings and in the parallel account in II Chron. 11.2, and in II Chron. 12.5ff., where he is active again on the occasion of Shishak's expedition, when his authority enjoined a solemn fast. In view of the well-known role of the prophet on such occasions in the ancient Near East (e.g. Joel), this may well be historical. Shemaiah seems to have been a Judaean prophet, and in the tradition in the Greek supplement in I K. 12.24o that Shemaiah and not Ahijah figured with Jeroboam in the mantle-rending incident we have surely a late Judaean adaptation. Whatever historical credence may be assigned to the otherwise obscure prophet Shemaiah, the historical basis of the tradition is probably the abatement in the civil war, which would in any case be induced by the expedition of Shishak in Rehoboam's fifth year (14.25–28), with which II Chron. associates Shemaiah, who is depicted as giving a divine word interpreting the historical situation as a divine chastisement, as here (see above, Introduction to this section).

24. The apparently archaic *n* in *tillāḥ*[a]*mūn* may be a case of dittography after *w*.

[a]G. von Rad, 'The Levitical Sermon in I and II Chronicles', *The Problem of the Hexateuch*, pp. 267–80.
[b]Reading the singular with Q.
[c]G[BL] reads 120,000.
[d]Certain MSS read *yhwh* for *'*[e]*lōhīm*.
[e]Reading with G *wayyišb*[e]*tū*, which has possibly been omitted by haplography after *wayyāšūbū* ('and drew back'). This suggests the further emendation, which, however, is not strictly necessary, of *lāleket* to *milleket*.

At 12.24 G, having followed MT in telling the story of the rise of Jeroboam, his acclamation by Ahijah of Shiloh, his flight to Egypt and return to his home town, the death of Solomon and accession of Rehoboam, the revolt of the Northern tribes at Shechem (but significantly omitting participation by Jeroboam), the reaction of Rehoboam towards military reprisals, which, however, were stopped by the oracle of Shemaiah, resumes with the statement of Solomon's death and the accession of Rehoboam and the appraisal of his reign in familiar Deuteronomistic terms (v. 24a according to Swete's text), and proceeds to retell the story of the origin and rise of Jeroboam to the abandonment of Rehoboam's expedition in a long passage (vv. 24b–z) which has no counterpart at this point in MT. The account in G, however, is composed of statements which occur at other places in Kings, though occasionally there is disagreement between G and MT as to details, time, place, and the significance of the incidents, as we may indicate by the following table:

24a. Solomon's death (=11.43), introduction of Rehoboam (cf. 14.21 ff., with variations).

24b. Origin and early career of Jeroboam (cf. 11.26–28, with variations).

24c. Flight from Solomon to Egypt (= 11.40).

24d–f. Jeroboam in Egypt, his marriage, return, fortification of his town, given here as *Sareira* (not represented in MT) cf. MT Zeredah.

24g–n. Jeroboam at *Sareira*; his wife, here named Anoth, consults Ahijah, though Shiloh is not named, as in MT, and she is not in disguise, as in MT; the prophecy of the death of Jeroboam's sick child and of the doom of his house, without any reason given (cf. 14.1–18, with variations, the Deuteronomistic reasons for the doom on Jeroboam's house not being given in G, which also omits any reference to the Exile, which MT includes at v. 15).

24n. Jeroboam assembles the tribes of Israel at Shechem; Rehoboam at Shechem.

24o. The incident of the rent robe, the prophet being Shemaiah, not Ahijah; this was at Shechem, apparently in the presence of Rehoboam (cf. the incident of the rent robe in Ahijah's encounter with Jeroboam before his flight to Egypt and on the road from Jerusalem while Jeroboam was an official of Solomon, 11.29–31).

24p–s. The rejection of Israel's petition to Rehoboam (cf. 12.3–14, where the counsel of the elders and young men to Rehoboam is given more fully).

24t–u. The defection of the tribes except Judah and Benjamin (cf. 12.16).

24x–z. Rehoboam's proposed expedition against the Northern tribes and Shemaiah's dissuasion (cf. 12.21–24, which gives more detail).

It is evident here that in G an independent Northern tradition is cited, but it has been worked over by a Judaean editor, who probably described Jeroboam's mother as a harlot (v. 24b), and assigned Ahijah no place in the early part of Jeroboam's career. As this certainly enhanced the authority of Jeroboam and reflected the real support he had in North Israel of the most conservative elements, this is certainly a North Israelite source. Instead of admitting this the Judaean editor transfers the incident to the assembly at Shechem, where Shemaiah, the Judaean prophet, is given the role of indicating that it was the will of Yahweh to condone the disruption, rather out of disapproval of the absolutism of Rehoboam than out of cordial sympathy for Jeroboam. Jeroboam reigned, that is to say, by the permissive will of Yahweh mediated by a Judaean prophet rather than by cordial divine sanction. The Judaean editor is also probably responsible for the tradition of Jeroboam's marriage with a daughter of the Pharaoh (v. 24e), which is probably a tradition influenced by the tradition of the marriage of Hadad of Edom with a daughter of the Pharaoh (11.19). Other details, representing genuine North Israelite tradition, are worth consideration.

2. SIGNIFICANT EVENTS OF JEROBOAM'S REIGN: 12.25–32

The matter of this passsage concerns events of real historical significance, e.g. the fortification of Shechem and Penuel (v. 25), the elevation of Dan and Bethel to the significance of national shrines to counteract the politico-religious influence of Jerusalem (vv. 26–30), and the institution of the New Year festival with its significance for the ideology of kingship, a month after that at Jerusalem (v. 32). Jeroboam's building and his cultic arrangements at Bethel were no doubt recorded in North Israelite archives, but not in the form in which they are communicated in vv. 25–32. Verse 25, which stands in isolation from the sequel, seems a scrap of a larger statement on

Jeroboam's capital, which was eventually fixed at Tirzah (14.17). Verses 26–32 are, rather, a résumé, almost certainly from a Judaean hand, as indicated by the reference to Rehoboam as 'their master' (v. 27). The specific mention of the Levites, whose exclusive status was not recognized in the cult at Bethel under Jeroboam, has been taken to indicate Deuteronomistic influence, but in view of the role that the Levites had played as the agents of David (see above, p. 296 n.[b]), the measures of Jeroboam may well be historical. The historical résumé in fact may well have come from Levitical circles in Jerusalem, who may also have been responsible for the remarkably objective account of Rehoboam's encounter with the assembly of Israel in Shechem, where their sympathies with the traditions of the old sacral confederacy are apparent. Noth (*op. cit.*, p. 271), who sees vv. 26–32 as the conclusion of vv. 1, 3b–20, emphasizes the affinity in spirit with the Story of the Davidic Succession in the critical attitude to the king of the Davidic house and regards the tradition of the disruption as emanating from a circle in Jerusalem which was influenced by the Succession Story. In this connection the statement of the disruption of the kingdom of Solomon 'to this day' in v. 19 is significant. Noth gives a *terminus ante quem* as 722, which must be accepted, but the statement may rather refer to an earlier date, when a reunification of the kingdom might have been expected, that is, within a generation of the secession, especially if we may accept the statement of war between Jeroboam and Rehoboam 'all their days' (14.30) as indicating that Rehoboam had not given up hope of reunifying the kingdom. In vv. 25–32, however, the source material has possibly been expanded by the Deuteronomistic compiler as an introduction to the following passage 12.33–13.32, as Noth suggests (*op. cit.*, p. 268). This is certainly true of v. 33, but in view of the significance of the New Year festival and the role of the king in it as the executive of the divine king, it is most likely that Jeroboam's establishment of this most important counterpart to the New Year festival in Jerusalem should be noted in conjunction with the foundation of the rival kingdom and so belong to the original source. The dating of the festival in the eighth month, however, i.e. after the spring equinox, as in Mesopotamia, is probably the contribution of the Deuteronomist, as is the animadversion on Jeroboam's officiating at the sacrifice in person. The fact that there is no mention of Shishak's expedition to Northern Israel, which is attested in the Pharaoh's inscription at Karnak and by the remains of his stele at

Megiddo, indicates how selectively matter for Jeroboam's reign has been used. The fact of this omission suggests that, whatever the original source may have been, what we have is a somewhat sketchy summary of events in Northern Israel by a Judaean editor or redactor, the activity of Shishak in Judah (I K. 14.25–26) being of more intimate interest. This is one of the outstanding instances of a significant political event in the history of Israel about which we should know little but for extra-biblical information.

12 [25]And Jeroboam fortified Shechem in the hill-country of Ephraim and dwelt therein, and went out from there and built Penuel. [26]And Jeroboam said to himself, Now will the kingdom revert to the house of David; [27]if this people goes up to sacrifice at the house of Yahweh in Jerusalem then will the heart of the[a] people turn to their master,[b] even to Rehoboam the king of Judah, and they will kill me [c]and return to Rehoboam the king of Judah.[c] [28][d]And he made two golden calves, and said to the people,[e] You have gone up long enough to Jerusalem. Behold your God, O Israel, who brought you up[f] out of the land of Egypt. [29]And he put the one in Bethel and he assigned the other to Dan. [30]And this matter became a sin to Israel,[g] and the people went [h]before the one to Bethel and[h] before the other to Dan. [31]And he made shrines on high places[i] and he made priests from the whole range of the people who were not of the Levites. [32]And Jeroboam made a feast in the eighth month on the fifteenth day of the month like the feast which was in Judah, which[j] he made in Bethel to sacrifice to the calves which he had made, and he posted in Bethel the priests of the high places which he had made.

12.25. Jeroboam did not actually build Shechem, as MT literally means, but he did fortify it. This accords with archaeological

[a]After G^{h} for MT 'this people'.

[b]I.e. Rehoboam and the house of David, but G^{BA} reads *yhwh w*^{e}*ʾel r*^{e}*ḥabʿām* ('to Yahweh and to Rehoboam') which reflects orthodox Jewish contempt for the cult of Bethel and Dan in implying that this was not the worship of Yahweh.

[c]G omits this phrase, which is strictly redundant.

[d]G^{h} omits MT *wayyiwwāʿaṣ hammelek* ('and the king took counsel'); G^{BL}, on the other hand, read *wayyēlek hammelek* ('and the king went'), which may be correct.

[e]Reading with G and L *ʾel-hāʿām* for MT *ʾ*^{a}*lēhem* ('to them').

[f]In Israelite sources this verb was doubtless singular *heʿel*^{e}*kā*, but has been written in the plural *heʿ*^{e}*lūkā* ('gods . . . who brought you up') for polemical reasons.

[g]So G^{L}, for MT, which omits 'to Israel'.

[h]So following the clue of G^{L} for MT, which omits the phrase. The statement of MT 'And the people went before the one to Dan' is obviously incomplete.

[i]The particle *ʾet* introducing the direct accusative must be omitted before the indefinite noun *bēt bāmōt*. Probably we should read the plural *bāttē bāmōt* for the singular in MT.

[j]Omitting *wayyaʿal ʿal-hammizbēaḥ*, which was obviously erroneously repeated here from v. 33a, G reads the relative particle *ʾ*^{a}*šer*.

evidence from Shechem, where Wright[a] attests repair of casemate walling *c.* 900 BC, with ceramic deposits which might be from the occupation of Jeroboam. Strictly, Shechem was in the tribal territory of Manasseh. Its location here 'in the hill-country of Ephraim' indicates that Ephraim was originally a geographic rather than an ethnic term, as in Josh. 20.7 and Judg. 4.5. The strategic significance of Shechem in the narrow neck of the pass from west to east by the *Wādī Fārʿa* and commanding the road through the hills of Manasseh to Bethshean is indicated by the fact that though the capital of Israel was shifted to Tirzah and Samaria those places were in the same vicinity within some seven miles of the old capital. Penuel, east of the Jordan at a ford of the Jabbok, where reputedly Jacob wrestled with the angel (Gen. 32.24ff.), is probably mentioned in the list of the conquests of Shishak, the contemporary of Jeroboam, as Per-nu-al. In the story of Gideon it is noted as a place with a strong tower or fort (Judg. 8.8f., 17), and is apparently a little east of Succoth (perhaps *Ḫirbet Deir ʿAllā*) and on higher ground. Jeroboam's fortification was designed doubtless to secure Gilead, which had remained loyal to David in Absalom's revolt. Merrill, followed by Albright and Glueck, identified Penuel with *Tulūl aḏ-Ḏahab* ('the Mounds of Gold'), so called from the yellow sandstone of which they are composed, standing on the Jabbok about five miles from its junction with the Jordan. Glueck locates Penuel particularly at the eastern mound, where he found Early Iron potsherds, and there is no reason to doubt this location. Gressmann[b] suggests that Jeroboam's occupation of Penuel may have indicated his withdrawal in the face of Shishak's invasion; so also van den Born (*op. cit.*, p. 83), who cites the analogy of Ishbaal's withdrawal to Mahanaim in the face of the Philistine menace in II Sam. 2.8. The fact that, on B. Mazar's feasible reconstruction of Shishak's campaign on the evidence of his inscription at Karnak,[c] Penuel is mentioned may suggest that Jeroboam's withdrawal occasioned the Pharaoh's eastern detour. The occupation of Penuel, however, was more probably designed to secure the influence of Israel over the remnants of David's empire in Transjordan, and to prevent the coercion of North Israelite elements there by Judah.

12.27. On 'their master', *'ᵃdōnēhem*, a plural of majesty, see p. 313 n.[b]. In this case Jeroboam was providing a substitute for the ark as

[a]G. E. Wright, *Shechem*, 1965, pp. 150ff.
[b]*Die älteste Geschichtsschreibung* . . ., p. 250.
[c]'The Campaign of Pharaoh Shishak to Palestine', *SVT* IV, 1957, pp. 57–66.

a symbol of the presence of the invisible God of Israel, probably his throne or footstool (Isa. 6.3, 5) a tradition perhaps already known at Shiloh in the days of the judges (I Sam. 4.4).[a]

12.28. The golden calves, misrepresented by orthodox Jewish opinion as idols, were rather the places where the presence of Yahweh was visualized, like the ark in the Temple in Jerusalem and the bull-pedestals of Baal-Hadad in Syrian sculpture, as pointed out by Albright, after H. T. Obbink.[b] The use of the symbol of the bull, the cult-animal of the Canaanite Baal, indicates syncretism between the worship of Yahweh and the Canaanite nature-cult, to which the language and imagery of many of the psalms refer, particularly those appropriate to the New Year festival.[c] This syncretism had been effected through the appropriation of the liturgies of the peasant's year, notably the New Year festival, when, on the evidence of the Ras Shamra texts, the triumph of Baal over the forces of chaos in nature was celebrated, together with his kingship.[d] On the evidence of such psalms as Pss. 2 and 110, the earthly king and his government were pledges of the kingship and order of God, hence this festival was of great significance in enhancing the status of the king, as Eichrodt[e] has perceived, though we believe that he has overemphasized the propagandist aspect of the conception of the kingship of God, which we maintain to be prior to, and independent of, monarchic propaganda in Israel. It was because of this peculiar propagandist potential of this festival and its 'myth' that Jeroboam established the cult at Bethel and Dan. We believe that it was in respect of the cult of God as King in the New Year festival at Bethel and the reflection of that ideology in the office of the king that

[a]The title *yhwh ṣ^{e}bā'ōt* was apparently specifically the title of God at Shiloh (I Sam. 4.4), though the conception of the ark as his throne or footstool in I Sam. 4.4 may reflect the later Jerusalem tradition. Possibly, however, through the association of Yahweh, whose presence was symbolized by the ark, with the New Year festival in the time of the judges in the Israelite adaptation of the Canaanite ideology of the kingship of Baal proper to that occasion, the ark may already have been associated with Yahweh as King. J. Gray, 'Gud som konge og nyttårsfesten. II, Den historiske anvendelse av nyttårfestens tema i Israel', *NTT* LXVIII, 1967, pp. 134–41.

[b]H. T. Obbink, 'Jahwebilder', *ZAW* XLVII, 1929, pp. 264–74.

[c]J. Gray. 'The Hebrew Conception of the Kingship of God: its Origin and Development', *VT* VI, 1956, pp. 268ff.; 'The Kingship of God in the Prophets and Psalms', *VT* XI, 1961, pp. 1–29.

[d]A. S. Kapelrud, 'Jahves tronstigningsfest og funnene i Ras Sjamra', *NTT*, 1940, pp. 38–58.

[e]*Theology of the Old Testament* I, 1961, pp. 195ff.

Amaziah in the time of Amos characterized Bethel as 'a royal shrine' and 'the shrine of the kingdom' (Amos 7.13). J. A. Soggin[a] does well to point out that Jeroboam's development of the cult at Bethel with its highlight, the New Year festival, was conditioned by the same situation as in Solomon's reign, the presence of an even greater proportion of Canaanites in his territorial state, with an important economic and military potential. The syncretism, however, also reflects the assimilation of significant elements of the Canaanite fertility cult by Israel, on which later Hosea was to animadvert. 'Behold your God' (actually, as the verb indicates, 'your gods') 'who brought you up out of the land of Egypt' is re-echoed in Ex. 32.4, 8 (J) at the incident of the golden calf at Sinai. The plural of the noun, which has significance only with reference to gods of Dan and Bethel, indicates that the Exodus passage, a later expansion of J, has been elaborated to cast aspersion on Jeroboam's cult.[b] The words ascribed to Jeroboam also summarize Israel's *Heilsgeschichte*, her declaration of faith in God active in her redemption. Similar words also introduce the Decalogue.

12.29. Bethel, modern *Beitīn*, 11 miles north of Jerusalem in Benjamin, lay in the path of pilgrims going south along the ridge of the central highlands to Jerusalem. The sanctuary, as suggested in 13.13, was at some distance from the town and is specifically to be located on the evidence of Gen. 12.8 at *Burj Beitīn*, about three-quarters of a mile south-east of *Beitīn*, where Byzantine building is still visible above ground and probably also the natural rock altar with limestone shelves forming natural steps, which may have suggested the tradition of Jacob's ladder (Gen. 28.12ff.).[c] Dan (*Tell al-Qāḍī*) was in the extreme north. On the basis of one of the fragments of the Baal-myth from Ras Shamra, where certain localities in Upper Galilee and southern Syria seem to be named, R. Dussaud has plausibly conjectured that at Dan, which was a Phoenician settlement before the Israelite occupation, the cult of Baal was long domiciled.[d] Besides being an important shrine at the boundary of northern Israel, where transactions with her neighbours might be ratified, the sanctuary of Dan was important from the time of the judges as an oracle-shrine (II

[a]J. A. Soggin, *Das Königtum in Israel*, BZAW CIV, 1967, p. 95.

[b]So Noth, *Exodus*, p. 246.

[c]For the stratification of the site after excavation see J. L. Kelso, *BASOR* 137, 1955, pp. 5–10.

[d]'Cultes cananéens au source du Jourdain d'après les textes de Ras Shamra', *Syria* XVII, 1936, pp. 283–95.

Sam. 20.18 G), as the association with ephod and teraphim suggests (Judg. 17f.). Jeroboam's concentration on the development of features of the Canaanite fertility cult to emphasize the kingship of God and the role of the king as his executive may have been designed to counteract the Levitical influence at the tribal sanctuary, and we may detect disparagement of the older cult by the royal priests in the mild though subtle mockery of the older cult in Judg. 17f., which emphasizes the origin of the cult-instruments in stolen silver and of the priesthood in a runaway Levite.[a]

12.30. Verse 30a is almost certainly a later gloss. The phrase 'the people went before the one . . .' has occasioned some doubt. Our opinion is that it means that the people made pilgrimage to the shrine where the symbol was set up, but it has also been suggested (Benzinger, Šanda, Kittel, Skinner, Noth) that an inaugural procession is indicated, to which we may cite the analogy of David's installation of the ark in Jerusalem with such a festal procession.

31. Houses on high places, local centres of the fertility-cult, are also imputed to Jeroboam. There is abundant evidence of many cult-centres in North Israel in the monarchy, e.g. Carmel in the time of Elijah, Gilgal and Beersheba (possibly 'the high places of Isaac' in Amos), and Mizpeh and Tabor (Hos. 5.1). The present verse is no doubt an effort of the Deuteronomist to impute this multiplicity of shrines to Jeroboam. The Deuteronomistic viewpoint is also thought to be reflected in the animadversion on Jeroboam's non-Levitical priests. But this may also reflect the viewpoint of Levitical circles in Jerusalem against the deliberate policy of Jeroboam to eliminate the Levites in the North as agents of the Davidic House (see above, p. 296 n.[b]). There is no ground for the AV translation 'from the lowest of the people' for *miqeṣōt hāʿām*; the evidence of Gen. 47.2, Ezek. 33.2, and particularly Num. 22.41, where Balaam looks upon the whole camp of Israel, indicates that the meaning is 'the mass' or 'whole range' of the people.

32. *ḥag* should be probably translated 'New Year festival', the Feast of Tabernacles on the eve of the New Year, which was *the* festival *par excellence*, *heḥāg*. The root in Arabic signifies 'pilgrimage', and this is probably implied in the Hebrew word also, this being one of the three feasts to which pilgrimage was obligatory. It corresponded to the similar festival in Jerusalem in the seventh

[a]M. Noth, 'The Background of Judges 17–18', *Israel's Prophetic Heritage*, ed. B. W. Anderson and W. Harrelson, 1962, pp. 68–85.

month, at which the Temple was dedicated. It has been suggested that there was no hard and fast time for this harvest festival in the early monarchy and that the establishment of the festival at Bethel in the eighth month might indicate a later harvest than in the south. The distance between Jerusalem and Bethel is not so marked as to occasion the difference of one month in harvest, and in fact rain is actually earlier at Bethel, which is higher than Jerusalem, so that this would occasion a somewhat earlier harvest. Actually the dating of the festival in the seventh month, reckoning from the vernal equinox as in Mesopotamia, may reflect exilic usage, the festival in pre-exilic times being according to the harvest, perhaps later as in that of Jeroboam. But Rehoboam's appearance at Shechem may have been to be confirmed as king of North Israel, having probably just acceded as king over Judah at the New Year festival, perhaps a day or two before, during the seven-day festival. Hence Jeroboam may have hastened to celebrate in the following month a counterpart of the Jerusalem festival which combined the sacrament of the covenant (cf. v. 28b), the essential element in the gathering of the sacral confederacy at Shechem in the days of the Judges, with the royal-divine ideology of the Canaanite New Year festival. The latter element particularly was vital to Jeroboam's own prestige as king. The precise dating, 'on the fifteenth day' of the eighth month, possibly reflects the later fixing of the Feast of Tabernacles after the exile (Lev. 23.39a, 41b), though this festival probably always coincided with the full moon (Ps. 81.3[4]) in the middle of the seventh or eighth month.

3. PROPHETIC TRADITION OF THE REIGN OF JEROBOAM: 12.33–14.18

The original stratum of this section consists of 12.33–13.32 and 14.1–6, 12, 17f.; 13.33f. and 14.7–11, 13–16 are Deuteronomistic comment.

The relationship between I K. 12.33–13.32 and the account of Josiah's reformation in II K. 23.15–20 is obvious, not only in the mention of Josiah in I K. 13.2, which is obviously a late accretion, but even more in the encounter between the prophets who shared the same grave (I K. 13.7–32), which was apparently a conspicuous monument at Bethel in Josiah's time. As to whether the tradition in I K. 12.33–13.32 influenced the account of Josiah's reformation at Bethel or was a later prophetic legend reconstructed in the light of events in Josiah's time, we have no doubt that the tradition was an ancient one, though attracting accretions throughout the ages, and that it influenced the account of Josiah's reformation at Bethel, as is apparent from the artificial way in which II K. 23.16–18 is introduced.

Wellhausen suggested that the incident of Amos, a prophet of Judah, at Bethel, underlay the tradition in I K. 12.33–13.32, and certainly both Amos (3.13–15; 4.5) and the man of God from Judah in I K. 13.1–32 denounced the cult and sanctuary at Bethel, proclaiming the ruin of the sanctuary. This is sufficient to suggest that in certain other details the tradition of Amos may have influenced that in I K. 12.33–13.32. Amos, however, unlike the man of God, denounced the cult and sanctuary at Bethel not as a rival to that in Jerusalem, but since it was divorced from the moral basis and content of true religion. But the denunciation of the Bethel cult, introduced as it was by the account of Jeroboam's rival cult at Bethel in I K. 12.26–32, and his exclusion of the Levites and his presumption to officiate in person, may reflect the influence of the Deuteronomistic compiler(s), to whom the cult at Bethel, from the relish with which its desecration by Josiah is described, was particularly abhorrent. Noth, who emphasizes that the naming of the king as Jeroboam is secondary (*op. cit.*, p. 293), attributes the tradition of the man of God's denunciation of the Bethel cult to prophetic circles, opposed to the cult in North Israel towards the end of the Northern Kingdom (*ibid.*, p. 294). In this case, the association with Jeroboam, who promoted the cult at Bethel as a rival to Jerusalem, may be part of the Deuteronomistic development of the original tradition. On the other hand, the resentment of Bethel and the New Year Festival at Jerusalem may reflect the feelings of conservatives in Jeroboam's time, who rightly saw it as a menace to the solidarity and traditional worship of Israel, which were given expression in this festival, which by this time was traditionally associated with the Feast of Tabernacles on the eve of the New Year (Deut. 31.10) in the Temple at Jerusalem, which, as housing the ark, was the real sanctuary of Israel. The insistence on the observance of this particular festival 'before Yahweh' in the early festal calendar in Ex. 23.10–19 (E) and the Ritual Code (Ex. 34.10–26, J) visualized the sacrament at the central sanctuary of the sacral confederacy in the pre-monarchic period as a precaution against the impairing of the solidarity and distinctive self-consciousness of Israel through the assimilation of local Canaanite features associated with the New Year festival at local shrines. In centralizing the cult, the reformation of Josiah which the Deuteronomic circles supported was simply implementing an earlier tradition, which was still familiar in the early monarchy on the evidence of the Ritual Code incorporated in the J source of the Pentateuch and the festal calendar in Ex. 23.10–19, which was later incorporated in E. We would suggest that the historical nucleus of I K. 13.1–6 was an incident in which a prophet from Judah denounced the cult at Bethel for such motives, quite possibly in the presence of Jeroboam himself, as he officiated. The authentication of a significant word of God by a portent (*mōpēt*)—not, however, necessarily immediate—is so well established in prophetic tradition that the proclamation of the portent in v. 3 must be admitted as original, though the account of its implementation in v. 5, which is intrusive, is probably secondary (so Noth, *op. cit.*, pp. 297f.). The reference to the desecration of the altar at Bethel by human bones (v. 2b) may be, as Noth suggests (*op. cit.*, pp. 293f.), primary, and the reference to this as the work of a Davidic king who shall burn the bodies of the priests of the 'high places' is secondary. Certainly the reference to Josiah is from the Deuteronomist. The incident of the paralysing of the arm of the king raised to direct the arrest of the man of God (v. 4) is also in our opinion secondary, though pre-Deuteronomistic, an expansion characteristic of prophetic legend, which Fichtner (*op. cit.*, p. 205) rightly compares to the annihilation by fire from heaven of the soldiers sent by Ahaziah to Elijah (II K. 1.9ff.) and the mauling by the two bears of the boys of Bethel who insulted Elisha (II K. 2.23). The historical nucleus is the courage and confidence of the man of God, another feature which the tradition shares with the incident of Amos at Bethel—but it has been elaborated in the hagiology of Bethel in the miracle in vv. 4, 6.

The incident in vv. 7–10, where the man of God rejects the king's invitation, or inducement, to hospitality, is joined, so far as content is concerned, with the sequel in vv. 11–32, where the prophet of Bethel, with fatal consequences, persuades the man of God to share a meal with him, an important factor both in vv. 7–10 and 11–32 being the prohibition of this through the word of God. For this reason, and through stylistic considerations, we now admit with Fichtner,[a] Noth[b] and M. A. Klopfenstein[c] that vv. 7–32 and

[a] *Ibid.*, pp. 203ff. [b] *Op cit.*, pp. 292ff.
[c] 'I Könige 13', *Parrhesia* (Barth Festschrift), 1966, ed. E. Busch, J. Fangmeier and M. Geiger, pp. 648ff.

probably also the original matter in 12.33–13.6 is a unity. In our commentary, however, to facilitate treatment, we shall break up the text into 12.33–13.10 and 13.11–32.

The unity of the basic tradition in 12.33–13.32 is obscured by the embellishments of prophetic legend throughout, to say nothing of Deuteronomic accretions by the compiler, such as the reference to 'Josiah' (v. 2) and to the province of 'Samaria' (v. 32), which must post-date 734, when the district of Samaria alone was left to Israel after Tiglath-Pileser III had incorporated Gilead, Galilee and Sharon as provinces of the Assyrian Empire, or even after Sargon's organization of the province of Samaria after the fall of Samaria in 722 and the revolt of 720. This unity is suggested by the style of the narrative, which, with its verbatim repetition of the main motif of the genuine divine commission 'by the word of Yahweh' (vv. 1, 2, 5, 9, 17, 18, 32) and the double invitation to a meal (vv. 7, 15) and the double refusal of the man of God, citing the divine command (vv. 8f.; 16f.), is reminiscent of the saga style, as in the patriarchal legends and particularly in the traditions of Elijah (e.g. the Horeb incident, 19.9–18, and the incident when Elijah called down fire to destroy the envoys of Ahaziah, II. K. 1.1–16, and the translation of Elijah, K. 2.1–18). There is unity of content also, which is apparent when we are not distracted by the secondary motif of the ineluctable divine commission of the prophet—another feature which may reflect the influence of the Amos tradition, e.g. Amos 3.6a, and particularly v. 8:

> The lion has roared;
> Who will not fear?
> The Lord God has spoken;
> Who can but prophesy?

Klopfenstein[a] finds this unity of theme in the effort of the prophet of Bethel to succeed where the king had failed, namely to nullify the prophetic word against the sanctuary of Bethel according to a primitive mechanical view of the quasi-magical operation of the word of God, by persuading him against his divine commission to take a meal. The view that it was possible to frustrate the purpose of God by the intervention of other factors and activities is indicated by the divine commission through Elisha to Gehazi to go on his healing mission without giving or returning greeting (II. K 4.29) and

[a]*Op. cit.*, pp. 646ff.; so also Noth, *op. cit.*, pp. 298, 300.

by Elisha's use of a new bowl in restoring the fertility of the water of the spring of Jericho (II K. 2.20). There are, however, possible explanations of the theme of the meal in relation to the denunciation of the cult of Bethel, which do equal justice to the essential unity of the passage.

The response of the man of God to the king's appeal to him to exercise the prophetic office of intercession—another feature in common with the Amos tradition (Amos 7.16)—could well be a pre-Deuteronomistic tradition. The meal and the present offered (v. 7), apart from being ordinary expressions of hospitality and respect, had the ulterior motive of associating the threatened party with the agent of God, who had the power of blessing through physical contact. The curse might thus be turned to a blessing according to the primitive view of the operation of both, cf. Jacob's present to Esau (Gen. 33.10f.). On the refusal of the man of God, the prophet of Bethel uses his prophetic status and alleged revelation to achieve what the king had been unable to do—and with fatal result.

This, true as it may be, still does not take full account of the monumental character of the tomb of the man of God from Judah, which was a notable feature of Bethel in the time of Josiah, and which attests the originality of the tradition of the death of the prophet as a testimony of the validity of his unwelcome word. We agree with Noth (*op. cit.*, pp. 295ff.) that this was central to the original tradition. It is for this reason that we persist in our view that, partially true as the above explanations may be, the real explanation, which implies the essential unity of the passage, is that the prophet of Bethel was testing the authority of his colleague. Like the king, he was disturbed, and was compelled to discover if he really had the authority of God and was not the agent of political opponents of the regime in North Israel, as Amos was suspected of being by Amaziah the priest (Amos 7.10–12). He concentrates on the alleged divine command not to eat or drink and to go back another way (v. 17), which the man of God had cited in rejecting the king's invitation (v. 9), which indicates the essential unity of the chapter. If the man of God could evade this word of God with impunity, this would reflect on the seriousness of his oracle of doom on the cult and sanctuary of Bethel, a matter in which the prophet of Bethel, both as prophet and as a member of the prophetic guild attached to the sanctuary (so Fichtner, *op. cit.*, p. 207), was vitally interested. The sudden death of the man of God, however it may have occurred, authenticated the oracle, so that his status and commission were recognized by the prophet of Bethel, who discharged the mourning rites and buried him in his family tomb (v. 30). The tomb became a local monument, like a *wālī* among the Arabs, the tomb of one regarded as a notable saint, or agent of God, or the possessor of the *baraka*, or blessing. As such it was distinguished among the tombs of Bethel in the time of Josiah (II K. 23.17), which denotes the antiquity of the tradition.

Like most incidents of such a striking character, the historical nucleus of the incident has been elaborated in tradition and has attracted various secondary elements. As developed locally at Bethel and in prophetic circles, the proclamation of the portent became a miracle (v. 5); the courage of the man of God in the discharge of his unpalatable mission in the presence of the king himself was embellished by the miracle of the paralysis of the king's arm (v. 4), and is accompanied by the miracle in reverse (v. 6). This is a familiar motif in prophetic legend, cf. Moses and the signs of the staff and serpent and the leprosy on his hand (Ex. 4.1–7), Gideon and the dew (Judg. 6.36–40) and Isaiah and the shadow (II K. 20.9–11). The manner of the sudden death of the man of God may also be an elaboration of the prophetic legend. A lion is not impossible near Bethel, especially if the man of God returned by the east side of the watershed, which is rocky, desolate country, but the behaviour of the lion is so unnatural as to prompt Gressmann's characterization '*ein rechter Märchenlöwe*' ('a real folk-tale lion'). It is possible that Amos' saying regarding the lion in his passage on the prophetic urge gave rise to the tradition which was further embellished didactically: the lion being the instrument of God's purpose, refraining from harming the ass or eating the body of the man, doing nothing more or less than what God requires (so Fichtner, *op. cit.*, p. 209; Noth, *op. cit.*, pp. 301f.), is here cited didactically in animadversion on the departure of the man of God from the strict command of God. We have noted the many features in common with the tradition of Amos at Bethel which may have affected the basic tradition of I K. 12.33–13.32. Apart from the Deuteronomistic epilogue, the specific naming of Josiah in v. 2b and the designation of the North Kingdom as Samaria (v. 32) are almost certainly Deuteronomistic, and possibly the inclusion of the incident in the history of the reign of Jeroboam. Here was a tradition congenial to the Deuteronomistic compiler(s), who used it to demonstrate that the cult of Bethel was foredoomed by God right from its development under Jeroboam.

(*a*) THE ORACLE OF THE MAN OF GOD FROM JUDAH ON THE CULT AT BETHEL: 12.33–13.10

Prophetic legend in saga style, transmitted by the Deuteronomistic compiler. 12.33 is a transitional passage, introducing 13.1–32. It has been adapted to the previous, originally independent, account (12.26–32). 13.1b is parenthetical; note that the king, who in the rest of the passage is anonymous, is here named Jeroboam.

12 [33]And he offered whole burnt offerings on the altar which he had made in Bethel on the fifteenth day of the eighth month at the feast[a] which he had devised of his own fancy,[b] and he made a feast for the Israelites and went up upon the altar to make his offering.

13 [1]Now behold a man of God came from Judah by the word of Yahweh to Bethel, and Jeroboam was standing by the altar to make a burnt offering. [2]And he cried out against the altar by the word of Yahweh and said, O altar, altar, thus says Yahweh, Behold a son shall be born to the house of David, Josiah by name, and he shall slaughter upon you priests of the high places who burn incense upon you, and he shall burn[c] human bones upon you. [3]And he gave a portent that day saying, This is the portent which Yahweh has declared, Lo the altar shall be rent and the residue of fat which is thereon shall be scattered. [4]And it came to pass, when the king heard the word of the man of God which he had proclaimed against the altar in Bethel, that Jeroboam stretched forth his hand from the altar saying, Seize him! And his hand which he had stretched forth against him shrivelled up and he could not withdraw it again to himself. [5]And the altar was rent and the residue of fat was scattered from the altar according to the portent which the man of God had given by the word of Yahweh. [6]And the king replied and said to the man of God, Please placate Yahweh your God (and intercede for me)[d] that my hand be restored to me. So the man of God placated Yahweh and the king's hand was restored to him and became as it was before. [7]And the king spoke to the man of God (saying), Come in with me and take nourishment and let me give you a gift. [8]And the man of God said to the king, If you were to give me half of your house I will not come with you nor will I eat bread nor drink water in this place, [9]for so did Yahweh command me with the word[e] saying, You shall not eat bread nor drink water nor return by

[a]G supplies the necessary antecedent 'at the feast' (*beḥāg*), which is corrupted to *baḥōdeš* in MT.

[b]So Q *millibbō* for MT *millibbōd*.

[c]Reading singular with G, S, and V for plural of MT, which would still be admissible as indicating the indefinite subject.

[d]This phrase is omitted in G^{BL} and L, which we should probably follow. It was probably introduced into MT as a theological gloss to soften the crudity of the phrase 'soften the face of Yahweh', see note.

[e]The verb 'commanded' requires the subject expressed here, Yahweh possibly being the expressed subject, though the separation of subject so far from object would not be usual. We follow G and S in reading *baddābār*, 'by the word' or 'in the word', i.e. the actual message committed to the prophet.

the way which you go. [10]So he went by another way and did not return by the way by which[a] he came to Bethel.

12.33. The nucleus of this passage, which mentioned the New Year festival as the occasion when the king officiated in person, was independent of 12.32 and was the introduction to the sequel. It has been worked over by the Deuteronomistic compiler in the light of 12.26–32 (see introduction to the section).

bādā' is cognate with Arabic *badā*, whence the noun *badā'* ('caprice') is derived. L. Kopf (*op. cit.*, p. 165) cites the usage in Neh. 6.8, the only other instance of the fact in the OT, and emphasizes the sense of 'creation' in the Arabic cognate.

13.1. The fact that the prophet is unnamed has already been noted. The designation 'man of God' probably signifies a somewhat obscure member of a prophetic guild, but may be used here to denote the particular divine commission of the man as distinct from the profession of the 'prophet'. Josephus[b] gives the name of the prophet as Yadon. This is possibly Hebrew *ya'adōn*, which may be, by metathesis, *'īdōn*, possibly that *'iddō* of II Chron. 13.22, whose 'legend' is cited as a source for the events of Abijah's reign. It is possible, however, that *'iddō* here may be a common noun rather than a proper name, *'ōdēd* being found as a common noun for 'soothsayers' or 'prophets' in the Aramaic inscription of Zakir king of Hamath and La'ash.[c] The word of Yahweh with which the man of God was charged was probably in the original incident a simple denunciation of the cult at Bethel, to be implemented by a portent, the destruction of the altar. This catastrophe may have been by earthquake or tremor, or it may have been the effect of fire on the stones, in which case it may have given rise to the tradition of a prophetic word. On the other hand, the prophetic portent may have been visualized in the indefinite future, the tradition of its immediate realization being secondary, but pre-Deuteronomistic, as indicated by the awkward insertion of v. 5. See introduction to the section. The tradition has been elaborated and particularized under Deuteronomistic influence in the light of Josiah's measures against Bethel in the reformation of 622. In this secondary development there is a much more mechanical view of the word of God which recalls the Deuteronomic test of the validity of prophecy in Deut. 13.

[a]*derek* is usually masculine, which would suggest the emendation of *bāh* to *bō*; the noun, however, is occasionally feminine.

[b]*Ant.* VIII, 9.1.

[c]M. Lidzbarski, *Ephemeris für semitische Epigraphik* III, 1915, pp. 1–11.

Jeroboam is depicted as standing 'on the altar', i.e. on the steps leading up to it. On *l^ehaqṭīr* with the general meaning 'to make burnt-offering' see on 11.8.

13.2. The naming of the reforming king Josiah is either a *vaticinium post eventum*, or, more probably, a later gloss. The sequel with its literal fulfilment in the Josianic reformation (II K. 23.16–18) suggests that the original tradition was reshaped in the light of later events, though it is possible that there was an original prophetic denunciation of the cult and altar of Bethel in the colourful language of v. 2, omitting the name of Josiah, which suggested the deliberate destruction of Bethel in the particular detail described in II K. 23.16–18. In the account of Josiah's desecration of Bethel the slaughter (*zbḥ*) of priests on the altar is introduced as an afterthought (II K. 23.20) under the influence of the present passage.

3. The use of *w^e* with the perfect *nātan* is late and suggests midrashic elaboration of the original word of God in v. 2. With *mōpēt* we are introduced to a word denoting, if not miracle, at least portent. It is found in parallelism with 'sign' (*'ōt*) in Ex. 7.3; Deut. 6.22; Ps. 78.43, etc., and with 'wonder' (*niplā'ā*) in Ps. 105.5, a token of God's immediate activity to the fulfilment of his purpose inexplicable to man through secondary causes. Here, as in Ex. 7.9, it is found with the verb *nātan* in the sense of giving a token in authentication of a prophetic mission, in both cases the miraculous being an element. The derivation is uncertain.

niqra' suggests the splitting of masonry, possibly by earthquake or by fire. If an immediate incident is denoted, as assumed in v. 5, cold water may have been spilt on the hot stones by accident or contrivance, or perhaps some piece of limestone softer than the rest had calcinated and caused a rift in the altar. The residue of fat (*dešen*), with which the ashes were saturated was that part of the sacrifice reserved to Yahweh, and so had to be very carefully disposed of in a 'clean' place (Lev. 1.16; 4.12; 6.10ff.). The portent involving the unceremonious scattering of the fat signified that the fat was 'common' and the sacrifice invalid.

4. Here is a further elaboration of the prophetic legend, in which miracle is peculiarly at home. Withering, lit. 'drying up', from the root *yābēš*, is the common expression for nervous paralysis until the Gospels, cf. Zech. 11.17. Nervous paralysis might be the natural result of a shock received by a mind which firmly believed in the power of imitative magic involved in the word of God, and such cases are commonly experienced in primitive societies in Africa or Australia. Biblical instances of miracle, however, are to be related to their peculiar literary sources, and this case, like most miracles outside the Pentateuch, is preserved in prophetic legend, which adduces yet more fatuous cases, e.g. Jonah and the great fish. The factual basis of the tradition may be the stretching forth of the hand to command arrest having no effect owing to the popular dread of the word of God in the mouth of the prophet.

13.6. *wayyaʿan*, taken in its usual meaning 'and he replied', implies an answer to an address. This might be the oracle which had so shocked Jeroboam, or it may have been the withering of his hand as a divine word in action, to which the king replied. In the Ras Shamra texts, however, the verb is often used in the sense of 'he spoke up' rather than 'he replied'. 'Placate Yahweh' (*ḥal-nāʾ ʾet-pᵉnē yhwh*) means literally 'Sweeten' (or 'make smooth') 'the face of Yahweh', probably going back to primitive usage, where some concrete symbol of the presence (*pᵉnē*) of Yahweh was smeared with oil, e.g. Jacob's pillar at Bethel (Gen. 28.18). The intercessory office of the prophet is well known, e.g. I Sam. 7.8; Amos 7.1–6, which is particularly significant with reference to the present passages.

7. 'Come in with me' (*bōʾā ʾittī habbayᵉtāh*) does not signify 'Come home', since a place in Bethel is visualized. Possibly Jeroboam had a house in Bethel; more probably the *liškā* or dining-hall of the sanctuary is visualized, which had been a feature of the sanctuary at Shiloh (I Sam. 1.18, G). On the significance of the meal and present as a means of sharing the *bᵉrākā* or divine blessing, see introduction to the section.

9. 'With the word' (so G and S) signifies that the ban on eating and drinking was part and parcel of the message which he was commissioned to deliver. On the significance of the uninterrupted discharge of the divine commission, see introduction to this section, pp. 321f.

(*b*) THE PROPHET OF JUDAH AND THE OLD PROPHET OF BETHEL: 13.11–32

See the introduction to the section, pp. 320ff.

13 [11]Now there was a certain[a] old prophet living in Bethel, and his sons[b] came[b] and told[b] him all that the man of God had done that day

[a]G[L], very feasibly, reads *ʾaḥēr* ('another') for MT *ʾeḥād*.
[b]Reading with G, S, L, and V plural throughout for MT singular.

in Bethel and[a] the words that he had spoken to the king, and they repeated them to their father. [12]And their father spoke to them saying,[b] Where is the way he went? And his sons showed him[c] the way taken by the man of God who came from Judah. [13]And he said to his sons, Harness me the ass. And they harnessed the ass for him, and he mounted it, [14]and went after the man of God and found him sitting under the terebinth and he said to him, Are you the man of God who came from Judah? And he said, I am. [15]And he said to him, Come to the house with me and eat bread. [16]And he said, I cannot go back with you or go with you,[d] nor will I eat bread nor drink water[e] in this place, [17]for I had a word along with the word of Yahweh, You shall not eat bread nor drink water there; you shall not go back again by the way which you go. [18]And he said to him, I also am a prophet like you, and an angel spoke to me with the word of Yahweh saying, Bring him back with you to your house that he may eat bread and drink water; and[f] he lied to him. [19]So he went back with him[g] and ate bread in his house and drank water. [20]And they were sitting at the table when the word of Yahweh came to the prophet who had brought him back, [21]and he cried out to the man of God who came from Judah saying, Thus says Yahweh, Because you have defied the word of God and have not kept the commandment which Yahweh your God gave you, [22]but have returned and eaten bread and drunk water in the place concerning which he spoke to you saying, You shall not eat bread nor drink water (there); your corpse shall not come into the grave of your fathers. [23]And it came to pass, after he had eaten bread and drunk water,[h] that he harnessed the ass for the prophet whom he had brought back. [24]And he went away, and a lion came upon him on the way and killed him, and his corpse was thrown down on the road, and the ass was standing by it, and the lion was standing by the body. [25]And behold men passed by and saw the body lying on the road and the lion standing by the body, and they came and told it in the city where the old prophet lived. [26]And the prophet who had brought him back from his journey heard and said, It is the man of God who defied the commandment of Yahweh, and Yahweh has given him to the lion and it has mauled him and killed him according to the word of Yahweh which he spoke to him. [27]And he spoke to his sons saying, Harness me the ass. And they harnessed it. [28]And he went and found his corpse lying on the road and the[i] ass and the lion standing by the corpse; and the lion had not eaten the corpse

[a]Reading 'and' with G[L], S, and V.
[b]Inserting 'saying' (*lē'mōr*) with G.
[c]Reading *wayyar'ūhū* after G, T, and L for MT *wayyir'ū* ('and they saw').
[d]Gh and L omit 'and go in with you'.
[e]Omitting 'with you' (*'itt[e]kā*) of MT after G and L.
[f]Reading the conjunction *w[e]* with G and S, as the syntax demands.
[g]Pointing the same consonants differently, G[BL] read 'and he brought him back' (*wayyāšeb 'ōtō*) for MT *wayyāšob 'ittō* ('and he returned with him').
[h]Inserting 'water' (*mayim*) with G, L, and V.
[i]So many MSS instead of the indefinite noun.

and had not mauled the ass. [29]So the prophet lifted up the corpse of the man of God and laid it on[a] the ass, [b]and the prophet brought him back to the city[b] to give him mourning rites and burial. [30]And he laid his corpse in his grave and they lamented for him (saying), Alas my brother! [31]And it happened that after he had buried him he said to his sons, When I die you shall bury me in the grave where the man of God is buried;[c] lay my bones by his bones.[c] [32]For the thing he proclaimed by the word of Yahweh against the altar which is in Bethel and against all the shrines of the high places which are in the cities of Samaria shall certainly come to pass.

13.11. Throughout this section the distinction between 'the man of God' from Judah and the prophet (*hannābī'*) from Bethel is consistently preserved. The significance of the distinction is not clear. Both seem to have been members of prophetic guilds. If the distinction was made first in the Judaean version of the tradition, 'man of God' (*'īš 'elōhīm*) might indicate specific divine authority whereas *nābī'* might be a derogatory term suggesting rather 'dervish', one given to 'prophetic' yoga to induce reception of the word of God. If the distinction was an element in the original tradition of Bethel, *nābī'* might indicate a member of a recognized prophetic guild whose status was probably authenticated by ecstatic propensities and 'man of God' a prophet whose affiliations were unknown and whose sole claim to prophetic status in the eyes of the people of Bethel was his ministry of the word of God unaccompanied by abnormal behaviour.

The repetition of the verb in *wayesapperūm* ('and they repeated them') has been suspect, and G, reading 'and they turned the attention' (lit. 'face') of their father, suggests Hebrew *wayyāsirū penē 'abīhem*. In view of the different objects of the verb in this sentence, however, we consider that the first verb might express the general narrative and the second the actual repetition of the prophet's words. The incident at the altar obviously happened at a distance from the town of Bethel, where the old prophet lived, and this suggests that the sanctuary was located at *Ḫirbet Burj Beitīn*, about three-quarters of a mile south-east of *Beitīn* (Bethel). The old prophet remained in the town, probably because of his age. Fichtner's view that his 'sons' are

[a]Reading *'al* with G for MT *'el*, a common scribal error in MT.
[b]So G for MT 'and he came into the city of the old prophet'.
[c]G and L read here 'by his bones lay me so that my bones may escape with his bones'. This is evidently influenced by the account of Josiah's reformation in II K. 23.18, but, as the whole passage is so influenced, this may well be the original meaning.

not his family but the members of the prophetic guild which acknowledged him as its head (*op. cit.*, p. 207) is possible, but not certain.

13.14. The use of the definite article with 'terebinth' (*hā' ēlā*) has been considered as indicating a well-known tree in the vicinity of Bethel, possibly that reputed to mark the grave of Deborah the nurse of Rebekah (Gen. 35.8). The vital objection to this view of Kittel and Skinner is that this tree is not *'ēlā* ('terebinth') but *'allōn* ('oak'), as noted by Šanda (I, p. 353), who cites Hos. 4.13, where the two are clearly distinguished. Šanda also cites an apparent case of a singular noun with the definite article signifying the indefinite noun in Gen. 14. This, however, is a case of a collective singular, which may also be the sense of *hā 'ēlā*.

15. On the motive of the prophet of Bethel, see introduction to the section, p. 322. There seems to be a double significance in the word *dābār* here. The word of God was the primary message with which the prophet was entrusted, the denunciation of the cult and shrine of Bethel, but together with this was the verbal injunction, literally interpreted, to abstain from food and drink in his mission.

17. The injunction of God may have been not to return by the same road as he had come, possibly to avoid molestation. But *derek* in such a context may mean 'mission' rather than 'road', and in this case the injunction would be not to be hindered or detained in his mission.

18. The prophet (*nābī'*) of Bethel admits common status with the 'man of God' in his words 'I also am a prophet as you'. The revelation claimed by the prophet of Bethel is admittedly not direct, but through an angel or messenger, *mal'āk*, unqualified by Yahweh, which is usual in the Pentateuch, particularly in E, and is paralleled in the Elijah narrative in I K. 19.5. In both instances we have North Israelite traditions, which may reflect here the theology of E in introducing an intermediary between God and man. In the present passage, however, the usage is perhaps a means of avoiding a deliberate lie in the name of God, which might have called down immediate wrath.

'He lied to him', introduced in MT without a conjunction, may be a later gloss, though *w* could easily have been omitted by haplography between *m* and *k*, both of which, particularly the latter, it closely resembles in the proto-Hebraic script.

20. *šulḥān*, generally translated 'table', has been taken to mean 'that which is spread out', from the root *šālaḥ* ('to send forth', 'let go free'), and to signify the primitive usage, still observed in Bedouin tents, of spreading a mat of leather or rush-plait on the ground to serve as a tablecloth. In the light of the Ras Shamra texts, however, where *ṯlḥn* ('a table') as distinct from *šlḥ* ('to send') is attested, this is no longer tenable. The revelation which now comes to the prophet of Bethel and which is authenticated by the sequel is no longer indirect, so is termed 'the word of God'.

13.21. *mārā* means 'to rebel', hence 'defy authority'. 'The command of God' means literally 'the mouth of God'. It required no divine insight to declare that the man of God had sinned in preferring indirect revelation through the prophet and his alleged 'angel' to the direct and specific command of God. The real revelation to the prophet of Bethel is that the body of the man of God will not come into his fathers' grave, i.e. he will die a violent death outside his own community. The reference is to family tombs, usually in this period cut in caves in the soft limestone in some wadi by the settlements, where the dead were laid out in an extended position. Hebrew burials in the monarchic period differ from early Bronze Age burials by a great economy of grave furniture, simple bowls as lamps with a second bowl inverted as a lid being a regular feature.

24. Lions of a small breed were known in Palestine and the Near East in Old Testament times (I Sam. 17.34; Amos 3.12, etc.), and are known to have become extinct only in the 12th century AD. The didactic nature of the passage is indicated, according to Gressmann,[a] by the fact that the lion did not harm the innocent ass, but only the disobedient prophet. The contrast between beast and man recalls the Balaam story, both stories probably borrowing the motifs of folk-lore. See further introduction to the section, p. 321.

29. Mourning rites, *mispēd* (lit. 'beating the breast') accompanied burial both before and after interment. This, as at present among Arab peasants, was a communal responsibility, indicated by the plural of the verb in v. 30. Valuable documentation of mourning rites in ancient Canaan is found in the stereotyped and anthropomorphic descriptions of mourning for Baal and for 'Aqht in the Ras Shamra texts, e.g. *UT* 67, VI, 10ff.

> Then the Kindly One, El, the Merciful
> Comes down from his throne, he sits on the footstool,
> And from the footstool he sits on the ground.
> He lets down his turban in grief;

[a] *Die älteste Geschichtsschreibung* . . ., p. 247.

On his head is the dust in which he wallows.
He tears asunder the knot of his girdle;
He makes the mountain re-echo with his lamentation,
And with his clamour the forest to resound.
Cheeks and chin he rends,
The humeral joint of his arm he scores;
The chest as a garden-plot,
Even as a valley-bottom his back he lacerates.
He raises his voice and cries:
Baal is dead! What is become of the Prince?
The son of Dagan (is dead)! What of the multitudes (of men)?

In similar terms the mourning of the goddess Anat is described, and finally

She weeps for him and buries him,
She puts him in the niche of the divinities of the earth.

Then follows a funeral feast. The proper integration of the defunct with the dead was a matter affecting the security of the community. The various elements in the extempore mourning chants which may be observed among the Arabs at the present day are the direct address to the defunct, 'Ah, my brother!' (cf. Jer. 22.18), complimentary references to the prowess of the defunct, and resignation to the will of God in his decease.

13.31. In seeking to share the burial of a man of God the prophet of Bethel, according to the reading of G and L, anticipates the actual circumstances of Josiah's reformation, where this tomb was spared desecration. The real motive was the desire to be associated with one who had been so strikingly authenticated as a prophet of God.

32. The reference to Samaria as a province obviously dates from at least after 734, see critical introduction to this section. More probably the usage reflects the situation after 722 and specifically in Josiah's reformation when local shrines (*bāttē habbāmōt*) were suppressed.

(*c*) DEUTERONOMISTIC EPILOGUE ON THE RELIGIOUS POLICY OF JEROBOAM: 13.33f.

After the prophetic legend the compiler resumes the theme of Jeroboam's religious policy, objecting particularly to the local priesthood. A transition is made in v. 33a, where it is remarked that not even the portents related in the preceding passage made any impression on the king.

13 [33]After this thing Jeroboam did not return from his evil way, but he still made priests of the high places from among the whole range of the people. Any who would, he would consecrate, and he became a priest[a] of the high places. [34]And this matter[b] vitiated the house[c] of Jeroboam to the extent of effacing and destroying it from off the face of the earth.

13.33. The stative participle with the definite article *heḥāpēṣ* ('any who would') refers to volunteers for the holy office. The phrase 'to fill the hand' (with the insignia of office) is well attested in Mesopotamian inscriptions. As these also use the phrase of handing one over to the enemy, 'hand over' in the sense of transmitting authority is the meaning. In the Old Testament the phrase is used of consecration, perhaps in symbolic transmission of authority, as in the case of Micah's Levite (Judg. 17.12) and of Moses' consecration of Aaron and his sons (Ex. 29.22).

34. The root meaning of *ḥāṭā'* is 'to miss the mark' or 'fail of one's object', and 'to sin' is merely the secondary meaning. The religious policy of Jeroboam is represented as crippling his house from the outset so that it is foredoomed to failure. 'Failure' is a better translation of *ḥaṭṭā't* than 'sin', see on I K. 1.21.

(*d*) AHIJAH'S DENUNCIATION OF JEROBOAM AND HIS HOUSE: 14.1–18

This is another instance of local prophetic tradition, probably associated, like 11.29–32a, with the prophetic circle at Shiloh, and having as its central figure Ahijah. The nucleus of the passage is vv. 1–6, 12f., 17f., the consulting of the prophet by Jeroboam's wife in disguise, and Ahijah's detection of her and his grim prophecy of the death of her son. It is likely, however, that the response of the prophet included the oracle of doom on the house of Jeroboam, whether this was prompted by the statement that this son would die (v. 13), or was the main message, followed by the response concerning the death of the boy, as Noth (*op. cit.*, p. 311) suggests. The latter view is supported by the graphic language of the oracle of doom on the house of Jeroboam in vv. 10f., which ends with the technical signature of the oracle of Yahweh. That Ahijah's oracle on the elevation of Jeroboam really emphasized the conditional favour of God, as in the

[a]Reading with G, L, V, and S *way^{e}hī kōhēn* for MT *wīhī kōh^{a}nē*.
[b]Reading with G, L, T, and S *haddābār* for MT *baddābār*.
[c]Reading with G and S *l^{e}ḥaṭṭā't l^{e}bēt* for MT *l^{e}ḥaṭṭa't bēt*.

Deuteronomistic elaboration in v. 38, is indicated by Jeroboam's apprehension, which prompted him to send his wife disguised to consult the prophet. This has been utilized by the Deuteronomist as a prophecy of the doom of the Northern kingdom founded by Jeroboam, and as a qualification of the promise of Ahijah to Jeroboam in I K. 11.29–32a, which was already, in the view of the Deuteronomist, regarded as conditional (I K. 11.37f.). This later hand is evident in vv. 7–9 (excluding 'Go, tell Jeroboam', in v. 7a and probably 'therefore', *lākēn*, in the beginning of v. 10, which is introduced after the Deuteronomistic insertion on the sins of Jeroboam in vv. 7–9), and particularly in the specific reference to the liquidation of Northern Israel and the subsequent deportations after the Assyrian conquest was complete in 720.

14 [1]At that time Abijah the son of Jeroboam fell sick. [2]And Jeroboam said to his wife, Rise up and disguise yourself and they will not know that you are the wife of Jeroboam, and go to Shiloh; behold there is Ahijah the prophet, he who spoke concerning me that I should be king[a] over this people. [3]Take then with you ten loaves of bread and seed-cakes and a jar of honey and go to him; he will tell you what will happen to the lad. [4]And the wife of Jeroboam did so and she arose and went to Shiloh and came to the house of Ahijah, and Ahijah could not see, for his eyes were set by reason of his old age.[b] [5]And Yahweh had said to Ahijah, Here comes Jeroboam's wife to seek a word from you concerning[c] her son, for he is sick. Thus and thus shall you speak to her. And it happened,[d] as she came in, that she was disguised, [6]and when Ahijah heard the sound of her feet as she came in[e] the door he said, Come in you, wife of Jeroboam. Why this disguise when I am sent to you with a harsh word?[f] [7]Go, tell Jeroboam, Thus says Yahweh, God of Israel, Inasmuch as I exalted you from among the people and appointed you a leader over my people Israel, [8]and tore the kingdom from the house of David and gave it to you, but you have not been as my servant David, who kept my commandments and who walked after me with his whole heart to do only that which was right in my eyes, [9]but have done evil more than all who were before you and have gone and made

[a]Reading *limlōk* with G^A, S, and V for MT *lemelek*.

[b]Reading the verbal noun (infinitive construct) *śīb* ('being old') for MT *śēbō* ('his grey hair').

[c]Reading *ʿal* for MT *ʾel*, though the latter is found in the sense 'pertaining to'.

[d]Reading *wayehī* with G^A and V.

[e]It is proposed to read *raglē habbāʾā* ('her feet as she entered') or, with G^A, *raglehā bebōʾā*. There is no strict need to read the definite article with the participle, however, as it may be analogous to the Arabic usage of participle without the article in the adverbial accusative of attendant circumstances, so we retain MT.

[f]G^A suggests that the masculine *qāše* be read here. MT feminine *qāšā*, however, is in order as an abstract used adverbially.

for yourself other gods and molten images to provoke me to anger and have cast me behind your back, [10]therefore I shall bring ill upon[a] the house of Jeroboam. I shall cut off him belonging to Jeroboam who pisses against the wall, to the very last in Israel, and I shall make an utter riddance of what is left of the house of Jeroboam as one clears away dung. [11]Him who belongs to Jeroboam who dies in the city shall the dogs eat, and him who dies in the country shall the birds of the heavens eat, for Yahweh has spoken. [12]And you, get up and go home. When your feet come into the city the boy will die, [13]and all Israel shall observe mourning rites for him and shall bury him, for this one alone belonging to Jeroboam will come into a grave, for there has been found in him in the family of Jeroboam something good towards Yahweh, God of Israel. [14]And Yahweh will raise up for himself a king over Israel who will cut off the house of Jeroboam [b]on that day. And also from now onwards [15]Yahweh will strike[b] Israel, and they shall be shaken[c] as a reed is shaken in the water and he shall pluck up Israel from off this good land which he gave to their fathers and will scatter them over the river because they have made their Asherah-symbols, provoking Yahweh to anger. [16]And he will give up Israel for the sins of Jeroboam which he committed and caused Israel to commit. [17]And Jeroboam's wife arose and went away and came to Tirzah; she was coming in to the threshold of the house when the lad died. [18]And they buried him, and all Israel mourned him, according to the word of Yahweh which he spoke through his servant the prophet Ahijah.

At this point G departs from MT and resumes with MT 14.21. MT 14.1–18 is represented by a variant account in G 12.24g–n (ed. Swete). Since this version is concerned solely with the visit of Jeroboam's wife (not in disguise) to Ahijah and the death of her son after the prophet's oracle, without any Deuteronomistic elaboration (cf. MT 14.7–10, 13–16), it is possibly the elaboration of a genuine local tradition. Such details as the fact that the home of Jeroboam is given here (v. 24k) as his home town Sareira (MT Zeredah) are probably from the original tradition, but other details are adventitious and less reliable, e.g. the name of Jeroboam's wife, *Anō* (v. 24g), who, according to this account (v. 24e), was the daughter of the

[a]Some MSS read, correctly, *ʿal*.

[b]The sense breaks down completely here and the versions give no assistance. The reading which we have followed, *bayyōm hahūʾ wᵉgam mēʿattā yakke*, is suggested by Kittel (HKAT, p. 119). The word *ze* in MT suggests that a gloss may be indicated or that the sense may have been 'the one now and others later', reading *wᵉze mēʿattā* for MT *ūme gam-ʿattā*. Since what immediately precedes in v. 14 refers to the end of the house of Jeroboam, *ze hayyōm* of MT can hardly refer to the death of Jeroboam's son, so that we are forced to a solution along the lines of Kittel's conjecture.

[c]Reading with Kittel *wᵉhitnōdᵉdū*, as suggested by the following verb.

Pharaoh Shishak, an obvious erroneous variant of the tradition of the marriage of Hadad of Edom with the Egyptian royal house. On the reliability or otherwise of this version see above pp. 310f. We would retain the reference to Ahijah's oracle on Jeroboam's elevation in v. 2b as part of the original tradition rather than, according to Noth, a Deuteronomistic note, since, as Noth observes, the object of the visit to the prophet was not so much information about the boy's recovery as an auspicious word with the effect of imitative magic. The emphasis was not so much on the prophet's clairvoyancy as on his dynamic influence on the future as an agent of God, of which his former oracle to Jeroboam had given evidence.

14.3. The humble gift of bread, cakes, and honey seems scarcely worthy of the royal donor or the prophet, and recalls the fourth part of a silver shekel which Saul and his lad proposed to offer Samuel (I Sam. 9.7f.). This may reflect the humble status of Ahijah among the dervishes of Shiloh, but it must be remembered that Jeroboam's wife was in disguise, and a richer gift would have excited suspicion. On the other hand, the gift may well have been simply a token, a substitute for the conventional meal which established fellowship between the parties, engaged their mutual interest and admitted one to a share in the prophet's 'blessing' (*berākā*). In I Sam. 9.7 food is first thought of when a visit to the prophet is considered. That had to be provided by the visitors, since that in possession of a man of God would be 'holy'. This point is missed by the elaboration of G that the seed-cakes were for the prophet's children. The meaning of *niqqūdīm* (AV 'cracknels') is uncertain. It may be cognate with Arab *naqada* ('to prick out'), hence 'cakes with perforation'. A surer indication, however, would seem to be the meaning of *nāqōd* indicating the speckled sheep among Jacob's herd (Gen. 30.32). 'Speckled cakes' might be sweet bread garnished with seeds on the crust, such as one sees in the East at the present day. The word for 'jar', *baqbuq*, an onomatopoeic word meaning generally 'bottle', does not seem appropriate for a receptacle for honey. *debaš* might indicate Arabic *dibs*, a more liquid preparation from grape-juice, used instead of sugar for sweetening in cooking. Generally, however, in the Old Testament it means actual honey, which is much thinner in consistency in the hot climate.

5. *dāraš* is the regular word for consulting an oracle.

6. *qāšā* after the passive *šālūaḥ* is adverbial, denoting the content, or effect, of the message with which the prophet was sent.

14.7. The use of *nāgīd* ('one who is set over against'), 'a leader', instead of 'king' is to be noted in this Deuteronomistic expansion of the oracle of Ahijah. 'My people' denotes the status of Israel as a sacral community rather than a political state, a status which had been periodically recognized by the assembly at Shechem when the covenant was sacramentally experienced.

9. Molten, or cast, images (*massēkōt*) probably refers to the bull-images of Bethel and Dan. The reference to the predecessors of Jeroboam is loose considering the fact that he was the first king of the separate kingdom of Northern Israel. It reflects the stock phraseology of the Deuteronomistic compiler, or, as van den Born suggests (*op. cit.*, p. 90), is an animadversion by him on Manasseh. The conjunction in *ūmassēkōt* is explicative.

10. The use of *hinnē* and the participle after *lākēn* ('therefore') introduces a prophetic threat in the imminent future, as regularly in the prophetic books. *maštīn b*^{e}*qīr* ('him who pisses against the wall'), denoting all males, is a typical example of the direct, graphic, uninhibited speech of the Israelite peasant, particularly of the prophets. The Akkadian verb *šānu*, with the same meaning, indicates that Hebrew used the form with the infixed *t*. The precise significance of the phrase *'āṣūr w*^{e}*'āzūb* is uncertain, and M. Noth[a] has written it off as a stereotyped expression the precise primary meaning of which has been lost. It has been taken variously as a legal term referring to men comprehensively as 'bond and free' (Gesenius), 'one who is affiliated with a tribe and has the right of protection and the stranger who has no such protection' (A. S. Yahuda), or 'a dependent and an independent freeman' (König), but, since the phrase refers to the royal families of Jeroboam and Ahab where it is used in the Old Testament, none of these can be the meaning if the phrase has retained any of its primary meaning. It has been suggested (Schwally) that it means 'under ritual taboo and ritually free', Jer. 36.5 being cited as evidence for *'āṣūr* as meaning 'under ritual taboo'. Here, however, G suggests that the word means simply 'under arrest'. E. Kutsch[b] rightly points out that the phrase in I K. 14.10; 21.21, and II K. 9.8 refers to the extirpation of a family, and suggests that, as the preceding phrase *maštīn b*^{e}*qīr* indicates, the reference is to all males of the royal family, those under parental restraint (*'āṣūr*) and those free from it (*'āzūb*). He takes the phrase *b*^{e}*yiśrā'ēl* to denote the original signifi-

[a] *Überlieferungsgeschichtliche Studien*, p. 75 n.2.
[b] 'Die Wurzel עצר im Hebräischen', *VT* II, 1952, pp. 57–69.

cance of the phrase as a legal term, but, since it is confined to the family, the origins of the usage go back to a very early stage of social development and so are lost in obscurity. This applies very well to I K. 14.10; 21.21; II K. 9.8, but does not explain the usage in Deut. 32.36; cf. II K. 14.26; 24.14, where the phrase is qualified by the adverb *'epes* ('except', 'only'). This suggests to P. P. Saydon[a] that the terms may not be, after all, antithetic, but synonymous, and he feasibly argues[b] that *'āṣūr* means 'hindered' or 'helpless', and *'āzūb* 'abandoned' or 'destitute'. The phrase is a popular usage describing the miserable survivors of a general catastrophe, the literal significance of the terms referring to the lowest class, who through their helplessness and destitution might be expected to be spared. Whatever the precise meaning originally, this has been lost in general usage, as Noth suggests.

The verb *bi'ēr* means 'to drive beasts to pasture', hence 'to drive away'. *'aḥarē* may be a noun, 'last descendants', rather than a preposition. The dung (*gālāl*) is doubtless that from the lower level of the native oriental peasant's house, the human inmates inhabiting a slightly higher level (Arab. *masṭaba*) with no partition. The lower level of such a house, no doubt, was the 'stable' visualized in the story of Jesus' birth.

14.11. The dogs, excluded from dwelling-houses, as among the Muslims, were the scavengers of the ancient East. Never regularly fed, they were ready at all times to devour any edible thing exposed in the streets. This graphic threat was made to Baasha (16.4) and to Ahab regarding Jezebel (21.24), in whose case it was literally fulfilled.

13. That this would be the only son of Jeroboam that all Israel would mourn stresses the fact that only in his case would all Israel recognize the claim of the royal family. Jeroboam's successor Nadab was to perish in civil war.

14. This verse indicates the deposition of Jeroboam's son Nadab by Baasha (15.25ff.) and the next verse the subsequent civil wars, which were endemic in Israel. That the assassin Baasha should be regarded as an agent of Yahweh does not condone violence and political opportunism, but emphasizes the preoccupation of the Hebrew mind with primary causes.

15. The simile of reeds moved by water is an excellent description

[a]*VT* II, 1952, pp. 371–4.
[b]After P. Joüon, *Mélanges de la faculté orientale à Beyrouth* IV, 1910, pp. 9–12.

of the intrigues and *coups d'état* which involved the people of Israel in her unhappy history until 722. The 'reed shaken in the wind' is a similar figure of instability in the graphic language of Jesus (Matt. 11.7; Luke 7.24). The dispersion 'beyond the river' (i.e. Euphrates) dates this passage to 734 at the earliest and probably after 720. The language and the view of this catastrophe as divine chastisement for the sins of Jeroboam are characteristic of the Deuteronomists, who, in the interests of Josiah's political and religious unification of the kingdom, were anxious to discredit the cult of Northern Israel.

14.17. This is the first mention of Tirzah, which became the capital of Northern Israel in the time of Baasha (see on 15.33). G is possibly nearer the truth here in reading Sareira (12.24n), though this is a corruption of Zeredah, the home of Jeroboam, so that for *tirṣātā* we should possibly read *ṣ*ᵉ*rēdātā*.

4. SYNCHRONISTIC HISTORY OF ISRAEL AND JUDAH: 14.19–16.34

This is the least interesting part of the books of Kings, covering the six decades between Solomon and Ahab. In this period the most significant features from a purely political point of view were the active intervention of the Aramaean kingdom of Damascus in the history of Israel, the beginning of which is noted in 15.16–20, and the reigns of Omri and Ahab (16.15–34), under which Israel was to occupy the north part of Moab and to enter into significant alliances with the Phoenicians and Aramaeans, the latter of which was to delay the effective advance of Assyria to the West for a lifetime. Such political matters do not concern the Deuteronomist except as they bear directly on his major theme. So the advent of Damascus in Israelite politics is noted in anticipation of the Aramaean wars which were the background of the ministry of Elisha, and the Phoenician alliance is touched upon in the marriage of Ahab with Jezebel (16.31), which serves to introduce his religious toleration (16.32) and the encounter with Elijah (ch. 18). But there is no attempt to assess the real historical significance of the reigns of Omri and Ahab. By contrast, the deviations of the kings of Israel and Judah from orthodoxy and their toleration of alien cults is noted in Deuteronomic language, and the violent changes of dynasty in North Israel are circumstantially described to emphasize the failure of Jeroboam and in anticipation of the end of the Northern kingdom in 722 BC. This selective treatment of history, and the fact that stereotyped editorial introductions and epilogues to reigns and Deuteronomistic animadversions on unorthodoxy occupy more than half the 70 verses of this section, indicate how strongly it bears the impress of the Deuteronomistic compiler.

(*a*) EDITORIAL NOTE ON THE DEATH OF JEROBOAM AND THE ACCESSION AND REIGN OF REHOBOAM OF JUDAH: 14.19–24

The obituary of the king of Israel and the summary reference to sources for the history of his reign, namely the Book of the Chronicles of the Kings of Israel, and the note of the accession of his son (vv. 19–20) are distinctive of the Deuteronomistic editor, the summary reference to other sources for the history indicating the predominating religious interest. The note of the accession of the king of Judah, his age at accession, the length of his reign, and his mother's name, with the appraisal of his reign according to Deuteronomic principles and in Deuteronomic language (vv. 21–24), are also characteristic of the work of the editor. The length of the reign of the king, however, is usually given in the notice of his accession, and not in the obituary. Here, owing to the peculiar circumstances of Jeroboam's accession, the subject of historical narrative, this is reserved for the epilogue, as in the case of Jehu (II K. 10.36). The notice of Rehoboam's accession and the length of his reign amplifies the bare notice of his accession in 11.43, from which the length of his reign is omitted for the same reason. The circumstances of the disruption of the kingdom preoccupied the attention of the Deuteronomistic compiler, who selected the incident for special treatment, not as part of the reign of Rehoboam but because of its significance as an instance of the judgement of God on Solomon's lapses (11.31–33). He has also considered that the elevation of Jeroboam, the immediate sequel to the eventful assembly, must be modified forthwith by the tradition of the rejection of Jeroboam (14.1–18) in anticipation of the decline and fall of the Northern Kingdom.

14 [19]And as for the rest of the acts of Jeroboam, his warfare, and his rule, they are written in the Book of the Chronicles of the Kings of Israel. [20]And the days which Jeroboam ruled were twenty-two years, and he slept with his fathers, and Nadab his son reigned in his stead.

[21]And Rehoboam the son of Solomon reigned in Judah. Rehoboam was forty-one[a] years old when he became king and he reigned seventeen[a] years in Jerusalem, the city which Yahweh had chosen to put his

[a]G[B] (12.24a) reads sixteen and twelve years. For the probability of MT see on v. 21.

name there out of all the tribes of Israel, and his mother's name was Naamah the Ammonitess. 22And Judah[a] did that which was evil in the sight of Yahweh and they provoked him to jealousy more than their fathers[a] did in the sins which they committed. 23And they also built for themselves high places and standing stones and Asherah-symbols on every high hill and under every green tree. 24And moreover there were sacral prostitutes in the land. They did according to all the abominations[b] of the nations which Yahweh had dispossessed before the Israelites.

14.19. For the sources of secular history in Israel, and the selective use of them by the Deuteronomistic compiler see Introduction, pp. 25ff.

20. Nadab is a hypocoristicon, or truncated form, of the theophoric name Nadabiah, which actually appears in one of the Lachish Letters (ed. H. Torczyner, No. iii). It is of the same type as Nathan and Ahaz, and signifies 'Yahweh has freely given' or 'Yahweh incites to noble deeds'.

21. The lower numbers of G are apparently influenced by the association of Rehoboam with 'the youngsters (*hayyᵉlādīm*) who had grown up with him' (12.8, with the suggestion that they were not his contemporaries but had grown up in his service; see comment *ad loc.*). In view of the youth of Solomon at his accession, his early marriage, customary in the Near East and, indeed, probably enjoined on the king according to the primitive association of royalty and virility, and the long reign of the king, it is quite likely that his eldest son was 41 before acceding. In this case the 40 years of Solomon's reign must be a round number.

The amplification on Jerusalem, though familiar Deuteronomistic phraseology, may in this context emphasize that a theology of Jerusalem with the Temple as the established seat of the Divine King had already developed with the conception of the king as the executive of the Divine King, to support the dynastic pretensions of the House of David, on which Rehoboam effectively relied (so Noth, *ad loc.*).

The names of the queen-mothers of Judah are faithfully given, since they had a regular status at court (e.g. 2.13) with the title

[a]G reads 'Rehoboam' for 'Judah'; cf. II Chron. 12.14, where, in the abridged version, Rehoboam is not named, but signified. Probably we should follow G here, emending the verb 'provoked' and the pronominal suffix in 'their fathers' to the singular.

[b]Omitting the definite article in the construct *tōʿᵃbōt* where it is a dittograph of the initial consonant *t*, though Noth's suggestion that *tōʿᵃbōt* is a marginal gloss is feasible.

hagg^e^bīrā (11.19; 15.13). The omission of any such notice in the case of the kings of Israel may indicate that affairs in Israel were peripheral to the interest of the Judaean editor. With the new significance of the hereditary principle the mother of the heir-apparent had a distinctive status. Perhaps the omission of any reference to the queen-mother in Northern Israel reflects the fact that the hereditary monarchy was never freely accepted there. Naamah ('Pleasant') was one of the women from the neighbouring peoples whom Solomon married and whom he indulged with their native cult in Jerusalem. The fact that his eldest son was born of an Ammonite mother indicates a cautious principle of political consolidation after David's conquests. Perhaps Ammon was the first object of Solomon's foreign *rapprochement*, owing to its position between the Israelite elements of Reuben and Gad, who were protected by no defensible frontier.

14.22. If 'Judah' is retained as subject of this sentence, the standard by which their sins are judged is that of Solomon and the Hebrews in the time of the judges, and the Deuteronomistic presentation of history in Joshua and Judges is presupposed. If after G and Chronicles we read Rehoboam as the subject, the same might still be true.

23. Specifically the sin deplored by the Deuteronomist is worship at local sanctuaries. There old local animistic beliefs and rites of imitative magic of the fertility-cult, served by ritual prostitutes, died hard. The standing stones (*maṣṣēbōt*) as a feature of these sanctuaries were symbols of the presence of the deity or memorials of the reception of a theophany. As such they had a recognized place in the religion of the Hebrew fathers in more primitive times (Gen. 28.18, 22; 31.13; 35.14, etc.), but with the establishment of the shrines of the confederacy (Shechem and Gilgal) and Jerusalem and Bethel these objects were more and more associated with the local nature shrines of Canaan, and were finally officially discredited in the Deuteronomic reformation. *'^a^šērīm* (singular *'^a^šērā*) occasionally signifies sacred poles, or stylized trees, as the apparatus of the fertility-cult (Deut. 16.21; Judg. 6.26; Jer. 17.2). These might be single or more numerous, hence AV 'groves'. Etymologically the word might seem to be connected with the root *'āšēr*, 'to be straight', but since the discovery of the Ras Shamra texts it is known that *Asherah* (Ugaritic *'aṯrt*) was the mother-goddess in the Canaanite fertility-cult, a fact which was already indicated by the theophoric names in the Amarna Tablets, e.g. Abdašerat. In II K. 21.7 there is a clear reference to a graven image (*pesel*) of Asherah set up by Manasseh in the Temple, so that it is likely that the sacred tree or pole of the local shrines of the fertility-cult were symbols of Asherah, the mother-goddess. Perhaps they symbolized the receptive and productive element in nature under the stimulus of rain, which was the province of the male party in the nature-cult, Hadad or Baal; see further on 15.13.

14.24. Nothing better illustrates the non-moral connotation of *qādēš* in Hebrew than the use of this word to denote sacred prostitutes, which were, as indicated by Deut. 23.18, of both sexes. It is not clear from this and similar passages, e.g. 15.12; 22.46[47]; II K. 23.7, that castrated sodomites are indicated, as Aquila's rendering assumes, though such were not unknown in Israel (Deut. 23.1[2]). Those persons were ministers of rites of imitative magic designed to promote fertility in nature. The administrative texts from Ras Shamra list such 'sacred persons' among various classes and professions at Ugarit at the end of the Bronze Age, but do not specify their functions. The incident of Judah and Tamar in Gen. 38.21ff. may suggest that from its original sacral connotation *q^e^dēšā* came to mean simply 'prostitute' in a general sense, but G. R. Driver[a] has argued convincingly that Tamar's being veiled, which common harlots, at least by Assyrian law, were not, indicates that she simulated a respectable woman who had dedicated herself for sacred prostitution. Hos. 4.14 seems to preserve the original sacral connotation of the term.

(*b*) THE HISTORY OF THE REIGNS OF REHOBOAM, ABIJAH AND ASA, KINGS OF JUDAH: 14.25–15.24

Here we are in touch with sober history in the account of the expedition of Shishak (14.25–28) and the war between Israel and Judah in the time of Asa and Baasha (15.16–22), and the matter is almost certainly taken directly from the Books of the Chronicles of the Kings of Judah. Deuteronomistic comment is mostly confined to obituaries on the kings with summary condemnation of their infidelity to Deuteronomic principles and notice of the accession of their successors, and a summary of the significance of their reigns from the same viewpoint (e.g. 14.29–15.15, 23–26). Here the Deuteronomistic matter is easy to discern. The historical sources are objectively presented, though in the selection of such matter the interest of the editor is apparent, particularly in the account of Shishak's invasion, which

[a]G. R. Driver, 'Problems of Interpretation in the Heptateuch', *Mélanges bibliques rédigés en l'honneur de André Robert*, 1957, pp. 70-73.

ignores his activity in the provinces and notes only the spoliation of the Temple.

(i) THE EXPEDITION OF SHISHAK AND THE REDUCTION OF JUDAH: 14.25–28

Though this matter is probably drawn from state archives and is objectively attested in an inscription of Shishak I on one of the pylons of the temple of Amon at Karnak (ancient Thebes),[a] a comparison of the present passage with the Egyptian source reveals the limitations of the Hebrew account. The Egyptian account, though no more than a list of localities, between 50 and 60 in Israel and about 100 in Judah, gives a more just indication of the scope of the expedition, of which II Chron. 12.2–4, in contrast to the present passage, gives a hint. The expedition may have been simply a show of arms to impose tribute on Israel and Judah. The Hebrew account, moreover, omits all reference to Shishak's activity in the Northern kingdom, where the Pharaoh, by his own account and on the evidence of a fragment of a stele of his set up in Megiddo[b], asserted his authority. Most of the present passage is occupied with a note on Solomon's gold shields, with which Rehoboam indemnified the Pharaoh, and his replacement of these with bronze shields, and the occasions on which these were used. This may indicate the limited interest of the Deuteronomistic editor. On the other hand, the preoccupation with the Temple may indicate Temple archives as a source, or at least one of the Temple personnel as the writer. The same may apply to 15.18; II K. 12.18; 14.14; 16.8, 17; 18.15–16; 24.13; 25.9–13, all of which refer to indemnities from, or plunder of, the Temple treasury.

The key to Shishak's campaign was the discovery of B. Mazar[c] that the Karnak inscription must be read *boustrophedon*. The progress of the Egyptian army, apparently without opposition, is noted from Gaza to Gezer, forces having been detached to scour the Negeb, where boundary points between the desert and the sown and tribal fortresses, many of them bearing clan-names familiar from the Books of Chronicles, were overrun as far as Arad east of Beersheba. The purpose of this is taken by Mazar to be to secure the rear of the main Egyptian force. We think it more likely to have been intended to

[a]Breasted, *ARE* IV, §§ 709–17.
[b]C. S. Fisher, *OIC* IV, 1929, figs. 7 A and B.
[c]B. Mazar, 'The Campaign of Pharaoh Shishak to Palestine', *SVT* IV, 1957, pp. 57–66.

distract Rehoboam of Judah while the main force operated in Israel, and also no doubt to replenish the Egyptian commissariat from the barley lands of the Negeb in view of the return journey to Egypt. The main force advanced from Gezer to Aijalon and up the Pass of Beth-horon, emerging on to the plateau at Gibeon. Since it proceeded north from here to the Jordan valley, passing probably near Shiloh, the Pharaoh probably received the tribute of Rehoboam by Gibeon. Penuel, Mahanaim, and other places on the lower Jabbok were the next objective, from which the expedition returned westwards by Tirzah on the *Wādī Fārʿa*, then northwards by the pass through the hills to 'the *ʿēmeq*', the eastern end of the great central plain, to Bethshean, then west to Shunem, Taanach, and Megiddo, where the Pharaoh signified his authority by setting up his statue, the base of which was recovered in excavations. From Megiddo he went through the famous pass, where ʿAruna is mentioned among other places, and south to Soco, east of modern *Ṭulkarm*, and so home by the coastal plain. Archaeological stations on this route such as Gezer, Gibeon, Megiddo, and *Tell Qasīleh* and *Tell Jerīsheh* at the ford of the Jarkon River (*Nahr al-ʿAwjā*) attest partial destruction, which would indicate that in the five years which had elapsed since the accession of Jeroboam the Pharaoh was not satisfied with the loyalty of his *protégé*.

14 [25]And it happened in the fifth year of king Rehoboam that Shishak[a] the king of Egypt came up against Jerusalem. [26]And he took the treasures of the house of Yahweh and the treasures of the palace; all[b] he took, and took all the shields of gold which Solomon had made. [27]And king Rehoboam made in place of them bronze shields and committed them[c] to the hand of the commanders of the guard who kept the door of the palace. [28]And it used to be that, whenever the king entered the house of Yahweh, the guard would carry them and bring them back into the guard-room.

14.25. On the dating of the accession of Rehoboam in 930 see Introduction, Chronology, pp. 70f. The fifth year of Rehoboam's reign, inclusive reckoning, would be 926.[d] On the significance of the

[a]The pointing is that of Q, for Egyptian Shoshenq.

[b]Omitting *wᵉ* of MT with certain MSS and with MT of the parallel account in Chronicles, and as the sense demands.

[c]Perhaps *w* consecutive and imperfect should be read, though in a catalogue rather than a sequence of events *w* with perfect is occasionally found. Possibly the consonants of MT ought to be pointed *wᵉhapqēd*, the infinitive absolute, which is occasionally used in such a catalogue for the finite verb (*GK* § 113, 4a).

[d]Cf. Breasted *ARE* IV, p. 348: 'probably about 926'.

sole reference to Jerusalem as Shishak's objective and its relevance to the source see critical introduction to this section. Shishak in his Karnak inscription mentions about 150 places both in Israel and Judah from north of the Plain of Esdraelon to the extreme south of the settled land in the Negeb, including such strategic centres as Megiddo and Taanach on the main pass through the Carmel range, Bethshean at the eastern end of the great central plain, Aijalon and Beth-horon respectively at the foot and head of 'the ascent of Beth-horon', and Etam south of Bethlehem near the head of the pass from the coastal plain by the *Wādī as-Sanṭ*, which the Philistines proposed to use in the campaign culminating in the fall of Goliath. Glueck finds evidence of this expedition in the burning of the first level at *Tell al-Ḫaleifeh* (Ezion-geber) on the shore of the Gulf of Aqaba,[a] but this extent of the campaign is not suggested in the inscription. The burning may be accidental, or represent a rebellion by the slave labourers on the occasion of Judah's embarrassment in Shishak's invasion. The heavy fortifications of the strategic cities of Judah at this time, generally associated with Rehoboam (II Chron. 11.5–12), may indicate his reaction to the loss of the Northern kingdom and the attack of Shishak.

14.27. *rāṣīm* (lit. 'runners') denotes professional soldiers. The term is first used in the Old Testament in II Sam. 15.1, then in I K. 1.5, to denote outrunners or a royal escort, but eventually came to denote the royal bodyguard (so also in 14.27, 28). Noth (*ad loc.*) feasibly suggests that, in view of the limited numbers of the royal bodyguard, the plural *śārīm* denotes rather the succession of single commanders, a view which is supported by the frequentative tenses of the verbs in v. 28, if not by MT *wᵉhipqīd*, which Noth takes as frequentative in v. 27. The bronze shields, like their gold, or gilt, predecessors (10.17, where they are said to have been deposited in the house of the Forest of Lebanon), were used for ceremonial purposes.

28. The rare word *tā'* is used of the guard-room only here, in the parallel account in II Chron. 12.11, and in the description of the Temple-complex in Ezek. 40.7ff. The root *ṯawa* ('to dwell') is well known in Arabic, and the noun *tā'* is attested in Syriac and Aramaic. It may have come into use in Hebrew as a survival of a North Mesopotamian dialect of Aramaic from patriarchal times, or from Aramaean professional soldiers of Solomon.

[a] *BASOR* 75, 1939, pp. 17ff.

(ii) OBITUARIES AND NOTES OF ACCESSIONS, WITH SUMMARIES OF THE REIGNS OF THE KINGS OF JUDAH FROM REHOBOAM TO ASA FROM THE STANDPOINT OF THE DEUTERONOMISTIC EDITOR: 14.29–15.15

From 15.1 the accession of a king is synchronized with the regnal year of his neighbour, and this is a regular feature of the Deuteronomistic framework of the Book of Kings to the fall of Samaria (see Introduction: the Sources). With his stereotyped appraisal of the religious policy of the king, the Deuteronomistic compiler in the case of Asa has incorporated older historical data regarding actual reform (vv. 12–15), possibly from a Temple chronicle.

14 [29]Now, as for the rest of the acts of Rehoboam and all that he did,
are they not written in the Book of the Chronicles of the Kings of Judah?
[30]And there was war between Rehoboam and Jeroboam all the time.
[31]And Rehoboam slept with his fathers and he was buried with his
fathers[a] in the city of David[b], and Abijah[c] his son reigned in his place.
15 [1]Now in the eighteenth year of the reign[d] of Jeroboam the son of
Nebat, Abijah[e] became king over Judah. [2]Three years[f] he reigned in
Jerusalem, and his mother's name was Maacah the daughter of
Absalom.[g] [3]And he walked in the way of all the sins of his father, which

[a]'With his fathers' is omitted in the parallel version in II Chron. 12.16, and at first sight it seems a dittograph of a phrase. But in the first instance the statement that Rehoboam 'slept with his fathers' refers generally in the popular idiom to his death, while in the second instance the reference is specifically to his burial alongside Solomon and David.

[b]G[BL] and the parallel passage in Chron. omit 'and his mother's name was Naamah the Ammonitess', cf. MT.

[c]The accounts of this king in the parallel version in Chronicles and in Josephus name him Abijah, while G has *Abiou* suggesting Abiyo, a variant of Abiyah. The form Abijam could only be explained as a theophoric where Yam was the divine element. Such a deity is now known from the Ras Shamra mythology, but such a name in the case of a Hebrew king was inconceivable. If, as is likely, the divine element is a form of Yahweh, the final *w* of Abiyo may be corrupted to *m*, which it closely resembles in the proto-Hebraic script.

[d]Reading *limlōk* with G for MT *lammelek*.

[e]See n.[c].

[f]G reads '6', *šš* for MT *šlš*. The parallel version in II Chron. 13 and Josephus, *Ant.* VIII, 6.3 supports MT.

[g]No Absalom (*'abīšālōm*) other than the son of David is known, and the only daughter of Absalom was Tamar (II Sam. 14.27). But as Absalom was one of the older sons of David, it is extremely unlikely that Rehoboam the son of Solomon, one of the younger sons of David, married the daughter of Absalom. Josephus (*Ant.* VIII, 9.1) offers the solution that 'daughter', as is possible, really means 'grand-daughter'. The notice of the local affinities of the father of the queen-mother, which is usual in the introduction to the reigns of the kings of Judah,

he had committed before him, and his mind was not wholly devoted to Yahweh his God as the mind of David his father. [4]Nevertheless, for the sake of David, Yahweh[a] gave him a light in Jerusalem[b] in raising up his son[c] after him to establish Jerusalem, [5]since David did that which was right in the eyes of Yahweh and did not turn from anything he had commanded him all the days of his life (except in the affair of Uriah the Hittite).[d] [6]And there was war between Rehoboam and Jeroboam all the days of his life.[e] [7]As for the rest of the acts of Abijah and all that he did, are they not written in the Book of the Chronicles of the Kings of Judah? And there was war between Abijah and Jeroboam. [8]And Abijah slept with his fathers, and they buried him in the city of David, and Asa his son [f]reigned in his place.

[9]Now in the twentieth[g] year of Jeroboam the king of Israel Asa became king over[h] Judah. [10]And he reigned forty-one years in Jerusalem and his mother's name was Maacah[i] the daughter of Absalom. [11]And Asa did that which was right in the eyes of Yahweh like David his father. [12]And he put away the ritual prostitutes from the land and removed all the images which his fathers had made. [13]And even his mother Maacah he removed from her position as the principal lady because she made a horrible image to Asherah, but Asa cut down her horrible image and

---

might support the reading 'Michaiah the daughter of Uriel of Gibeah', cf. II Chron. 13.2, though 'Maacah the daughter of Absalom' is given as the mother of Abijah in II Chron. 11.20–23. The omission of the notice of the home of the father of the queen-mother, or in this case her grandfather, may indicate that Absalom the son of David was denoted. There is no reason to believe that the name Absalom, though rare in the Old Testament, was not a common name, but the omission of the locality suggests the conclusion that we have adopted.

[a]Omitting 'his god' of MT with G^{BL}.

[b]Perhaps 'in Jerusalem' also should be omitted with G^{BL}, though in the early, precarious days of the divided monarchy the future of Jerusalem and the house of David, which were so closely bound up with each other, hung in the balance.

[c]G reads the plural.

[d]G omits this clause, which, indeed, has all the appearance of a later gloss.

[e]This phrase also in its present form would seem to have been influenced by 14.30, and is omitted in G^{BL}. It is possible that the sentence should be retained, with 'Abijah' for 'Rehoboam'.

[f]The fact that the mother of Abijah and of Asa is given as the same might suggest that 'brother' should be read here for MT 'son'. It is possible, however, that, since Abijah reigned such a short time, his mother 'Maacah' remained 'principal lady', the mother of Asa remaining obscure, hence unnamed. The present citation of her name as Maacah is possibly owing to the assumption that 'the principal lady' of v. 13 was the mother of Asa.

[g]G^{BL} read 'twenty-fourth', thus bringing this statement into agreement with its reading 'six' for MT 'three' as the length of Abijah's reign.

[h]Inserting *ʿal* with L.

[i]G^{BL} read *Ana* for Maacah of MT, feeling the difficulty of the fact that the mother of Asa was apparently the same as the mother of Abijah (v. 2), who is stated to be the father of Asa (v. 8).

burned it in the Kidron wadi. [14]But the high places were not abolished,[a] but the mind of Asa was wholly with Yahweh all his days. [15]And he brought into the Temple of Yahweh the dedications of his father and his own dedications, silver, and gold, and vessels.

14.30. No doubt there was a state of warfare between the two kingdoms under Rehoboam and Jeroboam, but since neither Kings, Chronicles, nor Josephus gives any specific details it is likely that this was rather an armed truce, both sides fortifying frontier fortresses.

15.1. The 18th year of Jeroboam's reign, reckoning inclusively from 930, was 913, see Introduction: Chronology.

2. Abijah's three years are reckoned inclusively, and might amount to no more than one complete year and parts of two official years, see Introduction: Chronology.

3. On *lēbāb* and *šālēm* see on 11.4. David is mentioned here, not as the natural father of Abijah, but as his ancestor.

4. Note the significance of the conceptions of God's covenant with the Davidic house and the choice of Jerusalem as a cult-centre as mutually complementary. As such they were propagated in the Psalms and accepted in the premonarchic Deuteronomistic history.

7. See textual n. The war between Jeroboam and Abijah is attested in full detail in II Chron. 13.3–20, and also in Josephus,[b] when apparently Abijah, trusting no doubt in the strength of his father's bases, took the initiative (II Chron. 13.4).

9. The accession of Asa in Jeroboam's 20th year indicates that the statement in vv. 1f. that his predecessor Abijah reigned three years, having become king in Jeroboam's 18th year, means that only one full year was included in the three. On the variant in G see p. 347 n.[f].

12. On ritual prostitutes see on 14.24. The masculine plural indicates females together with males. *gillūlīm* means, according to its etymology, 'sculptures in the round', but the pointing is that of *šiqqūṣīm* ('abominations').

13. On the status of 'the principal lady' (*hagg[e]bīrā*) in the realm see on 2.19 and 11.19, and on the possibility that 'Maacah' was the grandmother of Asa see p. 347 n.[g] above. The nature of *mipleṣet*

[a]G and S read 'he did not abolish', implying the reading *hēsīr* for MT *sārū*. Since the reformations of Jehoshaphat, Joash, Amaziah and Azariah-Uzziah are qualified in the same way as those of Asa here in MT, Noth rightly argues that the intransitive verb is used to spare the kings censure in the Deuteronomistic appraisal of them.

[b]*Ant.* VIII, 9.2.

presents a problem. As a noun it is found in the Old Testament only here, and as a verb in Job. 9.6, signifying an earthquake. In Job 21.6; Ps. 55.5[6]; Isa. 21.4, and Ezek. 7.18 the root denotes shock or terror; hence in the present passage it is probably an orthodox substitute for a concrete term. If that is so, however, it is remarkable that it is not found elsewhere in such a context. V, familiar with the gross sexual rites of the cult of Priapus, takes it as a phallic emblem, but there is no support for this view except the association with the cult of Asherah, the Canaanite mother-goddess. Asherah, now well known through the Ras Shamra texts, here denotes the mother-goddess of the Canaanite fertility cult; elsewhere in the Old Testament, 'the Asherah' denotes a wooden pole in the sanctuary (Deut. 12.3; II K. 23.6). The word is often translated in AV as 'the grove'. The *'ᵃšērā* represented the sacred tree, either natural or stylized, which, in the form of a palm tree flanked by rampant caprids which reach up to its fruits, is a familiar motif in Canaanite art.[a] That the tree symbolizes the mother-goddess is indicated by the relief on the lid of an ivory unguent-box from Minet al-Beida (fourteenth century BC), where the place of the tree is occupied by the mother-goddess, who offers plants to two rampant caprids.[b]

15.15. The Kidron wadi below the steep eastern escarpment of the city of David and its northern extension to the Temple hill was the natural dump for the city debris (II K. 23.6). The dedications (*qᵒdāšîm*) may be the bronze shields made by Rehoboam to replace the gold or gilt ones of Solomon, or dedications from local shrines other than Jerusalem (so Kittel, Montgomery), or perhaps spoils of war.

(iii) HOSTILITIES BETWEEN ASA AND BAASHA AND THE GENERAL POLITICAL CONSEQUENCES. THE STABILIZATION OF THE FRONTIER BETWEEN ISRAEL AND JUDAH: 15.16–22

16. Seems like an editorial introduction to the passage on the border-wars between Israel and Judah (vv. 16–22), the statement being repeated at v. 32, again probably by the editor, to indicate that the change of dynasty in Israel (vv. 25–29a) did not affect the situation. Having recorded the war with Baasha, with the momentary stabilization of the frontier in favour of Judah (v. 21) in his account of Asa's reign, on which he is already engaged, the compiler notes the

[a] J. Gray, *The Canaanites*, 1964, figs. 40, 42, 43, 44.
[b] C. F. A. Schaeffer, *Ugaritica* I, 1939, pl. 1.

death of Jeroboam's son Nadab and the accession of Baasha, still in the reign of Asa, at which point he repeats the statement of the war between Asa and Baasha.

The matter in vv. 16–22 is based on official annals of the kingdom of Judah, but has been developed as a historical narrative, in which form it was found and used by the compiler.

15 [16]Now there was war between Asa and Baasha the king of Israel
all their days. [17]And Baasha the king of Israel came up against Judah
and built Ramah that none might[a] go out or come in belonging to Asa
the king of Judah. [18]And Asa took all[b] the silver and gold which was
left[c] among the treasures of the Temple of Yahweh [c] and the treasures
of the palace[d] and gave them into the hands of his servants, and king
Asa sent them to Benhadad[e] the son of Tab-rimmon the son of Hezion
the king of Aram, whose seat was in Damascus, saying, [19]There is a
covenant between me and you and[f] between my father and your father.
Here I have sent to you an inducement[g] of silver and gold; go break
your covenant with Baasha the king of Israel that he may raise his siege
of me. [20]Benhadad listened to king Asa and sent the commanders of
his forces against the cities of Israel and they attacked[h] Ijon and Dan
and Abel-beth-Maacah and the whole of Chinneroth over and above[i]
all the land of Naphtali. [21]And it happened, when Baasha heard that,
that he stopped building Ramah and withdrew to Tirzah.[j] [22]And king

[a]Reading *h*^{e}*yōt* with G for MT *tēt* ('that he should not let any . . .'), which is also possible.

[b]G^{L} omits 'all'. Another possibility, though unsupported by the versions, is that *k*^{e}*lē* ('vessels') should be read for *kol*.

[c]This phrase is omitted in G^{h}.

[d]Reading Q *hammelek* for K *melek*.

[e]G reads consistently Benhadar, and so also certain Hebrew MSS. S, however, which shows generally a better understanding of the Semitic milieu of the OT, supports MT. The name Bar-Hadad is known in Aramaic inscriptions from the eighth century. S reads the name as Barhadad ('the son of H.') and it is generally thought that this was the native Aramaic form, of which Benhadad was a Hebraization.

[f]Reading 'and' with strong support from Hebrew MSS, versions and the parallel account in Chronicles.

[g]G and II Chron. 16.3 omit 'inducement' (*šōḥad*) of MT.

[h]G^{B} reads the plural for MT singular, which, however, is not impossible.

[i]G reads 'up to' (*ʿad* for MT *ʿal*). *ʿal*, however, may mean 'over and above', 'besides' and so be retained. The reading of G is a correction of *ʿal* taken in the physical sense 'above' by one who knew that Chinneroth in Lower Galilee was lower than most of Naphtali.

[j]Reading G and V *wayyāšob tirṣātā* for MT *wayyēšeb b*^{e}*tirṣā* ('and he dwelt in Tirzah'). The latter reading might indicate that Tirzah was occupied as capital first by Baasha, and the doubtful reading of MT at 14.17, where Tirzah is abruptly introduced for the first time, may support this view. This view, however, is not excluded by the reading which we adopt. Tirzah, north-east of Shechem on the hill road to the plain of Esdraelon, was occupied by the usurper Baasha, a man of Issachar, whose home was in that plain.

Asa made a proclamation to all Judah without exemption, and they carried away the stones and timbers of Ramah which Baasha had built, and with them king Asa built Geba[a] of Benjamin and Mizpah.

15.17. Ramah, on the high road between north and south, which followed the ridge of the central hills, is the present Arab village of *ar-Rām*, east of the present road, five and a half miles north of Jerusalem and just two and a half miles north of *Tell al-Fūl* (Gibeah of Saul). Since this was in Benjamin it was not Ramatha, the home of Samuel, which was in Ephraim and is to be located in the foothills north-east of Lydda. Ramah, as well as controlling traffic on the main north-south road, also controlled the head of the Descent of Beth-horon to the foothills of Ephraim and the coastal plain. Even with the occupation at Mizpah, the situation of Jerusalem as the capital of Judah was precarious, and only its sacral significance and its status as a crown possession on which the Davidic dynasty based its authority may have prevented Jerusalem being superseded at this time by either Bethlehem or Hebron.

18f. With Asa's overtures to Benhadad we are introduced to the power of the Aramaean kingdom of Damascus which was to play such a grim role in the subsequent history of Israel until the Aramaean state was liquidated by Assyria in 732. The short nominal sentence *b*^e^*rīt bēnī ūbēnekā* ('a covenant between me and you') is in itself ambiguous, being either optative or indicative. G^L^ takes it as optative ('May there be a covenant . . .'), which Noth (*ad loc.*) accepts, cf. W. Rudolph,[b] who assumes the omission of *k*^e^*rōt* before *b*^e^*rīt*, a feasible case of haplography. The mention of a covenant between the fathers of the principals, however, suggests that this is a statement of fact. This passage indicates that Abijah the father of Asa had an agreement with Damascus which Kings does not mention. It was probably this that enabled Abijah to attack and defeat Jeroboam, the Aramaeans possibly intervening at a critical moment when Jeroboam held the advantage (II Chron. 13.13–15). This is another instance of the limitations of the Book of Kings as objective history. Baasha also had an agreement with Damascus, of which Judah was well aware. It is not certain who took the initiative in this Aramaean alliance, but it is not impossible that Baasha sought support for his usurped power, an advantage not to be forgone by Aram. The theophoric Benhadad or Barhadad (see p. 351 n.[e]), borne by at least four kings of Aram

[a]G reads 'Gibeah of Benjamin'. See Commentary, p. 355 below.
[b]*ZAW* LXIII, 1951, p. 206.

and known from Aramaic inscriptions from the eighth century, indicates that the paramount deity in the Aramaean pantheon was Hadad, now well known from the Ras Shamra texts as the god manifest in winter storms, thunder, and rain, the Canaanite Baal. The name signifies 'the Thunderer', according to an Arabic cognate, which is also the meaning of *Rammānū*, known as the epithet of the same god in Assyria. The latter word, parodied by Hebrew scribes as 'Rimmon' ('pomegranate'), is also an epithet of Hadad, being found in the compound divine name Hadad-Rimmon, the fertility-god for whose temporary eclipse ritual mourning was held (Zech. 12.11). In the genealogy of Benhadad there is no mention of Rezon, the founder of the state of Damascus, though it has been thought that Hezion the grandfather of Benhadad was the same person as Rezon, both names being corruptions of an original form Hezron (so Thenius). Winckler again[a] follows G^{AL} as against G^{B} and MT and reads 'Hazael', suggesting that Hezion has evolved through an effort to combine Hazael with Rezon. These, however, are mere conjectures. Mazar's conjecture is more probable, namely that Hezion is original, and Rezon a royal title, the two being the same person. See on 11.23. Since probably over three-quarters of a century intervened between the rise of Rezon and Benhadad, we need not assume that there were no more rulers than three in Damascus. Indeed in the circumstances it is not likely that conditions were more stable in Damascus than in Israel, where the fourth king since David reigned in Judah, besides the three kings in Israel. The name Tab-rimmon may signify 'R. is bountiful' or 'R. is willing' (Syriac *ṭayyēb*). The name Bar-Hadad is attested as the name of a king of Aram in his inscribed dedication to Melqart in the Damascus stele published by M. Dunand.[b] In the second line, where Dunand does not hazard any reading, W. F. Albright[c] reads 'the son of Tabrimmon, the son of Hezion', but both Dunand[d] and R. de Vaux[e] emphatically declared that their examination of the fragmentary text finds this impossible. Dunand is thus led to the conclusion that this Bar-Hadad was the second of that name, the contemporary of Elisha.

15.20. The name Ijon survives in the present *Marj 'Uyūn*, a large village situated in an upland plain between the Rivers *Liṭānī* and

[a] *Alttestamentliche Untersuchungen*, 1892, pp. 60ff.
[b] *BMB* III, 1941, pp. 65–76.
[c] *BASOR* 87, 1942, pp. 23–29.
[d] *BMB* VI, 1942–3, pp. 41–45.
[e] *BMB* V, 1941, p. 8n.

Ḥesbānī. The ancient site has been located in the vicinity at *Tell Dibbīn*. Dan is *Tell al-Qāḍī* on the headwaters of the Jordan, and Abel-beth-Maacah ('the water-course of the house of Maacah', an Aramaean tribe which fought against Israel in the Ammonite campaign of David, II Sam. 10.6ff.) is probably *Ibil al-Qamḥ*, six miles west of Dan.[a] The inscription of Thothmes III names Chinnereth as a city of Galilee, to be located probably at *Tell al-ʿOreimeh* north of the harp-shaped plain just south of *aṭ-Ṭabġah*. The plural form Chinneroth, if correct, is interesting, and may denote several fertile bays of good land between the eastern escarpment of the mountains of Galilee and the lake shore. Naphtali was that part of Upper and Lower Galilee lying mainly east of the watershed between the Sea of Galilee and the Mediterranean, thus including the localities just mentioned. This area was debatable land between Aram and Israel throughout their history. Šanda (I, p. 389) rightly emphasizes the economic significance of the region, through which trade routes ran to Tyre and Sidon from the corn-land of the Hauran and over the fords of Jordan to Bethshean and the great central plain (Jezreel), and through the Plain of the Baṭṭuf to Acco, or through the Carmel range by Jokmeam or Megiddo to the coastal plain. The Aramaeans occupying Damascus were the middlemen of ancient Eastern commerce.

15.21. On Tirzah see p. 351 n.[j] and on v. 33. The omission of the action which Baasha would be bound to take in the Aramaean invasion is characteristic of the Deuteronomistic compiler's determination not to be distracted from the main object of his book, and also of his Judaean interest.

22. This was an extraordinary levy, *mas* but not *mas ʿōbēd* (see above on 5.27; 9.21). On the other hand, the king apparently had the power of compulsion. For the use of timber beams in stone building, see on 7.12. The location of the fortresses subsequently built by Asa is doubtful. Mizpah is variously identified with *Nabī Samwīl* and *Tell an-Naṣbeh*. The former is a most arresting feature about six miles north-west of Jerusalem, overlooking the approach from the coastal plain to the plateau north of Jerusalem either by the upper course of the Vale of Sorek (*Wādī aṣ-Ṣurār*) or by the Descent of Beth-horon. The latter is a good base on the north–south highway from which to control the Descent of Beth-horon. It is almost certainly the Mizpah which was the seat of Gedaliah after the fall of Jerusalem in 586, as

[a] Abel, *GP* II, p. 233.

Jer. 41.5f. suggests. Ceramic remains at both sites attest an occupation in the early monarchy. Our opinion is that both sites were known as Mizpah, which was, after all, a common noun meaning 'look-out post', and was applied to several sites in Palestine and Transjordan. The name might well have been used with a qualifying noun which dropped out through familiarity. There is a local analogy in the names Gibeʿah, Gebaʿ, and Gibeʿon, all variants of 'hill', within a radius of three miles. There seems little point in Asa, after his victory over Israel, fortifying Mizpah-*Nabī Samwīl*, which is actually a little to the south of Ramah, but much more point in pushing the frontier as far north as practically possible to Mizpah-*Tell an-Naṣbeh*, which is actually four miles north of Ramah and about two miles from Bethel. Geba (MT, cf. G. Gibeah) raises a similar problem. Gibeah, *Tell al-Fūl*, excavated by Albright, the stratification of which attests occupation and rebuilding at this time, is actually two and a half miles south of Ramah, and is open to the same objection as the identification of Mizpah in this passage with *Nabī Samwīl*. But Geba, three miles over the watershed east of Gibeah and a base for the campaign of Saul and Jonathan against the Philistines at Michmash (I Sam. 14), is much more likely, in view of the Israelite occupation of Jericho. It is mentioned in Isa. 10.29 as a stage in the Assyrian advance on Jerusalem and commanded the wadi leading down to Jericho and the national sanctuary of Gilgal (near *Ḫirbet al-Mafjar*), which was in Israelite territory. While part of the tribe of Benjamin was in Israel in the lower part of this valley and part on the plateau in the kingdom of Judah the situation was delicate and the fortification of Geba a necessity.

(iv) THE DEUTERONOMISTIC OBITUARY ON ASA AND THE NOTE ON THE ACCESSION OF JEHOSHAPHAT: 15.23f.

This includes, extraordinarily, a more intimate note on the physical health of Asa, possibly a later expansion, after the tradition in II Chron. 16.12. There it is stated that he was so afflicted because he had trusted the doctors more than Yahweh. This may be a variant of the tradition in II Chron. 16.7ff. of the rebuke of Asa by the prophet Hanani for relying on the Aramaeans in his war with Israel rather than on Yahweh (so Fichtner, *op. cit.*, p. 230).

15 [23]Now as for the rest of the acts[a] of Asa and all his might and[b]

[a]Omitting 'all' of MT with G as tautological with 'the rest'.
[b]G omits 'all'.

what he achieved and the cities which he built,[a] are they not written in the Book of the Chronicles of the Kings of Judah? But in the time of his old age[b] he was diseased in his feet. [24]And Asa slept with his fathers and was buried with his fathers in the city of David his father, and Jehoshaphat his son reigned in his place.

15.23. The successes of Asa's reign not mentioned in Kings included, no doubt, his repulse of an Egyptian force of Ethiopian mercenaries about Maresha, magnified in Hebrew tradition to a victory over 'Zerah the Ethiopian' with 1,000,000 infantry and 300 chariots (II Chron. 14.9–15[8–14]). The note on the king's disease, as the adverb 'only' (*raq*) suggests, is an afterthought. The disease of the king, though probably based on fact, is cited by the Deuteronomist as a qualification of his successes, which implied divine favour. G^L makes the implication explicit by adding, though without specification, that Asa's disease was the result of his evil-doing.

(*c*) THE FALL OF THE HOUSE OF JEROBOAM: 15.25–32

This is based on the royal annals of Israel, introduced by the Deuteronomistic notice of the accession of Nadab and the duration of his reign (v. 25) and the general condemnation of him from the same standpoint (v. 26) and his obituary, presented as the fulfilment of the divine doom pronounced on Jeroboam by Ahijah (vv. 29b–30, cf. 14.14), with the usual reference to other sources for the secular history of Israel and Nadab.

From this point until II K. 10 the Books of Kings are occupied wholly with the history of the Northern kingdom except for brief notices of affairs in Judah from annalistic sources, e.g. I K. 22.46–49 and II K. 8.16–24. This preoccupation with Northern affairs is owing partly to the limited significance of Judah, which was practically a vassal kingdom from the time of Ahab until the native revolt against Athaliah, with which the interest in Judah significantly revives in II K. 11. Another reason for the peculiar interest in Israelite affairs is the fact that most of the section I K. 15.25–II K. 10.36 is occupied with prophetic history (I K. 17.1–19.21; 21; II K. 1.1–2.25; 3; 4.1–6.23; 8.1–15; 9.1–28). The focus of attention on

[a]G^h omits 'the cities which he built', probably reckoning that these are included in the passage on Asa in Kings. In view of the statement in II Chron. 14.6f.[5f.], however, concerning Asa's fortifications throughout Judah, MT should be retained.

[b]G^L reads 'he did that which was evil and . . .', his disease according to Deuteronomic theology being the consequence of his sin.

the history of the Northern kingdom was also motivated by the Deuteronomistic presentation of the disorders of that kingdom as the divine retribution for the sin of Jeroboam and the prelude to the final catastrophe of 723/2.

15 [25]Now Nadab the son of Jeroboam became king over Israel in the second year of Asa king of Judah, and he reigned over Israel two years. [26]And he did that which was evil in the sight of Yahweh and he went in the way of his father and in his sins[a] in which he involved Israel. [27]And Baasha the son of Ahijah of the house of Issachar[b] made a conspiracy against him and Baasha struck him down at Gibbethon which belonged to the Philistines, while Nadab and all Israel were laying siege to Gibbethon. [28]And Baasha put him to death in the third year of Asa king of Judah and reigned in his place. [29]And it came to pass that, when he was king, he struck down all the house of Jeroboam; he did not leave any that breathed belonging to Jeroboam until he destroyed[c] him according to the word of Yahweh which he spoke through the agency of his servant Ahijah of Shiloh, [30]on account of the sins of Jeroboam which he committed and in which he involved Israel, with his provocation with which he provoked Yahweh God of Israel. [31]Now, as for the rest of the acts of Nadab and all that he did, are they not written in the Book of the Chronicles of the Kings of Israel? [32]And there was war between Asa and Baasha the king of Israel all their days.

15.25. On the chronology, Nadab and Asa reigning contemporaneously for parts only of two years (cf. 15.1, 2, 9), see Introduction: Chronology.

27. With the brief notice of the revolt of Baasha, the Annals of the Kings of Israel are again drawn upon. Baasha was a man of Issachar at the bottleneck of the plain of Jezreel between the ridge of Gilboa and the foothills of Lower Galilee. It may have been Baasha who first developed Tirzah on the hillroad from Shechem to the plain of Jezreel as the capital of Israel.

Gibbethon was occupied by the Philistines now and 24 years later (16.15) when Omri was acclaimed king. Its location, possibly at *Tell Mal'āt*, three miles west of Gezer and five miles north of Ekron (*Tell al-Muqanna*ʿ near ʿ*Āqir*)[d] in the Philistine country in the

[a]Reading plural with G and S for MT singular.

[b]G reads variously 'who was of *Beth Belaan* (or *Beth Beddama*)', and certainly Beth Issachar of MT is unique. One would suspect that Beth indicated a place name in Issachar, though none such except Bethshemesh occurs in the tribal list in Josh. 19.17–23. Nor does *Belaan* or *Beddama* suggest any known tribal division of Issachar, though possibly this was noted here.

[c]Pointing as the infinitive construct as the grammar demands.

[d]This is noted by J. Naveh, *IEJ* VIII, 1958, pp. 165–70, as the largest Iron Age settlement in Palestine.

original country of Dan, as Josh. 19.44 suggests, indicates that in spite of his short reign Nadab was vigorous enough to take the offensive beyond the mountains of the interior.

(*d*) THE RISE AND FALL OF THE HOUSE OF BAASHA: 15.33–16.14

This is the Deuteronomistic account of the reign of Baasha. Beginning with the familiar synchronism with the reign of his contemporary in Judah, and the length of his reign, the Deuteronomist condemns him in familiar, though vague, terms and describes his doom pronounced by the prophet Jehu the son of Hanani (15.34; 16.1,7), with his obituary (16.6), where, exceptionally in the case of kings of Israel, his grave is mentioned. The reign of his son Elah, with Judaean synchronism, is introduced (16.8), and after a circumstantial extract from the history of the kingdom of Israel (16. 9–11) describing the fall of Zimri, the Deuteronomistic epilogue closes the account of his reign.

The striking language in vv. 3f., which exceeds the stereotyped Deuteronomistic condemnation, as in 14.10f., is probably the relics of a prophetic source from North Israel on which the Deuteronomistic compiler drew. Verses 9–12a also may belong to this source, which reflects the same critical view of the monarchy in North Israel as finds expression in Hos. 8.4 and in the tradition of Elijah and part of that of Elisha. The importance of this source as a preface to the disaster of 723/2 in the plan of the Deuteronomistic History, and also its extent, explains the predominance of North Israelite affairs until II K. 10. The existence of such a source may be indicated by the note in II Chron. 20.34 of 'the chronicles of Jehu the son of Hanani, which are recorded in the Book of the Kings of Israel'. The prophetic work, we assume, may have been begun by Jehu or have been stimulated by his prophecy, going back to incorporate the tradition of Ahijah. See further Introduction, pp. 30ff.

15 [33]In the third year of Asa king of Judah, Baasha the son of Ahijah became king over all[a] Israel in Tirzah (and reigned) twenty-four years. [34]And he did evil in the sight of Yahweh and went in the way of Jeroboam in the sins[b] in which he involved Israel.

16 [1]And the word of Yahweh came to Jehu the son of Hanani

[a]G[BL] omit 'all', but as the verse notes the accession of the usurper Baasha his acceptance by *all* elements of Israel including the supporters of his rival Nadab has a definite point.

[b]G and S here, as in v. 26, read the plural for MT singular.

concerning Baasha saying, [2]Because I exalted you from the dust and made you a leader over my people Israel, yet you go in the way of Jeroboam and have involved my people Israel in sin, provoking me with their sins, [3]behold, I shall make a riddance[a] of Baasha and his house, and shall make his[b] house as the house of Jeroboam the son of Nebat. [4]Him belonging to Baasha who dies in the city shall the dogs eat and him belonging to him who dies in the open country shall the birds of the air eat. [5]And as for the rest of the acts of Baasha and what he did and his might, are they not written in the Book of the Chronicles of the Kings of Israel? [6]And Baasha slept with his fathers and he was buried in Tirzah, and Elah his son became king in his place. [7]And moreover the word of Yahweh came by the agency of the prophet Jehu the son of Hanani to Baasha and to his house because of[c] all the evil which he did in the sight of Yahweh, provoking him to anger with the work of his hands, that it might be as the house of Jeroboam in spite of the fact that he had struck it down.

[8]In the twenty-sixth year of Asa king of Judah, Elah the son of Baasha became king over Israel in Tirzah (and he reigned) two years. [9]And his servant[d] Zimri, the commander of half his chariot-force, made a conspiracy against him while he was in Tirzah drinking himself drunk in the house of Arza the royal chamberlain in Tirzah. [10]And Zimri came in and struck him down and he killed him in the twenty-seventh year of Asa king of Judah and reigned in his place. [11]Now it came to pass in his reign when he was installed on his throne he struck down all the family of Baasha; [e]he did not leave any belonging to him who pissed against the wall, or any of his kinsfolk or friends.[f] [12]And Zimri destroyed the whole family of Baasha[e] according to the word of Yahweh which he spoke to[g] Baasha by the agency of the prophet Jehu, [13]on account of all the sins of Baasha and the sins of Elah his son which they committed and in which they involved Israel, provoking Yahweh God of Israel with their vanities. [14]And as for the rest of the acts of Elah and all that he did, are they not written in the Book of the Chronicles of the Kings of Israel?

15.33. For chronology see Introduction: Chronology.

Tirzah was one of the 31 cities captured by Joshua according to Hebrew tradition (Josh. 12.24). According to MT of 14.17, Tirzah had already become the capital of the Northern kingdom, but in that

[a]G reads 'will stir up' (*mēʿîr*) for MT *mabʿîr*. The following preposition and the phraseology of 14.10, however, suggest the reading *mebaʿēr*.

[b]So G[BL] for MT 'your house'.

[c]Omitting 'and' of MT with several MSS and S.

[d]G[BL] omits the title.

[e]Omitted in G[BL], possibly by homoeoteleuton.

[f]Plural for MT singular, though a conjecture unsupported by the versions, is almost certain.

[g]G reads 'concerning' (*ʿal*), which is commonly corrupted to *'el*.

passage G casts doubt on this, and the specific mention of the place in association with the reigns of Baasha and Elah may indicate that it became the capital only under Baasha. It remained the capital until Omri transferred his administration to Samaria. Long disputed, the site seems now settled beyond doubt at *Tell al-Fārʿa*, a well-watered and strategically significant site about six miles north-east of Nāblus and Shechem, commanding communications from Shechem to Bethshean and to the Jordan Valley, an identification originally proposed by W. F. Albright.[a] The recent excavations of the Dominican fathers de Vaux and Stève have demonstrated occupation since the Neolithic Age (before *c.* 5000 BC) to the end of the Israelite kingdom. The burnt level which terminates the first stratum of the Iron Age occupation may indicate the civil disorders before Omri came to the throne (16.18). The reduction of the place from an important fortress to virtually an open town just at the time Samaria was built confirms the view that *Tell al-Fārʿa* was the old capital Tirzah.[b]

16.1. As in the case of Ahijah in the days of Jeroboam and Elijah and Elisha in the time of Ahab, the conservative spirit of Israel asserted itself in politics through a prophet. This Jehu the son of Hanani is cited in II Chron. 20.34 as the author of a history which was incorporated in 'the Book of the Kings of Israel'. The following oracle, in substance and language like Ahijah's denunciation of Jeroboam and his house (14.10f.), is a Deuteronomistic expansion of an original oracle, which contained vv. 3f. The prophet himself is an obscure figure. He is mentioned as encountering Jehoshaphat of Judah (II Chron. 19.2), but this was after the death of Ahab, over 50 years after his oracle to Baasha, which hardly sounds probable.

2. *nāgīd* (lit. 'one who is set over against') is used also of Jeroboam (14.7), and here as there implies a limitation of the authority of the ruler, *melek* having absolutist implications, cf. Arabic *malaka* ('to possess'). 'My people' (*ʿammī*) has a peculiar connotation for Israel. It denotes primarily the relationship of the community with its God as a kinship-group (*ʿam*), where the moral relationship of people and God is paramount. This relationship was sacramentally conserved in ancient Israel by the ceremonial renewal of the covenant in the

[a] *JPOS* XI, 1931, pp. 241ff.

[b] R. de Vaux and A. Stève, *RB* LIV, 1947, pp. 394–433, 573–89; LV, 1948, pp. 544–80; LVI, 1949, pp. 102–38; LVIII, 1951, pp. 393–430; R. de Vaux, 'Tirzah', *Archaeology and Old Testament Study*, ed. D. W. Thomas, 1967, pp. 371–83.

assembly of the sacral confederacy,[a] and indicates the tradition represented by the prophet. The use of *nāgīd* relative to the people of Yahweh probably reflects the upholding of the conception of charismatic authority over hereditary monarchy, which was a leading motif of the prophetic adaptation of the historical narrative of the Northern kingdom.

16.7. This verse seems at first sight secondary and a useless addition to vv. 1–4, but may be admitted as primary and genuine if we take *weʿal-ʾašer hikkā ʾōtō* as a concessive clause, 'in spite of the fact that he had struck it down'.[b] This, in so far as it was the fulfilment of the word of God through Ahijah, was considered meritorious. The concessive use of *ʿal* is common in Arabic.

9. 'His servant' signifies here primarily 'his retainer'. In Canaan of the Late Bronze Age there was a special class of military specialists in chariot warfare, whose status of *mariannu* with lands and privileges depended personally on the king. This modified feudal system was adapted to local exigencies in Israel under Saul, David, and his successors, and Zimri was one of these. The name Zimri seems Semitic, a hypocoristicon, or truncation, possibly of Zimri-el or Zimri-yahu, cf. Zimri-lim of Mari. The ending in *-i*, however, may signify a nickname. G. B. Gray suggests a connection with *zamrān* ('mountain sheep'), but this is unlikely. The affinity is more likely to be with Arabic *ḏamīr* ('courageous, mighty') which Tur Sinai finds in the phrase *zemīrōt belāyelā* in Job 35.10. We should find other instances in *ʿuzzī wezimrātī yāh* in Ex. 15.2; Isa. 12.2; Ps. 118.14; cf. Isa. 25.5, *zemīr ʿarīṣīm yeʿanne* ('he abases the might of tyrants'). The Ugaritic cognate proposed by U. Cassuto, quoted in *UT* 51 VII, 38f., is possible, but, we consider, unlikely. The name Arza or Arisu is doubtless derived from the root *rṣh* ('to be favourable'), and is a hypocoristicon. The name Arṣu, an appellative which has become a proper name, is known as one of the twin-gods manifest in the evening and morning star in the Roman imperial period at Palmyra, and as a divine attribute the root occurs in an Aramaic variant in the divine name *ʾarqaʾrešep* in a royal inscription from the eighth century at Zinjirli. On the title *ʾašer ʿal-habbayit* denoting the royal chamberlain, see on 4.6. His office may have been restricted to managing the royal demesne at Tirzah, as Noth (*ad loc.*) suggests.

[a]On the significance of *ʿam* with such sacral implications as opposed to the purely secular *gōy* see E. A. Speiser, *JBL* LXXIX, 1960, pp. 157–60.

[b]So Montgomery, ICC, pp. 282, 289.

16.11. 'Kinsfolk' (*gōʾalīm*) means primarily those who had the duty of rehabilitation of those who had lost status or liberty, primarily in the family, hence the secondary meaning 'kinsfolk'. The point here is that none should be left to discharge the duty of blood revenge as *gōʾēl haddām* (cf. Josh. 20.3; II Sam. 14.11).

13. 'Their vanities' (*habelēhem*), as in Deuteronomistic phraseology at v. 26, II K. 17.15 and Deut. 32.21, denotes gods other than Yahweh, or idols, who have no substance.

(*e*) THE RISE OF THE HOUSE OF OMRI: 16.15–34

This section is introduced by an editorial note on the accession of Zimri, synchronized with the reign of Asa in Judah, and with an epilogue from the same Deuteronomistic hand on his reign and delinquency (vv. 15a, 19–20). There is a similar introduction (v. 23) and epilogue to the reign of Omri (vv. 25–28) and to the reign of Ahab, with a Deuteronomistic preview of his reign (vv. 29–33). On each reign there is more detailed and objective historical matter based ultimately on the royal annals of the Northern kingdom for Zimri and Omri (vv. 15b–18), for the final success of Omri (vv. 21–22) and his reign (vv. 23b–24), and for a note of the rebuilding of Bethel in the reign of Ahab (v. 24). This, however, is expanded by circumstantial details, e.g. v. 24a, in the style of historical narrative. In the summary account of the reign of Ahab (16.31–34), which follows the introduction to his reign and the Deuteronomistic appraisal of it (16.29f.), the influence of the compiler is obvious in the selection of the note on Ahab's marriage with Jezebel in anticipation of the clash with Elijah and the prophetic oracle of doom on his house, which occupies so much of the sequel. In the note on the rebuilding of Jericho in Ahab's reign in face of the curse, taken to be prophetically communicated (16.34), we may see the same motivation.

16 [15]In the twenty-seventh year of Asa king of Judah Zimri became king for seven days in Tirzah, the people[a] being in the field against Gibbethon which belonged to the Philistines. [16]Now the people in camp heard that Zimri had made a conspiracy and had, moreover, struck down the king, so all Israel made Omri, the commander of the army, king over Israel that day in the camp. [17]Then Omri and all Israel with him went up from Gibbethon and laid siege to Tirzah.

[a]G reads 'and the army (lit. 'camp') of Israel . . .', possibly conscious of the fact that the people, strictly speaking, were not engaged at Gibbethon, since part of them supported Zimri and, later, Tibni. The army, however, was ideally 'the people of Yahweh', even though the days of the militant confederacy were past.

18And when Zimri saw that the city was taken he went into the residence of the palace-complex[a] and he set fire to the palace over himself and died, 19on account of his sins which he committed, doing evil in the sight of Yahweh, going in the way of Jeroboam in the sin which he committed, involving also Israel. 20And as for the rest of the acts of Zimri and the conspiracy he made, are they not written in the Book of the Chronicles of the Kings of Israel?

21Then were the people of Israel divided in half; half of the people followed Tibni the son of Ginath to make him king and half followed Omri. 22And the people who followed Omri proved stronger than[b] the people who followed Tibni the son of Ginath, and Tibni (and his brother Joram) [c] perished (at that time),[c] and Omri became king.[d]

23In the thirty-first year of Asa king of Judah, Omri became king over Israel (and reigned) twelve years; he reigned six years in Tirzah. 24And he bought the hill Shomron from Shemer for two talents of silver and he built up the hill and called the name of the city which he had built after the name of Shemer, the owner(s) of the hill, Shomron (Samaria). 25And Omri did evil in the sight of Yahweh, yea, he did more evil than any who were before him. 26And he walked in all the way of Jeroboam the son of Nebat and in his sins[e] in which he involved Israel, provoking Yahweh God of Israel to anger with his vanities. 27And as for the rest of the acts of Omri and all[f] that he did and his might which he realized, are they not written in the Book of the Chronicles of the Kings of Israel? 28And Omri slept with his fathers and was buried in Samaria, and Ahab his son reigned in his place.

29Now Ahab the son of Omri became king over Israel in the thirty-eighth year of Asa[g] king of Judah, and Ahab the son of Omri ruled

[a]According to MT here *'armōn*, being a construct, must signify some part of the palace. It is found elsewhere in the Old Testament as a residence, but it is generally taken in the present passage as a fortress (Kittel, Skinner, Montgomery) and is derived by Ginsberg from the root *rmy* ('to throw down'), i.e. the foundation, cf. Assyrian *rimītu* ('building') (E. A. Speiser, *JQR* XIV, 1924, p. 329). The root *rwm* is found in Ugaritic in the intensive, meaning 'to erect' a building (Gordon, *UT* 51 V, 114). Doubtless the building was fortified, but there is no reason to take the word in other than its usual sense of 'mansion, residence'. This is here singled out from the palace-complex of storehouses, administrative quarters etc., now well illustrated by the palaces of Mari, Ugarit and Samaria. There is thus no need to add the definite article to *'armōn* and to take it in apposition to *bēt hammelek*.

[b]There is no need to emend *'et* to *mē* before *hāʿām*, the verb *ḥāzaq* being found with a direct object (pronominal suffix) in Jer. 20.7 and II Chron. 28.20.

[c]So with G for the shorter MT.

[d]G reads 'after Tibni', which may be right, though Omri ruled simultaneously with Tibni.

[e]Q reads the singular. Following the MT consonants the plural should be read, as usual in this stock phrase.

[f]So with G and many Hebrew MSS.

[g]G^{BL} read 'in the second year of Jehoshaphat', since they reckon Omri's twelve years from the suppression of Tibni. This brings Ahab's accession down to the year after Asa's death, hence Jehoshaphat's second year discounting an accession year. G also inserts an account of Jehoshaphat's reign between vv. 28 and 29.

over Israel in Samaria twenty-two years. 30And Ahab the son of Omri[a] did that which was evil in the sight of Yahweh[b] more than any who was before him. 31And it happened that, as if it were a light matter that he walked in the sins of Jeroboam the son of Nebat, he took to wife Jezebel the daughter of Ethbaal king of the Sidonians, and went and served Baal and bowed down to him, 32and he erected a place of sacrifice to Baal, the temple of Baal which he built in Samaria. 33And Ahab made the Asherah and Ahab did even more to provoke Yahweh the God of Israel to anger than all the kings of Israel who were before him.

34In his days Hiel[c] the Bethelite built Jericho; at the cost of Abiram his eldest son did he found it, and at the cost of Segub his youngest son did he set the gates in place according to the word of Yahweh which he spoke through Joshua the son of Nun.

16.15. G^B states that Zimri reigned seven years. *yāmim* signifies both 'days' and 'years', but the sense of the passage indicates that the *coup d'état* of Zimri was quite ephemeral. On Gibbethon as an Israelite military objective and its location see on 15.27.

16. The statement that 'all Israel' made Omri king is obviously not literally true, since Zimri had a sufficient number of supporters in Tirzah to necessitate a siege by Omri, and for five years Omri's rule was disputed by Tibni and his followers. The name Omri is unique in Israel and has been thought to be of Arab origin, cf. ʿOmar, ʿAmr,[d] and Šanda (I, pp. 401ff.) suggests that he was the governor of Moab under Baasha. The family of Omri is not mentioned, which lends support to the view that Omri was one of the class of professional soldiers, perhaps of alien birth, who depended on the king. Against this view is the fact that he was elected by the army in the field, which, though officered to a considerable extent by professional soldiers not necessarily of Israelite birth, was still 'the people', i.e. the people of Yahweh. It is not likely that they would have chosen an alien, however able. A more probable view in our opinion is that the fact that Omri's lineage is not mentioned indicates that he was of Canaanite extraction from a community incorporated in Israel since the time of David and Solomon. Quite conceivably the predilection of Ahab for Jezreel (ch. 21) indicates that that was the ancestral home,[e] cf. the reference to the natural kinsmen of Ahab in Jezreel

[a]G^{BL} omit *ben ʿomrī* of MT.

[b]G^{BL} reads 'and did evil'.

[c]G reads, probably more correctly than MT, *'aḥī'ēl*, though in theophoric compounds with *'aḥī* the *'a* may be omitted, e.g. Hiram.

[d]Noth, *IP*, pp. 63, 222.

[e]Šanda, I, p. 402.

(II K. 9.11). In this case, the struggle between Omri and Tibni may have been a struggle between the Canaanite element in the state of Israel with their traditions of professional military service under the feudal system in the former Canaanite city-states and the Israelite element under Tibni. It is obvious, however, that Omri had the support of many Israelites also, 'the people' being divided. His supporters would include those Israelites assimilated to the Canaanite way of life, chiefly in the central plain.[a] This is the only case to which the prohibition against a foreigner as king (Deut. 17.15) is relevant. The derivation of the name Omri is uncertain. The fact that his unsuccessful rival was Tibni, and the ending of both names, suggests that these may have been nicknames, 'the man of the sheaf' (*'ōmer*) and 'the man of straw' (*teben*), but if this were so it is remarkable that the Assyrian records use the nickname in referring to Israel as *bīt Ḫumria*. The only philological clue is the Arabic root *'amara* ('to live'). The name may be a hypocoristicon of 'Omriyahu, possibly '(The) life (which) Yahweh (has given),' or 'Pilgrim (at the shrine) of Yahweh'.

16.18. On the significance of *'armōn* see p. 363 n.[a]. The subject of *wayyiśrōp* ('burned'), though probably the same as *wayyābō'* ('entered') and *wayyāmōt* ('died'), i.e. Zimri, is uncertain. In the singular the verb might have the indefinite subject.

19. This is probably an editorial addition in conformity with the general pattern of the assessment of the reigns of the kings of Israel in their obituaries. In seven days Zimri can have had little opportunity to 'go in the way of Jeroboam in the sin he committed, involving also Israel'.

20. The summary Deuteronomistic reference to the conspiracy of Zimri seems to imply a fuller account, of which the compiler has made only summary use in vv. 9–11.

21. The name Tibni, if not a nickname, may be paralleled by the Akkadian name Tabni-ea ('May Ea give a son'), cited by Šanda, and possibly by the Phoenician Tabnith. Affinities with these names are suggested by the fact that G and Josephus give the name as Tabni, of which Tibni may be a Jewish parody ('man of straw'). The feminine ending of Ginath suggests at first a place-name, the home of Tibni rather than his father. In the Amarna Tablets a place Gina is

[a]Cf. Soggin, *op. cit.*, p. 99, who, though admitting the inadequacy of the evidence, would see in the triumph of Omri the triumph of the professional army over the militia of Israel and their popularly acclaimed nominee.

mentioned, Engannim of the Old Testament, modern *Jenīn* on the southern edge of the great central plain. According to G, Tibni was supported by his brother Joram, whose name is certainly orthodox. The counter-movement to the rising of Omri, in so far as it maintained a balance of power for five years, is certainly significant. It is tempting to speculate on this as a movement of the religious community of Israel against the power of the army, now largely professional, or perhaps a protest by the older, more conservative elements against the younger men of the army. If Tibni's movement had a religious significance it is difficult to suppose that the Deuteronomist would not have treated the matter at greater length. The silence of Kings on this significant movement indicates its limitation as a secular history.

16.22. The phrase *wayyāmot tibnī* ('and Tibni died') is equivocal, signifying, especially if we read with G 'and his brother Joram', violent death or, as Noth thinks (*Könige*, *ad loc.*), a natural death. In the latter case, the shorter MT is to be preferred.

23. On the date of Omri's accession, cf. vv. 15ff., here reckoned from the 31st year of Asa, when he became sole ruler after the suppression of Tibni, see Introduction: Chronology.

24. The name 'Samaria' is that of G. Beyond the dating of Omri's reign (see Introduction: Chronology, pp. 64f.) this is the only specific communication of anything of political significance in his important reign. Nothing is indicated of what Omri's acquisition of a new capital signified, but from the fact that he was the first to give stability to a dynasty in Israel, it is obvious that by purchasing this virtually virgin site (mod. *Ṣebasṭīyeh*, some seven miles north-west of Nablus) Omri acquired a personal possession, as David acquired Jerusalem, in which he was free to develop a city-state within a state, and bequeath it to his descendants, so founding a dynasty.[a] The stormy history of Israel since the disruption of the kingdom of Solomon indicated that hereditary government was not cordially accepted, perhaps, as Alt suggests,[b] because the tradition of the sacral community regarded the authority of the king as *ad hoc*, like that of the ancient judges in a given crisis. Alt makes the further feasible suggestion that Omri, himself a Canaanite, selected for his capital a site with no Israelite associations in a Canaanite region. It is significant that the only cult for which provision was evidently made in Samaria

[a]See A. Alt, 'Der Stadtstaat Samaria', *KS* III, pp. 258–302.
[b]'Das Königtum in Israel und Juda', *VT* I, 1951, pp. 2ff.

was the cult of Baal, to whom Ahab built a temple (16.32), which was destroyed in Jehu's revolt (II K. 10.27). The marriage of Ahab to Jezebel of Tyre would tend to confirm this view. Shemer, from whom Omri bought the hill, might be a private individual, but the size and fertility of the hill and the form of the name (segholate and probably feminine) suggests a tribe or sept rather than an individual. A tribe Shemer is unknown in this region in the Old Testament. Perhaps it was a Canaanite community. Noth, however (*op. cit.*, p. 353), regards the citation of *šemer*, from whom Omri is said to have bought the hill (v. 24a), whether as an individual or as a Canaanite community (cf. *'ᵃdōnē hāhār*, 'the owners (?) of the hill'), v. 24b as a secondary explanatory gloss, *šōmᵉrōn* being actually the name of the hill before Omri's building, cf. *ṣīyōn*, *ṣalmōn*, *lᵉbānōn*, *ḥermōn*, *śiryōn*. Most of these are appellatives, so *šōmᵉrōn* may conceivably have meant 'the Ward Hill'.

16.26. Omri is sweepingly condemned in the familiar Deuteronomistic denunciation, which, however, names no specific sin. Thus sketchily in those few verses does the editor dismiss the most significant king of the Northern kingdom, who unified a divided kingdom, made the rule of Israel effective in at least the northern part of Moab, and so impressed Assyria, the greatest imperial power in the Near East of the time, that until the end of the kingdom, when the house he founded had been liquidated, they refer to Israel as 'the house of Omri'.

28. The name Ahab, like Omri, is unique in the Old Testament. It may signify, as Noth suggests,[a] 'The brother of the father', i.e. 'resembling the father'. Šanda's suggestion (I, p. 407) is also feasible that 'brother-father' refers to the social custom of levirate marriage, or may be complimentary to the brother of the father, regarding him as the godfather of the child. The name is attested in Assyrian and in Safaitic inscriptions. Another possible explanation is that the name reflects the relations of the father, Omri, to the kin-god of a community into which he had intermarried. He might consider this god as his 'brother', but his son having been born to a woman of his adoptive community, this 'brother' is now 'father' to his son. Another possibility is that Ahab was a throne-name indicating the admission of the prince to co-regency with his father.

31. It has been proposed to point the *h* in *hᵃnāqēl* ('is it a light matter?') as the definite article instead of the interrogative, thus

[a]*IP*, p. 222.

giving the participle the superlative sense, but this is unnecessary, the interrogative occasionally bearing a conditional sense, e.g. Ezek. 8.17. The name Jezebel (*'īzebel*) as pointed in MT is an obvious parody. The first perversion of the name may have been *'ī-zᵉbūl* ('No nobility'), for an original *'ī zᵉbūl* ('Where is the Prince?'), then with the scribal perversion of *zᵉbūl*, the title of Baal, to *zebel* ('dung'). *zᵉbūl* is known as an element in the divine name Baalzebul, and is now known as one of the stock titles of Baal in the Ras Shamra texts, meaning 'Prince'. The probable significance of the name, of which we conjecture the original pointing in Phoenician, *'ī-zᵉbūl*, is 'Where is the Prince (i.e. Baal)?' This was actually a cultic cry of those who mourned the eclipse of Baal as a vegetation deity in the Ras Shamra text,

> *'i 'al'iyn bʿl*
> *'i zbl bʿl 'arṣ.*[a]
> Where is Baal the Mighty,
> Where is the Prince, Lord of the Earth?

The name might reflect the birth of the princess in the summer, when such ritual was seasonable. The name of Jezebel's father Ethbaal or Ittobaal, as Josephus's spelling suggests,[b] is patient of a similar explanation. In the same text from Ras Shamra (*UT* 49, III, 20–21) the revival of Baal is anticipated with the cultic cry

> *kḥy 'al'iyn bʿl*
> *k'iṯ zbl bʿl 'arṣ.*
> For Baal the Mighty is alive!
> For the Prince, Lord of the Earth, exists!

This passage indicates that the name signifies 'Baal exists'.[c] Josephus designates Ethbaal 'king of the Tyrians and Sidonians'. Actually Ethbaal, like Hiram in Solomon's time, was king of Tyre, but the southern coastland of Phoenicia was at this time under Tyrian hegemony and the rulers entitled themselves king of the older settlement of Sidon, or rather, of the Sidonians, e.g. Hiram II in the eighth century, and Tabnith, *c.* 300.[d] According to Josephus, Ethbaal, or Ittobaal, who came to the throne probably just before Omri's *coup*

[a]Gordon, *UT* 49, IV, 40ff.
[b]*C. Apionem*, 1.18.
[c]Cf. Albright's opinion that *'iṯ* in the Ras Shamra texts signifies 'presence' rather than 'existence', *BASOR* 94, 1944, p. 31.
[d]Cooke, *NSI* 4.

d'état, ruled for 32 years, being dated by E. Meyer *c.* 887–856. Omri's Phoenician alliance, as well as supporting perhaps his Canaanizing policy in Israel, was dictated by the menace of the Aramaean states of inland Syria, particularly Damascus, which had taken districts in North Galilee from Israel in the time of Baasha (15.20). The Aramaeans were formidable commercial rivals both of the Phoenicians and Israel (cf. 20.34). The agricultural potential of a friendly power in Palestine was important for the Phoenician coastal towns (Acts 20.21), and the overseas trade of the Phoenicians provided markets for the wine and olive-oil of Palestine.

16.32 *mizbēaḥ* generally means 'altar'. If it has this meaning here the preposition *b*[e] must be understood, though, as often, not expressed before *bēt habbaʿal*. The word, however, may mean here 'place of sacrifice' in the wider sense, *bēt habbaʿal* being in apposition. Baal-worship was stimulated by the zeal of Jezebel. It may reflect the possible Canaanite origin of the family of Omri, though Ahab, significantly, named his children with Yahweh-theophorics. In the private domain of Samaria, Ahab was free to build the temple of Baal either for Jezebel, as Solomon provided shrines for his foreign wives in Jerusalem, or as an expression of his liberal policy, which was orientated to his Canaanite as well as to his Israelite subjects (11.7). On Asherah, the image or symbol of the mother-goddess of Canaan, see on 15.13.

34. No doubt the notice of the rebuilding of Jericho under Ahab (v. 34a) was recorded in the annals of Ahab's reign, like the 'cities which he built', for which we are referred to such a source in 22.39. It has been selected by the Deuteronomistic compiler, however, to bring Ahab under the curse pronounced in Josh. 6.26 upon the man who would rebuild Jericho, and the words of the curse are explained in the tradition of Hiel, which was probably secondary, cited by the Deuteronomist from popular tradition. Hiel is an abbreviation of Ahiel, the form in G. Jericho (*Tell as-Sulṭān*, about a mile and a half north-west of modern Jericho) was not quite deserted at this time, hence *bānā* signifies 'fortified' or 'built up'. The recent excavations at Jericho attest a considerable Iron Age occupation on the evidence mainly of remains of the period washed off the *tell*, but these are mainly from two centuries after the time of Ahab.[a] II Sam. 10.5 indicates a settlement at Jericho in the time of David, but an open settlement in the oasis may be indicated rather than a fortified settle-

[a]K. M. Kenyon, *Digging up Jericho*, 1957, pp. 263ff.

ment on the actual mound. MT means literally that the foundation of the city was laid in, or with, Abiram and the gate in, or with, Segub. The preposition *b*^e^ is ambiguous. It may conceivably be locative, the reference being to foundation sacrifices. This practice has been questioned,[a] and it is not easy to determine whether house-burials, usually of infants, in archaeological stations in Palestine are the evidences of foundation sacrifices or normal burials, it being known that among the fellahin of Upper Egypt still-born infants are buried in dwelling-houses. Citing such instances from his excavations at Gezer, Macalister[b] was able further to attest anthropomorphic figurines in bronze and silver buried under the foundation of houses at Gezer,[c] and lamps, which were probably lit to signify life, with inverted bowls, which have been found at various Palestinian sites.[d] Remains of foundation sacrifices, possibly bearing more directly on the present passage, were found in the burial of two new-born infants in jars within the gate-complex of *Tell al-Fārʿa* by Nāblus in the last phase of the Middle Bronze Age.[e] The fact that these burials were not associated with others, but were isolated in the open space 'within the gate', may support the conclusion that this is a case of foundation sacrifice.[f] Alternatively, in the present passage the preposition *b*^e^ could signify 'at the cost of' (*beth pretii*), indicating the belief that the natural death of the sons of the builder was the consequence of the curse upon the rebuilding of the ruined site of Jericho. This is associated in the present passage with the word of God through Joshua (Josh. 6.26). On the assumption that the passage in Joshua is later than that in Kings, it is suggested that the curse on the rebuilding of Jericho reflected common practice in the case of ancient ruins, and that the curse of Joshua was suggested by the fate of Hiel's sons. Infant mortality is high enough in the primitive East for popular opinion to find in the misfortunes of Hiel's family the literal fulfilment of such a curse. On the other hand, though the Joshua narrative in its literary form is later, there is no reason to doubt the antiquity of the oral tradition of the curse on Jericho, and such was the current belief in the automatic operation of the curse that it might have been literally carried out in the case of Abiram and Segub. Hiel of Bethel

[a] Watzinger, *Denkmäler Palästinas* I, 1933–5, p. 72.
[b] *Gezer* II, 1912, pp. 426ff., fig. 508.
[c] *Ibid.*, pp. 433ff., fig. 518.
[d] *Ibid.*, pp. 434ff., fig. 516.
[e] De Vaux and Stève, *RB* LVIII, 1951, Pl. V, tombs J and K, pp. 401–3.
[f] See further H. C. Trumbull, *The Threshold Covenant*, 1896, pp. 46ff.

might have volunteered to make this sacrifice, or he may have been some backward person or political suspect who was compelled to make this sacrifice to popular superstition. On the other hand, I. M. Blake[a] has feasibly suggested that 'the foundation and the gates' and 'the eldest and the youngest' sons of Hiel refer to the complete work and the complete disaster in the entire loss of his family, which Blake refers to contamination of the spring through temporary radiation, to which he relates Elisha's restoration of the fertility of the spring in II K. 2.19–22, on which see further. Almost certainly the rebuilding of Jericho was connected with the threat, and possibly the fact, of rebellion against Israel in Moab, see on II K. 3.5.

5. THE REIGN OF AHAB AND THE FALL OF THE HOUSE OF OMRI: I. 17.1–II. 10.31

In this section genuine historical sources are used in some detail (e.g. 20.1–34; 22; II K. 3.4–27; 6.24–7.20; 8.20–22; 9.1–10.14), but with prophetic adaptation and Deuteronomistic comments and notices throughout. The bulk of the section, however, is taken from sources dealing with Elijah and Elisha. Some of this matter is concerned with the role of these prophets in historical and social crises in Israel, e.g. ch. 18 (the ordeal on Carmel), ch. 19 (the sequel foreshadowing the prophetic support for Jehu and the commissioning of Elisha), ch. 21 (the incident of Naboth's vineyard), II K. 8.7–15 (Elisha and the *coup d'état* of Hazael), II K. 9.1–6 (Elisha and the *coup d'état* of Jehu). There is a great deal of other matter, however, which is concerned with more personal incidents on the career of these prophets, and is rather in the nature of hagiology, e.g. I K. 17.4–6 (Elijah miraculously fed in the famine), II K. 1.9–16 (Elijah calls down fire on the emissaries of Ahaziah), II K. 2.1–18 (Elijah's translation), 2.19–22 (Elisha and the waters of Jericho), 2.23–25 (Elisha and the children of Bethel), 4.1–7 (Elisha and the widow's oil), 4.8–37 (Elisha and the Shunammite's son), 4.38–41 (death in the pot), 4.42–44 (Elisha and the multiplication of food), 5 (Elisha and Naaman), 6.1–7 (Elisha and the floating axe), 6.8–23 (Elisha and the blinding of the Syrians). Here are traditions orally preserved by prophetic circles, eventually forming saga-cycles. The origin of these in such narrow communities is obvious from the limited and even trivial interest of most of these incidents. The absence of any moral tone in most of this matter is

[a] *PEQ*, 1967, pp. 86–97.

further indication of its humble origin from the dervish guilds, and it is significant that in the Elijah-Elisha passages, where miracle in the Old Testament, outside the Exodus tradition, is particularly at home, it is only in the latter category of passages that it predominates.

In his penetrating study of Elijah, G. Fohrer[a] distinguishes between sober narrative of the historical significance of Elijah, and popular traditions, which, in the fashion of hagiology, magnified the historical figure to legendary proportions, emphasizing the miraculous. The former is a compilation of separate traditions[b] which had been developed and transmitted in prophetic circles, possibly within the living memory of those who had known Elijah, the contemporary of Ahab (874–853), and his son Ahaziah (853–852). The tradition was fixed in the compilation, which may also be dated early, possibly in the lifetime of Elisha in the early eighth century.[c] The material naturally shows the influence of the compiler in the arrangement according to the theme of Elijah's protest against the proclivity to the cult of Baal, the Canaanite fertility cult (17.1; 18)[d] and that of the king's persecution of the prophet and worshippers of Yahweh (see especially ch. 19, with reflections in 17.3 and 18.7–14). In view of the early date of the compilation, however, there is no reason to doubt the historicity of this representation of the significance of Elijah,[e]

[a]*Elia*, 1957; 1968².

[b]Alt, 'Das Gottesurteil auf dem Karmel', *KS* II, 1953, pp. 135ff., regards these as independent traditions. Jepsen, *Nabi*, 1934, p. 64, assumes considerable effacement and transposition of the original traditions. Eissfeldt, *Der Gott Karmel*, 1953, pp. 32f., like Fohrer, emphasizes the unity of chs. 17–19 in MT.

[c]Fohrer, *op. cit.*, p. 42, suggests that it is as early as the end of the ninth century. Albright, *From the Stone Age to Christianity*, 1957², pp. 306–9, considers that the stories of Elijah could not have had a very long oral tradition since they so closely reflect historical circumstances which are known to have obtained in Israel, and were given their coherent form 'hardly later than the ninth century'.

[d]Fohrer, *op. cit.*, pp. 32–36, regards Elijah's warning through the drought in 17.1 and his announcement of the rain (18.1–2a, 16f., 41–46) as located at Jezreel and distinct from the ordeal on Carmel (18.3a–4). 17.1 is of course distinct from the ordeal on Carmel, but we are not convinced that the ordeal on Carmel is distinct from the breaking of the drought in 18.1–2a, 41–46. See commentary on 18.41–46.

[e]Fohrer, *op. cit.*, pp. 53f., questions the historicity of Elijah's dramatic protest against Ahab's liberal policy in religion, which, he claims, is unlikely on the scale on which it is presented, in view of what is known or can be inferred from the conditions of Ahab's reign. No doubt the ordeal on Carmel may have been less dramatic and the vindication of Yahwism less drastic than the slaughter of the priests suggests, and it may well be coloured by the tradition of Moses' rally of the people to a like decision after the incident of the golden calf (Ex. 32, esp. vv. 25–28). The boldness of the canonical prophets, however, and the prophetic denunciations of the earlier kings of Israel may be cited in support of the bold intervention

which, we think, simply reflects his mission set in just perspective by the next generation. The tradition of Elijah at Horeb in 19.1–18, about which Fohrer is, we think, unduly sceptical,[a] has also a historical significance in the mission of Elijah. Though in the nature of the case this reflects the intimate personal experience of the prophet, which nevertheless may have been communicated and publicly divulged through his disciple Elisha as the authority for the tradition of Elijah, the journey itself may have had public significance as an act of prophetic symbolism, indicating the significance of a return to the ancestral faith of Israel for which Elijah strove. So regarded, the incident was relevant both in the context of his protest against the amoral nature worship of Canaan, which is the subject of chs. 17f., and against the overriding of the rights of free Israelites traditionally sanctioned by Yahweh at Horeb, the theme of the incident of Naboth's vineyard in ch. 21. Since God's religious and social demands in the covenant, however, with the exception of the first commandment, are not mentioned in the Horeb incident, we should agree with Fohrer[b] that the incident is independent of the traditions in chs. 17f. before the compilation. We consider that, apart from its

---

of Elijah. The antipathy to, or at least apprehension of, the influence of the Canaanite Baal-cult was characteristic of the custodians of the religion of Israel for long before the time of Elijah, as is indicated in the insistence on the celebration of the three great annual festivals at the central shrine of the sacral confederacy of Israel specifically to counteract the influence of the Canaanite fertility cult. With the impetus to the latter given as a result of Ahab's Phoenician alliance and intensified as a result of the development of monotheistic tendencies in the cult of Baal, there is nothing improbable in Elijah's great attempt to rally the people to their ancestral faith. Indeed, if the persecution of the Yahwists, including the prophets, is to be taken seriously, as the recurrence of the theme in chs. 17–19 suggests, then the prophetic protest must belong to the tradition of the historical Elijah. This motif and that of the protest against the fertility cult certainly serve to give coherence to the collection of the traditions of Elijah, as Fohrer insists (*op. cit.*, pp. 53f.), but they are, we claim, more than literary devices. If the collection of these traditions is as early as Fohrer himself suggests, we are entitled to regard the great prophetic protest against religious syncretism and the subsequent persecution as reflecting the true perspective on the events in which Elijah was involved at a remove perhaps of only one generation.

[a]Noth, *PJB* XXXVI, 1940, pp. 7ff., however, argues for Horeb as a place of pilgrimage in the north-west Hejaz. Certainly Beersheba was an objective of pilgrimage from Israel about a century after Elijah (Amos 5.5; 8.14).

[b]Fohrer, *op. cit.*, pp. 88–93, justly emphasizes the distinctive contribution of Elijah, no mere reactionary, to extending the domain of Yahweh beyond the narrow limits of the militant sacral confederacy and its historical and social exigencies to the control of all forces in the sedentary life of Canaan, to the exclusion of Baal.

public significance as an act of prophetic symbolism and as a retreat in persecution, its real significance was the revelation that the communication of the will of God was not primarily in the spectacular phenomena traditionally associated with the desert mountain of God and preserved in psalms in the cult (cf. the hymnic introductions to the Song of Deborah (Judg. 5.4f.) and the Blessing of Moses (Deut. 33.2)), which rather removed God from the sphere of ordinary human activity and formalized man's response. Elijah's new insight was that God was accessible in intelligible communication to men, particularly prophets, in the ordinary course of daily affairs of men and communities. The specific commission to Elijah, which unfortunately has been coloured by the role that Elisha played in the rise of Hazael and Jehu, probably concerned the wider political context, where Elijah, like the later prophets, would be called upon to interpret events and perhaps even to direct particular agencies in the fulfilment of the will of God for Israel. The Horeb incident, however, remains incomplete with the omission of the commission to Elijah, which, whether general or particular, has been displaced by the commission to appoint Hazael and Jehu (19.15–18a), reflecting the practical measures in which Elijah was involved, whatever these may actually have been, and by the addition of the commission to anoint [*sic*!] Elisha (v. 16b). The significance of Syria in Elijah's future mission, to say nothing of the improbable part of the individual Hazael, must remain a mystery. In view of the association of Jehu with the austere Rechabites, however, Elijah's commission may have concerned a *rapprochement* with them in his campaign for the ancestral values in Israel. Indeed the historical significance of Elijah's journey to Horeb may have been either such a *rapprochement* or a testimony to such elements that, though determined to include the annual cycle of fertilty in the sphere of Yahweh, as chs. 17f. indicate, he was none the less staunch to ancestral Yahwism.

With this matter, the tradition of other independent incidents of historical significance in which Elijah was involved was associated in the compilation, as for instance his denunciation of Ahab in the incident of Naboth's vineyard (ch. 21) and of Ahaziah in his mission to consult Baal-zebul of Ekron after his accident (II K. 1.2–8, 17a). The call of Elisha (19.19–21) also commends itself as genuine, particularly as it differs from the commission to 'anoint' Elisha (19.16b), which is obviously coloured by the commission to anoint Hazael and Jehu, itself secondary to the account of those events in Elisha's time.

In the context of the compilation, the incident of Naboth's vineyard demonstrates that the amoral fertility cult of Canaan, against which Elijah protests in chs. 17f., diminishes the social responsibilities fostered by the covenant-sacrament in the cult of Yahweh, the breach of the first commandment in chs. 17f. opening the way to the breach of the sixth and tenth in ch. 21. The Elisha saga received its substantial form certainly before the disappearance of the Northern kingdom, since there is a consciousness of the distinction between Israel and Judah (19.3) and between Israel and Sidon (17.9), which would have been pointless after Assyria had stripped Israel of Galilee in 734. Since Elisha lived until the time of Jehoash (796–781), there is no good reason to doubt his part in the transmission of the Elijah-tradition as it has reached us. Further indication of the same conclusion is the sharpness of outline with which Elijah and Ahab are presented. The adherence of Ahab to the God of Israel in his countenancing of the royal steward Obadiah, and in his failure, or refusal, to stay the wrath of Elijah on the Baal-prophets, indicate a contemporary source rather than a late authority, to whom Ahab as the antagonist of Elijah was a monster of iniquity.

Apart from those traditions where the public significance of Elijah in the religious and social crises of his time is at once apparent, Fohrer segregates 'anecdotes' which relate to the prophet individually and not in his public function, and which in the compilation have been associated with one or another of the major incidents in his public activity. These are of a more popular character, and reflect the growth of a great historical figure to legendary proportions in popular tradition. Thus miracle is a regular feature of the passages. When Elijah, for instance, is sustained by the widow of Zarephath, her meal and oil never fails, despite the drought and dearth (17.14–16), and he raises her son from the dead (17.17–24); he is sustained with food by an angel on the way to Horeb (19.4–8); he calls down fire which consumes the emissaries of Ahaziah to Baal-zebul of Ekron (II K. 1.9–16). The tradition of the sustaining of the prophet at the Wadi Cherith (17.2–6) may also be of this character if MT *ʿōrebīm* ('ravens') is read rather than *ʿarābīm* ('Arabs'), which we prefer. This incident and that of the sojourn of Elijah with the widow of Zarephath, apart from the miracles, may belong to historical traditions of the persecution of Elijah (cf. esp. 17.3) and the other prophets of Yahweh, to which Elijah's encounter with Obadiah (18.2–15) also belongs. This, however, if it did form in detail part of the original tradition of Elijah, has been abridged by the compiler or the Deuteronomistic historian after him, being simply touched upon in two passages.

In the case of such a figure as Elijah, especially as he is presented in oral tradition, we must expect the miraculous, as for instance in the tradition of his translation (II K. 2.1–12), which is from the tradition of Elisha. We must also expect the greater figure of Elijah to attract to himself traditions which really belong to his successor. Thus the unfailing meal and oil in the hospitable house of the widow of Zarephath (17.8–16) is paralleled by Elisha's multiplication of the oil for the widow in II K. 4.1–7; the raising of the dead son of the hospitable widow of Zarephath (17.17–24) seems a doublet of the raising of the son of the hospitable lady of Shunem (II K. 4.18–37). Such cases, however, are confined to the less significant traditions of Elijah, Fohrer's 'anecdotes', which were thus probably combined with the historical tradition of Elijah, which we attribute to Elisha's authority, later than Elisha, that is to say, in the compilation.

Another feature which Fohrer (*op. cit.*, p. 48) has done well to note is the association in the Elijah tradition of motifs from the tradition of Moses. Thus, apart from Elijah's sustenance with bread in the morning and flesh in the evening (17.6), which Fohrer, rather forcedly as we think, associates with the manna and quails of the desert wandering (Ex. 16.8, 12 P), the ordeal on Carmel with the priests of Baal does suggest Moses' challenge to the Egyptian magicians (Ex. 7.8–13, 20–22; 8.22f., of which the last two passages are from the earlier narrative sources), while the challenge to Israel on Carmel and the grim sequel in the slaughter of the prophets of Baal down by the Kishon suggests the incident of the golden calf in Ex. 32 (E), and may reflect also Jehu's massacre of the devotees of Baal in the temple at Samaria (II K. 10.17–27). The reflection of the Moses tradition is, of course, obvious in the tradition of Elijah at Horeb (19.1–18), particularly in the actual theophany (vv. 9–13). The parallels here lie in the major historical traditions as apart from the 'anecdotes', and are thus likely to reflect a real aspect of the mission of Elijah as a new Moses, to vindicate the distinctive character of the people of God in religion and in the social order at a crisis when its identity in both respects was threatened by Ahab's liberalistic policy and his feudal absolutism after the Canaanite pattern.

It was the significance of Elijah at this critical juncture in the history in Israel which accounts for the inclusion in the Deuteronomistic History of so much of the Elijah tradition and the tradition of his successor Elisha, with the final triumph of Yahwism in the revolt of Jehu. The tradition proclaimed its own message without undue Deuteronomistic comment. In the introduction, however, the circumstances which prompted Elijah boldly to cite the great drought as a token of God's wrath on Ahab and that Yahweh alone and not Baal would send rain again (17.1; 18.1) are omitted, owing to the Deuteronomistic summary of the reign of Ahab and his religious policy (16.29–33, esp. 30–33).

(*a*) ELIJAH'S PUBLIC MINISTRY: PROCLAMATION OF THE GREAT DROUGHT AS A SIGN OF YAHWEH'S DISPLEASURE AT AHAB'S PROCLIVITY TO THE CULT OF BAAL: 17.1

17 [1]And Elijah the Tishbite, [a]of the settlers of[a] Gilead, said to Ahab, As Yahweh the God of Israel lives, before whom I stand, there will certainly be no dew nor rain these two years, and it will not be otherwise than I say.

17.1. On Tishbeh see note a below. The place has been identified since Byzantine times with *al-Istib*, eight miles north of the Jabbok in the immediate proximity of a shrine Mar Elias (St Elijah).[b] The drought is depicted as proclaimed by Elijah, presumably with divine authority, as an appropriate punishment for defection to the cult of Baal, the Canaanite god of rain and the power of providence in nature (cf. Amos 4.6–11).[c] This is confirmed by Ahab's accusation of Elijah 'the troubler of Israel' (18.17), who by his proclamation of the drought was considered by Ahab as responsible for it, possibly like Elisha in the famine in Samaria in II K. 6.24–33, esp. v. 31. The two main sources of moisture in Palestine are noted, the regular rains from October/November to March and the dew which condenses on the mountains of Palestine in the hot season and may be almost as heavy as a drizzle of rain in the higher regions about Hebron,

[a]G reads here 'E. the Tishbite, the prophet from Tishbeh in Gilead'. If Tishbeh is read, 'the Tishbite' is tautological, and possibly we should read 'E. the prophet from T. in Gilead', assuming a dittograph of *mittišbē*. 'Tishbeh' before Gilead in G is a feasible reading, since such elaboration may have been demanded by the fact that there was another Tishbeh in Naphtali near Kedesh (Tobit). Glueck suggested the reading *miyyābēš gilʿād* ('from Jabesh Gilead'), which is sufficiently close to MT to be feasible. In view of the fact that the wilder country in Gilead was an area of colonization we see no reason to alter MT except to point *tōšābē* as *tōšebē*, with the meaning 'settlers' or 'colonists' (see note on v. 1).

[b]Abel, *GP* II, p. 486.

[c]So Fohrer, *Elia*, p. 6.

Jerusalem and Bethel. A great drought is actually noted by Josephus,[a] quoting Menander's 'Acts of Ithobalus King of Tyre'. This is here stated to have lasted a year. Jewish tradition (Luke 4.25) states that the drought in Ahab's time lasted three and a half years. This is an obviously conventional figure, being half of a sabbatical period, but in view of the heavier condensation in the Lebanon the drought may have lasted longer in Palestine than in Phoenicia. Nevertheless, three whole years of drought in Palestine, as Fichtner well observes, on the authority of those experienced in local life (*op. cit.*, p. 265), would have annihilated all plant and animal life together with humanity. Actually 'the third year' of the drought in 18.1 could refer to a whole year and a small part of the first and third. Elijah's declaration on the drought is not simply a case of foretelling. Taken with the figure of the third year in 18.1, mention of two years indicates that it has already set in. The prophet cites it as a token of the wrath of God to Ahab, who, probably as much out of respect to his Canaanite subjects as through the influence of Jezebel, favoured the cult of Baal, whom the Canaanites, as indicated in the Ras Shamra texts, regarded as the power of providence in nature and the giver of rain. Elijah is to emerge again at the end of the drought to proclaim that Yahweh, and not Baal (it is implied) will give rain (18.1).

(*b*) ELIJAH'S PERSONAL EXPERIENCE IN THE GREAT DROUGHT: 17.2-16

17 [2]And the word of Yahweh came to Elijah[b] saying, [3]Go from here and
turn eastward[c] and hide yourself in the Wadi Cherith east of the Jordan,
[4]and it shall be that you shall drink of the wadi, and I have commanded
the Arabs[d] to feed you there. [5]And he went and did according to the word
of Yahweh and went and lived in the Wadi Cherith east of the Jordan.
[6]And the Arabs[d] brought him bread [e]in the morning[e] and flesh in the

[a]*Ant.* VII, 13.2.

[b]Reading *'el-'ēlīyāhū*, a simple case of haplography of MT.

[c]G omits 'turn eastward', which makes no difference to the grammar in the context.

[d]Reading *ʿarābīm* for MT *ʿōrebīm* ('ravens'), though there is no support in the Versions. We adopt this reading solely because of its congruity with the sequel, where Elijah is fed by an alien Phoenician woman. That he should also have experienced the humanity of Arabs (Bedouin) was perhaps a divine preparation for the emergence in the prophetic conscience of a larger humanity and a fuller apprehension of the sole sovereignty of God, such as is found in Amos (chs. 1–2) a century later.

[e]So with G^{BL} for MT 'bread and flesh in the morning and bread and flesh in the evening'.

evening and he would drink of the wadi. [7]And it came to pass after some days that the wadi went dry, for there had been no rain in the land. [8]And the word of Yahweh came to him saying, [9]Arise, go to Zarephath, which belongs to Sidon, and dwell there. See, I have ordered a widow-woman there to feed you. [10]And he arose and went to Zarephath and came to the gate of the city, and behold, there was a widow-woman picking up sticks, and he called to her and said, Bring me a little water in a vessel that I may drink. [11]And she went to get it, and he called after her[a] and said to her,[b] Bring me a piece of bread in your hand. [12]And the woman[c] said, As Yahweh your God lives! I have not a cake, but only a handful of meal in the jar and a little oil in the flask, and here I am gathering a couple of sticks and I shall come in and prepare it for myself and my son and we shall eat it and die. [13]And Elijah said to her, Have no fear. Go in and do as you have said. Only prepare me a little cake first and bring it out to me, and for yourself and your son you shall make (another) after, [14]for thus says Yahweh God of Israel, The jar of meal shall not fail nor the flask of oil give out until the day that Yahweh gives[d] rain upon the face of the ground. [15]And she went and did as Elijah had said, and she ate, she and he[e] and her house, day by day.[f] [16]The jar of meal failed not and the flask of oil did not give out, according to the word of Yahweh, which he spoke through Elijah.

17.3 The Wadi Cherith ('Cutting') is here explicitly located east of the Jordan, where, in fact, Eusebius locates it,[g] cf. E. Robinson's location at the *Wādī Qilt* south of Jericho. The east bank of Jordan differs from the west in the number of perennial wadis.[h]

4. On the pointing of *ʿrbm* see p. 378 n.[d]. Skinner's suggestion that the word should be pointed *ʿarābīm* ('Arabs') has been condemned as 'a rationalistic absurdity'.[i] We accept this reading because of the resulting congruity with the following episode of the charity of the Phoenician woman. The provision of meat twice daily by Bedouin seems at first sight highly abnormal, since they live mainly on milk

[a]So G.

[b]Reading with G[BL] *wayyōʾmer lāh qeḥī* for the irregular *liqeḥī*. The form of the imperative of *lāqaḥ* with initial *l* retained is found, however, in Ezek. 37.16 and Prov. 20.16, and in Ex. 29.1, where there is possibly a dittograph of *l* after *ly*.

[c]Reading *wattōʾmer hāʾiššā* with G.

[d]Reading Q *tēt*.

[e]So Q, supported by G[BL], T, and S.

[f]Reading *yōm yōm* for MT *yāmīm* ('for days' or 'for a year'), though the conjecture is unsupported by the versions.

[g]*Onomasticon*, p. 174.

[h]See N. Glueck, *The River Jordan*, 1946.

[i]Skinner, CB, p. 224.

and its by-products, with such meal as they secure by barter of their butter. Meat is eaten only when a beast is killed for a guest or in fulfilment of a vow. Our explanation is that in the severe drought feeble beasts were being killed off by the Bedouin. As crows are known to anticipate the death of such beasts, this might justify the MT reading, which has the unanimous support of the Versions. The feeding of the hero by beasts, on the other hand, is a well-known theme in folk-story. *gešem* signifies the heavy rain of late autumn and winter, which softens the earth, hardened by the summer drought, and makes cultivation and growth possible.

17.9 Zarephath, of which MT *ṣareptā* is the locative of direction, is known in accounts of Assyrian campaigns as *ṣariptu*, modern *Ras Ṣarafand* some seven miles south of Sidon. The movement of Elijah to Phoenician territory may indicate that he had already clashed with Ahab, as, indeed, 18.10ff. suggests. The definition of Zarephath as 'pertaining to the Sidonians' suggests a date before Assyria divested Israel of Galilee in 734. The position of widows and orphans without a breadwinner or male protector was precarious. Levirate marriage, i.e. with the brother of the deceased husband, was not designed primarily to relieve the widow, but to provide an heir to the name and property of the dead man. Thus a childless widow was the responsibility of the family, but a widow-mother, as the woman of Zarephath, had no such provision, save by charity. In the Ras Shamra legends such are the charge of a good government. This situation makes Elijah's dependance on the widow-mother more poignant. The verb *qāšaš* is possibly a denominational verb from *qaš*, 'straw' or dry twigs, withered, or 'scaled off', from the living plant.

12. *māʿōg* is derived from the root *ʿūg*, which describes the baking of a cake on dried dung used in place of charcoal (Ezek. 4.12), as among the Bedouin (*mall fī'l-jall*). Doubtless the meaning is a 'round cake', cf. Arab. *ʿāja* (Form II, V), 'to bend, be curved'. *kad* is used of the fairly large earthenware jars in which Gideon and his men carried their torches (Judg. 7.16) and of the jars of water from which Elijah had the trench filled at the ordeal on Carmel (18.34). It denoted the earthenware water-pot about a foot and a half high in which women carry water from the well (Gen. 24.14; Eccl. 12.6), but in the present passage it is a storage jar for meal. *ṣappaḥat* denotes the small water-jar which a warrior might carry in battle (I Sam. 26.11ff.), perhaps the lentoid jar of about one pint capacity with surrounding groove for a thong and pair of small handles familiar in excavations from the

Late Bronze and Early Iron Age in Palestine and known as 'pilgrim-flasks'.[a]

17.14 The unfailing supply, which was a motif in the ancient Near Eastern king-ideology, where the king was the dispenser of the water of life, e.g. Gudea of Lagash in a well-known sculpture,[b] has become a well-known motif in folk-lore, and is here an indication of the saga-character of the Elijah story. The factual basis may be that the generosity of the widow touched the conscience of her better-provided neighbours.

(*c*) THE REVIVAL OF THE WIDOW'S SON: 17.17–24

The woman here is apparently the same as the widow of Zarephath though Montgomery (ICC, p. 295) considers it odd that the destitute widow should have had a house with an upper chamber. This, however, would be a flimsy shelter such as may commonly be seen on the flat roof of an Arab peasant house to accommodate guests without infringing the privacy of the family in houses too small for the preservation of the intimacies of family life. This was necessary in the present case in order to observe the Semitic convention of hospitality without embarrassment, all the more so in the case of the unattached female.

17 [17]And it happened after these things that the son of the lady of the house fell ill, and his illness was so very grievous that he lost animation. [18]And she said to Elijah, What have I to do with you, O man of God, that[c] you have come to bring my sin to notice and to bring death upon my son? [19]So he said to her, Give me your son. And he took him from her bosom and took him up to the upper room where he was living and laid him on his bed. [20]And he cried to Yahweh and said, O Yahweh, my God, hast thou even brought calamity upon the widow with whom I am sojourning so as to bring death upon her son? [21]Then he stretched himself upon the boy three times and cried to Yahweh and said, Yahweh, my God, may the breath of this lad come back into him. [22]And Yahweh listened to the voice of Elijah and the lad's breath came back into him and he revived. [23]And Elijah took the boy and brought him down from the upper room into the house and gave him to his mother, and Elijah said, See, your son is alive. [24]And the woman said to Elijah, Now do I know that you are a man of God and the word of Yahweh is really in your mouth.

[a]On the technical words for vessels in the Old Testament and the various types found in local excavations see A. M. Honeyman, *PEQ*, 1939, pp. 81–89.

[b]A. Parrot, *The Arts of Mankind: Sumer*, 1960, pl. 264.

[c]Reading *kī* with ten Hebrew MSS.

17.18. The conception here is that the sickness of the child was the divine punishment for some obscure sin. Such a state was considered incompatible with the divine presence, of which the spirit (*rūaḥ*) in the man of God was the extension. The same attitude is illustrated in the case of Peter in Luke 5.8 ('Depart from me, for I am a sinful man, O Lord'), and the man with the unclean spirit in Capernaum in Mark 1.24 ('What have I to do with thee, thou Jesus of Nazareth? Art thou come to destroy us? . . .'). The very mention of the name of God, the Holy One, in a house so stricken, in so far as the name was an extension of the person, might occasion further suffering for sin not yet expiated (Amos 6.10). Another graphic instance of the incompatibility of the Holy and other than holy on the cruder, physical level is the case of Uzzah and the ark (II Sam. 6.6f.). *hazkīr* means 'to put in mind' (of God), with *ʿāwōn* as object, to make explicit what is implicit. *ʿāwōn* may be derived from *ʿāwā*, cognate with Arabic *ʿawā* ('to twist', hence 'pervert'), but is probably rather derived from the Hebrew cognate of Arabic *ġawā* ('to go astray').

19. The removal of the invalid to the airy upper chamber, clean of the household debris, was a matter of simple hygiene, and may have been the factual basis of the tradition of the healing of the lad, together with Elijah's invocation of Yahweh. Neither in this verse nor the sequel to it is it said that the lad was actually dead. As A. R. Johnson has pointed out,[a] *mōt* may signify a weak form of life. So *mēt* may indicate a temporary suspension of animation or deprivation of all the faculties rather than actual death, but, granted that it bears the last meaning in the causative *lehāmīt*, intention rather than result may be indicated by the infinitive construct. The detail of Elijah stretching himself upon the boy may be borrowed from the tradition of a similar cure by Elisha, also of a boy (II K. 4.34ff.). This is a case of contactual magic, such as is well known in the ancient East in Mesopotamia[b] and in Canaan, cf. the Ugaritic Legend of Krt, which mentions the transference of the sickness of the king into a clay image (*UT* 126, V, 26ff.). Generally the conception was that the sickness was thus transferred into the corresponding parts of an animal, e.g. a sheep; here *per contra* the health of Elijah is conveyed to the corresponding organs of the invalid. The exploitation of such primitive beliefs was really a potent factor in homoeopathic treatment, e.g. Paul's revival of Eutychus at Troas (Acts 20.9f.). Just as *mēt* does

[a] *Studies in Old Testament Prophecy*, ed. H. H. Rowley, 1950, pp. 86ff.
[b] G. Contenau, *Everyday Life in Babylon and Assyria*, 1954, p. 294.

not always signify actual death, the return of *nepeš* does not necessarily mean that the lad had been dead. The word means primarily 'breath', 'animation' rather than 'life'.

17.22. *wayyeḥī* again does not mean that he lived after he had been dead. *ḥayyīm*, which means life, means also 'full vitality' and occasionally 'health' rather than 'life', as in Syriac.[a] Hence our translation 'and he revived . . .', a sense which the Pael of the root regularly bears in Syriac, in the healing miracles in the Gospels.

24. *'emet* grammatically may either be in apposition to *debar yhwh* or adverbial 'really'. The latter is the sense, since if the woman admitted that the word of God was in Elijah's mouth she would not gainsay the truth of it.

(*d*) ELIJAH'S PUBLIC MINISTRY IN THE GREAT DROUGHT: THE ORDEAL ON CARMEL: 18.1–46

More particularly this episode is presented in three acts, Elijah's confrontation of Ahab through the agency of Obadiah, with the digression on Obadiah's succour of the prophets in time of persecution, drawn probably from a fuller account of the conflict (vv. 1–19), which originally was probably the prelude to ch. 17, the ordeal on Carmel (vv. 20–40), and Yahweh's vindication and its sequel (vv. 41–46).

The question of the unity of this passage has often been discussed. Alt,[b] who treats the chapter as independent of ch. 19, follows Gressmann[c] in seeing in ch. 18 two distinct traditions, first Elijah's encounter with Obadiah (vv. 2b–16) with the rain-inducing sequel (vv. 41ff.), and secondly the ordeal with the priests of Baal, where the combustion of the sacrifice on Carmel, and not rain, marks Yahweh's vindication (vv. 17–40). Alt regards v. 1, with its mention of rain, which is not mentioned again till v. 41, as an editorial introduction, whereby a false unity was imposed on the chapter. This view is followed and developed by G. Fohrer,[d] who sees in 18.1–2a, 16f. and 41–46 the continuation of Elijah's mission to Ahab asserting Yahweh's wrath on his proclivity to the cult of Baal betokened by the great drought in 17.1 and Yahweh's control of the rain, the action being located not at Carmel but by Jezreel. According to Fohrer, the

[a]See further A. R. Johnson, *op. cit.*, pp. 89ff.
[b]'Das Gottesurteil auf dem Karmel', *KS* II, pp. 135ff.
[c]*Die älteste Geschichtsschreibung*, p. 269.
[d]*Elia*, 1957, pp. 34–36.

encounter with Obadiah (18.2b–15) was originally independent, as was also the narrative of the ordeal on Carmel. Fichtner[a] distinguishes three main elements, the encounter between Elijah and Obadiah and Elijah's challenge to Ahab to meet him and see his authority in inducing rain (vv. 2b–16), the ordeal on Carmel (vv. 17–40), with vv. 31–32a as a later accretion and vv. 1–2a and vv. 41–46 on the theme of the drought and its end, which may belong to the first passage or, so far as vv. 41–46 is concerned, be independent. E. Würthwein[b] limits the ordeal on Carmel to vv. 21–39, with vv. 17f. as the secondary link between the first and second passages. There appears at first sight a stylistic difference between vv. 1–16 and vv. 17–40, but that is owing to the long periphrasis on Obadiah in v. 4 with its repetition in v. 13, and to the more dramatic character of the second passage. The latter requires some introduction such as we have in vv. 1–16, particularly in the courageous challenge by the lone Elijah, and, if vv. 17–40 are more dramatic, that is only what we expect in the main scene as apart from the introduction. The two parts, then, do not represent an inharmonious unity, but vv. 1–16 as it stands is obviously an introduction, as is indicated by so much in the passage that is of an explanatory nature, such as the explanation of how Elijah had access to Obadiah privately (vv. 5–7), and the note on Obadiah's sheltering of the prophets in Jezebel's persecution (vv. 3b–4), which is explanatory of v. 13. This indicates probably a fuller version of the Elijah legend, or possibly an independent prophetic legend that has survived in the present context. Verses 1–16 probably contain the original introduction to the Carmel incident in vv. 17ff., but it has been presented secondarily with a résumé from this fuller source. The composite version of ch. 18, however, is probably the work of a pre-Deuteronomistic editor from prophetic circles, so that we see no compelling reason to dissent from Eissfeldt, who regards the chapter as presented by the pre-Deuteronomistic compiler as a unity,[c] especially since we believe, contrary to Alt and Noth,[d] that the Baal of Carmel was not an obscure local deity, the destruction of

[a]Fichtner, *op. cit.*, p. 264, follows Fohrer in regarding the reference to the trench and the water in vv. 32b, 33b–35 and 38b as later accretions in oral tradition to enhance a miracle. Fichtner further dissociates the ordeal on Carmel in vv. 17–40 from the breaking of the drought in the rest of the chapter.

[b]*ZThK* LIX, 1962, pp. 131–44.

[c]*Der Gott Karmel*, 1953, pp. 32ff., so also D. R. Ap-Thomas, *PEQ*, 1960, pp. 147ff.; H. H. Rowley, 'Elijah on Mount Carmel', *BJRL* XLIII, 1960, pp. 190–219.

[d]*History of Israel*, p. 242 n.6.

whose shrine by fanatical Yahwists was the historical basis of the tradition of the ordeal, but the Canaanite Baal manifest in winter rain and the thunder and lightning which accompanied the 'fire of Yahweh' of v. 38.[a] Fohrer (*op. cit.*, p. 58) suggests that this was a local incident. His assumption is probably correct, that Carmel was a Phoenician region until the time of David, and he suggests that it may have reverted to Tyre with Solomon's concessions in Galilee at the adjacent district of Cabul (9.11–13). Or again, the region with its Canaanite Baal-shrine may always have been Phoenician and have been given to Israel on the marriage of Ahab and Jezebel, perhaps indeed as dowry, which might explain the phrase 'who eat at Jezebel's table' (v. 19). At any rate, the ordeal reflects the reaction of Elijah and his followers to the cult of Baal here, and apparently to the liberalism of local Israelites who saw nothing incompatible in the Canaanite nature-cult and their traditional allegiance to Yahweh. The latter ('the people') seem certainly to be addressed by Elijah in his famous question 'How long will you hobble on two crutches?' (v. 21). Fohrer nevertheless (*op. cit.*, p. 60) recognizes the universal significance of Baal. The reference to the prophets of Baal eating at Jezebel's table indicates official support at an important shrine of Baal, probably the oldest and most important in Palestine, on Carmel, the luxuriant vegetation of which, stimulated by the earliest precipitation of rain in the land, was naturally associated with the universal Canaanite Baal, who was, moreover, particularly associated by the Phoenician seafarers with headlands. What gives plausibility to the view of Alt is that there is no mention of rain in the scene of the ordeal (vv. 20–40), and, as Rowley has pointed out,[b] the lightning apparently fell from a clear sky, the cloud from the west not appearing till later. Our opinion is that this is too literalistic an interpretation, and disregards the art of the narrator. We believe that what actually happened was that the clouds appeared and massed as a result of Elijah's prayer in vv. 36–37 and 42ff., then the lightning which ignited his sacrifice. On the other hand, Dalman[c] attests lightning a day *before* the first heavy rain. The facts have been rearranged for dramatic effect in oral tradition in the pre-literary stage of the saga. The difficulty in this theory is that there is not

[a]So now R. Hillmann, *Wasser und Berg*, 1965, pp. 95ff., who follows Eissfeldt in contending that Baal on Carmel was the Tyrian Baal Shamayim, the expression of a monotheistic tendency in Syria.

[b]*Op. cit.*, p. 213.

[c]*Arbeit und Sitte in Palästina* I, p. 114.

sufficient time for the slaughter of the ministers of Baal between the igniting of Elijah's sacrifice and the hasty departure from Carmel before the rain fell. This difficulty may be obviated by supposing that Elijah left the slaughter of the prophets of Baal to his followers (so Šanda, who reads the Hiphil *wayyašḥīṭēm* for the Qal). Another possibility is that a later massacre of the devotees of Baal as a result of the vindication of the native faith of Israel was given a more immediate association with the ordeal on Carmel in pre-literary tradition. Again this may have been introduced under the influence of Jehu's massacre of the devotees of Baal in Samaria (II K. 10.18–24), which was the culmination of the reaction against the fertility cult initiated by Elijah, an instance of the greater figure attracting elements from the Elisha tradition. Here we consider the coming of rain as fundamental to all episodes in the chapter, Elijah's confrontation of Obadiah and Ahab, the ordeal, and the rainclouds, regarding the chapter as a literary unity, except perhaps the digression on Obadiah's succour of the prophets in Jezebel's persecution (vv. 3b–4), which is a *résumé* of a fuller source.

From vv. 10ff., 18 it is apparent that Elijah had already confronted Ahab and was known as a public figure. This indicates that what is extant of the Elijah story is a mere torso, as is further suggested by the abrupt way in which the prophet is introduced in ch. 17. The previous clash with Ahab might explain Elijah's retirement east of the Jordan and into Phoenicia.

18 [1]And it came to pass after many days that the word of Yahweh came to Elijah in the third year saying, Go, show yourself to Ahab that I may send rain upon the face of the ground. [2]And Elijah went to show himself to Ahab, and the famine was grievous in Samaria. [3]And Ahab called to Obadiah the royal chamberlain, and Obadiah feared Yahweh greatly. [4]And it happened that, when Jezebel cut off the prophets of Yahweh, Obadiah had taken a hundred prophets and hidden them by fives in the caves,[a] and he would feed them with bread and water. [5]And Ahab had said to Obadiah, Come, and let us traverse[b] the land to all[c] the springs of water and to all the wadis, if by chance we may

[a]There seems no sense in hiding a hundred prophets by fifty in the same cave. Apprehending this difficulty G^L read 'in two caves'. Montgomery, however, (ICC, p. 298) feasibly proposes to understand MT *m*ᵉ*ʿārā* collectively in the sense of 'cave-country'. We might further suggest the possibility that MT *ḥ*ᵃ*miššim* should be taken literally as 'fives'. Perhaps the final *m* is not the plural ending, but the adverbial enclitic as in *yōmām*, *'omnām*, etc.

[b]Reading *w*ᵉ*naʿ*ᵃ*bōr* with G and S.

[c]G^{BL} omits 'all' of MT.

find grass and save the horses and mules and not be deprived of our beasts. [6]So they divided the land between them to traverse it; Ahab went one way by himself and Obadiah went another way by himself. [7]And Obadiah was on the way when there was Elijah confronting him and he recognized him[a] and fell on his face and said, Is this you, my lord Elijah? [8]And he said to him, It is. Go, say to your master, Elijah is here. [9]And (Obadiah)[b] said, What have I committed that you should give your servant into the hand of Ahab to put me to death? [10]By the life of Yahweh your God there is no nation or realm where my master has not sent to seek you, and if they said, He is not here, he would take an oath of the realm and nation that they could not find you. [11]And now you yourself say, Go, tell your master, There is Elijah. [12]And if it happens that when I go from you the spirit of Yahweh carries you whither[c] I know not and I come and tell Ahab and he does not find you, then he will slay me, and your servant fears Yahweh from my youth. [13]Has it not been told my lord what I did when Jezebel slew the prophets of Yahweh, when I hid a hundred of the prophets of Yahweh by fives[d] in the caves, and fed them with bread and water? [14]And now you yourself say, Go, say to your master, There is Elijah, and he will slay me. [15]And Elijah said, As Yahweh (Lord) of Hosts lives before whom I stand, I shall surely appear before him today. [16]So Obadiah went to meet Ahab and told him, and Ahab[e] went to meet Elijah. [17][f]And it happened that, when Ahab saw Elijah,[f] Ahab said to him,[g] Is this you, you troubler of Israel? [18]And he said, I have not troubled Israel, but you and your father's house, in that you have forsaken [h]Yahweh your God[h] and gone after the Baals. [19]Now, then, send, gather to me all Israel to Mount Carmel and the dervishes of Baal, four hundred and fifty, and the dervishes of the Asherah, four hundred, who eat at Jezebel's table. [20]So Ahab sent through all Israel[i] and gathered all[j] the prophets to Mount Carmel. [21]And Elijah drew near to all the

[a]G reads 'and Obadiah hastened' (*way^emahēr* for MT *wayyakkīrēhū*).

[b]Reading 'Obadiah' with G and S.

[c]G inserts 'the land, which . . .' The preposition *'el* ('to') is more appropriate in the context than *'al* of MT.

[d]See p. 386, n.[a].

[e]G reads 'and Ahab ran and . . .'

[f]G[A] omits this clause, which is immaterial to the sense.

[g]G reads 'to Elijah' for MT 'to him'. This reading depends on the omission of the previous clause.

[h]So G for MT 'the commandments of Yahweh', which has a Deuteronomic ring. In view of the early date of the apodeictic 'commandments', especially that against apostasy and idolatry, and their *Sitz im Leben* in the assembly of the sacral community at Shechem since the period of the judges, MT might well be defended here.

[i]G and L omit MT *b^enē*, which is an awkward, though not impossible, reading. Certain Hebrew MSS propose an easier reading 'territory' (*g^ebūl*), which is somewhat too facile, though in the proto-Hebraic script a confusion between this word and *b^enē* is not impossible.

[j]So G and L for MT, which omits 'all'. The context supports G and L.

people[a] and he said, How long will you hobble on two crutches? If Yahweh is God follow him; and if Baal, follow him. And the people answered him not a word. [22]And Elijah said to the people, I am left as a prophet of Yahweh alone by myself and the prophets of Baal are four hundred and fifty men. [23]Now let them give us two oxen, and let them choose one ox and cut it up and put it on the wood, but let them set no fire (to it), and let me dress the other[b] ox and I shall set it upon the wood and I shall set no fire (to it). [24]And you call on the name of your god and I shall call on the name of Yahweh my God,[c] and it shall be that the god who answers by fire will be God. And all the people answered and said, What you say is good. [25]Then Elijah said to the prophets of Baal, You choose the one ox and dress it first, for you are the greater number, [d]and call upon the name of your god, but do not set fire (to it).[d] [26]So they took the ox which he had given them, and they dressed it, and called on the name of Baal [e]from the morning until noon,[e] saying, O Baal, answer us. But there was no sound nor did any answer, and they hobbled up on the altar which they had made.[f] [27]And it happened at noon, that Elijah ridiculed them and said, Call loudly, for he is a god. Perhaps he has to defecate, or perhaps he has occasion to withdraw, or perhaps he is on a journey; perhaps he is asleep and needs to be awakened. [28]And they cried loudly and gashed themselves according to their custom with knives and with lances to the effusion of blood. [29]And it happened, when noon was past, that they performed their dervish rites until the offering of the oblation, but there was no sound, and no one answered, nor (was there) any attention. [30]And Elijah said to all the people, Draw near to me. And all the people drew near to him. And he repaired the altar of Yahweh which was ruined. [31]And Elijah took twelve stones corresponding to the number of the tribes of (the sons[g] of) Jacob,[h] to whom was the word of Yahweh, saying, Israel will be your name. [32] So he built up the stones as an altar[i] in the name of Yahweh, and he made a trench about the altar such as would contain two seahs of seed. [33]And he arranged the wood and cut up the ox and laid it on the wood. [34]And he said, Fill four jars with water and let them pour it over the offering and over the wood. And he said, Do it again. And they did it again. And he said, Do it a third time. And they did it a third time. [35]And the water went about

[a]G[B] reads 'them all' (*kull[e]hem*).

[b]Reading *hā'aḥēr* with G for MT *hā'eḥād* ('the one').

[c]Inserting 'my God' with G and S, as the antithesis 'your God' in the previous clause suggests.

[d]S omits this clause.

[e]G[L] omits this clause.

[f]The sense demands the plural, which is, in fact, read by many MSS.

[g]G omits *b[e]nē*, which may be a gloss on 'tribes'.

[h]Certain MSS and G[BL] read 'Israel' for MT 'Jacob'. The relative clause following, however, demands the reading 'Jacob' of MT.

[i]G omits 'altar' of MT, possibly because 'stones' is not a construct. MT, however, is defensible, 'altar' being in apposition to 'the stones'.

the altar, and filled the trench also. [36a]And it happened, at the time when the evening sacrifice was offered,[a] that Elijah the prophet drew near and said, Yahweh, God of Abraham, Isaac, and Israel, let it be known today that thou art God in Israel and that I am thy servant and that I have done all these things at thy word. [37]Answer me, Yahweh, answer me, so that this people may know that thou, Yahweh, art God, and that thou hast turned their heart back again. [38]And the fire of Yahweh fell and consumed the offering and the wood and the stones and the dust, and licked up the water which was in the trench. [39]And all the people saw and fell on their faces and said, Yahweh is God, Yahweh is God. [40]And Elijah said to them, Seize the prophets of Baal; let no man of them escape. And they seized them, and Elijah made them go down to the stream Kishon and made them slaughter them[b] there. [41]And Elijah said to Ahab, Up, eat and drink, for there is the sound of the roar of the rain. [42]So Ahab went up to eat and drink, and Elijah went up to the top of Carmel, bowed himself to the ground, and put his face between his knees. [43]And he said to his lad, Up and look towards the sea. And he went up and looked, and said, There is nothing. And he said, Go back seven times.[c] [44]And it happened at the seventh time, that he said, Behold a little cloud like a man's hand coming up from the sea.[d] And he said, Up! and say to Ahab, Hitch up and go down that the rain may not stop you. [45]And it happened that, meanwhile, the sky grew black with clouds and wind, and there was a great rainstorm, and Ahab mounted his chariot and went to Jezreel. [46]And the hand of Yahweh was upon[e] Elijah, and he girded up his loins and ran before Ahab until you come to Jezreel.

18.1. On the length of the famine in Israel see on 17.1.

3. On the title and status of *'ᵃšer ʿal-habbayit* ('the royal chamberlain') see on 4.6.

4. This is the first explicit reference in Kings to associations of prophets, though 13.11ff. implies that such associations existed in the proximity of shrines; cf. I Sam. 10.5. It is also the first explicit reference to organized prophetic resistance to the assimilation of the Baal-cult. Ahijah's opposition to Solomon was as much on political grounds as on account of the resentment of the conservative elements to his religious innovations at Jerusalem. Protests against the assimila-

[a]This clause is omitted in G[h] and L, and may even be a gloss in the light of later ritual in the Second Temple, e.g. *minḥat-ʿāreb* ('the evening sacrifice', Dan. 9.21). But the verb *ʿᵃlōt* indicates that the *minḥā* was not the bloodless offering of the Second Temple, and so there may be a reference to a local North Israelite rite.

[b]So Šanda (*op. cit.*, p. 440) since Elijah's further transactions were on the height of Carmel far from the scene of the massacre.

[c]G inserts 'and the lad went back seven times', which, in the nature of the narrative, where ellipse is a feature of the saga style, is not strictly necessary.

[d]G[BA] read 'bringing up water' (*maʿᵃle mayim*) for MT *ʿōlā miyyām*.

[e]Reading *ʿal* with G for MT *'el*.

tion of the nature-cult of Canaan in its grosser external aspects had been voiced at the periodic assembly of the sacral community at Shechem, at least in the solemn renunciation of the worship of other gods and the use of idols. The dangers of assimilation of the grosser elements of the Canaanite fertility cult of Baal are reflected in the insistence in the early festal calendar Ex. 23.10–19 and the ritual code in Ex. 34.10ff. on the celebration of the great seasonal festivals of Unleavened Bread, Weeks and Tabernacles at the central shrine of the sacral confederacy ('before Yahweh') in the days of the judges. How much of the Canaanite tradition might be assimilated is evidenced in the imagery and also the ideology of the Kingship of God in the Israelite liturgy of the Feast of Tabernacles on the eve of the New Year, which was an adaptation of the Canaanite New Year liturgy, now attested in the Baal-myth of Ras Shamra. The real danger of a practical diarchy of Yahweh and Baal in Israel is indicated as late as a century after the time of Elijah, in Hosea. Now against the more positive policy of the Phoenician queen a protest is more vigorously and articulately voiced by the prophets of Yahweh, involving a crisis of which we have here but echoes.

On the generic sense of the singular *hamme'ārā* ('the cave') see p. 386 n.[a] above. This cave region might have been anywhere in the limestone hills of Palestine, but may well have been on Carmel, where the great number of caves, particularly in the *Wādī Muġārā* by Athlit on the western escarpment, afforded dwellings since the Palaeolithic Age.[a] The choice of Carmel, apart from its significance as a kind of Palestinian Zaphon, associated with the cult of Baal as a mountain and a headland, as the locus of the ordeal may have been dictated by the fact that the prophets of Yahweh were hiding in its caves and woods, which were well known as a place of refuge (Amos 9.3). On our reading 'by fives' for MT *ḥamiššīm* see p. 386 n.[a] above. The following *'īš* may be a gloss after *ḥamiššīm* had been misunderstood as 'fifty'.

18.5. Pasture for the royal stables was probably a priority claim throughout the Hebrew monarchy, cf. 'the king's mowings' (Amos 7.1), as it was for the imperial chariot-force in Syria in the Roman imperial period.[b]

[a]T. D. McCown and A. Keith, *The Stone Age on Mount Carmel*, 1939. On the traditional cave of the prophets on the Carmel Head see Abel, *GP* I, pp. 438ff.

[b]See the Syriac lawbook cited by W. R. Smith, *The Religion of the Semites*, 1894[3], p. 246 n.

18.6. That Obadiah shared this task with the king is indicative of his unique authority among Ahab's subjects. The personal authority of the king and his immediate representative, who doubtless bore the royal seal, was necessary to secure the precious fodder.

9. Obadiah's fear that Ahab would slay him is a reflection of the constitutional change in Israel, where the power of life and death over a nominally free Israelite now rested on the royal caprice.

10. 'Your God' implies the recognition of the close association of God and prophet. *gōy* is primarily a political term in contrast to *ʿam*, a religious community.[a]

12. The comings and goings of Elijah are related to the spirit of Yahweh (*rūaḥ yhwh*). This refers to abnormal activity. It might denote exceptional physical effort, as the running of Elijah from Carmel to Jezreel, where 'the hand of Yahweh' was upon him, or the prophet's exceptional astuteness in evading capture. It might refer more directly to the overmastering divine wisdom which made Elijah's escapes possible. Perhaps this transportation by the spirit of Yahweh suggested the experience to Ezekiel, where the expression occurs very often.

13. In *'ēt 'ašer ʿāśītī* ('what I did') after the passive *huggad* we have a case of the accusative after the passive of the verb with the agent suppressed, the passive being tantamount to an active with the indefinite subject.

15. The title *yhwh ṣebā'ōt* is regularly translated 'Yahweh (Lord) of Hosts'. It has been suggested that the stars as the heavenly host is the primary significance of *ṣebā'ōt* (e.g. Gen. 2.1, P), or that other gods, regarded as subordinate to Yahweh, are denoted.[b] Chronologically, however, the first occurrence of the title is in the account of the Philistine wars (I Sam. 17.45), where the reference is undoubtedly to Yahweh as God of the armies of Israel, and von Rad,[c] noting the association of the title with the ark, relates it to worship of Yahweh in the assembly of the sacral confederacy. On the evidence of the title in I Sam. 1.31; 4.4, we may fairly conclude that it was the title of Yahweh at Shiloh.[d] B. N. Wambacq,[e] however, while maintaining that the title first designated Yahweh as God of the armies of Israel, and, later, as

[a]See on this E. A. Speiser, *JBL* LXXIX, 1960, pp. 157–60.

[b]V. Maag, 'Jahwäs Heerscharen', *Schweizerische Theologische Umschau* XX, 3/4, 1950, pp. 75–100.

[c]*Theology of the Old Testament* I, pp. 18–20.

[d]Alt, 'Gedanken über das Königtum Jahväs', *KS* I, 1953, pp. 345ff.

[e]*L'épithète divine Yahwe Sebā'ōt: étude philologique, historique, et exégétique*, 1947.

God supreme over the forces of nature and the nations, holds that the title expresses more than its strict linguistic content, and with the latter part of this contention, at least in later sources, we would agree. This assumes that *yhwh ṣ^ebā'ōt* is an abbreviation for *yhwh 'ᵉlōhē ṣ^ebā'ōt*, but the relative frequency of the former and its use in earlier sources suggests that it is primary and that the latter is a later attempt at explanation once the significance of the former was forgotten. Hence Eissfeldt[a] concludes that *yhwh ṣ^ebā'ōt* is not a construct-absolute combination, but that the two nouns are in apposition, the second being the feminine plural of abstraction meaning 'Might'. We would emphasize the association with the militant sacral confederacy, which was properly *ṣ^ebā'ōt*, and, including its God, whose agent and expression it was, could be considered the extension, or self-articulation, of the divine person. This meaning of *yhwh ṣ^ebā'ōt* was very real to the conscience of Israel as long as the holy war was a real experience, but, with the passing of that phase, the primary meaning of the title was gradually lost and attained the general significance for which Wambacq contends.

18.17. 'The troubler of Israel' (*'ōkēr yiśrā'ēl*) denotes one who, like Achan in Joshua's invasion (Josh. 6.18; 7.25), is an infectious influence. The verb is found in Arabic denoting the pollution of water by mud. It is used to denote ritual disability which excludes a man from society, as Jacob was excluded from fellowship with the people of Shechem through the violence of Simeon and Levi (Gen. 34.30), and Israel's harmonious and successful co-operation with Yahweh was disrupted through Achan's breach of the tabu at the fall of Jericho (Josh. 6.18; 7.25), and of a man's separation from society occasioned by pain (Ps. 39.2[3]). It is also used of the disability brought on Israel by Jonathan's breach of the tabu imposed by Saul, for which the latter is held responsible (I Sam. 14.29). Fohrer[b] preserves the sense of an alienating influence, which is undoubtedly implied in the present passage, though in our opinion his rendering of the verb as *behexen* ('bewitch') is somewhat too specific. In the king's mouth, the charge probably implies that the antagonism of Elijah had brought wrath of Baal on Israel in the withholding of the rain, which in the Canaanite religion was particularly the province of Baal. Thus we find a unity of theme between vv. 1–16 and vv. 17ff., where Yahweh, and not Baal, is proved to be the giver of rain.

[a]'Jahwe Zebaoth', *Miscellanea academica Berolinensia*, 1950, pp. 128ff.
[b]*Elia*, 1968², pp. 12f.

18.18. The courage of Elijah before Ahab is indicated by his use of the *argumentum ad hominem.* On the significance and genuineness of 'commandments' in this context see p. 387 n.[h]. The plural 'Baals' indicates the various local manifestations of the paramount Canaanite fertility-deity Hadad, the Baal (lit. 'lord'). We consider that M. J. Mulder[a] is right in seeing in the Tyrian Melqart not a god strange to Palestine but a local manifestation of the familiar Canaanite Baal. The specification of the dervishes of Baal as 450 and the addition of 400 dervishes of Asherah are probably later redactional glosses prompted by the mention of dervishes of Baal in v. 22, as Fohrer (*op. cit.*, p. 11) suggests.

19. In 'all Israel' in this episode, the narrative is probably coloured by the tradition of a similar challenge to the sacral community in the covenant-sacrament, reflected in Gen. 35.2–5 and Josh. 24.[b]

The use of the same word *n^e^bî'îm* to denote the prophets of Yahweh and the devotees of Baal indicates that the two groups had certain features in common. From the case of Saul's encounter with the prophets, *n^e^bî'îm* (I Sam. 10.10; 19.23f.), and from the use of the verb *hitnabbē'*, the capacity for self-effacement in the service of God induced by, and resulting in, abnormal behaviour and extraordinary physical feats appears to be the common element. With this propensity, the *nābî'* may be the channel of popular expression before God, as in acts of imitative magic, as in the case of the Baal-devotees on Carmel, who sought on behalf of the community to promote a new effusion of life after rain by the release of the life-essence, their own blood. This was the distinctive aspect of 'prophecy' in the fertility-cult of Canaan, but it was also an aspect of prophecy in Israel in the worship of Yahweh, as in the many instances of prophetic symbolism, e.g. Zedekiah and his iron horns (ch. 22). The *nābî'*, however, by his ecstatic propensity could also express the will of God to the community by acting or speaking some reassuring oracle, or, as in the case of the 'canonical' prophets, some divine admonition. The apprehension of the will of God which this implied is expressed in the term *rō'e*, 'seer' (I Sam. 9.11). It was this aspect of prophecy which was distinctive of the higher forms of Hebrew prophecy, though this function of the prophets was not confined to Israel. In Mesopotamia a clear distinction is made between the *maḫḫu* ('ecstatic') and the *barū* ('seer'), though the *maḫḫu* can also communicate the will of God

[a]M. J. Mulder, *Baal in het Oude Testament*, 1962, pp. 27–29.
[b]So Eissfeldt, *ZAW* LVII, 1939, pp. 1–39.

in act and speech.[a] This may have been a feature of Canaanite prophecy also, as is suggested by the case of the ecstatic of Byblos who influenced the king in favour of Wen-Amon[b] and by Lucian's statement about priests and prophets of the Syrian goddess at Hierapolis as the media of oracles.[c] In the case of the cult of the Tyrian Baal-Melqart there may have been a development towards monotheism, which would explain the accentuation of the conflict with Yahweh in Israel under Jezebel. If this were so—and on the evidence of an inscribed piece of sculpture from the Roman period to Zeus Heliopolites Karmelos[d] Eissfeldt considers this probable—the Baal-devotees may have been the media of oracles in other spheres than that of nature. This is suggested by the fact that 'Baal of the Heavens' was accredited with direction in historical affairs through seers in the inscription of Zakir of Hamath in the beginning of the eighth century.[e] The mediation of the will of God in history, however, particularly in intelligible speech, and the interpretation of the divine will in the context of the people's history and destiny as a whole was the distinctive feature of Hebrew prophecy. To this, prophetic ecstasy in its physical aspects, which may not always have been present, was strictly ancillary. G. von Rad[f] justly makes the further distinction in Hebrew prophecy between the word of God in the wide context of world history, which dominated the consciousness and life of the great prophets, and the narrower vision of the 'false prophets', who were circumscribed in their intercessory office to secure the welfare of their people. This was the real issue between Jeremiah and Hananiah, both authentic prophets and earnest in their discharge of their office.

The ecstatic ministers of imitative magic were naturally numerous, the seer with insight into the will of God tending to be rather an individualist, as Šanda notes (I, p. 436). Mount Carmel as the place selected by Elijah for the celebrated ordeal with the Baal-devotees may have been chosen, as we have indicated, because his associates

[a]A. von Soden, 'Verkündigung des Gotteswillens durch prophetisches Wort in den altbabylonischen Briefen aus Mari', *Die Welt des Orients*, 1950, pp. 396–403; M. Noth, 'History and the Word of God in the Old Testament', *BJRL* XXXII, 1950, pp. 194–206.

[b]Golenischeff Papyrus, J. H. Breasted, *ARE* IV, pp. 278ff.

[c]H. A. Strong and J. Garstang, *The Syrian Goddess*, p. 36.

[d]M. Avi-Yonah, *IEJ* II, 1952, pp. 123ff.

[e]M. Lidzbarski, *Ephemeris für semitische Epigraphik* III, pp. 1–11.

[f]'Die falschen Propheten', *ZAW* LI, 1933, pp. 109–20.

were hiding there. Again, as a range rising abruptly from the coastal plain it may have been a favoured cult-centre of Baal, who, as the Ras Shamra texts indicate, was manifest in his control of the sea and winter rains. On the horizon of the Phoenician country, it was an ideal place for Elijah to throw down the gauntlet to Jezebel. Carmel was certainly known as a sanctuary in Roman times,[a] and is probably *Rōš Qdš*, which is listed after Acco in the Karnak lists of the Palestinian conquests of Thothmes III.[b] According to Alt[c] and Noth[d] the incident on Carmel was not an attack on the Baal-cult introduced by Jezebel, which, it is contended, was confined to Samaria, but the destruction of the shrine of the local god of Carmel by fanatical Yahwists. To be sure, such a local god, called indeed 'Carmel', is actually attested in the Roman period, being identified with Zeus of Heliopolis (Baalbek) in the inscription cited by Avi-Yonah (*op. cit.*). The identification of the god with Zeus, the senior God of the trinity of Baalbek, suggests that he was of more than merely local significance, and was, in fact, the high god who controlled thunder, lightning, and rain, and the consequent order in nature, Hadad of the Ras Shamra texts and later Baal of the Heavens, as Eissfeldt maintains.[e] It is contended that the worship introduced by Jezebel was that of Baal Melqart, 'the Lord of the City',[f] and to this view we have no objection. We doubt, however, if a distinction should be made between Baal Melqart and Baal Shamem. The city-god of Tyre, which depended on maritime trade, was surely the Canaanite Hadad, whose victory over the unruly Sea is celebrated in the Ras Shamra text, the same Baal Zaphon to whom Phoenician sailors saved from shipwreck set up a shrine near Pelusium.[g] The Baal worshipped on Carmel had more than a local significance. Headlands with variable winds and currents were notorious in ancient navigation, and it is appropriate that the Baal worshipped on Carmel should be Hadad, who subdued the unruly waters in Canaanite mythology, and pre-

[a]Tacitus, *Hist.* II, 78.

[b]Abel, *GP* I, pp. 350ff.

[c]'Das Gottesurteil . . .', *KS* II, pp. 135ff.

[d]*History of Israel*, p. 242 n.6.

[e]'Baʿalšamēm und Jahwe', *ZAW* LVII, 1939, pp. 1–31.

[f]F. C. Movers, *Die Phönizier* I, 1841, pp. 175ff., 385ff., and more recently A. Alt, *op. cit.*, and R. de Vaux, 'Les prophètes de Baal sur le mont Carmel', *BMB* V, 1941, pp. 1ff.

[g]Eissfeldt, *Baal Zaphon, Zeus Kasios, und der Durchzug der Israeliten durchs Meer*, citing Philo of Byblos, *Fragmenta Historiarum Graecarum* IV, ed. W. Müller, fr. 2.17, p. 568.

served order in nature, guaranteeing the life of vegetation, for which Carmel, the first part of Palestine to enjoy the rain from the sea, was famous (Amos 1.2).

18.21. Elijah treats the assembled Israelites as *hāʿām*, the religious community. The general sense of the phrase *pōseḥīm ʿal-štē hasseʿippīm* is beyond doubt, prevarication being connoted. The literal meaning is less certain. The verb *pāsaḥ* is used of the lame Mephibosheth (II Sam. 4.4), and in v. 26 is used of the ritual dance, which, on modern Arab analogy, would be a stiff, staccato hobble. The noun *sāʿīp* signifies a cleft in a rock (Judg. 15.8, 11; Isa. 2.21; 57.5), or a branch (Isa. 17.6; 27.10), cf. *seʿappā* (Ezek. 31.6, 8). From this noun the Piel *sēʿēp* is derived, meaning 'to lop off the branches'. If 'branches' is the root meaning, then the phrase might be a metaphor of a bird hopping among the branches, but if, as the noun in Judg. 15.8, 11 and Isa. 2.21 suggests, the root meaning is 'cleft', which is not incomprehensible in the case of a branch dividing itself from the main trunk or limb, then the phrase may mean, as Moffatt renders, 'hobbling between two forks' (at a cross-roads), though it should be noted against this view that the noun occurs not as a dual, but as a plural. De Vaux,[a] on the other hand, proposes to find in the verb the description of the rites of the Baal-devotees in v. 26, the dance referred to in Heliodorus's description of a native dance of Tyrian sailors,[b] a feature of which was the bending of the knees in a low squatting position (*epoklazontēs*) somewhat like that in a Cossack dance. This, de Vaux plausibly contends, was what was meant by 'bending the knee to Baal' (19.18), where the same verb *epoklazein* is used in G. In view of the meaning attested for *seʿippīm* we doubt if de Vaux is right in seeing in the phrase *pōseḥīm ʿal-štē hasseʿippīm* a reference to such a ritual dance. The phrase *štē hasseʿippīm* instead of the dual militates against any reference to the knees of the worshippers, and we prefer Fohrer's interpretation 'hobble on two crutches' (*op. cit.*, pp. 57f.), a reference to seeking the support both of Yahweh and Baal on the part of the people, with an animadversion also on Ahab's policy to respect both Israelite and Canaanite traditions in his kingdom.

22. Note the emphatic position of 'myself alone'.

23. Elijah offers his rivals their choice of the oxen as a guarantee that he will use no sleight of hand and that they will have no excuse

[a] *Op. cit.*, pp. 9–11.
[b] *Ethiop.* IV, 17.1.

that the victim was less fit for sacrifice, hence vitiating the efficacy of the ritual.

18.26. Note the vocative *h* with *ba'al*. The precise significance of the preposition *'al* is uncertain here. It may indicate 'about', 'by the side of', or even 'before',[a] or it may signify the ascent up to the altar by steps, in which case *way^epass^eḥū* would seem to mean that they hopped, or ceremonially hobbled, up the steps. We prefer the interpretation of de Vaux, however (see on v. 21), that a ritual dance about the altar is indicated. A local manifestation of Baal in Lebanon was Baal Marqad ('Baal of the Dance'). The circumambulation of the altar is attested in Ps. 26.6, cf. the circumambulation (*ṭawāf*) of the Ka'ba by the pilgrims at Mecca, also performed with unnatural motion.[b]

27. The taunt of Elijah that Baal may have a matter to think over (*śīaḥ lō*), if original, would imply a limitation comparable to that of man who is not free to take cognizance of all things but is excluded from certain fields by concentration on others. De Vaux, however,[c] would see a more specific reference to the Phoenician conception of Baal Melqart in the reference to his activity by *śīaḥ* and *śīg* and to his being on a journey. The usual interpretation of *śīg* as 'turning aside' assumes that this word is a variant of *sīg*. But the fact that *śīg* is a *hapax legomenon* in the Old Testament impairs the force of this interpretation. Actually *śīaḥ* and *śīg* occur in conjunction in the Hebrew text of Ben Sirach (13.26), where G renders simply *chrēmatizein* ('to be busy'), thus treating the two verbs as synonyms. Again he cites sources from the Roman period to demonstrate the conception of Heracles, the Tyrian Baal, as the originator of practical wisdom and invention. The journey seems to reflect the activity of the god with his worshippers in their trade and colonial enterprises in the western Mediterranean, which is indicated by the representation of the god on a sea-horse on the oldest Tyrian coins from the Persian period. The Phoenicians were already active overseas in the time of Elijah, Carthage being founded little more than a decade later in 841. Alternatively the journey may refer to an episode in the Baal-myth illustrated in the Ras Shamra text *UT* 75, where Baal before his eclipse as a vegetation-deity makes a journey to the desert marches to hunt 'the Devourers, the Voracious Ones', to whom he succumbs.

[a] So de Vaux, *op. cit.*, p. 9.
[b] R. F. Burton, *Pilgrimage to Medina and Mecca* II, 1926, pp. 165ff.
[c] *Op. cit.*, pp. 13–16.

G. R. Driver,[a] however, has probably found the solution in a pejorative reference to Baal's withdrawal for defecation. He proposes feasibly that the original reading was *šîaḥ* or *šûaḥ* ('to defecate'), with *śîg* ('to turn aside', or 'to do one's business', G. *chrēmatizein*, cf. G rendering of Ben Sirach 13.26 (Hebrew)) as a euphemistic gloss. This in turn suggested the reading *śiaḥ*, itself a euphemism for *šîaḥ* or *šûaḥ*, as rather obviously in the passage on Isaac seeking the privacy of the open country at nightfall in Gen. 24.63. Baal's sleeping and requiring to be awakened may refer to some ritual awakening of the God known in the fertility-cult and in any case is a scathing reference to the naïve anthropomorphism of the Baal-mythology, now so vividly illustrated in the Ras Shamra texts. De Vaux, however, is more probably right in seeing in this passage references to elements in the later development of the cult of the Tyrian Baal half a millennium after the Ras Shamra texts, making effective use of documentary material from the Roman period, supported in certain cases by Phoenician inscriptions from the second century BC and later. Thus, as the particular type of sacred dance referred to in our note on v. 26 is attested by Heliodorus (a native of Homs) of Tyrian sailors (cf. Herodian V, 5, 9), self-laceration in a Syrian cult is attested by Apuleius[b] and by Lucian in his description of the cult of the Syrian goddess, consort of Baal of the Heavens at Hierapolis (*Membij*).[c] A striking coincidence between this matter and the present passage is in Apuleius, where the self-laceration is followed by prophetic utterance.[d] The awakening of the god was also an element in the Near Eastern nature-cult in Egypt in the middle of the second millennium,[e] where it was apparently a daily rite, and in Tyre in the time of Hiram, the contemporary of Solomon,[f] where the reference is to a rite in the rededication of local temples in the late spring. We question, however, if de Vaux[g] is right in maintaining that this was an annual rite in the cult of Tyrian Baal, assuming that Baal Melqart as a vegetation deity was awakened from his sleep of winter. On the contrary, the Ras Shamra texts show that Baal was especially active in the rains and storms of winter, but

[a]G. R. Driver, 'Problems of Interpretation in the Heptateuch', *Mélanges bibliques rédigés en l'honneur de André Robert*, 1957, pp. 66–68.
[b]*Metamorphosis* VIII, 27.
[c]Garstang and Strong, *The Syrian Goddess*, p. 84.
[d]*Metamorphosis* VIII, 27ff.
[e]A. Erman, *Literature of the Ancient Egyptians*, 1927, p. 12.
[f]Josephus, *Ant.* VIII, 5.3, after Menander.
[g]*Op. cit.*, p. 17.

languished with the advent of summer. We should rather associate the rite of Carmel with the rousing of Baal *ad hoc*, being tantamount to the invocation of the presence of the god.

18.28. We believe that the self-laceration of the Baal-prophets was more than a mere *yoga*. Blood was the vital essence, and the blood-letting was a rite of imitative magic to prompt a liberal release of the vital rain and the life dependent on it. W. R. Smith's suggestion[a] that the effusion of the blood of the Baal-devotees established a bond between them and the god is not feasible, since this was already established by the blood of the third party, the victim. A more plausible suggestion, though in our opinion inferior to the interpretation of the rite as one of imitative magic, is that this was a substitute for human sacrifice.[b]

29. The denominative verb *hitnabbē'* denotes the externals of 'prophetic' experience, the dervish rites and the ecstatic behaviour, often indistinguishable from the conduct of a madman, which is occasionally denoted by the same verb (e.g. I Sam. 18.10; II K. 9.11; Jer. 29.26). On *minḥā* see p. 389 n.[a].

30. The fact of there being an altar to Yahweh on Mount Carmel which was countenanced by Elijah on this occasion is a significant indication of the late date of the Pentateuchal prohibition against plurality of places of sacrifice. It is considered (Kittel, Skinner, Eissfeldt) that the reference to an altar of Yahweh is a later interpolation to obviate the difficulty of Elijah using a local altar not dedicated to Yahweh, and van den Born (*op. cit.*, p. 111) finds it strange that an altar to Yahweh should have been found on Carmel, which was properly the seat of Baal. Strictly speaking, the reference to the repair of the ruined altar in v. 30 does not accord with Elijah's fashioning apparently of a new altar in vv. 31f., a difficulty felt by G, where the last clause of v. 30 appears after vv. 31f. This suggests that vv. 31–32a is a gloss by the Deuteronomistic compiler, reflecting his dogmatic view that Jerusalem was the only valid place of sacrifice (so Fohrer, *op. cit.*, p. 14n.). Carmel, however, is not a single peak, but a ten-mile long ridge, and there may well have been an altar to Yahweh on the south-east spur of the range, overlooking the scene of the victory of Deborah and Barak. Sanctuaries of both Yahweh and Baal in this region, where Israelites and Phoenicians had probably long come into contact, would be natural not only for worship, but

[a]*Religion of the Semites*, 1894², pp. 321ff.
[b]Skinner, CB, p. 232.

for business dealings involving oaths and pledges. The twelve stones in the Deuteronomistic expansion seen symbolical, rallying the consciousness of Israel as a twelve-tribe confederacy, which was primarily a religious community.

18.31. The use of 'Jacob', which it is proposed to omit or change to 'Israel' (see p. 388 n.[h]), must be retained here, as the latter half of the verse suggests.

32. The description of the trench as 'the content of two seahs of seed' has occasioned speculation. At first sight it seems to mean a hollow which would hold two seahs, or two-thirds of an ephah, and this is the interpretation which we accept. After Lev. 27.16 and Isa. 5.10, however, it has been held that the reference is to the amount of land which could be sown with two seahs of seed corn, i.e. the area enclosed by the trench.[a] The Mishnah defines *bēt sᵉʾā*, the area to be sown with a seah, as 900 square yards, so that if one took the latter interpretation the computation in the present passage would be enormous, and, in fact, out of all proportion to the four jars of water with which Elijah had the trench filled (vv. 33–35). The error has been made through pressing the literal meaning of *zeraʿ*, which means, to be sure, 'seed'. This, however, in our opinion, suggests the solution of the difficulty. We consider that *zeraʿ* should be taken literally, and suggest that in this particular the tradition of what Elijah did has been influenced in the pre-literary stage by familiarity with a peasants' rite of imitative magic where seed-corn was put in a trench and soaked with water to cause it to sprout, cf. the popular folk-chant from Bethlehem cited by Dalman:[b]

Water our parched seed (*zarʿana*)
Make our dry seed green.

34. On the vessel *kad*, the common water-pot, see on 17.12. The pouring of water over the sacrifice was ostensibly a guarantee against fraud, though it may be a feature developed by tradition from a rite of imitative magic, cf. the water-pouring over the altar on the Feast of Tabernacles at Jerusalem.[c] Patai would see in the four jars of water a rite of imitative magic to induce rain from one or other of the four points of the compass. The effective rain, however, came with

[a]So apparently R. B. Y. Scott, 'Weights and Measures of the Bible', *BA* XXII, 1959, p. 27.

[b]*Palästinische Diwan*, 1901, p. 56.

[c]R. Patai, 'The Control of Rain in Ancient Palestine'. *HUCA* XIV, 1939, pp. 251ff.

the prevailing moisture-laden wind from the west, and, in so far as details may be pressed, we consider it more likely that the reference was to the four directions of the land where rain was desired. One rationalistic commentator[a] suggested that not water, but naphthah or some such substance susceptible to spontaneous combustion was used. R. H. Kennett[b] went even further and suggested that a burnished reflector was also used. If such hypercriticism is worthy of reply we may object, with Rowley,[c] that the Baal-prophets would be especially vigilant, and would be as much *au fait* with such elementary science as Elijah. If one were in such a sceptical mood one could emphasize the command of Elijah to the people to draw near (v. 30), all kinds of sleight of hand being possible in a crowd. In such a case as this the nature of the source is to be taken into account. Whatever the basic historical facts, this is transmitted as prophetic saga.

18.36. On 'the time of the offering of the oblation' see p. 389 n.[a]. In the Second Temple[d] the *minḥā* was offered at the ninth hour (about 3 p.m.), cf. Mishnah, *Pesaḥim* 5. 1 ('between eight and a half and nine and a half hours'). In view of the native custom of starting the day's work before the daylight,[e] this probably marked the end of the serious work for the day, and so may be 'the evening oblation' of Dan. 9.21. This seems a genuine note, since the sequel on Carmel and the journey to Jezreel makes a later time in the day unlikely.

Elijah's appeal to the God of Abraham, Isaac, and Israel suggests familiarity with the patriarchal traditions which form the prelude to the history of Israel based on the *Heilsgeschichte*, or cult-legend of salvation, in the Pentateuch. Elijah's specific mention of Abraham and Isaac, who play hardly any part in the message of the pre-exilic prophets, may indicate topical interest in the E source of the Pentateuch, completed or nearing completion in the time of Elijah. By these words Elijah rallies Israel as the elect and covenanted community and emphasizes the gulf between the historical faith of Israel and the impersonal nature-cult of Canaan, though the whole episode emphasized the sovereignty of the God of Israel over the forces of nature also. We should emphasize the element of prayer, which we associate with the sequel in vv. 41 ff. (see critical introduction to ch. 18). Elijah's prayer may have been deliberately prolonged in

[a] Hitzig, *Geschichte des Volkes Israel*, 1869, p. 176.
[b] *Old Testament Essays*, 1938, pp. 103ff.
[c] 'Elijah on Mount Carmel', *BJRL* XLIII, 1960, pp. 211ff.
[d] Josephus, *Ant.* XIV, 4.3.
[e] Dalman, *Arbeit und Sitte* . . ., I, 2, pp. 597ff.

anticipation of rain. Elijah's appeal to God to let it be known that he was God's servant and did all things at his word corrects the impression, already perhaps part of the popular tradition, that he himself had special efficacy. It is, moreover, a feature of the tradition of the authentication of the divine authority of a prophet by a 'sign', or token of God's immediate activity.

18.38. The answer to Elijah's prayer was lightning (*'ēš yhwh*), which is the accompaniment of rain in the late autumn, e.g. the Baal-myth of Ras Shamra, *UT* 51, V, 68ff.:

> Moreover Baal will send abundance of his rain,
> Abundance of moisture with snow;
> He will utter his voice in the clouds,
> (He will send) his flashing to the earth with lightning.[a]

For lightning as the prelude to rain, cf. the Arab folk-saying, *'al-baraq ʿalāmat 'al-maṭar* ('the lightning is the announcement of the rain').[b] In popular tradition, however, this was associated with the conception of fire as the medium of the theophany, cf. Judg. 6.21; 13.20, also associated with the consumption of an offering. Under the spur of the Carmel range crowned by *Deir al-Muḥraq*, the reputed setting, is an outcrop of rock which to primitive imagination might resemble large stones fused together by heat. In local folklore this may have suggested the detail of the fire consuming the altar. There is no good reason to doubt this location. The well is necessary to explain the jars of water in time of drought, and there is an ancient road from the plain to this locality, which is necessary to explain the fact that Ahab was able to bring his chariot up (v. 44). The place where the Baal-devotees were massacred may well be located at the traditional site *Tell al-Qasīs* ('Mound of the Priest') by the Kishon (*Nahr al-Muqaṭṭaʿ*) in the plain below.

39. The cry of the people 'Yahweh is God' re-echoes the name of Elijah ('My God is Yahweh'), which may very well have been a name assumed to give point to his mission. This view is supported by the fact that Elijah is introduced abruptly at 17.1 without any patronymic. The exclamation probably re-echoes a cry long established in the cult, probably the occasion when Israel formally renounced all other gods and declared that Yahweh was their god (Josh. 24.18). This is re-echoed also in the great declaration of

[a]For philological notes in support of our translation see our *Legacy of Canaan*, 1965², pp. 49f.
[b]Dalman, *Arbeit und Sitte* . . . I, p. 114.

monotheism, *'ᵃnī 'ᵃnī hū' wᵉ'ēn 'ᵉlōhīm ʿimmādī* ('I, even I, am he, and there is no god beside me') (Deut. 32.39; Isa. 43.10, 13; 48.12).

18.40. Though the reading *wayyašḥīṭēm* might be more strictly correct in sense (so Šanda), the Qal of MT is not unintelligible, signifying that what was done was by Elijah's authority, he remaining up the mountain, as the sequel demands, while the massacre took place in the plain below. The success of the Yahwists was merely temporary. Even if the tradition of Elijah's flight to Sinai in ch. 19 is not in its chronological order, which it probably is, the issue was not decided in Israel until the *coup d'état* of Jehu (II K. 9–10), and the Baal-cult persisted in Judah until the assassination of Athaliah (II K. 11).

41. The verb *ʿᵃlē* need not imply that Ahab, any more than Elijah, had been down at the Kishon witnessing the massacre. The call of Elijah to Ahab to eat and drink may indicate that until then a fast had been observed, such as was customary on the occasion of intercession in drought (Joel 1.14) or some such other public calamity. The meal again might symbolize the renewed communion between Ahab, Elijah, and Yahweh. *hāmōn* expresses the sound as well as the movement of a crowd. Here it signifies the noise of the rain, either experienced in anticipation by the lively imagination of the prophet or perhaps the sound of the rising west wind, which was the herald of the storm.

42. The place of the sacrifice was thus below the summit, towards which Elijah now climbed, stopping short of the actual summit, however, to which he sends his lad to observe the signs of weather over the sea. These details would well fit the location of the sacrifice at *Bīr al-Muḥraq*.

The verb *gāhar* ('bowed') is found besides here only in the Elisha story, where the prophet stoops over the dead or sick child (II K. 4.34f.). The attitude of Elijah is different from that of Elisha, implying a squatting posture with the head between the knees. The similarity to certain postures of dervishes in their exercises has been remarked upon. We cannot agree with Jirku that this was a mourning rite observed by Elijah pending the coming of the rain.[a] It is true that the drooping of the head on the knees is an attitude of humiliation in the Tale of Sinuhe and the Ras Shamra texts, cited by Jirku,[b] but there is nothing there to indicate that this was a religious rite, as Jirku claims. The purpose was, we believe with Montgomery (ICC,

[a]So Fohrer, *Elia*, 1968², p. 19.

[b]' "Das Haupt auf die Knie legen" ', *ZDMG* CIII, 1953, p. 372.

p. 306), to induce concentration rather than, as T. H. Robinson suggests,[a] an act of imitative magic, where the prophet simulates a rain-cloud.

18.43. On the topography see on v. 42. The sevenfold journey of the lad to the top of the mountain suggests the saga. In the Ras Shamra texts, indefinitely repeated action is thus described, e.g. *UT*, Krt, 114–18:

Tarry a day, a second day,
A third, a fourth day,
A fifth, a sixth day. . . .
Then at sunrise on the seventh day. . . .

44. On the cloud from the sea see p. 389 n.[d]. 'Hitch up and go down . . .' indicates that Ahab must have been meanwhile up on the mountain, to which there was a road possible for a chariot.

45. The phrase *ʿad-kō weʿad-kō* is a *hapax legomenon*. *kō* has a local, and sometimes a temporal, significance. Here the phrase means 'meanwhile'. The momentary darkening and outburst of torrential rain is a well-known phenomenon in late autumn and winter in Palestine.

46. Elijah's outrunning Ahab's chariot to Jezreel is taken as an example of abnormal physical effort characteristic of the ecstatic experience of the prophet,[b] and this is supported by the statement that 'the hand of Yahweh was upon him', which regularly describes prophetic ecstasy in Ezekiel. It was indeed a strenuous physical effort, though not extraordinary. Jezreel (*Zerʿin*) was some 17 miles distant, and it is not impossible for a man to outstrip a horse and chariot over this distance, especially since the man runs cross-country in a straight line and the horse and chariot must pass slowly over rough ground and make certain detours. Moreover, after a long drought the earth would be gashed with great cracks and the sudden flush of rain down the dry watercourses would impose further obstacles, to say nothing of the mud. Footmen held a similar advantage over horses and chariots in the same locality and under the same conditions when Barak defeated Sisera. We cannot agree with D. R. Ap-Thomas[c] that this also was an act of imitative magic, Elijah, having by his crouching on Mount Carmel simulated a rain-cloud, now running eastwards to secure the diffusion of rain over the Plain of

[a] *History of Israel* I, p. 306.
[b] So most recently, Fohrer, *op. cit.*, p. 20.
[c] *PEQ*, 1960, p. 155.

Jezreel. We think it much more likely that, having won Ahab's sympathy in his triumph on Carmel, he now sought to exploit the situation in face of Jezebel's opposition in Jezreel, well knowing the support that Ahab needed against that dominant lady. Furthermore Elijah, through whose agency the rain was coming, wanted to exploit popular opinion in the queen's presence when the rain actually did come.

(*e*) JEZEBEL'S REACTION, ELIJAH'S FLIGHT, DESPAIR, AND REASSURANCE, AND THE CALL OF ELISHA: 19.1–21

On the unity of at least ch. 19 in the Elijah-saga with ch. 18, and on the influence of the tradition of Elisha in vv. 15f., see critical introduction to the Elijah-saga, p. 374. Certain commentators[a] have maintained that ch. 19, describing the flight and despair of Elijah immediately after his triumph on Carmel in ch. 18, belongs really to before ch. 17. It is unlikely, however, as Fichtner (*op. cit.*, p. 280) observes, that chs. 17–19 are strictly biographical, or, if the incidents are in chronological order, it is quite uncertain at what interval they followed one another. The present arrangement, culminating in the particular commission to Elijah to anoint Hazael, Jehu and Elisha (19.15f.), has probably suggested the inclusion of ch. 19 at this point. Since this really authenticated Elisha's mission, however, those verses in the tradition of ch. 19 and its inclusion towards the end of the Elijah cycle are probably due to the collector of the Elijah traditions, who, we suggest, was possibly Elisha himself or one associated with him.

In this passage it is suggested by most modern commentators that the divine question and Elijah's response in vv. 9b–10 are secondary in that position, though primary in vv. 13b–14, but such repetition is well-known in the saga convention and may be deliberate, in order to emphasize the isolation of Elijah and his zeal for Yahweh and the measure of his frustration.

19 [1]And Ahab told Jezebel all that Elijah had done and that[b] he
had slain all the prophets with the sword. [2]And Jezebel sent a messenger

[a]E.g. Jepsen, *Nabi*, 1934, p. 63, and Hölscher, *Eucharisterion* (Gunkel Festschrift) I, 1923, p. 190, who takes the arrangement as editorial, 19.1–3a betraying the editorial adaptation.

[b]MT *wᵉʾēt kol-* (*ʾašer hārag*) is obviously a dittograph of *ʾēt kol-* (*ʾašer ʿāśā*) earlier in the verse.

to Elijah saying, [a]If you are Elijah, I am Jezebel![a] So may god do[b] and more also[b] if about this time tomorrow I do not make your life as the life of one of them. 3 And he was afraid[c] and he rose up and went for[d] his life and came to Beersheba which belongs to Judah, and he left his lad there. 4 And he himself went in the desert a day's journey, and came and sat down under a single[e] broom-bush, and he made a request for himself that he might die, saying, Now it is too much, Yahweh; take my life, for I am no better than my fathers. 5 Then he lay down and slept there,[f] and lo, an angel touched him and said to him, Arise and eat. 6 And he looked, and behold, at his head was a cake baked on the coals and a flask of water, and he arose[g] and ate and drank, and lay down again. 7 And the angel of Yahweh came back a second time and touched him and said, Arise, eat, for the journey is too great for you. 8 And he arose and ate and drank, and went in the strength of that food forty days and forty nights to the mount of God, Horeb. 9 And he came there to a cave and spent the night there, and, behold, the word of Yahweh came to him and (Yahweh) said to him, What is your business here, Elijah? 10 And he said, I have been a very fanatic for Yahweh, God of Hosts, yet the Israelites have forsaken thy covenant, ruined thine altars, and slain thy prophets with the sword, and I alone am left and they have sought my life to take it. 11 And he said, Go forth and stand upon the mountain before Yahweh. And lo, Yahweh passed by, and a great wind and strong (rending the mountain and shattering the rocks before Yahweh), but Yahweh was not in the wind; and after the wind an earthquake, but Yahweh was not in the earthquake; 12 and after the earthquake, fire, but Yahweh was not in the fire; and after the fire a sound of thin silence. 13 And it happened, when Elijah heard, he wrapped up his face in his mantle and went out and stood at the mouth of the cave, and behold, a voice came to him saying, What is your business here, Elijah? 14 And he said, I have been a very fanatic for Yahweh, God of Hosts, yet the Israelites have forsaken thy covenant, ruined thine altars, and slain thy prophets with the sword, and I alone am left, and they have sought my life to take it. 15 Then Yahweh said unto him, Go, return the way you came to the wilderness of Damascus, and go in and anoint Hazael king over Aram. 16 And Jehu the son of Nimshi you shall anoint king over Israel, and Elisha the son of Shaphat from Abel-Meholah you shalt anoint a prophet in your place. 17 And it shall come

[a]G and L add here 'If you are Elijah and I am Jezebel'; see on v. 2.

[b]In view of the fact that Jezebel was probably pressing the universalistic claims of Baal-Shamayim, the singular should probably be read after G^B, the plural being the interpretation of her faith by orthodox Jewish scribes.

[c]Certain MSS and G and S support this reading *wayyīrāʾ* for MT *wayyarʾ* ('and he saw').

[d]Reading *ʿal* ('on account of') for *ʾel* ('to').

[e]Q *ʾeḥād* for MT (K) *ʾaḥat*, as in v. 5.

[f]Reading *šām* for MT *taḥat rōtem ʾeḥāḏ*, an inconvenient repetition, cf. G *hupokatō Rathmen*.

[g]Inserting *wayyāqom* with G.

to pass that him who escapes the sword of Hazael shall Jehu slay, and him who escapes from the sword of Jehu shall Elisha slay. [18] Yet shall I leave in Israel seven thousand, all the knees which have not bowed to Baal and every mouth which has not kissed him. [19]And he went thence and came upon Elisha the son of Shaphat ploughing with twelve yoke of oxen in front of him, he being with the twelfth, and Elijah went over to him and cast his mantle upon him.[a] [20]And he left the oxen and ran after Elijah and said, Let me kiss my father and my mother, that I may come after you. So he said to him, Go back again, but (remember) what I have done to you. [21]And he went back from following him and took the yoke of oxen and slaughtered them, and with the ox-tackle he boiled them,[b] and gave to the people, and they ate, and he arose and followed Elijah and served him.

19.2. Thenius, Klostermann and Kittel (BH[3]) admitted the reading of G and L, 'If you are Elijah, I am Jezebel!', which is accepted by Fohrer (*op. cit.*, p. 17) and Fichtner (*op. cit.*, p. 278). Stade, Schwally and Montgomery regarded it with reserve as feasible, but did not see how it was likely to have been omitted. Eissfeldt[c] notes that L presupposes a repetition of *lēʾmōr* introducing the subject of Jezebel's message and again before her oath. The first phrase then would be omitted by homoioteleuton. There is particular significance in the name 'Yahweh is my God!' and 'Where is the Prince (Baal)?', the latter heralding the resurrection of Baal the Mighty in the fertility cult of Canaan illustrated in the Ras Shamra texts (see above on the name Jezebel in 16.31).

3. The fact of Elijah's flight beyond Israel to the far south suggests at first sight that his triumph at Carmel was momentary. Events, however, may be telescoped in the tradition as it has reached us, and this episode may even be part of the earlier history of Elijah as a fugitive in remote places from the persecutions of Jezebel, like ch. 17. Not until the extirpation of the house of Omri was Yahwism to gain unquestionable ascendancy over Baalism. The description of Beersheba as 'belonging to Judah' indicates the consciousness of the political distinction between Israel and Judah and dates the source from at least before 722, see critical introduction to the Elijah cycle. Beersheba was practically the southern limit of sedentary occupation, and so it has remained except for periods when for commercial reasons the Nabataeans occupied and developed every possible

[a]Reading *ʿālāw* for *ʾēlāw*.
[b]Omitting *habbāśār* of MT with G.
[c]Eissfeldt, 'Bist du Elia, so bin ich Isebel (I K. xix, 1)', *SVT* XVI, 1967, pp. 65–70.

locality in the southern desert between the fourth century BC and the fifth AD, and when Jehoshaphat first in the late ninth century BC and then the Byzantines from the fifth to the seventh centuries AD settled it as a frontier province, and recently for strategic and economic reasons in the State of Israel, when greater transport facilities and modern methods of water supply have counteracted natural difficulties.

19.4. *rōtem* is broom, with a delicate white flower with maroon centre commonly found along the beds of wadis. We have noticed it as a feature of the wadis north-west of the Dead Sea, where it provides ample forage for bees. We should emphasize *'eḥād*, which has not so much the force of the indefinite article here as the meaning 'a single'. 'He requested his life to die' indicates the Semitic conception that life (*nepeš*, lit. 'life-breath') proceeded directly from, and belonged properly to, God, so that, though a man might wish to die, he was not at liberty to commit suicide, which was quite exceptional among primitive Semites.

5. *ze* in *hinnē-ze* is a demonstrative enclitic (*GK* 136d). The 'angel' (*mal'āk*, lit. 'messenger') as the divine intermediary is a marked feature of the E source of the Pentateuch, which was crystallizing at this time.

6. 'A cake baked on hot stones' (*'ūgat reṣāpīm*) refers to a round, flat cake of bread (see on 17.12), baked, as still among the Arabs in desert and villages, on hot stones in the ashes. In the desert, charcoal of dried camel dung is often used instead of hot pebbles.

8. Forty is the conventional round number of Semitic folk-lore, see on 11.42. Elijah's journey of 'forty days and forty nights' may be influenced by the tradition of Moses' sojourn of the same period on the Mount of God. Horeb, which simply means 'desert', is the holy mountain of E and D in the tradition of the Covenant and Law-giving, cf. 'Sinai' in J and P. The Sinai tradition is old in Israel, Sinai being given as the scene of the theophany in the Song of Deborah (Judg. 5.5). In this passage *ze sīnay* is taken as a late gloss, 'this is Sinai', but it is probable that *ze* is a corruption of *z* as an old relative pronoun here, cf. Ugaritic and Aramaic *d*ᵉ, and Arabic *d̲u* ('master of', 'he of'), and the phrase is probably original. This peak was probably an objective of pilgrimage from an early date,[a] and it served the same purpose now in the case of Elijah. Regarding the

[a]Noth, 'Der Wallfahrtsweg zum Sinai', *PJB* XXXVI, 1940, pp. 5ff. Noth, however, locates the holy mountain in the north-eastern Hejaz.

location of the holy mountain near Kadesh Barnea (*'Ain Qedeirāt*) rather than at the traditional *Jebel Serbal*, Mowinckel[a] finds that all the really concrete traditions of the desert wandering of Israel are attached to Kadesh, the source dealing with the southern location being a late interpolation in the early Kadesh tradition between Ex. 17 and Num. 20.[b] We have argued for a location of the desert wandering in the northern part of the Sinai desert, emphasizing the incident of the migrant quails, which must be located on the Mediterranean shore.[c] This location is supported by the topographical term *tih bany 'isra'īl* ('the desert of the B. Israel'), by which Usāmah ibn Munqidh[d] alludes to the desert hinterland between Egypt and Al-Arish, so also Yaqut and Al-Qazwini. This northern location of Sinai is supported by Hab. 3.3. The sanctity of the *Wādī Feirān* in the vicinity of the Mount Sinai of Christian tradition is attested by Nabataean inscriptions from 149–253 AD.[e] Diodorus Siculus (III, 42f.) and Strabo (XVI, 4, 8), drawing on the authority of Agatharchides, carry this tradition back to the second century BC. It is possible that the movements of Elijah or the tradition of them were influenced by the Moses tradition. Moses also received his call at Horeb (Ex. 3.1ff.).

19.9. The definite article with the singular *hamme'ārā* ('cave') is explained by Montgomery (ICC, p. 317) as the generic article ('the cave-region'), as in 18.4. Here, however, it seems rather to point to the tradition of a definite cave on the holy mountain, possibly that from which Moses saw the back of Yahweh (Ex. 33.21ff.). The tradition of Elijah at Horeb is strongly coloured by that of the theophany to Moses at Sinai, cf. v. 11, describing the 'passing' of God, cf. Ex. 33.19, already current in J.

10. *qānā'* is used of the enthusiasm of exclusive devotion. It amounts to fanatical intolerance as in the case of Jehu (II K. 10.16). It is also used of Yahweh's intolerance of other gods in worship of his people, his 'jealousy' (Ex. 20.5). G^{B}, L, and S read simply 'they have forsaken thee' for MT 'they have forsaken thy covenant', but the

[a]'Kadesj, Sinai, og Jahve', *NGT* XI, 1942, pp. 1–32, following Gressmann, *Mose und seine Zeit*, 1913, pp. 123ff.

[b]Mowinckel, *op. cit.*, pp. 14ff.; Gressmann, *op. cit.*, pp. 123f.

[c]'The Desert Sojourn of the Hebrews and the Sinai-Horeb Tradition', *VT* IV, 1954, pp. 148–54.

[d]*Kitāb al-i'tibār*, ed. P. K. Hitti, p. 14.

[e]B. Moritz, *Der Sinai-Kult in der heidnischer Zeit*, Abhandl. der königlicher Gesellschaft der Wissenschaften zu Göttingen, Phil-hist. Klasse, Band XVI, 1916.

particular covenantal relationship of people and Yahweh was the essence of the faith of which Elijah was the protagonist against the broad universalism which Jezebel sought to promote in the name of Baal.

In the reference to plurality of altars to Yahweh, Elijah obviously knows nothing of the Deuteronomic insistence on a single shrine. Is the reference to the slaughter of the prophets an indication of another lacuna in the Elijah story between the Carmel incident and the flight to Horeb? Or does it refer to the persecution mentioned in 18.4, 13? The complaint of Elijah that he is left alone is a typical case of hyperbole for the sake of emphasis, which is common in Semitic thought and speech.

19.11–18. The statement in v. 11 that Yahweh passed by may be secondary, suggested by Ex. 33.19 in the theophany to Moses. The significance of the theophany to Elijah at Horeb has been taken to be the revelation that the violent measures adopted by Elijah at Carmel were not the methods Yahweh desired of his servants. The meaning of the theophany seems to us rather to be an admonition to the prophet to expect, not the supernatural and spectacular inbreaking of Yahweh into history anticipated in the traditional liturgy of the cult with the accompaniments of storm, earthquake, and fire (e.g. Ps. 18.12 [13]; Judg. 5.4f.; Hab. 3.3ff.; Ps. 68.8 [9] etc.), but rather an intelligible revelation to find God's direction in the ordinary course of daily life and to communicate it regularly and constructively. The proleptic reference to the anointing of Hazael and Jehu may have been prompted by a reference to the prophet's duty to interpret the events of history as tokens of the will of God, in the fashion which became traditional in the great prophets, or even to utilize such contingencies to further the will of God in Israel. The reference, however, was most probably not particularly to Hazael or Jehu, but more general. There may, however, have been a reference to Syria, indicated by the direction to Elijah to go to the wilderness of Damascus (v. 15a) and to the Yahwistic party in Israel, eventually identified with Jehu, in the 'seven thousand' who had not bowed the knee to Baal (v. 18). In so far as Elijah may have contemplated the effecting of the divine purpose by drastic political means, the Horeb theophany may reflect his interpretation of an inner conflict to his successor and associate Elisha. The revelation of God in an intelligible communication rather than in the spectacular phenomena described marks an advance in man's conception of God as personally accessible and intelligible to man within the framework of human experience, anticipating the prophetic conception of the expression of the divine will in contemporary history and the divine revelation in Jesus Christ.

The participle *ʿōbēr* ('passing by') after *hinnē* is used for graphic effect.

19.11,13. The masculine adjective *ḥāzāq* ('strong') and participles *m^{e}pārēq* and *m^{e}šabbēr* ('rending' and 'shattering') after the adjective *g^{e}dōlā* ('great') agreeing with *rūaḥ* ('wind') indicate that MT *w^{e}ḥāzāq m^{e}pārēq hārīm ūm^{e}šabbēr s^{e}lāʿīm* is a later amplification (so Fohrer, *op. cit.*, p. 19n.). We cannot agree with Fohrer, however, that the divine question and Elijah's response in vv. 9b–10, which is repeated verbatim in vv. 13b–14, is a 'dogmatic gloss'. Such verbal repetition is a regular feature of the saga style. The wrapping of his face in his mantle indicates Elijah's apprehension of the presence of Yahweh, cf. Moses at the theophany on Sinai (Ex. 33.21ff.).

15. 'The wilderness of Damascus' has been taken as a gloss, and, indeed, G^{h} omits it. But there may well be a reference to a new place of refuge for Elijah, the desert edge east of the Lake of Tiberias in the lava region of *al-Lejā*, as Šanda suggests (I, p. 449), well known as a region of refuge. Here Elijah would be nearer the centre of affairs in which he had developed a new interest in Israel and Syria, and, incidentally, nearer his own home in Gilead. Perhaps this passage suggested to the Qumran sect the term 'wilderness of Damascus' as the name for their place of refuge. The realization that there were yet other protagonists for Yahwism besides himself no doubt influenced the prophet to return.

Elijah's commission to anoint is intelligible in the case of the two kings, Hazael and Jehu, but the anointing of his prophetic successor Elisha is extraordinary. There is no other case of the conferring of prophetic authority by anointing, though priests were anointed. It is possible that this marks, in the experience of Elijah, a new conception of the prophetic office, but, in effect, in the very circumstantial account of his commissioning, Elisha is not anointed, but has the prophetic authority conveyed according to ancient belief by contact with the prophet's mantle. For that matter Hazael was not anointed, but simply designated as king by Elisha (II, K. 8.13). This suggests that the verb *māšaḥ* here means 'to set apart', which was the real significance of the rite of anointing (see on 1.34).

The fact that Elijah did not personally anoint Hazael and Jehu suggests either that the Horeb experience fell at the end of his life, or that the actual commission to anoint Hazael and Jehu was a pious fiction to justify the high-handed methods of Elisha, who is in every respect a grosser type than Elijah. On the rise of Hazael, see on II K. 8.7, and on Jehu's revolt see on II K. 9–10. The name Jehu has the appearance of an exclamation *Yā hū'* ('Ah! it is he'), which either denoted his birth or reflected the acclamation of the epiphany of Yahweh in the cult. The name is possibly an abbreviation of *Yā hū' hā'ᵉlōhīm*, reflecting the public confession of the community when confronted with the choice of Yahweh or other gods. Noth[a] emphasizes the confession of faith implied in the name, aptly citing the great declarations of monotheism in Deut. 32.39 and in Isa. 43.10, 13; 48.12. There may even have been a reflection of the great crisis of the faith in the ordeal on Carmel, the family of Jehu so naming their son as a testimony of the part they played in that struggle and of Yahweh's vindication of Elijah. The name Elisha ('God is salvation') is attested on a seal (*c.* seventh century BC) from Amman,[b] and the name of his father Shaphat is doubtless a hypocoristicon of Shaphaṭyahu, and indicates the rule, or decision, of Yahweh. On Abel-Meholah, located by Eusebius in the Jordan Valley ten Roman miles south of Bethshean, see on 4.12.

19.17. In the anticipation of the Syrian wars as an instrument of divine discipline we have a foretaste of the view of the hand of God in history which characterizes the canonical prophets and was to help the faith of the people to survive the shock of Assyrian conquest. A certain difficulty is that the suffering inflicted by Hazael followed rather than preceded the rise of Jehu, a fact which may suggest that the episode falls in the lifetime of Elijah rather than Elisha, when the prophetic word would have been adjusted to fit the facts. The reference to those that Elisha shall slay is obscure, since there is no record of such a slaughter inspired by Elisha as the massacre of the Baal prophets at Carmel on the instigation of Elijah.

18. The 'seven' in the seven thousand loyalists is the conventional indefinite number of saga. In conjunction with the severe divine discipline mentioned in v. 17 we have here the conception, to become familiar in the message of Amos and Isaiah of Jerusalem, of the remnant of Israel through whom God's promise would be realized. Kissing of an image or symbol of a god is a well-known rite in primitive religion ancient and modern, evidenced by the efface-

[a] *IP*. pp. 143ff.
[b] I. Benzinger, *Hebräische Archäologie*, p. 228.

ment of the surface features of sacred objects of antiquity. The bowing of the knees may be an allusion to a peculiar type of dance, one feature of which was a squatting position, for which de Vaux cites evidence.[a]

19.19. Elisha was ploughing along with his community, cultivating probably on the run-rig system common among Palestinian peasants today. The eleven yoke of oxen were before him with their ploughmen in échelon. The note of Elijah going over (*wayyaʿᵃbōr*) the tilth is an intimate detail. The casting of the prophet's mantle upon his chosen successor is a rite of contactual magic, the mantle, since it was in intimate contact with a man's body, being thought to be imbued with his personality and power. The king's mantle was used as a substitute for his person in certain Assyrian rituals of purification,[b] and a prophet from Mari attests his personal commitment in an oracle by sending his robe.[c] In a Greek graffito from a Phoenician tomb of the third century BC at *Beit Jibrīn* a lover states that she has secured the garment of her beloved, believing that thereby she has secured power over his person.[d] So, by cutting off the skirt of Saul's mantle, David was probably regarded as having permanent power over Saul. This incident may be the origin of the cruder tradition of the miraculous properties of Elijah's mantle (II K. 2.14). The mantle, which was probably the distinctive garb of the prophet, as the rough woollen robe was of the later Muslim mystics (Sufis), was probably hairy (II K. 1.8; Zech. 13.4).

20. The answer of Elijah to Elisha's request to go and take leave of his parents is enigmatic. Fohrer (*op. cit.*, p. 22) takes it to signify a rebuke to Elisha, who had not realized the full significance of what Elijah had done to him in designating him as his successor with all the unconditional demands of the prophetic call. The sense is probably complicated here by the elliptic nature of direct speech. Probably the best sense is to take *kī* as an adversative particle, i.e. 'Go, but (remember) what I have done to you.' In any case, the emphasis is on the uncompromising nature of the call. The interpretation is supported by the hyperbolic demand of Jesus in similar circumstances (Matt. 8.21 f.; Luke 9.61).

21. Elisha's slaughter of the yoke of oxen and his cooking them in

[a] 'Les prophètes de Baal . . .'. pp. 9–11.

[b] R. Labat, *Le caractère religieux de la royauté assyro-babylonienne*, 1939, p. 354.

[c] A. Malamat, *SVT* XV, 1966, pp. 207–27.

[d] J. R. Peters and H. Thiersch, *Painted Tombs in the Necropolis of Marissa*, 1905, p. 57.

fire made from the tackle is a symbol of his break with the old life, and the meal is his rite of integration with Elijah, and his way of engaging his people in his new enterprise.

(*f*) PROPHETIC ADAPTATION OF HISTORICAL NARRATIVE OF THE SYRIAN WARS (continued in ch. 22): INCIDENTS OF THE SYRIAN WARS: 20.1–43

This chapter is quite different in character from the three preceding chapters and from the following, where the central figure is Elijah and the matter may be characterized, whatever its historical basis, as prophetic saga. Chapter 20 exhibits the features of historical narrative, particularly vv. 1–34. The central figure is the king of Israel, and there is no mention of Elijah or Elisha. The picture of the king is quite different from that in chs. 17–19 and 21. The attitude there is uncompromisingly hostile to Ahab. In ch. 20 the king is presented in a much more favourable light. In his extremity he refers his case to the elders of the people and is cordially supported in his resistance to the insulting demands of Benhadad (vv. 7ff.); when prophets are introduced they support the king (vv. 13ff., 22ff.), though one condemns his clemency (vv. 35–43), which, to be sure, had a political motive. In style, subject-matter, and general scope and viewpoint ch. 22 forms a unity with ch. 20, and there also Ahab, who, to be sure, is mentioned only once by name (v. 20), is presented as a strenuous king, ready to take the offensive in the interests of Israel. Here, too, the king has the support of nationalistic prophets, though emphasis is laid on the critical attitude of Micaiah ben Imlah. The role of Micaiah is emphasized, no doubt, in anticipation of the death of the king in the campaign of Ramoth Gilead, both being elaborated in prophetic tradition. In any case this instance of prophecy and fulfilment in the case of Ahab, whom prophetic tradition in the Elijah-saga presents in such a dark light, was something which the Deuteronomist was sure to emphasize.

The originality of Ahab in chs. 20 and 22 has been seriously questioned, and it must be noted that the name in 20.2, 13, 14 and 22.20 may well be intrusive, the 'king of Israel', as in II K. 6.24–7.20, with which ch. 20 has much in common, being anonymous. Since Jepsen,[a] it has been recognized that the king of Damascus contemporary with Ahab at the Battle of Qarqar in 853 was Hadadezer, who is mentioned in Assyrian inscriptions until 845 BC, by which time Ahab was

[a] *AfO* XIV, 1942, pp. 154–8.

certainly dead. This difficulty, which had already been felt by Luckenbill,[a] suggested to him that the campaigns of I K. 20, in which he did not question the part of Ahab, are to be dated to the beginning of Ahab's reign in the reign of Benhadad the predecessor of Hadadezer, a situation which scarcely accords with the strength of Omri, under whom in this case Israel would have been a vassal of Damascus. Kittel also[b] dates the events of I K. 20 before Qarqar, but assumes that the Assyrian record was mistaken in naming the Israelite king as Ahab. Jepsen[c] went on to suggest that the incident was in the reign of Joash of the House of Jehu, who was co-regent with Jehoahaz from 799 to 797 and sole king from 796 to 781, thus the contemporary of Benhadad III (II K. 13.24ff.), from whom he recovered cities lost by his father Jehoahaz (II K. 13.25, cf. I K. 20.26–34) and possibly also independence from Aramaean domination (II K. 13.7). Joash's decisive victory was at Aphek (II K. 13.17, cf. I K. 20.23–30). Fohrer,[d] who also finds 'Ahab' adventitious in chs. 20 and 22, finds no time for a campaign against Syria at Ramoth Gilead, as in ch. 22, in 853, when Ahab died, since the campaign where he was allied to Hadadezer at Qarqar in the early summer of the same year. It is also suggested that the only reason for an attack by Ahab on the Syrians at Ramoth Gilead could have been resentment at subordination to Damascus in that alliance, to which possibly, it has been suggested,[e] Ahab had been constrained in the campaign against Samaria mentioned in I K. 20, which has been dated three years before 853. Or, it is suggested, the heavy losses of Damascus at Qarqar, where she contributed the largest contingent of infantry, may have encouraged Ahab's attack. But in view of the Assyrian menace, which had been only momentarily halted at Qarqar, this would have been suicidal politics for a man of Ahab's ability, and actually Shalmaneser III in his account of Syrian campaigns in his tenth, eleventh and fourteenth years, implies that the coalition of Damascus, Hamath and the kings of Syria and Palestine remained unchanged, and indeed effective, to 845, though to be sure

[a]*AJSL* XXVII, 1910, pp. 253ff.

[b]*Geschichte des Volkes Israel* II, 1916^3, pp. 253ff.

[c]*Op. cit.*, p. 157.

[d]*Elia*, 1957, p. 66n.

[e]J. Skinner, *I and II Kings*, CB, p. 244. Mowinckel, *Acta Orientalia* X, 1931–2, p. 210, on inconclusive evidence, regards Ahab as a vassal of Damascus from 855 to just after the New Year of 852. Gressmann, *Die älteste Geschichtsschreibung*, pp. 277ff., associates the events of 20.1–34 with the building up of a common front against Assyria by Damascus, though he dates it earlier than 855.

he does not explicitly mention Ahab or Israel. Moreover, Ahab's contribution of the largest chariot force in the alliance in 853 (2,000) and 10,000 infantry certainly does not accord with the relative weakness of the subordinate king of Israel in I K. 20.1–34. The name Benhadad in ch. 20 may have been the throne-name of Hadadezer, cf. the king of Judah as 'the son of God', e.g. Ps. 2.7, but there is no actual evidence of reference in the inscriptions to the kings of Damascus by two names. Another fact that must militate against the identity of 'the king of Israel' in ch. 22 with Ahab is the statement in 22.40 that 'Ahab slept with his fathers'. This might refer to burial rather than death, but a careful study by B. J. Alfrink[a] shows that in this case this would be the only instance of the phrase being used of one who died by a violent death. Thus we now admit[b] that Ahab is adventitious in chs. 20 and 22.

Accepting the arguments of Jepsen, C. F. Whitley[c] attributes the identification of the unnamed king of Israel in chs. 20 and 22 with Ahab to the Deuteronomistic compiler.[d] Fichtner suggest that the Deuteronomist identified the king with Ahab because of his association in ch. 22 with Jehoshaphat. But Jehoshaphat was contemporary also with Jehoram of Israel, with whom he was associated in the Moabite campaign (II K. 3), with which I K. 22.1–18 has much in common.[e] We find it inconceivable that the Deuteronomist should have presumed to make this identification in the account of two such important events as the campaign at Ramoth Gilead and the death of the king and then immediately have referred the reader to the Book of the Chronicles of the Kings of Israel for the death of the king, evidently peacefully, which would contradict his presentation of the events in 22.1–38. We consider that the Deuteronomistic compiler found the identification with Ahab already made, and found this source con-

[a]B. J. Alfrink, 'L'expression "שכב עם אבותיו", *OTS* II, 1943, pp. 106–18, first pointed out by Hölscher, 'Das Buch der Könige, seine Quellen und seine Redaktion', *Eucharisterion* (Gunkel Festschrift) I, 1923, p. 185.

[b]See the first edition of this commentary, pp. 369f.

[c]'The Deuteronomic Presentation of the House of Omri', *VT* II, 1952, pp. 137–52.

[d]So also Fichtner, *op. cit.*, p. 297.

[e]The association with Jehoshaphat, if taken literally, would indicate the identity of the king of Israel with Ahab or Jehoram, whom J. M. Miller takes to be the king in question ('The Fall of the House of Ahab', *VT* XVII, 1967, pp. 307–24). In view of the close parallels between this passage and II K. 3 in the role of Jehoshaphat and the character of both passages as the prophetic adaptation of historical narrative, however, we may doubt the original historicity of Jehoshaphat in ch. 22.

genial to his general presentation of Ahab as meriting the end visualized in Elijah's oracle of doom (I K. 21.19). This association also has been made in the Deuteronomist's source.

Chapters 20 and 22 are claimed to be historical narrative, and Oesterley and Robinson[a] suggest that it is from a Book of the Acts of Ahab, a kind of dynastic history. If that were so, it must have been as critical of the kings as the Story of the Davidic Succession. The absolutism which Ahab affected, however, on the evidence of I K. 21, would scarcely have tolerated this candid criticism, nor does the theory accord with prophetic opposition to Ahab's reign. The passages, moreover, are not historical narrative, though they are in the style of that type of literature. Chapter 22 begins with a scene where the prophet Micaiah ben Imlah explains the support of the nationalistic prophets as the divine design to stultify the king, and it closes with the death of the king in fulfilment of Elijah's oracle. It is therefore really a prophetic narrative from prophetic circles. Chapter 20 is less obviously of this character, but it, too, emphasizes the role of the prophets in association with the king. When the king consults his elders and opposes involvement in foreign politics (20.7–12), he is supported by a prophet in his successful resistance (20.13–15, 22), but when the king spares his defeated enemy for diplomatic reasons he is condemned by a prophet (20.35–43). Both chapters, however, are probably prophetic narratives adapted from historical narrative, the original character of which is preserved particularly in 20.1–34. It was, we claim, at this stage that 'Ahab' was introduced.

It is claimed in support of the originality of Ahab in these passages that the Deuteronomistic compiler or any other hand which was so inimical to Ahab could not have represented him in such a favourable light as in 20.1–34 and ch. 22, which is claimed to describe Ahab's great courage and heroic death. We have already given our explanation of the prophetic representation of Ahab in ch. 20. In ch. 22, from first to last, he is depicted as a doomed man, stultified by nationalistic prophets to undertake a fatal campaign, wilfully ignoring the warning of Micaiah, wounded in spite of his disguise, trapped in the thick of the battle, when his wound might have been staunched behind the lines, and so bleeding to death as the victim of the ineluctable word of God which he had defied. For the prophetic circles from which ch. 22 emanated, such a figure could only be Ahab. The incident of the dogs licking the blood of the king from his chariot

[a]*Introduction to the Books of the Old Testament*, 1934, pp. 97ff.

(22.37f.) recalled Elijah's oracle of doom in 21.19, which further suggested the identity of the unnamed king with Ahab.

It is quite uncertain what king of Israel, if any, was killed at Ramoth Gilead, since Joram the son of Ahab was killed at Jezreel, though to be sure after being wounded at Ramoth Gilead, and Jehoahaz and Jehoash, the latter of whom was probably the 'king of Israel' in ch. 20, 'slept with their fathers' (II K. 13.9; 14.16). If the story is not apocryphal, it may refer to the death of a son of Ahab or some member of his family. The source of ch. 22, thus developed as a prophetic tradition, may be a historical narrative concerning such a person. The influence of the narrative of the joint expedition of Jehoram of Israel and Jehoshaphat of Judah is obvious. The king of Israel summons Jehoshaphat to join him in the expedition (22.4a, cf. II K. 3.7a), and Jehoshaphat replies, 'I am as you are, my people as your people, my horses as your horses' (22.7, cf. II K. 3.11). The latter narrative has probably shaped the development of the former at least up to this point. Chapter 20.1–34, like II K. 6.24–7.20, is developed from historical narrative of events in the beginning of the Israelite revival under Jehoash after Syrian domination, as indicated in the relative situations of Israel and Damascus at the beginning of operations in both passages. The precipitate withdrawal of the Syrians as far as the Jordan (II K. 7.15) may be a variant tradition of the withdrawal of the Syrians in ch. 20, especially if, as we believe after Yadin,[a] the Syrian base-camp was at Succoth at the mouth of the Jabbok and the rout of the Syrians was the result of an ambush in the *Wādī Fār'a*. The account of the second campaign at Aphek in 20.23–34, with the restoration of the Israelite cities in v. 34, is pure historical narrative of the reign of Joash, though introduced and concluded by prophetic traditions (vv. 23–25, 35–43).

(i) THE SYRIAN CAMPAIGN AND RELIEF OF SAMARIA: 20.1–22

20 [1]And Benhadad[b] the king of Aram gathered all his forces together and with him thirty-two kings, and horses and chariots, and came up and laid siege to Samaria and fought against it. [2]And he sent messengers to Ahab the king of Israel to the city. [3]And he said to him, Thus says Benhadad, Your silver and your gold are mine, and your

[a]Y. Yadin, 'Some Aspects of the Strategy of Ahab and David', *Biblica* XXXVI, 1955, pp. 332–51.

[b]G reads 'the son of *ʽΑδερ*'. The aspirate indicates that the first consonant in the Aramaic original was not ʼ, but *h*, so that we take the name as a corruption of Benhadad.

wives and your children[a] are mine also. 4And the king of Israel
answered and said, As you say, my royal master; I and all that I have
are yours. 5And the messengers returned and said, Thus says Benhadad,
Nay,[b] but I have sent to you saying, Your silver and your gold, your
wives and your children you shall give to me. 6Only, about this time
tomorrow I shall send my servants to you; they will search your palace
and the houses of your servants and it shall be that all that is pleasant
in their[c] eyes they shall put it in their hand and they shall take it away.
7Then the king of Israel called to all the elders[d] and said, Know and see
that this man seeks trouble, for he has sent to me for my wives and children, though I have not withheld from him my silver[e] and my gold.[e]
8And all the elders and all the people said, Do not listen or agree. 9So
he said to the envoys of Benhadad, Say to my royal master,[f] All the
terms which you sent to your servant in the first place will I fulfil, but
this matter I cannot fulfil. So the envoys went and took back an answer.
10And Benhadad sent to him and said, So may the gods do to me and
more also if the dust of Samaria is sufficient for handfuls[g] for all the
people who follow me. 11And the king of Israel answered and said, Say,
Let not him who girds on his armour boast as him who takes it off.
12And it happened that when he heard this word he was drinking, he
and the kings, in Succoth, and he said to his attendants, Attack. And
they attacked the city. 13And behold, a certain prophet came up to[h]
the king of Israel, and he said, Thus says Yahweh, Have you seen all
this great crowd? See, I shall give it into your hand today and you shall
know that I am Yahweh. 14And Ahab said, By whom? And he said,
Thus says Yahweh, By the squires of the commanders of the provinces.[i]
And he said, Who will clinch the fighting? And he said, You. 15And
Ahab[j] reviewed the squires of the commanders of the provinces, and
they were two hundred and thirty-two, and after them he reviewed[k]

[a]It is proposed to read 'daughters' (*ūb^{e}nōtekā*), which were in greater demand as booty than sons, but the masculine may be retained in the generic sense. G^{B} omits MT *haṭṭōbīm* ('the best').

[b]G reads 'I', which suggests Hebrew *'ānōkī*, of which the last syllable survives in MT *kī*, which is the adversative particle here.

[c]G, S, and V agree in reading 'their eyes' (*ʿēnēhem* for MT *ʿēnekā*).

[d]Reading with G^{B} 'the elders' (*hazz^{e}qēnīm*) for MT *ziq^{e}nē hā'āreṣ* ('the elders of the land').

[e]Reading after G^{BL} *w^{e}kaspī ūz^{e}hābī lō'*.

[f]G^{BL} read *la'^{a}dōnēkem* for MT 'to my royal master'. The latter, however, is in keeping with the vassal status of the king implied in his acquiescence in the first demand of Benhadad, and should be retained.

[g]G^{BL} have the interesting reading 'for foxes', indicating the pointing *šūʿālīm* for MT *š^{e}ʿālīm*.

[h]Omitting 'Ahab' of MT with G.

[i]G reads *en tois paidariois tōn archontōn tōn chorōn*. The last word is a mistake for *chōrōn*, 'regions', i.e. administrative districts.

[j]Adding 'Ahab' with G.

[k]Omitting 'all' of MT with G^{B}.

the people, every man of substance,[a] seven thousand.[b] 16And they came out at midday, and Benhadad was drinking to excess in Succoth, he and the kings, thirty-two kings, his auxiliaries. 17And the squires of the commanders of the provinces went forth first. And they sent to[c] Benhadad and told him, Some men have come out of Samaria. 18And he said, If they have come out in peace take them alive, and if they have come out to fight take them alive. 19But these came out of the city, the squires of the commanders of the provinces and the force which came after them. 20And each man struck down his antagonist, and the Aramaeans fled and Israel pursued them, and Benhadad the king of the Aramaeans escaped on a horse and horsemen along with him.[d] 21And the king of Israel came out and took[e] all[f] the horses and chariots and struck the Aramaeans a great blow. 22And the prophet came up to the king of Israel and said to him, Go, reinforce yourself, and take note and see what you should do, for when the year comes round the king of Aram will come up against you.

20.1. The name of 'the king of the Aramaeans', whose capital was Damascus, has three variants. In MT it is given as Benhadad, in G as *huios Ader*, and in the record of the Battle of Qarqar by Shalmaneser III, if the same king is meant, Adad-idri, i.e. Hadadʿezer. G has been taken to reproduce *ʿezer* in the second part of the name, but the rough breathing in the Greek does not reproduce Semitic ʿ, and, in fact, suggests the consonant *h*. G seems an obvious corruption of Benhadad. On the identity of Benhadad with Benhadad III of II K. 6.24, see introduction to this chapter. The title *melek ʾarām* is actually used by Benhadad III, who led seven kings out of a conspiracy of ten against Hamath (*ANET*, p. 501). It is used by the king himself on a stele he set up near Aleppo. The fact that his authority was so signalized here indicated that the title did refer to his authority over the Aramaeans so far North. That Aram undefined has this wider significance is indicated by the reference to 'all Aram' on the stelae from Safireh in

[a]Reading *b^enē ḥayil* after G. The low number suggests that only a section of the people is indicated, and not 'all the Israelites' as in MT.

[b]G^BL read 60 for MT 7,000. This is too small a number, and, if thousands are denoted, too large if only 'men of substance' are indicated.

[c]After G^A.

[d]G reads variously 'on a horse of a horseman' (*ʿal-sūs pārāš*), 'on a horse from the cavalry-mounts' (*ʿal-sūs mipp^erāšīm*), and 'on horseback with some horsemen' (*ʿal-sūs ʿim pārāšīm*).

[e]Reading with G *wayyiqqaḥ* for MT *wayyak* ('and he struck').

[f]Reading with G^B 'all'.

the same locality.[a] Jepsen[b] has made the feasible suggestion that the Aramaean hegemony of Damascus, so effective in the reign of Hadad-ezer, the contemporary of Ahab, and apparently effective, though to a minor degree, under Benhadad, was revived by his father Hazael. Possibly this was rather by force than by persuasion, as Hazael's campaigns in Palestine suggest. This would partly explain the failure of the allied army under Benhadad in I K. 20, especially if Damascus had limited the armament of her reluctant allies, as she had limited the forces of Jehoahaz (II K. 13.7), such reduced forces being possibly limited to personnel amenable to the policy of Damascus (see on II K. 10.32). The 32 kings of I K. 20.1 may be contrasted with the alliance of 10 states under the hegemony of Benhadad III in the Zakir inscription (*ANET*, p. 501), of which he enlisted 7, and is much higher than the whole number of Aramaean states in Greater Syria at Qarqar in 853, and must include Aramaean tribal sheikhs. Jepsen[c] is probably right in his suggestion that the hegemony of Damascus was based on the fact that her rulers were chiefly engaged in attracting and concentrating the Aramaean tribesmen between the desert and the sown and settling those who wished to settle. Damascus, the great oasis lying south-east of the southern extremity of the Anti-Lebanon, was the natural point of impact on the settled land of Syria for the powerful tribes of the North Arabian steppe, as is notably apparent in the Great Arab Revolt of 1916–18. The first expedition was intended to impress with the muster of Benhadad's vassal 'kings'. The second was organized for action. The basis of the new organization in v. 24 may be suggested by the organization of the kingdom of Damascus into 16 districts mentioned in the inscription of Tiglath-pileser III (*ANET*, p. 283), with the nucleus of the armed forces of his ten confederates and the better disciplined of his tribal confederates. The title 'king of Aram' refers to the authority of Damascus over the Aramaeans of the surrounding area. 'Aram' is an ethnic term and not geographic. The 'kings' are chiefs of various tribes or confederacies rather than rulers of Aramaean kingdoms in Syria. There were various occasions, as at Qarqar in 853, when the king of Damascus headed a large coalition of such rulers, but not even then were there ten kings under his leadership. The limitations

[a]H. Donner and W. Rollig, *Kanaanäische und aramäische Inschriften*, 1962, No. 222 A,5, pp. 41, 244.
[b]A. Jepsen, 'Israel und Damaskus', *AfO* XIV, 1942, pp. 167f.
[c]*Ibid.*, p. 168.

of a loose military organization of Aramaean tribesmen under their sheikhs was soon apparent in their desertion of the king (v. 25), and reorganization on professional military lines was demanded (v. 24). The readiness of the king of Israel to accept the first terms of Benhadad, harsh as they were (v. 3), suggests that he had suffered reverses in the provinces and that the country was overrun. It was probably the dispersion of the Aramaean tribal levies over the diversified country of Northern Israel which led to their desertion and the rally of Israel. The present narrative is in all probability a fragment of a much larger whole (see critical introduction to this section).

20.2. On 'Ahab' here and at vv. 13f. (cf. 22.20) as intrusive, a feature of prophetic adaptations of a historical narrative of the time of Joash, see introduction to this section.

3f. The claim of Benhadad to the possessions and family of the king of Israel denotes the vassal status of the latter, further indicated by the deferential address 'my royal master' (vv. 4, 9). The king of Israel assumes that a verbal acknowledgment of the claims of his suzerain would be sufficient, but a peremptory order by Benhadad convinces him that he means to exert his full authority, taking the king's family as hostages. The substance of the statement of the king of Israel in v. 7 is that he had not withheld tribute, that he should be liable to such an absolute demand. For the occasion in the beginning of the Israelite revival under Joash the son of Jehoahaz, see the critical introduction to this section.

5. *kī* is patient of a variety of meanings here. It may simply be recitative after *lē'mōr* ('saying'), but the general sense demands a stronger meaning. It may be a strong asseverative 'I did certainly send', 'it is true that I sent', the statement continuing 'but (moreover) I shall send . . .' That is to say, the king of Israel is not to be allowed merely to acknowledge his dependence, but is to be humiliated by the visit of Benhadad's officers. On the other hand, regard should be had to the statement in v. 4, 'I am yours and all I have'. To this the reply of Benhadad is, 'Nay, but I sent to you for your possessions and harem' (using *kī* in the adversative sense (*GK* § 163a)), 'only, I shall send my officers to fetch all they consider fit'. That is to say, in v. 5 Benhadad declines the king's offer to surrender his person, and apparently relents in demanding instead only his possessions and family. But his leniency is qualified by the demand that his officers should come and take what they deemed fit. The fact that Benhadad declined to take the king personally, but insisted on taking his family, indicates that he wanted the authority of the king with his subjects in an alliance, but proposed to take his family, probably as hostages.

20.7. The elders are the representatives of the free communities of Israel, hence MT *kol-ziqᵉnē hā'āreṣ* ('are the elders of the land') might possibly be read.

10. The sense of this verse is that Benhadad can reduce Samaria to dust and has sufficient men and more to carry the dust away in handfuls. The G variant (see p. 419 n.[g]) means that there will not be sufficient dust left to serve as fox-holes.

11. The Hebrew expression 'Let not him who girds on (his armour) boast as him that takes it off' is much shorter and more concise than in English, and was doubtless a popular aphorism. For the verbs as technical terms for arming and disarming cf. I Sam. 17.39 (*ḥāgar*) and Isa. 45.1 (*pātaḥ*). It is possible, however, that the reference is not to arming and disarming, but to putting on one's girdle in the morning and removing it at night.

12. *sukkōt*, which has generally been taken as 'field bivouacs', for the more regular *'ōhālīm*, is not attested in this sense except, questionably, here and in the account of David's campaign against Ammon in II Sam. 11. In both cases, Yadin[a] has convincingly contended that Succoth in the Jordan Valley by the mouth of the Jabbok (see on I K. 7.46) was the base camp of Benhadad and David. It may be noted that where the phrase recurs in v. 16, G(21.16) takes *sukkōt* as a place-name. Here the main force of the Syrians was poised to impose respect in Israel and Ammon, and, if need be, to strike at Samaria and other capitals and from here envoys were sent to summon them to tokens of their allegiance. The king of Israel apparently treated the summons as merely formal (v. 4). His formal and merely verbal acquiescence, however, did not satisfy Benhadad, who renewed his summons with more point, insisting on tribute and hostages to be given to his representatives within twenty-four hours (vv. 5f.), which implies negotiations at some distance. Refusal to comply is met with a threat of military force, Benhadad's reference to his army (v. 10) indicating a large army of which the king of Israel was apparently not precisely aware, which does not suggest that the force before Samaria was anything but at the most a strong escort of the envoys. Benhadad then ordered an attack on the city (v. 12), sending his chariotry and

[a] Y. Yadin, 'Some Aspects of the Strategy of Ahab and David', *Biblica* XXXVI 1955, pp. 332–51.

cavalry (vv. 21, 25) through the steep and tortuous *Wādī Fārʿa*, which leads from the Jordan Valley to Shechem, 7 miles east of Samaria. Here an Israelite striking force took them at a disadvantage. Yadin suggests that the specific mention of an attack at noon implies the deliberate timing of the attack according to the position of the Syrians in the wadi. The emphasis on the God of Israel as 'a God of the hills' (v. 23) indicates the importance of this difficult terrain in the *Wādī Fārʿa*, which Allenby's air force exploited in the harassing of the retreat of the Turkish Seventh Army in 1918. In his campaign against Ammon, especially after the nearly disastrous failure of the initial attack (II Sam. 10.7ff.), David took the precaution of concentrating the militia of Israel with the ark at Succoth at the mouth of the Jabbok to intercept Aramaean relief to Ammon, while Joab and the professional army ventured a direct attack on the capital of Ammon. *śīm* ('set') is used intransitively as in I Sam. 15.2 for 'to attack', cf. Ezek. 23.24, where it possibly means 'to besiege'. We may express the imperative as 'Set on!'

20.13–22. This passage has been suspected as an interpolation from a prophetic source, but, in describing the strategy by which the Israelites routed the Aramaeans, it is integral to the chapter and must be preserved.

13. The prophet, unnamed in MT, is identified by Josephus with Micaiah ben Imlah, but on insufficient grounds. In 'Have you seen?' introductory *h* must be pointed as the interrogative *hª*.

14. *naʿªrē śārē hammᵉdīnōt* (lit. 'the young men of the commanders of the provinces') suggests the usage of *nᵉʿārīm* as a mobile force of professional soldiers, who were employed in skirmishing in the encounter of Joab and Abner at Gibeon (II Sam. 2.14). De Vaux[a] notes the use of *naʿaruna* as a military term in Egypt, possibly referring to mercenaries recruited in Canaan. As young unmarried men they may have been employed as shock troops or commandos. Here they are obviously a military group, lesser feudal retainers of district commanders, under whom Omri had probably organized the realm for military purposes. Montgomery (ICC, p. 323) cites an analogous term *ġulām*, plural *ġulmān*, from Arabic sources for the history of the Crusades, where the word means 'squires' or young knights. In the present passage the young soldiers were probably less ostentatiously equipped than their seniors and so escaped detection as

[a] *Ancient Israel*, p. 221.

soldiers (v. 18), but were nevertheless a picked body of striking troops. In view of the military character of the 'squires', the district commanders (*śārē hamm^e^dīnōt*) can hardly be fiscal officers, heirs of the office of Solomon's officials in ch. 4, as Eissfeldt (*HSAT*, p. 537) suggests, unless they were a kind of armed police, who gathered in fiscal dues and escorted the fiscal officers of the provinces, as which they may have been calculated not to arouse the suspicions of the Syrians. *'āsar*, usually taken as 'to begin', means literally 'to bind', hence according to etymology and context, 'end', or 'close with', hence our rendering 'clinch'.

20.15. *pāqad* means 'to review, take stock of', i.e. to notice what is present and what is lacking, hence the Niphal of the verb means 'to be lost', cf. Arabic *faqada*. The limited number 232 indicates that the numbers were so small as to leave the enemy in doubt as to whether they intended serious warfare (vv. 17ff.). 'Men of substance' (*b^e^nē ḥayil*), see p. 420 n.[a], signifies men whose property and standing obliged them to serve in the field or to furnish men and equipment (see on 1.8). *wayyēṣ^e^'ū* may mean rather 'they emerged to view' from ambush in the *Wādī Fār'a*, and not 'they made a sortie', having left Samaria early in the morning to take up their positions at a point in the wadi most awkward for the Syrians.

20. *pršm* might mean 'horses' or 'horsemen'. In any case mounted cavalry is denoted, such as was now coming into vogue in Near Eastern warfare. Among the Western allies at Qarqar, Damascus contributed by far the largest contingent of mounted cavalry, numbering 1,200.

22. 'The turn of the year' (*t^e^šūbat haššānā*) can mean the recurrence of any part of the year. The chief crisis in the natural year in Palestine was the autumnal new year in the month Tishri, on the eve of the winter rains, the occasion of the natural and social rehabilitation (*šūb š^e^būt*) of the community (Ps. 126.4). II Sam. 11.1 is usually cited as referring to the turn of the year as the time for military expeditions. Since the late spring and summer was the regular season for military expeditions, when ripe corn was available in field and threshing-floor (Judg. 6.11; I Sam. 23.1), this has been taken to be 'the turn of the year'. In II Sam. 11.1, however, the reference is not general, but particular (note the definite article with 'kings'); hence we maintain that in the present passage the phrase refers simply to the coming round again of any time of the year, though here probably late spring is indicated.

(ii) THE SECOND ATTACK ON SAMARIA: 20.23–34

20 [23]And the servants of the king of Aram said to him, Their god[a]
is a god of the mountains,[b] therefore they have proved stronger than
we, but let us fight against them in the plain, and we shall certainly
prove stronger than they. [24]And do this; remove the kings each from
his place, and put officers in their place, [25]and number an army for
yourself like the army which deserted you,[c] horse for horse, and chariot
for chariot, that we may fight with them[d] in the plain, and we shall
certainly prove stronger than they. And he listened to what they said
and did so. [26]And it happened when the year came round that
Benhadad mustered the Aramaeans and came up to Aphek to fight
against Israel. [27]And the Israelites were mustered and provisioned[e] and
went to meet them, and the Israelites encamped over against them like
two flocks of goats, and the Aramaeans filled the land. [28]And a man of
God came up[f] to the king of Israel and said, Thus says Yahweh,
Because the Aramaeans have said, Yahweh is a mountain-god and not
a god of the valleys, I have given all this great multitude into your hand,
and you shall know[g] that I am Yahweh. [29]And they encamped over
against each other seven days and it happened on the seventh day that
it came to warfare, and the Israelites struck down of the Aramaeans
one hundred thousand[h] footmen in one day. [30]And the rest fled to
Aphek to the city, and the wall fell upon twenty-seven thousand[i] men
of the survivors, and Benhadad fled and came into the city into one
room after another. [31]And his servants said to him, See, we have heard
that the kings of the house of Israel are loyal to a covenant; let us then
put sackcloth on our loins and ropes on our heads[j] and surrender to
the king of Israel if by chance he may spare your life. [32]So they girt
themselves with sackcloth on their loins and ropes on their heads, and
came to the king of Israel and said, Your servant Benhadad says, May
my life be spared. And the king said, Is he yet alive? Then he is my
brother. [33]Now the men took this as a good omen[k] and they were

[a]G reads a much fuller text: 'A mountain-god is the God of Israel and not a god of the valley.'

[b]See previous note.

[c]Reading *mē'itt^{e}kā* for *mē'ōt^{e}kā*.

[d]Reading *'ittam* for *'ōtām* after the intransitive verb *nilḥam* ('to fight').

[e]G omits this word (*w^{e}kolk^{e}lū*), which may be a dittograph of the following *wayyēl^{e}kū*.

[f]Omitting MT *wayyō'mer* ('and he said') with S, certainly correct in view of the following *wayyō'mer*.

[g]Reading with G singular for MT plural.

[h]G^{L} reads 120,000.

[i]S reads 25,000.

[j]There is good MS authority for plural, read also by G. S, and V, as in v. 32.

[k]The imperfect of MT would signify that the envoys were looking for an omen. Perhaps the perfect should be read, indicating that they took the answer as an omen.

quick to take it as a definite indication[a] from him, and they said, Benhadad is your brother. And he said, Go in and bring him. So Benhadad came out to him, and (Ahab) had him come up into the chariot. [34]And he said to him, The cities which my father took from your father will I give back, and you may make a quarter for yourself in Damascus as my father made in Samaria. And I shall release[b] you from the vassal-treaty. So he made a covenant for him and let him go.

20.24. On the 'kings' in Benhadad's army see on v. 1. *paḥōt* is an Assyrian loanword, *bel piḫati* ('lord of a province'). It is found in 10.15 denoting fiscal officers, so Skinner concludes that civil, not military organization is implied here. This may be so, though a year was too short a time for the efficient working of the new system. The purpose of the new organization was military, and what is implied is command by regular officers probably on a territorial rather than on an ethnic basis. The latter system permitted divided policies and loose authority, where each tribal chief was traditionally free and might himself command, but was not bound to be obeyed by his free tribesmen. The new levy was not an undisciplined rabble of tribal volunteers, but troops picked and drilled by regional officers.

This almost certainly reflects the political consolidation of a Greater Syria under Benhadad III, a relic of which was possibly the stele of 'Bar-Hadad' near Aleppo.[c] In any case, the different constitution of the army on the two occasions indicates that the first expedition, with the contingents of vassals under their 'kings', was rather meant to impress, whereas the second was intended as a military expedition. The character of the first expedition would support the view that Benhadad did not invest Samaria, but lay at Succoth in the Jordan valley.

25. In 'the force which deserted you' (lit. 'fell away from you') there is reference to this liberty of action of the tribal units, who were besides easily distracted by the prospect of plunder.

26. The location of Aphek, the objective of the Aramaean army, is uncertain. Etymologically the word signifies a source of water,

[a]After certain MSS, Q, and the versions we should attach *h* as the pronominal suffix to the verb instead of taking it as the interrogative particle before *mimmennū* as in MT.

[b]It is proposed to emend *'ašallᵉḥekkā* to *tᵉšallᵉḥēnī* ('you shall send me'), though this has no support in the versions. Otherwise a change of subject is assumed, Ahab being understood as in EVV. In the sequel Ahab is certainly the subject of the verb *wayyikrōt* ('and he made (a covenant)'), though he is unnamed. But in support of our translation see p. 431.

[c]Dunand, *BMB* III, 1941, pp. 65–76, see above on 15.18.

and is the name of several localities, of which three enter seriously into the reckoning here: (1) The base of Philistine operations against Israel in the hills of Ephraim (I Sam. 4.1) and the Plain of Jezreel (I Sam. 29.1). This place, located between Ono, Soco, and Sharon in the lists of the Palestinian conquests of Thothmes III, corresponds to *Rās al-ʿAin*, the source of the River Jarkon (Arabic *Nahr al-ʿAwjā*), later known as Antipatris. (2) A locality in Asher (Josh. 19.30; Judg. 1.31), plausibly identified by Alt[a] with *Tell Kurdāneh* in the Plain of Acco at the source of the River *Naʿmīn*. (3) A locality on the plateau east of the south end of the Lake of Tiberias at the spring *ʿAin Fīq* on the Roman road from Damascus to Bethshean.[b] The first is out of the question in the present passage, since it implies that the Aramaeans commanded the plains of Jezreel and Sharon, which is most unlikely after the defeat of the previous year, nor is there any hint in Kings that the Plain of Jezreel was dominated by the Aramaeans. This difficulty is not felt by Gressmann, who locates Aphek somewhat vaguely in the Plain of Jezreel,[c] cf. Eissfeldt, who, with the Philistine campaign of I Sam. 29.1 in mind, locates it near Megiddo (*HSAT*, p. 537). The second location is unlikely, though it is just possible that the Aramaeans invaded from the towns which they held north of Safed (v. 34) by way of the upland rift from Safed by Ramah and *Majd al-Kurūm* to the Plain of Acco. Much more probable is the location at *al-Fīq*, east of the Lake of Tiberias on the direct way from Damascus to Israel and the traditional line of attack (cf. 22.3) through country open to Aramaean tribesmen who might be enlisted against Israel, and a frontier post. This is doubtless also the Aphek of II K. 13.17,[d] which we consider to be the source adapted in the present passage as a prophetic tradition. The plateau about *al-Fīq* might be described as 'plain' (*mīšōr*).

20.27. On the unusual Hothpaal with the passive rather than reflexive sense see *GK* § 54 b, h, l. *ḥªśīpē* ('flocks') is a *hapax legomenon*, possibly cognate with Arabic *ḥasafa* ('to drive sheep'), cited by Šanda.

29. Battles were often decided by the panic of one army, which was interpreted as divine intervention. Both armies here may have waited for omens of such divine interventions before they attacked. The pause before the engagement of the armies is reminiscent of the

[a] *PJB* XXIV, 1928, p. 59; XXV, 1929, p. 41n.
[b] Eusebius, *Onomasticon*, p. 22.
[c] *Op. cit.*, p. 278.
[d] Abel, *GP* II, p. 246.

skirmishing and single combats of the wars of early Islam, and may go back to the convention of tribal warfare, which was waged with economy of life in apprehension of the complication of the *lex talionis*. Seven is the conventional indefinite number in Semitic folklore and popular narrative, indicating, with 100,000 casualties, the popular nature of the tradition. This great number, in so far as it may be relevant to fact, probably refers to the total Aramaean force discomfited rather than to actual casualties. Even so there is probably liberal exaggeration, since not even in the Battle of Qarqar had Damascus more than 20,000 infantry. The collapse of the wall may have been because of undermining by the Israelites.

20.30. The refuge of Benhadad is described as *ḥeder beḥeder* (lit. 'a room in a room'). The phrase is found in a similar context in 22.25 and in II K. 9.2, where it refers to the anointing of Jehu in an inner chamber, cf. in the Ras Shamra texts, where privacy is denoted, 'in seven rooms, yea eight chambers' (*UT* ʿnt, V, 19–20, 35). This might be the sense here, but it might also mean that Benhadad moved from one chamber to another, for which Šanda (I, p. 482) cites the analogy *šānā bešānā, yōm beyōm* ('year by year', 'day by day'). In Ugaritic *b* may mean 'from' as well as 'in' or 'on', denoting the point of contact either in contact or separation. Communications between one house and another in the congested villages of Palestine greatly complicated the task of the police during the British Mandate.

31. On the covenantal implications of *ḥesed* ('loyalty') see on 2.7. The conception of merciful or humane dealing in human relations implied in the phrase *ʿāśā ḥesed ʿim* is secondary to the primary meaning of loyalty to a covenant. Benhadad may have been invoking a covenant between himself and the king of Israel, which would of course be a vassal-treaty in favour of Damascus as suzerain.

32. Coarse black cloth about the loins was the symbol of mourning or fast and penitence. In both cases it indicated a suspension of normal custom at a season of crisis when untoward supernatural influences were especially active. The rope on the head is explained by Šanda (I, 483) as possibly indicating the readiness of the defeated king to be the porter of the victor. He also cites the Assyrian custom of boring the cheeks or nose of the defeated enemy and passing a rope through, by which the victim was led in procession. We should rather explain the gesture in the light of the Bedouin custom whereby, in the negotiations for commutation in the convention of blood-revenge, the representative (*wakīl*) of the homicide appears before the avenger of blood in the attitude of a suppliant over whom he has the power of life and death, bareheaded, with the rope of his Bedouin headdress around his neck.[a]

20.33. On the reading *niḥašū* ('took it as an omen') see p. 426 n.[k] above.

ḥālaṭ is a *hapax legomenon*. According to Arabic etymology the meaning ought to be 'to seek a decision', or 'to seek to fix an omen', i.e. to take as a definite indication. See further p. 427 n.[a] on the reading *wayyaḥleṭūhā*. The definite article with 'chariot' is significant. Šanda (p. 484) plausibly assumes that Benhadad tendered his submission by symbolically putting his shoulder to the wheel of the chariot of the king of Israel, which is mentioned in the Aramaic inscription of Bar-Rekub[b] as a symbolic act of submission which survived through Byzantine times until the time of Sultan Abdul Hamīd at Istambul. By contrast Benhadad was honourably treated as an equal beyond his expectation. The account, with its elliptic style, indicates a first-hand source.

34. There is no mention of the Aramaeans taking territory from Omri, though specific towns in Upper Galilee were taken from Israel in the time of Baasha (15.20), who might be said to be Ahab's 'father' in the sense of his predecessor according to Semitic idiom. The districts may have been lost in the civil wars between Omri and Tibni for the first six years of Omri's reign. The association of the restoration of the cities lost by the father of the king of Israel with the victory of Aphek, however, most probably indicates Joash's restoration of those cities lost by his father Jehoahaz, cf. the annalistic note in II K. 13.25. The Aramaeans were keen traders between East and West, Damascus itself being an important caravan city. Their interest in the towns of Upper Galilee related to their desire to secure a route to the coast at Acco and to the trunk highway through the hills of Lower Galilee by the famous *via maris* from the northern end of the Lake of Galilee through the Plain of the *Baṭṭūf* and the *Wādī al-Melek* to Acco. The 'streets' were bazaars and residential quarters for particular nationalities, which were a feature of the life of Eastern cities, e.g. Jerusalem, with its Jewish and Armenian quarters, until quite recently. It was this commercial aggression, combined with other motives, that had led Omri to effect his alliance with Tyre.

The definite article with 'covenant' signifies the existing vassal-

[a]A. Jaussen, *Coutumes des Arabes au pays de Moab*, 1908, pp. 222–4.
[b]G. A. Cooke, *NSI* 63, 8–9.

treaty from which Benhadad now released the king of Israel. The clue to this solution is the recognition of the meaning of *b^e^* as 'from', as in Ugaritic. This may be a vestige of the dialect of Northern Israel. It is possibly this to which Benhadad refers in v. 31 in describing the kings of Israel as 'loyal to a covenant'. Another covenant is now made expressing the altered relations between the two parties, as is indicated by the preposition *l^e^*. A good example of a covenant whereby the stronger imposed restrictions on the weaker party is the vassal-treaty of Ashurnirari V (754–745), where the Aramaean king Matti'ilu of Arpad is bound by the strongest oaths to Assyrian allegiance.[a]

(iii) A PROPHETIC INCIDENT: 20.35–43

The genuineness of this passage is disputed. It is held that the different attitude to 'Ahab' from that in the rest of the chapter suggests a different source. That may well be so, though there is nothing improbable about the incident in its historical context. Such clemency to Benhadad, politic as it may have been, must have had its critics, particularly among narrowly nationalistic elements like the prophets.

It is probable, however, that the passage reveals both an original prophetic tradition and the elaboration of the Deuteronomist. The incident of the disobedient prophet and the lion, which strongly suggests the influence of the similar prophetic legend from the guild of Bethel in ch. 13, at least seems to come from prophetic circles. Again, we may note the different attitude to the prisoner of war. In v. 39 he is considered the perquisite of his captor, to whom compensation is due if he escapes. This reflects the actual situation, when the holy war was obsolete, and is certainly part of the original source. In v. 42, however, the prisoner is regarded as the exclusive property of Yahweh (*'īš ḥermī*) according to the conception of the holy war, which was revived in the Deuteronomic tradition as an aspect of the conception of Israel as a militant tribal confederacy.[b]

In the Deuteronomistic compilation, the passage, with the prophetic declaration on the forfeiture of 'Ahab's' life, leads up to the more pointed oracle of Elijah after the Naboth incident in ch. 21 (v. 19), with its fulfilment in ch. 22.

[a]E. F. Weidner, *AfO* VIII, 1932, pp. 17–34.
[b]G. von Rad, *Studies in Deuteronomy*, pp. 49ff.

20 [35]And a certain man of the sons of the prophets said to his friend in the word of God, Strike me. But the man refused to strike him. [36]And he said to him, Because you have not listened to the voice of Yahweh, see, you shall go from me and a lion shall strike you down. So he went from him, and a lion met him and struck him down. [37]And he found another man and said, Strike me, and the man struck him, striking him and wounding him. [38]Then the prophet went and waited for the king by the road,[a] and he concealed himself by a bandage over his eyes. [39]And as the king was passing he cried out to the king and said, Your servant went forth into the thick of the battle and there came a man, who turned aside and brought a man to me and said, Keep this man. If he is missing your life shall be forfeit for his life or you shall pay out a talent of silver. [40]And your servant was busy[b] here and there, and he vanished. Then the king of Israel said to him, Even so is your verdict. You have yourself decided. [41]And he quickly took the bandage from over his eyes, and the king of Israel recognized him as being one of the prophets. [42]And he said to him, Thus says Yahweh, Because you have let go from my hand[c] a man devoted to destruction for me, so shall your life be forfeit for his life, and your people for his people. [43]So the king of Israel went home[d] sullen and aggrieved and came to Samaria.

20.35. This is the first explicit mention of prophetic guilds ('sons of the prophets') in Kings, though ch. 13 implies that prophets tended to live in the vicinity of shrines and that there was a certain corporate sympathy among members of the profession. From this point onwards the guilds play a prominent part in the history and probably also in the transmission of traditions, especially of Elisha.

36. The punishment by means of the lion for disobedience to the word of God suggests the prophetic story in ch. 13. The definite article with *'aryē* is generic.

38. *'ᵃpēr* ('bandage') is a *hapax legomenon*, the sense in the context being in no doubt.

39. A talent of silver (see on 9.14) consisted of 2,500 shekels according to the Canaanite system, and possibly 3,000. This is one hundred times the price of a slave in the Book of the Covenant (Ex. 21.32). It was an exorbitant price for a poor man to pay, and the debt would have involved him in slavery. The prisoner being the property of the

[a]Reading *ʿal* for MT *'el*.

[b]G[BA] read 'was looking around', which has suggested *šōʿe* for MT *ʿōśē*, which would give excellent sense. The intransitive of *ʿāśā*, however, is attested in the sense of 'to be busy', and so MT may be defended.

[c]The Versions vary in reading *miyyādᵉkā* and *miyyādī*, both of which give good sense.

[d]Reading *'el* for MT *ʿal*.

captor, his loss by the man to whom he had been entrusted would have involved a technical breach of pledge, for which restitution was demanded according to what was probably an adaptation of Canaanite law in the Book of the Covenant (Ex. 22.7f., 10–13).[a] This view of the prisoner as the property of his captor implies a totally different conception of war from the time of the judges and Saul's Amalekite raid, when war was a holy office and the captive was the property of Yahweh. Verse 42 re-echoes the older conception in the prophet's extreme and fanatical statement of the case.

20.40. *ḥāraṣ* means 'to make sharp', hence it expresses decision, as in the cognate Assyrian root.

41. The king's recognition of the man as a prophet after the removal of the bandage over his eyes is held to indicate that the prophets made marks on themselves, perhaps tattoo marks. Zechariah 13.6 refers to wounds in front of a prophet, i.e. probably on his chest (lit. 'between his hands', cf. Arabic *bayna yaday*, 'in front'), and Isa. 44.5 refers to a devotee of Yahweh having a proprietary mark on his hand. Some such custom is probably denoted here, though possibly it was the features of the man that the king recognized.

42. War in the estimation of the prophet—or of the Deuteronomistic editor—was a holy service of Yahweh, to which warrior and arms were dedicated, and in consequence all spoils, animate and inanimate, were sacrosanct. Hence the prisoner could not be treated as common property, but, if not appropriated to the sanctuary, must be destroyed (Deut. 7.2; 20.16). The affinity of this prophetic story to Samuel's condemnation of Saul's fatal leniency to Agag (I Sam. 15) suggests that the story may be introduced under the influence of the Deuteronomist in anticipation of the end of 'Ahab' in ch. 22, which immediately follows ch. 20 in G.

43. The phrase *sar wᵉzāʿēp* ('sullen and aggrieved') is repeated in 21.4. *sārar* means 'to be stubborn, resentful'.

(*g*) THE ELIJAH CYCLE (continued from ch. 19): 21.1-29

(i) THE INCIDENT OF NABOTH'S VINEYARD: A SOCIAL CRISIS IN AHAB'S REIGN: 21.1–24

In this chapter we revert to an incident in which Elijah is a protagonist, at least in its final phase, and it is natural to regard it as

[a]For the probable date of this adaptation in the period of the Judges, see A. Alt, 'Die Ursprünge des israelitischen Rechts', *KS* I, pp. 278–333; ET, 'The Origins of Israelite Law', *Essays on Old Testament History and Religion*, 1966, pp. 79–132.

part of the Elijah narrative of chs. 17–19. In fact, G places it after ch. 19. In this case the objective historical matter from the account of the Syrian wars is conveniently grouped together, and the position of ch. 21 in MT is doubtless suggested by the oracle anticipating the death of Ahab, which is narrated in ch. 22. Chapter 21, however, differs from chs. 17–19 in that it presents the matter much more objectively than in the rest of the Elijah narrative.

Elijah is introduced only at the end as the organ of Yahweh's condemnation of Ahab and Jezebel in a prophetic oracle. Šanda[a] found that in style and in its presentation of Elijah as a prophet of doom in personal conflict with the king, ch. 21 has more affinity with II K. 1.2ff. than with chs. 17–19, a view with which we should not agree, because of the centrality of Elijah in the latter passage and the absence in ch. 21 of the motif of the persecution of the prophet, which predominates in II K. 1.9–16. Fohrer[b] notes the absence of the theme of the persecution of Elijah and the Yahwists, which recurs in chs. 17f. and predominates in ch. 19 and II K. 1.9–16. Ahab, moreover, is represented in a not unfavourable light with certain scruples, and is not the adversary of Yahwism as in chs. 17f. Thus J. M. Miller[c] would remove ch. 21 from the Elijah cycle. The Naboth incident, he argues, like the account of the death of Ahab in I K. 22, is associated with Ahab, hence also with Elijah, only secondarily by the redactor, subsequent to the Deuteronomistic compilation, and he suggests that in the original form of the tradition it concerned not Ahab but Jehoram. This thesis depends on the priority which Miller gives to the fulfilment of the prophecy in the historical narrative of Jehu's *coup d'état* in II K. 9. The religious policy with its social consequences attributed to Ahab may have been inherited by his son Jehoram, but it is more likely that the conflict with Israelite tradition should have been sharper in the first phase of the policy of the dynasty under the influence of the Phoenician affiance than in the time of Jehoram, who apparently felt bound to respect native Israelite tradition in removing his father's Baal symbol, as is acknowledged in II K. 3.2, though the cult of Baal was still established in the capital, Samaria. II K. 9.25, however, cites an oracle of Elijah against Ahab referring to the requital of the blood of Naboth *and his sons* in his ancestral plot at Jezreel. In two details this differs from the oracle in 21.19, namely the

[a]*Op. cit.*, I, p. 469.
[b]*Op. cit.*, pp. 39f.
[c]*Op. cit.*, pp. 313–7.

mention of Naboth's sons and the reference to the dogs licking Ahab's blood. This strongly suggests the originality of the oracle in 21.19, since, had the account of the Naboth incident in ch. 21 been secondary to II K. 9, this discrepancy would have been avoided. As it is, the discrepancy between the oracle in 21.19 and its fulfilment in II K. 9.25 and I K. 22.38 indicates an original tradition of the *ipsissima dicta* of Elijah at 21.19.

Fohrer[a] assumes that the centrality of Jezebel does not quite correspond to historical fact, but rather reflects the intense hatred of prophetic circles which transmitted the tradition. For her to contrive the judicial murder of Naboth within the letter of Hebrew law, she would have been, Fohrer declares, 'a world's wonder of learning and resource'. She may nevertheless have been advised by a subservient Israelite, though undoubtedly the decree for the fast would have been issued by Ahab himself. To this extent, then, we can agree with Fohrer that the predominant role of Jezebel reflects the prophetic version of the tradition. This is not to say, however, that Jezebel was not the motive force behind the injustice.

We should retain the passage as the prophetic version of a significant tradition of Elijah and Ahab, which retains, though not literally in every detail, a true reflection of the consequences of the policy of the house of Omri to effect a synthesis of Israelite and Canaanite tradition, of which the marriage of Ahab and Jezebel was symptomatic. It seems more natural that this episode should have preceded Elijah's commission of Elisha (19.16–21), which probably anticipates Elijah's demise.

The content of Elijah's denunciation and oracle of doom at the command of God is probably limited to v. 19. The rest of the passage (vv. 20–29) consists of a number of secondary statements from various sources. First there is the Deuteronomistic condemnation of Ahab in vv. 25f. Then one notices the repetition of the phraseology of the doom of the houses of Jeroboam and Baasha (vv. 21b, 24, cf. 14.7–11; 16.1–4), to which v. 22 should be added. The fact that Ahab, unlike Jeroboam and Baasha, was not the founder of a dynasty suggests that this is a secondary adaptation of the prophetic oracle of doom on the dynasty, and the indictment (v. 20a) which introduces the oracle of doom, which suggests the greeting of Ahab and the riposte of Elijah in their first encounter (18.17f.), makes the same im-

[a]*Op. cit.*, p. 56.

pression of Deuteronomistic expansion. The oracle on Jezebel in v. 23, which breaks the sequence of vv. 22–24, is possibly a fragment of a different tradition concerning Elijah, as is suggested by the reference to the oracle in II K. 9.36, and is probably a very late redactional insertion. The final passage on Ahab's submission and personal reprieve from the doom pronounced (vv. 27–29) should be seen as another late insertion. In our opinion, vv. 20–22, 24, vv. 27–29 and v. 23 are all late attempts to explain the fact that the proclamation that the dogs would lick the blood of Ahab in the very place where they licked the blood of Naboth was not literally fulfilled. One explanation was that this was in consequence of Ahab's contrition (vv. 27–29); another (vv. 21f., 24) emphasized the extinction of Ahab's house in the death of Jehoram (II K. 9.24–26) and the rest of Ahab's family (II K. 10.1–11). Actually the death of Jehoram at Jezreel, the scene of Naboth's judicial murder, generally fulfilled the oracle in v. 19b. Not yet satisfied, another redactor noted that in what concerned the dogs in the oracle there was an instance of prophecy and fulfilment in the case of Jezebel's death at Jezreel, the scene of Naboth's death (v. 23, cf. II K. 9.36). Those are secondary in the context, though the oracle on Jezebel may be a genuine old tradition. The genuineness of the oracle on Ahab in v. 19b is indicated by the care which the narrator takes to note that dogs licked Ahab's blood off his chariot by the Pool of Samaria (22.38).

21 [1]And it happened after these things[a] that Naboth of Jezreel had a certain vineyard[b] [c]which was in Jezreel[c] adjoining the palace of Ahab the king of Samaria. [2]And Ahab spoke to Naboth saying, Give me your vineyard that I may have it as a vegetable-garden, for it adjoins my house, and let me give you in its place a better vineyard, or[d] if you think fit, I will give you silver as the price of it. [3]But Naboth said to Ahab, God forbid that I should give you the heritage of my

[a]This phrase is omitted in G[h] in agreement with G's reading of ch. 21 after ch. 19.

[b]So G[BA], which better introduces the episode when the introductory phrase is omitted. See previous note.

[c]G omits this phrase, apparently as tautological after 'Naboth of Jezreel'. The phrase, however, qualifies not Naboth, but the vineyard. From the passage on the fulfilment of Elijah's prophecy that the dogs would lick the blood of Ahab where they had licked the blood of Naboth (v. 19) in the description of how the dogs licked the blood of Ahab off his chariot in Samaria, it was possible that the vineyard might be thought to be in Samaria, hence the phrase 'which was in Jezreel' is apparently an effort on the part of the redactor to clarify the position, as Eissfeldt maintains (*HSAT*, p. 538).

[d]Reading *'ō 'im* ('or if . . .') with S, of which MT *'im* is a haplograph.

fathers. [4a]So Ahab went to his house sullen and aggrieved on account of the word which Naboth of Jezreel had spoken to him saying, I will not give you the heritage of my fathers.[a] And he lay down on his couch and covered[b] his face, and did not eat food. [5]Then his wife Jezebel came to him and she said to him, Why so, that your temper is sullen and you eat no food? [6]And he spoke to her, Because I spoke to Naboth of Jezreel and said to him, Give me your vineyard for money, or,[c] if you wish, I shall give you another[d] vineyard in its place. And he said, I will not give you my vineyard. [7]And Jezebel his wife said to him, Now [e]is it you who exercises royal authority[e] over Israel? Rise up, eat food, and set your mind at ease. I shall give you the vineyard of Naboth of Jezreel. [8]So she wrote a letter in the name of Ahab and sealed it with his seal, and she sent the letter to the elders and to the freemen [f]who were in his city,[f] [g]the neighbours of Naboth.[g] [9]And she wrote in the letter saying, Proclaim a fast and give Naboth the seat at the head of the people. [10]And give two men, reprobates, a seat opposite him that they may testify against him saying, You cursed God and the king. And put him out and stone him to death. [11]And the men of his city, the elders and the freemen,[h] did as Jezebel had sent to them, [i]as it was written in the letter she sent to them.[i] [12]They proclaimed a fast and gave Naboth the seat at the head of the people, [13]and two reprobates came and sat opposite him and the reprobates testified against Naboth before the people saying, Naboth cursed God and the king. So they took him out of the city and stoned him with stones and he died. [14]And they sent to Jezebel saying, Naboth has been stoned and is dead. [15]And it came to pass, when Jezebel heard that [j]Naboth was stoned and was dead,[j] that she[k] said to Ahab, Rise up and take possession of the vineyard of Naboth of Jezreel, which he refused to give you for money, for Naboth is not alive, but[l] dead. [16]And it

[a]G^{BL} and L read 'and the spirit of Ahab was troubled', but the pleonastic style of MT suits the style of the context.

[b]Reading *way^{e}kas* with G and L for MT *wayyassēb*. V apparently read or understood the MT to imply 'to the wall'.

[c]G reads 'and' (*w^e*) for MT 'or' (*'ō*).

[d]Inserting *'aḥēr* in MT after G^{BA}, which is better, if not strictly necessary.

[e]G reads 'Is it thus that you exercise rule . . .', but MT 'You' for G 'thus' is emphatic.

[f]G^h and L omit this phrase. Either this or 'the neighbours of N.' seems to be a gloss.

[g]See previous note.

[h]Omitting MT *'^{a}šer hayyos^{e}bim b^e'irō* ('who were those dwelling in his city') with G^L.

[i]This clause, which appears pleonastic, is omitted in G^L. The Hebrew text from which this was translated might, however, be truncated by homoeoteleuton.

[j]This is another case where the versions G^L and S read a much shorter text, viz. 'that he was dead.' Here again the pleonastic style is a feature of the narrative.

[k]G^B omits 'Jezebel'.

[l]Certain MSS. read (*kī*) *'im*. The sense, however, is quite well conveyed by *kī* adversative alone.

happened that when Ahab heard that Naboth was dead, Ahab rose up to go down to the vineyard of Naboth of Jezreel to take possession of it. [17]Then the word of Yahweh came to Elijah the Tishbite saying, [18]Rise up, go down to confront Ahab the king of Israel who lives in Samaria; see he is in the vineyard of Naboth, which he has gone down to claim possession of. [19]And you shall speak to him saying, Thus says Yahweh, Have you done murder and moreover taken possession? And you shall speak to him saying, Thus says Yahweh, In the very place where the dogs[a] have licked the blood of Naboth[b] the dogs will lick your blood, even yours.[c] [20]And Ahab said unto Elijah, Have you caught up with me, O mine enemy? And he said, I have caught up with you. Because you have sold yourself do to evil in the sight of Yahweh,[d] [21]lo I shall bring[e] harm upon you and I shall make a riddance of you, for I shall cut off him belonging to Ahab that pisses against the wall, to the very last in Israel. [22]And I shall make your house as the house of Jeroboam the son of Nebat and as the house of Baasha the son of Ahijah on account of the provocation which you have caused and the sin in which you have involved Israel. [23]And concerning Jezebel also Yahweh spoke saying, The dogs will eat Jezebel all around Jezreel. [24]Him belonging to Ahab who dies in the city will the dogs eat, and him belonging to him[f] who dies in the country will the birds of the heavens eat.

21.1. The name Naboth may be derived from a root cognate with Arabic *nabata* ('to grow'), used of plants or men. It may signify 'offspring', being, perhaps, a hypocoristicon.[g]

This is the first occurrence of *hēkāl* in Kings in the sense of 'palace'. It is derived from the Sumerian *e-gallu* ('the great house'). The designation of Ahab as *melek šōmᵉrōn* ('King of Samaria') has been noted by Šanda as a feature of II K. 1, with which he would associate the present passage. The title is taken to reflect the situation after Tiglath-pileser III had divested Israel of Gilead, Galilee, and the Plain of Sharon in 734, but before that Tiglath-pileser had styled Menahem 'the king of Samaria'. The usage in the present passage probably reflects the situation of the crown possession of Samaria as the basis of the power of the house of Omri. It may reflect the consciousness that the house of Omri was not truly representative of the people of Israel.

[a]G^BL inserts 'and the swine', of which there is no trace in MT or in S or V.

[b]Hebrew grammar requires the insertion of the resumptive adverb *šām* in MT (so G).

[c]G and L add 'and the harlots shall wash in your blood', obviously influenced by 22.38.

[d]G and L add 'to provoke him to anger', which, in the Deuteronomistic tenor of the text, is likely.

[e]Q *mēbī'*. [f]Inserting *lō* with G and S and certain Hebrew MSS.

[g]See Noth, *IP*, p. 221.

Jezreel, Arab *Zer'īn*, at the foot of the north-west spur of the Gilboa ridge, gave its name to the great central plain (Greek, the Valley of Esdraelon), stretching from the sea to the Jordan. Commanding access from the east to the main part of this plain, it was occupied by Ahab, no doubt as a base of operations against Damascus about Ramoth Gilead. It may also have served as a winter resort for the king (18.45), and may have been the ancestral home of the Omrids, with whose collapse the place sank into insignificance. No trace of its former significance remains in the poor Arab village of *Zer'īn* but potsherds indicate its occupation in the Late Bronze Age (*c.* 1500–1200), the Iron Age, and the Roman period.

21.3. The exclamation *ḥālīlā-lī* expresses the conception that the course of action deplored was profane (*ḥālāl*), or wrong, in the eyes of God. The attitude of Naboth regarding his ancestral land reflects the solidarity of the family among the Palestinian peasants. Moreover the status of Naboth as a freeman, and probably a *gibbōr ḥayil* ('man of substance'), was bound up with his possession of his ancestral land. To have accepted Ahab's proposal, fair as it seemed, would have prejudiced his own status and that of his family, relegating them to the status of royal dependants. In the administrative texts from the palace of Ras Shamra we are familiar with grants of lands to certain classes and individuals at the king's discretion, usually with feudal or fiscal burdens.[a]

4. On *sar weza'ēp* ('sullen and aggrieved') see on 20.43. *miṭṭātō* need not mean 'bed', but rather 'couch', such as was used for feasting. The inlaid inscription of such a couch was found at Arslan Tash, part of the booty of Damascus once belonging to Hazael, which the Assyrians carried off.[b] On the reading 'and he covered his face' see p. 437 n.[b].

5. We take *leḥem*, which generally means 'bread' in Hebrew, in the general sense of 'food', cf. the verb *lḥm* ('to eat') in Ugaritic.

7. The answer of Jezebel is patient of a variety of interpretations. It may be interrogative, 'Is it you . . .?', or asseverative, 'You it is who . . .', or, in the latter sense it may be sarcastic, cf. V, '*grandis auctoritatis es et bene regis regnum Israel*'. The phrase *weyīṭab libbekā* usually means 'be content', *lēb* having the connotation of mind.

8. Šanda (I, p. 462) takes the plural *sepārīm* ('writings') in the singular sense, for which Hezekiah's letter in Isa. 37.14 may be cited as an

[a] G. Boyer, *Mission de Ras Shamra* VI; *Le Palais Royal d'Ugarit* III. *Textes accadiens et hourrites des archives est, ouest, et centrales.*

[b] A. G. Barrois, *Manuel d'Archéologie Biblique* I, 1939, pp. 501–7, figs. 196f.

analogy. Letters were usually written by a scribe or amanuensis in the name of a correspondent, who is usually depicted as speaking in the third person, and sealed in clay or wax with the seal of the sender. Many such seals have been found in Palestinian excavations, including the seal of 'Yotham' or 'Yatham', possibly Jotham, the son of Azariah either before or after he became king of Judah, at *Tell al-Ḫaleifeh*,[a] and a clay sealing 'Belonging to Gedaliah, the royal chamberlain' (*lgdlyhw 'šr ʿl hbyt*) found in the last phase of the Judaean city of *Tell ed-Duweir* (Lachish).[b] Other seals which signify ultimately royal authority are those of 'Shemaʿ the servant of Jeroboam', found at Megiddo,[c] and that of 'Eliaqim the servant of Yokin'.[d] 'Yokin' was quite possibly Jehoiachin the second last king of Judah.

The fiction of communal justice is noteworthy. Jezebel's reliance on the local elders and freeborn men of Jezreel suggests that Ahab was personally influential. This indicates perhaps that the persons in question had been long accustomed to follow the lead of the family of Ahab. This situation is readily intelligible if Ahab's family was from Jezreel, the modern Arab analogy suggesting that the influence of a powerful local family to whom all in a locality are in some degree attached is permanently dominant. This is the first specific mention of the freeborn (*ḥōrīm*) as a class. In Jer. 27.20; 39.6 the freemen, or nobles, of Judah (*ḥōrē yᵉhūdā*) are mentioned as among the chief victims of the Babylonian conquerors.

21.9. *qārā'* is used of a public proclamation of a fast, solemn assembly (Lev. 23.24; Joel 1.14) or general military levy. The occasion of the fast was no doubt some untoward circumstances locally, which, experienced or apprehended (cf. I Sam. 7.6), were alleged to be the result of some default of the community, which in this case was fixed by arrangement on Naboth. The occasion of the fast is plausibly suggested by van den Born (*op. cit.*, p. 123) to be the great drought of 17.1. It is suggested (Kittel, Skinner) that the place of Naboth at the head of the people is not a place of honour, as at a feast, but the place of the accused, and the two reprobates are set before him not to accuse but to support the accusation by false evidence (*wīʿīdūhū*). We agree with Šanda, however, in assuming that Naboth was given a place of honour. His title 'the Jezreelite' suggests to us that he was a representative figure, the head of an influential local family,

[a]Glueck, *BASOR* 79, 1940, pp. 13–15.
[b]S. H. Hooke, *PEFQS* 1935, pp. 197ff.
[c]D. Diringer in *Documents from Old Testament Times*, pp. 220f. [d]*Ibid.*, p. 224.

perhaps the equivalent of the *muḫtār* of the place, and in virtue of this status he was given the place 'at the head of the people'. As such an influential person he would often speak on public questions, and if we assume that he represented the family at Jezreel opposed to the family of Ahab, also from Jezreel, it is natural that he would speak somewhat freely of the rival family, through any one of whom his actions and words would, according to the ancient Semitic conception of the solidarity of the family, touch the king. The impairing of the power of 'a ruler of the people' by a curse is a capital offence according to Ex. 22.28 [27], where God is conjoined, as here, with the 'ruler'. In the mood that a community was in during a fast they were prepared to accept the fact that some individual had through his sin brought the community under the divine wrath. The punctilio with which the destruction of Naboth was contrived is grimly sadistic. He is condemned by the elders with a show of conservative Israelite democracy on the evidence of the two witnesses which custom required (cf. Deut. 17.6; 19.15; cf. Matt. 26.60), and he is stoned by the community (cf. Lev. 24.16). The property of rebels and public criminals in the ancient East reverted to the crown.

21.10. This is probably part of Jezebel's plan rather than her overt instructions to the people of Jezreel, and may be secondary in the narration. 'Reprobates' is our paraphrase of *bᵉnē bᵉlīyaʿal* (lit. 'sons of worthlessness'), *yaʿal* being a verbal noun from the verb *yāʿal* usually found in the Hiphil, *hōʿīl* ('it was of avail').

'You cursed (*bēraktā*, lit. "you blessed") Yahweh' employs euphemism, avoiding the use of 'curse' along with Yahweh, cf. Job 1.

The conjunction of Yahweh and the king is interesting. In such psalms as Pss. 2 and 110 the same ideology and language is applied to the king as is applied to God as king in his triumph over the powers of Chaos. The king is God's visible guarantee of his cosmic sovereignty, and this relationship is expressed by the father-son relationship of God and king. Jeroboam's insistence on the autumnal festival at Bethel, which was specifically the cult of God as king, indicates that he promoted the same political ideology in Israel as in Judah.

The stoning of Naboth was outside the city (according to II K. 9.25 in Naboth's own field) to avoid ritual pollution (Lev. 24.14; Num. 15.36). As in the case of Achan (Josh. 7.22ff.), Naboth's family suffers with him (II K. 9.26). Here again punctilious observance of Semitic custom rids Ahab of possible claimants to the confiscated property.

21.17. Elijah, as usual, is introduced with dramatic suddenness. He apparently confronts Ahab while the latter is formally taking possession of Naboth's vineyard. Elijah's prophecy that the blood of Naboth would be expiated on the very spot where he died was fulfilled, though not absolutely literally, in Jehu's slaughter of Ahab's son Joram in the field of Naboth at Jezreel (II K. 9.26). The blood of Joram was according to ancient Semitic belief the blood of his father Ahab. Probably vv. 1–16 is a plain narrative of the incident of Naboth's vineyard and vv. 17–19 a version from a different source of Elijah's oracle in its historical context, vv. 20–26 being Deuteronomistic elaboration of this oracle to extend it to the dynasty of Omri.

18. The verb 'go down', as always in the Old Testament, is very specific. Jezreel is only 375 feet above sea level, just before the great central plain of Palestine dips to below sea level. So one 'went down' to Jezreel practically from any district in West and Central Palestine. Samaria, from which Ahab 'went down', is almost 1340 feet above sea level. The mention of 'the king of Israel who is in Samaria' is generally taken to indicate that the king was actually in Samaria taking possession of the vineyard. The phrase, however, may be a sneer on the part of a conservative at the crown possession of Samaria, with no Israelite tradition, as the basis of power of Ahab and his house.

19. Elijah's 'word of God' to Ahab is an indictment (v. 19a) and an oracle of doom (v. 19b). The king is indicted for the infringement of two of the apodictic laws which were recognized in the Decalogue as basic in Israelite society, those condemning murder and forcible appropriation (*lō' taḥmōd*, AV 'Thou shalt not covet'), and on the analogy of apodictic laws in the Book of the Covenant, those were capital offences. Hence the oracle of doom is pronounced in the graphic language of v. 19b. The literal fulfilment of this prophecy is noted in the sequel to the death of Ahab describing how dogs licked his blood off his chariot by the pool of Samaria (22.38).

Elijah touches pointedly on the price, i.e. the vineyard, as the material advantage of Ahab's sin.

20. For the sense of *māṣā'* as 'to overtake in pursuit of' cf. 13.14; Josh. 2.22. Ahab apparently regards Elijah as the avenger of blood, who pursues his victim relentlessly.

21. 'Behold I shall bring' (*hinᵉnī mēbī'*) is the familiar formula introducing imminent judgement in the prophets. This verse and the following, like 14.10 (Ahijah's doom of Jeroboam) and 16.3 (Jehu's doom of Baasha and his house), the *ipsissima dicta* of which they re-echo, are probably from the pre-Deuteronomistic prophetic compiler; see above, pp. 30ff. Verse 23, the oracle on Jezebel, is certainly a typical short, colourful, and very pithy oracle, but it may be secondary, adapted to the actual fate of Jezebel, i.e. prophecy *post eventum.*

21.23. *ḥēl*, taken in G, G^L, and RV as 'rampart', is read as *ḥēleq* ('portion', 'territory') in S, V, and T. The latter reading is suggested by the statement in II K. 9.26 that Naboth's blood was expiated in the death of Joram in the field of Naboth, and may be a deliberate harmonization. G. R. Driver[a] defends MT, but proposes to take *ḥēl* as cognate with Arabic *ḥiyāl* ('by'). On this clue we propose to understand the word rather as a cognate of Arabic *ḥawla* ('round about'), referring to the dogs fighting for the fragments of mutilated flesh which they carry off to eat apart all round the town. *ḥēl* means 'precinct' or 'city-wall' in Ps. 122.7.

(ii) DEUTERONOMISTIC ASIDE ON AHAB (in same tone as vv. 20b–22): 21.25f.

21 [25]But there was none such as Ahab, who sold himself to do evil in the sight of Yahweh, incited[b] by Jezebel his wife. [26]And he committed great abomination in following idols, according to all that the Amorites did, whom Yahweh dispossessed before the Israelites.

25f. The tenor and language of this passage suggest the Deuteronomistic redactor, the introductory particle *raq* ('only') indicating a late addendum.

(iii) AHAB'S REACTION TO ELIJAH'S ORACLE: 21.27–29

This may be secondary to the tradition centring upon Elijah's oracle in v. 19b, being motivated by the consciousness that the fulfilment of the prophecy was deferred to the time of Joram (II K. 9.26). On the other hand, Ahab may have genuinely repented. He had so much respect for Israelite tradition that he had felt obliged to accept Naboth's refusal, and probably only acted, or allowed Jezebel to act, stung by her taunt that his rule was not effective. It may well be that Ahab did not know of the measures taken by Jezebel, as vv. 15f. suggest, and in fact may have been himself in Samaria when the tragedy was contrived at Jezreel.

[a]*JBL* LV, 1936, p. 109.
[b]Emending the vowels of MT *hēsattā* to *hēsītā.*

21 [27]And it happened that, when Ahab heard these words, he tore his clothes and put sackcloth on his body and fasted, and lay in sackcloth and went about quietly. [28]And the word of Yahweh came to Elijah the Tishbite saying, [29]Have you seen how Ahab is subdued before me? Because he is subdued before me, I shall not bring about[a] ill in his days; in his son's days shall I bring the harm upon his house.[b]

21.27. The mourning rites here are all familiar. The rending of one's garment, usually the tearing off of a broad strip from the neck down, and the wearing of coarse dark cloth, sackcloth, either over one's normal clothes or next to the skin as here, and the abstention from staple food, or from any food at all, and avoidance of normal exercise, here sitting or lying instead of standing, were all part of the suspension of normal activity practised at periods of social crisis, when the community was especially open to untoward supernatural influences. Here Ahab had particular reason to apprehend the vengeful spirit of Naboth, whose blood had not been duly 'covered'. His duty of mourning moreover was not a private precaution only, but a public duty, to avert the potential harm from the community which he represented. The adverb *'aṭ* ('softly, unobtrusively, quietly') is generally introduced by *l^e*, and is used of the gentle course of the waters of an irrigation channel (Isa. 8.6) and of the gentle treatment of the rebel Absalom (II Sam. 18.5), etc.

(*h*) PROPHETIC ADAPTATION OF HISTORICAL NARRATIVE OF THE SYRIAN WARS: 22.1–40

(i) THE CAMPAIGN OF RAMOTH GILEAD AND THE DEATH OF 'AHAB': 22.1–38

For the literary affinities of this passage see critical introduction to ch. 20. The prophetic adaptation culminates in the circumstances of the king's death in v. 38, related to the *ipsissima dicta* of Elijah's prophecy in 21.19.

The part of Jehoshaphat in vv. 4–18, as in II K. 3.11–14, may indicate elaboration by a Judaean editor, possibly the Deuteronomistic compiler himself, being suggested by the presence of Jehoshaphat as a vassal of the king of Israel in 22.29ff. At this stage, vv. 4–18 may have raised the incident of Micaiah and the other prophets to the level of a theological question on prophecy as a medium of influencing God by auto-suggestion or an objective revelation normative of

[a]Q *'ābī'*.
[b]G^BL omit MT 'upon his house'.

human conduct, which was interesting men at the end of the monarchy, together with the validity of the claim to the prophetic urge on the part of men who had contradictory messages to deliver. The situation recalls the conflict of Jeremiah and Hananiah (Jer. 28.1–17) at the period when we believe that the Deuteronomistic History was being compiled.

22 1And they sat still for three years without war between the
Aramaeans and Israel. 2Then it happened in the third year that
Jehoshaphat the king of Judah came down to the king of Israel.
3And the king of Israel said to his servants, Do you realize that Ramoth
Gilead belongs to us, and we hold our peace and do not take it from
the hand of the king of the Aramaeans? 4And he said to Jehoshaphat,
Will you go with me[a] to Ramoth Gilead to fight? And Jehoshaphat
said to the king of Israel, I am as you are; my people is as your people,
and my horses as your horses. 5And Jehoshaphat said to the king of
Israel, Consult now the word of Yahweh. 6So the king of Israel gathered
together[b] the prophets, about four hundred men, and said to them,
Shall I go to fight against Ramoth Gilead or refrain? And they
said, Go up, and Yahweh[c] will certainly give[d] it into the hand of the
king. 7And Jehoshaphat said, Is there not here besides any prophet of
Yahweh that we may enquire of him?[e] 8And the king of Israel said to
Jehoshaphat, There is yet one man of whom[e] we may enquire of
Yahweh, but I detest him because he does not prophesy good concerning me, but ill, Micaiah the son of Imlah. And Jehoshaphat said,
Let the king not say so. 9And the king of Israel called to a certain
officer and said, Quick! (and bring) Micaiah the son of Imlah. 10Now
the king of Israel and Jehoshaphat the king of Judah were sitting each on
his throne in uniform in the open place at the gate of Samaria, and all
the prophets were prophesying before them. 11And Zedekiah the son of
Chenaanah had made himself iron horns and he said, Thus says
Yahweh, With these you shall thrust the Aramaeans until you annihilate them. 12And all the prophets prophesied the same saying, Go
up to Ramoth Gilead and succeed, and Yahweh will give [f]into your
hand even the king of the Aramaeans.[f] 13Then the messenger who had

[a]G^BA read *'ittānū* ('with us').

[b]G reads, perhaps better, 'all' (the prophets).

[c]*yhwh* for MT *'ᵃdōnāy* is well attested in Hebrew MSS and in Aquila, Symmachus, Theodotion, and the Targum, but not in G.

[d]So G (*wᵉnātōn yittēn*) for MT *wᵉyittēn* . . . ('that he may give . . .' or 'and let him give . . .').

[e]Reading *mē'ittō* with many MSS for MT *mē'ōtō*.

[f]So G for MT *bᵉyad hammelek* ('into the king's hand . . .'), with the object omitted. Gressmann, however (*Die älteste Geschichtsschreibung* . . ., p. 280), would retain MT as designedly ambiguous. The fact that the king is unnamed and undefined makes this possible. Such ambiguity was a well-known feature of the Delphic oracle, e.g. the oracle to Croesus, 'If you cross the Halys you will destroy a mighty empire.' See also v. 15.

gone to call Micaiah spoke to him saying, [a]All the prophets have unanimously given[a] a favourable word to the king; let your word[b] be as the word of one of them and speak favourably. [14]And Micaiah said, As Yahweh lives! what Yahweh shall say to me that shall I speak. [15]And he came to the king, and the king said to him, Micaiah, shall we[c] go up to Ramoth Gilead to fight or refrain?[c] And he said to him, Go up[d] and succeed,[d] and Yahweh will give into your hand the king of the Aramaeans. [16]And the king said to him, How many times have I adjured you on oath to speak to me only the truth in the name of Yahweh. [17]Then he said,

> I saw all Israel scattered upon[e] the mountains
> As sheep without a shepherd,
> and Yahweh said,
> These have no master;
> Let them return each man to his own house in peace.

[18]Then the king of Israel said to Jehoshaphat, Did I not say to you, This man[f] does not prophesy good to me, but ill. [19]Then he said, No![g] Hear the word of Yahweh! I have seen Yahweh sitting upon his throne, and all the heavenly host standing in attendance on him at his right hand and at his left. [20]And Yahweh said, Who will stultify Ahab that he may go up and fall at Ramoth Gilead? And one said thus[h] and another said thus.[h] [21]And the spirit came forth and stood before Yahweh and said, I will stultify him. And Yahweh said, How? [22]And he said, I shall go forth and be a lying spirit in the mouth of all his prophets. And he said, You shall stultify (him) and bring the matter to effect. Go and do so. [23]And now, see, Yahweh has set a lying spirit in the mouth of all these your prophets, and Yahweh has spoken ill concerning you. [24]Then Zedekiah the son of Chenaanah came up to him and struck Micaiah on the cheek and said, By which way[i] did the spirit of Yahweh pass from me to speak with you?[j] [25]And Micaiah said, Behold, you shall see it on that day when you go from one chamber to another to hide yourself. [26]And the king of Israel said, Take Micaiah

[a]Reading with G *dibb^{e}rū kol-hann^{e}bī'īm* for MT *dib^{e}rē hann^{e}bī'īm* ('the words of the prophets'), which is qualified by the singular adjective *ṭōb*.

[b]So Q, Symmachus, T and S for MT (K) plural.

[c]G reads the singular here.

[d]The parallel version in II Chron. 18.14 gives the plural.

[e]S, T, and the parallel version in Chronicles read *ʿal* for MT *'el*.

[f]Adding *ze* ('this man') to MT, after G.

[g]G reads 'not so, not I' (*lō' kēn lō' 'ānōkī*), the second two words being probably a variant in the Hebrew text of the first two, which give the better sense.

[h]Reading *kākā* for *b^{e}kō*, with the parallel passage in Chronicles. The MT, however, is still possible.

[i]G reads 'What kind of spirit of the Lord spoke by you?', which is rather a paraphrase. The position of the verb *ʿābar* ('passed') in the sentence indicates that *'ē* is an interrogative adverb rather than an interrogative pronoun. The parallel passage in Chronicles makes this clear by inserting *hadderek* after *'ē-ze*.

[j]Reading *'ittāk* for the ungrammatical *'ōtāk* of MT.

and send him back to Amon the city-commandant and to Joash the king's son, [27]and say, Thus says the king, Put this man in prison and give him food of affliction to eat and let him drink[a] water of affliction until I come safe and sound. [28]And Micaiah said,

If you return safe and sound
Yahweh has not spoken by me.

[b]And he said, Hear, you people, all of you.[b]

[29]So the king of Israel and Jehoshaphat the king of Judah made the expedition to Ramoth Gilead. [30]And the king of Israel said to Jehoshaphat, I [c]shall disguise myself and go[c] into the battle and you put on my[d] robes. So the king of Israel disguised himself and went into the battle. [31]Now the king of Aram had ordered his chariot-commanders (the thirty-two of them)[e] saying, You shall not fight with small or great, but only with the king of Israel. [32]And it happened that, when the chariot-commanders saw Jehoshaphat, they said, That seems[f] the king of Israel. And they surrounded him[g] to fight, and Jehoshaphat cried out. [33]And it happened that, when the chariot-commanders saw that it was not the king of Israel, they turned back from following him. [34]And a man drew a bow at random, and struck the king of Israel between the scale-armour and the breast-plate, and he said to his chariot-driver, Turn your hand and take me out of the battle,[h] for I am grievously wounded. [35]And the conflict on that day mounted and the king was propped up in his chariot facing the Aramaeans until evening,[i] and he died at evening, and the blood of his wound poured down into the body of his chariot. [36] And a crier[j] went through the army about sundown saying, Each man to his city and to his land,[k] for the king is dead. [37]So they came[k] to Samaria and

[a]Adding 'let him drink' with G^L.

[b]This is omitted in G^{BL} and the direct speech is identical with the beginning of the Book of Micah (1.2). It is obviously a gloss by a late hand which wrongly considered the son of Imlah identical with the prophet Micah.

[c]So G^{BL}, S, and T for MT, which reads the verbs as imperative. The emphatic 'and you' following, and the subsequent statement that it was the king of Israel who disguised himself and went into battle indicates that the versions are right here.

[d]So G for MT 'your robes'.

[e]This phrase is missing in the parallel passage in Chronicles. It is an obvious gloss suggested by 20.1.

[f]G suggests this reading, which indicates that *'ak*, which means 'as' in Syriac, has this meaning here. Alternatively it may be a corruption of *k^e^* ('like').

[g]Reading with G and the parallel passage in Chronicles *wayyāsōbbū* for MT *wayyāsūrū* ('and they turned aside').

[h]So with G (*hammilḥāmā*) for MT *hammaḥ^a^ne* ('army'). The point of the story is that, though 'Ahab' was *hors de combat*, he remained with the army.

[i]Inserting 'until the evening' (*ʿad-hāʿereb*) with the parallel passage in Chronicles.

[j]Reading the masculine singular participle *hārōne* with G, S, V, and T for MT *hārinnā* ('cry'), as suggested by the masculine singular verb *wayyaʿ^a^bōr*.

[k]Reading with G *kī mēt hammelek wayyābō'ū* for MT *wayyāmot hammelek wayyābō'*. The corruption of *k* of *kī* to *w* of *wayyāmot* probably occurred in the proto-Hebraic script, where *k* and *w* are much alike.

buried the king in Samaria. [38]And they washed the chariot by the pool of Samaria, and the dogs licked his blood, and they washed the weapons,[a] according to the word of Yahweh which he had spoken.

22.1. It is natural to suppose that the three years' peace was the consequence of the Israelite victory and generous treatment of Benhadad described in ch. 20, but that is not certain, since the king of Aram is not named in ch. 22. This is a vestige of the historical chronicle adapted in the prophetic narrative.

At this point Chronicles, which ignores the history of the Northern kingdom since the civil war between Jeroboam and Abijah the son of Rehoboam (II Chron. 13.13–20), records the incident on the eve of the campaign to Ramoth Gilead and the death of the king, obviously because of the role played by Jehoshaphat. From the sequel, where 'Ahab' disguises himself and obliges Jehoshaphat to wear his clothes at Ramoth Gilead, and from Jehoshaphat's reply (v. 4) it seems that Jehoshaphat, if not actually a vassal, was at least the junior partner.

3. It is supposed that Ramoth Gilead, a key fortress dominating the approach to the heart of Israel by the eastern end of the Plain of Jezreel, had been ceded by Benhadad after his defeat by the king of Israel (ch. 20), but had not yet been handed over. That the king of Israel should not have pressed for this may indicate that he had the greater interest of Western unity at heart in view of the united front against Assyria. The general historical background, however, is vague. The location of Ramoth Gilead at *Ḥuṣn ʿAjlūn* near modern *Irbid*[b] is much more likely than *ar-Ramṭeh* in the open plain south of *Deraʿa*, which shows no trace of occupation before the Arab period. Glueck,[c] on the other hand, has proposed *Tell ar-Rāmīt*, about four and a half miles south-east of the large modern village of *ar-Ramṭeh* in northern Transjordan. The significance of Ramoth Gilead is indicated by the fact that it was a district centre in Solomon's administration (4.13, which see). The association of this centre with Bashan in that passage corroborates the more easterly location at *Ḥuṣn ʿAjlūn*.

ḥāšā, meaning properly 'to keep silence', is used to denote general inaction, cf. Judg. 18.9, where it is parallel to *neʿeṣal* (lit. 'to be slothful').

4. The fact that Jehoshaphat is apparently given a free choice to

[a]Reading *hazzᵉyānōt* for MT *hazzōnōt* (see on v. 38).
[b]Dalman, *PJB* 1913, p. 64; Albright, *BASOR* 35, 1929, p. 11; Abel, *GP* II, p. 430.
[c]*AASOR* XXV–XXVIII, 1945–49, 1951, pp. 96ff.

accompany the king of Israel seems to suggest that he was the member, though weaker, of a free alliance rather than a vassal with obligatory commitments. The reply, which at first sight would suggest the latter relationship, need not do so.

22.5. The verb *dāraš* (lit. 'to seek') is the regular term meaning 'to consult an oracle'.

6. The number 'about 400' may be an approximation suggested by the 450 prophets of Baal in the story of the ordeal on Carmel (18.19).

7f. The orthodox attitude of Jehoshaphat, who is used as a foil to the king of Israel, indicates Judaean influence in the transmission of the tradition; see critical introduction to this section.

8. The respective attitudes of the king of Israel and Jehoshaphat to Micaiah introduce us to the main conceptions of prophecy in ancient Israel. The former employed the prophets as agents of imitative magic in word and, in the case of Zedekiah, in symbolic action, and there was a whole corps of prophets willing to give him the moral support he required. Jehoshaphat, at least by implication, regarded the prophet not as an agent of the community in its efforts to influence God by autosuggestion, but as the instrument of the revelation of the will of God to the community. This passage significantly anticipates the difference and, indeed, antipathy between the great figures of prophecy such as Amos and the other canonical prophets and those termed by them 'false prophets', which is so accentuated in Jeremiah and the 'false prophets' (Jer. 23), particularly Hananiah (Jer. 27–29), whom von Rad[a] sees as an official prophet circumscribed by his office of intercession and reassurance, and limited by a merely national outlook, as against Jeremiah, whose experience of divine revelation made him independent of institutionalism and turned his vision outward to the action of God in world history. There is no other mention of Micaiah the son of Imlah, who was such an important figure in Hebrew prophecy. He was most likely a representative figure, probably associated with the protagonists of Yahwism of the circle represented earlier by Elijah and Elisha. If this incident had really concerned Ahab, Elijah, who outlived him, would surely have been introduced at this point.

9. *sārîs* in this passage, as in Gen. 37.36 (Potiphar), II K. 18.17 (the chief officer of the king of Assyria), II K. 20.18 (the chief officer of the king of Babylon), etc., is the Hebrew version, through

[a]'Die falschen Propheten', *ZAW* LI, 1933, pp. 109–20.

Aramaic, of the Akkadian *ša riši* (*šarri*) ('he who is at the head of the king'). The connection with *sārīs*, 'eunuch' (Isa. 56.3; Esth. 2.3, 14ff.) is probably fortuitous, the latter being possibly derived from a root 'to be impotent', of which Arabic *sarisa*, with this meaning, though not an exact phonetic equivalent, may be a corruption.

22.10. For *meluḇbāšīm* G gives 'in full panoply', which may well be the correct interpretation, the following *beḡādīm* ('robes') being possibly a dittograph and corruption of *beḡōren*. *gōren* in the sense of an open (lit. 'well-rubbed' according to Arabic etymology) public place in connection with the gate is probably genuine, as is suggested by a passage in the Ras Shamra texts (*UT* 2 'Aqht, V, 6ff.):

ytšʾu. yṯb. bʾap. ṯġr
tḥt. ʾadrm. dbgrn

> He rises to sit at the entrance to the gate,
> In the place of the notables who are in the public place.

This, rather than 'threshing-floor', is the meaning of *gōren* here, though the spacious threshing-floor would have been an apt place for an assembly of the kings described in the passage here. The Arabic verb *jarana* means 'to fray' or 'rub', and *al-jārūn* means 'the worn track'. Hence *grn* in the Ugaritic passage cited and in the present passage in Kings signifies a space rubbed by public concourse and so kept clear, as the open space inside gates attested in various archaeological sites in Palestine,[a] or perhaps where all tracks converged outside the city gate.

11. The name Zedekiah indicates that the prophet was a devotee of Yahweh, though a chauvinist. His act of prophetic symbolism may have been intended to reinforce the ancient tribal oracle to Joseph (Deut. 33.17):

> His horns are like the horns of the wild ox,
> With them he shall thrust the people all together to the ends of the land.

The *Sitz im Leben* of this and the other tribal oracles may have been the assembly of the sacral community at the central shrine, where the old covenantal association between Yahweh and Israel was periodically renewed. The gestures of the prophet are typical of prophetic symbolism adapted especially by Jeremiah and Ezekiel.

[a]See our article 'The *Goren* at the City Gate . . .', *PEQ*, 1953, pp. 118–23, in reply to Sidney Smith, 'On the Meaning of Goren', *PEQ*, 1953, pp. 42–5, and *PEQ*, 1946, pp. 5–14.

22.12. On the content of the prophecy see textual note.

13. The officer of the king holds the same view of the prophetic function as his master; it is an instrument of propaganda.

14. Šanda notes the significance of the imperfect *yō'mar*. The prophet has not yet received the word of God, cf. v. 17 *rā'ītī*, the perfect being used after conclusive revelation.

15. The first answer of Micaiah to the king, repeating the favourable oracle, which, no doubt, had been reported to him by the officer, is intended probably to emphasize the facility with which such moral support could be lent by the prophets. Of this function of the prophets as the vehicle of human aspirations and hopes Micaiah was well aware, and possibly, through default of revelation, he felt quite entitled to give this encouraging oracle on his own authority. It is to the credit of the king, however, that he did not remain satisfied with this response, but looked for something deeper 'in the name' (i.e. with the authority) of Yahweh.

17. This oracle, cast characteristically in verse and characteristically figurative, represents the word of God now received by the prophet, as the perfect *rā'ītī* ('I saw') indicates. The Arabic cognate of this verb means 'to think' or 'perceive intellectually' as well as 'to see' physically. The perception of the prophet, quickened by his mind which was accustomed to think in graphic imagery, may have convinced him that he actually saw what he describes.

The figure of the shepherdless flock has a particular significance, the shepherd being a common figure for the king in the ancient Near East in Mesopotamia and Israel (cf. Zech. 13.7); cf. the Homeric *poimenes laōn* ('Shepherds of the peoples').

'In peace' (*b^e^šālōm*) sounds strange after the proclamation of the defeat of the king. It is feasibly taken by Eissfeldt[a] to signify the end of the war. There may be a contrast between the violent end of the king and the survival of the common people.

19. On the first words of the reply of Micaiah see p. 446 n.[g]. The quickened perception of the prophet visualizes (*rā'ītī*) a scene in the heavenly court. Yahweh directs human affairs from his royal throne, a conception probably originally borrowed from Canaanite mythology, e.g. the Ras Shamra texts where El gives his decrees *ex cathedra* (cf. Zech. 3; Ezek. 1f.). Eissfeldt (*op. cit.*, p. 541) would see a further example in the vision of Isaiah (ch. 6), and the present passage indicates that this was chronologically possible. We would,

[a]*HSAT*, p. 541.

however, agree with Mowinckel[a] in deriving Isaiah's vision from the association of ideas in the cult of Yahweh as King manifest in the New Year festival. The 'host of heaven' (*ṣ*ᵉ*bā' haššāmayim*) occasionally refers to the heavenly bodies deified as in the Assyrian astral cults introduced to Judah by Ahaz and Manasseh (II K. 21.5; 23.4, 5, 12 etc.); it also may refer in other contexts (e.g. Gen. 2.1; Ps. 33.6; Isa. 34.4; 45.12; Jer. 33.22, etc.) to the stars as the armies of Yahweh innumerable, ordered, and obedient. The assault of 'the little horn' on the 'host of heaven' and the stars, in Dan.8.10 as also Rev. 12.4, refers to a myth where the dragon, or serpent, of Chaos menaces the celestials, the stars being regarded as animate warriors with Yahweh their captain. In the present passage, as in Ps. 103.21 and Luke 2.13, the phrase refers to heavenly beings as an organized force or army under Yahweh. The conception probably represents a fusion of the native Israelite idea of Yahweh as marshal of the host of Israel with that of God as king or governor of the forces of nature, which we consider to be adapted by Israel from Canaanite religion.

'To stand by' (lit. 'above') refers to the attitude of the subordinate, who stands while his superior sits or reclines on his divan.

22.20. Possibly there is prophetic ambiguity in the phrase *w*ᵉ*yippōl b*ᵉ*rāmōt gilʿād*, which may mean either 'that he may fall at R.G.' or 'that he may attack R.G.', cf. Josh. 11.7 (Joshua's attack on the Canaanites at Waters of Merom) and II Sam. 17.9. The fact that no clear distinction is made here between the positive and the permissive will of Yahweh in the case of the impending disaster is a sign of the early date of the passage. Micaiah is prepared to admit that the word of Yahweh encouraging the king to go on his expedition is genuine, and he reconciles this with his own deeper insight by explaining it as a means to the divinely appointed destruction of the king. 'The spirit' may be an instance of the generic definite article (cf. *happālîṭ*, Gen. 14.13), meaning 'a spirit',[b] and, in fact, it has been conjectured that *haśśāṭān* ('the adversary') should be read. This, however, is to assume a theology for which there is no evidence till post-exilic times, and to miss the real point of the passage. 'The spirit' is the supernatural, divinely inspired power of prophecy, which in the case of Zedekiah and his colleagues lured the king to destruction. This was an emanation, or extension, of the divine personality, and so may be personi-

[a] *He That Cometh*, p. 84 n.
[b] So Eissfeldt, *op. cit.*, p. 541.

fied. We may see here the germ of the conception of the Holy Spirit as a person of the Godhead, though at a very primitive level. It is the purpose of God which conditions the nature of the activity of the spirit for immediate harm or good. In this passage the spirit (here the gift of popular prophecy) is the supernatural and hence, according to ancient Semitic conceptions, divine influence which is instrumental in the ruin of 'Ahab', as it occasioned the melancholy of Saul, who had forfeited the divine blessing (I Sam. 16.14f.). The idea, familiar in Greek tragedy, that 'he whom God wishes to destroy he first makes mad', hence the instrument of his own destruction, was even more familiar to the ancient Hebrew, e.g. God hardened Pharaoh's heart (Ex. 4.21) and allowed Shimei to curse David (II Sam. 16.10), hence incurring a capital charge which was used against him at a convenient moment. On the sole mention of Ahab in this incident, a feature of the prophetic adaptation of the historical narrative, see introduction to ch. 20.

22.22. In the description of the spirit which inspired his colleagues as a spirit of falsehood, Micaiah is not denying the fact that they were under supernatural influence in the exercise of their prophetic, or dervish, powers, but he is expressing the fact that this was intended by the divine will to be the means of the king's delusion and destruction, and it is expressive of his own deeper conviction of the folly of his course and of the ultimate disaster.

25. The extremity of Zedekiah when he will run for refuge from one room to another (*ḥeder beḥeder*, cf. 20.30) will vindicate the authority of Micaiah. That is his pointed reply to the question of Zedekiah on the subject of relative prophetic authority.

26. However the king might ignore the oracle of Micaiah, he could not treat him with indifference. As a potential source of demoralization in Israel he is confined under custody of the city-commandant and Joash 'the son of the king', as Jeremiah was confined in the house of Malchiah 'the son of the king' in the time of Zedekiah (Jer. 38.6). This may refer literally to the sons of the king (Joash) and Zedekiah (Malchiah), or possibly members of the royal family at large, perhaps brothers of the king, or a son of the king by a concubine. On the other hand, the fact that the present passage and Jer. 36.26; 38.6 all refer to the confinement of a state prisoner suggests that this is a title, a theory which is supported, as de Vaux has pointed out,[a] by the fact that in a seal or seal-imprint from

[a] *Ancient Israel*, pp. 119f.

Palestine 'the son of the king' follows the proper name when one would expect an official title. 'The king's son' might have been one personally and absolutely responsible to the king and over whom the king had the power of life and death as the father over the son. Such a person might be a guarantee for the safe custody of the prisoner.

22.27. *šālōm* means here 'security', 'safety' (lit. 'wholeness') rather than 'peace'.

30. On the instructions of the king of Israel to Jehoshaphat see p. 447 n.[c]. The disguises of the kings, which drew the attack of the enemy on Jehoshaphat, may not have had that intention. 'Ahab' wished obviously to lead in the ranks, but the visible presence of the king was also necessary for purposes of morale, and this role was to be fulfilled by Jehoshaphat impersonating the king of Israel. The change of status and robes, on the other hand, may have been designed to avert the fate that had been prophesied by Micaiah. To avert the power of evil influences especially potent on the Babylonian sabbaths the ancient kings of Mesopotamia refrained from their usual activities and from wearing their royal robes on such occasions.

32. *'ak* may be an Aramaism, cf. Syriac *'ak* ('like'). When Jehoshaphat cried out his identity was known. G and the parallel passage in Chronicles add that he cried out in prayer, but it is more likely that he was known by his war-cry, his shout to the men of Judah, or by his dialect.

34. *l^etummō* means literally 'in his wholeness' (i.e. of heart), innocently, not knowing how vital his shot would be, cf. *hōl^ekīm l^etummām* ('going in their innocence', II Sam. 15.11), of Absalom's followers whom he involved in his rebellion.

d^ebāqīm means 'welding', 'joints', hence possibly the mobile scale-armour between the solid cuirass (*širyān*) and the abdomen and thighs. Scales of such armour have been found in excavations at Nuzu,[a] Ugarit,[b] and, nearer the time of 'Ahab', at *Tell ed-Duweir* (Lachish).[c] On the other hand, the Targum on Jer. 38.12 attests *midbaq* (*yād*) as 'armpit'. It was in raising his arm to cheer on his men that John Graham of Claverhouse, Viscount Dundee, was shot in the Battle of Killiecrankie.

The king's order to be taken behind the lines must be emphasized in view of the common assumption that he was determined to remain

[a] *BASOR* 30, 1928, pp. 2ff.
[b] C. F. A. Schaeffer, *Syria* XXVIII, 1951, p. 11.
[c] O. Tufnell, *Lachish III*, 1953, pl. 39, 7, 8, 9.

in his chariot facing the enemy (v. 35), to sustain the morale of his troops. Actually he fought incognito, and, brave though he may have been, his remaining wounded in the battle line was of necessity, since v. 35 indicates that it was impossible to turn in the press of chariots. Thus 'Ahab', who might have been successfully treated behind the lines, eventually died through loss of blood (v. 35), and the incident may have been emphasized in the prophetic compilation in order to emphasize the ineluctability of God's doom on Ahab pronounced by Elijah and Micaiah.

22.38. We regard this verse as the conclusion of the prophetic adaptation of the source. It overlooks the fact that the prophecy of Elijah referred to the expiation of the death of Naboth at Jezreel and the additional fact that this was fulfilled in Jehu's slaughter there of Ahab's son (II K. 9.21ff.; cf. I K. 21.29), though it does relate to the dogs licking the king's blood. The apparent reference to the harlots is strange. It formed no part of the prophecy of Elijah, and is apparently introduced to vilify 'Ahab'. The statement may be parenthetical, signifying that the public pool of Samaria was where the harlots washed (Skinner). On the other hand, there may be a reference to a superstitious practice. Blood was regarded in ancient Israel as the essence of life, and the king in the ancient East was the vehicle of divine blessing and the channel of fertility, so a rite of contactual magic may have been involved. Another possibility is that *zōnōt* may be a corruption of *zᵉyānōt*, 'armour' (so Stade after the Aramaic and Syriac versions). *zayin* in this sense is certainly attested in Aramaic, though not so far in Hebrew. Burney's[a] objection that the verb *rāḥaṣ* ('to wash') is never used of inanimate objects in biblical Hebrew is invalid, since the verb is used of the washing of sacrificial victims in Ex. 29.17; Lev. 1.9, 12; 8.21; 9.14. Thus we have no hesitation in seeing a reference to the washing of Ahab's weapons. The clause nevertheless is a later accretion. The pool of Samaria at this time has not been certainly identified. The city in the Israelite period was supplied with water from cisterns, which have been estimated to have sufficed for some 25,000 people in Omri's time.[b] Since the water-supply for these cisterns in Samaria was necessarily restricted, it is unlikely that any of the lime-plastered cisterns excavated in the citadel area was the pool where the chariot of the king was washed. This, as the word *bᵉrēkā* suggests, is more likely to have been some catchment area used

[a]*Notes on . . . Kings*, p. 259.
[b]J. W. Crowfoot, *Samaria-Sebaste* I, *The Buildings*, 1942, p. 4.

for washing of clothes and watering of animals outside the wall of the city, possibly in the area occupied by the modern Arab village of *Ṣebasṭiyeh*.

(ii) DEUTERONOMISTIC EPILOGUE ON AHAB AND NOTE OF HIS SUCCESSOR: 22.39f.

22 [39]Now as for the rest of the acts of Ahab and all that he did and the palace of ivory which he built, and all the cities which he built, are they not recorded in the Book of the Chronicles of the Kings of Israel? [40]And Ahab slept with his fathers, and Ahaziah his son reigned in his place.

22.39. Ahab's 'ivory palace' was, of course, of stone, the panelling and furniture being inlaid with ivory, as indicated by the discovery of ivory plaques of various shapes, for the most part carved in low relief with Phoenician renderings of Egyptian motifs and marked on the back with proto-Hebraic characters as sequence-numbers.[a] Such decoration was fashionable in the Iron Age in Palestine and the Near East generally (Amos 3.15), cf. an ivory plaque probably belonging to a couch looted from Damascus inscribed *lmrn ḥz'l* ('belonging to our lord Hazael'), found in an Assyrian palace at Arslan Tash in northern Syria,[b] and other pieces from Assyria.[c] The cities 'built' by Ahab mean generally those fortified by him, though most of the palace at Samaria was built by him, since Omri occupied the place for only six years, most of which would probably be devoted to fortification. Megiddo with the north stable-complex and other buildings (see on 9.15), and Hazor are other places where Ahab's work is well attested by archaeology.

(*i*) DEUTERONOMISTIC SUMMARY, WITH ISRAELITE SYNCHRONISM, OF THE REIGN OF JEHOSHAPHAT OF JUDAH, AND A NOTE OF THE ACCESSION AND REIGN OF AHAZIAH: 22.41–53 [41–54]

In this Deuteronomistic note there is incorporated a brief notice of the religious policy of Jehoshaphat (vv. 43–45, 47), his administration of Edom (v. 48), and his abortive maritime enterprise in the Red Sea (vv. 49–50), which probably comes from the annals of the Kingdom of Judah.

[a]J. W. Crowfoot, *Samaria-Sebaste* II, *Early Ivories*, 1938.

[b]A. G. Barrois, *Manuel d'Archéologie Biblique*, I, pp. 501–7, figs. 196f.

[c]R. D. Barnett, *The Nimrud Ivories*, 1957. M. E. L. Mallowan, *Iraq* XX, 1958, p. 104, attests 'a great ivory screen which once overlay the brick' of a wall of a palace founded under Adad-Nirari III at Nimrud (ancient Kalḫu).

(i) THE REIGN OF JEHOSHAPHAT: 22.41–50 [41–51]

22 [41]And Jehoshaphat the son of Asa became king over Judah in
the fourth year of Ahab[a] king of Israel. [42]And Jehoshaphat was thirty-
five years old when he became king and for twenty-five years he reigned
in Jerusalem, and his mother's name was Azubah the daughter of
Shilhi. [43]And he walked in all the way of Asa his father; he did not
turn aside from it, doing what was right in the eyes of Yahweh.
However, he did not abolish[b] the high places; the people continued to
sacrifice and burn incense at the 'high places'. [44]And Jehoshaphat made
peace with the king of Israel. [45]And as for the rest of the acts of Jehoshaphat and his power which he realized and the wars that he fought,[c]
are they not written in the Book of the Chronicles of the Kings of Judah?
[46]And what remained of sacral prostitutes, who survived in the days of
Asa his father, he drove out of the land. [47]And there was no king in
Edom, but a representative of the king.[d] [48]Jehoshaphat made[e] a
Tarshish-fleet[f] to go to Ophir for gold, but they did not go, for the
ships were wrecked at Ezion-geber. [49]Then Ahaziah the son of Ahab
said to Jehoshaphat, Let my subjects go with your subjects in the ships,
but Jehoshaphat would not consent. [50]And Jehoshaphat slept with his
fathers and was buried[g] in the city of David his father, and Jehoram
his son became king in his place.

22.41. On the date of Jehoshaphat's accession (871) see n. below and Introduction: Chronology, p. 66.

42. The note of the name of the queen-mother is a feature of the record of the kings of Judah. This was of interest in a polygamous society, where affinities were in consequence nationwide. It also reflects the status of the queen-mother as first lady (*hagg[e]bîrā*) in the state.

44. Jehoshaphat's peaceful relations with the king of Israel are noted as marking a termination of the continual hostility of the kingdoms since the disruption, cf. 14.30; 15.6 (Rehoboam and

[a]G[BL] notes the accession of Jehoshaphat after the note of the death of Omri and the accession of Ahab at 16.28, dating it in the eleventh year of Omri (885–874). Reckoning from 881, when Omri eliminated his rival Tibni, we date the accession of Jehoshaphat in 871, the fourth year of Ahab (see Introduction: Chronology).

[b]Reading *hēsîr* with G, S, and V, for MT *sārū* with *habbāmōt* as subject.

[c]G[B] omits MT *'[a]šer nilḥam* ('that he fought').

[d]Conjecturing *n[e]ṣîb melek* for MT *niṣṣāb melek* ('a deputy ruled'), which is asyndetic, but, in an obvious extract from state archives, not impossible.

[e]So Q for MT *'āśār*. Here there is perhaps a case of haplography, and both *'āśā* and *'āśār* may have originally stood.

[f]G[BL] read the singular, which the verb *hālak* seems to demand, though this, to be sure, should be feminine. The second predicate is taken by Q in the plural, so that the plural ending *w* may have dropped out after *k* of *hālak* and before the following *k* of *kî*, an easy error in the proto-Hebraic script.

[g]Omitting MT 'with his fathers' as a dittograph, so G[L].

Jeroboam); 15.7 (Abijah and Jeroboam); and 15.16, 32 (Asa and Baasha). The verb *wayyašlēm* signifies properly 'concord' rather than 'peace'.

22.46. *qādēš* is used collectively. On the function of sacred prostitutes see on 14.24.

47. This is the first mention of Edom since the note of the restoration of the monarchy of Edom with the return of Hadad (11.14ff.). It is remarkable that no mention should have been made of the re-establishment of the supremacy of Judah, but this is one more indication that Kings is not primarily secular history. The recovery of Judaean power in Edom was among 'the rest of the acts' of one or other of Solomon's successors. Judah's supremacy in Edom may have been the consequence of Jehoshaphat's *rapprochement* with Ahab, to support the Israelite occupation of the north part of Moab. The significance of the influence of Judah in Edom in support of Israel is apparent in the Moabite war of independence in the reign of Joram (II K. 3).

47f. It is possible that *neṣīb melek* (see p. 457 n.[d]) and not 'Jehoshaphat' (which may be omitted) is the subject of the verb *ʿāśā* (see p. 457 n.[e]).

48. The resumption of the Red Sea trade was a direct consequence of the re-establishment of the influence of Judah in Edom, itself a consequence of the alliance between Israel and Judah, of which the expedition of Israel, Judah and Edom in II K. 3.4–27 gives evidence. On Tarshish-ships, Ophir, and Ezion-geber see on 9.28; 10.22.

(ii) DEUTERONOMISTIC NOTICE OF THE REIGN OF AHAZIAH OF ISRAEL: 22.51–53 [52–54]

22 [51]Ahaziah the son of Ahab became king over Israel in Samaria in the seventeenth[a] year of Jehoshaphat king of Judah, and he reigned over Israel two years. [52]And he did evil in the sight of Yahweh and went in the way of his father and in the way of his mother and in the way[b] of Jeroboam the son of Nebat, who involved Israel in sin. [53]And he worshipped Baal and bowed down to him and provoked Yahweh God of Israel to anger according to everything his father had done.

51. On the chronology see n. below.

[a]G^BL read 'twenty-fourth', obviously adjusted to MT of II K. 1.17, which states that Ahaziah's successor Jehoram began his reign in the second year of Jehoram the son of Jehoshaphat, who reigned twenty-five years (22.42). This, however, is literally interpreted, whereas we believe II K. 1.17 to refer to the adoption of Jehoram as co-regent with his father Jehoshaphat in 853 (see Introduction: Chronology).

[b]G, perhaps better, reads 'in the sins' for MT 'in the way', the threefold repetition of which, though grammatically correct, is suspicious.

THE SECOND BOOK OF KINGS

For the division between I and II K., see below.

(j) ELIJAH'S DENUNCIATION OF AHAZIAH (II. 1.1, 2–8, 17), EXPANDED BY THE TRADITION OF THE FATAL ATTEMPT TO ARREST ELIJAH (vv. 9–16)

The beginning of II K., with an episode from the life of Elijah, raises the problem of the literary affinity of this passage and the following account of the translation of Elijah (ch. 2). The latter passage is obviously the prelude to the extracts from the Elisha-saga which follow, and the bulk of the former also has more in common with the popular version of Elisha's miracles than with the much more sober account of Elijah as the protagonist in the historical crises of his time. There may well be a nucleus of historical fact in Elijah's protest against Ahaziah's appeal to the oracle of Baal of Ekron (vv. 2–8, 17), but in the annihilation of the king's innocent emissaries by fire (vv. 9–16) there is a moral pointlessness, which relegates the tradition to the same category as Elisha's baneful curse upon the rude boys of Bethel (2.23f.). The present passage is possibly the elaboration of an actual incident in Elijah's life in the prophetic compilation noted above, pp. 372ff. Thus the early scholars who included this incident in II K. just before the Elisha-cycle were guided by a true critical instinct. The repetitive style of the narrative, especially in vv. 9–16, is characteristic of saga.

The episode is introduced by a historical note from the annals of Israel recording the rebellion of Moab after the death of Ahab. This rebellion is dealt with more fully in ch. 3 in the reign of Jehoram, and there have been various attempts to explain the short note, which seems out of context at II K. 1.1. Kittel (after Benzinger) suggests that it was the preface to a fuller account of the rebellion which once stood here, but was suppressed as tautological, since it was described in ch. 3. Šanda regards it as editorial, recorded as an instance of divine retribution on the sin of Ahab and the apostasy of Ahaziah recorded in I K. 22.52f. [53f.]. In this case the verse would be from the Deuteronomist, like I K. 22.50–53 [51–54], and it is noteworthy that G^B repeats the verse at the end of I K. On the other hand, 3.5 states somewhat vaguely that Moab rebelled after the death of Ahab 'against the king of Israel', whom it does not name, and then goes on to describe the punitive expedition of Jehoram. The present verse may be designed to specify that the revolt actually broke out in the reign of Ahaziah, one incident of whose short and inglorious reign is then described.

The account closes with a Deuteronomistic note on the accession of Jehoram and a reference to the annals of Israel for further information on the reign of Ahaziah.

(i) THE REVOLT OF MOAB: A SYNCHRONISTIC NOTE (see further on ch. 3): 1.1

1 [1]And Moab rebelled against Israel after the death of Ahab.

1.1. Here only a rough synchronism is possible with the data of Mesha king of Moab in his stele from Diban. Mesha speaks of Israelite domination of the northern part of Moab, specifically 'the land of Madaba' in the time of Omri and half the days of his son (or 'sons'), 'forty years'. Since the whole reign of Omri (12 years dating from 885, I K. 16.23) and that of Ahab (22 years, I K. 16.29) did not amount to 40, it seems that 'sons' rather than 'son' should be read in the inscription, the revolt taking place half-way between the accession of Ahab and the death of Jehoram, the last of the house of Omri, hence in the second year of Ahaziah just before his death. This would actually be in the 36th year after the accession of Omri. Since there is no indication when Omri extended his rule over the northern part of Moab, we may suppose that this was in the latter part of his reign, when he was undisputed ruler after the disappearance of his rival Tibni. On the other hand, it is not necessary to press the literal accuracy of the 'forty years' of the Moabite inscription, which may simply indicate a round number. Nevertheless it does support the suggestion of the present verse that the revolt broke out in the reign of Ahaziah.

pāša' is used here in its primary sense of 'rebel'. Signifying 'sin', its secondary sense, it denotes specifically deliberate defiance of what is known and admitted to be the will of God.

(ii) ELIJAH AND THE MISSION TO BAAL OF EKRON: 1.2–17a

1 [2]Now Ahaziah fell through the lattice in his upper chamber which was in Samaria, and he sickened and sent messengers and said to them, Go, consult the oracle of Baal 'Zebub' the god of Ekron (to know)

whether I shall recover from this sickness of mine.[a] [3]Then the angel of Yahweh said to Elijah the Tishbite, Rise up and go up to meet the messengers of the king of Samaria, and say to them, Is it for want of a God in Israel that you go to consult the oracle of Baal 'Zebub' the god of Ekron? [4]Now, therefore,[b] thus says Yahweh, From the bed upon which you have gone up you shall not come down, but you shall certainly die. And Elijah went off.[c] [5]And the messengers returned to him and he said to them, Why is it that you have returned? [6]And they said to him, A man came up to confront us and said to us, Go, return to the king[d] who sent you and say to him, Thus says Yahweh, Is it for want of a God in Israel that you send[e] to consult the oracle of Baal 'Zebub' the god of Ekron? Therefore from the bed upon which you have gone up you shall not come down, but you shall certainly die. [7]Then he said to them, What was the manner of the man who came up to confront you and spoke these words to you? [8]And they said to him, A shaggy man, girt with a leather belt on his loins. And he said, He is Elijah the Tishbite. [9]Then he sent to him a captain of fifty men and his fifty, and they came up[f] to him and[g] he was sitting on the top of a mountain, and he[h] said to him, O man of God, the king has said, Come down! [10]And Elijah answered and spoke to the captain of fifty, Yea, and[i] if I am a man of God may fire come down from heaven and consume you and your fifty. And fire came down from heaven and consumed him and his fifty. [11]And again he sent to him another captain of fifty and his fifty men, and he went up[j] and spoke to him, O man of God, this is the

[a]After G, S, V, and T, assuming haplography of the last letter in MT.

[b]In MT *welākēn*, the various MSS and recensions of G vary in reading or omitting the conjunction. Its inclusion connects the sequel more closely with what precedes and should be read here, though at other points in the repetitive narrative (e.g. vv. 6, 16) it is omitted in MT.

[c]At this point in the narrative there appears to be an ellipse of the narrative, since there is an abrupt transition from the divine revelation to Elijah and the narrative statement of the return of the emissaries of the king. Hebrew narrative, of course, was not unfamiliar with such an ellipse, but in this case it is likely that, in the repetitive style familiar in saga the narrative of the journey of the emissaries, using the *ipsissima dicta* of the divine revelation, is omitted in error.

[d]S reads 'the man' instead of 'the king'.

[e]G reads 'go' (*hōlēk*) for MT 'send' (*šōlēaḥ*), but, as the word of God is addressed not to the emissary but to the king, MT is preferable.

[f]S reads the plural.

[g]Reading *wehū'* with S and T for MT *wehinnē*, which, in any case requires a pronoun or pronominal suffix. Perhaps the original reading was *hinnēhū*, final *w* being omitted by haplography before *y*.

[h]G adds 'the captain of fifty', which is not strictly necessary.

[i]Certain MSS and S, V, and T omit the conjunction, which is omitted in the repetitive phrase in v. 12. It may, however, be retained to express the close connection of the prophet's rejoinder with the *ipsissima dicta* of what immediately precedes.

[j]Reading *wayyaʿal* with G^L for MT *wayyaʿan*. G^B and V omit the verb. Actually *wayyaʿan* is defensible, the word signifying in the Ras Shamra texts 'spoke up' as well as 'answered'.

order of the king, Haste and come down! [12]And Elijah answered and said to him,[a] Yea[b] and if I am a man of God[c] may fire come down from heaven and consume you and your fifty. And fire[d] came down from heaven and consumed him and his fifty. [13]And again he sent a third[e] captain of fifty and his fifty, and the third[f] captain of fifty[g] came and knelt on his knees before Elijah and entreated his favour and said to him, O man of God, may my life and the life of[h] your servants be precious in your sight. [14]See, fire has come down from heaven and consumed the former two captains of fifty and their fifties;[i] now may my life be precious in your sight. [15]And the angel of Yahweh said to Elijah, Go down with him,[j] fear not before them.[k] So he rose up and went down with him[j] to the king. [16]And he spoke to him, Thus says Yahweh, Because you have sent messengers to consult the oracle of Baal 'Zebub' the god of Ekron,[l] therefore from the bed upon which you have gone up you shall not come down, but you shall certainly die.[17]And die he did according to the word of Yahweh which Elijah spoke.[m]

1.2. The 'upper chamber' (*ʿᵃliyā*) was often little more than a shelter for privacy on the flat roof of an oriental house, as in the story

[a]This reading, supported by certain MSS and G and S, is preferable to MT 'to them'.

[b]For the inclusion of the conjunction after G^{L} see p. 461 n.[i] on v. 10.

[c]Reading *ʾîš ʾᵉlōhīm*, for MT *ʾîš hāʾᵉlōhīm*, though the latter might be admitted, the definite article having the force of quotation, 'the man of God (that you say I am)'. MT is supported by G^{A}.

[d]Omitting *ʾᵉlōhīm* after *ʾēš* with certain MSS and G, V, and T. 'Fire of God' as lightning was probably denoted, but *ʾᵉlōhīm* ('God') was probably added as an explanatory gloss.

[e]So with G^{L}, V, and T for MT *šᵉlīšīm*, The singular *šᵉlīšī* agreeing with *śar ḥᵃmiššīm* ('captain of fifty') is demanded by the third singular masculine pronoun in the following 'and his fifty'. The reading of S *šᵉlīšīt* 'a third time' is also possible.

[f]So MT, but *haššᵉlīšī* is omitted in S and read as *haššᵉlīšīm* in T, while V omits the word and the preceding *śar haḥᵃmīššīm*.

[g]Omitting MT *wayyaʿal* with G^{BL} and V.

[h]Omitting with G^{L} the ungrammatical *ʾēlle* and, with G^{B}, *ḥᵃmīššīm*, which likewise lacks the definite article.

[i]Certain MSS and G, V, and T omit 'and their fifties'.

[j]*ʾittō* ('with him') should obviously be read with certain MSS and with the Versions, for the ungrammatical MT *ʾōtō*.

[k]So G for MT *mippānāw* ('before him'), which, however, is perfectly intelligible.

[l]The phrase 'Is it for want of a God in Israel whose word you may consult?' may be omitted with G^{BL} as breaking the natural sequence of thought between the preceding clause introduced by *yaʿan ʾᵃšer* ('because') and the following clause introduced by *lākēn* ('therefore'). It may have been inserted by a scribal inadvertency as an echo of vv. 3, 6, the rest of the *ipsissima dicta* of which are repeated in the present verse. The phrase here, on the other hand, may be parenthetical.

[m]MT might stand, but a more natural alternative would be to read 'which he spoke through Elijah'.

of Elisha and the Shunammite lady (4.10). In the palace at Samaria it must have been much more pretentious, probably denoting the whole upper storey with balconies in the style of the North Syrian *bīt ḥillani* ('house with windows'). These terraces or balconies, however, were closed by screen-work (*śᵉbākā*), which admitted air but excluded strong light and the public gaze. Composed of many small pieces of jointed wood-work this lattice was easily broken, as in Ahaziah's mishap.

dāraš (lit. 'to seek') is used specifically of seeking divine revelation by consulting an oracle, cf. Amos 5.5.

It is suggested that Baal Zebub denoted the local god of Ekron who was associated with flies as the bearers of disease, and Josephus and the Greek versions render *Baal muiōn* ('Lord of Flies'). The element Zebub, however, is more probably a parody by the orthodox on *zᵉbūl* ('Prince'), now known from the Ras Shamra myths as the stock epithet of the Canaanite Baal, and it is significant that in the New Testament at Matt. 10.25; 12.24; Mark 3.22; Luke 11.15ff. the earliest and best texts support the reading Beelzebul as against the variant Beelzebub. Ekron, the northernmost of the Philistine cities, has been identified with *Tell al-Muqanna'* near *'Āqir*, about ten miles south-east of Jaffa; see on I K. 15.27. The cult of this Semitic deity in the Philistine city indicates the extent to which these aliens assimilated local culture. The worship of the local Canaanite Baal as the power giving life and health may have been established early in the Philistine settlement in Palestine, when, in the unsettled conditions of their occupation of their new homes, they suffered from new maladies of a local nature, which obliged them to placate the local god. An analogous case is the veneration of Yahweh at Bethel by the Assyrian military colonists in face of local troubles. There is no other reference in the Old Testament to this cult at Ekron.

1.3. The introduction of the 'angel of Yahweh' in intercourse between God and man is a feature of the E source of the Pentateuch, which is associated with Northern Israel in the eighth century. This is the time when the traditions of Elisha were crystallized, those of Elijah being at least half a century earlier. This suggests that the present passage reflects the theology of the contemporary E source, coming from the circles who transmitted the Elisha-cycle. It is not possible here to determine the form in which the 'angel' or 'messenger' of Yahweh was visualized. The word of Yahweh, conveyed with such force and compulsion that it seemed to be audible, may have suggested a personal messenger, who, reporting the very word of God, was regarded as the extension of the divine personality.

The designation of Ahaziah as 'the king of Samaria' probably reflects the conservative reaction in Israel to Omri's founding of a dynasty in defiance of democratic opinion in Israel on the basis of his crown possession of Samaria.

Note the causative use of *min*, cf. Isa. 50.2, *mē'ēn mayim*, 'because there is no water'.

Logically one negative should cancel another, but in Hebrew one reinforces the other, cf. Ex. 14.11; Eccles. 3.11, cf. *GK* 152y.

The use of *dibber* for *'āmar* throughout this chapter is one feature which singles it out from the rest of the Elijah-cycle.

1.4. On the retention of the conjunction *w*[e] before *lākēn* see p. 461 n.[b].

5. On the ellipse of a stage in the narrative before this verse see p. 461 n.[c]. This is further indicated by the reference to the personal pronoun without an antecedent in MT. The surprise of the king at the return of the emissaries suggests that the encounter with Elijah was not far from Samaria. The mention of Elijah on a hill-top indicates the same. The direct road to Ekron ran west from Samaria, emerging from the hills to the coastal plain about seven miles from Samaria. The encounter could well have been in the neighbourhood of Samaria.

7. *mišpāṭ*, derived from *šāpaṭ* ('to govern'), signifies primarily rule and order, hence 'disposition' or 'manner' in general.

8. *ba'al śē'ār* might signify 'a hairy man', i.e. with long hair and beard, or one clad in a rough, shaggy cloak, which was actually recognized as the insignia of a prophet (Zech. 13.4) and was the mantle of asceticism of John the Baptist (Matt. 3.4) and the Sufis of Islam. The girdle of leather or probably undressed skin was also part of the distinctive clothing of John the Baptist, possibly to signify his status as the forerunner of the Messiah, the status accorded to Elijah in popular tradition based on Mal. 4.5 [3.23].

9. The rank 'captain of fifty' indicates the organization of a professional standing army, a feature of the Hebrew monarchy.

10. *'îš 'elōhîm* ('man of God') in the peremptory address of the captain may be derogatory, as Šanda (II, p. 5) suggests, ranking Elijah with the numerous dervishes of the land. Note the word-play in *'îš 'elōhîm* and *'ēš 'elōhîm*, cf. similar suggestions through assonance in prophecy in Amos 8.2 (*qayiṣ-qēṣ*) and Jer. 1.11f. (*šāqēd-šōqēd*).

1.13. *nepeš* here has the meaning it generally has in the Old Testament of physical life.

(iii) DEUTERONOMISTIC EPILOGUE ON THE REIGN OF AHAZIAH: 1.17b–18

1 [17B] [a]And Jehoram his brother[b] reigned after him [c]in the second year of Jehoram the son of Jehoshaphat king of Judah,[c] for he had no son.[a] [18]And as for the rest of the acts of Ahaziah which he did, are they not written in the Book of the Chronicles of the Kings of Israel?

17. On the apparent chronological discrepancy in the dating of the accession of Jehoram of Israel in the second year of Jehoram of Judah and, according to 3.1, in the 18th year of Jehoshaphat of Judah, and on our solution in the co-regency of Jehoram of Judah in 853, the year of the Qarqar campaign, which was also the 17th year of Jehoshaphat, see Introduction: Chronology.

(*k*) ANECDOTES OF ELISHA AND HISTORICAL EPISODES FROM HIS TIME: 2.1–8.29; 13.14–21

In the matter concerning Elisha there are two main sources, first an Elisha-saga concerned with incidents in which Elisha was directly involved, and second, historical narrative where the main focus of interest is in the events in the wider perspective of history, in which Elisha was involved, but was not the main focus of interest. In the former, miracle plays a large part; in the latter, Elisha is a figure of credible historical proportions, usually reflecting the attitude of the conservative party in Israel towards the monarchy, as in his response to the king of Israel in the siege of Samaria (6.24–7.20) and his part in the revolt of Jehu (9.1ff.). In the more strictly historical narrative, history is related in the style of popular narrative, as notably in the account of the siege of Samaria (6.24–7.20). Both elements have been well categorized by Šanda (II, pp. 37ff.), whose classification we largely adopt in the following more detailed analysis of this matter.

[a]The historical note of the accession of Jehoram, with the synchronism with the reign of the king of Judah, is omitted in G^B, possibly because of the note on his accession in 3.1 and the apparent discrepancy of the latter with the synchronism here in v. 17 (see commentary).

[b]Inserting 'his brother' with G^L, Theodotion, S, and V.

[c]See n.[a] G^L omits.

I. Elisha among the sons of the prophets:

The translation of Elijah and the transmission of prophetic authority to Elisha, and the dividing of Jordan (2.1–18).
The restoration of the spring at Jericho (2.19–22).
The punishment of the boys of Bethel (2.23f.).
Death in the pot (4.38–41).
The feeding of 100 prophets of Gilgal (4.42–44).
The recovery of the axehead from Jordan (6.1–7).
The miraculous power of the bones of Elisha (13.20f.).

These anecdotes have certain common features. They are concerned with miracles and have generally no point beyond demonstrating the miraculous power and authority of Elisha. They concern the prophet in association with prophetic groups and are largely located at shrines where these groups lived, at Gilgal, Bethel, and by Jericho and the Jordan. In the Elijah-saga in I K. 17–19 the prophet is the great individualist and there is little trace of the relationship of Elijah to prophetic circles. In these anecdotes of Elisha this relationship is fundamental. It is hard to avoid the conclusion that the Elisha-saga took shape in these dervish circles, those at various shrines associated with Elisha possibly competing with one another in the local miracles which they related of the prophet, until eventually the various local traditions were collected, combined and recorded in the Elisha-saga as we now have it. Such historical sources as the story of Jehu's revolt (ch. 9) indicate that Elisha, like Elijah, was a figure of real historical significance, but, as the subject of hagiology in the group of anecdotes we have noted, he suffers in comparison with Elijah. This is no doubt owing to the fact that whereas the authority of Elisha gave the stamp of final authenticity to the traditions of his older contemporary Elijah, no single great figure did the same for him, but in their very zeal to enhance the reputation of Elisha the dervish fellowships actually impaired it by their emphasis on miracle for its own sake.

It will be noticed that we admit the story of Elijah's translation (ch. 2) into this group of the Elisha traditions. The element of miracle and the association with the prophetic communities suggest that it belongs here rather than with the stories of the great individualist Elijah in the Elijah-saga proper, where the element of miracle is strictly subordinate to the role of the prophet in historical crises. Actually ch. 2 is really the prelude to the Elisha-saga and concerns the transfer to him of the prophetic power and authority of Elijah.

II. Anecdotes of the individual Elisha:

The multiplication of the widow's oil (4.1–7).
Elisha and the Shunammite woman (4.8–37).

In both cases there are echoes of the Elijah-saga (I K. 17.8–24). This suggested to Benzinger and Winckler that these stories of Elisha are just doublets of the Elijah tradition. The real explanation may be that in both cases the association with a man of God was regarded as conferring the blessing (*b^erākā*) which he was admitted to enjoy, and that was held to be the reason for the relief experienced in want or sickness, which through repetition in oral tradition was expanded to the dimensions of miracle. In simple fact there is no reason to doubt that the two traditions are independent, but in details with which they were transmitted the earlier tradition of Elijah probably coloured the later one of Elisha, and to this extent we agree with Benzinger and Winckler. Whatever the source of these traditions of Elisha, they comprise in their extant form a distinct literary unit from a single hand, the distinctive feature being Aramaisms throughout, which will be noted in our commentary. There are certain other linguistic peculiarities noted by Šanda (II, pp. 79ff.). Here, as distinct from the first group of Elisha stories, the prophet is not associated with prophetic groups. Nevertheless in the first episode, which is not specifically located, the widow was the relict of a member of a prophetic community, who was known to Elisha (v. 1), and in the second Elisha is obviously a man of God (v. 9) who was in the habit of paying regular visits to Carmel (cf. 2.25), probably to a prophetic community there. The miraculous is prominent here as in the incidents regarding Elisha among the prophets; hence this section, too, may be from a prophetic guild on Carmel. The comparative isolation of this community from those in the south at Bethel or the two Gilgals may account for the dialectal peculiarities (Aramaisms) which characterize this section.

III. Elisha in the setting of contemporary history:

This matter may be subdivided as follows:

(*a*) Elisha in single incidents involving miracle in a setting credibly historical:

The healing of Naaman (ch. 5).

Elisha as the saviour of Israel from the Aramaeans (6.8–23, the blinding of the Aramaeans, to which on grounds of literary style and the common historical situation 6.24–7.20 should be added, though here no miracle is involved, but a prediction and its sequel, the death of the incredulous notable of Samaria, which is cited to enhance the prophetic authority of Elisha).

In these stories the historical situation is somewhat different. At the time of Naaman's mission there is peace, but a certain tension, between Israel and Damascus, and there have obviously been comparatively recent hostilities, whereas in 6.24 the Aramaeans actually lay siege to Samaria. There is, however, much in common. In neither case is Elisha associated with prophetic guilds, but has his house in Samaria, where he is apparently a conspicuous figure. In spite of such common ground it is probable that the story of the healing of Naaman is a tradition distinct from that of Elisha's part in the Aramaean invasion (6.8–23) and in the siege of Samaria (6.24–7.20), the second of which is characterized by certain precise reflections of actual historical background (e.g. the mention of the kings of the Hittites and Musri in Cilicia, 7.6). These traditions are distinct from the Elisha hagiology which stemmed from the prophetic guilds, and distinct also from the stories of Elisha and the widow and the Shunammite, with their distinctive Aramaisms. In view of the location of the prophet at Samaria, a Samarian source is not unlikely, and the sense of the historical situation in chs. 6 and 7 probably reflects the mature political views of Elisha shared by some personal associate such as his attendant Gehazi.

(β) Elisha in a minor incident in a historical situation, where secular history is treated at length and is the focus of attention, giving his practical advice and reassuring oracle in the Moabite campaign (3.4–27).

In this passage the activity of Elisha is limited to vv. 11–19, and the rest of the chapter describes the general course of the campaign and, with more detail, its termination, with the genuine ring of a good historical source. Opinions, however, vary as to the historical worth of the passage. Benzinger (II, p. 132) regards it as a somewhat fanciful reconstruction of history round the incident of the prophet, and even A. Weiser[a] in his appraisal of its worth admits the elements

[a] *Introduction to the Old Testament*, pp. 175ff.

both of legend and of history. We would agree with Eissfeldt,[a] who emphasizes the subsidiary role of Elisha in a primarily historical narrative. In the part played by Elisha, miracle is absent, and the oracle and practical advice which he gives are quite natural in the circumstances. Indeed, in the prophet's use of music to induce ecstasy a certain limitation is implied which would never have been admitted by the hagiographers, whose aim was to magnify the power of the prophet. The fact that Elisha subserves the interest of the state distinguishes this passage from those we have already noticed. This passage, in fact, is not really part of the Elisha-saga at all, but is a historical narrative in which Elisha as a prophet of Israel is mentioned incidentally as any other prophet might have been. So far is Elisha from being a central figure in this episode that he is described as the servant of Elijah (v. 11) of apparently recent memory. In this detail the narrative is probably true to historical fact, a further authentication being the unsuccessful termination of the campaign which is admitted (v. 27). Šanda (II, p. 81) conjectures that 3.4ff. is part of the historical narrative to which I K. 20 and 22 belong, and certainly there are many common elements. The narratives commonly refer to 'the king of Israel', whom they seldom name, as distinct from the king of Judah, Jehoshaphat, who is regularly named, and in both I K. 22 and II K. 3.4ff. the assumption is that the court prophets are deluders. Šanda's view is most feasible, that this is a continuation of the story of the house of Omri completed soon after the death of Elisha (*c.* 790), before legend had had time to magnify the prophet. A similar episode, where the prophet, true to his calling, directs a rite of imitative magic, is the story of Elisha on his death-bed and the king with 'the arrows of victory' (13.14–19). 13.4ff. and 13.14–19, and probably also 6.8–23 and 6.24–7.30, are historical narrative adapted by the same prophetic hand as adapted the historical narrative in I K. 20.1–34 and I K. 22 and the story of the revolt of Jehu when the doom of the house of Ahab was fulfilled.

(γ) Elisha as protagonist in high politics:
Elisha and the *coup d'état* of Hazael (8.7–15).

Here the role of the prophet, though important, is restrained. Summoned as a healer in the sickness of the king, presumably through his reputation after the healing of Naaman, he inspires the usurper Hazael by his oracle. The apparent fulfilment in these cases of the

[a] *The Old Testament. An Introduction*, p. 295.

oracles to Elijah at Horeb in I K. 19.15ff. raises the question of the priority of I K. 19.15ff. or II K. 8.7–15 and 9.1–6, and the balance of probability must rest in favour of the latter, since the commission to Elijah in the case of Hazael and Jehu was not fulfilled, and indeed the rise of those private individuals to the throne was hardly likely to have been foreseen as early as the time of Elijah. This passage, like 9.1–6, where Elisha's role is perhaps due to the prophetic editor of the historical narrative, we should exclude from the Elisha-saga and regard as part of a primarily historical work. In both instances there is a basis of historical fact, and it may even be argued that the restrained role of the prophet points to the historicity of his part in those events. Elisha, for instance, is not said to have anointed Hazael, but merely to have given him an oracle, a fact which may well suggest a near-contemporary source, while the circumstantial detail of Hazael's *coup* indicates intimate knowledge which may rest on the personal communication of Elisha. Nevertheless, whatever its historical basis, this matter has been coloured in communication by the style of saga, of which 'forty camel-loads of all the good things of Damascus' is an obvious feature.[a] This, too, belongs to the prophetic adaptation of the historical narrative of events in the time of the house of Ahab, though this aspect of the work does not obtrude itself except in the final passage in the account of Jehu's eradication of the family of Omri and Jezebel, when Elijah's oracle of doom is emphasized.

From the part which the prophet plays in the Elisha-saga proper, where he is a figure of supernatural stature, and from the stylistic features of lively dialogue, verbal repetition, and dramatic suspense to stimulate interest, it seems highly probable that the traditions of Elisha had a considerable period of oral development. They bear all the distinctive marks of the oral story-teller like the Arab *rāwī*. From the common features and viewpoint of the first group of Elisha stories we have noted, which depict Elisha as a wonder-worker among the sons of the prophets, there seems little doubt that the various local traditions from such circles were gathered together and possibly committed to writing by someone, himself from these circles, after the death of the prophet *c.* 790, probably a considerable time after his death, when he had grown to legendary proportions. The second group, with ch. 5, 6.8–23, and 6.24–7.20 in the third group, is distinguished from the first by Aramaisms, which are absent in the first group. Chapter 5, 6.8–23, and 6.24–7.20, depicting the role of

[a]Gressmann, *Die älteste Geschichtsschreibung*, p. 304.

Elisha in Samaria and in the Aramaean wars, stem from a different source, which we have proposed to find in circles in Samaria personally associated with the prophet. The emphasis on the miraculous, however, as in the story of the healing of Naaman (ch. 5) and in the blinding of the Syrians (6.8–23), may reflect the influence of the first group of Elisha traditions at a time when the first and the third groups were being combined. The second group also probably originated in Samaria, as is suggested by the story of the rehabilitation of the Shunammite woman (8.1–6), which is most naturally located at the capital. This passage, in fact, may give us a clue to the source of the second group of Elisha stories, with which the incident is organically connected. The incident is dated after the death of the prophet, when a certain biographical interest is indicated by the king's request, 'Tell me, I pray thee, all the great things that Elisha did' (8.4). Interest was stimulated because of the prophet's public reputation in the matter of such events in the history of Israel as are recorded in the third group of stories, but more precise information is sought from Elisha's personal attendant Gehazi, and it is significant that there is a direct reference to the revival of the Shunammite's son in the second group of Elisha stories. There seems little doubt that the source of this group of traditions was Gehazi, or some such personal associate of Elisha in Samaria, some considerable time after his death.

Since the third group of traditions deals with the Aramaean wars and reflects with considerable accuracy details of the political situation, the Elisha-saga, as far as concerns this matter, was completed before the fall of Damascus in 731. This was some 60 years after the death of the prophet, but the reference we have just cited from ch. 8 indicates that these events in which the prophet was involved were decidedly a living memory.

Such passages as 3.4ff. and 9.1–6, which are primarily historical, serve to set Elisha in proper historical perspective and to control the traditions regarding him in the Elisha-saga proper.

For reasons cited above we should retain the incident of Elisha at Damascus in the *coup d'état* of Hazael as historical, in spite of its saga features and its alleged artificial relation to the oracle to Elijah regarding Hazael. So long as the real motive of Elisha's alleged intervention in Aramaean politics in unknown, we cannot reject the tradition of his acclamation of Hazael, as Gressmann does, on the grounds of its improbability.

(i) THE TRANSLATION OF ELIJAH AND THE COMMISSION OF ELISHA: 2.1–18

For the inclusion of this tradition in the Elisha- rather than in the Elijah-cycle see critical introduction to this section, pp. 466f. The independence of the two traditions is indicated by the fact that the present passage ignores the passage in I K. 19 where Elijah designates Elisha as his successor by throwing his mantle upon him, and by the emphasis in 2.1–8 on the association of the older prophet with prophetic guilds, in contrast to the Elijah-saga proper, where the prophet is an individualist. Eissfeldt (*HSAT*, p. 544) points out that the incident interrupts the Deuteronomistic obituary on Ahaziah (II K. 1.18) and the editorial introduction of Joram (3.1–3), this suggesting that the passage is a late addition after the framework of the first compilation of Kings had been established, and so not an original element in the Elisha-cycle. The fact that the title 'the chariot of Israel and the horsemen thereof' is applied to Elisha in a tradition more securely anchored in an historical context (13.14) suggests that this was properly the title of Elisha, who was more involved in external politics than Elijah, and that the present story of Elijah's translation is really secondary to the tradition of his bequeathing of a double portion of the prophetic spirit to Elisha, as Eissfeldt suggests.

2 1 Now it happened, when Yahweh would take Elijah up to heaven
in the whirlwind, that Elijah and Elisha set out from Gilgal. 2 And
Elijah said to Elisha, Remain here, for Yahweh has sent me to Bethel.
And Elisha said, As Yahweh lives and you live, I shall not leave you.
So they went down to Bethel. 3 And the sons of the prophets who were
in Bethel came out to Elisha and said to him, Do you know that today
Yahweh is going to take your master from your head? And he said, I
also know it. Keep silence. 4 And Elijah said to Elisha,[a] Stay here, for
Yahweh has sent me to Jericho. And he said, As Yahweh lives and as
you live, I shall not leave you. And they came to Jericho. 5 And the
sons of the prophets who were at Jericho drew near to Elisha and said to
him, Do you know that today Yahweh is going to take your master from
your head? And he said, I also know it. Keep silence. 6 And Elijah
said to him, Stay here, for Yahweh has sent me to the Jordan. And he
said, As Yahweh lives and as you live, I shall not leave you. And the
two of them went on. 7 And fifty men of the sons of the prophets went
and stood over against them at a distance, and the two of them stood
by the Jordan. 8 And Elijah took his mantle and rolled it up[b] and struck

[a] So G, S, and V for MT *wayyōʾmer lō ēlīyāhū ʾ^{e}lišāʿ*.

[b] Reading *way^{e}gall^{e}lennā*, though this is unsupported by any Version. The MT verbal form *glm* is not attested elsewhere in the Old Testament, though Ezek. 27.24 attests the noun *g^{e}lōmīm* ('a wrap').

the water, and it was divided this way and that, and the two of them
crossed over on dry land. 9And it happened, when they crossed, that
Elijah said to Elisha, Ask[a] what I may do for you before I am taken
from you. And Elisha said, Well,[b] let me have a double portion of your
spirit. 10And he said, It is a hard thing you ask. If you see me taken
from you then[c] may it be so; and if you do not see (me taken) it will
not be so. 11And it happened that, as they were going on their way,
talking as they were going, behold, there was a fiery chariot and horses
of fire and they separated the two of them, and Elijah was taken up[d] to
heaven in the whirlwind. 12And Elisha saw it and he cried out, My
father! My father! the chariotry of Israel and the horsemen[e] thereof!
And he did not see him again. And he seized hold of his clothes and tore
them in two pieces. 13And he lifted up the mantle of Elijah which had
fallen off him and went back and stood on the bank of the Jordan,
14 [f]And he took the mantle of Elijah which had fallen from off him[f] and
struck the water[g] and said, Where is Yahweh the God of Elijah, even
he?[h] And he struck the water and it divided this way and that, and
Elisha crossed over. 15And the sons of the prophets who were in Jericho
over against him saw him and said, The spirit of Elijah has come to
rest upon Elisha. And they came to meet him and bowed down before
him to the ground. 16And they said to him, See, there are with your
servants fifty able men. Let them go now to seek your master, in case
the spirit of Yahweh has taken him up and cast him upon some mountain or into some valley.[i] But he said, You shall not send them. 17And
they insisted until he felt shame and said to them, Send them. So they
sent fifty men, and they searched three days, but did not find him.
18So they returned to him, he staying in Jericho. And he said to them,
Did I not tell you, Do not go?

2.1 The definite article with 'whirlwind' indicates that the writer is alluding to a well-known tradition regarding the translation of Elijah.

Gilgal, as indicated by the fact that Elijah and Elisha 'went down'

[a]G[B] omits 'ask', which gives quite good sense.

[b]G omits the conjunction before *y[e]hī*. The conjunction, however, connects the request of Elisha with the invitation of Elijah.

[c]Restoring the conjunction *w[e]* before *y[e]hī* after G[BA].

[d]Pointing MT *wayyaʿal* ('and he went up') as Hophal *wayyōʿal*, as suggested by G *anelēmphthē*.

[e]G and V read the singular.

[f]This phrase, or at least the relative clause in it, is possibly to be omitted as a scribal repetition of the phraseology of the preceding verse.

[g]G[L] and certain MSS of V read 'and it (the water) was not divided' (*w[e]lō' neḥ[e]ṣū*), which seems feasible in view of the response elicited from Elisha, 'Where is Yahweh the God of Elijah?'

[h]G[BA] transliterate *aphphō*, which may suggest the reading *'ēpō'* ('Where?'). It would be strange to find such a sudden change from one interrogative *'ayyē* to another in the scope of one verse.

[i]Following Q, as is demanded by the general sense of the passage.

(v. 2) to Bethel, cannot be the famous national shrine between Jericho and the Jordan. Actually the name is a common one in Palestine, signifying 'stone circle', and there are several sites *Jiljilīyeh* in the country. The one here denoted is generally located about eight miles north of Bethel. This, too, is lower than Bethel, but a journey from there to Bethel involves an ascent to higher ground between the two sites, so that eventually one does go down to Bethel. Šanda, however (II, p. 10), suggests a location further west of *Jiljilīyeh*, about six miles west of *Kefr Tulṯ*, about 16 miles north of Lydda. He associates the prophetic community at Gilgal with Baalshalisha (4.38–44), located at either *Ḫirbet Sarisīyeh* (Baithsarissa of Eusebius, *Onomasticon*) about 14 miles north of Lydda, or with *Kefr Tulṯ*.

2.3. Here and in this group of stories of Elisha we are introduced more intimately to the communities of prophets or dervishes who lived and practised in the vicinity of shrines. The community at the national shrine of Bethel was certainly numerous and influential, and was probably one of the main sources of the Elisha hagiology, as of the traditions of the denunciation of Jeroboam and the mishap of the prophet of Judah (I K. 13.).

5. This is the first mention of Jericho as the centre of one of those prophetic communities, which were generally associated with shrines. Jericho itself was not a cult-centre, and, indeed, until quite recently had lain largely desolate under a sacred ban. Doubtless the shrine to which the prophets were attached was Gilgal, to be located near *Ḫirbet Mafjar* about two miles north-east of *Tell as-Sulṭān* (ancient Jericho). This is still between Jericho and the Jordan, where the narrative in Josh. 4.19 demands the location. This site shows evidence of Iron Age occupation and agrees with Josephus's location[a] '50 stades from the ford of the Jordan' in contrast to the traditional location south-east of Jericho near the traditional site of the baptism of Jesus, where occupation does not antedate the Byzantine period.[b] Gilgal was a significant shrine in the early history of Israel, and as the tradition of the setting up of 12 stones (Josh. 4.20) indicates, it was a cult-centre of the 12-tribe amphictyony where the tribes east and west of the Jordan realized their solidarity.[c] It was associated with the work of Samuel as a judge (I Sam. 7.16) and was the place where the

[a] *Ant.* V, 1.4.

[b] A. M. Schneider, 'Das byzantinische Gilgal', *ZDPV* LIV, 1931, pp. 50ff.

[c] Cf. K. Mohlenbrink (*ZAW* LVI, 1938, pp. 238ff.), who regards Gilgal as first the shrine of an amphictyony of three tribes, Reuben, Gad and Benjamin.

kingship of Saul was formally consecrated (reading *n^eqaddēš* for MT *n^eḥaddēš* in I Sam. 11.14) after his relief of Jabesh-Gilead, and was the rallying-point for national resistance in Saul's Philistine wars (I Sam. 13.4–15) and the scene of the hewing of Agag in pieces before the Lord (I Sam. 15.33). Though the importance of the sanctuary at Gilgal probably waned with the passing of power from Benjamin to the house of David and the new significance of Jerusalem as the seat of the ark and the national shrine, it never quite lost its significance, and was probably always a centre of pilgrimage, a religious institution always in much favour among the Semites. It was certainly a place of pilgrimage in the middle of the eighth century and ranked with Bethel, the national shrine (Amos 4.4; 5.5; Hos. 4.15; 9.15; 12.11 [12]). The significance of this shrine as a conservatory of the traditions of the Hebrew occupation has been emphasized by Alt, Noth, H. J. Kraus, and K. Galling. It is feasibly suggested that the sacramental experience at the shrine of Gilgal has coloured the narrative of the conquest in Josh. 1–9 and Judg. 2.1–5.

2.8. The mantle (*'adderet*) was the long loose cloak, Arabic *ʿabāya*. Wonders associated with a certain locality tend to be repeated in tradition in connection with other great personalities and events associated with the same locality. In this case the crossing of the Jordan by Elijah and Elisha re-echoes the crossing of the Israelites under Joshua, which itself may be influenced by the tradition of the crossing of the Sea at the Exodus or be a rite in the amphictyonic sacrament at Gilgal.[a]

9. Elisha in asking for a double portion of the spirit which inspired Elijah was not seeking to excel his master, but to receive the double portion which by Hebrew law (Deut. 12.17) was the share of the eldest son. Elisha wished to be recognized and equipped as the true successor of Elijah.

11. The mention of the whirlwind with the definite article after the chariot and horses of fire suggests a necessary connection, and, as the former was a natural phenomenon, the latter may also have been. The whirlwind and sudden disappearance of Elijah suggests a dust-devil, which might accompany the sirocco east of the Jordan. Fire suggests the sirocco, and the visible progress of an accompanying dust-storm might be compared to horses and chariots. The comparatively late origin of this literary unit, on the other hand (see critical

[a]H. J. Kraus, 'Gilgal, ein Beitrag zur Kultusgeschichte Israels', *VT* I, 1951, pp. 190ff.

introduction to the section p. 472), should warn us against seeking a rationalistic interpretation, and the genesis of the tradition may simply be the elaboration of the title 'the chariotry of Israel and the horsemen thereof', originally the title of Elisha, now transferred to Elijah. Another explanation is that this may be a case of historification of a native myth or cult-legend. The horse was well known in antiquity as the cult-animal of the sun (cf. II K. 23.11), so that the story of Elijah may be fused here through local association with an old solar cult-legend. Again, the renewal of the power of the old prophet in his successor suggests the renewal of the power of the Phoenician nature-god in the local cultic variation of the phoenix-myth.[a] The element of fire, on the other hand, apart from the rationalistic and mythological explanations we have suggested, is a common motif in accounts of theophanies, e.g. Ex. 3.2; 24.17; Isa. 30.27; Hab. 3.3–5; Deut. 33.2. The theophany at the disappearance of Elijah may have been elaborated to emphasize the presence of God and so to enhance the authority to which Elisha fell heir.

2.12. 'My father' (*'ābī*) expresses respect and dependence.

rekeb is to be taken here probably as collective, 'chariotry' rather than 'chariot', and in 13.14 is expressive of the power that Elisha was recognized to be in Israel. Šanda (II, p. 12) felicitously cites the analogy of the title accorded by Muhammad to the great general Khālid ibn al-Walīd, 'The Sword of Allah'. We consider rather fanciful Fohrer's suggestion[b] that this expresses the conception that Elijah was now recruited to continue his struggle with God's heavenly host.

16. *b^enē ḥayil* is ambiguous. It may refer to strong, active men capable of endurance in the search for Elijah. It often means 'men of substance' able, and expected, to maintain themselves or substitutes in readiness for war. Such persons may be signified here if the prophets perhaps considered that Elijah had been kidnapped by Bedouin. The former possibility is the more likely. The prophets also consider the possibility that 'the spirit of Yahweh' had carried Elijah away and cast him on to some mountain or into some ravine. Here *rūaḥ yhwh* might refer to the sudden, and to ancients inexplicable, onset of a whirlwind. It might again refer to the ecstatic experience of Elijah under which he was not *compos sui* and so liable to come to

[a]R. de Vaux, 'Les prophètes de Baal sur le mont Carmel', *BMB* V, 1941, pp. 19f., citing Nonnos of Pannopolis and Lucian, *De Dea Syra*.

[b]*Elia*, 1968², p. 100.

harm in the broken country in the escarpment of Moab, where he might fall in a ravine or be exposed to hunger and thirst in the fierce heat of that vast depression.

(ii) THE RESTORATION OF THE SPRING AT JERICHO: 2.19–22

This episode is doubtless part of the Elisha hagiology of the prophetic community of Gilgal in the vicinity of Jericho. It is, we think, a ritual of release from the curse upon the site of Jericho, which was effected in conjunction with the rebuilding of the site under Ahab (I K. 16.34) in, or just before, the time of Elisha, and which has been elaborated by tradition, through local association, into a miracle of the prophet.

2 19And the men of the city said to Elisha, Behold, the situation of the city[a] is good, as my lord sees, but the water is bad and the land fails of fruition.[b] 20And he said, Take me a new dish and put salt into it. And they took it to him. 21And he went out to the source of the water and cast salt into it and said, Thus says Yahweh, I have refertilized the water. No longer shall death and barrenness come from it. 22So this water was refertilized[c] (and so it remains) to this day according to the word of Elisha which he spoke.

2.19. The spring on which the fertility of the land depended was the copious spring now called *'Ain as-Sulṭān* at the foot of the mound of ancient Jericho, with its record of occupation from the Neolithic Age till the late Iron Age. Since the unhappy division of Palestine after the end of the British Mandate the oasis of Jericho has greatly expanded, largely watered by the distribution of water from this spring. In a recent geological and hydrological survey of the Wilderness of Judah south of Jericho, it has been observed that certain springs are affected by radio-activity, which laboratory tests have demonstrated to cause sterility, which was noticed at Jericho in this passage. J. M. Blake in presenting this evidence[d] has cited similar instances from Kenya. This would be occasioned by contact of the

[a]G[L] reads 'this city', adding *hazzō't*, which is feasible but not strictly necessary.

[b]G[L] omits 'the land' and reads *m^ešakk^elīm*, agreeing with *mayim*, for MT *m^ešakkelet* agreeing with *hā'āreṣ*. In Mal. 3.11, however, the active participle of this verb (Piel) is used with *gepen* ('vine') to indicate failure of fruition, hence we retain MT.

[c]The verb is certainly *rāpā'* with final *aleph*, which is included in Q and in two MSS of MT.

[d]*PEQ*, 1967, pp. 86–97.

water with radio-active geological strata. The apparently sudden contamination and clearing of the water may have been due to geological shifts in that notoriously unstable area in the great rift valley, or even to such a slight factor as the shift of the water-table in a drought. This empirical fact, rather than Joshua's reputed curse, may have accounted for the dereliction of such an apparently favoured site as Jericho, which archaeology attested for about half a millennium, and the dereliction may have been the source of the tradition of Joshua's curse rather than vice versa. On the association of the effect of a curse through the waters of a region, cf. the oath of purgation taken by the elders of a community suspected of manslaughter by the source of a perennial wadi (Deut. 21.1–9), so that in case of perjury the curse would operate in all the land watered by the spring.

2.20. Blake has suggested that the salt may have been used rather to test the reaction of the water for infection, but the association with a 'new dish' indicates that it was an element in a rite of separation. Since the archaeological evidence attests the limited occupation of Jericho in the ninth century, Elisha may have been associated with these rites. When a city was destroyed the site was sown with salt to symbolize a complete break with the past.[a] Similarly offerings were removed from the realm of the profane by the ritual use of salt (Lev. 2.13; Num. 18.19; Ezek. 43.24) and the rubbing of a new-born child in modern Arab society, as in ancient times (Ezek. 16.4), signifies the division between the former 'unclean' state of the child and his normal status as a member of the society. So the use of salt in a new dish was part of the ritual separating Jericho and its vital spring from the realm of the 'holy' for common occupation, thought to have been forbidden under the sanction of the curse (Josh. 6.17, 26). Jericho, as the archaeological evidence indicates (see on I K. 16.34), had already been occupied to some extent in the Iron Age, but was probably thinly populated in consequence of the apprehension of the curse, so that it was not a prosperous community. The '*new* dish' is significant in magical ritual, in which it is necessary to use an article the virtue of which is unimpaired and which has not been subject to any influence which might counteract the magic rites, cf. new ropes in the Samson story (Judg. 16.11), a new cart for the ark (I Sam. 6.7; II Sam. 6.3), Ahijah's new mantle in his rite of prophetic

[a]Cf. Judg. 9.45, though in this case the rite may have been to counteract the influence of the blood of kindred shed by Abimelech. See A. M. Honeyman, 'The Salting of Shechem', *VT* III, 1953, pp. 192–5.

symbolism (I K. 11.29). The resettlement of Jericho must have been attended with many such rites in view of the consciousness of the ancient curse.

ṣ[e]*lōḥit* is a variant of *ṣallaḥat*, which in Prov. 19.24; 26.15 signifies a dish out of which one eats. This, however, in the usage of the ancient East may also have been the open cooking-pot (*ṣēlāḥā*, cf. II Chron. 35.13), which was set in the middle of the company for all to stretch forth the hand and take 'pot luck'.

2.21. *rāpā'* means regularly in Hebrew 'to heal'. Here, however, we maintain that it means specifically 'to restore to fertility', as in the case of the restoration of the fertility of the harem of Abimelech of Gerar (Gen. 20.17). In the 'Aqht text and associated fragments in the Ras Shamra texts we consider the participle of this verb to be used of the ancient king Dan'il and certain of his associates in connection with agricultural ritual.[a] It is well known that the king in primitive society was the channel of divine blessing to flock and field.

(iii) ELISHA AND THE RUDE BOYS OF BETHEL: 2.23–25

This is in every respect a puerile tale, and serves as a gauge of the moral level of the dervish communities from which the strictly hagiographical matter in the Elisha cycle emanated. In such circles miracles abounded and credulity flourished. There is no serious point in this incident, and it does not reflect much to the credit of the prophet. It is difficult to regard it otherwise than as, at the best, the memory of some catastrophe which happened to coincide with Elisha's visit to Bethel and was turned to account by the local dervish-community to awe their children. These prophets were not all celibate (II K. 4.1) and we may well suppose that familiarity bred contempt in the children of these men, whose extravagant eccentricities must have been a regular source of amusement. There is no doubt that the source of the tradition is Bethel, though the statement that the incident happened on Elisha's journey from Jericho after his restoration of the water and other incidents there betrays the hand of the compiler of the various local traditions.

2 [23]And he went up from there to Bethel, and as he was going up on the road little boys came out from the city and mocked him saying to him, Up, Baldy! Up, Baldy! [24]And he turned after them[b] and looked upon them and cursed them in the name of Yahweh, and there came out of the scrub two she-bears and lacerated forty-two boys of them.

[a]J. Gray, *The Legacy of Canaan*, 1965[2], p. 211.
[b]So G[BA] for MT 'behind him'.

25So he went from there to Mount Carmel and from there he went back to Samaria.

2.23. The reference could not have been to natural baldness, since the oriental, particularly a stranger on a journey as distinct from a slave or labourer at work, would not have had his head uncovered. Hence it was a kind of tonsure as a mark of the separation of the prophet from the profane sphere of life to the service of God. This was inferred by the boys, who knew Elisha as a prophet by his mantle, and were familiar with the tonsure, since many of them were themselves the progeny of prophets of Bethel and all were familiar with the conventions of the large dervish-community there.

24. The supposition that Elisha invoked the name of Yahweh to curse the boys, with such terrible consequences, is derogatory to the great public figure, and borders on blasphemy. That this passage is part of a prophetic saga rather than strict history is indicated by the number 42, the conventional nature of which is suggested by the 42 victims of Jehu (10.14) and by the 42 months of the supremacy of the beast in Revelation (13.5). In these cases 2 may be added to 40, the conventional indefinite number in Semitic folk-lore, to give the impression of accuracy, cf. 'fifty siller bells and nine' of Border ballads.

yaʿar signifies not 'forest' but rather *maquis*. Bears were known until quite recently in the Hermon massif. Montgomery cites the mention of bears in the vicinity of Shayzar on the Orontes by Usāma ibn Munqidh, who in his colourful memoirs frequently mentions lions also in his hunting exploits in the 12th century AD.

25. Perhaps the mention of Carmel and Samaria is not so much a description of the actual itinerary of Elisha on this occasion as an editorial note occasioned by his known association with those places. He was at Carmel when the Shunammite woman appealed to him (4.25) and at Samaria when he was visited by Naaman (ch. 5) and during the Aramaean siege of the city (ch. 6). Eissfeldt, on the other hand (*HSAT*, p. 545), suggests that an original 'Gilgal', north-east of Bethel, has been altered to Samaria in view of the sequel.

(iv) THE MOABITE EXPEDITION AND THE ADVENT OF ELISHA IN PUBLIC LIFE: 3.1–27

For the literary affinities of this primarily historical narrative, in which interest in Elisha is secondary, see literary introduction to this section.

The passage is introduced by the Deuteronomistic notice of the accession of Jehoram and the length of his reign (v. 1) and the assessment of his reign on Deuteronomistic principles (vv. 2ff). The synchronism with the reign of Jehoshaphat king of Judah (v. 1) rather than that of his son Joram, as in 1.17, is to be noted. The statements are not contradictory, since in Judah's involvement in Israelite politics Jehoram was probably co-regent with his father, who evidently withdrew from public life in favour of his son in 848, a year before his death. The different synchronisms, however, may point to two different sources, or possibly to the two different Deuteronomistic editions. The main body of the chapter is historical narrative, and the role of Jehoshaphat in insisting on prophetic guidance (v. 11) may indicate the prophetic adaptation of the historical narrative as in I K. 20 and 22 and a Judaean version of the narrative. The passage has been linked by various scholars since Wellhausen with the historical narrative in I K. 20 and 22. With the second of these passages the present has much in common, notably the insistence of Jehoshaphat on prophetic revelation. Here the ultimate source is certainly North Israelite, but the role of Jehoshaphat suggests a Judaean edition of the story, as in I K. 22, which may account for the expansion of the story in narrative style beyond archival details. The fact that in 3.11 a North Israelite knows Elisha only as the servant of Elijah, while Jehoshaphat is represented as vouching for him as a prophet of Yahweh, suggests a later Judaean revision of the North Israelite historical source.

(*a*) *The Deuteronomistic introduction to the reign of Jehoram of Israel*: 3.1–3

3 [1]Now Jehoram the son of Ahab became king over Israel in Samaria[a] in the eighteenth year of Jehoshaphat king of Judah, and he reigned twelve years. [2]And he did evil in the sight of Yahweh, but not like his father[b] and his mother, for he removed the stele[c] of the Baal which his father had made.[d] [3]Only he adhered to the sin[e] of Jeroboam the son of Nebat, in which he involved Israel, and did not depart from it.[f]

[a]G^BL omit *bᵉšōmᵉrōn* ('in Samaria').

[b]In the variant form of this passage in 1.18 G has 'like his brother', whom he immediately succeeded.

[c]G and V read the plural.

[d]In the variant version in 1.18 G adds 'and broke them in pieces'.

[e]MT reads the plural, but the singular pronominal suffix with *min* indicates that the singular is to be read. In the variant version in 1.18 the plural is consistently read.

[f]MT *mimmennā*, cf. G (1.18), which adds 'and the anger of Yahweh was kindled against him and against the House of Ahab'.

3.1. On the synchronism here and in 1.17 see introduction to this section.

2. What precisely the stele (*maṣṣēbā*) of Baal was is uncertain. E. Dhorme, however,[a] aptly cites the Zenjirli steles (*nṣb*) of Panammu,[b] which carried both an inscription and relief of the god Hadad. To this evidence we may add the stele (*nṣb*) with short inscription set up by Barhadad the king of Aram to Baal-Melqart, who is depicted on it in bas-relief.[c]

(β) *The Moabite expedition:* 3.4–27

3 [4]Now Mesha[d] the king of Moab was a hepatoscopist [e](and he used to render to the king of Israel one hundred thousand wether lambs and one hundred thousand shearling rams).[e] [5]And it came to pass, when Ahab was dead, that the king of Moab rebelled against the king of Israel. [6]And king Jehoram went forth at that time from Samaria and mustered all Israel, [7]and[f] he sent to Jehoshaphat[g] king of Judah saying, The king of Moab has rebelled against me. Will you go with me to Moab to the war? And he said, I will go. I will be as you, my people shall be as your people, my horses as your horses. [8]And he said, By what road shall we go up? And he said, By way of the steppe of Edom. [9]So the king of Israel and the king of Judah and the king of Edom went and they fetched a compass of a journey of seven days, and there was no water for the army or for the beasts which followed them. [10]And the king of Israel said, Alas! for Yahweh has called these three kings to give them[h] into the hand of the king of Moab. [11]Then Jehoshaphat[i] said, Is there not here a prophet of Yahweh that we may seek an oracle of Yahweh from him?[j] And one of the servants of the king of Israel an-

[a]*L'évolution religieuse d'Israël* I, 1937, pp. 161ff.

[b]G. A. Cooke, *NSI*, 61, 62.

[c]M. Dunand, 'Stèle araméenne dédiée à Melqart', *BMB* III, 1941, pp. 65–76.

[d]G reads *Mōsa*, suggesting Hebrew *mōšāʿ* ('deliverance'), and in his inscription Mesha indulges in a word-play to this effect (lines 3f.). The traditional MT spelling of the name is supported by the analogy of the names Medad and Methar, both derived from *p/w* stems, yet written with an initial *y*.

[e]We should probably omit this clause as a gloss on *nōqēd*, actually, we believe, 'a hepatoscopist', but misunderstood as 'a breeder of sheep' (see Commentary). The Versions have an addition to MT. T adds 'year by year' (*šānā bešānā*) and G^{BA} read *en tē epanastasi* ('in the uprising'), which makes no sense. The suggestion of A. D. Nock, quoted by Montgomery, is feasible, that the Greek *epanastasi* is a corruption of *hupanastasi*, which means 'rising up to yield one's place to another', hence 'subjection', but the original Hebrew which this renders is irrevocably lost.

[f]Omitting MT 'and he went' (*wayyēlek*) with G^L and V.

[g]We should possibly omit the name 'Jehoshaphat', reading simply 'the king of Judah'.

[h]G^L and V read 'us' (*'ōtānū*) for MT 'them' (*'ōtām*).

[i]G^L omits the name 'Jehoshaphat'.

[j]Reading with certain MSS. and the Versions *mē'ittō* for MT *mē'ōtō*.

swered and said, Elisha the son of Shaphat is here, who poured water on the hands of Elijah. 12Jehoshaphat[a] said, The word of Yahweh is with him.[b] And the king of Israel and Jehoshaphat[c] and the king of Edom went down to him. 13And Elisha said to the king of Israel, What business have I with you? Go to the prophets of your father.[d] And the king of Israel said to him, Nay, not so, for Yahweh hath called these three kings to give them into the hand of the king of Moab. 14Then Elisha said, Assuredly, as Yahweh of Hosts lives before whom I stand, were it not that I respect Jehoshaphat[e] the king of Judah, I would not regard you nor look at you. 15But now bring me a minstrel—for it happened[f] that, when a minstrel played, Yahweh took control of him. 16And he said, Thus says Yahweh, Make this wadi full of trenches. 17For thus says Yahweh, You shall not see wind, nor shall you see rain, yet that wadi shall be filled with water and you shall drink, both you and your armies[g] and your beasts. 18And as if this were a light thing in the eyes of Yahweh, he will give Moab into your hand. 19And you shall attack every fortified city[h] and you shall fell every good tree and stop up all wells of water, and every good plot you shall spoil with stones. 20And it came to pass in the morning at the time of the offering of the oblation, behold, there was water coming from the direction of Edom, and the land was filled with water. 21Now all Moab heard that the[i] kings had come up to fight against them, and they were called up, from every one that was girt with a girdle and upwards, and they took up position on the border. 22And when they rose up early in the morning, the sun was shining over the water and Moab saw the water over against them red as blood. 23And they said, This is blood. The kings have actually destroyed[j] one another, and each has struck down the other. Now, then, to the spoil, Moab! 24So they came to the camp of Israel, and Israel rose up and attacked Moab, and they fled before them, and they came ever on,[k] smiting Moab all the way. 25And they destroyed the cities and on every good plot each man cast a stone and they covered it, and they stopped up every well of water, and felled every good tree until Kir

[a]'Jehoshaphat' may possibly be omitted, cf. vv. 7, 11.

[b]Reading *'ittō* as in v. 11.

[c]Here G^B omits 'Jehoshaphat' and reads 'the king of Judah'.

[d]Omitting 'and the prophets of your mother' with G^B.

[e]G^L omits 'Jehoshaphat' again.

[f]As MT stands *w^ehāyā* must be taken in parenthesis as frequentative. In this case there would be no actual statement that the minstrel played on this occasion, with the consequences described, so it is natural to emend *w^ehāyā* to *way^ehī* ('and it came to pass'), though this is a purely conjectural emendation unsupported by the versions.

[g]Reading *maḥ^anēkem* with G^L for MT *miqnēkem* ('your flocks'). The MT reading is possible if we understand by *miqnēkem* beasts of burden, but, even so, the Lucianic reading is preferable.

[h]Omitting MT 'and every choice city' (*w^ekol-ʿīr mibḥōr*) with G^{BL}.

[i]G^L reads 'these kings'.

[j]Reading Niphal infinitive absolute *hēḥārōb* before the Niphal perfect.

[k]So G (*wayyābō'ū bō'* . . .) for the unintelligible and obviously corrupt MT.

'Haresheth' alone was left to Moab,[a] and the slingers surrounded it and attacked it. [26]And the king of Moab saw that the fighting was too hard[b] for him, and he took with him[c] seven hundred who drew the sword, to cleave a way through to the king of Aram,[d] but they were not able. [27]So he took his eldest son who was to reign in his place and offered him up as an offering upon the wall, and there was great dismay upon Israel, so they decamped from (their expedition) against him and returned to the homeland.[e]

3.4. On the orthography of Mesha see p. 482 n.[d].

nōqēd as applied to the king of Moab is here taken, as the sequel in MT indicates, as 'a breeder of small cattle', which are called *nāqōd* in Gen. 30. The discovery of the term applied to the chief priest at Ras Shamra in the Late Bronze Age (*UT* 62, 54ff.) raises the question whether, applied to Mesha and to Amos in Amos 1.1, it may not have a similar sacral significance, as I. Engnell maintains.[f] Following this clue M. Bič[g] suggests that the term, as suggested by the Akkadian verb *naqādu* ('to probe', i.e. liver in augury) may mean a hepatoscopist. The reputation of Mesha as an augurer might well have affected his enemies when he sacrificed his son on the wall of Kir 'Haresheth'. This may be the true interpretation of the term. The

[a]G supports MT, though interpreting the text differently, viz. 'until they left the stones of the ruined wall'. The immediate sequel and the pronominal suffix after the verb indicates that the reference is to the Moabite capital of Kir 'Haresheth'. In view of the fact that the invaders were repulsed from the city, which apparently stood intact, it is difficult to accept 'the stones thereof' as genuine. Hence it is simplest to suppose that the sense is 'until only Kir "Haresheth" remained' (*ʿad hiššā'ēr lebāddāh qīr ḥarešet*) or, as we propose, *ʿad hiššā'ēr lemō'āb raq qīr ḥarešet*, *lemō'āb* ('to Moab') being nearer MT *'abānīm* ('stones') and *raq* ('only') being omitted owing to its resemblance to *qīr*.

[b]Reading feminine singular of the verb, *ḥāzeqā*.

[c]Reading *'ittō* for MT *'ōtō*, which is clearly wrong, since there is no antecedent for the pronominal suffix as direct object.

[d]Reading *'arām*, a conjectural emendation, but extremely probable, it being nonsensical for the king of Moab and his desperate band to try to break through to the king of Edom, who was actually in alliance with the invaders. On the other hand, the king of Aram, who was hostile to Israel and still held Ramoth Gilead in the northern part of Transjordan, was a natural source of hope to Moab. A precedent for Aramaean interference in Israelite aggression in Transjordan when circumstances were less inviting was the Aramaean reinforcement of Ammon at David's siege of Rabbath Ammon. Kittel, followed by Olmstead, retains 'Edom' and emends *'el* ('to') to *ʿal* ('against').

[e]G[L], S, and V read 'to their land' (*le'arṣām*). This, however, is unnecessary, since MT *lā'āreṣ*, read also by G, indicates 'to the homeland', as in the case of the district of Judah in Solomon's fiscal list (I K. 4.19). The usage is paralleled in Assyrian inscriptions.,

[f]*Studies in Divine Kingship in the Ancient Near East*, 1943, p. 8.

[g]*VT* I, 1951, pp. 293ff.

word was obviously taken, probably later, as 'breeder of sheep', and the statement of the tribute in wether lambs and shearling rams added as a gloss, the extravagant round number of 100,000 of each supporting this hypothesis.

ṣāmer is best taken as an accusative of respect, referring to rams at their first shearing, i.e. in their second year at the beginning of their breeding life. Tribute of sheep seems actually to have been paid by Moab, cf. Isa. 16.1.

3.5. Reiterating in substance 1.1, which see.

7. On the general omission of the names of the kings in G^L see pp. 482 n.[i], 483 nn.[g,e]. The narrative style, as distinct from the archival style, of this passage favours the vaguer references in G^L to 'the king of Israel' and 'the king of Judah'. At some point, however, Jehoshaphat, whose reputation stood high, was given the credit of citing the authority of a prophet of Yahweh here and in the kindred narrative in I K. 22. The reply of Jehoshaphat to the king of Israel, 'I am as you are, my people as your people, my horses as your horses', is the same as in I K. 22.4. The reference to the 'king' of Edom is strictly an inaccuracy, there being no king in Edom at this time (I K. 22.47; II K. 8.20), and seems to us to indicate the later reworking of the history of the house of Omri in the later, rather free, historical narrative.

8. The 'way of the steppe of Edom' cannot be the well-watered western escarpment of Edom, but the desert marches to the east of the land. This is suggested by the length of the detour, a week from the place where the forces of Israel and Judah joined up with those of Edom. This view is supported by the fact that the Moabites appear to have seen the water secured by the allies towards the rising sun (v. 22). The direct line of attack from the north was blocked by Mesha's recovery and fortification of the strongpoints north of the Arnon (*Wādī Mūjib*), as we read in his inscription, and the southern frontier of Moab along the northern bank of the ravine of *Wādī al-Ḥeṣa* (the Zered) was so easily guarded that attack in force from that direction was out of the question. Hence a detour round the head of the *Wādī al-Ḥeṣa* was necessitated, which took the allies so far to the east that the water from a flash flood ran eastward from Edom (v. 20).

10. The conception that Yahweh had called the allies out for their own destruction again re-echoes the idea in I K. 22 that Yahweh has deliberately deluded Ahab by the nationalistic prophets to march to his own destruction.

3.11. Note the use of *dāraš* with the specific meaning of seeking an oracle. The pouring of water over one's hands, e.g. after a meal, is still a gesture of deference among the Arabs, as of a servant to his master, a son to his father, or a host to his guest. Elisha is introduced not as a prophet in his own right, but as the servant of Elijah. This indicates an early source, perhaps in the lifetime of the prophet, and certainly not long after his death, and may be part of the original North Israelite account of the campaign. On the other hand, the reply of Jehoshaphat (v. 12)—who, incidentally, in the scene at the gate of Samaria on the eve of the Ramoth Gilead campaign appears to be quite ignorant of Elijah—, in which Elisha is acclaimed as an accredited prophet of Yahweh, suggests a later revision of this matter, probably from a Judaean hand, to judge from the role assigned to the king of Judah.

12. 'And they went down' indicates the headquarters of the kings on some height which commanded a strategic view of the country and afforded them privacy. The army was encamped on the lower slopes of the wadi, where bushes nourished by ground water afforded fodder for the baggage animals and flocks driven along for food, and also brushwood for camp-fires.

13. The defiant reply of Elisha may be original, reflecting as it does the attitude of his master to the house of Ahab. His obvious character as a man of God gave him immunity from the king. Nevertheless, it probably reflects the prophetic adaptation of the historical narrative.

14. Elisha's respect for the king of Judah certainly suggests a secondary source, the Judaean revision of the original North Israelite matter.

On the title 'Yahweh of Hosts' see on I K. 18.15. Here doubtless the reference is to Yahweh militant with the armies of Israel.

Here is an instance of conditional *'im* after the oath expressing a strong negative.

15. On the reading 'and it happened' (*wayᵉhī* for MT *wᵉhāyā*) see textual note. The dependance of Elisha on music to induce ecstasy is a significant limitation which indicates an early and genuine source. Music for this purpose is associated with dervish activity in I Sam. 10.5.[a] It promoted a monotonous, rhythmic movement like the ritual dance of the Baal-priests at Carmel or the rhythmic swaying and

[a]Cf. Lucian, *De Dea Syra*, 43.

chanting of local dervishes at a *ḏikr*, or religious seance, among the Arabs, the ultimate effect of which is ecstasy.[a]

The 'hand (power) of Yahweh' indicates the possession of the prophet by the divine power to which he reacts totally, spiritually, mentally, and physically, the last reaction often authenticating his spiritual experience before his public.

3.16. Note the use of the infinitive absolute as an abrupt, impersonal declaration of the prophet at the moment of revelation. The repetition of *gēbîm* indicates that many trenches were to be made, i.e. 'trenches all over'. The presence of bushes along the line of the wadi would signify ground water, which is available in similar terrain in certain parts of the Negeb.[b] The expedient of tapping the water-table, however, to which Gressmann[c] takes this passage to refer, must surely have been obvious to all, and particularly to the men of Judah and Edom, and is hardly a matter for divine revelation. The flash flood, or *sayl*, which is mentioned in v.17, however, would be an exceptional prediction, and the trenches suggested by Elisha were probably to trap this flood water of which he felt so confident. Perhaps the time of year was favourable to such rainfall in the mountains of Edom and Elisha was prepared to wait for the consequences of the *sayl* in the steppe east of the more settled region of Edom.

17. The wind was the prevailing wind from the west, which causes a precipitation of rain in the mountains of Edom, which rise to over 5,000 feet, but diminishes in force and freshness in the eastern steppe, which is in a rain-shadow, so that no downpour (*gešem*) is experienced. Had the army been encamped on the western escarpment of Edom, both rain and wind would have been experienced. The experience of a flood in the circumstances as the result of a remote rainstorm must have heightened the sense of a miracle.

18. The perfect *nāqal* introduced by *w*e is conditional.

19. The adjective *mibṣār* means 'something cut off abruptly' so as to be isolated, and aptly describes a fortified city with walls rising sheer above a steep escarpment, a good example of which is the wall of *Ḥaram aš-Šarīf* at Jerusalem above the steep slope of the Kidron ravine. For the omission of *w*e*kol-ʿîr mibḥōr* see p. 483 n.[h]. In view

[a]For further instances of the use of music in prophecy see W. R. Smith, *The Prophets of Israel*, 1882, p. 391.

[b]N. Glueck, *Rivers in the Desert*, 1959, p. 100.

[c]*Die älteste Geschichtsschreibung*, p. 288.

of Glueck's discovery of over 60 fortified settlements of the Iron Age in Moab,[a] 'every fortified city' is no exaggeration. No doubt, however, the tightly organized defence of the land dated generally from after the revolt of Mesha. At this time the fortifications seem to have been concentrated on the borders of the land, so that after their victory on the south-eastern border the allies meet with no opposition until they reach the capital.[b] The felling of fruit trees in war was banned by Deuteronomic law (Deut. 20.19ff.), but the present case indicates that this law was not of general application, but applied only to Canaan in consideration of the neighbours with whom Israel had to live in a degree of mutual dependence. In remote Moab, however, the Israelites seem to have destroyed the fruit trees without compunction. Regarding the general application of this law, however, the injunction of the Caliph Abu Bakr to the first Muslim expeditionary force to Syria may be cited: 'Neither bark nor burn the date-palms; cut not down fruit trees nor destroy crops.' De Vaux, however, cites Assyrian sculptures as proof that this barbarity was actually practised (*BJ*, p. 132). The spoiling of 'every plot of good land' was not practicable on the rolling open plains in the heart of Moab, but only where the cultivable land was scarce, being confined to wadi beds in the south-east of the land. In the sequel there is no evidence of a penetration beyond the capital Kir 'Haresheth' on the edge of the escarpment in the south-west (modern Kerak).

3.20. As in I K. 18.29 there is reference to a daily offering *minḥā* at a certain time. There it is offered in the early evening, actually the afternoon, while here there is reference to an early morning offering, which in the worship of the Second Temple was made at dawn.[c]

The statement that 'the land was filled with water' suggests that the water was trapped in the trenches dug by Elisha's direction.

21. *ṣā'aq* in the Niphal, meaning 'to have a call addressed to one', is regularly used in the Old Testament to describe a general call to arms. The primitive Semite, like the modern Arab peasant, was chary of citing actual numbers, hence ages are denoted by appropriate features or activities. A very young child under 5 is described as 'chasing the hens from the door of the house', a girl of 10 or 11 as 'gathering sticks and carrying water', and one 13 or 14 as 'marriage-

[a] *AASOR* XVIII–XIX, 1939, pp. 60ff., XXV–XXVIII, 1951, pp. 371ff.

[b] On this subject and on the cities of Moab in general see A. H. van Zyl, *The Moabites*, 1960, pp. 61ff.

[c] *Tāmīd* 3.2.

able'.[a] Hence the age of a boy fit for military service is indicated by the wearing of a girdle as apart from running about with a loose shirt. This is about 11 or 12 among modern Arabs.

3.23. It seems odd that the red light of the rising sun on the water should have so deceived the Moabites, but it must be remembered that they had not known of the rain in the west nor of the trenches the allies had dug in the wadi. The confused movement of men and beasts about the water seen from a distance suggested hostilities. Montgomery (ICC, p. 365) suggests that the verb *ḥārab*, which means generally in Hebrew 'to be devastated', is here in the Niphal a denominative verb from *ḥereb* 'a sword', and is paralleled by the Arabic *ḥaraba* (Form III and IV), 'to fight', cf *ḥarb* ('war'). Probably it was the sudden and unusual activity in the allied camp rather than the impression of blood that encouraged the Moabites to think that fighting had broken out and to rush in to the spoil. The other explanation seems an elaboration by the narrator. On the other hand, the sight of the red light suggesting the semblance of blood might have been taken as a favourable omen to the Moabites, who were obviously poised for attack, such psychological factors being of great importance in warfare of that age. This may have been reported by Moabite prisoners of war, and so have been retained in the Israelite narrative.

25. On the corrupt text and conjectural emendation see p. 484 n.[a] above. The capital of Moab is termed *Qīr ḥāreś* or *Qīr ḥareśet* in Isa. 16.7, 11 and Jer. 48.31, 36, where one notes the variation on the final sibilant from *š* of the present passage. De Vaux suggests (*BJ*, p. 133) on the basis of G of Isa. 16.11 that the actual name of the fortress was *Qīr ḥadāšā* ('Newcastle') and that *Qīr ḥareśet* ('Sherdwall' or 'Sherdburg') was a Jewish parody. We doubt this, and suggest that the MT text of the name should be retained, meaning 'Wall', or 'Fortification of the Watch', 'Wartburg', *ḥereš* being cognate with Arabic *ḥarasa* ('to guard, keep watch'). The view of W. Borée[b] that the name means 'City of the sun' is open to the objection that the last consonant of the second element is not *s* but *ś* or *š*, not an insuperable difficulty, indeed, in view of possible dialectic variations, but still a difficulty. The site is identified with *Kerak* on an isolated spur of the

[a]See particularly H. Granqvist, *Marriage Conditions in a Palestinian Village* (Societas Scientiarum Fennica, Commentationes Humanarum Litterarum III, 8), 1931, pp. 35ff.

[b]*Die alten Ortsnamen Palästinas*, 1930, pp. 90, 105.

south-western escarpment of Moab, the name deriving from the Targum rendering of Qir Moab. Its strategic advantage was appreciated by the most adventurous of the crusading leaders, Reginald de Châtillon, whose castle, thanks to his fortification and the natural strength of the place, fell to Salaḥ ad-Din after the Crusading disaster at *Qurn Ḥaṭṭīn* only after a year of siege and famine in 1188.[a]

3.26. On the objective of the desperate bid by the king of Moab see p. 484 n.[d] above.

27. The supreme sacrifice of the crown prince was doubtless to the national god Chemosh, to whose anger Mesha attributes the subjection of his people in the time of Omri and Ahab. We have argued that this god was a local manifestation of the god Aṯtar, manifest in the Venus-star, and have adduced a notable instance of human sacrifice to this deity in Byzantine times.[b] In the present instance, as in the Mesha inscription, the attribution of the disasters of Moab to the displeasure of the god is significant, and the sacrifice of Mesha's son on the wall aimed at the transference of the anger of the god to the enemies outside. Done in view of the allies, it horrified them with the prospect of the vengeance of the local god thus drastically entreated, so that they hastily decamped. If *qeṣep* means 'anger', as regularly in biblical Hebrew, the precise meaning of the statement 'there was great wrath upon Israel' is not clear. This can hardly refer to the indignation of the Moabites, since there is no mention of their further action against the Israelites and their allies, and the only explanation is that it might refer to the anger of God or the anger of Chemosh, which was inferred from the apparently panic reaction and sudden withdrawal of the allies. Driver thinks it unlikely that it should be said that the allies involved should withdraw because of the anger of the god of Moab, but at that date nothing was more natural than that Chemosh should be considered effective in his own land, especially after the supreme sacrifice by Mesha. This agrees with the view in 5.17 that it was necessary for Naaman to take two mules' burdens of earth to Syria in order to worship Yahweh in a strange land. It is not necessary to postulate with Šanda (II p. 24) plague as the cause of their withdrawal, though, incidentally, anger (*qeṣep*) is a possible

[a]See further Abel, *GP* II, pp. 418f.; Glueck, *AASOR* XVIII–XIX, 1939, p. 98; A. H. van Zyl, *op. cit.*, pp. 69–71.

[b]J. Gray, 'The Desert God Aṯtar in the Literature and Religion of Canaan', *JNES* VIII, 1949, pp. 72–83.

corruption of 'plague' (*qeṭeb*). The view of G. R. Driver[a] is much more feasible, that the word has the nuance of the Aramaic, cf. Syr. *qeṣap*, *qeṣīpā'* ('sad') and the late Hebrew (Mishnah) *qeṣūpā* ('sorrow'). G. renders *qeṣep* by *metamelos* ('change of heart'), which might justify the rendering 'dismay'. This Aramaic nuance may be a vestige of the character of the dialect of North Israel, which we have noted in ch. 4.

(v) TWO MIRACLES OF ELISHA: 4.1–37

Recurrent Aramaisms, peculiarities of language, and the individual status of Elisha, who is not so closely associated with the prophetic guilds in this section, have suggested a different source from the anecdotes of Elisha and the sons of the prophets (see critical introduction to this section, pp. 466f.). In the first episode, however, the widow relieved by Elisha was the relict of a member of a prophetic community, who was apparently well known to Elisha (v. 1), and in the second Elisha is obviously a 'man of God' (v. 9), who was in the habit of visiting Carmel regularly, probably to see a community of prophets there. Thus the matter may stem from the prophetic group of Carmel.

(*a*) *The multiplication of the widow's oil*: 4.1–7

4 [1]And a certain woman of the wives of the sons of the prophets cried out to Elisha saying, Your servant my husband is dead, and you know that your servant feared Yahweh, and the creditor has come to take my two boys for himself as slaves. [2]And Elisha said to her, What shall I do for you? Tell me what you have in the house. And she said to him, Your handmaid has nothing in the house except a single pouring[b] of olive oil. [3]And he said to her, Go, borrow for yourself vessels from outside, from all your neighbours.[c] Get no lack of empty vessels. [4]Then come in and close the door upon yourself and your sons, and pour into[d] all these vessels and set aside that which is full. [5]And she went from him and closed the door upon herself and her sons; they brought (the vessels) to her and she poured out.[e] [6]And it happened that, when the vessels were full, she said to her sons, [f]Bring[f] me another vessel. And they said[f] to her, There is not another vessel. Then the oil gave out.

[a]*JTS* XXXVI, 1935, p. 293.

[b]MT *'āsūk* is a *hapax legomenon*, the meaning 'pot' being unattested. The connection with *nāsak* ('to pour') suggests that *'āsūk* may be a corruption of *mesek* as Burney suggests, or better *massāk*, in the proto-Hebraic script.

[c]Reading plural *šekēnayik* as Q suggests.

[d]So G for MT 'over' (*'al*).

[e]Reading Piel *meyaṣṣeqet* for Hiphil *mōṣāqet* of Q.

[f]Reading plural with G for singular of MT.

7Then she came and told the man of God, and he said, 'Go, sell the oil and pay your debt, and live,[a] you and your sons, on what is left.'

4.1. This verse throws an interesting sidelight on the social and economic life of the prophetic communities. Though their eccentric and devoted life must have involved them in certain deprivations, they had economic obligations from which the community did not relieve them. Perhaps like the Greek monastic communities some were idiorhythmic, as this community apparently was, while others, like that of Gilgal in vv. 38–41 and 42–44, were apparently coenobitic, though in these two last cases the common meal may have been a ceremonial one. Marriage also was permitted. In permitting the enslavement of the children of a debtor, Hebrew law in the Book of the Covenant (Ex. 21.7; cf. Isa. 50.1; Neh. 5.5) is at one with the Code of Hammurabi (§ 117). The form of this law in the Book of the Covenant puts it into the category distinguished by Alt[b] as casuistic law, which was adapted by Israel from Canaan in the days of the settlement.

2. *lᵉki*, like *šᵉkēnayki* in v. 3 and *nišyeki* and *bānayki* in v. 7, are Aramaic forms of the second singular feminine pronominal suffix. The form, however, is not consistently used in this passage.

4. It is emphasized that the miracle was performed in Elisha's absence. It was by the power of God and not by any sleight of hand. The unfailing vessel is a common motif in folk-lore and the present tradition recalls the incident in the Elijah-saga in I K. 17.8ff.

(β) *The birth and revival of the Shunammite woman's son:* 4.8–37

The birth of a child to an elderly parent as a reward for hospitality is a theme of saga also in the patriarchal narratives (Gen. 18.1–15). Gressmann[c] regards the themes of the birth of the child and his revival as part of two distinct traditions. But in view of v. 28 it is hard to maintain this thesis, for which there is no tangible evidence in the text. Gressmann notes the introduction of Gehazi to prepare for the entrance of Elisha, cf. Elijah's encounter first with Obadiah and then with the king in I K. 18, as a device of saga to heighten the drama of the entrance of the principal figure.

4 8And one day when Elisha was passing by[d] Shunem there was a

[a]Reading plural with G.
[b]'The Origins of Israelite Law', *Essays*, 1966, pp. 79–132.
[c]*Die älteste Geschichtsschreibung*, p. 393.
[d]Reading *ʿal* for MT *ʾel*, which is preferable with the verb *ʿābar* in the context.

great lady there, who prevailed on him to eat bread, and it came to be that whenever he passed he turned aside there to eat bread. [9]So she said to her husband, See, I know that this is a holy man of God who passes by us continually. [10]Let us make a little upper chamber with walls and put in a bed and a table and a chair and a lamp, and it will be that when he comes to us he may go apart there. [11]And it happened one day that he came there and went apart to the upper chamber and lay down there. [12]And he said to Gehazi his servant, Call this Shunammite lady. [a](And he called her, and she stood before him. [13]And he said to him,)[a] Say to her, See, you have shown all this solicitous deference to us. What can we do for you? Can we speak to the king for you, or to the commander of the army? But she said, I am settled among my own kinsfolk. [14]And he said, Then what can we do for her? Then Gehazi said, Nay, but she has no son and her husband is old. [15]And he said, Call her. So he called her and she stood at the doorway. [16]And he said, At this season according to the period of gestation you shall be embracing a son. And she said, Say not so, my lord,[b] do not delude your handmaiden. [17]And the woman conceived and bore a son at the[c] due season[d] as Elisha had told her. [18]Now the child grew up, and one day he went out to his father to the harvesters, [19]and he said to his father, O my head! my head! So his father said to the servant, Carry him to his mother. [20]And he took him up and brought him in to his mother and he lay on her knees until noon and died. [21]And she went up and laid him on the bed of the man of God and shut the door upon him and went out. [22]And she called to her husband and said, Send me, I beg you, one of the lads and one of the asses that I may run to the man of God and back again. [23]And he said, Why are you going[e] to him today? It is not new moon nor sabbath. And she said, All is well. [24]Then she saddled the ass and said to her servant, Drive on and go forward. Do not check the riding unless I tell you. [25]So she went and came to the man of God, to Mount Carmel. And it happened that, when the man of God[f] saw her at a distance, he said to Gehazi his lad, See, yonder is the Shunammite lady. [26]Now[g] run to meet her, and say to her, Is it well with you? Is it well with your husband? Is it well with your child? And she said, It is well. [27]And she

[a]Since these words interrupt the instructions of Elisha to Gehazi, and are in any case repeated in sense at v. 15, they should be omitted in v. 12.

[b]G[B] omits 'O man of God' of MT.

[c]MT *hazze* ('this') should probably be omitted in the narrative at this point as a scribal repetition of the oracle of Elisha at v. 16.

[d]*kāʿēt ḥayyā* is probably also an inadvertent repetition from the oracle in v. 16.

[e]*y* after the feminine singular participle gives a meaningless form, and is either repeated after the *y* in the Aramaic form of the pronoun *ʾatti*, in which case we should read *hōleket*, or is an Aramaic form of the second feminine singular perfect. The sense of the passage would preclude the latter.

[f]G[BA] read 'Elisha' for MT 'man of God'.

[g]We should probably add *w*[e] to the adverb *ʿattā*, which is read by certain MSS.

came to Elisha,[a] to the mountain, and she laid hold of his feet, and Gehazi came near to thrust her away, but Elisha[a] said, Leave her alone, for she is deeply embittered, but Yahweh has hidden it from me and has not told me. [28]Then she said, Was it I who asked a son of my lord? Did I not say, Do not deceive me? [29]Then he said to Gehazi, Gird up your loins and take my staff in your hand and go. If you meet any man do not greet him, and if any man greet you do not answer him, and you shall put my staff upon the face of the lad. [30]And the mother of the lad said, As Yahweh lives and as you live, I shall not leave you, and he arose and went after her. [31]And Gehazi went on before them and he laid the staff on the face of the boy, but there was neither sound nor response, so he came back to meet him and told him, The lad has not awakened. [32]Then Elisha went into the house, and[b] there was the lad lying dead on his bed. [33]And he went in and shut the door on the two of them and made intercession to God. [34]And he went up (on to the bed) and lay on the boy and put his mouth upon his mouth and his eyes upon his eyes and his hands upon his hands[c] and he crouched over him, and the flesh of the boy grew warm. [35]Then he went back and walked in the house once this way and once that way, and he went up (on to the bed) and crouched over the lad,[d] and the lad sneezed as many as seven times, and the lad opened his eyes. [36]Then he called to Gehazi and said, Call this Shunammite lady, and he called her, and she came in to him, and he said, Take up your son. [37]So she came and fell at his feet and prostrated herself to the ground, and she took up her son and went out.

4.8. Shunem was at the foot of the south-western slopes of *Jebel ad-Dāḥī*, the Hill of Moreh, where the Midianites were encamped before Gideon's attack. It is known that Elisha frequented Carmel, which, at the traditional site of Elijah's sacrifice (*Deir al-Maḥraq*) is about 15 miles from Shunem. Shunem is seven miles south of Tabor, which was the site of a sanctuary in the Israelite period (Hos. 5.1 and probably Deut. 33.19), which Elisha may also have frequented. Shunem, to be sure, is not on the direct road from Tabor to *Deir al-Maḥraq*, but the fact that the conspicuous hill, *Jebel ad-Dāḥī*, was crowned in Arab times with a *wālī* (saint's tomb) may indicate the ancient sanctity of the place, as indeed 'the Hill of Moreh' suggests, this name signifying a place of revelation, the seat of an oracle with possibly a prophetic community. If he had just visited this community

[a]So with G[BA] for MT *'īš hā'elōhīm*. Gehazi also was presumably a man of God, but even if he were not, the contrast between the confidence with which the woman treated him and Elisha indicates that the proper name should be read.

[b]S reads 'and he saw' in addition to MT at this point.

[c]*kappāyw* obviously should be read here for MT *kappāw*, after Q.

[d]The noun *hanna'ar* seems to be demanded instead of the pronominal suffix with the preposition.

Elisha would not actually need the Shunammite lady's hospitality, but it is stated that she 'constrained' (*wattaḥ^a^zeq*) him to accept refreshment, thus at once observing the ancient Semitic convention of hospitality to sustain her own credit and bringing herself within the range of the 'blessing' (*b^e^rākā*) which a man of God enjoyed.

4.9. The fact that Elisha is holy, i.e. ritually sacrosanct, made it unsafe for the Shunammite couple to entertain him in their common premises, hence an upper chamber was to be built for him.

10. The qualifying word *qīr* ('wall') means that this was not a temporary shelter, which is often erected as a guest-chamber on the roof (e.g. I Sam. 9.25). The walls ensured privacy, besides providing a permanent building, which was regularly furnished for eating (with a table) as well as sleeping, so that the menage of the family, of necessity ritually profane, would be completely safeguarded against the consequences of contact with the 'holy' man of God. Possibly *qōr* ('coolness') may be the original reading, cf. *ʿ^a^liyat hamm^e^qērā*, the 'cool upper chamber' of Eglon of Moab in Judg. 3.20. *m^e^nōrā* here does not mean a 'candlestick' (AV), but an ordinary open pottery saucer-lamp with pinched nozzle (Scots 'cruisie-light'). Some of these in the Israelite period had seven nozzles.

12. The tentative suggestion of *BDB* that the name Gehazi means 'valley of vision' is extremely unlikely. We think that it is more probably derived from a cognate of the Arabic *jaḥida* ('to be avaricious'). This might, as the termination of Gehazi suggests, be a nickname, perhaps a reflection of the incident in 5.20ff., where Gehazi extorts the reward which Elisha had waived. This story, on the other hand, may be a popular attempt to explain the name. *l^e^* in *laššūnammīt* and *lāh* may be a case of the direct object introduced by *l^e^*, characteristic of Aramaic.

13. *ḥārad* normally means 'to tremble' or 'to be in a panic'. We maintain that in this passage it means more than 'to be careful' or even 'to show anxious care' (EVV). It indicates a real fear of infringing the sanctity of the man of God, which had prompted the solicitous provision of an upper chamber for him, hence we render 'to show solicitous deference'. The Hebrew verb seems to have something of the connotation of the possible Arabic cognate *ḫarida* ('to be bashful').

The influence of Elisha with the king indicates that he was more than the erstwhile servant of Elijah, who had emerged into public life in the Moabite campaign in ch. 3. The incident is to be dated at a later period, probably when the prophet's home was in Samaria. The suggestion of Elisha that he should speak to the king or the commander of the army on behalf of the woman can only mean that there were certain state burdens on the community for fiscal and military purposes, imposed regionally by Solomon (e.g. I K. 4) and retained after the disruption of the kingdom. As a *gibbōr ḥayil*, a man of property and substance, the elderly husband of the lady would be liable for the provision and equipment of men for military service. This may be the purport of the lists of bowmen and slingers from certain localities in the kingdom of Ugarit among the administrative texts from Ras Shamra.[a] Perhaps this is all that is intended by the prophet, but the lady apparently assumes that further favour is indicated, and she replies that she enjoys the protection of her clan (*ʿam*). This truly reflects the temper of the ancient Israelite peasantry, which, as the modern Arab peasantry, were settled in kin-groups, where social obligations were clearly defined and seriously accepted, the rights of each being safeguarded by all.

4.16. The demonstrative *hazze* probably signifies 'such and such'. The following phrase *kāʿēt ḥayyā* is confined to this passage and the promise of the birth of Isaac in Gen. 18.10, 14. In all three cases *ḥayyā* is an adjective. We may question the Massoretic pointing, however, and read *keʿēt ḥayyā*, taking *ḥayyā* as a noun, the phrase meaning 'according to the time of gestation,' i.e. the quickening and development of life in the womb. The noun *ḥayyā* is found in Isa. 57.10, *ḥayyat yādēk māṣāʾt* ('thou hast found revival of thy power'). *kāzab* ('to lie') means 'to excite delusive hopes' in Job 41.9[1], *tōḥaltō nikzebā* ('his hope is delusive) cf. *miqsam kāzāb* ('a delusive divination'), Ezek. 13.7.

18. The plural 'reapers' (*qōṣerīm*) need not indicate the reapers of the Shunammite, though he was a man of substance who probably did employ others. The reference is to the whole community which was reaping, each family its own strip, among whom were the Shunammite and his reapers.

21. The placing of the dead child in the prophet's chamber may have been intended by his mother as a reproach to Elisha, as the sequel suggests. On the other hand, Gressmann[b] has rightly emphasized the significance of closing the door, in the light of modern Arab

[a] *UT* 321; C. Virolleaud, 'Les villes et les corporations du royaume d'Ugarit', *Syria* XXI, 1940, pp. 123–51.

[b] *Die älteste Geschichtsschreibung*, p. 293.

peasant custom, to retain the *nepeš* or life-essence, now dissociated from the body. The association of the body of the subject in this intermediate stage between life and death, the ultimate state of which was finalized by burial, with the objects associated with the man of God, supercharged as he was with the divine *rūaḥ*, gave a hope that the fact of final death might be averted.

4.23. 'New moon' (*ḥōdeš*) and sabbath (*šabbāt*) are similarly associated in Amos 8.5; Hos. 2.11 [13] and Isa. 1.13ff., and Meinhold[a] concludes that the sabbath in Israel was the Babylonian *šappatu*, the day on which the moon 'rested' from waxing, i.e. the full moon day, on which the gods might be propitiated. The fact that new moon and sabbath are associated in the life of Israel, however, and that both involved suspension of normal business (Amos 8.5), does not mean that the sabbath in Israel was a lunar occasion. In fact, falling with mathematical regularity every seventh day, it was not. The fact that the seventh day sabbath observance was a distinctive rite of the sacral community Israel, as in the Decalogue (Ex. 20.8; Deut. 5.12), the Ritual Code (Ex. 34.12) and the Book of the Covenant (Ex. 23.12), indicates a deliberate attempt to counteract the influence of Canaan in the observance of rites of suspense at lunar phases.[b] Such lunar phases are actually noted in ritual texts from Ras Shamra.[c] On such occasions in Mesopotamia on the 7th, 14th, 19th, 21st and 28th of the month the king on behalf of the community suspended his normal activities and behaviour to evade untoward supernatural influences to which the community was thought to be peculiarly open at such crises. The significance of the sabbath in pre-exilic Israel as a humanitarian or sacramental occasion related to God's exaltation as King and Creator, noted respectively in addenda to the primitive Decalogue in Deuteronomy and Exodus, is uncertain. The journey of the Shunammite from her home to Carmel would normally have been postponed to a rest day. The fact of its being undertaken on a work day immediately excited the apprehension of her husband, which had to be allayed by her 'All is well!' (*šālōm*). Believing as she did that by her precautions death was not finalized, she was careful that these should not be undone by inauspicious words of lamentation by which her husband would have responded to the news.

[a]'Die Enstehung des Sabbats', *ZAW* XXIX, 1909, pp. 81–112.

[b]So S. Mowinckel, *Le Décalogue*, 1927, pp. 75–98.

[c]Gordon, *UT* 3 and possibly 9, and other unpublished material from the season 1961, on which the writer has worked by courtesy of Professor Schaeffer.

4.24. The 'great lady' of Shunem personally harnesses the ass. She is a substantial peasant.

25. On the association of Elisha with Carmel see p. 467.

The preposition *minneged* (lit. 'over against') means here 'at a distance'.

26. Again as in v. 23 the lady shrugs off enquiries with '*šālōm!*' This is designedly ambiguous, and may be taken either as her greeting to Gehazi or as an expression of her faith, 'All is going to be well'. Her business is with none other than Elisha.

27. *napšā mārā*, as the sequel shows, means not 'She is sad' but 'She is embittered'.

28. The emphasis is on 'ask'. The birth of a son was not what the lady herself had asked; it was what Elisha had promised on his own initiative. *šālā* in the Hiphil means, we maintain, 'cause to be at ease', i.e. lull into complacency, a *hapax legomenon* in this sense in the Old Testament.

29. The dispatch of Gehazi with the staff of Elisha, considering the effective result of his mission, was intended by Elisha, no doubt, as a pledge of his personal engagement and a guarantee of his prophetic assurance, as in the case of the prophet in the Mari text who sent some of his hair and the hem of his robe for the purpose. It was a means of allaying the mother's impatience. The staff as the vehicle of a man's power and prestige is instanced in the case of Judah's pledges to Tamar, where the staff is given with his signet ring as a pledge (Gen. 38.18). The staff of Moses also was the vehicle of the spirit through him in the miracles attributed to him (Ex. 4.1–4; 17.8–13). The sending of Gehazi on what was to be a fruitless errand may also be a literary convention to heighten the effect of Elisha's personal appearance and success. The waiving of the normal convention of greeting by the way indicates the extreme urgency of the mission, an injunction which was cited by Jesus on his dispatch of the 70 disciples (Luke 10.4).

30. The faith of the woman is fixed on Elisha.

31. *qōl* means 'audible response' and *qešeb* 'sign of attention'.

33. The mere magical means employed by Gehazi are contrasted with the prayer of Elisha in the revival of the boy.

34. The crouching (*ghr*, found here and at I K. 18.42, which see) over the lad and the contact of hands, mouth, and eyes suggests a rite of contactual magic whereby the properties of one party were transferred to another. Doubtless this was a popular elaboration of the tradition reflecting popular belief and practice of the time. Popular tradition might also have exaggerated the unconsciousness of the boy to actual death. The revival of the boy with prayer and personal bodily contact is a striking repetition of the revival of the widow's son in the Elijah-saga (I K. 17).

4.35. Elisha's walking about in the house was probably an act of relaxation after intense physical and spiritual concentration which had temporarily exhausted him. In this respect it is a revealing sidelight on the prophetic exercise of intercessory prayer.

The sneezing of the child is an intimate fact which may well go back to a personal account by Gehazi. The 'seven times' rather indicates popular elaboration of the fact. The sneezing was the material token of 'life' (lit. 'breath') in the boy, cf. breath in the nostrils in the animation of Adam (Gen. 2.7).

(vi) 'DEATH IN THE POT': 4.38–41

Part of the Elisha hagiology (see Introduction, pp. 466f.).

4 38Then Elisha returned to Gilgal, and the famine was in the land,
and the sons of the prophets were in session before him, and he said to
the lad, Set on the great pot and boil broth for the sons of the prophets. 39And one[a] went out to the country to gather herbs, and he
found a wild vine and he picked wild gourds from it, as much as his
skirt would hold, and he came and sliced them into the pot of broth,
for they[b] did not know about them. 40Then they poured out for the[c] men
to eat. And it happened, when they were eating the broth, lo[d] they
cried out and said, Death in the pot, man of God! And they could not
eat. 41And he said, Then take meal. And he cast[e] it into the pot, and
he said, Pour out for the people, and let them eat. So there was no
harm in the pot.

38. The identity of Gilgal is again in question. Dalman, in a disquisition on the wild gourds,[f] takes it to be Gilgal by Jericho. That raises the question of the identity of the gourds, which Dalman notes as a plant with powerful laxative properties common in the district of Jericho. If vv. 38–41 is located in the same community as

[a]G omits, thus taking Elisha as the subject, though the subject might still be indefinite.

[b]G^{L}, S and V read singular.

[c]So probably for the indefinite noun in MT.

[d]Reading *w*ᵉ*hinnē* with G^{BA} for MT 'they' (*w*ᵉ*hēmmā*).

[e]G, S, and T read imperative here. V feels the want of a verb in the narrative tense corresponding to the imperative *q*ᵉ*ḥū*, and reads 'and they took (it)' (*wayyiq*ᵉ*ḥū*). In the swiftly moving Hebrew narrative there is often ellipsis of a verb and here also it is not strictly necessary to insert *wayyiq*ᵉ*ḥū*.

[f]*Sacred Sites and Ways*, 1935, pp. 81ff.

vv. 42–44, the location of Baalshalisha mentioned in the latter passage with the settlement of the prophets would suggest that this Gilgal is identical with the *Jiljilīyeh* near the Arab town of *Qalqīliyeh* and six miles west of *Kefr Ṯulṯ*, possibly biblical Baalshalisha. The two episodes, however, may simply be juxtaposed in Kings and not be really associated with the same locality, though it is likely that they are.

It is possible to take the definite article in 'the famine' generically, but it is more likely to refer to the notorious seven-year famine of Elisha's lifetime (8.1ff.).

The episode has suggested that the prophetic community at Gilgal was coenobitic, but the common meal may have been occasioned by the temporary presence of Elisha, as in an Arab community when a guest comes. In the meal at Gilgal the association at the common meal had the purpose of making possible the communication of the blessing (*b*e*rākā*) of the great prophet. The fact that Elisha himself directs the preparation of the meal either indicates that he was acknowledged head of the community as long as he was present or that the particular brew was designed to have some exciting physical effect.

4.39. *śāde* in both cases where it is used in this passage denotes not the cultivated field but the open country, *gepen śāde* being a wild vine, which is not a grapevine, since its gourds were sliced into the pot. It has been thought by Dalman to be *citrullus colocynthus*, which produces yellow fruits like small melons, which are pungent and purgative, and if eaten in great quantity may indeed be fatal. The man who gathered the gourds put them in the skirt of his mantle, which, like the modern Arab, he gathered up by one corner, thus making a large pocket.

40. 'Death in the pot' may have meant no more than our jocular remark if food is ill seasoned, 'I'm poisoned'. The harm was doubtless done through excessive use of the gourds with defect of more regular fare, which Elisha supplied with the meal. He at least does not seem to take the objection seriously. The exclamation 'Death in the pot!' however, in a primitive community was an ill-omened remark which had to be counteracted, as it was by the casting of meal into the pot, probably with some word of better omen. It is interesting to know that West Highland folklore still retains the tradition of the use of meal, either sprinkled dry on one or an oatcake broken over one, as a charm against supernatural influence.

(vii) THE FEEDING OF A MULTITUDE: 4.42–44

Possibly, though not certainly, associated with vv. 38–41.

4 42 Now a man came from Baalshalisha[a] and brought to the man of
God bread of[b] the firstfruits, twenty loaves[c] of barley [d]and plants of his
orchard,[d] and he said, Give it to the people that they may eat. 43 And his
servant said, What? should I set this before a hundred men? And he
said, Give it to the people that they may eat, for thus says Yahweh,
They shall eat and have some left over. 44 So he set it before them and
they ate and had some left over according to the word of Yahweh.

4.42. On the location of Baalshalisha see on 2.1, cf. 'the land of Shalisha' north of Lydda in the western foothills of the hill-country of Ephraim in Saul's search for the strayed asses (I Sam. 9.4).

The firstfruits (*bikkūrīm*) were offered to Yahweh (Lev. 23.20). This being so, the provision brought by the man of Baalshalisha may have been appropriated by Elisha on the authority of Yahweh (cf. v. 43) as the elements of a special sacramental meal.

In the case of MT *wᵉkarmel bᵉṣiqlōnō,b* in the second letter-complex has been misunderstood as a preposition and *wᵉkarmillō*, possibly *mikkarmillo*, has been in consequence misplaced. We take *biṣqᵉlōn* as a diminutive of *bṣql*, now recovered in a Ras Shamra text *UT* I 'Aqht, I 61–66:

ydn(dn')il ysb p'alth
bṣql yph bp'alt
bṣ(q)l yph byġlm
bṣql y(ḥb)q wynšq
'aḥl 'an bṣ(ql)
ynpʿ bp'alt bṣql
ypʿ byġl 'ur

Dn'il investigates, he goes round his tilth;
He sees a plant in the tilth,
A plant he sees in the scrub.
He embraces the plant and kisses it.
Ah me for the plant!
Would that the plant might grow tall in the tilth,
Would that the herb might flourish in the scrub!

[a]G reads *Bethsareisa*.

[b]G[B] omits 'bread' (*leḥem*), which does not affect the context grammatically.

[c]G[L] omits *leḥem* of MT, but even if this is omitted, which is possible, it must still be understood.

[d]Reading *ūbiṣqᵉlōn karmillō* for MT *wᵉkarmel bᵉṣiqlōnō*. Following G[A], which reads *bakellet* for MT *bᵉṣiqlōnō*, a *hapax legomenon*, Lagarde proposed *bᵉqalʿātō* ('in his pouch'). In this case *karmel* would have to be taken in the sense of 'fresh fruit', which is actually attested in Lev. 2.14; 23.14. The quantity, however, makes this reading most unlikely. For our reading, based on a text from Ras Shamra, see Commentary on v. 42.

The recurrence of *bṣql* in clauses where it is an obvious noun and the parallel in the last bicolon with *'ūr* ('herb') sets the meaning of the problematic *biṣqᵉlōn* in the present passage beyond doubt.

4.43. The physical inadequacy of 'this among so many' is transcended here, as in the feeding of the multitudes in Galilee (Matt. 14.13–21; 15.32–39; Mark 6.30–44; 8.1–10; Luke 9.10–17), by the fact that it subserves the divine purpose. As there the blessing of Jesus lifts the purely material to a higher plane, so the 'word of Yahweh' makes the meal of the prophets a sacrament. The comparative restraint of this tradition of the satisfying of 100 men with 20 loaves and orchard fruits is remarkable compared with the feeding of 5,000 and/or 4,000 with five loaves and two fishes or seven loaves and a few small fish. The Old Testament passage again does not particularize like the Gospels on the quantity left over. In both cases the real point is that the sacrament is in itself satisfying.

(viii) THE HEALING OF NAAMAN AND ITS SEQUEL, THE CURSE ON THE AVARICIOUS GEHAZI: 5.1–27

On the literary affinity of this passage and its possible provenance see literary introduction to the Elisha-cycle. The curse on Gehazi is possibly a later expansion to account for the name Gehazi, which, we suggest on Arabic analogy, means 'avaricious'. Gressmann, however,[a] implies the unity of the passage, pointing out the dramatic rhythm and balance of the whole, where Naaman is depicted as proud when he is sick and humble when he is healed; the noble pagan is a leper at the outset, while Gehazi the servant of Elisha is a leper at the end. A similar antithesis is that of the unselfishness of Elisha and the avarice of Gehazi. This, however, may be the effect of the final literary revision of the traditions.

(a) *The healing of Naaman:* 5.1–19

5 [1]Now Naaman the commander of the army of the king[b] of Aram was a great man before his master and well respected, for by him Yahweh had given victory to Aram, but the man was[c] stricken with leprosy. [2]Now the Aramaeans had gone out in raiding parties and they had brought as a captive from the land of Israel a little Hebrew maid, and she waited on Naaman's wife. [3]And she said to her mistress, If

[a]*Die älteste Geschichtsschreibung*, p. 297.

[b]G^{BA} omits 'king', which does not affect the grammar of the context.

[c]G^{L} omits MT *gibbōr ḥayil*, which seems superfluous in the sense of 'a man of property able for war'. In the sense of 'mighty man of valour', which is also possible, it may be retained.

only my master were before the prophet who is in Samaria then would he cleanse him from his leprosy. 4And one went in[a] and told[a] his[a] master saying, Thus and thus said the girl from the land of Israel. 5And the king of Aram said, Go, come and I shall send a letter to the king of Israel. And he went and took with him ten talents of silver and six thousand shekels of gold and ten changes of clothing, 6and had brought the letter to the king of Israel saying, And now as this letter reaches you I have sent to you my servant Naaman, so cleanse him of his leprosy. 7And it happened, when the king of Israel read the letter, that he rent his clothes and said, Am I God to give life and death that this man sends to me to cleanse a man from his leprosy? But consider rather and see that he seeks occasion against me. 8And it happened that, when Elisha[b] heard that the king[c] had torn his clothes, he sent to the king saying, Why have you torn your clothes? Let him come to me that he may know that there is a prophet in Israel. 9So Naaman came with his horses and chariot and stood at the door of Elisha's house. 10And Elisha sent a messenger to him saying, Go, wash seven times in the Jordan and your flesh will be made clean again.[d] 11Then was Naaman angry and went off saying, I thought, To (such a person as) me he will surely come out and stand and call in the name of Yahweh his God, and wave his hand towards the place and cleanse the leprosy. 12Are not Abana[e] and Pharpar, rivers of Damascus, better than all the rivers of Israel? May I not go[f] and wash in them and be clean? And he turned and went away in a rage. 13But his servants drew near and spoke to him and said, My father, if[g] the prophet had enjoined some great thing upon you, would you not be doing it? How much the more when he has bidden you, 'Wash and be clean'. 14So he went down and dipped himself seven times in the Jordan according to the word of the man of God, and his flesh became again like the flesh of a young boy, and he was clean. 15And he went back to Elisha,[h] he and all his company, and went in and stood before him and said, See, now I know that there is no God in all the earth except in Israel, so now take a present from your servant. 16Then (Elisha) said, As Yahweh lives, before whom I stand, I will not take it. And he pressed him to accept, but he refused. 17And Naaman said, Then if (you will) not (agree), let two mules' burdens of earth be given to your servant, for your servant shall no more make whole burnt offerings and sacrifices to other gods, but only to Yahweh. 18For this thing may Yahweh pardon your servant. When my master

[a]G reads the feminine singular throughout for MT masculine singular, which may be retained, however, the indefinite subject being understood.

[b]G^B omits *'īš hā'ᵉlōhīm* of MT.

[c]G^L and S omit 'of Israel' of MT.

[d]Reading *wᵉṭāhēr* with S for MT *ūṭᵉhār*.

[e]Q and T read *'ᵃmānā* for MT *'ᵃbānā*, supported, and perhaps suggested to the Massoretes, by S. of S. 4.8.

[f]So G.

[g]Inserting *'im* into MT after *'ābī* with G^L.

[h]So G^{BA} for MT *'īš hā'ᵉlōhīm*.

comes into the temple of 'Rimmon' to worship there and leans on my arm, and I bow down in the temple of 'Rimmon',[a] then let Yahweh pardon your servant in this matter. [19]So he said to him, Go in peace! And he went from him a certain space.

5.1. Naaman is attested as a proper name in the administrative texts from Ras Shamra[b] and as an epithet of royal personages, namely, Krt[c] and 'Aqht.[d] In the form Nuʿman it was also used extensively among the Arabs before Islam. It was an epithet of Adonis, and the name Naaman may be a hypocoristicon, or truncated theophoric. On the other hand, it might simply be a name of fair omen, 'Gracious, Pleasant', cf. Ḥasan, Jamīl ('Handsome').

The idiom *nāśā' pānīm* ('to show favour', lit. 'to lift up the face') refers to the gesture of the king stretching forth his sceptre and touching the face of a suppliant bowed to the ground before him and raising the face up, e.g. Esth. 8.3f.

tešūʿā, a variant of *yešūʿā*, meaning here 'victory', is derived from the verbal root *ysʿ*. The Arabic cognate *wasiʿa* means 'to be wide', hence the Hiphil of the Hebrew cognate, the form in which the verb regularly occurs, means 'to make a clearance', 'rid of cramping circumstances', in a physical sense primarily, e.g. when Jonathan and his armour-bearer cleared the Philistine garrison off the point of vantage near Michmash (I Sam. 14.45). 'Salvation' in the spiritual sense, preserving something of the primary physical connotation of 'relief', is secondary.

Naaman's leprosy (*ṣāraʿat*) was obviously not of that kind which debarred him from society, so that it was an embarrassing skin disease, but not as serious as leprosy proper, for which ancient ritual law prescribed isolation (Lev. 13.45f.). The disease of Naaman must have been what Herodotus (I, 138) calls *leukē* as distinct from *leprē*.

2. This was a period of uneasy peace between Aram, with its capital at Damascus, and Israel, which was liable to be disrupted by border raids by bands (*gedūdīm*), probably by semi-nomad Aramaean tribesmen, who sold their booty in the market of Damascus.

3. Here Elisha is termed not 'man of God', as regularly in the hagiology emanating from the prophetic communities, but *nābī'*, the mediary of God's creative word. He is not associated here with

[a]Omitting MT *behištaḥawāyātī bēt rimmōn* as a dittograph.
[b]*UT* 10, 5; 64, 41; 80, I, 21; 311, I, 26; IV, 2.
[c]*UT*, Krt, 40, 61; 128, II, 20.
[d]*UT*, 2 'Aqht VI, 45.

any prophetic community, but lives in his own house at Samaria, where he had the opportunity to interpose the word of God in affairs of state. His status is therefore much higher and more influential than among the various local prophetic communities.

'āsap with a personal object, meaning 'to heal', or 'cleanse', is attested in the Old Testament only in this episode. If the verb occurred only once in the sense 'to heal' we should have proposed that it was a corruption of *'āsā*, found in this sense in Aramaic, but it occurs thrice in this passage, which makes the MT reading more certain. A verb *'āsap* is, of course, well attested with an impersonal object, e.g. wrath, light, peace, meaning 'to rid, remove'. In its present context the verb suggests Akkadian *ašāpu* ('to practise exorcism'). The sibilants, to be sure, do not correspond, but this may be explained by the fact that the verb is a loanword from Akkadian or by the conscious effort of the writer to reproduce the border dialect of the Hebrew girl, which probably resembled Aramaic.

5.5. So far there has been no mention of the king of Aram, this being a feature of the swiftly moving narrative.

The royal mission to the king of Israel recalls similar correspondence between kings in the Amarna Tablets on the same subject. In his letter to Amenhotep III,[a] Tušratta of Mitanni states that he has sent the statue of Astarte of Nineveh, which was held to have healing propensities, to the Pharaoh, and he mentions that it had been sent also in the previous generation. The amount of silver and gold seems an exaggeration. On the weights see on I K. 9.14; 10.16.

6. The contents of the letter are cited, though the preliminary greetings are omitted, as is indicated by the formula 'and now . . .' introducing the main business of the letter. This is the common pattern of letters in the ancient East.

'My servant' (*'abdī*) indicates a high officer of the king, possibly, though not necessarily, bound to him in feudal status, see on I K. 1.2.

7. The indignant question of the king 'Am I God to give death and life?' indicates that, as the letter conveys, the request had been made directly to him with no actual mention of the prophet. In so far as the king of Aram had taken any regard of the prophet he had probably regarded him as a servant of the king through whom the royal virtue of healing was exercised.[b]

[a]Knudtzon, *Die El-Amarna Tafeln*, 23, 15ff.

[b]On the ancient conception of the king as the channel of divine blessings see our analysis of the Canaanite material in 'Canaanite Kingship in Theory and

Taking the appeal to be directed to himself, the king of Israel, who is unnamed throughout, concludes that the king of Aram, also unnamed, is seeking an occasion for war. The usage of the Hithpael *hit'annā* here is a *hapax legomenon* in the Old Testament, but the word is attested in the verbal noun *tō'ᵃnā* in Judg. 14.4. The root is cognate with Arabic *'anā*, used impersonally meaning 'the time is opportune'.

5.9. Naaman comes to Elisha's house with all the pomp of his status, which, from the sequel, we gather not to be the seemly approach to a prophet. The fact that Naaman was able to drive up in his chariot to the house of Elisha indicates either that Samaria under Omri and Ahab had been more spaciously laid out than the normal eastern city, or, more probably, that Elisha lived either in an isolated house, or in the proximity of the official quarters, and not in the normally congested quarters of the populace.

10. Elisha's response to this approach is to stand on his own dignity and send a messenger to deal with Naaman. This was a somewhat exacting test of the faith of Naaman, and from the brusqueness of the prophet's reply and the content of it, Naaman might well be excused for taking it as a studied insult. The sevenfold immersion recommended by Elisha reveals the saga-form of the tradition.

11. The position of *'ēlay* is emphatic, meaning 'to a person like me'. The infinitive absolute *yāṣō'* ('come out') also emphasizes the fact that Naaman regarded it the duty of Elisha, whom he regarded as his social inferior, to come out to him. Naaman also expected some physical gesture and an invocation of the name of Yahweh, a simple ritual and 'myth', with the principle of which he was familiar. 'The place' is ambiguous. Šanda maintains that *māqōm* indicates not the place affected by the 'leprosy', but the place where Naaman was standing, and etymologically that is what one would expect. Kittel and others, again, take it to mean the place of the sanctuary, as if, presumably, the prophet were accompanying his invocation of Yahweh by a beckoning gesture. There is the further possibility that in spite of the definite article the word should be translated 'some particular place', to which the disease, according to the primitive conception of the time, was expected to be exorcised. On this use of the definite article cf. Gen. 14.13, etc., *GK* § 126r. The use of the

---

Practice', *VT* II, 1952, pp. 207ff. The belief in the healing efficacy of the royal touch was well established in antiquity, e.g. the Emperor Vespasian, and with respect to scrofula, persisted in England until the eighteenth century, when Dr Johnson records being 'touched' by Queen Anne.

word to denote the affected part of the body is actually attested in Lev. 13.19.

5.12. Abana, if the reading is correct, would be the only mention of such a river. Q and T read Amana, which is possibly correct, the river, the modern Baradā, being named from the mountains where it rises, known in Assyrian records[a] as Ammana (cf. S. of S. 4.8), probably the Anti-Lebanon immediately north-east of Damascus. Pharpar is probably *Wādī al-Aʿwāj*, which rises in Hermon and flows, like the Barada, into swamps south-east of Damascus. The name probably survives in *Wādī Barbar*, a tributary of this stream.

14. In the use of the verb *šūb* we have an instance probably of a pregnant meaning, the flesh of Naaman 'was restored and became' as the flesh of a child. L. Kopf, however,[b] would take the verb to mean 'become' on the analogy of Arab *ʿāda*, which means primarily 'to return', but is attested by Arab lexicographers as a synonym of *ṣāra* ('to become').

15. This striking confession of monotheism, recalling the *šahāda*, or testimony, of Islam, is the more striking as coming from an Aramaean, yet is naïvely inconsistent with this request for two mules' burdens of earth so that he might worship Yahweh in Damascus. His reason consented to monotheism but convention bound him practically to monolatry. Eissfeldt has argued that there was already a tendency to monotheism in the cult of Baal-shamaim in Syria,[c] so that Naaman was the more prepared to confess that the one God was Yahweh.

berākā (lit. 'blessing' or 'virtue' as the consequence of blessing) means 'present' here. The secondary meaning signifies the communication of the blessing which is manifest in the possession of the means of giving.

17. *wālō'* indicates a suppressed protasis 'Then if you won't', and implies the view that Elisha would have conferred a favour by accepting the present, in place of which Naaman asks him to do him the favour of consenting that he take two burdens of Israelite land.

18. *laddābār hazze* anticipates *baddābār hazze* at the end of the sentence and may be a dittograph, but in view of the length of the sentence it may be retained.

Rimmon ('pomegranate') is probably a Jewish parody of Ram-

[a]D. D. Luckenbill, *AA* I, § 720.
[b]*VT*, VIII, 1958, p. 206.
[c]'Baʿalšamēm und Jahwe', *ZAW* LVII, 1939, pp. 1ff.

mān, the title of Hadad, the Syrian Baal, manifest in winter storm, rain and thunder, cf. Assyr. *Ramānu* ('the Thunderer', from *ramānu*, 'to roar, crash'). The identity of 'Rimmon' with Hadad and his significance in the religion of the Aramaeans of Damascus is confirmed by the theophoric name Benhadad, borne by several Aramaean kings, and Tabrimmon the father of Benhadad, the contemporary of Asa of Judah (I K. 15.18). This deity was Baal-shamaim whose cult at this time showed a marked tendency to monotheism. On the location of the temple in question, on the site of the Umayyad Mosque at Damascus, see on I K. 11.23.

5.19. The presumed noun *k^ebārā*, found only in the phrase *kib^erat hā'āreṣ*, is of uncertain derivation. The phrase in Gen. 35.16 and 48.7 indicates a short distance, hence can hardly be cognate with Akkadian *kibratu*, which indicates a quarter of the earth. In the phrase *kbrt mṣ' šmš* in a Phoenician inscription from Ma'sub, G. Hoffmann[a] finds a parallel to the phrase in Kings, which he takes to mean that which is visible between the seer and the horizon. Here as in the Assyrian usage the word means 'direction'. We may suggest a connection with *bārar* ('to be clear'), *k^e* being the preposition, hence *kib^erat hā'āreṣ* may mean 'about (a certain) space of land'.

(β) *The curse on Gehazi:* 5.20–27

This may be a later expansion of the preceding tradition, motivated by the object of explaining the name Gehazi ('avaricious') and attributing to Elisha the power that Moses had to impose as well as to heal leprosy (cf. Num. 12.10ff.), see Commentary on v. 27.

5 20Now Gehazi the lad of Elisha[b] said, See, my master has spared
this Aramaean[c] in not taking from him what he brought. Nay, but, as
Yahweh lives, I will run after him and take something from him.
21So Gehazi went after Naaman, and Naaman saw him[d] running after
him, and he got down from his chariot to meet him and he said, Is all
well? 22And he said, All is well. My master has sent me saying, See
now, here have come to me two lads from the hill-country of Ephraim
from the sons of the prophets. Give them a talent of silver and two
changes of clothes. 23And Naaman said, Please take two talents. And
he pressed him[e] and bundled up two talents of silver in two bags and
two changes of clothes and gave them to two of his servants, and they

[a]Cited by Cooke, *NSI*, p. 49.

[b]Omitting *'īš hā'elōhīm* ('the man of God') of MT with G^BA.

[c]Omitting MT 'Naaman', though this is conjectural and unsupported by the versions.

[d]Reading *wayyir'ēhū* with G for MT *wayyir'e*.

[e]The sense demands the reading *wayyipṣar bō* ('and he pressed him') for MT *wayyipros*, cf. 2.17.

carried them before him. [24]And they[a] came to the citadel, and he took them from them and deposited them in his house and dismissed the men and they went off. [25]Then he came and presented himself before his master, and Elisha said to him, Where have you come from, Gehazi? And he said, Your servant has not gone anywhere. [26]Then he said to him, Did not[b] my heart go with you[c] when a certain man turned from his chariot to meet you? Have you now taken[d] the money [e]to buy orchards[e] and olive-trees and vineyards and sheep and oxen and menservants and maidservants? [27]So the leprosy of Naaman shall cleave to you and to your seed for ever. And he went forth from his presence stricken with leprosy like snow.

5.20. The strong asseverative is to be noted after *kī 'im*, cf. Judg. 15.7; Jer. 51.14. In the latter instance, as in the present passage, this is preceded by an oath. After the oath *kī* is often used independently as a strong asseverative. In the instances cited, however, the compound *kī 'im* seems to imply the contradiction to an unexpressed clause, e.g. 'he is going away, but I will run after him', thus preserving its usual adversative sense. In this case the verb *raṣtī* is to be explained as a perfect of certitude akin to the 'prophetic perfect', as Burney suggests.[f]

21. The use of *nāpal* (lit., 'fall') is noteworthy here, being paralleled by the usage in Gen. 24.64 to denote descent from a camel. The present deference of Naaman to even the servant of Elisha contrasts strongly with the hauteur with which he drove up to Elisha's door and expected him to come out and meet him as an inferior.

23. The usage of the Hiphil *hō'il* here is paralleled in 6.3; Judg. 19.6 and II Sam. 7.29. The sense is literally 'Consent!'

ḥārīṭ is found in the Old Testament only here and in the list of women's finery in Isa. 3.22, where it means 'satchels', possibly for perfumes.

[a]Reading plural of the verb with G.

[b]The reading *h^alō'* is suggested for MT *lō'*, and the interrogative sense is correct. But here and in Amos 7.14 the question may be asked without the interrogative particle before the negative, see G. R. Driver, *ExpT* LXVII, 1955, pp. 91f.

[c]Inserting *'imm^ekā* with G.

[d]Reading with G and V *ha'attā lāqaḥtā* for MT *ha'ēt lāqaḥat* ('Is it a time to take'), which, however, might be defended by supposing Elisha to mean that the occasion of the manifestation of the power of God in the healing miracle and what that portended was not the time to be thinking of such mundane matters. The time when Naaman was so visibly impressed with the power of the God of Israel was not an occasion to be marred by the material cupidity of Gehazi (Burney, *Notes . . on Kings*, p. 283).

[e]Reading *liqnōt bō gannīm* for MT *w^elāqaḥat b^egādīm* ('and to obtain clothes') as suggested by the reference to agricultural property in the sequel.

[f]*Op. cit.*, p. 281.

5.24. *ʿōpel* means etymologically a 'tumour' or 'swelling' (e.g. I Sam. 5.6), so that it might conceivably denote a hill or mound. Here, however, the definite article suggests some feature more specific than a hill, hence we suggest that it was the citadel of Samaria, crowned by the inner wall and palace of Omri and Ahab, though 'the Ophel' at Jerusalem may refer rather to the 'bulge' eastward from the north end of the south-east hill (Neh. 3.27). Possibly in the use of 'the Ophel' here we have a parallel to *al-Qasba* ('the castle', or quarters of the Arab ruling class) in North African towns in contrast to *al-Ḥāra* ('the quarter' of the Jews). This might indicate that Gehazi, like Elisha, lived in the palace-complex or its immediate vicinity, consonant with Elisha's status as a royal seer. The meaning of 'Ophel' as a fortified area of limited extent, a citadel, is further indicated in the reference of Mesha in the Moabite Stone to such a fortification.

26. On the use of *lōʾ* in the interrogative sense without the interrogative particle see p. 509 n.[b]. *libbī* ('my heart') indicates the cognition of the prophet. The passage may be roughly rendered, as Burney suggests,[a] 'Was I not present in spirit?'

27. The phrase 'smitten with leprosy like snow' (*meṣōrāʿ kaššeleg*) is the description of Moses' leprosy (Ex. 4.6f.), and it may well be that this feature of the episode is suggested to the author of the saga by the tradition of Moses.

(ix) THE RECOVERY OF THE AXE-HEAD FROM THE JORDAN: 6.1–7

On the provenance of the tradition and its affinities see critical introduction to the Elisha-cycle. When the episode is appreciated as part of the Elisha-hagiology from a popular source the element of miracle is expected.

> 6 [1]Now the sons of the prophets said to Elisha, See, the place where we are dwelling before you is too cramped for us. [2]Let us go to the Jordan and take thence a beam apiece to make[b] for ourselves a place

[a]*Op. cit.*, p. 283.

[b]G^L and S omit MT *šām* ('there'), which leaves open the question of the location of the new dwellings. The MT signifies that the prophets sought a new settlement by the Jordan, but in the jungle growth of that low depression by the river (*az-zawr*) settlements were not practicable because of malaria. It is more likely that timber was cut there for additional buildings in the oasis of Jericho in the vicinity of the shrine of Gilgal. These would be light shelters, which sufficed in the heat and rain-shadow of the Jordan Valley. We therefore omit MT *šām* with G^L and S and take the second *šām* as referring to the new buildings in which the prophets proposed to live.

to dwell. So he said, Go. [3]And one said, Please go with your servants. So he said, I will go. [4]So he went with them, and they came to the Jordan and hewed down the trees. [5]And one of them was felling his beam when the iron blade fell into the water, and he cried out saying, Alas, master, and it was borrowed too. [6]Then the man of God said, Where did it fall? So he showed him the place, and he cut a stick and cast it in there, and the iron floated. [7]And he said, Take it up. So he put out his hand and took it.

6.1. Elisha seems here to be living in the prophet-community, which must have been near the Jordan, probably about Jericho (2.5, 19–22), attached to the shrine of Gilgal. Šanda, however (II, p.48), cautiously points out that *l^epānekā* need not necessarily imply that Elisha lived with the prophets, the phrase, like Arabic *bimaẓẓarik* (lit. 'in seeing thee') being simply deferential.

2. On the location of the new buildings see p. 510, n.[b].

3. On *hō'ēl* ('Please!', lit. 'Consent!') see on 5.23.

4. The trees which the prophets felled by the Jordan were of the proportion of beams rather than heavy timber, such not being required for the light shelters in the hot, dry Jordan Valley. The smaller trees such as willow, tamarisk, acacia, and plane grow in profusion on the immediate banks (*az-zawr*) of the Jordan. This luxuriant jungle-growth (*g^e'ōn hayyardēn*) is proverbial in the Old Testament as the haunt of wild beasts, e.g. lions (Jer. 49.19; 50.44; Zech. 11.3) and, until recently, wild pig.

5. MT *w^e'et* standing before the apparent nominative *habbarzel* ('the iron') can be paralleled by such usage in Jer. 36.22; Ezek. 17.21; 35.10; 44.3, which suggests that it is normally a late usage. *GK* § 117m explains it as the enclitic introducing the accusative after some word understood, e.g. 'Behold'. Klostermann proposed to read *'et* in the sense of 'blade', which was accepted by Benzinger and Kittel, but in the Old Testament *'ēt* means a 'ploughshare', and, in view of the instances above cited of *'et* used to emphasize a noun, this interpretation is perhaps unnecessary.

6. The factual basis of the 'miracle' of the floating axe-head may be that Elisha with a long pole or stick probed about the spot indicated (an important point in the text) until he succeeded either in inserting the stick into the socket, or, having located the hard object on the muddy bottom, moved it until the man was able to recover it. In the circles in which the Elisha-hagiology took shape simple instances of prophetic sagacity were soon exaggerated to miracles. The point that impressed the man who lost the axe was that he had appealed to Elisha and his faith had been justified, by whatever means the axe-head had been recovered. If this was simply a case of practical sagacity on the part of the prophet, its elevation to miracle may be apologetic for the practical ineptitude of the man who lost the axe and had not the resource to try to recover it.

(x) ELISHA AND THE ARAMAEAN INVASION: 6.8–23

Here, as in the story of Naaman, Elisha is depicted in the setting of contemporary history, though he is still rather a figure of legend or saga, cf. the role of Elisha in the siege of Samaria in the following section (vv. 24–33), with which this passage has affinities in language and the general historical setting.

Šanda (II, pp. 49ff.) argues at length that, since the king of Israel and his forces were apparently confined to Samaria and the Aramaeans were able to penetrate unhindered to Dothan within about 12 miles of Samaria, a late date is indicated, when Israel was confined to Samaria and practically stripped of chariotry (7.13). Thus he would associate 6.8–23 and 6.24–7.20 and date the whole soon after 797, though earlier than the passage dealing with the healing of Naaman (ch. 5), since the good relations between Israel and Aram in that incident suggest a period after the hostilities in 6.8ff. We admit his arguments for the late date of 6.24–7.20, but would dissociate the events there from those in 6.8–23. Here and in ch. 5 the king of Aram is not named and there is no means of accurate dating. The reference in 6.23 to the 'bands' (*gedūdīm*) of Aramaeans suggests not full-scale war but border raids, such as that in which the Hebrew girl had been captured (5.2). These may have been undertaken not by the army of Aram but by semi-nomad Aramaeans loosely federated with Damascus. Such raids might be comparatively easily contained, especially if conducted without much organization. Their frequency and their regular repulse (v. 10) suggests raids on this scale rather than regular war, which would surely have occasioned many incidents which would have left their impression on Scripture. The apparent vision of the horses and chariots of fire (v. 17) and the blinding of the Aramaeans (v. 18, cf. Gen. 19.11) certainly suggests saga rather than sober history, but the historical basis of the tradition of the vision of the horses and chariots and the bringing of the enemy into Samaria may have been an ambush in the hills which ring the Plain of Dothan, in which the chariot-force of Israel closed the exit from the plain and shadowed the Aramaeans, while Elisha guided them southwards into another ambush where the main force of Israel awaited them in the vicinity of Samaria, perhaps in the natural amphitheatre to the north of the city. Elisha's disclosure to his lad may refer to the ambush at Dothan, and his prayer that the Syrians should be blinded may be the hope that not until the final disclosure near Samaria should they be aware that they were being shadowed. This and his organization of an efficient intelligence service, through his general mobility and many local contacts, and the diplomatic advice to spare the prisoners, may have been the actual role of Elisha in an actual Aramaean raid. If the raiders had been semi-nomad tribesmen, the clemency of the king and the common meal (the convention of bread and salt) would have been effective in pacifying the raiders and others associated with them, especially if they were of the free tribes of the border without any fixed allegiance to Damascus. Had the party been from the regular army of Damascus, one cannot imagine that they would have been spared, and the indignity would certainly not have been unavenged. However that may be, the vagueness of the reference to historical circumstances, the focus of interest on the prophet, and the element of miracle here and in ch. 5 suggest a different source and different historical conditions from 6.24–7.20, and such common features as are present are probably due to the compiler who combined the traditions, probably soon after 797 BC.

Regarding the date of the episode, Šanda would rule out the reign of Hazael in view of the intimate relations between him and Elisha (8.7ff.), but this passage visualizes enmity between Hazael and Israel (8.12), and, if the reference to the king in 6.8–12 is correct, those very relations between the house of Hazael and Elisha might account for the allegation that the secrets of the king's bedchamber were relayed to Elisha (v. 12). A date in the reign of Hazael or his son Benhadad is probable, more particularly in the reign of Jehu. Until the death of Jehoram the son of Ahab, Israel, strengthened by the alliance with Judah, was able to take the offensive against Aram at Ramoth Gilead east of the Jordan, but with the revolution under Jehu this alliance was weakened and Aram under Hazael passed over to the offensive (10.32ff.). This activity of Hazael was apparently motivated by his determined opposition to Assyria, to whom Jehu had submitted in 841, after the temporary Assyrian withdrawal from the west in 839, which may be taken as the *terminus post quem* for the events described in the passage, with the proviso that the reference to the king of Aram in 6.8–12 may not be correct and the incident be simply a nomad raid.

6 [8]Now the king of Aram was at war with Israel and he took counsel with his servants saying, Towards such and such a place shall we set an ambush.[a] [9]But Elisha[b] sent to the king of Israel saying, Be careful not to go past this place, for there the Aramaeans are in ambush.[c] [10]And the king of Israel sent to the place of which Elisha[b] had told him, warning him, and he saved himself there not (merely) once or twice. [11]So the mind of the king of Aram was troubled on account of this matter, and he called to his servants and said to them, Will you not tell me who of our people[d] is for the king of Israel? [12]And one of his servants said, There is no one, my lord, but Elisha the prophet who is in Israel tells the king of Israel the words which you speak in your bedchamber. [13]Then he said, Go and see where he is that I may send and take him. And it was told him[e] saying, He is in Dothan. [14]So he sent there horses and chariots and a strong force and they came by night and surrounded the city. [15]And when the man of God[f] rose early the following morning[g] and went out there was an army surrounding the city with horses and chariots, and his lad said to him, Ah, master, how shall we fare? [16]And he said, Do not fear, for those who are with us are more than those with them.[h] [17]Then Elisha made intercession and said, Yahweh, open his eyes that he may see. And Yahweh opened [i]the eyes of the lad[i] and let him see, and there was the mountain full of horses and chariots of fire around Elisha. [18]And they came down to him, and Elisha prayed to Yahweh and said, Strike, I pray thee, this people with blindness. And

[a]Reading after Thenius, Benzinger, and Kittel *nēḥābē'* for MT *tḥnti*, presumably a scribal error for *tnḥti* ('my going down'). Thenius's emendation is suggested by G[L], S, and V.

[b]So G for MT *'īš hā'ᵉlōhīm* ('the man of God').

[c]The only possible pointing of the MT here is *nōḥᵉtīm* ('going down'), which, to be sure, would be an Aramaism appropriate in this passage. The same root might be the original reading in the last word in v. 8, though here we prefer Thenius's suggestion *nēḥābē'*.

[d]G[L], L, and V read 'Who betrays me?', suggesting *mī mᵉgallēnī*, which is read by Klostermann, Benzinger, and Kittel. Böttcher proposed a different pointing in MT *miššellānū*, viz. *mašlēnū* ('misleading us'), citing the Hiphil of the root *šālā* of 4.28. But there the verb means 'to lull into a false complacency', which is hardly the sense here. Kittel suggests that *mᵉgallēnū* or *mᵉgallēnī* has dropped out by haplography after *miššellānū*, and this is perhaps more likely than that *g* should have been mistaken for *š*.

[e]G, S, and V read *wayyāggīdū* ('and they told him'), which does not materially affect the sense.

[f]G[BA] read 'Elisha'.

[g]Reading *mimmoḥᵃrat* with Klostermann, Benzinger, and Burney for MT *mᵉšārēt* ('servant'). The adverbial phrase is found commonly after the verb *hiškīm* in the Old Testament in combination with *babbōqer* ('in the morning'), which should probably be read for MT *lāqūm* as suggested by G[L]. V ignores *lāqūm*.

[h]Reading *'ittām* for the meaningless MT *'ōtām* ('them', accusative).

[i]G reads simply 'his eyes'.

Yahweh[a] struck them with blindness according to the word of Elisha.
[19]And Elisha said to them, This is not the way and this is not the city.
Come after me and let me guide you to the man you seek. And he
guided them to Samaria. [20]And it came to pass, when they came to
Samaria, that Elisha said, O Yahweh, open the eyes of these men that
they may see. And Yahweh opened their eyes and they saw, and there
they were in the midst of Samaria. [21]And the king of Israel said to
Elisha[b] when he saw them, Shall I strike them down,[c] my father?
[22]But he said, You shall not strike them. Would you strike down him
whom you have not[d] taken with sword or bow? Set bread and water
before them that they may eat and drink and go to their master. [23]And
he made a great feast for them, and they ate and drank, and he sent
them away and they went to their master, and the bands of Aramaeans
came no more into the land of Israel.

6.8. 'His servants' (*ʿabādāw*) here obviously refers to high officials, privy counsellors, but includes also high-ranking army officers, who, as feudal retainers, could be strictly termed the king's servants. On the text of the end of the verse and v. 9 see p. 514 nn.[a,b].

9. Such a mobile person as Elisha, who travelled about the land visiting the prophetic communities, would naturally be well informed on current affairs and topography.

10. In *wehizhīrō wenišmar* ('and he warned him and he saved himself') the perfects with *w* consecutive are best taken as frequentatives. G[BL] omit *wehizhīrō*. If MT is correct here, the form of the pronominal suffix may be noted as North Palestinian.

11. *sāʿar* is very strong; the mind (lit. 'heart') of the king was in a whirl, like a whirlwind (*seʿārā*).

On *miššellānū* see p. 514 n.[d].

The preposition *'el* in the sense of 'supporting' is found in Jer. 15.1; Ezek. 36.9; Hag. 2.17.

12. In view of the Israelite prisoners, such as the Hebrew maid of Naaman's wife, and others who, perhaps, became concubines of the king and his officers, there might well have been a leakage of secrets from the bedchamber, if not of the king, at least of the leaders of the raid. This has been a regular source of information to the enemy in

[a]G[L] and V read 'Yahweh', which is wanting in MT.

[b]G[B] omits *'el 'elīšāʿ* of MT.

[c]Reading with G[BA], S, and T the infinitive absolute and imperfect *hahakkē 'akke* for MT *ha'akke 'akke*.

[d]Reading *lō'* with G[L], which is wanting in MT. It was regular to strike down prisoners of war, and, as Burney (*Notes on . . . Kings*, p. 287) well observes, the failure to do so was the subject of the prophetic rebuke to Ahab in I K. 20.42. The slaughter in cold blood of an enemy against whom the king had not proved himself in battle, however, would not redound to the glory of the king.

recent wars. The mention of Elisha in the defeat of Aramaean attempts seems rather to reflect the confidence of Israel than the fear of the Aramaeans, though the incident of Naaman, if it preceded this incident, would establish the reputation of Elisha among the Aramaeans.

6.13. Certain MSS read *'ēpō* for MT *'ēkō*, but MT with the same meaning may be retained as one of the Aramaic or North Palestinian features in this narrative. The termination of the name Dothan indicates that it may be a dual, cf. Arabic dual in the nominative. This is confirmed by G, which reads Dothaim, and by Gen. 37.17, where the form is Dothain. The place, in a plain somewhat higher than the Plain of Esdraelon, commands the pass between the southern end of the Carmel range and the hills of Manasseh leading from the coastal plain to the Plain of Esdraelon. It was thus on one of the trunk highways between Damascus and Egypt, cf. Gen. 37.17. Šanda has based his theory of the late date of this passage on the fact that Israel was so reduced that the Aramaeans were able to penetrate as far as Dothan without opposition. The force, however, was not the whole force of the Aramaeans and the journey, presumably from the southern end of the Sea of Galilee, was made by night. Still, the fact remains that this force did penetrate to Dothan within 12 miles of Samaria itself, which indicates that the frontier could not have been effectively held, and Ramoth Gilead must have been in the hands of Aram.

15. See p. 514 n.[g] above.

17. We have suggested in our introduction to this passage that the sight of horses and chariots of fire, if not the elaboration of the stratagem, may be based on some phrase heard by the lad in the prayer of Elisha, or it may take its origin from the lad's figurative description of a psychological experience with Elisha, an analogy being Muhammad's vision, under great emotional stress, of a giant figure on the horizon, which he took to be the archangel Gabriel. It may, on the other hand, reflect the title by which Elisha was known (13.14), and, if this title by which according to 2.12 Elisha acclaimed Elijah at the moment of their parting really applied originally to Elijah, might reflect the confidence the lad felt in Elisha as the successor of Elijah, the story of whose assumption he had probably often heard from Elisha.

18. Note the usage of *gōy* ('people') as distinct from *'am*, a religious community ('people-cum-God').

sanwērīm, found in the Old Testament only here and in Gen. 19.11, is taken as the phonetic modification of a Shaphel, or causative variation, of the verbal root *nwr* ('to be bright'). The hypothetical verb *sanwar* may mean 'to dazzle' or may perhaps be a euphemism 'to make dark', as Burney suggests.[a] This can hardly be said to be a very convincing explanation. The rescue of the servants of God by the miraculous blinding of their adversaries here as in the story of Lot at Sodom (Gen. 19.11) is a typical motif of saga.

6.19. *zō*, also found in I K. 14.5; Judg. 18.4; II Sam. 11.25; Ezek. 40.45; Eccles. 2.2, 24; 5.15, 18; 7.23; 9.13, may be an Aramaic or North Palestinian form of the demonstrative adjective.

The mention by Elisha of 'the man you seek', though the mission of the Aramaeans has not so far been mentioned to him, puts this episode out of the category of history into that of legend or hagiology.

22. On the text and general interpretation see p. 514 n.[d].

23. *kārā* in this context must mean 'he made a feast' (*kērā*). This is a *hapax legomenon* in the Old Testament, and is possibly cognate with Akkadian *kirētu*, a feast', to which one brings guests (*karū*). The reference to *g*^{e}*dūdē 'a*$^{}$*rām* ('bands of Aramaeans') (cf. 5.2) indicates that, in spite of the reference to the king in vv. 8–12, the incident rather concerned a border raid, possibly by semi-nomad auxiliaries.

(xi) ANECDOTES FROM THE SIEGE OF SAMARIA IN THE LIFETIME OF ELISHA: 6.24–7.20

It is difficult to avoid the impression that here are several originally independent anecdotes, e.g. the appeal of the woman to the king in the case of the cannibal compact and the dramatic disclosure of the king's fasting (6.24–31), Elisha's jeopardy (vv. 31–33), his prophecy of relief and of the fate of the disbelieving officer and its fulfilment, which is the prophet's vindication in his hour of danger (6.31–7.2, 17–20), and the story of the lepers and the relief of the famine (7.3–16). These incidents, probably taken from a fuller historical narrative, have been selected and combined to serve as a basis for prophetic biography. The famine brings Elisha into imminent danger of the king's wrath, and the crisis is accentuated by the incident of cannibalism. The famine occasions the prophecy of relief, and the means of relief is elaborated in the story of the lepers, so that the story of Elisha brings unity to the whole.

From certain details in this passage which seem historically

[a] *Notes on . . . Kings*, p. 286.

genuine, Šanda (II, pp. 49ff.) has drawn certain conclusions as to the date of the events and the composition of the passage. Since the kings of the Syro-Hittite states and Cilician Musri are known to have been in alliance with Damascus against Assyria in 853, 849, and in 846, is it unlikely that the events date from earlier than 842. The mention of Benhadad the king of Aram (6.24) indicates a date after the death of Hazael, which we date between 813 and 806 (see below on 13.22). After the violent usurpation of Jehu in 841 and his ready submission to Assyria, Israel, bereft of her Judaean ally, was a ready prey to the aggressive Hazael, who tolerated no Assyrian vassals in his proximity. The situation of Israel, thrown back on Samaria and almost stripped of horses and chariots (7.13), suggests a time after the depredations of Hazael (10.32f.) and specifically in the time of Benhadad III, who reduced Israel in the time of Jehoahaz (13.3) and stripped her of all but a token force of chariots (13.7). The Aramaean withdrawal from Samaria, however, in so far as it may not be a minor incident exaggerated by tradition, may herald the revival of Israelite power towards the end of the reign of Joash the son of Jehoahaz (13.17, 19), which was consummated by the victories of Jeroboam II (14.25). Šanda advances the plausible argument that the Aramaean suspicion of the kings of the Hittites and Musri indicates a date shortly after the accession of Benhadad in 797, since he was soon after that in alliance with these Syro-Hittite states against Zakir of Hamath, the loyal vassal of Assyria, according to the Aramaic inscription of Zakir[a] and the inscription of Adadnirari III (812–783).

6 [24]And it came to pass after this that Benhadad the king of Aram gathered all his army and went up and besieged Samaria. [25]And there was a great famine in Samaria and they[b] were pressing it hard until an ass's head cost eighty shekels of silver and a quarter of a kab of carob beans[c] five shekels of silver. [26]Now the king of Israel was passing along

[a]A. Dupont-Sommer, *Les Araméens*, 1949, pp. 45–48; M. Lidzbarski, *Ephemeris für semitische Epigraphik* III, pp. 1–11.

[b]The Syriac text expresses the subject after *hinnē*, which, however, may be omitted if it may be readily inferred from the context. See S. R. Driver, *Moods and Tenses*, § 135 (6).

[c]Reading *ḥarūbīm* with Cheyne (*Expositor*, X, 1899, p. 32), cf. II K. 18.27 and possibly Isa. 1.20. The EVV reading 'doves' dung' is based on the arrangement of MT *ḥryywnym* as *ḥry ywnym*. Bochart proposed that this was the popular name for some vegetable such as roasted chickpeas, citing the analogy of Arabic *ḥarwu 'l-ʿaṣāfīr* ('sparrow's dung') for a certain herb. There is, in fact, a plant known in Arabic as *ḥara' al-ḥamām* ('doves' dung'). The Massoretes suspected the text, as is indicated by Q (*dibyōnīm*, 'doves' droppings'). Klostermann proposed *ḥarṣannīm* ('grapestones'), cf. Num. 6.4. Winckler, more venturesome, questioned the reading 'ass's

on the wall, and a woman cried out to him saying, Help, my lord the
king! 27 And he said, If[a] Yahweh does not help you, from where may I
bring you relief? From the threshing floor, or from the winevat? 28 And
the king said to her, What is amiss with you? And she said, This woman
said to me, Give your son that we may eat him today and we shall eat
my son tomorrow. 29 So we boiled my son and ate him. Then I said to
her another day, Give your son that we may eat him, but she hid her
son. 30 And it came to pass that, when the king heard the words of the
woman, he tore his clothes as he stood[b] on the wall, and the people
saw, and there was sackcloth on his flesh within. 31 And he said, So may
God do to me and more also if the head of Elisha the son of Shaphat
remains upon him this day. 32 Now Elisha was sitting in his house, and
the elders were sitting with him—now the king[c] had sent a man from his
presence—and before the messenger came to him he said to the elders,
Do you see that this murderous fellow has sent to take off my head? See,
when the messenger comes, shut the door and hold it against him. Is not
the sound of his master's feet behind him? 33 While he was yet speaking
with them, there was the king[d] coming down to him, and he said, See,
this is the disaster from Yahweh. What yet may I expect from Yahweh?
7 1 Then Elisha said, Hear[e] the word of Yahweh. Thus says Yahweh, About this time tomorrow a seah[f] of fine flour shall cost a shekel
and two seahs[f] of barley shall cost a shekel in the gate of Samaria.
2 And the retainer upon whose arm the king[g] leant retorted to the man
of God[h] and said, Yes, and if[i] Yahweh makes shutters in heaven will

---

head' (*rō'š ḥ^{a}mōr*) and proposed *ḥōmer tīrōš* ('a homer of new wine'), and for *ḥiryyōnīm* of MT he proposed *ḥōrī* ('white meal'), postulating a dittograph of *y* and taking the ending *-ōnīm* as a dittograph of *biš^{e}mōnīm*. The simplest emendation is that of Cheyne, but the Arabic analogy suggests that 'doves' dung' as a botanical term may be the correct reading.

[a] The sense we expect is 'If Yahweh does not help you . . .', which suggests that *'al* of MT is a corruption of *'im lō'*. In conditional sentences, however, it is not unknown in Hebrew for the protasis to be put as a jussive, e.g. Ps. 45.12, *yit'āw* . . . ('should he desire then . . .'); Ps. 104.20, *tāšet-ḥōšek wīhī lay^{a}lā* ('If thou makest darkness then it is night'). Thus in the present passage *'al* is the natural negative before the jussive in the protasis.

[b] Reading *ʿōmēd* with G^L for MT *ʿōbēr* ('passing').

[c] Reading *hammelek* with G^L, which is not in MT.

[d] Reading *melek* for MT *mal'āk*, cf. 7.17.

[e] G reads singular for MT plural. The latter may indicate that the elders who were with Elisha were cited as witnesses of the message, which was, as the reading of G indicates, properly for the king.

[f] Here, and throughout where MT reads *s^e'ā* and *sā'tayim, mē'ā* and *mā'tayim* ('100,200' sc. measures) have been proposed, but the versions support MT, and the measure *s^e'ā* is well known.

[g] Reading with certain MSS *hammelek* for MT *lammelek*.

[h] G^{BA} read *'et-'^{e}līšāʿ* ('Elisha') for MT *'et-'īš-hā'^{e}lōhīm*, while S omits it.

[i] Reading *w^{e}hinnē* with G^L for MT *hinnē*, the conjunction continuing the thought of Elisha's statement.

this come to pass? And he said, Look, you shall see it with your eyes,
but shall not eat of it.
[3]Now there were four men, lepers, at the entrance to the gate and
they said to each other, Why are we sitting here till we die? [4]If we say,
Let us go into the city, then the famine is in the city and we shall die
there, and if we sit here then we shall die here. Come now, let us desert
to the camp of Aram; if they let us live we shall live, and if they kill us
we shall but die. [5]So they rose at dusk to come to the camp of Aram and
they came to the edge of the camp of Aram, and behold, there was no
man there. [6]For the Lord had caused the army of Aram to hear the
sound of chariots and the sound [a]of horses and the sound[a] of a great
army, and they said to one another, Behold, the king of Israel has
hired against us the kings of the Hittites and the kings of Musri[b] to
come against us. [7]So they rose and fled in the dusk and they abandoned
their tents and their horses and their asses [c]in the camp just as they were,[c]
and they fled for their life. [8]And these lepers came to the edge of the
camp and they went into a certain tent and they ate and drank and took
from it silver and gold and clothing and went and hid it; and they came
back and went into another tent and took some from there and went
and hid it. [9]Then they said one to another, We are not doing right. This
is a day of good news and we are hushing it up. If we wait till the morning light then punishment will overtake us. So now,[d] come, and let us
go and tell the king's household. [10]So they came and called the gate-
keepers[e] of the city, and they told them saying, We came to the camp of
Aram and see, there was no man there nor any human voice, but the
horses were tethered and the asses were tethered, and their tents[f] just
as they were. [11]So the gatekeepers called[g] and told the household of the
king within. [12] And the king arose in the night and said to his servants,
Let me tell you what the Aramaeans have done to us. They know that
we are famished and they have gone out of the camp to hide[h] in the
open country[i] saying, When they come out of the city we shall take
them alive and enter the city. [13]And one of his servants answered and
said, Let them[j] take then five of the remaining horses[k]—see! they are all

[a]Reading the conjunction *w*^{e} before *qōl* with G, S, and T.

[b]Reading *hammuṣrīm* for MT *miṣrayim* and *hammiṣrīm* of V, and T.

[c]Reading *bammaḥ*^{a}*ne* with G^{BA} and T for MT *hammaḥ*^{a}*ne*, and *hēmmā* for MT *hī'*, with G^{L}.

[d]For MT *w*^{e}*ʿattā* 6QK reads *ʿattā*, agreeing with S. G and T support MT, and V omits (*w*^{e}) *ʿattā*.

[e]Reading *šōʿ*^{a}*rē* with S and T for MT *šōʿēr*. G reads *šaʿar*.

[f]The reading *'oh*^{o}*lēhem* or *w*^{e}*hā'*^{o}*hālīm* is demanded by the context, the former being supported by G.

[g]The plural is obviously demanded and is written in certain MSS.

[h]The verb should end in a final ', cf. MT final *h*.

[i]Following Q.

[j]G and S omit the conjunction and V reads the first person plural.

[k]In this very corrupt text it seems obvious that the phrase *'*^{a}*šer niš'*^{a}*rū bāh* ('that were left in it') occurred only once in the original text. G, S, and V admit the first incidence of the phrase, reading *pō* ('here') for *bāh* ('in it'), but omit it at the second

which are left here of the multitude of Israel which are sound—and let us
send and see. 14So they took two horsemen[a] and the king sent (them)
after the army of Aram saying, Go and see. 15So they went after them to
the Jordan, and there was all the way full of clothing and vessels which
the Aramaeans had thrown away in their haste.[b] And the emissaries
returned and told the king. 16So the people went out and plundered the
camp of Aram, and a seah[c] of fine flour cost a shekel and two seahs[d] of
barley cost a shekel according to the word of Yahweh. 17Now the king
appointed the retainer upon whose arm he leant to take charge of the
gate, and the people trampled him down in the gate, and he died as
the man of God had said[e] when the king came down to him. 18So it
happened as Elisha[f] had declared to the king saying, Two seahs[g] of
barley shall cost a shekel and a seah[g] of fine flour shall cost a shekel
about this time tomorrow in the gate of Samaria. 19And the retainer
had retorted to the man of God and said, Yes, if Yahweh makes
shutters in heaven will this you have said come to pass? And (Elisha)
had said, Behold you shall see it with your eyes, but shall not eat thereof. 20And so it happened to him, for the people trampled him down in
the gate and he died.[h]

---

incidence as a dittograph. There is an obvious dittograph of the following phrase *hinnām k^{e}kol-h^{a}mōn yiśrā'ēl*, which G, S, and V omit at the second incidence. MT suggests two possibilities: one, retaining only the second incidence of *'^{a}šer niš'^{a}rū pō* (for MT *bā*, after G) and the first incidence of *hinnām k^{e}kol-h^{a}mōn yiśrā'ēl* and taking *tāmmū* in the sense 'they are exhausted' (cf. Gen. 47.15, 18, J; Lev. 26.20, H; Num. 14.33, J; Jos. 8.24; 10.20; Deut. 2.14, 15, 16; I K. 14.10, etc.), to render 'Let them take five of the remaining horses—behold they are as all the multitude of Israel who are left here in that they are finished—and let us send and see.' The second possibility, which we prefer, is to omit *'^{a}šer niš'^{a}rū bā* in the first incidence and *hinnām k^{e}kol-h^{a}mōn yiśrā'ēl* in the second, and assuming corruption of *m* to *k* in the proto-Hebraic script in MT *k^{e}kol*, to continue: *hinnām mikkol-h^{a}mōn yiśrā'ēl '^{a}šer niš'^{a}rū pō* (so G for MT *bā*) *'^{a}šer tāmmū* . . ., rendering: 'Let them take five of the remaining horses—see! they are all which are left here of all the multitude of Israel which are sound—and let them send and see.' Burney (*Notes on . . . Kings*, p. 292) on the basis of the Targum, attempts a bold reconstruction, 'Send men and let them take five of the horses which survive' (*šil^{e}ḥū '^{a}nāšīm w^{e}yiq^{e}ḥū ḥ^{a}miššā min-hassūsīm hanniš'ārīm*); 'if they live, lo, they are as the multitude of Israel that survive here' (*'im yiḥyū hinnām k^{e}kol-h^{a}mōn yiśrā'ēl '^{a}šer niš'^{a}rū pō*), 'and if they perish they are as all the multitude of Israel who are consumed' (*w^e'im yō'b^{e}dū hinnām k^{e}kol-h^{a}mōn yiśrā'ēl '^{a}šer tāmmū*). This depends on too much that is not suggested by MT.

[a]Reading *rōk^{e}bē* with G for MT *rekeb*.

[b]Omitting the definite article with Q, though the consonants of MT might be retained, pointed as Niphal infinitive construct.

[c]See p. 519 n.[f]. [d]See p. 519 n.[f].

[e]Omitting MT *'^{a}šer dibber* with S and V as a dittograph.

[f]G reads 'Elisha' for MT *'īš hā'^{e}lōhīm*.

[g]See p. 519 n.[f].

[h]6QK must have added, as the space in the fragment indicates, *kid^{e}bar 'īš hā'^{e}lōhīm*, which is supported by two MSS of V, but by no other version.

6.24. The reference here to a general levy of all the forces of Aram seems to suggest that the preceding passages had been concerned only with one of several small-scale raids. The phrase 'after this' need not necessarily connect with the preceding passage, but with some other matter which has been omitted by the compilers. The Benhadad in question could only have been Benhadad III the son of Hazael, under whom Israel was brought to the nadir of her fortunes under Jehoahaz, before the revival under Jehoash and Jeroboam II (see introduction to this section). The mention of the Aramaean king by name contrasts with the vague reference to 'the king of Aram' in the preceding passage.

25. Kittel (HKAT, p. 213), also Burney (*op. cit.*, p. 288) and van den Born (*op. cit.*, p. 151), assume that the famine was that announced by Elisha (8.1ff.) and was the occasion of the Aramaean attack. This we think unlikely, since the invaders lived off the land and apparently fared quite well, as is indicated by the provisions they abandoned in their camp (7.7ff.). The famine was confined to Samaria and was the consequence of the investment of the city, as the verse suggests.

On EVV 'ass's head' and 'doves' dung' see p. 518 n.[c]. An ass's head at an exorbitant cost is recorded by Plutarch,[a] and the sale of vermin and refuse for food is a familiar feature in ancient sieges. There is, however, no account of doves' dung being sold as food which is not possibly influenced by the biblical story, cf. Josephus's statement that the Jews at the siege of Jerusalem were reduced to eating dung.[b] It is possible, of course, that the doves' dung may have been sold as fuel or as a substitute for salt,[c] and this is the view of Gressmann,[d] but we prefer the reading of Cheyne *ḥ^a^rūbīm* ('carob pods'), or the interpretation of Bochart that 'doves' dung' was the popular name for some food such as roast chickpeas.

This is the only mention in the Old Testament of the measure *qab*, but it is stated in the Talmud to be a sixth of a seah, or two litres.

26. The king of Israel throughout this passage, as in the preceding, is unnamed. He was either Jehoahaz or Joash.

hôšîʿā ('help') denotes relief from all that restricts the vitality of a man, first physically, as here, then spiritually. See on 5.1.

[a] *Artaxerxes*, 24.
[b] *War* V, 13.7.
[c] Josephus, *Ant.* IX, 4.4.
[d] *Die älteste Geschichtsschreibung*, p. 302.

6.27. On the use of the jussive in the protasis of a conditional sentence see textual note.

28. Cannibalism under stress of famine or siege was well known in antiquity and is not unfamiliar in the Old Testament, e.g. Deut. 28.56f.; Ezek. 5.10; Lam. 2.20; 4.10, etc.; it is also recorded in Josephus (*War* VI, 3.4). Cases are attested in an Assyrian text from the time of Ashurbanipal and in an Egyptian papyrus cited by A. Oppenheim.[a]

30. With a fine sense of the dramatic the narrator reveals the sackcloth which the king wore beneath his regalia, and the sympathy with the people in their suffering which that symbolized. Here, as in few instances in the Old Testament outside the liturgy of the Psalms, the status of the king as the embodiment of the people is graphically illustrated.

31. The king's threat to the life of Elisha has occasioned speculation. It is thought (Kittel, Burney) that Elisha by predicting a famine (8.1) has been held by the king to be responsible. That begs the question of the identity of the present famine, which was apparently merely local as the result of the siege of Samaria, with that of 8.1ff., which was general. Another suggestion is that Elisha, in inspiring the prolonged resistance of Samaria, was responsible for the sufferings of the inhabitants. Skinner suggests that the king's exasperation at Elisha was directed against Yahweh (cf. v. 33), by oracles in whose name Elisha had encouraged resistance. The real reason may be that the king apprehended riots and sought to divert attention from himself to Elisha.

32. The fact that the local elders keep company with Elisha suggests that his circle was that of the conservative elements in Israel apart from the royal retainers in the crown possession of Samaria.

ben hamᵉraṣṣēaḥ means literally 'the son of the murderer', and might refer to the son or grandson of Jehu. But, as Jehu's *coup d'état* was instigated by Elisha, that is improbable. The phrase means probably merely 'murderer'. 'Hold the door against him', lit. 'press him (*ūlᵉḥaṣtem 'ōtō*) with the door'.

33. The king 'came down' from the palace, which occupied the highest point of the hill of Samaria.

There are two possible interpretations of *mā-'ōḥīl 'ōd layhwh* ('what may I yet expect from Yahweh'). The king admits, like Amos later (3.6), that calamity is from Yahweh. Why, then, should he wait

[a] '"Siege-documents" from Nippur', *Iraq* XVII, 1955, pp. 69–89.

upon, or hope from, Yahweh any longer? His break with Yahweh will be expressed by his rough handling of the prophet. On the other hand, this may indicate a scruple on the part of the king. He pauses to reflect that the present sufferings are inflicted by Yahweh and asks what, if he carried out his threat to Elisha, he might yet have to expect from Yahweh. On the preposition *l*ᵉ in the sense of 'from', as in Ugaritic, cf. *hū' šā'ūl layhwh* in parallelism with *'ᵃšer šā'altī mēʿimmō* (I Sam. 1.28); *bēn mayim lāmayim* (Gen. 1.6).[a]

7.1. The *sᵉ'ā* was one-third of an ephah, roughly equivalent to a bushel.

The 'gate' was the open place inside the city gate where public business was done.

2. On *šālīš*, the title of a feudal retainer, originally the third man, the shield-bearer, in the chariot with the driver and the warrior, see on I. K. 9.25. The office is eventually that of a royal aide-de-camp, e.g. Naaman, 'on whose arm the king leant' (5.18).

The opening of 'windows' or 'roof-shutters' (*'ᵃrubbōt*) in heaven is mentioned in the passage in the Baal-myth of Ras Shamra describing the building of the temple of Baal (*UT* 51, V, 123ff.), where it is explicitly stated to be for the purpose of inducing rain, a fact which points to a rite of imitative magic. Possibly the royal aide-de-camp hints here that the Baal-cult would have been more effective than the cult of Yahweh in the present emergency. The particle *hinnē* is best taken as 'if'. This remark gives some substance to the claim of Kittel, Burney, and van den Born that the famine was a general one caused by drought rather than a local famine in Samaria as the result of the siege.

3. The nature of the skin trouble of the 'lepers' is not apparent, but from the fact that they have access to the city at will (v. 4) we conclude that their disease was of the same kind as Naaman's.

4. *nāpal 'el* (lit. 'to fall away to') is the technical term 'to desert' (e.g. I Sam. 29.3).

6. It is hard to believe that, with the situation so much in their favour, the Aramaeans should have fled in panic at the fancied sound of an army. It seems more likely that a rumour had reached them of the activity of 'the kings of the Hittites' and of Musri, and it is not impossible that this rumour had been fomented by one of the prophets by the authority of Elisha. The message might well have been conveyed in the form of the sentence, 'a sound of chariots and a

[a]See *UT*, § 10, for a similar usage of *l* in Ugaritic.

sound of horses, etc'. Yet some such sudden panic there must have been if we may accept as literal the statement that the Aramaeans abandoned their silver, gold, and chariot-horses. The Aramaeans could not have been ignorant of the fact that it was such an appeal of Asa of Judah which brought their countrymen first to Israel (I K. 15.18). On the 'kings of the Hittites' and Musri in Cilicia see I K. 10.28f.

7.7. The horses that the Aramaeans abandoned must have been chariot-horses, which presumably they had not time to harness.

9. *kēn* is a noun, 'right', e.g. 17.9. It is also found as an adjective, e.g. Gen 42.11, *kēnīm 'aⁿaḥnū* ('we are true men').

'āwōn, from the root *'āwā*, Arabic *ġawā*, 'to go astray', means primarily aberration, then guilt, and secondarily, as here and in Gen. 4.13; Ex. 28.38; Isa. 40.2; 53.6; Ps. 69.28[27], the consequences of sin, i.e. 'punishment'. The verb *māṣā'* which means normally 'to find'. means also 'to light upon', and occasionally, as here, 'to overtake, catch up with', cf. I K. 13.14. It is used with *haṭṭā't* ('sin') as its subject in Num. 32.23.

13. On the interpretation of this notoriously corrupt and difficult passage see p. 520, n.[k]. A further complication is the ambiguity of the verb *tāmam*, 'to be finished, exhausted' and 'to be perfect, sound'.

14. The 'riders' were more mobile than chariots as scouts in the rough terrain of Palestine.

15. The line of the retreat of the Aramaeans to the Jordan is not specified, but it probably lay by way of Bethshan rather than by Shechem and the *Wādī Fār'a*. *kēlīm* may mean 'weapons', but it is more likely that, in view of the danger the Aramaeans apprehended, they retained these and jettisoned their vessels as well as clothing, both possibly part of their plunder.

18–20. The full verbatim repetition of the encounter between Elisha and the royal aide-de-camp may be secondary matter from the Deuteronomistic editor, for whom the criterion of prophecy was its fulfilment, or, if original, it may indicate the way in which the prophetic anecdotes, though dealing with the stuff of history, were told over with due emphasis on the prophetic word and its fulfilment.

(xii) THE RESTITUTION OF THE LAND OF THE SHUNAMMITE LADY: AN ECHO OF THE TIME OF ELISHA: 8.1–6

This is an incident after the death of Elisha, but serves to accredit the acts of the prophet, which had already become the theme of oral saga (v. 4), for which the authority was Gehazi, the servant of Elisha. This in itself would serve to isolate the passage from the rest of the Elisha-saga, further evidence of which Eissfeldt (*HSAT*, p. 553) adduces from the fact that Gehazi, though a leper according to ch. 5 or an addendum to the main passage there, moves without restriction in society in the present passage. This, however, is not a strong argument, since according to ch. 5 Naaman, though afflicted with a similar skin disease, enjoyed a like freedom, and the story of Gehazi's affliction is probably a late, etymologizing addendum to the main part of the Naaman-anecdote.

8 [1]Now Elisha had spoken to the woman whose son he had revived saying, Rise up and go, you and your household, and sojourn in some place, for Yahweh has proclaimed a famine, yes, and it shall come upon[a] the land seven years. [2]So the woman rose and did[b] according to the word of the man of God,[c] [d]and she went with her household and sojourned in[d] the land of the Philistines seven years. [3][e]And it happened that, at the end of seven years,[e] the woman returned from the land of the Philistines, and she came[f] to appeal to the king for[g] her house and land.[h] [4]Now the king was speaking to Gehazi the servant of Elisha[i] the man of God saying, Tell me all the great things that Elisha did. [5]And it happened that, as he was telling the king how he had revived the dead (lad), behold, there was the woman whose son he had revived appealing to the king for her house and land, and Gehazi said, My lord king, this is the woman and this is her son whom Elisha revived.

[a]Reading probably *ʿal* for *ʾel* of MT, which, however, is not impossible, and is read by 6QK, S, and T, and probably G, though it is equivocal.

[b]6QK reads *wattēlek* ('and she went'). See n.[d].

[c]G^{BA} reads 'Elisha' for MT *ʾîš hāʾelōhîm.*

[d]After a lacuna in 6QK *ʾel-ʾereṣ* for MT *beʾereṣ* indicates that *wattēlek* must be read in the lacuna, which leaves no room for *wattaʿaś* of MT. Nor is there room for *hîʾ ûbētā* of MT, the verb *wattāgor* ('and she sojourned') being excluded in the lacuna in 6QK by the preposition *ʾel* (*ʾereṣ*). The resultant text of 6QK, *wattāqom hāʾiššā wattēlek kidebar ʾîš hāʾelōhîm ʾel-ʾereṣ pelištîm* ('and the woman rose and went according to the word of the man of God to the land of the Philistines'), is one notable instance where this second-century text is shorter than MT.

[e]6QK omits, as the length of a lacuna in the fragment indicates. This, however, is possibly a scribal error of haplography through homoeoteleuton of *šebaʿ šānîm* ('seven years').

[f]G^{BA} and S read *wattābōʾ* ('and she came') for MT *wattēṣēʾ* ('and she went out', or 'and she came forth', i.e. from the crowd). 6QK, however, supports MT.

[g]Reading *ʿal* for MT *ʾel*, as in the same phrase in v. 5. 6QK, however, supports MT.

[h]Here is a lacuna in 6QK, which may have contained either a fuller text than MT or a vacant space not indicated in MT.

[i]Inserting 'Elisha' with G. 6QK reads simply 'Elisha', which is read by one MS of G, omitting 'the man of God'.

[6]So the king interrogated the woman, and she told him the story. So the king appointed her a certain officer saying, Restore all her property and all the produce of the land from the day she left[a] the land until now.

8.1. *gūr* properly indicates the status of a *gēr*, a protected stranger in an alien community. Here it simply means to live abroad for a season in the intention of returning to enjoy one's rights and property in one's native land. The estate of the Shunammite, in her absence, had become crown property. Whether such land was held in trust by the crown or not is uncertain. There is no means of telling whether the appointment of a royal steward was a regular procedure or an exception. The lands so left were probably held in trust by the crown, but in this case the husband of the Shunammite, who owned the land, had died, being already old before they left (4.14), and his widow had to make good her claim. From the analogous case of Naomi in the Book of Ruth we know that the land might revert to the nearest kinsman. There was, of course, a general reversion of property in Israel at the end of each seven-year period (Ex. 21.2; Deut. 15.1ff.). In fact, the idea of seven years' drought may have been suggested by the fact that the Shunammite waited till the seventh year (the year of release) before claiming her estate.

In *qārā'* . . . *lārā'āb* ('has proclaimed a famine') the particle *l* may be used to introduce the accusative, e.g. Isa. 53.11; 61.1; Jer. 40.2; Pss. 69.5[6]; 86.9; Job 19.28. This usage, familiar in Aramaic, is stated by *GK* (§ 117n) to be a late solecism, and most of the passages we have cited are certainly late. The regularity of the usage in Aramaic, however, suggests that it may have been more common in classical Hebrew than is generally recognized and may be a survival of an earlier substratum of Aramaic in Hebrew. Here it may be an Aramaism or a feature of the North Palestinian dialect, another case of which in the same verse is the second singular feminine of the pronoun *'atty*.

In *qārā'* we have a case of the perfect of the imminent future, the so-called 'prophetic perfect'.

4. This verse very significantly indicates an awakening of interest in the great deeds of Elisha, already the subject of oral tradition, one of the sources of which was Gehazi, the personal attendant of Elisha.

6. On *sārīs* see on I K. 22.9. In the present case in the transaction with a woman *sārīs* may well have its literal meaning 'a eunuch'.

[a]Reading infinitive construct with third feminine singular pronominal suffix for MT perfect.

(xiii) ELISHA AND THE COUP D'ÉTAT OF HAZAEL: 8.7–15

For the literary affinities of this passage see critical introduction to the Elisha-cycle, pp. 469ff.

The incident, of course, dates before 6.24–7.20, since the Benhadad of that episode was the son of Hazael. It must be dated between 845, when the record of the fourteenth campaign of Shalmaneser III names Hadadezer as king of Damascus (*ANET*, p. 280), and 841, when Hazael is named as king (*ibid*). But the Assyrian records mention no Benhadad as the immediate predecessor of Hazael, as 8.7–15 suggests. Hadadezer might still have been succeeded by Benhadad before Hazael succeeded, as 8.15 states, but for so brief a time as to pass unnoticed in Assyrian records. A difficulty is raised by the notice in the annals of Shalmaneser (*ANET*, p. 280) that Hadadezer 'met his fate' (*šadāšu ēmid*) and Hazael the son of a nobody took the throne. Weidner[a] has demonstrated that this phrase, whatever its precise meaning, meant that Hadadezer died a violent death, which might, though not necessarily, be supported by 8.15. In this case, the identification of the king of Damascus in 8.7–15 would seem to be wrong. In our opinion, however, 8.15 does not necessarily state that Hazael smothered Benhadad, but that when the king's bed-screen was changed in the morning Benhadad was dead, the manner of his death not being stated. It may be noted also that the Assyrian records, which laconically associate the violent death of Hadadezer and the usurpation of Hazael, still do not state that it was Hazael who slew Hadadezer. Events in Syria between 845 and 841 may well be telescoped in the Assyrian note of the death of Hadadezer and the accession of Hazael owing to the tendency which Olmstead has noted in Assyrian records to give such a résumé of the situation before the contemporary events they record (see above, p. 61). Thus the assassin of Hadadezer may have been Benhadad the predecessor of Hazael in a situation which recalls the brief reigns of the Israelite usurpers Zimri (I K. 16.9–18) and Shallum (II K. 15–9–14), who were themselves killed after their ephemeral reign.

> **8** 7Then Elisha came to Damascus, and Benhadad the king of Aram was ill, and it was told him saying, The man of God has come here. 8And the king said to Hazael, Take a present in your hand and go to meet the man of God and seek an oracle of Yahweh from him[b]

[a] *AfO* XIII, 1940, pp. 233f.
[b] Reading *mē'ittō* for MT *mē'ōtō* with certain MSS.

saying, Shall I recover from this illness of mine?[a] [9]So Hazael went to meet him and he took a present in his hand consisting of[b] every good thing of Damascus, forty camel-loads, and he came and stood before him and said, Your son Benhadad the king of Aram has sent me to you saying, Shall I recover from this illness of mine?[a] [10]And Elisha said to him, Go say to him,[c] Life to you!—though Yahweh has revealed it to me that he shall certainly die. [11d]And he stiffened his features and was appalled[e] until he (Hazael) was put out of countenance,[d] and the man of God wept. [12]And Hazael said, Why does my lord weep? And he said, Because I know what you shall do to the Israelites;[f] you shall send fire upon their strongholds, their young men you shall slay with the sword, their little ones you shall dash in pieces, and their pregnant women you shall rip up. [13]Then said Hazael, But what is your servant, who is but a dog,[g] that he should do this great thing? Then Elisha said, Yahweh has revealed to me that you shall be king over Aram. [14]So he went from Elisha and came to his master and he said to him, What did Elisha say to you? And he said, He said to me, Life to you! [15]But it happened the next day, when one took the netting and dipped it in water and spread it before his face, that he died. And Hazael became king in his place.

8.7. The introduction of the passage with *w* consecutive implies a prelude to the coming of Elisha to Damascus. It does not connect with the preceding story of the restoration of the Shunammite's property, since that narrative most naturally presupposes the death of the prophet (v. 4). The occasion of the visit of Elisha to Damascus is generally held to be a summons from Benhadad, his reputation being established after the healing of Naaman. The text naturally, though not necessarily, suggests that his visit merely happened to

[a]As in 1.2 we should read *mēḥolyī hazze*. In late Hebrew *mēḥolyī ze* would be regular, but in biblical Hebrew it is suspect. *h* has been omitted after *y*, in the proto-Hebraic script.

[b]Reading *mikkol-* with G[L] and S for MT *w[e]kol-*.

[c]Reading *lō* ('to him') with 18 Hebrew MSS, Q and the Versions except G[B], which omits MT *lō'* ('not'), which is an obvious scribal effort to make the first part of Elisha's statement agree with the prediction of the king's death. This reading is supported by the report of the oracle in v. 14.

[d]This passage, which is very difficult, is omitted in S.

[e]Pointing *wayyiššōm*, as suggested by Klostermann after V, for MT *wayyāśem* ('and he put').

[f]Reading *'attā* with G[L] for *rāʿā*, which comes in a very awkward position after the relative clause and wanting the definite article of the antecedent.

[g]G adds *hammēt*, a 'dead dog' being a self-designation of the utmost deference, cf. I Sam. 24.14; II Sam. 9.8; 16.9, but in view of the use of *keleb* without qualification in deferential address in the Amarna Tablets, e.g. Knudtzon, *Die El-Amarna Tafeln*, no. 60. etc., and the Lachish Letters (ed. H. Torczyner, *Lachish* I, ii, v, vi) the MT may be defended.

coincide with the sickness of the king. Elisha may have sought temporary refuge there, having incurred the wrath of King Jehoram. The fact that a present is offered (v. 8) after and not before Elisha's arrival in Damascus indicates that he had not been summoned to treat the king.

8.8. A declaration or oracle of Yahweh is 'sought'. Note the technical term *dāraš*. This involved a direct answer to the question, Shall I recover . . .? The meaning of *ḥāyā* is ambiguous. It may mean 'live' or 'recover one's health'. Doubtless it was meant in the former sense by Benhadad, but it was used in the latter sense by Elisha in his reply (v. 10).

9. A gift of 'every good thing of Damascus' was a costly one, including fruits of this fair oasis, which Muhammad compared with Paradise, and the varied merchandise of a great caravan-city, an emporium of desert-borne trade between Egypt, Syria, South Arabia, and Mesopotamia. Nevertheless this is still an exaggeration, the conventional indefinite number 40 revealing the saga, of which hyperbole is a feature.

'He stood before him' (*wayyaʿamōd lepānāw*) indicates a deferential attitude, as in the case of Naaman after his cure (5.15).

'Your son' indicates dependence upon Elisha as 'father'.

10. The text as we have taken it (see p. 529, n.[c]) seems to imply a deliberate misleading of the king by Elisha, who knowingly conceals the revelation of the king's death, which he nevertheless communicates to Hazael. MT *lō'* represents a very early, pre-Massoretic attempt to avoid this implication, and, as the easier reading, is suspect. Two interpretations are possible without implying deliberate deception. If *lō* is read, Elisha may mean that the king's illness, to which he had referred in his message to ask if he would recover health, was not fatal, though he knows with the certainty of revelation that the king is foredoomed to death by some other agency not here revealed. The consonantal text of MT, *l'*, may, on the other hand, be read *lū'* or, following the consonantal variant, *lū*, the optative particle. The response which the prophet communicated to Hazael to transmit to the king, *ḥāyō tiḥye*, might then reflect the loyal greeting to the king *yeḥī hammelek* ('Life to the king!'). This would be a case of oracular ambiguity, which is more familiar in the classical than in the Semitic world, though conceivable there. The prophet, who already had his suspicions of Hazael's ambitions, may have thus been testing the extent of his commitment by his revelation in the order to wish the king well, and again by his communication of the revelation that the king would die. C. J. Labuschagne[a] has suggested that *ḥāyō tiḥye* is indirect speech, the subject of the verb being Hazael, which we consider unlikely in default of a conjunction introducing the noun clause. An ambiguous reference to Hazael himself or to the king is possible, however, in Hazael's communication of the oracle as direct speech in v. 14, when there is in fact a double ambiguity, the loyal wish of the acclamation by the prophet of Hazael himself as king, and the affirmative response to the king's enquiry if he would recover.

8.11. See p. 529 n. e. There are two possible interpretations, one, that Elisha 'looked fixedly' (*wayyaʿamēd 'et-pānāw*) at Hazael, the second, that his features became rigid, as one in a trance experiencing second sight. On either interpretation the meaning of the Hiphil of *ʿāmad* is unusual, though not unintelligible. The analogy of the Arabic *ʿamada li* or *ʿamada 'ilā*, which indicates determination and intensity of purpose, suggests the former. The stiffening of the features, on the other hand, seems to indicate another stage in the revelation, and this is the interpretation we follow. The subject of *bōš* is obviously Hazael, since the subject of the next verb is specifically mentioned. Hazael was embarrassed before the fixed stare of Elisha and his appalled look at the prospect which he saw in vision. Perhaps his announcement of the recovery, then death, of the king had been designed by the prophet in view of his plans involving Hazael to test the reaction of Hazael, whose face revealed to the prophet not only his ambition, but his ruthless character and the consequences for Israel. Perhaps the announcement of the king's recovery was intended simply as a gauge of the disappointment of the ambitious Hazael. In non-literate society men become adept at reading the mind in the features in personal interview, as among the Bedouin.

12. The barbarities of border warfare among the Semites, where women and children were not spared, are noticed by Amos in his oracle on Ammon (1.13). The cruelties experienced by Gilead (and Galilee) at the hands of Damascus (Amos 1.3) probably included the severities of Hazael.

13. On the 'dog' as a term of self-abasement in ancient etiquette see p. 529 n.[g]. It is noteworthy here that Elisha does not anoint Hazael (cf. I K. 19.15), but only, wittingly or unwittingly, abets his ambition by revealing that he shall be king.

14. On the ambiguity of the response see on v. 10.

15. Hazael's usurpation is noted in Assyrian inscriptions, which

[a] *ZAW* LXXVII, 1965, pp. 327f.

refer to him as 'the son of a nobody', the regular designation of a usurper, but there is nothing in this verse which of necessity signifies that he murdered the king, though that is a possible interpretation. As Ewald already saw, the subject of *wayyiqqaḥ*, *wayyiṭbōl*, and *wayyiprōś* may be indefinite. The meaning of *makbēr* is 'net-work', cf. *k^{e}bārā*, 'a sieve' (Amos 9.9). It was apparently a feature of bedding, e.g. *k^{e}bīr hā'izzīm*, which David's wife spread over the place where his head should be (I Sam. 19.13, 16). Thus AV 'coverlet' is improbable, though a possible emendation would be *marbēd* ('blanket'). If it had been the purpose to suffocate the king, however, this would have been as effective dry as wet. We should retain MT *makbēr* in the sense of 'netting', woven of rough goathair like David's *k^{e}bīr hā'izzīm*, with the bristly hairs between the meshes, as in Bedouin tent-cloth. This would serve as a mosquito-net and, if soaked, as an air-conditioner. The point is that one came in and took the netting away as usual to be freshly soaked and hung up again, and, on doing so, he noticed that the king had died. On this interpretation Elisha's prophecy of the king's recovery was unfulfilled, but this is not the only case of an unfulfilled prophecy in the history of Israel, and if this is the correct interpretation it would certainly authenticate the passage. In this case there is no detailed account of how Hazael actually seized the throne.

(xiv) EDITORIAL MATTER FROM THE DEUTERONOMIST ON THE REIGNS OF JEHORAM AND AHAZIAH OF JUDAH AND JORAM OF ISRAEL: 8.16–29

This includes an extract from the Annals of Judah (vv. 20–22). The fact that the contents of vv. 28–29a are stated in more detail in 9.14b–15a suggests that the latter passage is the original one, probably the summary of an earlier introduction to Jehu's revolt, which was adapted here as the end of the editorial introduction to the reign of Ahaziah.

8 16And in the fifth year of Joram the son of Ahab the king of Israel, Jehoshaphat being then king of Judah,[a] Jehoram the son of

[a]G and S omit MT *wīhōšāpāṭ melek y^{e}hūdā*, obviously understanding the name as a genitive. If this is so, the number of the year of Jehoshaphat's reign has been lost in the text. Since the reference is to the accession of J(eh) oram of Israel, the date is 848, actually before the death of Jehoshaphat in 847, Jehoram of Judah having become co-regent with Jehoshaphat in 853 (see Introduction: Chronology). The reference to Jehoshaphat in 8.16 may then be a secondary note to explain that Jehoshaphat virtually abdicated in favour of Jehoram in 848 (see Introduction: Chronology).

Jehoshaphat the king of Judah began to reign. [17]He was thirty-two years old when he became king and he reigned eight years in Jerusalem. [18]And he walked in the way of the kings of Israel just as the house of Ahab did, for he had the daughter of Ahab to wife, and he did that which was evil in the sight of Yahweh. [19]But Yahweh would not destroy Judah for the sake of David his servant, as he had promised him to give a lamp before him[a] always. [20]In his days Edom revolted from the control of Judah and they made a king over themselves. [21]So Joram crossed over to Zair with all his chariot-force, and he rose up by night and attacked Edom,[b] who had surrounded him, and with him[c] were the chariot-commanders, and the people fled home. [22]And Edom has been in revolt from the control of Judah to this day. Then at that time Libnah revolted. [23]And as for the rest of the acts of Joram and all that he did, are they not written in the Book of the Chronicles of the Kings of Judah? [24]And Joram slept with his fathers and was buried with his fathers in the city of David and Ahaziah his son became king in his place.

25 In the twelfth year of Joram the son of Ahab the king of Israel, Ahaziah the son of Jehoram the king of Judah[d] became king. [26]Ahaziah was twenty-two years old when he became king and he ruled one year in Jerusalem, and his mother's name was Athaliah the daughter of Omri king of Israel. [27]And he went in the way of Ahab and did that which was evil in the eyes of Yahweh just as the house of Ahab, [e]for he was affianced to the house of Ahab.[e] [28]And he went with Joram, the son of Ahab, to war with Hazael the king of Aram at Ramoth[f] Gilead, and the archers[g] wounded Joram. [29]And King Joram came back

[a]Reading with Klostermann *l^e^pānāw* for MT *l^e^bānāw*, the sons themselves being 'the lamp.'

[b]The statement that Joram 'smote' Edom seems to contradict the statement in v. 22 that the revolt of Edom was effective. Hence it is suggested that for MT we should read 'and Edom, who had surrounded him, smote him' (*wayyakkēhū 'edōm hassōbēb 'ēlāw*). We agree with Eissfeldt (*HSAT*, p. 555) that in agreement with the mention of the effective revolt of Edom in v. 22 a Jewish reverse is indicated. This, however, is toned down in the text, which simply records that Joram, who had been encircled, broke out at night with his chariot-commanders, leaving the army to a *sauve qui peut*.

[c]Reading with Kittel *w^e'ittō* for MT *w^e'ēt*.

[d]'The king of Judah' is omitted in G^B. In this passage, however, there is point in such qualifying phrases, since 'Jehoram' and 'Joram' are variants of the same name, with the possibility of confusion.

[e]The phrase is omitted in G^B and is, strictly, tautological after the statement in v. 26 that Ahaziah's mother's name was Athaliah of the house of Omri. This, however, is a mere archival detail of the name of the queen-mother. Verse 27 emphasizes the conduct of the king, which was influenced by the conduct of his mother and her family.

[f]G^L reads 'Ramath' for MT 'Ramoth', which is supported by MT 'Ramah' in v. 29.

[g]Reading *hārōmīm* for MT *'arammīm* ('the Aramaeans'). In the parallel account in II Chron. 22.5 MT has *hārammīm*, which G translates as 'archers', suggesting to Klostermann an original *hāmmōrīm*, which is possible. The same meaning, however, may be obtained from *hārōmīm*, cf. *rōmē qešet* (Ps. 78.9; Jer. 4.29).

to be healed at Jezreel of the wounds which the archers[a] had inflicted[b] upon him at Ramah when he fought against Hazael the king of Aram; and Ahaziah the son of Jehoram the king of Judah[c] went down to see Joram [d]the son of Ahab[d] in Jezreel because he was ill.

8.16. On the chronology see Introduction: Chronology, and p. 532 n.[a]. The names of the two kings are just orthographic variations of the same name. In the introduction to the reign of Jehoram there is no mention of the name of his mother, which is regular in the case of the kings of Judah. Šanda makes the feasible suggestion that she was dead before Jehoram's accession, which supports the view that the point in mentioning the king's mother was that on his accession she became the head of the harem and the first lady in the land with the official status of *haggᵉbīrā*; see above, p. 106. Jehoram's eight years expired in 841, the year that Jehu became tributary to Shalmaneser III. This is a significant date in Hebrew chronology, since it is the first year of Jehu, the last year of his victims Joram of Israel and Ahaziah of Judah, whose reign is given as one year (v. 26), obviously incomplete, and the last year of the reign of Jehoram of Judah.

18. Jehoram's wife, here stated to be a daughter of Ahab, was the notorious Athaliah (v. 26; ch. 11). The statement in v. 26 that she was the daughter of Omri need not be at variance with this statement, as in Semitic idiom 'daughter' might mean 'female descendant'. In v. 26 G^{L} boldly harmonizes by rendering 'daughter of Ahab', while it is to be noted that S in II Chron. 21.6 reads 'sister of Ahab' for MT 'daughter of Ahab'. Since Ahaziah the son of Athaliah was 22 when he became king in 841, Athaliah must have been born no later than 878, four years before the death of Omri. Thus while she may have been a daughter of Ahab and the grand-daughter of Omri, she could well have been the daughter of Omri, brought up as a young orphan at the court of her brother Ahab and particularly under the influence of Jezebel, as H. J. Katzenstein suggests,[e] thus giving the impression that she was a daughter of Ahab. We may see in her marriage, probably at an early age, to Jehoram, the contrivance of the masterful Jezebel.

[a]See p. 533 n.[g].

[b]Reading perfect *hikkūhū* for MT imperfect *yakkūhū*, *h* closely resembling *y* in the proto-Hebraic script. The parallel account in II Chron. 22.6 supports this reading.

[c]This phrase is omitted in G^{B}, but on its significance in this passage to avoid confusion between the contemporaries Jehoram or Joram see on v. 25.

[d]This phrase must also be retained to distinguish between the two kings.

[e]H. J. Katzenstein, 'Who were the Parents of Athaliah?', *IEJ* V, 1955, pp. 194–7.

8.19. This passage, in the familiar language of royal propaganda, re-echoes the conception inculcated in the royal psalms of the covenant of Yahweh with the house of David, cf. Nathan's oracle (II Sam. 7.12–17). On the lamp as the symbol of life see on I K. 11.36.

20. The statement that the Edomites made a king over themselves in the sole reign of Jehoram of Judah seems to contradict 3.9, where there was a king in Edom in the joint expedition of Joram of Israel and Jehoshaphat. We must suppose that 'the king of Edom' is an inadvertent reference to the royal deputy (*n*[e]*ṣīb melek*) who held office then in Edom (I K. 22.47). It was probably the failure of this expedition against Moab, coupled with the activity of Assyria in the west between 850 and 841, which encouraged Edom to revolt from Judah.

21. Zair, which Montgomery (ICC, p. 396) takes to be Zoar of Gen. 13.10 at the south end of the Dead Sea, may be Zior of Josh. 15.54, about five miles north-east of Hebron. In this case either the Edomites must have invaded Judah or this place must have been the base for Jehoram's operations. On the interpretation that Jehoram saved himself and his chariot-force by a desperate night sortie and left the infantry to shift for themselves see p. 535 n.[b]. On the phrase 'to their tents' see on I K. 12.16.

22. 'To this day' seems to betray a hand later than the time of Uzziah, in whose reign Elath, strictly in Edomite territory, was in Judaean hands (14.22). It seems impossible that Judah should have held this isolated place on the north-eastern shore of the Gulf of Aqaba unless Edom was under subjection. The fact is, however, that no complete occupation of Edom was ever again effected.

Libnah ('White') is generally identified with *Tell aṣ-Ṣāfī* ('Gleaming Mound') located in the western foothills of the Shephelah dominating the entrance to *Wādī as-Sanṭ* (Vale of Elah). The *tell* was occupied continuously from *c.* 1700 to the Seleucid period.[a] An alternative site is proposed by W. F. Albright[b] at *Tell Burnāṭ* about six miles further south, which was occupied in the Early Bronze and Iron Ages. So near the Philistine plain, this was a frontier town and never quite part of Judah. The revolt of Libnah was probably part of a joint attack on Judah by Arabs and Philistines, which II Chron. 21.16f. records. Šanda (II, p. 74) notes that periods of Judaean strength and power over Edom coincided with peace with the Arabs and Philistines, according to Chronicles. In Jehoshaphat's ascend-

[a]Abel, *GP* II, pp. 369f.
[b]*BASOR* 15, 1924, p. 9.

ancy, for instance, the Arabs and Philistines were at peace with Judah (II Chron. 17.11), cf. Edomite revolts against Judah and the hostility of the Arabs and Philistines (II Chron. 21.16; 26.7). The bone of contention was the trade-routes through the Negeb to the Red Sea and the Hejaz. The supremacy of Judah over Edom made Judah economically dominant in the Negeb and obliged the Arabs and Philistines to be content with a modest share of the trade, but when Edom revolted the others followed, if possible, to break the domination of Judah in the south.

8.26. On 'the daughter of Omri' see comment on v. 18. The verbal element in the name Athaliah is derived by Noth[a] from the Akkadian *etēlu* ('to be manly'). In view of the names *ʿaṯal* and *ʿaṯalan* from the Northern Hejaz, we suggest rather an Arabic derivation *ʿaṯala* ('to be abundant, bulky'), the name referring, perhaps to a robust child.

27. The noun *ḥātān* means a son-in-law, and it has been suggested that Athaliah the mother of Ahaziah was a daughter not of Ahab (cf. v. 18), but of Omri (v. 26). This is to press the literal meaning of *bat* and *ḥātān* too much. We suggest that, in accordance with Arabic usage, *ḥātān* refers generally to relationship by marriage, but see on v. 18.

28. It is not clear whether the statement that Ahaziah went with Joram to war against Hazael means that he was personally involved in the campaign of Ramoth Gilead. The statement that he 'went down' to see Joram at Jezreel when he was wounded might refer to his journey from Jerusalem or from Ramoth Gilead. His personal involvement in the campaign at Ramoth Gilead would not be surprising in view of the active support of Judah under Jehoshaphat in the campaign at Ramoth Gilead in I K. 22 and in Joram's Moabite campaign. Now, however, since the successful revolt of Moab, Judah might have done a better service by remaining as a potential adversary of Moab in the south. Moreover, in Judah itself there was an explosive situation which might well have demanded the presence of the king and his troops. Only seven years earlier, according to II Chron. 21.4, Jehoram on becoming sole ruler put his six brothers to death with other prominent men in Judah. We agree with Šanda (II, p. 72) in seeing in this the drastic suppression of native protest against the pro-Israelite policy of Jehoshaphat and Jehoram and against the influence of Athaliah, a protest which was to be more effectively expressed later in the revolt against Athaliah (11.4ff.),

[a] *IP*, p. 191.

We should therefore take the statement that Ahaziah 'went with' Joram in his campaign against Hazael to indicate the direction of Judaean politics rather than the personal involvement of Ahaziah in the Aramaean war.

(*l*) THE REVOLT OF JEHU: 9.1–10.31

It strikes one as remarkable in view of the emphasis on the commission to Elijah to anoint Jehu (I K. 19.16) that his successor Elisha plays such a minor part in the actual revolt. He does not even anoint Jehu personally, but is represented as sending one of his prophetic associates to do so (9.1–6, 11), and thereafter neither Elisha nor any of the prophets is ever mentioned in the actual *coup d'état*. This and the fact that the account of the actual revolt (9.15ff.) begins with a statement as if *de novo* of facts already well known and recorded in vv. 1ff. that Joram was at war with Hazael at Ramoth Gilead, where he had been wounded and had returned to recuperate at Jezreel (vv. 14–15a; cf. 8.28f.), might suggest two different sources. After v. 15a, however, the narrative is resumed in the same racy style and tenor, the catastrophe of the drama at Jezreel linking up with the prophetic call at Ramoth Gilead by the emissary of Elisha, by the citation of Elijah's prophecy on the death of Jezebel (9.36f.; cf. 10.10, 17). The unity, however, is, we think, imposed by a compiler, either the Deuteronomist or an earlier compiler from prophetic circles. It is possible that there are indeed two sources reflecting the two aspects of the revolt against the house of Ahab, the religious reaction inspired by the prophets and the political, where a military group took the initiative, using Rechabite fanatics, to the exclusion, apparently, of prophetic elements. The extant account in chs. 9–10 possibly consists of the prophetic account of Jehu's rising in 9.1–14a and incorporates in the sequel the secular source. The apparent inactivity of the prophets in the actual course of the revolt might, of course, be owing to revulsion of feeling against Jehu either as an Assyrian tributary at a later date in the eighth century, when nationalist feeling prevailed under Jeroboam II or Pekah, or as a bloodthirsty political adventurer, in which light Hosea saw him (Hos. 1.4–5). The more natural explanation, however, would appear to be the two-source theory which we have propounded, unity being given to the whole by the prophetic compiler. Possibly his contribution was the insertion of Elisha and the emphasis on the prophetic call and the note of the fulfilment of Elijah's prophecy in 9.25f., 36f. On the other hand, the prophecy against the house of Ahab could hardly have failed to be exploited by Jehu and his party, so that this may well also belong to the secular source. Here again historical narrative has been overworked by the prophetic tradition as in I K. 20; 22; II K. 3. Noth[a] may well be right in including this prophetic redaction in I K. 20; 22; II K. 9.1–10.27 in the account of the prophetic intromission in the accession in Israel in I K. 11.29–39; 12.21–24; 14.1–18 (cf. II K. 9.9).

The story is told with great dramatic power, and stands in the saga tradition. The value of suspense is appreciated, as in the secret anointing of Jehu (v. 6) and his open acclamation, which is deferred till v. 12. Similarly the final catastrophe of the house of Omri is suspended in the narrative, which describes the ride of Jehu, the watchman's report, the sending of one messenger, then another, to Jehu, and finally the fatal sortie of the king himself (vv. 16ff.). The details of Jezebel, again, who found time for cosmetics in face of death (vv. 30ff.), serve to heighten the effect of her end and to give an insight into her character. The actions of Jehu, too, are calculated to serve as a character-study as well as a record of events. In such a narrative one might expect historical accuracy to be sacrificed to dramatic effect, and possibly this may be so in the matter of the spot where Joram fell, given as Naboth's plot (v. 21). The narrator, however, preserves his sense of historical perspective in avoiding the temptation to make vengeance for Naboth and the fulfilment of Elijah's prophecy (I K. 21.19) the main motive of Jehu. It was primarily the influence of the Phoenician Jezebel in religion and society that the resurgents opposed (v. 22).

There were a number of causes of hostility to the house of Ahab expressed in the revolt of Jehu. The extensive building of Ahab, so well attested in the fine bonded masonry of the palace and citadel of Samaria, Hazor, and in at least the northern stable-complex of Megiddo,[b] must have taxed the economy of Israel, while the campaigns against the Aramaeans and Moabites took toll of her manpower. The lack of success in those campaigns, particularly that in Moab, contributed to the general dissatisfaction, indicating, according to the conceptions of the day, that the divine blessing (*b^e^rākā*) had passed from Joram and his house. Šanda (II, pp. 91–93) supposes that Elisha, who knew Aramaean politics and the temper of

[a] *Überlieferungsgeschichtliche Studien*, p. 80.

[b] Y. Yadin, 'New Light on Solomon's Megiddo' *BA* XXIII, 1960, pp. 62–68.

Hazael, wished to break off the fruitless border war with Aram and form a united front against Assyria, whose advance to the west Hazael apprehended and was ready to resist. In Jehu, however, such hopes were disappointed. Too sanguinary in internal politics, he was too ready to submit to Shalmaneser III, and rendered tribute in the first year of his reign. In his declaration in the name of Yahweh 'I have anointed you over the people of Yahweh, even over Israel', the emissary of Elisha expresses the conservative dissatisfaction with the dynasty of Omri and the assertion of charismatic leadership of the sacral community *'am yhwh*, which was an ideal of the prophetic circle which adapted the historical narrative of North Israel. The revolt of Jehu was stimulated by a probable revulsion of feeling earlier against the house of Ahab in Judah, which, however, had been bloodily suppressed by Jehoram, the husband of the notorious Athaliah (II Chron. 21.4). The connection of Jehu's party with this abortive rising partly explains the readiness with which Jehu killed Ahaziah of Judah.

There are certain editorial features in this historical narrative, e.g. 9.7–10, from the prophetic adaptation, cf. I K. 14.10f.; 16.3f.; 21. 21, 24, and 10.28–36, which condemn the religious policy of Jehu according to Deuteronomistic principles.

(i) JEHU ANOINTED: 9.1–6

9 [1]And Elisha the prophet called one of the sons of the prophets and said to him, Gird your loins and take this flask of oil in your hand and go to Ramoth[a] Gilead. [2]And when you come there look out there Jehu the son of Jehoshaphat the son of Nimshi, and go in and rouse him from among his fellows and take him into an inner chamber. [3]Then take the flask of oil and pour it on his head and say, Thus says Yahweh, I have anointed you as king over[b] Israel. And you shall open the door and flee and shall not wait. [4]So the lad went[c] to Ramoth Gilead. [5]And when he came, there were the commanders of the army sitting, and he said, I have a matter with you, commander. And Jehu said, With whom of us all? And he said, With you, commander. [6]So he rose and went inside, and he poured the oil on[b] his head and said to him, Thus says Yahweh, the God of Israel, I have anointed you as king over[b] the people of Yahweh, over[b] Israel.

9.1 The name Jehu is borne by a prophet before the better-known

[a]Cf. p. 533 n.[f], on 8.28.

[b]Reading with a number of Hebrew MSS *'al* for MT *'el* ('to'), as the sense demands.

[c]Omitting MT *hanna'ar hannābī'* ('the lad, the prophet'). Possibly the original text was *na'ar hannābī'* ('the prophet's lad').

king (I K. 16.1). It is of the same type as Abihu and Elihu,[a] the first syllable being probably an abbreviation of Yahweh. The name 'Yahweh is (God)' may have been given by the parent of Jehu in sympathy with Elijah and in commemoration of his decisive action and vindication on Carmel, when the people had responded *yhwh hū' hā'elōhīm*. The name certainly indicates the conservative circles from which Jehu came. Jehoshaphat ('Yahweh will judge') signifies the same. If Nimshi was the name of Jehu's grandfather, he was presumably more prominent than Jehoshaphat, since the latter is not mentioned when Jehu is named 'the son of Nimshi' in 9.20. Nimshi may be the name of Jehu's clan, but it is attested as the name of an individual in fiscal dockets from Samaria in the time of Jeroboam II. The name probably originated as a nickname 'the weasel', cf. Arabic *nims*.[b]

9.2. On *ḥeder beḥeder* see on I K. 20.20; 22.25.

3. On the significance of the rite of anointing as a setting-apart see on I K. 1.34. Probably in the conception of the conservative elements in Israel this was only valid when the person to be anointed had evidenced his possession of the *berākā*, or blessing, by some natural ability or aptitude, while the anointing of a prince simply because he was the son of the king was held to be an abuse of the rite. Joram's lack of success was a sign that he no longer enjoyed the *berākā*, while the obvious popularity of Jehu among his brother-officers (v. 13) indicated that the *berākā* was his in portion, to be confirmed and amplified by the rite of anointing. Here the sacred rite was fittingly dispensed by a prophet as one who possessed the spirit of Yahweh, as in the case of Samuel with Saul (I Sam. 10) and David (I Sam. 16), though Samuel was also a priest. The tradition of the sacral confederacy in the North recognized possession by the spirit as the characteristic of leadership in kings as in judges.

5. The commanders were 'sitting', possibly 'in session' as a council of war. Possibly the appearance of the prophet was a preconcerted signal for dénouement of the military plot.

6. *'am*, as distinct from *gōy*, signifies the religious community, even apart from the qualifying *yhwh*. Whether part of the secular historical narrative or the prophetic redaction, it indicates the traditional Israelite reaction against the liberal cosmopolitan policy of the house of Omri.

[a]Noth, *IP*, 143.
[b]So Noth *IP*, p. 230.

(ii) THE WORDS OF THE PROPHET TO JEHU ON THE THEME OF RETRIBUTION ON THE SINS OF AHAB CHARACTERISTIC OF THE PROPHETIC ADAPTATION OF THE HISTORICAL NARRATIVE: 9.7–10a

The words re-echo I K. 14.10f. and I K. 21.21ff. (cf. v. 10); see Introduction to I K. 21.

9 7And you shall strike[a] down the house of Ahab your master and I
will take vengeance[b] for the blood of my servants the prophets[c] from
Jezebel. 8And all the house of Ahab shall perish,[d] and I shall cut off him
that belongs to Ahab who pisses against the wall, to the last man in Israel.
9And I will make the house of Ahab as the house of Jeroboam the son
of Nebat and as the house of Baasha the son of Ahijah. 10And Jezebel
the dogs shall eat in the field of Jezreel and none shall bury her.

(iii) THE ACCLAMATION OF JEHU: 9.10b–14a

9 10BAnd he opened the door and fled. 11Then Jehu went out to the
servants of his master and they said[e] to him, Is all well? Why did
this mad fellow come to you? And he said to them, You know your-
selves the man and his talk. 12And they said, It's a lie! Tell us. So he
said, Thus and thus he said to me saying, Thus says Yahweh, I have
anointed you as king over[f] Israel. 13So they hastened and took each
man his cloak, and put it under him on the top of the steps and they
sounded the trumpet and said, Jehu is now king. 14So Jehu the son of
Jehoshaphat the son of Nimshi conspired against[f] Joram.

9.10. The latter half of the verse continues the narrative interrupted at v. 7 by the expansion of the prophet's message, in which we would see a vestige of the prophetic adaptation of the historical narrative.

11. 'The servants of his master' signifies that Jehu and his brother officers were feudatories of the king.

Here, as in Hos. 9.7 and Jer. 29.26, the passive participle *m^{e}šuggā'* is used to describe a prophet with respect to his ecstatic propensity. The word may be connected with the Arabic verb *saja'a*, which expresses the cooing of pigeons, and secondarily the recital of rhymed

[a]G reads 'and you shall cut off' (*w^{e}hikrattā*), which is a feasible reading rather more Deuteronomistic in style in the context, and almost identical with MT (*w^{e}hikkītā*) with *r* for *y*.

[b]G reads the second person, which again is quite feasible.

[c]Omitting as tautological 'and the blood of all the servants of Yahweh', though there is no evidence for this in the Versions.

[d]G reads 'and from (the hand of)' (*ūmiyyad*) for MT *w^e'ābad*, which S and V support by reading, though in the Hiphil and with change of person, *w^e'ōbīd*.

[e]Reading the plural with certain Hebrew MSS and G, S, V, and T.

[f]Reading *'al* for MT *'el*.

prose, of which the Qur'an is the best example. The sometimes inarticulate mutterings of the prophet under intense emotional strain or spiritual preoccupation may have suggested the cooing of a pigeon. On the other hand, the word may be connected with the Assyrian *šēgu* ('to howl' or 'rage'), referring to the more extreme abandon of the prophet or 'howling dervish'. Secondarily perhaps the word may have come to designate the ecstasy of the prophet, the frequent extravagances of whom were not noticeably different from the behaviour of a madman, hence the use of the word to express 'madman' in general, e.g. Deut. 28.34, and the behaviour of David, who feigned madness at Gath (I Sam. 21.13ff.). The term in the present passage is derogatory (cf. I Cor. 14.23) and indicates on the one hand the comparatively low esteem in which the meaner members of the prophetic guilds were held and on the other the contempt of the professional soldiers for these 'men of God', (cf. 1.9, 11). This passage is often cited along with such passages as Jer. 29.26, where the denominative verb *hitnabbē'* is used of madness, in support of the theory that ecstasy was an essential feature of Hebrew prophecy. Ecstasy has, on the other hand, been denied, at least in the case of the canonical prophets. Certainly what impresses us is the sanity rather than the abnormality of these great figures, but Isaiah and Jeremiah, to say nothing of Ezekiel, went to great extremes of eccentricity in the inculcation of their message. In our opinion the truth is that ecstasy was indeed a characteristic of Hebrew prophecy, but that this varied in degree from the wild and often pointless behaviour and utterance of the 'sons of the prophets', who might be described as *m*[e]*šuggā'im*, to the devoted absorption of the great prophets in their divine mission, in the discharge of which their self was sublimated and their conscious self-repression subserved the great revelations of the divine will which had mastered them.

'His talk' is a somewhat general rendering of *śîḥō*. Here it might indicate the muttering speech of a man speaking to himself in his preoccupation or conning over a lesson or prayer, cf. Job 15.4; Ps. 119.97.

9.12. *šeqer* means a deliberate lie, as in Jeremiah's reply to the charge that he was deserting to the Babylonians (Jer. 37.14).

13. The setting of the officers' cloaks under Jehu indicates submission to his authority, cf. Jesus' triumphal progress from Bethany (Matt. 21.8). This is another instance of the clothes representing the man, cf. David's cutting off the skirt of Saul's robe (I Sam. 24.4f.), or communicating the personality, cf. the designation of Elijah's successor (I K. 19.19, which see).

In *ʿal-gerem hammaʿalōt* ('on the top of the steps'), *gerem* is a *hapax legomenon*. On the analogy of Aramaic usage, later attested, de Vaux (*BJ*, p. 155), after Gesenius, Ewald, and Keil, takes it to mean 'on the steps themselves', i.e. just where he was on the steps, the pile of cloaks forming a throne. Graetz offered the attractive emendation *merōm* ('the height', i.e. top), where MT *g* would be an easy corruption of *m* in the proto-Hebraic script. *gerem* is attested in G^B, which transliterates, while Aquila renders literally 'on the bony part . . .' We prefer to retain *gerem* as a rare architectural term connecting it with the Arabic verb *jarama* ('to cut off, complete'), meaning that with which the steps are finished off, the landing.

The use of the trumpet (*šōpār*) was a feature of the declaration of Yahweh's Kingship at the New Year festival (Ps. 47.5[6]), and of the accession-ceremony of the kings, e.g. Solomon (I K. 1.34) and Joash (11.14). On the significance of the acclamation *mālak X* with reference to the assumption of rather than the state of kingship, and its relevance to the phrase *yhwh mālak* in the Psalms which we consider enthronement psalms, see on I K. 1.11.

9.14. *hitqaššēr* means primarily 'to bind oneself', and secondarily 'to conspire', i.e. to bind as confederates by oath.

(iv) RÉSUMÉ OF THE GENERAL POLITICAL SITUATION: 9.14b–15a

This fragment, itself perhaps a précis, served no doubt as the original introduction to the reign of Jehu. The editor adapted it at 8.28f. in his introduction of Ahaziah of Judah, who was associated with the death of Joram, and in consequence of its appearance at that point it was omitted before the account of the call of Jehu at the beginning of ch. 9. It is reintroduced at this point at vv. 14b–15a to account for the absence of Joram when Jehu was anointed and acclaimed king at Ramoth Gilead. In agreement with this explanation of the appearance of the passage at this point the suggestion of Graetz should be noted that 'Jehu' should be read instead of 'Joram' in the statement that 'Joram kept Ramoth Gilead'. This is probably taken from a fuller historical narrative. If Ahab was really killed in the presumably vain attempt to take Ramoth Gilead, as I K. 22 states, it is odd that the recovery of such an important place by Israel before the event of II K. 9 is not noted in the Bible. This must be an additional argument for the original relation of the events of I K. 22 to a later period than the reign of Ahab. Mowinckel ('Die Chronologie . . .', p. 212) is probably right in seeing a connection between this Ramoth Gilead campaign and the Assyrian attack on Damascus in 841 following the change of dynasty with the accession of Hazael. In this case the 'king of Israel' may be Jehoram, and the episode a variant tradition of the account of the wounding of Jehoram at Ramoth Gilead and his death at Jezreel in II K. 9.14ff., as J. M. Miller[a] argues.

The wounding and withdrawal of Joram and the command of Jehu probably confirmed men in the conviction that the *b^erākā* had passed from the king to his commander.

9 14B Now Jehu[b] was warden in Ramoth[c] Gilead, he and all Israel, against attack by Hazael the king of Aram, 15 Jehoram the king having gone back to be healed at Jezreel from the wounds which the archers[d] had inflicted[e] upon him when he fought with Hazael the king of Aram.

9.14b. Šanda feasibly suggests (II, p. 95) that Hazael, seeing no help against Assyria materializing from Israel, whose weakness was emphasized in her failure to subdue the Moabite revolt (ch. 3), took the offensive to capture Ramoth Gilead, where Jehu, in the absence of Joram, was in charge of the defence (*hāyā šōmēr*).

'All Israel' is a survival of the term referring to Israel as an army consecrated to the service of Yahweh, the God of the sacral community. Here it indicates either the prophetic adaptation of the historical narrative or the Deuteronomistic compilation.

(v) JEHU'S SLAUGHTER OF JORAM AND AHAZIAH: 9.15b–28

A continuation of the historical narrative from v. 14a, the prophetic adaptation being evident in the reference to the 'harlotries of Jezebel . . .' in v. 22 and the emphasis on the fulfilment of Elijah's prophecy against Ahab in the incident of Naboth's vineyard (vv. 21b, 25f.).

9 15B And Jehu said, If you are truly with me[f] let no survivor go out

[a] 'The Fall of the House of Ahab', *VT* XVII, 1967, pp. 314f.
[b] So with Graetz for MT 'Joram.'
[c] See p. 533 n.[f].
[d] So with G[L] for MT *'^arammīm* ('Aramaeans'); see on 8.28 (p. 533 n.[g].).
[e] Reading perfect for MT imperfect as in 8.29.
[f] Reading with G *'im yēš napš^ekem 'ittī* for MT, which omits *'ittī*. This reading is suggested by certain MSS which read *'im yēš 'et-napš^ekem*. The last reading may well be right, cf. Gen 23.8 *'im yēš 'et-napš^ekem liqbōr 'et-mētī* ('If you agree with me to bury my dead').

from the city to go to tell (the news) in Jezreel. [16]Then Jehu mounted
his chariot and went to Jezreel, for there Joram was lying, and Ahaziah
the king of Judah had come down to see Joram. [17]Now the watchman
stood on the tower at Jezreel and he saw the company of Jehu as he
came on and he said, I see a company. And Joram said, Take a rider
and send him to meet them that he may say, Is all well? [18]So the horseman went to meet him, and he said, Thus says the king, Is all well? But
Jehu said to him, What concern of yours is it whether all is well? Turn in
behind me. So the watchman reported saying, The messenger came to
them,[a] but has not come back. [19]So he sent another rider and he came
to them and said, Thus says the king, Is all well?[b] But Jehu said, What
concern of yours is it whether all is well? Turn in behind me. [20]So the
watchman reported saying, He came to them too,[c] but does not come
back, and the driving is as the driving of Jehu the son of Nimshi, for he
drives with abandon. [21]Then Joram said, Yoke! So they yoked his
chariot and Joram king of Israel and Ahaziah king of Judah went out,
each in his chariot, and they went forth to meet Jehu, and they encountered him in the plot of Naboth of Jezreel. [22]And it happened that,
when Joram saw Jehu, he said, Is all well, Jehu? But Jehu said, How
can all be well[d] while[e] the harlotries of Jezebel your mother and her
sorceries are so rife? [23]So Joram turned his hand and fled, saying to
Ahaziah, Treachery, Ahaziah! [24]Then Jehu drew a bow to full stretch
and hit Joram between the shoulders, and the arrow came out from his
heart and he fell on his knees in his chariot. [25]And he said to Bidkar
his armour-bearer, Up! throw him into the plot (of the field)[f] of
Naboth of Jezreel, for I remember when I and you[g] were driving
chariot-teams[h] in the retinue of Ahab his father and Yahweh imposed

[a]Reading ʿ^{a}*dēhem*.

[b]Reading with certain Hebrew MSS and G^{BL} and T *h^{a}šālōm*.

[c]We should read probably ʿ^{a}*dēhem* or ʿ^{a}*lēhem*, but ʿ*ad l^{e}* is attested in the Old Testament, though it is probably a later usage. Another possibility is to point MT ʿ*ad* as ʿ*ōd* with the meaning 'in addition, too', 'he also came to them . . .', cf. the use of ʿ*ōd* with this meaning in Ugaritic, *UT* 52.67, and probably also 75.11, 46.

[d]Klostermann and Kittel, followed by RV, postulate a dittograph of *h* in MT *mā-haššālōm*, translating 'What peace?'. We should retain MT, however, reading the consonants of *mā-h^{a}šālōm* as a quotation of the question of the emissary of Joram, 'What is the meaning of the question, Is all well? So long as . . .?'

[e]After G Klostermann reads ʿ*ōd*, '(the many harlotries . . .) are still (practised)'. We should retain MT ʿ*ad* in the sense of 'during, while', cf. Judg. 3.26; Jonah 4.2, etc.

[f]Possibly omitting MT *ś^{e}dē*, which is never mentioned in the frequent references to the plot (*ḥelqat*) of Naboth.

[g]Reading with G^{L}, S, and V *kī zōkēr ʾ^{a}nī kī ʾ^{a}nī w^{e}ʾattā rōk^{e}bīm* . . . for MT *kī z^{e}kōr ʾanī wāʾattā ʾēt rōk^{e}bīm*. . . .

[h]See previous note. ʾ*ēt* may either be omitted as a dittograph after ʾ*attā* or, less probably, taken as the preposition 'with'. MT *ṣ^{e}mādīm* ('chariot-teams') would signify that Jehu and Bidkar were driving different chariot-teams. The word, if vocalized as a passive participle *ṣ^{e}mīdīm*, would mean 'paired together' in the same chariot-team.

this oracle upon him. [26]Surely I saw yesterday the blood of Naboth and the blood of his sons, says Yahweh, and shall requite it to you in this very plot, says Yahweh. So now, up! throw him into the plot according to the word of Yahweh. [27]And Ahaziah king of Judah saw this and fled towards Beth-hag-gan and (Jehu) pursued after him saying,[a] Him also! So they wounded him[a] in his chariot at the ascent of Gur, which is by Ibleam, and he fled to Megiddo and died there. [28]So his retainers drove him to Jerusalem and they buried him in his tomb with his fathers[b] in the city of David.

9.15b. On the reading and the feasibility of MT see p. 544 n.[f] *nepeš* here means 'enthusiasm'.

The mention of *pālīṭ* ('a survivor') suggests that Jehu visualized a loyalist reaction, which, however, did not materialize.

laggīd, as the Massoretic pointing suggests, may be a scribal error for *l*[e]*haggīd* ('to tell'), but the *h* may have been elided, as in colloquial speech.

17. The *migdāl*, or tower, may have been an independent feature within the town of Jezreel, but it was more likely to be incorporated in the wall, certainly to the east, where the plain falls abruptly away to the *ʿēmeq* (lit. 'deepening') of Jezreel proper.

šipʿā is rendered 'dust' in G^B, G^L attesting this interpretation and also 'company' in the composite rendering 'dust of the company'. The word is well attested in the sense 'abundance', e.g. of water (Job 22.11; 38.34), horses (Ezek. 26.10), and camels (Isa. 60.6), so that there is little reason to doubt MT, though Kittel proposes 'dust'.

20. The driving of Jehu is described as *b*[e]*šiggāʿōn* ('with abandon') from the same root as *m*[e]*šuggāʿ*, used of the prophet in v. 11, which see. T renders *b*[e]*nīaḥ* ('quietly'), which is also the interpretation of Josephus,[c] who renders 'J. drove rather leisurely and in good order'. It is difficult to see how this meaning was obtained from a Hebrew text anything like MT, unless we read for *b*[e]*šiggāʿōn b*[e]*lī ʿāwōn* ('unswerving'), taking *ʿāwōn* in its primary physical sense, cf. Arabic *ġawā* ('to go astray'), *šg* being a possible corruption of *ly* in the proto-Hebraic script.

21. Here, as in I K. 13.14, etc., *māṣā'* means not 'to find as the result of search', but 'to light upon, fall in with'.

[a]So G for MT *gam-'ōtō hakkūhū* ('Smite him too'), which requires the *w* consecutive with the imperfect *wayyakkūhū* in the sequel. This may have fallen out through haplography, but we follow G, taking *gam-'ōtō* as a brusque order with the ellipse of the imperative, and emending *hakkūhū* to *wayyakkūhū*.

[b]G^{BL} omit MT *ʿim 'ᵃbōtāw*.

[c]*Ant.* IX, 6.3.

9.22. On text see p. 545 nn.[d, e].

The 'harlotries' (*zᵉnūnē*) of Jezebel refers to ritual prostitution as a rite of imitative magic in the fertility cult of the Canaanite Baal. Her 'sorceries' (*kᵉšāpehā*) may refer to seductive arts, i.e. the allurement which those rites had for the common man. In Nahum 3.4, where Nineveh is personified as a harlot, the noun is found associated, as in the present passage, with *zᵉnūnīm*. Gressmann[a] sees here a reference to the use of amulets of the fertility-goddess, which were a common feature of Canaanite life on the evidence of the many 'Astarte plaques' in clay and metal from various archaeological sites in Palestine. The word also indicates sorcery for prognostication, e.g. Jer. 27.9, where those who practise such arts are listed together with prophets, diviners, and dreams. It is noteworthy, as Gressmann observes,[b] that vengeance for Naboth is strictly secondary to the religious motivation of the revolt. This on the theme of the oracle of doom on the reigning house and its fulfilment is a feature particularly of the prophetic adaptation of the historical narrative. From that amoral cult of Canaan and the Phoenician ideology of absolute monarchy stemmed such social abuses as the Naboth incident.

23. From this passage, where the singular *yādō* should probably be written for MT dual *yādāw*, it appears that Joram was so far from suspecting Jehu that he went without a driver. Thus in vv. 17, 19, and 22 the question was not 'Do you come in peace?', but 'Is all well?' (i.e. at Ramoth Gilead).

24. The phrase *millē' yādō baqqešet* is taken by Rashi as 'he drew the bow with all his might', which amounts to the same as 'to the full stretch of his arm', but on the analogy of II Sam. 23.7 *yimmālē' barzel wᵉʿēṣ ḥᵃnīt* ('he is armed with iron and a wooden spear') we must consider it possible that *millē' yādō* may simply mean 'he seized' or 'armed himself'.

25. It is not certain that *bidqar* was a proper name. S translates it *bar dᵉqar* (lit. 'the son of stabbing'), which Šanda (II, p. 98) renders *Lanzenknecht*, this reading assuming that *b* is an abbreviation for *ben*. This person, however, was the *šālīš*, or third person in the chariot besides the driver and the warrior, and as his part was to hold the shield and arms of the warrior, aggressive warfare such as S implies was no part of his work. Hence we conclude that *bidqar* was a proper name. On the office of *šālīš* in the Israelite army, where, as in the Hittite and Assyrian armies, there were three men to a chariot, see

[a] *Die älteste Geschichtsschreibung* . . ., p. 314. [b] *Ibid.*, p. 311.

on 7.2, 17, 19, where the king's *šālīš* is a kind of aide-de-camp, and 15.25, where the aide-de-camp of Pekahiah was his assassin and successor Pekah. Jehu refers to a time some 20 years before, when he and Bidkar had driven chariot-teams in Ahab's retinue when Elijah declared the famous oracle after Naboth's death, though it may be noted that Elijah is not actually cited here.[a] At that time Jehu was presumably a young man who was still a driver and not yet promoted to a warrior's place in the chariot.

Though the literal rendering of *śā'* from *nāśā'* ('to take up') is quite intelligible, we favour the view of L. Kopf[b] that, as the Arabic *našā*, Hebrew *nāśā'* combined with another verb has the inchoative sense.

9.26. *rā'ītī* here means 'I have noticed' rather than 'I have seen'. The oracle here differs from I K. 21.19, 'In the very place where the dogs have licked the blood of Naboth the dogs will lick your blood.' This would suggest that I K. 21.19 and the present passage belong to different sources.

It is significant that there was no resistance to Jehu on the part of Joram's subjects, which supports our view that they had lost faith in him and believed that the *berākā* had passed from the house of Omri.

27. Ahaziah was marked down by Jehu as brother-in-law of Joram and so as a possible avenger. Beth-hag-gan (lit. 'the House of the Garden') was Engannim (Josh. 19.21), modern *Jenīn*, seven miles south of Jezreel, as the further mention of Ibleam (modern *Tell Belʿameh*) indicates. This place is only one mile farther south. Wounded here, the hapless Ahaziah, knowing that he cannot depend on the speed of his chariot among the hills north of Samaria, turns and heads for Megiddo 11 miles to the north-west, where his progress would be faster along the edge of the great central plain. There was a great chariot-depot, evidenced by three stable-complexes in use at this time,[c] and as the chariot-force consisted of professional soldiers feudatory to the king, there was always the hope that Megiddo was still loyal to Joram. This was probably so, as Ahaziah was taken into Megiddo, but only to die there.

[a] Noting this, J. M. Miller, *op. cit.*, pp. 316f., argues for the priority of II K. 9 to the tradition of the oracle of Elijah against Ahab in I K. 21, where, he argues, Ahab and Elijah are secondary. I K. 21 is admittedly overworked in prophetic tradition, but for the probability of the social crisis in Israel in Ahab's time see above, Introduction to I K. 21.

[b] 'Arabische Etymologien und Parallelen', *VT* VIII, 1958, p. 187.

[c] Y. Yadin, *BA* XXIII, 1960, pp. 62–68.

9.28. The use of the Hiphil of *rākab* in the sense of putting the dead man in the chariot and driving him to Jerusalem is somewhat unusual, though not unintelligible. The same usage occurs in the account of Josiah's death, which may have coloured the tradition of the death of Ahaziah at Megiddo.

(vi) SYNCHRONISTIC NOTICE OF THE ACCESSION OF AHAZIAH: 9.29

This, as Kittel contends, is probably one of the earliest attempts to adjust an apparent discrepancy in Hebrew chronology. In 8.25 the accession of Ahaziah is given as the 12th year of Joram (841), in which both died. But there the duration of Ahaziah's reign is given as one year (v. 26). This could not have been a full year. Some editor, however, takes this last statement literally and so states that Ahaziah acceded in Joram's 11th year.

9 [29]And in the eleventh year of Joram the son of Ahab, Ahaziah became king over Judah.

(vii) THE END OF JEZEBEL: 9.30–37

This is a continuation of the historical narrative interrupted at v. 28. The author of the narrative, or perhaps the hand which combined the prophetic and secular traditions, which we distinguish in this chapter, is obviously interested in the fulfilment of Elijah's oracle on the house of Omri, though, apart from the later editorial interpolation in I K. 21.23, there is no reference to Jezebel in Elijah's oracle on Ahab in I K. 21. 19, nor is it said that the blood of Naboth shall be expiated in the plot of Naboth. The first mention of this as the scene of the retribution is in the account of the death of Joram (9.26). The fact is that the deaths of Joram and Jezebel were taken as fulfilments of the oracle of Elijah, but in the transmission of the tradition they were made to conform particularly in detail.

9 [30]Then Jehu came to Jezreel. Now Jezebel had heard and she blackened her eyes with kuhl and adorned her head and looked through the window. [31]And when Jehu came into the city[a] she said, Is it well, you Zimri, who murdered his master? [32]And he lifted up his face[b] to

[a]Reading *bāʿīr* with G for MT *baššaʿar* ('into the gate').
[b]G^L and S read 'eyes' for 'face'.

the window[a] and said, Who is with me?[b] Now two or three eunuchs looked out to him. [33]So he said, Throw her down! So they threw her out and some of her blood bespattered the wall and the horses, and they trampled[c] her. [34]Then he went in and ate and drank and said, See now to this accursed woman and bury her, for she is a king's daughter. [35]So they went to bury her, but found nothing of her except the skull and the feet and the palms of her hands. [36]And they went back and reported to him, and he said, That is the word of Yahweh which he spoke by his servant Elijah the Tishbite saying, In the plot of Jezreel the dogs shall eat the flesh of Jezebel, [37]and the body of Jezebel shall be as dung upon the face of the land [d]in the plot of Jezreel,[d] so that they shall not say, This is Jezebel.

9.30. *wattāśem bappūk ʿēnehā* refers to the touching of the eyelashes and lids with kuhl as a setting to the eyes. *pūk*, known also from Jer. 4.30, is Arabic *kuhl*, the substance of which is sulphide of antimony, which is applied as powder mixed with oil and is widely used among modern Arab women as a cosmetic. It is the Assyrian *guḫlu* mentioned among Hezekiah's tribute to Sennacherib. We question whether this means literally 'she put her eyes in kuhl', and propose that the verb is a homonym of *śīm* ('to put'), a cognate of Arabic *šāma* (*y*), which is used to describe feet *covered* with dust, cf. *šāma*, 'a mark' on a person, 'a black mole', hence our rendering 'she blackened her eyes with kuhl'. It is uncertain whether Jezebel looked through the lattice-work or appeared at an open window, in view of Jehu's possible question 'Who are you?' It could be, however, in view of the privacy in which oriental women were kept, that Jehu, though he saw the lady at an open window (here *ḥallōn* and not *śebākā*), might never actually have seen her face before. Her toilet suggests that she meant now to be seen.

[a]G^BL read in addition to MT 'and saw her'.

[b]This rendering of *ʾittī* is well enough attested in the Old Testament to be feasible here. G, however, reads 'Who are you? Come down with me', cf. G^L, which reads 'to me' in the last phrase. This suggests a double tradition of the reading *ʾatty* and *ʾittī*. 'Come down' suggests a fuller Hebrew text, which may include both *ʾatty* (the Aramaic or North Israelite form of the classical Hebrew *ʾatt*) and *ʾittī*. Klostermann suggested that the Greek *katabathi* was the translation of Hebrew *tērédī*, which was a corruption of *tārībī*, hence he suggests the reading *mī ʾatty tārībī ʿimmī* ('Who are you that you would contend with me?'). It is true that *ʿimmī* is practically a synonym of *ʾittī*, which would be less suitable in the context, but it is too far from MT, though the same objection does not apply to *tārībī* for *tērédī*, if we may assume a Hebrew original for G 'Come down'.

[c]Reading with the Versions plural for singular of the verb in MT, but the consonants of MT may be retained.

[d]The phrase seems redundant and may be omitted with G^L.

9.31. Jezebel greets Jehu with a question rather than with the customary assurance *šālōm* ('we are at one'). There is defiance in her greeting, especially in her reference to the deed and precedent of Jehu. The instance of Zimri was well chosen for invective, since he killed Elah and the survivors of the house of Baasha, but reigned only seven days (I K. 16.9–15).

32. On *sārīs* see on 8.6. Here the meaning is undoubtedly 'eunuchs' as attendants in the harem.

33. The root *šāmaṭ*, with cognates in Syriac and Arabic, means 'to let drop', and is familiar in the noun *šemiṭṭā*, the letting drop, or remission, of debts at the end of seven years (Deut. 15.1, 9), 'the year of release' (*šenat haššemiṭṭā*).

34. The meal is something more than a show of the callous indifference of Jehu to the grim events just recorded. As Montgomery, after Ehrlich, remarks, it is a typical Semitic communal meal which shall serve to bind Jehu and the community together, serving at once as a test of the support of the local notables in the enterprise of Jehu and at the same time guaranteeing them the goodwill of Jehu. *pāqad* means 'to review' or 'take stock of'. Here it indicates ascertaining what had happened to Jezebel and disposing of her remains.

'This accursed woman' (*hā'arūrā hazzō't*) is not mere invective, but means literally one who had manifestly lost the *berākā*, or 'blessing,' and was in consequence under the divine curse.

It was now a matter of personal interest for the new king to accord the honours of a royal burial to Jezebel's remains.

35. *bāh* means 'of her', *be* being used in a partitive sense as occasionally in Ugaritic. See *UT* § 10.1, cf. Deut. 8.7, *yōṣe'īm babbiq'ā ūbāhār*.

36f. On the question of the oracle and its agreement with other versions of the oracle of Elijah see introduction to this section.

37. *whyt*, vocalized in MT as *wehāyetā*, may be vocalized *wehāyat*, as Burney[a] suggests, this being an old form of the third feminine singular perfect, cf. Arabic, and may be paralleled by similar forms in *l/h* verbs., e.g. Lev. 25.21; 26.34; Jer. 13.19; Ezek. 24.12.

There is, as Montgomery recognizes (ICC, p. 407), possibly a word-play between 'dung' (*dōmen*) and *zebel* (meaning also 'dung' as in the Arabic cognate) in the Hebrew parody of an original element *zebūl* in the name of the queen. See on I K. 16.31.

[a] *Notes on . . . Kings*, p. 301.

(viii) THE EXTERMINATION OF THE HOUSE OF OMRI: 10.1–11

The historical narrative continued.

10 1Now Ahab had seventy descendants in Samaria, so Jehu wrote
letters and sent to Samaria to the commanders of the city,[a] to[b] the
elders and to those who brought up the children[c] of Ahab saying, 2So
now, when this letter reaches you, seeing that you have with you your
master's children and the chariots and horses and fortified cities[d] and
armour, 3look out the best and fittest of your master's sons and set him
on the throne of his father and fight for your master's house. 4And they
were exceedingly afraid and said, See, the two kings did not stand
before him. How then shall we stand? 5So they sent the royal chamberlain, the city commandant, the elders, and the guardians to Jehu
saying, We are your servants, and all that you bid us will we do. We
will not make anyone king. That which seems best to you, do. 6So he
wrote them a second[e] letter saying, If you are for me and listen to what
I say, take the heads of the family[f] of your master and bring them[g] to
me tomorrow to Jezreel. [h]Now the royal family comprised seventy
persons whom[i] the notables of the city were rearing.[h] 7And it happened
that, when the letter reached them, they took the royal family and
slew them,[j] seventy persons, and they put their heads in baskets and
they sent them to him in Jezreel. 8And the messenger came and told
him saying, They have brought the heads of the royal family. And he
said, Put them in two heaps at the opening of the gate until the morning.
9And it happened in the morning that he went out and stood still and
said to all the people, You are loyal to the right. See, I conspired
against my master and slew him, and whoever has slain all these,
10know now that there shall not fall to the ground a single word of
Yahweh which Yahweh has spoken against the house of Ahab, but
Yahweh has done what he declared by his servant Elijah. 11So Jehu slew

[a]Reading *hāʿîr* ('the city' i.e. Samaria) for MT 'Jezreel' since Jehu directed those events from Jezreel.

[b]Reading *w^{e}'el* before *z^{e}q'ēnîm* with certain MSS, G^{BL}, S, and V, . . . *hāʿîr w^{e}'el* being corrupted to MT *yizr^{e}ʿēl*.

[c]*hā'ōm^{e}nîm* ('who brought up') of MT requires a direct object after it, hence we read *'et-b^{e}nē* or *b^{e}nē* with G^{L}.

[d]Reading plural with certain MSS and the Versions for MT singular.

[e]*šēnît* of MT might be retained in the adverbial sense, 'a second time', but we prefer to read *šēnî* with certain Hebrew MSS and G in agreement with *sēper*.

[f]Omitting MT *'an^{e}šē* with G^{L}, S, and V as a possible gloss on *rā'šē*, meaning ambiguously 'heads' or 'chiefs'. For *b^{e}nē* certain MSS read *bēt*, which might mean 'palace' or 'family'.

[g]Reading with G, S, and T *w^{e}hābî'û* or perhaps *wah^{a}bî'ûm* for MT *ûbō'û* ('and come').

[h]This sentence is tautological and may be a later intrusion.

[i]If the clause noted in n.[h] is read, the best reading is that of G^{L} which reads the relative particle *'^{a}šer* for *'et* before *g^{e}dōlē*.

[j]Reading *wayyišḥāṭûm* with G^{BL} and S for MT *wayyišḥ^{a}ṭû*.

all those remaining of the family of Ahab in Jezreel, and all his kinsmen[a] and his familiars and his priests until there was left to[b] him no survivor.

10.1. The revolution could only be complete with the capture of Samaria, which, as bought by Omri, was the crown possession of his house, and the foundation of the power of the dynasty. Since Jehu in his letters (vv. 2 and 3) refers to the sons of Joram, it is maintained (Stade) that the mention of the 70 sons of Ahab in v. 1 is a later gloss.[c] Since the actual massacre included the kinsmen of Ahab (reading *gō'ᵃlāw* for *gᵉdōlāw* with G^L in v. 11), it is likely that *bᵉnē 'aḥ'āb* refers broadly to the family of Ahab, including the brothers of Joram and all descendants of Ahab. Elsewhere in this section where the king is unnamed, *bᵉnē hammelek* signifies the royal family in general. The number 70 is, of course, a round number. Šanda (II, p. 105) cites the 70 sons of Gideon in Judg. 8.30; 9.2, the 70 souls who came with Jacob to Egypt (Gen. 46.27), and the 70 'brothers' (i.e. male members of the family) of the Aramaean King Panammu who were murdered by a usurper,[d] to which we may add the 70 brothers slain by Baal in the Ras Shamra myth (*UT* 75, II, 47–50) who are probably identical with the '70 sons of Aṯerat', the Canaanite mother-goddess (*UT* 51, VI, 46). These instances indicate that 70 is a conventional indefinite number and denotes here all the male stock of the old royal house. This is another instance of the influence of the saga-form on the historical narrative.

Jehu's letters were addressed to the professional soldiers, the commanders of the city, who were feudal barons owing their status solely to the king, to the local elders, who represented the people and the native traditions of Israel, though in Samaria, a crown-possession of the house of Omri, this independent status must have been rather nominal, and, thirdly, to the *'ōmᵉnīm*, those who were entrusted with the guardianship and rearing of the younger members of the royal family. The conventional interpretation of *'ōmᵉnīm* as 'foster-parents' is suggested by *'ōmenet* in Ruth 4.16. Bearing in mind the statement that Wisdom was the *'āmōn* of God in creation (Prov. 8.30), we may

[a]Reading with G^L *gō'ᵃlāw* for MT *gᵉdōlāw* ('his notables') cf. I K. 16.11 in the narrative of Zimri's massacre of the house of Baasha.

[b]Reading with T *hiššā'ēr* for MT *hiš'īr* ('he left'), the consonants of which, however, might be retained with the third singular masculine pronominal suffix, *śārīd* ('survivor') in that case being the object.

[c]So also Eissfeldt, *HSAT*, p. 557.

[d]G. A. Cooke, *NSI* 62.

suppose that the *'ōmenīm* were those entrusted with the education of the young princes in statecraft and general empirical wisdom, a necessary discipline, since if they did not form a kind of privy council, as Malamat feasibly supposes (see on I K. 12.8), they were all potential rulers, for whom such education was necessary, since the most promising of the princes was often chosen as co-regent with his father.

On the text see p. 552 nn. [a, b, c].

10.2. *weʿattā* introduces the strictly business part of the letter after the formal greetings. The fact that the business of the letter brought by Naaman to the king of Israel (5.6) is introduced by the same formula indicates that this was the regular form of a letter, which is, in fact, attested by No. 4 in the Lachish Letters.

In referring to the horses and chariots, Jehu seems to challenge on behalf of the popular party the professional soldiers, those elements in Israel who owed their status solely to the king, who is referred to as their 'master' (*'adōnīm*). This bold challenge would doubtless impress his correspondents with his confidence and the strength of his party even more than if he issued a peremptory summons to surrender. At the same time it left the way open for an honourable surrender.

5. On the official 'who was over the palace' (*'ašer ʿal-habbayit*), the royal chamberlain or vizier, see on I K. 4.6. The different classes here mentioned probably correspond to those mentioned in v. 1, in which case 'the commanders of the city' there are the royal chamberlain, who was presumably the city-governor and commander of the palace guard, and the city commandant.

6. See p. 552 n.[f]. The pleonastic *'anešē* and possibly also *benē* for *bēt* may be due to the consciousness of the ambiguity of *rā'šē*, 'heads' or 'chiefs'. It has been suggested that Jehu spoke with deliberate ambiguity, but this is improbable, since on the reception of the message that his order had been carried out he ordered the heads to be heaped up at the gate.

7. *dūdīm* elsewhere in the Old Testament means earthenware pots, but all the versions agree in translating the word here by 'baskets', which are more fitting receptacles for the heads.

8. The root *ṣbr* is found in the Ras Shamra texts meaning 'to gather, or mass', and is used of an assembly. The grim order of Jehu could often be paralleled in the history of the Near East from Jehu's time till the Tartar invasions. The Assyrian kings, especially Ashurnasirpal and Shalmaneser III, repeatedly boast of pyramids of heads heaped up before the city gates to intimidate the inhabitants and discourage rebellion.

10.9. The precise meaning of Jehu's statement is uncertain, depending on the interpretation of *ṣaddīqīm 'attem*. This is generally taken in the sense 'you are innocent', which is a possible meaning of the adjective, though not the primary one. The declaration is then taken as an instance of the cynicism of Jehu, who exonerates the people from the massacre of the old royal family, though he admits liability for the slaughter of Joram, and hints his horror at the mass murders in Samaria, which he then proceeds to justify by citing the oracle of Elijah. Šanda (II, p. 107) suggests that *ṣaddīq* here means 'impartial', and that Jehu is appealing to the people to judge of the relative guilt of himself and the people of Samaria, though he cites Elijah's oracle to justify both. Burney[a] takes *ṣaddīq* in the same sense, but interprets the statement as Jehu's exculpation of the massacre in Samaria. 'The inference is therefore clear to fair-minded men that this is no case of the unscrupulous securing of his own interests by a single individual, but that circumstances are working together to bring about the destruction of the house of Ahab.' We suggest that *ṣaddīq* be taken in a sense nearer its root meaning as signifying conformity to a norm, in the case of Israel 'loyal' or 'right' with Yahweh. It is significant here that Jehu is appealing to the people of Yahweh, the fulfilment of whose word through his prophet Elijah they might naturally applaud. In agreement with this interpretation we take *mī* not as interrogative, but as an indefinite relative pronoun and subject of the verb *deʿū* in the following verse.

10. Note the singular *debar* with the partitive *min*. There is no need to read a plural *dibᵉrē* with G[L] and V, the singular with partitive *min* being an idiom both in Hebrew and Arabic for 'a single . . .', e.g. I Sam. 14.45, *'im yippōl miššaʿarat rō'šō* ('there shall not fall a single hair of his head'), cf. Qur'an Surah 6, 59 *wamā tasquṭu min waraqatin illā yaʿlamuhā* ('there falls not a single leaf but that he knows it'), cf. *GK*, § 119 10 n.

11. On the reading *gō'alāw* ('kinsmen') see p. 553 n.[a]. For the role of the *gō'ēl* see on I K. 16.11. With the appeal to the oracle of Elijah, Jehu seeks authority for completing the extirpation of the family of Ahab at Jezreel. The reference here to Ahab's kinsmen probably indicates that Jezreel was the home of the family of Omri before his elevation to the throne.

[a] *Notes on . . . Kings*, p. 303.

(ix) THE MASSACRE OF THE ROYAL FAMILY OF JUDAH: 10.12–14

10 [12]Then he rose up and[a] went to Samaria and he was at Beth Eked of the Shepherds[b] on the way, [13]and he[c] met the brothers of Ahaziah king of Judah and he said, Who are you? And they said, We are the brothers of Ahaziah and have come down to greet the royal family and the sons of the queen. [14]And he said, Seize them alive. So they seized them alive and they slew them by the well of Beth Eked, forty-two men, nor did he leave any of them.

10.12. *bēt ʿēqed hārōʿīm* may mean 'the meeting-place of the shepherds', *ʿaqada* meaning in Arabic (as in Hebrew) 'to tie', but also 'to meet together' (Vth form). This may have been a gathering-place for shepherds who, like the Bedouin until the recent history of Palestine, brought their flocks over after harvest to pasture on the arable land. During this season those who pastured on the plain of Esdraelon may have had their permanent camp in the hills of Manasseh just south of the plain, where Eusebius attests a place *Beït Qad* about three miles north-east of *Jenīn* in the locality which the present passage seems to demand. The philology of *ʿēqed* suggests the possibility that the place may have been a market centre, lit. 'house of agreement or bargain', as Gaza and Beersheba are still for the Bedouin of the Negeb.

13. It is most reasonable to suppose with Stade that the Judaean princes would not have prosecuted their journey from Samaria had they, as the position of this passage indicates, left after the massacre there. Skinner suggests that they had passed through Samaria before the massacre and were on their way back from Jezreel. But in this case they would have known of the death of Joram and Ahaziah. Stade[d] therefore rejected the passage as a fictitious interpolation, but Šanda (II, p. 110) retains it, also de Vaux (*BJ*, p. 161), who accepts the view that it it is out of its chronological order at this point. This is the probable explanation, though in favour of Stade's view is the obviously conventional number 42, which is apparently at home in legend (the number of the children mangled by the bears in 2.24) and myth (the number of months of the reign of the beast in Rev. 13.5).

bᵉnē hammelek means the royal family in general, and *bᵉnē haggᵉbīrā* the actual children of the queen and the late king.

[a]Omitting MT *wayyābōʾ* (' and came') with G^{BL}.
[b]Reading *wᵉhūʾ bᵉbēt ʿēqed* . . . as suggested by G^{L} and S.
[c]G^{L} and V omit 'Jehu' of MT. [d]*ZAW* V, 1885, pp. 276ff.

(x) THE MASSACRE OF THE BAAL-WORSHIPPERS IN SAMARIA: 10.15–27

10 [15]And when he went from there he met with Jehonadab the
Rechabite coming to meet him and he greeted him and said to him,
Is[a] your heart straight with my heart as my heart is straight with your
heart? And Jehonadab said, It is. [b]And Jehu said,[b] Then if it is, give me
your hand. So he gave him his hand and he made him come up into the
chariot to him. [16]And he said, Come with me and look upon my zeal for
Yahweh. So he drove[c] him in his chariot. [17]And he came to Samaria
and struck down all the survivors of the house[d] of Ahab in Samaria until
he had destroyed[e] them according to the word of Yahweh which he
had spoken to Elijah. [18]Then Jehu gathered all the people together and
said to them, Ahab served Baal a little, but Jehu will serve him much.
[19]So now summon to me all the prophets of Baal, all his worshippers,[f]
and all his priests, let not one be wanting, for I have a great sacrifice to
Baal; whosoever is wanting shall not live. But Jehu acted in guile in
order that he should destroy all the worshippers of Baal. [20]Then
Jehu said, Sanctify a solemn assembly for Baal. And they made the proclamation. [21]And Jehu sent through all Israel, and all the worshippers
of Baal came,[g] there was no man left who did not come, and they came
to the temple of Baal, and the house of Baal was filled from one end
to the other. [22]Then he said to the keeper of the wardrobe, Bring out
vestments for all the worshippers of Baal. So he brought out the vestments. [23]Then Jehu and Jehonadab the Rechabite went into the
temple of Baal, and he said to the worshippers of Baal, Seek out and
see that there are here with you none of the worshippers of Yahweh,
but only worshippers of Baal. [24]So they went in to make sacrifices and
whole burnt offerings, but Jehu had set eighty[h] men outside, and had

[a]Reading *h*^{a}*yēš l*^{e}*bab*^{e}*kā ʾet-l*^{e}*babī yāšār* with G^{BL} as suggested by the following clause *kaʾ*^{a}*šer l*^{e}*bābī ʿim l*^{e}*bāb*^{e}*kā*.

[b]Reading *wayyōʾmer yēhūʾ* with G, as the sense demands.

[c]Reading singular with G and S.

[d]Certain MSS and S read *l*^{e}*bēt*, though this would be sufficiently understood from MT.

[e]We should probably read the Hiphil infinitive construct here.

[f]Possibly 'all his worshippers' (*kol-ʿ*^{a}*bādāw*) is out of place here, only leaders, prophets, and priests of the Baal-cult being summoned in the first instance (v. 19), and charged to proclaim and sanctify a solemn assembly (v. 20). The reading, however, is attested in G^{L}, where the phrase comes after *kōh*^{a}*nāw*.

[g]Omitting *w*^{e} with G and V in agreement with the general Hebrew usage in such a context.

[h]There are the usual variant versions of the numbers, G^{L} giving 3,000, and S 380. MT is to be preferred, since the larger number would have deterred the worshippers of Baal from attending the worship. Suspicious as they must have been of Jehu, it was essential to his plan that the executioners should mingle unobtrusively with the people.

given the order, Whoever lets a man escape[a] of the men I bring into[b] your hands his life shall be forfeit for his life. [25]And it came to pass, when he had finished making the burnt offering, that Jehu said to the guards and the officers, Come in and strike them down. Let no one go forth. So they smote them with the edge of the sword and they cast them[c] out into [d]the third court,[d] and they went on to the inmost shrine of the temple of Baal, [26]and they brought out the standing symbol[e] of the temple of Baal and burned it. [27] [f]And they pulled down the altar of Baal and they pulled down the house of Baal[f] and they made it a place for defecation (and so it is) to this day.

[a]The Niphal *yimmālēṭ* of MT raises great difficulty. MT might be translated 'Any man of the men I have brought in who escapes is your liability' (lit. 'on your hands'), but on this reading the third masculine singular pronominal suffix in the first *napšō* in the phrase *napšō taḥat napšō* ('his life for his life') has no antecedent. Hence we point the first verb as Piel after Thenius, Klostermann, etc.

[b]*ʿal-yᵉdēkem* might mean 'your liability', but according to the reading we have just adopted the meaning is probably 'into your hands', the original preposition probably being *ʾel*.

[c]Reading *wayyašlīkūm*, the transitive verb having no object in MT. The haplograph probably occurred in the proto-Hebraic script, where *m* and *w* are very similar. It is possible, as Klostermann thought, that the object underlies the MT in the following words *hārāṣīm wᵉhaššālīšīm*, which, as they occur already in v. 25, are unlikely here, hence Klostermann proposed to read after *wayyašlīkū ʾarṣā hāʾᵃšērā* ('They cast the *ashera* to the ground'), which must be seriously considered.

[d]As Klostermann's emendation suggests, we expect a note of the place where whatever was cast out was cast. Hence we suggest the reading *haḥᵃṣērā haššālīšīt* ('unto the third court'). This is the outer, or large, court of the tripartite temple known from the excavation of the Baal-temple at Ras Shamra and from the description of Solomon's temple, and the reading is suggested to us by the mention of the inmost shrine. The slaughter obviously took place inside the second court or hall of the temple, and to clear a way for their progress Jehu's guardsmen threw the bodies out into the outer, or public, court.

[e]The versions and two Hebrew MSS read the singular, which is suggested by the singular pronominal suffix in *wayyiśrᵉpūhā*. Exception is taken to this reading on the grounds that the *maṣṣēbā* ('standing symbol' (was of stone, and *ʾᵃšērā*, the wooden pole or stylized tree of the fertility-cult, is proposed, this further ruling out the emendation proposed by Klostermann cited in n.[c]. To this there are two objections. According to the etymology of *maṣṣēbā* this signifies any standing object and may refer to a wooden image; secondly, granted that the *maṣṣēbōt* of the fertility-cult were generally of stone, the simplest way to shatter a massive piece of stone was to heat it and then throw cold water over it, as the local Arabs did with the Moabite Stone. Hence the only modification of MT that we suggest is to read the singular for the plural *maṣṣēbōt*.

[f]The mention of the destruction of *maṣṣᵉbat baʿal* after the description of its destruction in the previous verse is suspect, and the whole clause *wayyittᵉṣū ʾet-maṣṣᵉbat habbaʿal* is suspect before the following clause *wayyittᵉṣū ʾet-bēt habbaʿal*. In the Versions, however, it is the second clause which is suspect, being omitted in G^B. This suggests that the first clause is substantially genuine, but, assuming that it was the *maṣṣēbā* that was burnt in v. 26, we should probably read *mizbaḥ* ('altar') for *maṣṣᵉbat* of MT. If one of these clauses must be rejected it is, as G^L suggests, the second, the enclosure of the Baal-temple being left as a place of defecation, which demanded a certain privacy.

10.15. It must strike all readers as obvious that the presence of Jehonadab with Jehu at Samaria would at once arouse suspicion of his professed patronage of the Baal-cult; hence de Vaux suggests (*BJ*, p. 162) plausibly that the incident is displaced in its present context. The procession of Jehu through the country with Jehonadab in his chariot was probably a gesture to rally all conservative elements in Israel and convince them that his *coup d'état* was more than the fulfilment of personal ambition.

Jehonadab, whose designation *ben Rēkāb* denotes his tribe rather than his father, was according to Jer. 35 the founder of an ascetic order which maintained the austerity of the desert, drinking no wine, practising no cultivation, and building no stone houses. It is generally held that these taboos were a protest against Israel's assimilation of the way of the settled land. Some semblance of support is given to this view by the fact that the emergence of the order coincided with the militant Yahwistic reformation of Jehu as the consummation of the struggle between the worship of Yahweh and Baal associated with Elijah. Apart from the association with Jehu, however, there is no evidence that the Rechabites practised their asceticism as a conscious religious protest like the Nazirites. They were, according to I Chron. 2.55, a Kenite clan. They are probably mentioned in I Chron. 4.12, where *rēkāb* should be read for *rēkāh*, and here they are significantly associated with *ʿīr hannāḥāš* ('Copper-city'). As Kenites they maintained the primitive forms of the worship of Yahweh, whom they worshipped probably before Israel.[a] As metal-workers and artificers jealously guarding their trade secrets they refused to settle down to the sedentary life, where their craft might have been learnt by their clients. The ban on wine might have had the same motive, since this is a notorious loosener of the tongue. The severe Yahwism of the Kenites and their itinerant life along the ancient trade-routes is illustrated in the case of Heber the husband of Jael (Judg. 4.17–22; 5.24–27). Their modern counterpart in a social and economic respect are the nomad tinker-clans *Nawwār* and *Sulayb*, who live in tents and have no proprietary rights of land.

'He blessed him' is a synonym with 'he greeted him'. By the greeting *šālōm* one associates another with oneself in the blessing one hopes for or is conscious of possessing. On a recent visit to Palestine the

[a] H. H. Rowley, *From Joseph to Joshua*, 1950, pp. 152 ff., with relevant bibliography.

writer experienced a striking illustration of this principle *per contra*, when an embittered Arab returned his *salām ʿalaykum* with 'the curse of Allah'. The handclasp is the physical expression of unity invoked by the greeting *šālōm*. The handclasp is the ritual and *šālōm* the myth.

10.16. *qin'ā* denotes exclusive devotion, and often, as here, fanaticism.

17. Ahab rather than Joram is mentioned because of his greater notoriety and the fact that he had built the Baal-temple at Samaria (I K. 16.32), but chiefly because the oracle of Elijah, on which Jehu based his actions, was directed against him and through him on his family. This is indicated by his explicit reference to the oracle.

18. Jehu may have intended a word-play for the satisfaction of himself and his associates between the verb *ʿābad* ('to worship') and *'ibbad* ('to destroy'), 'Ahab worshipped Baal a little, but I shall thoroughly destroy him', cf. the collocation of the two verbs in v. 19 *l^e^maʿan ha'^a^bīd et-ʿōb^e^dē baʿal* ('in order to destroy the worshippers of Baal'). The reference to the limited extent to which Ahab worshipped Baal is probably true to fact. All his children who are named bear Yahweh-theophorics, and his Baal-temple in Samaria was probably in deference to his Canaanite subjects and for his Phoenician queen and her retinue primarily, like similar alien cult-places for the wives of Solomon in Jerusalem. The king probably gave mere lip-service to Baal.

19. On the prophets, or ecstatics, of Baal see on I K. 18.19.

The Arabic *faqada* means 'to lose', a meaning which the Hebrew cognate has, apparently, only in the Niphal. Since the Qal in Hebrew means 'to review' or 'take stock of', the Arabic sense may be the primary one also in Hebrew, the verb in its usual sense 'to review' meaning 'to find out one's loss'.

In *zebaḥ gādōl lī* there is probably a *double entendre*, *zebaḥ*, Arabic *ḏabaḥa* meaning primarily 'slaughter' and secondarily 'sacrifice'.

ʿoqbā ('guile') is a derivative from the verb *ʿāqab* ('to circumvent'), on which the narrative of Jacob and Esau turns. In that case, however, there is an instance of popular etymology. Actually in the truncated theophoric *yaʿ^a^qōb ('ēl)*, the verbal element, as suggested by South Arabian usage, means 'help'.

20. For MT *qadd^e^šū* ('sanctify') S and T read *qir^e^'ū* ('call'). *qiddēš*, even if it were not original here, at least expresses the familiar Semitic conception of the worshipping community brought into a state of ritual compatibility with the deity, his precincts, and cultic personnel.

The verb may explain the noun *ʿaṣārā*, the assembly so constituted and as such 'restrained' or precluded from contact with the profane. Another possible explanation of *ʿaṣārā* is that it was an assembly convoked under solemn imprecation, any outside the 'closed' circle of which was liable to punishment under the curse.

10.21. The phrase 'from one end to another' (*pe lāpe*) is found only once more in the Old Testament, in 21.16, from one end of Jerusalem to another.

22. *meltāḥā* ('wardrobe'), a *hapax legomenon*, the meaning of which, however, is quite clear from the sequel, has been taken as a loan-word from Assyrian *maltaktu*. Now the root has probably been found in one of the administrative texts from the palace at Ras Shamra.[a] The same root *'ilḥ* probably lies behind the verse in Jer. 38.11, as Eissfeldt suggests,[b] dealing with Ebed-melek's rescue of Jeremiah with rags obtained from *'el-taḥat hā'ōṣār*. Here we may read *'eltaḥat hā'ōṣār*, 'the vestment department of the store'. The conception of special clothes being necessary in the approach to the deity is familiar in the Old Testament (cf. Gen 35.2; Ex. 19.10) and beyond Israel. The king Dan'il in the Ras Shamra legend 'Aqht wears such a special veil or loincloth in his sojourn in the temple, and pilgrims to Mecca wear the *iḥrām*, or sacred shift, when they enter the sacred bounds. Among the various classes listed in administrative lists from Ras Shamra we have suggested[c] that *yṣḥm*, who are listed with singers (*šrm*) and sculptors of images (*pslm*), are makers of sacred vestments, the word being cognate with Arabic *naṣaḥa*, 'to sew' (for interchange of *y* and *n* cf. Ugaritic *ytnm*, Hebrew *nᵉtînîm*).

25. The natural sense of *kᵉkallōtō* is that Jehu himself was sacrificing. In view of the subsequent desecration, the end may have justified the means. The pronominal suffix, however, may denote the officiating priest or even be a corruption of the *m* of the third masculine plural suffix, there being a great similarity of *m* to *w* in the proto-Hebraic script. In view of the unconscionable treachery of Jehu, however, we find no difficulty in referring the sacrifice to him.

On *rāṣîm*, originally 'outrunners', later 'guardsmen', see note on I K. 1.5. On *šālîš* see on II K. 7.2; 9.25.

On MT *hārāṣîm wᵉhaššālîšîm* see p. 558 nn.[c, d].

[a]C. Virolleaud, *Le palais royal d'Ugarit* II, ed. C. F. A. Schaeffer, no. 109, a list of garments which went out from the *m'ilḥ* (*spr npṣm dyṣ('a) bm'ilḥ*).

[b]'The Alphabetic Cuneiform Texts from Ras Shamra published in *Le palais royal d'Ugarit*, II, 1957', *JSS* VI, 1960, p. 46.

[c]*The Legacy of Canaan*, 1965², p. 213.

In the difficult *ʿad-ʿîr bêt habbaʿal*, which cannot mean 'to the city of the temple of Baal', Klostermann proposed to read *d^ebîr* (inmost shrine') for *ʿîr*. Undoubtedly this is the sense, but the MT *ʿîr* may still be right. In a similar scene of massacre in a temple in the Baal-mythology of Ras Shamra the Ugaritic cognate *ġr* seems to bear the sense of inmost recess, or shrine, of the temple, e.g. *UT*, ʿnt II, 3ff.:

kl'at ṯġrt bht ʿnt
wtqry ġlmm bšt ġr

Anat has closed the gates of the temple,
Gathering (her) ministrants into the inmost recesses of the penetralia.

The word may be a cognate of the Arabic *ġawr* ('a hollow'), cf. *muġāra* ('cave'), a reminiscence of a primitive rock sanctuary. These details of the Baal-temple of Samaria are rightly taken by Šanda (II, p. 124) as an indication of a contemporary, or near-contemporary, source, since the description would have been impossible some 40 years after the destruction of the shrine.

10.27. On the nature and fate of the *maṣṣēbā* see p. 558 nn.[e, f]. *maḥ^arā'ōt* is a *hapax legomenon* in the Old Testament meaning 'the place of *ḥ^arī'* ('dung'), which is found also once in 6.25. There is an Arabic cognate *maḥrā'a*. The Massoretes gave the noun euphemistically the vowels of *mōṣā'ot* ('excrement'), so actually Q for MT *mōhār'ōt*.

(xi) EPILOGUE TO THE REIGN OF JEHU: 10.28–31

This is mainly from the Deuteronomistic compiler, consisting of a general assessment of the reign of Jehu, applauding him for his repression of the Baal-cult, but condemning him for his toleration of the cult at Dan and Bethel, the specific sin of Jeroboam, and noting his death and the accession of his son. Space is found, too, to explain how it was that the house of Jehu lasted for four generations, culminating in the glorious reign of Jeroboam II. The Deuteronomistic epilogue in vv. 28–31 seems to be from two different editors, the shorter one in vv. 28f. and the longer in vv. 30f.

An excerpt from the Chronicles of Israel is added, giving a general reference to the Israelite defeats at the hand of Aram east of the Jordan.

10 [28]So Jehu destroyed Baal out of Israel. [29]Nevertheless from the sins of Jeroboam the son of Nebat, in which he involved Israel, Jehu did not turn away,[a] even the golden calves which were in [b]Bethel and

[a]As the syntax suggests, all v. 29b is a later gloss.

[b]Reading *b^ebêt'ēl* with certain MSS and the versions, cf. *b^edan* in the same v.

which were in Dan.[a] 30 And Yahweh said unto Jehu, Because you have done well in doing what was right in my eyes and[b] all that was in my heart you have done to the house of Ahab, your sons to the fourth[c] generation shall sit upon the throne of Israel. 31 But Jehu did not take heed to walk in the law of Yahweh the God of Israel with all his heart; he departed not from all the sins of Jeroboam in which he involved Israel.

6. SYNCHRONISTIC HISTORY OF ISRAEL AND JUDAH: 10.32–17.41

This is continued from I K. 16.34.

(*a*) EPILOGUE TO THE REIGN OF JEHU AND OBITUARY NOTICE: 10.32–36

This is a Deuteronomistic résumé of the Israelite defeats at the hands of Aram east of the Jordan, specifically from the south-east to the north-east (vv. 32f.), followed by a Deuteronomistic notice of the death of Jehu and reference to other sources for his history (vv. 34–36).

10 32 In those days Yahweh began to dock Israel[d] and Hazael defeated them in all the marches of Israel, 33 from the Jordan eastward, [e]with all the land of Gilead, the people of Gad, and Reuben, and Manasseh[e] from Aroer which is by the Wadi of Arnon, even Gilead and Bashan.

34 And as for the rest of the acts of Jehu and all that he did and all his might, are they not written in the Book of the Chronicles of the Kings of Israel? 35 And Jehu lay down with his fathers, and they buried him in Samaria, and his son Jehoahaz became king in his place. 36 Now the years that Jehu reigned over Israel were twenty-eight years in Samaria.

10.32. The reign of Jehu heralded a period of eclipse for Israel in Near Eastern politics. It began with his submission to Shalmaneser III in 841, when Hazael successfully held Damascus against Assyria. Šanda suggested that Ramoth Gilead had been restored to Israel by Aram in the hope that she might join a united front against Assyria,

[a]As the syntax suggests, this is a later gloss.

[b]Reading *wekol*, assuming the omission of *w* before *k*, which it closely resembles in the proto-Hebraic script.

[c]Reading *ribbēʿīm* ('pertaining to the fourth') for *rebīʿīm* ('fourth'), cf. 15.12.

[d]In MT *leqaṣṣōt beyiśrāʾēl* the preposition may have a partitive significance, as in the Ras Shamra texts, see on 9.35. The reading of V, however, must be noted: *lāqūṣ beyiśrāʾēl* ('to loathe Israel').

[e]A gloss.

but since Israel refused to do so Aram attacked Ramoth Gilead, as was happening when Jehu made his *coup*. Hazael could scarcely have attacked Jehu immediately after the latter submitted to Shalmaneser in 841, since he lost 1,121 chariots in that year, hence his successful attacks on Transjordan must be dated in the latter part of Jehu's reign, *c*. 824–815.[a] This period until the renewal of Assyrian interest in the West under Adadnirari III (810–783), specifically before his reduction of Damascus and the Philistine coast in his fifth year (806 BC) (*ANET*, p. 282), was the period of Israel's eclipse by Aram, to which 6.24–7.20 is probably to be dated. Jepsen[b] has noted that, in contrast to Hadadezer, who is noted in Assyrian inscriptions as the head of an alliance of Syrian states in all his activities against Assyria, Hazael is mentioned as apparently opposing Assyria alone. If this were literally so, it would explain Hazael's campaign in Palestine in order to secure his rear in his opposition to Assyria. On Hazael's campaign in the Philistine plain see on 12.17f. [18f.]. On the other hand, Hazael's son Benhadad III held the hegemony of most of Syria (see on I K. 20.1), which was probably a legacy from Hazael. This hegemony probably differed from that of Hadadezer in that the earlier confederacy was one of autonomous states, whereas that under Hazael was contrived under compulsion, Hazael probably using the Aramaean tribes, over whom Damascus seemed to have particularly strong influence, to secure his interest in the Syrian states, whose armed forces he limited to those amenable to his own policy. This policy is indicated by the fact that Benhadad III was able at will to substitute for the general levies of his allies against Israel under their own rulers a force commanded entirely by professional officers (I K. 20.24). The limitation of the armaments of the confederates is indicated by his limitation of the forces of Jehoahaz of Israel to fifty horsemen, ten chariots and 10,000 foot (II K. 13.7), and the exploitation of the Aramaean element in the policy of Damascus is indicated by the intention of Rezin of Damascus, who had already gained Israel in his common front against Assyria, to supplant Ahaz of Judah by an Aramaean ruler (Isa. 7.6). The sole mention of Hazael in Assyrian records may reflect this new nature of the hegemony of Damascus.

10.33. Šanda plausibly argues (p. 119) that since Joram had not been able to retake the land lost to Moab under Mesha and had been

[a]So Šanda, II, p. 120.
[b]*AfO* XIV, 1942, p. 159.

forced to invade by the east of Edom (ch. 3), the region about Aroer on the Arnon must have been recovered in the early part of Jehu's reign, presumably before Hazael had recovered from the Assyrian invasion and investment of Damascus in 841. This, he suggests, may be 'all his might', to which v. 34 refers. Hence he would date the stele of Mesha before that date. It is possible, however, that with the cession of Ramoth Gilead, Hazael may have recovered the northern part of Moab for Israel and handed it over as an inducement to join the common front against Assyria. However this may be, the Transjordanian lands were now lost to Israel until they were recovered by Jeroboam II. Aroer, mentioned as by the Arnon in Deut. 2.36; 3.12, etc., is given as the southern limit of the territory of Sihon (Josh. 12.2) and of the tribes of Reuben (Josh. 13.16) and Gad (Josh. 13.9, cf. II Sam. 24.5). The place is located at *'Arā'ir* just to the north of the *Wādī Mūjib* (Arnon) about ten miles east of the Dead Sea, where there are sherds of the third millennium and of the Iron Age and the remains of an Iron Age fortress.[a]

(*b*) THE REIGN OF ATHALIAH AND THE ACCESSION OF JOASH: 11.1–20

Already on the death of Jehoshaphat Jehoram had had to face conservative opposition in Judah, which resented the close involvement of Judah in the politics of Israel under the house of Omri. Jehoram silenced the opposition for the moment with the execution of his own brothers and sundry other notables of Judah under whom nationalist feeling sought to find expression (II Chron. 21.4). On the death of Ahaziah the queen-mother Athaliah, herself from the household of Ahab and the notorious Jezebel, sought to anticipate a nationalist rally under a prince of the royal house by a massacre of the heirs-apparent. For the moment she was successful in her repression and ruled for six years. Meanwhile the nationalist opposition, represented by the Temple priesthood, sheltered the young prince Joash, who had been rescued by the sister of Ahaziah from the massacre of Athaliah. At an opportune moment a *coup d'état* was effected which had both popular support and the support of the priesthood and the professional soldiers in the capital, and Athaliah was killed and Joash set on the throne.

Such a movement was not the work of the minority, and, as the drastic action of Jehoram (II Chron. 21.4) indicates, there was a

[a]N. Glueck, 'Explorations in Eastern Palestine', *AASOR* XIV, 1934, pp. 49ff.

considerably body of public opinion against the pro-Israelite policy of the ruling house and the religious innovations of Jehoram's wife Athaliah. Indeed, had there not been a strong party in Judah opposed to the royal house and their liaison with the house of Omri, Jehu would hardly have ventured to slay king Ahaziah and the other members of the royal family of Judah. The conservative reaction in Judah was greatly strengthened by events in Jehu's *coup* in Israel, and the extreme measures of Athaliah are a gauge of the strength of the opposition. The popular reaction to Athaliah must be borne in mind when we consider the narrative of her death and the accession of Joash. Though the priesthood played such a notable part with the aid of the professional soldiers in Jerusalem, this was not simply the revolt of a class of officials and the palace guard, and this is apparent from the narrative itself, which mentions the activity of 'the people of the land'.

Since Stade, critics have generally held that two sources are involved, as indicated by the double mention of the death of Athaliah. According to vv. 13ff., she had already appeared in the Temple at the coronation of Joash, and was escorted out and into the palace, where she was killed (v. 16), while in vv. 18b–20 after the installation of the young king in the palace, Athaliah's death in the palace is reported (v. 20). This of itself we consider insufficient evidence for two sources, since vv. 16 and 20 agree on the death of Athaliah in the palace, and either v. 16 may be proleptic of v. 20 or v. 20 may be a circumstantial amplification of v. 16. In vv. 13–18a the queen-mother's name is spelt in the short form *Athalyah*, while in vv. 1–12 and 18b–20 the longer form *Athalyahu* is used. But in vv. 1–4, dealing with Athaliah's reign before the *coup d'état*, both forms are found, so that this argument is unconvincing. Much is made of the fact that in vv. 4–12 and 18b–20 the initiative is with the priests in the Temple to the virtual exclusion of the people, while the people play a leading role in vv. 13–18a, and it is suggested that in vv. 1–12, 18b–20 we have a priestly source, whereas in vv. 13–18a the source is a popular one. This has been questioned by W. Rudolph,[a] who reduces the incidences of 'the people of the land' in vv. 13–18a most drastically, though, in our opinion, somewhat arbitrarily, in default of support from the Versions. Hence we adhere to the theory of a priestly source in vv. 4–12, 18b–20 and a popular one in vv. 13–18a. The former, it is

[a]'Die Einheitlichkeit der Erzählung vom Sturz der Atalja (2 Kön 11)', *Bertholet Festschrift*, 1950, pp. 473–8.

claimed, represents the revolution in its political, the latter in its religious aspect. This is probably true in the main, but the two accounts are complementary rather than divergent. It is not sufficient to say with Šanda (II, p. 135) that the only mention of 'the people' (actually 'the people of the land') in vv. 1–12, 18b–20 is in v. 20 and 'the people of the land' in v. 13 is a gloss, since the recent history of Judah and Israel and the tradition even in the priestly compilation of Chronicles (II Chron. 23.1f.) shows that the priests, if they did take the initiative in the elevation of Joash, were simply the leaders of public opinion. It is not necessary to postulate a great representative gathering of the people from all over the realm on this occasion, since the people (*hā'ām*) might signify the worshipping community, though, we may add, we think it most likely that the occasion would be the New Year festival, of which an element was the celebration of the enthronement of Yahweh, which was the appropriate occasion for the accession of the king. This was *heḥāg*, 'the festival' *par excellence*, at which people from the provinces could be present without exciting undue suspicion. Hence it is not true to say that the people are excluded from the priestly account of the *coup d'état*. Nor does the second account in vv. 13–18a exclude the priests from the leading role. Nevertheless the former account emphasizes the political aspect of the revolution, the element of intrigue with the professional military elements, and the leading role of the Temple personnel, while the second makes explicit what we could only conjecture from the former, the popular support for the *coup*. Here also (v. 18a) the religious aspect of the revolt is emphasized. The accounts, therefore, are generally complementary, the second making explicit what is implicit in the first, namely the popular support for the action of the priests, and the details of Athaliah's death, which is barely and generally stated in the first.

Nevertheless there are certain discrepancies which point to two distinct sources. In vv. 13–18a the death of Athaliah is after the anointing of Joash, but before the covenant with God and the people; in vv. 4–12, 18b–20 it is after these events, when the excitement had died down.

So far as we may reconstruct, the priestly source is somewhat vague on the death of the queen-mother, which it locates in the palace after the installation of Joash there. In the popular account Athaliah tries unsuccessfully to intervene in the anointing of Joash in the Temple, and is escorted out of the sacred precinct by the guard through the horse-entrance to the palace, where she is killed; when, it is not specified. The destruction of the temple of Baal was not carried out between the anointing and installation of Joash as the present order of the MT indicates. Hence we suppose that the whole *coup* was effected during the seven-day New Year festival. On that occasion the accession of the king as a reflection of the divine assumption of kingly power was a feature, and another distinctive feature was the renewal of the divine covenant, the covenant with the house of David being fused with the covenant with Israel.[a] This took place at a later stage in the festival, towards the end of which the destruction of the Baal temple or precinct was well in hand, though the concise nature of the narrative in vv. 13–18a gives a false impression that the events were simultaneous. The posting of a guard in the Temple (18b), which Burney[b] takes to indicate that the queen was not yet killed, was probably a precaution against spiteful desecration of the shrine of Yahweh by the personnel of Athaliah's Baal-cult, the queen herself being taken out of the Temple under military escort.

11.1–12, 18b–20 has affinities in style and viewpoint with ch. 12, and Wellhausen[c] feasibly postulates a priestly source including 16.10ff. and ch. 22, which had as its theme the history of the Temple, its cult, and the priesthood. The general objection to this view, however, is the fact that 12.6ff. admits the inefficiency and remissness of the priests in the upkeep and repair of the Temple, which is not likely to have been admitted by a priestly author. Kittel, on the other hand, suggests (HKAT, pp. 243ff.) that chs. 11f. are from the History of the Kings of Judah, but he is uncertain whether the sources are in their original form or have been worked over. We think, however, that we may still postulate a priestly source, probably reflecting the sober and self-critical mood of the priests in and after the Deuteronomic reformation. Since the Josianic reformation was as much a constitutional as a religious reformation, this may have been the time at which the two sources in ch. 11 were combined, the fragment of the popular source in vv. 13–18a being introduced to do credit to the role of the people, or 'the people of the land' (*'am hā'āreṣ*), who play a similar part in the Josianic reformation (ch. 23), of which the fragment in 11.13–18a with its sequence of events, the

[a]M. Noth, 'Jerusalem and the Israelite Tradition', *The Laws in the Pentateuch*, pp. 134 ff.; H. J. Kraus, *Die Königsherrschaft Gottes im Alten Testament*, 1951, pp. 115 ff.

[b]*Notes on . . . Kings*, p. 308.

[c]*Einleitung in das AT*, ed. F. Bleek, 1878, pp. 257ff.

covenant of the king and the popular iconoclasm, is a close counterpart. Whatever their origin, both sources in ch. 11 are not annalistic, but historical narrative, of which there was already a prototype in Judah in the Story of the Davidic Succession (II Sam. 9.20–I K. 2.46) and in Israel in the historical narratives of the house of Ahab (I K. 20.1–34; 22.1–38), of certain events in the Syrian wars (e.g. II K. 6.24–7.20), and of the revolt of Jehu (chs. 9f.). In the Judaean narratives, however, apart from the Story of the Davidic Succession, attention is focused on events rather than on personalities and the interplay of character and motive, with the result that, though quite dramatic, they lack the vivacity of the Israelite narratives, which no doubt owe much to prophetic adaptation, and were probably much influenced by the dramatic representation of history in the E narrative of the Pentateuch, which was produced simultaneously with the events so graphically narrated of Ahab's reign and immediately after.

The incident is elaborated in II Chron. 23, where the role of the professional soldiers is played by Levites, and the account in Kings in its extant state has been influenced by this priestly reconstruction.

(i) THE REIGN OF ATHALIAH: 11.1–3

11 [1]Now Athaliah the mother of Ahaziah saw[a] that her son was dead, so she arose and destroyed all the seed royal. [2]But Jehosheba the daughter of king Joram, the sister of Ahaziah, took Joash the son of Ahaziah[b] and smuggled him away from among the royal family who were being put to death, [c]and put[c] him and his wet-nurse in the bedchamber, and hid[d] him from Athaliah, and he was not put to death. [3]And he was with her in the Temple of Yahweh, hidden away for six years, and Athaliah ruled over the land.

11.1. The reign of Athaliah is not introduced or rounded off with the usual editorial notes and comments; this shows that it was regarded as a usurpation, the bloody nature of which spoke for itself. On the significance of her massacre see critical introduction to this section (p. 565).

[a]Omitting *w* before the perfect of the verb with Q, the Versions, and the parallel account in II Chron. 22.10.

[b]G reads 'her brother' (*'āḥîhā*) for *'ᵃḥazyā* ('Ahaziah'), which does not materially alter the sense.

[c]Cf. Q Hophal participle *mûmātîm*, MT *mmwttym* possibly being a corruption, first through a dittograph of a following *wattittēn*, as in the parallel passage in II Chron. 22.11.

[d]G, S, and V read the third singular feminine, though MT might be defended on the assumption that the third plural masculine expresses the indefinite subject.

11.2. Jehosheba is stated in II Chron. 22.11 to have been the wife of the priest Jehoiada, which is very probable from the fact that she was able to keep the child in her private chambers in the Temple. She was no doubt the half-sister of Ahaziah, the daughter of Joram by another mother than Athaliah. The name, a compound of Yahweh, and *šebaʿ* ('oath') is given in a variant form in Chronicles, Jehoshabeath, of which Elisabeth is a variant. Doubtless when the child could no longer be concealed in the bed-chamber he would escape detection as one of the priest's children or perhaps as a devotee like the young Samuel at the sanctuary of Shiloh.

gānab is used in the sense of kidnapping in Deut. 24.7 and in the case of Joseph in Gen. 40.15, and almost certainly has this sense in the Decalogue (Ex. 20.15; Deut. 5.19), cf. Ex. 21.16, where this is explicit, the crime being a capital offence.[a]

The parallel account in Chronicles reads *wattittēn* ('and she put') before 'him and his nurse'. The 'nurse' would not be suitable as an object to *wattignōb*.

The fact of the young children of the king being out with sundry foster-mothers would facilitate Jehosheba's frustration of the bloody design of Athaliah.

(ii) THE PRIESTLY ACCOUNT OF THE ACCESSION OF JOASH: 11.4–12

11 [4]Then in the seventh year Jehoiada sent and took the captains of hundreds[b] of the Carites and the guards and brought them to him in the Temple of Yahweh and made a covenant with them and swore them in in the Temple of Yahweh[c] and showed them the prince. [5]And he gave them their orders saying, This is what you shall do. The third part of you, who come in on the sabbath and stand guard in the palace,[d] [7]and the two detachments of you, all who come out on the

[a]See further A. Alt, 'Das Verbot des Diebstahls im Dekalog', *KS* I, 1953, pp. 333–40.

[b]Q points the word as if *y* were not written. It has been suggested that the *y* is written simply to avoid hiatus between the *aleph* and the following vowel, cf. the modern Arab pronunciation of *mā'un* ('water').

[c]G^B and S omit 'in the Temple of Yahweh'.

[d]Omitting v. 6 'and the third part at the gate Sur' (cf. II Chron. 23.5 'of the foundation') 'and the third part at the gate behind the guards, and you shall keep guard on the Temple in relays'. This is probably, as Wellhausen suggested, a redactional gloss suggested by the mention of a third part in v. 5, but ignoring 'the two detachments' in v. 7, which continues the sense of v. 5 normally and gives an intelligible text. Probably the particularization on the two gates and

sabbath and stand guard in the Temple of Yahweh,[a] [8]you shall form a ring about the king all around, each man with his weapons in his hand, and whoever comes within the ranks shall be slain; and be with the king when he goes out and when he comes in. [9]So the captains of hundreds[b] did all that Jehoiada the priest commanded and each took his men, those who came in on the sabbath together with those who came out on the sabbath, and they came to Jehoiada the priest. [10]Then the priest gave the commanders of the hundreds[b] the spears[c] and the shields which had been king David's, which were in the Temple of Yahweh. [11]And the guards stood, each man with his weapons in his hand, from the right wing of the Temple to the left wing, around the altar and the Temple.[d] [12]Then he brought out the prince and put the symbol of dedication upon him and the testimony,[e] and made him king [f]and anointed[f] him, and they clapped their hands and said, Life to the king!

11.4. The Carites are mentioned in MT again only at II Sam. 20.23 with *pelētī*, where Q reads *kerētī*, who are familiar as the royal bodyguard traditionally recruited from among the Philistines. It is known, however, that Psammetichus of Egypt (663–609) employed Carians from Cilicia as his bodyguard,[g] and possibly the kings of Judah in the latter part of the ninth century did the same. It is, however, more probable that the word is a scribal error for *kerētī*. On *rāṣīm* see on I K. 1.5.

---

relative positions of the troops there denotes a well-informed early glossator. The gate 'Sur' is unknown and the last word in v. 6 *massāḥ* is also an enigma. The best suggestions, in our opinion, are that of Haupt, who posits a Hebrew cognate of Arabic *nasaḫa* ('to replace'), and that of W. Rudolph, *op. cit.*, pp. 474f., that *haššaʿar (hā) ʾaḥēr* should be read for MT *baššaʿar ʿaḥar*, and the following *hārāṣīm* treated as a gloss, giving the meaning 'the other gate', that is of the Guards, cf. the two gates mentioned in vv. 16, 19. Rudolph's further proposal that *ṣūr* is a corruption of *sūs* ('horse'), presumably in the proto-Hebraic script, may be seriously considered in the light of vv. 16, 19.

[a]Omitting 'to the king' of MT.

[b]See p. 570 n.[b].

[c]Reading plural for MT singular with G, S, and V and the parallel account in Chronicles, though in the form *ḥanītōt* rather than *ḥanītīm* of II Chron. 23.9.

[d]Omitting 'about the king' after S, which reads 'they surrounded the altar and the house of the king'. Probably 'the king' indicates a misunderstanding of 'house' (= temple). Perhaps, as Burney suggested (*Notes*, p. 311), *ʿal-hammelek* was introduced before *sābīb*, which was displaced from before *lammizbēaḥ welabbayit*. 'The king' is out of place here, since Joash was only brought out of the Temple in v. 12.

[e]For MT *ʿēdūt* and the proposed variants *haṣṣeʿādōt*, 'bracelets' (Wellhausen) and *ʿadāyōt*, 'ornaments' (Klostermann after Kimchi), see note.

[f]Reading singular with G for MT plural.

[g]Herodotus II, 154.

11.5. In this and the following two verses there is great obscurity in MT, which disappears as soon as v. 6 is set aside as a gloss. In vv. 5 and 7, which, as the conjunction and the grammar of v. 7 suggest, should be read continuously, the meaning is fairly obvious. The guard in Temple and palace was changed on the sabbath, one-third going into barracks and guard duty in the palace, and two-thirds coming out of barracks and off guard duty in the palace and mounting guard in the Temple. Jehoiada selected the change of guard for the *coup d'état*, when troop movements would occasion no comment and when it was possible to concentrate all the divisions of the guards of the capital in the Temple, thus denuding Athaliah of the means of resistance. On the view that v. 6 is an early gloss see textual note.

This passage suggests that the sabbath, in the end of the ninth century was regularly observed. On the sabbath in Israel as a weekly occasion see on 4.23.

6. On the omission of v. 6 and on textual points in it see p. 570 n.[d].

7. 'And the two parts' (*ūštē hayyādōt*) follows on naturally from the mention of one-third in v. 5. Note the usage of *yād*, lit. 'hand', for 'part', cf. Gen. 47.24; II Sam. 19.44; Neh. 11.1.

8. *śedērōt* is presumably a variant spelling of *sedērōt* and probably refers to the ranks of the guardsmen, though Šanda takes it to refer to the colonnades or 'ranks' of pillars between the Temple court and the palace, where Athaliah was killed (v. 16). Against this view is the fact that she was not killed when she reached the colonnade, but was escorted outside the Temple and was killed in the palace at a time not specified here.

10. 'The shields and spears' (see p. 571 n.[c]) belonging to David suggests the statement of II Sam. 8.7 that David dedicated gold, or gilded, shields which he took from the servants of Hadadezer of Zobah in the Ammonite campaign. These, however, had been pillaged by Shishak (I K. 14.26), being replaced with bronze shields (I K. 14.27). From that passage (v. 28) we learn that the guards bore those shields when the king visited the Temple. Hence on this occasion they were issued to the guards, either ostensibly in preparation for a visit by Athaliah or in anticipation of the anointing of Joash. In II Sam. 8.7 there is no mention of spears in David's dedication, and it may be that we should follow MT in reading the singular, and that Ewald was right in supposing that the spear was David's own. The spear signifies authority, e.g. Saul's spear in I Sam. 26.7, cf. the Ras

Shamra text (*UT* 125.47) where the son of King Krt on an important mission carries his spear, presumably as a mark of royal status. Hence we may suppose that David's spear would be given to the new king, or it may have been given to the commander-in-chief to signify the delegation of the authority of the king in war. Ewald further insists that the guardsmen obviously did not come to the Temple unarmed, hence the handing out of weapons to them was influenced by the account in II Chronicles, where the unarmed Levites were so armed. The passage we have cited from I K. 14.28, however, indicates that the shields in the Temple and possibly also spears were regularly used by the guards on duty. These may have been specially consecrated weapons for use only in the sacred precinct, though we may doubt if they were as ancient as the time of David.

11.11. The guards seem to have formed a semicircle about the porch of the Temple and the altar which stood before it. See further p. 571 n.[d].

12. *nēzer*, root *nāzar*, whence 'Nazirite', is best translated 'symbol of dedication', leaving its identity with the diadem an open question. Noth[a] and de Vaux[b] note the identity of *nēzer* with the golden flower (*ṣîṣ*), the symbol of dedication, on the turban of the high priest (Ex. 39.30; Lev. 8.9). This symbol, along with the bracelet (*ṣᵉʿādā*), both, no doubt, of gold, were the royal insignia of Saul (II Sam. 1.10), and this suggested to Wellhausen that here *hāʿēdūt* should be emended to *haṣṣᵉʿādōt*, since the phrase 'and he set on him' (*wayyittēn ʿālāw*) is allegedly not suitable to the object *hāʿēdūt* ('the testimony'). This objection, however, is hardly valid, since, even if the phrase does not mean, as it may, the momentary laying of a written document on the person of the king, as phylacteries are bound to the foreheads of orthodox Jews, it may still mean imposing a responsibility. Actually in Ps. 132.12, which deals with the covenant of Yahweh with the house of David, *ʿēdōt* is found in parallelism with *bᵉrît*, which in turn is associated with *nēzer* in another royal psalm, 89.39 [40]. This indicates that *ʿēdūt* ('testimony') was a feature of the coronation ritual and is specifically associated with the covenant of Yahweh with the Davidic king. The covenant, as we learn from the *locus classicus*, the oracle of Nathan (II Sam. 7.12–16), contained both promise of divine grace and obligations upon the king, and from Ps. 132.12 (*ʿēdōt zū ʾalammᵉdēm*, 'the testimonies which I teach them') it seems obvious that *ʿēdūt* or *ʿēdōt* signified specifically the king's obliga-

[a]*Exodus*, pp. 225f. [b]*Ancient Israel*, p. 465.

tions in the covenant. Here we agree with A. R. Johnson[a] as against G. von Rad,[b] Mowinckel[c] and H. J. Kraus,[d] who emphasize the element of divine promise. In support of this interpretation the use of *ʿdy*, from a by-form of the verb *ʿūd*, may be noted in the vassal-treaty of Bar-Ga'ya' with Mattiel,[e] where the word means 'treaty', involving friendship promised and loyalty in response. G. Widengren, studying these passages, would identify *ʿēdūt* here with the whole law, which he takes to be entrusted to the king, the possession and declaration of the law by Joshua (Josh. 24.25–28) and by Agrippa I in AD 41[f] being a reflection of pre-exilic usage.[g] The status of Joshua and the other greater judges, however, as leaders of all Israel is an idealization of the situation by the Deuteronomistic compiler at the end of the monarchy or in the Exile, so that this is not necessarily a reflection of the function of the pre-exilic king. Noth[h] may well be right in seeing in Joshua really one of the minor judges, who was a hereditary custodian of the law, which may be the basis of the tradition in Josh. 24.25–28 cited by Widengren. Von Rad alleges an analogy to, and possibly the prototype of, the element of *ʿēdūt* in the coronation ritual in Israel in the Egyptian usage of communicating to the king on his accession the title-deeds and conditions of his office, together with his throne names, in a formal protocol. But no Egyptian text explicitly associates such a protocol with the five new throne-names (*nekbet*) which were communicated at the coronation,[i] though these contain the elements of divine promise to the king and emphasis on his responsibilities, as in royal accession-oracles to the king of the Davidic house (e.g. Pss. 2; 110) and as is implied in *ʿēdūt*. Further and more explicit reference to such quasi-legal authority for the rule of the king in Israel is in Ps. 2.6ff., which refers to the recitation of *ḥōq*, the written decree declaring the king the adopted son of God (Ps. 2.7f.), a relationship which involves responsibilities

[a]*Sacral Kingship in Ancient Israel*, 1955, p. 21 and n.; *Myth, Ritual and Kingship*, p. 210.

[b]'Das judäische Königsritual', *TLZ* LXXII, 1947, cols. 211–16; *The Problem of the Hexateuch*, pp. 222–31.

[c]*The Psalms in Israel's Worship* I, pp. 62ff.

[d]*Psalmen* II, pp. 886f.

[e]H. Donner and W. Röllig, *Kanaanäische und aramäische Inschriften*, I, 1962, 223, B, 2.

[f]Mishna, *Soṭa* 7.8.

[g]'King and Covenant', *JSS* II, 1957, pp. 12ff.

[h]'God, King and Nation in the Old Testament', *The Laws in the Pentateuch*, p. 162, n.1.

[i]K. A. Kitchen, *Ancient Orient and Old Testament*, 1966, p. 107, citing particularly H. W. Fairman and B. Grdseloff, *JEA* XXXIII, 1947, p. 15.

as well as privileges. MT *ʿēdūt*, which is supported unanimously by the versions, is accepted by a number of scholars.[a] H. G. May[b] also accepts MT, but, with less relevance, we think, sees an analogy in Mesopotamian myth and presumably also in ritual in the laying of the 'tablets of destiny' on the breast of Kingu by Tiamat. The emendation of Wellhausen is accepted by Kittel, Burney, Skinner, Gressmann, Smith and Goodspeed, while Klostermann's reading *hāʿᵃdīyōt* ('the ornaments', sc. regalia) is accepted by G. R. Driver.[c]

The order, coronation, presentation with the testimony, and finally anointing is noted by Šanda (II, p. 130) as the procedure at the investiture of Aaron (Ex. 29.6f.; Lev. 8.9–12).

On the acclamation of the new king *yᵉḥī hammelek* ('life to the king!') see on I K. 1.25.

(iii) THE POPULAR, AS DISTINCT FROM THE PRIESTLY, ACCOUNT OF THE DEATH OF ATHALIAH AND THE ACCESSION OF JOASH: 11.13–18a

11 13Now Athaliah heard the sound[d] of the people, so she came to the people in the Temple of Yahweh. 14And she saw that there was the king standing by the pillar[e] according to custom and the com-

[a]W. E. Barnes, CB, 1928, *ad loc.*; T. H. Robinson, *History of Israel* I, p. 351 and n.; G. von Rad, *loc. cit.*; S. Mowinckel, *The Psalms in Israel's Worship* I, pp. 62ff.; Montgomery, ICC, pp. 420f.; A. R. Johnson, *Sacral Kingship in Ancient Israel*, 1967[2], p. 23n.; and tentatively de Vaux, *Ancient Israel*, p. 103, where the relevant evidence is excellently marshalled.

[b]*JBL* LVII, 1938, p. 181.

[c]*JTS* XXXVI, 1935, pp. 293ff.

[d]*hārāṣīn* ('of the guards') of MT should be excluded, this being possibly a gloss introduced to connect this independent account of the accession of Joash with the priestly account. Burney (*Notes on . . . Kings*, p. 311) suggests that the plural ending in *n* is an Aramaism and so points to a later gloss. It may simply be a scribal error for *m* in the proto-Hebraic script.

[e]MT 'by the pillar' has the support of the parallel account in II Chron. 23.13, where the third masculine singular pronominal suffix is added. In the account of Josiah's covenant with the people it is stated that he stood *ʿal-ʿomdō*, which might simply mean 'in his place', cf. II Chron. 34.31; Neh. 8.7. In II K. 11.14 only V of all the Versions supports the reading *ʿal-hāʿōmed*, translating 'on a tribunal,' which Gressmann and Noth accept. This reading might be authenticated by the reading of G at II K. 16.18, where there is an allusion to 'the base of the tribunal' (*mūsad haššebet = themelion tēs kathēdras*), which was removed by Ahaz in the Temple area. If this reading is correct, the removal of the royal tribunal would be fittingly symbolic of the vassalage of Ahaz. MT, however, might signify one of the pillars Jachin and Boaz, as Eissfeldt (*HSAT*, p. 560), Kittel (HKAT, p. 250) and Widengren ('King and Covenant', *JSS* II, 1957, p. 6) think. This is supported by II Chron. 23.13, which states that the king was standing 'by his pillar at the entrance (to the Temple)'. This supports our conjecture that the pillars Jachin and Boaz symbolized the association of God and the king. See further on 11.14 and I K. 7.21.

manders[a] by the king and all the people of the land rejoicing and sounding of[b] trumpets, and Athaliah rent her robes and cried out, Conspiracy! Conspiracy! [15]Then Jehoiada the priest ordered [c]the captains of hundreds[c] who were set over[d] the army and said to them, Take her out [e]between the ranks,[e] and any who follows her let him be put to death[f] with the sword. For the priest said, Let her not be put to death in the Temple of Yahweh. [16]So they escorted her and she came by the way of the horse entrance into the palace, and she was put to death there. [17]Then Jehoiada made the covenant between Yahweh and the king and the people, that they should be a people belonging to Yahweh,[g] and between the king and the people.[g] [18]And all the people of the land came to the temple of Baal and pulled it down;[h] and his altar[i] and images they broke in pieces thoroughly, and as for Mattan the priest of Baal they slew him before the altar.[j]

11.13. Note the short form of the name Athaliah in this passage.

14. On 'the pillar' (or perhaps 'platform') see p. 575 n.[e]. The coronation inscription of Thothmes II[k] mentions 'the station of the king' in the Temple of Amon, the occupancy of which signified that

[a]Omitting MT *w^ehah^aṣōṣ^erot* ('and the trumpets'), which, as an impersonal noun, is unsuitable, and may be a dittograph of *bah^aṣōṣ^erōt* later in the verse.

[b]It is unlikely that 'the people of the land' should have been equipped with trumpets, and we suggest pointing MT *tōqēaʿ* as the verbal noun *toqaʿ*.

[c]Burney, after Stade, regards *śārē hammēʾōt* as a gloss representing the effort to harmonize the priestly and popular account of those events. This is not supported by any Hebrew MS or Version, and is conditioned too much by the two-source theory, which must be supported by the evidence of the text.

[d]Reading the more common *p^eqīdē* for the passive *p^eqūdē* of MT, as suggested by G.

[e]MT, with the sense 'between', i.e. 'within', the ranks, is supported by most of the Greek versions, though others feel a difficulty and, like S and V, read 'outside the ranks', guided probably by the general sense rather than the MT. Burney assumes a gloss after the account in the priestly source. The presumed prepositional phrase *ʾel-mibbēt* is unique, though perhaps comparable to *l^emibbēt* in Num. 18.7.

[f]Reading Hophal jussive *yūmat* with the Versions and the parallel passage in Chronicles for MT *hāmēt*, the infinitive absolute Hiphil with the imperative or jussive sense with indefinite subject understood, which is quite feasible.

[g]This phrase is omitted in G^L and the parallel account in Chronicles, but since the only covenant so far mentioned was the Davidic covenant between Yahweh and the king, the covenant between king and people is a significant feature in the adoption of the new king, as the incident at Shechem in the time of Rehoboam clearly indicates (I K. 12.1ff.). See further n. on v. 17.

[h]Reading *w^eʾet* with G, T, and the parallel account in Chronicles for MT *ʾet*, a case of haplography after the final *w* in the previous word.

[i]Q and G read *mizb^eḥōtāw*, but we follow the clue of the pronominal suffix, reading the singular. See n.[h].

[j]Reading singular with S, V, and T, for MT, and G, plural.

[k]Breasted, *ARE* II, § 140.

the god had found a legitimate king. The parallel account at II Chron. 23.13 indicates that the pillar was at the entrance to the Temple, which rather indicates Jachin or Boaz. If these are giant cressets symbolizing the abiding presence of Yahweh, one of them might have been associated with Yahweh and the other with the king of the house of David as the temporal manifestation of the cosmic reign of God. Whether or not we may so discriminate, the article indicates that it was customary (*kammišpāṭ*) for the king on such solemn appearances to the people to stand by one of the pillars, cf. 23.3, which agrees with MT in the present passage. Trumpets are a natural instrument of acclamation, but in this context they may reflect in the accession of the king of Judah the ritual of trumpet-blowing in the theophany of Yahweh as king in the New Year festival.

'Commanders' (*śārīm*) is read in the parallel passage in Chron., but here G and V point the word as *šārīm* ('singers'), a tradition apparently known to the Chronicler, who assigns the singers a place in the coronation. The singers would certainly find opportunity for their art in one of the psalms appropriate to a coronation, but in the present circumstances it is doubtful whether such an opportunity was afforded.

It is doubtful in this passage whether we should discriminate between 'the people' (*hā'ām*) and 'the people of the land' (*'am-hā-'āreṣ*). The latter term is used in rabbinical writings as a term of contempt signifying simple people or provincials as distinct from the intellectual and spiritual leaders of Judaism in, or under the influence of, Jerusalem. This usage originated no doubt with the self-consciousness of the restored Jewish community over against the local population of Palestine, both Jews and non-Jews, who cared little for Zionist aspirations or ritual exclusiveness. In the pre-exilic period, however, *'am-hā'āreṣ* are the real representatives of the tradition of the sacral community in Israel. Noting the intervention of the *'am-hā'āreṣ* at crises in the Davidic monarchy, as in the present passage, Würthwein[a] took the term to denote the assembly of free men in Judah associated with the old general military levy over against the feudal administration of Jerusalem as a crown estate. They thus, according to Würthwein, represented the democratic principle, which was reasserted in their acclamation of the new king, as they had

[a]E. Würthwein, *Der* Amm ha'arez *im AT*, BWANT IV, 17, 1936; cf. earlier studies by E. Gilleschewski, *ZAW* XL, 1922, pp. 137ff.; K. Galling, *AO* XXVIII, Heft 3/4, 1929, pp. 32ff.; and R. Gordis, *JQR* XXV, 1935, pp. 242ff.

once confirmed Saul's authority by their acclamation. J. A. Soggin,[a] too, notices that of the few kings of Judah commended by the Deuteronomistic historian, Joash, Amaziah, Uzziah and Josiah were supported by *ʿam-hāʾāreṣ* against the royal 'servants' in the crown-possession of Jerusalem, who had evidently been suborned to support rival claimants to the throne and actually assassinated Joash (12.20) and Amon (21.23) and probably also Amaziah (14.19), as is indicated by the accession of his son Uzziah with the support of 'all the people of Judah' (14.21). The same cleavage between Judah at large and the feudal retainers in Jerusalem is also noted in the case of two other kings approved by the Deuteronomistic historian, Asa and Jehoshaphat, who, like Amaziah (II Chron. 25.5ff.) relied by preference on the support of the general military levy throughout the kingdom (II Chron. 14.7; 17.13ff.). This leads Soggin to the feasible conclusion that *ʿam-hāʾāreṣ* denotes the representatives of the sacral community loyal to the Yahwistic tradition, which was expressed in the covenant-sacrament. E. Nielsen[b] regards the assertion of the rights of the representatives of the people in Judah as an adaptation and development of the tradition of the sacral community, which was properly at home in the North, but Soggin[c] regards it rather as the survival of the covenant tradition of all Israel, including Judah. From 23.35; 25.19 it is apparent that *ʿam-hāʾāreṣ* were representatives of the freemen of Judah rather than the people in general, as Alt[d] maintains, equating the 60 of the *ʿam-hāʾāreṣ* deported in 25.19 with *nišē māti*, local notables deported with unsatisfactory rulers in Assyrian inscriptions of the eighth century. As the subject of the general fiscal levy in 23.35, the *ʿam-hāʾāreṣ* denotes the sacral community in Judah consisting of all of full status, usually indicated by the possession of property, probably in practice represented by the local notables.

11.16. 'The horse entrance' to the palace was apparently related to, but not identical with, the Horse Gate mentioned in Jer. 31.40

[a]J. A. Soggin, 'Der judäische ʿam-hāʾāreṣ und das Königtum in Juda', *VT* XIII, 1963, pp. 187–95. Without specifically mentioning *ʿam-hāʾāreṣ*, K. H. Bernhardt, *Das Problem der altorientalischen Königsideologie*, SVT VIII, 1961, pp. 173ff., emphasizes the limitation on the royal authority in Judah by the priests as the representatives of the traditions of the covenant-community, which were also kept alive in Judah by the presence of the ark in the Temple, and was also represented by the popular intervention in the above-mentioned crisis in the history of the Davidic monarchy.

[b]E. Nielsen, *Shechem*, 1955, p. 345.

[c]Soggin, *Das Königtum in Israel*, BZAW CIV, 1967, pp. 106f., n. 4.

[d]*KS* II, 1959, p. 237 n.

and Neh. 3.28 as at the south-east angle of the Temple area and the north-east angle of the palace-complex. It was probably outside the Temple area, unlike the gate of the (foot) guards, through which Joash was taken into the palace (v. 19), cf. I K. 14.27. The *hapax legomenon śîm yādayim lᵉ* should be noticed. This does not necessarily mean that violent hands were laid on Athaliah, but rather that the forces escorted her or made way for her. This is important as bearing on the time of her death in the palace after some interval, in agreement with v. 20.

11.17. Here for the first time in this fragment from the popular account of these proceedings 'the covenant' is mentioned. The definite article suggests customary procedure, though that does not necessarily follow. G. Widengren[a] thinks of a transaction such as David's covenant with Israel at Hebron (II Sam. 5.3), but there is no evidence that this was regular in Judah, and there is no mention of a similar covenant between David and Judah at Hebron, though the fact that he became king at Hebron, which was a notable shrine of Yahweh, probably involved a covenant. G. Fohrer in his careful study of the covenant between king and people in Israel[b] in the case of David at Hebron, Saul, the present case and Josiah's covenant, as well as the usage in Israel and Judah generally, notes variations in practice. The present instance is, moreover, a special case, since the Davidic succession had been broken by Athaliah's usurpation, which necessitated a formal renewal of the Davidic covenant. We should insist on recognizing various elements in the transaction in which Joash was involved, which is represented as a threefold covenant, that between Yahweh and the king, that between the people and Yahweh, and that between king and people. The first is a renewal of the Davidic covenant and royal obligations, which we have seen reason to equate with the 'testimony' (*ʿēdūt*) in our note on v. 12. This we take to be the customary practice, to which the definite article probably refers. The second is a renewal of the covenant traditionally associated with Sinai, and according to this passage the emphasis lay on the responsibilities of the community, the act of self-rededication as the people of God. The transaction follows the pattern of the renewal of the covenant in Deut. 27 and Josh. 24, of which the renunciation of the strange gods by the people of Jacob in Gen. 35.2–4 is probably a reflection, all these instances being located

[a] 'King and Covenant', pp. 21ff.
[b] *ZAW* LXXI, 1959, pp. 1–22.

at Shechem. This was imposed on king and community because of the strange worship which Athaliah had introduced into the Temple. The occasion was probably the New Year festival, a feature of which was the epiphany of Yahweh as King, an apt occasion for the formal accession of the king, who was God's guarantee of order in the community. Since it was the occasion of a great pilgrimage (*ḥag*) to the central shrine, this was of all occasions the best fitted for the nationalist revolution, when the presence in force of people from the provinces or their representatives (*ʿam hāʾāreṣ*) would occasion less suspicion. We may well suppose that there was some significance in the revolt in the seventh year from the accession of Athaliah. In the interim, no doubt, plans were matured, and through local agents trusted supporters from the provinces were prepared for a final concentration on Jerusalem in support of Jehoiada. The third phase of the covenant transaction according to the text was the covenant between king and people. This part of the text is not represented in the parallel account in Chronicles, but this is no valid objection, since Chronicles is late and the social structure of the community was so different then. The transaction was a political and constitutional one, and the Chronicler was familiar with the community as a theocracy. In support of MT and the originality of this transaction we may cite the covenant between David and the elders of Israel at Hebron (II Sam. 5.3), the abortive agreement between Rehoboam and the community of Israel at Shechem (I K. 12.1ff.), and the covenant between Josiah and the people (II K. 23.3), which must have been distinct from the Davidic covenant at his accession, since it took place in his 18th year.

11.18. With the destruction of the Baal Temple the revolution follows the same lines as that of Jehu in Samaria, with, however, less calculated bloodshed. We have no evidence of the precise nature or indeed of the location of the Baal shrine, which may, in fact, have been no more than a sacred enclosure and altar open to the sky except perhaps for a small inner shrine or 'holy of holies'. It may have stood in the court of the Temple or, as Šanda suggested (II, p. 137), that of the palace. The mention of 'images' (*ṣᵉlāmīm*) here makes explicit what is implicit in the account of Jehu's iconoclasm in Samaria, where the general word *maṣṣēbōt* is used (10.26f.). On the evidence of 11.18 we seem entitled to take *maṣṣēbōt* in the sense of 'images' rather than 'standing stones', which, in any case, are not normally burnt. It is significant of the limited extent of Athaliah's success and the universal opposition to her religious policy that only two victims of the insurgents are mentioned, Athaliah and her priest Mattan, a situation contrasting strongly with that in Israel in Jehu's revolt. This suggests that the practice of the fertility-cult of Canaan against which the prophets inveigh was rather the artless observation of local seasonal rituals and rites of imitative magic on the part of the peasants, the great appeal of which was rather that, associated with the burial places of notable ancestors (the real significance of *bāmōt*), they gave communities and clans the opportunity to realize their solidarity. When the systematic Baal-cult of Phoenicia was introduced with all its ideological complications, which militated against all the traditions of Israel, men in Israel and Judah were ready to oppose it resolutely. In attacking elements of the fertility-cult the prophets were attacking the system at its roots.

Skinner implies by his note on the name Mattan (CB, p. 341), that it was specifically Phoenician. It is, in fact, the truncation ('Gift') of a very common Semitic name, e.g. Mattaniah, the original name of King Zedekiah (24.17) and others (I Chron. 25.4, 16; Neh. 11.17, 22, etc.). The hypocoristicon Mattan is now attested on a seal from Lachish.[a]

(iv) THE CONTINUATION OF THE PRIESTLY ACCOUNT OF THE ELEVATION OF JOASH: 11.18b–20

11 18BAnd the priest set officers over the Temple of Yahweh. 19And he took the captains of hundreds, and the Carites, and the guards and all the people of the land, and they took the king down from the Temple of Yahweh and they came into the palace by the gate of the guard, and he took his seat[b] upon the throne of the kings. 20And all the people of the land rejoiced, and the city was quiet; and they killed Athaliah with the sword in the palace.

11.19. The mention of 'the people of the land' here only in the priestly source may be a harmonizing gloss of the editor.

The verb 'they brought down', as usual in the Old Testament, is an accurate reflection of the topography, the palace on the northern part of the south-eastern hill being lower than the Temple area to the north.

20. Note the general reference to the violent death of Athaliah 'in the palace', which, however, is strictly not at variance with the statement in v. 16 that Athaliah came into the palace by the horse entrance and was put to death there. Even if that means that she was

[a] *BASOR* 86, 1942, pp. 24ff.
[b] G reads *wayyōšībūhū* ('and they made him sit').

killed at the entrance that was still part of the palace-complex. Where the two accounts of the death of Athaliah seem to be at variance is in the apparent order of events. The popular account mentions her death before the covenant and after she has come into the Temple when Joash was being acclaimed king by the pillar, whereas in the priestly account it is mentioned after the installation of Joash in the palace. The apparent variance is owing mainly to the focus of interest. The popular account is obviously religiously orientated and is eager to pass on to the threefold covenant (v. 17) and the destruction of the Baal-temple (v. 18), whereas the priestly source notes carefully the stages of the political *coup d'état*. We submit that, after noting Athaliah's appearance in the Temple, v. 16 simply notes that she was escorted out into the palace by the horse entrance, the statement about her death being, we think, anticipatory, and the interest of the writer moving on to the covenant. She was for the moment held in custody in the palace until the ceremonies were over, it not being seemly that such an occasion be marred by bloodshed, which might have evoked a curse, cf. the general custom of an amnesty at a coronation in the ancient Near East.

Possibly in the rejoicing of the people of the land and the silence of Jerusalem there is a contrast between the people of Judah and the city, which, as a royal demesne inhabited to a large extent by dependants on the palace, was expected to rally to Athaliah's support, an apprehension which apparently prompted Jehoiada to post a guard over the Temple while Joash was being installed in the palace.

(*c*) THE REIGN OF JOASH: 11.21–12.21 [12.1–22]

This chapter is composed from a variety of sources. The latest is the Deuteronomistic notice of the accession of Joash, the synchronism with the reign of Jehu of Israel, the length of his reign, his mother's name, and the typical Deuteronomistic appraisal of his reign (vv. 11.21–12.3 [12.1–4]) and his obituary from the same hand (vv. 19–21 [20–22]), summarized from the royal annals of Judah. The bulk of the chapter is occupied with the fiscal arrangements for the maintenance of the Temple fabric. This may be from a literary history of the kingdom of Judah based on state archives, as Noth suggests,[a] selectively drawn upon by the Deuteronomistic compiler, one of whose dominating interests was the Temple. We should posit such a literary

[a] *Überlieferungsgeschichtliche Studien*, pp. 75ff.

history, but emphasize priestly authorship, which would account for the detail where the Temple and events there are involved. We cannot agree with Wellhausen's view that there was a separate Temple history, from which this and similar passages were drawn, in view of the wider interest in such passages as 11.1–12, 18b–20 and chs. 22f. in political issues such as the constitution and the fortunes of the house of David, but we do admit priestly authorship. See further on passages dealing with the Temple, Introduction, pp. 32f. above. The notice of Joash's war-indemnity to Hazael (vv. 18f. [19f.]) is probably from the same source, owing its selection and its position to the fact that he drew on Temple funds for this purpose.

(i) DEUTERONOMISTIC INTRODUCTION TO, AND PREVIEW OF, THE REIGN OF JOASH: 11.21–12.3 [12.1–4]

11[21] Joash was seven years old when he became king. **12**[1] Joash became king in the seventh year of Jehu[a] and reigned forty years in Jerusalem, and his mother's name was Zibiah from Beersheba. [2]And Joash did what was right in the eyes of Yahweh all his days,[b] for Jehoiada the priest directed him.[3] Only, the 'high places' were not abolished; the people still sacrificed and burnt offerings on the high places.

12.1. The synchronism with the reign of Jehu precludes Montgomery's view, which dates Joash's reign from the death of his father, ignoring the interregnum of Athaliah. We admit, however, that the 40 years of his reign may be designedly general, and so include the six years of Athaliah.

The name of Joash's mother Zibiah ('Gazelle') is appropriate to one from Beersheba, the capital of the southern steppe-land and still a market town for the Bedouin in spite of the development of modern light industry under Israeli enterprise.

12.2. On the interpretation of this verse see p. 583, n.[b] below.

yārā, used in the Hiphil, means 'to direct by revelation' and

[a]We should probably follow G^L in inverting the order of the first two sentences, reading in the order *biš*^{e}*nat-šebaʿ l*^{e}*yēhūʾ mālak y*^{e}*hōʾāš* (12.1) *ben šebaʿ šānīm y*^{e}*hōʾāš b*^{e}*mol*^{e}*kō* (11.21), thus restoring the normal order in such editorial introductions to the reigns of the kings of Judah.

[b]G^L reads *hayyāmīm* for MT *yāmāw*, obviously thinking of the assertion in II Chron. 24.15–22 that the conduct of Joash deteriorated after the death of Jehoiada. On this reading the antecedent of the relative clause is *hayyāmīm*. But the antecedent may also be Joash, as Burney suggests (*Notes*, p. 312), or *ʾ*^{a}*šer* may mean 'because', cf. Gen. 30.18; 31.49; 34.13; I Sam. 15.15; I K. 3.19; 8.33, etc. See *GK* § 158b. Ewald's argument is sound that MT should be defended, the Deuteronomistic redaction of Kings knowing nothing of the declension of Joash from his early standards of conduct, and holding him up as exemplary (14.3).

secondarily 'to direct' or 'teach'. The latter is the sense here and generally in late literature such as Proverbs and Wisdom Psalms.

(ii) MAINTENANCE OF THE TEMPLE FABRIC: 12.4–16 [5–17]

12 4 Now Joash said to the priests, All the money of the devotions
which is brought into the Temple of Yahweh, [a]the assessment of each
man according to his assessment[a] and[b] all the silver which anyone
undertakes to contribute to the Temple of Yahweh, 5 let the priests take
for themselves, each from his business assessor, and let them repair the
dilapidation of the Temple with regard to everything where any
dilapidation is found. 6 But it happened that in the twenty-third year of
king Joash the priests had not repaired the dilapidation of the Temple.
7 Then king Joash summoned Jehoiada the priest and the priests and
said to them, Why are you not repairing the dilapidation of the Temple?
Now do not take silver from your business assessors, but give it up for
the dilapidation of the Temple. 8 So the priests agreed to take[c] no
silver from the people and not to repair the dilapidation of the Temple.
9 Then Jehoiada the priest took a single chest[d] and bored a hole in the
lid of it and set it by the doorpost[e] on the right as one entered the
Temple of Yahweh, and the priests who kept the threshold put therein
all the silver which was brought into the Temple of Yahweh. 10 And it
happened that, when they saw that there was much silver in the chest,
the royal scribe came up with the chief priest and they emptied[f] it and

[a] Reading *ʿērek* ('assessment', cf. Lev. 27.2ff.) for MT *ʿōbēr* ('current') after G^{BL}, omitting *nap*^{e}*šōt* as a gloss with Stade, Kittel and Burney, and reading *k*^{e}*ʿerkō* for MT *ʿerkō*, which is a conjecture. Alternatively we might retain MT *ʿōbēr*, assuming metathesis of *ʿōbēr* (here 'who passes in') and *ʾīš*, and read *kōper napšō* ('a ransom for himself') for MT *kesep napšō* (cf. Ex. 30.12f., *w*^{e}*nāt*^{e}*nū ʾīš kōper napsō* . . . *ze yitt*^{e}*nū kol-hāʿōbēr ʿal-happ*^{e}*qūdīm*, 'and they shall give, each man a ransom for himself . . . this they shall give, each man who comes under the census'), but it is possible that MT has been corrupted by the passage in Exodus, which is very much later.

[b] Reading *w*^{e}*kol* for *kol*, assuming a haplograph of *w*, which resembled *k* in the proto-Hebraic script.

[c] Pointing *qaḥat* for MT *q*^{e}*ḥat*.

[d] *ʾ*^{a}*rōn* is vocalized as a construct, but in the context it must be absolute.

[e] For MT *mizbēaḥ* ('altar'), which is impossible in the context unless in the general sense 'place of slaughter', this not being at the entrance to the Temple, G^{A} simply transliterated, reading *ammasbē*. This suggested to Stade the reading *maṣṣēbā* which is followed by Kittel. Klostermann suggested *m*^{e}*zūzā* ('doorpost'), which seems the obvious sense, but *maṣṣēbā*, a standing stone or slab, would not exclude the meaning 'doorpost'. W. McKane ('A note on II Kings 12.10', *ZAW* LXXI, 1959, pp. 260–5), after A. M. Honeyman (*JTS* XXXVII, 1936, pp. 57ff.), supports the reading *mizbēaḥ* in the general sense, *sap* being the threshold-altar.

[f] Reading *way*^{e}*ʿārū* after the parallel account in Chronicles for MT *wayyāṣūrū* ('and they bundled it up'). Eissfeldt (*FuF* 1937, p. 163) after Torrey (*JBL* LV, 1936, pp. 247ff.) takes *ṣūr* as a byform of *yāṣar*, the *yōṣēr* of Zech. 11.13 being a Temple official who melted down contributions of precious metal for the Temple treasury. This is a possible interpretation here, and is adopted by Montgomery (ICC, p. 430).

counted the silver that was found in the Temple of Yahweh. [11]And they gave the silver that was weighed out into the charge of the masters of works who had been appointed[a] in the Temple of Yahweh, and they disbursed it to the carpenters and builders who worked in the Temple of Yahweh, [12]and to the masons and stone-hewers to buy[b] wood and hewn stone to repair the dilapidation of the Temple of Yahweh and for all the expenses for the Temple to repair it. [13]But there were not to be made in the Temple of Yahweh[c] cups of silver, snuffers, sprinkling-bowls, trumpets, any vessels of gold or vessels of silver from the silver that was brought into the Temple of Yahweh, [14]but they gave it to the masters of works and they repaired the Temple of Yahweh with it. [15]And they did not call to account the men into whose charge they gave the silver to give to those who did the work, for they dealt honestly. [16]Silver for guilt-offering, silver for sin-offering, was not brought into the Temple of Yahweh; it was to be the priests'.

12.4. For the textual difficulties in this passage see p. 584 n.[a]. *q°dāšīm* is of wide reference and could include obligatory offerings, votive offerings, and freewill offerings (*nᵉdābōt*). In the first class MT seems to visualize the poll-tax of a half-shekel, which was incumbent on every Israelite as a redemption tax for his life (see note just cited). But the texts which make this explicit, viz. Ex. 13.2, 12f.; 30.12–30, are post-exilic, and it is not certain that II K. 12.4 has not been influenced in transmission by later practice. It is unlikely that the dues included the value of the guilt-offering (*'āšām*) and the sin-offering (*ḥaṭṭā't*), which were the perquisites of the priests (v. 16). These, however, were the subject of assessment in the Second Temple (Lev. 5.15, 18). The redemption of vows is included, which were fixed according to age and sex (Lev. 27.2ff.), and finally the freewill offerings *nᵉdābōt*, which occur to a man spontaneously (lit. 'come up upon his heart').

'ērek (from verb *'ārak*, 'to arrange') is used technically of assessment in the same connection with Temple dues in Lev. 27.2ff., guilt- and sin-offerings (Lev. 5.15, 18), and civil taxation (II K. 23.35). The assessment in the last case, however, might have been based on the religious tax.

5. *lāhem* may be an instance of the ethic dative. The sense is 'let the priests themselves gather the tax'.

[a]Reading *mupqādīm* with Q or *pᵉqīdīm* ('overseers'), a possible gloss on *'ōśē hammᵉlā'kā*.

[b]Omitting *w* before *liqnōt* with G.

[c]G^L omits *bēt yhwh* of MT with G^L, but the point here may be that the casting of metal into vessels within the privacy of the Temple was now forbidden to prevent misappropriation of funds.

makkār ('assessor') has been misunderstood in modern translations, which derive it from *nākar* ('to be familiar'). It is formally a vocational word and *m* is not a preformative but a root letter, the meaning being literally 'trader', cf. Akkadian *tamkaru.* A Temple official of minor grade is indicated by the fact that in administrative texts from Ras Shamra (*UT* 82, 83, 113) *mkrm* are listed along with priests and other temple personnel. The last text is of particular relevance to the present passage, since *mkrm* are listed with priests (*khnm*), temple prostitutes (*qdšm*), and silver-casters (*nsk ksp*). The *makkārīm* were perhaps business assessors who helped the priests to fix the cost of sacrificial animals and offerings in kind, etc., at their market value (cf. Matt. 21.12). This was their primary function, though they may have invested the moneys of the Temple, both common and private, in current trade.[a]

bedeq ('breach') is a collective singular.

12.6. The 23rd year of the reign, not the life, of Joash is denoted. At the age of 30 he obviously wanted to emancipate himself and the state from priestly domination. At that time Jehoiada was probably aged and incapable, and Joash took the opportunity of priestly negligence in the maintenance of the Temple to reassert the authority of the palace.

7. The first step taken by Joash to eliminate the *makkārīm* of the priests was to instal a treasure-chest at the entrance to the Temple and to make the repair of the Temple fabric a priority.

8. The next step was to relieve the priests of the responsibility of the repairs.

9. On alternative readings for MT *mizbēaḥ* see p. 584 n.[e].

The priestly keepers of the threshold, according to 25.18, were three in number, and one, Shallum, is named in Jer. 35.4; cf. Jer. 52.24, where the three keepers of the threshold are mentioned with the chief priest and the second priest, an indication of the significance of the office. The defence of the sacred precinct against all profane intrusion was an important matter both to Temple personnel and to the public, the significance of which may be gauged by the inscriptions, on the screen of the inner court of Herod's Temple, banning intrusion by Gentiles on pain of death.

10. The third step taken by Joash to reassert the royal authority in the Temple was to associate a royal fiscal officer ('the scribe')

[a]On further possible activities of *makkārīm* see J. Gray, *The Legacy of Canaan*, 1965[2], p. 214.

with the chief priest in the summing and possibly minting of the collection. In view of the fact that Jehoiada is termed throughout simply 'the priest', the title 'the chief priest' (*hakkōhēn haggādōl*) may reflect the post-exilic usage here and in 22.4, 8 and 23.4. At Ugarit, however, in the fourteenth century there was a chief priest *rb khnm.*

This sytem of collection and repair of the Temple is mentioned again in 22.3–7, which seems to have influenced the present passage, which is largely a verbal repetition of it.

On *wayyāṣūrū* and variant readings see p. 584 n.[f].

The mention of *nsk ksp* ('casters of silver') in the administrative texts from Ras Shamra might authenticate the view of Torrey and Eissfeldt that *ṣūr* is a byform of *yāṣar* (see note just cited). The bullion was presumably cast into ingots, which were then stamped, counted, and stored. There is, of course, no question of coined money, which came into use among the Lydians and Ionian Greeks in the middle of the sixth century BC and was adopted by the Persian Empire. As early as the ninth century regular weights of pure metal were stamped with the marks of private traders and, later, of Lydian, Ionian, and Aegean states as a guarantee of sterling. Presumably the same usage was followed in the Temple treasury, and if *makkār* has any connection with the verb *nākar* it might signify one who set a distinctive mark upon the metal. The fact that a *makkār* was attached to each priest, however, suggests that they were rather financial assessors, who acted as arbiters when the priest received his dues.

12.11. As *hammupqādīm* or *happ*ᵉ*qīdīm* indicates, if this is not a gloss, *'ōśē hamm*ᵉ*lā'kā* (lit. 'those who did the work') are not tradespeople, but rather masters of works, actually Temple officials, see also I K. 5.16 [30]; 9.23.

13. A further control on the priestly manipulation of Temple revenues was the ban on manufacturing utensils of precious metal in the Temple. By renewing the Temple utensils too often the priests might misappropriate treasure. There seems definite point in retaining *bēt yhwh*, since such work done in the Temple made the control of the weight of metal difficult. For the various utensils and their uses see on I K. 7.50.

15. *'*ᵉ*mūnā* is used here in its proper sense of 'reliability', 'good faith' rather than faith as opposed to works, cf. the oft-cited text Hab. 2.4 (EVV 'the just shall live by his faith').

16. The sin-offering (*ḥaṭṭā't*), which has special prominence in the P legislation (see Lev. 4), refers mainly to ritual offences, which may be unwitting as well as known. Outside P and Ezek. 40.39; 44.27ff.; 45.22ff., which are post-exilic, but possibly reflect earlier usage, the present passage and Micah 6.7 ('shall I give . . . the fruit of my body as a sin-offering for my life?'), if the present passage is not a post-exilic gloss, are singular evidence in the pre-exilic period for the practice. The guilt-offering *'āšām* is not easy to distinguish from the sin-offering (*ḥaṭṭā't*) on the basis of Lev. 5, since it, too, relates to ritual offences witting and unwitting, though chiefly the latter. This unclear distinction is attributed by von Rad[a] to the rather summary systematization in the late P law of earlier usage and terminology, which differed at various shrines in the monarchic period and earlier. In the only reliable pre-exilic source for *'āšām*, regarding the offering of the *'āšām* when the Philistines returned the ark (I Sam. 6.3, 8), *'āšām* was clearly a restitution-offering, equivalent to our 'damages'. In this case, however, the offence was against the property of Yahweh, so that possibly the *'āšām* was the offering for any infringement of the holy. Lev. 5 visualizes both aspects of the *'āšām*. The real distinction between the two offerings is probably that the latter related to cases where restitution was possible. This element is mentioned in Num. 5.5ff., where restitution was made to a man, his family, or, failing both, the priest. Here and in Lev. 5.16, where a fifth part of the value of the offering is given to the priest, there is a connection with the present passage where both offerings, or the value of them, probably assessed by the *makkār*, were the perquisite of the priest.

(iii) SECULAR POLITICS OF THE REIGN OF JOASH: 12.17f. [18f.]

For the character of this section and its source see critical introduction to the chapter and general literary Introduction, pp. 32f.

12 [17]Then Hazael the king of Aram made an expedition and fought against Gath and took it and Hazael turned to come up against Jerusalem. [18]But Joash the king of Judah took all the dedications which Jehoshaphat and Jehoram and Ahaziah his fathers, the kings of Judah, had dedicated and all his own dedications, even all the gold which was to be found among the treasures of the Temple of Yahweh and in the palace, and sent it to Hazael the king of Aram and he went away from Jerusalem.

12.17. The present position of this passage is no absolutely reliable indication of the date of Hazael's expedition, but it may neverthe-

[a] *Old Testament Theology* I, p. 259.

less preserve a sound tradition. If the campaign was soon after Joash's reform of Temple finance in his twenty-third year (813), this was the first year of Jehoahaz the son of Jehu. Hazael may have taken this occasion before the vassal treaty of Israel with Assyria was renewed to secure his rear in view of war with Assyria. Or the campaign may have been soon after the death of Shamsi-Adad V in 811. At any rate, it must have been before 806, when Adadnirari III reduced Damascus. The campaign of Adadnirari against the Philistine plain in that year would restore the situation disrupted by Hazael. Hazael, who has already been noted in 10.32f. as overrunning Israel and docking her of her Transjordanian territory as far south as the north bank of the Arnon (*Wādī Mūjib*), extended his raids down the coastal plain to Gath, from which he menaced Jerusalem. Gath has been variously identified with *Tell aš-Šeiḫ Aḥmed al-ʿAreineh* at the eastern edge of the coastal plain between Lachish and Ashkelon, some five miles from Lachish (*Tell ad-Duweir*), and *Tell aṣ-Ṣāfī* on a spur of the Shephelah commanding the way to the interior by the Vale of Elah (*Wādī as-Sanṭ*). On the location of Gath at the latter site see on I K. 2.39. Hazael's motives in his advance on Gath are uncertain. He may have decided that to drive in between Jerusalem and Lachish, the second city of the kingdom, was the most effective means of reducing Judah, but the fact that he was so easily bought off by Joash suggests that he was not seriously interested in reducing Judah. His real purpose may have been to dominate the trade-routes of the Negeb by controlling the western terminal towards Gaza, the Aramaeans being keen traders. Hazael's domination of the Philistine plain led to the campaigns in that area by Adadnirari III in 806 (*ANET*, p. 282). According to II Chron 24.24f., this incident was dated at the end of the reign of Joash, just before his death.

The Temple served the purpose of a state treasury (so Waterman, see on I K. 6.2). This, however, was only incidental, the personal treasure of the house of David being in the palace, as v. 19b suggests, and the Temple, housing the ark, being the central sanctuary.

(iv) THE DEUTERONOMISTIC EPILOGUE ON THE REIGN OF JOASH AND THE NOTICE OF HIS ASSASSINATION: 12.19–21 [20–22]

12 [19]And as for the rest of the acts of Joash and all that he did are they not written in the Book of the Chronicles of the Kings of Judah? [20]Now his retainers rose up and made a conspiracy and they struck

Joash down at the barracks [a]as he was going down the ramp.[a] [21]And Jozacar[b] the son of Shimeath and Jehozabad the son of Shomer his retainers struck him down and he died, and they buried him with his fathers in the city of David, and Amaziah his son reigned in his place.

12.20. The report of Joash's death in Kings takes no account of motives. From what is probably a genuine tradition in II Chron. 24.25 Joash suffered because he had antagonized the priests, especially through the stoning to death of Zechariah the son of Jehoiada in the Temple precinct (v. 21, cf. Matt. 23.35). The reason for this drastic act is stated (vv. 18ff.) to have been the outspoken criticism of the apostasy of the king to the fertility-cult. It seems more likely that the rift between palace and Temple opened with the stringent financial control which Joash imposed on the priests (II K. 12.5–17). No doubt after the death of Jehoiada his son Zechariah, less statesmanlike but more enthusiastic, used Joash's observance of seasonal festivals and rituals related to the agricultural year to incite opinion against him. II Chron. 24.24ff. connects the death of Joash closely with his humiliation by Aram. This might have been exploited by the priestly faction as an indication that the *berākā* had passed from him and, though there is no mention of it, his son may have been now appointed as co-regent. See on 14.1. The account in Kings gives no indication of a popular reaction against Joash, who was murdered by two of his retainers, no doubt suborned to do the deed, but by whom it is uncertain. The status of these 'servants' or retainers is uncertain. They may have been of the palace staff, but were more probably professional soldiers. The role of these royal retainers in the politics of the kingdom at this time is highly significant, Athaliah and Joash both perishing by their hand. As mercenaries those men had their price and were ready tools of any party. In the doubtful text of v. 21

[a]The text is obviously corrupt. G[B] omits *hayyōrēd* of MT and the other Greek versions give no help, reading 'the house of Maala' and giving Gaala for *sillā'* of MT. This may suggest that *sillā'* is a corrupt dittograph for *millō'* (so Kittel, HKAT, p. 256). S offers a more promising approach, suggesting the reading *wehū' yōrēd sela'* ('as he was going down to Sela'). Klostermann conjectures the reading *bemōrad millō'* ('at the descent of Millo') for MT *hayyōrēd silla'*, a reading most feasible if we take *millō'* as a garrison or barracks, cf. *bēt millō'* (Judg. 9.6). Our own preference is for Thenius's reading *mesillā* for MT *sillā'* together with the reading suggested by S, e.g. *wehū' yōrēd mesillā* ('as he was going down the ramp'). The ramp may have been a raised causeway leading into the palace by the Horse Gate at the north-east corner of the palace and citadel on the Ophel, where Athaliah had met her end.

[b]The names of the assassins, both variants of the same name, throw suspicion on MT, and almost certainly we should prefer MS authority for the name of the first as Jozacar.

bēt millō' seems to indicate the locus of the crime. G. A. Smith[a] takes the reference to be to the Millo, already known as part of the fortification of Jerusalem at the north end of the south-east hill, but we doubt this. *bēt millō'* is found only once more in the Old Testament, in Judg. 9.6, where it is complementary to *baʿalē šekem* ('the men of Shechem') in the account of Abimelech's rising. There it seems to indicate a garrison, *bēt* referring to the occupants, and in so far as the term in the present passage refers to a building, we propose to take it as the quarters of the garrison or 'barracks'.

12.21. The account in II Chron. 24.26 states that the first assassin was the son of Shimeath, an Ammonitess, and the second of Shimrith, a Moabitess. The addition of the nationalities is hard, if not impossible, to understand, but the feminine forms are explicable on the grounds that the first, with its feminine ending, was wrongly taken as a feminine, and the second was altered on the assumption that that, too, was a feminine. A more serious discrepancy is that II Chron. 24.25 states that Joash was slain in his bed, a statement which may cast further doubts on the doubtful text of II K. 12.20. A further discrepancy is the explicit statement in II Chron. 24.25 that Joash was buried in the city of David, though not in the tombs of the kings, cf. II K. 12.21, where the statement that he was buried 'with his fathers' indicates that he was buried in the royal tombs. The Chronicler is usually well informed about events and details in Jerusalem, but here he may be considering Joash an apostate with Manasseh and Amon, who were buried in the Garden of Uzza (II K. 21.18, 26).

(*d*) NORTH ISRAELITE HISTORY CONTEMPORARY WITH THE REIGN OF JOASH: 13.1–25

This section covers the reigns of Jehoahaz (vv. 1–9) and Jehoash (vv. 10–25) and is drawn from various sources.

The reigns of both kings have the usual Deuteronomistic introduction (vv. 1–2, 10–11) with synchronisms with the regnal year of the king of Judah and the length of the reigns of Jehoahaz and Joash respectively and a general condemnation of both for perpetuating the sins of Jeroboam. The introduction to the reign of Jehoahaz has secondary matter of the same nature attached to the Deuteronomistic passages (vv. 4–6, which similarly condemns Jehoahaz, but admits that Yahweh yielded to the intercession of Israel and raised up a liberator

[a] *Jerusalem* II, p. 112.

for them, which strongly suggests the Deuteronomistic framework of the Book of Judges). The reigns of both have in general terms, though not in detail, the usual Deuteronomistic epilogue (vv. 8f., 12f., cf. 14.15f.), noting sources for the rest of the acts of the kings, their burial in Samaria and the accession of their sons.

Significant political events and conditions of their times are noted in brief excerpts from the Book of the Chronicles of the Kings of Israel (vv. 3, 7, 22–25), the background being the Aramaean domination under Hazael and Benhadad. This matter is also furnished with moralizing comment (v. 23, cf. vv. 4–6), which in the style of the Deuteronomistic comments on the events in the Book of Judges relates the relief of Israel to Yahweh's choice of the race since the time of the patriarchs. This comment, which seems like a Deuteronomistic afterthought, is prompted by the success at the end of the reign of Jehoahaz and the victories of Jeroboam II. The view, however, is that the doom of Israel is but postponed. The respite granted to Israel did not prompt her to discard the worship of Jeroboam or elements of the Canaanite nature-cult (v. 6), so that, though Yahweh did not cast them from his presence, that calamity was merely 'not yet' (v. 23, which is probably an editorial gloss).

Finally there are two incidents concerning Elisha, which stand in marked contrast to the rest of the matter in this chapter by their length, both being full, rounded narratives with a wealth of circumstantial detail. The first of these (vv. 14–19) depicts Elisha in the setting of contemporary history, introducing him on his deathbed, with great verisimilitude, in an act of imitative magic, from which the prophetic symbolism associated with the later prophets was developed. Here, as in other matter of this type which we have already considered, Elisha is presented in historical proportions and miracle is absent. The passage is an instance of the Deuteronomist's selection from prophetic tradition to introduce a significant phase of the history of the decline and fall of Samaria, namely the relief from Aramaean oppression which culminated in Jeroboam's successes. This is represented as a divinely-appointed respite. It is probably designed to show Elisha as the liberator mentioned in v. 5, as Noth maintains.[a] The second anecdote of Elisha (vv. 20f.) is of the nature of hagiology, recording a miracle at the prophet's tomb. This tomb, as the tombs of holy men still among the Arab peasants, was doubtless an objective of pilgrimage and probably had its custodians. It may

[a] *Überlieferungsgeschichtliche Studien*, p. 84.

have been located near a settlement of the 'sons of the prophets', probably at Gilgal near Jericho, as the mention of the Moabite raiders (v. 20) indicates. Hence again we have a local dervish-circle as the probable source of an anecdote in the Elisha-hagiology, where the element of miracle is properly at home. The purpose of the introduction of this passage is not clear, and it is probably added simply to round out the traditions of Elisha.

These various elements are but loosely composed, and a comparison of the epilogues on the reign of Joash at 13.12f. and 14.15f. indicates that the latter is primarily Deuteronomistic and is probably the real epilogue to the reign of the king. The account of the abortive challenge to Joash by his contemporary Amaziah of Judah, though it owes its place in 14.8–14 to its date in the reign of Amaziah, which is the subject of ch. 14, is most probably an excerpt from the annals of the northern kingdom and stood originally after the account of the revival of Israel under Joash at the end of ch. 13 (vv. 24f.), being followed there by the Deuteronomistic epilogue (14.15ff.). After the transference of 14.8–14 with the Deuteronomistic epilogue on Joash (14.15f.), a later hand supplemented the deficiency of the epilogue in ch. 13 by inserting 13.12f., rather anomalously, immediately after the Deuteronomistic introduction to the reign of Joash.

(i) THE DEUTERONOMISTIC INTRODUCTION TO THE REIGN OF JEHOAHAZ OF ISRAEL: 13.1–2

13 [1]In the twenty-third year of Joash the son of Ahaziah the king of Judah, Jehoahaz the son of Jehu became king [a]over Israel[a] in Samaria (and reigned) for seventeen years. [2]And he did evil in the sight of Yahweh, following after the sin[b] of Jeroboam in which he involved Israel, without turning from it.

13.1. Since Jehu became king in 841 and reigned 28 years (10.36) to 814, the reference here to the accession of Jehoahaz in the 23rd year of Joash in 813 allows for an accession-year, which the Judaean scribe, familiar with the custom in Judah, mistakenly assumed in Israel. See Introduction on Chronology, pp. 68f.

(ii) THE POLITICAL SITUATION: 13.3

A general Deuteronomistic note on the historical situation, continued in v. 7.

[a]G^B omits 'over Israel'.

[b]The pronominal suffix in the last word of the sentence indicates that the singular should be read for MT plural.

13 [3]And the anger of Yahweh was kindled against Israel, and he delivered them into the hand of Hazael the king of Aram and into the hand of Benhadad the son of Hazael without intermission.

13.3. This is obviously a living memory to the author of the oracle on Damascus in Amos 1.3, 5 and is possibly to be dated before the prophet, who, according to the superscription to the Book of Amos, was not active before the time of Jeroboam II. See further on v. 7.

The last statement prompts the memory of relief from Aramaean domination at the end of Joash's reign and the virtues of Jeroboam, which may have coincided with a revival of certain aspects of ancient Israelite religious practice, and so have merited notice. See on v. 5.

(iii) COMMENT OF DEUTERONOMISTIC CHARACTER IN QUALIFICATION OF THE FINAL STATEMENT IN THE PREVIOUS VERSE: 13.4–6

13 [4]But Jehoahaz placated Yahweh and Yahweh heard him, for he had regard to the oppression of Israel, how the king of Aram oppressed them. [5]So Yahweh gave Israel a deliverer and he extricated them[a] from under the power of Aram, and the Israelites dwelt in their tents as beforetime. [6]Nevertheless they did not turn aside from the sin[b] of[c] Jeroboam in which he involved[d] Israel; they walked[e] therein, and the Asherah also remained standing in Samaria.

4. On *wayᵉḥal . . . 'et-pᵉnē yhwh* see on I K. 13.6. The reading 'Jehoahaz' may well be doubted in view of the statement in v. 22 that Hazael oppressed Israel all the days of Jehoahaz. The original reading was doubtless 'Jehoash', under whom the recovery began (v. 25). In this case, the passage vv. 4–6 is misplaced after the corruption.

5. The phraseology is reminiscent of the framework of the Book of Judges. *mōšīaʿ* is used here in its primary sense of 'making room' or 'giving relief'. The identity of the deliverer is a matter of dispute. Winckler suggested the Assyrian King Adadnirari III (810–783),[f] who invaded Syria in the fifth year of his reign (806), besieged Damascus, and laid the king, called in his inscription *mar'i* (his Aramaic title, 'my lord'), under tribute, a view which has recently

[a]Reading *wayyōṣī'ēm* after G[L] for MT *wayyēṣᵉ'ū* ('they went out') for which G[BA] and S read singular.

[b]Reading singular for MT plural, as suggested by the pronominal suffix in *bāh*.

[c]Omitting *bēt* of MT with certain MSS and S.

[d]Reading final *aleph* with Q, assuming haplography of final *aleph* either before the following *aleph* or after *y* in the proto-Hebraic script.

[e]The context demands the plural, which is read by G[A] and T.

[f]So, more recently, B. Mazar, *BA* XXV, 1962, p. 115.

found favour with H. Schmökel,[a] W. Hallo[b] and M. Haran;[c] cf. S. A. Cook,[d] who also suggests Zakir of Hamath, who records his frustration of 'Bar-Hadad (Benhadad of the Old Testament) the son of Hazael' and his Aramaean allies either before or, more probably, after Adadnirari's expedition.[e] Zakir, however, was on the defensive, the attack of Bar-Hadad and his allies being designed to coerce Zakir into an alliance against Assyria. While Zakir's resistance no doubt relieved Israel momentarily, he could hardly be said to be *mōšîaʿ*. The language of a similar editorial comment in 14.26f. suggests that in v. 5 Jeroboam may be meant (so Šanda, Kittel, Skinner, Montgomery). The main objection to this view is that this relief is apparently a response to the supplication of Jehoahaz (v. 4), whereas relief did not come until the time of Joash and Jeroboam. In the present context the inclusion of the Elisha passage at vv. 14–19 so long after the last mention of the personal activity of the prophet (ch. 8) and actually after the mention of his death (8.4) surely indicates that for the Deuteronomistic editor the deliverer was Elisha, who inspired the nationalist revival like the charismatics in the Deuteronomistic presentation of history in the Book of Judges, and particularly like Deborah (so van den Born).

The reference to Israel dwelling 'in their tents as aforetime' is interesting. It is a notorious fact in the history of Palestine as illustrated by archaeology that the insecurity of the country generally precluded settlement in the plains, compelling settlement to be concentrated on villages clustered on hill-tops and in fortified towns. Šanda (II, p. 153) therefore suggests that the peace now brought to Israel made it possible again for the people to live in open settlements in their ploughlands, presumably during the season of spring grazing and summer activity among their crops, when the villagers do live in light shelters.

The tent-dwelling might possibly, on the other hand, refer to the revival of the seven-year pilgrimage to the central sanctuary, where Israel, in tents for the period of the feast, renewed the covenant, formally renouncing Canaanite practices, though in effect certain of

[a]*Geschichte des alten Vorderasiens*, 1957, p. 259, n. 4.

[b]'From Qarqar to Carchemish in the Light of New Discoveries', *BA* XXIII, 1960, p. 42.

[c]'The Rise and Decline of the Empire of Jeroboam ben Joash', *VT* XVII, 1967, pp. 267f.

[d]*CAH* III, 1925, p. 367.

[e]M. Lidzbarski, *Ephemeris für semitische Epigraphik* III, pp. 1–11.

these remained. It is noteworthy that Amos (4.4; 5.5) attests that pilgrimage to Gilgal, one of those sanctuaries, was in high favour in his time, when the material aspect of the *Heilsgeschichte* seemed to find its authentication in the victories of Jeroboam. M. Haran takes this phrase to refer to the peace between Israel and Aram imposed by the subjection of both by Adadnirari III (*op. cit.*, pp. 267f.).

13.6. According to this verse the reformation of Jehu in Samaria had not been so thorough after all, since there was still an Asherah.

(iv) THE POLITICAL SITUATION: 13.7

An excerpt from the Annals of Israel, continued from v. 3.

13 [7]For he left not to Jehoahaz any strength[a] except fifty horsemen and ten chariots and ten thousand footmen, for the king of Aram had destroyed them and made them as dust at a threshing.[b]

7. The conjunction *kī*, if it belonged to the historical source in v. 7, indicates that the verse lacks its introduction. Jepsen (*op. cit.*, p. 159) suggests that the introduction was v. 22, which records Hazael's oppression during the whole reign of Jehoahaz. The fact that Jehoahaz' death is recorded in v. 9 suggests that this is likely. On the other hand, the conjunction may be editorial, amplifying the general statement of v. 3, in which case v. 22 might be displaced from after v. 7. It is impossible to tell whether the 50 horsemen were the teams and trainers of the horses of the ten chariots or whether they were mounted horsemen, the ten chariots including their horses and teams of three men to a chariot. The disproportionate size of the infantry force suggests that the repression of Aram had not resulted so much in a reduction of all the armed forces, but only of the chariotry, since the infantry now numbered no less than the 10,000 infantry which Ahab had at Qarqar in 853.

(v) THE DEUTERONOMISTIC EPILOGUE ON THE REIGN OF JEHOAHAZ AND INTRODUCTION TO THE REIGN OF JOASH: 13.8–11

13 [8]And as for the rest of the acts of Jehoahaz and all that he achieved and his might, are they not written in the Book of the Chroni-

[a]Reading *ʿōṣem*, cf. Arabic *ʿiṣma* ('defences'), assuming omission of *ṣ* by haplography before *m* in the proto-Hebraic script.

[b]G^L reads v. 23 here with a certain degree of plausibility, since, after the account of the reign of Joash, we apparently revert in v. 22 to the reign of his predecessor Jehoahaz. Verse 22, however, mentions the oppression under Jehoahaz in order, by contrast, to emphasize the deliverance under Joash, to which v. 23 also serves as a prologue.

cles of the Kings of Israel? [9]And Jehoahaz lay down with his fathers and they buried him in Samaria and his son Joash became king in his place.

[10]In the thirty-seventh[a] year of Joash king of Judah, Jehoash the son of Jehoahaz became king [b]over Israel[b] in Samaria for sixteen[c] years. [11]And he did evil in the eyes of Yahweh, not turning from all the sin[d] of Jeroboam the son of Nebat in which he involved Israel, and walking therein.

(vi) SECONDARY REDACTIONAL EPILOGUE ON THE REIGN OF JOASH: 13.12–13

(Displaced from after v. 25: see introduction to 13.1–25)

13 [12]And as for the rest of the acts of Joash and all that he achieved, and his might, and[e] how he fought with Amaziah the king of Judah, are they not written in the Book of the Chronicles of the Kings of Israel? [13]So Joash lay down with his fathers [f]and Jeroboam sat upon his throne,[f] and Joash[g] was buried in Samaria with the kings of Israel.

(vii) ELISHA'S FINAL ACTS OF IMITATIVE MAGIC AND PROPHETIC ORACLE: 13.14–19

This episode is detached by the Deuteronomistic compiler from its context at the end of the saga of Elisha depicting the prophet in the setting of contemporary history (see critical introduction), and placed in its present context as a prelude to the account of the Israelite recovery from the oppression of Aram.

13 [14]Now Elisha was sick with his illness of which he was to die, and Joash the king of Israel went down to him and wept over his face and said, My father, my father, the chariotry of Israel and the horsemen thereof! [15]And Elisha said to him, Take a bow and arrows. So he brought him a bow and arrows. [16]Then he said to the king,[h] Lift up your hand on the bow. So he lifted up his hand, and Elisha put his hands over the king's hands. [17]Then he said, Open the window eastwards. So (the king) opened it. Then Elisha said, Shoot! So he shot. And

[a]According to 13.1; 14.1 Joash, if the verse refers to his accession as sole king, should have acceded in the 39th year of Joash of Judah, which is actually read by certain MSS of G with an obvious attempt at harmonization. The note of his elevation in the 37th year of his Judaean contemporary, however, may refer to his designation as heir apparent in 799 or his elevation to co-regency with his father, who died in 797.

[b]Omitted in G^A.

[c]S reads *šālōš* (i.e. 'thirteen years') for MT *šēš*.

[d]Reading singular for MT plural with most of the MSS of G, which is suggested by the pronominal suffix in *bāh*.

[e]Adding the conjunction *w*[e] with G and S.

[f]G^L omits these words, which are unique in the epilogues of Kings of Israel.

[g]G^L omits.

[h]Reading *lammelek* with G and omitting *yiśrā'ēl* of MT.

he said, The arrow of Yahweh's deliverance, and the arrow of deliverance against Aram, and you shall defeat Aram in Aphek[a] until you annihilate them. [18]Then he said, Take the arrows. So he took them. And he said to the king,[b] Strike on the ground. So he struck three times and stopped. [19]And the man of God was angry with him and said, [c]Would that you had struck[c] five or six times. Then you would have defeated Aram until you had annihilated them. But now you shall defeat Aram three times.

13.14. 'And he went down' indicates perhaps the home of Elisha in Samaria, cf. 6.33, but it might also indicate the ancestral home of Elisha at Abel-Meholah in the eastern foothills of central Palestine ten miles south of Bethshean. Neither locality, however, would suit the location of the tomb of Elisha in the following anecdote, which mentions Moabite raids. Gilgal by Jericho would be a more suitable locality, being accessible to the Moabites across the fords of the Lower Jordan. Since Elisha had already been associated with the prophetic community here we presume that he had fallen ill on one of his visits and had died there. Since burial in Palestine must quickly follow death, the prophet was buried there rather than with his ancestors at Abel-Meholah. The prophetic community was no doubt eager to have the honour of his tomb, and his burial at a hallowed site like Gilgal reconciled his kinsmen to his burial there. The nature of the anecdote in vv. 20f. suggests this association with such a prophetic circle, with which hagiology in the Elisha-cycle is particularly associated.

'My father, my father' indicates not only affection but respect for the authority of the prophet. Presumably the revival of Israel had begun, probably with the hasty withdrawal of Aram from Samaria (7.6ff.) in the time of Benhadad. Since Elisha had inspired resistance then and had foretold the relief of the siege, his credit stood high with the royal family. The obvious respect of Joash for Elisha explains his interest in the whole of the Elisha tradition after the death of the prophet (8.4). The particular acclamation of Elisha as 'the chariotry of Israel and the horsemen thereof' recalls Elisha's acclamation of Elijah at his translation (2.12), and may be the origin of what appears to be a miraculous apparition of horses and chariots in Elisha's encounter with Aramaean marauders at Dothan (6.17).

[a]The mention of Aphek is rather too specific, though perhaps at the time an Israelite army was meeting an Aramaean attack there on the main line of approach, cf. I K. 20.26. It reads like a gloss, though none of the versions questions MT here.

[b]Reading *lammelek* with L and omitting *yiśrā'ēl* of MT.

[c]Reading with G and V *lū hikkītā* for MT *l*^{e}*hakkōt*.

13.16. *rākab* is interesting in this context. In the Hiphil it signifies 'to cause to get up' as a man into a chariot or on to a horse, hence 'to lift up'. In the Ugaritic text *UT* Krt, 74–75 it is found in the Qal in parallelism with the cognate of the Hebrew *ʿālā* describing the ascent of the king to the parapet of his palace. R. de Langhe in his analysis of the Hebrew evidence justly concludes that the primary meaning is simply 'to mount', 'go up'.[a] Elisha's putting his hands on those of the king was designed to give the king reassurance that the power, or divine blessing (*berākā*) of the prophet as the vehicle of the 'spirit of Yahweh' was being communicated to him. In the sequel, however, the king could not share the dynamic faith and enthusiasm of the prophet.

17. The shooting of the arrows in the direction of Aram recalls a similar ritual in the cult in ancient Egypt. This and the striking of them on the ground is an act of imitative magic designed originally to influence the deity by auto-suggestion, but adapted by the great prophets, e.g. Hosea, Isaiah, Jeremiah, and Ezekiel, in their prophetic symbolism, to arrest the minds of the people and to impress them with the certainty of what they proclaimed. We may question to what extent the great prophets themselves shared the primitive belief in the force of imitative magic. We must be careful to appraise even the prophets in their own context of time and place. We must, however, remember that the function of a prophet was not only to present the wishes of the people to God, but, more specifically, to mediate the will of God to the people. Hence acts of prophetic symbolism, though primarily designed to implant an idea in the mind of the deity, were used by the great prophets to reveal that idea to men. In the present instance, however, it is possible that the prophet was testing the king. Emphasizing the rite of imitative magic, the prophet bids the king further strike the ground with the arrows. This the king does perfunctorily, humouring the dying man rather than sharing his conviction, of which the act of imitative magic was an expression, and so he fails in the test. The act of imitative magic, moreover, emphasizes the immediate relation of contemporary politics to the divine economy, and in treating it lightly the king revealed himself as a materialist, whose vision was limited by mere political factors. Possibly Elisha feared a conciliatory policy towards Aram such as the man of God upbraided in the case of the king of

[a]'De Betekenis van het Hebreeuwse Werkwoord רכב', *Handelingen van het XVIIIe Vlaamse Filologencongres*, 1949, pp. 89–96.

Israel in I K. 20.35–43. Such a *rapprochement* with Aram indicates an involvement in secular politics which the prophets consistently condemn, cf. the Syro-Ephraimite crisis in the days of Isaiah. For a similar rite of imitative magic Montgomery aptly cites Joshua's pointing his javelin at Ai (Josh. 8.18ff.). Such rites of imitative magic could be cited profusely from the Old Testament and other literature from the ancient Near East.[a]

(viii) THE HEALING TOUCH OF THE BONES OF ELISHA: 13.20f.

An anecdote from the Elisha hagiology of the prophetic community of Gilgal (?)

13 [20]Now Elisha had died and they had buried him, and raiding bands of the Moabites used to come into the land [b]at the end of the year.[b] [21]Now they were burying a man, and behold they saw a raiding band, and they threw the man into the tomb of Elisha and went their way,[c] and when the man touched the bones of Elisha he came to life and rose up on his feet.

13.20. By raiding at the end of the year in late summer the Moabites, like the Midianites of Gideon's time (Judg. 6.11), found plenty to loot on the threshing-floors and storage-pits. The reduced state of Israel after the campaigns of Hazael and Benhadad no doubt encouraged the Moabites. On the other hand, when the Aramaeans were preoccupied with Adadnirari's campaigns they may have incited the Moabites to create diversions in Israel to keep Israel on the defensive in their rear.

(ix) THE POLITICAL SITUATION IN THE REIGN OF JEHOAHAZ: 13.22

From the Annals of Israel, continued at v. 24.

The verse is displaced either from between vv. 3 and 7 or from after v. 7 (see on v. 7), the displacement being occasioned by the

[a]E.g. A. Lods, 'Le rôle des idées magiques dans la mentalité israélite', *Old Testament Essays*, ed. D. C. Simpson, 1927.

[b]Reading *kᵉbō' haššānā* after G[L], the simplest reading of an impossible phrase in MT, *bā' šānā*. The Vulgate reading 'in that year' suggests the reading *bāh bᵉšānā*, an Aramaism, which is actually read in S. Kittel reads on the authority of no version, *šānā baššānā* ('year by year'). We take *bō'* in the reading we accept as indicating the end of the year, cf. *bō' haššemeš* ('sunset'), as opposed to *ṣē't haššānā* ('the beginning of the year'). The season then would be late summer.

[c]Reading plural for MT singular, as the context demands.

resumption of annalistic narrative in v. 24 after the incorporation of the passages from the Elisha tradition (vv. 14–19; 20f.) and before the secondary redactional comment in v. 23.

13 [22]And Hazael the king of Aram oppressed Israel all the days of Jehoahaz.[a]

13.22. If this statement is taken literally, it would suggest that Hazael reigned till 797, when Jehoahaz died. But since Hazael was a man of standing when he usurped the throne *c.* 841, this is unlikely. The last reference to Hazael by name in the Assyrian records is in 838, in the account of the twenty-first campaign of Shalmaneser III (*ANET*, p. 280), and the next king of Damascus to be mentioned is *mar'i* in the account of the fifth campaign of Adadnirari III (806). This does not preclude the identity of the king of Damascus with Hazael, since *mar'i* is a title ('my lord'), but in view of the general nature of the statement in 13.22, we consider it more likely that Hazael died soon after his campaign in Palestine between 813 and 806 (see on 12.18).

(x) SECONDARY REDACTIONAL COMMENT ON THE PREVIOUS VERSE: 13.23

13 [23]But Yahweh was gracious to them and had pity on them and turned towards them because of his covenant with Abraham, Isaac, and Jacob, and would not destroy them nor did he cast them from his presence.[b]

23. The mention of the covenant with the patriarchs is significant. The pre-exilic prophets knew only of the covenant with Israel after the Exodus, which for them is the beginning of the history of Israel. This might suggest that the present verse and other matter like it is late. But the sympathy for Israel is hardly what we expect after the main Deuteronomistic compilation, though the temporary grace of Yahweh might have been the redactor's explanation of the revival

[a]G[L] adds 'and Hazael took the Philistine (lit. 'the stranger') out of his hand from the western sea to Aphek'. The reading was accepted by Wellhausen and Stade, but has been rejected by critics since Šanda after Rahlfs on the grounds that Philistine rule never extended to Aphek on the plateau at the south-east end of the Sea of Galilee, and that Lucian misunderstood *yam hāʿarābā*, which refers generally, e.g. 14.25, to the Dead Sea. *yam hāʿarābā* could, nevertheless, mean Western Sea, and in Lucian's *ton allophulon*, translated 'Philistine', we see Hebrew *haggōy* as a corruption of *haggālīl*, 'Galilee', and so would regard Lucian's reading as so extraordinary as to be treated seriously.

[b]Omitting *ʿad-ʿattā* ('until now') with G[BA] as a later gloss.

under Joash and Jeroboam. If, on the other hand, this verse is early, it might reflect the knowledge of the E source of the Pentateuch, which carried the covenant and promise back to patriarchal times.

(xi) THE POLITICAL SITUATION AND NOTICE OF THE REVIVAL UNDER JOASH: 13.24–25

From the Annals of Israel, continued from ch. 22.

13 [24]Then Hazael the king of Aram died and his son Benhadad became king in his place. [25]And Joash the son of Jehoahaz recovered from the hand of Benhadad the son of Hazael the cities which he had taken from the hand of Jehoahaz his father in war. Three times did Joash defeat him and he recovered the cities of Israel.

The Israelite recovery was no doubt connected with the renewed Assyrian attacks on Damascus under Adadnirari III (810–783), beginning with his victory over *mar'i* ('my lord') of Damascus.[a]

13.24. On the date of the death of Hazael see on 13.22.

25. The Israelite recovery under Joash must surely have been the subject of fuller record than this brief notice of the threefold victory over Benhadad and the recovery of the cities lost by Jehoahaz. The latter success suggests the notice of the favourable reversal of fortune in I K. 20, which is the prophetic adaptation of a historical narrative describing two campaigns in the reign of Joash, who was in that version the generally anonymous 'king of Israel', wrongly identified with Ahab. See above, pp. 417f.

(*e*) THE REIGN OF AMAZIAH OF JUDAH: 14.1–22

This is composed of four different elements. There are two sources, the annals of the kingdom of Judah for the notice of Amaziah's campaign against Edom (v. 7) and the account of his death and the succession of his son Azariah, or Uzziah (vv. 18–22), and another historical source which describes in narrative style and fullness Amaziah's abortive challenge to Joash of Israel and its disastrous sequel (vv. 8–14). The obvious sympathy with Joash and the contempt for Amaziah and the definition of Bethshemesh as 'which belongs to Judah' (v. 11) point clearly to a North Israelite source and a date before 722. This passage is incorporated into its present context *en bloc*, being terminated by the Deuteronomistic notice on the reign and death of Joash of Israel (vv. 15f.). It is generally held that this

[a]Luckenbill, *ARE* I, §§ 734f.

passage is a continuation of the Annals of Israel from 13.25, but it is much fuller and more detailed than mere annals, being rather historical narrative like the narrative of the campaign against Ramoth Gilead (I K. 22), apart from its prophetic adaptation.

Such historical narrative is a notable feature of North Israelite literature at this time and suggests to us that someone wrote the history of those times under the influence of the E narrative of the Pentateuch, which was composed at this period.

The foregoing matter is interspersed with Deuteronomistic and later redactional comment.

The reign of Amaziah is introduced with the typical Deuteronomistic formula synchronizing his accession with the regnal years of his Israelite contemporary, age at accession, the length of his reign, his mother's name, and the appraisal of his reign by Deuteronomistic standards (vv. 1–6). In the notice of the death of the king the Deuteronomistic editor refers to other, annalistic, sources for the history of Amaziah (v. 18), but instead of the usual Deuteronomistic epilogue a citation from the Annals of Judah describes the extraordinary circumstances of the death of Amaziah and the accession of his son Azariah (vv. 19–22). Finally there is a redactional note to the effect that Amaziah outlived Joash of Israel by 15 years (v. 17). This seems to be motivated by the realization that in what immediately precedes (vv. 8–16) the reader may tend to forget that the theme of 14.1–22 is not the reign of Joash of Israel but that of Amaziah of Judah.

(i) THE DEUTERONOMISTIC INTRODUCTION TO THE REIGN OF AMAZIAH: 14.1–6

14 [1]In the second year of Joash the son of Jehoahaz king of Israel Amaziah the son of Joash king of Judah became king. [2]He was twenty-five years old when he became king, and he reigned twenty-nine years in Jerusalem, and the name of his mother was Jehoaddan[a] from Jerusalem. [3]And he did that which was right in the eyes of Yahweh, but not like David his father; he did according to all that Joash his father had done. [4]Nevertheless the 'high places' were not abolished; the people still sacrificed and burned offerings at the 'high places'. [5]And it happened that, when the royal power was firmly in his grasp, he struck down his retainers who had slain the king his father. [6]But the sons of the assassins he did not put to death, according to what was written in the book of the law of Moses, as Yahweh commanded,

[a]So Q and Chronicles with S, V, T, and Josephus, *Ant.* IX, 9.1, for MT Jehoaddin, which is supported by G. Jehoaddan is more likely and intelligblei ('Y. has increased delight' or 'May Y. increase delight').

saying, The fathers shall not be put to death[a] because of the children nor the children be put to death[a] because of the fathers, but each man shall be put to death[a] because of his own sin.

14.1. On the apparent chronological discrepancy here see Introduction on Chronology, pp. 65f. Amaziah may have been adopted as co-regent in 798, the second year of the co-regency of Joash of Israel. This was probably connected with the reverses against the Aramaeans, the *b^{e}rākā* ('blessing') having manifestly passed from Joash, who was murdered, probably at the instigation of the priests. Joash may have been obliged to appoint Amaziah as co-regent as the price of his use of the Temple treasure to buy off the Aramaeans.

2. The name, probably Jehoaddan (see p. 603 n.[a]), signifies 'Y has given', or 'May Y give (sexual) pleasure', cf. *ʿednā* ('pleasure') in Sarah's exclamation on the annunciation of the birth of Isaac (Gen. 18.12).

3. Montgomery suggests that the lack of a conjunction before *k^{e}kōl ʾ^{a}šer ʿāśā yōʾāš* ('according to all that Joash had done') indicates that 'only not as David his father' is an early interpolation. This does not follow, and in the case of a contrast the second clause is often stated without a conjunction.

5. Amaziah according to ancient Semitic custom avenged the blood of his father upon the assassins.

6. Such a notable observance of the law, eventually enshrined in Deut. 24.16, but doubtless part of a more ancient local code, cannot be allowed to pass unnoticed by the Deuteronomistic compiler. This is the second reference in Kings to the book of the law of Moses, doubtless the lawbook found in the Temple in the 18th year of Josiah (22.8ff.). The first reference is in a Deuteronomistic passage at I K. 2.3.

(ii) AMAZIAH'S EDOMITE CAMPAIGN: 14.7

From the Annals of Judah.

14 [7]He it was who defeated Edom in the Valley of Salt[b] to the number of ten thousand, and took possession[c] of the Rock by war, and called the name of it Joktheel (as it is) to this day.

[a]So Q cf. G, S, V, and T, which read the Qal without, however, materially affecting the sense.

[b]The article of MT should probably be omitted as in Q and MT of II Sam. 8.13.

[c]Reading *wayyitpōś* for MT *w^{e}tāpaś*, an error of haplography, *w* and *y* closely resembling each other, especially at the stage of development of the script at the period of the Qumran scrolls.

14.7. Montgomery, who was very sensitive to the features of archival style, notes the emphatic use of the pronoun, here in the third person, comparing the use of the first personal pronoun, in the same emphatic position, in Mesha's inscription (ICC, p. 239).

The identity of the Valley of Salt is in question. The general view is that it was the depression of the Araba just south of the Dead Sea, from which, presumably, it takes its name. The alternative location, the *Wādī Milḥ* east of Beersheba, would suggest that Edom was actually strong enough to invade Judah, which is just possible after the reduction of Judah by Aram at the end of the reign of Joash and the internal troubles evidenced by his assassination. The account in II Chron. 25.5ff., however, indicates that the initiative was taken by Judah, hence the Valley is more normally identified with the north part of the Araba which was reached by Amaziah from Beersheba, probably by the Pass of Akrabbim, a less likely location being *ʿAin Meliḥī* in the *Wādī al-Jīb*, which drains into the Araba just west of Petra. The round number 10,000 probably refers rather to the number of the defeated army than to the number slain.

Selaʿ ('rock, crag, cliff') is a common noun of frequent occurrence in Hebrew. In certain passages, e.g. Judg. 1.36; II K. 14.7; Isa. 16.1, it appears to be a proper name, though it is generally used with the definite article. In Judg. 1.36, a site in the Araba south of the Dead Sea is required by the context, where it is associated with the Ascent of Akrabbim, and this would also satisfy the requirements of II K. 14.7. It is not improbable, however, that more than one place was so designated. Generally, however, and probably in Isa. 16.1, Sela signifies the capital of Edom, the celebrated Petra ('the Rock') about 50 miles south-south-east of the Dead Sea in the impressive sandstone canyon of the *Wādī Mūsā*, where Eusebius (*Onomasticon*) locates Joktheel. In view of the fact that what was probably the main objective of Amaziah, the port of Elath on the Gulf of Aqaba, remained untaken till the time of Azariah we may doubt whether Amaziah occupied Petra, where, Eusebius apart, there is no trace of the name Joktheel, which would certainly have occurred again had it referred to such an important place as Petra, the capital of Edom. As it is, the name Joktheel recurs only in Josh. 15.38 among settlements in Judah between the Negeb and the Shephelah, which is obviously of no relevance here. It has been suggested that the verbal element in Joktheel, as indicated by the form *yᵉqūtīʾēl* in I Chron. 4.18, may be a jussive of a verb cognate with the Arabic *qūt* ('to nourish').

We prefer the suggestion of Šanda (II, p. 165), that the verb is rather a cognate of Arabic *qatā* ('to destroy'). Another possible connection is with Arabic *qatta* ('to acquire property').

Amaziah's campaign, in which II Chron. 25.6 includes a North Israelite contingent, was probably occasioned by Edomite activity after the Judaean reverse when the Aramaeans penetrated to Gath. Simultaneously with this attempt to control the western terminal of the trade-route from Arabia through the Philistine country at the expense of Judah, Edom sought to secure control of Elath. In the tripartite interest of Judah, Edom, and the Philistines in the trade-route to Elath on the Red Sea, the least reverse or success of any one party had its inevitable repercussions in the politics of the other two. The independence of Edom at this time is attested in the Assyrian inscriptions and in the oracle on Edom in Amos 1.11ff.

(iii) THE ABORTIVE CHALLENGE OF AMAZIAH TO JOASH OF ISRAEL: 14.8–14

From the historical narrative of Northern Israel (see critical introduction to ch. 14, pp. 602f. above).

14 [8]Then Amaziah [a]the king of Judah[a] sent envoys to Jehoash the son of Jehoahaz the son of Jehu the king of Israel saying, Come let us look each other in the face. [9]And Jehoash the king of Israel sent to Amaziah the king of Judah saying, The thistle [b]which was in Lebanon[b] sent to the cedar which was in Lebanon saying, Give your daughter to my son to wife. Then the wild beast of the countryside [b]which was in Lebanon[b] passed by and trod down the thistle. [10]You have indeed defeated Edom and your self-esteem has lifted you up [c]to glorify yourself.[c] Glorify yourself indeed, but remain at home. Why[d] would you provoke calamity and fall, you and Judah with you? [11]But Amaziah would not listen, so Jehoash the king of Israel went on campaign and they looked each other in the face, he and Amaziah the king of Judah, at Bethshemesh which belongs to Judah. [12]And Judah was defeated before Israel, and they fled, each man to his home. [13]And as for Amaziah

[a]Reading *melek yᵉhūdā* with S, the qualifying title being natural in a North Israelite source.

[b]The phrase 'which was in Lebanon', though attested in all the versions, seems awkward here. Possibly it was used to qualify only 'the cedar' and appeared with 'the thistle' by a scribal error, after which it was used with 'the beast' by a further scribal error.

[c]Reading *lᵉhikkābēd*, omitted by haplography.

[d]MT *wᵉ* is best omitted with G[A] and certain MSS of the Vulgate, cf. the parallel passage in Chronicles.

[a]the king of Judah,[a] Jehoash the king of Israel took him at Bethshemesh and came[b] to Jerusalem and broke down a piece of the wall of Jerusalem from the Gate of Ephraim to the Gate of the Corner, four hundred cubits, [14]and he took[c] all the gold and the silver and all the vessels which were found in[d] the Temple of Yahweh and among the treasures of the palace, and hostages, and returned to Samaria.

14.8. The phrase 'let us look each other in the face', if it occurred only here, might be ambiguous, meaning possibly to meet and discuss matters of common interest on equal terms, the one not abasing himself and only looking the other in the eye when the latter had 'lifted his face'. In this case it might denote a *rapprochement* between Israel and Judah after the disruption of relationship after the extirpation of the house of Ahab. The recurrence of the phrase in v. 11, however, referring to the battle of Bethshemesh, suggests that the words are a challenge to arms. There is no reason to suppose with Šanda (II, p. 165) on the basis of the fable in v. 9 that Amaziah had sought an Israelite princess for his son.

9. The point of this homely fable, cf. that of Jotham, also of trees (Judg. 9.7–15), needs no elaboration. It may be matched by homely sayings as pregnant and even more brief among the Arabs, e.g. 'The mule says the horse was his father'. Note the generic definite article in *haḥōaḥ*, *hā'āreṣ* and *ḥayyat haśśāde*.

10. The Hithpael of *gārā* is attested in the Old Testament. The Qal is cognate with Akkadian *gāru* ('to attack') and is possibly attested in Ugaritic (*UT* Krt 110, 211). In Hebrew it is found in the Piel meaning 'to stir up strife'; hence the Hithpael means 'to rouse oneself to strife', the following preposition *b*^{e} signifying the object of hostility.

11. The qualification of Bethshemesh 'which belongs to Judah' is probably correctly taken as an indication of a Northern source before 722,[e] but it may simply serve to distinguish the place from Bethshemesh in Naphtali in Upper Galilee (Judg. 1.33; Josh. 19.38) and another place of the same name just south of Bethshean, modern *'Ain aš-Šamsīyeh*.

[a]G^{B} omits 'the king of Judah', but cf.v.8. We question the propriety of MT 'the son of Joash the son of Ahaziah' in a North Israelite text relating to Judah. S omits the words.

[b]Reading singular with Q, G^{BA}, and S.

[c]The sense demands the reading *wayyiqqaḥ* for MT *w*^{e}*lāqaḥ*. G omits MT *kol*-.

[d]Reading *b*^{e}*bēt* with certain MSS.

[e]So S. A. Cook, *JBL* LI, 1932, p. 284.

Joash came against Jerusalem, like Hazael, the Seleucid armies, Cestius Gallus, and the Crusaders, down the coastal plain. It is difficult to see why, when Joash held Bethel some 11 miles north of Jerusalem at its most vulnerable point, he should have troubled to come down the coast; hence there seems justice in Šanda's view (II, p. 166) that there was a frontier dispute just north of Bethshemesh, Judah having possibly sought to push the frontier north after the withdrawal of the Aramaeans. Possibly, however, the main objective of Joash was not Judah but the Philistine country in the Shephelah, if he hoped, like the Aramaeans, to control the western terminal of the trade-route from Elath. Here the parallel account of the Edomite war in Chronicles is interesting. According to II Chron. 25.6ff. Amaziah had an Israelite contingent in his army, but sent them back before invading Edom. Presumably the anger of these men, which Chronicles records, was the frustration of the hopes of Joash of sharing the mercantile advantages which success in this campaign would open up; hence his desire to compensate himself with control of the western terminal of the Red Sea trade. The same source states that this force in returning fell upon 'the cities of Judah from Samaria to Beth-horon' (II Chron. 25.13), which confirms Šanda's view that in the period of Israelite weakness in the Aramaean domination under Jehoahaz Judah had, in fact, pushed her border north in the foothills north of the Shephelah. In clearing the lower end of the vital passes to the interior, Joash secured control of the lower end of the Vale of Sorek which led from the coastal plain to Jerusalem. Bethshemesh, where the *Wādī aṣ-Ṣurār* (Vale of Sorek) crosses the north-south depression of the Shephelah, was one of Solomon's administrative centres (I K. 4.9). It has been excavated and proved to have been occupied from the Chalcolithic Age till Islam, its settlement flourishing particularly up till the beginning of the Iron Age (*c.* 1200).[a] Josephus[b] dates this campaign in the 14th year of Amaziah.

14.13. In *wayyiprōṣ b^e ḥōmat* . . . ('and he broke down the wall'), *b^e* may signify 'in' or may be partitive as occasionally in Ugaritic (*UT* §10, 5, with examples).

It is natural to locate the Ephraim Gate in the north wall, but the position is not further specified, and of course the statement that Jehoash demolished 200 yards of wall between the Ephraim Gate and

[a] A. Mackenzie, 'The Excavations at Ain Shems', *PEF Annual* I–III, 1911–12; E. Grant, *Beth Shemesh, Ain Shems Excavations* 1928–33.

[b] *Ant.* IX, 9.3.

the Corner Gate does not necessarily mean that this was the actual distance between the two gates. More precisely, Neh. 12.39 (cf. 8.16) locates the Ephraim Gate in the north wall of the monarchic period after David (Josephus' first wall) just west of Hezekiah's northward extension ('another wall outside' the wall he repaired, apparently after Jehoash's damage, II Chron. 32.5), which was apparently built to enclose the Second Quarter (Mishneh), if we are right in reading the ungrammatical *šaʿar hayᵉšānā* of Neh. 12.39, which lay north of the Ephraim Gate and south-west of the Fish Gate, in or by the Central Valley, as *šaʿar hammišne* ('the Mishneh Gate'). The Corner Gate is mentioned again in a text referring to Jerusalem before 586, Jer. 31.38, from immediately after that date, declaring that 'the city shall be built . . . from the Tower of Hananel and to the Gate of the Corner.' Also from the post-exilic period, probably before Nehemiah's reconstruction just after the middle of the fifth century, and visualizing the city before the disaster of 586, Zech. 14.10 describes its extent 'from the Benjamin Gate to the place of the First Gate, to the Corner Gate, and from the Tower of Hananel to the King's Winepresses'. Whether the 'King's Winepresses' is accepted as genuine, referring to rock-hewn presses by the King's Garden just beyond the mouth of the central valley, or, as has been suggested,[a] 'the royal tombs' should be read, with slight emendation, the southern extremity of Jerusalem is indicated, which points to the Tower of Hananel as the northern extremity. This suggests that the Benjamin Gate of Zech. 14.10 was the eastern extremity, possibly identical with the Sheep Gate or the Prison Gate (better 'the Inspection, or Muster Gate') of Neh. 12.39. The fact that the Tower of Hananel with the Sheep Gate and the Tower of the Hundred were built by the priests in Nehemiah's reconstruction indicates the northern and eastern limits of the Temple area. Hence the Corner Gate is to be located in the west, being the extremity of the city in that direction, where it is located by Simons at the site of the Turkish Citadel by the Jaffa, or Hebron, Gate.[b] This to be sure would accord with Josephus' classic description of the earliest north wall of Jerusalem, which, like the fortification of the south-west hill (which he mistakenly regards as Zion) he ascribes to David (*War* V.4). Excavations in the Turkish Citadel by C. N. Johns, while not revealing any building which might be dated before the Hellenistic period, to which he was

[a] J. Simons, *Jerusalem in the Old Testament*, 1952, p. 208 n.2.
[b] *Ibid.*, p. 233.

the first to ascribe the wall round the south-west hill,[a] which Bliss and Dickie had dated to the Davidic monarchy, produced quantities of pottery of the seventh century. More also was found by Dr Kenyon in the filling of what was apparently the fosse of a wall running east from the vicinity of the Citadel to the Muslim Sacred Precinct, like the wall described by Josephus as the earliest north wall of Israelite Jerusalem.[b] Here there is a distinctive cross-valley running from the west to join the north-south central valley, and the south bank of this would be the natural line of fortification of the north of Jerusalem.[c] This seems to be supported by Josephus' statement that the strength of 'the first wall' was increased by valleys. With the reservation that the seventh-century pottery found out of stratification in the Citadel and in Dr Kenyon's soundings in the Muristan, south-east of the Church of the Holy Sepulchre, may denote only open settlements, and that a wall of the Jewish monarchic period along the south bank of the cross valley is not yet proved by archaeology, we may tentatively accept Josephus' north wall here as strategically feasible, though later than David and even Solomon. In Zech. 14.10, which describes the extent of the city from east to west as from the Benjamin Gate to the Corner Gate, 'the place of the First Gate', which lies between, probably denotes rather 'the Principal Gate' in the north wall, or the Ephraim Gate.

This north wall, probably built after Solomon, from the site of the Citadel on the south-west hill to the south-west of the north-east hill where the palace and Temple stood, presupposes a wall running south from the present Turkish Citadel and then east. Here the natural line southwards would be that of the present wall of the Old City. Here also Dr Kenyon guided excavations in 1964 in the grounds of the Armenian patriarchate, and found sufficient masonry and pottery from the Jewish monarchy[d] to make it feasible that the south wall on the south-west hill enclosed the summit, perhaps running eventually north-east to join the west wall of the city of the Jebusites and David at the north-west of the south-east hill. The west and

[a]C. N. Johns, 'The Citadel, Jerusalem', *QDAP* XIV, 1950, 139–47.

[b]K. M. Kenyon, *PEQ*, 1962, pp. 84–6.

[c]L. H. Vincent discusses fragments of ancient walling along this line (*Jérusalem de l'Ancien Testament* I, 1954, pp. 52–64), but only one, with affinites with masonry from the acropolis of Samaria in Ahab's time (early ninth century) (*op. cit.*, fig. 13), is conceivably from the Davidic dynasty.

[d]A. D. Tushingham, *PEQ*, 1967, p. 72, notes debris of the seventh century on bare rock, associated with quarrying, as in the site of the Muristan.

south wall on the south-west hill would thus correspond to the direction, and perhaps even nearly to the location, of the present Turkish wall. Actually the south wall of the extension to the south-west hill seems to be indicated in II Chron. 26.9, which states that 'Uzziah built towers in Jerusalem at the Corner Gate and at the Valley Gate and at the turning of the wall'. The 'turning of the wall' may indicate a point south-east of the Corner Gate by the Turkish Citadel, where the wall turned north-east to link up with the north-west angle of the fortifications of the city of David on the south-east hill. This is the only text where the Corner Gate and the Valley Gate are mentioned together, and we suspect that the conjunction has the explicative force ('the Corner Gate, that is to say, the Valley Gate'). Nehemiah 3.13, in the enumeration of the gates in a counter-clockwise direction, states that 1,000 cubits were repaired between the Valley Gate and the Dung Gate. This does not necessarily indicate the precise distance between the two gates, but it does indicate the direction and position of the Dung Gate roughly on the site of the present Dung Gate, or Gate of the Moors, on the slope of the south-west hill just west of the central valley, or possibly on the site of the Maccabaean gateway discovered by Crowfoot at the north-west corner of the south-east hill, though to be sure no work earlier than the Hellenistic age was discovered here.[a]

Montgomery (ICC, p. 441) well observes that, since Uzziah had only to repair and refortify the north wall with towers (II Chron. 26.9), only a partial demolition or dismantling of towers and battlements by Joash is indicated.

14.14. *b^e nē hatta^c a rūbōt* is a *hapax legomenon* in the Old Testament, being *hat*, found only here and in the parallel passage in II Chron. 25.24. The sense is easily guessed from the verb *ʿārab* ('to take or give in pledge'). It is the only recorded instance of hostages in the Old Testament. Šanda (II, p. 168) feasibly suggests that the hostages were pledges for war-indemnity for which palace and Temple funds did not suffice so soon after the indemnity paid to the Aramaeans in the reign of Joash (12.14[18]).

It is not certain whether the palace and Temple treasures were taken by Joash as war indemnity or by pillage. De Vaux[b] takes the latter view.

[a] J. W. Crowfoot and G. M. Fitzgerald, *PEF Annual*, V, 1927, pp. 12ff.
[b] *Ancient Israel*, pp. 255, 322, 377.

(iv) THE DEUTERONOMISTIC EPILOGUE TO THE REIGN OF JEHOASH OF ISRAEL: 14.15f.

Displaced with vv. 8–14 from the account proper of the reign of Jehoash ending at 13.25.

14 [15]Now as for the rest of the acts of Jehoash and all[a] that he did
and his might[b] in his war with Amaziah, king of Judah, are they not
written in the Book of Chronicles of the Kings of Israel? [16]So Jehoash
lay down with his fathers and was buried in Samaria with the kings of
Israel, and his son Jeroboam became king in his place.

(v) SYNCHRONIZATION OF THE REIGN OF AMAZIAH WITH THE DEATH OF JEHOASH: 14.17

A secondary redactional note whereby the reader is reminded that, in spite of the focus of interest in Jehoash of Israel and the use of an Israelite source, the real subject of the section for the Deuteronomistic compiler is Amaziah of Judah.

14 [17]Now Amaziah the son of Joash the king of Judah survived
Jehoash the son of Jehoahaz king of Israel by fifteen years.

(vi) DEUTERONOMISTIC REFERENCE TO OTHER SOURCES FOR AMAZIAH'S REIGN: 14.18

This statement, which generally introduces the Deuteronomistic epilogue to the reign of a king, breaks off here, the notice of the king's death being communicated in vv. 19–22 by the citation of the Annals of Judah.

14 [18]Now as for the rest of the acts of Amaziah [c]and all that he did,[c]
are they not written in the Book of the Chronicles of the Kings of
Judah?

(vii) THE DEATH OF AMAZIAH AND THE ADVANCEMENT OF AZARIAH (UZZIAH): 14.19–22

From the Annals of Judah.

14 [19]And they made a conspiracy against him in Jerusalem and he
fled to Lachish, and they sent after him to Lachish and they put him to
death there. [20]And they carried him on horses, and he was buried in
Jerusalem with his fathers in the city of David. [21]And all the people of
Judah took Azariah, he being sixteen years old, and they made him
king in the place of his father Amaziah. [22]He it was who built up Elath
and restored it to Judah after the king slept with his fathers.

[a]Adding *wᵉkol-* to MT with ten MSS and S.
[b]Omitting *wᵉ* of MT with G and V.
[c]Adding *wᵉʾet-kol-ʾăšer ʿāśā* with G.

14.19. The movers of the plot against Amaziah are not named. The specific mention of the advancement of Azariah by 'all the people of Judah' suggests that the plot against Amaziah was the work of a relatively small party, probably in Jerusalem. Šanda (II, p. 169) thinks of a military rising. De Vaux[a] thinks that the movement was inspired by the priests, incensed at the spoliation of the Temple treasury after Amaziah's disastrous political adventure against Jehoash. The fact that the influence of the antagonists of Amaziah was so effective at Lachish, the second city of Judah, a powerful bastion on the south-west of the kingdom, rather suggests that these were military.

Lachish is now located practically beyond doubt at *Tell ad-Duweir*, a conspicuous mound about four miles south-south-west of *Beit Jibrīn* (Eleutheropolis), which fits the statement of Eusebius[b] that Lachish, in his day a small village, was seven Roman miles from Eleutheropolis on the way to Daroma (modern *ad-Duweimeh*). The excavations of the late J. L. Starkey revealed occupation from the Chalcolithic Age (caves) to the Greek period, with fortifications and a city-gate of the Solomonic period or of the time of Rehoboam, who is said (II Chron. 11.9) to have fortified the city, which already had a massive wall, glacis, and fosse and counterscarp from the Middle Bronze Age. Another feature, of the Judaean period, was a great palace-fort, which dominated the mound. The significance of the place as the second city of Judah is indicated by a seal-impress from the end of the Monarchy with the legend 'Belonging to Gedaliah who is over the house' (i.e. the royal chamberlain), not improbably the Gedaliah who was left as high commissioner under the Babylonians in 586. The identity of the site with biblical Lachish is further strongly suggested, if not conclusively proved, by 21 inscribed potsherds found mostly in the charred debris of a guardroom in the chambered gateway. In one of these the correspondent, either the officer of an outpost or a political agent, reports to the city commandant that the signals of Azekah (*Tell az-Zakarīyeh*, some 11 miles north of *Tell ad-Duweir*) are no longer to be seen, so he is now observing the signals of Lachish.[c]

20. It is suggested by various scholars after Winckler, but with-

[a] *Ancient Israel*, p. 377.
[b] *Onomasticon*, p. 120.
[c] H. Torczyner and others, *Lachish*, *I*, *The Lachish Letters*: O. Tufnell, *Lachish III*, *The Iron Age*.

out the support of any of the versions, that 'and they carried him on horses' is displaced from before 'and he fled' in v. 19, but Šanda (II, p. 169) is probably right in seeing a reference to a solemn funeral cortège to Jerusalem.

14.21. 'All the people of Judah' probably indicates that the forces against Uzziah's or Azariah's father Amaziah were not the priests, but rather the feudal administrators and professional army in Jerusalem. 'All the people of Judah' may be *ʿam-hāʾāreṣ*, who, as well as the priests, represented the tradition of the sacral community, and so the democratic tradition of Israel, by which the new king was adopted by popular acclamation. See on 11.14. On the chronology of the period see Introduction, Chronology, pp. 65f., 72f. This verse is not taken directly from the Annals of Judah, but combines two distinct facts therefrom, first that Azariah (Uzziah) was made co-regent with his father at the age of 16 (791), having been born when his father was 17 (cf. 14.1), and second that he was raised to the sole monarchy by popular acclaim (766).

22. Azariah's administration falls into two periods, that of his co-regency (791–766) and that of his sole rule (766–740). The recovery and refortification of Elath on the Gulf of Aqaba is from the latter period.

(*f*) THE REIGN OF JEROBOAM II OF ISRAEL: 14.23–29

(i) THE DEUTERONOMISTIC INTRODUCTION TO THE REIGN OF JEROBOAM: 14.23f.

14 [23]In the fifteenth year of Amaziah the son of Joash king of Judah, Jeroboam the son of Joash king of Israel became king in Samaria (reigning) forty-one years, [24]and he did evil in the sight of Yahweh, not turning from all the sins of Jeroboam the son of Nebat, who made Israel to sin.

23. This verse is a potent source of confusion in Old Testament chronology, the problem being solved by the realization that the Deuteronomistic editor has misleadingly associated two different facts. The 15th year of Amaziah was 781, when Jeroboam II became sole ruler, while his 41 years' reign is reckoned from 794, when he became co-regent with his father Joash, a measure which might well have been dictated to Joash in his involvement in the wars of liberation against Aram. On the chronological problems of Jeroboam's reign see on 15.1 and Introduction, Chronology, pp. 72f.

(ii) THE REIGN AND ACHIEVEMENTS OF JEROBOAM: 14.25

From the Annals of Israel, freely adapted by the Deuteronomist, who emphasizes the revival of Israel as the fulfilment of prophecy.

Here and in the Deuteronomistic epilogue on the reign of Jeroboam (v. 28) the revival of Israel and the expansion of her influence to Syria is mentioned rather summarily. Nothing illustrates the limitations of the Books of Kings as objective history and emphasizes their theological orientation better than this summary, almost perfunctory, treatment of the reign of Jeroboam II, which witnessed such a remarkable recovery of the power of Israel to the high degree of national prestige and material prosperity attested in the Book of Amos.

14 [25]He it was who restored the bounds of Israel from the approaches of Hamath to the Sea of the Steppe according to the word of Yahweh the God of Israel, which he spoke through his servant Jonah, the son of Amittai, the prophet from Gath-hepher.

14.25. On the localities, which are more ideal than actual, being, in the north, the limit of Solomon's influence, see on I K. 4.21[5.1]. The campaigns of Jeroboam east of the Jordan recovered (Ashtaroth) Karnaim and Lodebar (*al-Idbar* east of *Umm Qeis*) according to Amos 6.13. II Chron. 26.8 mentions tribute of the Ammonites to Azariah and grazings which he had in the plain west of Amman, hence it seems that Azariah co-operated with Jeroboam. and, indeed, as Šanda points out (II, p. 171), neither Kings nor Amos betrays any tension between Israel and Judah at this time.

The prophet Jonah of Gath-hepher, who was obviously a patriot of the type of the prophets who bade Ahab 'Go up to Ramoth Gilead and succeed!' or like Elisha, who encouraged Joash by acts and words of imitative magic on his death-bed, is otherwise unknown. If, as Jepsen maintains,[a] the oracles in Zech. 9.1–6 against Damascus and Hadrach, the neighbouring region to Hamath, are from the monarchic period, this might be a relic of 'the word of Yahweh' through Jonah, which might confirm the view that v. 28 referred to Jeroboam's establishment of Israelite control of Hamath and Damascus, as in the time of David and Solomon, but cf. our textual note *ad loc.* It is on him, that quite unhistorically, the writer of the late Book of Jonah fathers his work. His home village plays no part in the history of Israel, being merely noted in the territory of Zebulun (Josh. 19.13),

[a] *ZAW*, LVII, 1939, pp. 242f.; *AfO* XIV, 1942, p. 171.

by which it is feasibly located at the considerable Arab village of *al-Mešhed* just north of Nazareth, where the putative tomb of the prophet, round which Arab legend has gathered, is locally venerated.

(iii) REDACTIONAL COMMENT ON THE REVIVAL UNDER JEROBOAM: 14.26f.

As in the Book of Judges, the success of Jeroboam is regarded as a season of grace rather than as the material achievement of the king; this betrays the Deuteronomistic origin of this comment.

14 [26]For Yahweh saw the extremely bitter[a] affliction of Israel, none being spared, nor any helper for Israel. [27]But Yahweh did not declare for the blotting out of the name of Israel from under the heavens, so he delivered them by the hand of Jeroboam the son of Joash.

14.26. On *ʿāṣūr weʿāzūb* see on I K. 14.10.

27. There is probably a reference here to an oracle, or oracles, of encouragement, to which reference has been made in the allusion to the prophet Jonah of Gath-hepher (v. 25).

(iv) DEUTERONOMISTIC EPILOGUE ON THE REIGN OF JEROBOAM AND SUMMARY: 14.28f.

This perhaps includes an exaggerated reference to Jeroboam's success against Aram.

14 [28]And as for the rest of the acts of Jeroboam and all that he achieved and his might in war [b]with Damascus, and how he turned away the wrath of Yahweh from Israel,[b] are they not written in the Book of the Chronicles of the Kings of Israel? [29]And Jeroboam slept with his fathers, even the kings of Israel, and Zechariah his son became king in his place.

28. The MT is indefensible except on the assumption that the Deuteronomistic editor, living more than a century and a half after the liquidation of the Aramaean state of Damascus, is generalizing widely without any regard to historical detail. *hēšīb* in the sense of

[a]Reading *hammar* after G, S, and V for the pointless 'rebellious' of MT.

[b]Reading as conjectured by Burney (*Notes*, pp. 320ff.), *ʾašer nilḥam ʾet-dammeśeq waʾašer hēšīb ʾet-ḥamat yhwh beyiśrāʾēl* for the obviously corrupt MT (*ʾašer nilḥam*) *waʾašer hēšīb ʾet- dammeśeq weʾet-ḥamāt līhūdā beyiśrāʾēl* '(how he fought) and how he restored Damascus and Hamath, which belonged to Judah (to be) in Israel'. To say nothing of the difficulty of the prepositions before Judah and Israel, which this translation barely meets, the statement conflicts with the facts of history (see note). S feels this difficulty and omits any mention of Judah, and emends *beyiśrāʾēl* ('in Israel') to *leyiśrāʾēl* ('to Israel').

'he brought back' might be supposed to refer to the restoration of the control which David had exercised over Damascus, but which Solomon had not been able to maintain. Hamath *may* have been a vassal of David under a nominee of the house of Judah (see on I K. 4.21[5.1]), as the name Joram (II Sam. 8.10) may signify, and the recurrence of the Yahweh theophoric Yaubidi the king of Hamath in 720 BC may indicate a reassertion of the suzerainty of the house of David (*hēšīb līhūdā*) at the initiative of Israel (*b^eyiśrā'ēl*) in the co-operation of Israel and Judah under Jeroboam and Uzziah-Azariah, which to be sure the Old Testament does not contradict. In that case, however, it would be strange if Chron. omitted such a spectacular revival of the power of Judah. Indeed, the ideal limits of the domain of Israel in the time of Solomon (I K. 8.65) and Jeroboam (Amos 6.14) reached only 'to the entering in of Hamath', i.e. the Biqʿa between the Lebanon and Anti-Lebanon south of Hamath. The revival of Israel at this time was made possible by the increased interest of Assyria in Syria from the fifth year of Adadnirari III (806), through his reign (810–783), and under Shalmaneser IV (782–772), who made an expedition against Damascus in 773, and particularly in the reign of Tiglath-pileser III (743–726). Haran (*op. cit.*, pp. 226–79) has argued that Jeroboam's revival must post-date the Syrian expedition of Ashurdan III in 772 and that it probably fell in the weak reign of Ashurnirari V (755–45). This view, however, is based on the assumption that Jeroboam reduced Damascus and Hamath to the status of Israelite dependencies. This depends on the doubtful MT at v. 28 (see textual n.). Jeroboam's successful campaigns against Damascus might be dated soon after Syria had felt the brunt of the Assyrian attacks in 773 and 772, rather than in the recession of Assyrian power after 755, which permitted the revival of Damascus.

(*g*) THE REIGNS OF AZARIAH AND JOTHAM OF JUDAH: THE DECLINE OF ISRAEL: 15.1–38

This section is composed of three elements, one extract, much briefer than the significance of Azariah's reign warrants, derived from the Annals of Judah (v. 5), and more extracts, also brief, from the Annals of Israel from the short reign of Zechariah the son of Jeroboam to the successful *coup d' état* of Hoshea (vv. 10, 14, 16, 19f., 25, 29f.), which the Deuteronomistic editor notices in order to emphasize the approaching ruin of Israel. In the scanty reference to the state archives in this not insignificant period, including the reign of Azariah, who established Judah's control of the Negeb to the Gulf of Akaba (II Chron. 26), and the last quarter-century of the history of the Northern kingdom, with the political crises which are the background of the work of Amos, Hosea, and Isaiah, and in the disproportionate space devoted to summaries and the appraisals of the various reigns from the formalistic Deuteronomistic viewpoint, the theological bias of Kings is particularly evident.

(i) THE DEUTERONOMISTIC INTRODUCTION TO THE REIGN OF AZARIAH: 15.1–4

15 [1]In the twenty-seventh year of Jeroboam king of Israel, Azariah the son of Amaziah king of Judah became king. [2]He was sixteen years old when he became king and he reigned in Jerusalem for fifty-two years, and his mother's name was Jecoliah from Jerusalem. [3]And he did that which was right in the sight of Yahweh according to all that Amaziah his father had done. [4]Nevertheless he did not abolish[a] the 'high places'; the people still sacrificed and made burnt offerings at the 'high places'.

15.1f. On our view that Azariah was adopted as co-regent or heir-apparent at the age of 16 in 791 see on 14.21. The synchronism in v. 1 refers to his accession as sole ruler in 766. See Introduction, Chronology, pp. 65f., 72f.

(ii) THE KING'S DISEASE AND THE CO-REGENCY OF JOTHAM: 15.5

From the Annals of Judah.

15 [5]And Yahweh touched the king and he was smitten with leprosy until the day he died, but he lived [b]in his palace released from obligations,[b] and Jotham the son of the king was royal chamberlain, governing the people.[c]

5. On the disease of the king, not so serious as leprosy, cf. Naaman's case; see on 5.1. The king was nevertheless unable to discharge his sacral functions, and so Jotham was appointed regent. On the

[a]Reading *hēsīr* with G[BA], S, and V for MT *sārū* ('were abolished').

[b]Reading with Klostermann *bētōh ḥopšīt*, i.e. preserving the consonants of the MT, but reading *h* as the old pronominal suffix third singular masculine instead of the definite article of *ḥopšīt*, the termination of which is not nominal but adverbial, a difficulty felt by the scribes, since ten MSS have the ending *-ūt*, also G, which transliterates, cf. II Chron. 26.21, where the consonantal text has *u* but the pointing is *i*. See note.

[c]Here we follow the reading of the Hexaplar Syriac for MT *ʿam hāʾāreṣ*.

designation 'over the palace' (*'al-habbayit*) see on I K. 4.6. The functions of Jotham as *šōpēṭ* no doubt included judicial cases, but *šāpaṭ* means generally 'to rule, govern', as in the Ras Shamra texts, where (e.g. *UT* 51, IV, 43f.) *špṭ* and *mlk* are synonyms. The recognition of the root *šāpaṭ* as synonymous with *mālak* is of great importance in recognizing psalms and passages in the prophets relevant to the kingship of Yahweh.

The name Jotham signifies 'Yahweh is perfect'.

It is generally held that the leper king, released perforce from his regular functions and routine, was confined in a kind of 'isolation ward', *bēt haḥopšīt* being taken to signify lit. 'the house of isolation'. On the assumption of this interpretation Y. Aharoni made the attractive suggestion that the small palace of this period which he excavated at *Rāmat Rāḥēl* on the highest point between Jerusalem and Bethlehem is indeed Azariah's isolation quarters, but excavations in 1961 proved that the palace was later than Azariah.[a] If this is the meaning of *bēt haḥopšīt* (better, in our opinion, *ḥopšūt*), this is a *hapax legomenon* in the Old Testament. Evidence is cited from the Ras Shamra texts, where the emissaries of Baal are sent to the underworld and bidden:

rd. btḫpṯt 'arṣ
tspr. byrdm. 'arṣ

Go down into the corruption of the underworld,
Be numbered among those that go down into the underworld.
(*UT* 51, VIII, 7; 67, V, 15)

It will be noted that there is no word-divider between *bt* and *ḫpṯt*, not that this rules out the reading *bt ḫpṯt*. Here, however, it is not a question of isolation quarters, but, as the sequel shows, of the filth, ruin, and general loathsomeness of the underworld, and we would follow T. H. Gaster[b] in connecting the word not with Hebrew *ḥopšī*, but with Arabic *ḫabaṯa* ('to be filthy'), taking the initial *b* as the preposition and the following *t* as the preformative of the abstract *tḫpṯt* ('corruption'). The generally accepted interpretation of the Hebrew phrase, however, remains a possibility. From I Sam. 17.25 it is apparent that the Hebrew word *ḥopšī* means 'free from burdens', hence we prefer to follow Kimchi in the present passage, taking the reference to indicate release, albeit perforce, from the royal functions. Kimchi, however, took *ḥopšīt* as a noun. He took *bēt* as meaning 'in

[a] *BA* XXIV, 1961, pp. 116ff.
[b] *Thespis*, 1950, p. 448.

the condition of', which is possible. On Klostermann's reading, which we prefer, taking *ḥopšit* as an adverb, see p. 618 n.[b]. Azariah was allowed to live in his own palace in freedom from his public functions, but also possibly from the usual restrictions on such afflicted persons, just as Naaman's leprosy did not exclude him from the royal presence or even from worship in the Temple of Hadad. It may be added that, if, as is probably the case, the ossuary discovered by E. L. Sukenik with an Aramaic inscription 'Hither were brought the bones of Uzziah king of Judah—do not open'[a] were really the remains of Uzziah, these must have been easily distinguishable, probably from their isolation, though the king was buried with his fathers in the city of David (v. 7); cf. II Chron. 26.23, which suggests that Azariah's burial was apart from the other royal burials.

(iii) THE DEUTERONOMISTIC EPILOGUE ON THE REIGN OF AZARIAH AND THE INTRODUCTION TO THE REIGN OF ZECHARIAH THE SON OF JEROBOAM: 15.6–9

15 [6]And as for the rest of the acts of Azariah and all that he achieved, are they not written in the Book of the Chronicles of the Kings of Judah? [7]So Azariah slept with his fathers and they buried him with his fathers in the city of David, and Jotham his son became king in his place.

[8]In the thirty-eighth year of Azariah king of Judah, Zechariah the son of Jeroboam became king over Israel in Samaria for six months. [9]And he did that which was evil in the sight of Yahweh just as [b]his fathers had done;[b] he did not turn away from the sins of Jeroboam the son of Nebat in which he involved Israel.

15.8. The date (754) is from the year 791, when Azariah became co-regent with his father Amaziah.

(iv) THE DEATH OF ZECHARIAH: 15.10

An excerpt from the Annals of Israel (cf. v. 15).

15 [10]And Shallum the son of Jabesh (or a man of Yasib) conspired against him and struck him down [c]at Ibleam[c] and killed him and became king in his place.

[a]*PEFQS*, 1931, pp. 217ff.

[b]S reads 'his father had done', but in view of the general condemnation of the kings of Israel the plural must be read with MT.

[c]Reading *b*^{e}*yibl*^{e}*ʿām* with G^{L} for MT *qābāl ʿām* ('before people'), a reading barely possible since *qābāl* is Aramaic rather than Hebrew and *ʿām* would require the definite article.

15.10. There is a certain poetic justice here in that the last of the house of Jehu was killed at Ibleam, near which Jehu had so brutally massacred princes of the royal house of Judah when he usurped the throne of Israel (10.14).

(v) THE DEUTERONOMISTIC EPILOGUE ON THE REIGN OF ZECHARIAH AND THE INTRODUCTION TO THE REIGN OF SHALLUM: 15.11–13

15 [11]And as for the rest of the acts of Zechariah, see they are written in the Book of the Chronicles of the Kings of Israel. [12]That was the word of Yahweh which he spoke to Jehu saying, Your sons to the fourth generation[a] shall sit upon the throne of Israel. And so it was.

[13]Shallum; the son of Jabesh (or a man of Yasib),[b] became king in the thirty-ninth year of Azariah[c] and he reigned a complete month in Samaria.

12. As usual the Deuteronomistic editor especially notes the fulfilment of prophecy, here of the oracle at 10.30.

13. The name Shallum, a passive, signifies perhaps 'the requited' or 'he for whom compensation has been made', an allusion, probably, to the discharge of a vow of the parents.

Taking MT Jabesh as a place-name rather than as a personal name, Šanda (II, p. 182) suggests that the reaction against the house of Jehu came from Transjordan (Jabesh-Gilead) with the support of Damascus, but see on v. 16. The Assyrian records note this usurpation, terming Shallum 'the son of a nobody' (*apal la manman*).

yeraḥ yāmīm (lit. 'a month of days') may indicate a full month, or the qualifying word *yāmīm* may simply indicate that *yeraḥ* in an unpointed text means 'month' and not 'moon'.

(vi) THE USURPATION OF MENAHEM: 15.14

From the Annals of Israel, continued at v. 16.

15 [14]And Menahem the son of Gadi went up from Tirzah and came to Samaria and struck down Shallum the son of Jabesh (or the man of Yasib) in Samaria and killed him and became king in his place.

14. The name Menahem, a Piel participle, means 'comforting', i.e. comforting the parents in old age, or as Noth suggests,[d] consoling

[a]Reading *bānekā ribbēʿīm* for MT *rebīʿīm* here, cf. 10.30 and p. 563 n.[c].
[b]For MT *yābēš*, assuming scribal metathesis, see on v. 16.
[c]So with certain Hebrew MSS. and G, V, and T for MT *ʿuzzīyā*.
[d]*IP*, p. 222.

them for the death of an earlier child. Gadi might mean a Gadite, but may be a hypocoristicon of Gadiyahu ('Yahweh is my luck'), as suggested by Šanda (II. p. 183) on the analogy of the Punic name Gadi'el. Tirzah (*Tell al-Fārʿa*, see on I K. 14.17) was apparently the centre of the power of Menahem, who was probably a man of Manasseh, in whose territory Tirzah lay. See further note on v. 16.

(vii) THE DEUTERONOMISTIC EPILOGUE ON THE REIGN OF SHALLUM: 15.15

15 [15]And as for the rest of the acts of Shallum and his conspiracy which he made, behold they are written in the Book of the Chronicles of the Kings of Israel.

15.15. 'The rest of the acts of Shallum' could not have amounted to much in the space of a month. This indicates the conventionality of the Deuteronomistic introductions and epilogues to the reigns of the kings.

(viii) THE PROGRESS OF MENAHEM IN THE CIVIL WAR: 15.16

From the Annals of Israel, continued from v. 14.

15 [16]Then Menahem overpowered Tappuah[a] and all who were in it, and its territory, from Tirzah, for they did not open up[b] (the city) to him, and he struck it[c] down and[d] all its pregnant women[e] he ripped up.

16. Tappuah, some 14 miles south-south-west of Tirzah, was on the border between Manasseh and Ephraim, the settlement belonging to the latter and the lands to the former (Josh. 17.8). Menahem's severe treatment of the inhabitants of Tappuah is unparalleled in inter-tribal warfare in Israel, and matched only by the Ammonite barbarities mentioned by Amos (1.13). After the fall of the house of Jehu the tribes asserted their right to choose a king in protest against the hereditary principle. The contending parties were Ephraim and Manasseh, as Isa. 9.19–21 seems to suggest. In the vicinity of Tappuah

[a]Reading *tappūaḥ* with G[L] for MT *tipsaḥ*, Thapsacus on the Euphrates, which is quite out of the question.

[b]Reading *pātᵉḥū lō* with G[BA], S, and V for MT *pātaḥ*, which might be retained on the assumption that the singular indicated the indefinite subject.

[c]Reading *wayyakkehā* after G[BA] for MT *wayyak*, which has no object, since the noun which follows is the object of *biqqēaʿ* ('ripped up').

[d]Adding the conjunction *wᵉ* with G, S, and T, as is demanded after the addition of the pronominal suffix to the preceding verb.

[e]Omitting initial *h* as a dittograph before *h* of *hārōtehā*.

about two miles distant, was a place Yasib, mentioned in G of Josh. 17.7 as on the spring of Tappuah,[a] which, we suspect, was the home of Shallum, this being concealed in the MT, which designates Shallum as *ben yābēš*. This explains, in our opinion, why Tappuah, otherwise so insignificant, was the object of Menahem's savagery.

(ix) THE DEUTERONOMISTIC INTRODUCTION TO THE REIGN OF MENAHEM: 15.17f.

15 [17]In the thirty-ninth year of Azariah king of Judah, Menahem the son of Gadi became king over Israel for ten years in Samaria. [18]And he did evil in the sight of Yahweh; he turned not away from all[b] the sins of Jeroboam the son of Nebat in which he involved Israel in[c] his days.

15.17. The dating (753) is from 791, when Azariah became co-regent with his father. Menahem did not immediately succeed Shallum, the civil war lasting perhaps several months, see Introduction, Chronology, p. 73.

(x) MENAHEM'S SUBMISSION TO ASSYRIA: 15.19f.

From the Annals of Israel.

15 [19]Pul king of Assyria came against the land and Menahem gave Pul a thousand talents of silver that his hand[d] should be with him [e]to confirm the kingdom in his hand.[e] [20]And Menahem paid the silver; Israel, that is to say all the men of property, had to give fifty shekels of silver each for the king of Assyria, and the king of Assyria withdrew and did not stay there in the land.

19. The Assyrian king was Tiglath-pileser III (743–726), who is actually named Pul in a Babylonian kinglist,[f] and is Poros of the kinglist in Ptolemy's chronology, this being his throne-name in assuming the throne of Babylon in 729. An inscription of Tiglath-pileser[g] mentions the tribute of Menahem. The date is uncertain, but probably late in the reign of Menahem (see Introduction, Chron-

[a]Abel, *GP* II, 1938, pp. 475f. This may or may not be the place *ysb* mentioned in the ostraca from Samaria (J. W. Jack, *Samaria in Ahab's Time*, 1929, p. 80).

[b]Reading *mikkol-* with certain Hebrew MSS, G[BA], and T for MT *mēʿal*, a scribal error in dictation.

[c]Omitting *kol* with G.

[d]Reading singular with G and S for MT dual.

[e]This is wanting in G[B], see note below.

[f]*ANET*, p. 272.

[g]A. H. Layard, *Discoveries among the Ruins of Nineveh and Babylon*, 1856, p. 526; A. L. Oppenheim, *ANET*, pp. 282ff.

ology, pp. 59f.). The advent of Tiglath-pileser in the politics of Syria and Palestine marked a decisive stage in a vigorous policy of Assyrian penetration to the confines of Egypt. A tight control was established over vassal states in the west, which were eventually liquidated, as Damascus in 732, or severely docked, as Israel when her northern and eastern provinces were annexed in 734 (v. 29).

Menahem's 1,000 talents tribute is compared by Šanda with the 2,300 talents of silver exacted from the king of Aram by Adadnirari III in 806[a] and 30 talents of gold and 800 talents of silver, the indemnity of Hezekiah to Sennacherib in 701.[b] Menahem's ready submission earned him a certain relief. The phrase 'that his hand might be with him' (*lihyōt yādō 'ittō*) is ambiguous, meaning either that Menahem enlisted Assyrian support or that he gave the tribute as a token of his readiness to accord with Assyrian policy. The final phrase supports the former interpretation, and indeed, in view of the bitter opposition to Menahem in Israel (vv. 16, 26), this is most likely, though the phrase in question is not in G^B.

15.20. *yāṣā'* in the Hiphil is generally regarded as strange in combination with *'al* before *yiśrā'ēl*, and Klostermann proposed to read *wayeṣaw* for MT *wayyōṣē'*, continuing *menaḥēm 'et-kol-yiśrā'ēl we'et-kol-gibbōrē haḥayil* and omitting *'et-hakkesep* as introduced after the presumed corruption of *wayeṣaw* to *wayyōṣē'* ('Menahem [commanded] all Israel and all the men of property [to give the king of Assyria fifty shekels]'), cf. Burney. But Šanda has aptly cited the analogy of Arabic *ḫarāj* ('land-tax'), from *ḫaraja* ('to go out'), but meaning in the Xth form (causative reflexive) 'to impose the land-tax'. We may treat the preposition as the *'al* of liability, translating 'he paid the silver; Israel . . . had to give . . .' D. J. Wiseman[c] has noted that 50 shekels was the average price of a slave at Kalḫu in the following century.

(xi) THE DEUTERONOMISTIC EPILOGUE ON THE REIGN OF MENAHEM AND THE INTRODUCTION TO THE REIGN OF PEKAHIAH: 15.21–24

15 [21]And as for the rest of the acts of Menahem and all that he did, are they not written in the Book of the Chronicles of the Kings of Israel? [22]And Menahem slept with his fathers, and Pekahiah his son became king in his place.

[a] *ANET*, pp. 281f.
[b] *Ibid.*, p. 288.
[c] D. J. Wiseman, *Iraq* XV, 1953, p. 135.

[23]In the fiftieth year of Azariah king of Judah, Pekahiah the son of Menahem became king over Israel in Samaria for two years.[24] And he did evil in the sight of Yahweh; he did not turn away from the sins of Jeroboam the son of Nebat in which he involved Israel.

15.23. The date, again from the time when Azariah became co-regent in 791, is 742, two years after the death of his father Menahem (15.17). If the information of the Deuteronomist is correct, two years may have elapsed until Assyria sanctioned the succession of Pekahiah.

(xii) PEKAH'S REVOLT: 15.25

From the Annals of Israel.

15 [25]And Pekah the son of Remaliah his aide-de-camp conspired against him and struck him down in Samaria in the residential quarter of the palace,[a] and with him fifty Gileadites, and he killed him and became king in his place.

25. The name Pekah (*peqaḥ*) is a hypocoristicon of Pekahiah ('Yahweh is open-eyed, i.e. alert', or 'Y. has opened the eyes'). The name is now attested on a jar from Hazor, stratum V, the level destroyed by Tiglath-pileser in 734.[b]

On *šālīš* see on I K. 9.22; II K. 7.2.

On *'armōn* signifying part only of the palace, probably the residential part, see on I K. 16.18.

The 50 Gileadites suggests that Pekah himself was probably from Gilead.

(xiii) THE DEUTERONOMISTIC EPILOGUE ON THE REIGN OF PEKAHIAH AND THE INTRODUCTION TO THE REIGN OF PEKAH: 15.26–28

15 [26]And as for the rest of the acts of Pekahiah and all that he did, behold they are written in the Book of the Chronicles of the Kings of Israel.

[a]Omitting *'et-'argōb wᵉ'et-hā'aryē* of MT, which, as Stade suggested (*ZAW* VI, 1886, p. 160), are displaced from the list of places in Gilead taken by Tiglath-pileser in v. 29, being perhaps a gloss there. The scribe, glancing at his exemplar, has noticed 'Gilead', which is mentioned in v. 25 and v. 29 and has mistakenly copied certain place-names from v. 29 at v. 25, or a gloss on v. 29 may have been written too near v. 25, where the word 'Gilead' occasioned its inclusion here. Argob is mentioned in I K. 4.13 as a district in Bashan, and Stade feasibly suggests that *hā'aryē* is a scribal corruption of *ḥawwōt yā'īr*, known as a group of settlements in the same region. The brilliant conjecture of Klostermann deserves to be noted, *'et-'arbaʿ mᵉ'ōt gibbōrāw* ('together with his four hundred warriors',) presumably his body-guard. The fifty Gileadites certainly suggests an attack on more than one man in his residential quarters.

[b]Y. Yadin, *Hazor* II, 1960, pp. 73ff.

27In the fifty-second year of Azariah king of Judah, Pekah the son of Remaliah became king over Israel in Samaria (and ruled) for twenty years. 28And he did evil in the sight of Yahweh; he did not turn away from the sins of Jeroboam the son of Nebat in which he involved Israel.

15.27. See Introduction, Chronology, pp. 64f., where we propose that the accession was in 740, but the reckoning 20 years is from an unmentioned abortive rising *c.* 750. This is the first of the notorious chronological difficulties in the history of Israel and Judah from now until Hezekiah's time. This 'partisan dating' is, we believe, the clue to solution of apparent chronological inconsistencies in the following chapters. (See further Introduction, Chronology, pp. 67f.).

(xiv) THE ASSYRIAN INVASION OF 734 AND THE INTERNAL POLITICS OF ISRAEL: 15.29f.

From the Annals of Israel.

15 29In the days of Pekah king of Israel, Tiglath-pileser king of Assyria came and took Ijon, Abel-beth-Maacah, Janoah, Kedesh, Hazor, and Gilead and Galilee, all the land of Naphtali, and deported them to Assyria. 30And Hoshea the son of Elah conspired against Pekah the son of Remaliah and defeated him and killed him and became king in his place [a]in the twentieth year of Jotham the son of Azariah.[a]

29. This campaign is attested thrice over in (1) an Assyrian building inscription, (2) Tiglath-pileser's royal annals, and (3) a fragment from another annalistic text.[b] These are all undated and it is not clear that they refer to the same expedition, but, in spite of difference of details, all mention the appointment of Idi-ba'li as warden of the desert marches. (1) mentions *Ya-u-ḫa-zi* of Ya-u-da-a, Ahaz of Judah, as the mention of the kings of Ammon, Moab, Edom, and Gaza along with him indicates.[c] The devastation of Israel's northern

[a]This passsage, in apparent variance with II K. 15.33, where Jotham is said to have reigned sixteen years, is omitted in G^L, which, however, is notoriously conscious of such difficulties and given to simplification and harmonization. Here apparently was such a glaring inconsistency that only omission would suffice. S is conscious of the difficulty, but writes two for 20, which still does not meet the case, since it is at least six years too early. The 20 years refers to the period after Jotham became co-regent with Azariah in 750 (see Introduction, Chronology, pp. 67f.), hence we should defend MT.

[b]Luckenbill, *ARA* I, §§ 800ff., 772, 8.15–19.

[c]It is often stated that Azariah of Judah is also mentioned in Tiglath-pileser's Annals (Luckenbill, *ARA*, I, c 770), but the person in the inscription, which refers to events after the death of Azariah of Judah and in the time of Ahaz, was the king of Yaudi in northern Syria, as the localities in the context indicate.

and eastern provinces (15.29f.) is apparently mentioned in (2), which refers to certain localities in Galilee, including Ḥinatuni at the western end of the Plain of *Baṭṭūf*, Qana on the northern edge of the plain (Cana of Galilee), Merum (*Meirūn* near Safed), and Aruna (*Yarūn* according to Abel,[a] biblical Iron), Samaria and its immediate vicinity only being left to Israel. (3) mentions explicitly Gilead (Gil'zu), and Galilee, Abilakku (Abel-beth-Maacah?), and 'the whole wide (land of) (Haza'i)li,'[b] and the appointment of Assyrian governors. This inscription is either after 731 referring to an expedition in 732, since it refers to Hoshea's overthrow of Pekah, which was effected in 731, or if the loss of Gilead and Galilee was in 734, as is frequently stated, there is a certain telescoping of the history of Assyria in the west at that time. The mention of Menahem in this inscription is a doubtful reading, but, if it were genuine, it would be explicable on the assumption of telescoping.[c] A third Assyrian province created at this time was Du'ru, the Plain of Sharon with its administrative centre at Dor (modern *Ṭanṭūra*), the administrative centre of Galilee being Megiddo, which gave its name to the province.

The reduction of Galilee is attested by the destruction of the great frontier fortress of Hazor in northern Galilee, where a layer of carbon has sealed off the furniture of the houses of the Israelite city in Stratum V,[d] and by the destruction of Megiddo Level III and the rebuilding of the city with a large fort or watch-tower as the most conspicuous feature of Level II.

Of the first five towns mentioned, Ijon, Abel-beth-Maacah, Kedesh, and Hazor are certainly located in northern Galilee, which suggests that Janoah is here, too. The name Ijon survives in the modern Lebanese village of *Marj ʿUyūn* just north of the Israeli frontier settlement of Metulla, and is probably to be located specifically at *Ḫirbet Dibbīn* at a strong spring just north of the modern settlement. Abel-beth-Maacah is the conspicuous mound of *Tell Ibil* on an isolated tongue of land just south of Metulla, taking its name no doubt from the Aramaean tribe of Maacah (9.6), whose watering-

[a]*GP* II, p. 104.

[b]I.e. Damascus. The reading is now certainly attested in two fragments from Nimrud, D. J. Wiseman, *Iraq* XVIII, 1956, pp. 117–29, and H. W. F. Saggs, *Iraq* XVII, 1955, pp. 131–3. The conjecture '(Naphta)li' must therefore be discarded.

[c]On the accuracy of Assyrian annals for contemporary events and for telescoping and résumé of earlier annals in later redactions, see above, p. 61.

[d]Y. Yadin, *Hazor I*, 1958, pp.22f.; II, 1960, p. 63.

place (*'ābēl*) and stronghold it was. Kedesh also retains its name in *Qadeis* ten miles north of Safed and seven miles north-north-west of Hazor on the Mandatory frontier road. Hazor (*Tell al-Qedaḥ*, also called *Tell Waqqāṣ* from the wadi which runs past it) is now well known from the excavations of Yadin and his colleagues. In this context Janoah may be located at *Yanūḥ*, about seven miles east of Tyre, though the comparative isolation of this site from the other identifiable sites makes the location less certain.

15.30. With this note of the accession of Hoshea must be compared the claim of Tiglath-pileser III :'They overthrew their king Peqaḥa and I placed Ausi (Hoshea) as king over them'.[a] The first claim confirms the Old Testament in admitting the initiative of Hoshea, but the second suggests, what is not admitted in the Old Testament, that he was the representative of a pro-Assyrian party, the same, no doubt, as had backed Menahem.

On the chronological note, which we relate to Jotham's co-regency in 750, see p. 626 n.[a] and Introduction, Chronology, pp. 67f.

(XV) THE DEUTERONOMISTIC EPILOGUE TO THE REIGN OF PEKAH: 15.31

15 [31]And as for the rest of the acts of Pekah, and all that he did, see, they are written in the Book of the Chronicles of the Kings of Israel.

(XVI) THE REIGN OF JOTHAM: 15.32–38

This section includes a few historical notes from the Annals of Judah (vv. 33b, 37) set in the stereotyped Deuteronomistic introduction and epilogue.

15 [32]In the second year of Pekah the son of Remaliah king of Israel, Jotham the son of Azariah[b] king of Judah became king. [33]He was twenty-five years old when he became king and he reigned six[c] years in Jerusalem, and the name of his mother was Jerusha the daughter of

[a]Luckenbill, *ARA* I, § 817.

[b]So with G^{BA} for MT Uzziah. Azariah is the usual form of the name in Kings, as Uzziah is in Chronicles and Isaiah. In view of the frequency of both names we think it unlikely that one was the original name and the other a throne-name. We think it likely that Azariah ('Yahweh has helped' or 'May Y. help') was the king's throne name or perhaps the name assumed when he became co-regent in 791, while Uzziah ('Y. is my strength') may have been assumed when he became sole king in 766 or on the thirtieth anniversary of his reign, which, in Egyptian royal ritual, was marked by the *djed* festival signifying renewal of kingship. The influence of Egyptian courtly etiquette and ritual is noted by Gunkel in his study on the Psalms (*Die Psalmen*, 1926).

[c]Reading *šēš* for *šēš ʿeśrē* ('sixteen') a mistake made possibly when cyphers instead of words were used. See further Introduction, Chronology, p. 70.

Zadok. 34And he did right in the eyes of Yahweh according to all that Uzziah[a] his father did. 35Nevertheless he did not abolish[b] the 'high places'; the people still sacrificed and made burnt offerings at the 'high places'. He it was who built the upper gate of the Temple of Yahweh. 36And for the rest of the acts of Jotham and all[c] that he did, are they not written in the Book of the Chronicles of the Kings of Judah? 37In those days Yahweh first sent against Judah[d] Rezin[e] king of Aram and Pekah the son of Remaliah king of Israel.[f] 38And Jotham slept with his fathers and was buried with his fathers in the city of David his father and Ahaz his son became king in his place.

15.32. The name Jotham ('Yahweh is perfect') is attested in a seal found in the last Jewish stratum in Glueck's excavations at *Tell al-Ḫaleifeh* (Ezion-geber),[g] which may have belonged to a representative of Jotham either as king or as regent of Azariah, who restored this region to Judah (14.22). Glueck suggests that the seal may have been the governor's seal of office, but, in view of the design of a ram and a small human figure before it, it may have been used by an official responsible for royal flocks and the return of wool to Jotham, cf. the mention of tribute of lambs from this region in Isa. 16.1.

33. On the reading 'six' for MT 16 and its agreement with the chronology of the period see p. 628 n.[c] and Introduction, Chronology, p. 70.

yᵉrūšā' ('Jerusha') may mean 'Taken possession of', but the final *aleph* is suspicious, and we should take the name as the hypocoristicon of *yᵉrūšā'ēl* ('Strengthened by God'), taking the verb as the imperfect passive of *rāšā'*, cognate with Arabic *rašā'* ('to be firm'). The father so congratulated himself on the birth of the child. Zadok may have been the hereditary priest in Jerusalem. The prominence of the father of Jerusha and his family's monopoly of the name Zadok is suggested by the fact that it is not necessary to name her home, as is generally done in the case of the queen-mother.

35. In contrast to the reserve of Kings on the achievements of Jotham, II Chron. 27.4 notes Jotham's fortifications throughout

[a]We read the MT form of the name, though the regular form in Kings, Azariah, is read by G^A and certain other MSS of G.

[b]Reading *hēsīr* with G, S and V for MT *sārū*.

[c]Inserting *wᵉkol-* with many Hebrew MSS and G, S, and V.

[d]G^BA omits 'against Judah', which is intelligible, but much inferior to MT.

[e]G. reads *rᵉṣōn* or *raṣōn*, but the Assyrian version is *Raḫianu*, which supports the termination of Hebrew *Rasyon*, so that Rezin may be retained.

[f]Adding 'king of Israel' with S, which seems to be demanded by the fact that his colleague Rezin is designated king of Aram.

[g]N. Glueck, *Rivers in the Desert*, pp. 167f., fig. 5.

the country, presumably in preparation for resistance to Rezin and Pekah, who were already raiding Judah (15.37), and his success in war with Ammon. His fortification of the Ophel is noticed, too (II Chron. 27.3), probably also a defence measure against the Syro-Ephraimite menace. Jotham's building of the upper gate of the Temple is noted in true annalistic style and is probably drawn from an annalistic source. The gate is not certainly identified, though 'the Upper Gate of Benjamin which was in the Temple' is mentioned in Jer. 20.2, and in Ezek. 9.2 'the Upper Gate that faces north' is mentioned. This may be the Benjamin gate at the north-east of the Temple area (Zech. 14.10); see on 14.13.

15.37. This is another excerpt from the Annals of Judah. The attacks of Rezin and Pekah are specifically associated with the reign of Ahaz in the crisis which brought Isaiah into political life (Isa. 7), but their pressure had already begun in the time of Jotham. Montgomery (ICC, p. 456) notes the use of the Hiphil of *šālaḥ* in the sending of plagues, e.g. Ex. 8.17; Amos 8.11.

(*h*) THE REIGN OF AHAZ: 16.1–20

There are three main subjects in this section, and, we think, three literary elements. The general political situation is described with specific note of Ahaz's involvement in it (vv. 5–9). The dry factual, annalistic style is unmistakable, and the section is certainly based on the Annals of Judah. It was not, however, directly drawn from them, otherwise we should have had more detail about the invasion of Judah by Rezin and Pekah. There seems a telescoping of history in this section, which passes almost immediately from the height of the power of Rezin to the bald statement about his death (v. 9). There is evidence of redaction in the note on the presence of Aramaeans at Elath 'to this day' (v. 6), so that the section seems to be a late presentation of the salient facts of Ahaz's reign based on the Annals of Judah rather than a direct citation from these Annals. The section vv. 10–18 is generally taken as a separate unit, concerning religious affairs and Temple installations. Benzinger thought of this as part of a history of the Temple. But both Šanda (II, p. 207) and Kittel (HKAT, p. 270) think that if this were so, the author being a priest, we might have had a more outspoken criticism of Ahaz. Šanda thinks of this section rather as part of a fragmentary history of Ahaz's reign. If this were so, the letter of Ahaz to Tiglath-pileser (v. 7) might also be part of it. Our own opinion, the absence of criticism of Ahaz notwithstanding, is that vv. 5–9 are a résumé of the reign of Ahaz from the Deuteronomistic compiler, whose interest was in the Temple, probably because he was of priestly family. He used early annalistic material, but his telescoping of the political events of Ahaz's life indicates that his main interest lay in the sphere of the cult. Besides the annalistic source and the compiler's version of the reign of Ahaz based on this (vv. 5–9) with his excursus on Ahaz's ritual innovations (vv. 10–18), there is the customary Deuteronomistic introduction to the reign of Ahaz (vv. 1–4) and epilogue (vv. 19f.). The condemnation of the apostasy of Ahaz in the Deuteronomistic introduction (vv. 3ff.) possibly explains the absence or suppression of criticism of the king in vv. 10–18.

(i) THE DEUTERONOMISTIC INTRODUCTION TO THE REIGN OF AHAZ: 16.1–4

16 [1]In the seventeenth year of Pekah the son of Remaliah, Ahaz the son of Jotham king of Judah became king. [2]Ahaz was twenty years old when he became king and he reigned for sixteen years in Jerusalem, and he did not do what was right in the sight of Yahweh his God like his father David, [3]but he walked in the way of the kings of Israel, and moreover he passed his son through the fire according to the abominations of the peoples whom Yahweh dispossessed before the Israelites. [4]And he sacrificed and burned offerings in the 'high places' and on the hills and under every green tree.

16.1f. The 17th year of Pekah, reckoning inclusively from his first unsuccessful bid for power in 750, is 734, when we consider that Ahaz became co-regent with Jotham at the age of 20. His reign for 16 years, however, refers to his rule from the time he was recognized as sole king by his Assyrian overlord in 730 till 715. For the relevance of his co-regency in 734 to the chronology of Hezekiah in 18.2 see Introduction, Chronology, p. 68. We calculate that Hezekiah was born in 738 when his father was 16.

3. This is the first instance in the history of Judah of this practice, which is repeatedly mentioned as an act of apostasy in the times of stress at the end of the monarchy of Israel (17.17) and in Judah under Manasseh (21.6; 23.10). That actual burning of human victims, and no token rite, was practised is indicated explicitly in Jer. 19.5. The site of these rites was in the Valley of Hinnom (23.10: Jer. 7.31; 19.2ff.), where Tophet ('the Firepit') was. The rite was, we think, specifically associated with the cult of Melek-ʿaṯṯar (misvocalized as *mōlek* or *milkōm*), which survived at Jerusalem from pre-Israelite times. See above on I K. 11.5. H. Schmidt[a] and Eissfeldt contend that Ahaz's offering was exceptional in the danger of the Syro-Ephraimite crisis, like Mesha's offering of his eldest son in the siege of his capital.

(ii) RÉSUMÉ OF THE POLITICAL SITUATION IN THE REIGN OF AHAZ: 16.5–9

This is probably by a priestly redactor, possibly the Deuteronomistic compiler, incorporating material from the Annals of Judah.

The cursory nature of this résumé and the length and detail of the following passage on Ahaz's religious innovations (vv. 10–18) emphasize the limitations of the Books of Kings as objective history, and again we see the selective principle on which the Deuteronomist used his sources. By contrast Isa. 7.1ff. gives a much fuller picture of the Syro-Ephraimite crisis in Judah and introduces the fact, which Kings totally ignores, of the project to supplant Ahaz by an Aramaean puppet Ben Tabeal (Isa. 7.6).

16 5Then Rezin king of Aram and Pekah the son of Remaliah king of Israel made an expedition to Jerusalem to fight, and they laid siege to Ahaz,[b] and he could not[c] fight for it.[d]

6At that time the king of Edom[e] recovered Elath for Edom[e] and he cleared the Jews from Elath,[f] and Edomites came to Elath and have lived there to this day.

7And Ahaz sent servants to Tiglath-pileser king of Assyria saying, I am your servant and son, so come up and deliver me from the hand of the king of Aram and from the hand of the king of Israel, who have risen up[g] against me. 8And Ahaz took the silver and the gold which were found in the Temple of Yahweh and in the treasury of the palace and sent it as an inducement to the king of Assyria. 9And the king of Assyria heard his appeal and the king of Assyria made an expedition against Damascus and took it and deported its people to Nineveh (lit. the city), and put Rezin to death.

[a]*Die grossen Propheten*, 1923, p. 2.

[b]S reads *ʿālehā*, ('against it') as Isa. 7.1, for MT *ʿal-'āḥāz*. This, however, deprives the pronominal subject of the verb in the following clause of an antecedent.

[c]MT *w^e lō' yāk^e lū l^e hillāḥēm* ('and they were not able to fight') seems contradicted by the general sense of the context. Hence we follow the clue of Isa. 7.1 and read the singular *yākōl l^e hillāḥēm*.

[d]Reading *ʿālehā* as in Isa. 7.1.

[e]On the clue of MT in reading 'Edomites' later in the v. we read *'^e dōm* for *'^a rām*, a very slight change of one similar consonant, Rezin being inserted in MT after the corruption to *'^a rām*.

[f]Reading Elath for MT Eloth in agreement with the general punctuation.

[g]Pointing *qāmīm* for MT *qōmīm*.

16.5. It is nowhere said that the object of the Syro-Ephraimite campaign in Judah was to coerce Judah into an anti-Assyrian alliance, though that was probably its purpose, to judge from the inveterate enmity of Rezin to Assyria evidenced in the Annals of Tiglath-pileser.[a]

6. On the reading Edom for Aram see p. 632 n.[e]. In the excavation of *Tell al-Ḫaleifeh* Glueck found change of Hebrew occupation in the seal of Jotham from the last Jewish stratum and from the next a store-room of storage jars stamped on their handles with a seal 'Belonging to Qausanal'. This name is a theophoric of Qaus, well known as the national god of Edom.[b]

This is the first mention of the designation 'Jews', i.e. subjects of the kingdom of Judah.

7. This verse continues the record of v. 5, the appeal to Assyria following the inability of Ahaz to fight for his capital. The appeal is in the form of a letter in which Ahaz declares his submission to Tiglath-pileser ('I am your servant'), and his dependence on him ('I am your son', cf. 13.14, where Joash addresses Elisha as 'my father').

8. The 'inducement' (*šōḥad*, lit. 'bribe') sent by Ahaz to Tiglath-pileser was more than *ex gratia*, and Tiglath-pileser records the tribute of Ya-u-ha-zi (Jehoahaz, of which Ahaz is a hypocoristicon) of Ya-u-da-a (Judah) among the tribute of other Aramaean states in Syria, but not yet of Damascus or Israel.[c]

9. *qīr* is not mentioned in G as the place to which the subjects of Rezin were deported, and it is suggested that it is an interpolation in the text suggested by Amos 1.5, where the oracle on Damascus declares that the Aramaeans shall be deported to *qīr* (*qīrā*). We regard this as a common noun, 'the city', i.e. the Assyrian capital Nineveh, cf. Istambul, a corruption of *eis tēn polin* ('to the city'). The Assyrians regularly referred to their holy city of Ashur as 'the City', and the deportation to 'the City' may refer to dedication of prisoners of war. There is, we think, no connection with *qīr* named in Amos 9.7 as the original home of the Aramaeans. This we regard as a corruption of *qᵉrāqīr*, cf. Arabic broken plural, meaning 'waterholes' or oases of the North Arabian steppe. A depopulation of the district of Damascus, probably preceding the final defeat of Rezin, is mentioned by Tiglath-pileser in his Annals.[d]

[a]Luckenbill, *ARA* I, §§ 774–9.
[b]Glueck, *Rivers in the Desert*, pp. 165–8.
[c]Luckenbill, *ARA* I, §§ 800ff.
[d]*Ibid.*, §§ 777–9.

(iii) AN EXCURSUS OF THE DEUTERONOMISTIC COMPILER OR A PRIESTLY REDACTOR ON AHAZ'S SUBMISSION TO TIGLATH-PILESER AND HIS CONSEQUENT RELIGIOUS INNOVATIONS: 16.10–18

16 10And king Ahaz went to meet Tiglath-pileser king of Assyria at Damascus,[a] and he saw the altar which was in Damascus, so king Ahaz sent to Uriah the priest the fashion and construction of the altar just as it was made. 11And Uriah the priest constructed the altar according to all the specifications which king Ahaz had sent from Damascus;[b] [c]even so did Uriah the priest until king Ahaz came from Damascus.[c] 12And the king came from Damascus, and the king saw the altar, and the king made offering[d] for the altar and offered a holocaust for it. 13And he sent up the smoke of his whole burnt-offering and (he offered) his meal-offering, and he made his libation and sprinkled the blood of his communion-offerings on the altar. 14And as for the bronze altar[e] which was before Yahweh, he brought it forward from the front (or east) of the Temple, from between the altar and the Temple of Yahweh, and he put it beside the altar[f] to the north. 15And king Ahaz ordered him[g] (i.e. Uriah the priest),[g] saying, Burn the morning holocaust upon the great altar, and the evening offering and the king's holocaust and his offering and all the people's[h] holocaust and their offering and their libations; and you shall sprinkle upon it all the blood of the holocaust and all the blood of sacrifice, and the bronze altar shall be for me to inquire by. 16So Uriah the priest did according to all that king Ahaz bade him.[i] 17And king Ahaz cut off the panels[j] of the bases and removed [k]the[l] basin from off them,[k] and he took down the 'sea' from upon the bronze oxen which were under it and he set it on a

[a]*dammeśeq* for MT *dummeśeq*, cf. II Chron. 28.23.

[b]G^L omits 'Damascus', of which there is rather too much repetition.

[c]Omitted in G^B owing to homoeoteleuton.

[d]Reading Hiphil for Qal of MT, a conjecture supported by no version, but suggested by the sequel *ʿal-hammizbēaḥ*. G^B omits *wayyiqrab ʿal-hammizbēaḥ*, an error through homoeoteleuton.

[e]Grammar demands that the definite article be omitted in Hebrew before the construct *mizbaḥ*.

[f]This must be the altar which Ahaz had had made, and G^L adds 'which he had made'.

[g]The pronominal suffix *-ēhū* (for MT *-ehū*) to the first verb indicates that *'et-'ūrīyā hakkōhēn* has been added as an early gloss.

[h]Omitting MT *hā'āreṣ* with G^BL.

[i]Reading *ṣiwwāhū* with G and S for MT *ṣiwwā*, which wants an object.

[j]Omitting the definite article before *misgᵉrōt*, as demanded by the grammar, cf. G and S.

[k]V omits this clause, and is supported by MT(K), which reads *wᵉ* before *'et*, which indicates that the verb *wayᵉqaṣṣēṣ* has the sequel also as an object, but the Massoretic pointing indicates that the conjunction should be omitted.

[l]Omitting MT *wᵉ* before *'et*, see previous n.

pavement of stone. [18]And [a]the barrier of the sabbath[a] which they had built in the Temple and the king's entrance into the court[b] he removed[c] from[d] the Temple of Yahweh because of the king of Assyria.

16.10. Ahaz's visit to Tiglath-pileser at Damascus was to proffer his submission. The date is early in the reign of Ahaz as sole king, since according to an Assyrian eponym-list Damascus fell in 732, the year of Ahaz's accession as sole king pending confirmation by Assyria. At the expedition of Tiglath-pileser to Syria and Palestine in 734, when he mentions 'Yauḥazi of Yauda' as a tributary, Ahaz must have been regent and more active than his father Jotham. This is remarkable, since if Jotham became co-regent with Azariah in 750 at the age of 25 (15.33) he must have been only 41 in 734, hence the designation of Ahaz as co-regent in 734 may indicate that Jotham was in weak health, which is indeed confirmed by his early death in 732. Under these circumstances the burden of administration may have devolved upon Ahaz before his actual accession, as the Assyrian inscription suggests. Ahaz's adoption of a particular type of altar and his reorganization of the cult (vv. 12–18) were not a mere matter of aesthetic taste as Šanda (II, p. 205) and Skinner (CB, pp. 369ff.) suggest, but an expression of subservience to Assyria.[e] In Uriah the priest we have a point of contact with Isaiah (8.2). He was cited as a witness by the prophet before the final fall of Damascus in 732. *d^emūt* indicates the style or fashion of the altar, the general impression it made, as *tabnīt* indicates the technicalities of the construction.

12. The meaning of *ʿal* is doubtful. Normally it would mean sacrifice 'upon' the altar, but it may also mean 'on account of', 'for' the

[a]G reads *themelion tēs kathedrās* (*mūsad haššebet*) for MT *myysak haššabbāt* (Q *mūsak haššabbāt*), the barrier, or grille, of the sabbath. The G reading suggests the podium of a throne or tribunal, which may have been used by the king on ceremonial occasions, perhaps at his presentation or his anointing, cf. 11.14, where the reading *ʿōmed* for *ʿammūd* may possibly be authenticated by the reading of G in the present passage. We retain MT, however, in view of a reference to a gate in the Temple which was kept closed except on sabbaths and new moon days, when it was opened to admit the king (Ezek. 46.1f.). The use of the root *sūk* in the sense of putting up a barrier is attested in Job 3.23 and 38.8.

[b]Reading *haḥ^aṣērā* ('into the . . . court') for the awkward *haḥīṣōnā* ('to the outside'), a pure conjecture.

[c]Reading *hēsīr*, which is a pure conjecture, for MT *hēsēb* ('he reorientated', or 'moved around').

[d]*mibbēt*, a pure conjecture, for MT *bēt*, which, if genuine, would mean 'in the Temple'. The verb *hēsīr*, however, demands the sense 'from the Temple'.

[e]So Kittel, *Geschichte der Hebräer* I, 1888, pp. 294f.; Gressmann, *ZAW* XLII, 1924, p. 324; T. H. Robinson, *History of Israel* I, p. 377; cf. de Vaux, *Ancient Israel*, p. 410, who believes that the prototype was a Syrian altar.

altar. Since the sprinkling of blood upon the new altar is mentioned specifically after the gamut of sacrifices and offerings (v. 13), it seems obvious that the consecration of the new altar was not effected until the sprinkling of the blood, hence we conclude that the sacrifices were for its dedication.

16.13. This is a *locus classicus* for sacrifice in the Temple. The *ʿōlā* was the holocaust, or whole burnt-offering, which was entirely consumed on the altar; the *minḥā* was properly the bloodless offering of produce of the earth, though it was also used with a general significance for sacrifice, see on v. 15; *nesek* was the libation of wine or oil; and *šᵉlāmīm* were the sacrifices, part of which was eaten by the worshippers and part devoted to God to effect the communion of God and the worshippers. The blood of this offering sprinkled on the altar consecrated it as a place where God and his worshippers might meet. The third singular masculine pronominal suffix does not indicate the king's offerings as apart from the people's, though there was such a distinction (v. 15), but that the king himself officiated, as Solomon did at the dedication of the Temple (I K. 8.63ff.).

14. The bronze altar which stood east of the entrance to the Temple between the great altar and the porch of the Temple is mentioned in I K. 8.64, where it is taken as intrusive, since it is not mentioned among the bronze-work of Hiram.[a] The designation of the new site of the bronze altar as north of the new altar suggests that *mēʾēt pᵉnē habbayit*, its old site, means east of the Temple.

15. The evening offering (*minḥā*) is mentioned in the story of the ordeal on Carmel (I K. 18.29). In II K. 3.20 the morning offering is mentioned, and that is also termed *minḥā*. The practice of the bloody offering (*ʿōlā*) in the morning and the bloodless offering (*minḥā*) in the evening, or, strictly speaking, in the afternoon, is the daily practice in the priestly legislation in Ex. 29.38–42 and Num. 28.2–8, where the offering is called 'the perpetual' (*hattāmīd*), and, as far at least as concerns the bloody offering in the morning, is visualized in Ezek. 46.13–15. Here the reconstruction of the cult, though the various features have, in certain cases, a new significance, is based on pre-exilic usage. In the present passage the distinction between the king's sacrifices and those of the people is interesting, and recalls the practice in Ezek. 46, where the king's sacrifices on sabbaths and new moon days are distinct from the daily offerings presented on behalf of the whole community. Doubtless in the present passage the double

[a]So W. R. Smith, *Religion of the Semites*, 1894², n. L.

sacrifices of king and people were because of the particular solemnity of the occasion, which may well have been fixed to coincide with a Sabbath or new moon day. The use of *haqṭēr* with *ʿōlā* as object indicates that there can be no question of incense here, but that the verb means 'to send up in smoke', a meaning which would be much more appropriate in other Deuteronomistic references to the local sacrifices at the 'high places'. We must not imagine, however, that there was no incense-offering in pre-exilic times. As de Vaux has pointed out,[a] the mention of *lᵉbōnā* in Jer. 6.20 and 41.5, the incense altars from the Late Bronze Age strata of excavations at Bethshean and Taanach, the more recent find of a South Arabian seal at Bethel from the ninth or eighth century BC, and the mention of an incense-offering in the Elephantine papyri, which reflect the pre-exilic cult in Palestine, are clear evidence to the contrary.

The old bronze altar was now reserved for the consulting of entrails (*lᵉbaqqēr*). This usage of the Piel of *bāqar* is not attested in the Old Testament, though in Lev. 27.33 it is used meaning 'to discriminate' between good and evil. The sense of discriminating seems fundamental, as suggested by the Arabic cognate *baqara* ('to split, rip open'). A possible usage of the verb in augury is in an omen text from Ras Shamra.[b] We have translated *wʿbdm tbqrnn skn* at the end of this text 'then let the devotees seek out a substitute',[c] but admit the possibility of the translation 'then let the devotees divine danger'. Ahaz's practice of divination was a feature of his addiction to Assyrian usages. Divination by entrails or by the behaviour or expression in the eyes of a dying victim is well attested in Mesopotamian texts and by clay models of animals' livers from excavations in Mesopotamia and Palestine. A full description of such divination at Harran in the Middle Ages is given by an-Nadīm (*al-Fihrist*).

16.17. On the wheeled laver-bases (*mᵉkōnōt*) and the cross-pieces (*misgᵉrōt*) see on I K. 7.27ff., and on the 'sea' (*hayyām*) and the bronze oxen supporting it see on I K. 7.23ff. The oxen were appropriated by Ahaz for the sake of their bronze, and the huge basin which they supported was now set in stone paving, which must have been much more convenient, if much less artistic and imposing.

18. On 'the barrier of the sabbath' and its variant in G 'the base of the tribunal' and our explanation of the MT in the light of the

[a] *Ancient Israel*, p. 431.
[b] C. Virolleaud, *Syria* XXVIII, 1951, pp. 25–27, text III.
[c] *The Legacy of Canaan*, 1965², p. 194.

royal Sabbath ceremonial described in Ezek. 46.1f., which probably reflects pre-exilic practice, see p. 635 n.[a]. All that enhanced the dignity of the king in Judah was abolished by order of Tiglath-pileser, who thus emphasized the status of his vassal. The further reference to the king's entrance supports this interpretation. Ahaz made other innovations at the instance of, or to ingratiate himself with, Tiglath-pileser.

(iv) THE DEUTERONOMISTIC EPILOGUE TO THE REIGN OF AHAZ: 16.19f.

16[19]And as for the rest of the acts of Ahaz [a]and all[a] that he did, are they not written in the Book of the Chronicles of the Kings of Judah? [20]Then Ahaz slept with his fathers and was buried[b] in the city of David, and Hezekiah his son became king in his place.

(*i*) THE REIGN OF HOSHEA, THE FALL OF ISRAEL, AND THE ASSYRIAN RESETTLEMENT: 17.1–41

This section is composed of a historical source which gives very briefly the salient facts of the last nine years of the kingdom of Israel, culminating in the great deportation to Mesopotamia (vv. 3–6); there follows a statement of the Assyrian resettlement of the land (vv. 24–28). The reign of the last king of Israel, Hoshea, is introduced by the stereotyped Deuteronomistic formula (vv. 1f.) with but slight modification, and there is an epilogue, probably Deuteronomistic, on the final fall of Samaria and the deportation of the inhabitants in vv. 18, 21–23. The national calamity is the occasion for a long section where the Deuteronomist represents the events as the just retribution for Israel's apostasy to the Canaanite fertility-cult and her obdurate disregard of the admonitions of her prophets (vv. 7–17, 19–20). It is generally held that vv. 29–34a is another comment from the Deuteronomistic redactor on the foreign cults of the Assyrian settlers, qualifying the statement that the cult of Yahweh was reintroduced at Bethel among the Assyrian colonists (vv. 27–28), and perhaps a further comment on this passage from a later redactor still is vv. 34b–40, which modifies the statement in v. 33 that the Assyrian colonists in addition to their alien cults feared Yahweh, dwelling on

[a]Inserting *wᵉkol-* with certain Hebrew MSS, G, S, and T.

[b]Omitting MT *ʿim ʾᵃbōtāw* ('with his fathers') as tautological after *wayyiškab ʿim ʾᵃbōtāw*.

the deliverance from Egypt, the covenant and prohibition against idolatry, traditions which the new settlers flagrantly flout. We suspect, however, from the absence of any criticism of the Bethel-cult, that vv. 29–34a are not from a Deuteronomistic hand, but from a local priestly authority, which was responsible probably for vv. 24–28. In v. 41, on the other hand, which refers to the persistence of the worship of Yahweh alongside alien cults, we seem to have the remark of a redactor earlier than the hand of vv. 29–34a.

Of this matter, vv. 3–6 could conceivably be drawn from the Annals of Israel, at least up to the siege of Samaria in v. 5, but the fact of the capture of the city and the deportation to certain places in Mesopotamia and the Iranian escarpment in v. 6 cannot come from such a source, and, in fact, we may question whether state archives were kept recording the intrigues of Hoshea in the last precarious years of Israel, the last three of which were occupied in the final desperate resistance of Samaria. Behind vv. 3–5 there is a nucleus of recorded historical fact, as is suggested by the similarity of vv. 5f. to 18.9–11. The latter passage is a citation probably from the Annals of Judah, which could not allow such a significant event as the fall of Samaria to pass unnoticed. We suggest that, where the two passages agree, the primary source is the Israelite one, and where they differ, namely in Hoshea's Egyptian intrigues, stated to be the occasion of his removal three years before the fall of Samaria (vv. 3f.), the source is the Annals of Judah. The passage vv. 3ff., however, leaves much to be desired as a historical record, and the problem is complicated by the fact that Sargon II, the successor of Shalmaneser V, to whom the fall of Samaria is ascribed in II K. 18.9f., claims the reduction of the city as his exploit in his annals of his seventh year (715) and in a display inscription from the end of his reign. For the view that both the biblical statement of the fall of Samaria to Shalmaneser and the subsequent resettlement and Sargon's claim to have reduced and resettled the place are telescoped accounts of events from 725 to 715, and that Sargon emphasized his part in the final reduction of Samaria after the revolt of 720 and ignored its fall under Shalmaneser in 723/2, see Introduction, Chronology, pp. 60f.

The captivity of Hoshea during the latter stages of the siege of Samaria is not an insuperable difficulty, since in any case those of his subjects who had forced him to break with Assyria were sufficiently determined to defend the city without Hoshea, who was from the outset a creature of Assyria. The king may have gone out of the city to meet Shalmaneser, relying on his accepting his explanation that he had withheld his tribute not of his own free will but under pressure of his subjects.

The second historical source, vv. 24–28, in so far as it deals with the Assyrian resettlement of the district of Samaria after the deportation, is obviously not from the Annals of Israel. Nevertheless the local interest and detailed knowledge argue an authoritative hand and one interested in his people's fate and their ancient homeland. The interest, however, is religious rather than political, hence we think of a priestly author, perhaps the actual Israelite priest sent back to Bethel by the Assyrian king (now Sargon), or one of his assessors (see on vv. 27–28) or of his family. Had the section come from a contemporary Judaean source or from the Deuteronomist, the opportunity would not have been lost of animadverting on the cult of Bethel, which is so stigmatized in Deuteronomistic passages throughout Kings. By the same token we should regard the excursus on the worship of the Assyrian colonists in vv. 29–33 as stemming from the priestly historian of Bethel who was the author of vv. 24–28, rather than from the Deuteronomistic redactor, as is generally held. The hand of the Deuteronomist, however, is manifest in the selection of this matter concerning the cult of Bethel from the original source. In claiming vv. 29–33 for a Deuteronomistic redaction, Šanda (II, p. 235) emphasizes the designation of the native Israelites as 'Samaritans' (*šōm^e^rōnīm*) instead of 'Israelites' (*b^e^nē yiśrā'ēl*). This we consider no valid objection, for, since Tiglath-pileser stripped the Northern kingdom of Galilee and the region of Megiddo, the plain of Sharon, and Gilead, Samaria and district (Samerina of the Assyrian records) was the whole extent of the kingdom. Again, we are not told how long after the deportation the cult of Bethel was revived, therefore the priest and his family who were now sent back were perhaps a new generation who had never known the province by any other designation. If, as may well be, this person after the lapse of almost a generation was responsible for the statement on the fate of Samaria and the Israelites in vv. 5f., and possibly for vv. 3f., the vagueness of this last passage and the loose parenthesis of vv. 3b–4a may be explained. It is true that the natives are designated 'Israel' in v. 7, but we suggest that a priestly historian from Bethel may have been influenced here by a Judaean source, which appears in almost verbatim repetition in 18.9–11.

(i) THE DEUTERONOMISTIC INTRODUCTION TO THE REIGN OF HOSHEA: 17.1f.

17 [1]In the second[a] year of Ahaz king of Judah, Hoshea the son of Elah became king in Samaria (and ruled) over Israel nine years.[2] And he did evil in the sight of Yahweh, but not as the kings of Israel who were before him.

17.1. On the chronological problem we propose that Hoshea, according to Tiglath-pileser's annalistic account of his campaign of 732, was appointed vassal king of Samaria in 732, but was not able to establish himself there in the face of heavy anti-Assyrian opposition till 731, the second year of Ahaz and the 20th of Jotham (i.e. since Jotham's co-regency in 750/49, 15.30). This suggests 732 as the year of Ahaz's accession. But 16.1 already gives the year of his adoption as co-regent as 734, while, if Hezekiah acceded in 714 at the New Year festival following the death of Ahaz (18.13), and Ahaz reigned 16 years (16.2), his accession is in 730. Our solution is that there are three different chronological systems here. Ahaz was adopted as co-regent with Jotham in 734 shortly before his death (15.32; 16.1). Since Tiglath-pileser III was then in Palestine he did not formally accede as an independent king, cf. Tiglath-pileser's curtailment of the royal dignity implied in 16.18. Nevertheless Tiglath-pileser accorded him some recognition of authority in 731, and Northern Israelite records, drawn upon in 17.1f., regard this as his formal accession. But not till 730 was Ahaz free to assume his royal authority according to traditional custom in Judah at the New Year festival. It is from this date that his reign runs in the Annals of Judah. The reference to the accession of Hoshea in the second year of Ahaz' reign (731), suggests that the latter, which we consider to be Ahaz' recognition by Tiglath-pileser, was at the end of one year and the accession of Hoshea at the beginning of the next, thus only after a few months.

2. The mitigation of the regular Deuteronomistic criticism of a king of Israel is interesting. The political involvements of Hoshea's short and troubled reign left him no time for religious matters. His comparative virtue according to Deuteronomistic principles was a virtue of necessity.

[a]Reading 'second' for MT 'twelfth', a mistake arising when the number was indicated by a cypher. The date is 731, see Introduction, Chronology, p. 70.

(ii) SHORT RÉSUMÉ OF THE REIGN OF HOSHEA, THE FALL OF SAMARIA, AND THE DEPORTATION OF ISRAELITES: 17.3–6

Verses 3f. probably from the Annals of Israel, vv. 5f. from the Annals of Judah (cf. 18.9–11), both summarized, with vv. 3b–4a in loose parenthesis, possibly by a priestly historian from Bethel, possibly by the Deuteronomist.

17 [3]He it was against whom Shalmaneser king of Assyria came up (now Hoshea had become his vassal and rendered tribute to him). [4]But the king of Assyria had detected intrigue in Hoshea, who had sent envoys to Sais, to[a] the king of Egypt, and had not sent tribute to the king of Assyria as (he had done) year by year and the king of Assyria put him under arrest and held him bound in prison. [5]And the king of Assyria made an expedition against the whole land and went up against[b] Samaria and besieged it for three years. [6]In the ninth year[c] of Hoshea the king of Assyria took Samaria and deported Israel to Assyria and settled them in Halah and the Habor region, the river of Gozan, and in the mountains[d] of Media.

17.3. We regard the position of the pronominal suffix as emphatic on the analogy of similar usage of *hū'* in annalistic sources. Here the theme is the reign of Hoshea, which was chiefly notable for the expedition of Shalmaneser which culminated in the fall of Samaria. On the problem of possibly two expeditions, and the solution of the difficulty, in which, after Benzinger, we take 3b–4a as in parenthesis, with vv. 3f. and 5f. coming ultimately from two different sources, as Winckler proposed, see critical introduction to this chapter. The problem is complicated by the paucity of the records for the reign of

[a]Reading *'el-sō' 'el-melek miṣrayim*, as proposed by Albright (*BASOR* 171, 1963, p. 66). So' has been commonly taken to be Sib'e, thought to be the *turtanu* of Egypt defeated by the Assyrians at Rapʿa in 720. The reading Sib'e, in the inscription of Sargon (*ANET*, p. 185) has been proved to be *reʿeh*, an unknown Egyptian general (R. Borger, 'Das Ende des ägyptischen Feldherrn Sib'e = סוא', *JNES* XIX, 1960, pp. 49–53). The Egyptian ruler in the Delta at this time was Tefnakhte (726–16), but in II K. 17.4 So' may indicate rather his capital Sais (Egyptian *s'w*), which was mistaken by later Hebrew scribes for the name of the king. This led to the omission of *'el* before *melek* by haplography after *'el* before *sō'*, or omitted after *sō'* had been misunderstood as the name of the king. See further H. Goedicke ('The end of So, King of Egypt', *BASOR* 171, 1963, pp. 64–66).

[b]*ʿal* is probably omitted after *wayyaʿal*.

[c]Reading with certain Hebrew MSS *baššānā* for MT *bišenat* as demanded by grammar.

[d]G evidently found MT *ʿārē* ('cities') an unsuitable meaning, rendering *orē*, which is either a transliteration or, more probably, we think, the translation of *hārē* ('mountains').

Shalmaneser V (727–722). One expedition is probably indicated, in 725 (see critical introduction). Josephus also mentions an expedition against the Phoenician cities in 725, the revolt of which after the death of Tiglath-pileser III in 727 was probably the opportunity which the Israelites took to withhold tribute.

Hebrew Shalmaneser is a corrupt version of Assyrian *Šulman ašāridu* ('S. is exalted'), final *d* being omitted in Hebrew by haplography after *r*.

The vassal status of Hoshea is indicated by his designation as *ʿebed*. On *minḥā* in the sense of 'tribute' see on I K. 5.1.

On the assumption that *sō'* is a personal name, various identifications have been proposed. Among these, Shabaku, whom Manetho lists as the father of Tirhakah (689–664), may be discarded as too late. Winckler avoided this difficulty of So, unknown among the rulers of Egypt, by supposing that *miṣrayim* was *muṣriri*, the North Arabian kingdom associated with Hejazi tribes such as Thamud in Sargon's seventh campaign (715). But Hoshea's intrigues against Assyria would be more likely to interest Egypt, so Winckler's identification of *miṣrayim* may be dismissed. E. F. Weidner[a] proposed that *sō'* denoted Silḫu, or Silḫeni, named as 'king of the land of *muṣri*' in an inscription concerning a campaign in Sargon's sixth year,[b] whom he took to be Osorkon, Osorkon IV according to W. von Bissing, but he is too late. On the view that *sō'* denotes Sais, the capital of the XXIVth Dynasty in the Delta, and that the Pharaoh was Tefnakhte, and the slightly emended text, see p. 642, n.[a].

Superficially it might seem that Shalmaneser must have been in possession of Samaria if he could arrest Hoshea. On our solution, assuming that Hoshea, at variance with his more patriotic subjects, sought to make a personal peace with Shalmaneser, see critical introduction to this chapter. *ʿāṣar* could mean disciplinary action, but in view of its meaning 'to arrest' in Jer. 33.1; 36.5, it is likely that that is the meaning here.

5. The three years' siege of Samaria is a tribute to the defensive building of Omri and Ahab, who surrounded the city with a strong, well-built wall, little of which, however, has been traced, and an inner wall laid in rock-hewn foundation-trenches round the palace and citadel on top of the hill. The latter was probably not built

[a] *AfO* XIV, 1941, pp. 45ff.
[b] Luckenbill, *ARA* II, §§ 104–11.

originally for defence, but was later developed for this purpose.[a] The date is 723–22. On the date of the fall of Samaria and the apparent discrepancy between the biblical statement and Sargon's inscriptions see Introduction, Chronology, pp. 60f. In deporting rebels and settling their lands with military colonists from other provinces Sargon was following the policy of Tiglath-pileser III. By a similar policy and by fostering vassal rulers in the Philistine plain, he was either providing a buffer zone against Egypt or building up a bridgehead for an eventual Assyrian attack on Egypt.[b] Of the localities in which the deportees were settled Halah and Gozan are probably the Chalchitis and Gausanitis of Ptolemy (5.8.14), the former on the west bank of the Tigris near the mouth of the Lower Zab, and the latter the old Aramaean city of *Tell Ḥalāf*, excavated by A. von Oppenheim (*Tell Ḥalāf*, 1931). The 'mountains of Media' (see p. 642 n.[d]) may indicate a settlement of the Israelites as garrison troops, in which capacity they were employed by the native Egyptian rulers before the Persian period at Elephantine and Asswan, and later by Ptolemy I in Libya.[c] Doubtless those settled at Gozan and Halah, nearer the Assyrian homeland, would be those whose allegiance was suspect. This very scanty account of the fall of Samaria is supplemented by Sargon's 'Display Inscription': 'Samaria I besieged and captured; 27,290 of its inhabitants I carried away; 50 chariots I collected from them; the rest I allowed to keep their property; I set my governor over them, and imposed the tribute of the former king upon them.'[d] The comparatively small number of chariots in proportion to the deportees is actually quite considerable when we reflect that since the loss of Galilee, Sharon, and Gilead only the immediate neighbourhood of Samaria is in question. Since those that remained were sufficiently spirited and numerous to join Aramaeans of Syria in a revolt headed by Ilu-bi'di of Hamath in 720, on the suppression of which Babylonian settlers were planted in Palestine, we may question if the 27,290 may not refer to the total population of the province rather than to those actually deported, or if we must take the statement literally it may be that the population of the

[a]Crowfoot and Kenyon, *Samaria-Sebaste I: the Buildings*.

[b]See further E. F. Weidner, *AfO* XIV, 1941, pp. 40ff.; A. Alt, 'Neue assyrische Nachrichten über Palastina', *ZDPV* LXVII, 1945, pp. 128–46 = *KS* II, 1959, pp. 226–41.

[c]Josephus, *Contra Apionem* II, 44; J. Gray, *Cyrenaican Expedition of the University of Manchester*, 1952, ed. A. Rowe, 1956, pp. 43–56.

[d]Luckenbill, *ARA* II, § 5.

province of Samaria included many refugees from other districts taken by Tiglath-pileser in 734. It is stated on the authority of Israelite archives that Menahem levied tax on 60,000 men of property (15.19f.) while the realm was intact. Allowing, then, for a considerable number of refugees in Samaria, the 27,290 might reasonably comprise a third of that number with another 7,000 of their families. It is interesting to note that 27,290 is almost a quarter of the population of Palestine before the end of the British mandate.

(iii) COMMENT BY THE LATER DEUTERONOMISTIC REDACTOR ON THE END OF THE STATE OF ISRAEL: 17.7–17

17 [7]And [a]Yahweh was angry with Israel,[a] because the Israelites had
sinned against Yahweh their God who had brought them up from the
land of Egypt from under the hand of Pharaoh king of Egypt, and had
feared other gods, [8]and walked in the statutes of the peoples whom Yahweh had driven out before the Israelites [b](and of the kings of Israel
whom they made).[b] [9]And the Israelites uttered words which were not
right against Yahweh their God and constructed for themselves 'high
places' in all their cities from the watchman's tower to the fortified
city.[10]And they set up for themselves stelae and Asherah-symbols on
every high hill and under every green tree. [11]And they sent up the
smoke of their sacrifices there at every 'high place' just as the peoples
whom Yahweh had sent into exile from before them, and they did evil
things so that they provoked Yahweh to anger. [12]Indeed they worshipped
graven images, regarding which Yahweh had said to them, You shall
not do this thing. [13]So Yahweh testified against Israel and Judah
through [c]every prophet and seer[c] saying, Turn back from your evil
ways and keep my commandments and[d] my statutes according to the
whole law which I commanded your fathers and which I transmitted
to you through my servants the prophets. [14]But they did not hearken,
but stiffened their necks more[e] than their fathers, who did not rely on
Yahweh their God; [15]but they spurned his statutes and his covenant
which he made with their fathers and his testimonies which he adjured
upon them, and walked after inanity and became inane, and after the
peoples who were round about them, regarding whom Yahweh had

[a]The subject of *way^{e}hī* in MT is apparently the fact of the collapse of Israel stated in v. 6, but the verb demands a more direct subject, hence we adopt the reading of G^{L} *'ap yhwh ʿal-yiśrā'ēl* after *way^{e}hī*.

[b]This phrase is omitted in S, suggesting that it was recognized as a redactional gloss.

[c]Reading singular *nābī'* and attaching *w^{e}* to the sequel, *kol-nābī' w^{e}kol-ḥōze*.

[d]Adding *w* with certain Hebrew MSS, G, S, and T, assuming haplography after the final *y* of the previous word.

[e]Reading with G and S *mēʿōrep* for MT *k^{e}ʿōrep*, assuming corruption of *m* to *k* in proto-Hebraic script.

commanded them not to do as they did. [16]And they forsook all the commandments of Yahweh their God and made for themselves a molten image, even two calves, and they made an Asherah-symbol, and bowed down to the whole host of heaven and worshipped Baal. [17]And they made their sons and daughters pass through the fire, and practised divination and prognostication and they sold themselves to do evil in the sight of Yahweh so that they provoked him.

17.7. The philosophy of sin and retribution is characteristically Deuteronomistic, as is the language of the whole section, which recalls Jeremiah's indictment of the apostasy of his contemporaries, and indeed stigmatizes the same particular sins as the prophet. The sins of Israel in violation of the covenant are emphasized in the context of the *Heilsgeschichte* of the deliverance from Egypt, cf. the prelude to the Decalogue (Ex. 20.2), the revelation of the will of God, subsumed under the first commandment 'Thou shalt have no other gods before me' (Ex. 20.3), and the occupation of the promised land (v. 8). In the recitation of the *Heilsgeschichte* as a prelude to the violation of God's demands on his people the Deuteronomist is re-echoing the experience of the sacrament of the covenant from the days of the settlement of Israel in Palestine, cf. Josh. 24, which also reflects this experience.

8. The reference to the foreign cults introduced by royal decree interrupts the chronological sequence of the sins of Israel and must be treated as an early gloss, as is suggested by the omission of the phrase in S.

9. *hippē'* is a *hapax legomenon* in the Old Testament, and is taken in EVV as a by-form of the better-attested *ḥāpā* ('to conceal'), so G ('to cloak'), Rashi, Kimchi, and most moderns. A better sense is obtained, if with G. R. Driver[a] after V. Scheil, we take *ḥāpā'* as cognate with the Akkadian *ḫapu* ('to utter'), a meaning which is supported by S and T. For *kēn* meaning 'right', cf. 7.9, and, of something said, cf. Ex. 10.29; Num. 36.5, and the affirmative response cf. Josh. 2.4. With the adoption of Canaanite principles after the settlement in Palestine, Israel also practised the rites of the fertility-cult, with its stelae symbolizing Baal and the symbols of the mother goddess Asherah.

11. The infinitive construct *lᵉhakʿīs* ('to provoke') signifies not the intention but the inevitable effect, cf. Isa. 6.9ff.

12. Another principle of the Decalogue (Ex. 20.4) is violated with

[a] *The People and the Book*, ed. A. S. Peake, 1925, p. 89.

the making of images in the round (*gillūlīm*). This is not a matter of artless observation of rites of the local fertility-cult thought to be vital to agriculture, but a deliberate sin.

17.13. The inclusion of Judah in the doom of Israel here and at v. 19 indicates an exilic date, as does also the reference to the ignoring of the prophets' call to turn from their evil ways. *šūb*, however, is most distinctive of the pre-exilic canonical prophets.

14. Another element in the *Heilsgeschichte* is remembered, the obstinacy of the people Moses led through the wilderness. *he'ᵉmīn* does not mean 'to believe about', but 'to rely on'. The reference is to the reluctance of the generation of the Exodus to trust Yahweh and his agent Moses and to commit themselves to their divinely appointed destiny, and the implication is that their descendants have been equally reluctant to commit themselves to the will of God according to the admonitions and promises of the prophets. The frantic political expedients in the last phase of the history of Israel, of which Hosea (12.2) complains, attest the lack of faith of the people, cf. Isa. 7.9 *'im lō' ta'ᵃmīnū kī lō' tē'āmēnū* ('no faith, no stability').

15. The moral delinquencies of Israel, which are notably lacking here, are no doubt implied in the neglect of the statutes and covenant. The testimonies which are solemnly laid upon Israel (*'ēdᵉwōtāw 'ᵃšer hē'īd bām*) imply, according to the general usage of the phrase *hē'īd bᵉ*, a disability, and, in our opinion, visualize the principles laid upon Israel with solemn curses to which the people said 'Amen!' in the covenant sacrament so graphically described in Deut. 27. All the solemn prohibitions in the list in Deut. 27.15–26 except the first, which is against idolatry, concern social, hence moral, evils. *hebel*, usually translated 'vanity', means primarily, as the Arabic cognate suggests, 'vapour, breath', e.g. Prov. 21.6, which compares wealth accumulated through lies to 'vapour driven away', and Isa. 57.13, where *hebel* in the physical sense is parallel to *rūaḥ* in the sense of 'wind'. The notion of delusion or unreality underlies the use of *hebel* to describe the life of the Gentiles (II K. 17.15), or of the man who is indifferent to the divine law (Ps. 94.11), or has deliberately rejected discipline and whose life is haphazard and futile, the prey of chance rather than governed and stabilized by the moral law. It describes the state in which there is no discrimination between righteous and wicked, wise and foolish, as in Eccl. 2.17; 8.14. Specifically *hebel* refers to idolatry (Jer. 16.19) or to idols or pagan gods (Deut. 32.21; I K. 16.13, 26; Ps. 31.6 [7]; Isa. 57.13; Jer. 2.5; 8.19; 10.8; 14.22;

51.18; Jonah 2.8[9]). In Jer. 51.17f., there is a word-play, the graven image being said to be without *rūaḥ* and to be *hebel*.

17.16. Finally the specific sin of Jeroboam is apparently stigmatized, the setting up of molten calf-images at Dan and Bethel in direct defiance of the specific prohibition in the Decalogue. 'The two calves', however, may be a later insertion, as is suggested by the fact that *massēkā* is singular, though it might still be collective. The worship of 'the host of heaven' refers to the astral cult introduced probably from Mesopotamia, where it was much affected. The first mention of it in Israel is in the middle of the eighth century when Amos (5.26) animadverts on Sakkuth and Kaiwan, the Mesopotamian Jupiter and Saturn. We may well suppose that the Assyrian astral cult was imposed as a symbol of subjection under Menahem and Hoshea, though there is no specific mention of this. It was much more prominent in Judah in the seventh century under Manasseh (21.5), its abolition being part of the reformation of Josiah (23.4, 5, 12). The mention in 23.12 of 'the altars which were upon the roof of the upper chamber of Ahaz' suggests that the astral cult was introduced to Judah by Ahaz as a symbol of his Assyrian vassalage (16.10ff.), the cult being appropriately practised on the roofs of houses (Jer. 19.13; Zeph. 1.5).

17. On the passing of children through the fire, first mentioned historically in the reign of Ahaz, see Commentary on 16.3. This, like the worship of the host of heaven, was more particularly practised in Judah towards the end of the monarchy. In times of perplexity, such as the decline of Israel and Judah, men resort naturally to various means of ascertaining the pattern of the future, hence divination in its various forms flourished when Assyria and then Babylon cast their shadow over Palestine. Divination, though it is not confined to those later times in Israel, may nevertheless have been encouraged partly by the perplexity of the people, and partly stimulated by Assyrian and Babylonian religion, where divination flourished. As far as we may distinguish between *qāsam* and *niḥēš*, the former may be connected with divination by entrails or by the section of a liver, as suggested by the possible connection of the Hebrew word with Arabic *qasama* ('to divide'). The sense, on the other hand, may be akin to the Arabic *qismat Allāh*, the portion divided, or allotted, to each man by God. In the Old Testament passages dealing with *qesem* the sense is general, signifying the search into one's future or fate, e.g. 'fate is upon the lips of the king' (*qesem 'al-śipᵉtē melek*, Prov.

16.10). Ezek. 21.21[26] does not really help. Montgomery (ICC, p. 469), doubtless thinking of the Arabic practice of divination by arrows, for which the tenth form of the verb *qasama* is used, suggests that the word in Ezek. 21.21[26] indicates this type of divination, especially as arrows are mentioned. The fact, however, that questions put to *t^erāpīm* and hepatoscopy are also mentioned indicates that these methods as well as divination by arrows are subsumed under the general term *qāsam*. *niḥēš*, found frequently in parallelism with *qāsam*, has also so far defied satisfactory explanation, being used of hydromancy (Gen. 44.5) and for listening for a portentous word (I K. 20.33). There can scarcely be a connection with *nāḥāš* ('a serpent'), and the Arabic *nāḥiša* ('ill-luck') seems rather derived from the cognate of the Hebrew verb than *vice versa*. The connection with *n^eḥōšet* ('copper') seems at first sight hardly possible. There was, however, a time when the knowledge of metal-working, whereby an object of use and form was produced from formless ore, was a caste-secret and the object of general superstitious fear, as evidenced by the part played by metal (usually iron) as a prophylactic against supernatural influences in folklore. A relic of the association of metallurgy with the occult may survive in the general belief in the clairvoyant skill of gipsy tinkers.

(iv) A COMMENT OF THE DEUTERONOMISTIC COMPILER: 17.18

This is distinct from the second Deuteronomistic redaction (vv. 7–17, 19–20) in that, while the latter refers to the exile of Judah, v. 18 refers only to the fall of the Northern kingdom and the reduction of the people to Judah.

17 [18]And Yahweh was very angry with Israel and he removed them from his presence, and there was left none but the tribe of Judah alone.

(v) THE SIN AND RETRIBUTION OF JUDAH: 17.19f.

Possibly a continuation of the excursus by the second Deuteronomist (the redactor) (so Kittel), but possibly also a secondary comment independent of vv. 7–17, and in qualification of v. 18.

17 [19]Judah also failed to keep the commandments of Yahweh their God, and walked in the statutes of Israel which they had made. [20]And Yahweh rejected all the seed of Israel and afflicted them, and gave them into the hand of spoilers[a] until he cast them out from his presence.

[a]MT is to be preferred, as a quotation from Judg. 2.14, to the reading of G *šōsēhem* ('those who spoiled them').

(vi) COMMENT ON THE END OF ISRAEL BY THE DEUTERONOMISTIC COMPILER: 17.21–23

Here the sins of Israel are not particularized as in the comment of the Deuteronomistic redactor in vv. 7–17, but are referred to generally, their immediate consequence being the political disruption of the kingdom, which gave opportunity for the sins of Jeroboam, in which he involved Israel, which are the cause of the final collapse of the Northern kingdom.

17 [21]For he rent[a] Israel from the house of David and they made Jeroboam the son of Nebat king, and Jeroboam seduced[b] Israel from following Yahweh and involved them in great sin. [22]And the Israelites walked in all the sins of Jeroboam which he committed; and they did not turn from them. [23]So that finally Yahweh removed Israel from his presence, even as he had declared by all his servants the prophets, and Israel was deported from their land to Assyria (where they are) to this day.

(vii) ADDENDUM TO THE ANNALS OF ISRAEL ON THE ASSYRIAN RESETTLEMENT OF ISRAEL: 17.24–28

Possibly from an account by a priest of the restored cult of Bethel.

17 [24]Then the king of Assyria brought people from Babylon, from Cuthah, from Avvah, from Hamath, and from Sibraim,[c] and he settled them in the cities of Samaria in place of the Israelites, and they possessed Samaria and dwelt in its cities. [25]And it happened in the beginning of their settlement there that they did not fear Yahweh, so Yahweh sent against them lions and they killed some of them. [26]So they said to the king of Assyria, The peoples whom you have deported and settled in the cities of Samaria do not know the way of the God of the land, so he has sent against them lions, and, behold, they kill them since they do not know the way of the God of the land. [27]Then the king of Assyria gave the order, saying, Send certain[d] of the priests whom you

[a]G^L reads the Niphal for MT Qal, guided by the third plural subject of the following verb. The passage, however, refers to the oracle of Ahijah to Jeroboam I (I K. 11.32), 'I will rend the kingdom out of the hand of Solomon'. The disruption was God's punishment for sin, hence the active Qal must be kept. The disruption was a divine discipline, but, far from submitting, Israel in her obstinacy appointed a king and followed too eagerly in his ways.

[b]Reading with certain Hebrew MSS, Q, and G *wayyaddaḥ* for the *hapax legomenon wayyadda'*.

[c]Conjecturing Sibraim (cf. Ezek. 47.16), a town in northern Syria, as the association with Avvah and Hamath suggests, for MT Sepharvaim, which is not satisfactorily identified.

[d]Reading *'aḥādīm mēhakkōhanīm* ('certain of the priests'), assuming haplography of *īm*, see Commentary.

deported from there that they may go and settle there, and let them instruct[a] them in the way of the God of the land. [28]So one of the priests whom they had deported from Samaria came and settled at Bethel and instructed them how to fear Yahweh.

17.24. It is not certain when after the fall of Samaria the resettlement took place. In an inscription relating to his first year (721), Sargon records the suppression of a rising in southern Mesopotamia and the deportation of people from those regions to 'Ḫatti-land,'[b] which is the west generally, including Syria and Palestine. In Sargon's second year he had to crush a rising in the west headed by Ilubi'di (also called Yaubi'di) of Hamath, in which Samaria was involved,[c] and in his seventh year (715) he records the suppression of an Arab revolt and the settlement of captives in Samaria.[d]

Cuthah, known as the centre of the cult of Nergal, the Mesopotamian deity who slew men in the mass by plague or war, is generally located at *Tell Ibrāhīm* north-east of Babylon. *Kūthīm* survived as a Jewish term of abuse for Samaritans, and in the ninth century AD the Arab historian al-Balādhūrī in his account of the Muslim conquest of Palestine refers to the *Kushīyīn* of the mountains of Samaria.

Avvah might as well be associated with Hamath on the Orontes as with Babylon and Cuthah in southern Mesopotamia, and in 18.34, where the spelling is *ʿiwwā*, it is mentioned with Syrian localities including Hamath. Various localities have been suggested, e.g. Ammia of the Amarna Tablets, which Winckler locates near Gebel (Byblos), 'Imm east of Antioch (Sachau), and Tell Kefr ʿAya on the upper Orontes,[e] while Šanda (II, p. 225) thinks rather of an Elamite city, perhaps ʿAma conquered by Sargon in 710.

Hamath on the middle Orontes rivalled Damascus in power, though until the fall of Damascus she apparently did not strenuously oppose the Assyrian invasion. In 720 Hamath assumed the hegemony of the west Semitic rebels, for which the city was burnt, the king, Ilubi'di, killed, and 800 of the inhabitants recruited for Sargon's chariot-force and cavalry.[f]

[a]Consistently with our emendation to *'ᵃḥādīm* we read *wᵉyōrūm*, hence avoiding the difficulty felt by G[L], S, and V, where the singular is read for MT *wᵉyēlᵉkū wᵉyēšᵉbū*. The plural *wᵉyōrūm* is supported by G[BA] and T.

[b]Luckenbill, *ARA* II, § 4.

[c]*Ibid.*, § 5.

[d]*Ibid.*, §§ 17–18.

[e]Dhorme, Abel, *GP* II, p. 256.

[f]Luckenbill, *ARA* II, § 55.

Sepharvaim of MT seems to be Sibraim of Ezek. 47.16, where, as Sepharvaim of II K. 18.34; 19.13, taken by the Assyrians shortly before Sennacherib's expedition of 701, it is noted with Syrian cities. The place is named Šabara'in in the Babylonian Chronicle.[a] On this view it seems that a dittograph of *y* has occurred, *w* being then written for the first *y*, cf. the form Sepharyam in v. 31. It is held by others that 'Sepharvaim' was the Babylonian Sippar. The difficulty here is that it is listed with Avva and Hamath in Syria. Winckler therefore proposed that these two cities were inserted by the redactor from the lists of Assyrian conquests in 18.34 and 19.13.

šōmᵉrōn is, of course, the Assyrian designation of the new province of Samaria and district, called in Assyrian records Samerina.

17.25. To 'fear the Lord' is the Hebrew idiom for 'to worship' him, cf. Arabic *'ittaqā 'llāha* (lit. 'to seek protection against Allah'), so 'to show piety towards Allah'.

Lions are known in Palestine to biblical writers, e.g. Amos, Jeremiah, etc., and in the Middle Ages, e.g. to Usāma ibn Munqidh of Shayzar, who hunted them in the Valley of the Orontes. It is suggested by H. Schmidt[b] that the lions were attracted by unburied carcases in the ruined Israelite settlements. The depopulation itself would encourage their encroachment.

26. *mišpāṭ* here signifies the duly regulated order maintained by authority, here of Yahweh in his own land. Authority or rule is always implied in the root *šāpaṭ* and its derivatives; see above on 15.5.

27. Surely one priest was too few to instruct the new settlers. On our emendation of *'eḥād* to *'ᵃḥādīm* see p. 650 n.[d]. 'Certain' (*'ᵃḥādīm*) suggests careful selection, necessary in view of the revolts of the remanent Israelites in 720 and 715.

28. The mention of a single priest at Bethel does not rule out our reading of the plural *'ᵃḥādīm* in v. 27. There various priests are indicated, whose duty it was to instruct the inhabitants of the various districts. In v. 28 the reference is to the incumbent at the chief sanctuary as the supreme authority. An analogy for this supreme priestly authority is indicated in the colophons to the Baal-myth of Ras Shamra in the authority of *'atnprln*, the chief priest, for the version of these liturgical texts, where the verb is *lmd* ('teach').

[a] R. W. Rogers, *Cuneiform Parallels to the Old Testament*, 1912, p. 210.
[b] *Die grossen Propheten*, p. 7.

(viii) FURTHER DETAILS OF THE RELIGION OF THE ASSYRIAN COLONISTS: 17.29–33

These qualify the immediately preceding statement of the reintroduction of the cult of Yahweh. They are taken probably from an account by the same hand, one of the restored priests, but are possibly a comment by the Deuteronomistic redactor.

17 [29]And each people made its own god and they set them in the shrines[a] of the 'high places' which the people of Samaria had made, each nation in their cities where they dwelt. [30]And the men of Babylon made Sarpanitu,[b] and the men of Cuthah made Nergal, and the men of Hamath made Asherah,[c] [31]and the people of Avva made the altar[d] (of their god) and Atargatis,[e] and the men of Sibraim[f] burned their children in the fire to the Lordship of Melek[g] and to Anammelek, the gods of Sibraim.[h] [32]And they feared Yahweh, but they made for themselves from their whole number priests of the 'high places' and they acted for them in the shrines of the 'high places'. [33]They feared Yahweh, but they worshipped their own gods in the regular manner of the peoples from among whom they had been deported.[i]

17.29. The use of the participles with the auxiliary verb 'to be' expresses the recurrence of the practices (*GK* § 116r), and also probably the fact that this was going on in several localities. *wayyannîḥû* may signify that they laid up the idols, or brought them to rest. In view of the occurrence of the noun *nḫt* meaning 'dais' as a parallel to 'throne' (*ks'e*) in the Ras Shamra texts (*UT*, ʿnt IV, 46–47), cf. Arabic *nāḫa* ('to level'), the verb may mean that the idols were set up on their pedestals or platforms. The root occurs also, we claim, in Isa. 11.10, where we suggest that *wᵉhāyᵉtā mᵉnūḥātō kābōd* should be translated 'and his dais shall be glory'.

[a]Reading plural for MT singular, as suggested by V.

[b]Assuming that *sukkōt* of MT is a corruption of *ṣarpānīt* and *bᵉnōt* a dittograph of the second half of Sarpanitu, see Commentary.

[c]Assuming an orthodox Jewish parody (*'ašēmā*, 'guilt') of *'ašērā*, see Commentary.

[d]Assuming deliberate metathesis by an orthodox scribe for *mizbēaḥ* ('altar') and subsequent scribal corruption in MT, see Commentary.

[e]Assuming an original *ʿaṯtarʿatta*, perhaps in its Aramaic form *ʿaṯtarqatta'*, *tartaq* being an unintentional corruption. See Commentary.

[f]Reading the place-name as in Ezek. 47.16, see Commentary on v. 24.

[g]The conjecture of W. F. Albright, however, should be noted, that Adadmelek should be read.

[h]The name here approximates more closely to the form in Ezek. 47.16.

[i]The verb may be pointed as the Hophal, in which case *'ōtām* ('them') would have to be omitted, but we prefer to retain MT, taking the subject of *higlū* as indefinite, the phrase being tantamount to a passive.

šōmerōn here is the Assyrian designation of the province.

17.30. The association with Babylon has suggested that the deity was Ṣarpanitu, the consort of Marduk, the city-god of Babylon. This goddess was popularly titled Zir-banitu ('seed-creating'). The first element of MT *sukkōt benōt* suggests Sakkuth of Amos 5.26, but this deity was Ninib, and the association with Babylon suggests that we might have expected Marduk here, and, in fact, Stade has suggested Marduk-Banit. There is nothing in the consonants of MT which would suggest Marduk, though the second element may be a corruption of the end of Ṣarpanitu.

Nergal, the city-god of Cuthah, was originally associated with fire and the heat of the sun, and then with war, hunting, and disasters which destroyed men in the mass. The consort of Ereshkigal, mistress of Hell, he had as his cult-animal the lion. One of his titles is 'lord of weapons and the bow', cf. 'Resheph of the arrows'.[a]

'Ashima' seems a deliberate misvocalization of Asherah, the name of the Canaanite mother goddess. Of similar significance may be *'ašemat šōmerōn*, by which the contemporaries of Amos swear (Amos 8.14). Greek sources from the Roman imperial period, however, attest a deity *Simi* or *Seimios*, who may be named in the composite divine name Ashembethel in the Elephantine papyri. Here, however, the first element may be a dialectic variation of *šēm* ('name').[b]

31. No such Mesopotamian deity as Nibhaz (MT) is known, and an Elamite origin has been conjectured (Hommel). This is unlikely, since the worshippers are probably Syrian. More probably the word is a corruption in the early text, or possibly a wilful Jewish distortion of *mizbēaḥ* ('altar'), which is known to have been deified and so the object of worship, cf. the deification of 'the house of God' (*bēt 'ēl*) attested in the Elephantine papyri.[c]

No such deity as Tartak (MT) is known. Probably Atargatis was intended (see p. 653 n.[e]), a composite figure combining the attributes of Aṯtar, or his female counterpart, the Venus-star, and Anat, the most active goddess in the Syrian fertility-cult.[d]

[a]See M. Jastrow, *The Religion of Babylonia and Assyria*, 1898, pp. 65–68; E. Dhorme, *Les Religions de Babylonie et d'Assyrie*, 1945², pp. 38–44.

[b]A. Vincent, *La religion des judéo-araméens d'Éléphantiné*, 1937, pp. 566, 654–6, 662–76; Montgomery, ICC, p. 475.

[c]A. E. Cowley, *Aramaic Papryi of the Fifth Century BC*, 1923, pp. 18ff.; Montgomery, ICC, pp. 474f.

[d]J. Garstang, *The Syrian Goddess* (translation and commentary of Lucian, *De Dea Syra*); Montgomery, ICC, pp. 474ff.

The consonants of MT *'adrammelek* may be better pointed *'adarmelek* 'the Lordship of Melek'. The *melek* element may be either the title of an unnamed local deity of Sibraim or of the god Aṯtar, the Venus-star, whose specific title was *melek*.[a] Albright's proposal to read Adadmelek is also feasible.[b]

Anammelek means, possibly, 'Anu (the Mesopotamian sky-god) is king'. There is no specific reference to the burning of children in the cult of Anu in Mesopotamia; hence we suggest that this indicates a syncretism between the cult of Mesopotamian Anu and West Semitic Melek, the Venus-star Aṯtar, to whom human sacrifice was made.[c]

17.32. On *miqeṣōtām*, 'from their whole number', without any discrimination in favour of any priestly caste like the Levites, see Commentary on I K. 12.31; 13.33.

(ix) COMMENT ON THE WORSHIP OF THE ASSYRIAN COLONISTS: 17.34–40

This note, by a late redactor, is prompted by the statement that the worship, or fear, of Yahweh survived alongside the alien cults. We should add to the generally accepted section vv. 34b–40 the beginning of v. 34, which, like v. 40, mentions the persistence of the former ways of the settlers.

> **17**[34] Until this day they do according to their former manner;[d] they do not fear Yahweh and they do not act according to his[e] statutes and ordinances[e] and the law or the commandment which Yahweh laid upon the children of Jacob, whom he named Israel, [35]with whom Yahweh made a covenant and charged them saying, You shall not reverence other gods, nor bow down to them, nor serve them, nor sacrifice to them, [36]but Yahweh your God,[f] who brought you up from the land of Egypt with great might and with an outstretched arm, him shall you reverence and to him shall you bow down and to him you shall sacrifice. [37]And the statutes, and ordinances, and the law, and the commandment which he wrote for you you shall keep and do it for ever, and you shall not reverence other gods. [38]And the covenant which he[g]

[a]J. Gray, 'The Desert God ʿAṯtar in the Literature and Religion of Canaan', *JNES* VIII, 1949, pp. 78–80.

[b]*Archaeology and the Religion of Israel*, pp. 162–4.

[c]M. Jastrow, *op. cit.*, pp. 88f.; J. Gray, *op. cit.*, pp. 78–81.

[d]Reading *kemišpāṭām hārī'šōn* with G^{L} and B^{BA}, cf. v. 40.

[e]Sense demands the third masculine singular pronominal suffix for third masculine plural of MT.

[f]Adding *'elōhēkem* with G^{L} and V as in v. 39. The severely formal rhetorical style of the passage compels uniformity in phraseology.

[g]Reading third masculine singular for MT first singular, with G, and V, and in agreement with the rest of the passage.

made with you you shall not forget, nor shall you reverence other gods, [39]but Yahweh your God shall you reverence, and he will deliver you out of the hand of all your enemies. [40]But they did not listen, but continued to act according to their former manner.

This whole passage is thoroughly Deuteronomistic in thought and solemn rhetorical style. Unlike the first Deuteronomist, the compiler, the author of this section does not animadvert on the defection to the sins of Jeroboam or to any particular sin except worshipping other gods in defiance of the law of God. The language is general, stereotyped and repetitive, and loftily aloof from the actual situation.

(x) ANOTHER COMMENT ON THE ACCOUNT OF THE SYNCRETISTIC RELIGION OF THE INHABITANTS OF THE PROVINCE OF SAMARIA: 17.41

This is from a later period than the account in question, which occurs in vv. 29–33, but independent of vv. 34–40, which does not admit that Yahweh was reverenced at all.

17 [41] And these peoples reverenced Yahweh and served their graven images, also their children and their children's children as their fathers did, so they do to this day.

IV

JUDAH ALONE: II KINGS 18–25

1. THE REIGN OF HEZEKIAH: 18.1–20.21

In contrast to the preceding section, where significant reigns like that of Jeroboam II (14.23–29) are passed over by the Deuteronomistic compiler with the scantiest reference to events of real political importance, for which the reader is directed to historical sources (e.g. vv. 25, 28), the account of the final phase of the history of Judah is much more full and detailed, though still deficient in historical perspective. The narrative now expands, though it is not free from the limitations characteristic of the Deuteronomistic compilation, the major interests of which are fully apparent in the uneven treatment of this eventful reign. As in the account of the reign of Ahab, which totally ignores such a significant event as the Battle of Qarqar, the account of Hezekiah's reign omits any reference to his intrigues among the vassals of Assyria in the coastal plain and the drastic reduction of his territory which resulted from this disastrous venture of Hezekiah into power politics, which is so fully described in the records of Sennacherib. For more detailed information of the extent and nature of Hezekiah's reformation, for instance, we should gladly have foregone the half-chapter on his boil. With Hezekiah, in spite of the space devoted to his reign, the Deuteronomistic compiler stimulates only to disappoint our curiosity, and for a true appraisal of the actual historical significance of his reign we are obliged to use the factual Assyrian records and the often indirect references in the Books of Isaiah and Micah.

The reign of Hezekiah is introduced (18.1–8) and concluded (20.20f.) with the familiar Deuteronomistic summary, synchronism and reference to other historical sources. There is what appears to be a citation from the Annals of Judah referring to the fall of Samaria and the transplanting of deportees (vv. 9–11), with a further Deuteronomistic comment on these events (v. 12). Then after a general historical introduction which notes very summarily the beginning and end of Sennacherib's campaign of 701 (18.13–16), the account suddenly expands into a narrative, apparently of two embassies from Sennacherib's field headquarters to Hezekiah in Jerusalem, demanding his surrender (18.17–37; 19.9b–13), Hezekiah's reaction (19.1–5; 14–19), the encouraging oracle(s) of Isaiah (19.6f., 20–34, of which we believe that the composite passage 19.21–31 is secondary), accounts of the Assyrian withdrawal and the fulfilment of the oracle in 19.6f. (19.36, 35 and 37). This is followed by passages from prophetic tradition concerning Isaiah in his relations with Hezekiah, in the sickness of the king (20.1–11) and the Babylonian delegation (20.12–19) (for analysis, see below, pp. 696, 701f.), in which the dominant figure is no longer Hezekiah, as in 19b–35, but Isaiah. The space devoted to Hezekiah is comparable to that given to Ahab and his house, where the length of the treatment and the content is due to the fact that the annalistic matter and the narrative of the secular history of the period is amplified by prophetic biography, which originated and was transmitted in the circle of the prophet's associates. This analogy raises the question as to how far this section in Kings actually depends on prophetic biography. Indeed, the close verbal correspondence and the order of 18.13, 17–20.19 with Isa. 36–39 poses the problem as to whether the passage in Kings is from prophetic biography used by the compiler of Kings as a background to the history of the period or a historical source used by the editor of Isaiah as a background to the words and work of the prophet.

Quite simply it may be stated that the fact that the same order is observed in both Kings and Isaiah in spite of the loose chronological arrangement[a] and the variety of sources, suggests that both cannot be drawn independently from a common source, but that one is dependent on the other. The fact, that this matter in the Book of Isaiah, which seems at first sight prophetic biography, including Isaiah's oracles in certain crises of Hezekiah's reign, stands where it does in a prose context at the end of the compilation mainly comprised of the poetic oracles and traditions of Isaiah of Jerusalem would indicate, as Šanda (II, p. 315) suggests, that it may well have been

[a]II K. 20.1–19 || Isa. 38.1–8, 21f.; 39.1–8 probably antedates II K. 18.13 || Isa. 36.1 and II K. 18.17–19.37 || Isa. 36.2–37.38.

a later addendum to the main Isaianic tradition. Moreover, the annalistic note of Sennacherib's expedition in the 14th year of Hezekiah, which serves as a prelude to the account of his reign in both Kings and Isaiah, certainly indicates the priority of the version in Kings, which is supported by the abridgement of the annalistic digest of II K. 18.13–16 in Isaiah. We would still maintain, however, that the matter belongs mainly to the Isaiah legend, though we agree with Šanda that its place at the end of the collection of the oracles and biographical traditions of Isaiah of Jerusalem indicates that it was secondary matter on the periphery of the Isaiah-cycle, which was incorporated into the Book of Isaiah after its inclusion in the Deuteronomistic compilation of Kings.

Closer study of the passage 18.17–19.37, however, indicates that the matter is by no means simple. The passage has been held by most critics since Stade[a] to consist of two parallel versions, 18.17–19.9a, 36f., and 19.9b–35, a notable exception being Šanda,[b] whose view that the passage is to be taken literally as referring to two different delegations has not commanded wide consent among critics. The two accounts differ in the tradition of the reason for Sennacherib's so very abrupt withdrawal. The former credits Isaiah with knowledge of internal conditions in the Assyrian homeland (19.7, on which the historical note on the death of Sennacherib by the hand of two of his sons [19.37], evidently disappointed since the designation of a younger son Esarhaddon as heir apparent, is probably a commentary). The latter version attributes the dramatic relief of Jerusalem, promised by Isaiah, to the sudden desolation wrought in the camp of the Assyrians by 'the angel of Yahweh' (19.35). The reason for this sudden expansive treatment of what may only be a single phase in the reign of Hezekiah in the Deuteronomistic History lies mainly in the subject matter, the themes of the inviolability of Zion, the site of the Temple and throne of the divine king, a doctrine developed in the liturgy of the New Year festival during the monarchy, which was maintained by the Deuteronomistic compiler, and that of prophecy and fulfilment (see Introduction, pp. 11–13) in the tradition which associated Isaiah with this crisis. A further explanation of the exceptionally full treatment of this phase of the reign of Hezekiah lies in the nature of the sources. Here Hezekiah is presented as a model of piety and deference to prophetic guidance, which explains the inclusion of the relatively

[a]B. Stade, *ZAW* IV, 1884, pp. 173ff.
[b]Šanda, *op. cit.*, II, pp. 289ff.

lengthy treatment in narrative prose of the episodes of Hezekiah's illness (20.1–11; Isa. 38.1–8, 21f.), which is supplemented by the psalm in Isa. 38.9–20, and the Babylonian embassy (20.12–19; Isa. 39).

In II K. 18.13–16, the substantial correspondence with the annals of Sennacherib[a] indicates close reliance on an annalistic source, though the narrative style and summary of details indicates adaptation by the Deuteronomistic compiler. This passage undoubtedly refers to Sennacherib's third campaign in 701 BC, the only expedition which he records against Hezekiah. On that occasion Hezekiah was stripped of all but Jerusalem and possibly his family, or crown, possessions, being pent up in the city 'like a caged bird' and obliged to pay a heavy indemnity, as 18.14f. states.

18.17ff., on the other hand, apparently visualizes a successful resistance by Hezekiah, with Jerusalem remaining untaken. The reason given for Sennacherib's withdrawal, trouble in the homeland culminating in his death at the hand of his sons (19.7, 37), suggests that this passage may refer to a later expedition towards the end of Sennacherib's reign, though in fact no such expedition against Hezekiah or Tirhakah is recorded by Sennacherib. It has been claimed that the reference to 'Tirhakah king of the Sudan' in 19.9 relates the incident of the Assyrian delegation in the sequel to the end of Hezekiah's reign rather than to Sennacherib's expedition of 701 BC. This is not a new view, having been first advanced by the Assyriologists Winckler[b] and R. W. Rogers,[c] but it has recently received fresh currency since Laming Macadam's interpretation of epigraphic evidence from Kawa by Dongala in the Sudan, which, he claims, proves that Tirhakah (689–664) would have been too young to take the field against Sennacherib in 701.[d] This view has, however, been

[a]Luckenbill, *ARA* II § 233f.; A. L. Oppenheim, *ANET*, pp. 287ff.

[b]Winckler, *Alttestamentliche Untersuchungen*, 1892, pp. 28ff.

[c]R. W. Rogers, 'Sennacherib and Judah', *Wellhausen Festschrift*, 1914, pp. 319ff.

[d]Laming Macadam, *The Temples of Kawa I: The Inscriptions*, 1949, followed by W. F. Albright, *BASOR* 130, 1953, pp. 8ff.; 140, 1956, pp. 25ff.; J. Bright, *History of Israel*, 1960, pp. 282ff., and the present writer in the first edition of this book, pp. 602ff. Apparently influenced rather by the chronological note on Hezekiah's accession in II Kings 18.1 than by difficulties which Macadam's findings raised over the age of Tirhakah in 701, H. H. Rowley, 'Hezekiah's Reform and Rebellion', *BJRL* XLIV, 1962, pp. 420ff., follows de Vaux, *BJ*, p. 212, and Noth, *History of Israel*, 1960^2, p. 268, in taking the mention of Tirhakah as an inaccuracy, he being simply cited as the best known of the Sudanese dynasty in an obscure period of Egyptian history. It is further proposed by T. H. Robinson, *History of Israel*, I,

questioned by J. Leclant and J. Yoyotte[a] in a review of Macadam's book. Their interpretation of the relevant evidence is that the Sudanese dynasty (the XXVth Egyptian Dynasty) had already penetrated northwards to dispute supremacy in the Delta with the XXIVth dynasty. The predecessor of Tirhakah, his brother Shabatkah, may have acceded as early as 701 and reigned till 689, when Tirhakah succeeded him. Tirhakah was summoned to the Delta in the second year of his reign, when he was thus old enough to be of political and military significance. Thus Tirhakah may well have been engaged against Sennacherib in the end of his campaign of 701–700 BC, as 19.9 states, though the reference to him as 'king' is an anachronism. The passage, however, is accurate in describing him as 'of the Sudan'. Thus the mention of Tirhakah in 19.9 need not of itself indicate two campaigns of Sennacherib in the West.

In the accounts of the Assyrian delegation, Hezekiah's reaction and Isaiah's oracle(s) in 18.17–19.7 and 19.9b–34, with their respective conclusions in 19.36f. and 19.35, there is undoubted agreement despite variations the chief of which are the poetic oracles of Isaiah in 19.21–28 and 29.31. This could just possibly be a case of the fusion of traditions concerning two different episodes, but there are certain considerations which point to parallel traditions of the same episode, probably in the only known Assyrian expedition against Hezekiah in 701 BC. If from a literary point of view 18.17–19.37 were a historical passage, then there would be a serious doubt of its reference to the same episode and certainly to the historical situation of 701 noted in the historical passage in 18.13–16. But 18.17–19.37, despite the proportion of prose narrative, is not of the literary genre of history, but belongs rather to popular anecdotal tradition centring on the prophet Isaiah and 'the good king Hezekiah' and the general theological theme of God's vindication of his honour and the inviolability of Zion, the place of his throne, a theme familiar in cult-liturgy and re-echoed on occasion by the prophets, especi-

---

1932, p. 459, Montgomery, ICC, p. 483, N. H. Snaith, 'Kings', *IB* III, p. 292, and Rowley, *op. cit.*, pp. 41ff., that the date of Hezekiah's revolt in I K. 18.13 should be emended from 'the fourteenth year' to 'the twenty-fourth year'. This would be a simple error in cyphers, but seems to the writer to raise more questions than it solves in the general chronology of the period (see above, p. 74).

[a]J. Leclant and J. Yoyotte, 'Notes d'histoire et de civilisation éthiopiennes', *Bulletin de l'Institut Français d'Archéologie Orientale du Caire*, LI, 1952, pp. 15–27.

ally Isaiah of Jerusalem.[a] We have already noted the view that this matter stands on the periphery of the authentic tradition of Isaiah of Jerusalem (see above, pp. 658f.), which probably accounts for the discrepancies between the parallel accounts in II K. 18.17–19.7, 36f. and 19.9b–35 and 18.13–16. When the literary character of 18.13–16 and 18.17–19.37 respectively, with their different interests and emphases, is appreciated, there is no longer any insuperable difficulty in referring the whole to the Assyrian invasion of 701 BC. Indeed, despite the triumphant note in the account of the withdrawal of Sennacherib, which is the theme of the prophet's assurance, the fact remains that in all passages Hezekiah was reduced and humiliated, and what is celebrated in 18.17–19.37 is not a Jewish victory but a profound relief at the withdrawal of Sennacherib after the reduction of the whole kingdom and the confinement of Hezekiah to Jerusalem. If we seek for a historical nucleus in 18.17–19.37, it may be found in v.9 in the suggestion that the occasion of the Assyrian delegation to Jerusalem was to warn Hezekiah, who had probably submitted, not to be encouraged by the démarche of Egypt, to which 18.21 may also refer.

Though there is now general consent among scholars that 18.17–19.7, 36f., possibly including 19.8–9a, and 19.9b–35 are two parallel versions of Sennacherib's delegation to Hezekiah, there is difference of opinion as to where 18.17–19.7 ends and 19.9b–35 begins. Stade, noting the substance of Isaiah's oracle in v. 7 that Sennacherib would 'hear a rumour' and withdraw, takes the statement in v. 9a that Sennacherib heard of Tirhakah's advance to be the actualization of this oracle. In this case he takes the verb *wayyāšob* in the last clause of v. 9, not with the following verb in the sense 'and he again (sent)', but as meaning 'and he returned', this being the conclusion of 18.17–19.7, to which vv. 36f. may be a later historical comment. This view seems to be supported by I Q Is[a] 37.9, which adds *wayyišmaʿ* before *wayyāšob*, which is supported by LXX. According to this view the end of 18.17–19.7 and the beginning of the parallel version of Sennacherib's delegation have been fused together in v. 9, with subsequent adaptation of the text, including the omission of 'to his own land' after *wayyāšob*. Alternatively, *wayyāšob* in v. 9b (MT) has been

[a]G. Fohrer, *Introduction to the Old Testament*, 1968, pp. 234f.; *Das Buch Jesaja*, Band 2, 1967², p. 159, emphasizes this character of II K. 18.17–19.37, which he characterizes as 'prophetic midrash' or 'edifying legend'. On a more accurate form-critical delimitation of this composite passage and appraisal of the components see the excellent form-critical study by B. S. Childs, *Isaiah and the Assyrian Crisis*, 1967.

taken with the following verb *wayyišlaḥ* in the sense 'and he again sent' as the introduction to the parallel version in 19.9b–35. The problem of the end and beginning respectively of the first and second versions will probably never be solved to the satisfaction of all critics. There will, however, be agreement on the fact that v. 9 serves as a bridge between the two accounts of the delegation of Sennacherib. *wayyāšob* in v. 9b may well have belonged at the end of the former version at this point, but it may have been adapted as the beginning of the second after the combination of the two. The note on the return of the Rabshakeh to Sennacherib, now at Libnah, not Lachish (v. 8), may be the secondary introduction of a historical note to explain what the compiler assumed to be a second delegation. Thus we take both vv. 8 and 9 to be editorial bridges between the two versions of the same delegation. The mention of Libnah, *Tell aṣ-Ṣāfī* on the western edge of the foothills of Judah, in conjunction with the report of the advance of 'Tirhakah the king of the Sudan' (19.9), despite its association with a context in 18.17–19.37, which is not of the literary category of history, probably preserves a genuine historical tradition. It agrees in two important points with Sennacherib's own account of the campaign in that Eltekeh, where the important battle took place, is in the vicinity of Libnah and the Assyrian annals mention, though not by name, 'the king of the Sudan (Kush)'. There is thus no difficulty in associating the context of 19.8f. with the historical situation of 701 summarized in 18.13–16. It may describe the first diplomatic contact between the Assyrians and Hezekiah. This would explain the apparent discrepancy between the statement of Hezekiah's capitulation in the Assyrian annals and in 18.14f. and the fact that in 18.17–19.37 he apparently did not capitulate. The submission at Lachish in 18.14 may have been subsequent to the delegation, the note 'from Lachish' in 18.17 being possibly an inaccuracy, influenced by the mention of Lachish in 18.14. The sparing of Jerusalem may actually have been the result of Hezekiah's policy in hesitating to submit while as yet the potential of Egyptian and Sudanese aid was uncertain (18.21), while at the same time not embarrassing Sennacherib's army in the flank and the rear. Hezekiah's enforced, yet convenient, neutrality may explain how when he was stripped of so much of his kingdom he was allowed to retain Jerusalem, which tradition in 18.17–19, 37 claimed as a vindication of the cultic theme of the inviolability of Zion.

Though we would emphasize that in view of the literary character of 18.17–19.37, which differs from the historical summary in 18.13–16, we cannot expect the same accurate rendering of the historical situation, it is not on that account to be assumed that the passage has no historical relevance. Here a valuable contribution has been made by B. S. Childs (*op. cit.*) on the basis of form-criticism, in which he has succeeding in differentiating the two versions in 18.17–19.7, 36 and 19.9b–35 in respect of form and theological content, drawing out the implications admitted by G. Fohrer that the first version is more circumstantial, with the reflection of an actual historical situation. This Childs finds in the speeches of the Assyrian officer, which characterize and largely occupy the first version in contrast to the second, which is characterized by the prayer of Hezekiah (19.15–19) and prophetic oracles (19.21–28; 29–31 and 32f.). It is noteworthy that in the second version only one argument of the Assyrian officer (19.10–13; cf. 18.30, 32b–35) is used of the four in the first version (18.19–21, 23f.: Egyptian aid is a delusion; vv. 22, 35: How can the Jews trust Yahweh, whose rural sanctuaries Hezekiah has abolished? Sennacherib may claim that his successes are evidence of the favour of Yahweh; vv. 31–32a: Join in my good fortune . . . live and not die!; and 30, 32b–35: Yahweh will be no more effective to deliver Jerusalem than the gods of other conquered peoples had been effective). This undoubtedly sets the second version into the category of Fohrer's 'edifying legend'.

Noting the significance of the opening of the speech of the Assyrian officer in 18.19a as the formal introduction to an official communication, Childs draws attention to the style of the succeeding communication, which differs strikingly from what the introduction leads one to expect. It is not strictly a communication from Sennacherib, but a series of arguments in diplomatic disputation in which the envoy is given liberty to exploit the reaction of his hearers as he may see opportunity. Childs adduces a formal analogy in the notice of just such a delegation from Tiglath-pileser III to the King of Babylon in revolt, who heard the demands and arguments of the envoys, and their attempts to split the opposition, behind his barred city-gate.[a] The content of the Assyrian's arguments, too, bears the stamp of historical verisimilitude both in the appraisal of the political situation and the assumption of the implications of Hezekiah's abolition of the rural sanctuaries of Yahweh, which we see no good reason to

[a]H. W. F. Saggs, ' "The Nimrud Letters", 1952—Part I', Iraq, XVII, 1955, pp. 21–56; ' "The Nimrud Letters", 1952—Part II', *ibid.*, pp. 126–60.

doubt, as involving an offence against Yahweh. This reflects Assyrian logic and is a cunning appeal to popular misgivings, since the local sanctuaries were undoubtedly in favour, probably through long association with families in Israel and notable kinsmen whose tombs ('high places') there, as of those who had possessed the divine blessing, were probably visited like the *wālī* among the Arabs.

The respective roles of the prophet and Hezekiah differ in the two versions, though both reflect a common tradition. In the first, Hezekiah performs the rites of a fast and resorts to the Temple (19.1), from which he sends officials and priests to Isaiah (v. 2) to implore his prophetic office in intercession (v. 4), an aspect of the prophetic office well attested until the time of Isaiah (I Sam. 12; Amos 7.1–6) and at the end of the monarchy (Jer. 7.16; 37.3ff.; Joel). Here it is not stated that Isaiah interceded nor that an oracle was sought. Instead, the prophet gives an oracle reassuring Hezekiah that the Assyrians would withdraw as the result of a rumour. It is not certain what the content of that may be. The reference to the withdrawal 'to his own land' (v. 7) may indicate domestic trouble, which, originating with Sennacherib's designation of a younger son Esarhaddon as his co-regent, cost him his life at the hands of his disappointed elder sons, of which v. 37 is aware. This, however, was later in the reign of Sennacherib, and may be either from the circle who preserved the tradition of Isaiah or even from the Deuteronomistic compiler himself, reflecting the theme of prophecy and fulfilment. Apart from the actual control of the oracle, the reassurance of the prophet, and certainly his intercessory role, has historical verisimilitude. The role of Hezekiah, though it reflects to his credit as a reformer and one duly dependent on God's means of grace, does not exceed that of any other king in such an extremity, in fasting and seeking the intercessory office of the prophet. So far the passage exhibits none of the features of Fohrer's 'edifying legend' and does reproduce a historical situation with considerable verisimilitude. The well-marshalled argument of the Assyrian officer, however, obviously does not depend on archival tradition and, likely enough in itself and probable in substance, may still reflect in its present form the composition of the Deuteronomistic compiler, who thus provided a background to the edifying legend in 19.9b–35, with its theme of the prophetic oracle (19.21–28) that God would take vengeance for the affront, or blasphemy, of the Assyrian, with which, as a parallel version of the same incident in prophetic tradition, he was familiar.

The second version, with its account of Hezekiah's pious reaction and the citation of his prayer (19.15–19), with its animadversion on the Assyrian's affront to Yahweh in alleging that he is no more effective than the gods of the conquered peoples (vv. 10–13, cf. 18.33–35) and its Deuteronomic monotheism, which recalls the great lyrics on the subject in Deutero-Isaiah,[a] bears the clear stamp of 'edifying legend', which singles out the conduct of Hezekiah as exemplary. Hezekiah has become the type of the righteous king whose heart is perfect before God, so far removed from the Hezekiah of II K. 18.13ff.[b] The prophet is here introduced not as bidden by the king to intercede, but as sending, evidently unprompted, an oracle assuring the king that his prayer in extremity has been heard. This reproduces the convention of the fast-liturgy, where the Plaint of the Sufferer, of which Hezekiah's prayer is an adaptation, culminates in a reassuring oracle (e.g. Ps. 60.6–9 [8–11]). In this context the actual content of the oracle is not so precise as vv. 21–28, 29–31, or 32f., nor indeed so full, so that it is likely that those passages are secondary, inserted at this point, where Isaiah is introduced, owing to their standing on the periphery of the Isaiah tradition and dealing with the theme of the inviolability of Zion as the site of the throne of Yahweh, a theme well established in pre-exilic cult-tradition. This theme, which is common to all three oracle-groups, vv. 21–28, 29–31 and 32f., is suggested by the Assyrian officer's citation of Hezekiah's claim in 19.10, cf. 18.30. The oracle on the deliverance of Zion in vv. 21ff. may well be drawn from the liturgy of the New Year festival, to which one should relate Ps. 46 on the same theme. The liturgy of this festival, with its theme of the triumph of God as King over the forces of Chaos, continually fostered the faith of Judah in extremity and in turn often reflected deliverance in historical crises, a notable instance being probably Nahum's effusion on the downfall of Nineveh, which P. Humbert[c] feasibly takes as that prophet's contribution to the liturgy of the first New Year festival after the fall of Nineveh in 612 BC. This cultic experience of the sovereignty of God, on which Isaiah had already animadverted in his Immanuel oracle, citing the theme of the New Year liturgy in Ps. 46 in the historical crisis of 734, by which Israel again rallied her faith in 701, may be the real source of the tradition of God's vindication of his honour and the preservation

[a]As O. Procksch, *Jesaja* I, 1930, p. 452, noted.
[b]Childs, *op. cit.*, p. 100.
[c]P. Humbert, 'Le problème du livre de Nahoum', *RHPR* XII, 1932, pp. 1–15.

of Zion expressed in II K. 19.9b–35. The character of the second version, developed as 'edifying legend', is sustained in the conclusion in v. 35 in the tradition of the miraculous destruction of the whole Assyrian army in a single night.

The theology of the second variation is much more mature than in the first. The theme is no longer simply the earnest prayer of the prophet or king for the relief of Jerusalem, but rather the vindication of the honour of Yahweh as the one living and true God in the face of Assyrian affronts. This is the subject of Hezekiah's prayer (19. 15–19) and the oracle in vv. 21–28, especially vv. 22f. This passage then may well have been incorporated by the exilic Deuteronomistic redactor as distinct from the compiler to whom we owe 18.17–19.7, 36f.

In ch. 19, after Isaiah intervenes with an assurance that Hezekiah's prayer is heard (v. 20), the passage continues with what is apparently a long poetic oracle (vv. 21–28), but which may really consist of several small units, and the declaration of a 'sign' (vv. 29–31). From the examples of prophecy known to us, we may expect Isaiah to have conveyed his oracle as verse, so that his *ipsissima dicta* may reasonably be sought in the poetic section 19.21–34. On the other hand, the sober prose oracle which is attributed to Isaiah in 19.6f. has nothing in form and practically nothing in content in common with the vivid figures in the lively poetic oracles in vv. 21–34. There is, however, nothing in these which, to judge from what may be genuinely oracles of Isaiah of Jerusalem in the Book of Isaiah, may not be his.[a] Šanda (II, p. 296) distinguishes between the taunt-song on the king of Assyria (19.21b–28), which alone de Vaux (*BJ*, p. 202) relates to 701, though admitting the Isaianic style of the rest, and the reassuring oracle on Jerusalem and Judah (vv. 29–31) and the final comprehensive oracle (vv. 32–34) referring to the withdrawal of the king of Assyria and Yahweh's protection of his city 'for David's sake'. These, however, may be elements of the same sustained oracle. In the reference to the economic hardship in vv. 29f., it is hard to avoid the conclusion that this relates to the dereliction of the land denuded by Sennacherib's campaign of 701. Our conclusion is that, though vv. 21–34 may be a sustained poetic oracle of Isaiah, it is more likely to be a series of oracles traditionally associated with the Assyrian wars of his time by the prophetic group associated with him, who preserved his oracles. They were probably genuinely Isaiah's, but not certainly

[a]For instance, the encouraging oracles in Isa. 7.3–9 in the crisis of 734 BC.

so, and the oracles may not all have been declared at the same time.

The difference in emphasis which we have noted in the sections 18.13–19.7 and 19.9b–35 is undoubtedly owing to the fact that in the first passage the Deuteronomistic compiler has elaborated on historical tradition and the redactor in the latter on an edifying legend and cult-tradition.

The final section on the reign of Hezekiah (20.1–19 || Isa. 38–39, with a slight modification in order and lacking the prayer of Hezekiah [Isa. 38.9–20], which is a psalm of the type Plaint of the Individual Sufferer) falls into two episodes, the sickness of Hezekiah and the reassuring oracle of the prophet with the sign of the receding shadow (20.1–11 || Isa. 38.1–8, 21f.), which may be two independent traditions, and the incident of the Babylonian delegation and the prophet's rebuke of Hezekiah (20.12–19 || Isa. 39). These two incidents are related in the text, the Babylonian delegation having as a pretext congratulations on the recovery of the king from illness (20.12b || Isa. 39.1b), but we suspect that this is an artificial attempt of the editor to associate two distinct episodes. If the king's illness were so trivial as to be healed by a fig-plaster, it is not likely that the news penetrated to southern Mesopotamia. The date of the king's illness is uncertain. It seem probable that the episode is put towards the end of the account of Hezekiah's reign because of the statement that he 'was sick unto death' (20.1), and the mention of the 14th year of his reign of 29 years (18.2) may have suggested the tradition that the prophet in the name of God guaranteed him 15 more years (20.6).

The date of the embassy of Merodach-baladan (Marduk-apal-idinna) is uncertain. This inveterate rebel seized the throne of Babylon at the beginning of the reign of Sargon II in 720 and held it till he was expelled by Sargon in 709. He took refuge in the marsh-land at the head of the Persian Gulf and emerged again on the death of Sargon, when he succeeded in occupying Babylon for some nine months in 703 before he was finally expelled. The embassy may have been connected with the rebellion in the west mentioned in Isa. 20.1, when Sargon dispatched an expedition to Ashdod to suppress a revolt fomented by Egypt in his eleventh year, i.e. 711 (Isa. 20);[a] or, it may have been in 703 or 702 before, rather than after, the revolt of Hezekiah and his allies in 701, as the present arrangement of MT suggests. The remarkable difference of the prophet's attitude to the

[a]Luckenbill, *ARA* II, § 30.

house of David, on the exile of which in Babylon he animadverts (20. 17f.; cf. 19.34; Isa. 9.6f. [5f.]; 11.1), indicates that if this tradition did relate to Isaiah, it was retouched either in the Exile or, as Šanda suggests (II, p. 314), towards the end of the seventh century by someone of Jeremiah's circle. The centrality of the prophet in this chapter indicates that this is part of a prophetic biography of Isaiah, though, as its place in the Book of Isaiah suggests, it is from the periphery of the Isaianic tradition.

(*a*) THE DEUTERONOMISTIC INTRODUCTION TO THE REIGN OF HEZEKIAH: 18.1–8

18 1Now[a] in the third year of Hoshea the son of Elah king of Israel, Hezekiah the son of Ahaz king of Judah was designated king. 2He was twenty-five years of age when he became king and he ruled in Jerusalem for twenty-nine years, and his mother's name was Abijah[b] the daughter of Zechariah. 3And he did right in the sight of Yahweh according to all that David his father had done. 4He it was who abolished the 'high places' and broke in pieces the standing stones and cut down the Asherah-symbols[c] and cut up small the bronze serpent which Moses made, for until those days the Israelites were in the habit of sacrificing to it and they called[d] it Nehushtan. 5He trusted in Yahweh the God of Israel and after him there was none like him among all the kings of Judah, nor any that were before him. 6And he adhered to Yahweh; he did not turn away from following him, but he kept his commandments, which Yahweh commanded Moses. 7And Yahweh was[e] with him, and[f] in all his expeditions he was successful, and he revolted against the king of Assyria and did not serve him. 8He defeated the Philistines as far as Gaza [g]and its vicinity,[g] both watchmen's tower and fortified city.

18.1. According to the dating of the attack upon, and fall of, Samaria (723–2) relatively to the careers of Hoshea and Hezekiah (17.1, 6, which see), Hoshea must have acceded in 731 and Hezekiah have been designated heir-apparent in 729. Probably appointed by Tiglath-pileser in 732, Hoshea was either not able to establish himself until 731, or the dating of his reign from this year is from a Judaean scribe, who reckoned with an accession-year.

[a]Omitting MT *wayehī* with S and V.

[b]Reading the form as given in the parallel passage in II Chron. 29.1. MT *'abī*, however, may be an abbreviation.

[c]Reading plural *'ašērōt* with one Hebrew MS and G, S, and V.

[d]Reading plural with G^L, S, and T, though the singular of MT might be retained, signifying the indefinite subject.

[e]Reading *weyhwh hāyā* for MT *wehāyā yhwh*, which might, however, be retained expressing frequency, so Burney (*Notes on . . . Kings*, p. 338).

[f]Inserting the conjunction with G^B, S, and V.

[g]Reading *weʿad-gebûlehā* after two Hebrew MSS and G.

18.2. Here the age of Hezekiah is his age when he became sole ruler in 714. Only on this reckoning, Hezekiah being born in 738, may this statement be reconciled with the statement that his father was 20 when he became co-regent in 734. See further Introduction, Chronology, p. 74.

4. This reads like an excerpt from an annalistic source. It has been thought that the reference to the religious reforms of Hezekiah in v. 22 reflects the reforms of Josiah, and it is maintained[a] that this is supported by the fact that Isaiah does not mention any such reformation under Hezekiah. That might well be, but there is no reason to suppose that the nationalist policy of Hezekiah did not have as its religious aspect the centralization of the cult. There is no indication in Kings of any appeal by Hezekiah to Israelites remaining in the north in his presumed centralization of the cult, as in II Chron. 29–31, but, since there is no mention in the account of Josiah's reformation of the abolition of the brazen serpent, this at least might stand to the credit of Hezekiah, and there is no good reason to deny him the credit of the reformation described in this verse, though we should emphasize the limited scope of Hezekiah's reformation compared with that of Josiah. See further, p. 717.

The responsibility of Moses for the making of the bronze serpent is probably merely traditional, this indicating the antiquity of this cult-symbol at Jerusalem. The story of its role as a prophylactic against serpents in Num. 21.6–9 (E) is an aetiological myth. The traditional association with Moses either simply indicates its antiquity or is an attempt to legitimize it, since it was a legacy of the pre-Israelite cult of Jerusalem,[b] of which Zadok in the time of Solomon was perhaps the hereditary priest.[c] The serpent is a well-known feature in the Canaanite fertility-cult, being specifically associated with the mother-goddess Asherah in pendant reliefs from the Late Bronze Age at Ras Shamra[d] and on clay-moulded incense-altars of the pre-Israelite period at Bethshan,[e] and possibly represented entwined round the lower limbs of a robed female figure at *Tell Beit Mirsīm*.[f] This association may have suggested the role played by the

[a]By Duhm, *Das Buch Jesaia*, 1914^3, pp. 234ff., and H. Schmidt, *Die grossen Propheten*, 1923, p. 9.
[b]So H. H. Rowley, 'Zadok and Nehushtan', *JBL* LVIII, 1939, p. 123.
[c]Mowinckel, *Ezra den Skriftlærde*, 1916.
[d]*Syria* XIII, 1932, pl. IX.
[e]A. Rowe, *The Four Canaanite Temples of Bethshan*, 1940, pl. LVIII.
[f]Albright, *AASOR* XVII, 1938, pp. 42ff., pl. 214.

serpent in the story of the fall of man through Eve in Gen. 3. A small bronze serpent was actually found near the 'high place' of Gezer in what Macalister reported as an Early Bronze Level.[a] It is uncertain whether Nehushtan signifies a serpent (*nāḥāš*) or, as we think more probable, a bronze object (*n^{e}ḥōšet*), such as the silver-plated bronze cult-standard with relief and incised design of a human face flanked by two serpents, probably Asherah, found in the Late Bronze Age sanctuary at Hazor.[b]

18.5. The phrase *wa'^{a}šer hāyū l^{e}pānāw* ('and who were before him') comes in somewhat awkwardly, and seems a later addition, as appears from the fact that David at least has been forgotten among Hezekiah's predecessors.

7. The statement of Hezekiah's uniform success reflects the Deuteronomistic opinion of the merits of a reformer rather than the actual course of history, in which the king's political projects against Assyria met with frustration and his realm was severely docked in consequence. Here is evidence of the beginning of the legend of the good king Hezekiah, which is used in 19.9b–35, and in II Chron. 32.

8. This statement, as is suggested by the emphatic position of the personal pronoun, which is a feature of the archival style, is probably drawn from the Annals of Judah. Hezekiah's activity in conjunction with anti-Assyrian elements in the Philistine plain had been devoted to removing Assyrian nominees, best known of whom was Padi of Ekron, who was held in custody in Jerusalem. Gaza had once determinedly opposed Sargon under Hanno, but latterly was held for Assyria by a loyal vassal Ṣilli-Bel, who was rewarded by territory stripped from Judah by Sennacherib after his campaign of 701.

(*b*) THE FALL OF SAMARIA AND THE DEPORTATION OF ISRAEL: 18.9–11

Probably from the Annals of Judah, introduced by a chronological note by the compiler.

18 [9]In the fourth year of king Hezekiah, that is, the seventh year of Hoshea the son of Elah king of Israel, Shalmaneser king of Assyria made an expedition against Samaria and laid siege to it, [10]and took[c] it; at the end of three years in Hezekiah's sixth year, that is, the ninth year of

[a]R. A. S. Macalister, *The Excavation of Gezer* II, 1912, p. 399, fig. 488.
[b]Y. Yadin and others, *Hazor* II, 1960, pp. 117f., pl. CLXXXI.
[c]Reading singular with G, Symmachus, S, and V for MT plural, and taking it with v. 9 as the sequel in v. 10 requires.

Hoshea king of Israel, Samaria was captured. [11]And the king of Assyria deported Israel to Assyria and settled[a] them in Halah and on the Habor, the river of Gozan and in the mountains[b] of Media.

18.9. The reckoning is from the year 729/8, in which Hezekiah was designated heir-apparent, the fourth year from which by inclusive reckoning was 726/5, when the Assyrian records attest an expedition by Shalmaneser V, the destination unspecified. That was the seventh year of Hoshea's reign reckoning inclusively from 731.

10. On the view that Samaria fell to Shalmaneser in 723/2, and the basis of Sargon's claim to have reduced the city, see Introduction, Chronology, pp. 60–62.

11. See on 17.6.

(*c*) DEUTERONOMISTIC COMMENT ON THE FATE OF ISRAEL: 18.12

18 [12](Because they did not listen to the voice of Yahweh their God, but transgressed his covenant, all that Moses the servant of Yahweh commanded, nor listened, nor did it.)

(*d*) HISTORICAL DIGEST OF SENNACHERIB'S CAMPAIGN OF 701: 18.13–16

From the Annals of Judah, but compiled possibly by a priest, as the interest in the Temple (v. 16) suggests.

18 [13]Now in the fourteenth year of King Hezekiah, Sennacherib king of Assyria made an expedition against all the fortified cities of Judah and took them. [14]And Hezekiah king of Judah sent to the king of Assyria at Lachish saying, I have done wrong. Withdraw from me and[c] whatever you impose on me I will bear. So the king of Assyria imposed on Hezekiah king of Judah three hundred talents of silver and thirty talents of gold. [15]And Hezekiah gave all the silver which was to be found in the Temple of Yahweh and in the palace treasury. [16]At that time Hezekiah cut up the doors of the Temple of Yahweh and the doorposts which Hezekiah king of Judah had overlaid, and he gave them to the king of Assyria.

13. This is one of the cardinal dates in the chronology of the Hebrew monarchy, since we have in the annals of Sennacherib[d] a synchronism with the firm chronology of Assyria. The date of the expedition, Sennacherib's third, is 701, hence Hezekiah acceded as sole king

[a]Reading *wayyannīḥēm* with the versions for MT *wayyanḥēm* ('and he led them').
[b]Reading *hārē* with G for MT *ʿārē* ('cities'), see 17.6.
[c]Inserting *wᵉ* before *'et* with G[L], S and V.
[d]Luckenbill, *ARA* II, §§ 233ff.

in 714, and any reference to an earlier date for his reign (e.g. the synchronism with the reign of Hoshea in v. 1) refers to his designation as heir-apparent in 729. It should be noted, however, that a number of scholars,[a] in dating Hezekiah's reign from 727 according to the synchronism with the reign of Hoshea, assume a scribal error in v. 13 of *'arbaʿ ʿeśrē(h)* for *'arbaʿ w^{e}ʿeś^{e}rīm* ('14' for '24'), which would refer to 704 or 703, when, it is contended, Hezekiah prepared for the revolt preceding Sennacherib's campaign in 701. A certain lapse of time before Sennacherib's punitive expedition is natural, though we doubt if the situation would have been allowed to develop so long as three years, and the reference in v. 13 is explicitly to Sennacherib's campaign and the reduction of Judah, that is, to the end of the campaign in 701 and not to Hezekiah's preparation. Besides, we find other grave chronological difficulties (see Introduction: Chronology) in dating Hezekiah's accession as sole king so early.

The fortified cities in question were mainly in the frontier region. According to Sennacherib's account of this expedition, Hezekiah and his allies had interfered with his nominees in the centres in the Philistine plain; hence his main objective was that region and the frontier area between Judah and the plain, particularly fortified places commanding the passes to the interior, such as Timnah, Eltekeh, and Bethshemesh in the Vale of Sorek (*Wādī aṣ-Ṣurār*), Libnah (cf. 19.8), Azekah, Soco, and Jarmuth in the Vale of Elah (*Wādī as-Sanṭ*), and Lachish, the great bastion of Judah in the south-western foothills, where his headquarters were fixed. Many more places were taken, Sennacherib mentioning 46 major, and an unspecified number of minor, places. The confinement of Hezekiah in Jerusalem 'as a bird within its cage', which Sennacherib claims, refers possibly not to a siege, which neither the Old Testament nor the Assyrian records claim, but to his overrunning of the country and stripping from Hezekiah all but his immediate neighbourhood and his crown possessions, and assigning these as new Assyrian provinces to his vassals such as Mitinti of Ashdod, Padi of Ekron, and Ṣilli-Bel of Gaza. Since there is no mention in the Old Testament of the deportation of 200,150 men of the people of Judah, which Sennacherib claims, the reference is probably to the population of the districts overrun and now taken from Judah. Possibly the number

[a]T. H. Robinson, *History of Israel* I, p. 456; Montgomery, ICC, p. 483; Snaith, 'Kings', *Interpreter's Bible* III, p. 292; Rowley, 'Hezekiah's Reform and Rebellion', *BJRL* XLIV, 1962, pp. 411ff.

ought to be 2,150.[a] Olmstead,[b] in noting instances of exaggeration in later editions of Assyrian royal annals and display inscriptions, suggests that 150 may be more realistic, those being no doubt local notables.

18.14. Lachish (see on 14.19) is known from Sennacherib's palace reliefs at Nineveh[c] as his headquarters, probably during this campaign. The siege and defence of the city is forcibly depicted, with the Assyrian victory as its culmination. Sennacherib is depicted on his throne receiving the submission and tribute of the conquered, who are led as prisoners of war on foot and with the rest of the booty on ox-wagons. R. D. Barnett[d] emphasizes the protracted siege of Lachish, indicated by the arrow-heads of bone-splinters found outside the walls, which indicates that the supply of metal was running short. He also emphasizes the significance of Lachish as a base from which to intimidate and control the Philistine plain and to operate against a relief force from Egypt. We note that this passage in Kings makes no mention of Hezekiah's successful defiance of Sennacherib in Jerusalem.

ḥāṭā' in this context has a double meaning. From Sennacherib's point of view it means a grave offence against his authority; from the point of view of Hezekiah it means an error of judgement.

nāśā' here, as in its use in prophecy, means the imposition and assumption of a burden.

There is a striking, if not absolute, agreement in the figures here with the statement in Sennacherib's account of his expedition in 701 that he imposed on Hezekiah a tribute of 30 talents of gold and 800 talents of silver. The discrepancy is only partly accounted for by the assumption that the Old Testament reckoned heavy talents and the Assyrian inscription reckoned light talents. But this does not explain the absolute agreement in the matter of the gold talents. Possibly the 300 talents of silver was the amount available in stamped ingots, and the extra mentioned in the Assyrian inscription is that obtained from other sources, such as the despoliation of the Temple and the palace treasury. Again, the 30 talents of gold and 300 of silver may be the amount of the tribute which the priestly compiler knew to have been taken from the Temple treasury, the surplus being drawn from the

[a] So A. Ungnad, *ZAW* LIX, 1943, pp. 199–202.
[b] *Assyrian Historiography*, p. 8.
[c] In British Museum: inscription in Luckenbill, *ARA* II, § 156.
[d] 'The Siege of Lachish', *IEJ* VIII, 1958, pp. 161–4.

palace. A possible clue to the weight of precious metal taken by the Assyrians is an official two-thirds mina weight of Shalmaneser V (727–22 BC; *ANEP*, Pl. 119), which would give a talent of 59.82 kg, according to R. B. Y. Scott.[a] The Assyrian records mention many other commodities sent by Hezekiah, which indicate the amenities of court life in Jerusalem of that day. Sennacherib's annals mention a levy made on the family and harem of Hezekiah, which pointedly emphasized his vassal status.

18.16. The *hapax legomenon ʾōmᵉnōt*, if genuine, means 'supports', and must in the context denote doorposts. Ehrlich proposed to read *māginnōt* ('shields'), thinking doubtless of the case of Rehoboam (I K. 14.26).

(*e*) ONE ACCOUNT OF HEZEKIAH'S DEFIANCE OF SENNACHERIB, STIMULATED IN HIS EXTREMITY BY AN ORACLE FROM ISAIAH: 18.17–19.7

A historical narrative of the first contact of Hezekiah with the Assyrians in 701, freely rendered by the Deuteronomistic compiler (see pp. 662ff.).

18 [17]Then the king of Assyria sent [b]the commander-in-chief and the High Chamberlain and[b] the chief aide-de-camp from Lachish to Jerusalem[c] to king Hezekiah with a strong force[d] [e]and they went up and came to Jerusalem,[e] and they halted at the conduit of the Upper Pool, which was by the embankment of the Fuller's Field. [18]And [f]they summoned the king,[f] and Eliakim the son of Hilkiah the royal chamberlain went out to them with Shebna the scribe and Joah the son of Asaph the royal herald. [19]And the chief aide said to them, Say now to Hezekiah, Thus says the Great King, the king of Assyria, What security is this in which you trust? [20]You think that mere words[g] of

[a]'Weights and Measures of the Bible', *BA* XXII, 1959, p. 32.

[b]The account in Isa. 36 omits *tartān wᵉʾet-rab-sārīs wᵉʾet-*, and the sequel, which visualizes only *rab šāqē*, supports this text.

[c]Isa. 36 reads *yᵉrūšālayᵉmā* immediately after *millākīš*.

[d]Pointing as the absolute *bᵉḥayil*.

[e]These words are omitted in Isa. 36, but the dittograph of them in the present passage indicates their originality. The text continues in Isa. 36 with *wayyaʿamōd*, which suggests that the singular should be used in the verbs in the present passage if we omit mention of any Assyrian officers but *rab šāqē*.

[f]Isa. 36 omits these words, and in view of the fact that the message of the delegation was conveyed to the king by his officers (II K. 18.37; 19.1) it seems that the text of Isaiah should be followed here.

[g]Reading plural with G.

mouth are counsel and strength for war. So[a] now on whom do you rely that you have rebelled against me? 21 [b]See, you have relied on this crushed reed of a staff, Egypt, which, if one lean upon it, will go into his hand and pierce it, just so is Pharaoh king of Egypt to all who rely on him. 22 And if you say[c] to me, Our trust is in[d] Yahweh our God, is this not he whose 'high places' and altars Hezekiah has abolished, saying to Judah and Jerusalem, Before this altar shall you bow down in Jerusalem? 23 So now make wager with my lord the king of Assyria, and let me give you two thousand horses if you can put riders on them. 24 How then will you repulse[e] one of the least of my lord's servants, you who rely upon Egypt for chariots and cavalry? 25 And[f] now is it without Yahweh that I have undertaken this expedition against this place to destroy it? Yahweh it was who said to me, Make an expedition against this land and destroy it. 26 And Eliakim [g]the son of Hilkiah and Shebna and Joah[g] said to the chief aide, Speak to your servants in Aramaic, for we understand it, and do not speak with us in the dialect of Judah in the hearing of the people on the wall. 27 But the chief aide said,[h] Is it to[i] your master and you that my master has sent me to speak these words? Is it not to[j] the men who are sitting on the wall that that they may eat their own dung[k] and drink their own piss[l] with you. 28 Then the chief aide stood and shouted with a loud voice in the dialect of Judah[m] and said, Hear the words[n] of the Great King, the king of Assyria. 29 Thus says the king, Do not let Hezekiah deceive you, for he cannot deliver you.[o] 30 And do not let Hezekiah direct your trust

[a]Inserting *w*ᵉ before *ʿattā* with G^BAL.

[b]G^L, L, and S and Isa. 36 omit *ʿattā* of MT.

[c]G, S, and Isa. 36 (MT) read singular, but the Qumran Isaiah (1 QIs^a) supports MT, which we accept.

[d]We might have suspected the corruption of *ʿal* to *ʾel*, but the latter is used in v. 30, though Isa. 36 reads *ʿal*.

[e]Omitting *paḥat* ('provincial governor') as a dittograph and corruption of *ʾaḥad*.

[f]Inserting *w*ᵉ before *ʿattā* with certain Hebrew MSS, G^BAL, S, and Isa. 36.

[g]Isa. 36 omits the words. It would be natural to associate others with Eliakim, however.

[h]Isa. 36 omits MT 'to them', a reading supported by the singular pronominal suffixes which follow.

[i]The reading of Isa. 36 *haʾel* for MT *haʿal* is preferable on account of the preposition.

[j]We prefer to read *ʾel* for MT *ʿal*, though Isa. 36 also reads *ʿal*.

[k]The pointing of MT in Isa. 36 indicates the pointing in the present passage as *ḥᵃrēhem*, MT being pointed in Q as if read *ṣōʾātām* ('their excrement').

[l]The pointing of *šynyhm*, which should probably be *šēnēhem*, is given euphemistically in Q with the vowels of *mē raglēhem* ('the water of their legs').

[m]Omitting MT *wayᵉdabbēr* with certain Hebrew MSS, V, and Isa. 36.

[n]Reading plural with G, V, and Isa. 36 for singular of MT.

[o]Omitting *miyyādō* ('from his hand') of MT with certain Hebrew MSS, G^AL, S, V, and T. If these words are retained the pronominal suffix of *miyyādō* must be altered to *y*.

to Yahweh saying, Yahweh will deliver us and[a] this city[b] will not be given into the hand of the king of Assyria. [31]Do not listen to Hezekiah, for thus has the king of Assyria said, Join in my good fortune and surrender to me, and eat each his own vine and fig tree, and drink each the water of his own cistern [32]until I come and take you to a land like your own land, a land of corn and must, a land of bread and vineyards[c], a land of olives[d] and oil and honey, and live and not die, and do not listen to Hezekiah lest[e] he move you saying, Yahweh will deliver us. [33]Did the gods of the peoples deliver[f] each one his own land from the hand of the king of Assyria? [34]Where are the gods of Hamath and Arpad? Where are the gods of Sibraim and [g]where were the gods of the land of Samaria[g] that they should deliver Samaria from my hand? [35]Who among all the local gods is there who has [h]delivered his land[h] from my hand that Yahweh should deliver Jerusalem from my hand? [36]And the people were silent[i] and answered him not a word, for it was the king's order, Do not answer him. [37]Then Eliakim the son of Hilkiah the royal chamberlain came with Shebna the scribe and Joah the son of Asaph the royal herald to Hezekiah with their clothes torn and they reported to him the words of the chief aide.

19 [1]And it happened, when King Hezekiah heard it, that he tore his clothes and covered himself in sackcloth and came into the Temple of Yahweh. [2]And he sent Eliakim the royal chamberlain and Shebna

[a]G[BA] and Isa. 36 (MT) omit *w*[e] before *lō'* in MT, but 1 QIs[a] supports MT in the present passage.

[b]Certain Hebrew MSS and MT of Isa. 36 omit *'et*, taking *hāʿîr* as the subject of the Niphal *tinnātēn*, but 1 QIs[a] agrees with MT of the present passage. In this case the Niphal must be the passive with the agent suppressed, tantamount to the active verb with the indefinite subject (see *GK* 221b).

[c]This whole passage is omitted in Isa. 36, and it seems that the compiler has expanded a little here in order to describe Palestine.

[d]If the words of MT are read here we should probably follow S and V and read *zayit w*[e] (*yiṣhār*).

[e]MT *kî* . . . meaning 'for Hezekiah would move you', though not unintelligible, is inferior to the reading of Isa. 36 *pen* . . . 'lest . . .'

[f]Isa. 36 omits the infinitive absolute and attaches the interrogative particle directly to *hiṣṣîlū*.

[g]Omitting *hēnaʿ w*[e]*ʿiwwā* of MT with G[BL] and Isa. 36. The Targum takes them as the Hiphil of *nūaʿ* and the Piel of *ʿāwā*, meaning 'he sent them wandering and caused them to stray', cf. Symmachus on the parallel passage in Isa. 37.13 *anestatōse kai etapeinōse* ('displaced and humiliated them'), reading *ʿinnā* (for MT *ʿiwwā*). G[L] and L read instead *w*[e]*'ayyē '*[e]*lōhē 'ereṣ šōm*[e]*rōn* ('and where are the gods of the land of Samaria?'), which is suggested by the immediate sequel. In any case a reference to Samaria is obviously natural so soon after the fall of the Northern kingdom rather than a reference to more distant places.

[h]Reading singular *hiṣṣîl* and *'arṣō* with G[L] and S for MT plural *hiṣṣîlū* and *'arṣām*. The plural pronominal suffix would demand the plural *'*[a]*rāṣōt* in the context.

[i]Reading *wayyaḥ*[a]*rîšū* with Isa. 36. It is interesting to note that the 1 QIs[a] has the same reading as MT, which we reject.

the scribe and the elders of the priests covered with sackcloth to Isaiah the prophet the son of Amoz. [3]And they said to him, Thus says Hezekiah, A day of distress and chastening and contumely is this day,

For children have come to the birth,
And there is no strength to bring forth.

[4]It may be that Yahweh your God will hear[a] the words of the chief aide whom the king of Assyria his master has sent to reproach the living God, and will punish him for the words which Yahweh your God has heard, so undertake intercession for the remnant which are still here. [5]So the servants of King Hezekiah came to Isaiah. [6]And Isaiah said to them, Thus shall you say to your master, Thus says Yahweh, Fear not because of the words which you have heard, with which the flunkeys of the king of Assyria have blasphemed me. [7]See I will put a spirit in him and he shall hear a rumour and shall withdraw to his own land, and I shall cause him to fall by the sword in his own land.

18.17. The *tartanu* was the commander-in-chief of the Assyrian army, an officer who led the expedition to the Egyptian border in the reign of Sargon (Isa. 20.1).

rab sārīs, in Hebrew 'chief eunuch', is the title of a senior military officer in Jer. 39.3, 13. It has been suggested that *rab sārīs* may be a corruption, perhaps wilful, of the Assyrian title *rab ša rēši* (lit. 'the chief of the head'), perhaps the chief of the king's bodyguard. *sārīs*, however, is a well-known official title at the Israelite court, and there is no reason to suppose that there were not corresponding officials in the Assyrian court.

rab šāqē may either be 'chief butler', but no longer designating the literal services of a butler, or 'chief officer', *rab šāqū*.

Lachish is depicted in Sennacherib's relief from Nineveh as his headquarters in his expedition of 701 (see on v. 14), and a place as strategically sited as Lachish (*Tell ad-Duweir*) in the south of the Shephelah, was a natural base for operations against Judah, the Philistine plain, and the Egyptian border. Traces of the siege depicted on Sennacherib's reliefs (probably in 701) have been found in weapon-heads of the period, armour scales, and the crest-socket for a helmet-plume from the roadway leading up to the gate of the city.[b] The expedition, or embassy with armed escort, from Lachish would agree with Sennacherib's account of his advance first along the coast

[a]Omitting MT *kol* ('all') with certain Hebrew MSS, G[AL], S, and Isa. 37.
[b]O. Tufnell, *Lachish III, The Iron Age*, p. 55.

and the coastal plain of southern Palestine. A detachment from the main expedition on their way through the plain, however, may be visualized, resulting in the first contact between the Assyrians and Hezekiah before Hezekiah's surrender to Sennacherib at his headquarters at Lachish (v. 14), which may have suggested 'Lachish' in the secondary passage in the present context.

The Assyrian delegation was apparently backed with some force, though it is questionable if it was more than an escort. There is no mention of military action, such as blockade and circumvallation, which Sennacherib mentions in his account of the expedition against Jerusalem in 701.

The location of the canal of the Upper Pool by the 'highway' of the Fuller's Field has been much disputed. The first point to be observed is that the same location is given for the memorable meeting of Ahaz and Isaiah (Isa. 7.3). There are various views which associate the Upper Pool with a lower one connected by a canal. The Upper Pool has been connected with the Pool of Siloam, and the presumed lower one with *Birket al-Ḥamrā*, which is now an orchard, at the lower end of the Tyropoeon Valley. The view that *Birket al-Ḥamrā* was the Upper Pool and the presumed lower one was an unknown pool above En Rogel (*Bīr Ayyūb*) outside the city wall south of Ophel (de Vaux), seems unlikely in view of the remoteness of the point from the palace and administrative centre of the city. The view of G. A. Smith[a] is that the channel was the well-known channel, mostly open, running along the contour of the south-eastern hill above the Kidron Valley from *'Ain Umm ad-Darāj* (Gihon) to *Birket al-Ḥamrā*, for which he claims the support of Neh. 3.16 for a constructed pool at Gihon. This is supported by Vincent,[b] who cites the rock-cuttings of the enlarged basin around the now subterranean spring of Gihon. The difficulty here seems to be 'the highway', if this is what *m^esillā* means here. In view of the fact that the northern limit of the city until the time of David was just north of the spring, it might be that 'the Great North Road' was indeed here. Or *m^esillā* may mean rather a ramp, cf. *sōl^elā* (19.32), such as is probably visualized as leading to the Horse Gate immediately north of the Spring of Gihon (11.16; II Chron. 23.15; Jer. 31.40; Neh. 3.28). Or, it might mean an 'embankment' for a dam just below the Spring of Gihon, where it may have been fed from one of the lateral sluices from the canal along

[a] *Jerusalem* I, pp. 106ff.
[b] L. H. Vincent, *Jérusalem de l'Ancien Testament* I, 1954, p. 200.

the south-east hill. Here the Assyrian envoy would be near the palace and administrative quarter of the city and would be audible not only to those who manned the wall, now to be located much lower down the eastern slope of the south-eastern hill[a], but also to those in the houses clustering on their terraces and buttresses on the steep slope above the wall. If, as seems likely from the Hebrew text, a certain show of military power was made, even a small force would not naturally camp here, but by the northern or western wall of Jerusalem, where they could occupy ground not lower, but actually higher than the city. Here the main highway that connected Jerusalem with the outside world in Hezekiah's time would run out of the Ephraim Gate (see on 14.13), and a reminiscence of the present incident seems to be contained in Josephus's reference to the area just north of the north-west angle of the present old city as 'the camp of the Assyrians'.[b] The present passage implies that the canal was, at least partly, outside the city wall, but the Upper Pool need not have been outside. If it were a catchment basin it would be outside, but J. Simons[c] claims that Isa. 7.3 implies that Ahaz's meeting with Isaiah was where the conduit flowed *into* the Upper Pool, which must have been inside the city. In the north the Patriarch's Bath just north-west of the present Jaffa Gate, or the Mamilla Pool still further west of the Jaffa Gate (the north-west angle of the city in Hezekiah's time) have been proposed,[d] but, as Simons suggests, these might have been catchment basins, but, so far beyond the wall, could not have been the Upper Pool of Isa. 7.3. Dalman[e] suggested that the Upper and implied Lower Pools were not connected by any canal, but were two independent pools in two different parts of the city, though the designation Upper and Lower City is not attested until Josephus, as Simons points out.[f] Actually, apart from the spring of Gihon, which fed *Birket al-Ḥamrā* by the open conduit on the eastern side of Ophel, probably from the time of Solomon, as R. Weill suggests,[g] the natural catchment area for the Temple and the higher (northern) part of the city, which developed west of the Temple, was the depression, still called *'Arḍ al-birkeh*, north-west of the present Damascus Gate at the head of the valley which bisected the new part of the city from north to south and was called, by a mistranslation of the Hebrew original in

[a]K. M. Kenyon, *PEQ*, 1963, p. 9. [b]*War* V, 7.3; 12.2.
[c]*Jerusalem in the Old Testament*, 1952, p. 334.
[d]G. B. Gray, ICC on Isa. 7.3, and Šanda II, pp. 250–3.
[e]*PJB* XIV, 1918, p. 66. [f]*Op. cit.*, p. 337 n.
[g]*La Cité de David* II, 1947, pp. 58ff.

Josephus, the Tyropoeon Valley.[a] The flood-water from this basin might have been led by canal into the upper city by the then 'great north road' ('the highway') and ponded in the valley about the south-western corner of the Temple area, a point most convenient to Temple, palace, and upper city. The Lower Pool would then be the Pool of Siloam (the *miqwā* of Isa. 22.11). which now received the water which used to run into 'the old pool' (Isa. 22.11), i.e. *Birket al-Ḥamrā*. The Fuller's (better Washerman's) Field (*śᵉdē kōbēs*), known only from this passage and its parallel in Isa. 36.2 and from Isa. 7.3, can only be located relatively to the canal which fed the Upper Pool and the 'highway', or possibly 'ramp', or 'embankment'. It obviously had a connection with the water, and, as *śᵉdē* indicates, was beyond the wall. Our conclusion is that Dalman's view must be rejected for lack of evidence, and that Simons' view that 'the end of the conduit of the Upper Pool' need not indicate the inflow to the Upper Pool. We propose that it indicates the end of the conduit *from* the Upper Pool, i.e. the basin of the Spring of Gihon. Admittedly, the more natural meaning would be as Simons suggests, but the curious usage might indicate the common source of the canal because it was diverted as need arose into the *Birket al-Ḥamrā*, which was used for irrigation, or into the depression at the south-west corner of the city, where water was poured in emergency and where Hezekiah was later to lead his tunnel. The point of divergence was where Ahaz was supervising when Isaiah confronted him (Isa. 7.3), and this must be also where the Assyrian envoy delivered his message, being attracted there, in spite of the distance from the palace, by curiosity to know whether the water had been diverted, which would give an indication of how well-prepared, or determined, Hezekiah was to withstand siege. In this case, we would suggest that *mᵉsillā* means not highway, but 'embankment', and that it denotes the embankment either damming 'the Old Pool', or *Birket al-Ḥamrā*, which, being clear of the city, may have been used by washermen, or the embankment between the Lower Pool, or Pool of Siloam (Isa. 22.11), and the lower *Birket al-Ḥamrā*. In this case there may indeed be a con-

[a]This conspicuous feature of ancient Jerusalem is unnamed before Josephus, unless it is the 'Outer Valley' of the Copper Scroll from Qumran, i.e. that on the western extremity of the ancient settlement on the south-eastern hill. The adjective *haḥyṣwn*' ('outer') is plausibly conjectured by J. M. Allegro (*The Treasure of the Copper Scroll*, 1960, pp. 153ff.) to have been mistaken by the redactors of Josephus for a noun spelt in the same way, but derived from a root *ḥwṣ* attested in Aramaic meaning 'to bind', hence 'to coagulate', e.g. cheese or curds.

nection between *kōbēs* and *rōgēl*, in the place name En Rogel, though this is merely hypothetical.

18.18. Eliakim is honourably mentioned in Isa. 22.20ff. as the person destined to succeed Shebna as royal chamberlain. On the three offices see on I K. 4.2.

19. 'Great King' was the self-designation of the kings of Assyria.

20. The meaning of this problematic verse is probably that the diplomatic talk of Egypt was no more than mere talk and no adequate substitute for strategy and military power. Sennacherib, like Isaiah (chs. 18–20; 30.1–7; 31.1–5), had truly taken the measure of Egypt, and with the invasion of Egypt under Sennacherib's son Esarhaddon[a] the goal of Assyrian policy in the west was attained.

21. The reference to Egypt as a 'crushed reed-cane' (*qāne rāṣūṣ*) is repeated in Ezek. 29.6, which suggests that this was the subject of a popular proverb. The truth of the observation of the Assyrian was bitterly experienced by Judah right until her final collapse.

22. The reference to Hezekiah's reformation and his centralization of the cult is often held to be a reflection of Josiah's reforms. Such measures, with a political as well as a religious aspect, were, however, normally suggested by the collapse of the last of Northern Israel in 722 (see further critical introduction to this section). The Assyrians could not fail to take note of these reforms, owing to the relevance to their subjects in the northern provinces of Palestine.

23. *hitʿārēb* is taken in AV as 'to give pledges', which the verb means in the Pentateuch, and in RV as 'to make a wager' (lit. presumably 'to pledge stakes in a wager'), cf. Prov. 20.19; 24.21, 'to enter into contract with', cf. *ʿārēb* in the Qumran *Manual of Discipline* (vi. 22), *ʿārēb ʾet-hōnō*, 'to share one's wealth' (*ibid.* vi. 17; vii.24f.; viii.23). The taunt reflects the contempt of the foremost military tacticians of the day for the forces of Hezekiah as mere militia-men, not only inadequate in numbers, but inexperienced in mobile warfare.

25. The claim that the Assyrians had progressed by the permissive will of Yahweh repeats the sentiment of Isa. 10.5ff., that Assyria is the rod of the anger of Yahweh, without, naturally, regarding this as merely incidental.

26. The linguistic ability of the Assyrian officer in Hebrew and Aramaic, though notable, is natural in the officer of an Empire whose

[a]Luckenbill, *ARA* II §§ 584ff.

subjects in western Asia and even in Mesopotamia were so largely Aramaean. Illustrative of this fluency of the Assyrian chancellory in Aramaic is a letter from one Assyrian officer, Beletir, to another, Pir-Awur, in the reign of Assurbanipal (664–626).[a] The use of Aramaic as a Semitic *koinē* in the Near East is further indicated by Aramaic-Akkadian bilingual texts from the Babylonian period and from the Aramaic papyrus letter from Saqqara from one Adon, ruler of a principality in the Philistine plain or in Syria appealing to the Pharaoh for help against the Babylonian invaders, probably in 605.[b] The reference to Hebrew as Jewish probably indicates the dialect of the court of Jerusalem and the inhabitants of the south, in contrast to which the dialect of Northern Israel, as is apparent from parts of the Elisha-saga, shows Aramaic affinities.

18.27. On the pointing of MT *ḥªrēhem* and *šēnēhem* see p. 676 nn.[k, l].

30. On the text and grammar of *lō' tinnātēn 'et-hā-'īr* see p. 677 n.[b].

31. *'ªśū 'ittī bᵉrākā* is taken by RV after the Targum as 'make your peace with me' (so Burney). Montgomery, evidently following the Targum, takes *bᵉrākā* (=*šālōm*) in the sense of 'greeting', in which sense it is used in its verbal form. 'Greeting', however, is a secondary meaning of both *bᵉrākā* and *šālōm*. In greeting, the person either communicates the blessing (*bᵉrākā*) or wellbeing (*šālōm*) he enjoys or indicates his wish to be associated with the person greeted in the blessing he evidently enjoys. In the present instance Sennacherib, confident that his star was in the ascendant (that he had the *bᵉrākā*), summons the Jews to acknowledge that fact; resistance can only set them outside the pale of the *bᵉrākā*, or blessing, reflected from Sennacherib.

32. The prospect of enjoyment of their goods until the Assyrians should resettle the Jews reveals at once the brutal frankness of the Assyrians, their confidence in their power, and their callousness to any but material values. The mention of wine (see p. 677 n.[c]) indicates mountainous regions, possibly in the foothills of Anatolia and the Iranian escarpment, where deported peoples were settled as frontier garrisons, cf. 17.6. The promise of olives, however, could not apply to any part of the Assyrian Empire except the Mediterranean region, and certainly not to the Assyrian homeland or the Iranian

[a]A. Dupont-Sommer, 'L'ostracon araméen d'Assur', *Syria* XXIV, 1944–5, pp. 24–61.

[b]A. Dupont-Sommer, 'Un papyrus araméen d'époque saïte découvert à Saqqarah', *Semitica* I, 1948, pp. 43–68.

escarpment with their continental climates.[a] Letters from the palace at Nimrud (ancient Kalḫu) somewhat earlier than this indicate that the Assyrians provided with some solicitude for the settlement of such deportees, providing native wives for Aramaeans who were settled in Assyria.[b] Saggs suggests that the request for the parley in Aramaic rather than Hebrew may have been in apprehension of the effect of such seductive inducements to the people of Jerusalem.

18.34. On the text and especially on the hypothetic place-names Hena and Ivva, see p. 677 n.[g]. Arpad, modern *Tell Erfad*, north of Aleppo, was the capital of an Aramaean state which had joined an anti-Assyrian coalition of Simirra, Damascus, and the remaining Israelites under Ilubi'di of Hamath in 720, when it had been crushed by Sargon. Arpad had first been conquered by Tiglath-pileser III in 743–40. The gods of these Syrian peoples could not be expected to deliver Samaria; hence Lucian's reading 'where are the gods of Samaria?' is demanded before the final phrase.

19.1. The king's rending of his robes and donning of sackcloth may have initiated a public fast, in which the royal emissaries also put on sackcloth. In this interim period of suspense from normal activity marked by the wearing of sackcloth, the king withdraws from public life into the Temple. The intercessory prayer, which was a feature of the fast, devolves in this narrative on Isaiah (v. 4), where a fast-liturgy like those in Joel and Amos 7.1–6 is expected of the prophet. These details and the diplomatic arguments of the Assyrian envoy directed to the people of Jerusalem, which have an analogy in a siege of Babylon (see above, p. 664), indicates the historical verisimilitude of 18.17–19.7 in the parallel. In the parallel account the fast-liturgy is put into the mouth of the king (vv. 15–19), which, if not without historical verisimilitude in view of the function of the ancient king, is probably adapted from the role of Isaiah in the first account.

2. The emergence of Isaiah is the first appearance of a canonical prophet in the historical books of the Old Testament, which are remarkably silent on the role of the canonical prophets in the history of Israel.

3. The appeal of Hezekiah is in couplets, probably under stress of emotion. The statement:

[a]D. Baly, *The Geography of the Bible*, 1957, p. 103.

[b]H. W. F. Saggs, 'The Nimrud Letters, 1952—Part III', *Iraq* XVIII, 1956, pp. 40ff.

Children have come to the birth (lit. 'breaking out'),
But there is no strength for the birth,

probably repeats a popular proverb. There may be a pointed allusion to the frustrated spirit of the people in not being able to carry through the revolt against Assyria.

19.4. *tᵉpillā* is essentially intercessory prayer. The remnant here is not the spiritual nucleus of Israel as in Isa. 6.13, but the people of Judah truncated after the loss of all except Jerusalem and its environs.

6. Isaiah's riposte to the blasphemy (*'ᵃšer giddᵉpū*) of Sennacherib's officials is to refer to them as *naʿᵃrē*, which refers to their subservience, with also, possibly, the nuance of their rashness and inexperience of the deeper workings of Providence. *naʿar* is found in the administrative texts of Ras Shamra indicating a feudal retainer.

7. Here, as ever, where it does not denote wind, *rūaḥ* is the invasive supernatural influence which either raises a man's natural functions and abilities to the plane of the extraordinary or occasions behaviour which contravenes his normal way of life (e.g. Saul's madness) or logical expectation. Panic in its various degrees was thought by the Hebrews to be the consequence of the operation of the spirit (*rūaḥ*) of God.

(*f*) THE BRIDGE BETWEEN THE TWO PARALLEL ACCOUNTS OF HEZEKIAH'S DEFIANCE OF SENNACHERIB: 19.8 (probably originally including 9a)

One of these is apparently associated with the Assyrian delegation from Lachish and the other with that from Libnah. The mention of Lachish, however, here and in 18.17, may indicate an adjustment of the text after the arrangement of 18.17–19.37 after 18.13–16, with the note on Hezekiah's final surrender to Sennacherib at Lachish (18.14). The phrase 'for he heard that he had decamped from Lachish' may be such an editorial adjustment. Verse 9a, ending with *wayyāšob*, especially as suggested by 1 Q Isᵃ, which reads *wayyišmaʿ wayyāšob* ('and he heard and returned') may have been the original ending to the first account, but it has been adjusted to bridge, with v. 8, the gap between the first and second accounts. See Introduction to the section, pp. 662f.

19 [8]And the chief aide returned and found the king of Assyria fighting against Libnah, for he had heard that he had decamped from Lachish.

19.8. On Libnah, which we locate at *Tell aṣ-Ṣāfī*, commanding the entrance to the Vale of Elah (*Wādī as-Sanṭ*), see on 8.22.

nāsaʿ means 'to pull up', e.g. tent-pegs (Isa. 33.20; Job 4.21, reading *yeṯēdām* for MT *yitrām*), hence 'to decamp', or 'to journey on'.

(*g*) THE PARALLEL ACCOUNT OF THE ASSYRIAN SUMMONS TO HEZEKIAH AND HIS REACTION, ENCOURAGED BY AN ORACLE FROM ISAIAH: 19.9–20

This is from the edifying legend of the good king Hezekiah. The oracle of Isaiah assures Hezekiah that his prayer is heard (v. 20) and is probably amplified by the oracle on the inviolability of Jerusalem (vv. 32–34), with v. 35 as a later historical comment. If this oracle really belongs to the incident of 701 BC, the content of the 'rumour' is uncertain. As it is, it has been associated with the domestic troubles and assassination of Sennacherib (cf. 19.37) by the addition of v. 7b, a later adjustment.

19 9And he heard about[a] Tirhakah the king of the Sudan, saying, He has come forth to fight with you, and he again[b] sent messengers to Hezekiah saying, 10Thus shall you say to Hezekiah king of Judah, Do not let the God in whom you trust deceive you saying, Jerusalem shall not be given into the hand of the king of Assyria. 11See, you have heard what the kings of Assyria have done to all the lands, destroying them utterly. And will you be delivered? 12Did the gods of the peoples whom my fathers destroyed deliver them, Gozan, Harran, Rezeph, the people of Beth Adini and[c] those in Telassar[d]? 13Where[e] is the king of Hamath, and the king of Arpad?[f] 14Then Hezekiah took the letter[g] from the hand of the envoys and read it,[h] and went up to the Temple of

[a]Reading *ʿal* for MT *ʾel* with Isa. 37.9.

[b]MT definitely understands a second delegation, reading as it does *wayyāšob wayyišlaḥ*, which was read also by G. This reading is questioned by the reading *wayyišmaʿ* in the parallel passage in Isa. 37.9, and, in reading *wayyišmaʿ wayyāšob*, 1Q Is[a] may have preserved the original tradition of the end of the first account in the withdrawal after Sennacherib had heard the rumour mentioned in v. 7. As it stands, however, followed by *wayyišlaḥ*, this, too, represents the editorial adjustment of the parallel accounts in 18.17–19.7 and 19.9b–35.

[c]G^L reads 'and', which seems feasible.

[d]MT *teläʾššār* is not questioned in any text or version, but the known site of Til Bašir has been suggested (de Vaux), this being the capital of Bit Adini.

[e]Reading *ʾayyē* for MT *ʾayyō* as in Isa. 37.

[f]Omitting *ūmelek lāʿīr* after G^B, for which *melek laʿaš* has been suggested; *separwayim hēnaʿ weʿiwwā* are also to be omitted as a mere echo of 18.34.

[g]The singular pronominal suffix in *wayyipreʿšēhū* indicates that the singular should be read as in G^L.

[h]See previous note.

Yahweh, and Hezekiah spread it out before Yahweh. 15And Hezekiah
prayed before Yahweh and said, O Yahweh God of Israel who sittest on
the cherub-throne, thou alone art God for all the kingdoms of the
earth. Thou hast made heaven and earth. 16Incline thine ear, O
Yahweh, and hear; open thine eyes, O Yahweh, and see; and hear all[a]
the words of Sennacherib, which he has sent[b] to reproach the living
God. 17It is true, O Yahweh, that the kings of Assyria have utterly
destroyed the peoples and their lands, 18and have put[c] their gods into
the fire, for they were not gods, but works of men's hands, wood and
stone, and destroyed them. 19Now then, Yahweh our God, save us from
his hand that all the kingdoms of the earth may know that thou,
Yahweh, art God alone.

20 Then Isaiah the son of Amoz sent to Hezekiah saying, Thus
says Yahweh God of Israel, Inasmuch as you have prayed to me
regarding Sennacherib king of Assyria I have heard (your prayer).

On Tirhakah and the possibility of his activity in 701 BC, see Introduction to this section, pp. 660f.

19.11. It is objected by Šanda that the Assyrians did not lay cities under the sacred ban, which the root *ḥrm* literally signifies, hence he would emend MT *leha ḥarīmām* to *leha ḥarībām* as in v. 17 (MT). The present usage in MT, however, may be a secondary one, 'to devastate', since the devotion of a captured city, e.g. Jericho, involved total destruction.

12. All these places were Aramaean centres on the western frontier of Assyria. On Gozan (*Tell Ḥalaf*) see on 17.6. Harran was a centre of the cult of Sin the Moon-god from the third millennium BC. As the name signifies, it was a centre of the caravan trade between Mesopotamia, Anatolia, and Syria. Rezeph is generally identified with *Reṣafa*, once an important caravan city, the last stage before the Euphrates on the route from Damascus to Raqqa on the Euphrates via Palmyra, which is still covered with extensive Byzantine remains.[d] E. Forrer,[e] however, notes that though *Reṣappa* is mentioned as the seat of an Assyrian governor in the reign of Adadnirari and Shamsi-Adad VI neither of these kings had incorporated the district later occupied by Roman *Reṣafa*, which was only brought under Assyrian dominion under Shalmaneser III in 856; but in this expansion there is no mention of *Reṣappa*. Actually on the basis of commercial documents *Reṣappa* is to be located between *Tille* and *Isana* between

[a]Inserting *kol-* with many MSS, S, V, T, and Isa. 37.
[b]Reading *šālaḥ* with G, S and V for MT *šelāḥō*.
[c]Reading infin. absol. *wenātōn* after Isa. 37.
[d]R. Fedden, *Syria*, 1946, pp. 126ff.
[e]*Die Provinzeinteilung des assyrischen Reiches*, 1920, pp. 12ff.

the *Jebel Sinjar* and the Tigris. *b^{e}nē ʿeden* signifies the inhabitants of *Bīt Adini*, an Aramaean kingdom on both banks of the middle Euphrates at its great western bend, with its capital at *Til Bašir*, of which Telassar of MT is possibly a corruption.[a] The regions had been subjected and had suffered transportations before the end of the ninth century.

19.13. Hamath and Arpad had been subjugated in 740 and a fresh revolt had been crushed in 720. Dussaud's proposal to read *laʿaš* for *lāʿīr* cannot be accepted, since *laʿaš* was the region over which the king of Hamath ruled.

14. The letter of Sennacherib, as the verb 'spread it out' indicates, was probably on papyrus or leather in Aramaic script and language.

15. From the reference to the cherub-throne of Yahweh we may reasonably infer that Hezekiah in virtue of his sacral status was visualized as in the Holy of Holies, or at least before it, where the ark between the cherubs symbolized the presence of Yahweh. See on I K. 6.19ff.

(*h*) A COLLECTION OF TYPICAL ORACLES FROM THIS PERIOD: 19.21–35

Probably all these are from Isaiah in the reign of Hezekiah, or from the Isaianic circle, but on the periphery of the authentic Isaianic tradition.

(i) AN ORACLE ON SENNACHERIB IN THE FORM OF A TAUNT-SONG IN THE *QĪNĀ* MEASURE: 19.21-28

19 21This is the word which Yahweh has spoken concerning him.
Despised and mocked you
Has the virgin daughter of Zion,
Shaken the head after you
Has the daughter of Jerusalem.
22Whom have you insulted and blasphemed,
And against whom have you raised your voice?[b]
And lifted your eyes aloft?
Against the Holy One of Israel.
23[c]By your envoys you have insulted my Lord, and said,[c]
with my mass[d] of chariotry

[a]So de Vaux, *BJ*, p. 200.

[b]The metre demands a shorter half-couplet, which might be secured at the sacrifice of the sense by omitting either *ʿal-mī* or *qōl*.

[c]This line, which is prosaic and contains no parallelism, seems a gloss by which the editor connected the oracle with the preceding prose passage.

[d]Reading *b^{e}rōb* with Q, the versions, and Isa. 37 for MT *b^{e}rōkb*.

[a]I have done mightily[a];
I have climbed the mountain-tops,
The utmost heights of Lebanon,
[b]And cut down its tall cedars
Its choice[c] fir trees,
And have come to its remotest lodge,[d]
Its forest-like orchard-land.
24 I am he who has dug and drunk
Strange waters,
That I may dry up with the soles of my feet
All the rivers of Egypt.[e]

25 Have you not heard?
From afar I wrought it,
From days of old fashioned it:[f]
Now I have brought it about
That you have been[g] for the demolition[h] to ruined heaps
Of fortified cities.

26 Their inhabitants, powerless,
Were dismayed and confounded;
They were as herbage on the field[i]
And green grass,
Even as the weeds on the housetop
[j]Blasted before the east wind.[j]
[k]Your rising up 27 and your sitting down is before me,[k]
And your going out and your coming in I know.

[a]Here a half-couplet is necessary to complete the line, and we follow Graetz after G^L in restoring *ʿāśītī ḥayil*.

[b]Reading *wā'ekrōt* for MT *we'ekrōt*.

[c]Reading *mibḥar* with certain Hebrew MSS. and Isa. 37 for MT *mibḥōr*.

[d]Isa. 37, however, and also 1 Q Is[a] probably, read *m^{e}rōm qiṣṣō* ('its utmost height').

[e]MT *y^{e}'ōrē māṣōr* ('rivers of the fortress') or, as V suggests, 'dammed rivers', are not really intelligible, hence after Kimchi we accept the emendation assumed by most moderns *miṣrayim* for *māṣōr*.

[f]Reading *y^{e}ṣartīhā* for MT *wīṣartīhā*, taking *w* as a dittograph of the preceding *m* in the proto-Hebraic script.

[g]Reading *watt^{e}hī* with G for MT *ūt^{e}hī*, the past tense being suggested by the verbs in the sequel *ḥattū* and *hāyū* (v. 26).

[h]Reading *l^{e}has'ōt* with Isa. 37 for MT *lahšōt*.

[i]G^L, S, and T read *k^{e}ʿēśeb* and *kaḥ^{a}ṣīr*, but we may dispense with *k^{e}*, treating the figure as metaphor.

[j]Reading *š^{e}dūpā lip^{e}nē qādīm*, as proposed by Thenius and now strikingly confirmed by the Qumran Isa. 37, *nišdāp lip^{e}nē qādīm* for MT *ūš^{e}dēpā lip^{e}nē qāmā* ('blasted before it has grown up').

[k]Reading *l^{e}pānay qūm^{e}kā* for *lip^{e}nē qāmā* at the end of v. 26, where *lip^{e}nē qādīm* dropped out through haplography. The reading, suggested by Wellhausen, is now corroborated through 1 Q Is[a], where *qūm^{e}kā* is read, though not *l^{e}pānay*.

> [28]Because you have raged against me[a]
> And your storming[b] is[c] in my ears,
> So I will put my hook in your nose,
> My bridle in your lips,
> And I will send you back by the way
> You have come.

19.21. Note the two constructs, the first in apposition to the second, cf. *'ēšet ba'^{a}lat 'ōb* (I Sam. 28.7), see *GK* § 130e.

For the shaking, or wagging, of the head as a gesture of contempt and derision, cf. Ps. 22.7[8]: 109.25; Job 16.4, etc.

22. The *qinā* measure of the piece requires only two beats in the second half of the line, see p. 688 n.[b].

23. See p. 688 n.[c] for the omission of the line *b^{e}yad mal'ākekā ḥēraptā '^{a}dōnāy wattō'mer*, from the oracle, if not from the text. The passage of some of the mountainous country in Syria and Palestine with chariots was no mean feat and is the subject of special mention in Sennacherib's inscription.[d]

yark^{e}tē is generally taken as 'remotest recesses'. Isaiah 14.13–15, however, which contrasts the high aspirations of the king of Babylon to 'sit enthroned on the mount of the divine assembly on the summit of Zaphon' (*yark^{e}tē ṣāpōn*) with his abasement to the bottom of the pit (*yark^{e}tē bōr*), indicates that *yark^{e}tē*, though dual and referring properly to the sides, or lateral extremities, has come to mean extremities in any direction; hence here height or summit.

The timber-felling expeditions of Mesopotamian kings are often mentioned in their inscriptions, and were the theme of legend in the Humbaba incident in the Gilgamesh epic. There is also an echo of the present passage in Isa. 14.8, 'The fir-trees rejoice because of you, even the cedars of Lebanon; since you are laid low no feller is come up against us.'

If genuine the phrase *m^{e}lōn qiṣṣō* must mean 'its remotest lodge', referring to a temporary shelter for lumber-men, or perhaps a watch-tower, or even a summer shelter in a high terrace plot. The last is suggested by the parallel *karmillō* ('its orchard-land'), and we note the use of *m^{e}lūnā* signifying such a summer shelter in a vegetable-plot in Isa. 1.8.

[a]Omitting MT *w^{e}'ēt hitraggez^{e}kā 'ēlay* in v. 27b as a dittograph of the following *ya'an hitraggez^{e}kā 'ēlay*.
[b]Reading *še'ōn^{e}kā* for MT *ša'^{a}nan^{e}kā* ('your ease').
[c]MT *'ālā* should probably be omitted *metri causa*.
[d]Luckenbill, *ARA* II, § 236.

19.24. *qartī* has been derived from *qārar* ('to be cool, refreshed'), but it is better derived from *qūr* ('to dig a well', *māqōr*).

On the reading *miṣrayim* ('Egypt') for MT *māṣōr* see p. 689 n.[e]. The fact that Sennacherib did not penetrate to the Delta ('the rivers of Egypt') may suggest either that the MT *māṣōr* must be read, though it is difficult to see the sense, or that this oracle is later than the time of Sennacherib, as it may well be. On the other hand, *w* before *'aḥrīb* is not *w* consecutive, so that the matter referred to is not a matter of history, but of prospect, to which, in fact, the whole course of Assyrian politics in the west was tending.

25. Here begins the reply of Yahweh to the imperious boast of Assyria. The recent successes are but incidental to the purpose of God undertaken from of old (*l^emērāḥōq, 'ōtāh 'āśītī*) and shaped by his creative will (*y^eṣartīhā*) to its consummation. This statement of predestination is a distinctive feature of Deutero-Isaiah, and the conception of Assyria as a mere instrument of divine policy re-echoes Isa. 10.5ff.

Note the use of the preposition *l^e* in conjunction with *min* in *l^emērāḥōq* and *l^emīmē*. The preposition is used alone to signify 'from' as well as 'to, for' in the Ras Shamra texts, where *min* is unknown, e.g. *rd lks'i* ('come down from the throne').

On the reading *watt^ehī*, which we adopt see p. 689 n.[g]. The achievements of Assyria are admitted.

nāṣā, of which *niṣṣīm* ('ruined') is the Niphal participle, is attested in the Old Testament only here and in Jer. 4.7 in a similar phrase *'ārayik tiṣṣenā mē'ēn yōšēb* ('thy cities are ruined without inhabitant').

26. *qiṣ^erē yād* (lit. 'short of hand') may signify natural weakness or reduction through defeat by Assyria. The phrase recalls the rhetorical question *h^aqāṣōr qāṣ^erā yādī mipp^edūt* ('Am I powerless to redeem') (Isa. 50.2).

On the reading *š^edūpā lip^enē qādīm*, suggested by the Qumran Isa., see p. 689 n.[j]. The figure of man's achievements perishing as verdure before the sirocco is a familiar one in Scripture, e.g. Isa. 40.8.; Ps. 102.4[5].

27. See p. 689 n.[k].

28. The figure may be that of a wild beast caught in a trap and led off with a hook in its nose and muzzled, cf. Ezek. 19.4, but the reference is rather to the barbarous Assyrian custom of so humiliating their defeated enemies, cf. Ezek. 38.4.

(ii) A REASSURING ORACLE PROMISING RELIEF AFTER DISTRESS: 19.29–31

Formally this is not metrical, but there is a certain rhythm and a parallelism in thought. The unity of this oracle with vv. 21–28 is doubtful in view of the formal difference, but it may well be Isaianic, as is suggested by the fact that in two other oracles of Isaiah where relief is promised, Isa. 7.14–16 and Isa. 20, a three-year interval is figuratively suggested as here.

19 [29]And this will be a sign for you.
Eat this year the aftergrowth and in the second year the random growth,[a]
And in the third year sow and reap,
And plant vineyards and eat their fruit;
[30]So shall the survivors of the House of Judah
Again take root below and bear fruit above,
[31]For from Jerusalem shall go forth a remnant
and survivors from the mountain of Zion.
The zeal of Yahweh [b]of Hosts[b] shall do this.

19.29. The sign (*'ōt*) here is not, as occasionally in the Old Testament, a miracle. There is a close connection between the token of the self-sown seed, which sustains men until regular agriculture is possible again, and the role of the remnant of Judah as the custodians of the nation's future, which verges on the allegorical. It may well be that this is an oracle from this period promising to the oppressed provincials a future based on the Jews of the capital (v. 31), which had survived the Assyrian invasion. Another interpretation is that the prophet gives an indication of the time of the final deliverance. Wetzstein has reckoned that the Assyrians robbed the Jews of the harvest in 701, obliged them to eat the aftermath, and also prevented ploughing and sowing in the autumn of the year, without which the next crop would not reach maturity. It was not till 699 that a regular crop could be expected.

The infinitive absolute (*'ākōl*) may represent any part of the finite verb, here probably the imperative, as is suggested by the imperatives

[a]Reading *šāḥīs* with Isa. 37.30. This word, otherwise unknown in the Old Testament, may be cognate with Arabic *šahasa*, the second form of which means 'to miss the target'. Hence *šāḥīs* may mean corn from seed which has fallen in waste places, e.g. among rocks and thorns, where it would not normally be harvested. Such corn run wild is a common feature in the rough terrain of Palestine.

[b]So Q, many Hebrew MSS, the versions, and Isa. 37.

zire'ū, *qiṣ^erū*, and *niṭ^e'ū*, for which, however, G^{BA} reads infinitive absolutes.

sāpīaḥ is known from Lev. 25.5, 11 as the self-sown corn from the seed which is left undisturbed by ploughing in the Sabbatical year. Etymologically it means 'poured out', hence 'overplus', 'abundance', e.g. the epithet of the first Abbassid Caliph *as-Saffāḥ* ('the Liberal') which secondarily became associated with his liberality in shedding the blood of his political rivals.

19.31. On *šāḥīs* ('random growth') see p. 692 n.[a].

The conception of the remnant is characteristic of Isaiah of Jerusalem, also the final clause, which rounds off the oracle of salvation at Isa. 9.6 as a kind of signature theme.

(iii) AN ORACLE, PROBABLY FROM ISAIAH, AMPLIFYING THE DIVINE ASSURANCE GIVEN IN V. 20: 19.32f.

19 32 Wherefore thus says Yahweh regarding the king of Assyria:
He shall not come to this city
And shall shoot no arrow there,
Nor bring up shield against it,
Nor cast ramp against it.
33 By the way he came[a] he shall go back,
And to this city he shall not come.
Oracle of Yahweh.

32. The reference to the failure of Sennacherib to attack Jerusalem agrees with the biblical account of the mission of the *rab šāqē*, but not with Sennacherib's inscription of his campaign of 701, where he explicitly mentions at least a rampart of circumvallation if not a ramp for battering-rams. This suggests that the oracle may refer, as Šanda suggested (II, p. 298), to the later campaigns under Esarhaddon or Ashurbanipal, which bypassed Jerusalem, proceeding through the coastal plain towards Egypt. Alternatively the oracle may relate to the time of Hezekiah's rebellion before his final surrender.

The details of assault are well illustrated in Sennacherib's reliefs of the siege of Lachish from his palace in Nineveh, where battering-rams advance up ramps under a screen of raw hides and the covering fire of archers, who advance shooting from behind a screen of interlocked shields.

33. *n^e'ūm yhwh* indicates the end of an oracle, though the sequel would naturally connect with vv. 32f.

[a]Reading with certain Hebrew MSS, the versions, and Isa. 37 *bā'* for MT *yābō'*.

(iv) A FRAGMENT OF AN ORACLE, POSSIBLY CONNECTED WITH THE PRECEDING: 19.34

This couplet may have become displaced from the oracle in vv. 32f., which mentions the shield-screen under which the Assyrians used to attack. Yahweh would be the shield of his city. On the other hand the mention of *gnn* in v. 34, the root of *māgēn* ('shield'), may have suggested the juxtaposition of two independent oracles to the editor.

19 [34]But I will shield this city to deliver it for my sake and for the sake of my servant David.

(v) MIDRASH ON THE PRECEDING ORACLES: 19.35

19 [35a]And it came about that night[a] that the angel of Yahweh went forth and struck in the army of Assyria 185,000, and they rose in the morning, and there they were, all dead corpses.

19.35. There is no evidence for a plague of this magnitude in the army of Sennacherib elsewhere than here and in the parallel passage in Isa. 37. Herodotus, however (II, 141), records a local temple-tradition that one night while the army of Sennacherib lay in the vicinity of Pelusium mice infested his camp and nibbled the quivers, bowstrings and leather shield-handles, thus occasioning a speedy withdrawal of the Assyrians. This still does not corroborate the Old Testament statement that 185,000 perished in a single night. Both the Old Testament tradition and the story in Herodotus, however, may be variant accounts of an actual historical fact. The two are not irreconcilable, as mice are notorious bearers of plague, cf. the mouse-symbols with which the Philistines returned the ark after they had been 'smitten with boils' (I Sam. 5.6ff.; 6.1ff.).

(*i*) HISTORICAL COMMENT, PROBABLY ON THE ORACLE ON SENNACHERIB'S WITHDRAWAL (v. 7): 19.36f.

19 [36]And Sennacherib king of Assyria decamped and went his way and returned and stayed at Nineveh. [37]And it happened, as he was prostrating himself in the temple of Nusku[b] his god, his sons[c] Adrammelech and (Nebu)sharezer [c]struck him down with the sword, but

[a]Isa. 37 omits this phrase.

[b]No such god as Nisroch (MT) is known, and it has been suggested that the deity was either Marduk or Nusku. Since the murder probably took place at Nineveh, as the text suggests, it is more likely that the latter rather than the former, who was the city-god of Babylon, was the one. This is nearer the MT.

[c]Almost certainly a divine name is missing in the first part of the name. Eusebius on this period states that 'Nergilus' succeeded Sennacherib and was killed

they themselves escaped into the land of Urartu, and Esarhaddon his son became king in his place.

19.36. On the reading Nusku for MT Nisroch see p. 694, n.[b]. Nusku was the fire god, the son of Sin the moon god and his consort Ningal, and was regarded as an intermediary between the great gods and men, and is so mentioned in Assyrian inscriptions.[a] His cult, though native to southern Mesopotamia, was practised also in the north, especially at Harran and its vicinity.[b] The main difficulty is that neither our text nor the Assyrian records state where Sennacherib was murdered, otherwise we might have a more certain clue to the identity of the god. On the assumption that Marduk is denoted, J. P. Lettinga[c] cites the fact that the statue of Marduk had been removed from Babylon to Ashur in 689,[d] where Lettinga would locate the assassination. This is probable, since the king was buried here.[e] The city-god of Ashur was Ashur, and in the LXX versions of MT Nisroch (Esdrach, Esthrach, Asrach), Lettinga would see a version of the compound name Ashur-Marduk, citing by analogy the name Antart (Anat-Astarte) from Egypt in the 13th century, to which we may add Atargatis (Aṯtar-Anat).

Adrammelech may be a scribal corruption of Adadmelek ('Adad is king'), see on 17.31, or of Arad-maliki ('servant of M.'), as Šanda suggests. The names of the assassins are not disclosed in Mesopotamian records. The extant records from Assyria speak only once of the violent death of Sennacherib,[f] though Esarhaddon alludes to the disappointment of his elder brothers when Sennacherib designated him as king, and to the civil war which ensued, and to his pursuit of his defeated enemies to Hanigalbat,[g] which was in the direction at

---

by his son 'Adramelus'. This corroborates the MT Adrammelech, and may suggest that the name of his accomplice according to the Old Testament tradition was Nergalsharezer, as Hitzig suggested. But on the other hand the tradition which is reflected in Q and in Isa. 37.38 that the consonants *bnyw* stood after MT Sharezer suggests that the original reading of the name may have been Nabusharezer, (assuming metathesis), which is known as the name of the eponym for the year of Sennacherib's assassination (681).

[a]E. Dhorme, *Les religions de Babylonie et d'Assyrie*, pp. 59, 111ff.
[b]G. A. Cooke, *NSI*, 1903, pp. 186–91.
[c]'A note on II Kings xix, 37', *VT* VII, 1957, pp. 105ff.
[d]Luckenbill, *ARA* II, § 712.
[e]E. F. Weidner, *AfO* XIII, 1940, p. 215.
[f]Luckenbill *ARA* II, §§ 795ff.
[g]A. L. Oppenheim in *ANET*, p. 289.

least of Urartu (Armenia, Ararat). The Babylonian Chronicle[a] and an inscription of Nabonidus note that Sennacherib perished by the hand of one of his sons. II Chron. 32.21 states that the deed was done by *mīṣī'ē mē'āw* ('certain issues of his bowels'), a remarkable correspondence with the inscription of Nabonidus, which calls the assassin *maru ṣit libbišu* ('a man the issue of his inside'), which indicates that the Chronicler knew the Babylonian tradition if not the source. It is not certain whether the two assassins mentioned in the present passage were brothers, as Meissner suggests,[b] or father and son, 'Nergilus' (Nergalsharezer) and 'Adramelus' (Adrammelech), as Eusebius states.[c]

(*j*) ISAIAH'S ROLE IN HEZEKIAH'S SICKNESS: 20.1–11

This section is composed possibly of two distinct traditions, that of the sickness of Hezekiah, Isaiah's two oracles and the healing of the king (vv. 1–7), and that concerning the sign of the receding shadow (vv. 9–11); v. 8, which connects with v. 5, is possibly a redactional bridge between the two different traditions. It is notable in this connection that in vv. 9–11 the form of the king's name is *y^{e}ḥizqīyāhū*, as distinct from *ḥizqīyāhū*, which is used in vv. 1–7 and 8. Moreover, if this section is a unity, it is remarkable that there is no mention of the fulfilment of the prediction that the king would go up to the Temple on the third day, a fact that suggests to us that there was no clear tradition of the occasion of the sign.

(i) TWO ORACLES OF ISAIAH TO HEZEKIAH IN HIS SICKNESS AND THE HEALING OF THE KING: 20.1–7

The date is unknown (see above, p. 668 and on 20.12). The reference to 15 years to be added to the life of the king possibly suggested a connection with the foregoing incident, which is traditionally dated in the 14th year of the king, i.e. 701. The reference in v. 12 to the recovery of Hezekiah as the occasion of the Babylonian delegation, though possible, is probably an editorial gloss.

20 [1]In those days Hezekiah was mortally ill, and Isaiah the son of Amoz the prophet came to him and said to him, Thus says Yahweh,

[a]Rogers, *Cuneiform Parallels to the Old Testament*, 1912, p. 215.
[b]'Neue Nachrichten über die Ermordung Sanheribs', *Preuss. Akad. der Wiss., Sitz.-Bericht. phil.-hist. Kl*, 1932, pp. 250ff.
[c]*Chronica* I 27.25–29.

Give last injunctions to your family for you shall die and not recover.
[2]Then he turned his face to the wall and prayed to Yahweh saying,
[3]Ah! Yahweh, remember how I have walked before thee in truth and
with a whole heart and have done that which was good in thine eyes.
And Hezekiah wept sorely. [4]And it came about that [a]Isaiah had not
gone out to the middle court[ab] when the word of Yahweh came to him
saying, [5]Go back and say to Hezekiah [a]the prince of my people,[a] Thus
says Yahweh the God of David your father, I have heard your prayer and
have regarded your tears. See [a]I will heal you; on the third day you
shall go up to the Temple of Yahweh.[a] [6]And I will add to your days
fifteen years and shall deliver you [c]and this city[c] from the hand of the
king of Assyria and shall shield this city [d]for my own sake and for the
sake of my servant David.[d] [7]And Isaiah said, Take a cake of figs. And
they took it and applied it to the inflammation and he recovered.[e]

20.1. 'In those days' is quite vague, and does not help to date the incident. The formal introduction of Isaiah as 'the son of Amoz the prophet' does not sound as if this passage was originally related to what precedes. Our translation of *ṣaw* as 'give last injunctions' is prompted by the Arabic usage of *waṣā* (form II) in the sense of making a will, or giving parting injunctions, which Montgomery cites (ICC, p. 512). *ṣaw* may be a *p'w* verb cognate with this Arabic verb rather than from *ṣiwwā* here and in I K. 2.1, or the *l'h* verb *ṣiwwā*, apart from that meaning 'to order', may be a byform of this. No doubt this amounted to the designation of a successor and provision for the rest of the family. This may have been the occasion on which Manasseh was designated as successor at the age of 12, in which case the date would be 695 (see Introduction, Chronology, p. 74).

2. The turning of the face to the wall was perhaps a symbolic act of renunciation of the world and turning to God alone.

3. 'A whole heart' (*lēbāb šālēm*) indicates a conscience wholly unimpaired and at one with God.

4. The middle court was that between palace and Temple, 'the other court' of I K. 7.8, the Temple proper having but one court (I K. 7.12), see further reference to the two courts of the Temple in 23.12.

[a]This is omitted in Isa. 38.

[b]Reading *heḥāṣēr*, cf. certain Hebrew MSS, Q, and the versions, for MT *hāʿîr*.

[c]This is omitted from the first hand of G in Isa. 38. It may be a dittograph of the same words later in the verse.

[d]These words are omitted in Isa. 38 (MT), but are included in 1 QIs[a].

[e]G and S read 'that he might recover' (*wᵉyeḥī*), which anticipates the sequel (vv. 8–11), which this reading assumes to be a unity with vv. 1–7.

The modification in the word of God to Isaiah recalls the experience of Micaiah ben Imlah in I K. 22.

20.6. If, as we hold, Hezekiah became king in 714 at the age of 25, and his illness was the occasion in which Manasseh was nominated king at the age of 12 in 695, Isaiah's prediction of another 15 years may be no more than a vague reference to the normal life of a man. The menace to Hezekiah and Jerusalem throughout his reign, when Assyria had stripped him of all but his capital and immediate environs, was real enough to evoke the prophecy, which need not limit the incident to 701, the occasion of 18.17–19.37. Here is a new context for the oracle in 19.34, which indicates uncertainty in the Isaiah tradition.

7. The use of figs to draw ulcers is attested by Pliny,[a] and in two veterinary texts from Ras Shamra 'a matured fig-cake with matured raisins and bean-flour' (*dblt yṯnt wṣmqm yṯnm wqmḥ bql*) is prescribed to be injected into the nose of a horse (*UT*, 55.28; 56.33). It must be admitted that after the high-sounding oracle of Isaiah this homely prescription sounds rather ludicrous, and it may be an affected editorial gloss, a suspicion corroborated by the place it occupies at the end of the psalm in Isa. 38, which is called 'Hezekiah's prayer' and its omission in the parallel account in Chronicles. On the meaning of *ḥāyā*, 'to recover', 'gain perfect health' rather than 'to live' see on I K. 17.22.

(ii) INTRODUCTION (POSSIBLY EDITORIAL) TO THE INCIDENT OF THE SIGN OF THE RECEDING SHADOW: 20.8

20 [8]Then Hezekiah said to Isaiah, What is the[b] sign that Yahweh will heal me and that I shall go up to the Temple of Yahweh on the third day?

(iii) THE SIGN OF THE RECEDING SHADOW: 20.9–11

20 [9]And Isaiah said, This shall be the sign for you from Yahweh that Yahweh will do this thing of which he has spoken. Will the shadow advance[c] ten steps or recede ten steps? [10]And Hezekiah said, It is easy for the shadow to decline ten steps. Not so, but let the shadow recede ten steps. [11]Then Isaiah the prophet called to Yahweh and he

[a] *Hist. Nat.* XXII, 7.
[b] Reading *hā'ōt* for MT *'ōt*.
[c] Reading *h^a yēlēk* with T.

caused the shadow to recede on the steps (on which the sun[a] had gone down on the upper chamber[b] of Ahaz) backward ten steps.

20.9. The first point to be noted here is that there was no question of a sundial. Already in the parallel passage in Isa. 38.8 in G the MT phrase *ʿeśer maʿalōt bemaʿalōt ʾāḥāz* is queried. We might thus expect that the problematic *maʿalōt ʾāḥāz* was some building. Now 1 QIs[a] supports this conjecture in reading *ʿalīyat ʾāḥāz* for MT *maʿalōt ʾāḥāz*, by which we should probably understand a shrine for astral worship introduced by Ahaz to the Temple precinct, erected on some roof-top in the Temple-complex.[c] The sign itself is patient of several explanations. The commonly accepted view is that this was a miracle, and no adequate explanation is given except that Isaiah's word coincided with an eclipse of the sun which he was in some way able to predict. Such a phenomenon occurred in the lifetime of Hezekiah on January 11th, 689. But such an interpretation depends on the view that 'sign' (*ʾōt*) signifies, as often it does, 'miracle'. The *ʾōt* elsewhere in Isaiah, however, is not the miraculous, but some natural phenomenon, which nevertheless is the token of some fundamental truth. We have just read of the 'sign' of two seasons' famine which would precede deliverance as tokens of the fulfilment of Isaiah's message of hope (19.29–31). In agreement with the significance of the 'sign' in Isaiah, e.g. Immanuel (7.11ff.), his walking about Jerusalem naked (20.3ff.) and the two years of famine, we expect this 'sign' also to reflect the message of the prophet. Now, from the position which the account of this 'sign' occupies in Kings especially, where it appears with all the semblance of a midrashic expansion after the statement that Hezekiah had recovered (v. 7), we may suspect its relevance in the context. If we treat the application of the poultice as a prosaic comment which is really not relevant to Isaiah's encounter with Hezekiah, then the 'sign' follows the prophet's promise of favour 'for my servant David's sake' (v. 6), and to this the sign in its original form may be relevant. Isaiah may have amplified his oracle by asking Hezekiah to note the shadow cast by the sun on the steps of a building erected by Ahaz as an astral shrine on some building in the

[a]Inserting *haššemeš* as subject of *yāredā*, of which the masculine *ṣēl* cannot be the subject.

[b]Reading *ʿalīyat* with 1 QIs[a], G in Isa. 38 also visualizing a building in reading *tous deka anabathmous tou oikou tou patros sou* ('the ten steps of your father's house'). The reading *ʿalīyat* is confirmed by the gloss in 23.12.

[c]S. Iwry, 'The Qumran Isaiah and the End of the Dial of Ahaz', *BASOR* 147, 1957, pp. 27–33.

Temple area and to have asked him if the shadow could be drawn back. This may have been then stated to be symbolic of God's abiding favour to the house of David, and such a usage would agree with Isaiah's general use of the 'sign'. Or it may be that the lengthening shadow and the impossibility of its being drawn back was really associated with Isaiah's first oracle to the king that he would not recover (v. 1), and when Hezekiah did recover the tradition may have arisen that the shadow had been drawn back. Stemming, as the chapter does, from the circle which preserved the traditions of the prophet, the historical nucleus of the tradition is likely to be elaborated in this way out of the regard in which the prophet was held. We must further remember that, as its position at the end of the Book of Isaiah of Jerusalem indicates, it is not in the main stream of the Isaianic tradition. We may well suspect that, whatever undoubted historical nucleus the story may contain, that has almost certainly been expanded in prophetic legend to the proportions of the miraculous. An analogous case is the incident of 'the sun and the moon over Gibeon' in the story of Joshua's invasion (Josh. 10.12–14). Here the prayer of Joshua, in verse quoted from the Book of Yashar (vv. 12b–13a), is only for a prolongation of night and a delay of daylight in order that he might surprise the enemy by a night attack, (v. 9), conditions which might have been fulfilled by a cloudy morning or even by the speed of his advance. In the prose adjunct, however (vv. 13b–14), those perfectly natural conditions have been raised to the proportions of a miracle, the sun being arrested in mid-sky and there being no day like it before or after.[a] So in the 'sign' of the shadow we must carefully discriminate between the original facts or words of the principals and the tradition in which those are eventually communicated. A 'miracle', that is to say, cannot be considered apart from the nature of the literary source in which it is recorded. In the present instance the pattern of the tradition recalls that of the staff of Moses being turned to a serpent and reverting to its original nature and that of Gideon's fleece, both of which authenticate the word of God.

(*k*) THE DELEGATION OF MERODACH-BALADAN: 20.12–19

This section is probably out of place chronologically, probably relating to an incident either between 714 and 709, perhaps in 711,

[a]B. J. Alfrink, 'Het "stilstaan" van zon en maan in Jos. 10.12–15', *Studia Catholica* XXIV, 1949, pp. 238–69.

or in 703–2 (see critical introduction to this section, p. 668), so earlier than the immediately preceding passage, to which it is artificially attached by the editor in v. 12b, where it is stated that the delegation had as its pretext congratulation to Hezekiah on his recovery.

20 12At that time Merodach[a]-Baladan the son of Baladan king of
Babylon sent letters and a present to Hezekiah, for he had heard that
Hezekiah was ill. 13And Hezekiah was gratified[b] by them and he showed
(the delegates) all his store-house, the silver and the gold, the balsam
and the aromatic oil, and his armoury, and all that was found among
his treasures; there was nothing which Hezekiah did not show them in
his palace and in all his kingdom. 14Then Isaiah the prophet came to
king Hezekiah and said to him, What did these men say, and from
where do they come to you? And Hezekiah said, They came from a
distant land, Babylon. 15And he said, What have they seen in your
house? And Hezekiah said, They have seen everything in my house.
There was nothing which I did not show them among my treasures.
16Then Isaiah said to Hezekiah, Hear the word of Yahweh, 17Behold
the days are coming when all that is in your house and whatever your
fathers have stored up to this day will be carried to Babylon. Nothing
will be left, says Yahweh. 18And of your sons who shall issue from your
loins, [c] whom you beget, they shall take and they shall be eunuchs in
the palace of the king of Babylon. 19And Hezekiah said to Isaiah, The
word of Yahweh which you have spoken is good. And he said, Is it not
so if all is secure and well in my days?

20.12. Marduk-apal-idinna (Merodach-Baladan) revolted from Assyria and ruled independently in Babylon from 720 to 709, when he was suppressed by Sargon and fled to a refuge in the impassable marshes of Lower Mesopotamia. He emerged again on the death of Sargon and ruled in Babylon for nine months in 703. His delegation to Hezekiah was more than the courtesy visit that the present passage suggests, and is more likely to be associated with political activity in the west, either that which occasioned Sargon's expedition in 711 against Egypt and her allies, or before the revolt of Hezekiah and his allies in 701 BC. Apparently Isaiah, who opposed participation (Isa. 20) succeeded in keeping Hezekiah neutral in 711.

minḥā, which we have already met with in the sense of 'ritual offering' (16.13, 15) and 'tribute' (I K. 5.1; II K. 17.3, 4), means

[a]Reading Merodach-B. with Isa. 39 for MT Berodach-B.

[b]Reading *wayyiśmaḥ* with certain Hebrew MSS, G, S, V, T, and Isa. 39 for MT *wayyišmaʿ*.

[c]Reading *mimmēʿekā* with 1 QIs^a for MT *mimm^{e}kā* ('from thee').

here obviously 'present' (cf. Gen. 32.14, 19, 21, 22; 43.11, 15, 25, 26). For *sᵉpārīm* ('letters') *sārīsīm* was conjectured by Duhm, and G feels the same want of a personal antecedent to 'he showed them' (*wayyar'ēm*) in v. 13, since it inserts 'and ambassadors' (*kai presbeis*) after 'letters'. We think it probable that *kī šāmaʿ kī ḥālā ḥizqīyāhū* ('for he heard that Hezekiah had been sick') is an editorial insertion to connect this episode with the sickness of Hezekiah.

20.13. *bēt nᵉkōt* is found in the Old Testament only here and in the parallel passage in Isa. 39, and is probably an Assyrian loanword, cf. *bīt nakamti* ('a treasure-house').

bᵉśāmīm ('spices'), which were used for cosmetics (Esth. 2.12; S. of S. 5.13) and for preparing the oil of consecration (Ex. 25.6; 35.8) and for burial rites, where they were burnt (II Chron. 16.14), were included in the gifts brought to Solomon by the Queen of Sheba (I K. 10.2, 10), and suggest that the wealth of Hezekiah was largely drawn from his control of the vital trade-route with South Arabia at the head of the Gulf of Aqaba.

In Isa. 39 the inclusion of the definite article before *šemen* indicates a misunderstanding of the following *ṭōb*, which is not an adjective here, but a noun cognate with Arabic *ṭayb* ('perfume'). The word also occurs in Jer. 6.20; S. of S. 7.10. *ṭb* is also enumerated with scent (*npš*) and silver and gold in an offering-text from Ras Shamra (*UT* 5), where the provision of a sacrificial meal was the obligation of the royal family.

Skinner suggests that the armoury may have been the house of the Forest of Lebanon, which is mentioned as the arsenal (Isa. 22.8). A good indication of the wealth of Hezekiah is given in the list of tribute which Sennacherib records in the record of his expedition of 701. Besides 30 talents of gold and 800 of silver, he lists precious stones, antimony, large cut slabs of red stone, couches of ivory (inlay), *nimedu*-chairs with ivory inlay, elephant-hides, ebony, box-wood *inter alia*, including singing girls and ladies of his harem. If the statement of Hezekiah's display of his wealth is true the Babylonian delegation must surely have been before 701.

17. The prediction of the exile of the royal family to Babylon is surely a case of later retouching of matter traditionally associated with Isaiah, and may be a trace of the compilation of the Book of Isaiah of Jerusalem in the Exile after the deportation of Jehoiachin in 597.

19. The response of Hezekiah, which seems at first sight to be selfish and shortsighted, may simply reflect the attitude of the modern Arab, who, if asked about his welfare, answers 'Praise be to Allah' (*al-ḥamdu lillāhi*), and, if the victim of adversity, will still answer *al-ḥamdu lillāhi*, adding generally in this case (*'alā kulli ḥālin*) ('in any condition'). The king was following a primitive instinct in that, while accepting the adverse oracle, he felt that the last word must be auspicious.

hᵃlō' 'im šālōm . . . yihyeh looks as if it may be a conflation of two different readings, *hᵃlō' šālōm yihyeh* ('will all not be well?') and *'im šālōm yihyeh* ('if only all will be well'). The MT, however, may be understood as we translate 'is it not so if . . .?', reflecting back to the statement that 'the word of Yahweh is good'.

(*l*) THE DEUTERONOMISTIC EPILOGUE TO THE REIGN OF HEZEKIAH: 20.20f.

A REFERENCE TO HIS PUBLIC WORKS IN THE ANNALS OF JUDAH

20 [20]And as for the rest of the acts of Hezekiah and all his might and how he made the pool and the conduit and brought the water to the city, are they not written in the Book of the Chronicles of the Kings of Judah? [21]And Hezekiah slept with his fathers and Manasseh his son became king in his stead.

20.20. In view of the activity of Assyria in the coastal plain towards Egypt and from the strenuous efforts of Isaiah to keep Judah out of power politics (e.g. chs. 18,20) and the brief reference to his religious reforms, which may have had the aim of religious, if not political, unification of the Israelites who remained with his own subjects of Judah, there is no king the loss of whose annals is more grievous than Hezekiah.

The pool and the conduit by which water was brought into the city might refer to the conduit running along the eastern side of the south-eastern hill of Jerusalem from Gihon (*'Ain Umm ad-Darāj*) to *Birket al-Ḥamrā* just below the Pool of Siloam, or to be diverted at need into the depression on the site of the Pool of Siloam, or the celebrated tunnel from the Spring of Gihon to the Pool of Siloam. The former, with its lateral sluices for irrigation of terraces in the Kidron valley, was largely exposed and was the work of peace, to which Jerusalem was unaccustomed since the age of Solomon.[a] Its diversion to the site of the Pool of Siloam was in use by the time of Ahaz (Isa. 7.3, see above, pp. 679ff.), hence the reference is to the

[a]R. Weill, *La Cité de David* II, 1947, p. 58.

tunnel to the pool of Siloam. II Chron. 32.30 states that 'Hezekiah also stopped the spring of the upper waters of Gihon and brought them straight down on the west side of the city of David', and Ecclus. 48.17 is likewise unequivocal: 'Hezekiah fortified his city, and brought in water into the midst of them. He dug the sheer rock with iron and built up a well for waters.' Assuming that Hezekiah's defence measures noted in Isa. 22 were carried through in haste, Montgomery (ICC, p. 511) questions whether the Siloam tunnel was completed by Hezekiah in 701. Since that passage refers to the ponding of the water of 'the lower pool' (Isa. 22.10), it would seem that 'the lower pool' must be distinguished from 'the old pool', which, from its location 'between the two walls' (i.e. the south-eastern and south-western walls of Jerusalem or perhaps the old Jebusite wall on the west of the south-eastern hill and a new Israelite wall which enclosed the two pools), cannot be other than *Birket al-Ḥamrā*. Hence the Pool of Siloam was 'the lower pool', the main water supply of the old city on the south-eastern hill, as distinct from 'the upper pool' of II K. 18.17 and Isa. 7.3, which we would identify with the enlarged basin at the Spring of Gihon.[a] The work is described in an inscription cut in the rock-face just before the exit at the Pool of Siloam as having been cut by gangs of miners working from either end. An overlap is mentioned just where the two gangs were about to meet, and this is still to be observed. The length of the tunnel is given as 1,200 cubits and the depth underground 100 cubits. Vincent estimates that this considerable engineering work occupied some nine months. The excavations of Miss K. M. Kenyon and Père de Vaux above *'Ain Umm ad-Darāj* now show that the water of Gihon was brought by a short tunnel within the Jebusite wall like similar works on an even more impressive scale, but in softer rock, at Megiddo, Gezer, and Gibeon, which were probably constructed in the period of racial movement and general insecurity at the end of the Late Bronze Age and the beginning of the Iron Age (*c.* 1200).

2. THE REIGNS OF MANASSEH AND AMON: 21.1–26

The account of the reigns of these two notorious apostates mainly consists of Deuteronomistic introductions (vv. 1, 19) and epilogues

[a]On the general hydraulics of ancient Jerusalem see R. Weill, *La Cité de David* II, 1947, ch. IV; G. A. Smith, *Jerusalem* I, 1908, pp. 101ff.; L. H. Vincent, *Jérusalem Antique* I, 1912, pp. 134ff.; J. Simons, *Jerusalem in the Old Testament*, 1952, pp. 157–94, and above, pp. 679ff.

(vv. 17f., 25f.) and extended appraisals of the religious significance of the reigns. The preoccupation with the religious apostasy of Manasseh and Amon, in spite of the significant involvement of Manasseh in the politics of his Assyrian overlord, indicates the hand of the Deuteronomist, who designed this section as a prelude to the account which follows of the reformation of Josiah (22.3–23.24), which carried into effect the principles of the Deuteronomic school. In ch. 21 there is a trace of the Deuteronomistic redaction as well as of the first compilation. The original compiler does not visualize the collapse of the kingdom of Judah (e.g. vv. 1–7, 16–22, 25f.). This includes the normal Deuteronomistic introductions and epilogues and general appraisal of the respective reigns. The redactor in vv. 8–15, qualifying the last sentence in vv. 1–7, visualizes the destruction of Jerusalem as divine retribution for idolatry. In the detailed note on the death of Amon the compiler probably cites the Annals of Judah (vv. 23f.).

(*a*) THE DEUTERONOMISTIC INTRODUCTION TO THE REIGN OF MANASSEH AND GENERAL APPRAISAL (continued at v. 16): 21.1–7

21 1Manasseh was twelve years old when he became king and he
reigned fifty-five years in Jerusalem, and his mother's name was
Hephzibah. 2And he did evil in the sight of Yahweh according to
the abominations of the peoples whom Yahweh had driven out before
the Israelites. 3And he apostatized and built the 'high places' which
his father Hezekiah had destroyed and he set up an altar[a] to Baal
and made an Asherah-symbol as Ahab king of Israel had done, and
he prostrated himself to the whole heavenly host and served them.
4And he built[b] altars[c] in the Temple of Yahweh, regarding which
Yahweh had said, In Jerusalem will I set my name. 5And he built altars
to the whole heavenly host in the two courts of the Temple of Yahweh.
6And he passed his son[d] through the fire and practised augury and
divination and practised necromancy and wizardry; he did many evils

[a]Reading singular with G for plural of MT. The reference is to Ahab's provision of an altar to Baal and an Asherah-symbol in Samaria (I K. 16.32 ff.).

[b]Objection is taken to the use of *w* with the perfect *bānā*, and the infinitive absolute *banō* is proposed. This is possible, but Stade (*ZAW* V, 1885, p. 291ff.) proposes that cases of the perfect with *w*, when not frequentative, are glosses, and this section has every evidence of overworking. Montgomery, on the other hand (*JBL* LIII, 1934, pp. 311–19) regards this usage as a feature of the cataloguing style of archives.

[c]G reads singular for MT plural.

[d]For the perfect with *w* see n.[b]. G and Chronicles, in reading plural *bānāw* for MT *b*e*nō*, obviously regard the perfect with *w* as frequentative, and this is possible.

in the sight of Yahweh to provoke him[a] to anger. [7]And he put the graven image of Asherah which he had made in the Temple concerning which Yahweh had said to David and to his son Solomon, In this Temple and in Jerusalem, which I have chosen out of all the tribes of Israel, I will set my name for ever.

21.1. The reference is to the designation of Manasseh as co-regent, or heir-apparent, at the age of 12 in 695. His reign of 55 years, reckoned from this date, is the longest in the history of Israel. The name signifies 'he causes to forget', cf. Menahem ('he consoles'), cf. Nehemiah, Nahum. Such names may reflect, as Noth suggests[b] consolation for the loss of an earlier child, or perhaps the joy of the mother in her child, which causes her to forget the pain of childbearing. Hephzibah is another name which reflects the joy of the family in the child.

3. Like v. 2, the first part of this verse refers generally to the apostasy of Manasseh to the Canaanite fertility-cult suppressed by Hezekiah, and specifically to Manasseh's official cult of Baal and Asherah, the mother-goddess, probably in the Temple area in Jerusalem, as vv. 4 and 7 (the former perhaps an editorial expansion) suggest. In thus establishing this cult officially in the capital Manasseh was following the sin of Ahab (I K. 16.32ff.). Finally the writer animadverts on the astral cults. On the worship of 'the host of heaven', which, as in the case of Ahaz, reflected the status of Manasseh as an Assyrian vassal, see on 17.16. Frequent references in Deuteronomy and particularly in Zeph. 1.5 and in Jer. 8.2, etc., indicate the prevalence of the cult under Manasseh.

4. On the significance of Yahweh's setting his name in Jerusalem see on I K. 8.16. The reference is to the building of the Temple as a place where the name of Yahweh could be invoked and his presence thus, according to ancient Semitic ideas, be realized. This verse, as indicated by the perfect *bānā* with *w*, may be a later gloss.

5. It is objected (Burney, Skinner, Eissfeldt) that there is no mention in the account of the Temple in I K. 6ff. to two courts in the Temple, and it is suggested that the second court ('the middle court' of 20.4, according to Q and the versions) is actually that of the palace, which was in the same complex as the Temple area. The Temple 'blue-print' in Ezek. 40ff., which, though exilic, is generally held to

[a]Adding the pronominal suffix *-ō* with many Hebrew MSS, the Versions, and the parallel account in Chronicles. The *w* is omitted by haplography before the *w* at the beginning of the following word.

[b]*IP*, p. 222.

reflect the pre-exilic Temple, mentions an outer and an inner court (vv. 19f.). Notwithstanding, we regard the verse as a later gloss, perhaps reflecting the form of the second Temple, which had two courts; cf. 23.12, which is probably a later gloss.

21.6. On the passing of one's son through the fire, a rite of the cult of the Venus-star Melek, as we believe, see on 16.3. *ʿōnēn* is a perfect Poʿel of the root *ʿnn*. It has been explained as divining by the observation of the clouds, *ʿanānīm*,[a] or as the crooning of diviners, from Arabic *ġanna* ('to hum', of persons or insects). Wellhausen[b] relates it generally to Arabic *ʿanna* ('to appear'), the Hebrew verb thus meaning 'to interpret phenomena'. This type of divination, with prognostication in general, is associated in Isa. 2.6 with the Philistines. On *niḥēš* see on 17.17. The *locus classicus* for the practice of *'ōb* and *yiddeʿōnīm* is I Sam. 28.3ff., where Saul consults the witch (*baʿalat 'ōb*) of Endor. *baʿalat 'ōb* ought to mean 'the controller of *'ōb*', this word being possibly a collective, since the woman gave Saul the choice of whomsoever she would call up. In I Sam. 28.3 the feminine plural *'ōbōt* is used, these, with *yiddeʿōnīm*, being said to have been abolished by Saul. Possibly *'ōb* is derived from a cognate of Arabic *'āba* (*w*) ('to return'), meaning those who return from the dead, as Samuel appeared to Saul at Endor. *yiddeʿōnīm* means either those who profess to possess familiar spirits or the familiar spirits themselves. In the original usage the terms probably refer to ghosts and familiar spirits, and secondarily to those who are their mediums, or to the practice of divination by this means.

7. From the use of *pesel* ('a graven image') it is obvious that Asherah was a goddess and not an inanimate object. Asherah is now known from the Baal-myth in the Ras Shamra texts as the consort of El, the senior god of the Canaanite pantheon, and mother of the gods.

(*b*) LATE DEUTERONOMISTIC QUALIFICATION OF THE PRECEDING SECTION, VISUALIZING THE DESTRUCTION OF JERUSALEM AND THE EXILE AS RETRIBUTION FOR THE SINS OF JUDAH: 21.8–15

21 [8]And I shall no more let the foot of Israel wander from the land which I gave to their fathers, if only they will be careful to do all that I have commanded them according to all the law which my servant

[a]E. Dhorme, *L'évolution religieuse d'Israël*, 1937, pp. 229ff.
[b]*Reste arabischen Heidentums*, 1897², p. 204.

Moses commanded them. 9But they did not listen, and Manasseh led them astray to do more wickedly than the peoples whom Yahweh had destroyed before the Israelites. 10And Yahweh spoke through his servants the prophets saying, 11Because Manasseh the king of Judah has done these abominations, doing more evil than the Amorites had done, who were before him, and caused Judah also to sin by his idols, 12therefore thus says Yahweh God of Israel, Behold I shall bring ill upon Jerusalem and Judah at which the two ears of him who hears of it[a] shall tingle. 13And I shall stretch over Jerusalem the line[b] of Samaria and the plummet of the house of Ahab, and I shall wipe out Jerusalem as one wipes out a dish, wiping it out [c]and turning it[c] upside down. 14And I shall cast off the remnant of my portion and shall give them into the hand of their enemies, and they will be a plunder and a spoil to all their enemies, 15because they have done evil in my sight and have provoked me to anger from the day when their fathers came out of Egypt to this day.

21.8. This Deuteronomistic homily is prompted by the statement that Yahweh has chosen Jerusalem and the Temple as the place where he shall put his name for ever (v. 7). The phrase 'for ever' obviously requires modification in the light of the destruction of the Temple and the Exile, hence the homily on the conditional grace of God, which shows its secondary character by recapitulating largely the sins already mentioned in vv. 1–7.

13. The line (*qaw*) and plummet (*mišqōlet*) might indicate respectively reapportionment irrespective of old family claims and rebuilding (e.g. Isa. 44.13; Zech. 1.16; Job. 38.5), but in Isa. 34.11 'the line of desolation' (*qaw tōhū*) and 'the stones of chaos' (*'abene bōhū*) suggest destruction without reconstruction. Perhaps the figure is taken from the periodic testing of building, necessary in a land subject to earthquake and subsidence, where as normally in the case of dwelling-houses no foundations were dug, with the consequent demolition of bulging walls; cf. Amos's lesson from the plumb-line (Amos 7.8), which, like the present passage, is pervaded by the consciousness of sin and inexorable judgement.

haṣṣallaḥat is a case of the definite article denoting a single object not definitely known yet present to the consciousness under given circumstances, cf. *hā'aryē* (I K. 20.36), *happāliṭ* (Gen. 14.13), and

[a]Reading singular *šōmeʿāh* with Q, certain Hebrew MSS, and the Versions for the plural with masculine singular suffix *šōmeʿāw* of MT.

[b]Pointing *qaw* for MT *qāw*.

[c]Reading infinitive absolute of both verbs for third masculine singular perfect of MT.

probably *hāʿalmā* in Isa. 7.14. In the present instance the definite article probably indicates a well-known popular proverb.

21.14. *nāṭaš* is a forcible verb, used of skinning an animal, and is commonly used of Yahweh's abandoning, e.g., his sanctuary at Shiloh (Ps. 78.60). Israel is depicted as cast off on her land, *niṭṭešā ʿal-ʾadᵉmātāh* (Amos 5.2). The actual phrase of the present passage *nāṭaštī ʾet-naḥᵃlātī* is used in Jer. 12.7.

(*c*) THE FIRST DEUTERONOMISTIC APPRAISAL OF THE REIGN OF MANASSEH AND EPILOGUE (continued from v. 7): 21.16–18

21 16Moreover Manasseh shed innocent blood copiously until he filled Jerusalem from end to end, besides his sin[a] in which he involved Judah, doing evil in the sight of Yahweh.

17And as for the rest of the acts of Manasseh and all that he did, and the sin[b] that he committed, are they not written in the Book of the Chronicles of the Kings of Judah? 18And Manasseh slept with his fathers and was buried [c]in the garden of his palace,[c] in the enclosure of Uzza, and Amon his son reigned in his place.

16. The 'innocent blood' may refer to child sacrifice to Aṯtar the Venus-star, whose title was Melek (cf. v. 6; 16.3 and I K. 11.5), but probably refers to Manasseh's persecution of the prophets, suggested by the fact that, in contrast to prophetic activity since the middle of the ninth century and from the time of Josiah, there is total silence in the long reign of Manasseh. Tradition maintains that Isaiah was sawn asunder at this time (Heb. 11.37), but the persecution would not be limited to such outstanding figures, but would be directed against many lesser men, who, in representing the true tradition of Israel's faith in Yahweh, were loyal nationalists, and as such noxious to Manasseh as an Assyrian vassal. This status of Manasseh is indicated in two Assyrian inscriptions. Esarhaddon (680–669) mentions Ma-na-si-i of Ia-u-da along with the kings of Tyre, Edom, Moab, Gaza, Ashkelon, Ekron, Ashdod, Ammon, and other principalities in Syria and elsewhere as present at Nineveh during building operations, presumably responsible for contingents of their subjects in the Assyrian public works.[d] Ashurbanipal (668–626) also mentions him by name, together with most of the local kings of Esarhaddon's

[a]The Versions read the plural, but the singular of MT may be used collectively.

[b]Here also G^L, S, and T read the plural though the singular of MT may be retained as a collective.

[c]G^L omits, see n. on v. 18.

[d]A. L. Oppenheim in *ANET*, p. 291.

inscription, as accompanying him to Egypt when he finally defeated Tirhakah and reduced Thebes.[a] On this occasion these kings were either in command of units of their own nationals or were hostages for the loyalty of their subjects in the Assyrian rear.

21.18. The 'garden', or rather 'enclosure' (root *gnn*, 'to screen off') of Uzza is mentioned as a burial-ground only in the case of Manasseh and his son Amon. As these were notorious apostates, addicted to astral worship and 'passing children through the fire', probably as a rite in the cult of Aṯtar-Melek, the Venus-star, called in Arabic Uzza, we have proposed to see in 'the enclosure of Uzza' a precinct of the cult of this deity.[b] If *gan bētō* is genuine, which G^L will not admit, it is likely that the precinct in question is to be located in the palace-complex. Otherwise we have suggested that it is to be identified with 'the garden (or enclosure) of the king' (*melek*), which again we take as the enclosure of this deity. From Neh. 3.15 it is known that this feature was by the Pool of Siloam and it is suggestive that this is near the confluence of the Kidron Valley with the Valley of Hinnom (*Wādī ar-Rabābī*), where human sacrifice to Melek was practised (II Chron. 28.3; Jer. 32.35). It is contended, on the other hand, that the reason for the change of burial-place in the case of Manasseh and Amon was simply lack of room in the old royal necropolis at the southern extremity of the old city on the south-eastern hill.[c] It is pointed out that the situation is noted in II Chron. 32.33, which states that Hezekiah was buried 'in the ascent (*maʿalē*) of the sepulchres of the sons of David', by which Vincent[d] understands an upper storey in a tomb, and Simons[e] a monumental avenue leading to the tombs of the reigning kings, itself flanked by tombs of non-reigning members of the royal house. It is certainly significant that the burial of Hezekiah should be noted in Chronicles in this exceptional way and that there is no longer any reference to kings buried in the city of David. The view that the enclosure or walled precinct (*gan*) of Uzza was in the palace-complex adjacent to the Temple seems to be supported by Ezek. 43.7–9, where reference is made to the encroachment of palace on Temple and the defiling of the holy precinct by the funerary monuments (*pigerē malekēhem, bāmōtām*)

[a] Luckenbill, *ARA* II, § 876.

[b] 'The Desert God ʿAṯtar in the Literature and Religion of Canaan', *JNES* VIII, 1949, p. 80.

[c] So J. Simons, *Jerusalem in the Old Testament*, 1952, pp. 206–8.

[d] *RB* XXX, 1921, pp. 422ff.

[e] *Op. cit.*, p. 207.

of the kings. Wellhausen suggested that Uzza was a contracted form of Uzziah, which we think unlikely, though Eissfeldt (*HSAT*, p. 587) is apparently inclined to accept this view, regarding the place as an extension which King Uzziah made to the palace.

(*d*) THE DEUTERONOMISTIC INTRODUCTION AND APPRAISAL OF THE REIGN OF AMON: 21.19–22

21 [19]Amon was twenty-two years of age when he became king, and he ruled in Jerusalem two years, and his mother's name was Meshullemeth the daughter of Haruz from Jotbah. [20]And he did evil in the sight of Yahweh as his father Manasseh had done. [21]And he walked in all the way his father had walked and served the idols which his father had served and bowed down to them. [22]And he forsook Yahweh the God of his fathers and did not walk in the way of Yahweh.

21.19. From the chronology of his successors it is apparent that Amon was not elevated to co-regency in the reign of his father, who died in 641 at the age of 65. The failure of Manasseh to appoint a co-regent in spite of his age is the first lapse of this custom in Judah since Azariah (Uzziah) became co-regent with Amaziah in 791, and is a significant token of the status of Judah as a vassal kingdom of Assyria. So careful were the rulers of Assyria that there should be no leader round whom national resistance might rally that Manasseh is found twice as a hostage, probably, for the loyalty of his people, in Nineveh and Egypt. Thus we may understand why no co-regent was appointed.

The ethnic affinity of Haruz is thought by Montgomery to be Arab, the name being attested in inscriptions from Sinai and the Hejaz; he cites, however, a Phoenician instance of the name. The locality Jotbah, given as two stages from Ezion-Geber in Num. 33.34, hence feasibly identified with *aṭ-Ṭaba*, a site at a spring about 20 miles north of Aqaba, suggests that the family of Meshullemeth was indeed of Arab or Edomite origin.

(*e*) THE DEATH OF AMON: 21.23f.

From the Annals of Judah.

21 [23]Now the retainers of Amon conspired against him and killed the king in his palace. [24]But the people of the land struck down all those who had conspired against king Amon and the people of the land made his son Josiah king in his place.

23. Joash perished also by the hand of two of his retainers (12.20f.), who may have been the tools of the priestly party, whom the king's fiscal policy had antagonized. The reason for Amon's death is not mentioned. N. M. Nicolsky[a] suggests that with the decline of Assyrian power Egypt was already pushing her influence in Palestine, as the 29-year-old menace of Psammetichus to Ashdod (Herodotus II, 147) indicates (cf. possibly Jer. 2.18, 36f.), so that the assassins of Amon may have been Egyptian agents, and the 'people of the land', who set Josiah on the throne, may have opposed a pro-Egyptian party in the interests of national independence. A. Malamat[b] notes the coincidence of the death of Amon in 640–639 with the suppression of revolt in the west by Ashurbanipal in 639 immediately after the great revolt of Elam in 642–639 BC. Ashurbanipal certainly advanced as far as Acco and may have been prompted to settle Elamites and Persians in Samaria as a preventative measure, if Ashurbanipal is to be identified with 'Osnappar', to whom such a settlement is attributed in Ezra. 4.9f. Malamat therefore concludes that the assassination of Amon represented a revulsion against his pro-Assyrian policy, but that the action of 'the people of the land' was taken in apprehension on the advance of Ashurbanipal. This would account for the fact that Ashurbanipal makes no mention of an expedition against Judah. It would be strange, however, if the nationalists were the retainers of the king rather than 'the people of the land', and we prefer Nicolsky's view that the retainers were suborned to remove the pro-Assyrian Amon by Egyptian agents.

21.24. The conspirators miscalculated, since the people rose against them and placed Josiah on the throne. The antagonism between the 'servants' of the king and 'the people of the land' is significant in view of the probability that the latter term refers to the free Israelite subjects of the realm or their representatives (see above on 11.14), and the former to the feudal retainers of various degree of the king in his crown property of Jerusalem. The same social distinction may be observed in the repeated reference to Jerusalem and Judah.

(*f*) THE DEUTERONOMISTIC EPILOGUE ON THE REIGN OF AMON: 21.25f.

21 [25]And as for the rest of the acts of Amon which he did, are they not written in the Book of the Chronicles of the Kings of Judah? [26]And

[a]'Pascha im Kulte des jerusalemischen Tempels', *ZAW* XLV, 1927, p. 184.

[b]A. Malamat, 'The Historical Background of the Assassination of Amon, King of Judah', *IEJ* III, 1953, pp. 26–29. The same view was tentatively proposed by Noth, *History of Israel*, 1960[2], p. 272, and by F. M. Cross and D. N. Freedman, 'Josiah's Revolt against Assyria', *JNES* XII, 1953, pp. 56–58.

they buried[a] him in his tomb in the enclosure of Uzza, and Josiah his son reigned in his place.

21.26. According to MT, Amon was buried in a new tomb prepared for himself. G^L reads 'his father's tomb', but, as new ground had been broken for Manasseh in the enclosure of Uzza, it is unlikely that congestion would be felt already. Josiah also was buried 'in his own tomb'.

3. THE REIGN AND REFORMATION OF JOSIAH: 22.1–23.30

Between the formal Deuteronomistic introduction (22.1–2) and epilogue (23.25, 28) to Josiah's reign this section consists of a very circumstantial account of the finding of a law-book in the Temple and the reformation which was apparently inspired and directed by it (22.3–23.24).

Within this narrative account of the reformation there is at least one main element of secondary matter. The response of Huldah the prophetess, who was consulted after the discovery of the lawbook, is elaborated in 22.16–20, where the fall of Jerusalem and the destruction of the Temple is visualized. The statement here that Josiah will come to the grave in peace (v. 20) seems at first sight to be from before Josiah's violent death at Megiddo. That may well be, but it may, like the reference to the final disaster of 586, be later, from one who was interested in the *šālōm*, or well-being, of the kingdom rather than of the individual king. Some response of Huldah is certainly to be expected here in the pre-exilic compilation, but this is so much worked over by the exilic redactor that earlier and later matter is impossible to distinguish.

Another passage generally taken as secondary is the account of Josiah's desecration of the shrine of Bethel (23.14ff.) and his sparing of the prophet's tomb (23.16–20). We cannot dismiss this matter so summarily as Pfeiffer does[b] on the assumption that Josiah had no jurisdiction over the province of Samaria. The limitation of the suppression of local sanctuaries 'from Geba to Beersheba' (23.8) would appear to be the strongest argument for the view that the Bethel incident is an interpolation. This, however, merely refers to a phase in the first main stage of the reformation, of which, we

[a]G, S, V, and T read the plural. The singular of MT, however, may denote the indefinite subject.

[b]*Introduction to the Old Testament*, 1941, pp. 181, 402.

believe, the whole passage gives a telescoped account. In the rapid decline of the fortunes of Assyria, perhaps even before the fall of Nineveh in 612, an application of the principles of Josiah's reformation to the Northern province was possible without fear of reprisal. Just how seriously the tradition of Josiah's activity in Bethel must be taken is indicated by Alt's view[a] that the inclusion of Bethel and Ophrah in the tribe of Benjamin rather than Joseph (Josh. 18.22f.) is to be dated to this period,[b] and, indeed, the passages in question in Joshua cannot well refer to any other period before or since Josiah's reign. Notwithstanding the historicity of the events, the incident is suspect as a later interpolation by the use of *w^e* copulative with the perfect,[c] cf. the reference to Bethel in 23.4 (see *ad loc*).

It seems likely, too, that the passage dealing with arrangements for Temple repairs (22.4b–7) has been worked over, being influenced by 12.12ff., 15ff., the phraseology of which it repeats.

The question of the sources of the narrative of Josiah's reformation is not easy to decide. Since the events are so near the date of the first Deuteronomistic compilation of Kings before the fall of Jerusalem, it is natural to assume that the Deuteronomist should expatiate on matter which was so congenial to his principles, and that he would require no source for what was a matter not only of personal interest, but of personal recollection.

Here, however, we should note the observation of T. Oestreicher[d] that a distinction must be drawn between the historical narrative of the finding of the lawbook, the covenant dispensed by Josiah, and the passover (22.3–23.3, 21–25) and the account of the actual reforms of Josiah (23.4–20). These are limited to the purging of the Temple of the fertility-cult and astral worship, which symbolized servitude to Assyria, and the suppression of local cult-centres first in Judah and then in the Assyrian province of Samaria, and are as much political as religious measures. They represent, moreover, only part of the whole Deuteronomic law, with which we believe Josiah's law-book to be identical. Here, surely, we have reality as distinct from ideal,

[a]'Judas Gaue unter Josia', *KS* II, pp. 276–88.

[b]So Noth, *Das Buch Josua*, 1953[2].

[c]Budde ('Das Deuteronomium und die Reform König Josias', *ZAW* XLIV, 1926, p. 194), however, feasibly suggests that the many instances of this usage throughout this section are a sign not of late redaction, but of hasty insertion by the compiler from other sources which are not elaborated, or marginal notes which have eventually crept into the text.

[d]*Das deuteronomische Grundgesetz*, 1923.

and we agree with Oestreicher that, as the style indicates, 23.4–20, redactional matter excepted, is based on the Annals of Judah. The historical narrative, on the other hand (22.3–23.3, 21–25), is directly from the Deuteronomist, the compiler himself or one of his circle among the Temple personnel. Also from the Annals of Judah is the account of the death of Josiah (23.29f.).

Besides the influence of the second Deuteronomist, the redactor, in the response of Huldah (22.16–20) and possibly in the elaboration at least of the Bethel incident (23.15–20), this appears again in the statement that the wrath of God was irrevocable in spite of the reformation, resulting in the rejection of Jerusalem (vv. 26f.), and the appraisal of Josiah (v. 25) possibly belongs to the same source.

In this section of Kings, then, we are in the mainstream of the Deuteronomic tradition, and in order to understand the scope and significance of the reformation under Josiah it is necessary to determine, if possible, the origin of that tradition.

The law-book found in the Temple in the 18th year of Josiah (22.3) has been identified with the nucleus of the Book of Deuteronomy since the time of Jerome,[a] and, given a new status by the critical study of De Wette in 1805, this theory with modifications has prevailed among critical scholars with few exceptions, who claim a post-exilic date for Deuteronomy.[b] The fact that the principles of the legal nucleus of the Book of Deuteronomy are carried into effect, at least as far as concerns the renunciation of the local fertility-cult and the suppression of local cult-centres in favour of 'the place that Yahweh had chosen to put his name in', indicates a close correspondence between Josiah's law-book and the nucleus of Deuteronomy.[c]

[a]E. Nestle, *ZAW* XXII, 1902, pp. 170ff., 312ff.

[b]E.g. R. H. Kennett, *Deuteronomy and the Decalogue*, 1924; G. Hölscher, *ZAW* XL, 1922, pp. 161–255; and more recently G. A. Berry, *JBL* LIX, 1940, pp. 133ff.

[c]This, however, is, in our opinion greatly exaggerated by H. H. Rowley (*The Growth of the Old Testament*, p. 30) in his statement: 'In one respect only did the reform not implement the provisions of Deuteronomy, and the account in 2 Kings draws special attention to this. . . . It notes that the country priests did not come to minister in Jerusalem (2 Kings xxiii. 9), and so even here points to Deut. xviii. 6ff.' The matter is not quite so simple, and it is significant that the account of Josiah's reformation makes no reference to social legislation in Deuteronomy, nor the constitutional limitation of the royal authority (Deut. 17.14ff.), nor the provisions for the holy war, etc. Only the principles of the purity of the cult are mentioned, with the fact of the covenant and passover, as Alt has emphasized ('Die Heimat des Deuteronomiums', *KS* II, pp. 252ff., so Noth, 'Die Gesetze im Pentateuch', *Gesammelte Studien zum Alten Testament*, 1957, p. 66; *The Laws in the Pentateuch* . . ., p. 46 n.122).

From the fact that the law-book found in the Temple was read publicly with apparently full comprehension twice in a part of the same day (22.8, 10) it is most unlikely that it was as full as the canonical Deuteronomy. The reference to the said law-book as 'the book of the law' (*sēper hattōrā*) would seem to limit it to the legal portion of the canonical Deuteronomy, excluding the introductory discourse (chs. 1–11) and epilogue (chs. 31–34), and the Song and the Blessing of Moses (chs. 32, 33). The specific reference to the tribal gathering at Shechem (ch. 27) may also be omitted. This leaves chs. 12–26, and the blessings and curses in ch. 28, which made such an impression on Josiah (22.11–13). This matter may be still further reduced, as Eissfeldt suggests,[a] by reckoning with doublets in the legal portion of Deuteronomy (chs. 12–26) and passages like 16.21–17.7, which interrupt the subject of the context and are evidence of later redaction. Though the introductory discourse in Deuteronomy should no doubt be omitted from the nucleus of the book, which was identical with the law-book of Josiah's reformation, we think that some sort of historical introduction as Deut. 1–11 presents it was probably part of the law-book. The relation between the *Heilsgeschichte* (the recital of Yahweh's salvation of his people from the Exodus to the settlement in the Promised Land) and the law, which is exemplified in the Decalogue and in the repeated references to the experience of Israel in Egypt and her deliverance in the strictly legal portion of Deuteronomy (chs. 12–26), is fundamental as the basis of Yahweh's claim to the obedience of his people and as the ground of their faith in his abiding favour. This, then, could not well have been omitted in the Josianic law-book, to which no doubt it formed the preamble, though in a reduced form, and probably not so extensive as Pfeiffer supposes in admitting Deut. 4.49; 6.1–8.20, and 10.12–11.25 to the law-book.[b]

The date of the original Deuteronomy is of vital importance for a true assessment of the Josianic reformation. Three views may be taken into serious consideration. The first is that the book was written *ad hoc* in the reign of Josiah immediately before the reformation, its discovery by Hilkiah being a pious fraud. In this case, however, the provision for the services of rural Levites (Deut. 18.6f.), which was not observed in the reformation (cf. 23.9), would scarcely have been introduced by the priests of the Temple, who were obviously anxious

[a] *Einleitung* . . . pp. 191ff.; *The Old Testament* . . ., pp. 225f., 231f.
[b] *Introduction to the Old Testament*, p. 187.

to maintain their distinctive status. Sellin once[a] related the book to Hezekiah's reform (18.4) and centralization of the cult in Jerusalem (18.22), but, though there seems no adequate reason to doubt that reform did take place under Hezekiah, there is no evidence that it was based on such a law-book. This, however, may have been the occasion when a collection and revision of the traditions of Israel was begun, which was to come to light in the law-book which supported the reformation of Josiah. To this subject we shall revert. Finally there is the view that the original Deuteronomy, the law-book of the Josianic reformation, was from the early monarchy or even from the time of the judges.[b] This view is most important. Surely if the original Deuteronomy had been a product of Jerusalem in the time of Hezekiah or Josiah, to say nothing of later, the author would not have localized the giving and solemn reception of the law at Shechem. The attitude to the king in Deut. 17.14–20 most closely reflects the democratic tradition of the northern tribes (I K. 12.1–17 and especially Hos. 3.4; 8.4, 10; 13.11), especially as Deut. 17.15 evidently visualizes not hereditary monarchy,[c] as in Judah, but the designation of the king according to God's choice, indicated probably in the charisma, in the sacral assembly. Hence we think it probable that soon after the fall of the Northern kingdom a collection of Northern Israelite traditions, crystallized formerly in the sacrament of the renewal of the covenant in the old assembly of the sacral confederacy at Shechem, had been made, possibly by Israelites who had found refuge in Judah. This may have stimulated the reformation of Hezekiah, who may have had hopes of reuniting his subjects of Judah with the Israelites remaining.[d] This collection, which, we believe, was an excerpt from a much larger whole, in which the *Heilsgeschichte* probably occupied a much fuller space more proportionate to its place in the canonical Deuteronomy, was modified in the light of practical difficulties in the centralization of the cult under Hezekiah and Josiah. We must not, however, expect exact correspondence between Josiah's reformation and the law-book, which we accept as the legal nucleus of Deuteronomy. What we know of Deuteronomy is the result of a good deal of redactional elaboration and the account

[a]*Introduction to the Old Testament*, 1923, p. 74.

[b]T. Oestreicher, *Das deuteronomische Grundgesetz*, 1923; A. C. Welch, *The Code of Deuteronomy*, 1924; *Deuteronomy: the Framework and the Code*, 1932; E. Robertson, *The Old Testament Problem*, 1950.

[c]The reference to the dynasty in Deut. 17.20 is probably a Judaean adaptation of the North Israelite tradition. [d]So A. C. Welch, *Post-Exilic Judaism*, 1935, pp. 23ff.

of Josiah's reformation in Kings shows correspondence with Deuteronomy only in as far as concerns the cult. In view of this situation the caution of Budde[a] is warranted, that the law-book had never the force of statutory law, nor was this probably ever visualized, but it was a programme, which, in effect, could not be fulfilled in all its details. This is evidenced by the modification in the provision made for the provincial Levites. It was found impracticable to admit them to the holy office, as Deut. 18.6f. laid down, so a compromise was made by admitting their right to perquisites from offerings according to Deut. 18.3–5.[b]

We may ask why, in his reformation in Judah, Josiah should have revived a legal tradition from Northern Israel.

Apart from the possible appeal to the remanent Israelites, we may conclude from the fact that this ancient law was invoked as authority for the suppression of local places of worship, primarily in Judah, that the popularity of these was so great that no legislation from the Jerusalem priesthood could break it. For the rural shrines were also sanctuaries of Yahweh served by Levites, who were recognized as 'brethren' of the priests of the Temple (23.9), even though the cult there, with its emphasis on seasonal rituals, incorporated elements of Canaanite nature-worship. Moreover, those cult-centres were placed where people of the various districts had long been accustomed to realize the solidarity of kinship, like Samuel and his people at the local sanctuary of Ramah (I Sam. 9.12ff.), and David and his kinsfolk at Bethlehem (I Sam. 20.29). In many cases these cult-places were doubly hallowed because notable common ancestors were occasionally buried there and commemorated by their standing stones on burial-mounds (*bāmōt*) as, probably, in the sanctuaries at Gezer and Hazor.[c] To break this attachment a divine directive was invoked in the law of the old tribal amphictyony, forgotten in Judah, but part of the Northern Israelite tradition, and so having the force of fresh authority in the south. To give this law its full force, of course, it was necessary to present it in its full context, hence the renewal of the covenant, and the passover, which was already associated with the

[a] *ZAW* XLIV, 1926, p. 188.

[b] Budde (*op. cit.*, p. 202) emphasizes the impractibility of admitting all the Levites to the Temple service at the time of their concentration by Josiah in Jerusalem, but he suggests that after a while they were sent home, and it was then possible to employ visiting Levites according to Deut. 18.7f.

[c] Y. Yadin and others, *Hazor* I, pp. 85ff., Pl. XXVIII; XXIX, 1; XXX, 1; R. A. S. Macalister, *Gezer* II, fig. 485.

original context of the law. It may be, in fact, that this great communal meal of all Israel was designed to reconcile men to the loss of the communal meals at local sanctuaries, whereby the solidarity of the clans was realized. The fact that both the inauguration of Josiah's reform and the nucleus of the Book of Deuteronomy (12–28) is cast in the convention of the covenant-sacrament[a] of the sacral confederacy in the days of the settlement suggests a connection between the lawbook which prompted Josiah's reformation and the nucleus of Deuteronomy.

Though this is, we think, the explanation of Josiah's use of an old tradition from Northern Israel, we may still ask if the king did not at the same time intend to reunite the Northern Israelites with his own subjects of Judah on the basis of this tradition. The main difficulty in this view is that the covenant dispensed to the people by Josiah in the tradition of Moses (cf. Ex. 24.3–8) and Joshua (Josh. 24) is said to have been with the elders of Judah and Jerusalem (23.1), as Noth emphasizes.[b] But, if the covenant on the basis of the law-book was made in 622, when the book was found, Samaria was still an Assyrian province, with which Josiah did not presume to interfere until later, perhaps even not until the fall of Nineveh in 612. He may, however, as early as 622 have visualized a reunification of all Israel. The mention of Judah and Jerusalem as the parties to the covenant, on the other hand, may simply reflect the hand of the Judaean scribe. In this connection we may note throughout this passage the conspicuous absence of the theme of Yahweh's covenant with the Davidic house. Since the time of Solomon and the development of the Temple cult in Jerusalem, while the tradition of the *Heilsgeschichte*, Yahweh's covenant with Israel, and the law, had not been abandoned, the emphasis had come to rest more and more upon the Davidic covenant and the divine choice of Jerusalem. The Temple, though it was the new shrine of all Israel under Solomon,

[a]This pattern, discerned in Ex. 19 and Josh. 24, and in the Qumran Manual of Discipline i. 16–ii.18 in the light of imperial vassal-treaties best known from the Hittite archives of the fourteenth and thirteenth centuries, is emphasized as suggesting the structure of Deut. 4.44–30.20 by K. Baltzer (*Das Bundesformular*, 1960) and G. von Rad (*Deuteronomy*, 1966, pp. 21–23). The expansion of laws as covenant-obligations in this context by explanatory and hortatory passages, though containing later Judaean, and even exilic, matter, probably also reflects practice in the covenant-convention from earliest times and through the monarchy, as noticed by J. J. Stamm (*The Ten Commandments in Recent Research*, 1967), and H. Graf Reventlow (*Gebot und Predigt im Dekalog*, 1962).

[b]*The Laws in the Pentateuch* . . ., p. 46.

was so only ideally after the disruption of the kingdom, and was then practically a royal chapel, as Joash (12.4ff.), Ahaz (16.10–16), and Manasseh (21.4f.) had pointedly shown. Now under Josiah in his 18th year the attempt of Hezekiah to provide in the Temple a real central shrine for all elements of Israel may have been remembered and followed. In any case, even apart from the possible appeal to Northern Israelite sentiment, which may have been more ideal than realistic, the suppression of the local cult-centres in Judah demanded some such expedient as the renewal of the old ideal of the sacral confederacy based on the covenant-sacrament at the central sanctuary.

The time was ripe for national self-assertion expressed in the progressive steps of Josiah's reformation. Though Nineveh did not fall till 612, the decline had already been apparent under Ashurbanipal, who had to suppress a rising under his own brother in southern Mesopotamia in 650–648. In 625 Nabopolassar, an Aramaean, had successfully asserted his independence as king of Babylon, and Assyria, distracted on her southern front, was further crippled by repeated onslaughts by the Medes from the Iranian plateau, the Lydians from Anatolia, and by inroads of Scythian barbarians from beyond the Caucasus. So Judah saw the dawning of the day of freedom, though Josiah proceeded cautiously step by step before venturing into the Assyrian province of Samaria. We are, however, not well enough informed of the chronological sequence of these events in Palestine for a positive reconstruction, since the history of the period is probably telescoped in the account in Kings.

(*a*) THE DEUTERONOMISTIC INTRODUCTION TO THE REIGN OF JOSIAH: 22.1–2

22 [1]Josiah was eight[a] years old when he became king, and he reigned thirty-one years in Jerusalem, and his mother's name was Jedidah the daughter of Adaiah from Bozkath. [2]And he did right in the sight of Yahweh and walked in the whole way of David his father;[b] he did not turn to the right or left.

22.1. There is no need to emend the number to 18 with Klostermann

[a]Two MSS of G add 10, thus making Josiah 18 when he became king. This reading is probably prompted by grammatical preciosity, the numerals from 2 to 10 taking the noun in the plural. There are certain exceptions to this rule, however, such nouns as *yōm*, *šānā*, *'īš*, *nepeš*, etc., being found almost invariably in the singular after numerals from 2 to 10, see *GK* § 134e and f.

[b]The normal editorial formula omits the conjunction, which in this case is a dittograph in MT after *w* of the pronominal suffix in the preceding word.

after two MSS of G (see p. 720 n.[a]). Jehoiakim the son of Josiah being 25 when he acceded (23.36), must have been born when Josiah was 14 or 15, which was not impossible. The first duty of a Semite is to perpetuate his name in posterity, the more so if he is of the royal line. Since the death of Josiah may now be accurately dated, thanks to the Babylonian Chronicle of Nabopolassar in 609, he acceded in 639. We have calculated that Manasseh died in 641. Hence either Amon or Josiah acceded without an accession year. In the circumstances of the death of Amon Josiah was probably elevated immediately in 639.

Bozkath is listed in Josh. 15.39 between Lachish (*Tell ad-Duweir*) and Eglon (probably *Tell al-Ḥesy*) to the south-east of Lachish, which suggests a location at one of the *tells* in the foothills or plain between the two, perhaps *Tell an-Najila*, *Tell al-Quneitra*, or perhaps *Tell aš-Šeiḫ Aḥmed al-ʿAreineh*.

(*b*) THE FINDING OF THE LAW-BOOK: 22.3–15

Historical narrative, probably from the compiler or one of the Deuteronomistic circle, probably a priest of Jerusalem (continued at v. 20a).

While recognizing that the ancient tradition of the covenant community which is expressed in Deuteronomy and Josiah's reformation was much more vital in the life of the Northern kingdom, where the old sanctuaries of the sacral community had been in the days of the settlement, it must be emphasized that the latest central shrine of the community was Jerusalem. Here, as Weiser has stressed in his study of the Psalms,[a] the tradition of the covenant was preserved in the most important religious festival, the Feast of Tabernacles at the New Year season, throughout the monarchy, which was also the occasion when the Kingship of God was celebrated. Moreover, as von Rad[b] has urged, the traditions of the old covenant community had experienced a resurgence in Judah under the *ʿam hāʾāreṣ*, the heads of families in the provinces of Judah, in protest first against the alliance of the Davidic House with the House of Ahab, with its political absolutist tendencies and religious syncretism (ch. 11) and the effort of the professional soldiers and royal retainers in Jerusalem to determine the government and policy of the kingdom (21.23f.). It

[a] *The Psalms*, 1962, pp. 35–52.
[b] *Studies in Deuteronomy*, 1953, pp. 60–69.

was they who had set Josiah on the throne (21.24); and their influence is again seen at the end of his life, when they set his son Jehoahaz on the throne (23.30).

It is clear that in his covenant and reformation (ch. 23), Josiah came to terms with those heirs of the covenant tradition in Judah. This would explain the dual aspect of his reformation, political unification and national resistance to Assyria, and religious reform and consolidation. With the decline of Assyria, the time for the former was ripe: since the organization of practically all Judah as an Assyrian province since Hezekiah's abortive rebellion in 701, the latter was necessary to reassert the Jewish self-consciousness, which had already apparently protested against effacement at the death of Amon, possibly by pro-Egyptian officials among his retainers. Both aspects of this movement in Judah in Josiah's time are expressed in what von Rad aptly calls the 'militant piety' of Deuteronomy.[a] The holy war in the book of Deuteronomy, with the various practices associated with it, is an element of genuine antiquity, being in fact one of the most distinctive expressions of the solidarity of the sacral community Israel in the days of the settlement, as it was in early Islam, where it was one of the 'pillars of the faith'. But the prominence of the theme in Deuteronomy in exhortations (e.g. Deut. 6.18; 7.1ff., 16–26; 11.23ff.,; 12.29; 19.1), with the conventions of the holy war, both ancient and brought up to date (e.g. Deut 20; 21.10, 14; 23.10–14; 24.5; 25.17–19), suggests to von Rad, following E. Junge,[b] that here we have a clue to the Judaean circles which gave the distinctive development to the traditions of Israel in the book of Deuteronomy.

In view of the role of the Levites in Deuteronomy, B. Mazar[c] has emphasized the political as well as the religious role of the latter, which has been stressed by Alt.[d] Mazar[e] notes their settlement

[a]*Deuteronomy*, 1966, p. 25.

[b]*Der Wiederaufbau des Heereswesens des Reiches Juda unter Josia*, 1937.

[c]'The Cities of the Priests and Levites', SVT VII, 1960, pp. 193–205, on the basis of the list of Levitical settlements in Josh. 21.

[d]'Festungen und Levitenorte im Lande Juda', *KS* II, 1953, pp. 310–16, where it is contended that the placing of the Levites was for strategic purposes under Josiah, cf. Albright (*Archaeology and the Religion of Israel*, 1953^3, pp. 123ff.), who dates the settlement as in Josh. 21 mainly under David and for military purposes. Mazar dates the settlement of Levites specifically in the end of David's reign, possibly when Solomon was co-regent and during Solomon's reign. It may have been continued in Rehoboam's fortification of his frontiers after the disruption of the kingdom, as II Chron. 11.13–17 suggests. See further on this question *à propos* of Josh. 21, J. Gray, *Joshua, Judges, Ruth*, 1967, pp. 26–31.

[e]*Op. cit.*, pp. 199–205.

throughout the kingdom, especially in frontier areas, where doubtless they served to counteract the political and religious influence of the Canaanites in the early monarchy (I Chron. 26.30). Such elements, with the local notables of Judah (*ʿam hāʾāreṣ*), were the natural custodians of the traditional ideals of the sacral community on which Josiah might rely for a nationalist revival after the Assyrian domination since 701 and for a military revival since the reduction of feudal forces which that involved. Thus, as developed in Judah, with the new prominence given to the theme of the holy war, Deuteronomy relates closely to the revival under Josiah. We think, however, that it reflects rather the aims of the priests and Levites who gave expression to the policy of the 'people of the land'. The limited role of the Levites in the account of Josiah's reform (23.9) indicates a compromise between Josiah and his supporters throughout the country, a concession, no doubt, to the higher priesthood in the capital.

22 3And it came about in the eighteenth year of king Josiah[a] that the king sent Shaphan the son of Azaliah the son of Meshullam the scribe to the Temple of Yahweh saying, 4Go up to Hilkiah the chief[b] priest, and let him melt[c] the silver which has been contributed to the Temple of Yahweh which the warders of the threshold have gathered from the people, 5and let them give it into the charge of the masters of works who are appointed over the Temple of Yahweh that they may give it to those who undertake the work which is in the Temple of Yahweh for the repair of the Temple, 6to the craftsmen, the builders, and the stone-hewers,[d] and for the purchase of timber and hewn stone to repair the dilapidation of the Temple. 7But let no account be taken with them of the silver which is given into their charge, for they deal honestly. 8And Hilkiah the chief[b] priest said to[e] Shaphan the scribe, I have found the book of the law in the Temple of

[a]G^{BL} adds 'in the eighth month', and G^{A} 'in the seventh month'. Obviously they retain a tradition that the reformation was inaugurated at the New Year festival, and this is not unlikely. As the occasion when the people of the provinces made the pilgrimage to Jerusalem it was a fitting occasion for the covenant (23.3) and if, as we believe, this was a revival of the tradition of the old sacral confederacy (cf. Deut. 31.10) the New Year Feast of Tabernacles was the *Sitz im Leben*.

[b]In this rare occurrence of the title *hakkōhēn haggādōl*, which became current in post-exilic times, *haggādōl* is suspect as an exilic gloss, the more so as at vv, 10, 12, 14 Hilkiah is termed simply 'the priest' cf. on 12.10, pp. 586f. But the title is supported by the title *kōhēn hārōʾš* as distinct from *kōhēn hammišne* in 25.18.

[c]Reading *weyattēk* with G^{L}, V, and T for MT *weyattēm* ('and let him sum up the whole amount'), a sense not otherwise attested. Thenius after G^{BA} reads *waḥatōm* ('and seal it up' i.e. 'stamp it'), which is feasible, though further from MT. The reading we adopt is supported by *hittīkū* in v. 9.

[d]Reading *gōzerīm* for *gōderīm* ('masons'), which is already expressed in *bōnīm*.

[e]Reading *ʾel* for MT *ʿal* with certain Hebrew MSS and the Versions.

Yahweh. And Hilkiah gave the book to Shaphan, and he read it. [9]And
Shaphan the scribe came to the king and reported to the king and said,
Your servants melted the silver which was found in the Temple and gave
it into the charge of the masters of works who are appointed in the
Temple of Yahweh. [10]And Shaphan the scribe told the king saying,
Hilkiah the priest gave me a book. And Shaphan read it before the
king. [11]And it came about that, when the king heard the words of the
law-book, he tore his robes. [12]And the king ordered Hilkiah the priest
and Ahikam the son of Shaphan and Achbor the son of Micaiah, and
Shaphan the scribe and Asaiah the king's minister, saying, [13]Go
consult the oracle of Yahweh on my behalf [a]and on behalf of the
people who are left in Israel and in Judah[a] on account of the words of
this book which has been found, for great is the wrath of Yahweh
which is kindled against us because our fathers have not listened to
the words of this book to do according to all that is written in it.[b] [14]So
Hilkiah the priest and Ahikam and Achbor and Shaphan and Asaiah
went to Huldah the prophetess the wife of Shallum the son of Tikvah
the son of Harhas[c] the keeper of the robes, who lived in Jerusalem in
the Second Quarter, and they spoke to her. [15]And she said to them,
Thus says Yahweh God of Israel, Say to the man who sent you to
me . . .

22.3. According to II Chron. 34.3, Josiah's campaign against the fertility-cult in Jerusalem began in the 12th year of his reign (628). This may well be, but his iconoclasm in 'Ephraim and Manasseh' at this time, though not impossible, in the decline of Assyrian power, is unlikely in view of the statement of II K. 23.8, which limits Josiah's initial activity to 'from Geba to Beersheba'. The account in Chronicles, in mentioning two stages of the reformation in 628 and 622, does appear to preserve an important fact, that the religious reformation proceeded in stages, first the purging of the Temple and the immediate neighbourhood of Jerusalem, then the suppression of local cult-centres throughout Judah, including regions taken from Hezekiah by Sennacherib and now claimed again for Judah, when Assyria was too embarrassed to protest. This stage was associated with the finding of the law-book and the covenant. This evoking no response from Assyria, a third stage may well have been the extension of the reformation to Bethel and the north, which, with the pre-

[a]Cf. II Chron. 34.21 *ūbeʿad hanniš'ār beyiśrā'ēl ūbīhūdā*, where the singular of the participle implies the reading *hāʿām*, as in Kings, hence our reading *ūbeʿad hāʿām hanniš'ār beyiśrā'ēl ūbīhūdā*.

[b]Reading with G^L *ʿālāw* for MT *ʿālēnū*, cf. II Chron. 34.21 *ʿal-hassēper hazze*.

[c]The name in the MT form is peculiar and defies etymological explanation. It is given as Hasrah in Chronicles, which may be the proper form, being connected with the root *ḥāsēr*, and may indicate that his mother had lacked milk.

occupation of Assyria with Nabopolassar and the Medes and northern enemies from 625 till her final collapse in 612, was quite practicable. In his account of the decisive stage of the reformation which came upon the finding of the law-book, in which he is so vitally interested, the Deuteronomistic compiler has probably telescoped these three stages of the reformation. Shaphan means 'rock-badger', and is one of several apparently animal names in this passage, which seems to suggest that they were fashionable at this period; see further on vv. 12, 14.

On the office of scribe see on I K. 4.3.

The name *'aṣalyāhū* ('Azaliah') is connected by Noth[a] with the Arabic verb *'aṣula* ('to be distinguished'), cf. Ex. 24.11 *'aṣīlē bené yiśrā'ēl* ('the notables of the Israelites').

22.4. On the title 'chief priest' see p. 723 n.[b].

On the reading *weyattek* see p. 723 n.[c], and on the officials in this and in vv. 5, 6, 7 see on 12.12ff.

8. The definite article with *tōrā* ('law') after *sēper* ('book') is possibly an instance of the demonstrative significance of the article, generally limited to certain stock phrases, e.g. *hayyōm*, *hallayelā*, *haššānā*, see *GK* § 126a. On the other hand, Hilkiah may have assumed the law to go back to written authority. The book was no doubt a roll, probably written on prepared skin, like the Qumran scrolls, though papyrus also was in use then, as indicated by the impress on clay seals from Lachish.[b]

9. Strict grammar would require the use of the preposition *le* and the genitive after the phrase *wayyāšeb dābār*, but the construction is according to sense, the compound phrase being tantamount to the transitive verb *'ānā*.

10. The reading this second time was certainly aloud, which is the proper meaning of *qārā'*, cf. Qur'an ('that which is recited'). In the Qur'an many passages are introduced with the divine imperative to the Prophet *'iqra'* ('recite', not 'read'). It was the death of so many of the reciters of the Qur'an in the wars of reclamation after the death of Muhammad which first occasioned the collection and first editing of the Qur'an as a book which might be read.

11. The king's rending of his robes, as well as indicating his own genuine contrition, probably anticipated, if it did not inaugurate, a solemn fast.

[a] *IP*, p. 193.
[b] D. Diringer, *PEQ*, 1941, pp. 102–4.

22.12. Achbor means 'a mouse', and may be an instance of an animal name apparently in vogue at this time, like Shaphan ('rock-badger') and Huldah ('mole'); cf. Hagab, 'locust'.[a] It may be that the prevalence of such names at this time was a riposte to the banning of Yahweh theophorics in the families of certain determined opponents of the cults of Manasseh. On the other hand, it may be that these animals evoked more admiration in ancient Israel than with us; cf. the Homeric figure of the courage of a fly. Another possible explanation is that the names are caritative in the case of Achbor, a mother's pet name, or nicknames, not necessarily derogatory.

13. On the specific meaning of *dāraš*, 'to consult an oracle', see on 1.2.

On the text see p. 724 n.[b]. If the MT *kātūb ʿālēnū* is read, L. Kopf[b] is probably right in citing the Arabic *kataba ʿalā* (Qur'an, Surah 5.32), signifying 'written injunction as evidence against the transgressor'.

MT mentions only Judah, see p. 724 n.[a]. The inclusion of Israel, which we adopt after Chronicles, is probably influenced in retrospect by the memory of the later phase of Josiah's reformation in the Assyrian province of Samaria.

14. The status of the prophetess Huldah is interesting in view of the fact that both the canonical prophets Jeremiah and Zephaniah were already active at that time. It was probably felt that such independent spirits would give an answer which the priests considered *ultra vires*, whereas Huldah, the wife of a minor Temple official, would give the divine authority to what they sought without embarrassing them. Budde[c] suggests that Jeremiah's sympathy with the reformation, involving as it did the suppression of local sanctuaries and the consequent degradation of local priests, explains the bitter hostility which he encountered from his kinsmen in the Levitical community of Anathoth, some four miles north-north-east of Jerusalem.

On the name Harhas, for which we should probably read Hasrah, see p. 724 n.[c]. On the office of keeper of the ritual vestments, see on 10.22 on the similar office in the Baal-temple in Samaria.

The 'Second Quarter' (*hammišne*) of Jerusalem is generally accepted as the northern extension of the old Jebusite city, which

[a] D. Diringer, *Lachish* III, pp. 331–9; also Ezra 2.46.
[b] VT VIII, 1958, p. 180.
[c] ZAW XLIV, 1926, p. 205.

probably developed as a residential area for palace and Temple personnel after the building of the Temple. At the time of Josiah it would be located west of the palace and Temple over the depression of the upper Tyropoeon Valley, 'the Mortar' (*hammaktēš*).

(*c*) THE RESPONSE OF HULDAH: 22.16–20a

This is so developed by the Deuteronomistic redactor that the original oracle is no longer distinguishable, though it was probably a threat (v. 16) modified by a vague promise of grace to Josiah, beginning at v. 18 and probably ending at v. 19, as the words 'oracle of Yahweh' (*neʾūm yhwh*) suggest.

22 [16]Thus says Yahweh, See I shall bring calamity upon[a] this place and its inhabitants, all the words of the book which the king of Judah has read, [17]because they have forsaken me and sent up the smoke of sacrifice to other gods in order to provoke me to anger with all the work of their hands, and my wrath shall be kindled against this place and shall not be quenched. [18]But to the king of Judah who sends you to consult the oracle of Yahweh thus shall you say, Thus says Yahweh God of Israel, As for the words which you have heard, [19]inasmuch as your heart has been susceptible and you have humbled yourself before Yahweh in listening to what I have spoken against this place and its inhabitants that they should be for devastation and curse, and have torn your robes and wept before me, I also have heard; oracle of Yahweh. [20A]Therefore I will gather you to[b] your fathers, and you shall be gathered safely to your tomb[c] and your eyes shall not look upon all the evil which I shall bring upon this place [d]and its inhabitants.[d]

22.16. 'calamity . . . even all the words of the book . . .' indicates the consequences of the curses on transgression of the law in Deut. 28.15ff.

20. It seems reasonable to suppose that the prediction of Josiah's death *bešālōm* was part of the original response of Huldah in so far as a date after the violent death of Josiah seems precluded. The late redactor of the passage, however, may be visualizing the major disaster of the liquidation of the state, Josiah still dying and being buried while the state was intact (*bešālōm*). Fohrer[e] cites this verse as

[a]Reading *ʿal* with the Versions and the parallel passage in Chronicles for MT *ʾel*.
[b]Reading *ʾel* with certain Hebrew MSS, the Versions, and the parallel passage in Chronicles for MT *ʿal*.
[c]Reading the singular *biqebūrāteḵā* with the Versions.
[d]Inserting *weʿal-yōšebāw* with G[L] and the parallel version in Chronicles, *yōšebāw* having dropped out through a scribal error due to the following word *wayyāšibū*.
[e]*Elia*, p. 50 n.

evidence that the first Deuteronomistic compilation was completed in the reign of Josiah, before his violent death in 609.

(*d*) THE INAUGURATION OF THE REFORMATION, THE PUBLIC READING OF THE LAW AND THE COVENANT: 22.20b–23.3

Historical narrative from a priestly source, probably the Deuteronomistic compiler, continued from the oracle of Huldah in its pre-redactional form in vv. 16–20a with the account of the Passover and the general reference to reforms in Judah in 23.21–25.

22 20BSo they reported the word to the king.

23 1Then the king sent and gathered to himself all the elders of Judah and Jerusalem. 2And the king went up to the Temple of Yahweh and all the men of Judah and all the inhabitants of Jerusalem with him [a]and the priests and the prophets[b] and all the people both small and great,[a] and he read in their ears all the words of the book of the covenant which was found in the Temple of Yahweh. 3And the king stood by the pillar[c] and made the covenant before Yahweh to walk after Yahweh, keeping[d] his commandments and his testimonies and his statutes whole-heartedly and sincerely, establishing the words of this covenant which were written in this book, and all the people committed themselves to the covenant of set resolve.

23.1. The elders were the heads of families representing the people on this memorable occasion as the heirs of the old sacral community. Note the specific mention of Jerusalem apart from Judah *à propos* of the view that a distinction must be made between the inhabitants of Jerusalem as a crown estate and 'the people of the land'; see on 11.14.

2. The subject of *wayyiqrā'* ('read') is ostensibly the king. The in-

[a]The phrase *wᵉhakkōhᵃnīm wᵉhannᵉbī'īm wᵉkol-hāʿām lᵉmiqqāṭōn wᵉʿad-gādōl* should probably be omitted, as suggested by the parallel passage in Chronicles.. The versions, however, support its inclusion in the present passage. As the preposition *'ittō* indicates, the king was accompanied. 'The men of Judah and the inhabitants of Jerusalem' doubtless indicates their representatives.

[b]For MT *hannᵉbī'īm* Chronicles reads *hallᵉwīyīm* ('the Levites'), which may reflect post-exilic usage. This reading is supported by certain Hebrew MSS, which may reflect the reading of Chronicles. The Levites, however, had a definite status in pre-exilic Israel, particularly in the covenant-sacrament in earlier times, which was now re-enacted, and as custodians of the tradition of Israel and agents of the Davidic dynasty in the early monarchy throughout the territorial state under David and Solomon particularly (see above, pp. 722f.). The prophets also, of course, had a status both in cult and community, e.g. Huldah, so prophets would be as appropriate as Levites in this transaction. Both, however, may be omitted in the context, see n.[a].

[c]On the question of *hāʿammūd* or *hāʿōmed* see on 11.14. In the present passage Chronicles reads *ʿomdō* ('his platform').

[d]Omitting initial *w*, as suggested by G^B.

definite subject could be denoted, but in view of the role of Joshua (Josh. 8.34:24), Ezra (Neh. 8.2f.), and Moses (Ex. 24.3–8), and of the function prescribed for the king to administer the law in Deut. 17.18–20, it is probable that Josiah himself read it out aloud on this occasion.[a] This is the first time that the book is termed 'the book of the covenant', and is one more feature which connects it with the nucleus of Deuteronomy and with the sacrament of the renewal of the covenant, in which the recitation of the law and its endorsement was an important element (Deut. 27).

23.3. The only explicit precedent for such a covenant was that in which Joash was involved at his accession. The present case, however, was not the accession of Josiah. In the case of Joash, though he probably assumed the obligations of the covenant, indicated in the handing over of 'the testimony' (*hāʿēdūt*), he was to a degree making a concession to subjects. Here, however, Josiah, as emphasized by Noth,[b] was mediating the covenant according to the traditional role of Moses (Ex. 24.3–8) and Joshua (Josh. 24). G. Fohrer,[c] rightly in our opinion, notes the emphasis on the old type of covenant in the assembly of the sacral confederacy, with which the Northern Israelites were familiar, as distinct from the divine covenant with the Davidic dynasty, with which the people of Judah were familiar. As in the sacrament of the renewal of the covenant at Shechem, a formal renunciation of alien elements in religion is an important part of the transaction. The phraseology 'to keep his commandments, testimonies, and statutes with all his heart and with all his being' is characteristically Deuteronomic. The phrase *wayyaʿamōd babberīt* (lit., 'stood in the covenant') suggests to us the Arabic *'iʿtamada ʿalā* ('to rely upon', hence 'to commit oneself to'), and *ʿamada ʾilā* ('to resolve'), cf. *ʿamdān* ('of set purpose'), which inspires our translation. The meaning may, however, be more literal, indicating that the people sat or squatted when the book was read and stood up as a sign of assent when the covenant was executed.

(*e*) THE REFORMATION: 23.4–15

This passage is probably a telescoped account by the compiler resting ultimately on the Annals of Judah.

[a]Cf. Mishnah, *Soṭa* 7.8, cited by G. Widengren, 'King and Covenant', *JSS* II, 1957, pp. 1–32.

[b]'Die Gesetze im Pentateuch', *Gesammelte Studien*, pp. 61ff.; *The Laws in the Pentateuch*, p. 46.

[c]'Der Vertrag zwischen König und Volk in Israel', *ZAW* LXXI, 1959, pp. 1–22.

23 4Then the king ordered Hilkiah the chief[a] priest and the second
priest[b] and the warders of the threshold to put out of the Temple of
Yahweh all the equipment made for Baal and Asherah and all the
heavenly host, and he burned them outside Jerusalem in the limekilns[c]
of Kidron, and took the dust of them to Bethel. 5And he suspended the
priests whom the kings of Judah had appointed to burn sacrifice[d] at the
'high places' in the cities of Judah and around Jerusalem and those
who burned sacrifices to Baal, to the sun, and to the moon, and to
the zodiacal signs, and to all the heavenly host. 6And he brought out the
Asherah-symbol from the Temple of Yahweh outside Jerusalem to the
Wadi of Kidron and burned it in the Wadi of Kidron and ground it to
powder and cast the dust of it on the graves[e] of the common people.
7And he broke down the houses of the ritual prostitutes which were in
the Temple of Yahweh where the women wove robes[f] for the Asherah-
figure. 8And he brought all the priests from the cities of Judah and
desecrated the 'high places' where the priests had burned sacrifices[g]
from Geba right to[h] Beersheba, and he broke down the shrine[i] of the
gate-genii[j] which were at the entrance of the gate of Joshua the city-
commandant, which were at the left as one entered[k] the city-gate. 9But
the priests of the 'high places' did not go up to the altar of Yahweh in
Jerusalem, but they ate portions[l] among their colleagues. 10And he

[a]On the inclusion of the adjective *gādōl* see on 22.4.

[b]Probably, as 25.18 suggests, the singular should be read.

[c]Reading *miśrepōt* ('burning-places', hence limekilns) after Klostermann, suggested by G^{L} *en tō empurismō*, for MT *śademōt* ('flat plots', singularly inappropriate to the ravine of the Kidron below the Temple).

[d]Reading *leqaṭṭēr* with G^{L}, S, and for the obviously corrupt MT *wayeqaṭṭēr*.

[e]Reading plural with G^{L}, S, V, and T for the singular *qeber*, which might just possibly be used collectively.

[f]Reading *kuttonīm* for MT *bāttīm* ('houses'), as suggested by G^{L} (*stolās*) and the transliteration *chettieim* in G^{BA}. One MS of G, however, and Theodotion support the MT, transliterating. Šanda, therefore suggests that *bāttīm* is cognate with the Arabic *batt* ('woven garment'), and that MT is possibly to be read *baddīm*. This is accepted by G. R. Driver, *JBL* LV, 1936, p. 107.

[g]Reading *šām* for MT *šāmmā(h)*, though the final otiose *h* is often used in the Qumran biblical MSS.

[h]Reading *we'ad* for MT *'ad* after the literalism of G, S, and T.

[i]Reading *bēt* for MT *bāmōt* ('high places') after G.

[j]For MT *še'ārīm* Hoffmann proposed *śe'īrīm* ('satyrs'), cf. II Chron. 11.15 (a cult instituted by Rehoboam) and Lev. 17.7. Obviously guardian deities of the threshold of the gate were intended, who were also propitiated probably in the Passover rite of smearing the lintel and doorposts. We personally prefer the reading *šō'arīm* ('gate-keepers'). Perhaps the allusion is to the bull-colossi which represent the guardian genii of the entrance in Assyrian palaces.

[k]Reading *bā' ša'ar* after G^{L} and T, the preposition being generally omitted before the objective after a verb of motion in Hebrew.

[l]The reference here is to a privilege enjoyed by the rural priests, hence we take the reference to be their perquisites from the meat of the sacrifices, cf. Ex. 29.26; Lev. 8.29, etc., hence we prefer Kuenen's emendation *miṣwat, miṣwōt* ('statutory perquisites'), cf. Neh. 13.5, or *menāyōt* ('portions'), for *maṣṣōt* ('unleavened cakes'),

desecrated the furnace[a] which was in the Valley of ben Hinnom[b] for passing[c] one's son or one's daughter through the fire to Melech.[d] 11And he abolished the horses which the kings of Judah had provided for the sun at the entrance[e] to the Temple of Yahweh towards the chamber of Nathan-melech the chamberlain, which was in the purlieus, and the chariot[f] of the sun he burned in the fire. 12And also the altars which were on the roof,[g] which the kings of Judah had made, and the altars which Manasseh had made in the two courts of the Temple of Yahweh the king demolished [h]and beat them up small on the spot[h] and threw out the dust of them into the Wadi of Kidron. 13And the king polluted the 'high places' which were east of Jerusalem, which lay on the south of the Mount of Olives,[i] which Solomon the king of Israel had built for Ashtoreth[j] the 'abomination' of the Sidonians and for Chemosh the 'abomination' of Moab, and for 'the king', the 'abomination' of the Ammonites. 14And he smashed the standing-stones and cut down the Asherah-symbols and filled their places with men's bones. 15And as for the altar which was in Bethel, the 'high place' made by Jeroboam the son of Nebat, who caused Israel to sin, that altar and the 'high place', he demolished [k]and smashed up the stones of them, beating them[k] to dust, and he burned the Asherah.

In the proto-Hebraic script there is practically nothing to distinguish *ṣ* and *ny* if the latter are written closely together. Such portions, however, at least of the bloodless meal-offering, were eaten with unleavened bread (*maṣṣōt*) (Lev. 6.14–18), to which I Sam. 2.36 may literally refer.

[a]*tepet* should possibly be read, as G suggests, MT having the vowels of *bōšet* ('shame') substituted.

[b]Reading with Q, certain Hebrew MSS, and the Versions *ben h.* for MT *b*[e]*nē h.*

[c]Omitting MT *l*[e]*biltī* with two Hebrew MSS and G[BA], as suggested by the preposition *l*[e] before the following infinitive construct, which, with *l*[e]*biltī* of MT, would be a *hapax legomenon.*

[d]Assuming that MT uses the vowels of *bōšet* with the consonants of Melek, the title of the god manifest in the Venus-star.

[e]Reading with G, S, and V *m*[e]*bō'* for MT *mibbō'*.

[f]Reading singular with G for plural of MT.

[g]Omitting MT *ʿ*[a]*līyat 'āḥāz* as a late gloss (so Kittel, Stade), this being supported by the following relative clause 'which the kings of Judah had made'. Šanda, on the other hand, would retain the phrase and omit the article from *haggāg*, taking 'the upper chamber of Ahaz' to be an observatory.

[h]Reading after Ehrlich *way*[e]*diqqēm šām* for the impossible MT *wayyāroṣ miššām* ('and broke in pieces from there') *r* closely resembling *d*, and *ṣ q* in the proto-Hebraic script. Benzinger proposed *wayyōṣī'ēm miššām* ('and brought out from there'), which is better supported by the Versions. Ehrlich's emendation, however, is nearer MT in the proto-Hebraic script. Kimchi's suggestion *wayyāreṣ* ('and he banished'), with an impersonal object, does not recommend itself.

[i]A deliberate misvocalization in MT, *mašḥīt* ('destroyer') for *mišḥā* ('oil').

[j]The second part of the name is vocalized in MT with the vowels of *bōšet*.

[k]Reading with G *way*[e]*šabbēr 'et-'*[a]*bānāw* for the unlikely MT *wayyiśrōp 'et-habbāmā* ('and he burned the "high place"'). It is unlikely that *habbāmā* should be so soon repeated in the verse, and the sequel supports Ehrlich's reading. We should further read MT *hēdaq* as the infinitive absolute *hādēq*.

23.4. On the question of 'the chief priest' and 'the second priest' see pp. 723 n.[b] and 730 n.[b]. The chief priest and the second priest are individually named in Jer. 52.24, where they are mentioned, as here, together with the warders of the threshold.

On the reading *miśr^{e}pōt qidrōn* for *šad^{e}mōt qidrōn* see p. 730 n.[c]. M. R. Lehmann[a] offers a new interpretation. He reads *šad^{e}mōt* as *š^{e}dēmōt*, which has, he supposes, developed from *ś^{e}dē mōt*, 'fields of Mot', the Canaanite god of drought and sterility, the phrase being alleged in the Ras Shamra text (*UT*, 52, 10–11). Here Ugaritic *š*, however, would correspond to Hebrew *š*, which presents a difficulty which Croatta and Soggin[b] barely avoid by postulating in MT *šad^{e}mōt* a borrowing from Ugaritic literature. The best support for Lehmann's theory is that in Isa. 16.8, Hab. 3.17, and Jer. 31.40 *š^{e}dēmōt*, though apparently a feminine, is followed by the verb in the masculine singular, which would be intelligible if the word were originally *ś^{e}dē mōt*. Apart from the last passage, which, like II K. 23.4, refers to the Kidron Valley, the word does not, as Lehmann supposes, refer to barren land or imply pagan cults. In Deut. 32.32 and Isa. 16.8 it is associated with vines, as also in the Ugaritic text cited by Gordon. Such evidence would lead us to postulate a meaning 'terraces', possibly derived from some lost root *šādam*, 'to level', whence the general meaning 'field', i.e. for corn, as in Hab. 3.17. In Jer. 31.40 in a similar passage dealing with the Kidron Valley as a place of burial and burning MT has *š^{e}rēmōt*, probably a corruption of *šad^{e}mōt* or *š^{e}dēmōt*. Perhaps in these two passages the word is to be connected with *śīd* ('lime') and read *m^{e}śīdōt* ('limekilns').

The statement that 'he took the dust of them to Bethel', introduced, as it is, with *w* before the perfect, a late usage, seems a later addition, and is in any case a rather impracticable operation.

5. The introduction of the officials of the alien cults at this stage between the destruction of the equipment of these cults (v. 4) and the ejection of the Asherah cult from the Temple (v. 6) suggests an intrusion, which is supported by the late usage of *w^{e}* with the narrative perfect in *w^{e}hišbīt*. *k^{e}mārīm* is a derogatory reference, being reserved for priests of pagan cults. *mazzālōt* (lit. 'stations', cf. Arabic *nazala*, 'to alight', hence 'to camp') may refer to the constellations, but

[a] *VT* III, 1953, pp. 361–71.

[b] J. S. Croatta and J. A. Soggin, 'Die Bedeutung von שדמות im Alten Testament', *ZAW* LXXIV, 1962, pp. 44–50.

probably, as Akkadian *manzaltu*, refers to the stations or signs of the Zodiac, as Aquila's translation suggests.

The consciousness of a distinction between Jerusalem and its neighbourhood and the land of Judah may be noted. Alt,[a] in studying local administration in various phases of the settlement of the area, particularly under the Babylonian and Persian domination, concludes that new administrative divisions tended to respect traditional limits, and Judah proper was the country from Bethlehem to just north of Hebron, as distinct from Jerusalem, the crown possession of the house of David, with its strategic northern extension to Mizpah just south of Bethel. In the latter, Josiah was free to do as he cared. In abolishing local cult-centres in the former he was overriding local liberties. More particularly in his thesis that the topographical list in Josh. 15.21–62 really represents the administrative division of the realm of Josiah, which was reorganized on the same traditional principles, he maintains that Judah proper was limited to the districts of Bethlehem and Bethsur.[b] It is uncertain how far the reformation of Josiah extended beyond these strict limits of Judah proper. One would imagine that the political incorporation of the Philistine plain, which Alt plausibly posits, would, from its short duration, leave little scope for thorough religious reform. On this subject a Hebrew ostracon from the excavation of a small fortress on the coast near Yibneh confirms that Josiah actually extended his realm to the sea.[c] There is no reason to doubt the historicity of the Bethel incident, considering the fact that it was only two miles from Mizpah in Judah, though the date of this remains uncertain. The political organization of Josiah visualized in Josh. 15.21–62 must have been in project rather than in effect in view of the death of Josiah in 609. Alt argues that this drastic abolition of local cult-centres in Judah and the centralization of the cult in Jerusalem was not a

[a]'Bemerkungen zu einigen judäischen Ortslisten', *KS* II, pp. 291ff.

[b]'Judas Gaue unter Josia', *KS* II, pp. 285–7.

[c]See J. Naveh, 'A Hebrew Letter from the 7th Century BC', *IEJ* X, 1960, pp. 129–39, pl. 17. This ostracon, which is a letter of a peasant appealing against the commandant Hoshaʿyah for the return of a garment taken in distraint in default of contribution of corn in harvest, is a striking illustration of the operation of one of the laws in the Book of the Covenant (Ex. 22.26; cf. Deut. 24.10–13; Amos 2.8) and might suggest that Josiah's religious reformation also extended to the Philistine plain, particularly if the reference to a period of rest from work denoted the weekly Sabbath. The law, however, which enjoined the return by nightfall of a garment taken in pledge or distraint, is part of the casuistic law in the Book of the Covenant which Alt ('The Origins of Israelite Law') feasibly takes to be the Israelite application of general Canaanite law and custom.

natural political measure, but is intelligible only in the light of the religious sanction of the Deuteronomic law. Josiah was able to take this step, upon which his predecessors had not successfully engaged, because the bond between the king and Judah outside the city-state of Jerusalem had been broken since Sennacherib's conquest and provincial reorganization in 701.[a]

23.6. There is no reason to doubt that the Asherah was an image of the Canaanite mother-goddess. The deep ravine of the Kidron Valley, falling away steeply from the hill on which the Temple stood, was the natural dumping-ground for refuse from the Temple, which would be swiftly swept away by the winter floods of the wadi, which used to serve as a sewer for the northern part of the Arab city. Rubbish might also be burned here, and the lower slopes of the western escarpment of the Mount of Olives are still marked by tombs of priestly families of the Greek period, the higher slopes being occupied by common Jewish graves, many of which, since the division of Jerusalem in 1948, are now desecrated. From the last phase of the monarchic period the rock-hewn tomb of a royal chamberlain and his slave-wife at the village of Silwan is notable. This may possibly be Shebna or Shebaniah, the chamberlain of Hezekiah, on whose rock-hewn tomb Isaiah animadverts (Isa. 22.15ff.).

7. The masculine *qᵉdēšīm* is here used to denote ritual prostitutes of both sexes, who functioned in rites of imitative magic in the fertility-cult. On the reading *kuttᵒnīm* see p. 730 n.[f]. The robes were probably for those serving Asherah as well as for the image. On ritual garments see on 10.21.

8. The provincial priests are now concentrated in the central sanctuary, as Deut. 18.6–8 generally visualizes, but, contrary to Deut. 18.6f., they were not admitted to the holy office, and, whereas Deut. 18.6 visualizes an occasional visit or voluntary migration to the central sanctuary, Josiah gave the rural priests no option, but, at least for the time being, concentrated them in Jerusalem, observing, however, the Deuteronomic provision for the perquisites of the Levites (Deut. 18.3–5). Regarding the correspondence between Deuteronomy and the Josianic reformation, it must be remembered that there is no mention of the application of any Deuteronomic measures except in the cult, much in the Deuteronomic system being now no longer practicable, e.g. the holy war and many social observances. The careful note on the modification of the status of the

[a] 'Die Heimat des Deuteronomiums', *KS* II, pp. 257ff.

rural priests from what was visualized in Deuteronomy, however, does emphasize the connection between that book and the law-book of Josiah. At the same time, as against the view of the production of the law-book *ad hoc*, it suggests that the book had been produced before it was applied by Josiah, who found it necessary to modify the prescription concerning the rural priests. This minor status and restricted privilege seems to be indicated where the degradation of the family of Eli is visualized in I Sam. 2.36 ('Put me, I pray thee, into one of the priests' offices that I may eat a piece of bread'). 'From Geba to Beersheba' describes the limits of the Kingdom of Judah. The former may be either *al-Jibʿ* one and a half miles east of *ar-Rām* (Rama of I K. 15.22), as that passage indicates, or Gibeah of Saul (*Tell al-Fūl*) two miles south of *ar-Rām* and about three miles north of the Damascus Gate in Jerusalem. Beersheba is mentioned in Amos 5.5 (cf. 8.14) as a shrine to which the Israelites from the Northern kingdom made pilgrimage. The Chronicler apparently had Beersheba in mind in referring to Josiah's desecration of provincial shrines in 'Simeon' (II Chron. 34.6). Beersheba is associated in patriarchal tradition with Isaac, and we think that the shrine was 'the "high place" of Isaac' (Amos 7.9). This limitation of the reformation has been taken to throw suspicion on the references to the extension of Josiah's activity to Bethel in vv. 4 and 15ff., and both passages are further suspect owing to the usage of *w*ᵉ with the narrative perfect. There is, however, no reason to doubt that eventually, probably after 622, Josiah took this step, encouraged by the failure of Assyria to respond to his defiant rejection of the astral cult in Jerusalem and the assertion of his authority over the Philistine plain.

23.9. See p. 730. n.[1]. If *maṣṣōt* instead of *miṣwat*, *miṣwōt*, or *mᵉnāyōt is* read the reference is presumably not to the eating of unleavened bread (*maṣṣōt*) alone, but to the parts of the offering which accompanied the unleavened bread (Lev. 6.14–18).

10. Topheth of EVV, actually a common noun, as the definite article suggests, is feasibly explained by W. R. Smith[a] as the fireplace, by which he visualizes a framework set on the fire to hold the victim. He suggests that the word is Aramaic, cf. Syriac *tfīyā* and Arabic *'uṯfīya*, a stand, sometimes simply of large stones, set about the fire on the ground. If this is really an Aramaic form, the Hebrew cognate may be *šāpat*, used in 4.38 and Ezek. 24.3 of setting a pot on the fire. Granted the Aramaic form of the root, the Aramaism may be

[a] *The Religion of the Semites*, 1894², pp. 372ff., 377n.

explained otherwise than by Smith's assumption of Aramaean influence in the time of Ahaz, under whom child sacrifice is first mentioned in Judah (16.3). The Aramaism may be rather explained, on the ground that it was a rite of the cult of Melek-Aṯtar, the Ammonite god, whose cult, though probably already established in pre-Israelite Jerusalem, is noted among the cults sponsored by Solomon for his foreign harem. It must be admitted, however, that what is known of the dialects of Moab and Ammon in this period indicates that they were akin to Hebrew in phonetics, rather than to Aramaic. This gruesome hearth was located in the Valley of 'the son of Hinnom' (so Josh. 18.16), called in Josh. 15.8 simply the Valley of Hinnom, which is given as the boundary between Judah to the west and Benjamin (including Jebusite Jerusalem) to the east. These references indicate not the Kidron Valley, which W. R. Smith seems to visualize,[a] but the broad space where the *Wādī ar-Rabābī* (the Valley of Hinnom) turns east to join the Kidron Valley just north of *Bīr 'Ayyūb* (probably En Rogel), which, J. Simons[b] justly observes, was better adapted than the restricted space further up these valleys for a ritual assembly.

23.11. This is the only indication in the Old Testament that the horse was sacred to the sun, but W. R. Smith[c] notes the sacrifice of four horses (a chariot team) cast into the sea at the annual festival of the sun at Rhodes in the early Roman imperial period. Evidence from Palestine in the Israelite period of the horse as sacred to the sun may be the terra cotta figurine from the ninth century at Hazor of the horse's head with the solar emblem of the cross within a disc on its forehead.[d] The connection of the horse with the sun may be owing to its eastern provenance with the Aryan invasions *c.* 1800, cf. the Sumerian term for 'horse', 'the ass of the East'. From the Aramaean inscriptions from Zenjirli in the eighth century, when Assyrian influence was being felt, it is known that the sun was worshipped along with Baal-Hadad, as now in Judah under Manesseh and Amon. The chariot associated with the sun suggests the Assyrian title of the sun-god *rākib narkabti* ('chariot-rider').[e] A relic of this cult-object may be the winged wheels between which a deity sits on a coin

[a]*Op. cit.*, p. 272.
[b]*Jerusalem* . . ., pp. 11ff.
[c]*Op. cit.*, p. 293.
[d]Y. Yadin, *BA* XXI, 1958, pp. 46f., fig. 16.
[e]M. Jastrow, *The Religion of Babylonia and Assyria*, 1898, p. 461.

stamped YHD (Jehud) from the Persian period near Gaza.[a] In the Aramaic inscriptions from Zenjirli[b] a deity Rekub'el is mentioned, always before Shemesh, which may indicate a minor deity as charioteer of the sun-god. The sun-cult in the Temple is attested in Ezek. 8.16.

The name Nathan-melech is ambiguous. The second element may be a title either of Yahweh or of ʿAṯtar ('Molech' or 'Milcom').

On the ambiguity of *sārîs* see on I K. 22.9.

liškā is found in I Sam. 9.22 of a dining-hall adjoining the local sanctuary of Ramath. In Jer. 35.2–4 it signifies a room appropriated to one of the Temple personnel where Jeremiah offers the Rechabites wine, cf. Ezek. 40.17, where *l*ᵉ*šākōt* are chambers of priests, Levites, singers, and other Temple staff.

parwār, if, as generally supposed, a Persian word, indicates the hand of a later redactor in the present passage. The word is used in Aramaic, but not before the Persian period. In Persian it means an open pavilion; hence it may signify here a verandah, which would not be quite contrary to the Aramaic meaning 'suburb' or 'adjunct'.

23.12. On *ʿ*ᵃ*līyat 'āḥāz*, which is a gloss influenced by 20.11, where it suggests the correct reading, now supported by 1 QIs[a], see on 20.11. The roof altar as a place of sacrifice to Baal is mentioned in Jer. 32.29, and is strikingly attested by the worship of the king in the Ras Shamra text (*UT*, Krt, 60–84 ∥ 156–175). In the latter case, however, the king is in a state of ritual seclusion, hence the place of sacrifice 'on the rampart of the wall' is not perhaps the normal place of sacrifice to Baal. The roof was particularly appropriate to the worship of the heavenly bodies (Jer. 19.13; Zeph. 1.5). On the two courts of the pre-exilic Temple see on 20.4 and 21.5. The present passage is probably a late gloss suggested by 21.5, and the late usage of *w*ᵉ with the narrative perfect supports this assumption. On the reading *way*ᵉ*diqqēm šām* see p. 731 n.[h].

13. The compound prepositional phrase *ʿal-p*ᵉ*nē* may mean 'opposite' in any direction, e.g. Josh. 15.8 of the hill west of Jerusalem over the Valley of Hinnom. In the present passage it means the hill opposite Jerusalem to the east, 'in front of' meaning, as generally in the East, one's orientation to the rising sun. This is the earliest reference to the Mount of Olives, MT *har hammašḥît* being probably

[a]G. F. Hill, *Catalogue of the Greek Coins of Palestine in the British Museum* (*Galilee, Samaria, and Judaea*), 1914, p. 181, n.29.
[b]G. Cooke, *NSI*, 61, 62.

a parody of *har hammišḥā*, which, however, according to regular Old Testament usage, means 'mountain of anointing'. V translates *mons offensionis*, of which a trace survives as the name of the top south of the summit of the Mount of Olives *Jebel Baṭn al-Hawa* ('the mountain of the belly of the infernal abyss'). The reflection is probably upon the alien cults located here, see on I K. 11.7.

23.15. This ill-constructed sentence is suspect also by the usage of *w*[e] with the narrative perfect. On the reading *way*[e]*šabbēr 'et-'*[a]*bānāw* see p. 731 n.[k]. We further suggest reading the infinitive absolute *hādēq* for MT *hēdaq*.

(*f*) A FURTHER ELABORATION OF JOSIAH'S DESECRATION OF BETHEL: 23.16–20

This section reflects the interest of the Deuteronomists in the fulfilment of prophecy (cf. I K. 13). A different hand is at work here from that of the redactor in v. 15, who has already noted the destruction of the altar of Bethel, and the section may be from the Deuteronomistic redactor.

23 [16]Then Josiah turned and saw the tombs which were there in the hill[a] and he sent and took the bones from the tombs and burned them on the altar and desecrated it according to the word of Yahweh which the man of God proclaimed [b]when Jeroboam stood at the festival by the altar, and he turned and lifted his eyes upon the tomb of the man of God[b] who proclaimed these things; [17]and he said, What is that monument that I see? And the men of the city said to him, This is the tomb[c] of the man of God who came from Judah and proclaimed these words which you have carried into effect on the altar at Bethel.[d] [18]So he said, Let him be. Let no one move his bones. So they spared his bones with the bones of the prophet[e] from Samaria. [19]Moreover, all the shrines of the 'high places' which were in the cities of Samaria, which

[a]G reads *bā'īr*, but the tombs of common people were not in the city, but usually on some nearby rocky escarpment, where the soft limestone might be easily fashioned into a tomb, or natural caves so adapted. This is a common feature of sites of ancient occupation in Palestine. Hence MT must be retained.

[b]This is added by G, the passage, probably a complete line in ancient MSS, having dropped out, the scribe's eye playing him false because of the two phrases *'*[a]*šer qārā'* before and after the omission.

[c]We should expect *qeber* to be in the construct, but it is just possible to retain the definite article of MT with *qeber* before the definite *'īš hā'*[e]*lōhīm*, rendering with Montgomery, 'The tomb? That of the man of God. . . .'. *GK* (§ 127g) posits the ellipse of *qeber*, translating, 'the grave is the grave of the man of God. . . '. We prefer the reading of G[L], however *ze qeber* . . ., *z* resembling *r* at the end of the preceding word, after which it was omitted by scribal error.

[d]Reading *b*[e]*bēt-'ēl* with certain Hebrew MSS for MT *bēt'ēl*.

[e]Omitting MT *bā'*, see on v. 18.

the kings of Israel had made, provoking Yahweh[a] to anger, Josiah abolished, and he treated them according to all that he had done at Bethel. [20]And he slew all the priests of the 'high places' which were there by the altars and burned human bones upon them and returned to Jerusalem.

23.16. On the reading *bāhār* and ancient local burial see p. 738 n.[a].

The redactor shows a curious interest in the literal fulfilment of prophecy, which is a feature of the Deuteronomistic compilation of Kings, cf. Deut. 18.21f. The reference is to the incidents in I K. 13.

17. *ṣīyūn* ('monument') is found in connection with burial only in Ezek. 39.15, where, to be sure, it is used not of regular burial, but of a mark set up by the bones of a dead man protruding from the ground until a proper burial may be arranged. The tomb of the prophet obviously bore some conspicuous mark, which is all that *ṣīyūn* signifies. The pillar, or standing stone (*maṣṣēbā*) set up at Rachel's grave (Gen. 35.20) may have been such a memorial.

18. Neither in I K. 13 nor elsewhere is there any reference to a prophet coming from Samaria to Bethel, and, in fact, the city of Samaria was not founded in the time of Jeroboam I, to which the other incident refers. Hence we suppose that *bā'* is written loosely here through the influence of the clause concerning the prophet of Judah (*'ašer bā' mīhūdā*) and ought to be omitted. We suppose that *šōmerōn* in this late passage refers not to the city, but anachronistically to the Northern kingdom, and the prophet is the old prophet of Bethel of I. K. 13.

20. We note that only in the late elaboration of the account of Josiah's reformation is there any mention of the bloody elimination of the priests of the 'high places' of the Northern province, an enormity which would have reflected no credit to Josiah.

(*g*) THE GREAT PASSOVER, GENERAL REFORMS, AND APPRAISAL OF JOSIAH: 23.21–25

Historical narrative continued from v. 3.

23 [21]And the king commanded all the people saying, Keep a Passover to Yahweh your God as it is written in this book of the covenant. [22]Indeed there was no celebration such as this Passover since the days of the judges who governed Israel nor all the days of the kings

[a]Inserting *'et-yhwh* after the transitive verb with G, S, and V.

of Israel and the kings of Judah. [23]Only in the eighteenth year of king Josiah was this Passover kept to Yahweh in Jerusalem.

24 And moreover Josiah drove out the exponents of necromancy and of familiar spirits, and the household figurines, and the idols, and all the abominations which were seen in the land of Judah and in Jerusalem, in order to establish the words of the law which were written in the book which Hilkiah the priest found in the Temple of Yahweh.

25 And like him there was no king before him, he turning to Yahweh with all his will, and with all his being, and with all his strength according to all the law of Moses, and after him arose none like him.

23.21. The etymology of *pesaḥ* is uncertain. It has been connected with *pāsaḥ* ('to hobble', e.g. I K. 18.21); hence, it is suggested, 'to jump', as the angel of destruction 'jumped' the houses of the Israelites on the night of the Exodus. A more recent view is that of B. Couroyer[a] that it is an Egyptian word meaning 'blow, stroke', i.e. that which Yahweh struck in the last plague of Egypt. Both these views depend on the association with the escape from Egypt, which is really secondary. De Vaux[b] rightly emphasizes that the rite has all the appearance of a nomad custom, probably much older than the Exodus. The word may be connected with the Akkadian *pasāḫu* ('to appease'), which has been suggested, and the rite may have been connected, as de Vaux suggests (*ibid.*), with the migration of the nomad shepherds to their spring grazings. In this case the rite would come into A. van Gennep's categories of *rites de passage*, connected with a change of season or locality, which primitive man never underwent without prophylactic rites. It may be that the health of the animals was provided for in this way in view of the lambing and the possible ill effects of the lusher grazings after the poor pickings of winter. We offer the suggestion that the word is cognate with the Arabic verb *fasaḥa* ('to be clear'). One immediately thinks of the celebration of the feast on the night of the full moon in the middle of the spring month Abib, and the Arabic verb does denote atmospheric clearness, usually of dawn. It denotes also clearness of milk, and we suggest that this is the significence of *pesaḥ*, the rites of *pesaḥ* being designed to mark the time when the milk of the ewes and goats is clear of impurities after birth, and it is safe both hygienically and ritually for human consumption. Whatever the etymology of *pesaḥ* and the origin of the rite, it was eventually invested in Hebrew

[a]'L'origine égyptienne du mot "Pâque" ', *RB* LXII, 1955, pp. 481–96.
[b]*Ancient Israel*, p. 489.

tradition with a historical significance as a sacrament of the great deliverance from Egypt.

In the earliest description of the Passover, in J (Ex. 12.21–27), it is noteworthy that there is no association with the Feast of *maṣṣōt* (Unleavened Bread), which in turn is described independently of the Passover in the earliest passage where it is noted, in E (Ex. 23.15), where it is a feast to which, like the Feasts of Weeks and Tabernacles, pilgrimage (*ḥag*) is made to a central shrine. It will be noted that in Josiah's Passover there is no mention of *maṣṣōt*.

In Deut. 16.1–8, where the Passover is combined with the Feast of Unleavened Bread and dated not on a given day, but generally in the month Abib, it is generally claimed by critics that vv. 1, 2, 4b–7, which describe the Passover, are originally independent of vv. 3, 4a, 8, which refer properly to the Feast of Unleavened Bread. The main grounds of this separation of the feasts is that vv. 1, 2, 4b–7 refer to the Passover apparently as a one-day festival, the meal being eaten at night at a central sanctuary and the people dispersing next morning 'to your tents'. The ordinance for the Feast of Unleavened Bread, on the other hand (vv. 3, 4a, 8), visualizes a seven-day feast. It is possible, however, that what the dispersal 'to your tents' signifies is not, as often, 'home', but the reference may be to the worshippers living in tents by the sanctuary for a seven-day feast including Unleavened Bread and indicate the end of the ritual.[a] There is no doubt that the Passover as a nomadic festival was artificially associated with the Feast of Unleavened Bread, which was connected with the rites of desacralization of the new crop at the beginning of the barley harvest, and that in this passage we have evidence of this combination of traditions. In emphasizing the difference between this ordinance for the Passover in Deut. 16.1, 2, 4b–7 and the Passover rites in other early traditions, the young of cattle as well as sheep and goats being not roasted, but boiled (Deut. 16.7), Nicolsky[b] argues that this is determined by Josiah's centralization of the rite in the Temple which had facilities for boiling such ample sacrifices. This, of course, could apply to any local sanctuary, e.g. Shiloh in I Sam. 2.13–15, and leaves the question of the association of Passover and Unleavened Bread in Josiah's festival unsolved.

The earliest texts on Passover describe it as the feast of a family or a limited community and not as a pilgrimage involving general

[a] J. Pedersen, *Israel* III–IV, pp. 387ff.

[b] 'Pascha im Kulte des jerusalemischen Tempels', *ZAW* XLV, 1927, pp. 242–4.

pilgrimage to a central shrine. The novelty of Josiah's Passover, on the other hand, consists in the elevation of the Passover to the status of a pilgrimage feast celebrated at the central sanctuary with a real national significance.

It will be noted that neither this passage nor the account of the limited reformation of Hezekiah in 18.4 takes any account of the Passover attributed to Hezekiah by II Chron. 30. This seems, then, to be a reflection of Josiah's Passover, though A. C. Welch[a] treats it seriously without any question. W. Rudolph[b] argues that the Passover ordinance which prescribes the celebration of the festival at the central sanctuary (Deut. 16.5ff.) was not formulated till after Hezekiah's time and so militates against the historicity of the tradition of Hezekiah's passover. This is not so self-evident as Rudolph supposes. It is true that the promulgation of the nucleus of the Deuteronomic law is probably to be dated to the time of Josiah's reformation, but it may still represent Northern traditions which were brought to Judah by refugees from the North in Hezekiah's reign. Again, there is no reason to doubt that, as II Chron. 30.1a, 5a states, Hezekiah sent an appeal to the Israelites in Samaria and Galilee and that he may even have projected a public Passover in Jerusalem as a national manifesto (II Chron. 30.1b, 5b). But in view of the fact that the Passover is not mentioned in the account of Hezekiah's reformation in Kings and of the explicit statement of II K. 23.22 that there was no precedent for Josiah's passover since the time of the judges, it is questionable if Hezekiah was able to hold such a Passover at Jerusalem as II Chron. 30 describes.

The Deuteronomistic account of Josiah's Passover exasperates us by its silence as to the specific motive for the innovation. Nicolsky (*op. cit.*) would see in the celebration of Josiah's Passover, which was probably already associated with the deliverance from Egypt,[c] an assertion of nationalist feeling at a time when there was a danger of Judah exchanging Assyrian for Egyptian vassalage, which was what actually happened in 609. Certainly, as he points out, Egypt under Psammetichus I (671–617) was already challenging Assyria in Palestine, as the tradition of the 29 years' menace to Ashdod

[a] *Post-Exilic Judaism*, pp. 23ff.

[b] *Chronikbücher*, HAT, ed. Eissfeldt, 1955, p. 299.

[c] Mowinckel latterly saw an innovation in the association of the Passover with the whole theme of the Exodus instead of with only certain elements in that theme. The association of the Passover with the whole theme of the Exodus in the J source of the Pentateuch he regards as secondary and owing to the influence of D.

(Herodotus II, 147) suggests. He makes the feasible suggestion that danger of Egyptian domination was the major problem confronting Judah on the accession of the young Josiah. If that were so, and if the institution of the Passover by Josiah in Jerusalem were designed as an anti-Egyptian demonstration, it is odd that the anti-Egyptian party who put Josiah on the throne should have waited 18 years for this demonstration.[a]

A. S. Kapelrud[b] has recently suggested that the Passover with its theme of the great deliverance from Egypt as a preliminary to the covenant was given special prominence to counteract Assyrian influence in the New Year festival. In view of the Israelite development of the latter with its predominant theme of the Kingship of God from an earlier Canaanite New Year liturgy, the Feast of Tabernacles at the autumnal New Year had certainly become sufficiently coloured by Israelite experience to withstand undue influence from the analogous Assyrian festival. The triumph of God as King over the menacing forces of chaos, which was characteristic of this occasion, was further particularized by the experience of the covenant and its ritual and social obligations, which was also associated with this occasion, as Deut. 31.10 indicates.[c] We should emphasize the theme of the Kingship of God developed from the Canaanite New Year liturgy with remarkably persistent use of Canaanite imagery. This association in Israelite worship, with danger of assimilation of Canaanite religion, is surely reflected in the insistence of the early calendar in Ex. 23.10–19 (E) and the Ritual Code (Ex. 34.10ff. J) that this festival should be kept 'before the Lord God of Israel', that is to say at the central assembly of the

[a]Nicolsky further suggests that the Passover in the Temple was a prophylactic ritual to protect the Temple and its personnel from the wrath of God apprehended because of the contamination of alien cults. He bases his theory on Zeph. 1, though we consider that he overdraws his evidence for the conception of a night of wrath comparable to the passage of the angel of destruction on the night of the Passover in Egypt. The evidence of the Passover as a festival in the centralized cult emphasizes the significance of the rite as a sacrament of deliverance and as a rite effecting the solidarity of the community, and it is hard to see how a national assembly of this nature was necessary to effect a prophylactic rite for the Temple, especially as it was preceded by probably several months of purging of alien contaminations.

[b]A. S. Kapelrud, 'The Role of the Cult in Old Israel', *The Bible in Modern Scholarship*, ed. J. P. Hyatt, 1965, pp. 51ff.

[c]Thus Weiser and von Rad are right in seeing the New Year festival as the occasion for the sacramental celebration of the covenant, though in our opinion they err in the exclusive emphasis they lay upon that element in the festival.

sacral confederacy, which at such an assembly asserted its solidarity on the basis of the experience of the sovereign grace and power of God in the great deliverance and the covenant. As Deut. 31.10 indicates, the covenant-sacrament was the main theme of this festival 'every seventh year', though we believe that this did not exclude the theme of the Kingship of God. Otherwise we believe that the emphasis in the annual festival was laid on the Kingship of God, though this did not exclude the theme of the covenant and its obligations, which Mowinckel recognized as an element in the annual festival, which he thought of as Yahweh's Enthronement Festival.[a]

Finally, the persistence of the theme of the Kingship of God at the New Year festival in Nahum (e.g. 1.15[2.1], cf. Isa. 52.7), on which Deutero-Isaiah could rebuild (cf. especially Isa. 52.7 and the hymns of praise to God as Lord of history) indicates the permanent significance of the theme of the Kingship of God in the liturgy of the autumn festival in Israel, which was sufficiently strongly impregnated with Israelite tradition to resist assimilation to the ideology of the Assyrian New Year festival where it differed from that in Israel. The new emphasis given to the Passover in Josiah's reformation has undoubtedly a nationalistic significance, though there is no evidence that as a public sacrament in the Temple at Jerusalem it was more than a unique inaugural rite.

Mowinckel[b] maintained that Josiah's Passover was the occasion of his covenant. Now the *Sitz im Leben* of the covenant, as Mowinckel himself emphasized, was the autumnal New Year festival, and this is supported on this occasion by the addition of G to 22.3 'in the seventh (*var. lect.* eighth) month'. Thus, on Mowinckel's assumption, the Passover, which, by all traditions was a spring festival, must have been detached from its proper *Sitz im Leben* and have been made the ritual of the sacrament of the deliverance from Egypt, which was the historical context of the law. This is a matter which cannot well be determined, though we prefer to regard the Passover as being celebrated in the spring as marking the end of the main phase of Josiah's reformation which had been inaugurated by the covenant in its traditional context in the New Year festival in autumn. Originally limited to comparatively small kinship groups (*mišpāḥōt*) as a domestic festival, it now became a great national festival, and, even though properly associated, as Mowinckel once contended, with only

[a]S. Mowinckel, *Le Décalogue*, 1927, pp. 119ff.
[b]*Psalmenstudien* II, 1922, pp. 204–6.

one phase of the Exodus tradition, was still sufficiently associated with that tradition to be a fitting sacrament of the great deliverance and an apt expression of national solidarity.

Josiah's Passover, however, is stated to be not an absolute innovation and we are referred back to the days of the judges. Now, according the the Deuteronomistic schematization of the Israelite invasion of Palestine, the last time that Israel was together for each family or kinship group to observe this domestic occasion in one place was when Israel under Joshua crossed the Jordan in the spring and paused at Gilgal by Jericho, which became the first shrine of all Israel in Palestine. It is uncertain if the Passover noted in Josh. 5.10–12 was really an element in the popular cult at the shrine of Gilgal, where the sacrament and cult-legend of the *Heilsgeschichte*, culminating in the occupation of the Promised Land, and later the covenant tradition, was at home.[a] It may be, after all, a mere incidental note indicating the time of the conquest in the Deuteronomistic account, with nothing really to do with the sacrament of the Exodus and Conquest at the shrine of Gilgal. But whatever its original significance in this context, it was now under Josiah made an essential element in the sacrament of the great deliverance from Egypt.

23.24. On *'ōbōt* and *yiddeʿōnīm* see on 21.6. *terāpīm* were used in divination (Ezek. 21.26; Judg. 17.5; 18.14, 17; I Sam. 15.23; Hos. 3.4; Zech. 10.2), and they may have this significance here. They were apparently figurines or household gods (Gen. 31.19ff., though not, we believe, in I Sam. 19.13ff., where we agree with Albright in translating *terāpīm* as 'rags'). Possibly the many figurines with the features of Asherah and Astarte found at Palestinian sites and used, we believe, in rites of imitative magic to promote fertility rank as *terāpīm*. *gillūlīm* (root *gll*, 'to roll') are images in the round.

(*h*) NOTE BY THE REDACTOR ON THE IRREVOCABLE WRATH OF GOD: 23.26–27

23 [26]But Yahweh did not turn from the heat of his great anger, for his anger was hot against Judah on account of all the provocative acts whereby Manasseh provoked him. [27]So Yahweh said, I will remove

[a]G. von Rad, 'Das formgeschichtliche Problem des Hexateuch', *Gesammelte Studien zum AT*, pp. 52–55; *The Problem of the Hexateuch*, pp. 45–48, who regards the occasion as the Feast of Weeks; H. J. Kraus, 'Gilgal . . .', *VT* I, 1951, pp. 181–99, who regards it as the Feast of Maṣṣoth at the beginning of the barley harvest, when the crossing of the Jordan, which both assume to be an important element in the ritual of the sacrament of the deliverance and conquest, was practicable before the rising of Jordan with the melting snow from Hermon.

Judah also from my presence just as I removed Israel, and I will reject this city which I have chosen, Jerusalem, and the Temple, concerning which I said, My name shall be there.

(*i*) REFERENCE TO THE SECULAR SOURCES FOR THE HISTORY OF JOSIAH'S REIGN: 23.28

This is a feature of the Deuteronomistic epilogue to the reigns of kings, but in this case the note of the king's death and burial (vv. 29f.) is made in citation of the Annals of Judah.

23 28Now as for the rest of the acts of Josiah and all that he did, are they not written in the Book of the Chronicles of the Kings of Judah?

23.28. At this point we may deplore the restricted use which the compiler made of the Annals, which would contain a description of Josiah's provincial organization, which, according to Alt,[a] is preserved in Josh. 15; 18; 19, to which Noth[b] would add Josh. 13, which he takes to reflect Josiah's reorganization of Transjordan. The truth of this thesis is suggested by the inclusion of Bethel and Ophrah in Benjamin (Josh. 18.22f.) instead of in Joseph, their traditional affinity, the inclusion of the Philistine Ekron, Ashdod, and Gaza in Judah (Josh. 15.45–47), and the fact that Josiah could contest the Pharaoh's march through Palestine at Megiddo (II K. 23.29), which had been the administrative centre of the Assyrian province of that name, which included all Galilee and the great central plain. Unfortunately we have no indication of the chronology of this attempt to revive the united monarchy as under David and Solomon, but conceivably Josiah's progress was gradual, beginning with the cleansing of the Temple from astral cults which were symbols of Assyrian domination, then, when no opposition was met, by the recovery of land in Judah which had been taken by Sennacherib from Hezekiah, with the incorporation of areas in the Philistine plain such as Ekron and Ashdod, where the Assyrians were always careful to have vassals in office with military settlers. The desecration of Bethel unfortunately cannot be dated, but, as it lay but two miles beyond the frontier of Judah, it was a natural step. Since there is no mention of suppression of local sanctuaries in the north except 'in the cities of Samaria' (II K. 23.19), i.e. in the Assyrian province of that name, it is unlikely that Josiah had time to do more than claim Galilee and what territory it was practicable to claim in Trans-

[a]'Judas Gaue unter Josias', *KS* II, pp. 276ff.
[b]*ZAW* LX, 1944, pp. 49ff.

Jordan. To a large extent the topographical lists in Josh. 13; 15; 18; 19 represent Josiah's programme rather than his achievement.

(*j*) THE DEATH AND BURIAL OF JOSIAH: 23.29f.

From the Annals of Judah.

23 [29]In his days Pharaoh Necho, king of Egypt, made an expedition against the king of Assyria by the river Euphrates and king Josiah went to meet him and he slew him at Megiddo when he saw him. [30]And his retainers drove him dying from Megiddo and brought him to Jerusalem, and they buried him in his tomb, and the people of the land took Jehoahaz the son of Josiah and anointed him and made him king in the place of his father.

23.29. This is a very perfunctory statement of important historical events. Not only does the statement that 'Josiah went to meet' Necho leave us uncertain whether he went with hostile intent, or to parley, or at Necho's summons as to a recalcitrant vassal of his Assyrian suzerain,[a] but the circumstances of Josiah's death are uncertain also. The statement that Necho 'made an expedition *against* the king of Assyria' is contradicted by Josephus[b] and by the Babylonian Chronicle,[c] from which the following summary of events may be reconstructed. In 629 in southern Mesopotamia the Assyrian army was repulsed before Babylon, and in 625 Nabopolassar was proclaimed king. For the next decade Assyria was on the defensive, and this situation encouraged the Medes under Cyaxares to attack, apparently independently of the Babylonians. In 614 the Medes captured and plundered Ashur, the old capital of Assyria, and united with the Babylonians in an attack on Nineveh, which fell in 612. Now Necho, who had been a vassal of Assyria, attempted to retrieve the situation, ostensibly for Assyria, but actually to anticipate Babylonian control of Syria and Palestine and a possible advance on Egypt herself. Supported by Egypt, an Assyrian king Ashuruballiṭ maintained a token state in Harran, which in turn fell to the Medes and Babylonians in 610. Still Egypt maintained her support, based apparently on the fortress of Carchemish, commanding an important crossing of the Euphrates (cf. II Chron. 35.20, which is usually taken as a confusion with the disastrous Egyptian campaign of 605 in Jer. 46.2). In the summer of the 17th year of Nabopolassar's reign (609) an Egyptian

[a]So A. C. Welch, *ZAW* XLIII, 1925, p. 255.
[b]*Ant.* X, 5.1.
[c]C. J. Gadd, *The Fall of Nineveh*, 1923.

army advanced over the Euphrates and made a great, though unsuccessful, effort to retake Harran. So far the Babylonian Chronicle. Obviously Josiah saw in Necho's advance a menace to his designs for a reunited Hebrew state, and advanced to meet him at Megiddo.[a] Herodotus (II, 159) seems to retain a tradition of this action, which he locates at *Magdōlos*, referring to Necho's subsequent fortification of *Kadytis* in Syria. Locations for these places have been suggested at Migdal just north of Gaza and at Gaza. Probably Herodotus really meant Megiddo and Kadesh on the Orontes. The account in II Chron. 35.20–24 is much more circumstantial, stating that Josiah went to oppose Necho at the strategic pass of Megiddo, but Necho endeavoured to dissuade him from hostility, seeking only passage to the north. Josiah, however, knowing that this would only frustrate his designs for political independence, persisted, and was slain in battle. From details in the Babylonian Chronicle this encounter is certainly to be dated in the early summer of 609, actually in, or just before, Tammuz, i.e. June-July.[b] In the present passage in Kings it is possible that the preposition *ʿal* before *melek ʾaššūr* is a scribal error for *ʾel*, as the Babylonian Chronicle and Josephus demand, though it might still mean 'on behalf of', but the probable explanation is that the Deuteronomistic compiler has simply misunderstood the general political situation.

23.30. Our translation of *mēt* as 'dying' rather than 'dead' is suggested by the statement in II Chron. 35.23f. '. . . and the king said to his retainers, Take me away, for I am badly wounded. His retainers therefore took him out of that chariot and put him in the second chariot that he had, and they brought him to Jerusalem, and he died. . . .' On the burial of the kings of Judah after Hezekiah see on 21.18. On 'the people of the land' see on 11.14. From v. 36 it emerges that the people of the land preferred Jehoahaz to his older brother Eliakim (Jehoiakim), who was, in fact, a half-brother (cf. vv. 31, 36). From what we know of Jehoiakim it is likely that Jehoahaz was a man of stronger character than his older brother, who seems to have been an unprincipled political adventurer, who sought his future in submission to whatever major power seemed at the moment likely to prove victorious.

[a]F. M. Cross and D. N. Freedman, *JNES* XII, 1953, pp. 56–58, suggest that Josiah opposed the Egyptians in support of Nabopolassar, but there is no evidence for this.

[b]D. J. Wiseman, *Chronicles of Chaldaean Kings (626–556) in the British Museum*, 1956, pp. 62ff.

4. THE REIGN AND REMOVAL OF JEHOAHAZ: 23.31–35

(a) THE DEUTERONOMISTIC INTRODUCTION TO THE REIGN OF JEHOAHAZ: 23.31f.

23 [31]Jehoahaz was twenty-three years old when he became king, and he reigned three months in Jerusalem, and his mother's name was Hamital[a] the daughter of Jeremiah from Libnah. [32]And he did evil in the sight of Yahweh according to all that his fathers had done.

23.31. Jehoahaz was the throne-name of the king, or would have been had he survived till his formal accession at the New Year festival in Tishri. His private name, as we learn from Jeremiah's dirge over him, was Shallum (Jer. 22.10ff.).

The statement that Jehoahaz reigned three months is confirmed by the Babylonian Chronicle, which states that Necho's campaign in 609 in northern Mesopotamia lasted from Tammuz (June-July) to Elul (August-Sept.),[b] the death of Josiah taking place on Necho's journey northwards and the deposition of Jehoahaz on his return. From the revolt of Libnah from Judah under Jehoram (8.22) it appears that Libnah, probably *Tell aṣ-Ṣāfī*, on a spur of the Shephelah dominating the coastal plain south-west of Jaffa and the way to the interior by the Vale of Elah (*Wādī as-Sanṭ*), maintained a doubtful loyalty to Judah, so that Josiah's marriage with the daughter of a local notable may have had a political purpose.

The name Hamital contains as its first element the kin-name 'husband's father' (i.e. the god of the husband's people) and *ṭal*, which is taken by Noth[c] as 'dew'. This we think unlikely. We regard it as a dialectic form of Hebrew *ṣēl* ('shadow', 'protection'), cf. *Ṣilli-bēl*. The form *ṭal* for *ṣel* is attested in the Aramaic copy of the Behistun inscription from Elephantine. The element *ṭal* occurs in the name Abital (II Sam. 3.4), the mother of the fifth son of David.

Jehoahaz could not have had much opportunity to do evil 'according to all that his fathers had done', and this seems an inference on the part of the Deuteronomist from his miserable fate. His sin, however, may have been that he was too ready to go to Necho at Riblah,

[a]Reading Hamital as in 24.18 and the consonantal text of Jer. 52.1 and with Hebrew MSS, G and V for MT Hamutal. The kin-name *ḥamu* demands the pronominal suffix.

[b]Wiseman, *op. cit.*, pp. 62ff.

[c]*IP*, pp. 39, 79.

possibly to seek confirmation of his authority. In this case the people of the land had made a great error of judgement.

(*b*) THE REMOVAL OF JEHOAHAZ AND THE ELEVATION AND RULE OF JEHOIAKIM AS AN EGYPTIAN VASSAL: 23.33–35

From the Annals of Judah.

23 33And Pharaoh Necho put him into custody[a] at Riblah in the land of Hamath [b]so that he should not reign in Jerusalem,[b] and he imposed upon the land an indemnity of 100 talents of silver and (?)[c] talents of gold. 34And Pharaoh Necho made Eliakim the son of Josiah king in place of his father Josiah and he changed his name to Jehoiakim, and he took Jehoahaz and brought[d] him to Egypt, and he died there. 35And Jehoiakim gave the silver and the gold to Pharaoh; he just assessed the land to give the silver as Pharaoh had ordered, of every one according to his assessment he exacted [e]the silver and the gold[e] to give to Pharaoh Necho.

23.33. Riblah was the headquarters also of Nebuchadrezzar in 586 (25.6, 20). Lying about 20 miles south of Hama in the gap giving access from the coast to the interior and access to the south by the Biqʿa, it was admirably adapted as headquarters for an invading force. Its proximity to Kadesh on the upper Orontes suggests that *Kadytis* of Herodotus II, 159 was not Gaza, but Kadesh, hence his *Magdōlos* is more likely to be a corruption of Megiddo than to denote Migdol north of Gaza (see on v. 29).

ʿānaš is found meaning 'to fine' in Ex. 21.22; Deut. 22.19; Amos 2.8, etc. The present passage is the only case where it signifies a war indemnity. The amount is only a third of Sennacherib's exaction from Hezekiah, and possibly indicates a conciliatory attitude on the

[a]G and II Chron. 36.3 read *wayᵉsīrēhū* ('and he removed him'), which is quite feasible, if less explicit than MT *wayyaʾasᵉrēhū*. The sequel demands that Necho kept Jehoahaz in custody.

[b]If the phrase is original here and not influenced by the parallel account in Chronicles *mimᵉlōk* rather than *bimᵉlōk* should be read, as Q, G, V and T suggest, the preposition *min* having the privative sense.

[c]From other notes of tribute, e.g. Hezekiah's tribute to Sennacherib (18.14), the ratio of gold to silver should be 1:10, hence a numeral is expected before *kikkar* in MT. G^L and S read *wᵉʿeśer kikkᵉrē* . . . ('and 10 talents . . .'). G^BA, retaining MT *kikkar*, read *mēʾā* ('100 . . .').

[d]Reading with G^BA *wayyābēʾ* for MT *wayyābōʾ* ('and he came'), supported by G^L and Chronicles, which read *wayᵉbīʾēhū*.

[e]Omitting 'even the people of the land' as an explanatory gloss. *ʾet-hakkesep wᵉʾet-hazzāhāb* ('the silver and the gold'), should probably also be omitted, since *nāgaś* normally takes only a personal object.

part of Necho, highly advisable in view of the fact that his controversy with Babylon was not yet decided.

23.34. Conciliation of Jewish opinion may also have suggested the throne-name of Necho's nominee Jehoiakim, though the change of his name by the Pharaoh has its own significance. In the days of independence the king on his accession received an assuring oracle (e.g. Ps. 110) and his new name was of this character. That is to say, it was conferred by God. Now the name is conferred by the Pharaoh, who, to be sure, was considered a god incarnate in Egypt. This act of itself emphasized the vassal status of Judah. The fate of Jehoahaz is referred to in the dirge of Jeremiah (22.10ff.), where he is called by his private name Shallum.

35. The particle *'ak* is properly taken by Montgomery as 'simply', 'just'. *'ērek* is used for valuation for taxation in 12.5 and of valuation in the case of trespass-offerings in Lev. 5.15, 18, 25. Here the tax seems to have been universally exacted and not, as in the case of Menahem's tribute to Tiglath-pileser III (15.19), from the men of property alone. This may be indicated by the gloss 'the people of the land', which may denote all responsible men of Judah, ideally members of the sacral community, but it may also, as in 25.19 and in the Assyrian phrase *nišē māti*, denote local notables as representatives of the people. *nāgaś* means 'to harry, drive'. It is found meaning 'to exact tribute' in Dan. 11.20. It is noteworthy that there was no longer anything in the treasury of palace or Temple on which to draw for the tribute, as in the case of Hezekiah's tribute to Sennacherib.

5. THE END OF THE KINGDOM OF JUDAH: 23.36–25.21

For this period of 23 years covering the reigns of the last three kings of Judah the Annals of Judah are used up till Nebuchadrezzar's final engagement with Necho in Palestine (24.7), an event which is dated by Josephus on the authority of Berossus[a] and by the Babylonian Chronicle[b] in 601. Up to this point the reign of Jehoiakim is introduced and generally assessed by the familiar Deuteronomistic formula (23.36f.) and closed with the Deuteronomistic epilogue (24.5f.). In this period the expedition of Nebuchadrezzar is mentioned with the submission of Jehoiakim and his revolt after three years, probably

[a] *Ant.* X, 6.1.
[b] D. J. Wiseman, *op. cit.*, pp. 70ff.

from an annalistic source (24.1), and the note on the failure of Egypt to advance into Palestine (v. 7) is probably from the same source. The statement on the harassing of Judah by raiding parties from beyond Jordan (24.2–4), in so far as it visualizes the final destruction of Judah, and sees them as the manifestation of the irrevocable wrath of God, is obviously not directly from an annalistic source, though it may rest ultimately on such a source. The homiletic tone indicates the Deuteronomist, and the certainty of the final ruin of Judah indicates the exilic redactor. For the 12 years that elapsed from the revolt of Jehoiakim from Babylon in 598, which, surprisingly enough, is barely mentioned (v. 1), without details of Nebuchadrezzar's punitive raid, until the final collapse of Judah and the continuation of the history of the Jews who remained under Gedaliah (25.22–26) and the fate of Jehoiachin in Babylon until his release in 561 (25.27–30), the Deuteronomistic redactor of the Exile writes of contemporary events of which he had personal knowledge and, except in the Gedaliah incident, required no independent sources. It is noteworthy that this second Deuteronomist uses the same formula of introduction to, and general assessment of, the reigns of Jehoiachin (24.8f.) and Zedekiah (24.18f.) as the Deuteronomistic compiler used for the earlier kings. This, however, is natural in the case of one who was consciously rounding off the earlier work. An indication of spontaneous composition in the final section of Kings (24.8–25.30) independent of other sources is the continuous narrative style as distinct from the staccato statements of facts which characterize annalistic sources in the first compilation. There are, however, passages in this section incorporated from other sources, e.g. 25.16f., the description of the pillars Jachin and Boaz, which with Jer. 52.20–23, which is much fuller, is drawn from a more ancient source describing the furniture of the Temple, and the incident of Gedaliah (25.22–26), which is probably a summary from a fuller source used in Jer. 40.7–41.18. In the latter passage the relative fullness of the account in Jeremiah is explained by the fact that the events happened in Palestine and were therefore known more intimately to those interested in the work of Jeremiah. The exilic redactor of Kings, possibly in Mesopotamia, had not the opportunity of such knowledge of what happened in Palestine, so made a summary of the passage in Jeremiah, or of its original. The passage 24.13 is obviously an anachronistic account of the spoliation of the Temple at the final destruction of Jerusalem 11 years later, and v. 14, being a rough duplicate of the description of those deported with Jehoiachin in v. 16, must be a later addition.

There is no clear indication of the point at which the first Deuteronomistic compilation ended and the exilic continuation began. The fact that after the bare mention of Jehoiakim's revolt against Nebuchadrezzar (24.1) nothing more is mentioned in Kings about this significant event till the siege of Jerusalem under his son Jehoiachin would seem to suggest a break in the records. Since the Babylonian Chronicle dates the siege of Jerusalem precisely from Chislev (December) 598 to Adar (March) 597, and Jehoiachin reigned only three months (24.8), the siege must have begun before Jehoiakim's death or there must have been an interval between the death of Jehoiakim and the accession of Jehoiachin. Of this there is no mention in Kings, so that a definite break in the records is indicated between the outbreak of the revolt of Jehoiakim in 598 and the siege of Jerusalem under Jehoiachin from December 598 to March 597. This seems to us to indicate that the first Deuteronomistic compilation ended between the outbreak of the revolt and the death of Jehoiakim, and after a certain hiatus the history was continued after the Exile, possibly by the redactor. This is suggested by the fact that the fall of Jerusalem is dated in the eighth year of Nebuchadrezzar (24.12), the first dating in Kings by foreign chronology.

This view is confirmed by the obscurity surrounding the actual death of Jehoiakim. In what purports to be the last citation from the Book of the Chronicles of the Kings of Judah (24.5), the death of Jehoiakim is mentioned (v. 6), but no detail of burial is given as is usual in the Deuteronomistic epilogues. In II Chron. 36.6 it is stated that Nebuchadrezzar actually arrested Jehoiakim with the intention of taking him to Babylon. Nothing is said here of his death and burial in MT, though G on the passage states that he was buried in the enclosure of Uzza (see on 21.18). If this was at the confluence of the Kidron and Hinnom Valleys, this would accord with Jeremiah's prediction (Jer. 22.19) that Jehoiakim would be 'buried with the burial of an ass' and 'cast forth beyond the gates of Jerusalem'. Josephus[a] states that Jehoiakim, convinced by Jeremiah's assurances of the peaceful intentions of Babylon, submitted to Nebuchadrezzar after his revolt, but was put to death and thrown outside the wall unburied. Thereafter Nebuchadrezzar deported 3,000 from Jerusalem, including Ezekiel, a tradition which agrees with the

[a] *Ant.* X, 6.3.

statement in Dan. 1.2 that there was a deportation in the reign of Jehoiakim. Without committing ourselves to one tradition or another, we may say that this uncertainty confirms our opinion that the first work of the Deuteronomist, the compilation of Kings, ended before the death of Jehoiakim, and the sequel is from a later hand, which, however, modelled the epilogue on Jehoiakim on the style of the compiler, even to the extent of the reference to the Annals of Judah.

This is the period of the activity of the prophet Jeremiah, and there are passages which are repeated in the Book of Jeremiah. The most notable case is 24.18–25.21, which is reduplicated in Jer. 52.1–27, even to the extent of the repetition of the formal introduction to, and assessment of, the reign of Zedekiah (24.18=Jer. 52.1) and the statement 'thus Judah was deported from his own land' (25.21 = Jer. 52.27). The stylistic break after Jer. 51 and the rubric in Jer. 51.64b 'thus far are the words of Jeremiah' indicate that Jer. 52 is an appendix ending the book; cf. II K. 18.13–20.19 at the end of Isaiah of Jerusalem (Isa. 36–39). There can be no question but that 24.18–25.21 is prior to Jer. 52.1–27, though occasionally the latter has preserved the better text. Jer. 52.28–30 adds a list of deportees which is not included in the roughly parallel passage in Kings, and this suggests that there were written records available for this period, which the Deuteronomistic reviser could have consulted had he wished. After this significant addition to this passage in Kings, Jer. 52.31–34 continues with the account of the fate of Jehoiachin in exile, repeating II K. 25.27–30. Here again there is a significant addition in the explicit mention of the death of Jehoiachin (v. 34), this being merely implied in II K. 25.30. The Gedaliah incident (II K. 25.22–26) is described also, but much more fully and circumstantially in Jer. 40.7–41.18. The verbal correspondence between the two passages indicates that that in Kings is a summary of the original source which was used much more fully in Jeremiah.

(*a*) THE DEUTERONOMISTIC INTRODUCTION TO THE REIGN OF JEHOIAKIM: 23.36f.

23 [36]Jehoiakim was twenty-five years old when he became king, and he reigned eleven years in Jerusalem, and his mother's name was Zebudah[a] the daughter of Pedaiah from Rumah. [37]And he did evil in the sight of Yahweh according to all that his fathers did.

[a]So Q, cf. K *z^ebiddā*; probably, as certain MSS suggest, the daghesh should be omitted from *d*. Both forms in that case would be passives, but in view of the occurrence of the masculine form *zābūd* in I K. 4.5 Q is to be preferred.

23.36. Here we have two firm dates, thanks to synchronism with Babylonian records. Since the Babylonian Chronicle of Nabopolassar dates the expedition of Necho in 609, from Tammuz to Elul,[a] which would coincide with the three months' reign of Josiah's successor Jehoahaz (23.31), Jehoiakim's reign probably dates from the New Year festival in 608 to 598. Now neither the Old Testament nor the Babylonian Chronicle of Nebuchadrezzar records details of Jehoiakim's final revolt. The Old Testament gives Jehoiachin a reign of three months (24.8), which ended with the fall of Jerusalem in Adar (March) 597 according to the Chronicle of Nebuchadrezzar.[b] Hence Jehoiachin succeeded in December–January, probably after the siege of Jerusalem began, in 597, so that a few months had elapsed since the death of Jehoiakim in 598. There is nothing in the Old Testament to contradict this conclusion and, indeed, it is supported by the traditions in Chronicles and Josephus, which we have cited in the critical introduction to this section and by the vagueness of Kings on the reign of Jehoiakim. Our explanation of the silence of Scripture on such a significant lapse of royal authority is that the first compilation of Kings was completed in the reign of Jehoiakim and the account of the final phase of the history of Judah resumed after a certain interval by the exilic editor.

z^ebūdā means 'gifted', and may have some reference to 'dowry', cf. Syrian *zebdā*' ('dowry'), cf. the masculine form I K. 4.5. Rumah is probably to be located at *Ḫirbet Rūma* north of *Saffūrīyeh* on the southern edge of the Plain of *Baṭṭūf*.[c] This was in the Assyrian province of Megiddo. The name of Zebudah's father, Pedaiah ('Yahweh has redeemed'), possibly indicates that his family had been spared in the deportation under Tiglath-pileser III (734), when the grandfather of Pedaiah, whose name he bore, was born.

(*b*) THE SUBMISSION OF JEHOIAKIM TO NEBUCHADREZZAR: 24.1

From the Annals of Judah.

24 [1]In his days Nebuchadrezzar king of Babylon made a campaign, and Jehoiakim became a vassal to him for three years, then he turned and rebelled against him.

24.1. According to Jer. 46.2, Necho again marched north in the

[a]D. J. Wiseman, *Chronicles of Chaldaean Kings*, pp. 62ff.
[b]Wiseman, *op. cit.*, pp. 72ff.
[c]Abel, *GP* II, p. 438.

fourth year of Jehoiakim (605), which was not strictly the first official year of Nebuchadrezzar, as Jer. 25.1 states, but the year of the death of his father Nabopolassar. Necho was defeated by Nebuchadrezzar at Carchemish, the Babylonian Chronicle[a] bearing out the accuracy of the statement in Jer. 46.2. Formally acceding in 604, Nebuchadrezzar apparently followed up this victory by making his authority more effective in Syria and Palestine as far as the border of Egypt. The Babylonian Chronicle dates this expedition in 604, explicitly mentioning the destruction of a city, probably Ashkelon.[b] This is mentioned by Josephus,[c] who notes that Nebuchadrezzar acceded in the fourth year of Jehoiakim and at the same time passed on from Carchemish after the defeat of Necho to the Egyptian border. This, however, was in the year 605, and Josephus does not allow for the regnal year of Nebuchadrezzar nor for the interruption of his campaigns in the west by his return to Babylon to 'take the hands of Marduk' on his father's death in 605. Judah apparently remained free from Babylonian invasion, since Jehoiakim paid tribute for three years, as the present passage states. Unfortunately in this laconic and isolated excerpt from the Annals of Judah it is not stated from what date Jehoiakim paid tribute, but Josephus[d] states that the tribute was withheld in Nebuchadrezzar's fourth year, the eighth of Jehoiakim, when a punitive expedition was sent against Judah. This would be 601, when, in fact, the Babylonian Chronicle records an encounter with Egypt somewhere in Palestine. Egyptian resistance was now much stiffer, and the Babylonians withdrew after a bitter and inconclusive battle. Unfortunately this, in our opinion, was about the point at which the first Deuteronomist, the compiler, laid down his pen, and, with the exception of the somewhat vague statement in v. 7, there are no more citations from the annalistic source. If the three years' vassalage of Jehoiakim dates from 601, as we think likely, we must suppose either that he had been under tribute from 604 and, pending the result of the Babylonian-Egyptian action in 601, had withheld tribute, which was re-imposed by Nebuchadrezzar in 601, or that while matters were inconclusive between Babylon and Egypt Jehoiakim had been left independent for the meanwhile, which we think more likely. After paying tribute

[a]Wiseman, *op. cit.*, pp. 66–69.
[b]Wiseman, *op. cit.*, pp. 68ff.
[c]*Ant.* X, 6.1.
[d]*Ant.* X, 6.1.

for three years till 599, Jehoiakim withheld the tribute. Since the Babylonians did not invest Jerusalem till December (Chislev) 598, the Aramaean raids on Judah may be dated in this interim, to distract Judah until the Babylonians could mount an attack. The significance of Judah in this situation between Babylon and Egypt at this time must be noted. Judah, normally off the beaten track of imperial powers, was now important on the flank and rear of a Babylonian attack on Egypt, and as a potential ally of Egypt was a power to be conciliated, as Nebuchadrezzar, we believe, treated her from 604 to 601. But, after she had shown signs of sympathy with Necho in 601, Nebuchadrezzar could no longer afford to leave her independent, so he imposed tribute, after which it is significantly stated in what is perhaps the last citation in Kings from the Annals of Judah that 'the king of Egypt came no more out of his land . . .' (v. 7).

(*c*) A NOTE ON THE ARAMAEAN RAIDS ON THE EVE OF THE EXPEDITION OF NEBUCHADREZZAR IN 598/7: 24.2–4

Probably from the Deuteronomistic redactor, as indicated by the homiletic note and anticipation of the final collapse of the state, but there is a nucleus of historical fact in the notice of the Aramaean raids.

24 [2]And Yahweh[a] sent against him raiding-parties of Chaldaeans and of Aramaeans[b] and of Moab and Ammonites, and he sent them against Judah to destroy them according to the word of Yahweh, which he spoke through his servants the prophets. [3]It was just according to the command of Yahweh against Judah, to remove them[c] from before his presence for the sins of Manasseh according to all that he had done, [4][d](and also the innocent blood which he shed and filled Jerusalem with innocent blood)[d] and Yahweh refused to forgive.

24.2. This was apparently the occasion when the Rechabites were obliged to take refuge in Jerusalem (Jer. 35.11). In that passage the Aramaeans are mentioned and also the Chaldaeans, who are

[a]G^B omits the subject, which in this case must be the subject of the previous sentence, Nebuchadrezzar. This may well be the original reading, and is adopted by Stade and Eissfeldt, 'Yahweh' being in this case an insertion suggested by the sequel.

[b]Perhaps with S we should read *'ᵉdōm* for *'ᵃrām*, as the association with Moab and Ammon indicates. On the other hand, the Chaldaeans (*kaśdīm*) may have been Aramaean kinsmen of the Neobabylonian dynasty from Mesopotamia used by Nebuchadrezzar as garrison troops in the West, and so *'ᵃram* may be retained.

[c]Reading *lahᵃsīrō* with G and V for MT *lᵉhāsīr*.

[d]This has all the appearance of a secondary expansion.

taken there as the army of Nebuchadrezzar. As the passage in Kings suggests, the 'Chaldaeans' were either detachments of the regular Babylonian army or, as Skinner (CB, p. 428) suggests, Babylonian garrisons stationed in Syria, now directed by Nebuchadrezzar to harass Judah with irregulars from beyond Jordan. They may well have themselves been Aramaean Kaldu. akin to the ruling caste in Babylon.

24.3. The adverb *'ak* has a certain limiting sense, meaning 'exclusively' or 'utterly', e.g. *'ak śāmēaḥ*, 'utterly rejoicing' (Deut. 16.15), *'ak nᵉkā'īm*, 'utterly stricken' (Isa. 16.7), and *'ak šeqer*, 'nought but lies' (Jer. 16.19). *'ak* has the significance of German *eitel*.

(*d*) EPILOGUE ON THE REIGN OF JEHOIAKIM: 24.5f.

This is in the style of the Deuteronomistic compiler, but possibly from the exilic redactor.

24 [5]And as for the rest the acts of Jehoiakim and all that he did, are they not written in the Book of the Chronicles of the Kings of Judah? [6]And Jehoiakim slept with his fathers, and Jehoiachin his son became king in his place.

5. This is the last explicit reference in Kings to the Books of the Chronicles of the Kings of Judah, though v. 7 probably comes from the same source.

(*e*) REFERENCE TO THE GENERAL POLITICAL SITUATION IN PALESTINE: 24.7

Probably from the Annals of Judah.

24 [7]And the king of Egypt came no more out of his country, for the king of Babylon had taken from the Wadi of Egypt to the River Euphrates all that belonged to the king of Egypt.

This general note is hard to date, but in view of the statement of the Babylonian Chronicle that a battle was fought in Palestine in 601, the reference is unlikely to be to any time before that, such as the Egyptian defeat at Carchemish in 605. It is, in our opinion, the last citation from the Annals of Judah, though this is not explicitly stated.

(*f*) INTRODUCTION TO THE REIGN OF JEHOIACHIN: 24.8f.

Probably by the Deuteronomistic redactor in the style of the Deuteronomistic compiler.

24 [8]Jehoiachin was eighteen years old when he became king, and he reigned three months in Jerusalem, and his mother's name was Nehushta the daughter of Elnathan from Jerusalem. [9]And he did evil in the sight of Yahweh according to all that his father had done.

24.8. Jehoiachin ('Y. establishes' or 'Let Y. establish'), for which *Yakukina* of the fiscal dockets from the palace of Nebuchadrezzar at Babylon (see on 25.30) is an Akkadian version, is given as *Yochin* in two jar-handle stamps from *Tell Beit Mirsīm* and another of the same from Bethshemesh inscribed *'lyqm nʿr ywkn*, the name being probably a variant of Jehoiachin.[a] In Jer. 24.1; 28.4; 29.2 the name is given as Jechoniah, abbreviated to Coniah in Jer. 22.24, 28; 37.1, which means 'Y. is firm'. The alteration of the name in the prophet seems to signify faith in the stability of God apart from the incidents of history or the stability of king or dynasty.

(*g*) THE FALL OF JERUSALEM AND THE DEPORTATION OF JEHOIACHIN AND HIS NOTABLES: 24.10–12

From the historical narrative of the exilic Deuteronomistic redactor (continued at v. 15).

24 [10]At that time the officers[b] of Nebuchadrezzar king of Babylon came up[c] to Jerusalem, and the city came under siege. [11]And Nebuchadrezzar king of Babylon came against the city when his officers were besieging it. [12]And Jehoiachin king of Judah surrendered[d] to the king of Babylon, he and his mother and his courtiers and commanders and officers, and the king of Babylon took him[e] in the eighth year of his reign.

10. The arrival of Nebuchadrezzar on the eve of the surrender is quite natural. The general political situation in Palestine was not sufficiently critical, with Egypt out of the field, to warrant the king's personal presence until then.

12. This is the first instance in Kings of an event in the history of Israel dated by a foreign era. The dating in the eighth year of Nebuchadrezzar is surely from a Jew in Mesopotamia. In Jer. 52.28

[a]Albright, *JBL* LI, 1932, pp. 77ff.

[b]Certain Hebrew MSS, G, and S omit *ʿabᵉdē* ('officers') of MT, taking Nebuchadrezzar as the subject, and pointing *ʿlh* of MT as *ʿālā* ('went up'). If this is correct the following verse must refer to a parallel tradition of the initial activity of Nebuchadrezzar's officers, he himself arriving for the final phase of the siege.

[c]Retaining the MT and pointing *ʿlh* with certain Hebrew MSS and Q as *ʿālū*.

[d]The presence of the queen-mother indicates that *'el*, not *ʿal*, must be read.

[e]G[AL] read *'ōtām* ('them'); the singular, referring to the king, might be expected to include the others.

the date is given as the seventh year of Nebuchadrezzar. The date in Kings is more reliable, reckoning from 604, when Nebuchadrezzar formally acceded. The date of this event in 597 agrees with 25.27, which states that the relief of Jehoiachin in exile in the regnal year of Evil-Merodach (561) took place in the 37th year of Jehoiachin's exile, the reckoning in all cases being inclusive. The Palestinian authority in Jeremiah, familiar with the accession system in Judah, assumed that Nebuchadrezzar did not formally accede till the next New Year festival (i.e. 603). In effect his father died in 605, as we know from the new fragment of the Babylonian Chronicle,[a] so that Nebuchadrezzar's accession was in 604. On the fate and number of the notables of Jerusalem see vv. 15f.

(*h*) AN ANACHRONISTIC NOTE ON THE SPOLIATION OF THE TEMPLE AND ON THE DEPORTATION OF THE PEOPLE: 24.13f.

The secondary nature of this matter is indicated by the fact that it is an obvious interruption of the historical narrative of the Deuteronomistic redactor between vv. 12 and 15, and by the fact that it is redundant in view of the account of the deportation in the narrative in vv. 15ff.

24 [13]And he took out of it all the treasure of the Temple of Yahweh and the treasure of the palace and cut up all the gold furnishings which Solomon king of Israel had made in the Temple of Yahweh, just as Yahweh had said. [14]And he deported all Jerusalem, and all the commanders, and all the men of property, ten[b] thousand in captivity,[c] and all the artisans and the smiths, leaving none but the poorest of the people of the land.

24.13. This spoliation is flatly contradicted by Jer. 27.19ff. The reference to the spoliation of the Temple being according to the word of God has no place in the narrative of the Deuteronomistic redactor either here or in the account of the final fall of Jerusalem, but is drawn from Jer. 27.22 at a time later than the main Deuteronomistic redaction of Kings, when the edition of Jeremiah was familiar, about the end of the Exile or even later.

14. The first statement that 'all Jerusalem' were deported stamps this verse immediately as secondary and inaccurate. The number,

[a]Wiseman, *op. cit.*
[b]Reading *ʿaśeret* with Q.
[c]Reading *gōlā* with G^L, S, V, and T for MT *gōle*, the active participle.

too, is obviously a round one reckoned on the basis of the 8,000 and more of v. 16, on which see note. In the late source of v. 14 'the people of the land' probably means peasantry.

(*i*) THE DEPORTATION OF JEHOIACHIN AND SOME OF HIS SUBJECTS IN 597, AND THE ELEVATION OF ZEDEKIAH: 24.15–17

Historical narrative from the Deuteronomistic redactor continued from v. 12.

24 [15]And he deported Jehoiachin to Babylon and he led off into exile the queen-mother and the wives of the king, and his chamberlains and the chief[a] men of the land from Jerusalem to Babylon, [16]and all the men of property, even seven thousand, and the artisans and the smiths, even a thousand, all able men, warriors, and the king of Babylon brought them into exile in Babylon. [17]And the king of Babylon made Mattaniah his uncle king in his place, and he changed his name to Zedekiah.

24.15. Note the mention of the queen-mother next to the king, indicating her status as superior to the wives of the king. The chief men of the land (*'ēlē hā'āreṣ*) were probably provincial notables, heads of communities or clans.

16. The men of property (*'anᵉšē haḥayil*) were such as, in virtue of their property, were liable for personal military service and/or for the equipment of a certain number of others for war, see on I K.1.8. Montgomery has well noted the collective singular *ḥārāš* ('artisans') and *masgēr* ('smiths', lit. metal-fusers, cf. Arabic *sajara*, 'to roast in an oven') as indicative of the solidarity of the guilds. The guild-system is well exemplified in certain administration texts from Ras Shamra, where the subjects of the realm are grouped for taxation and conscription by their crafts, e.g. *UT* 300, 400. The numbers of the deportees are still not convincing, 7,000 and 1,000 suggesting rather approximations on the part of a later redactor, and the authority of Jer. 52.28 (3,023) is to be preferred. Montgomery (ICC, p. 556) supposes that the lower figure refers to men, which, with families, would bring the number up to, and even beyond, the 8,000 and more of Kings. In Jer. 52.28, however, the numbers are given as persons (*nepeš*), which would rather indicate all persons. The figures of Jeremiah probably represent the authority of a mature contem-

[a]Reading *'ēlē* with Q, though K has possibly preserved the original root of the word with medial *w* ('to be first').

porary as distinct from that of the exilic redactor, who may still, of course, have been one of the deportees sufficiently mature to take accurate note.

24.17. In spite of the designation of Mattaniah-Zedekiah in II Chron. 36.10 as the brother of Jehoiachin, the statement of v. 18 that his mother's name was Hamital the daughter of Jeremiah of Libnah indicates that he was a son of Josiah and the uterine brother of Jehoahaz and so the uncle of Jehoiachin, as Jer. 25.1, G of II Chron. 36.10, and I Chron. 3.15 [16] indicate. As in the conferment of the throne-name Jehoiakim by Necho (23.34), the present case indicates in the actual name a respect for Jewish traditions, though the vassal status of the king was emphasized. See further on 23.34.

(*j*) INTRODUCTION TO THE REIGN OF ZEDEKIAH AND ASSESSMENT OF ITS RELIGIOUS SIGNIFICANCE: 24.18–20a

Composed after the pattern of the Deuteronomistic compiler, but with a homiletic note on the main event, the revolt against Babylon, which reveals the Deuteronomistic redactor.

24 [18]Zedekiah was twenty-one years old when he became king and he reigned eleven years in Jerusalem, and his mother's name was Hamital[a] the daughter of Jeremiah from Libnah. [19]And he did evil in the sight of Yahweh according to all that Jehoiakim had done, [20A]for this came about because of the anger of Yahweh upon Jerusalem and Judah to the end that he should cast them forth[b] from his presence.

18. The reign of Zedekiah is reckoned from his official accession according to Jewish custom at the New Year festival after Nebuchadnezzar had nominated him king after March 597, hence from 596.

19. The thought seems to be that Yahweh had consented to the sin of Zedekiah because he had already doomed Israel for her earlier sins.

(*k*) THE REVOLT AND FALL OF JERUSALEM, AND THE FATE OF ZEDEKIAH: 24.20b–25.7

The historical narrative of the Deuteronomistic redactor.

24 [20B]And Zedekiah rebelled against the king of Babylon.

25 [1]And it came to pass in the ninth year[c] of his reign in the tenth

[a]Reading the consonantal text in preference to Q, see p. 749 n.[a].
[b]Reading infinitive construct *hašlīk* for MT perfect *hišlīk*.
[c]Reading with certain Hebrew MSS and Jer. 52.4 *baššānā*.

month on the tenth day of the month that Nebuchadrezzar king of Babylon came in person with all his army against Jerusalem and he encamped against it, and they built against it a wall of circumvallation. [2]And the city came under siege until the eleventh year of king Zedekiah (in the fourth month)[a] [3]on the ninth of the month, and the famine was sore in the city and there was no food for the people of the land. [4]And the city was penetrated [b](and it came to pass when Zedekiah)[b] and all the men of war [b](saw that)[b] [b](they fled and left the city)[b] by night[c] by way of the gate between the two walls which were above the King's Garden, but the Chaldaeans were against the city round about, and they went[d] by way of the steppe-land. [5]And the Chaldaean army pursued the king and caught up with him in the plains of Jericho, and all his army had scattered from him. [6]So they seized the king and took him up to the king of Babylon at Riblah, and he[e] took process with him. [7]And he[f] slew the sons of Zedekiah before his eyes, then blinded the eyes of Zedekiah, and bound him in fetters of bronze, and brought him to Babylon.

24.20b. The narrative passes with a single step to the final revolt of the Jews and the swift reprisal of the Babylonians, and we are left in ignorance of the circumstances which prompted the revolt. Alt[g] had little doubt that there was more than a coincidence between the outbreak of the revolt and the accession of the vigorous Pharaoh Apries (Hophra of Jer. 44.30) in 588, who undertook a naval expedition, apparently successful, against Sidon and Tyre.[h] Unfortunately no details of this expedition are given in the Greek sources and there is no note of the date. There seems, however, to have been rather more than the mere potential of an Egyptian advance into Palestine at this time, according to the statement in Jer. 37.5 that the advance of an Egyptian army forced the Babylonians to raise the siege of Jerusalem.

25.1. The 19-month siege of Jerusalem in the reduced strength of Judah is not wholly explicable by the natural strength of the site and

[a]The context indicates that something has dropped out of the MT; the lacuna is filled up from Jer. 39.2 and 52.6, *baḥōdeš hāreḇīʿī*.

[b]Here again there is an obvious lacuna, as is indicated by the want of a predicate to 'all the men of war', and again the lacuna is filled from Jer. 39.4, cf. Jer. 52.7, where the text is less full and the king is not mentioned.

[c]Reading *layelā* with Jeremiah for MT *hallayelā* ('the night').

[d]Reading plural *wayyēlekū* with certain Hebrew MSS, G[L], S, and Jer. 52.7.

[e]Reading singular *wayedabbēr* with many Hebrew MSS G[L], S, V, T, and Jer. 39.5 and 52.9 for MT plural.

[f]Reading singular with G, S, V, and Jer. 39.6 and 52.10.

[g]*Israel und Aegypten*, 1909, p. 100.

[h]Herodotus II, 161; Diodorus Siculus I, 69; so E. Otto, *Ägypten, der Weg des Pharaonenreiches*, 1958, p. 243.

the defences of the city, but corroborates the statement of Jer. 37.5 concerning an Egyptian diversion. A further explanation is that Nebuchadrezzar, contrary to the statement in the present passage, was not present in person, but had sent his subordinates to Jerusalem with part of his forces while he remained at his headquarters at Riblah on the Orontes, perhaps coping with local rebellion in the Lebanon, as the rather vague Brisa inscription[a] indicates, and perhaps apprehending attack from the coast by Apries, if his expedition mentioned by Herodotus and Diodorus had already taken place. The revolt broke out in 588, the ninth year of Zedekiah reckoning inclusively from 596 (see on 24.18), the months being reckoned from Nisan according to the Babylonian system familiar to the redactor in the Exile. The siege therefore began in Ṭebet (December/January) 588. Montgomery (ICC, p. 567) is not accurate in his reference to a sherd from Lachish 'of the ninth year', presumably of Zedekiah. The inscription (Letter X) is actually 'on the ninth', which is more likely to refer to the day of the month than the year of the king, the Lachish Letters not being official annals, but military or political dispatches. The wall of circumvallation was a feature of the siege of Jerusalem under Titus also. The word *dāyēq* is known only here and in Jer. 52.4, and in Ezek. 4.2; 17.17; 21.22 [27]; 26.8, where it is in parallelism with *sōlelā* ('siege-ramp'). It is tempting to relate the word to the Arabic *ḍāqa, yāḍīq* ('to be straitened'), but the dentals do not correspond and the word is more likely to be cognate with the Arabic *zāqa, yāzīq* ('to put a collar on to a shirt)'. A collar is no unapt description of a wall of circumvallation, which the adverb *sābīb* supports. Part of the policy of the Babylonians, as of Vespasian and Titus in AD 66–70, was to subjugate the country, a wise precaution in a land so admirably adapted for guerilla warfare, and so seal off Jerusalem. The preoccupation with the Shephelah fortresses of Azekah and Lachish[b] suggests apprehension of an attack from Egypt.

25.2. Reckoning the reign of Zedekiah from the New Year festival in 596 (see on 24.18), the 11th year of the king on inclusive reckoning was 586.

3. On the accurate date 'in the fourth month', i.e. Tammuz (June/July) after the Babylonian reckoning from Nisan see p. 763 n.[a]. The famine in the city was intensified by the fact that for two harvest seasons the Babylonians had been in the land eating up the

[a] A. L. Oppenheim in *ANET*, p. 307.
[b] Jer. 34.7, cf. *The Lachish Letters*, No. IV.

crop, and latterly by their circumvallation had prevented any produce from reaching the city.

25.4. On the deficient text and its restoration from Jer. 39 and 52 see p. 763, n.[b]. The recent demonstration that the wall round the south-western hill was not pre-exilic suggests that 'the two walls' were either the convergence of the walls round the south-eastern hill, with an extension over the central valley to include the pool of Siloam and 'the old pool' (*Birket al-Ḥamrā*; see on 18.17), as Isa. 22.11 suggests, though no trace of this western extension has been found, or, the narrow corridor to the postern at the south-east angle of the city, giving direct access to the Kidron valley above its confluence with the Central Valley and the Valley of Hinnom, where the King's Gardens were located. We prefer the latter location, which is particularized by Weill's discovery of the corridor, or 'two walls' and 'the stairs leading down from the city of David',[a] which, according to Neh. 3.15; 12.39, were just east of the Fountain Gate, which we take to be a small gate, or postern, communicating with the Pool of Siloam. The worship of Melech (misvocalized Molech) in this vicinity may indicate that the 'King' in 'the King's Garden' was not the king of Judah, but the deity. This was, however, thanks to the outflow of water from the reservoir and the Kidron canal with its lateral sluices, a prolific orchard-land, which it is still, and a natural place for the royal gardens. The precise meaning of *derek hāʿarābā* is uncertain. The second word may mean 'steppe-land', referring to the semi-desert region east of Jerusalem, which, being in the rain-shadow, rapidly degenerates almost to desert. On the other hand, on the analogy of the Arabic *ʿAraba* referring to the depression between the Dead Sea and the Gulf of Aqaba, the word may denote the Jordan depression south of Jericho, which is, in fact, called *ʿarebōt yerēḥō*, in which case *derek hāʿarābā* would mean 'towards the Jordan-depression'. We prefer the former interpretation.

5. *ʿarebōt yerēḥō* refers to the semi-desert plains south of Jericho beyond the reach of irrigation, which, however, afford quite good seasonal grazing for nomads' herds, with occasional oasis-cultivation, as, for instance, at the 'home farm' of the Qumran community at *ʿAin Fešḫa*. The scattering of Zedekiah's forces indicates the desperate situation. As a Babylonian vassal he probably never commanded the whole-hearted allegiance of any but his personal retainers, now less significant than formerly, so now the remnants of his army were

[a]R. Weill, *La Cité de David*, II, pp. 36–39, 40ff., Pl. VIIB.

determined to seek a future for themselves as isolated 'commandos' in a terrain which afforded abundant refuge; witness the continued resistance of Jewish nationalists here after AD 70 till the fall of Masada in 73, and the administration of the rebel Bar Kochba recently so graphically attested in letters from his secretaries recovered in the desert region north of Engedi.

25.6. The phrase *wayᵉdabbēr 'ittō mišpāṭ* indicates that Zedekiah had the semblance of a fair hearing, but as a rebel against his suzerain who had, in fact, appointed him to preserve order under his authority, the result was not in doubt.

7. The death of Zedekiah, who was still in his early thirties, is not recorded here, but Ezekiel has a brief reference to his death in Babylon after his graphic description of the escape of Zedekiah by night from Jerusalem (Ezek. 12.12f.).

(*l*) THE SACK OF JERUSALEM AND THE DEPORTATION: 25.8–15

The historical narrative of the Deuteronomistic redactor continued.

25 [8]In the fifth month, on the seventh[a] of the month, that is the nineteenth year of[b] Nebuchadrezzar king of Babylon, Nebuzaradan commander of the guards, minister of the king of Babylon, came to Jerusalem. [9]And he burned the Temple of Yahweh and the palace and all the houses of Jerusalem.[c] [10]And all the army of the Chaldaeans [d]which was with[e] the commander of the guards[d] broke down the walls of Jerusalem all round. [11]And Nebuzaradan commander of the guards deported the rest of the people who were left in the city and the deserters who had deserted to the king of Babylon[f g]. [12]And of the poorest of the land the commander of the guards left as vinedressers and ploughmen. [13]And the Chaldaeans broke up the bronze pillars of the Temple[h] of Yahweh

[a]G^L and S read '9th', obviously influenced by the rite of mourning for the destruction of Jerusalem and the Temple on the 9th of Ab after the destruction of the Temple on that day by Titus in AD 70. Jer. 52 reads '10th'.

[b]G^{BA} and S rightly omit MT *melek* before Nebuchadrezzar.

[c]MT *wᵉ'et-kol-bēt gādōl śārap bā'ēš* ('and every notable's house he burned with fire') should probably be omitted.

[d]The phrase may be omitted as a gloss.

[e]If [d–d] is retained the grammar demands that we insert *'et* ('with') or *lᵉ* ('belonging to') before *rab ṭabbāḥīm* ('the commander of the guards').

[f]Reading *'el* for MT *'al*, or possibly, after Jer. 39, *'ēlāw* for MT *'ālāw* instead of MT *'al -hammelek bābel* ('against the king of Babylon').

[g]MT *wᵉ'ēt yeter hehāmōn* ('and the rest of the crowd') here and in Jer. 39.9 should probably be omitted as tautological and excessive. The passage, however, may be genuine if with Jer. 52.15 *hā'āmōn* ('master-craftsmen') is read instead of MT *hehāmōn*.

[h]Reading with certain Hebrew MSS *bᵉbēt* or possibly *lᵉbēt* as in Jer. 52.17.

and the laver-stands[a] and the bronze 'sea' which was in the Temple of Yahweh and took the bronze of them to Babylon. [14]And they took the pots and shovels and snuffers and spoons and all the bronze vessels which they used in the service. [15]And the commander of the guard took away the firepans and sprinkling-basins, that which was of gold in gold, and that which was of silver in silver.

25.8. The date of the fall of Jerusalem is 586 reckoning inclusively from Nebuchadrezzar's formal accession in 604. Here, as in the case of the first capture of Jerusalem, Jer. 52.29 dates the event apparently a year earlier than Kings, i.e. the 18th year of Nebuchadrezzar. Knowing that Nebuchadrezzar ruled from 604, the western editor of Jeremiah presumes that as in Judah this was an accession year, the actual rule beginning in 603. Here again the Mesopotamian provenance of the conclusion of Kings is indicated. On the question of the actual day see p. 766 n.[a].

The title means lit. 'chief of the slaughterers', i.e. chief cook, as G translates (*archimageiros*), cf. Gen. 37.36, or 'chief executioner'.

12. *yōgᵉbīm* in the sense 'farmers', given in T, is used only here and in Jer. 52.16. The etymology is unknown, but a connection with *gūb* ('to dig'), properly 'to dig out a well', is suggested, which is not very convincing. In a parallel account of the same dealings in Jer. 39 it is stated in v. 10 *ūmin-hāʿām haddallīm ʾᵃšer ʾēn lāhem mᵉʾūmā hišʾīr nebūzarʾᵃdān rab-ṭabbāḥīm bᵉʾereṣ yᵉhūdā wayyittēn lāhem kᵉrāmīm wīgēbīm*, Theodotion and Jerome reading the last word as *gēbīm* ('wells'). It is possible that this was the original text of the passage in Kings also, though the reading *gēbīm* is not what is normally expected with vinedressers or vineyards.

13. On the bronze furnishings and vessels of the Temple see on I K. 7.15ff. Jer. 52.17–23 gives a more detailed account of the sack of the Temple, including the 12 bronze bulls under the great 'sea', which, the writer has apparently forgotten, were removed by Ahaz (16.17).

(*m*) A DIGRESSION DESCRIBING THE PILLARS YACHIN AND BOAZ: 25.16f.

This matter is given in Jer. 52.20–23 with more technical accuracy and detail. It is probably from an independent description, or inventory, of the Temple and its furnishings.

[a]Possibly *hakkīyōrōṯ* ('lavers') should be read.

25 [16]The pillars, two items, and the 'sea', one item,[a] and the laver-bases which Solomon made for the Temple of Yahweh, the bronze of all these pieces of equipment was beyond weight. [17b]Eighteen cubits was the height of one pillar, and a capital of bronze was upon it, and the height of the capital was five[c] cubits,[d] and the trellis-work and pomegranates on the capital round about was all of bronze, and the same for the second pillar, [e]as far as concerned the trellis-work.[e]

25.16f. On the pillars, etc., see on I K. 7.15ff. Jer. 52.21 adds the fact that they were hollow and four inches thick.

(*n*) REPRISALS ON LEADING PERSONALITIES IN JUDAH: 25.18–21

This section probably ended the redactor's historical narrative of the final collapse of the state of Judah, as v. 21 ('So Judah was deported from her land') suggests. What follows, then, is in the nature of postscript or appendix.

25 [18]And the commander of the guards took Seraiah the chief priest and Zephaniah the second[f] priest and the three warders of the threshold. [19]And from the city he took one officer, the one in command of the men of war, and five[g] men of those who saw the king's face, who were found in the city, and the scribe, the chief of the army, who mustered the people of the land, and sixty men from the people of the land who were found in the city. [20]And Nebuzaradan the commander of the guards took them and brought them to the king of Babylon at Riblah. [21]And the king of Babylon struck them down and slew them at Riblah in the land of Hamath. So Judah was deported from her land.

18. Probably those executions were exemplary, certain leading men of the nationalist resistance party being selected from various sections of the people. The priests in those days of vassalage were the champions of nationalism. Seraiah was the grandson of Hilkiah the priest (I Chron. 6.13f. [5.39f.]), who presented the celebrated law-

[a]Reading with Jer. 52.20 *'eḥād* for MT *hā'eḥād*.

[b]Perhaps after Jer. 52.21 we should read *w^ehāʿammūdīm* ('and the pillars') here.

[c]Reading with Jer. 52.22 *ḥāmēš* for MT *šālōš* ('three'), I K. 7.16 also reading 'five'.

[d]Reading with Q as Jer. 52.22 *'ammōt*, as grammar demands, for MT *'ammā*.

[e]Since this phrase *ʿal-haśś^ebākā* occurs also in Jer. 52.23, the passage may be a corruption of the fuller text there, *wayyihyū hārimmōnīm tišʿīm w^ešiššā rūḥā kol-hārimmōnīm mē'ā ʿal-haśś^ebākā sābīb* ('and the pomegranates were 96 on a side and all the pomegranates upon the net-work round about were a hundred').

[f]Reading *hammišne* with Jer. 52.24.

[g]Jer. 52.25 reads *šibʿā* ('seven') for MT *ḥ^amiššā* ('five'). Since these are simply those who did not escape and not the whole number of a kind of privy council, there is no means of settling the correct reading.

book to Josiah. Though Seraiah himself was executed, his son Jehozadak was spared, but was deported (I Chron. 6.15 [5.41]). This is the first instance of the title *kōhēn hārō'š*, which denotes the chief priest in Chronicles and Ezra, cf. *hakkōhēn haggādōl* (22.4; 23.4; Zech. 3.1). *kōhēn mišne* might mean 'a priest of the second rank', but probably the reading of Jer. 52 should be followed, *kōhēn hammišne* there meaning 'the second priest'; see on 23.4.

25.19. The precise function of 'those who saw the king's face' is uncertain. They were probably privy councillors, like the seven princes of Persia and Media in Esth. 1.14. The partitive *min* before the participle suggests that there were more than the five ('seven' in Jer. 52) singled out for execution. These were only 'those who were found in the city', i.e. who did not escape, perhaps by reason of age. *śar haṣṣābā'* if it is original here, cannot mean, as it normally does, a commander, but the scribe who kept the conscription lists and dealt with the mobilization of the free Israelites (*'am hā'āreṣ*) as distinct from the standing army of professional soldiers. Tablets listing the bows and slings, including probably the men to use them, demanded from various localities, families, and guilds in the realm of Ugarit have been found at Ras Shamra (*UT*, 113, 321). The 60 representatives of the third class, 'the people of the land', were probably provincial notables, elders, or heads of families. Here again we should note the distinction between 'the people of the land', indicating the people in general, the heirs of the sacral community, and the official class in the feudal system in the army or the civil bureaucracy in Jerusalem, which held its status from the king.

21. The last clause of this sentence is the climax and conclusion of the theme of the Deuteronomistic redactor's continuation of the historical narrative of the Deuteronomistic compiler of Kings. This is the real end of the book and the rest consists of two appendices.

Appendix I

THE MIZPAH INCIDENT: 25.22–26

A comparison with the much fuller account in Jer. 40.7–41.18 indicates that the latter is much better informed of the circumstances of the incident and the various personalities and their motives, as we should expect of a tradition emanating from those actually involved. The Deuteronomistic redactor knows this matter only at second hand, and his account is quite obviously a summary. The main facts for him are the murder of Gedaliah and the Babylonians at Mizpah and the flight of the Jewish community to Egypt, the other notable centre of the Exile, and practically all other matter narrated in Jeremiah is omitted. This, and in contrast the intimate knowledge of events in Babylon in the following passage (vv. 27–30), together with the dating of events just before the fall of Jerusalem by the regnal years of Nebuchadrezzar, points clearly to a Mesopotamian origin.

25 22 And as for the people that were left in the land of Judah, whom
Nebuchadrezzar king of Babylon had left, he appointed as governor
over them Gedaliah the son of Ahikam the son of Shaphan. 23 And all
the commanders of the forces, they and [a]their men,[a] heard that the
king of Babylon had appointed Gedaliah, and they came to Gedaliah
to Mizpah, including Ishmael the son of Nethaniah, and Johanan the
son of Kareah, and Seraiah the son of Tanhumeth of Netophah, and
Jaazaniah the son of the Maachathite, they and their men. 24 And
Gedaliah swore to them and their men, and said to them, Do not be
afraid of the officials[b] of the Chaldaeans; settle down in the land and
serve the king of Babylon that it may be well with you. 25 But it happened
in the seventh month that Ishmael the son of Nethaniah the son of
Elishama of the royal lineage came and ten men with him, and they
struck down Gedaliah[c] and the Jews and the Chaldaeans who were
with him in Mizpah. 26 And all the people, both small and great, and
the commanders of the forces rose up and came to Egypt, for they were
afraid of the Chaldaeans.

[a] Reading *w*^{e}*'an*^{e}*šēhem* with one Hebrew MS, G, S, T, and Jer. 40.7 for MT *w*^{e}*hā'*^{a}*nāšīm*.

[b] Here for MT *mēʿab*^{e}*dē* V and Jer. 40.9 read *mēʿ*^{a}*bōd* ('to serve').

[c] Omitting MT *wayyāmōt* ('and he died'). Jer. 41.2 has a much fuller text and reads *wayyāmēt* ('and he killed'). In the context of the résumé of the passage in Kings *wayyāmōt*, though not impossible, is awkward before the following accusative.

25.22. The moderate politics of Gedaliah agree with the fact that his father Ahikam the son of Shaphan supported Jeremiah's counsel of non-resistance (Jer. 26.24). We are probably brought into intimate contact with Gedaliah through a clay seal-impression from the last phase of Jewish occupation at *Tell ad-Duweir* (Lachish) with the legend 'Belonging to Gedaliah who is over the house' (*lgdlyhw 'šr ʿl hbyt*).[a] The title is that of the royal chamberlain, see on 15.5. The Babylonian king sought at once the development of the new province and the conciliation of its inhabitants through a native governor of reliable allegiance. Jer. 40.10 indicates that Gedaliah's office was mainly fiscal.

23. It is not clear whether the army commanders and their forces had been operating in the country during the siege of Jerusalem or had escaped from the city on its fall, perhaps on the night that Zedekiah left the city. In any case they had maintained themselves in a land well provided with what D. Baly[b] calls 'areas of refuge'. One of these was doubtless the area round Qumran and Engedi, which served this purpose in the two great revolts against Rome in AD 66–70 and 132–5, and from Jer. 40.11 we learn that other parties from Judah found refuge in Ammon, Moab, and Edom. On the location of Mizpah of this passage at *Tell an-Naṣbeh* about nine miles north of Jerusalem on the present main road to Ramallah and Nablus see on I K. 15.22. The fact that, though practically every archaeological site in Judah proved to have been destroyed at this time, *Tell an-Naṣbeh* was undisturbed[c] is a further indication that this was Gedaliah's Mizpah. It is tempting to identify Netophah with *Beit Neṭṭīf*, but the location of this place about three miles east of *Tell az-Zakarīyeh* towards the Vale of Elah is too far from Bethlehem, with which the place is associated in the post-exilic settlement of Judah (Ezra 2.22; Neh. 7.26). Alt[d] on Byzantine evidence suggested its location at an Iron Age site *Ḫirbet Badd Falūḥ* about three miles south of Bethlehem on the way to Tekoa, a spring in the vicinity *ʿAin an-Naṭūf* probably preserving the name. The region between Bethlehem and the Dead Sea, with its rare and secluded settlements, was a natural 'area of refuge'. The fact that the name of Jaazaniah's father is not given, but only his *kunya*, or by-name, may indicate that he was not of

[a]S. H. Hooke, 'A Scarab and Sealing from Tell Duweir', *PEFQS*, 1935, pp. 195–6, Pl. XI.

[b]*The Geography of the Bible*, 1957, pp. 191f., 223, 228f.

[c]Albright, *The Archaeology of Palestine*, 1956[2], pp. 141f.

[d]*PJB* 1932, pp. 12, 47–54, cited by Abel, *GP* II, p. 399.

known family in Judah. He may have been from Abel-beth-Maachah in Northern Galilee (modern *Tell Ibil*), and in this case would either be the descendant of one from there who had taken refuge in Judah on the reduction of his homeland to an Assyrian province by Tiglath-pileser III, or his father may have taken service with Josiah on the latter's extension of his power to the northern provinces between 622 and 609. On the other hand, he may have been from the clan of Maacah, which is enumerated in the kinship of Caleb, hence Kenizzite, in southern Judah in I Chron. 2.48. The name Jaazaniah is attested on an agate seal from a tomb of the Middle, or more probably, Late Iron Age at *Tell an-Naṣbeh*.[a] The legend is *ly'znyhw ʿbd hmlk* ('Belonging to Ja'azaniah the servant of the king'). The substance and design of the seal (fighting cock) may indicate that Jaazaniah was not merely a steward in charge of a royal estate, to whom seals with such a legend normally belong, but a high-ranking officer. Of the four persons known to bear this name in the Old Testament, Badè points out that only Jaazaniah of the present passage is mentioned after the fall of Jerusalem and only he is associated with Mizpah, so it is not improbable that the seal is his.

25.24. Though Nebuchadrezzar had appointed a native governor, there were Babylonian officials in the land, and apparently even with Gedaliah at Mizpah (v. 25).

25. Nothing is known of Ishmael or his father except in connection with this episode. His being 'of the royal lineage' need not astonish us when we consider that the kings of Judah were polygamous.

26. Besides Israelites and Aramaeans settled as mercenaries at Yeb and Asswan in this period, as their distinctive names in the Elephantine papyri indicate, there was a considerable civilian settlement from Judah in the Delta region, to which Isa. 19.18f. refers.[b] Hebrew traditions, literary and religious, were collected and committed to writing in Egypt as in Mesopotamia, which eventually appear in the G variation of the MT.

[a]W. F. Badè, *ZAW* LI, 1933, pp. 150–6, with illustration.

[b]Cf. Josephus, *Ant.* XIII, 3.1, which refers to Jewish sanctuaries in the time of Ptolemy Philometor (181–145) and *ibid.* 3.3, which refers to a temple built at the same time on the petition of the priest Onias 'like the one at Jerusalem but smaller and poorer', which Sir Flinders Petrie claimed to have found at *Tell al-Yahūdīyeh* about 20 miles north of Cairo.

Appendix II

THE ALLEVIATION OF THE LOT OF THE CAPTIVE KING JEHOIACHIN: 25.27–30

We cannot agree with von Rad that the mention of this incident is an indication of a modified Messianic hope, an ideal of royalty which was expressed in the liturgy, e.g. Psalms, Isa. 9.2–7[1–6]; 11.1–9. See Introduction, pp. 39f. Significant as the survival and release of Jehoiachin was in the prospects of Israel, the specific mention of it may have been motivated by the primitive superstition that to close the book on a despondent note was to bring the future under the same evil influence, whereas to close it on an auspicious note was to open up a brighter prospect. The same dread of the infectious influence of evil and the curse, especially at the beginning of an enterprise, led Evil-Merodach on his accession in 561 to release Jehoiachin from prison, no doubt as part of a general amnesty customary on such an occasion. This was evidently regular in Mesopotamia, and is attested at Mari in the eighteenth century[a] and in Assyria in a letter to Esarhaddon cited by I. Engnell;[b] see further on 12.4. The note on the relief of Jehoiachin implies rather the prospect of grace for Israel after her delinquency and punishment in accordance with the general pattern of the Deuteronomistic History, most clearly apparent in the book of Judges. This section also has a close verbal parallel in Jer. 52.31–34, of which it is the original. Jer. 52.34, however, adds that Jehoiachin enjoyed the favour of the king of Babylon 'until the day of his death', this being merely implicit in II K. 25.30, which mentions 'all the days of his life'. Probably Jehoiachin did not live long after 561, and the fact that the main redaction of the Books of Kings was completed then or very soon after is suggested by the silence concerning the new hope for Israel with the rise of Cyrus the Great and his victory over Babylon in 538.

[a]G. Dossin, 'Un rituel du culte d'Istar provenant de Mari', *RA* XXXV, 1938, pp. 1–13.

[b]I. Engnell, *Studies in Divine Kingship*, 1943, p. 77.

25 [27]And it came to pass in the thirty-seventh year of the exile of
Jehoiachin king of Judah, in the twelfth month, on the twenty-seventh[a]
day of the month, Evil-Merodach king of Babylon, in the year when he
became king, lifted up the head of Jehoiachin king of Judah and
brought him out[b] of the prison. [28]And he spoke kindly to him and
set his seat above the seats[c] of the kings who were with him in Babylon,
[29]and he changed his prison clothes and ate food continually in his
presence all the days of his life. [30]And as for his allowance, a regular
daily allowance was given to him from[d] the king all the days of his life.

25.27. The precise dating by day and month is a feature of the work of the exilic community in Mesopotamia, cf. Ezekiel, where, as here, events touching the Jewish community are dated from the deportation of Jehoiachin, the date 561, the formal accession of Evil-Merodach, being the 37th year from 597 reckoning inclusively.

28. Note the expression of the abstract, here used adverbially, by the feminine plural.

29. The other kings with Evil-Merodach in Babylon were presumably political prisoners or hostages for the good conduct of their subjects.

30. *ʾarūḥā*, found in the Old Testament only here and in the parallel passage in Jer. 52.34, in Jer. 40.5, and in the well-known proverb in Prov. 15.17, 'Better is a portion of herbs with love, than a stall-fed ox with hatred', is cognate with Akkadian *iaraḫtu*, probably meaning 'portion of corn', and possibly with *arḫītu*, which has been associated with the root *arḫ* ('month'), hence possibly means 'monthly portion'. The last statement in Kings is strikingly confirmed by the excavations of R. Koldewey at Babylon. From one of a complex of small rooms below the floor-level of the citadel of Nebuchadrezzar a number of cuneiform tablets were extracted which actually record rations served out to various foreigners from Egypt and Western Asia, including Philistines and Jews, many of whom were artisans, like those who, 24.15f. states, had been deported with the notables. Of the Jews, Jehoiachin is actually named as receiving rations in dry and liquid measure; '½ PI for Yakukinu, the son of the king of Yakudu' and '½ SILA for the five sons of Yakudu at the hand of

[a]Jer. 52.31 reads 'twenty-fifth', and, to complicate the matter, G of Jer. 52.31 reads 'twenty-fourth', while one Hebrew MS of II K. 25.27 reads 'twenty-eighth'.

[b]Reading *wayyōṣēʾ ʾōtō* with Jer. 52.31, though this is not strictly necessary.

[c]G, S, and T read the plural, but, since 'seats' has a distributive sense, the noun may be retained in the singular. See *GK* § 124, final remark.

[d]G may be right here in reading *mibbēt* ('from the house') for MT *mēʾēt*.

Qan'amu'.[a] It has been suggested by Weidner that the small rooms in which these were found were the actual apartments where Jehoiachin and his notables were confined, but they are more likely to have been store-rooms, as Koldewey himself suggested.[b]

[a]E. F. Weidner, 'Jojachin, König von Juda, in babylonischen Keilschrifttexten', *Mélanges syriens offerts à M. René Dussaud* II, 1939, pp. 933–35.
[b]*Das wieder erstehende Babylon*, 1925, p. 99.

BIBLIOGRAPHY

ABEL, F. M., *Géographie de la Palestine*, 2 vols., Paris, 1933–8 (abbrev. *GP*)

ABBOT, N., 'Pre-Islamic Arab Queens', *AJSL* LVIII, 1941, pp. 1–22

AHARONI, Y., 'The Date of the Casemate Walls in Judah and Israel and their Purpose', *BASOR* 154, 1959, pp. 35–9

'Excavations at Ramat Raḥel', *BA* XXIV, 1961, pp. 98–118

AHLSTRÖM, G. W., *Psalm 89, eine Liturgie aus dem Ritual des leidenden Königs*, Lund, 1959

ALBRIGHT, W. F., 'Gilgames and Engidu, Mesopotamian Genii of Fecundity', *JAOS* XL, 1920, pp. 307–35

'The Site of Mizpah in Benjamin', *JPOS* III, 1923, pp. 110–21

'Egypt and the Early History of the Negeb', *JPOS* IV, 1924, pp. 131–61

'Researches of the School in Western Judaea', *BASOR* 15, 1924, pp. 2–11

'The Administrative Divisions of Israel and Judah', *JPOS* V, 1925, pp. 17–54

'The Site of Tirzah and the Topography of Western Manasseh', *JPOS* XI, 1931, pp. 241–51

'The Discovery of an Aramaic Inscription relating to King Uzziah', *BASOR* 44, 1931, pp. 8–10

The Archaeology of Palestine and the Bible, New York, 1935[3]

'The Seal of Eliakim and the latest Preëxilic History of Judah, with some Observations on Ezekiel', *JBL* LI, 1932, pp. 77–106

'The Chaldaean Conquest of Judah, a Rejoinder', *JBL* LI, 1932, pp. 381–2

The Excavation of Tell Beit Mirsim, II: The Bronze Age (AASOR XVII), New Haven, 1938

From the Stone Age to Christianity: Monotheism and the Historical Process, Baltimore, 1948[2]

'Two Cressets from Marisa and the Pillars of Jachin and Boaz', *BASOR* 85, 1942, pp. 18–27

Archaeology and the Religion of Israel, Baltimore, 1953[3]

'A Votive Stele Erected by Ben-Hadad I of Damascus to the God Melcarth', *BASOR* 87, 1942, pp. 23–9

The Excavation of Tell Beit Mirsim, III: The Iron Age (AASOR XXI–XXII), New Haven, 1943

The Archaeology of Palestine, Pelican A 199, Harmondsworth, Middlesex, 1956[2]

'New Light from Egypt on the Chronology and the History of Judah' *BASOR* 130, 1953, pp. 4–11

'Further Light on Synchronisms between Egypt and Asia in the Period 935–685 BC', *BASOR* 141, 1956, pp. 23–7

'A note on Early Sabaean Chronology', *BASOR* 143, 1956, pp. 9–10

'The Nebuchadnezzar and Neriglissar Chronicles', *BASOR* 143, 1956, pp. 28–33

'The High Place in Ancient Palestine', *SVT* IV, 1957, pp. 243–58

ALFRINK, B. J., 'L'expression שָׁכַב עִם אֲבוֹתָיו', *OTS* II, 1943, pp. 106–18

'Het "still staan" van zon en maan in Jos. 10.12–15', *Studia Catholica* XXIV, 1949, pp. 238–69

ALLEGRO, J. M., *The Treasure of the Copper Scroll*, London, 1960

ALT, A., *Israel und Aegypten* (BWAT I.6), 1909

'Das System der Stammesgrenzen im Buche Josua', *Sellin Festschrift*, 1927, pp. 13–24, *Kleine Schriften zur Geschichte des Volkes Israel* (abbrev. *KS*) I, Munich, 1953, 193–202

'Die Ursprünge des israelitischen Rechts', *Berichte über die Verhandlungen der sächsischen Akademie der Wissenschaften zu Leipzig, Phil.-hist. Klasse*, 86 Band, Heft 1, Leipzig, 1934, *KS* I, pp. 279–332; ET, 'The Origins of Israelite Law', *Essays on Old Testament History and Religion* (cited as *Essays*), Oxford, 1966, pp. 79–132

'Das Verbot des Diebstahls im Dekalog', *KS* I, pp. 333–40

'Die Staatenbildung der Israeliten in Palästina', *Reformationsprogramm der Universität Leipzig* 1930, *KS* II, 1959, pp. 1–65; ET, 'The Formation of the Israelite State in Palestine', *Essays*, pp. 171–237

'Das Grossreich Davids', *TLZ* LXXV, 1950, cols. 213–20, *KS* II, pp. 66–75

'Israels Gaue unter Salomo', *Alttestamentliche Studien Rudolf Kittel zum 60. Geburtstag dargebracht*, 1913, pp. 1–19, *KS* II, pp. 76–89

'Die Weisheit Salomos', *TLZ* LXXVI, 1951, cols. 139–44, *KS* II, pp. 90–99

'Verbreitung und Herkunft des syrischen Tempeltypus', *PJB* XXXV, 1939, pp. 83–99, *KS* II, pp. 100–15

'Das Königtum in den Reichen Israel und Juda', *VT* I, 1951, pp. 2–22, *KS* II, pp. 116–34; ET, 'The Monarchy in Israel and Judah', *Essays*, pp. 239–59

'Das Gottesurteil auf dem Karmel', *Festschrift Georg Beer zum 70 Geburtstag*, 1935, pp. 1–18, *KS* II, pp. 135–49

'Tiglathpilesers III erster Feldzug nach Palästina', *KS* II, pp. 150–62

'Das System der assyrischen Provinzen auf dem Boden des Reiches Israel', *ZDPV* LII, 1929, pp. 220–42, *KS* II, pp. 188–205

'Jesaja 8.23–9.6: Befreiungsnacht und Krönungstag', *Festschrift A. Bertholet*, Tübingen, 1950, pp. 29–49; *KS* II, pp. 206–25

'Neue assyrische Nachrichten über Palästina', *ZDPV* LXVII, 1945, pp. 128–46, *KS* II, pp. 226–41
'Die Territorialgeschichtliche Bedeutung von Sanheribs Eingriff in Palästina', *PJB* XXV, 1930, pp. 80–9, *KS* II, pp. 242–9
'Die Heimat des Deuteronomiums', *KS* II, pp. 250–75
'Bemerkungen zu einigen judäischen Ortslisten des Alten Testaments', *Beiträge zur Biblischen Landes- und Altertumskunde* LXVIII, 1951, 193–210, *KS* II, pp. 289–305
'Festungen und Levitenorte im Lande Juda', *KS* II, pp. 306–15
'Völker und Staaten Syriens im frühen Altertum', *AO* XXXIV, Heft 4, 1936, *KS* III, 1959, pp. 20–48
'Neues über Palästina aus den Archiv Amenophis IV', *KS* III, pp. 169–75
'Menschen ohne Namen', *AO* XVIII, 1950, pp. 9–24, *KS* III, pp. 198–213
'Die syrische Staatenwelt vor dem Einbruch der Assyrer', *ZDMG* LXXXVIII, 1934, pp. 233–58, *KS* III, pp. 214–32
'Zelte und Hütten', *Bonner biblische Beiträge* 1, *Nötscher Festschrift*, 1950, pp. 16–25, *KS* III, 233–42
'Jerusalems Aufstieg', *ZDMG* LXXIX, 1925, pp. 1–19, *KS* III, pp. 243–57
'Der Stadtstaat Samaria', *Berichte über die Verhandlungen der sächsischen Akademie der Wissenschaften zu Leipzig, Phil.-hist. Klasse*, Band 101, Heft 5, 1954, *KS* III, 258–302
'Archäologische Fragen zur Baugeschichte von Jerusalem und Samaria in der israelitischen Königszeit', *Wissenschaftliche Zeitschrift der Ernst-Moritz-Arndt-Universität Greifswald. Gesellschaft- und sprachwissenschaftliche Reihe* Nr. 1, Jahrgang V, 1955–6, pp. 33–42, *KS* III, pp. 303–25
'Der Anteil des Königtums an den sozialen Entwicklung in den Reichen Israel und Juda', *KS* III, pp. 348–72
AP-THOMAS, D. R., 'Elijah on Mount Carmel', *PEQ* 1960, pp. 146–55
AUERBACH, E., *Wüste und gelobtes Land* (2 vols.), Berlin, 1932–6

BADÈ, W. F., 'The Seal of Jaazaniah', *ZAW* LI, 1933, pp. 150–6
BAILLET, M., MILIK, J. T., and de VAUX, R., *Discoveries in the Judaean Desert* III, Oxford, 1962
BALTZER, K., *Das Bundesformular*, Neukirchen, 1960
BALY, D., *The Geography of the Bible*, New York, 1957
BARNES, W. E., 'The Peshitta Version of 2 Kings', *JTS* VI, 1905, pp. 220–32
Kings, Cambridge Bible, 1908
BARNETT, R. D., *The Nimrud Ivories*, London, 1957
'The Siege of Lachish', *IEJ* VIII, 1958, pp. 161–4
BARR, J., *The Semantics of Biblical Language*, Oxford, 1961

BARROIS, A. G., *Manuel d'Archéologie Biblique*, I, 1939, II, 1953, Paris
BAUMGARTNER, W., *Israel und die altorientalische Weisheit*, Tübingen, 1933
van BEEK, G. W., 'A Radio-carbon Date for Early South Arabia', *BASOR* 143, 1956, pp. 6–9
and JAMME, A., 'An Inscribed South Arabian Clay Stamp from Bethel', *BASOR* 151, 1958, pp. 9–16
'South Arabian History and Archaeology', *The Bible and the Ancient Near East*, ed. WRIGHT, G. E., London, 1961, pp. 229–48
BEGRICH, J., *Die Chronologie der Könige von Israel und Juda*, Tübingen, 1929
BENTZEN, A., *Studier over det zadokidiske praesteskabs historie*, Copenhagen, 1931
BENZINGER, I., *Die Bücher der Könige*, Freiburg, 1899 (cited by author's name only)
BERNHARDT, K. H., *Das Problem der altorientalischen Königsideologie* (SVT VIII), 1961
BERRY, G. R., 'The Code found in the Temple', *JBL* XXXIX, 1920, pp. 44–51
'The Date of Deuteronomy', *JBL* LIX, 1940, pp. 133–9
BEYER, G., 'Das Festungssystem Rehoboams', *ZDPV* LIV, 1931, pp. 113–34
BEYERLIN, W., 'Gattung und Herkunft des Rahmens im Richterbuch', *Tradition und Situation*, ed. WÜRTHWEIN, E., and KAISER, O., Göttingen, 1963, pp. 1–29
'Geschichte und heilsgeschichtliche Traditionsbildung im Alten Testament', *VT* XIII, 1963, pp. 10ff.
BIČ, M., 'Der Prophet Amos—ein Hepatoscopos', *VT* I, 1951, pp. 293–6
BIRKELAND, H., *Die Feinde des Individuums in der israelitischen Psalmenliteratur*, Oslo, 1933; ET, *The Evildoers in the Book of Psalms*, 1955
BLACK, M., 'Aramaic Documents. The Milqart Stele. The Zakir Stele', *Documents from Old Testament Times*, ed. THOMAS, D. W., London, 1958
and ROWLEY, H. H., *Peake's Commentary on the Bible* (rev.), London, 1962
BLAKE, I. M., 'Jericho (Ain es-Sultan): Joshua's Curse and Elisha's Miracle—One Possible Explanation', *PEQ* 1967, pp. 86–97
BLISS, F. J., *A Mound of Many Cities*, London, 1898
and DICKIE, A. C., *Excavations at Jerusalem, 1894–7*, London, 1898
BOER, P. A. H. de, 'Vive le Roi', *VT* V, 1955, pp. 225–31
BORÉE, W., *Die alten Ortsnamen Palästinas*, Hildesheim, 1930
BORGER, R., 'Das Ende des ägyptischen Feldherrn Sib'e=סוא' *JNES* XIX, 1960, pp. 49–53
van den BORN, A., *Koningen uit de grondtext vertaald en uitgelegd*, Roermond and Maaseik, 1958 (cited by author's name only)
BOYER, G., see NOUGAYROL, *Mission de Ras Shamra* VI, Paris, 1955
BREASTED, J. H., *Ancient Records of Egypt* (5 vols.), Chicago, 1906–7
BRIGHT, J., *Early Israel in Recent History Writing*, London, 1956

A History of Israel, London, 1960
'Modern Study of Old Testament Literature', *The Bible and the Ancient Near East*, ed. WRIGHT, G. E., London, 1961, pp. 13–31
BROWN, F., DRIVER, S. R., and BRIGGS, C. A., *A Hebrew and English Lexicon of the Old Testament. . .* , Oxford, 1929, rev. 1957
BÜCHLER, A., 'Die Grundbedeutung der hebräischen Wurzel קדר', *ZAW* XXXII, 1912, pp. 56–64.
BUDDE, K., 'Das Deuteronomium und die Reform König Josias', *ZAW* XLIV, 1926, pp. 177–224
BÜLOW, S., and MITCHELL, R. A., 'An Iron Age II Fortress on Tel Nagila', *IEJ* XI, 1961, pp. 101–110
BURKITT, F. C., *Fragments of the Books of Kings according to the Translation of Aquila from a MS formerly in the Geniza at Cairo*, London, 1897
BURNEY, C. F., 'Kings I and II', *Hastings' Dictionary of the Bible*, Edinburgh, 1899
Notes on the Hebrew Text of the Books of Kings, Oxford, 1903
BURROWS, M., *What Mean These Stones?*, New Haven, 1941
BURTON, R. F., *Pilgrimage to Medina and Mecca* (2 vols.), London, 1924–26

Cambridge Ancient History, ed. by BURY, J. B., COOK, S. A., ADCOCK, F. E., vol. III, 1925, chs. i–iv, SMITH, S., 'Assyria'; revised ed. by EDWARDS, I. E. S., GADD, C. J., and HAMMOND, N. G. N., vol. II, ch. xxxiv, 1965, EISSFELDT, O., 'The Hebrew Kingdom'
CAUSSE, A., *Du groupe ethnique à la communauté religieuse: le problème sociologique de la religion d'Israël*, Strasbourg, 1937
CHILDS, B. S., *Isaiah and the Assyrian Crisis*, London, 1967
CLARK, W. E., 'The Sandalwood and Peacocks of Ophir', *AJSL* XXXVI, 1920, pp. 103–19
CLERMONT-GANNEAU, C., *Recueil d'archéologie orientale* (8 vols.), Paris, 1888–1924
CONTENAU, G., *La civilization phénicienne*, Paris, 1926, 2nd ed. 1949
La civilization des Hittites, Paris, 1948
Everyday Life in Babylonia and Assyria, ET, London, 1954
COOK, S. A., *The Religion of Ancient Palestine in the Light of Archaeology*, London, 1930
'Salient Problems in Old Testament History', *JBL* LI, 1932, pp. 273–99
The Old Testament, a Reinterpretation, London, 1936
COOKE, G. A., *A Text-book of North Semitic Inscriptions*, London, 1903 (cited as *NSI*)
COUROYER, B., 'L'origine égyptienne du mot "Pâque"', *RB* LXII, 1955, pp. 481–96
COWLEY, A. E., *Aramaic Papyri of the Fifth Century BC*, London, 1923
CROATTA, J. S., and SOGGIN, J. A., 'Die Bedeutung von שדמות im Alten Testament', *ZAW* LXXIV, 1962, pp. 44–50

CROSS, F. M., and FREEDMAN, D. N., 'Josiah's Revolt against Assyria', *JNES* XII, 1953, pp. 56–8

CROSS, F. M., 'A New Qumran Biblical Fragment related to the Original Hebrew underlying the Septuagint', *BASOR* 132, 1953, pp. 15–26

'The Oldest Manuscripts from Qumran', *JBL* LXXIV, 1955, pp. 165–72

and MILIK, J. T., 'Explorations in the Judaean Buqêah', *BASOR* 142, 1956, pp. 5–17

and WRIGHT, G. E., 'The Boundary and Province Lists of the Kingdom of Judah', *JBL* LXXIV, 1956, pp. 202–26

CROWFOOT, J. W., and FITZGERALD, G. M., *Annual of the Palestine Exploration Fund* V, 1927

and CROWFOOT, G. M., and SUKENIK, E. L., *Samaria-Sebaste II, Early Ivories*, London, 1938

and KENYON, K. M., and SUKENIK, E. L., *Samaria-Sebaste I, The Buildings*, 1942; *III, The Objects*, 1957

DALMAN, G., *Palästinische Diwan*, Leipzig, 1901

Arbeit und Sitte in Palästina (7 vols.), Gütersloh, 1928–42

Aramäische Dialektproben, Leipzig, 1927[2]

Sacred Sites and Ways, ET, London, 1935

DAWSON, W. R., and PEET, T. E., 'The so-called Poem on the King's Chariot', *JEA* XIX, 1933, pp. 167–74

DHORME, E., *L'évolution religieuse d'Israël* I, Paris, 1937

DICKIE, A. C., see BLISS, F. J.

DIRINGER, E., 'On Ancient Hebrew Inscriptions discovered at Tell ed-Duweir (Lachish) I, II', *PEQ* 1941, pp. 38–56, 89–109

'Hebrew Documents: Seals and Weights', *Documents from Old Testament Times*, ed. THOMAS, D. W., London, 1958, pp. 218–30

DONNER, H., and RÖLLIG, W., *Kanaanäische und aramäische Inschriften* (3 vols.), Wiesbaden, 1962–64

DORNSEIFF, F., 'Ägyptische Liebeslieder, Hohelied, Sappho, Theokrit', *ZDMG* XL, 1936, pp. 589–601

DOUGHTY, C. M., *Travels in Arabia Deserta*, London, 1936

DRIVER, G. R., 'The Modern Study of Hebrew Language', *The People and the Book*, ed. PEAKE, A. S., pp. 73–120

'Notes on the Psalms', *JTS* XXXVI, 1935, pp. 147–56

'Studies in the Vocabulary of the Old Testament. VIII', *ibid.*, pp. 293–301

'Linguistic and Textual Problems: Isa. XL–LXVI', *ibid.*, pp. 396–406

Problems of the Hebrew Verbal System, London, 1936

'Two Forgotten Words in the Hebrew Language', *JTS* XXVIII, 1927, pp. 285–7

DRIVER, S. R., *A Treatise on the Use of the Tenses in Hebrew*, London, 1892[3]

DUNAND, M., 'Stèle araméenne dédiée à Melqart', *BMB* III, 1941, pp. 65–76; VI, 1942–3, pp. 41–5
DUNCAN, J. G., see MACALISTER, R. A. S.
DUPONT-SOMMER, A., 'L'ostracon araméen d'Assur', *Syria* XXIV, 1944–5, pp. 24–61
'Un papyrus araméen d'époque saïte découvert à Saqqarah', *Semitica* I, 1948, pp. 43–68
Les Araméens, Paris, 1949
DUSSAUD, R., 'Samarie au temps d'Achab', *Syria* VI, 1925, pp. 314–38; VII, 1926, pp. 9–29
Topographie historique de la Syrie antique et mediévale, Paris, 1927
'Cultes cananéens au source du Jourdain d'après les textes de Ras Shamra', *Syria* XVII, 1936, pp. 283–95

EICHRODT, W., *Theologie des Alten Testaments* (3 vols.), Stuttgart, 1933–9; ET of 5th/6th ed., *Theology of the Old Testament* (2 vols.), London, 1961, 1967
EISSFELDT, O., 'Könige', *HSAT* I, 1922
'Jahwe als König', *ZAW* XLVI, 1928, pp. 81–105
Baal Zaphon, Zeus Kasios, und der Durchzug der Israeliten durchs Meer, Halle-Saale, 1932
Einleitung in das Alte Testament, 1956²; ET, *The Old Testament: an Introduction*, London, 1965
'Molk als Opferbegriff im Punischen und Hebräischen und das Ende des Gottes Moloch', *Beiträge zur Religionsgeschichte des Altertums* Heft 3, 1935
'Baʿalšamēm und Jahwe', *ZAW* LVII, 1939, pp. 1–31
'Israelitisch-philistäische Grenzverschiebung von David bis auf die Assyrerzeit', *ZDPV* LXVI, 1943, pp. 115–28
'Jahwe Zebaoth', *Miscellanea Academica Berolinensia*, 1950
Der Gott Karmel, Berlin, 1953
'Bist du Elia, so bin ich Isebel (1 K. xix, 1)', SVT XVI, 1967, pp. 65–70
ENGNELL, I., *Studies in Divine Kingship in the Ancient Near East*, Uppsala, 1943
ERBT, W., *Die Hebräer*, Leipzig, 1906
ERMAN, A., *The Literature of the Ancient Egyptians*, ET, London, 1927
EULER, K. F., 'Königtum und Götterwelt in den altaramäischen Inschriften Nordsyriens', *ZAW* LVI, 1938, pp. 272–313
EUSEBIUS, *Onomasticon*, ed. KLOSTERMANN, E., 1904

FEDDEN, H. R., *Syria—an Historical Appreciation*, London, 1946
FINEGAN, J., *Light from the Ancient Past—The Archaeological Background of the Hebrew-Christian Literature*, Princeton, 1946

FICHTNER, J., *Die altorientalische Weisheit in ihrer israelitisch-jüdischen Ausprägung* (BZAW LXII), 1933

Das erste Buch von den Köningen (Die Botschaft des Alten Testaments), ed FRICKE, K. D., Stuttgart, 1964

FINKELSTEIN, J. J., 'Ammiṣaduqa's Edict and the Babylonian "Law Codes"', *JCS* XV, 1961, pp. 91–104

FISHER, C. S., *The Excavation of Armageddon* (OIC Communications IV) Chicago, 1929

FOHRER, G., 'Der Vertrag zwischen König und Volk in Israel', *ZAW* LXXI, 1959, pp. 1–22

Elia, Zürich, 1957; 1968²

Einleitung in das Alte Testament: see SELLIN, E.

FORRER, E., *Die Provinzeinteilung des assyrischen Reiches*, Teil I, 1920

FRAZER, J. G., *Folklore in the Old Testament* (3 vols.), London, 1918

FRANKEN, H., 'The Excavations at Deir ʿAllā in Jordan', *VT* X, 1960, pp. 386–93

FRANKFORT, H., *Kingship and the Gods*, Chicago, 1948

FREEDMAN, D. N., and CROSS, F. M., 'Josiah's Revolt against Assyria', *JNES* XII, 1953, pp. 56–8

'Old Testament Chronology', *The Bible and the Ancient Near East*, ed. WRIGHT, G. E., London, 1961, pp. 203–14

FRIEDRICH, J., 'Eine altphönizische Inschrift aus Kilikien', *FuF* XXIV, 1948, pp. 77–9

GADD, C. J., *The Fall of Nineveh*, London, 1923

Ideas of Divine Rule in the Ancient Near East, London, 1948

'Inscribed Prisms of Sargon II from Nimrud', *Iraq* XVI, 1954, pp. 173–201

GALLING, K., 'Die israelitische Staatsverfassung in ihrer vorderasiatischen Umwelt', *AO* XXVIII, Heft 3/4, 1929

GARDINER, A. H., 'The Astarte Papyrus', *Studies Presented to F. Ll. Griffith*, London, 1932, pp. 74–85

Ancient Egyptian Onomastica (3 vols.), London, 1947

GASTER, T. H., *Thespis*, New York, 1950

GARSTANG, J., see LUCIAN of SAMOSATA

The Heritage of Solomon, London, 1934

GELB, I., 'Two Assyrian Kinglists', *JNES* XIII, 1954, pp. 209–30

van GELDEREN, C., *Die Boeken van Koningen* (3 vols.), Kampen, 1936–47

GENSENIUS, W., *Hebrew Grammar*, ed. KAUTZSCH, E., ET, COWLEY, A. E., 1910²

GILLESCHEWSKI, E., 'Der Ausdruck עם הארץ im AT', *ZAW* XL, 1922, pp. 137–42

GLASER, E., *Skizze der Geschichte und Geographie Arabiens von den ältesten Zeiten bis zum Propheten Muhammad*, Berlin, 1890

Glueck, N., 'Explorations in Eastern Palestine I', *AASOR* XIV, 1934; II, *ibid.* XV, 1935; III, *ibid.* XVIII–XIX, 1939
'The First Campaign at Tell el-Kheleifeh', *BASOR* 71, 1938, pp. 3–18; 'The Second Campaign . . .', *ibid.* 75, 1939, pp. 8–22; 'The Third Season . . .', *ibid.* 79, 1940, pp. 2–18
'Three Israelite Towns in the Jordan Valley: Zarethan, Succoth, Zaphon', *BASOR* 90, 1943, pp. 2–23
Das Wort hesed im alttestamentlichen Sprachgebrauch als menschliche und göttliche gemeinschaftsgemässe Verhaltungsweise (BZAW XLVII), 1927; ET, *Hesed in the Bible*, New York, 1968
The Other Side of the Jordan, New Haven, 1940
The River Jordan: being an illustrated account of the earth's most storied river, London, 1946
Rivers in the Desert, London, 1959
Goedicke, H., 'The End of So, King of Egypt', *BASOR* 171, 1963, pp. 64–6
Gooding, D. W., 'Temple Specifications: a Dispute in Logical Arrangement between the MT and the LXX', *VT* XVII, 1967, pp. 143–72
'The Septuagint's Rival Versions of Jeroboam's Rise to Power', *ibid.*, pp. 173–89
Goodspeed, J., 'The Shulammite', *AJSL* L, 1934, pp. 102–4
Gordis, R., 'Sectional Rivalry in the Kingdom of Judah', *JQR* XXV, 1935, pp. 237–55
Gordon, C. H., *Ugaritic Handbook*, Rome, 1947
Ugaritic Literature, Rome, 1949
'Azitawadd's Phoenician Inscription', *JNES* VIII, 1949, pp. 108–15
Ugaritic Manual, Rome, 1955
Ugaritic Textbook, Rome, 1965
Grant, E., *Beth Shemesh, Ain Shems Excavation 1928–33* (Biblical Studies), Haverford, 1931–4
Granqvist, H., *Marriage Conditions in a Palestinian Village* (Societas Scientiarum Fennica, Commentationes Humanarum Literarum III, 8), Helsinki, 1931
Gray, G. B., *Studies in Hebrew Proper Names*, London, 1896
Sacrifice in the Old Testament: its Theory and Practice, Oxford, 1925
Gray, J., 'The Canaanite God Horon', *JNES* VIII, 1949, pp. 27–34
'The Desert God 'Aṯtar in the Literature and Religion of Canaan', *JNES* VIII, 1949, pp. 72–83
'Cultic Affinities between Israel and Ras Shamra', *ZAW* LXII, 1950, pp. 207–20
'The Period and Office of the Prophet Isaiah in the Light of a New Assyrian Tablet', *ExpT* LXIII, 1952, pp. 263–5
'Canaanite Kingship in Theory and Practice', *VT* II, 1952, pp. 139–220
'Tell el-Far'a, a "Mother" in Ancient Israel', *PEQ* 1952, pp. 110–13

'A Metaphor from Building in Zephaniah ii. 1', *VT* III, 1953, pp. 404–7
'The *Goren* at the City Gate: Justice and the Royal Office in the Ugaritic Text 'Aqht', *PEQ* 1953, pp. 118–23
'The Hebrew Conception of the Kingship of God: its Origin and Development', *VT* VI, 1956, pp. 268–85
The Legacy of Canaan (SVT V), 1957; 2nd ed., 1965
'The Kingship of God in the Prophets and Psalms', *VT* XI, 1961, pp. 1–29
Archaeology and the Old Testament World, Edinburgh, 1962
Joshua, Judges, Ruth (Century Bible, ed. Rowley, H. H., and Black M.), London, 1967
'Gud som konge og nyttårsfesten', *NTT* LXVIII, 1967, pp. 121–44
Gressmann, H., *Mose und seine Zeit*, Göttingen, 1913
Könige, Die Schriften des AT in Auswahl, Göttingen, 1921
Die älteste Geschichtsschreibung und Prophetie Israels, Göttingen, 1921[2]
'Die neugefundene Lehre des Amen-em-ope und die vorexilische Spruchdichtung Israels', *ZAW* XLII, 1924, pp. 272–96
Altorientalische Texte und Bilder zum Alten Testament, Berlin, 1926–7
Grollenberg, L. H., *Atlas van de Bijbel*, Amsterdam, 1954; ET, ed. Rowley, H. H., *Atlas of the Bible*, Edinburgh, 1957
Guillaume, A., *Prophecy and Divination*, London, 1938
Gunkel, H., *Die Psalmen*, Göttingen, 1926
Einleitung in die Psalmen, Göttingen, 1933
Guy, P. L. O., *New Light from Armageddon* (OIC Publications IX), 1931

Haldar, A., *Associations of Cult Prophets among the Ancient Semites*, Uppsala, 1945
Hallo, W., 'From Qarqar to Carchemish in the Light of New Discoveries', *BA* XXIII, 1960, pp. 34–61
Hänel, J., 'Die Zusätze der Septuaginta in Reg. 2.35a–o und 46a–l', *ZAW* XLVII, 1929, pp. 76–9
Haran, M., 'The Rise and Decline of the Empire of Jeroboam ben Joash', *VT* XVII, 1967, pp. 266–97
Harding, G. L., see Lachish, I, II
The Antiquities of Jordan, London, 1959
Heidel, W. A., *The Day of Yahweh*, New York, 1929
Hempel, J., *Die althebräische Literatur und ihr hellenistisch-jüdisches Nachleben*, Potsdam, 1930–34
Das Ethos des Alten Testaments (BZAW LXVII), 1938
Geschichte und Geschichten im Alten Testament bis zum persischen Zeitalter, Gütersloh, 1964
Herodotus, ed. Godley, A. D., Loeb Classical Library (4 vols.), 1921–4
Herrmann, S., 'Die Königsnovelle in Ägypten und Israel', *Wissenschaft-*

liche Zeitschrift der Karl Marx-Universität Leipzig, III, 1953–4, pp. 51–62

HERTZBERG, H. W., 'Die Entwicklung des Begriffes mišpat im AT', *ZAW* XL, 1922, pp. 256–87; XLI, 1923, pp. 16–76

HILL, G. F., *A Catalogue of Greek Coins of Palestine in the British Museum*, London, 1914

HILLMANN, R., *Wasser und Berg*, Halle (Saale), 1965

HOCART, A. M., *Kingship*, London, 1926

HOGARTH, D. G., *Kings of the Hittites*, London, 1926

HÖLSCHER, G., 'Das Buch der Könige, seine Quellen und seine Redaktion', *Eucharisterion* (Gunkel Festschrift) I, 1923, pp. 158–213

Die Anfänge der hebräischen Geschichtsschreibung (Sitzungsberichte der Akademie, Heidelberg, Philos.-hist. Klasse), 1942

HONEYMAN, A. M., 'Hebrew סף, "Basin, Goblet" ', *JTS* XXXVII, 1936, pp. 56–9

'Some Developments of the Hebrew Root *by*', *JAOS* LXIV, 1944, pp. 81–2

'The Pottery Vessels of the Old Testament', *PEQ* 1939, pp. 76–90

'The Evidence for Regnal Names among the Hebrews', *JBL* LXVII, 1948, pp. 13–25

'Phoenician Inscriptions from Karatepe', *Le Muséon* LXI, 1948, pp. 43–57

'The Salting of Shechem', *VT* III, 1953, pp. 192–5

HOOKE, S. H. (ed.) *Myth and Ritual. Essays on the Myth and Ritual of the Hebrews in relation to the Culture Pattern of the Ancient Near East*, London, 1933

(ed.) *The Labyrinth. Further Studies in the relation between Myth and Ritual in the Ancient World*, London, 1935

'A Scarab and Sealing from Tell Duweir', *PEFQS* 1935, pp. 195–7

The Origins of Early Semitic Ritual, London, 1938

(ed.) *Myth, Ritual, and Kingship. Essays on the Theory and Practice of Kingship in the Ancient Near East and in Israel*, Oxford, 1958

HUMBERT, P., 'Le problème du livre de Nahoum', *RHPR* XII, 1932, pp. 1–15

INGE, C. H., see LACHISH II

IWRY, S., 'The Qumran Isaiah and the End of the Dial of Ahaz', *BASOR* 147, 1957, pp. 27–33

JACK, J. W., *Samaria in Ahab's Time*, Edinburgh, 1929

JACOB, E., *Théologie de l'Ancien Testament*, Strasbourg, 1955; ET, *The Theology of the Old Testament*, London, 1958

JASTROW, M., *The Religion of Babylonia and Assyria*, Boston, 1898

JAUSSEN, A., *Coutumes des Arabes au pays de Moab*, Paris, 1908

JEPSEN, A., *Nabi. Soziologische Studien zur alttestamentlichen Literatur und Religionsgeschichte*, Munich, 1934
'Kleine Beiträge zum Zwölfprophetenbuch II', *ZAW* LVII, 1939, pp. 242–55
'Israel und Damaskus', *AfO* XIV, 1942, pp. 153–72
Die Quellen des Königsbuches, Halle, 1956²
'Noch einmal zur israelitisch-jüdischen Chronologie', *VT* XVIII, 1968, pp. 31–46
JEREMIAS, A., *Das AT im Lichte des alten Orients*, 4th ed., 1930; ET of 2nd ed. of 1906: *The Old Testament in the Light of the Ancient East*, 2 vols., ed. JOHNS, C. H. W., London, 1911
JIRKU, A., ' "Das Haupt auf die Knie legen". Eine ägyptisch-ugaritisch-israelitische Parallele', *ZDMG* CIII, 1953, p. 372
JOHNS, C. N., 'The Citadel, Jerusalem', *QDAP* XIV, 1950, pp. 139–47
JOHNSON, A. R., 'The Role of the King in the Jerusalem Cultus', *The Labyrinth* . . . ed. HOOKE, S. H., London, 1935, pp. 113ff.
The One and the Many in the Israelite Conception of God, Cardiff, 1942, 2nd ed., 1961
The Cultic Prophet in Ancient Israel, Cardiff, 1944, 2nd ed., 1962
'Jonah 2.3–10: a Study in Cultic Fantasy', *Studies in Old Testament Prophecy*, ed. ROWLEY, H. H., Edinburgh, 1950, pp. 82–102
Sacral Kingship in Ancient Israel, Cardiff, 1955, 2nd ed., 1967
'Hebrew Conceptions of Kingship', *Myth, Ritual and Kingship*, ed. HOOKE, S. H., Oxford, 1958, pp. 204–35
JOSEPHUS, trans. WHISTON, W., ed. MARGOLIOUTH, D. S., London, 1906
JUNGE, E., *Der Wiederaufbau des Heereswesens des Reiches Juda unter Josia* (BWANT IV), 23, 1937

KAHLE, P., *The Cairo Geniza*, London, 1959²
'Der gegenwärtige Stand der Erforschung der in Palästina neu gefundenen hebräischen Handschriften', *TLZ* LXXIV, 1949, cols. 91–4
KAPELRUD, A. S., 'Jahves tronstigningsfest og funnene i Ras Sjamra', *NTT* XLI, 1940, pp. 38–58
'The Role of the Cult in Old Israel', *The Bible in Modern Scholarship*, ed. HYATT, J. P., Nashville, 1965, pp. 44–56
KATZENSTEIN, H. J., 'Who were the Parents of Athaliah?', *IEJ* V, 1955, pp. 194–7
KAUTZSCH, E., see GESENIUS
Die heilige Schrift des AT. (2 vols.), ed. BERTHOLET, A., Tübingen 1922–3⁴
KENNEDY, A. R. S., 'Weights and Measures', *Dictionary of the Bible* IV, ed. HASTINGS, J., Edinburgh, 1902, pp. 901–13
KENNETT, R. H., *Deuteronomy and the Decalogue*, London, 1924
Old Testament Essays, Cambridge, 1938

KENYON, K. M., *Digging up Jericho*, London, 1957
Archaeology in the Holy Land, London, 1960
'Excavations in Jerusalem, 1961', *PEQ* 1962, pp. 72–89
'Excavations in Jerusalem, 1962', *ibid.*, 1963, pp. 7–21
'Excavations in Jerusalem, 1963', *ibid.*, 1964, pp. 7–18
'Excavations in Jerusalem, 1964', *ibid.*, 1965, pp. 9–20
'Excavations in Jerusalem, 1965', *ibid.*, 1966, pp. 73–88
'Excavations in Jerusalem, 1966', *ibid.*, 1967, pp. 65–73
Jerusalem: Excavating 3000 Years of History, London, 1967
See CROWFOOT, J. W.

KING, L. W., *Bronze Reliefs from the Gates of Shalmaneser*, London, 1915

KITCHEN, K. A., *Ancient Orient and Old Testament*, London, 1966

KITTEL, R., *Die Bücher der Könige* (Handkommentar zum AT, ed. NOWACK, W.), Göttingen, 1900 (cited as HKAT)
Biblia Hebraica, ed. ALT, A. and EISSFELDT, O. (Kings by KITTEL, R. and NOTH, M.), Stuttgart, 1934[3]

KJAER, H., and SCHMIDT, A., 'The Excavation of Shiloh', *JPOS* X, 1930, pp. 87–174

KLOPFENSTEIN, M. A., '1 Könige 13', *Parrhesia, Karl Barth zum 80. Geburtstag*, ed. BUSCH, E., FANGMEIER, F., and GEIGER, M., Zürich, 1966, pp. 639–72

KLOSTERMANN, A., *Die Bücher Samuelis und der Könige, Kurzgefasste Kommentäre*, ed. STRACK, H. L. and ZÖCKLER, O., Nördlingen and Munich, 1887
see EUSEBIUS, *Onomasticon*

KNUDTZON, J. A., *Die el-Amarna Tafeln* (2 vols.), Leipzig, 1908–15

KOEHLER, L. and BAUMGARTNER, W., *Lexicon in Veteris Testamenti Libros*, Leiden, 1953; *Supplementum*, 1958

KOLDEWEY, R., *Das wieder erstehende Babylon*, Leipzig, 1925[4]

KOPF, L., 'Das arabische Wörterbuch als Hilfsmittel für die hebräische Lexicographie', *VT* VI, 1956, pp. 286–302
'Arabische Etymologien und Parallelen zum Bibelwörterbuch', *VT* VIII, 1958, pp. 161–215; IX, 1959, pp. 247–87

KORNFELD, W., 'Der Symbolismus der Tempelsäule', *ZAW* LXXIV, 1962, pp. 50–7

KRAELING, E. G., *The Brooklyn Museum Aramaic Papyri*, New Haven, 1953

KRAUS, H. J., *Die Königsherrschaft Gottes im Alten Testament* (Beiträge zur historischen Theologie XIII), Tübingen, 1951
'Gilgal, ein Beitrag zur Kultusgeschichte Israels', *VT* I, 1951, pp. 181–99
Gottesdienst in Israel. Studien zur Geschichte des Laubhüttenfest (Beiträge zur evangelischen Theologie XIX), Munich, 1954; ET, *Worship in Israel*, Oxford, 1966
Psalmen (Biblischer Kommentar Altes Testament XV, 2 vols.), Neukirchen, 1959–60

Kutsch, E., 'Die Wurzel עצר im Hebräischen', *VT* II, 1952, pp. 57–69
Salbung als Rechtsakt im Alten Testament und im alten Orient (BZAW LXXXVII), 1963

Labat, R., *Le caractère religieux de la royauté assyro-babylonienne*, Paris, 1939
Labuschagne, C. J., 'Did Elisha Deliberately Lie?—A Note on II Kings 8.10', *ZAW* LXXVII, 1965, pp. 327f.
Lachish, I, *The Lachish Letters*, Torczyner, H., with Harding, G. L., Starkey, J. L., and Lewis, A., London, 1937
II, *The Fosse Temple*, Tufnell, O., Inge, C. H., and Harding, G. L., London, 1940
III, *The Iron Age*, Tufnell, O. with contributions by Murray, M. A. and Diringer, D., London, 1953
IV, *The Bronze Age*, Tufnell, O., London, 1958
Lamon, R. and Shipton, G. M., *Megiddo I* (OIC Publications XLII), Chicago, 1939
de Langhe, R. 'De Betekenis van het Hebreeuwse Werkwoord רכב', *Handelingen van het XVIIIe Vlaamse Filologencongres*, 1949, pp. 89–96
Layard, A. H., *Discoveries among the Ruins of Nineveh and Babylon*, London, 1856
Leclant, J., and Yoyotte, J., 'Notes d'histoire et de civilisation éthiopiennes', *Bulletin de l'Institut Français d'Archéologie Orientale du Caire* LI, 1952, pp. 15–27
Lehmann, M. R., 'A New Interpretation of the Term שדמות', *VT* III, 1953, pp. 361–71
Lettinga, J. P., 'A Note on II Kings xix, 37', *VT* VII, 1957, pp. 105–6
Lewy, J., *Die Chronologie der Könige von Israel und Juda*, Giessen, 1927
Lidzbarski, M., *Ephemeris für semitische Epigraphik* (3 vols.), Giessen, 1902–15
Liver, J., 'The Chronology of Tyre at the Beginning of the First Millennium BC', *IEJ* III, 1953, pp. 113–20
Lods, A., 'Le rôle de la tradition orale dans la formation des récits de l'Ancien Testament', *RHR* LXXXVIII, 1923, pp. 51–64
'La divinisation du roi dans l'Orient méditerranéen et ses répercussions dans l'ancien Israël', *RHPR* X, 1930, pp. 209–21
Israël des origines au VIIIe siècle, Paris, 1930; ET, *Israel from its Beginnings to the Middle of the Eighth Century*, London, 1953
La Religion d'Israël, 1939
'Une tablette inédite de Mari', *Studies in Old Testament Prophecy*, ed. Rowley, H. H., Edinburgh, 1950
Loud, G., *The Megiddo Ivories* (OIC Publications LII), Chicago, 1939
Lucian of Samosata, *De Dea Syra*, translation and comment. Strong, H. A. and Garstang, J., *The Syrian Goddess*, London, 1913
Luckenbill, D. D., *Ancient Records of Assyria and Babylonia* (2 vols,.) Chicago, 1927

Lurje, W., *Studien zur Geschichte der wirtschaftlichen und sozialen Verhältnisse im israelitisch-jüdischen Reiche* (BZAW XLV), 1927
Lyon, D. G., Reisner, G., and Fisher, C. S., *Harvard Excavations at Samaria* (2 vols.), Cambridge, Mass. and London, 1924

Maag, V., 'Jahwäs Heerscharen', *Schweizerischen Theologischen Umschau* XX, 3/4 (Köhler Festschrift), 1950, pp. 75–100
Macadam, M. F. L., *The Temples of Kawa I: The Inscriptions*, London, 1949
Macalister, R. A. S., *Excavations in Palestine, 1898–1900*, London, 1902
The Excavation of Gezer (3 vols.), London, 1912
A Century of Excavation in Palestine, London, 1912
and Duncan, J. G., *Excavations on the Hill of Ophel, Jerusalem*, 1923–5 (PEF Annual IV), 1926
McCown, T. D., and Keith, A., *The Stone Age on Mount Carmel*, London, 1939
McEwan, C. W., 'The Syrian Expedition of the Oriental Institute of the University of Chicago', *AJA* XLI, 1937, pp. 8–16
McKane, W., 'A Note on II Kings 12.10', *ZAW* LXXI, 1959, pp. 260–5
Mackenzie, D., 'The Excavations at Ain Stems, 1911', *PEF Annual* I, 1911, pp. 41–94; 'The Excavations at Ain Stems, 1912–13'; *PEF Annual* II, 1913
Maisler, B. (now Mazar), *The Excavations at Tell Qasile. A Preliminary Report*, Jerusalem, 1951
Malamat, A., 'The Historical Background of the Assassination of Amon, King of Judah', *IEJ* III, 1953, pp. 26–9
'Doctrines of Causality in Hittite and Hebrew Historiography: a Parallel', *VT* V, 1955, pp. 1ff.
'Aspects of the Foreign Policies of David and Solomon', *JNES* XXII, 1963, pp. 1–17
'Organs of Statecraft in the Israelite Monarchy', *BA* XXVIII, 1965, pp. 34–65
'Prophetic Revelation in New Documents from Mari and the Bible', SVT XV, 1966, pp. 207–27
Marcus, R., and Gelb, I. J., 'A Preliminary Study of the New Phoenician Inscription from Cilicia', *JNES* VII, 1948, pp. 194–8
'The Phoenician Stele Inscription from Cilicia', *JNES* VIII, 1949, pp. 116–20
Margoliouth, D. S., *The Relations between Arabs and Israelites prior to the Rise of Islam*, London, 1924
Maspero, 'Manuel d'hiérarchie égyptienne', *Journal Asiatique* 8 sér., 11, 1888, pp. 250–80
Matouš, L., *Die lexikalischen Tafelserien der Babylonier und Assyrer in der Berliner Museum* I, *Gegenstandslisten*, Berlin, 1953
Mauchline, J., 'I and II Kings', *Peake's Commentary*, rev. Rowley, H. H., and Black, M. (edd.), London, 1962, pp. 338–56

MAZAR, B. (formerly MAISLER), 'The Campaign of Pharaoh Shishak to Palestine', SVT IV, 1957, pp. 57–66
'The Cities of the Priests and Levites', SVT VII (Congress vol.), 1960, pp. 193–205
'The Aramean Empire and its Relations with Israel', *BA* XXV, 1962, pp. 98–120
MEEK, T. J., *Hebrew Origins*, New York, 1936, 1960³
van der MEER, P., *The Chronology of Ancient Western Asia and Egypt* (*Documenta et Monumenta Orientis Antiqui*), Leiden, 1947, 1955²
MEINHOLD, J., 'Die Entstehung des Sabbaths', *ZAW* XXIX, 1909, pp. 81–112
MEISSNER, B., 'Neue Nachrichten über die Ermordung Sanheribs', *Preussische Akad. der Wissenschaften, Sitzungsberichten Phil.-hist. Klasse*, 1932, pp. 250–62
MENDELSOHN, I., 'Guilds in Ancient Palestine', *BASOR* 90, 1940, pp. 17–21
'State Slavery in Ancient Palestine', *BASOR* 85, 1942, pp. 14–17
MENDENHALL, G. E., *Law and Covenant in Israel and the Ancient Near East*, Pittsburgh, 1955 (also *BA* XVII, 1954, pp. 26–46; 49–76)
MEYER, E., *Geschichte des Altertums*, Stuttgart, 1921–31
MILIK, J. T. and BARTHÉLEMY, D., *Discoveries in the Judaean Desert I, Qumran Cave I*, Oxford, 1955
and CROSS, F. M., 'Explorations in the Judaean Buqêah', *BASOR* 142, 1956, pp. 5–17
Dix ans de découvertes dans le Désert de Juda, Paris, 1957, ET with revision and expansion *Ten Years of Discovery in the Wilderness of Judaea*, London, 1959
BENOIT, P., and de VAUX, R., *Discoveries in the Judaean Desert II, Les Grottes de Murabba ʿat* (2 vols.), Oxford, 1961
BAILLET, M., and de VAUX, R., *Discoveries in the Judaean Desert III*, Oxford, 1962
MILLER, J. M., 'The Fall of the House of Ahab', *VT* XVII, 1967, pp. 307–24
MÖHLENBRINK, K., 'Die Landnahmesagen des Buches Josua', *ZAW* LVI, 1938, pp. 238–68
MONTET, P., *L'Égypte et la Bible*, Cahiers d'Archéologie Biblique, No. 11, Neuchâtel, 1959
MONTGOMERY, J. A., *Arabia and the Bible*, Philadelphia, 1934
'The Year Eponymate in the Hebrew Monarchy', *JBL* XLIX, 1930, pp. 311–9
'Archival Data in the Book of Kings', *JBL* LIII, 1934, pp. 46–52
'The Supplement at the End of 3 Kingdoms 2 [I Reg. 2]', *ZAW* L, 1932, pp. 124–9
Kings (ICC), Edinburgh, 1951 (cited as ICC)

Moran, W. L., 'A Note on the Treaty Terminology of the Sefîre Stelas', *JNES* XXII, 1963, pp. 173–6
Morgenstern, J., 'The Three Calendars of Ancient Israel', *HUCA* I, 1924, pp. 13–18
'A Chapter in the History of the High-Priesthood', *AJSL* LV, 1938, pp. 1–24, 183–97, 360–76
Moritz, B., *Der Sinai Kult in der heidnischen Zeit* (Abhandlungen der königl. Gesellschaft der Wissenschaften zu Göttingen, Philos.-hist. Klasse, Band XVI), 1916
Mowinckel, S., 'Om nebiisme og profeti', *NTT* X, 1906, pp. 185ff., 330f.
Psalmenstudien (6 vols.), Oslo, 1921–4; photographic reproduction (2 vols.), Oslo, 1961
Ezra den Skriftlærde, Kristiania, 1916
' "Die letzte Worte Davids" II Sam. 23. 1–7', *ZAW* XLV, 1927, pp. 30–58
Le Décalogue, Paris, 1927
'Die Chronologie der israelitischen und jüdischen Könige', *Acta Orientalia* X, 1932, pp. 161–277
'Hat es ein Israelitisches Nationalepos gegeben?', *ZAW* LIII, 1935, pp. 130–52
'Til uttrycket "Jahves tjener" ', *NTT* XLIII, 1942, pp. 24ff.
'Kadesj, Sinai, og Jahve', *NGT* XI, 1942, pp. 1–32
Han som Kommer, Copenhagen, 1951, ET, *He that Cometh*, Oxford, 1956
Offersang og Sangoffer, Oslo, 1951; ET, *The Psalms in Israel's Worship* (2 vols.), Oxford, 1962
Mulder, M. J., *Ba'al en het Oude Testament*, The Hague, 1962
Muss-Arnolt, W., *A Concise Dictionary of the Assyrian Language*, Berlin, 1905
Myres, J. L., 'King Solomon's Temple and Other Buildings and Works of Art', *PEQ* 1948, pp. 14–41

Naveh, J., 'A Hebrew Letter from the 7th Century BC', *IEJ* X, 1960, pp. 129–39
'More Hebrew Inscriptions from Meṣad Hashavyahu', *IEJ* XII, 1962, pp. 27–32
Nestle, E., 'Miscellen', *ZAW* XXII, 1902, pp. 170–2, 305–17
Nicolsky, N. M., 'Pascha im Kulte des jerusalemischen Tempels', *ZAW* XLV, 1927, pp. 171–90, 241–53
'Das Asylrecht in Israel', *ZAW* LXVIII, 1930, pp. 146–75
Nielsen, E., *Shechem*, Copenhagen, 1955
North, C. R., 'The Religious Aspects of Hebrew Kingship', *ZAW* L, 1932, pp. 8–38
Noth, M., *Die israelitischen Personennamen im Rahmen der gemeinsemitischen Namengebung* (BWANT III 10), Stuttgart, 1928 (cited as *IP*)

Das System der zwölf Stämme Israels (BWANT IV 1), Stuttgart, 1930 (cited as *Zwölf Stämme*)

'Geschichte und Gotteswort im Alten Testament', *Bonner Akademische Reden* III, Krefeld, 1949; ET, 'History and the Word of God in the Old Testament', *BJRL* XXXII, 1950, pp. 194–206

Die Welt des Alten Testaments, Berlin, 1957[3]; ET, *The Old Testament World*, London, 1966

Überlieferungsgeschichtliche Studien. Die sammelnden und bearbeitenden Geschichtswerke im AT (Schriften der Konigsberger gelehrten Gesellschaft, 18 Jahrgang, geisteswissenschaftliche Klasse, Heft 2), Tübingen, 1957[2]

Geschichte Israels, Göttingen, 1950, 1956[3]; ET, *The History of Israel*, London, 1958, rev. ed., 1960

'Jerusalem und die israelitische Tradition', *OTS* VIII, 1950, pp. 28–46

Das Buch Josua (Handbuch zum AT 1.7), Tübingen, 1953[2]

and Thomas, D. W. (edd.), *Wisdom in Israel and the Ancient Near East* (SVT III), Leiden, 1955

'Die Bewährung von Salomos "Göttlicher Weisheit"', *op. cit.*, pp. 225–37

'Das alttestamentliche Bundschliessen im Lichte eines Mari-textes', *Mélanges Isidore Lewy*, Brussels, 1955, pp. 233–44; *Gesammelte Studien*, pp. 142–54; ET, 'Old Testament Covenant-making in the Light of a Text from Mari', *The Laws in the Pentateuch*, pp. 108–17

'Gott, König, Volk im Alten Testament', *ZTK* XLVII, 1956, pp. 157–91; *Gesammelte Studien*, pp. 188–229; ET, 'God, King and Nation in the Old Testament', *The Laws in the Pentateuch*, pp. 145–78

Gesammelte Studien zum Alten Testament (Theologische Bücherei Altes Testament, Band 6), Munich, 1957; ET, *The Laws in the Pentateuch and Other Studies*, Edinburgh, 1966

Amt und Berufung im Alten Testament, Bonn, 1958

Das zweite Buch Mose (Das Alte Testament Deutsch 5), Göttingen, 1959; ET, *Exodus*, London, 1962

'The Background of Judges 17–18', *Israel's Prophetic Heritage*, ed. Anderson, B. W., and Harrelson, W., New York and London, 1962, pp. 68–85

Könige (Biblischer Kommentar), Neukirchen-Vluyn, 1964ff.

Biblia Hebraica. See Kittel, R.

Nougayrol, J., *Mission de Ras Shamra* VI, ed. Schaeffer, C. F. A., *Le palais royal d'Ugarit III. Textes accadiens et hourrites des archives est, ouest et centrales*, Paris, 1955

Nowack, W., 'Deuteronomium und Regum' (BZAW XLI, Marti Festschrift), 1925, pp. 221–31

Obbink, H. T., 'Jahwebilder', *ZAW* XLVII, 1929, pp. 264–74

O'Callaghan, R. T., *Aram-Naharaim*, Rome, 1948

OESTERLEY, W. O. E. and ROBINSON, T. H., *Hebrew Religion: its Origin and Development*, London, 1937²
History of Israel (2 vols.), London, 1932
An Introduction to the Books of the Old Testament, London, 1934
OESTREICHER, T., *Das deuteronomische Grundgesetz*, Gütersloh, 1923
OLMSTEAD, A. T., 'The Fall of Samaria', *AJSL* XXI, 1906, pp. 179–82
Assyrian Historiography: a Source Study (University of Missouri Studies, Social Science Series III), 1916
History of Assyria, New York, 1923
A History of Palestine and Syria, New York, 1931
OPPENHEIM, A. L., 'Akkadian Historical Texts', *ANET*, pp. 266–317
' "Siege Documents" from Nippur', *Iraq* XVII, 1955, pp. 69–89
ORLINSKY, H. M., 'Qumran and the Present State of Old Testament Text Studies: the Septuagint Text', *JBL* LXXVIII, 1959, pp. 26–36
'The Textual Criticism of the Old Testament', *The Bible and the Ancient Near East*, ed. WRIGHT, G. E., London, 1961
OTTO, E., *Ägypten, der Weg des Pharaonenreiches*, Stuttgart, 1958

PARROT, A., *Ninive et l'Ancien Testament*, Neuchâtel and Paris, 1953; ET, *Nineveh and the Old Testament*, London, 1956
Samarie, capitale du royaume d'Israël, Neuchâtel and Paris, 1955; ET, *Samaria the Capital of the Kingdom of Israel*, London, 1958
Le Temple de Jérusalem, Neuchâtel and Paris, 1954; ET, *The Temple of Jerusalem*, London, 1957
Mission archéologique de Mari II, *Le Palais*, 2, *Peintures murales*, Paris, 1958
The Arts of Mankind: Sumer, London, 1960
PATAI, R., 'The Control of Rain in Ancient Palestine', *HUCA* XIV, 1939, pp. 251–86
PEAKE, A. S. (ed.), *The People and the Book*, London, 1925
PEDERSEN, J., *Israel: its Life and Culture* I–II, Copenhagen, 1926; III–IV, 1940, 1947²
'Passahfest und Passahlegende', *ZAW* LII, 1934, pp. 161–75
PEET, T. E., *Egypt and the Old Testament*, London, 1922
and DAWSON, W. R., 'The So-called Poem on the King's Chariot', *JEA* XIX, 1933, pp. 167–74
PETERS, J. R. and THIERSCH, H., *Painted Tombs in the Necropolis of Marissa*, London, 1905
PETRIE, W. M. F., *Egypt and Israel*, London, 1911
Beth-Pelet I, London, 1930
PFEIFFER, R. H., *Introduction to the Old Testament*, New York, 1948²; abridged version, *The Books of the Old Testament*, London, 1957
PHILO of Byblos, ed. MÜLLER, W., *Fragmenta Historiarum Graecarum* III, Paris, 1849

POEBEL, A., 'The Assyrian Kinglist from Khorsabad', *JNES* I, 1942, pp. 247–306, 460–92; II, 1943, pp. 56–90

POSENER, G., *Princes et pays d'Asie et de Nubie. Textes hiératiques sur des figurines d'envoûtement du Moyen Empire*, Brussels, 1940

PRITCHARD, J. B., *Palestinian Figurines in relation to certain Goddesses known through Literature*, New Haven, 1944

(ed.), *Ancient Near Eastern Texts relating to the Old Testament* (abbrev. *ANET*), Princeton, 1950

The Ancient Near East in Pictures relating to the Old Testament (abbrev. *ANEP*), Princeton and London, 1955

The Ancient Near East: an Anthology of Texts and Pictures (abridgement of the preceding two vols.), Princeton and London, 1958

Hebrew Inscriptions and Stamps from Gibeon, Philadelphia, 1959

'More Inscribed Jar-handles from el-Jib', *BASOR* 160, 1960, pp. 2–6

von RAD, G., 'Die falschen Propheten', *ZAW* LI, 1933, pp. 109–20

Das Formgeschichtliche Problem des Hexateuchs (BWANT IV, Heft 26), 1938; *Gesammelte Studien zum Alten Testament*, Munich, 1958, pp. 9–86; ET, 'The Form-critical Problem of the Hexateuch', *The Problem of the Hexateuch and Other Essays*, Edinburgh, 1966, pp. 1–78

'Der Anfang der Geschichtsschreibung im alten Israel', *Archiv für Kulturgeschichte*, Band 32, 1944, pp. 1–42; *Gesammelte Studien . . .*, pp. 148–88; ET, 'The Beginnings of Historical Writing in Ancient Israel', *The Problem of the Hexateuch*, pp. 166–204

'Das judäische Königsritual', *TLZ* LXXII, 1947, cols. 211–16

Deuteronomium-Studien, Göttingen, 1948; ET, *Studies in Deuteronomy*, London, 1953

Theologie des Alten Testaments (2 vols.), Munich, 1957, 1960; ET, *Old Testament Theology* (2 vols.), Edinburgh, 1962, 1965

Gesammelte Studien zum Alten Testament (Theologische Bücherei Altes Testament, Band 8), Munich, 1958; ET, *The Problem of the Hexateuch and Other Essays*, Edinburgh, 1966

'Die deuteronomische Geschichtstheologie in den Königsbüchern', *Gesammelte Studien . . .*, pp. 169–204; ET, 'The Deuteronomic Theology of History in I and II Kings', *The Problem of the Hexateuch*, pp. 205–21

Das fünfte Buch Mose: Deuteronomium, Göttingen, 1964; ET, *Deuteronomy*, London, 1966

RAHLFS, A., *Studien zu den Königsbüchern*, *Septuaginta-Studien* Heft I, 1904

Luciens Rezension der Königsbücher, *Septuaginta-Studien* Heft III, 1911

Septuaginta (2 vols.), Stuttgart, 1935

REISNER, G. A., see LYON

REVENTLOW, H. GRAF, *Gebot und Predigt im Dekalog*, Gütersloh, 1962

ROBERTS, B. J., *The Old Testament Text and Versions*, Cardiff, 1951

ROBERTS, C. H., *Two Biblical Papyri in the John Rylands Library*, Manchester, 1936

ROBERTSON, E., *The Old Testament Problem*, Manchester, 1950

ROBINSON, H. W., *The Old Testament: its Making and its Meaning*, London, 1937

ROBINSON, T. H., 'The History of Israel', *A Companion to the Bible*, ed. MANSON, T. W., Edinburgh, 1939, pp. 204–67

see OESTERLEY

ROGERS, R. W., *Cuneiform Parallels to the Old Testament*, New York, 1912

ROST, L., *Die Überlieferung von der Thronnachfolge Davids* (BWANT III 6), Stuttgart, 1926

'Sinaibund und Davidsbund', *TLZ* LXXII, 1947, cols. 129–34

ROTHENBERG, B., 'Ancient Copper Industries in the Western Arabah', *PEQ* 1962, pp. 5–71

ROWE, A., *A Catalogue of Egyptian Scarabs, Scaraboids, Seals, and Amulets in the Palestine Archaeological Museum*, Cairo, 1936

The Four Canaanite Temples of Bethshan, Philadelphia, 1940

ROWLEY, H. H., 'The Meaning of the Shulammite', *AJSL* LVI, 1939, pp. 84–91

'Zadok and Nehushtan', *JBL* LVIII, 1939, pp. 113–41

The Growth of the Old Testament, London, 1950

'The Prophet Jeremiah and the Book of Deuteronomy', *Studies in Old Testament Prophecy*, ed. ROWLEY, H. H., Edinburgh, 1950, pp. 154–74

'Melchizedek and Zadok (Gen. 14 and Psalm 110)', *Festschrift für Alfred Bertholet*, ed. BAUMGARTNER, W., Tübingen, 1950, pp. 461–72

(ed.), *Studies in Old Testament Prophecy*, Edinburgh, 1950

(ed.), *The Old Testament and Modern Study*, Oxford, 1951

From Joseph to Joshua, London, 1950

'Elijah on Mount Carmel', *BJRL* XLIII, 1960, pp. 190–219

'Hezekiah's Reform and Rebellion', *BJRL* XLIV, 1962, pp. 395–431

ROWTON, M. B., 'Manetho's Date for Ramses II', *JEA* XXXIV, 1948, pp. 57–74

'The Date of the Founding of Solomon's Temple', *BASOR* 119, 1950, pp. 20–2

RUDOLPH, W., *Chronikbücher* (HAT), ed. EISSFELDT, O., Tübingen, 1955

RYCKMANS, G., *Les noms propres sud-sémitiques* (3 vols.), Louvain, 1934–5

SAGGS, H. W. F., 'The Nimrud Letters, 1952: I', *Iraq* XVII, 1955, pp. 21–56; 'The Nimrud Letters, 1952: II', *ibid.* pp. 126–60; 'The Nimrud Letters, 1952: III', *Iraq* XVIII, 1956, pp. 40–56

ŠANDA, A., *Die Bücher der Könige* (2 vols.), Münster, 1911–12 (cited by volume only)

SAYDON, P., 'The Meaning of the Expression עָצוּר וְעָזוּב', *VT* II, 1952, pp. 371–4

SCHAEFFER, C. F. A., *Ugaritica* I, Paris, 1939
Stratigraphie comparée et chronologie de l'Asie Occidentale, London, 1948
Reprises des fouilles de Ras Shamra-Ugarit, Paris, 1955
See NOUGAYROL and VIROLLEAUD
SCHMIDT, H., *Die grossen Propheten* (Die Schriften des AT in Auswahl II 2), Göttingen, 1923
SCHMÖKEL, H., *Geschichte des alten Vorderasiens* (Handbuch der Orientalistik, ed. SPULER, B., I, ii, Part 3), Leiden, 1957
SCHNEIDER, A. M., 'Das byzantinische Gilgal', *ZDPV* LIV, 1931, pp. 50ff.
SCOTT, R. B. Y., 'The Pillars Jachin and Boaz', *JBL* LVIII, 1939, pp. 143–7
'Solomon and the Beginnings of Wisdom in Israel', *Wisdom in Israel*, SVT III, ed. NOTH, M. and THOMAS, D. W., 1955
'Weights and Measures of the Bible', *BA* XXII, 1959, pp. 22–40
'Weights, Measures, Money, and Time', *Peake's Commentary on the Bible*, rev. ed. ROWLEY, H. H. and BLACK, M, London, 1962
SEEBASS, H., 'Zur Königserhebung Jeroboams I', *VT* XVII, 1967, pp. 325–33
SELLIN, E., *Tell Ta'annek*, Vienna, 1904
Einleitung in das Alte Testament, ed. ROST, L., Heidelberg, 1950; 10th, rev. ed., FOHRER, G., 1965; ET, *Introduction to the Old Testament*, London, 1923, rev. ed., Nashville, 1968
SETHE, K., *Die Ächtung feindlicher Fürsten, Völker und Dinge auf altägyptischen Tongefässscherben des mittleren Reiches* (Abhandlungen der Preussischen Akademie der Wissenschaften, Philos.-hist. Klasse), 1926
SIMONS, J., *Jerusalem in the Old Testament*, Leiden, 1952
SIMPSON, D. C., *Old Testament Essays*, London, 1927
SKINNER, J., *I and II Kings* (Century Bible), London, n.d. (c. 1893) (cited as CB)
SMITH, G. A., *Jerusalem* (2 vols.), London, 1907–8
The Historical Geography of the Holy Land, London, 1935[26]
SMITH, H. P., *Samuel* (ICC), Edinburgh, 1899
SMITH, S., *Babylonian Historical Texts*, London, 1924
'Assyria', *Cambridge Ancient History* III, Cambridge, 1925, chs. 1–4
'A Preliminary Account of the Tablets from Atchana', *AJ* XIX, 1939, pp. 38–48
'On the Meaning of *Goren*', *PEQ* 1953, pp. 42–5
SMITH, W. R., *The Prophets of Israel*, London, 1882
Lectures on the Religion of the Semites, London, 1889; 1894[2]; (with introduction and notes by COOK, S. A.), London, 1927[3]
The Old Testament and the Jewish Church, London, 1892[2]
SNAITH, N. H., 'Kings', *Interpreter's Bible* III, London, 1954
von SODEN, W., 'Leistung und Grenze sumerischer und babylonischer Wissenschaft', *Die Welt als Geschichte* II, Berlin, 1936, pp. 417–64

'Verkündigung des Gotteswillens durch prophetisches Wort in den altbabylonischen Briefen aus Mari', *Die Welt des Orients*, Göttingen, 1950, pp. 396–403

SOGGIN, J. A., 'Der judäische ʿam-hā' āreṣ und das Königtum im Juda', *VT* XIII, 1963, pp. 187–95

Das Königtum in Israel (BZAW CIV), 1967

SPEISER, E. A., '"People" and "Nation" of Israel', *JBL* LXXIX, 1960, pp. 157–63

STADE, B., 'Der Text des Berichtes über Salomos Bauten, I Kö. 5–7', *ZAW* III, 1883, pp. 129–77

'Anmerkungen zu 2 Kö. 10–14', *ZAW* V, 1885, pp. 275–97

'Anmerkungen zu 2 Kö. 15–21', *ZAW* VI, 1886, pp. 156–89

STAMM, J. J., *Der Dekalog im Lichte der neuerer Forschung*, Bern, 1958; ET, of 2nd ed. 1962, *The Ten Commandments in Recent Research*, with additions by ANDREWS, M. E., London, 1967

STARKEY, J. L., 'Tell Duweir', *PEFQS* 1933, pp. 190–9

'Excavations at Tell Duweir, 1933–4', *PEFQS* 1934, pp. 164–75

'Excavations at Tell Duweir, 1934–5', *PEFQS* 1935, pp. 198–207

'Excavations at Tell Duweir, 1935–6', *PEFQS* 1936, pp. 178–89

'Lachish as illustrating Biblical History', *PEFQS* 1937, pp. 171–9

'Excavations at Tell Duweir', *PEQ* 1937, pp. 228–41

see LACHISH I

STÈVE, A. M., see de VAUX, R.

STRONG, H. A., see LUCIAN of SAMOSATA

SUKENIK, E. L., 'Funerary Tablet of Uzziah, King of Judah', *PEQ* 1931, pp. 217–21

see CROWFOOT, J. W.

SWETE, H. B., *The Old Testament in Greek* (3 vols.), Cambridge, 1914

TADMOR, H., 'The Campaigns of Sargon II of Assur', *JCS* XII, 1958, pp. 22–40, 77–100

TAYLOR, C., *Hebrew-Greek Cairo Genizah Palimpsests from the Taylor-Schechter Collection*, Cambridge, 1900

THACKERAY, H. St J., 'The Greek Translators of the Four Books of Kings', *JTS* VIII, 1907, pp. 262–78

THIELE, E. R., *The Mysterious Numbers of the Hebrew Kings*, Chicago, 1951

THOMAS, D. W., 'Napath-Dor: a Hill Sanctuary', *PEFQS* 1935, pp. 89–90

'"*The Prophet*" *in the Lachish Ostraca*', London, 1946

and NOTH, M., (ed.), *Wisdom in Israel and the Ancient Near East* (SVT III), Leiden, 1955

'Again "the Prophet" in the Lachish Ostraca', *Von Ugarit nach Qumran: Festschrift für Otto Eissfeldt*, ed. HEMPEL, J., and ROST, L., Berlin, 1958

(ed.), *Documents from Old Testament Times*, Edinburgh, 1958
(ed.), *Archaeology and Old Testament Study*, London, 1967
Thureau-Dangin, F., 'Trois contrats de Ras Shamra', *Syria* XVIII, 1937, pp. 249–51
Torrey, C. C., 'The Foundry of the Second Temple at Jerusalem', *JBL* LV, 1936, pp. 247–60
Torczyner, H., see Lachish I
Trumbull, H. C., *The Threshold Covenant*, London, 1896

Unger, M. F., *Israel and the Aramaeans of Damascus*, London, 1957
Ungnad, A., 'Die Zahl der von Sanherib deportierten Judäer', *ZAW* LIX, 1942/43, pp. 199–202

de Vaux, R., 'Les prophètes de Baal sur le Mont Carmel', *BMB* V, 1941, pp. 1–20
and Stève, A. M., 'La première campagne de fouilles à Tell el-Farʿah, près Naplouse. Rapport préliminaire', *RB* LIV, 1947, pp. 394–433
(suite), *ibid.*, pp. 573–89
'La seconde campagne de fouilles à Tell el-Farʿah, près Naplouse. Rapport préliminaire', *RB* LV, 1948, pp. 544–80
(suite), *RB* LVI, 1949, pp. 102–38
'La troisième campagne de fouilles à Tell el-Farʿah, près Naplouse. Rapport préliminaire', *RB* LVIII, 1951, pp. 393–430
'Les Livres des Rois', *La Sainte Bible* (*Jerusalem*), Paris, 1958 (cited as *BJ*)
'Les Livres de Samuel', *ibid.*
Les Institutions de l'Ancien Testament I, Paris, 1958; II, 1960; ET, *Ancient Israel: its Life and Institutions*, London, 1961
Benoit, P., and Milik, J. T., *Discoveries in the Judaean Desert II. Les Grottes de Murabbaʿat* (2 vols.), Oxford, 1961
Baillet, M., and Milik, J. T., *Discoveries in the Judaean Desert III*, Oxford, 1962
Vincent, A., *La religion des judéo-araméens d'Éléphantiné*, Paris, 1937
Vincent, L. H., *Jérusalem de l'Ancien Testament* (2 vols.), Paris, 1954-1956
Virolleaud, C., 'Les villes et les corporations du royaume d'Ugarit', *Syria* XXI, 1940, pp. 123–51
Mission de Ras Shamra VI, ed. Schaeffer, C. F. A., *Textes en cunéiformes alphabétiques des archives est, ouest et centrales, Le palais royal d'Ugarit* II, Paris, 1957

Walker, W., *All the Plants of the Bible*, London, 1960
Wambacq, B. N., *L'épithète divine Jahweh Sᵉbaoʾt: étude philologique, historique et exégétique*, Paris and Bruges, 1947
Waterman, L., 'The Damaged "Blueprints" of the Temple', *JNES* II, 1943, pp. 284–94

WATZINGER, C., *Denkmäler Palästinas*, Leipzig, 1933–5
WEIDNER, E. F., 'Jojachin König von Juda in babylonischen Keilschrifttexten', *Mélanges syriens offerts à M. René Dussaud* II, pp. 933–35, Paris, 1939
'Texte—Worte—Sache: 4. *šadâšu emêdu*', *AfO* XIII, 1940, pp. 233–4
'Silkan(ḫe)ni, König von Musri, ein Zeitgenosse Sargons II', *AfO* XIV, 1941–4, pp. 40–53
'Die Königsliste aus Khorsabad', *AfO* XIV, 1941–4, pp. 362–9
WEILL, R., *La Cité de David* (2 vols.), Paris, 1920, 1947
WEISER, A., *Einleitung in das Alte Testament*, Göttingen, 1949²; ET, *Introduction to the Old Testament*, London, 1961
WELCH, A. C., *The Code of Deuteronomy*, London, 1924
Deuteronomy: the Framework and the Code, London, 1932
Post-exilic Judaism, Edinburgh, 1935
WELLHAUSEN, J., *Skizzen und Vorarbeiten* (6 vols.), Berlin 1884–99:
I: *Abriss der Geschichte Israels und Judas*, 1884
II: *Die Composition des Hexateuchs und der historischen Bücher des Alten Testaments*, 1899³, pp. 263–301
III: *Reste arabischen Heidentums*, 1897²
Prolegomena zur Geschichte Israels, 1886³; ET, *Prolegomena to the History of Ancient Israel*, reprint, New York, 1957
WEVERS, J. W., 'Double Readings in the Books of Kings', *JBL* LXV, 1946, pp. 307–10
WHITLEY, C. F., 'The Deuteronomic Presentation of the House of Omri', *VT* II, 1952, pp. 137–52
WHYBRAY, R. N., *The Succession Narrative. A Study of II Sam. 9–20; I Kings 1 and 2*, London, 1968
WIDENGREN, G., 'Psalm 110 och det sakrala kungadömet i Israel', *UUÅ* 1941: 7, 1, Uppsala and Leipzig, 1941
'King and Covenant', *JSS* II, 1957, pp. 1–32
WINCKLER, H., *Alttestamentliche Untersuchungen*, Leipzig, 1892
WISEMAN, D. J., 'Two Historical Inscriptions from Nimrud', *Iraq* XIII, 1951, pp. 21–6
The Alalakh Tablets (British Institute for Archaeology at Ankara), London, 1953
'A Fragmentary Inscription of Tiglathpileser III from Nimrud', *Iraq* XVIII, 1956, pp. 117–29
Chronicles of Chaldaean Kings (626–556 BC) in the British Museum, London, 1956
Illustrations from Biblical Archaeology, London, 1958
WOLFF, H. W., 'Das Kerygma des deuteronomistischen Geschichtswerks', *ZAW* LXXIII, 1961, pp. 171–86
WOOLLEY, C. L., 'Excavations at Atchana-Alalakh 1938', *AJ* XIX, 1939, pp. 1–37

A Forgotten Kingdom, Harmondsworth, Middlesex, 1953

van der Woude, A. S., 'Das Hiobtargum aus Qumran', SVT IX, 1963, pp. 322–33

Wright, G. E., 'Lachish—Frontier Fortress of Judah', *BA* I, 1938, pp. 21–30

'Solomon's Temple Resurrected', *BA* IV, 1941, pp. 17–31

and Filson, F. V., *The Westminster Historical Atlas to the Bible*, London, 1945

The Old Testament against its Environment, London, 1950

God who Acts, London, 1952

'Deuteronomy', *Interpreter's Bible* III, London, 1953

and Cross, F. M., 'The Boundary and Provincial Lists of the Kingdom of Judah', *JBL* LXXV, 1956, pp. 206–26

Biblical Archaeology, London, 1957

(ed.), *The Bible and the Ancient Near East. Essays in Honor of William Foxwell Albright*, London, 1961

'The Archaeology of Palestine', *The Bible and the Ancient Near East*, pp. 73–112

'More on King Solomon's Mines', *BA* XXIV, 1961, pp. 59–62

Shechem, London, 1965

Wright, W. A., *A Short History of Syriac Literature*, London, 1894

Würthwein, E., *Der* Amm ha'arez *im AT* (BWANT IV 17), 1936

Der Text des Alten Testaments. Eine Einführung in die Biblia Hebraica von Rudolf Kittel, Stuttgart, 1952; ET, *The Text of the Old Testament*, Oxford, 1957

Yadin, Y., 'Some Aspects of the Strategy of Ahab and David', *Biblica* XXXVI, 1955, pp. 332–51

with Aharoni, J., Amiran, R., Dothan, T., Dunayevsky, I., and Perrot, J., *Hazor I, an account of the First Season of Excavations, 1955*, Jerusalem, 1958

'Solomon's City-wall and Gate at Gezer', *IEJ* VIII, 1958, pp. 80–6

'New Light on Solomon's Megiddo', *BA* XXIII, 1960, pp. 62–8

with Aharoni, J., Amiran, R., Dothan, T., Dunayevski, J., Perrot, J., and Angress, S., *Hazor II. An Account of the Second Season of Excavations, 1958*, Jerusalem, 1960

van Zyl, A., *The Moabites*, Leiden, 1960

MAPS

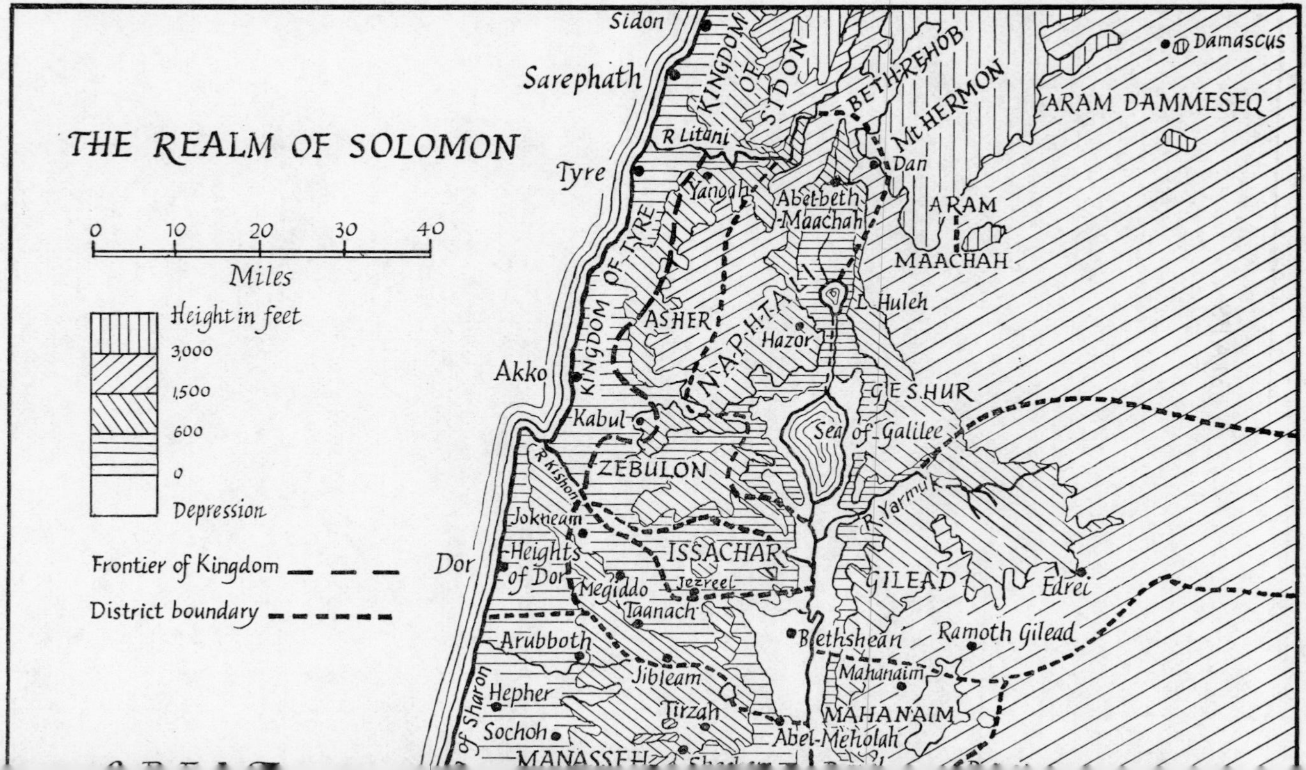
THE REALM OF SOLOMON
0 10 20 30 40
Miles
Height in feet
3,000
1,500
600
0
Depression
Frontier of Kingdom
District boundary
Sidon
Sarephath
Tyre
Akko
Dor
KINGDOM OF SIDON
R Litani
BETH-REHOB
Mt HERMON
ARAM DAMMESEQ
Damascus
Dan
ARAM
MAACHAH
Abel-beth-Maachah
Yanoah
KINGDOM OF TYRE
ASHER
NAPHTALI
Hazor
L. Huleh
GESHUR
Sea of Galilee
Kabul
R Kishon
ZEBULON
R Yarmuk
Jokneam
ISSACHAR
Heights of Dor
Megiddo
Jezreel
Taanach
GILEAD
Edrei
Arubboth
Bethshean
Ramoth Gilead
Jibleam
Mahanaim
Hepher
Tirzah
MAHANAIM
of Sharon
Sochoh
Abel-Meholah
MANASSEH

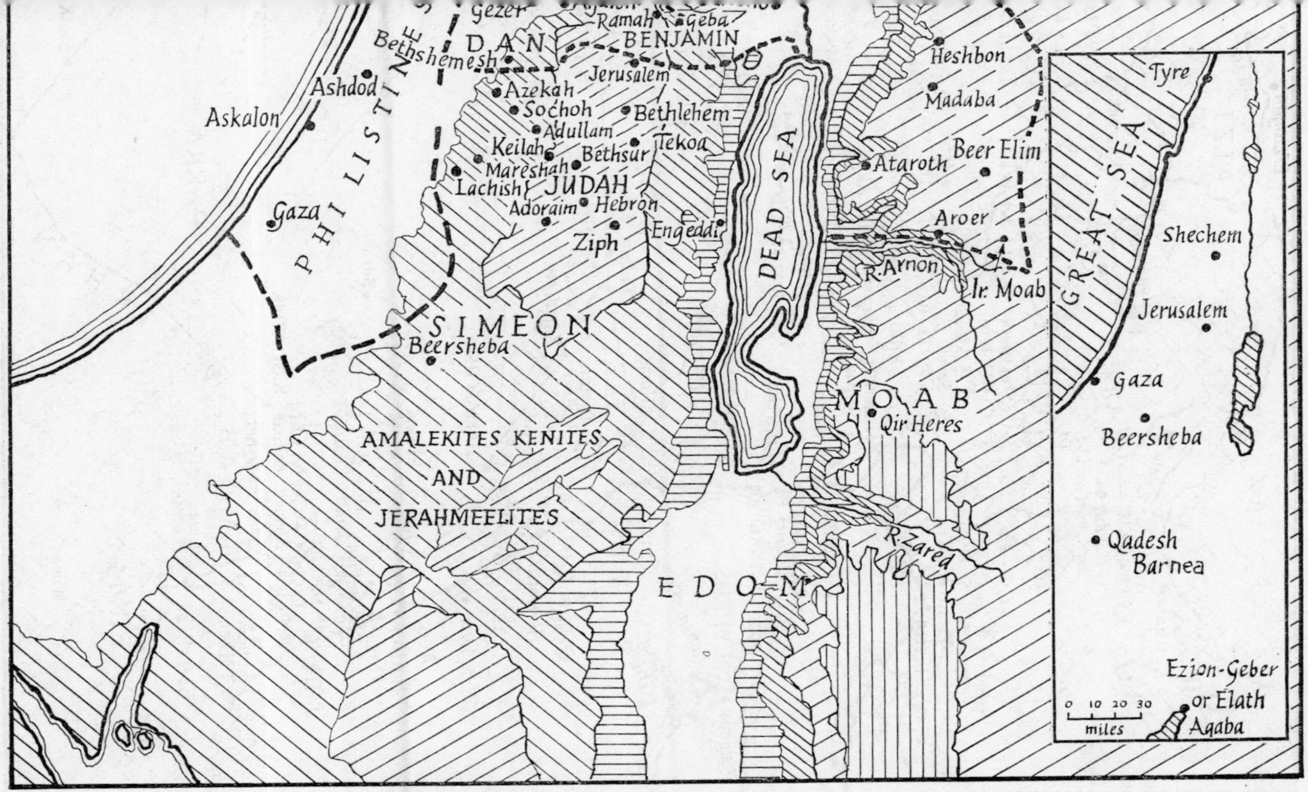
Gezer
Ramah
Geba
DAN
BENJAMIN
Bethshemesh
Ashdod
Askalon
PHILISTINES
Jerusalem
Azekah
Sochoh
Adullam
Bethlehem
Keilah
Bethsur
Tekoa
Mareshah
Lachish
JUDAH
Adoraim
Hebron
Engeddi
Ziph
Gaza
SIMEON
Beersheba
DEAD SEA
Heshbon
Madaba
Beer Elim
Ataroth
Aroer
R. Arnon
Ir. Moab
MOAB
Qir Heres
AMALEKITES KENITES
AND
JERAHMEELITES
EDOM
R. Zared
Tyre
GREAT SEA
Shechem
Jerusalem
Gaza
Beersheba
Qadesh
Barnea
Ezion-Geber
or Elath
Aqaba
0 10 20 30
miles

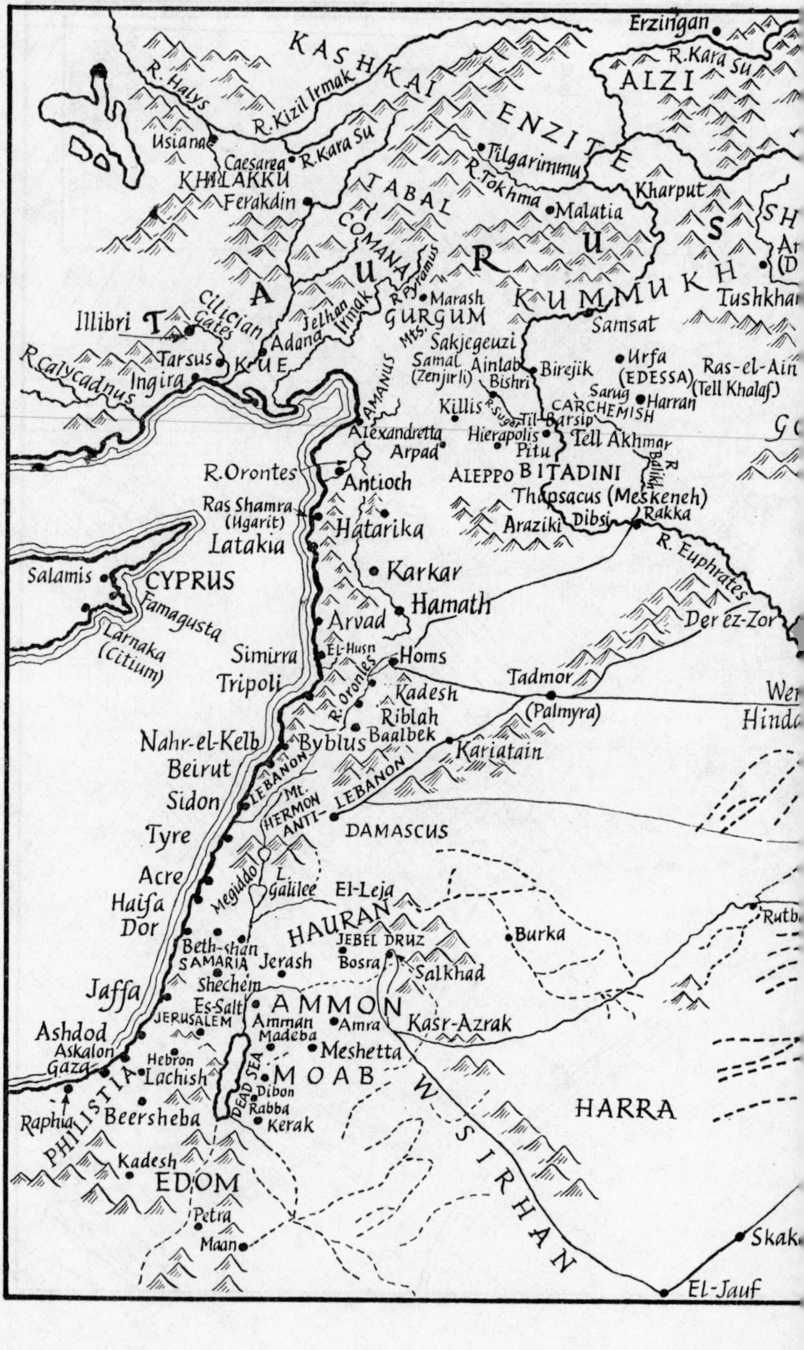
Erzingan
R. Kara Su
ALZI
KASHKAI
ENZITE
R. Halys
R. Kizil Irmak
Usiana
Caesarea
R. Kara Su
Tilgarimmu
KHILAKKU
R. Tokhma
TABAL
Malatia
Kharput
Ferakdin
COMANA
S
U
R
A
U
T
KUMMUKH
Tushkha
R. Pyramus
Marash
Cilician Gates
Jelhan Irmak
GURGUM
Samsat
Illibri
Adana
Mts.
Sakjegeuzi
Tarsus
KUE
Samal (Zenjirli)
Aintab
Birejik
Urfa (EDESSA)
Ras-el-Ain (Tell Khalaf)
R. Calycadnus
Ingira
AMANUS
Bishri
Sarug
Harran
CARCHEMISH
Killis
R. Sajur
Til-Barsip
Alexandretta
Hierapolis
Tell Akhmar
Arpad
Pitu
R. Balikh
R. Orontes
Antioch
ALEPPO
BITADINI
Thapsacus (Meskeneh)
Ras Shamra (Ugarit)
Hatarika
Araziki
Dibsi
Rakka
Latakia
R. Euphrates
Salamis
CYPRUS
Karkar
Famagusta
Hamath
Arvad
Der ez-Zor
Larnaka (Citium)
Simirra
El-Husn
Homs
R. Orontes
Tripoli
Tadmor
Kadesh
(Palmyra)
Riblah
Nahr-el-Kelb
Byblus
Baalbek
Kariatain
Beirut
LEBANON
ANTI-LEBANON
Sidon
Mt. HERMON
DAMASCUS
Tyre
Acre
L. Galilee
El-Leja
Haifa
Megiddo
Dor
HAURAN
Burka
Beth-shan
JEBEL DRUZ
SAMARIA
Jerash
Bosra
Shechem
Salkhad
Jaffa
Es-Salt
AMMON
JERUSALEM
Amman
Amra
Kasr-Azrak
Ashdod
Madeba
Meshetta
Askalon
Hebron
Gaza
Lachish
MOAB
DEAD SEA
Dibon
Raphia
PHILISTIA
Beersheba
Rabba
Kerak
HARRA
W. SIRHAN
Kadesh
EDOM
Petra
Maan
El-Jauf
Skak
Rutb

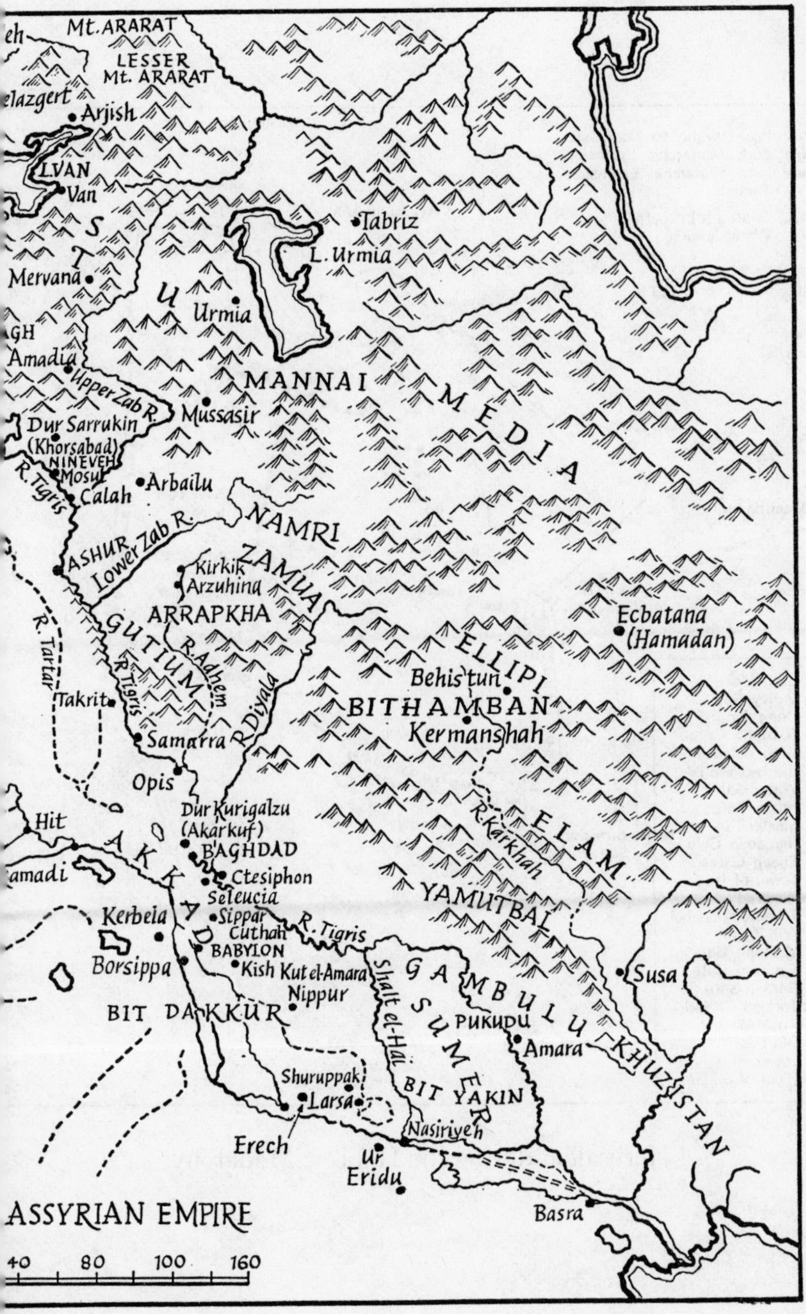

Mt. ARARAT
LESSER Mt. ARARAT
Arjish
L. VAN
Van
Mervana
Tabriz
L. Urmia
Urmia
Amadia
Upper Zab R.
MANNAI
MEDIA
Mussasir
Dur Sarrukin (Khorsabad)
NINEVEH
Mosul
R. Tigris
Arbailu
Calah
NAMRI
ASHUR
Lower Zab R.
ZAMUA
Kirkik
Arzuhina
ARRAPKHA
GUTIUM
R. Adhem
R. Tigris
R. Tartar
Takrit
R. Diyala
Samarra
Opis
Ecbatana (Hamadan)
ELLIPI
Behis'tun
BITHAMBAN
Kermanshah
Hit
Dur Kurigalzu (Akarkuf)
BAGHDAD
AKKAD
R. Karkhah
ELAM
Ctesiphon
Seleucia
Sippar
Cuthah
R. Tigris
YAMUTBAL
Kerbela
BABYLON
Borsippa
Kish
Kut el-Amara
Shatt el-Hai
GAMBULU
Susa
Nippur
BIT DAKKUR
SUMER
PUKUDU
Amara
KHUZISTAN
Shuruppak
Larsa
BIT YAKIN
Nasiriyeh
Erech
Ur
Eridu
Basra
ASSYRIAN EMPIRE
40
80
100
160

Legend:

- ═ ═ Pre–Davidic to Manasseh
- □□□ Early Monarchic Extension
- ■■■ Late Monarchic Extension
- — Turkish
- ⌇760⌇ Contours in metres
- ⌇ Water course

metres
0 — 250

Map labels:

Ard al-Birkeh

Herod Gate

Mount of Olives

Damascus Gate

Stephen Gate

New Gate

780

to Mamilla Pool

Golden Gate

Dome of the Rock

Patriarchs Bath

Palace and Temple of Solomon

Jaffa or Hebron Gate

CENTRAL VALLEY

Zion Gate

Siloam Village

Spring of Gihon

Birket as Sultan

Pre Davidic and Davidic City

Hill of Offence

KIDRON RAVINE

760

740

720
700
680
660
640
620

VALLEY OF HINNOM
Wadi ar-Rababi

740
720

Numbered key:

① Corner or Valley Gate
② Dung Gate
③ Fountain Gate
④ Gate 'Between the two Walls'
⑤ Water Gate
⑥ Horse Gate
⑦ Muster? or Benjamin Gate
⑧ Sheep Gate
⑨ Tower of the Hundred
⑩ Tower of Hananel
⑪ Fish Gate
⑫ Mishnah Gate
⑬ Ephraim Gate
⑭ Garden Gate
⑮ Turkish Citadel
⑯ Aqsa Mosque
⑰ Old Pool
⑱ Lower Pool (Pool of Siloam)

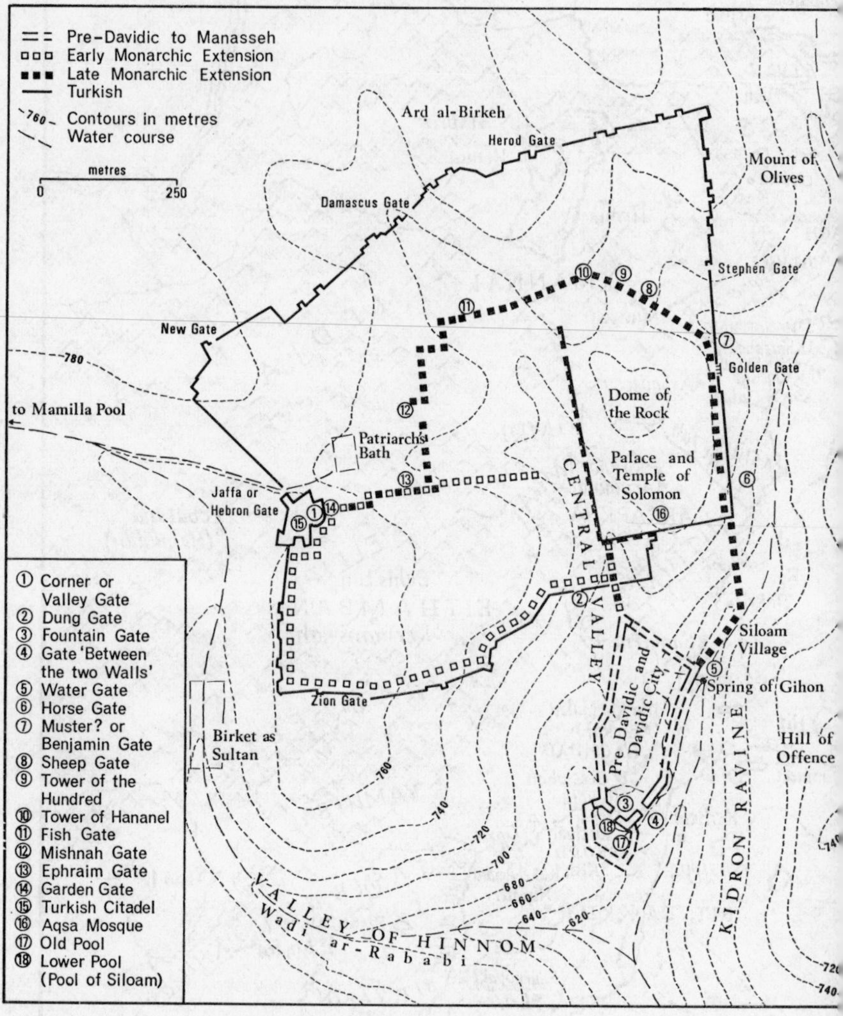

Jerusalem during the Hebrew Monarchy